Relationship Section

Rotated Alphabetical Terms Section

Term Clusters Section

Margin Index: To use, bend pages of book backward and follow margin index to pages with black edge markers.

THESAURUS

OF PSYCHOLOGICAL INDEX TERMS

Alvin Walker, Jr., Editor

EIGHTH EDITION

Library of Congress Cataloging-in-Publication Data

Thesaurus of psychological index terms. — 8th ed. / Alvin Walker, Jr., editor,
p. cm.
ISBN 1-55798-402-6
1. Subject headings—Psychology. 2. Psychology—Abstracting and indexing. I. Walker, Alvin, 1959– .
Z695.1.P7T48 1997
025.4915—dc21 97-3383
CIP

750 First Street, N.E., Washington, D.C. 20002-4242

Printed in the United States of America
ISBN 1-55798-402-6

Table of Contents

Preface v

History of the *Thesaurus* vii

Development of the Eighth Edition ix
Table 1-New 1997 Postable Index Terms x
Table 2-New 1997 Non-Postable Index Terms xii
Table 3-Other Term Changes xv

User Guide xvi
General Information xvi
Relationship Section xvi
Rotated Alphabetical Terms Section xviii
Term Clusters Section xviii

Search Guide xx
Introduction xx
Searching in *Psychological Abstracts (PA)* xxi
Searching on Electronic Systems xxi
Electronic Thesaurus xxi
Explode Feature xxi
Saved Searches xxi
Major Terms xxii
Adjusting Your Search Retrieval xxii
Searching using Content Classification Codes xxii
Searching using Age Groups xxii
How to contact us xxiii

Appendix A—Sample Journal Record xxiv

Appendix B—Sample Book/Chapter Record xxv

Appendix C—PsycINFO Content Classification System xxvi

Appendix D—Master Quick Reference Guide for Searching xxvii

Relationship (Hierarchical) Section 1

Rotated Alphabetical Terms Section 265

Term Clusters Section 357

Preface

The *Thesaurus of Psychological Index Terms* is a reference tool for use with the PsycINFO®, PsycLIT®, and ClinPSYC® databases or *Psychological Abstracts*. The *Thesaurus* has been developed by the PsycINFO Department of the American Psychological Association. The 8th edition is one more effort in PsycINFO's mission to advance scientific and professional knowledge in and about psychology and related disciplines by providing the best access to psychological information, thus ensuring high user satisfaction. As with all previous editions, many changes in this edition are in direct response to our users' needs, and we remain committed to continuing to provide you with a high quality reference product. For a brief history of the development of the *Thesaurus*, including the most recent terminology included in this edition, refer to **Table 1** and **Table 2** on pages x-xiv.

We suggest a brief orientation to the *Thesaurus* to help you become acquainted with how to use this new edition. A small investment of time spent familiarizing yourself with the features of this edition can result in better search retrieval.

Review the **USER GUIDE** on pages xvi-xix to learn how to read an index term entry. The **USER GUIDE** explains the components of term hierarchies, and also provides introductory details about other useful sections of the *Thesaurus*.

In the **RELATIONSHIP SECTION** on pages 1-264 you will find an alphabetical listing of controlled vocabulary (also referred to as "descriptors" or "index terms") complete with hierarchical structures providing information on broader, narrower, and related concepts. This section is useful for information on dates terms entered the vocabulary as well as definitions of term usage.

Consider using the **ROTATED ALPHABETICAL TERMS SECTION** on pages 265-356 when you have a general idea of the terminology you wish to use, but are unsure of the exact wording for the controlled vocabulary. This section serves as an index to terminology found in the **RELATIONSHIP SECTION** and is also useful when you want to see how many terms are embedded with a particular concept or word.

The **TERM CLUSTERS SECTION** lists terms grouped according to broad subject categories. Each broad cluster is divided into meaningful subcluster subject areas. Use this section to introduce yourself to a range of terms which may be relevant to your research topic.

In the front matter, the section entitled **SEARCHING USING THE THESAURUS** provides a brief introduction to electronic database searching. This section is followed by **APPENDICES** which you will find helpful as quick reference guides when executing a search.

Best wishes for your research!

The Thesaurus Management Team

History of the *Thesaurus*

Psychology has multiple roots in the older disciplines of philosophy, medicine, education, and physics. As a result, the vocabulary of the psychological literature is characterized by considerable diversity. As the field of psychology has grown, each new generation of psychologists has added to the vocabulary in attempting to describe their studies and perceptions of behavioral processes. This uncontrolled evolution of the psychological vocabulary has contributed to complex literature search and retrieval problems.

In response to these problems, the American Psychological Association developed the first edition of the *Thesaurus of Psychological Index Terms* in 1974. This controlled vocabulary was designed to provide a means of structuring the subject matter of psychology and to serve as an efficient indexing and retrieval tool. Since the publication of the first edition, the PsycINFO indexing staff has charted trends and newly emerging areas of interest reflected in the psychological literature as a way of updating and revising the *Thesaurus*. The eighth edition of the *Thesaurus* represents a concerted effort to provide a more valuable tool for researchers, practitioners, information science providers, students, and others interested in the field of psychology.

First Edition (1974)

Term selection was the first step in the development of the 1974 edition. The 800 index terms used by *Psychological Abstracts* (PA) prior to 1973 and a list of the frequencies of the occurrence of single words in titles and abstracts in PA over a 5-year period were taken as the starting points. In addition, phrases and terms were obtained from keyword-in-context (KWIC) lists produced from 10,000 titles of journal articles, books, separates, and dissertations. Inclusion/exclusion rules were developed, with a resulting list of about 3,000 potential terms reviewed by subject matter specialists for final selection. These terms were arranged to express interrelationships, including use, used for, broader, narrower, and related categories.

Second Edition (1977)

The first major revision of the *Thesaurus*, which included 204 new terms, was published in 1977. Some 180 never-used terms from the original *Thesaurus* were deleted, and a rotated alphabetical term section was added to make it faster and easier to find index terms.

Third Edition (1982)

The second major revision of the *Thesaurus*, which included 240 new terms, was published in 1982. The most significant change introduced in the third edition was the development of scope notes or definitions for over 1,300 terms. In addition, superscript dates were added to all terms to indicate the date of inclusion in the *Thesaurus* vocabulary.

Fourth Edition (1985)

The third major revision of the *Thesaurus* included 247 new terms and over 162 new and revised scope notes. Posting notes (PN) were added to each index term to indicate the number of times the terms had been used for indexing. Dates were added to each index term to show in what year it was added to the Thesaurus vocabulary. Also, each postable index term was given a unique five-digit code that can be used in online searching as an alternative to entering the term text.

Fifth Edition (1988)

An important change occurred during the fourth major revision—incorporation of all nonpostable terms into the Rotated Alphabetical Terms Section. These terms appeared in nonbold italic print and were marked with a star (★). Over 250 postable terms and 100 nonpostable terms were added to the vocabulary. In addition, over 100 new scope notes were added and over 75 scopes notes were revised. Because the *Thesaurus* had been in use for many years, an extensive hierarchy reconstruction project was begun with the intention of continuing the process in revisions of future editions.

Sixth Edition (1991)

The fifth major revision of the *Thesaurus* included the addition of 238 new postable terms and 100 new nonpostable terms. Over 50 scope notes were rewritten and 120 new scope notes were added to the vocabulary. In a continuing effort to make the *Thesaurus* more useful, the Relationship Section was enhanced by the addition of down arrows (↓) in each main term's hierarchy next to narrower and related terms that also have narrower terms. Term Clusters were developed to present a collection of index terms based on conceptual similarity to assist users unfamiliar with the *Thesaurus* vocabulary. As in earlier editions, revision of existing hierarchical relationships continued.

Seventh Edition (1994)

The 20-year anniversary edition of the *Thesaurus* was marked with many changes to the Relationship Section of the *Thesaurus*. Approximately 220 new postable terms and 115 new nonpostable terms were added, and nearly 110 new scope notes were added to the existing 1,970 scope notes. These included scope notes for terms new to the seventh edition as well as terms from previous editions. Revision of almost 2,000 hierarchies also occurred to increase their accuracy and to ensure consistent relationships. The hierarchies for array terms, conceptually broad terms identified with a slash (/), were reconstructed for the first time since the inception of the *Thesaurus* and the slash was removed. Posting notes were updated to indicate how many times each postable term was used to index a record through June 1993. A new "Neuropsychology and Neurology" cluster was added to the Term Clusters Section complete with 7 subclusters. Finally, the Rotated Alphabetical Terms section was completely revised so that nonpostable terms appeared for the first time with their "Use" reference.

Development of the Eighth Edition (1997)

NEW TERMS

Since the publication of the seventh edition, 254 new postable index terms and 191 nonpostable index terms have been added to the eighth edition. The new terms represent concepts and terminology expressed in the psychological and behavioral literature as well as the literature found in fringe areas of psychology, e.g., social work, education, sociology, and medicine. In addition, new terminology was developed for classic psychological concepts requiring appropriate controlled vocabulary. These additions to the vocabulary brings the total number of postable and nonpostable index terms to 7,726.

The criteria for index term inclusion involved: (1) the frequency of the term's occurrence in the psychological literature, (2) the term's potential usefulness in providing access to a concept, (3) the term's relationship to or overlap with existing *Thesaurus* terminology, (4) user feedback and need, and (5) lack of potential application problems by indexing staff. Every term has been researched extensively and integrated into the hierarchies in the Relationship Section. The Rotated Alphabetical Terms Section has been updated with the new terms as well. See **Table 1**, **Table 2**, and **Table 3** on pages x-xv for a listing of all new postable index terms, nonpostable index terms, and other significant term changes.

OTHER CHANGES

Term Hierarchies

Extensive revision of hierarchical relationships occurred during the development of this edition. Hierarchies were examined to ensure accuracy, completeness, and consistency. In a continuation of our efforts to examine hierarchical structures with each edition, over 200 hierarchies were revised to minimize any misleading and redundant relationships as well as to maintain a coherent and cohesive vocabulary structure.

Scope Notes

Approximately 115 new scope notes (SNs) have been added to the existing 2,026 scope notes in the seventh edition (1994). Scope notes were added to terms with ambiguous meanings, terms that need to be differentiated from existing terms, or terms with restricted indexing usage. In addition, as part of our pledge to provide better definitive notes with index terms, each of the existing 2,026 scope notes was examined. As a result, over 225 scope notes were rewritten or revised to improve clarity, to broaden or restrict the term's range of application, or to accommodate new 1997 terms.

Nonpostable Terminology

In an effort to provide additional entry points into the *Thesaurus* vocabulary, and to direct users more efficiently to preferred terms "used for" indexing, approximately 200 new nonpostable terms were added to this edition—50 percent more than were added to previous editions.

Posting Notes

Primarily as an aid to psychologists, researchers, librarians, and students, each postable index term in the Relationship Section appears with a posting note (PN) reference indicating how many times that index term has been used in the indexing process at the time of this publication. These posting notes are based on cumulations of term usage through June 1996. Index terms with posting notes (PN) = 0 are new 1997 terms that have been added to this edition. These terms have 0 postings because they have not been used in the indexing process as of the January 1997 publication date, and have yet to accumulate any postings.

Change in Status Terms

Terms with very low postings, obsolete and out-of-date terms, and terms that have undergone change in usage in the field of psychology were identified for a change in status during this revision. Close to 60 terms changed from a postable to nonpostable status and are referred to a synonymous term or a term of broader scope. See **Table 3** for a full listing of these changes.

Terms Used for Handicapped Populations

All index terms that contained the word "handicapped" (e.g., Multiply Handicapped) were reviewed during this revision and changed to "disability" terms (e.g., Multiply Disabled) to reflect changing terminology in the literature.

Table 1—New Postable Terms

Abandonment
Abuse of Power
Abuse Reporting
Academic Self Concept
Acoustics
Adlerian Psychotherapy
Adult Day Care
Adult Learning
Agreeableness
Aids (Attitudes Toward)
Aids Dementia Complex
Alaska Natives
Alternative Medicine
Anger Control
Anxiety Disorders
Anxiety Management
Assisted Suicide
Autoeroticism
Behavioral Ecology
Behavioral Sciences
Bonobos
Boundaries (Psychological)
Buddhists
Budgets
Cancer Screening
Canids
Catholics
Chaos Theory
Child Abuse Reporting
Chinese Cultural Groups
Christians
Chromaticity
Chronic Fatigue Syndrome
Chronic Mental Illness
Citalopram
Client Participation
Client Records
Client Transfer
Client Treatment Matching
Cognitive Assessment
Cognitive Processing Speed
Collective Unconscious
Color Saturation
Commonwealth of Independent States
Community Development
Computer Assisted Design
Conscientiousness
Constant Time Delay
Craving
Cross Cultural Communication
Cross Cultural Psychology
Debates
Decision Support Systems
Declarative Knowledge
Determinism
Direction Perception
Disability Discrimination
Disabled Personnel
Discourse Analysis
Dissociative Identity Disorder
Drug Distribution
Drug Legalization
Eating Disorders
Educational Attainment Level
Educational Quality
Educational Reform
Educational Therapy
Enabling
Enactments
English as Second Language
Erotomania
Experiential Learning
Explicit Memory
Exposure Therapy
Eye Movement Desensitization Therapy
False Memory
Family Life Education
Family Work Relationship
Fantasy
Felids
Five Factor Personality Model
Folk Psychology
Gender Identity Disorder
Geriatric Assessment
Geriatric Psychiatry
Global Amnesia
Goal Setting
Grasping
Group Development
Hardiness
Health Care Administration
Health Care Seeking Behavior
Health Complaints
Health Screening
Health Service Needs
Helplessness
Higher Order Conditioning
Hindbrain
Hindus
HIV Testing
Home Care Personnel
Homeless Mentally Ill
Human Computer Interaction
Human Machine Systems
Human Machine Systems Design
Human Nature
Huntingtons Disease
Hypermedia
Hypertext
Hyponatremia
Hypothalamic Pituitary Adrenal System
Impulse Control Disorders
Ingroup Outgroup
Inhibited Sexual Desire
Inlaws
Integrated Services
Integrity
Internalization
International Class of Diseases
Interpersonal Psychotherapy
Japanese Cultural Groups
Jews
Job Knowledge
Ketamine
Kirton Adaption Innovation Inven
Korean Cultural Groups
Latent Inhibition
Leadership Qualities
Life Sustaining Treatment
Lifestyle Changes
Listening (Interpersonal)
Literacy Programs
Maintenance Therapy
Military Psychologists
Mirroring
Misdiagnosis
Moclobemide
Monogamy
Motion Parallax
Movement Therapy
Multiculturalism
Munchausen Syndrome by Proxy
Music Perception
Muslims
Narratives
Natural Selection
Need for Approval
Need for Cognition
Negative Therapeutic Reaction
Neo Personality Inventory
Neurokinins
Neuropsychological Rehabilitation
News Media
Nicotine Withdrawal
Obesity (Attitudes Toward)
Object Recognition
Openness to Experience
Oppositional Defiant Disorder
Organizational Characteristics
Outreach Programs
Owls
Pain Measurement
Parental Expectations
Parental Investment
Parenting Skills
Patient Selection
Planned Behavior
Political Psychology
Positive And Negative Symptoms
Positivism (Philosophy)
Postmodernism
Prepulse Inhibition
Procedural Knowledge
Product Design
Professional Competence
Progressive Supranuclear Palsy
Prompting
Prospective Studies
Protective Services
Protestants

Continued on next page

Table 1—New Postable Terms, Cont'd

Psychiatric Evaluation
Psychiatric Symptoms
Psychological Assessment
Psychological Needs
Psychotherapeutic Neutrality
Quality of Services
Reading Development
Reflectiveness
Rehabilitation Education
Relationship Termination
Relativism
Religious Experiences
Religious Groups
Repressed Memory
Reputation
Resistance
Resource Allocation
Response Cost
Retirement Community
Retrospective Studies
Right to Treatment
Risk Management
Risk Perception
Risperidone
Ritanserin
Romance
Sample Size
School Transition
Science Achievement
Self Fulfilling Prophecies
Self Preservation
Separation Reactions
Serotonin Reuptake Inhibitors
Sertraline
Sex Recognition
Sexual Addiction
Sexual Fantasy
Sexual Orientation
Sexual Risk Taking
Shopping
Singing
Somatoform Pain Disorder
Spirit Possession
Sports Spectators
Supervisor Employee Interaction
Supportive Psychotherapy
Sustained Attention
Teleconferencing
Tempo
Test Coaching
Traumatic Brain Injury
Treatment Planning
Tricyclic Antidepressant Drugs
Twelve Step Programs
Vascular Dementia
Vietnamese Cultural Groups
Virtual Reality
Visuospatial Ability
Visuospatial Memory
Warning Labels
Warnings
Whiplash

Table 2—New Nonpostable Terms

Affairs (Sexual)
  USE Extramarital Intercourse
AIDS Testing
  USE HIV Testing
Alanon
  USE Alcohol Rehabilitation
Alateen
  USE Alcohol Rehabilitation
Alcohol (Grain)
  USE Ethanol
Allocation of Resources
  USE Resource Allocation
Anankastic Personality
  USE Obsessive Compulsive Personality
Antiadrenergic Drugs
  USE Sympatholytic Drugs
Assessment (Cognitive)
  USE Cognitive Assessment
Assessment (Psychological)
  USE Psychological Assessment
Atrial Fibrillation
  USE Fibrillation (Heart)
Attainment Level (Educational)
  USE Educational Attainment Level
Baldness
  USE Alopecia
Baptists
  USE Protestants
Big Five Personality Model
  USE Five Factor Personality Model
Bipolar Affective Disorder
  USE Manic Depression
Biracial Children
  USE Interracial Offspring
Boundary Violations (Sexual)
  USE Professional Client Sexual Relations
Brain Injury (Traumatic)
  USE Traumatic Brain Injury
Breakup (Relationship)
  USE Relationship Termination
Breast Cancer Screening
  USE Cancer Screening
Cardiac Arrest
  USE Heart Disorders
Cardiac Surgery
  USE Heart Surgery
Cervical Sprain Syndrome
  USE Whiplash
Child Molestation
  USE Pedophilia
Chiroptera
  USE Bats
Client Compliance
  USE Treatment Compliance
Client Dropouts
  USE Treatment Dropouts
Commercials
  USE Television Advertising
Compulsivity (Sexual)
  USE Sexual Addiction
Computer Conferencing
  USE Teleconferencing
Consumer Product Design
  USE Product Design
Contour Perception
  USE Form and Shape Perception
Control (Emotional)
  USE Emotional Control
Control (Locus of)
  USE Internal External Locus of Control
Control (Self)
  USE Self Control
Control (Social)
  USE Social Control
Corrective Lenses
  USE Optical Aids
Course of Illness
  USE Disease Course
Coyotes
  USE Canids
Criminal Interrogation
  USE Legal Interrogation
Cultural Factors
  USE Sociocultural Factors
Cultural Pluralism
  USE Multiculturalism
Customer Satisfaction
  USE Consumer Satisfaction
Data Pooling
  USE Meta Analysis
Demonic Possession
  USE Spirit Possession
Desertion
  USE Abandonment
Disclosure (Self)
  USE Self Disclosure
Discrimination (Social)
  USE Social Discrimination
Educational Environment
  USE School Environment
Educational Theory
  USE Theories of Education
EMDR
  USE Eye Movement Desensitization Therapy
Emotional Needs
  USE Psychological Needs
Emotionality (Animal)
  USE Animal Emotionality
Employee Supervisor Interaction
  USE Supervisor Employee Interaction
Episcopalians
  USE Protestants
ESL
  USE English as Second Language
Evaluation (Psychiatric)
  USE Psychiatric Evaluation
Excitation (Physiological)
  USE Physiological Arousal
Eye Accommodation
  USE Ocular Accommodation
Factual Knowledge
  USE Declarative Knowledge
Fairbairnian Theory
  USE Object Relations
Fans (Sports)
  USE Sports Spectators
Fetal Exposure
  USE Prenatal Exposure
Fraternal Twins
  USE Heterozygotic Twins
Functional Knowledge
  USE Procedural Knowledge
GABA Agonists
  USE Gamma Aminobutyric Acid Agonists
GABA Antagonists
  USE Gamma Aminobutyric Acid Antagonists
Galanin
  USE Peptides
Gamblers Anonymous
  USE Twelve Step Programs
Gaussian Distribution
  USE Normal Distribution
Gender Role Attitudes
  USE Sex Role Attitudes
Gender Roles
  USE Sex Roles
Gipsies
  USE Gypsies
Habitats (Animal)
  USE Animal Environments
Halcion
  USE Triazolam

Continued on next page

Table 2—New Nonpostable Terms, Cont'd

Harassment (Sexual)
 USE Sexual Harassment
Heart Beat
 USE Heart Rate
Home Health Aides
 USE Home Care Personnel
Hospital Addiction Syndrome
 USE Munchausen Syndrome
Huntingtons Chorea
 USE Huntingtons Disease
Hypoactive Sexual Desire Disorder
 USE Inhibited Sexual Desire
Hypothesis Testing (Cognitive)
 USE Cognitive Hypothesis Testing
ICD
 USE International Class of Diseases
Imaginativeness
 USE Openness to Experience
Incorporation (Psychological)
 USE Internalization
Individual Psychotherapy (Adlerian)
 USE Adlerian Psychotherapy
Information Processing Speed
 USE Cognitive Processing Speed
Interagency Services
 USE Integrated Services
Intercultural Communication
 USE Cross Cultural Communication
Interethnic Communication
 USE Cross Cultural Communication
Intergenerational Transmission
 USE Transgenerational Patterns
Interpersonal Competence
 USE Social Skills
Intersexuality
 USE Hermaphroditism
Job Family Relationship
 USE Family Work Relationship
Jungian Psychotherapy
 USE Analytical Psychotherapy
Latency (Response)
 USE Response Latency
Length of Stay
 USE Treatment Duration
Lions
 USE Felids
Lutherans
 USE Protestants

Manager Employee Interaction
 USE Supervisor Employee Interaction
Marital Fidelity
 USE Monogamy
Marriage and Family Education
 USE Family Life Education
Maternal Investment
 USE Parental Investment
Mental Health Service Needs
 USE Health Service Needs
Mentally Ill Homeless
 USE Homeless Mentally Ill
Methodists
 USE Protestants
Methyldiphenylhydramine
 USE Orphenadrine
Misarticulation
 USE Articulation Disorders
MMPI
 USE Minn Multiphasic Personality Inven
Mood Disorders
 USE Affective Disturbances
Narcotics Anonymous
 USE Twelve Step Programs
Negative and Positive Symptoms
 USE Positive and Negative Symptoms
Neutrality (Psychotherapeutic)
 USE Psychotherapeutic Neutrality
Olfactory Impairment
 USE Anosmia
Opioid Antagonists
 USE Narcotic Antagonists
Organizational Policy Making
 USE Policy Making
Outgroup Ingroup
 USE Ingroup Outgroup
Oxidopamine
 USE Hydroxydopamine (6-)
Paroxysmal Sleep
 USE Narcolepsy
Paternal Investment
 USE Parental Investment
Patient Care Planning
 USE Treatment Planning
Patient Dropouts
 USE Treatment Dropouts
Patient Participation
 USE Client Participation
Patient Records
 USE Client Records
Patient Transfer
 USE Client Transfer

Patient Treatment Matching
 USE Client Treatment Matching
Persistent Mental Illness
 USE Chronic Mental Illness
Person Centered Psychotherapy
 USE Client Centered Therapy
Personnel Turnover
 USE Employee Turnover
Perversions (Sexual)
 USE Sexual Deviations
Political Debates
 USE Debates
Political Involvement
 USE Political Participation
Polyphagia
 USE Hyperphagia
Population Density
 USE Social Density
Population Shifts
 USE Human Migration
Practical Knowledge
 USE Procedural Knowledge
Presbyterians
 USE Protestants
Presidential Debates
 USE Debates
Prostate Cancer Screening
 USE Cancer Screening
Pseudohermaphroditism
 USE Hermaphroditism
Pseudomemory
 USE False Memory
Psychic Healing
 USE Faith Healing
Psychogalvanic Reflex
 USE Galvanic Skin Reflex
Psychotherapy (Individual)
 USE Individual Psychotherapy
Psychotic Symptoms
 USE Psychiatric Symptoms
Pulmonary Disorders
 USE Lung Disorders
Pygmalion Effect
 USE Self Fulfilling Prophecies
Pygmy Chimpanzees
 USE Bonobos
Quaalude
 USE Methaqualone
Quality of Education
 USE Educational Quality
Rapid Heart Rate
 USE Tachycardia
Readiness Potential
 USE Contingent Negative Variation

Continued on next page

Table 2—New Nonpostable Terms, Cont'd

Reading Aloud
USE Oral Reading
Recurrence (Disorders)
USE Relapse (Disorders)
Reenactments
USE Enactments
Renal Diseases
USE Kidney Diseases
Renal Transplantation
USE Organ Transplantation
Resilience (Psychological)
USE Hardiness
Rhombencephalon
USE Hindbrain
Rogerian Therapy
USE Client Centered Therapy
Rural Development
USE Community Development
Safety Warnings
USE Warnings
Saturation (Color)
USE Color Saturation
Second Order Conditioning
USE Higher Order Conditioning
Service Quality
USE Quality of Services
Set (Response)
USE Response Set
Sexual Compulsivity
USE Sexual Addiction
Sexual Identity (Gender)
USE Gender Identity
Skin Cancer Screening
USE Cancer Screening
Sleeplessness
USE Insomnia
Songs
USE Music
Sound Waves
USE Acoustics
Student Adjustment
USE School Adjustment
Suffocation
USE Anoxia
Survival Instinct
USE Self Preservation
Tigers
USE Felids
Treatment Client Matching
USE Client Treatment Matching
Treatment Seeking Behavior
USE Health Care Seeking Behavior
True False Tests
USE Forced Choice (Testing Method)
Upward Mobility
USE Social Mobility
Urban Development
USE Community Development
Visual Spatial Ability
USE Visuospatial Ability
Visual Spatial Memory
USE Visuospatial Memory
Warning Signs
USE Warnings
Winnicottian Theory
USE Object Relations
Withdrawal (Drug)
USE Drug Withdrawal
Work Family Relationship
USE Family Work Relationship
Work Satisfaction
USE Job Satisfaction
X Rated Materials
USE Pornography
Xenophobia
USE Stranger Reactions

Table 3—Change in Status Terms

The following terms changed from postable to nonpostable status. Consult the Relationship Section for the appropriate "Use" term.

Adrenolytic Drugs
Adventitiously Handicapped
Aldolases
Allport Vernon Lindzey Study Values
Anxiety Neurosis
Appetite Disorders
Asthenic Personality
Aurally Handicapped
Authoritarian Rebellion Scale
Blacky Pictures Test
Butrylperazine
Carbonic Anhydrase
Cardiotonic Drugs
Chloralose
Chlorisondamine
Color Pyramid Test
Congenitally Handicapped
Deanol
Dieldrin
Differential Personality Inventory
Dissociative Neurosis
Handicapped
Handicapped (Attitudes Toward)
Henman Nelson Test Mental Ability
Homatropine
Huntingtons Chorea
Kupfer Detre Self Rating Scale
Leiter Adult Intelligence Scale
Lithium Bromide
Man Machine Systems
Man Machine Systems Design
Medics
Mephenesin
Minnesota Teacher Attitude Survey
Multiple Personality
Multiply Handicapped
Narcoanalytic Drugs
Nonmetallic Elements
Onomatopoeia and Images Test
Opinion Attitude and Interest Survey
Otosclerosis
Paraldehyde
Phenylglycodol
Physical Handicaps (Attitudes Toward)
Physically Handicapped
Psychogenic Pain
Psychopathy
Quinidine
Rauwolfia
School and College Ability Test
Sensorially Handicapped
Sensory Handicaps (Attit Toward)
Shuttle Box Grids
Shuttle Box Hurdles
Speech Handicapped
Temporal Spatial Concept Scale
Thyroid Extract
Transistors (Apparatus)
Trifluopromazine
Vane Kindergarten Test
Visually Handicapped
Volt Meters
White AB Scale

User Guide

General Information

Word Form Conventions

Conventions dealing with singular and plural word forms, direct and indirect entries, abbreviations, acronyms, homographs, and punctuation have been used to ensure standardization of the *Thesaurus* vocabulary. For example, noun forms are preferred entries, with the plural form used when the term is a noun that can be qualified (e.g., **Computers**, **College Students**, or **Employment Tests**) and the singular form when the term refers to processes, properties, or conditions (e.g., **Learning, Grief,** or **Rehabilitation**). Direct entry or natural word order is preferred when a concept is represented by two or more words (e.g., **Mental Health** vs "Health, Mental" or **Artificial Intelligence** vs "Intelligence, Artificial").

Some terms that would exceed the 36 character limit if completely spelled out are abbreviated (e.g., **Minn Multiphasic Personality Inven** and **Rotter Intern Extern Locus Cont Scal**). A selected number of acronyms are also used, such as **DOPA**, **REM Sleep**, and **ROTC Students**. In cases where ambiguity may occur and to clarify the meaning of homographs, qualifying expressions are included in parentheses (e.g., **Culture (Anthropological)**, **Conservation (Ecological Behavior)**, and **Reconstruction (Learning)**.

Term Relationships

The terms in the Relationship Section are displayed to reflect the following relationships:

USE. Directs the user from a term that cannot be used (nonpostable) to a term that can be used (postable) in indexing and searching. The **Use** reference indicates preferred forms of synonyms, abbreviations, spelling, and word sequence:

Facilitated Communication
Use Augmentative Communication

UF (Used For). Reciprocal of the **Use** Reference. Terms listed as **UF** (used for) references represent some but not all of the most frequently encountered synonyms, abbreviations, alternate spellings, or word sequences:

Augmentative Communication 94
UF Facilitated Communication

B (Broader Term) and **N (Narrower Term).** Reciprocal designators used to indicate hierarchical relationships:

Academic Achievement 67
B Achievement 67

Achievement 67
N Academic Achievement 67

R (Related Term). Reciprocal designator used to indicate relationships that are semantic or conceptual, but not hierarchical. Related term references indicate to searchers (or indexers) terms that they may not have considered, but may be related to their topic of interest:

Achievement Motivation 67
R Fear of Success 78

Relationship Section

Each *Thesaurus* term is listed alphabetically and, as appropriate, is cross-referenced and displayed with its broader, narrower, and related terms (i.e., subterms). Since the beginning of the database in 1967, PsycINFO's indexing vocabulary has been updated periodically with new terms. The date of the term's inclusion in the *Thesaurus* appears as a two-digit superscript. Each postable subterm in a main term's hierarchy also has its date of inclusion shown. Eleven dates can be found: '67, '71, '73, '78, '82, '84, '85, '88, '91, '94 and '97. It is important to note that new terms added to the vocabulary are not "mapped back" to older records to which they are conceptually relevant.

The subject code **(SC)** gives the unique five-digit code associated with the term, and can be used to retrieve records instead of entering the term text on some online search systems.

Each postable index term in the Relationship Section appears with a posting note **(PN)** reference indicating how many times that term has been used in the indexing of PsycINFO/PsycLIT records. Posting notes in this edition are based on cumulations of term usage through June 1996. Terms that have an indicator PN=0 are new 1997 terms that have been added to this edition and have yet to accumulate any postings. These terms will appear in the next edition of the *Thesaurus* with appropriate posting notes.

Many terms that have ambiguous meanings, applications unique to the PsycINFO database, or usage patterns that have changed over time have scope notes (**SN**). In many cases, a scope note provides a definition and/or information on proper use of the term. The scope note always refers to the one term with which it is associated and does not necessarily have implications for the subterms displayed in the term's hierarchy. The following are examples of some of the scope notes found in the Relationship Section:

Definition and usage	**Social Isolation** [67] **SN** Voluntary or involuntary absence of contact with others. Used for human or animal populations.
Change in usage	**Brain Lesions** [67] **SN** Not defined prior to 1982. From 1982 limited to experimentally induced lesions and used primarily for animal populations.
Mandatory application	**School Age Children** [73] **SN** Ages 6-12 years. Used in noneducational contexts. Application of terms designating age is mandatory for ages 0-17.
Change in status	Appetite Disorders **SN** Term discontinued in 1996. Use APPETITE DISORDERS to access references from 73-96.

Nonpostable index terms, those not used in the indexing process, are shown in nonbold print with an appropriate **USE** reference. Nonpostable terms are provided as points of entry into the *Thesaurus* vocabulary.

The following example from the Relationship Section illustrates a nonpostable term entry:

Nonpostable Index Term	Working Memory
Use Term (postable index term)	**USE** Short Term Memory [67]

Finally, the Relationship Section has been enhanced by the use of down arrows (↓) in front of any narrower (**N**) or related (**R**) terms that have narrower terms themselves. This feature alerts the user to consider another more specific hierarchical level. The PsycINFO database is indexed to the level of specificity in a given document. In using the Relationship Section and in choosing index terms, consider following any main term's subterms (**N** and **R** terms only) to its lowest level of specificity by turning to the page in the *Thesaurus* where the narrower (**N**) or related (**R**) subterm appears as a main entry to determine if more specific terminology is available. See **Table 4** for a sample of an index term entry in the Relationship Section.

Table 4—Postable Index Term Example

The following example from the Relationship Section illustrates the various components that may be included in the hierarchy of a postable index term:

Postable Index Term (with date of entry)		**Multivariate Analysis** [82]
Posting Note and Subject Code	**PN**	560 **SC** 32513
Scope Note	**SN**	Any statistical technique designed to measure the influence of many independent variables acting simultaneously on more than one dependent variable.
Used for (nonpostable term)	**UF**	Canonical Correlation
Broader Term	**B**	Statistical Analysis [67]
Narrower Terms (Down arrow indicates more specific terms)	**N**	↓Factor Analysis [67] Multiple Regression [82] Path Analysis [91]
Related Terms (Down arrow indicates more specific terms)	**R**	Analysis of Covariance [73] Analysis of Variance [67] ↓Statistical Correlation [67] ↓Statistical Regression [85]

Rotated Alphabetical Terms Section

Many terms represent concepts not expressed in a single word, therefore postable and nonpostable *Thesaurus* terms in this section are listed in alphabetical order by each word contained within them. The Rotated Alphabetical Terms Section is useful in finding all *Thesaurus* terms that have a particular word in common. This display groups related terms when they may otherwise be separated in the alphabetical Relationship Section. It is important to note that this section should be used in conjunction with the Relationship Section since hierarchies, scope notes, posting notes, and term dates do not appear. A term containing three words will appear in three locations in the Rotated Alphabetical Terms Section as illustrated below:

Academic Underachievement
College **Academic** Achievement
Acalculia

Achievement Potential
College Academic **Achievement**
Mathematics **Achievement**

Collective Behavior
College Academic Achievement
College Dropouts

Nonpostable index terms (terms not used for indexing) are represented in nonbold print followed by the appropriate **"Use"** term in italics. Each word of the term, just like the postable terms above, appear in different locations depending on how many words are contained in the index term as illustrated below:

Illumination
Illumination Therapy *USE Phototherapy*
Autokinetic **Illusion**

Hormone **Therapy**
Illumination Therapy *USE Phototherapy*
Implosive **Therapy**

Some *Thesaurus* terms have unusual spellings because of a term length limitation of 36 characters, e.g., **Mental Retardation (Attit Toward)** or **Minn Multiphasic Personality Inven**. The shortened word contained in these terms will appear in alphabetical order as if the word were spelled out completely:

Mental Illness **(Attitudes** Toward)
Mental Retardation **(Attit** Toward)
Middle Class **Attitudes**

Minks
Minn Multiphasic Personality Inven
Minnesota Teacher Attitude Inventory

Term Clusters Section

Clusters are collections of index terms that are related to one another conceptually rather than hierarchically, and are displayed together under broad subject categories. This section is useful for viewing all terms in each cluster collectively.

Clusters provide an entry point into the *Thesaurus* vocabulary by allowing a large group of similar terms to be scanned easily and efficiently, and helping the user translate their search vocabulary into *Thesaurus* vocabulary. In a sense, the clusters present an "index" to the indexing vocabulary found in the Relationship Section.

It is important to note the Clusters Section should not be used alone, but in conjunction with the Relationship Section. Useful details regarding particular index terms can be found in the Relationship Section such as scope notes, posting notes, hierarchies, dates for term inclusion, and links to additional search terms.

Not every index term will appear in the Term Clusters Section. Terms appear under nine broad cluster subject areas. The nine subject areas are meant to present index terms for selected subject areas that are frequent in psychological research, but do not cover all subject areas in psychology. There are approximately 3,100 postable index terms in the Clusters Section. Terms may appear in more than one broad cluster area, and also in more than one subcluster under any broad area, if appropriate. The Term Clusters and Subclusters are listed in **Table 5** on the following page.

Table 5—Term Cluster/Subcluster Subject Areas

Disorders Cluster
- Antisocial Behavior & Behavior Disorders
- Diagnosis
- Disorder Characteristics
- Learning Disorders & Mental Retardation
- Physical & Psychosomatic Disorders
- Psychological Disorders
- Speech & Language Disorders
- Symptomatology

Educational Cluster
- Academic Learning & Achievement
- Curricula
- Educational Personnel & Administration
- Educational Testing & Counseling
- Schools & Institutions
- Special Education
- Student Characteristics & Academic Environment
- Student Populations
- Teaching & Teaching Methods

Geographic Cluster
- Africa
- Antarctica
- Asia
- Central America
- Europe
- Latin America
- North America
- Pacific Islands
- South America
- West Indies

Legal Cluster
- Adjudication
- Criminal Groups
- Criminal Offenses
- Criminal Rehabilitation
- Laws
- Legal Issues
- Legal Personnel
- Legal Processes

Neuropsychology & Neurology Cluster
- Assessment & Diagnosis
- Electrophysiology
- Neuroanatomy
- Neurological Disorders
- Neurological Intervention
- Neurosciences
- Neurotransmitters & Neuroregulators

Occupational & Employment Cluster
- Career Areas
- Employee, Occupational & Job Characteristics
- Management & Professional Personnel Issues
- Occupational Groups
- Organizations & Organizational Behavior
- Personnel Management

Statistical Cluster
- Design, Analysis & Interpretation
- Statistical Reliability & Validity
- Statistical Theory & Experimentation

Tests & Testing Cluster
- Academic Achievement & Aptitude Measures
- Attitude & Interest Measures
- Intelligence Measures
- Nonprojective Personality Measures
- Perceptual Measures
- Projective Personality Measures
- Testing
- Testing Methods

Treatment Cluster
- Alternative Therapies
- Behavior Modification
- Counseling
- Hospitalization & Institutionalization
- Medical & Physical Treatment
- Psychotherapy
- Rehabilitation
- Treatment (General)
- Treatment Facilities

Search Guide

Introduction

Using the *Thesaurus of Psychological Index Terms* to search PsycINFO, PsycLIT, ClinPSYC, and *Psychological Abstracts* (PA) can enhance the precision of your retrieved references and guide you to closely related topics that you may otherwise have missed. The standardized vocabulary in the *Thesaurus* eliminates the need to worry about phraseology used by authors to describe a concept. For effective searches and development of comprehensive search strategies, follow the steps outlined below:

1. Select a search topic

   Example: "I'm interested in high school students and AIDS."

2. Specifically define the concepts of the topic using single or multiple word phrases and develop a list of synonyms that represent the concepts. This can include independent and/or dependent experimental variables and/or a population. A properly defined concept can result in an efficient search with precise retrieval of highly relevant articles, and will also reduce the need to scan and eliminate irrelevant references. The following example shows a more specific and defined topic.

   Example: "I'm interested in AIDS educational and prevention programs for high school students."

3. Look up your concepts in the *Thesaurus of Psychological Index Terms*. Start in any of the three sections, choosing terms on the basis of your topic and familiarity with *Thesaurus* vocabulary (see User Guide).

   The Term Clusters Section includes clusters of index terms grouped into 9 categories (see Table 5 on page xix for a full list). The 9 categories present descriptors for selected subject areas that are found frequently in psychological research, but do not cover all subject areas. Consult this section if you are unfamiliar with the vocabulary or need a guide to related concepts in a particular area of psychology.

   The Rotated Alphabetical Terms section is helpful in finding terms that include a particular word, even if the searcher is unsure of the word order. Terms that have similiar words or concepts embedded in them can be viewed easily using this section.

   The Relationship Section, the heart of the *Thesaurus*, includes scope notes to describe how terms are used, as well as posting notes, subject codes, term dates, and the critical *used for, broader, narrower,* and *related* terms. The most important things to look for in the Relationship Section are the narrower terms and the dates for main term entry (for articles indexed after that date). It is important to note each descriptor's year of entry to the *Thesaurus* (indicated by a two-digit superscript number appended to each term in the Relationship Section) because new terminology is not "mapped back" to older records to which they are conceptually relevant.

   To retrieve articles relevant to terms before their inclusion in the *Thesaurus*, consider their broader concepts as index terms or use free-text strategies to find records added to the database before the starting date.

   Also note each entry's posting note, which is a rough guide to the number of articles you can expect to find using that term.

It is important to remember that all PsycINFO databases are indexed to each article's level of specificity. For example, an author who calls an experimental population "high school students" will find this article indexed under "**High School Students**", not the broader and less specific term, "**Students**". Therefore, any applicable narrower terms should be added as synonyms to the list of index terms in your search. Related terms may also closely match a search topic, and should be considered carefully when formulating a strategy.

Examples:

a. Acquired Immune Deficiency Syndrome (This is the term PsycINFO uses for AIDS.)

b. Educational Programs or Health Education or AIDS Prevention (These terms can be used to describe the concept of educational and prevention programs.)

c. High School Students or High Schools or Secondary Education (These terms form the context of high school education.)

Searching in *Psychological Abstracts* (PA)

Look up the previous *Thesaurus* terms in the annual *PA* Subject Volume Indexes from your years of interest—typically the most recent year first—and work backward. Start with the terms you consider most relevant to your search. If all the terms are of equal relevance, begin with the one with the fewest postings. You will find a short key phrase to describe each article indexed with that term. Select the most relevant phrases, then note the volume, which is printed on the spine of the index, and the abstract number, which is listed after each phrase in the index.

A separate Brief Subject Index appears at the back of each monthly issue of *PA* as a guide to that issue's contents only. No phrases are included in this index. The Brief Subject Index allows access to the current literature otherwise available only in the annual Volume Indexes published at the end of each year.

The final step in the search is to look up the abstracts themselves in the individual monthly issues of *PA*, using the volume and abstract numbers as a guide. Read the abstracts, then copy the citations of the ones of interest in order to locate the complete articles. Abstracts should never be used as substitutes for original articles.

Searching on Electronic Systems (Online or CD-ROM)

Each vendor system that carries PsycINFO, PsycLIT, or ClinPSYC operates differently, yet each has the capability to limit a search to the descriptor or index term field. Online and CD-ROM search systems give you the opportunity to manipulate your search statement to provide precision and recall in retrieval. Formulate your topic and refer to the *Thesaurus* for appropriate terminology, then consult **Appendix D**, a quick reference guide to all vendor systems, to determine how to enter index terms as descriptors. Also, refer to **Appendix D** for other specific field names and search examples.

Electronic systems allow the use of Boolean logic in a search, which is difficult to do in a manual search of *PA*. Use the Boolean logical operators **AND, OR**, and **NOT** to combine terms. Once satisfactory sets have been formed, each search system allows customization of the format of the retrieved records to meet special preferences. The search system's documentation describes this procedure in detail.

Example of Boolean Logic

(Shaded Areas Indicate Retrieval)

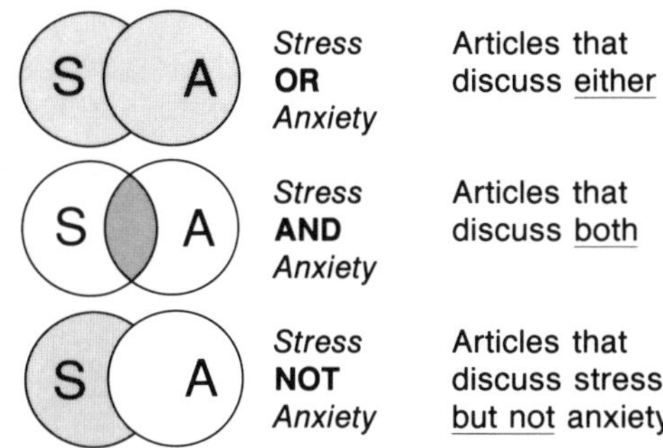

Stress **OR** *Anxiety*	Articles that discuss either
Stress **AND** *Anxiety*	Articles that discuss both
Stress **NOT** *Anxiety*	Articles that discuss stress but not anxiety

Example:

Acquired Immune Deficiency Syndrome

AND (Educational Progams **OR** Health Education **OR** AIDS Prevention)

AND (High School Students **OR** High Schools **OR** Secondary Education)

ELECTRONIC THESAURUS: For added convenience in searching, DIALOG, Silverplatter, Ovid Online, and DIMDI offer an electronic thesaurus, and the PsycLIT and ClinPSYC systems offer an on-disc thesaurus that can automatically display terms along with their broader, narrower, and related concepts. This feature can help reduce typing and enhance the speed of a search, especially when several narrower terms need to be entered, by allowing users to move from term to term and finding new appropriate search terms with ease.

EXPLODE FEATURE: The Explode feature is available on some search systems. See the Master Quick Reference Guide **Appendix D** for the systems that make this feature available. When a search system's explode command is evoked, the system will automatically search the index term and all of its narrower terms. It is important to note that some terms listed as narrower to an index term may have narrower terms of their own—"narrowers of narrowers." In the *Thesaurus*, narrower terms that have narrower terms of their own are marked with a down-arrow. To achieve comprehensive retrieval, they must be exploded as well.

SAVED SEARCHES: Saved Searches are stored sets of index terms in popular subject areas that save valuable search time. See **Table 6** on page xxii for a full listing of search topics currently available. When a Saved Search is invoked, the index terms will be searched automatically, and the resulting sets can be manipulated. On DIALOG and Data-Star,

Table 6—Saved Search Topics

TOPIC	DIALOG	DATA-STAR
Psychiatric Patients	?EX SBMDIS/USER 3471	..EXEC CL=MDIS
Substance Abuse	?EX SBABUSE/USER 3471	..EXEC CL=ABUS
Learning Disabilities	?EX SBLDIS/USER 3471	..EXEC CL=LDIS
Communication/Language/ Speech Disorders	?EX SBCDIS/USER 3471	..EXEC CL=CDIS
Racial and Ethnic Groups	?EX SBRACE/USER 3471	..EXEC CL=RACE
Tests and Measurements	?EX SBTEST/USER 3471	..EXEC CL=TEST
Mental Health Personnel	?EX SBMHPRS/USER 3471	..EXEC CL=MHPR
"Talking" Therapies	?EX SBTHRPY/USER 3471	..EXEC CL=THRP
Developing Countries	?EX SBWORLD/USER 3471	..EXEC CL=WRLD

Saved Searches can be executed at any time during a search session. Enter the command exactly as it appears below. Do not substitute your own user number for the "3471" in the DIALOG examples. Saved Searches for Silverplatter, Ovid, and NISC CD-ROM vendor systems are available free from PsycINFO. Please contact PsycINFO's User Services Department for details.

MAJOR TERMS: Index terms applied to PsycINFO, PsycLIT, or ClinPSYC records that represent the primary focus of the reference are designated as "major." Many systems allow for searching of major terms. See the Master Quick Reference Guide **Appendix D** for each system's label for searching major terms, if applicable.

Adjusting Your Search Retrieval

If your search retrieves too many records, try making your search more specific by adding another concept. If nearly all of your records appear relevant, but there are still too many, consider restricting your retrieval to recent publication years or English-language material.

If you retrieve too few records, consider dropping a concept, adding synonymous terms, or eliminating restrictions to specific fields.

Content Classification Code Searching

PsycINFO uses a content classification system that divides the psychological literature into 22 major or broad categories and 134 subcategories. Content classification codes can be searched in most systems. Use of the content classification system in searching can shorten online time and screen out undesired references. Content classification codes are particularly useful to retrieve records from a broad subject area in which many different index terms may have been used. Classification codes generally limit a search, since only one or two codes are assigned to each record. Keep in mind, however, that a classification code search usually does not retrieve everything in the database that is relevant to a respective topic. A well-constructed search will always include relevant descriptors.

Search classification codes at their broad level. Using the first two digits of a category retrieves the entire category and enables the search to be executed throughout the entire year range of the database. If more specific information is needed, search one or more four-digit subcategories. Four-digit subcategories were added in 1976; therefore, a search on a four-digit subcategory will limit retrieval to records added in 1976 and later. A list of the content classification codes appears in **Appendix C**.

Age Group Searching

All electronic systems use 4 specific identifying tags for human populations. A record may have more than one age group tag. ELDERLY is a subset of ADULT.

AGE	AGE GROUP TAG (AG)
0-12	CHILD
13-17	ADOLESCENT
18+	ADULT
65+	ELDERLY

Consult the Master Quick Reference Guide **APPENDIX D** for information on how to search the age group (AG) field.

If a more specific age range is desired in a search, choose appropriate descriptors from the table below. On the left side of **Table 7**, find the age range, then select one or more index terms from the appropriate column for the setting, i.e, nonschool or school related.

Table 7—Age Descriptors

AGE RANGE	NON-SCHOOL-RELATED	SCHOOL-RELATED
0-1 month	NEONATES [67]	
2-23 months	INFANTS [67]	
0-12 years	CHILDREN [67]	
2-5 years	PRESCHOOL AGE CHILDREN [67]	NURSERY SCHOOL STUDENTS [73] KINDERGARTEN STUDENTS [73] PRESCHOOL STUDENTS [82]
6-12 years	PREDELINQUENT YOUTH [78] SCHOOL AGE CHILDREN [73]	ELEMENTARY SCHOOL STUDENTS [67] INTERMEDIATE SCHOOL STUDENTS [73] PRIMARY SCHOOL STUDENTS [73] MIDDLE SCHOOL STUDENTS [85]
10-12 years	PREADOLESCENTS [88]	
13-17 years	ADOLESCENTS [67] JUVENILE DELINQUENTS [73] MALE DELINQUENTS [73] FEMALE DELINQUENTS [73] ADOLESCENT MOTHERS [85] ADOLESCENT FATHERS [85]	MIDDLE SCHOOL STUDENTS [85] JUNIOR HIGH SCHOOL STUDENTS [71] VOCATIONAL SCHOOL STUDENTS [73] HIGH SCHOOL STUDENTS [67]

How to Contact Us

Professional information specialists are available to answer questions and give assistance in search strategy formulation via our toll free line: *(800) 374-2722*. This free service is available in North America, 9:00 a.m. to 5:00 p.m., U.S. Eastern time, Monday through Friday.

For those who do not have toll free access, our User Services Department can be contacted at *(202) 336-5650*, FAX *(202)* 336-5633, TTY *(202) 336-6123*, or E-mail at *psycinfo@apa.org*.

Information on ordering documents, subscriptions, vendor system documentation, journals covered in PsycINFO, and search aids can also be found on PsycINFO's World Wide Web site:

http://www.apa.org/psycinfo/psycinfo.html.

Appendix A—Sample PsycINFO Journal Record

Vendor Record Number ←	22208009	
	83-08275	→ ***Psychological Abstracts* Volume and Abstract #**
Document Title ←	Cost of relapse in schizophrenia.	
	Weiden, Peter J.; Olfson, Mark	→ **Author(s)**
Affiliation of First Author ←	St Luke's-Roosevelt Hospital Ctr, Dept of Psychiatry, Schizophrenia Program, New York, NY, US	
	Schizophrenia Bulletin	→ **Journal Name**
Issue Citation and Page Number ←	1995 Vol 21(3) 419-429	
International Standard Serial Number ←	ISSN: 05867614	
	Journal Announcement: 9603	→ **Journal Announcement (PsycINFO Volume and Issue #)**
Document Language ←	Language: English	
	Document Type: JOURNAL ARTICLE	→ **Document Type**
Population Age Tags ←	Composite Age: ADULT	
	Estimated the yearly number of neuroleptic responsive multiple-episode schizophrenia inpatients in the US who are discharged to outpatient treatment and determined the cohort at risk for future relapse and rehospitalization. Monthly relapse rates are estimated to be 3.5% per month for patients on maintenance neuroleptics and 11.0% per month for patients who discontinued their medication. Postdischarge noncompliance rates in community settings are estimated to be 7.6% per month. An estimated 257,446 multiple-episode schizophrenia patients were discharged from short-stay inpatient units in the US during 1986. The estimated aggregate baseline inpatient cost for the index hospitalizations of this cohort was $2.3 billion (1993 dollars). Within 2 yrs after discharge, the aggregate cost of readmission approached $2 billion. (PsycLIT Database Copyright 1996 American Psychological Assn, all rights reserved)	→ **Document Abstract**
Major Descriptors ←	Major Descriptors: *COSTS AND COST ANALYSIS; *RELAPSE (DISORDERS); *SCHIZOPHRENIA; *PSYCHIATRIC HOSPITAL READMISSION; *NEUROLEPTIC DRUGS	
	Minor Descriptors: DRUG THERAPY; ADULTHOOD; TREATMENT COMPLIANCE: OUTPATIENT TREATMENT	→ **Minor Descriptors**
Descriptor Searching Codes ←	Descriptor Codes: 12045; 43660; 45440; 41410; 15380; 33710; 01150; 54153; 35970	
	Identifiers: postdischarge cost of loss of neuroleptic efficacy & noncompliance & rates of relapse & rehospitalization, neuroleptic responsive schizophrenic patients	→ **Descriptive Key Phrase**
Classification Heading ←	Section Headings: 3213-SCHIZOPHRENIA & PSYCHOTIC STATES; 3340-CLINICAL PSYCHOPHARMACOLOGY	

Appendix B—Sample PsycLIT Book/Chapter Record

FIELD NAME	SAMPLE BOOK RECORD
Accession Number	AN: EDITED BOOK 95-279019-000
Book Title	TI: Exploring young children's concepts of self and other through conversation
Author	AU: Sperry,-Linda-L. (Ed.); Smiley,-Patricia-A. (Ed.)
Author Affiliation	IN: Indiana State U, Terre Haute, IN, US
Publisher	PB: Jossey-Bass Inc, Publishers; San Francisco, CA, US; 94 pp.
Publication Year	PY: 1995
Series Title	SE: New directions for child development, No. 69.
ISBN(s)	IS: 0-7879-9939-3 (paperback)
Language	LA: English
Chapters Selected/Total	CH: 6 chapters selected from 6
Audience Type	AT: P1; Psychology: Pre-Professional/Undergraduate
Update	UD: 9603
Descriptors	DE: SELF-CONCEPT; CONVERSATION-; SOCIAL-COMPARISON; INFANTS-; PRESCHOOL-AGE-CHILDREN; OBSERVATION-METHODS; EARLY-CHILDHOOD-DEVELOPMENT; CONCEPT-FORMATION
Classification Code	CC: 2840; 28
Population	PO: Human
Age Group	AG: Child
Content Representation	CR: (from the editor's notes) The purpose of this volume is to explore very young children's conceptions of "self" and "other." The authors share a common approach...[*content representation continues*]
Table of Contents	TC: (Abbreviated) Editors' notes (by) Linda L. Sperry and Patricia A. Smiley 001- <<SEE CHAPTER>> Learning about self and other during requests/ Patricia A. Smiley and Joelle K. Greene 002- <<SEE CHAPTER>> What language reveals about children's categories of personhood/ Nancy Budwig and Angela Wiley...[*table of contents continues*]

FIELD NAME	SAMPLE CHAPTER RECORD
Accession Number	AN: CHAPTER 95-279019-005 <<SEE PREVIOUS CHAPTER>> <<SEE NEXT CHAPTER>>
Chapter Title	TI: Self in relation to other: Preschoolers' verbal social comparisons within narrative discourse.
Author	AU: Mintz,-Judith.
Author Affiliation	IN: U Chicago, Dept of Psychology, Chicago, IL, US
Parent Book	BK: Exploring young children's concepts of self and other through conversation. New directions for child development, No. 69. (Linda L. Sperry, Patricia A. Smiley, Eds.) pp. 61-73. Jossey-Bass Inc, Publishers, San Francisco, CA, US; 94 pp.<<SEE BOOK>>
Publication Year	PY: 1995
ISBN	IS: 0-7879-9939-3 (paperback)
Language	LA: English
Audience Type	AT: P1; Psychology: Pre-Professional/Undergraduate
Document Type	DT: 9300: Experimental Material
Update	UD: 9603
Descriptors	DE: SOCIAL-COMPARISON; STORYTELLING-; PSYCHOSOCIAL-DEVELOPMENT; PRESCHOOL-AGE-CHILDREN; CHILDHOOD-; SELF-CONCEPT
Classification Code	CC: 2840; 28
Population	PO: Human
Age Group	AG: Child
Content Representation	CR: (from the chapter) in conversational stories about personal experiences, young children and co-narrators use social comparisons to represent and mutually construct an understanding of themselves ...[*content representation continues*]
References	RF: References

Appendix C—Content Classification System

NOTE: This classification code system was designed to describe the content of the PsycINFO database, not the field of psychology.

2100 General Psychology
- **2140** History & Systems

2200 Psychometrics & Statistics & Methodology
- **2220** Tests & Testing
  - **2221** Sensory & Motor Testing
  - **2222** Developmental Scales & Schedules
  - **2223** Personality Scales & Inventories
  - **2224** Clinical Psychological Testing
  - **2225** Neuropsychological Assessment
  - **2226** Health Psychology Testing
  - **2227** Educational Measurement
  - **2228** Occupational & Employment Testing
  - **2229** Consumer Opinion & Attitude Testing
- **2240** Statistics & Mathematics
- **2260** Research Methods & Experimental Design

2300 Human Experimental Psychology
- **2320** Sensory Perception
  - **2323** Visual Perception
  - **2326** Auditory & Speech Perception
- **2330** Motor Processes
- **2340** Cognitive Processes
  - **2343** Learning & Memory
  - **2346** Attention
- **2360** Motivation & Emotion
- **2380** Consciousness States
- **2390** Parapsychology

2400 Animal Experimental & Comparative Psychology
- **2420** Learning & Motivation
- **2440** Social & Instinctive Behavior

2500 Physiological Psychology & Neuroscience
- **2510** Genetics
- **2520** Neuropsychology & Neurology
- **2530** Electrophysiology
- **2540** Physiological Processes
- **2560** Psychophysiology
- **2580** Psychopharmacology

2600 Psychology & the Humanities
- **2610** Literature & Fine Arts
- **2630** Philosophy

2700 Communication Systems
- **2720** Linguistics & Language & Speech
- **2750** Mass Media Communications

2800 Developmental Psychology
- **2820** Cognitive & Perceptual Development
- **2840** Psychosocial & Personality Development
- **2860** Gerontology

2900 Social Processes & Social Issues
- **2910** Social Structure & Organization
- **2920** Religion
- **2930** Culture & Ethnology
- **2950** Marriage & Family
  - **2953** Divorce & Remarriage
  - **2956** Childrearing & Child Care
- **2960** Political Processes & Political Issues
- **2970** Sex Roles & Womens Issues
- **2980** Sexual Behavior & Sexual Orientation
- **2990** Drug & Alcohol Usage (Legal)

3000 Social Psychology
- **3020** Group & Interpersonal Processes
- **3040** Social Perception & Cognition

3100 Personality Psychology
- **3120** Personality Traits & Processes
- **3140** Personality Theory
  - **3143** Psychoanalytic Theory

3200 Psychological & Physical Disorders
- **3210** Psychological Disorders
  - **3211** Affective Disorders
  - **3213** Schizophrenia & Psychotic States
  - **3215** Neuroses & Anxiety Disorders
  - **3217** Personality Disorders
- **3230** Behavior Disorders & Antisocial Behavior
  - **3233** Substance Abuse & Addiction
  - **3236** Criminal Behavior & Juvenile Delinquency
- **3250** Developmental Disorders & Autism
  - **3253** Learning Disorders
  - **3256** Mental Retardation
- **3260** Eating Disorders
- **3270** Speech & Language Disorders
- **3280** Environmental Toxins & Health
- **3290** Physical & Somatoform & Psychogenic Disorders
  - **3291** Immunological Disorders
  - **3293** Cancer
  - **3295** Cardiovascular Disorders
  - **3297** Neurological Disorders & Brain Damage
  - **3299** Vision & Hearing & Sensory Disorders

3300 Health & Mental Health Treatment & Prevention
- **3310** Psychotherapy & Psychotherapeutic Counseling
  - **3311** Cognitive Therapy
  - **3312** Behavior Therapy & Behavior Modification
  - **3313** Group & Family Therapy
  - **3314** Interpersonal & Client Centered & Humanistic Therapy
  - **3315** Psychoanalytic Therapy
- **3340** Clinical Psychopharmacology
- **3350** Specialized Interventions
  - **3351** Clinical Hypnosis
  - **3353** Self Help Groups
  - **3355** Lay & Paraprofessional & Pastoral Counseling
  - **3357** Art & Music & Movement Therapy
- **3360** Health Psychology & Medicine
  - **3361** Behavioral & Psychological Treatment of Physical Illness
  - **3363** Medical Treatment of Physical Illness
  - **3365** Promotion & Maintenance of Health & Wellness
- **3370** Health & Mental Health Services
  - **3371** Outpatient Services
  - **3373** Community & Social Services
  - **3375** Home Care & Hospice
  - **3377** Nursing Homes & Residential Care
  - **3379** Inpatient & Hospital Services
- **3380** Rehabilitation
  - **3383** Drug & Alcohol Rehabilitation
  - **3384** Occupational & Vocational Rehabilitation
  - **3385** Speech & Language Therapy
  - **3386** Criminal Rehabilitation & Penology

3400 Professional Psychological & Health Personnel Issues
- **3410** Professional Education & Training
- **3430** Professional Personnel Attitudes & Characteristics
- **3450** Professional Ethics & Standards & Liability
- **3470** Impaired Professionals

3500 Educational Psychology
- **3510** Educational Administration & Personnel
- **3530** Curriculum & Programs & Teaching Methods
- **3550** Academic Learning & Achievement
- **3560** Classroom Dynamics & Student Adjustment & Attitudes
- **3570** Special & Remedial Education
  - **3575** Gifted & Talented
- **3580** Educational/Vocational Counseling & Student Services

3600 Industrial & Organizational Psychology
- **3610** Occupational Interests & Guidance
- **3620** Personnel Management & Selection & Training
- **3630** Personnel Evaluation & Job Performance
- **3640** Management & Management Training
- **3650** Personnel Attitudes & Job Satisfaction
- **3660** Organizational Behavior
- **3670** Working Conditions & Industrial Safety

3700 Sport Psychology & Leisure
- **3720** Sports
- **3740** Recreation & Leisure

3800 Military Psychology

3900 Consumer Psychology
- **3920** Consumer Attitudes & Behavior
- **3940** Marketing & Advertising

4000 Engineering & Environmental Psychology
- **4010** Human Factors Engineering
- **4030** Lifespace & Institutional Design
- **4050** Community & Environmental Planning
- **4070** Environmental Issues & Attitudes
- **4090** Transportation

4100 Intelligent Systems
- **4120** Artificial Intelligence & Expert Systems
- **4140** Robotics
- **4160** Neural Networks

4200 Forensic Psychology & Legal Issues
- **4210** Civil Rights & Civil Law
- **4230** Criminal Law & Criminal Adjudication
- **4250** Mediation & Conflict Resolution
- **4270** Crime Prevention
- **4290** Police & Legal Personnel

Appendix D—PsycINFO ONLINE/ PsycLIT on CD-ROM Master Quick Reference Guide

The chart on the following two pages is a guide to the command syntax required to search Psyc-INFO and PsycLIT record fields on the online and CD-ROM vendor systems available at the time of this edition's publication.

The far-left column of the chart contains Psyc-INFO and PsycLIT field names. To find a field's corresponding label and search syntax, read across the field's row to the appropriate vendor column.

On PsycLIT, the syntax for subject searching of titles, descriptors, and classification codes is identical for journal articles, book chapters, and books, since these fields are common to the three types of records. Another source of chapter/book subject information is the content representation field, which is unique to chapter and book records, serving the same purpose as the journal-article abstract.

For complete information about searching, users should consult the *PsycINFO User Manual* or contact PsycINFO User Services to obtain vendor-specific documentation or searching information.

PsycINFO/PsycLIT MASTER QUICK REFERENCE GUIDE

PsycINFO/PsycLIT	NISC		DataStar		DIALOG	
FIELD NAME	**LABEL**	**SEARCH EXAMPLES**	**LABEL**	**SEARCH EXAMPLES**	**LABEL**	**SEARCH EXAMPLES**
Accession Number	ID	id=83-03187	.AN.	03222 adj 77-$2.an.	AN=	s an=77-03185
Title	TI	ti=affective style ti=proactive near3 organization	.TI.	electrical$2 adj stimulat$4.ti. cultur$2 same change$1.ti.	/TI	s hand()preference?/ti s dysfunct?(2n)famil?/ti
Author	AU	au=siever, l	.AU. ROOT	baumeister-r$.au. root vandenbos-g.au.	AU= E AU=	s au=baumeister, r? e au=siever, l
Author Affiliation	AF	af=st lawrence u	.IN.	u adj oregon same eugene.in.	CS=	s cs=(u()oregon(f)eugene)
Journal Name	JT SO	jt=american psychologist so=(eating and disorder*)	.SO. ROOT	new-england-journal-of-medicine.so. root social-work.so.	JN= E JN= SO=	s jn=journal of applied social? e jn=topics in early childhood s so=(private()practice)
Book Publisher	SO	so=mit press				
Publication Year	PY	py=1995 py=1990-1997 py=198?	.YR.	yr=93 85.yr. ..L 4 yr>92	PY=	s py=1993 s py=1985:1993 s s1/1990:1993
ISSN	IS	is=0112-3599	.IS.	0095-8964.is.	SN=	s sn=0219029
ISBN	IS	is=3-922016-71-5				
Update Code	UP	up=9606 up=97* up=(9601 or 9602 or 9603)	ED=	ed=90 ..L 5 ed>85	UD=	s ud=9103 s ud=9001:9999 s ud=91?
Language	LA	la=dutch la=english	.LG.	lg=en ge.lg. ..L 6 lg=fr	LA=	s la=french s s3/eng
Publication Type	PT	pt=journal article pt=literature review	.PT.	pt=j pt=10 pt=r	DT=	s dt=journal article s dt=dissertation s dt=review
Composite Age	AG	ag=adolescent	.AG.	adolescent.ag.	AG=	s ag=adult
Abstract		eating near mood*	.AB.	special adj education.ab. social$2 with perception$1.ab.	/AB	s diazepam/ab s guilt?(f)conscience/ab s wisc()r/ab
Book/Chapter Content Representation		helping adj behavior				
Descriptors						
All	KT	kt=assisted suicide	.DE.	military.de. concept-formation.de. impression-management	/DE	s schizophrenia/de s achievement motivation s child()relations/de s death "and" dying
Exploded (with narrower terms)	KT	kt=exp academic achievement		not available	!	s counseling!
Major	KM	km=depression [emotion]	.MJ.	professional-ethics.mj. accidents.mj. child adj relations.mj.	/DE*	s memory disorders/de* s phencyclidine/de*
Fixed Word/Phrase			.W..DE.	neurosis.w..de.	/DF	s health/df
Major Fixed Word/Phrase			.W..MJ.	personality.w..mj.	/DF*	s personality/df*
Descriptor Code			.SC.	01360.sc.	DC=	s dc=45440
Key Phrase	KP	kp=(corporate near2 culture)	.ID.	art same education.id.	/ID	corporate()moral?/id s computer(1n)litera?/id
Content Classification	CC	cc=3920 cc=(32* or 33*)	.CC.	3570.cc. 22#.cc. (32# or 33#).cc.	SH=	s sh=3570 s sh=32 s sh=(32 or 33)
Human/Animal	PO	po=human po=animal	H=Y H=N	..L 7 h=y ..L 8 h=n	/HUMAN /ANIMAL	s s1/human s emotion?/animal

DIMDI		SilverPlatter		OCLC-EPIC		OVID*	
LABEL	**SEARCH EXAMPLES**	**LABEL**	**SEARCH EXAMPLES**	**LABEL**	**SEARCH EXAMPLES**	**LABEL**	**SEARCH EXAMPLES**
ND=	find nd=77.3.7523	AN=	an=77-03185	NO	f no 79-05912	.AN.	63-10011.an.
/TI	find ft=substance abuse/ti find ft=child? # alcoholic?/ti	in TI	skinner box* in ti visual acuity in ti	TI	f ti social skill# f ti attention? n1 model#	.TI.	face recognition.ti. down? syndrome.ti.
AU= DISPLAY	find au=levy ? display au=siever, l?	in AU	gallo-robert* in au maslow-a* in au	AU= S AU=	f au=zotter d? s au=loftus e	.AU.	root siever.au. smith alan j.au. wilson william-$.au.
CS=	find cs=harvard medical school	in IN	george mason in in	CS	s cs johns hopkins	.IN.	case western.in
JT=	find jt=american journal of psychiatry find jt=diss?	in JN	journal-of-applied-social* in jn	SO= S SO=	f so=human development f so=psychology & aging s so=psychometri?	.JN. .JW.	psychobiology.jn behavior science$.jn. root american journal of.jn. brain.jw.
		in PB	plenum in pb			.PB.	wiley.pb.
PY=	find py=1992 find py>1985	PY=	py>=1989 py1987-1992 py=1985	YR	f yr 1990-1991 f yr 1987	.YR. ..L LIMIT TO	1994.yr. ; 1993.yr. ..L/1 yr=1994 limit 1 to yr=1993
SS=	find ss=0002953x	IS=	is=00219029	SN	f sn 0093-5301	.IS.	0065-1400.is.
		in IS	0-306-43318-4 in is			.IB.	0-8039-8603-3.ib.
ED=	find...(search)... and ed>01.88	UD=	ud=9103 ud>=9001 ud=9101-9112	UD	f ud 9301 f ud 9205-9301 f ud 9301-9912	..L LIMIT TO	..L/1up=y limit 1 to latest update limit 2 to up=9401-9412
LA=	find la=germ find la=engl	LA=	la=french la=english	LN=	f ln=swedish f ln=english f de motivation and ln=spanish	.LG. ..L LIMIT TO	fre.lg. ..L/1 en=-y limit 1 to english language
DT= DTC	find dt=review find...(search)...and dt=journal article find dtc=11	in DE	literature-review in de bibliography in de	DT	f dt bibliography f dt literature review	.PT. LIMIT TO	chapter.pt. ; journal article.pt. limit 1 to literature review
		AG=	ag=elderly	AG	f ag child	.PO. LIMIT TO	child.po. limit 1 to adult
/AB	find ft=diagnostic interview schedule/ab find ft=special education/ab find social? ? (perception; impression)/ab	in AB	methylphenidate in ab behavior* near modif* in ab mmpi 2 in ab	AB	f ab over (w1) counter f ab living will	.AB.	heroin addict$.ab. motor processes.ab. healing.ab.
		in CR	maternal employment in cr single parent* in cr			.CR.	trauma.cr. computer vision.cr.
CT= /CT	find ct=drug abuse find ct=?depression? ind ct=death a?d dying find ct=aged ?attitudes toward? find ct=disorders? find ft=drug abuse/ct	in DE	schizophrenia in de achievement-motivation in de child relations in de	DE	f de brain f de aged attitudes toward f de prisoners w1 war	.HW.	motor processes.hw. dysfunctional family.hw. military.hw.
CT DOWN	find ct down drug abuse	exp	exp psychotherapy		not available	exp	exp measurement/
				MJ	f mj schizophrenia f mj personnel	*/	*professional ethics/ *accidents/ *memory disorders/
CT=	find ct=color	in DE	health- in de [hyphen required]	DE=	f de=memory	.DE. .SH. /	psychotherapy.de. neurosis.sh. memory/
				MJ=	f mj=happiness	*/	*diabetes/
CC	find cc=15220			DE	f de 12510		
/UT	find ft=college students/ut	in KP	acquired immun* in kp factor* vailidity in kp computer near2 litera* in kp	ID	f id cognitive process? f id caregive?	.ID.	hearing impaired.id. mother$.id. freud's.id.
SC= SH=	find ft=33.4 find sc=23.2.3 find sc down 33 find sh=gerontology	CC=	cc=3570 cc=22	CC	f cc 22 f cc 3340 f cc (32 or 33)	.CC.	32.cc. 321.cc. 3800.cc.
PPS=	find PPS=animals	PO=	po=human po=animal	PO	f de memory and po human f ab fatigue and po animal	..L LIMIT TO	..L/1 hu=y ; ..L/1 hu=n limit 1 to animal

*Most commands selectable via pull-down menus.

RELATIONSHIP SECTION

Abandonment 97
PN 0 **SC** 00005
SN Loneliness, anxiety, and emotional and psychological loss of support resulting from desertion or neglect. Used for human populations.
UF Desertion
R Attachment Behavior 85
↓ Child Abuse 71
Child Neglect 88
Dependency (Personality) 67
↓ Emotional States 73
Loneliness 73
↓ Relationship Termination 97
Separation Anxiety 73
↓ Separation Reactions 97

Abdomen 73
PN 131 **SC** 00010
B Anatomy 67

Abdominal Wall 73
PN 7 **SC** 00020
B Muscles 67

Abducens Nerve 73
PN 17 **SC** 00030
UF Nerve (Abducens)
B Cranial Nerves 73

Ability 67
PN 2695 **SC** 00070
SN Conceptually broad array term referring to the skills, talents or qualities that enable one to perform a task. Use a more specific term if possible.
UF Aptitude
Skills
Talent
N Academic Aptitude 73
↓ Cognitive Ability 73
↓ Communication Skills 73
↓ Employee Skills 73
Learning Ability 73
↓ Nonverbal Ability 88
↓ Reading Skills 73
Self Care Skills 78
Social Skills 78
R Ability Grouping 73
Ability Level 78
↓ Achievement Potential 73
↓ Competence 82
Creativity 67
Gifted 67
Intelligence 67
↓ Performance 67

Ability Grouping 73
PN 288 **SC** 00040
SN Grouping or selection of individuals for instructional or other purposes based on differences in ability or achievement.
R ↓ Ability 67
Ability Level 78
Academic Aptitude 73
↓ Education 67
Educational Placement 78
Grade Level 94
Special Education 67

Ability Level 78
PN 797 **SC** 00050
SN Demonstrated level of performance. Used in academic, cognitive, perceptual, or occupational contexts.
R ↓ Ability 67
Ability Grouping 73
Adaptive Testing 85

Ability Tests
Use Aptitude Measures

Ablation
Use Lesions

Abortion (Induced)
Use Induced Abortion

Abortion (Spontaneous)
Use Spontaneous Abortion

Abortion Laws 73
PN 55 **SC** 00110
B Laws 67
R Induced Abortion 71

Abreaction
Use Catharsis

Absenteeism (Employee)
Use Employee Absenteeism

Absorption (Physiological) 73
PN 54 **SC** 00140
B Physiology 67
R Bioavailability 91
↓ Cells (Biology) 73
Intestines 73
Skin (Anatomy) 67

Abstinence (Drugs)
Use Drug Abstinence

Abstinence (Sexual)
Use Sexual Abstinence

Abstraction 67
PN 847 **SC** 00160
SN Process of selecting or isolating a certain conceptual aspect from a concrete whole.
B Thinking 67
N ↓ Imagery 67
R Divergent Thinking 73

Abuse of Power 97
PN 0 **SC** 00165
B Power 67
R Authority 67
Coercion 94
↓ Dominance 67
↓ Leadership 67

Abuse Potential (Drugs)
Use Drug Abuse Liability

Abuse Reporting 97
PN 0 **SC** 00180
N Child Abuse Reporting 97
R Battered Females 88
↓ Child Abuse 71
Elder Abuse 88
Informants 88
↓ Laws 67
Partner Abuse 91
Physical Abuse 91
Privileged Communication 73
Professional Ethics 73
↓ Sexual Abuse 88

Academic Achievement 67
PN 14935 **SC** 00190
UF Gradepoint Average
Scholastic Achievement
School Achievement
B Achievement 67

Academic Achievement — (cont'd)
N Academic Overachievement 67
Academic Underachievement 67
College Academic Achievement 67
Mathematics Achievement 73
Reading Achievement 73
Science Achievement 97
R Academic Achievement Motivation 73
Academic Achievement Prediction 67
Academic Aptitude 73
Academic Failure 78
Academic Self Concept 97
↓ Education 67
Educational Attainment Level 97
School Graduation 91
School Learning 67
School Transition 97

Academic Achievement Motivation 73
PN 1312 **SC** 00200
B Achievement Motivation 67
R ↓ Academic Achievement 67
Academic Self Concept 97

Academic Achievement Prediction 67
PN 2570 **SC** 00210
SN Prediction of future academic achievement based on results of tests, inventories, or other measures.
B Prediction 67
R ↓ Academic Achievement 67

Academic Aptitude 73
PN 1177 **SC** 00220
SN Potential ability to perform or achieve in scholastic pursuits.
UF Aptitude (Academic)
Scholastic Aptitude
B Ability 67
Achievement Potential 73
R Ability Grouping 73
↓ Academic Achievement 67
↓ Education 67
↓ Nonverbal Ability 88
Reading Ability 73
Student Admission Criteria 73
Verbal Ability 67

Academic Environment 73
PN 238 **SC** 00230
SN Physical setting or emotional climate where formal instruction takes place.
B Social Environments 73
N Classroom Environment 73
↓ School Environment 73

Academic Failure 78
PN 659 **SC** 00233
B Failure 67
R ↓ Academic Achievement 67
Academic Underachievement 67

Academic Grade Level
Use Grade Level

Academic Overachievement 67
PN 460 **SC** 00240
SN Academic achievement greater than that anticipated on basis of one's scholastic aptitude score or individual intelligence.
UF Overachievement (Academic)
B Academic Achievement 67

Academic Records
Use Student Records

Academic Self Concept 97
PN 0 **SC** 00248

Academic Self Concept — (cont'd)
B Self Concept [67]
R ↓ Academic Achievement [67]
Academic Achievement Motivation [73]
Self Confidence [94]
Self Efficacy [85]
Self Perception [67]

Academic Specialization [73]
PN 1548 SC 00250
SN Concentration of effort or interest in a special area of knowledge or discipline at an institution of learning.
UF College Major
Specialization (Academic)
R Educational Aspirations [73]
Professional Specialization [91]

Academic Underachievement [67]
PN 1403 SC 00260
SN Academic achievement less than that expected based on one's scholastic aptitude score or individual intelligence.
UF Underachievement (Academic)
B Academic Achievement [67]
R Academic Failure [78]
↓ Failure [67]

Acalculia [73]
PN 67 SC 00270
SN Form of aphasia involving impaired ability to perform simple arithmetic calculations.
UF Dyscalculia
B Aphasia [67]
R ↓ Learning Disabilities [73]

Accelerated Speech
Use Speech Rate

Acceleration Effects [73]
PN 144 SC 00290
SN Behavioral, physiological, or psychological effects resulting from acceleration onset/offset or the effects of changes in acceleration rate. Used for both human and animal populations.
R ↓ Aviation [67]
Decompression Effects [73]
Flight Simulation [73]
↓ Gravitational Effects [67]
Physiological Stress [67]
Spaceflight [67]

Acceptance (Social)
Use Social Acceptance

Accessory Nerve
Use Cranial Nerves

Accident Prevention [73]
PN 368 SC 00330
B Prevention [73]
R ↓ Accidents [67]
Risk Management [97]
↓ Safety [67]
↓ Transportation Accidents [73]
Warning Labels [97]
↓ Warnings [97]

Accident Proneness [73]
PN 143 SC 00340
R ↓ Accidents [67]
↓ Safety [67]

Accidents [67]
PN 540 SC 00350
N Home Accidents [73]
Industrial Accidents [73]
Pedestrian Accidents [73]

Accidents — (cont'd)
N ↓ Transportation Accidents [73]
R Accident Prevention [73]
Accident Proneness [73]
↓ Disasters [73]
Driving Under The Influence [88]
↓ Hazardous Materials [91]
Hazards [73]
↓ Injuries [73]
↓ Safety [67]
Warning Labels [97]
↓ Warnings [97]

Acclimatization (Thermal)
Use Thermal Acclimatization

Accomplishment
Use Achievement

Accountability [88]
PN 156 SC 00385
SN Liability and/or responsibility for specified results or outcomes of an activity over which one has authority.
B Responsibility [73]
R Blame [94]
↓ Competence [82]
Consumer Protection [73]
Criminal Responsibility [91]
↓ Management [67]
Professional Liability [85]
↓ Professional Standards [73]
Quality Control [88]
Quality of Care [88]

Accountants [73]
PN 193 SC 00390
UF Certified Public Accountants
B White Collar Workers [73]

Accreditation (Education Personnel) [73]
PN 64 SC 00400
SN Professional licensing or certification of teachers, school psychologists, or other educational personnel, usually required for employment.
UF Teacher Accreditation
B Professional Certification [73]
Professional Licensing [73]
R ↓ Education [67]
Educational Quality [97]
Professional Examinations [94]

Accreditation (Educational Programs)
Use Educational Program Accreditation

Acculturation
SN Term discontinued in 1982. Use ACCULTURATION or CULTURAL ASSIMILATION to access references from 73–81.
Use Cultural Assimilation

Acetaldehyde [82]
PN 53 SC 00415
SN First oxidation product of primary alcohol metabolism. Acetaldehyde has narcotic properties.
UF Acetic Aldehyde
Ethanal
Ethylaldehyde
R ↓ Alcohols [67]
↓ Carbohydrate Metabolism [73]
↓ Dopamine Metabolites [82]

Acetazolamide [73]
PN 20 SC 00420

Acetazolamide — (cont'd)
B Diuretics [73]
Enzyme Inhibitors [85]
R ↓ Anticonvulsive Drugs [73]

Acetic Aldehyde
Use Acetaldehyde

Acetylcholine [73]
PN 587 SC 00430
B Cholinergic Drugs [73]
Cholinomimetic Drugs [73]
Neurotransmitters [85]
R Acetylcholinesterase [73]
↓ Choline [73]
Cholinergic Nerves [73]

Acetylcholinesterase [73]
PN 202 SC 00440
B Esterases [73]
R Acetylcholine [73]
Cholinesterase [73]

Acetylsalicylic Acid
Use Aspirin

Aches
Use Pain

Achievement [67]
PN 2626 SC 00470
UF Accomplishment
Attainment (Achievement)
Success
N ↓ Academic Achievement [67]
Occupational Success [78]
R ↓ Achievement Measures [67]
↓ Competence [82]
↓ Failure [67]
↓ Performance [67]

Achievement Measures [67]
PN 1847 SC 00490
SN Tests designed to measure knowledge and/or skills acquired from learning, experience, or training.
UF Tests (Achievement)
B Measurement [67]
N Iowa Tests of Basic Skills [73]
Stanford Achievement Test [73]
Wide Range Achievement Test [73]
Woodcock Johnson Psychoed Battery [94]
R ↓ Achievement [67]
Criterion Referenced Tests [82]

Achievement Motivation [67]
PN 3038 SC 00500
SN Need that drives an individual to improve, succeed, or excel.
UF NAch
Need Achievement
B Motivation [67]
N Academic Achievement Motivation [73]
R ↓ Achievement Potential [73]
Fear of Success [78]
↓ Needs [67]

Achievement Potential [73]
PN 103 SC 00510
SN One's general ability to achieve in any area, including academic.
UF Potential (Achievement)
N Academic Aptitude [73]
R ↓ Ability [67]
↓ Achievement Motivation [67]

Achilles Tendon Reflex [73]
PN 13 **SC** 00520
B Reflexes [71]

Achromatic Color [73]
PN 95 **SC** 00530
SN Visual quality which lacks hue and saturation, consequently varying only in brilliance. Includes variations from black through gray to white.
B Color [67]
R ↓ Chromaticity [97]
Color Saturation [97]

Acids [73]
PN 455 **SC** 00550
N ↓ Amino Acids [73]
Ascorbic Acid [73]
Aspirin [73]
Dihydroxyphenylacetic Acid [91]
↓ Fatty Acids [73]
Heparin [73]
Homovanillic Acid [78]
Hydroxyindoleacetic Acid (5-) [85]
Kainic Acid [88]
Lactic Acid [91]
Lysergic Acid Diethylamide [67]
Nicotinic Acid [73]
↓ Nucleic Acids [73]
Taurine [82]
Uric Acid [73]
R ↓ Drugs [67]
↓ Solvents [82]

Acoustic Nerve [73]
PN 78 **SC** 00570
UF Auditory Nerve
Nerve (Acoustic)
B Cranial Nerves [73]

Acoustic Reflex [73]
PN 306 **SC** 00580
SN Bilateral contraction of stapedius muscles when a loud sound is presented.
UF Intra Aural Muscle Reflex
Stapedius Reflex
B Reflexes [71]
R Startle Reflex [67]

Acoustic Stimuli
Use Auditory Stimulation

Acoustics [97]
PN 0 **SC** 00591
SN Structural properties of auditorially perceived stimuli or sounds.
UF Sound Waves
R ↓ Auditory Perception [67]
↓ Auditory Stimulation [67]
Noise Effects [73]
↓ Speech Characteristics [73]
↓ Stimulus Parameters [67]

Acquaintance Rape [91]
PN 103 **SC** 00593
SN Rape perpetrated by a person or persons known to the victim.
UF Date Rape
B Rape [73]
R ↓ Human Courtship [73]
Social Dating [73]

Acquired Immune Deficiency Syndrome [88]
PN 3438 **SC** 00595
UF AIDS
B Human Immunodeficiency Virus [91]
Syndromes [73]

Acquired Immune Deficiency Syndrome — (cont'd)
R AIDS (Attitudes Toward) [97]
AIDS Dementia Complex [97]
AIDS Prevention [94]
HIV Testing [97]
↓ Venereal Diseases [73]
Zidovudine [94]

Acrophobia [73]
PN 42 **SC** 00600
SN Fear of heights.
B Phobias [67]

ACTH (Hormone)
Use Corticotropin

ACTH Releasing Factor
Use Corticotropin Releasing Factor

Acting Out [67]
PN 431 **SC** 00620
SN Behavioral manifestation of those impulses and desires that are unacceptable or irreconcilable with an individual's conscience. When such behavior becomes maladaptive, socially or personally, it is classified as an acting out disorder.
B Symptoms [67]
R ↓ Behavior Disorders [71]
↓ Emotionally Disturbed [73]
Enactments [97]

Active Avoidance
Use Avoidance Conditioning

Activism (Student)
Use Student Activism

Activist Movements [73]
PN 282 **SC** 00650
SN Doctrines or practices emphasizing direct, vigorous action (usually political) in support of or opposition to one side of a controversial issue.
B Social Movements [67]
N Student Activism [73]
R Black Power Movement [73]
Civil Rights Movement [73]
Homosexual Liberation Movement [73]
School Integration [82]
↓ Social Integration [82]
Womens Liberation Movement [73]

Activities of Daily Living [91]
PN 448 **SC** 00655
SN Basic personal care skills such as eating, bathing, dressing, and other personal hygenic skills used to measure functional ability in the elderly and the emotionally and physically disabled. Compare DAILY ACTIVITIES.
R Activity Level [82]
Daily Activities [94]
↓ Disabled [97]
Geriatric Assessment [97]
Habilitation [91]
Hygiene [94]
Independent Living Programs [91]
Physical Mobility [94]
↓ Rehabilitation [67]
Self Care Skills [78]

Activity Level [82]
PN 4285 **SC** 00660
SN General energetic state of an organism, frequently used as a measure of drug effects but not restricted to this application.
B Motor Processes [67]
R Activities of Daily Living [91]
Daily Activities [94]

Activity Level — (cont'd)
R ↓ Motivation [67]
Physical Mobility [94]
Rotational Behavior [94]

Activity Therapy
Use Recreation Therapy

Actualization (Self)
Use Self Actualization

Acupuncture [73]
PN 276 **SC** 00690
B Alternative Medicine [97]
Physical Treatment Methods [73]

Acute Alcoholic Intoxication [73]
PN 29 **SC** 00700
SN Temporary mental disturbance marked by muscle incoordination and paresis as the result of excessive alcohol ingestion.
B Alcohol Intoxication [73]
Brain Disorders [67]
Toxic Disorders [73]
R Toxic Encephalopathies [73]

Acute Paranoid Disorder
Use Paranoia (Psychosis)

Acute Psychosis [73]
PN 191 **SC** 00710
SN Use ACUTE PSYCHOTIC EPISODE to access references from 73–87.
UF Acute Psychotic Episode
Brief Reactive Psychosis
Psychotic Episode (Acute)
B Psychosis [67]
N Acute Schizophrenia [73]
R Postpartum Depression [73]

Acute Psychotic Episode
SN Term discontinued in 1988. Use ACUTE PSYCHOTIC EPISODE to access references from 73-87.
Use Acute Psychosis

Acute Schizophrenia [73]
PN 534 **SC** 00730
B Acute Psychosis [73]
Schizophrenia [67]
R Postpartum Depression [73]

Adaptability (Personality) [73]
PN 429 **SC** 00740
SN Ability to be flexible and to maximize functioning in the face of environmental changes. See ADJUSTMENT for terms relating to the process of adapting.
UF Flexibility (Personality)
B Personality Traits [67]
R ↓ Adjustment [67]
Agreeableness [97]
Coping Behavior [67]
Hardiness [97]
Openness to Experience [97]

Adaptation [67]
PN 907 **SC** 00750
SN Physiological or biological modification of an organism or its morphology in response to the physical environment. For psychological, social, or emotional adaptation, use ADJUSTMENT or one of its narrower or related terms.
UF Readaptation
N Environmental Adaptation [73]
↓ Sensory Adaptation [67]
Thermal Acclimatization [73]

Adaptation (Dark)
Use Dark Adaptation

Adaptation (Environmental)
Use Environmental Adaptation

Adaptation (Light)
Use Light Adaptation

Adaptation (Sensory)
Use Sensory Adaptation

Adaptation (Social)
Use Social Adjustment

Adaptive Behavior [91]
PN 192 **SC** 00793
SN Behaviors indicating ability to take care of personal needs, function socially, and control problem behavior. Primarily used for disabled or disordered populations.
B Behavior [67]
R ↓ Adjustment [67]
↓ Disabled [97]
↓ Mental Disorders [67]
↓ Mental Retardation [67]
↓ Mentally Retarded [67]
↓ Rehabilitation [67]
Self Care Skills [78]
Social Skills [78]
Special Education [67]

Adaptive Testing [85]
PN 98 **SC** 00795
SN Testing method, usually using a computer, in which test items of varying difficulty levels are selected according to the degree to which the examinee's previous answers were correct.
UF Tailored Testing
B Testing Methods [67]
R Ability Level [78]
Computer Assisted Testing [88]
Item Analysis (Statistical) [73]
↓ Test Construction [73]

Addiction [73]
PN 334 **SC** 00800
B Behavior Disorders [71]
N ↓ Alcoholism [67]
↓ Drug Addiction [67]
Sexual Addiction [97]
R Craving [97]
↓ Drug Abuse [73]
↓ Drug Usage [71]
Pathological Gambling [88]

Addisons Disease [73]
PN 12 **SC** 00810
B Adrenal Gland Disorders [73]
Syndromes [73]
R ↓ Tuberculosis [73]

Adenosine [73]
PN 320 **SC** 00820
B Nucleic Acids [73]

Adjectives [73]
PN 343 **SC** 00830
B Form Classes (Language) [73]

Adjudication [67]
PN 2887 **SC** 00840
SN Process of judicial decision-making. Use ADJUDICATION to access references to juries from 67-84.
UF Courts
Juvenile Court
Sentencing

Adjudication — (cont'd)
UF Verdict Determination
B Law Enforcement [78]
N Court Referrals [94]
R Case Law [85]
Criminal Conviction [73]
↓ Criminal Justice [91]
Criminal Responsibility [91]
Juries [85]
Jury Selection [94]
Legal Decisions [91]
↓ Legal Evidence [91]

Adjunctive Behavior [82]
PN 49 **SC** 00845
SN Noncontingent appropriate or inappropriate behavior that is maintained by an event which acquires its reinforcing characteristics as the result of some other ongoing reinforcement contingency.
B Behavior [67]
N Polydipsia [82]
R ↓ Operant Conditioning [67]
Pica [73]

Adjustment [67]
PN 5618 **SC** 00850
SN Conceptually broad array term referring to a state of harmony between internal needs and external demands and the processes used in achieving this condition. Use a more specific term if possible. Differentiate from ADAPTATION, which refers to physiological or biological adaptation.
N ↓ Emotional Adjustment [73]
Occupational Adjustment [73]
School Adjustment [67]
Social Adjustment [73]
R Adaptability (Personality) [73]
Adaptive Behavior [91]
Person Environment Fit [91]
Well Being [94]
Work Adjustment Training [91]

Adjustment Disorders [94]
PN 15 **SC** 00855
SN Maladaptive reaction to psychosocial stressors which impairs social or occupational functioning. Usually a temporary condition that remits after new levels of adaptation are obtained or stressors have been removed.
B Mental Disorders [67]
R Coping Behavior [67]
↓ Emotional Adjustment [73]
Emotional Trauma [67]
Occupational Adjustment [73]
Posttraumatic Stress Disorder [85]
School Adjustment [67]
Social Adjustment [73]
↓ Stress [67]
Stress Reactions [73]

Adler (Alfred) [67]
PN 250 **SC** 00860
SN Identifies biographical or autobiographical studies and discussions of Adler's works.
R Adlerian Psychotherapy [97]
Individual Psychology [73]
↓ Psychologists [67]

Adlerian Psychotherapy [97]
PN 0 **SC** 00865
SN Use INDIVIDUAL PSYCHOTHERAPY to access references from 91-96.
UF Individual Psychotherapy (Adlerian)
B Psychoanalysis [67]
Psychotherapy [67]
R Adler (Alfred) [67]
Individual Psychology [73]

Administration (Test)
Use Test Administration

Administrators
Use Management Personnel

Administrators (School)
Use School Administrators

Admission (Hospital)
Use Hospital Admission

Admission (Psychiatric Hospital)
Use Psychiatric Hospital Admission

Admission Criteria (Student)
Use Student Admission Criteria

Adolescence [84]
PN 58378 **SC** 00920
SN Mandatory age identifier used for ages 13-17. Where appropriate, more specific index terms (e.g., HIGH SCHOOL STUDENTS) are used in addition to this age identifier. The other two age identifiers are ADULTHOOD and CHILDHOOD.
R ↓ Adolescents [67]
Preadolescents [88]

Adolescent Attitudes [88]
PN 1775 **SC** 00925
SN Attitudes of, not toward, adolescents.
B Attitudes [67]
R ↓ Adolescents [67]

Adolescent Development [73]
PN 2529 **SC** 00930
SN Process of physical, cognitive, personality, and psychosocial growth occurring from age 13 through 17. Use a more specific term if possible.
B Human Development [67]
R ↓ Adolescents [67]
↓ Childhood Development [67]
↓ Developmental Age Groups [73]
↓ Developmental Stages [73]
↓ Physical Development [73]
↓ Psychogenesis [73]
Sex Linked Developmental Differences [73]
Sexual Development [73]

Adolescent Fathers [85]
PN 90 **SC** 00932
SN Fathers aged 13-17 years.
UF Teenage Fathers
B Adolescents [67]
Fathers [67]
R Adolescent Pregnancy [88]

Adolescent Mothers [85]
PN 613 **SC** 00935
SN Mothers aged 13–17 years. Consider also UNWED MOTHERS.
UF Teenage Mothers
B Adolescents [67]
Mothers [67]
R Adolescent Pregnancy [88]

Adolescent Pregnancy [88]
PN 475 **SC** 00936
UF Teenage Pregnancy
B Pregnancy [67]
R Adolescent Fathers [85]
Adolescent Mothers [85]
↓ Social Issues [91]

Adolescent Psychiatry [85]
PN 180 **SC** 00937

Adolescent Psychiatry — (cont'd)
B Psychiatry [67]
R Adolescent Psychotherapy [94]

Adolescent Psychology [73]
PN 80 SC 00940
SN Branch of developmental psychology devoted to the study and treatment of adolescents. Use a more specific term if possible.
B Developmental Psychology [73]

Adolescent Psychotherapy [94]
PN 102 SC 00945
B Psychotherapy [67]
R Adolescent Psychiatry [85]
↓ Child Psychotherapy [67]

Adolescents [67]
PN 27228 SC 00950
SN Ages 13–17 years. Used in noneducational contexts. Application of terms designating age is mandatory for ages 0–17.
UF Teenagers
Youth (Adolescents)
B Developmental Age Groups [73]
N Adolescent Fathers [85]
Adolescent Mothers [85]
R Adolescence [84]
Adolescent Attitudes [88]
Adolescent Development [73]
↓ College Students [67]
High School Graduates [78]
High School Students [67]
Junior High School Students [71]
↓ Juvenile Delinquents [73]
Preadolescents [88]
Predelinquent Youth [78]
Vocational School Students [73]
Young Adults [73]

Adopted Children [73]
PN 490 SC 00960
B Adoptees [85]
Family Members [73]
R ↓ Adoption (Child) [67]
↓ Children [67]
Interracial Adoption [94]

Adoptees [85]
PN 160 SC 00965
SN Anyone who has been formally adopted as a dependent. Limited to human populations.
N Adopted Children [73]
R ↓ Adoption (Child) [67]
Interracial Adoption [94]

Adoption (Child) [67]
PN 574 SC 00970
B Legal Processes [73]
N Interracial Adoption [94]
R Adopted Children [73]
↓ Adoptees [85]
Adoptive Parents [73]
Child Welfare [88]

Adoptive Parents [73]
PN 300 SC 00980
B Parents [67]
R ↓ Adoption (Child) [67]
Interracial Adoption [94]

Adrenal Cortex Hormones [73]
PN 117 SC 00990
B Hormones [67]
N Aldosterone [73]
Corticosterone [73]
Cortisone [73]
Deoxycorticosterone [73]

Adrenal Cortex Hormones — (cont'd)
N ↓ Glucocorticoids [82]
Hydrocortisone [73]
Prednisolone [73]
R ↓ Adrenal Glands [73]
↓ Adrenal Medulla Hormones [73]
↓ Corticosteroids [73]
↓ Stress [67]

Adrenal Cortex Steroids
Use Corticosteroids

Adrenal Gland Disorders [73]
PN 38 SC 01010
B Endocrine Disorders [73]
N Addisons Disease [73]
Cushings Syndrome [73]
R ↓ Endocrine Sexual Disorders [73]
↓ Pituitary Disorders [73]

Adrenal Gland Secretion [73]
PN 64 SC 01020
B Endocrine Gland Secretion [73]

Adrenal Glands [73]
PN 391 SC 01030
B Endocrine Glands [73]
N Hypothalamo Pituitary Adrenal System [97]
R ↓ Adrenal Cortex Hormones [73]

Adrenal Medulla Hormones [73]
PN 30 SC 01040
B Hormones [67]
N Norepinephrine [73]
R ↓ Adrenal Cortex Hormones [73]

Adrenalectomy [73]
PN 329 SC 01050
B Endocrine Gland Surgery [73]

Adrenaline
Use Epinephrine

Adrenergic Blocking Drugs [73]
PN 884 SC 01070
UF Beta Blockers
B Drugs [67]
N Alpha Methylparatyrosine [78]
Dihydroergotamine [73]
Hydroxydopamine (6-) [78]
Phenoxybenzamine [73]
Propranolol [73]
Yohimbine [88]
R ↓ Antihypertensive Drugs [73]
↓ Ergot Derivatives [73]
↓ Sympathetic Nervous System [73]
↓ Sympatholytic Drugs [73]
↓ Tricyclic Antidepressant Drugs [97]

Adrenergic Drugs [73]
PN 313 SC 01080
UF Adrenolytic Drugs
B Drugs [67]
N ↓ Amphetamine [67]
Dextroamphetamine [73]
Ephedrine [73]
Epinephrine [67]
Methoxamine [73]
Tyramine [73]
R ↓ Catecholamines [73]
Serotonin [73]
↓ Sympathetic Nervous System [73]
↓ Sympathomimetic Drugs [73]

Adrenergic Nerves [73]
PN 241 SC 01090

Adrenergic Nerves — (cont'd)
UF Nerves (Adrenergic)
B Autonomic Nervous System [67]

Adrenocorticotropin
Use Corticotropin

Adrenolytic Drugs
SN Term discontinued in 1997. Use ADRENOLYTIC DRUGS to access references from 73–96.
Use Adrenergic Drugs

Adult Attitudes [88]
PN 3766 SC 01122
SN Attitudes of, not toward, adults.
B Attitudes [67]
R ↓ Adults [67]

Adult Children
Use Adult Offspring

Adult Day Care [97]
PN 0 SC 01125
SN In home- or center-based care of physically or mentally disabled adults during daytime hours, providing personal, social, and homemaker services.
R Day Care Centers [73]
Elder Care [94]
Home Care [85]
Home Visiting Programs [73]
Long Term Care [94]

Adult Development [78]
PN 1808 SC 01127
SN Process of physical, cognitive, personality, and psychosocial growth occurring from age 18. Use a more specific term if possible.
B Human Development [67]
R Adult Learning [97]
↓ Adults [67]
↓ Aged [73]
↓ Developmental Age Groups [73]
↓ Developmental Stages [73]
Mentor [85]
Middle Aged [73]
Physiological Aging [67]
↓ Psychogenesis [73]
Young Adults [73]

Adult Education [73]
PN 1282 SC 01130
SN Formal or informal education for adults, including but not limited to basic education, high school equivalency, vocational education, correspondence courses, continuing education, nondegree coursework, and lifelong learning programs.
UF High School Equivalency
B Education [67]
N ↓ Continuing Education [85]
R Adult Learning [97]
Literacy Programs [97]
Reentry Students [85]

Adult Learning [97]
PN 0 SC 01133
B Learning [67]
R Adult Development [78]
↓ Adult Education [73]
↓ Continuing Education [85]
Reentry Students [85]

Adult Offspring [85]
PN 1550 SC 01135
SN Ages 18 or older.

Adult Offspring — (cont'd)
UF Adult Children
Grown Children
B Adults [67]
Family Members [73]
Offspring [88]
R Empty Nest [91]

Adultery
Use Extramarital Intercourse

Adulthood [84]
PN 287638 **SC** 01150
SN Mandatory age identifier used for ages 18 or older. Where appropriate, more specific index terms (e.g., MIDDLE AGED) are used in addition to this age identifier. The other two age identifiers are ADOLESCENCE and CHILDHOOD.
R ↓ Adults [67]

Adults [67]
PN 4225 **SC** 01160
SN Ages 18 years or older. Used in noneducational contexts. Applied only if age is important to the research focus.
B Developmental Age Groups [73]
N Adult Offspring [85]
↓ Aged [73]
Middle Aged [73]
Young Adults [73]
R Adult Attitudes [88]
Adult Development [78]
Adulthood [84]

Advance Directives [94]
PN 35 **SC** 01163
SN Declaration of personal wishes through legal documents or written instructions pertaining to future medical care if one becomes incapacitated.
UF Living Wills
R Assisted Suicide [97]
↓ Client Rights [88]
↓ Death and Dying [67]
Euthanasia [73]
↓ Legal Processes [73]
Life Sustaining Treatment [97]
Palliative Care [91]
Terminally Ill Patients [73]
Treatment Refusal [94]
Treatment Withholding [88]

Advance Organizers [85]
PN 166 **SC** 01165
SN Structural overview of material to be taught to facilitate incorporation of new material into that previously learned or known.
UF Structured Overview
B Instructional Media [67]
Teaching Methods [67]
R ↓ Learning Strategies [91]
Study Habits [73]

Adventitiously Disabled [97]
PN 0 **SC** 01167
SN Persons with disabilities resulting from illness or injury during developmental or adult years. Use ADVENTITIOUSLY HANDICAPPED to access references from 73–96.
UF Adventitiously Handicapped
B Disabled [97]
R Congenitally Disabled [97]

Adventitiously Handicapped
SN Term discontinued in 1997. Use ADVENTITIOUSLY HANDICAPPED to access references from 73–96.
Use Adventitiously Disabled

Adverbs [73]
PN 50 **SC** 01180
B Form Classes (Language) [73]

Advertising [67]
PN 1729 **SC** 01190
N Television Advertising [73]
R Brand Names [78]
Brand Preferences [94]
↓ Consumer Research [73]
Marketing [73]
↓ Mass Media [67]
Product Design [97]
Public Relations [73]
↓ Quality of Services [97]
Retailing [91]

Advocacy [85]
PN 346 **SC** 01195
SN The process of defending or pleading the cause of another individual or group.
UF Child Advocacy
R Child Welfare [88]
↓ Civil Rights [78]
Empowerment [91]
↓ Government Policy Making [73]
Legislative Processes [73]
Right to Treatment [97]

Aerobic Exercise [88]
PN 289 **SC** 01197
B Exercise [73]
R Health Behavior [82]
Physical Fitness [73]
Weight Control [85]

Aerospace Personnel [73]
PN 312 **SC** 01200
UF Aircraft Crew
Aviation Personnel
Flight Attendants
Navigators (Aircraft)
B Professional Personnel [78]
N Aircraft Pilots [73]
Astronauts [73]
R ↓ Business and Industrial Personnel [67]
Engineers [67]
Physicists [73]
Scientists [67]

Aesthetic Preferences [73]
PN 1062 **SC** 01210
B Preferences [67]
R Aesthetics [67]
Interior Design [82]

Aesthetics [67]
PN 813 **SC** 01220
SN Scientific or philosophical study of beauty or judgments of beauty. Also, the aesthetic qualities themselves.
R Aesthetic Preferences [73]
↓ Arts [73]
Interior Design [82]

Aetiology
Use Etiology

Affairs (Sexual)
Use Extramarital Intercourse

Affection [73]
PN 365 **SC** 01250
UF Liking
B Emotional States [73]
R ↓ Interpersonal Interaction [67]
Intimacy [73]
Love [73]

Affection — (cont'd)
R Physical Contact [82]
↓ Psychosexual Behavior [67]
Romance [97]
Sexuality [73]

Affective Disorders
Use Affective Disturbances

Affective Disturbances [67]
PN 3670 **SC** 01260
UF Affective Disorders
Mood Disorders
B Neurosis [67]
N ↓ Major Depression [88]
↓ Mania [67]
↓ Manic Depression [73]
Schizoaffective Disorder [94]
Seasonal Affective Disorder [91]
R Alexithymia [82]
↓ Anxiety Disorders [97]

Affective Education [82]
PN 390 **SC** 01265
SN Curriculum aimed at changing emotional and social behavior of students and enhancing their understanding of such behavior.
UF Humanistic Education
B Curriculum [67]
R Self Actualization [73]
↓ Self Concept [67]
Social Skills [78]

Affective Psychosis [73]
PN 288 **SC** 01270
B Psychosis [67]
N Involutional Depression [73]
R ↓ Manic Depression [73]

Afferent Pathways [82]
PN 741 **SC** 01275
SN Collections of fibers that carry neural impulses toward neural processing areas from sensory mechanisms or other processing areas.
UF Sensory Pathways
B Neural Pathways [82]
N ↓ Lemniscal System [85]
Spinothalamic Tracts [73]
R Dorsal Horns [85]
↓ Efferent Pathways [82]
↓ Receptive Fields [85]
↓ Sensory Neurons [73]

Afferent Stimulation [73]
PN 116 **SC** 01280
SN Sensory stimulation causing nerve impulses to be carried toward the brain, spinal cord, or sensory relay and processing areas.
UF Afferentation
B Stimulation [67]
R ↓ Nervous System [67]
↓ Perceptual Stimulation [73]
↓ Stereotaxic Techniques [73]
↓ Surgery [71]

Afferentation
Use Afferent Stimulation

Affiliation Motivation [67]
PN 563 **SC** 01300
SN Need for association with others and formation of friendships.
UF Need for Affiliation
B Motivation [67]
R ↓ Needs [67]

Affirmative Action [85]
PN 132 **SC** 01305

Affirmative Action — (cont'd)
SN Programs or policies designed to actively recruit females and minority group members for employment or higher education, in an effort to correct underrepresentative distributions of these groups relative to the general population.
R Age Discrimination [94]
↓ Civil Rights [78]
Disability Discrimination [97]
Employment Discrimination [94]
Minority Groups [67]
↓ Personnel [67]
↓ Personnel Management [73]
↓ Personnel Recruitment [73]
↓ Personnel Selection [67]
Race and Ethnic Discrimination [94]
Sex Discrimination [78]
↓ Social Discrimination [82]
Social Equality [73]

Afghanistan [88]
PN 7 **SC** 01307
B Asia [73]

Africa [67]
PN 1731 **SC** 01310
N Algeria [88]
Angola [88]
Benin [91]
Botswana [88]
Cameroon [91]
Congo [91]
East Africa [88]
Egypt [82]
Ethiopia [82]
Ghana [88]
Guinea [91]
Ivory Coast [88]
Kenya [82]
Liberia [91]
Libya [88]
Malawi [91]
Mali [91]
Morocco [88]
Mozambique [88]
Niger [91]
Nigeria [82]
Rwanda [91]
Senegal [88]
Sierra Leone [88]
Somalia [91]
South Africa [82]
Sudan [88]
Swaziland [91]
Tanzania [82]
Tunisia [91]
Uganda [88]
West Africa [88]
Zaire [88]
Zambia [82]
Zimbabwe [88]
R Madagascar [91]
Mauritius [91]
Middle East [78]

African Americans
Use Blacks

Aftercare [73]
PN 504 **SC** 01320
SN Continuing program of rehabilitation designed to reinforce and maintain the effects of treatment and to help clients adjust to their environment after hospital release.
B Treatment [67]
R Discharge Planning [94]
Maintenance Therapy [97]
Outpatient Commitment [91]
↓ Outpatient Treatment [67]

Aftercare — (cont'd)
R Partial Hospitalization [85]
Posttreatment Followup [73]
↓ Treatment Planning [97]

Aftereffect (Perceptual)
Use Perceptual Aftereffect

Afterimage [67]
PN 240 **SC** 01340
SN Persistence of sensory excitation, usually visual, after cessation of stimulation. This temporary illusory sensation is due to physiological changes in the receptor cells.
UF Successive Contrast
B Perceptual Aftereffect [67]

Age Differences [67]
PN 28924 **SC** 01360
SN Age comparisons of behavioral, developmental, and cognitive variations between individuals or groups. Used for human or animal subjects. Consider also DEVELOPMENTAL DIFFERENCES to access references prior to 1982.
UF Developmental Differences
R Animal Development [78]
Cohort Analysis [88]
↓ Development [67]
↓ Developmental Age Groups [73]
Generation Gap [73]
Grade Level [94]
↓ Human Development [67]
↓ Physical Development [73]
↓ Psychogenesis [73]

Age Discrimination [94]
PN 10 **SC** 01363
SN Use SOCIAL DISCRIMINATION to access references from 82-93.
B Social Discrimination [82]
R Affirmative Action [85]
Aged (Attitudes Toward) [78]
Aging (Attitudes Toward) [85]
↓ Civil Rights [78]
Employment Discrimination [94]
↓ Prejudice [67]
Stereotyped Attitudes [67]

Age Regression (Hypnotic) [88]
PN 44 **SC** 01365
SN Technique used to recapture early or past life experiences by guiding clients back through their history, usually year by year.
B Hypnosis [67]
Hypnotherapy [73]
R Early Experience [67]
Early Memories [85]
Enactments [97]
False Memory [97]
Life Experiences [73]
↓ Psychotherapeutic Techniques [67]
Repressed Memory [97]

Aged [73]
PN 34013 **SC** 01370
SN Ages 65 years or older. Use GERIATRICS or GERONTOLOGY to access references from 67–72.
UF Old Age
Senescence
Senior Citizens
B Adults [67]
N Very Old [88]
R Adult Development [78]
Aged (Attitudes Toward) [78]
↓ Aging [91]
Elder Abuse [88]
Elder Care [94]
Geriatric Patients [73]

Aged — (cont'd)
R Geriatrics [67]
Gerontology [67]
Homebound [88]
Physiological Aging [67]
↓ Senile Dementia [73]

Aged (Attitudes Toward) [78]
PN 842 **SC** 01372
B Attitudes [67]
R Age Discrimination [94]
↓ Aged [73]
↓ Aging [91]
Aging (Attitudes Toward) [85]
Geriatrics [67]
Gerontology [67]
Physiological Aging [67]
Very Old [88]

Agencies (Groups)
Use Organizations

Aggressive Behavior [67]
PN 6502 **SC** 01390
UF Agonistic Behavior
Fighting
B Social Behavior [67]
N ↓ Animal Aggressive Behavior [73]
Attack Behavior [73]
Coercion [94]
↓ Conflict [67]
R ↓ Behavior Disorders [71]
Conduct Disorder [91]
Cruelty [73]
Retaliation [91]
↓ Social Interaction [67]
Torture [88]

Aggressiveness [73]
PN 1160 **SC** 01400
B Personality Traits [67]

Agility (Physical)
Use Physical Agility

Aging [91]
PN 925 **SC** 01413
N Physiological Aging [67]
R ↓ Aged [73]
Aged (Attitudes Toward) [78]
Aging (Attitudes Toward) [85]
↓ Developmental Age Groups [73]
↓ Developmental Stages [73]
Geriatric Psychiatry [97]
Geriatric Psychotherapy [73]
Geriatrics [67]
Gerontology [67]
↓ Human Development [67]
Life Expectancy [82]
Middle Aged [73]
Very Old [88]

Aging (Attitudes Toward) [85]
PN 270 **SC** 01415
SN Attitudes toward the aging process. Includes attitudes toward one's own physical aging and psychological and social maturation.
B Attitudes [67]
R Age Discrimination [94]
Aged (Attitudes Toward) [78]
↓ Aging [91]
↓ Physical Development [73]
Physiological Aging [67]
↓ Psychosocial Development [73]
Self Perception [67]

Aging (Physiological)
Use Physiological Aging

Agitated Depression
SN Use DEPRESSION (EMOTION) to access references from 73-87.
Use Major Depression

Agitation 91
PN 123 **SC** 01440
SN State usually characterized by restlessness, anxiety, and anguish.
R Akathisia 91
↓ Anxiety 67
Distress 73
Restlessness 73

Agnosia 73
PN 224 **SC** 01450
SN Inability to recognize, understand, or interpret sensory stimuli in the absence of sensory defects. Also, the selective loss of knowledge of specific objects due to emotional disturbance, as seen in schizophrenia, hysteria, or depression.
B Aphasia 67
Perceptual Disturbances 73
N Anosognosia 94
Prosopagnosia 94

Agonistic Behavior
Use Aggressive Behavior

Agoraphobia 73
PN 1366 **SC** 01480
SN Excessive fear of being alone, or being in public places or situations (e.g., in crowds or elevators) from which there is no easy escape or where help cannot be obtained in the event of an incapacitating reaction or panic.
B Phobias 67

Agrammatism
Use Aphasia

Agraphia 73
PN 148 **SC** 01490
SN Inability to write (letters, syllables, words, or phrases) due to an injury to a specific cerebral area or occasionally due to emotional factors.
B Aphasia 67
R ↓ Learning Disabilities 73

Agreeableness 97
PN 0 **SC** 01495
SN Extent to which an individual is altruistic, sympathetic to others and eager to help versus being egocentric and skeptical of others' intentions.
B Personality Traits 67
R Adaptability (Personality) 73
Cooperation 67
Cynicism 73
Egocentrism 78
Empathy 67
Likability 88
Openmindedness 78
↓ Tolerance 73

Agricultural Extension Workers 73
PN 60 **SC** 01500
SN Government employees (usually local, county, or state) who assist with agricultural matters, distribute educational materials, and provide services pertaining to agriculture.
UF County Agricultural Agents
Extension Workers (Agricultural)
B Government Personnel 73
R ↓ Agricultural Workers 73

Agricultural Workers 73
PN 374 **SC** 01510

Agricultural Workers — (cont'd)
UF Farmers
Laborers (Farm)
B Nonprofessional Personnel 82
N Migrant Farm Workers 73
R Agricultural Extension Workers 73
↓ Business and Industrial Personnel 67

AIDS
Use Acquired Immune Deficiency Syndrome

AIDS (Attitudes Toward) 97
PN 0 **SC** 01516
B Physical Illness (Attitudes Toward) 85
R Acquired Immune Deficiency Syndrome 88
AIDS Prevention 94
↓ Human Immunodeficiency Virus 91

AIDS Dementia Complex 97
PN 0 **SC** 01514
SN Use ACQUIRED IMMUNE DEFICIENCY SYNDROME and DEMENTIA to access references from 88–96.
B Dementia 85
R Acquired Immune Deficiency Syndrome 88
↓ Human Immunodeficiency Virus 91

AIDS Prevention 94
PN 347 **SC** 01517
SN Health related programs or services directed toward those at risk for HIV/AIDS. Includes prevention of HIV/AIDS and personal risk through health behavior and lifestyle characteristics.
B Prevention 73
R Acquired Immune Deficiency Syndrome 88
AIDS (Attitudes Toward) 97
Condoms 91
Health Behavior 82
↓ Health Education 73
Health Promotion 91
HIV Testing 97
↓ Human Immunodeficiency Virus 91
Sexual Risk Taking 97

AIDS Testing
Use HIV Testing

Air Encephalography
Use Pneumoencephalography

Air Force Personnel 67
PN 968 **SC** 01530
B Military Personnel 67
R National Guardsmen 73

Air Traffic Accidents 73
PN 146 **SC** 01540
B Transportation Accidents 73
R Air Traffic Control 73
Air Transportation 73
↓ Aviation Safety 73

Air Traffic Control 73
PN 227 **SC** 01550
B Aviation Safety 73
R Air Traffic Accidents 73
Air Transportation 73
↓ Transportation Accidents 73

Air Transportation 73
PN 127 **SC** 01560
B Transportation 73
R Air Traffic Accidents 73
Air Traffic Control 73

Air Transportation — (cont'd)
R ↓ Aircraft 73
Public Transportation 73
Spacecraft 73

Aircraft 73
PN 159 **SC** 01570
UF Airplanes
N Helicopters 73
R Air Transportation 73
Aircraft Pilots 73

Aircraft Crew
Use Aerospace Personnel

Aircraft Pilots 73
PN 1194 **SC** 01580
UF Aviators
Pilots (Aircraft)
B Aerospace Personnel 73
R ↓ Aircraft 73
Astronauts 73
↓ Aviation Safety 73

Airplanes
Use Aircraft

Akathisia 91
PN 108 **SC** 01595
SN The inability to remain in a sitting posture or motor restlessness often resulting from heavy doses of tranquilizing drugs.
R Agitation 91
Restlessness 73
↓ Side Effects (Drug) 73
↓ Symptoms 67

Akinesia
Use Apraxia

Alanines 73
PN 25 **SC** 01610
B Amino Acids 73
N ↓ Phenylalanine 73

Alanon
Use Alcohol Rehabilitation

Alarm Responses 73
PN 238 **SC** 01620
SN Behavioral, emotional, or physiological reactions to actual or perceived physical threat. Used primarily for animal populations.
R ↓ Animal Defensive Behavior 82
Animal Distress Calls 73
Animal Escape Behavior 73
↓ Animal Ethology 67
↓ Fear 67
Startle Reflex 67
Tonic Immobility 78

Alaska 73
PN 112 **SC** 01630
B United States 67
R Arctic Regions 91

Alaska Natives 97
PN 0 **SC** 01635
SN Native populations residing in Alaska, including Aleuts and American Indians.
B Ethnic Groups 73
R American Indians 67
Eskimos 73
Minority Groups 67
Tribes 73

Alateen
Use Alcohol Rehabilitation

Albinism [73]
PN 54 **SC** 01640
B Genetic Disorders [73]
R ↓ Eye Disorders [73]
↓ Skin Disorders [73]

Albino Rats
Use Rats

Alcohol (Grain)
Use Ethanol

Alcohol Abstinence
Use Sobriety

Alcohol Abuse [88]
PN 2244 **SC** 01660
UF Problem Drinking
B Alcohol Drinking Patterns [67]
Drug Abuse [73]
N ↓ Alcoholism [67]
R ↓ Alcohol Intoxication [73]
Alcohol Withdrawal [94]
Blood Alcohol Concentration [94]
Codependency [91]
Drug Abuse Liability [94]
Polydrug Abuse [94]

Alcohol Dehydrogenases [73]
PN 51 **SC** 01670
B Dehydrogenases [73]
R ↓ Alcohols [67]

Alcohol Drinking Attitudes [73]
PN 909 **SC** 01680
SN Attitudes toward the use or abuse of alcohol.
UF Drinking Attitudes
B Drug Usage Attitudes [73]
R Sobriety [88]

Alcohol Drinking Patterns [67]
PN 5115 **SC** 01690
UF Drinking (Alcohol)
B Drinking Behavior [78]
Drug Usage [71]
N ↓ Alcohol Abuse [88]
↓ Alcohol Intoxication [73]
Social Drinking [73]
R ↓ Alcoholism [67]
Blood Alcohol Concentration [94]

Alcohol Education
Use Drug Education

Alcohol Intoxication [73]
PN 1054 **SC** 01700
UF Drunkenness
Intoxication (Alcohol)
B Alcohol Drinking Patterns [67]
N Acute Alcoholic Intoxication [73]
Chronic Alcoholic Intoxication [73]
R ↓ Alcohol Abuse [88]
↓ Alcoholism [67]
Blood Alcohol Concentration [94]
Driving Under The Influence [88]
↓ Toxic Disorders [73]
Toxic Psychoses [73]

Alcohol Rehabilitation [82]
PN 2992 **SC** 01705

Alcohol Rehabilitation — (cont'd)
SN Treatment for alcoholism or alcohol abuse which may include detoxification, psychotherapy, behavior therapy, Alcoholics Anonymous, and medication. Use DRUG REHABILITATION to access references from 73–81.
UF Alanon
Alateen
B Drug Rehabilitation [73]
N Alcoholics Anonymous [73]
Detoxification [73]
R Alcohol Withdrawal [94]
Rehabilitation Counseling [78]
Sobriety [88]

Alcohol Withdrawal [94]
PN 56 **SC** 01707
SN Processes and symptomatic effects resulting from abstinence from alcohol. Used for both human and animal populations. Use DRUG WITHDRAWAL to access references from 73–93.
B Drug Withdrawal [73]
R ↓ Alcohol Abuse [88]
↓ Alcohol Rehabilitation [82]
↓ Alcoholic Psychosis [73]
↓ Alcoholism [67]
Detoxification [73]
Sobriety [88]

Alcoholic Beverages [73]
PN 462 **SC** 01710
UF Beverages (Alcoholic)
N Beer [73]
Liquor [73]
Wine [73]
R Beverages (Nonalcoholic) [78]
↓ Drinking Behavior [78]
Prenatal Exposure [91]

Alcoholic Hallucinosis [73]
PN 41 **SC** 01720
B Alcoholic Psychosis [73]
Hallucinosis [73]
N Delirium Tremens [73]
Korsakoffs Psychosis [73]

Alcoholic Psychosis [73]
PN 66 **SC** 01730
B Organic Brain Syndromes [73]
Psychosis [67]
N ↓ Alcoholic Hallucinosis [73]
R Alcohol Withdrawal [94]
↓ Nutritional Deficiencies [73]
Toxic Psychoses [73]

Alcoholics Anonymous [73]
PN 349 **SC** 01740
SN A self-supporting, informal, international fellowship whose primary purpose is to help members achieve sobriety.
B Alcohol Rehabilitation [82]
Twelve Step Programs [97]
R ↓ Community Services [67]

Alcoholism [67]
PN 11925 **SC** 01750
B Addiction [73]
Alcohol Abuse [88]
N Korsakoffs Psychosis [73]
Wernickes Syndrome [73]
R ↓ Alcohol Drinking Patterns [67]
↓ Alcohol Intoxication [73]
Alcohol Withdrawal [94]
Fetal Alcohol Syndrome [85]
↓ Nutritional Deficiencies [73]
Sobriety [88]
↓ Toxic Disorders [73]

Alcohols [67]
PN 1359 **SC** 01760
B Drugs [67]
N Ephedrine [73]
Ethanol [73]
Isoproterenol [73]
Methanol [73]
Methoxamine [73]
Propranolol [73]
Tetrahydrocannabinol [73]
Trihexyphenidyl [73]
R Acetaldehyde [82]
Alcohol Dehydrogenases [73]
Blood Alcohol Concentration [94]
↓ Solvents [82]

Aldolases
SN Term discontinued in 1997. Use ALDOLASES to access references from 73–96.
Use Enzymes

Aldosterone [73]
PN 76 **SC** 01780
B Adrenal Cortex Hormones [73]
Corticosteroids [73]

Alexia [82]
PN 108 **SC** 01785
SN Inability to read which may be the result of neurological impairment. In a less severe form, often referred to as dyslexia.
UF Word Blindness
B Dysphasia [78]
N Dyslexia [73]
R ↓ Reading Disabilities [67]

Alexithymia [82]
PN 406 **SC** 01788
SN Affective and cognitive disturbances characterized by impaired fantasy life and an inability to verbalize or differentiate emotions. These disturbances overlap diagnostic categories and appear generally in psychosomatic patients.
B Mental Disorders [67]
R ↓ Affective Disturbances [67]

Algebra
Use Mathematics

Algeria [88]
PN 26 **SC** 01795
B Africa [67]

Algorithms [73]
PN 893 **SC** 01800
SN Set of well-defined rules established for step-by-step solution of problems in a finite number of steps.
B Mathematics (Concepts) [67]
R Computer Programing [94]

Alienation [71]
PN 1181 **SC** 01810
SN Withdrawal or estrangement from persons, objects, or positions of former attachment; feelings of detachment from self or avoidance of emotional experiences.
B Emotional States [73]
R Anomie [78]
Depersonalization [73]
↓ Separation Reactions [97]

Alkaloids [73]
PN 190 **SC** 01820
UF Homatropine
Opium Alkaloids
Quinidine
Rauwolfia
B Drugs [67]

Alkaloids — (cont'd)
N Apomorphine 73
Atropine 73
Bromocriptine 88
Caffeine 73
Cocaine 73
Codeine 73
Ephedrine 73
↓ Gamma Aminobutyric Acid Antagonists 85
Heroin 73
Mescaline 73
Morphine 73
Nicotine 73
Papaverine 73
Peyote 73
Physostigmine 73
Pilocarpine 73
Quinine 73
Reserpine 67
Scopolamine 73
Strychnine 73
Theophylline 73
Tubocurarine 73
R ↓ Anti Inflammatory Drugs 82
Curare 73
↓ Ergot Derivatives 73

Allergens
Use Antigens

Allergic Disorders 73
PN 165 **SC** 01830
B Immunologic Disorders 73
N Allergic Skin Disorders 73
Drug Allergies 73
Food Allergies 73
Hay Fever 73
R Anaphylactic Shock 73

Allergic Skin Disorders 73
PN 15 **SC** 01840
B Allergic Disorders 73
Skin Disorders 73
R ↓ Dermatitis 73
Eczema 73
Neurodermatitis 73

Alligators
Use Crocodilians

Allocation of Resources
Use Resource Allocation

Allport Vernon Lindzey Study Values
SN Term discontinued in 1997. Use ALLPORT VERNON LINDZEY STUDY VALUES to access references 73–96.
Use Attitude Measures

Alopecia 73
PN 56 **SC** 01880
SN Baldness or the loss of hair.
UF Baldness
Hair Loss
B Skin Disorders 73
R ↓ Genetic Disorders 73
Hair 73

Alpha Methylparatyrosine 78
PN 113 **SC** 01887
UF Alpha Methyltyrosine
B Adrenergic Blocking Drugs 73
Antihypertensive Drugs 73
Tyrosine 73

Alpha Methyltyrosine
Use Alpha Methylparatyrosine

Alpha Rhythm 73
PN 579 **SC** 01890
SN Electrically measured impulses or waves of low amplitude and a frequency of 8-13 cycles per second usually observable in the electroencephalogram during wakeful rest.
B Electrical Activity 67
Electroencephalography 67

Alphabets 73
PN 93 **SC** 01900
SN Systems for writing a language.
B Written Language 67
N Initial Teaching Alphabet 73
↓ Letters (Alphabet) 73
R Orthography 73

Alprazolam 88
PN 380 **SC** 01903
B Benzodiazepines 78
Minor Tranquilizers 73
Sedatives 73

Alternative Medicine 97
PN 0 **SC** 01904
B Treatment 67
N Acupuncture 73
Faith Healing 73
Folk Medicine 73
Vitamin Therapy 78
R Biofeedback Training 78
Holistic Health 85
↓ Hypnotherapy 73
Medical Treatment (General) 73
Meditation 73
↓ Organic Therapies 73
Phototherapy 91
↓ Physical Treatment Methods 73
Preventive Medicine 73
↓ Shock Therapy 73
Transcultural Psychiatry 73

Alternative Schools
Use Nontraditional Education

Altitude Effects 73
PN 155 **SC** 01910
B Environmental Effects 73
R ↓ Aviation 67
↓ Gravitational Effects 67

Altruism 73
PN 856 **SC** 01920
SN Consideration for well-being of others as opposed to self-love or egoism. Used for human or animal populations.
B Personality Traits 67
Prosocial Behavior 82
R Assistance (Social Behavior) 73
Charitable Behavior 73
Sharing (Social Behavior) 78

Aluminum 94
PN 13 **SC** 01930
B Metallic Elements 73

Alzheimers Disease 73
PN 4763 **SC** 01940
B Organic Brain Syndromes 73
Presenile Dementia 73
R Picks Disease 73
↓ Senile Dementia 73

Amantadine 78
PN 73 **SC** 01945
UF Amatadine
B Antibiotics 73

Amantadine — (cont'd)
B Antitremor Drugs 73
R Parkinsons Disease 73

Amatadine
Use Amantadine

Amaurotic Familial Idiocy 73
PN 21 **SC** 01950
UF Familial Idiocy (Amaurotic)
Idiocy (Amaurotic Familial)
Tay Sachs Disease
B Genetic Disorders 73
Lipid Metabolism Disorders 73
Mental Retardation 67
Neonatal Disorders 73

Ambiguity (Stimulus)
Use Stimulus Ambiguity

Ambiguity (Tolerance)
Use Tolerance for Ambiguity

Ambition
Use Aspirations

Ambivalence 73
PN 151 **SC** 01990
B Emotional States 73

Amblyopia 73
PN 161 **SC** 02000
SN An optically uncorrectable loss of visual acuity without apparent organic change or defect.
B Eye Disorders 73
R ↓ Refraction Errors 73
Strabismus 73

Ambulatory Care
Use Outpatient Treatment

Amenorrhea 73
PN 100 **SC** 02010
SN Absence or abnormal cessation of the menses.
B Menstrual Disorders 73

Amentia
Use Mental Retardation

American Indians 67
PN 1793 **SC** 02030
SN Native populations of North and South America and the Caribbean Islands, with the exception of Eskimos.
UF Indians (American)
Native Americans
B Ethnic Groups 73
R Alaska Natives 97
Minority Groups 67
Tribes 73

American Samoa 91
PN 10 **SC** 02035
B South Pacific 78

Amine Oxidase Inhibitors 73
PN 7 **SC** 02040
B Enzyme Inhibitors 85
N ↓ Dopamine Antagonists 82
Iproniazid 73
Isocarboxazid 73
Lysergic Acid Diethylamide 67
Nialamide 73
R ↓ Monoamine Oxidase Inhibitors 73

Amines [73]
PN 447 **SC** 02060
UF Chlorisondamine
B Drugs [67]
N Amitriptyline [73]
Atropine [73]
Bufotenine [73]
Chlordiazepoxide [73]
Chlorimipramine [73]
Chlorpromazine [67]
Chlorprothixene [73]
Cocaine [73]
Diphenhydramine [73]
Galanthamine [73]
Guanethidine [73]
Histamine [73]
Hydroxylamine [73]
Imipramine [73]
Mecamylamine [73]
Meperidine [73]
Methylphenidate [73]
Orphenadrine [73]
Phenethylamines [85]
Phenoxybenzamine [73]
Physostigmine [73]
Puromycin [73]
Scopolamine [73]
Serotonin [73]
↓ Sympathomimetic Amines [73]
Thalidomide [73]
Trihexyphenidyl [73]
Tryptamine [73]
R ↓ Amino Acids [73]

Amino Acids [73]
PN 751 **SC** 02070
B Acids [73]
N ↓ Alanines [73]
↓ Aspartic Acid [73]
Cysteine [73]
DOPA [73]
Folic Acid [73]
Gamma Aminobutyric Acid [78]
Glutamic Acid [73]
Glutamine [73]
Glycine [73]
Histidine [73]
Leucine [73]
Methionine [73]
↓ Neurokinins [97]
Proline [82]
↓ Tryptophan [73]
↓ Tyrosine [73]
R ↓ Amines [73]
Nerve Growth Factor [94]
↓ Neurotransmitters [85]
↓ Proteins [73]

Aminotransferases
Use Transaminases

Amitriptyline [73]
PN 880 **SC** 02090
UF Elavil
B Amines [73]
Tranquilizing Drugs [67]
Tricyclic Antidepressant Drugs [97]

Amnesia [67]
PN 1787 **SC** 02120
SN Systematic and extensive loss of memory caused by organic or psychological factors. The loss may be temporary or permanent, and may involve old or recent memories. Compare FORGETTING and MEMORY DECAY.
B Dissociative Patterns [73]
Memory Disorders [73]
N Fugue Reaction [73]
Global Amnesia [97]

Amnesia — (cont'd)
R False Memory [97]
Forgetting [73]
↓ Memory [67]
Repressed Memory [97]

Amniocentesis
Use Prenatal Diagnosis

Amniotic Fluid [73]
PN 29 **SC** 02130
B Body Fluids [73]

Amobarbital [73]
PN 152 **SC** 02140
UF Amobarbital Sodium
Amytal
B Barbiturates [67]
CNS Depressant Drugs [73]
Hypnotic Drugs [73]
Sedatives [73]

Amobarbital Sodium
Use Amobarbital

Amphetamine [67]
PN 2377 **SC** 02160
UF Amphetamine (dl-)
Amphetamine Sulfate
Benzedrine
B Adrenergic Drugs [73]
Appetite Depressing Drugs [73]
CNS Stimulating Drugs [73]
Dopamine Agonists [85]
Sympathomimetic Amines [73]
Vasoconstrictor Drugs [73]
N Dextroamphetamine [73]
Methamphetamine [73]
R Phenethylamines [85]

Amphetamine (d-)
Use Dextroamphetamine

Amphetamine (dl-)
Use Amphetamine

Amphetamine Sulfate
Use Amphetamine

Amphibia [73]
PN 65 **SC** 02200
B Vertebrates [73]
N Frogs [67]
Salamanders [73]
Toads [73]

Amplifiers (Apparatus) [73]
PN 39 **SC** 02210
B Apparatus [67]

Amplitude (Response)
Use Response Amplitude

Amputation [73]
PN 84 **SC** 02230
B Surgery [71]
N Mastectomy [73]
R Phantom Limbs [73]
↓ Prostheses [73]

Amputees [73]
PN 98 **SC** 02240
B Physically Disabled [97]

Amygdaloid Body [73]
PN 1293 **SC** 02250

Amygdaloid Body — (cont'd)
B Basal Ganglia [73]
Limbic System [73]
R Medial Forebrain Bundle [82]

Amytal
Use Amobarbital

Anabolism [73]
PN 11 **SC** 02280
SN Constructive part of metabolism concerned especially with macromolecular synthesis.
B Metabolism [67]

Anabolites
Use Metabolites

Anaclitic Depression [73]
PN 31 **SC** 02290
SN Syndrome of withdrawal characterizing infants separated from their mothers for a long period of time.
B Major Depression [88]
R Attachment Behavior [85]
Object Relations [82]
↓ Parental Absence [73]
↓ Separation Reactions [97]

Anagram Problem Solving [73]
PN 280 **SC** 02300
B Problem Solving [67]
R Anagrams [73]

Anagrams [73]
PN 32 **SC** 02310
SN Words or phrases made by rearranging letters of other words or phrases (e.g., leader from dealer).
B Vocabulary [67]
R Anagram Problem Solving [73]

Analeptic Drugs [73]
PN 53 **SC** 02320
UF Antagonists (CNS Depressant Drugs)
CNS Depressant Drug Antagonists
B CNS Stimulating Drugs [73]
N Bemegride [73]
Bicuculline [94]
Picrotoxin [73]
Strychnine [73]
R Barbiturate Poisoning [73]
Caffeine [73]
↓ Cholinomimetic Drugs [73]
↓ Heart Rate Affecting Drugs [73]
Methylphenidate [73]
Pentylenetetrazol [73]
Theophylline [73]

Analgesia [82]
PN 1401 **SC** 02325
SN Pain insensitivity chemically or electrically induced or occurring as a natural phenomenon (e.g., Kiesow's area on the inner cheek).
B Pain Perception [73]
R ↓ Analgesic Drugs [73]
↓ Anesthesia (Feeling) [73]
↓ Endorphins [82]
Enkephalins [82]
Pain Management [94]
Pain Measurement [97]

Analgesic Drugs [73]
PN 759 **SC** 02330
UF Anodynes
Pain Relieving Drugs
B Drugs [67]
N Aspirin [73]
Atropine [73]

Analgesic Drugs — (cont'd)
N Carbamazepine [88]
Codeine [73]
Dihydroergotamine [73]
Heroin [73]
Meperidine [73]
Methadone [73]
Morphine [73]
Papaverine [73]
Pentazocine [91]
Phencyclidine [82]
Procaine [82]
Quinine [73]
Scopolamine [73]
R Analgesia [82]
↓ Anesthetic Drugs [73]
↓ Anti Inflammatory Drugs [82]
↓ CNS Depressant Drugs [73]
↓ Hypnotic Drugs [73]
↓ Narcotic Drugs [73]
↓ Pain [67]
Pain Management [94]
↓ Sedatives [73]

Analog Computers [73]
PN 18 SC 02340
SN Electronic, mechanical, or electromechanical machines that measure continuous electrical or physical magnitudes (e.g., automobile speedometer) rather than operating on discrete digits.
B Computers [67]

Analogy [91]
PN 186 SC 02345
R Connotations [73]
↓ Figurative Language [85]
Inference [73]
Logical Thinking [67]
Metaphor [82]
↓ Reasoning [67]

Analysis [67]
PN 1191 SC 02370
SN Conceptually broad array term referring to the process of examination of a complex problem, its elements, and their relations. Use a more specific term if possible.
N Behavioral Assessment [82]
Causal Analysis [94]
Cohort Analysis [88]
↓ Content Analysis [78]
Content Analysis (Test) [67]
↓ Costs and Cost Analysis [73]
Error Analysis [73]
Item Analysis (Test) [67]
Job Analysis [67]
Risk Analysis [91]
↓ Statistical Analysis [67]
Systems Analysis [73]
Task Analysis [67]
R Analysis of Covariance [73]
Analysis of Variance [67]
Multidimensional Scaling [82]

Analysis of Covariance [73]
PN 368 SC 02350
B Variability Measurement [73]
R ↓ Analysis [67]
Analysis of Variance [67]
Multiple Regression [82]
↓ Multivariate Analysis [82]

Analysis of Variance [67]
PN 1028 SC 02360
UF ANOVA (Statistics)
B Variability Measurement [73]
R ↓ Analysis [67]
Analysis of Covariance [73]
Multiple Regression [82]

Analysis of Variance — (cont'd)
R ↓ Multivariate Analysis [82]
↓ Statistical Regression [85]
Variance Homogeneity [85]

Analysts
Use Psychoanalysts

Analytic Psychology
Use Jungian Psychology

Analytical Psychotherapy [73]
PN 402 SC 02390
SN Form of psychotherapy based on work of C. G. Jung. The unconscious, personal and collective, is disclosed through free association and dream analysis. Therapeutic goals include integration of conscious and unconscious for growth and personality development and a life of fuller awareness.
UF Jungian Psychotherapy
B Psychotherapy [67]
R Archetypes [91]
↓ Collective Unconscious [97]
Jung (Carl) [73]
↓ Jungian Psychology [73]

Anankastic Personality
Use Obsessive Compulsive Personality

Anaphylactic Shock [73]
PN 12 SC 02400
SN Immunologic or allergic reaction to antigens such as drugs or foreign proteins to which a hypersensitivity has been established by previous contact.
UF Protein Sensitization
Sensitization (Protein)
B Immunologic Disorders [73]
R ↓ Allergic Disorders [73]
Shock [67]

Anatomical Systems [73]
PN 15 SC 02410
SN Conceptually broad array term referring to anatomically related structures (e.g., vascular system). Use a more specific term if possible.
B Anatomy [67]
Systems [67]
N ↓ Cardiovascular System [67]
↓ Digestive System [67]
↓ Endocrine System [73]
↓ Musculoskeletal System [73]
↓ Nervous System [67]
↓ Respiratory System [73]
↓ Urogenital System [73]

Anatomically Detailed Dolls [91]
PN 27 SC 02415
SN Dolls used in a general play setting or for evaluation and assessment purposes in a therapeutic or legal context.
B Toys [73]
R ↓ Child Abuse [71]
Childhood Play Behavior [78]
Clinical Judgment (Not Diagnosis) [73]
Doll Play [73]
↓ Sexual Abuse [88]

Anatomy [67]
PN 1131 SC 02420
SN Conceptually broad array term referring both to the science of anatomy and the actual structure or morphology of an organism. Use specific anatomical or neuroanatomical terms if possible.
N Abdomen [73]
↓ Anatomical Systems [73]
Back (Anatomy) [73]
↓ Body Fluids [73]

Anatomy — (cont'd)
N Breast [73]
↓ Cells (Biology) [73]
Face (Anatomy) [73]
Feet (Anatomy) [73]
Hair [73]
Hand (Anatomy) [67]
Head (Anatomy) [73]
Neck (Anatomy) [73]
Palm (Anatomy) [73]
Scalp (Anatomy) [73]
↓ Sense Organs [73]
Thigh [73]
↓ Tissues (Body) [73]
R Morphology [73]
Neuroanatomy [67]
↓ Physiology [67]

Ancestors [73]
PN 13 SC 02430
UF Great Grandparents
B Family Members [73]
N Grandparents [73]
↓ Parents [67]

Androgen Antagonists
Use Antiandrogens

Androgens [73]
PN 442 SC 02440
B Sex Hormones [73]
N Testosterone [73]
R Antiandrogens [82]
Antiestrogens [82]

Androgyny [82]
PN 633 SC 02445
SN Combination of masculine and feminine personality characteristics in one individual.
B Personality Traits [67]
R Femininity [67]
Gender Identity [85]
↓ Human Sex Differences [67]
Masculinity [67]
Sex Roles [67]

Anemia [73]
PN 117 SC 02450
B Blood and Lymphatic Disorders [73]
R ↓ Genetic Disorders [73]
Sickle Cell Disease [94]

Anencephaly [73]
PN 9 SC 02460
B Brain Disorders [67]
Mental Retardation [67]
Neonatal Disorders [73]

Anesthesia (Feeling) [73]
PN 168 SC 02470
N Hysterical Anesthesia [73]
R Analgesia [82]
↓ Physical Disorders [97]
↓ Sense Organ Disorders [73]
↓ Tactual Perception [67]

Anesthesiology [73]
PN 70 SC 02480
B Medical Sciences [67]

Anesthetic Drugs [73]
PN 483 SC 02490
B Drugs [67]
N ↓ General Anesthetics [73]
Hexobarbital [73]
Ketamine [97]
↓ Local Anesthetics [73]
Pentobarbital [73]

Anesthetic Drugs — (cont'd)
N Phencyclidine [82]
Procaine [82]
R ↓ Analgesic Drugs [73]
↓ Anticonvulsive Drugs [73]
↓ Barbiturates [67]
↓ CNS Depressant Drugs [73]
↓ Hypnotic Drugs [73]
↓ Muscle Relaxing Drugs [73]
↓ Narcotic Drugs [73]
↓ Sedatives [73]

Aneurysms [73]
PN 65 SC 02500
B Cardiovascular Disorders [67]

Anger [67]
PN 1582 SC 02510
UF Rage
B Emotional States [73]
N Hostility [67]
R Anger Control [97]
Hate [73]
Jealousy [73]
Tantrums [73]

Anger Control [97]
PN 0 SC 02520
B Emotional Control [73]
R ↓ Anger [67]
↓ Behavior Modification [73]
↓ Behavior Therapy [67]
Explosive Personality [73]
Self Control [73]

Angina Pectoris [73]
PN 92 SC 02530
B Heart Disorders [73]
R Myocardial Infarctions [73]

Angiography [73]
PN 33 SC 02540
B Roentgenography [73]

Angiotensin [73]
PN 331 SC 02550
B Peptides [73]
Vasoconstrictor Drugs [73]
R Captopril [91]

Anglos [88]
PN 279 SC 02553
B Ethnic Groups [73]
R Whites [82]

Angola [88]
PN 1 SC 02555
B Africa [67]

Angst
Use Anxiety

Anguish
Use Distress

Anhedonia [85]
PN 107 SC 02575
SN Loss or absence of ability to experience pleasure.
B Symptoms [67]
R Dysthymic Disorder [88]
↓ Neurosis [67]
Pleasure [73]
↓ Schizophrenia [67]

Animal Aggressive Behavior [73]
PN 3975 SC 02580

Animal Aggressive Behavior — (cont'd)
B Aggressive Behavior [67]
Animal Social Behavior [67]
N Animal Predatory Behavior [78]
Attack Behavior [73]
Muricide [88]
Threat Postures [73]
R Animal Dominance [73]
Territoriality [67]

Animal Assisted Therapy [94]
PN 9 SC 02585
SN A type of therapy based on the human-animal companion bond used in an effort to assist in restoring feelings of hope, self worth, responsibility, and communication.
UF Pet Therapy
B Psychotherapeutic Techniques [67]
R ↓ Animals [67]
Geriatric Psychotherapy [73]
Interspecies Interaction [91]
Pets [82]
↓ Rehabilitation [67]

Animal Behavior
Use Animal Ethology

Animal Biological Rhythms [73]
PN 331 SC 02600
SN Rhythmic and periodic variations in behavioral or physiological functions of animals. Use BIOLOGICAL RHYTHMS to access references from 67–72.
UF Biological Clocks (Animal)
B Animal Ethology [67]
Biological Rhythms [67]
N Animal Circadian Rhythms [73]
R Animal Sexual Receptivity [73]
Estrus [73]
Hibernation [73]

Animal Breeding [73]
PN 2257 SC 02610
SN Propagation (or reproduction) of a species in its natural environment or in captive settings. Includes birth rate and breeding success. Compare ANIMAL DOMESTICATION, EUGENICS, and SELECTIVE BREEDING.
UF Breeding (Animal)
N Selective Breeding [73]
R Animal Captivity [94]
Animal Domestication [78]
↓ Animal Mating Behavior [67]
↓ Animal Sexual Behavior [85]
Animal Strain Differences [82]
↓ Animals [67]
Assortative Mating [91]
↓ Genetics [67]
Litter Size [85]
↓ Sexual Reproduction [73]

Animal Captivity [94]
PN 98 SC 02615
UF Captivity (Animal)
Zoo Environment
B Animal Environments [67]
R ↓ Animal Breeding [73]
Animal Domestication [78]
Animal Rearing [91]
Animal Welfare [85]

Animal Circadian Rhythms [73]
PN 1771 SC 02620
SN Diurnal cyclical variations or patterns of behavioral or physiological functions of animals. Use BIOLOGICAL RHYTHMS to access references from 67–72.
UF Circadian Rhythms (Animal)
Daily Biological Rhythms (Animal)

Animal Circadian Rhythms — (cont'd)
B Animal Biological Rhythms [73]
R Animal Nocturnal Behavior [73]

Animal Coloration [85]
PN 223 SC 02625
SN Physical aspect of body color.
R Animal Courtship Displays [73]
↓ Animal Defensive Behavior [82]
↓ Pigments [73]

Animal Communication [67]
PN 1074 SC 02630
B Animal Social Behavior [67]
Communication [67]
N Animal Distress Calls [73]
R Animal Scent Marking [85]
↓ Animal Vocalizations [73]
↓ Vocalization [67]

Animal Courtship Behavior [73]
PN 756 SC 02640
UF Courtship (Animal)
B Animal Sexual Behavior [85]
Animal Social Behavior [67]
N Animal Courtship Displays [73]
R Animal Mate Selection [82]
↓ Animal Mating Behavior [67]

Animal Courtship Displays [73]
PN 220 SC 02650
UF Courtship Displays (Animal)
B Animal Courtship Behavior [73]
Animal Social Behavior [67]
R Animal Coloration [85]
↓ Animal Mating Behavior [67]
Territoriality [67]

Animal Defensive Behavior [82]
PN 1394 SC 02652
SN Innate protective responses that occur in presence of predator or other threatening stimulus.
UF Defensive Behavior (Animal)
B Animal Ethology [67]
N Animal Escape Behavior [73]
Threat Postures [73]
R Alarm Responses [73]
Animal Coloration [85]
Animal Distress Calls [73]
Attack Behavior [73]
Instinctive Behavior [82]
Tonic Immobility [78]

Animal Development [78]
PN 1904 SC 02655
SN Conceptually broad array term. Use a more specific term if possible.
B Development [67]
R Age Differences [67]
↓ Animals [67]
↓ Motor Development [73]
Neural Development [85]
Perceptual Motor Development [91]
↓ Physical Development [73]
↓ Prenatal Development [73]

Animal Distress Calls [73]
PN 249 SC 02660
UF Distress Calls (Animal)
B Animal Communication [67]
Animal Vocalizations [73]
R Alarm Responses [73]
↓ Animal Defensive Behavior [82]
Instinctive Behavior [82]

Animal Division of Labor [73]
PN 141 SC 02670

Animal Division of Labor — (cont'd)
UF Division of Labor (Animal)
B Animal Social Behavior 67
Division of Labor 88
R Animal Dominance 73

Animal Domestication 78
PN 123 SC 02677
SN Adaptation of wild animals to life and breeding in tame conditions according to the interests of human society. Compare ANIMAL BREEDING, EUGENICS, and SELECTIVE BREEDING.
UF Domestication (Animal)
R ↓ Animal Breeding 73
Animal Captivity 94
Pets 82
Selective Breeding 73

Animal Dominance 73
PN 1512 SC 02680
UF Dominance (Animal)
Pecking Order
B Animal Social Behavior 67
Dominance 67
R ↓ Animal Aggressive Behavior 73
Animal Division of Labor 73
Animal Scent Marking 85
Dominance Hierarchy 73
Territoriality 67

Animal Drinking Behavior 73
PN 1688 SC 02690
UF Drinking Behavior (Animal)
B Animal Ethology 67
Drinking Behavior 78
R Licking 88
Polydipsia 82
Sucking 78
Thirst 67
Water Intake 67

Animal Emotionality 78
PN 736 SC 02696
UF Emotionality (Animal)
R Animal Motivation 67
↓ Emotional Responses 67

Animal Environments 67
PN 4735 SC 02700
SN Physical and social conditions of an animal's existence or habitat.
UF Habitats (Animal)
B Social Environments 73
N Animal Captivity 94
R Animal Rearing 91
↓ Animals 67
Place Conditioning 91

Animal Escape Behavior 73
PN 646 SC 02710
UF Escape Behavior (Animal)
B Animal Defensive Behavior 82
R Alarm Responses 73

Animal Ethology 67
PN 2367 SC 02720
SN Study of animal behavior especially in relation to ecology, evolution, neuroanatomy, neurophysiology, and genetics. Used for the discipline or the ethological processes themselves. Use a more specific term if possible.
UF Animal Behavior
Ethology (Animal)
B Behavior 67
N ↓ Animal Biological Rhythms 73
↓ Animal Defensive Behavior 82
Animal Drinking Behavior 73
Animal Exploratory Behavior 73
Animal Feeding Behavior 73

Animal Ethology — (cont'd)
N Animal Foraging Behavior 85
Animal Grooming Behavior 78
Animal Hoarding Behavior 73
Animal Homing 91
Animal Nocturnal Behavior 73
Animal Open Field Behavior 73
↓ Animal Parental Behavior 82
Animal Play 73
Animal Sex Differences 67
↓ Animal Sexual Behavior 85
↓ Animal Social Behavior 67
↓ Animal Vocalizations 73
Hibernation 73
Imprinting 67
Licking 88
Migratory Behavior (Animal) 73
Nest Building 73
Species Recognition 85
Territoriality 67
R Alarm Responses 73
Animal Motivation 67
↓ Animals 67
Echolocation 73
Instinctive Behavior 82
Stereotyped Behavior 73
Tool Use 91

Animal Exploratory Behavior 73
PN 1455 SC 02730
SN Use EXPLORATORY BEHAVIOR to access references from 67-72.
B Animal Ethology 67
Exploratory Behavior 67
R Animal Foraging Behavior 85
Instinctive Behavior 82
Neophobia 85
Spontaneous Alternation 82

Animal Feeding Behavior 73
PN 4054 SC 02740
UF Feeding Behavior (Animal)
B Animal Ethology 67
R Animal Foraging Behavior 85
Animal Maternal Behavior 73
Animal Paternal Behavior 91
↓ Food Intake 67
Hunger 67
Sucking 78

Animal Foraging Behavior 85
PN 1090 SC 02743
UF Foraging (Animal)
B Animal Ethology 67
R Animal Exploratory Behavior 73
Animal Feeding Behavior 73
Animal Predatory Behavior 78

Animal Grooming Behavior 78
PN 577 SC 02745
UF Grooming Behavior (Animal)
B Animal Ethology 67
R Licking 88

Animal Hoarding Behavior 73
PN 176 SC 02750
UF Hoarding Behavior (Animal)
B Animal Ethology 67

Animal Homing 91
PN 50 SC 02755
SN Returning accurately to one's home or natal area from a distance.
UF Homing (Animal)
B Animal Ethology 67
R Instinctive Behavior 82
Migratory Behavior (Animal) 73
Territoriality 67

Animal Human Interaction
Use Interspecies Interaction

Animal Innate Behavior
SN Term discontinued in 1982. Use ANIMAL INNATE BEHAVIOR or ANIMAL INSTINCTIVE BEHAVIOR to access references from 73-81 and 67-81, respectively.
Use Instinctive Behavior

Animal Instinctive Behavior
SN Term discontinued in 1982. Use ANIMAL INSTINCTIVE BEHAVIOR or ANIMAL INNATE BEHAVIOR to access references from 67-81 and 73-81, respectively.
Use Instinctive Behavior

Animal Licking Behavior
Use Licking

Animal Locomotion 82
PN 1342 SC 02775
SN Any form of motor activity resulting in bodily propulsion.
B Motor Processes 67

Animal Mate Selection 82
PN 744 SC 02778
SN Ethological processes surrounding the choice of mate for sexual reproduction.
UF Mate Selection
R ↓ Animal Courtship Behavior 73
↓ Animal Mating Behavior 67
↓ Animal Sexual Behavior 85
Assortative Mating 91
↓ Genetics 67
↓ Sexual Reproduction 73

Animal Maternal Behavior 73
PN 2153 SC 02780
UF Maternal Behavior (Animal)
B Animal Parental Behavior 82
R Animal Feeding Behavior 73
Animal Maternal Deprivation 88
Animal Paternal Behavior 91
Animal Rearing 91
Licking 88

Animal Maternal Deprivation 88
PN 108 SC 02785
SN Consider using ANIMAL MATERNAL BEHAVIOR prior to 1988.
R Animal Maternal Behavior 73
Animal Rearing 91
↓ Social Isolation 67

Animal Mating Behavior 67
PN 4199 SC 02790
UF Coitus (Animal)
Copulation (Animal)
Mating Behavior (Animal)
B Animal Sexual Behavior 85
Animal Social Behavior 67
N Animal Sexual Receptivity 73
R ↓ Animal Breeding 73
↓ Animal Courtship Behavior 73
Animal Courtship Displays 73
Animal Mate Selection 82
Assortative Mating 91
Nest Building 73
Pheromones 73
↓ Sexual Reproduction 73

Animal Models 88
PN 1679 SC 02797

Animal Models — (cont'd)
SN Experimentally induced simulations of human conditions in animals designed to investigate the etiology and characteristics of diseases, psychological and psychiatric disorders, or learning processes.
B Models 67
R ↓ Animals 67
↓ Experimental Design 67
↓ Experimentation 67

Animal Motivation 67
PN 1357 **SC** 02800
B Motivation 67
R Animal Emotionality 78
↓ Animal Ethology 67
↓ Animals 67
Instinctive Behavior 82

Animal Navigation
Use Migratory Behavior (Animal)

Animal Nocturnal Behavior 73
PN 108 **SC** 02820
UF Nocturnal Behavior (Animal)
B Animal Ethology 67
R Animal Circadian Rhythms 73

Animal Open Field Behavior 73
PN 1545 **SC** 02825
SN Spontaneous animal behavior studied in relatively unrestricted laboratory environments. Prior to 1985 also used for spontaneous animal behavior in natural environments.
UF Open Field Behavior (Animal)
B Animal Ethology 67

Animal Parental Behavior 82
PN 649 **SC** 02828
SN Nurturance and care of offspring performed by male and/or female parents.
UF Parental Behavior (Animal)
B Animal Ethology 67
Animal Social Behavior 67
N Animal Maternal Behavior 73
Animal Paternal Behavior 91
R Animal Rearing 91
Parental Investment 97

Animal Paternal Behavior 91
PN 107 **SC** 02829
B Animal Parental Behavior 82
R Animal Feeding Behavior 73
Animal Maternal Behavior 73
Animal Rearing 91

Animal Play 73
PN 373 **SC** 02830
UF Play (Animal)
B Animal Ethology 67
R ↓ Animal Social Behavior 67

Animal Predatory Behavior 78
PN 1245 **SC** 02834
UF Predatory Behavior (Animal)
B Animal Aggressive Behavior 73
R Animal Foraging Behavior 85
Attack Behavior 73
Instinctive Behavior 82
Threat Postures 73

Animal Rearing 91
PN 300 **SC** 02836
SN Conditions or environment in which animals are bred, nourished, and raised. Compare ANIMAL PARENTAL BEHAVIOR.
R Animal Captivity 94
↓ Animal Environments 67

Animal Rearing — (cont'd)
R Animal Maternal Behavior 73
Animal Maternal Deprivation 88
↓ Animal Parental Behavior 82
Animal Paternal Behavior 91

Animal Scent Marking 85
PN 227 **SC** 02837
UF Scent Marking (Animal)
R ↓ Animal Communication 67
Animal Dominance 73
Pheromones 73
Territoriality 67

Animal Sex Differences 67
PN 2579 **SC** 02840
SN Animal behavioral, developmental, and physiological/anatomical differences between the sexes.
UF Sex Differences (Animal)
B Animal Ethology 67
R Sex 67
Sex Recognition 97

Animal Sexual Behavior 85
PN 1319 **SC** 02845
SN Any form of sexual behavior in animals.
B Animal Ethology 67
N ↓ Animal Courtship Behavior 73
↓ Animal Mating Behavior 67
R ↓ Animal Breeding 73
Animal Mate Selection 82
Instinctive Behavior 82
Sex 67

Animal Sexual Receptivity 73
PN 1123 **SC** 02850
UF Lordosis (Animal)
Sexual Receptivity (Animal)
B Animal Mating Behavior 67
R ↓ Animal Biological Rhythms 73
Estrus 73

Animal Social Behavior 67
PN 5056 **SC** 02860
B Animal Ethology 67
Social Behavior 67
N ↓ Animal Aggressive Behavior 73
↓ Animal Communication 67
↓ Animal Courtship Behavior 73
Animal Courtship Displays 73
Animal Division of Labor 73
Animal Dominance 73
↓ Animal Mating Behavior 67
↓ Animal Parental Behavior 82
R Animal Play 73
Interspecies Interaction 91
Physical Contact 82

Animal Strain Differences 82
PN 1823 **SC** 02863
SN Anatomical, physiological, and/or behavioral variations between members of different subspecies or strains. Use GENETICS and ANIMAL BREEDING together to access references from 73-81. Compare SPECIES DIFFERENCES.
UF Strain Differences (Animal)
R ↓ Animal Breeding 73
↓ Genetics 67

Animal Tool Use
Use Tool Use

Animal Vocalizations 73
PN 2573 **SC** 02870
UF Vocalizations (Animal)
B Animal Ethology 67
Vocalization 67

Animal Vocalizations — (cont'd)
N Animal Distress Calls 73
R ↓ Animal Communication 67
Echolocation 73

Animal Welfare 85
PN 177 **SC** 02875
R Animal Captivity 94
Experimental Ethics 78

Animals 67
PN 2943 **SC** 02880
SN Conceptually broad array term. Use a more specific term if possible (e.g., VERTEBRATES, MAMMALS, DOGS).
N Female Animals 73
Infants (Animal) 78
↓ Invertebrates 73
Male Animals 73
↓ Vertebrates 73
R Animal Assisted Therapy 94
↓ Animal Breeding 73
Animal Development 78
↓ Animal Environments 67
↓ Animal Ethology 67
Animal Models 88
Animal Motivation 67
Biological Symbiosis 73
Interspecies Interaction 91
Pets 82
Species Differences 82

Animism 73
PN 71 **SC** 02890
SN Ascribing life to inanimate objects. Also, the Piagetian stage of development in which children ascribe emotional attributes and intentions to inanimate objects.
B Philosophies 67
R Ethnology 67
Myths 67
Taboos 73

Ankle 73
PN 15 **SC** 02900
B Joints (Anatomy) 73
R Feet (Anatomy) 73
Leg (Anatomy) 73

Anniversary Events 94
PN 2 **SC** 02905
SN Annual occurrence of a specific date that marks a notable event or experience. Includes aspects of both positive or negative reactions to the event or experience.
UF Anniversary Reactions
B Experiences (Events) 73
R Autobiographical Memory 94
Early Experience 67
Early Memories 85
Life Experiences 73
Life Review 91
Reminiscence 85

Anniversary Reactions
Use Anniversary Events

Annual Leave
Use Employee Leave Benefits

Annual Report 73
PN 37 **SC** 02920
SN Mandatory term used as a document type identifier.

Anodynes
Use Analgesic Drugs

Anomie [78]
PN 167 **SC** 02940
SN Sense of alienation or despair resulting from the loss or weakening of previously held values. Also, a state of lawlessness or a lack of normative standards within groups or societies.
B Social Processes [67]
R Alienation [71]
Personal Values [73]
Social Values [73]

Anonymity [73]
PN 159 **SC** 02945
SN Unknown, unacknowledged, or concealed personal identity.
R Privileged Communication [73]
Secrecy [94]
Self Disclosure [73]
↓ Social Perception [67]

Anorexia Nervosa [73]
PN 2651 **SC** 02950
SN Syndrome in which the primary features include excessive fear of becoming overweight, body image disturbance, significant weight loss, refusal to maintain minimal normal weight, and amenorrhea. This disorder occurs most frequently in adolescent females.
B Eating Disorders [97]
Underweight [73]
R Bulimia [85]
↓ Nutritional Deficiencies [73]
↓ Psychosomatic Disorders [67]

Anorexigenic Drugs
Use Appetite Depressing Drugs

Anosmia [73]
PN 126 **SC** 02970
SN Loss of the sense of smell.
UF Olfactory Impairment
B Sense Organ Disorders [73]
R ↓ Olfactory Perception [67]

Anosognosia [94]
PN 23 **SC** 02975
SN Lack of awareness of, or refusal or failure to deal with or recognize that one has a mental or physical disorder.
B Agnosia [73]
R Coping Behavior [67]
Denial [73]
Illness Behavior [82]

ANOVA (Statistics)
Use Analysis of Variance

Anoxia [73]
PN 368 **SC** 02990
SN Absence or reduction of oxygen in body tissue.
UF Asphyxia
Hypoxia
Suffocation
B Symptoms [67]
R ↓ Ischemia [73]
↓ Respiratory Distress [73]

Antabuse
Use Disulfiram

Antagonism
Use Hostility

Antagonists (CNS Depressant Drugs)
Use Analeptic Drugs

Antarctica [73]
PN 55 **SC** 03020

Anthropologists [73]
PN 28 **SC** 03030
B Professional Personnel [78]
R Scientists [67]
Sociologists [73]

Anthropology [67]
PN 601 **SC** 03040
SN Science dealing with the study of the interrelations of biological, cultural, geographical, and historical characteristics of the human species. Use a more specific term if possible.
B Social Sciences [67]
R Ethnography [73]
Ethnology [67]
Folk Psychology [97]

Anti Inflammatory Drugs [82]
PN 126 **SC** 03041
SN Agents which reduce inflammation by acting on body mechanisms, without directly antagonizing the causative agent.
UF Antipyretic Drugs
B Drugs [67]
N Aspirin [73]
↓ Glucocorticoids [82]
↓ Neurokinins [97]
R ↓ Alkaloids [73]
↓ Analgesic Drugs [73]
↓ Enzymes [73]
↓ Hormones [67]
Hydrocortisone [73]
Prostaglandins [82]
↓ Steroids [73]

Antiadrenergic Drugs
Use Sympatholytic Drugs

Antiandrogens [82]
PN 80 **SC** 03042
SN Substances capable of preventing the normal effects of androgenic hormones on responsive tissues by antagonistic effects on tissue or by inhibiting androgenic effects.
UF Androgen Antagonists
B Drugs [67]
R ↓ Androgens [73]
↓ Estrogens [73]
↓ Steroids [73]

Antianxiety Drugs
Use Tranquilizing Drugs

Antibiotics [73]
PN 198 **SC** 03050
B Drugs [67]
N Amantadine [78]
Cycloheximide [73]
Penicillins [73]
Puromycin [73]
R Antineoplastic Drugs [82]

Antibodies [73]
PN 367 **SC** 03060
B Globulins [73]
R Antigens [82]
Blood Serum [73]
↓ Drugs [67]
Gamma Globulin [73]
Immunization [73]
↓ Immunoglobulins [73]
↓ Neurotoxins [82]

Anticholinergic Drugs
Use Cholinergic Blocking Drugs

Anticholinesterase Drugs
Use Cholinesterase Inhibitors

Anticipation (Serial Learning)
Use Serial Anticipation (Learning)

Anticoagulant Drugs [73]
PN 24 **SC** 03100
B Drugs [67]
N Heparin [73]

Anticonvulsive Drugs [73]
PN 828 **SC** 03110
SN Use ANTICONVULSIVE DRUGS or ANTIEPILEPTIC DRUGS (including DIPHENYLHYDANTOIN, or PRIMIDONE) to access references from 73–81.
UF Antiepileptic Drugs
Paraldehyde
B Drugs [67]
N Carbamazepine [88]
Chloral Hydrate [73]
Clonazepam [91]
Diphenylhydantoin [73]
Nitrazepam [78]
Oxazepam [78]
Pentobarbital [73]
Phenobarbital [73]
Primidone [73]
Valproic Acid [91]
R Acetazolamide [73]
↓ Anesthetic Drugs [73]
↓ Antispasmodic Drugs [73]
↓ Barbiturates [67]
↓ Benzodiazepines [78]
↓ CNS Depressant Drugs [73]
↓ Convulsions [67]
↓ Epilepsy [67]
↓ Hypnotic Drugs [73]
↓ Muscle Relaxing Drugs [73]
↓ Narcotic Drugs [73]
↓ Sedatives [73]
↓ Spasms [73]
↓ Tranquilizing Drugs [67]

Antidepressant Drugs [71]
PN 4787 **SC** 03120
UF Deanol
B Drugs [67]
N Bupropion [94]
Citalopram [97]
Fluoxetine [91]
Fluvoxamine [94]
Iproniazid [73]
Isocarboxazid [73]
Lithium Carbonate [73]
Methylphenidate [73]
Mianserin [82]
Moclobemide [97]
Molindone [82]
Nialamide [73]
Nomifensine [82]
Paroxetine [94]
Phenelzine [73]
Pheniprazine [73]
Pipradrol [73]
Sertraline [97]
Sulpiride [73]
Tranylcypromine [73]
Trazodone [88]
↓ Tricyclic Antidepressant Drugs [97]
Zimeldine [88]
R ↓ CNS Stimulating Drugs [73]
↓ Lithium [73]
↓ Monoamine Oxidase Inhibitors [73]

Antiemetic Drugs [73]
PN 74 **SC** 03140

Antiemetic Drugs — (cont'd)
UF Antinauseant Drugs
B Drugs [67]
N Chlorpromazine [67]
Chlorprothixene [73]
Fluphenazine [73]
Perphenazine [73]
Piracetam [82]
Prochlorperazine [73]
Promethazine [73]
Sulpiride [73]
R ↓ Cholinergic Blocking Drugs [73]
↓ Hypnotic Drugs [73]
Nausea [73]
↓ Sedatives [73]
↓ Tranquilizing Drugs [67]
Vomiting [73]

Antiepileptic Drugs
SN Term discontinued in 1982. Use ANTIEPILEPTIC DRUGS (including DIPHENYLHYDANTOIN, or PRIMIDONE) or ANTICONVULSIVE DRUGS to access references from 73–81.
Use Anticonvulsive Drugs

Antiestrogens [82]
PN 23 SC 03155
SN Substances capable of preventing the normal effects of estrogenic hormones on responsive tissues by antagonistic effects on tissue or by inhibiting estrogenic effects.
UF Estrogen Antagonists
B Drugs [67]
R ↓ Androgens [73]
Antineoplastic Drugs [82]
↓ Estrogens [73]
↓ Steroids [73]

Antigens [82]
PN 177 SC 03158
SN Substances such as microorganisms or foreign tissues, cells, proteins, toxoids, or exotoxins having the ability to induce antibody formation.
UF Allergens
Immunogens
R Antibodies [73]
Blood Groups [73]
↓ Immunoglobulins [73]
Interleukins [94]

Antihistaminic Drugs [73]
PN 207 SC 03160
B Drugs [67]
N Chlorprothixene [73]
Cimetidine [85]
Diphenhydramine [73]
Mianserin [82]
Orphenadrine [73]
Promethazine [73]
R Histamine [73]
Hydroxyzine [73]
↓ Hypnotic Drugs [73]
↓ Sedatives [73]

Antihypertensive Drugs [73]
PN 190 SC 03170
B Drugs [67]
N Alpha Methylparatyrosine [78]
Captopril [91]
Chlorpromazine [67]
Clonidine [73]
Guanethidine [73]
Hexamethonium [73]
Hydralazine [73]
Iproniazid [73]
Mecamylamine [73]
Methyldopa [73]
Pargyline [73]
Pheniprazine [73]

Antihypertensive Drugs — (cont'd)
N Phenoxybenzamine [73]
Quinpirole [94]
Reserpine [67]
R ↓ Adrenergic Blocking Drugs [73]
↓ Diuretics [73]
↓ Ganglion Blocking Drugs [73]
↓ Heart Rate Affecting Drugs [73]
↓ Hypertension [73]
↓ Hypnotic Drugs [73]
↓ Muscle Relaxing Drugs [73]
↓ Sedatives [73]
↓ Tranquilizing Drugs [67]
↓ Vasodilator Drugs [73]

Antinauseant Drugs
Use Antiemetic Drugs

Antineoplastic Drugs [82]
PN 79 SC 03179
SN Drugs used in the prevention of the development, maturation, or spread of neoplastic cells.
B Drugs [67]
R ↓ Antibiotics [73]
Antiestrogens [82]
↓ Hormones [67]
Interferons [94]
↓ Neoplasms [67]
↓ Steroids [73]

Antiparkinsonian Drugs
Use Antitremor Drugs

Antipathy
Use Aversion

Antipsychotic Drugs
SN Term discontinued in 1982. Use ANTIPSYCHOTIC DRUGS (from 73–81) or the specific tranquilizing or neuroleptic drug to access references prior to 1982. From 1982, see the specific tranquilizing drugs, neuroleptic drugs, or other appropriate drug classes.
Use Neuroleptic Drugs

Antipyretic Drugs
Use Anti Inflammatory Drugs

Antischizophrenic Drugs
SN Term discontinued in 1982. Use ANTISCHIZOPHRENIC DRUGS (from 73–81) or the specific tranquilizing or neuroleptic drug to access references prior to 1982. From 1982, see the specific tranquilizing drugs, neuroleptic drugs, or other appropriate drug classes.
Use Neuroleptic Drugs

AntiSemitism [73]
PN 242 SC 03220
B Racial and Ethnic Attitudes [82]
Religious Prejudices [73]
R Holocaust [88]
Jews [97]
Judaism [67]
↓ Prejudice [67]
Racism [73]

Antisocial Behavior [71]
PN 1795 SC 03230
UF Deviant Behavior
Sociopathology
B Behavior [67]
N Child Neglect [88]
↓ Crime [67]
Cruelty [73]
Elder Abuse [88]
Emotional Abuse [91]
Juvenile Delinquency [67]

Antisocial Behavior — (cont'd)
N Partner Abuse [91]
Patient Abuse [91]
Persecution [73]
Physical Abuse [91]
Recidivism [73]
Runaway Behavior [73]
↓ Sexual Abuse [88]
Terrorism [82]
Torture [88]
↓ Violence [73]
R Antisocial Personality [73]
↓ Behavior Disorders [71]
Erotomania [97]
Explosive Personality [73]
Impulse Control Disorders [97]
↓ Prosocial Behavior [82]
Psychopathology [67]
↓ Sexual Deviations [67]
↓ Social Behavior [67]

Antisocial Personality [73]
PN 812 SC 03240
SN Personality disorder characterized by conflict with others, low frustration tolerance, inadequate conscience development, and rejection of authority and discipline. Prior to 1997, consider PSYCHOPATHY.
UF Psychopath
Psychopathy
Sociopath
B Personality Disorders [67]
R ↓ Antisocial Behavior [71]
Aspergers Syndrome [91]
↓ Autism [67]
↓ Criminals [67]
Juvenile Delinquency [67]
Narcissistic Personality [73]

Antispasmodic Drugs [73]
PN 5 SC 03250
SN Drugs that prevent or reduce spasms usually by relaxation of smooth muscle.
B Drugs [67]
N Atropine [73]
Chlorprothixene [73]
Meperidine [73]
Orphenadrine [73]
Papaverine [73]
Trihexyphenidyl [73]
R ↓ Anticonvulsive Drugs [73]
↓ Cholinergic Blocking Drugs [73]
↓ Muscle Relaxing Drugs [73]
↓ Spasms [73]

Antitremor Drugs [73]
PN 167 SC 03260
SN Drugs that diminish skeletal muscle tone through action on the central nervous system.
UF Antiparkinsonian Drugs
B Drugs [67]
N Amantadine [78]
Diphenhydramine [73]
Levodopa [73]
Nomifensine [82]
Orphenadrine [73]
Trihexyphenidyl [73]
R ↓ Decarboxylase Inhibitors [82]
Parkinsons Disease [73]
Tremor [73]

Antitubercular Drugs [73]
PN 8 SC 03270
B Drugs [67]
N Iproniazid [73]
Isoniazid [73]
R ↓ Tuberculosis [73]

Antiviral Drugs 94
PN 5 SC 03280
B Drugs 67
N Zidovudine 94

Antonyms 73
PN 53 SC 03290
B Semantics 67
Vocabulary 67
R Words (Phonetic Units) 67

Ants 73
PN 344 SC 03300
B Insects 67
R Larvae 73

Anxiety 67
PN 14946 SC 03310
SN Apprehension or fear of impending actual or imagined danger, vulnerability, or uncertainty. Prior to 1988, also used for anxiety disorders.
UF Angst
Anxiousness
Apprehension
Worry
B Emotional States 73
N Mathematics Anxiety 85
Performance Anxiety 94
Social Anxiety 85
Speech Anxiety 85
Test Anxiety 67
R Agitation 91
↓ Anxiety Disorders 97
Anxiety Management 97
↓ Fear 67
Fear of Success 78
Guilt 67
Jealousy 73
Panic 73
Panic Disorder 88
↓ Phobias 67
Shame 94
↓ Stress 67

Anxiety Disorders 97
PN 0 SC 03315
SN Disorders characterized by anxiety or dread without apparent object or cause. Symptoms include irritability, anxious expectations, pangs of conscience, anxiety attacks, or phobias. Use ANXIETY NEUROSIS to access references from 73–96. Prior to 1998, consider also ANXIETY.
UF Anxiety Neurosis
Generalized Anxiety Disorder
B Mental Disorders 67
N Castration Anxiety 73
Death Anxiety 78
Obsessive Compulsive Neurosis 73
Panic Disorder 88
↓ Phobias 67
Posttraumatic Stress Disorder 85
Separation Anxiety 73
R ↓ Affective Disturbances 67
↓ Anxiety 67
Anxiety Management 97
Fear of Success 78
Guilt 67
Hypochondriasis 73
Mathematics Anxiety 85
Performance Anxiety 94
Social Anxiety 85
Speech Anxiety 85
Test Anxiety 67

Anxiety Management 97
PN 0 SC 03318
R ↓ Anxiety 67
↓ Anxiety Disorders 97
↓ Behavior Modification 73

Anxiety Management — (cont'd)
R ↓ Behavior Therapy 67
↓ Cognitive Techniques 85
Cognitive Therapy 82
↓ Relaxation Therapy 78
Stress Management 85

Anxiety Neurosis
SN Term discontinued in 1997. Use ANXIETY NEUROSIS to access references from 73–96.
Use Anxiety Disorders

Anxiety Reducing Drugs
Use Tranquilizing Drugs

Anxiolytic Drugs
Use Tranquilizing Drugs

Anxiousness
Use Anxiety

Aorta 73
PN 17 SC 03360
B Arteries (Anatomy) 73

Apathy 73
PN 83 SC 03380
UF Indifference
B Emotional States 73
R Hopelessness 88
↓ Separation Reactions 97

Apes
Use Primates (Nonhuman)

Aphagia 73
PN 45 SC 03400
SN Not eating, the refusal to eat, or an inability to swallow foods or fluids.
B Pain 67
Symptoms 67
R ↓ Eating Disorders 97

Aphasia 67
PN 2673 SC 03410
SN Partial or complete impairment of language comprehension, formulation, or use due to brain damage.
UF Agrammatism
Word Deafness
B Brain Disorders 67
Language Disorders 82
N Acalculia 73
↓ Agnosia 73
Agraphia 73
↓ Dysphasia 78
R ↓ Learning Disabilities 73
↓ Perceptual Disturbances 73

Aphrodisiacs 73
PN 16 SC 03420
R ↓ Cannabis 73

Aplysia
Use Snails

Apnea 73
PN 154 SC 03430
SN Temporary absence of breathing or prolonged respiratory failure.
B Respiratory Distress 73
Respiratory Tract Disorders 73
N Sleep Apnea 91
R ↓ Neonatal Disorders 73
Sudden Infant Death 82

Apomorphine 73
PN 1287 SC 03440
UF Apomorphine Hydrochloride
B Alkaloids 73
Dopamine Agonists 85
Emetic Drugs 73
Hypnotic Drugs 73
Narcotic Drugs 73

Apomorphine Hydrochloride
Use Apomorphine

Apoplexy
Use Cerebrovascular Accidents

Appalachia 73
PN 96 SC 03470
SN A mountainous eastern North American geographic region.
B United States 67

Apparatus 67
PN 3391 SC 03480
SN Set of materials, instruments, or equipment designed for specific operation in any setting. Use a more specific term if possible.
UF Devices (Experimental)
Equipment
Experimental Apparatus
Transistors (Apparatus)
Volt Meters
N Amplifiers (Apparatus) 73
Audiometers 73
Cage Apparatus 73
Cameras 73
↓ Computer Peripheral Devices 85
↓ Computers 67
Electrodes 67
Generators (Apparatus) 73
Incubators (Apparatus) 73
Keyboards 85
↓ Mazes 67
Metronomes 73
Microscopes 73
Oscilloscopes 73
Polygraphs 73
Shuttle Boxes 73
Skinner Boxes 73
Sonar 73
↓ Stimulators (Apparatus) 73
Tachistoscopes 73
↓ Tape Recorders 73
Timers (Apparatus) 73
Transducers 73
Vibrators (Apparatus) 73
R ↓ Augmentative Communication 94
↓ Television 67

Apparent Distance 73
PN 97 SC 03490
SN Subjective perception of distance as opposed to actual distance, based on comparison of retinal and familiar sizes.
B Distance Perception 73

Apparent Movement 67
PN 749 SC 03500
SN Subjective perception of movement in the absence of real physical movement.
UF Stroboscopic Movement
B Motion Perception 67
N Autokinetic Illusion 67

Apparent Size 73
PN 220 SC 03510
SN Subjective perception of size as opposed to real or actual size.
UF Size (Apparent)
B Size Discrimination 67

Apperception 73
PN 27 **SC** 03520
SN Process of assimilating new perceptions and relating them to existing body of knowledge.
R ↓ Attention 67
↓ Perception 67

Appetite 73
PN 452 **SC** 03530
SN Indicates an instinctive or acquired motivation, impulse, or desire stemming from internal physiological conditions. Compare HUNGER.
B Physiology 67
N Hunger 67
R ↓ Appetite Depressing Drugs 73
Craving 97
Dietary Restraint 94
↓ Eating 67
Eating Attitudes 94
↓ Eating Disorders 97
Satiation 67

Appetite Depressing Drugs 73
PN 126 **SC** 03540
UF Anorexigenic Drugs
B Drugs 67
N ↓ Amphetamine 67
Dextroamphetamine 73
Fenfluramine 73
Phenmetrazine 73
R ↓ Appetite 73

Appetite Disorders
SN Term discontinued in 1997. Use APPETITE DISORDERS to access references from 73–96.
Use Eating Disorders

Applied Psychology 73
PN 358 **SC** 03560
SN Broad discipline in which psychological principles and theories are used to solve practical problems.
B Psychology 67
N ↓ Clinical Psychology 67
Community Psychology 73
Consumer Psychology 73
Counseling Psychology 73
↓ Educational Psychology 67
Engineering Psychology 67
Environmental Psychology 82
Industrial Psychology 67
Military Psychology 67
Political Psychology 97
Social Psychology 67
Sport Psychology 82

Apprehension
Use Anxiety

Apprenticeship 73
PN 77 **SC** 03580
B Personnel Training 67
R ↓ Experiential Learning 97
Mentor 85

Approval (Social)
Use Social Approval

Apraxia 73
PN 389 **SC** 03600
SN Inability to execute complex coordinated movements resulting from lesions in the motor area of the cortex but involving no sensory impairment or paralysis.
UF Akinesia
B Movement Disorders 85
Symptoms 67

Apraxia — (cont'd)
R Parkinsonism 94
↓ Speech Disorders 67

Aptitude
Use Ability

Aptitude (Academic)
Use Academic Aptitude

Aptitude Measures 67
PN 2059 **SC** 03630
SN Tests designed to assess capacities or potential abilities in performing tasks, skills, or other acts which have not yet been learned.
UF Ability Tests
School and College Ability Test
Tests (Aptitude)
B Measurement 67
N Army General Classification Test 67
Coll Ent Exam Bd Scholastic Apt Test 73
Differential Aptitude Tests 73
General Aptitude Test Battery 73
Graduate Record Examination 73
Modern Language Aptitude Test 73

Arabs 88
PN 198 **SC** 03635
SN Persons of Arabic-speaking descent residing in countries other than the country of their origin.
UF Palestinians
B Ethnic Groups 73
R Minority Groups 67

Arachnida 73
PN 216 **SC** 03640
UF Spiders
B Arthropoda 73

Arachnophobia
Use Phobias

Archetypes 91
PN 103 **SC** 03650
SN Unconscious representation of inherited collective experience on which the personality is built. Anima, animus, and the shadow are major archetypes. Consider JUNGIAN PSYCHOLOGY to access references from 73-90.
B Collective Unconscious 97
R Analytical Psychotherapy 73
↓ Imagery 67
Jung (Carl) 73
↓ Jungian Psychology 73
Myths 67
Unconscious (Personality Factor) 67

Architects 73
PN 58 **SC** 03670
B Business and Industrial Personnel 67

Architecture 73
PN 517 **SC** 03680
B Arts 73
N Interior Design 82
R Computer Assisted Design 97
↓ Environment 67
↓ Environmental Planning 82
Religious Buildings 73
Urban Planning 73

Arctic Regions 91
PN 13 **SC** 03685
R Alaska 73

Arecoline 73
PN 70 **SC** 03690

Arecoline — (cont'd)
UF Arecoline Hydrobromide
B Cholinomimetic Drugs 73
R Bromides 73

Arecoline Hydrobromide
Use Arecoline

Argentina 82
PN 113 **SC** 03706
B South America 67

Arguments 73
PN 267 **SC** 03710
B Conflict 67
Interpersonal Communication 73
R Debates 97

Arithmetic
Use Mathematics

Arm (Anatomy) 73
PN 316 **SC** 03730
B Musculoskeletal System 73
R Elbow (Anatomy) 73
Hand (Anatomy) 67
Shoulder (Anatomy) 73
Wrist 73

Army General Classification Test 67
PN 7 **SC** 03740
B Aptitude Measures 67

Army Personnel 67
PN 955 **SC** 03750
B Military Personnel 67
R Draftees 73
National Guardsmen 73

Arousal (Physiological)
Use Physiological Arousal

Arousal (Sexual)
Use Sexual Arousal

Arrest (Law)
Use Legal Arrest

Arrhythmias (Heart) 73
PN 159 **SC** 03790
B Heart Disorders 73
N Bradycardia 73
Fibrillation (Heart) 73
Tachycardia 73

Arson 85
PN 104 **SC** 03795
UF Firesetting
B Crime 67

Art 67
PN 959 **SC** 03800
SN Products of aesthetic expression. Not used as a document type identifier.
UF Artwork
B Arts 73
N Crafts 73
Drawing 67
Painting (Art) 73
Photographic Art 73
Sculpturing 73

Art Education 73
PN 471 **SC** 03810
B Curriculum 67

Art Therapy 73
PN 980 **SC** 03820
SN Therapy that uses the creative work of clients for emotional expression, sublimation, achievement, and to reveal underlying conflicts.
B Creative Arts Therapy 94
R Educational Therapy 97
Movement Therapy 97
Recreation Therapy 73

Arterial Pulse 73
PN 345 **SC** 03830
UF Pulse (Arterial)
R Blood Circulation 73

Arteries (Anatomy) 73
PN 131 **SC** 03840
UF Coronary Vessels
Retinal Vessels
B Blood Vessels 73
N Aorta 73
Carotid Arteries 73

Arteriosclerosis 73
PN 38 **SC** 03850
B Cardiovascular Disorders 67
N Atherosclerosis 73
Cerebral Arteriosclerosis 73
R ↓ Blood Pressure Disorders 73

Arthritis 73
PN 311 **SC** 03860
UF Rheumatism
B Joint Disorders 73
N Rheumatoid Arthritis 73
R ↓ Infectious Disorders 73

Arthropoda 73
PN 31 **SC** 03870
B Invertebrates 73
N Arachnida 73
↓ Crustacea 73
↓ Insects 67

Articulation (Speech) 67
PN 1175 **SC** 03880
SN Production of speech sounds resulting from vocal tract movements.
B Speech Characteristics 73
Verbal Communication 67
R Phonetics 67
Pronunciation 73

Articulation Disorders 73
PN 374 **SC** 03890
SN Speech disorders involving the substitution, omission, distortion, and addition of phonemes.
UF Misarticulation
B Speech Disorders 67
N Dysarthria 73

Artificial Insemination
Use Reproductive Technology

Artificial Intelligence 82
PN 1065 **SC** 03895
SN Study and application of computers to simulate and perform functions of human information processing.
B Computer Applications 73
N ↓ Expert Systems 91
Neural Networks 91
R Automated Speech Recognition 94
Automation 67
↓ Cognitive Processes 67
↓ Computers 67
Cybernetics 67
Decision Support Systems 97

Artificial Intelligence — (cont'd)
R Human Machine Systems 97
Intelligence 67
Robotics 85

Artificial Limbs
Use Prostheses

Artificial Pacemakers 73
PN 34 **SC** 03910
UF Pacemakers (Artificial)
B Medical Therapeutic Devices 73

Artificial Respiration 73
PN 30 **SC** 03920
UF Lifesaving
B Physical Treatment Methods 73
R Respiration 67
↓ Respiratory System 73
↓ Respiratory Tract Disorders 73

Artistic Ability 73
PN 193 **SC** 03930
B Nonverbal Ability 88
N Musical Ability 73
R Creativity 67

Artists 73
PN 920 **SC** 03940
B Personnel 67
N Musicians 91
Writers 91

Arts 73
PN 247 **SC** 03950
SN Conceptually broad term referring to all forms of the arts, including the performing arts. Use a more specific term if possible.
UF Performing Arts
N ↓ Architecture 73
↓ Art 67
Dance 73
↓ Literature 67
↓ Music 67
↓ Theatre 73
R Aesthetics 67
Postmodernism 97

Artwork
Use Art

Asbestos
Use Hazardous Materials

Asceticism 73
PN 16 **SC** 03970
B Philosophies 67
Religious Practices 73
R Religion 67
↓ Religious Beliefs 73

Ascorbic Acid 73
PN 77 **SC** 03980
UF Vitamin C
B Acids 73
Vitamins 73

Asia 73
PN 448 **SC** 04000
N Afghanistan 88
Bangladesh 82
Hong Kong 78
India 67
Iran 73
Iraq 88
Israel 67
Japan 67

Asia — (cont'd)
N Jordan 88
↓ Korea 73
Lebanon 88
Middle East 78
Nepal 91
Pakistan 82
↓ Peoples Republic of China 73
Saudi Arabia 85
↓ Southeast Asia 73
Sri Lanka 88
Syria 88
Taiwan 73
Turkey 73
Union of Soviet Socialist Republics 67
R Commonwealth of Independent States 97

Asian Americans
SN Term discontinued in 1982. Use ASIAN AMERICANS to access references from 78-81.
Use Asians

Asians 82
PN 2312 **SC** 04007
SN Populations of Asian descent residing in countries other than the country of their origin. (For those residing in their own country use the appropriate country name). Use ASIAN AMERICANS to access references from 78–81.
UF Asian Americans
Orientals
B Ethnic Groups 73
N Chinese Cultural Groups 97
Japanese Cultural Groups 97
Korean Cultural Groups 97
Vietnamese Cultural Groups 97
R Minority Groups 67
Race (Anthropological) 73

Aspartic Acid 73
PN 395 **SC** 04010
B Amino Acids 73
Neurotransmitters 85
N N-Methyl-D-Aspartate 94

Aspergers Syndrome 91
PN 55 **SC** 04015
UF Autistic Psychopathy
B Personality Disorders 67
Syndromes 73
R Antisocial Personality 73
↓ Autism 67

Asphyxia
Use Anoxia

Aspiration Level 73
PN 264 **SC** 04030
SN Level of expectations for future achievement.
R ↓ Aspirations 67

Aspirations 67
PN 615 **SC** 04040
SN Individual desires to achieve goals and ideals. Use a more specific term if possible.
UF Ambition
N Educational Aspirations 73
Occupational Aspirations 73
R Aspiration Level 73
Goal Setting 97
↓ Goals 67
↓ Motivation 67

Aspirin 73
PN 83 **SC** 04050
UF Acetylsalicylic Acid
B Acids 73

Aspirin — (cont'd)
B Analgesic Drugs 73
Anti Inflammatory Drugs 82

Assassination (Political)
Use Political Assassination

Assertiveness 73
PN 1629 **SC** 04070
B Personality Traits 67
R Assertiveness Training 78
Empowerment 91
Extraversion 67
↓ Resistance 97

Assertiveness Training 78
PN 879 **SC** 04072
SN Training in the social skills required to be able to refuse requests; to express both positive and negative feelings; to initiate, engage in, and terminate conversation; and to make personal requests without suffering from excessive stress.
B Human Potential Movement 82
R Assertiveness 73
↓ Behavior Modification 73
Communication Skills Training 82
Human Relations Training 78
Social Skills Training 82

Assessment
Use Measurement

Assessment (Cognitive)
Use Cognitive Assessment

Assessment (Psychological)
Use Psychological Assessment

Assessment Centers 82
PN 176 **SC** 04082
SN Centers specializing in standardized, systematic behavioral evaluation process used to make selection, promotion, development, counseling, and career planning personnel decisions.
R Occupational Guidance 67
↓ Personnel Evaluation 73
Personnel Placement 73
Personnel Promotion 78
↓ Personnel Selection 67

Assimilation (Cultural)
Use Cultural Assimilation

Assistance (Social Behavior) 73
PN 1523 **SC** 04100
SN Act of rendering aid or help. Limited to human populations.
UF Helping Behavior
B Interpersonal Interaction 67
Prosocial Behavior 82
R Altruism 73
Charitable Behavior 73
↓ Help Seeking Behavior 78
Social Support Networks 82

Assistance Seeking (Professional)
Use Health Care Utilization

Assisted Suicide 97
PN 0 **SC** 04105
SN Provision of support and/or means that gives a patient the power to take his or her own life.
B Suicide 67
R Advance Directives 94
↓ Death and Dying 67
Euthanasia 73
Life Sustaining Treatment 97

Assisted Suicide — (cont'd)
R Palliative Care 91
Professional Ethics 73
Terminally Ill Patients 73
Treatment Refusal 94
Treatment Withholding 88

Association (Free)
Use Free Association

Associationism 73
PN 38 **SC** 04120
SN Theory which holds that learning and mental development consist mainly of combinations and recombinations of irreducible mental elements. Also, the basis for theories that explain learning in terms of stimulus and response.
B History of Psychology 67

Associations (Contextual)
Use Contextual Associations

Associations (Groups)
Use Organizations

Associations (Word)
Use Word Associations

Associative Processes 67
PN 1956 **SC** 04160
SN Development or maintenance of learned or cognitive connections (associations) between events, sensations, ideas, memories, or behavior as the result of functional relationships, similarity-contrast, or spatial-temporal contiguity.
B Cognitive Processes 67
N Cognitive Contiguity 73
Connotations 73
Contextual Associations 67
Isolation Effect 73
R Cognitive Generalization 67
Connectionism 94
Cues 67
Word Associations 67
Word Recognition 88

Assortative Mating 91
PN 46 **SC** 04165
SN Nonrandom mating between unrelated individuals with similar characteristics. Used for human or animal populations.
UF Assortive Mating
R ↓ Animal Breeding 73
Animal Mate Selection 82
↓ Animal Mating Behavior 67
Family Resemblance 91
↓ Genetics 67
Human Mate Selection 88
Phenotypes 73
Population Genetics 73
↓ Psychosexual Behavior 67

Assortive Mating
Use Assortative Mating

Asthenia 73
PN 42 **SC** 04170
SN Physical weakness, lack of strength and vitality, or a lack of concentration.
B Symptoms 67
N Myasthenia 73
R Neurasthenic Neurosis 73

Asthenic Personality
SN Term discontinued in 1997. Use ASTHENIC PERSONALITY to access references from 73–96.
Use Personality Disorders

Asthma 67
PN 907 **SC** 04190
B Dyspnea 73
R ↓ Immunologic Disorders 73
↓ Psychosomatic Disorders 67

Astrology 73
PN 80 **SC** 04200
R ↓ Parapsychology 67
Superstitions 73

Astronauts 73
PN 78 **SC** 04210
B Aerospace Personnel 73
R Aircraft Pilots 73
↓ Military Personnel 67
Spacecraft 73

Asylums
Use Psychiatric Hospitals

At Risk Populations 85
PN 5948 **SC** 04225
SN Groups or individuals considered in danger of developing a physical, mental, emotional, behavioral, or other disorder due to adverse internal or external factors.
UF High Risk Populations
Risk Populations
R Coronary Prone Behavior 82
Predisposition 73
Premorbidity 78
Susceptibility (Disorders) 73

Ataractic Drugs
Use Tranquilizing Drugs

Ataraxic Drugs
Use Tranquilizing Drugs

Ataxia 73
PN 201 **SC** 04250
SN Loss of coordination of voluntary muscular movement.
UF Dysmetria
B Movement Disorders 85
Symptoms 67
R Hyperkinesis 73

Atheism 73
PN 28 **SC** 04260
B Religious Beliefs 73

Atherosclerosis 73
PN 78 **SC** 04270
B Arteriosclerosis 73

Athetosis 73
PN 22 **SC** 04280
SN Nonprogressive, developmentally-evolving disorder arising from basal ganglia damage in the full term brain characterized by postural reflex impairments, involuntary movements, and dysarthria with preservation of sensation, ocular movement, and frequently, intelligence.
B Brain Disorders 67
Movement Disorders 85
R Cerebral Palsy 67

Athletes 73
PN 2331 **SC** 04287
N College Athletes 94
R Athletic Participation 73
Athletic Performance 91
Athletic Training 91
↓ Sports 67

Athletic Participation 73
PN 881 SC 04290
B Participation 73
Recreation 67
R ↓ Athletes 73
College Athletes 94
↓ Extracurricular Activities 73
↓ Sports 67

Athletic Performance 91
PN 454 SC 04300
UF Sport Performance
B Performance 67
R ↓ Athletes 73
Athletic Training 91
College Athletes 94
↓ Sports 67
Teams 88

Athletic Training 91
PN 147 SC 04305
UF Sport Training
Training (Athletic)
R ↓ Athletes 73
Athletic Performance 91
Coaches 88
College Athletes 94
↓ Education 67
↓ Extracurricular Activities 73
↓ Sports 67
Teams 88

Atmospheric Conditions 73
PN 311 SC 04310
UF Barometric Pressure
Climate (Meteorological)
Weather
B Environmental Effects 73
R Pollution 73
↓ Temperature Effects 67
Thermal Acclimatization 73

Atomism
Use Reductionism

Atria (Heart)
Use Heart Auricles

Atrial Fibrillation
Use Fibrillation (Heart)

Atrophy (Cerebral)
Use Cerebral Atrophy

Atrophy (Muscular)
Use Muscular Atrophy

Atropine 73
PN 453 SC 04350
UF Hyoscyamine (dl-)
Methylatropine
B Alkaloids 73
Amines 73
Analgesic Drugs 73
Antispasmodic Drugs 73
Cholinergic Blocking Drugs 73
Narcotic Drugs 73
Sedatives 73

Attachment Behavior 85
PN 1932 SC 04355
SN Formation of and investment in significant relationships. Usually refers to the emotional and biological attachment of human or animal infants to caretaking figures.
UF Bonding (Emotional)
B Behavior 67

Attachment Behavior — (cont'd)
R Abandonment 97
Anaclitic Depression 73
Dependency (Personality) 67
Emotional Development 73
Erotomania 97
Intimacy 73
Love 73
Object Relations 82
↓ Parent Child Relations 67
Postpartum Depression 73
Separation Anxiety 73
Separation Individuation 82
↓ Separation Reactions 97
Stranger Reactions 88

Attack Behavior 73
PN 655 SC 04360
SN Forceful, assaultive behavior. Used for human or animal populations.
B Aggressive Behavior 67
Animal Aggressive Behavior 73
R ↓ Animal Defensive Behavior 82
Animal Predatory Behavior 78
Instinctive Behavior 82
Retaliation 91

Attainment (Achievement)
Use Achievement

Attainment Level (Education)
Use Educational Attainment Level

Attempted Suicide 73
PN 2361 SC 04380
UF Parasuicide
Suicide (Attempted)
B Behavior Disorders 71
Self Destructive Behavior 85
R Suicidal Ideation 91
↓ Suicide 67
Suicide Prevention 73

Attendance (School)
Use School Attendance

Attendants (Institutions) 73
PN 244 SC 04400
UF Hospital Attendants
Residential Care Attendants
B Paramedical Personnel 73
R Prison Personnel 73
↓ Psychiatric Hospital Staff 73

Attention 67
PN 7374 SC 04410
SN Condition of perceptual or cognitive awareness of or focusing on some aspect of one's environment. Compare ATTENTION SPAN and VIGILANCE.
B Awareness 67
N Divided Attention 73
↓ Monitoring 73
Selective Attention 73
↓ Sustained Attention 97
Vigilance 67
R Apperception 73
Attention Span 73
Concentration 82
Distraction 78
Human Channel Capacity 73
Listening (Interpersonal) 97
↓ Perception 67
Rotary Pursuit 67
Signal Detection (Perception) 67
Time On Task 88
↓ Tracking 67

Attention Deficit Disorder 85
PN 1745 SC 04412
SN Deficit in the ability to sustain attention. Consider also HYPERKINESIS.
R Attention Span 73
Distractibility 73
Hyperkinesis 73
Impulsiveness 73
↓ Mental Disorders 67
Minimal Brain Disorders 73
Oppositional Defiant Disorder 97

Attention Span 73
PN 269 SC 04413
SN Temporal duration of concentration or amount of material grasped during exposure to stimuli or information. Compare ATTENTION.
B Sustained Attention 97
R ↓ Attention 67
Attention Deficit Disorder 85
Conceptual Tempo 85
Distraction 78
Vigilance 67

Attitude Change 67
PN 4237 SC 04430
SN Significant alteration in individual or group attitudes or opinions.
UF Opinion Change
R ↓ Attitudes 67
Brainwashing 82

Attitude Formation 73
PN 475 SC 04440
SN Process of developing an opinion or attitude, especially as influenced by psychological, emotional, social, and experiential factors.
R ↓ Attitudes 67

Attitude Measurement 73
PN 607 SC 04460
SN Projective, physiological, self-report, or other approaches to the assessment of attitudes.
B Measurement 67
R ↓ Attitude Measures 67
↓ Attitudes 67
Likert Scales 94

Attitude Measures 67
PN 2603 SC 04470
SN Instruments or devices used in the assessment of attitudes.
UF Allport Vernon Lindzey Study Values
Minnesota Teacher Attitude Inventory
Opinion Attitude and Interest Survey
Opinion Questionnaires
Opinion Surveys
B Measurement 67
N Parent Attitude Research Instrument 73
Wilson Patterson Conservatism Scale 73
R Attitude Measurement 73
↓ Attitudes 67
Likert Scales 94
↓ Preference Measures 73
Semantic Differential 67

Attitude Similarity 73
PN 903 SC 04480
R ↓ Attitudes 67

Attitudes 67
PN 8518 SC 04500
SN Conceptually broad array term referring to a mental position or feeling toward certain ideas, facts, or persons. Use a more specific term if possible.
UF Beliefs (Nonreligious)
Opinions
N Adolescent Attitudes 88

Attitudes — (cont'd)
N Adult Attitudes 88
Aged (Attitudes Toward) 78
Aging (Attitudes Toward) 85
Child Attitudes 88
Childrearing Attitudes 73
↓ Client Attitudes 82
Community Attitudes 73
Computer Attitudes 88
↓ Consumer Attitudes 73
Counselor Attitudes 73
Death Attitudes 73
↓ Disabled (Attitudes Toward) 97
↓ Drug Usage Attitudes 73
Eating Attitudes 94
↓ Employee Attitudes 67
Employer Attitudes 73
Environmental Attitudes 78
Family Planning Attitudes 73
Health Attitudes 85
↓ Health Personnel Attitudes 85
Homosexuality (Attitudes Toward) 82
Job Applicant Attitudes 73
Marriage Attitudes 73
Obesity (Attitudes Toward) 97
Occupational Attitudes 73
↓ Parental Attitudes 73
↓ Political Attitudes 73
Psychologist Attitudes 91
Public Opinion 73
↓ Racial and Ethnic Attitudes 82
↓ Sex Role Attitudes 78
Sexual Attitudes 73
↓ Socioeconomic Class Attitudes 73
Stereotyped Attitudes 67
Student Attitudes 67
↓ Teacher Attitudes 67
Work (Attitudes Toward) 73
R Attitude Change 67
Attitude Formation 73
Attitude Measurement 73
↓ Attitude Measures 67
Attitude Similarity 73
Attribution 73
↓ Cognitions 85
Hedonism 73
Impression Formation 78
Irrational Beliefs 82
Labeling 78
Planned Behavior 97
↓ Prejudice 67
↓ Religious Beliefs 73
Stigma 91
Superstitions 73
World View 88

Attorneys 73
PN 560 SC 04510
UF Lawyers
B Legal Personnel 85
R ↓ Law Enforcement Personnel 73
Law Students 78

Attraction (Interpersonal)
Use Interpersonal Attraction

Attribution 73
PN 8521 SC 04525
SN Perception of causes of behavior or events or of dispositional properties of an individual or group.
B Social Perception 67
R ↓ Attitudes 67
Blame 94
Causal Analysis 94
Impression Formation 78
Inference 73
Internal External Locus of Control 67

Attribution — (cont'd)
R Learned Helplessness 78
Self Fulfilling Prophecies 97

Atypical Paranoid Disorder
Use Paranoia (Psychosis)

Atypical Somatoform Disorder
Use Dysmorphophobia

Audiences 67
PN 477 SC 04530
SN Groups of spectators or listeners.
N Sports Spectators 97
R Observers 73

Audiogenic Seizures 78
PN 74 SC 04536
B Convulsions 67
R ↓ Auditory Stimulation 67

Audiology 73
PN 118 SC 04540
SN Scientific study of hearing, including: anatomical and functional properties of the ear; hearing disorders and their assessment and treatment; and the rehabilitation of hearing-impaired persons. Consider also AUDIOMETRY and SPEECH AND HEARING MEASURES.
B Paramedical Sciences 73

Audiometers 73
PN 18 SC 04550
B Apparatus 67

Audiometry 67
PN 1017 SC 04560
SN Specific procedures or audiometric tests used to measure hearing acuity and range in the diagnosis and evaluation of hearing impairments. Consider also AUDIOLOGY and SPEECH AND HEARING MEASURES.
UF Bekesy Audiometry
N Bone Conduction Audiometry 73
R Auditory Acuity 88
↓ Auditory Stimulation 67
↓ Perceptual Measures 73

Audiotapes 73
PN 342 SC 04570
SN Tape recordings of sound used in both educational and noneducational settings. Not used as a document type identifier.
B Audiovisual Communications Media 73

Audiovisual Aids (Educational)
Use Educational Audiovisual Aids

Audiovisual Communications Media 73
PN 172 SC 04590
B Communications Media 73
N Audiotapes 73
↓ Educational Audiovisual Aids 73
Film Strips 67
↓ Motion Pictures 73
Photographs 67
Radio 73
↓ Television 67
Television Advertising 73
Videotapes 73

Audiovisual Instruction 73
PN 250 SC 04600
B Teaching Methods 67
N Televised Instruction 73
Videotape Instruction 73
R ↓ Educational Audiovisual Aids 73

Audition
Use Auditory Perception

Auditory Acuity 88
PN 61 SC 04615
SN The ability or capacity of a listener to perceive fine detail. Consider AUDITORY THRESHOLDS or AUDITORY DISCRIMINATION to access references prior to 1988.
UF Hearing Acuity
B Auditory Perception 67
Perceptual Discrimination 73
R ↓ Audiometry 67
Auditory Discrimination 67
Auditory Localization 73
Auditory Thresholds 73

Auditory Cortex 67
PN 387 SC 04620
UF Cortex (Auditory)
B Temporal Lobe 73

Auditory Discrimination 67
PN 2616 SC 04630
SN Distinguishing between sounds of different intensity, frequency, pattern, complexity, or other characteristics.
B Auditory Perception 67
Perceptual Discrimination 73
R Auditory Acuity 88

Auditory Displays 73
PN 38 SC 04640
SN Presentations of patterned auditory stimulation.
B Auditory Stimulation 67
Displays 67

Auditory Evoked Potentials 73
PN 2274 SC 04650
B Evoked Potentials 67
R ↓ Cortical Evoked Potentials 73

Auditory Feedback 73
PN 256 SC 04660
SN Return of information on specified behavioral functions or parameters by means of auditory stimulation. Such stimulation may serve to regulate or control subsequent behavior, cognition, perception, or performance. Also, the process of hearing one's own vocalizations, especially as pertains to regulating the parameters of one's speech.
B Auditory Stimulation 67
Sensory Feedback 73
N Delayed Auditory Feedback 73

Auditory Hallucinations 73
PN 280 SC 04670
B Hallucinations 67

Auditory Localization 73
PN 553 SC 04680
SN Subjective determination of the specific spatial location of a sound source or relative locations of sound sources.
UF Localization (Sound)
Sound Localization
B Auditory Perception 67
Perceptual Localization 67
R Auditory Acuity 88

Auditory Masking 73
PN 782 SC 04690
SN Change in perceptual sensitivity to an auditory stimulus due to the presence of a second stimulus in close temporal proximity.
B Masking 67
R ↓ Auditory Stimulation 67

Auditory Nerve
Use Acoustic Nerve

Auditory Neurons 73
PN 154 **SC** 04710
B Sensory Neurons 73

Auditory Perception 67
PN 6370 **SC** 04720
SN Awareness, detection, or identification of sounds.
UF Audition
Listening
B Perception 67
N Auditory Acuity 88
Auditory Discrimination 67
Auditory Localization 73
↓ Loudness Perception 73
Music Perception 97
↓ Pitch Perception 73
Speech Perception 67
R Acoustics 97
Auditory Thresholds 73
↓ Ear Disorders 73
Listening (Interpersonal) 97
Pattern Discrimination 67
↓ Rhythm 91

Auditory Stimulation 67
PN 6701 **SC** 04730
UF Acoustic Stimuli
Noise (Sound)
Sound
B Perceptual Stimulation 73
N Auditory Displays 73
↓ Auditory Feedback 73
Dichotic Stimulation 82
Filtered Noise 73
↓ Loudness 67
↓ Pitch (Frequency) 67
White Noise 73
R Acoustics 97
Audiogenic Seizures 78
↓ Audiometry 67
Auditory Masking 73
Bone Conduction Audiometry 73
↓ Speech Processing (Mechanical) 73

Auditory Thresholds 73
PN 1232 **SC** 04740
SN The minimal level of auditory stimulation, the minimal difference between any auditory stimuli, or the minimal stimulus change that is perceptually detectable.
B Thresholds 67
R Auditory Acuity 88
↓ Auditory Perception 67
↓ Perceptual Measures 73

Augmentative Communication 94
PN 147 **SC** 04750
SN Communication that is supported by keyboards, typewriters, books, gestural systems, or other devices to enable individuals with communication or speech disorders to communicate effectively.
UF Facilitated Communication
B Communication 67
N ↓ Manual Communication 78
R ↓ Apparatus 67
↓ Communication Disorders 82
↓ Medical Therapeutic Devices 73
↓ Speech Disorders 67
Speech Therapy 67

Aura 73
PN 46 **SC** 04760

Aura — (cont'd)
SN Sensations experienced immediately prior to the onset of a seizure, migraine headache, or other nervous system disorder symptoms. Also, the patient's recognition of the beginning of an epileptic attack. Use PARAPSYCHOLOGY or PARAPSYCHOLOGICAL PHENOMENA to access references on psychic auras and halos.
B Symptoms 67
R ↓ Epilepsy 67

Aurally Disabled 97
PN 0 **SC** 04765
SN Persons with varying degrees of hearing loss due to ear disorders or an organic defect of the sensorineural pathways. Use AURALLY HANDICAPPED to access references from 73–96.
UF Aurally Handicapped
B Sensorially Disabled 97
N ↓ Deaf 67
Partially Hearing Impaired 73
R Cochlear Implants 94
↓ Communication Disorders 82
↓ Ear Disorders 73
Hearing Disorders 82
Sensory Disabilities (Attit Toward) 97

Aurally Handicapped
SN Term discontinued in 1997. Use AURALLY HANDICAPPED to access references from 73–96.
Use Aurally Disabled

Auricles (Heart)
Use Heart Auricles

Auricular Fibrillation
Use Fibrillation (Heart)

Australia 73
PN 1816 **SC** 04800
R ↓ South Pacific 78

Austria 73
PN 159 **SC** 04810
B Europe 73

Authoritarianism 67
PN 1774 **SC** 04820
SN Complex of personality characteristics expressed as antidemocratic social attitudes, rigid attachment to traditional values, uncritical acceptance of authority, and intolerance of opposing views.
UF Domination
B Personality Traits 67
R Dogmatism 78
↓ Dominance 67
Egalitarianism 85
Openmindedness 78

Authoritarianism (Parental)
Use Parental Permissiveness

Authoritarianism Rebellion Scale
SN Term discontinued in 1997. Use AUTHORITARIANISM REBELLION SCALE to access references from 73–96.
Use Nonprojective Personality Measures

Authority 67
PN 581 **SC** 04845
SN Ability or vested power to influence thought, attitudes, and behavior.
R Abuse of Power 97
Coercion 94
↓ Dominance 67
↓ Leadership 67

Authority — (cont'd)
R Omnipotence 94
↓ Power 67
↓ Social Influences 67
↓ Status 67

Authors
Use Writers

Autism 67
PN 2146 **SC** 04850
B Mental Disorders 67
N Early Infantile Autism 73
R Antisocial Personality 73
Aspergers Syndrome 91
Autistic Children 73
Autistic Thinking 73
Developmental Disabilities 82

Autistic Children 73
PN 1958 **SC** 04860
B Emotionally Disturbed 73
R ↓ Autism 67
↓ Childhood Psychosis 67
↓ Children 67
Early Infantile Autism 73

Autistic Psychopathy
Use Aspergers Syndrome

Autistic Thinking 73
PN 13 **SC** 04870
B Thinking 67
Thought Disturbances 73
R ↓ Autism 67

Autobiographical Memory 94
PN 61 **SC** 04875
SN Personal memories of past events that have occurred over the course of one's life. Compare REMINISCENCE and LIFE REVIEW.
B Memory 67
R Anniversary Events 94
Early Experience 67
Early Memories 85
Life Experiences 73
Life Review 91
Reminiscence 85

Autobiography 73
PN 327 **SC** 04880
SN Recorded account of one's own life. Not used as a document type identifier.
B Biography 67

Autoeroticism 97
PN 0 **SC** 04890
SN Use MASTURBATION to access references from 73–96.
R Eroticism 73
Masturbation 73
Narcissism 67
↓ Psychosexual Behavior 67

Autogenic Training 73
PN 378 **SC** 04900
SN Physiological form of psychotherapy based on studies of sleep and hypnosis and the application of yoga principles.
B Psychotherapeutic Techniques 67
Psychotherapy 67
R Biofeedback Training 78
↓ Relaxation Therapy 78

Autohypnosis 73
PN 176 **SC** 04910
SN Practice, process, or hypnotic state resulting from self-induced hypnosis.

Autohypnosis — (cont'd)
UF Self Hypnosis
B Hypnosis 67
R Catalepsy 73

Autoimmune Disorders
Use Immunologic Disorders

Autokinetic Illusion 67
PN 249 SC 04930
SN Apparent movement of a fixated light in a dark field.
UF Illusion (Autokinetic)
B Apparent Movement 67
Visual Perception 67

Automated Information Coding 73
PN 45 SC 04940
B Automated Information Processing 73
R ↓ Computers 67

Automated Information Processing 73
PN 412 SC 04950
UF Information Processing (Automated)
N Automated Information Coding 73
↓ Automated Information Retrieval 73
Automated Information Storage 73
R ↓ Communication Systems 73
↓ Computers 67
↓ Data Processing 67
↓ Expert Systems 91
Information 67
Information Systems 91

Automated Information Retrieval 73
PN 208 SC 04960
UF Information Retrieval (Automated)
B Automated Information Processing 73
N Computer Searching 91
R Automated Information Storage 73
↓ Computers 67
Databases 91
Information Services 88
Information Systems 91

Automated Information Storage 73
PN 75 SC 04970
B Automated Information Processing 73
R ↓ Automated Information Retrieval 73
↓ Computers 67
Databases 91
Information Systems 91

Automated Speech Recognition 94
PN 33 SC 04975
SN Machine or other apparatus used in the automatic recognition and understanding of human speech.
UF Automatic Speaker Recognition
B Speech Processing (Mechanical) 73
R ↓ Artificial Intelligence 82
↓ Computer Applications 73
↓ Expert Systems 91
Speech Perception 67

Automatic Speaker Recognition
Use Automated Speech Recognition

Automation 67
PN 306 SC 04980
SN Use of mechanical and/or electronic devices to automatically control the operation of an apparatus, system, or process.
R ↓ Artificial Intelligence 82
↓ Computers 67

Automatism 73
PN 68 SC 04990

Automatism — (cont'd)
SN An act or movement performed without conscious control.
B Symptoms 67

Automobile Accidents
Use Motor Traffic Accidents

Automobile Safety
Use Highway Safety

Automobiles 73
PN 204 SC 05020
B Motor Vehicles 82
R Drivers 73

Autonomic Ganglia 73
PN 15 SC 05050
UF Celiac Plexus
Hypogastric Plexus
Myenteric Plexus
Postganglionic Autonomic Fibers
Preganglionic Autonomic Fibers
Stellate Ganglion
Submucous Plexus
B Autonomic Nervous System 67
Ganglia 73
R ↓ Peripheral Nervous System 73

Autonomic Nervous System 67
PN 938 SC 05060
B Peripheral Nervous System 73
N Adrenergic Nerves 73
Autonomic Ganglia 73
Cholinergic Nerves 73
↓ Parasympathetic Nervous System 73
↓ Sympathetic Nervous System 73
R Autonomic Nervous System Disorders 73

Autonomic Nervous System Disorders 73
PN 48 SC 05070
B Nervous System Disorders 67
R ↓ Autonomic Nervous System 67

Autonomy (Government) 73
PN 33 SC 05080
R Government 67

Autonomy (Personality)
Use Independence (Personality)

Autopsy 73
PN 91 SC 05090
R ↓ Diagnosis 67
↓ Medical Diagnosis 73
Psychological Autopsy 88

Autoregulation
Use Homeostasis

Autoshaping 78
PN 337 SC 05106
SN Learned behavior or the experimental paradigm involving a Pavlovian pairing of a reinforcer and a stimulus independent of the subject's behavior until the subject makes a response to the stimulus. At that point the reinforcer is made contingent on the acquired response to the stimulus, thereby bringing the response under operant control.
B Conditioning 67
R Noncontingent Reinforcement 88
↓ Reinforcement 67

Autosome Disorders 73
PN 55 SC 05110

Autosome Disorders — (cont'd)
B Chromosome Disorders 73
N Crying Cat Syndrome 73
Downs Syndrome 67
Trisomy 21 73
R Autosomes 73

Autosomes 73
PN 27 SC 05120
B Chromosomes 73
R ↓ Autosome Disorders 73

Autotomy
Use Self Mutilation

Aversion 67
PN 618 SC 05130
UF Antipathy
Dislike
B Emotional States 73
N Hate 73
R Disgust 94

Aversion Conditioning 82
PN 1378 SC 05135
SN Conditioning paradigm in which aversive effects are paired with external stimuli resulting in an aversion to the stimuli. Also, the learned aversion itself.
UF Odor Aversion Conditioning
Taste Aversion Conditioning
B Conditioning 67
N Covert Sensitization 88
R Aversive Stimulation 73

Aversion Therapy 73
PN 449 SC 05140
SN Form of behavior therapy designed to eliminate undesirable behavior patterns through learned associations with unpleasant or painful stimuli. Also known as aversive conditioning therapy.
B Behavior Therapy 67
N Covert Sensitization 88
R Counterconditioning 73
↓ Shock Therapy 73

Aversive Stimulation 73
PN 1409 SC 05150
SN Presentation of a noxious stimulus. Also, any noxious stimuli (i.e., stimuli that an organism attempts to avoid or escape from). Compare PUNISHMENT.
B Stimulation 67
R ↓ Aversion Conditioning 82
Covert Sensitization 88

Aviation 67
PN 554 SC 05160
N Flight Instrumentation 73
Spaceflight 67
R Acceleration Effects 73
Altitude Effects 73
↓ Aviation Safety 73
↓ Gravitational Effects 67

Aviation Personnel
Use Aerospace Personnel

Aviation Safety 73
PN 105 SC 05170
B Safety 67
N Air Traffic Control 73
R Air Traffic Accidents 73
Aircraft Pilots 73
↓ Aviation 67
↓ Transportation Accidents 73

Aviators
Use Aircraft Pilots

Avoidance [67]
PN 1812 **SC** 05190
UF Escape
R Avoidance Conditioning [67]
Neophobia [85]
↓ Resistance [97]

Avoidance Conditioning [67]
PN 6244 **SC** 05200
SN Learned behavior or the operant conditioning procedure in which the subject learns a behavior that prevents the occurrence of an aversive stimulus. Compare ESCAPE CONDITIONING.
UF Active Avoidance
Conditioning (Avoidance)
Passive Avoidance
B Operant Conditioning [67]
R Avoidance [67]

Avoidant Personality [94]
PN 17 **SC** 05205
SN Personality disorder characterized by excessive social discomfort, extreme sensitivity to negative perceptions of oneself, pervasive preoccupation with being criticized or rejected in social situations, and low self esteem.
B Personality Disorders [67]
R Social Anxiety [85]
Social Phobia [85]

Awareness [67]
PN 1663 **SC** 05210
SN Conscious realization, perception, or knowledge.
B Consciousness States [71]
N ↓ Attention [67]
Body Awareness [82]
R Metacognition [91]
Sensory Gating [91]

Axons [73]
PN 161 **SC** 05220
B Neurons [73]

Azidothymidine
Use Zidovudine

AZT
Use Zidovudine

Babbling
Use Infant Vocalization

Babies
Use Infants

Babinski Reflex [73]
PN 2 **SC** 05250
B Reflexes [71]

Baboons [73]
PN 492 **SC** 05260
B Primates (Nonhuman) [73]

Babysitting
Use Child Care

Back (Anatomy) [73]
PN 116 **SC** 05270
B Anatomy [67]

Back Pain [82]
PN 658 **SC** 05275

Back Pain — (cont'd)
B Pain [67]
R Chronic Pain [85]
↓ Physical Disorders [97]

Background (Family)
Use Family Background

Backward Masking
Use Masking

Baclofen [91]
PN 58 **SC** 05293
B Muscle Relaxing Drugs [73]

Bacteria
Use Microorganisms

Bacterial Disorders [73]
PN 49 **SC** 05300
B Infectious Disorders [73]
N Bacterial Meningitis [73]
Gonorrhea [73]
Pulmonary Tuberculosis [73]
↓ Tuberculosis [73]
R Pneumonia [73]
Rheumatic Fever [73]

Bacterial Meningitis [73]
PN 10 **SC** 05310
B Bacterial Disorders [73]
Meningitis [73]

Bahama Islands [73]
PN 16 **SC** 05330
B West Indies [73]

Balance (Motor Processes)
Use Equilibrium

Baldness
Use Alopecia

Ballet
Use Dance

Bangladesh [82]
PN 62 **SC** 05355
B Asia [73]

Bannister Repertory Grid [73]
PN 23 **SC** 05360
B Nonprojective Personality Measures [73]

Baptists
Use Protestants

Barbados [91]
PN 10 **SC** 05370
B West Indies [73]

Barbital [73]
PN 59 **SC** 05380
B Barbiturates [67]
CNS Depressant Drugs [73]
Hypnotic Drugs [73]
Sedatives [73]

Barbiturate Poisoning [73]
PN 4 **SC** 05390
B Toxic Disorders [73]
R ↓ Analeptic Drugs [73]
↓ Barbiturates [67]

Barbiturates [67]
PN 220 **SC** 05400

Barbiturates — (cont'd)
B Drugs [67]
N Amobarbital [73]
Barbital [73]
Hexobarbital [73]
Methohexital [73]
Pentobarbital [73]
Phenobarbital [73]
Secobarbital [73]
Thiopental [73]
R ↓ Anesthetic Drugs [73]
↓ Anticonvulsive Drugs [73]
Barbiturate Poisoning [73]
↓ CNS Depressant Drugs [73]
↓ Hypnotic Drugs [73]
Primidone [73]
↓ Sedatives [73]

Bargaining [73]
PN 507 **SC** 05410
B Negotiation [73]

Barium [73]
PN 9 **SC** 05420
B Metallic Elements [73]

Barometric Pressure
Use Atmospheric Conditions

Baroreceptors [73]
PN 57 **SC** 05440
UF Pressoreceptors
B Neural Receptors [73]
Sensory Neurons [73]
Sympathetic Nervous System [73]

Barrett Lennard Relationship Invent [73]
PN 10 **SC** 05450
B Nonprojective Personality Measures [73]

Barron Welsh Art Scale [73]
PN 6 **SC** 05460
B Nonprojective Personality Measures [73]

Basal Ganglia [73]
PN 1579 **SC** 05470
UF Corpus Striatum
B Ganglia [73]
Telencephalon [73]
N Amygdaloid Body [73]
Caudate Nucleus [73]
Globus Pallidus [73]
Putamen [85]
R Extrapyramidal Symptoms [94]
Nucleus Basalis Magnocellularis [94]
Progressive Supranuclear Palsy [97]
Substantia Nigra [94]

Basal Metabolism [73]
PN 39 **SC** 05480
SN The amount of heat produced by the body to maintain life processes at the lowest level of cell activity in the waking state.
B Metabolism [67]

Basal Readers
Use Reading Materials

Basal Skin Resistance [73]
PN 12 **SC** 05500
SN Baseline or minimum electrical current generated or conducted by the body as measured on the skin surface during a resting state.
B Skin Resistance [73]

Baseball [73]
PN 169 **SC** 05510

Baseball — (cont'd)
B Recreation 67
Sports 67

Basic Skills Testing
Use Minimum Competency Tests

Basketball 73
PN 297 **SC** 05520
B Recreation 67
Sports 67

Bass (Fish) 73
PN 23 **SC** 05530
B Fishes 67

Bats 73
PN 227 **SC** 05550
UF Chiroptera
B Mammals 73

Battered Child Syndrome 73
PN 32 **SC** 05560
SN Behavioral pattern, including inability to relate to others and feelings of rejection, characteristic of infants and children who have been abused.
B Child Abuse 71
Syndromes 73
R Physical Abuse 91

Battered Females 88
PN 551 **SC** 05561
SN Use FAMILY VIOLENCE to access references from 85-87.
B Human Females 73
R ↓ Abuse Reporting 97
↓ Family Violence 82
Partner Abuse 91
Physical Abuse 91
Shelters 91

Bayes Theorem
Use Statistical Probability

Bayley Scales of Infant Development 94
PN 14 **SC** 05575
B Developmental Measures 94
R ↓ Intelligence Measures 67

Beavers 73
PN 11 **SC** 05580
B Rodents 73

Beck Depression Inventory 88
PN 161 **SC** 05588
B Nonprojective Personality Measures 73

Bedwetting
Use Urinary Incontinence

Beer 73
PN 87 **SC** 05590
B Alcoholic Beverages 73

Bees 73
PN 432 **SC** 05600
B Insects 67
R Larvae 73

Beetles 73
PN 148 **SC** 05610
B Insects 67
R Larvae 73

Behavior 67
PN 4488 **SC** 05670

Behavior — (cont'd)
SN Conceptually broad array term referring to any or all aspects of human or animal behavior. Use a more specific term if possible.
N Adaptive Behavior 91
↓ Adjunctive Behavior 82
↓ Animal Ethology 67
↓ Antisocial Behavior 71
Attachment Behavior 85
Childhood Play Behavior 78
Choice Behavior 67
Classroom Behavior 73
Conservation (Ecological Behavior) 78
↓ Consumer Behavior 67
Coping Behavior 67
Coronary Prone Behavior 82
↓ Drinking Behavior 78
↓ Driving Behavior 67
↓ Exploratory Behavior 67
Health Behavior 82
Illness Behavior 82
Instinctive Behavior 82
↓ Psychosexual Behavior 67
Self Defeating Behavior 88
↓ Self Destructive Behavior 85
↓ Social Behavior 67
Stereotyped Behavior 73
Voting Behavior 73
Wandering Behavior 91
R Behavior Change 73
↓ Behavior Disorders 71
↓ Behavior Modification 73
↓ Behavior Problems 67
↓ Behavior Therapy 67
Behavioral Assessment 82
Behavioral Contrast 78
↓ Behavioral Sciences 97
Behaviorism 67
Human Nature 97
Planned Behavior 97

Behavior Analysis
Use Behavioral Assessment

Behavior Change 73
PN 2106 **SC** 05620
SN Detectable changes in behavior due to psychotherapeutic, behavioral or other intervention, or spontaneous occurrence.
R ↓ Behavior 67
↓ Behavior Modification 73
Lifestyle Changes 97
Personality Change 67

Behavior Contracting 78
PN 239 **SC** 05624
SN Therapeutic technique involving a formal written contract, usually between two parties, which explicitly states the relationship between a particular behavior and its consequences (sanctions). Viewed as a structural means of scheduling reinforcement between the two parties, it is used as a method of controlling contingencies of reinforcement.
R ↓ Behavior Modification 73
↓ Behavior Therapy 67

Behavior Disorders 71
PN 3278 **SC** 05630
SN Disorders characterized by persistent and repetitive patterns of behavior that violate societal norms or rules or that seriously impair a person's functioning. Compare BEHAVIOR PROBLEMS.
N ↓ Addiction 73
Attempted Suicide 73
↓ Drug Abuse 73
↓ Homicide 67
Juvenile Delinquency 67
Self Mutilation 73

Behavior Disorders — (cont'd)
R Acting Out 67
↓ Aggressive Behavior 67
↓ Antisocial Behavior 71
↓ Behavior 67
↓ Behavior Problems 67
Body Rocking 73
Conduct Disorder 91
↓ Crime 67
Faking 73
Fecal Incontinence 73
Hair Pulling 73
↓ Mental Disorders 67
Oppositional Defiant Disorder 97
Pathological Gambling 88
↓ Self Destructive Behavior 85
↓ Symptoms 67
Thumbsucking 73
Urinary Incontinence 73

Behavior Modification 73
PN 6607 **SC** 05640
SN Use of classical conditioning or operant (instrumental) learning techniques to modify behavior.
B Treatment 67
N ↓ Behavior Therapy 67
Biofeedback Training 78
Classroom Behavior Modification 73
↓ Contingency Management 73
Fading (Conditioning) 82
Omission Training 85
Overcorrection 85
↓ Self Management 85
Time Out 85
R Anger Control 97
Anxiety Management 97
Assertiveness Training 78
↓ Behavior 67
Behavior Change 73
Behavior Contracting 78
Behavioral Assessment 82
Cognitive Restructuring 85
Cognitive Therapy 82
Communication Skills Training 82
Constant Time Delay 97
Counterconditioning 73
↓ Operant Conditioning 67
↓ Prompting 97
↓ Relaxation Therapy 78
↓ Self Help Techniques 82
Self Monitoring 82
Social Skills Training 82
Stress Management 85

Behavior Problems 67
PN 6469 **SC** 05650
SN Disruptive or improper behaviors that generally fall within societal norms and do not seriously impair a person's functioning. Compare BEHAVIOR DISORDERS.
UF Disruptive Behavior
Misbehavior
Misconduct
N Tantrums 73
R ↓ Behavior 67
↓ Behavior Disorders 71
Conduct Disorder 91
↓ Crime 67

Behavior Therapy 67
PN 6333 **SC** 05660
SN Therapeutic approach that may employ classical conditioning, operant learning techniques, or other behavioral techniques, in an attempt to eliminate or modify problem behavior, addressing itself primarily to the client's overt behavior, as opposed to thoughts, feelings, or other cognitive processes.

Behavior Therapy — (cont'd)
B Behavior Modification [73]
Psychotherapy [67]
N ↓ Aversion Therapy [73]
↓ Exposure Therapy [97]
Implosive Therapy [73]
Reciprocal Inhibition Therapy [73]
Response Cost [97]
Systematic Desensitization Therapy [73]
R Anger Control [97]
Anxiety Management [97]
↓ Behavior [67]
Behavior Contracting [78]
Counterconditioning [73]
Eye Movement Desensitization Therapy [97]
Paradoxical Techniques [82]
Rational Emotive Therapy [78]

Behavioral Assessment [82]
PN 1912 **SC** 05671
SN Objective identification of response units and their controlling environmental and organismic variables for the purpose of understanding, analyzing, or changing behavior. Primarily used for human populations.
UF Behavior Analysis
B Analysis [67]
Psychological Assessment [97]
R ↓ Behavior [67]
↓ Behavior Modification [73]
Educational Program Evaluation [73]
↓ Empirical Methods [73]
Mental Health Program Evaluation [73]

Behavioral Contrast [78]
PN 235 **SC** 05674
SN Change in response rate or latency following a change in reinforcement of one component of multiple operant discrimination schedules of reinforcement.
R ↓ Behavior [67]
↓ Reinforcement [67]
Response Frequency [73]
Response Latency [67]
Stimulus Discrimination [73]

Behavioral Ecology [97]
PN 0 **SC** 57450
SN Study, usually based on naturalistic observations, of the interaction between the environment and the behavior of organisms within that environment.
R ↓ Ecological Factors [73]
Ecological Psychology [94]
Ecology [73]
Environmental Psychology [82]

Behavioral Genetics [94]
PN 64 **SC** 57405
SN Scientific discipline concerned with the role of genes and gene action in the expression of behavior. Includes analysis of whole populations for specific traits, e.g., intelligence. Used for the scientific discipline or the behavioral genetic processes themselves.
B Genetics [67]
R Biopsychosocial Approach [91]
↓ Genetic Disorders [73]
Genetic Dominance [73]
Genetic Recessiveness [73]
Nature Nurture [94]
Population Genetics [73]
Psychobiology [82]
Sociobiology [82]

Behavioral Health
Use Health Care Psychology

Behavioral Medicine
Use Health Care Psychology

Behavioral Sciences [97]
PN 0 **SC** 05680
SN Group of scientific disciplines dealing with human and animal action and behavior. Use SOCIAL SCIENCES to access references from 73–96.
B Social Sciences [67]
N ↓ Psychology [67]
R ↓ Behavior [67]
↓ Sociology [67]

Behaviorism [67]
PN 1212 **SC** 05690
B History of Psychology [67]
R ↓ Behavior [67]
Positivism (Philosophy) [97]
Skinner (Burrhus Frederic) [91]
Watson (John Broadus) [91]

Bekesy Audiometry
Use Audiometry

Belgium [73]
PN 200 **SC** 05710
B Europe [73]

Beliefs (Nonreligious)
Use Attitudes

Beliefs (Religion)
Use Religious Beliefs

Belize [88]
PN 7 **SC** 05725
B Central America [73]

Bem Sex Role Inventory [88]
PN 48 **SC** 05727
B Nonprojective Personality Measures [73]

Bemegride [73]
PN 19 **SC** 05730
B Analeptic Drugs [73]

Benactyzine [73]
PN 25 **SC** 05740
B Cholinergic Blocking Drugs [73]
Tranquilizing Drugs [67]

Benadryl
Use Diphenhydramine

Bender Gestalt Test [67]
PN 363 **SC** 05770
B Projective Personality Measures [73]
R ↓ Neuropsychological Assessment [82]

Benign Neoplasms [73]
PN 19 **SC** 05800
B Neoplasms [67]

Benin [91]
PN 6 **SC** 05805
B Africa [67]

Benton Revised Visual Retention Test [73]
PN 35 **SC** 05810
B Intelligence Measures [67]
R ↓ Neuropsychological Assessment [82]

Benzedrine
Use Amphetamine

Benzodiazepine Agonists [94]
PN 42 **SC** 05821
R ↓ Benzodiazepines [78]

Benzodiazepine Antagonists [85]
PN 305 **SC** 05822
R ↓ Benzodiazepines [78]

Benzodiazepines [78]
PN 2053 **SC** 05824
B Drugs [67]
N Alprazolam [88]
Chlordiazepoxide [73]
Clonazepam [91]
Diazepam [73]
Flurazepam [82]
Lorazepam [88]
Midazolam [91]
Nitrazepam [78]
Oxazepam [78]
R ↓ Anticonvulsive Drugs [73]
Benzodiazepine Agonists [94]
Benzodiazepine Antagonists [85]
↓ Hypnotic Drugs [73]
↓ Minor Tranquilizers [73]
↓ Muscle Relaxing Drugs [73]
↓ Sedatives [73]
↓ Tranquilizing Drugs [67]

Bereavement
Use Grief

Bermuda [91]
PN 0 **SC** 05825
B West Indies [73]

Beta Blockers
Use Adrenergic Blocking Drugs

Between Groups Design [85]
PN 23 **SC** 05828
SN Experimental design in which the subjects serve in only one treatment condition. Includes designs of matched or correlated groups and randomized groups.
B Experimental Design [67]

Beverages (Alcoholic)
Use Alcoholic Beverages

Beverages (Nonalcoholic) [78]
PN 127 **SC** 05833
UF Coffee
Tea
R ↓ Alcoholic Beverages [73]
↓ Drinking Behavior [78]
Nutrition [73]

Bias (Experimenter)
Use Experimenter Bias

Bias (Response)
Use Response Bias

Biased Sampling [73]
PN 127 **SC** 05860
SN Inadequate selection of subject samples resulting in an inaccurate representation of the larger population.
B Sampling (Experimental) [73]
R Experiment Volunteers [73]

Bible [73]
PN 244 **SC** 05870
B Religious Literature [73]
R ↓ Christianity [73]

Bible — (cont'd)
R Judaism [67]
↓ Religious Beliefs [73]

Bibliography [67]
PN 1584 SC 05880
SN Mandatory term used as a document type identifier.
R Literature Review [67]

Bibliotherapy [73]
PN 262 SC 05890
SN Use of reading as adjunct to psychotherapy.
B Treatment [67]
R Poetry Therapy [94]

Bicuculline [94]
PN 33 SC 05895
SN Use GAMMA AMINOBUTYRIC ACID ANTAGONISTS to access references from 85-93.
B Analeptic Drugs [73]
Gamma Aminobutyric Acid Antagonists [85]

Big Five Personality Model
Use Five Factor Personality Model

Bile [73]
PN 11 SC 05900
B Body Fluids [73]
R Taurine [82]

Bilingual Education [78]
PN 395 SC 05907
SN Education in one's native language as well as the majority language of the country in which one is educated or education in two languages.
B Education [67]
R Bilingualism [73]
English as Second Language [97]
Foreign Language Learning [67]
Foreign Languages [73]
Multicultural Education [88]
↓ Multilingualism [73]
↓ Teaching [67]

Bilingualism [73]
PN 1527 SC 05910
B Multilingualism [73]
R Bilingual Education [78]
Code Switching [88]
Cross Cultural Communication [97]
English as Second Language [97]
↓ Language [67]
Language Proficiency [88]

Binge Eating [91]
PN 182 SC 05915
SN Eating excessive quantities of food often after stressful events. Compare BULIMIA.
B Eating [67]
R Bulimia [85]
↓ Eating Disorders [97]
↓ Symptoms [67]

Binocular Vision [67]
PN 1080 SC 05920
B Visual Perception [67]

Binomial Distribution [73]
PN 47 SC 05930
B Statistical Probability [67]
R ↓ Statistical Sample Parameters [73]

Bioavailability [91]
PN 49 SC 05935

Bioavailability — (cont'd)
SN The degree and rate at which a drug enters the bloodstream and is circulated to specific organs or tissues, as measured by drug concentrations in body fluids or by pharmacologic or therapeutic response.
UF Bioequivalence
R Absorption (Physiological) [73]
↓ Biochemistry [67]
↓ Drug Dosages [73]
↓ Drug Therapy [67]
↓ Drugs [67]
↓ Metabolism [67]
↓ Pharmacology [73]

Biochemical Markers
Use Biological Markers

Biochemistry [67]
PN 3591 SC 05940
SN Study of the biological and physiological chemistry of living organisms. Used for the scientific discipline or the biochemical processes themselves.
B Chemistry [67]
N ↓ Neurochemistry [73]
R Bioavailability [91]
Biological Markers [91]
↓ Physiology [67]

Bioequivalence
Use Bioavailability

Biofeedback [73]
PN 1067 SC 05945
SN Provision of immediate ongoing information regarding one's own physiological processes.
B Feedback [67]
N Biofeedback Training [78]
R ↓ Conditioning [67]
↓ Reinforcement [67]
↓ Stimulation [67]

Biofeedback Training [78]
PN 2030 SC 05946
SN Self-directed process by which a person uses biofeedback information to gain voluntary control over processes or functions which are primarily under autonomic control. Used in experimental or treatment settings with human subjects.
B Behavior Modification [73]
Biofeedback [73]
R ↓ Alternative Medicine [97]
Autogenic Training [73]

Biographical Data [78]
PN 621 SC 05948
SN Information identifying an individual's background, life history, or present status. Not used as a document type identifier.
R Biographical Inventories [73]
Demographic Characteristics [67]
↓ Educational Background [67]
↓ Family Background [73]
Life Experiences [73]
Patient History [73]

Biographical Inventories [73]
PN 95 SC 05950
SN Sets of items listing information on an individual's background. Not used as a document type identifier.
B Inventories [67]
R Biographical Data [78]

Biography [67]
PN 377 SC 05960

Biography — (cont'd)
SN Recorded account of a person's life. Also used as a document type identifier.
B Prose [73]
N Autobiography [73]
R Narratives [97]
Psychohistory [78]

Biological Clocks (Animal)
Use Animal Biological Rhythms

Biological Family [88]
PN 154 SC 05975
SN The genetic family members of a person in contrast to adoptive or foster families.
UF Birth Parents
Natural Family
B Family [67]
Family Members [73]
R Family of Origin [91]

Biological Markers [91]
PN 375 SC 05977
UF Biochemical Markers
Clinical Markers
R ↓ Biochemistry [67]
Interleukins [94]
↓ Medical Diagnosis [73]
Physiological Correlates [67]
Predisposition [73]
Prognosis [73]
↓ Screening [82]
Susceptibility (Disorders) [73]

Biological Psychiatry [94]
PN 9 SC 05978
SN A branch of psychiatry focusing on biological, physical, and neurological factors in the etiology and treatment of mental and behavioral disorders.
B Psychiatry [67]
R Neurobiology [73]
Neuropsychiatry [73]
Psychobiology [82]

Biological Rhythms [67]
PN 428 SC 05980
SN Rhythmic and periodic variations in physiological and psychological functions. Used for human or animal populations.
N ↓ Animal Biological Rhythms [73]
Human Biological Rhythms [73]
Sleep Wake Cycle [85]
R Lunar Synodic Cycle [73]
Seasonal Variations [73]

Biological Symbiosis [73]
PN 212 SC 06000
SN Intimate relationship between organisms of two or more kinds, particularly one in which the symbiont benefits from the host. Includes parasitic behavior. Limited to animal populations.
UF Parasitism
Symbiosis (Biological)
R ↓ Animals [67]
↓ Biology [67]
Interspecies Interaction [91]

Biology [67]
PN 1171 SC 06010
SN Branch of science dealing with living organisms. Used for the scientific discipline or the biological processes themselves.
B Sciences [67]
N Botany [73]
Neurobiology [73]
Sociobiology [82]
Zoology [73]
R Biological Symbiosis [73]

Biology — (cont'd)
R Biosynthesis [73]
Phylogenesis [73]
Psychobiology [82]

Biopsy [73]
PN 33 SC 06020
B Medical Diagnosis [73]
R ↓ Surgery [71]

Biopsychosocial Approach [91]
PN 207 SC 06024
SN A systematic integration of biological, psychological, and social approaches to the study, treatment, and understanding of mental health and mental disorders.
UF Biopsychosocial Model
R Behavioral Genetics [94]
Holistic Health [85]
Interdisciplinary Treatment Approach [73]
Psychobiology [82]
Systems Theory [88]

Biopsychosocial Model
Use Biopsychosocial Approach

Biosynthesis [73]
PN 69 SC 06030
SN Formation of chemical compounds of relatively complex structure from nutrients by enzyme-catalyzed reactions in living cells.
B Metabolism [67]
R ↓ Biology [67]

Bipolar Affective Disorder
Use Manic Depression

Bipolar Mood Disorder
Use Manic Depression

Biracial Children
Use Interracial Offspring

Birds [67]
PN 4149 SC 06040
UF Fowl
B Vertebrates [73]
N Blackbirds [73]
Budgerigars [73]
Canaries [73]
Chickens [67]
Doves [73]
Ducks [73]
Geese [73]
Penguins [73]
Pigeons [67]
Quails [73]
Robins [73]
Sea Gulls [73]
R Owls [97]

Birth [67]
PN 1553 SC 06050
UF Childbirth
Parturition
N Natural Childbirth [78]
Premature Birth [73]
R Birth Injuries [73]
Birth Rites [73]
Birth Trauma [73]
Birth Weight [85]
Childbirth Training [78]
Labor (Childbirth) [73]
Midwifery [85]
Obstetrical Complications [78]
Perinatal Period [94]
↓ Pregnancy [67]
↓ Sexual Reproduction [73]

Birth Control [71]
PN 982 SC 06060
UF Contraception
Population Control
B Family Planning [73]
N ↓ Contraceptive Devices [73]
Rhythm Method [73]
Tubal Ligation [73]
Vasectomy [73]
R Condoms [91]
Induced Abortion [71]
Overpopulation [73]
Premarital Intercourse [73]
Sexual Abstinence [73]
↓ Sterilization (Sex) [73]

Birth Control Attitudes
Use Family Planning Attitudes

Birth Injuries [73]
PN 52 SC 06070
SN Physical injuries (such as brain damage) received during birth, mostly in, but not limited to, breech births, instrument deliveries, neonatal anoxia, or premature births. Used for both human and animal populations.
UF Injuries (Birth)
B Injuries [73]
R ↓ Birth [67]
Birth Trauma [73]
↓ Neonatal Disorders [73]
Obstetrical Complications [78]

Birth Order [67]
PN 1468 SC 06080
B Family Structure [73]

Birth Parents
Use Biological Family

Birth Rate [82]
PN 104 SC 06087
SN Ratio of the number of live births to the number of individuals in a human population within a specified time period.
R Fertility [88]
↓ Population [73]

Birth Rites [73]
PN 56 SC 06090
UF Circumcision
B Rites of Passage [73]
R ↓ Birth [67]

Birth Trauma [73]
PN 52 SC 06100
SN Stress, as experienced by infants, of being born and bombarded with external stimuli that may have negative influences on subsequent psychological development. Limited to human populations.
R ↓ Birth [67]
Birth Injuries [73]

Birth Weight [85]
PN 451 SC 06105
UF Low Birth Weight
B Body Weight [67]
R ↓ Birth [67]
Neonates [67]
Premature Birth [73]

Bisexuality [73]
PN 450 SC 06110
B Homosexuality [67]
Psychosexual Behavior [67]
R Lesbianism [73]
Male Homosexuality [73]

Bisexuality — (cont'd)
R Pedophilia [73]
Transsexualism [73]
Transvestism [73]

Bitterness
Use Taste Perception

Black Power Movement [73]
PN 32 SC 06130
B Social Movements [67]
R ↓ Activist Movements [73]

Blackbirds [73]
PN 161 SC 06140
B Birds [67]

Blacks [82]
PN 7590 SC 06150
SN Populations of black African descent. May also be used to refer to population groups in Africa when cultural or ethnic comparisons are studied. Use NEGROES to access references from 67–81.
UF African Americans
Negroes
R ↓ Ethnic Groups [73]
Minority Groups [67]
Race (Anthropological) [73]

Blacky Pictures Test
SN Term discontinued in 1997. Use BLACKY PICTURES TEST to access references from 73–96.
Use Projective Personality Measures

Bladder [73]
PN 39 SC 06170
B Urogenital System [73]

Blame [94]
PN 77 SC 06175
SN To assign fault or responsibility for an event, state, or behavior, or the condition of fault or responsibility for something believed to deserve censure.
R Accountability [88]
Attribution [73]
Guilt [67]
↓ Responsibility [73]
Shame [94]
↓ Social Perception [67]

Blind [67]
PN 2321 SC 06180
B Visually Disabled [97]
N Deaf Blind [91]
R ↓ Vision Disorders [82]

Blink Reflex
Use Eyeblink Reflex

Block Design Test (Kohs)
Use Kohs Block Design Test

Blood [67]
PN 1581 SC 06200
B Body Fluids [73]
N ↓ Blood Plasma [73]
R Blood Alcohol Concentration [94]
↓ Blood and Lymphatic Disorders [73]
Blood Groups [73]
Blood Volume [73]
↓ Heart [67]

Blood Alcohol Concentration [94]
PN 46 SC 06205

Blood Alcohol Concentration — (cont'd)
R ↓ Alcohol Abuse 88
↓ Alcohol Drinking Patterns 67
↓ Alcohol Intoxication 73
↓ Alcohols 67
↓ Blood 67
Driving Under The Influence 88
Drug Usage Screening 88

Blood and Lymphatic Disorders 73
PN 218 SC 06210
UF Blood Disorders
Hematologic Disorders
Lymphatic Disorders
B Physical Disorders 97
N Anemia 73
Hemophilia 73
Leukemias 73
Malaria 73
Porphyria 73
Rh Incompatibility 73
Sickle Cell Disease 94
R ↓ Blood 67

Blood Brain Barrier 94
PN 7 SC 06215
SN Functional barrier between brain blood vessels and brain tissues.
R Blood Circulation 73
↓ Blood Flow 73
↓ Blood Vessels 73
↓ Brain 67
↓ Cardiovascular System 67
Cerebrospinal Fluid 73
↓ Neurochemistry 73

Blood Cells 73
PN 118 SC 06220
B Cells (Biology) 73
N Erythrocytes 73
↓ Leucocytes 73

Blood Circulation 73
PN 136 SC 06230
UF Circulation (Blood)
R Arterial Pulse 73
Blood Brain Barrier 94
↓ Blood Flow 73
Blood Volume 73
Cerebral Blood Flow 94

Blood Coagulation 73
PN 18 SC 06240
UF Coagulation (Blood)

Blood Disorders
Use Blood and Lymphatic Disorders

Blood Donation
Use Tissue Donation

Blood Flow 73
PN 659 SC 06270
N Cerebral Blood Flow 94
R Blood Brain Barrier 94
Blood Circulation 73
Blood Volume 73

Blood Glucose
Use Blood Sugar

Blood Groups 73
PN 69 SC 06300
SN Genetically determined classes of human erythrocytes based on specific antigens for which the groups are named.

Blood Groups — (cont'd)
R Antigens 82
↓ Blood 67
Erythrocytes 73
↓ Genetics 67

Blood Plasma 73
PN 2831 SC 06310
UF Plasma (Blood)
B Blood 67
N Blood Serum 73

Blood Platelets 73
PN 837 SC 06320
UF Platelets (Blood)

Blood Pressure 67
PN 2166 SC 06330
N Diastolic Pressure 73
Systolic Pressure 73
R ↓ Blood Pressure Disorders 73
Blood Volume 73
Cardiovascular Reactivity 94
Cerebral Blood Flow 94
↓ Vasoconstrictor Drugs 73
↓ Vasodilator Drugs 73

Blood Pressure Disorders 73
PN 12 SC 06340
B Cardiovascular Disorders 67
N ↓ Hypertension 73
Hypotension 73
Syncope 73
R ↓ Arteriosclerosis 73
↓ Blood Pressure 67
Vasoconstriction 73
Vasodilation 73

Blood Proteins 73
PN 76 SC 06350
B Proteins 73
N Hemoglobin 73
↓ Immunoglobulins 73
Serum Albumin 73

Blood Serum 73
PN 1237 SC 06360
UF Serum (Blood)
B Blood Plasma 73
R Antibodies 73

Blood Sugar 73
PN 275 SC 06370
UF Blood Glucose
B Glucose 73

Blood Transfusion 73
PN 35 SC 06380
UF Transfusion (Blood)
B Physical Treatment Methods 73
R Hemodialysis 73
Tissue Donation 91

Blood Vessels 73
PN 27 SC 06390
B Cardiovascular System 67
N ↓ Arteries (Anatomy) 73
Capillaries (Anatomy) 73
Veins (Anatomy) 73
R Blood Brain Barrier 94

Blood Volume 73
PN 102 SC 06400
R ↓ Blood 67
Blood Circulation 73
↓ Blood Flow 73
↓ Blood Pressure 67

Blue Collar Workers 73
PN 867 SC 06410
SN Employees whose unskilled, semiskilled, or skilled occupations involve physical labor.
UF Laborers (Construct and Indust)
B Business and Industrial Personnel 67
N Industrial Foremen 73
Skilled Industrial Workers 73
Unskilled Industrial Workers 73
R Technical Service Personnel 73

Boarding Schools 88
PN 60 SC 06412
SN Elementary or secondary residential educational institutions for students enrolled in an instructional program. Primarily used for non-disordered populations.
B Schools 67
R Institutional Schools 78

Boards of Education 78
PN 78 SC 06416
SN Governing bodies responsible for managing public school systems.
R ↓ Education 67
Educational Administration 67
↓ School Administrators 73

Body Awareness 82
PN 297 SC 06425
SN Perception of one's physical self or body at any particular time.
B Awareness 67
R ↓ Body Image 67
Self Perception 67
↓ Somesthetic Perception 67

Body Fluids 73
PN 72 SC 06430
B Anatomy 67
N Amniotic Fluid 73
Bile 73
↓ Blood 67
Cerebrospinal Fluid 73
Mucus 73
Saliva 73
Sweat 73
Urine 73
R ↓ Physiology 67

Body Height 73
PN 265 SC 06440
UF Height (Body)
B Body Size 85
R Physique 67

Body Image 67
PN 1797 SC 06450
SN Mental representation of one's body according to feedback received from one's body, the environment, and other people.
N ↓ Body Image Disturbances 73
R Body Awareness 82

Body Image Disturbances 73
PN 348 SC 06460
SN Distortions in the evaluative picture or mental representation an individual has of his/her body.
B Body Image 67
N Koro 94
Phantom Limbs 73
R Castration Anxiety 73
↓ Surgery 71

Body Language 73
PN 253 SC 06470

Body Language — (cont'd)
SN Type of nonverbal communication in which thoughts, feelings, etc., are expressed through bodily movement or posture.
B Interpersonal Communication 73
Nonverbal Communication 71
R Gestures 73
Posture 73

Body Rocking 73
PN 48 **SC** 06480
UF Rocking (Body)
B Symptoms 67
R ↓ Behavior Disorders 71

Body Rotation
Use Rotational Behavior

Body Size 85
PN 547 **SC** 06485
SN Used for human or animal populations. For human populations consider also PHYSIQUE or SOMATOTYPES.
B Size 73
N Body Height 73
↓ Body Weight 67
R Physique 67

Body Sway Testing 73
PN 38 **SC** 06490
B Measurement 67
R ↓ Neuropsychological Assessment 82

Body Temperature 73
PN 1206 **SC** 06500
UF Temperature (Body)
B Physiology 67
N Skin Temperature 73
Thermoregulation (Body) 73
R Hypothermia 73

Body Types
Use Somatotypes

Body Weight 67
PN 3331 **SC** 06520
UF Weight (Body)
B Body Size 85
N Birth Weight 85
Obesity 73
↓ Underweight 73
R Obesity (Attitudes Toward) 97
Physique 67
Weight Control 85

Bolivia 88
PN 9 **SC** 06522
B South America 67

Bombesin 88
PN 71 **SC** 06523
B Peptides 73

Bonding (Emotional)
Use Attachment Behavior

Bone Conduction Audiometry 73
PN 31 **SC** 06530
B Audiometry 67
R ↓ Auditory Stimulation 67
↓ Perceptual Measures 73

Bone Disorders 73
PN 65 **SC** 06540
B Musculoskeletal Disorders 73
N Osteoporosis 91

Bone Marrow 73
PN 99 **SC** 06550
B Tissues (Body) 73
R Bones 73

Bones 73
PN 42 **SC** 06570
B Connective Tissues 73
Musculoskeletal System 73
R Bone Marrow 73
Jaw 73
Spinal Column 73

Bonobos 97
PN 0 **SC** 06575
SN Members of the species Pan panicus. Although not members of the chimpanzee species, Bonobos are often referred to as pygmy chimpanzees.
UF Pygmy Chimpanzees
B Primates (Nonhuman) 73
R Chimpanzees 73

Bonuses 73
PN 19 **SC** 06580
B Employee Benefits 73
R Salaries 73

Book 67
PN 7192 **SC** 06590
SN Mandatory term used as a document type identifier.

Books 73
PN 457 **SC** 06600
SN Refers to books as a means of communication, as distinct from the document type identifier BOOK.
B Printed Communications Media 73
N ↓ Textbooks 78
R Reading Materials 73

Borderline Mental Retardation 73
PN 77 **SC** 06610
SN IQ 71–84.
B Mental Retardation 67
R Psychosocial Mental Retardation 73

Borderline Mentally Retarded
Use Slow Learners

Borderline States 78
PN 2480 **SC** 06624
SN Personality disorder or other mental disorder characterized by instability of mood, interpersonal behavior, or personal identity and possible transient psychotic episodes; also, state in which individual has not broken with reality but may become psychotic if exposed to unfavorable circumstances (e.g., borderline schizophrenia).
B Mental Disorders 67
R ↓ Neurosis 67
↓ Personality Disorders 67
↓ Psychosis 67

Boredom 73
PN 220 **SC** 06630
B Emotional States 73
R Monotony 78

Botany 73
PN 27 **SC** 06640
B Biology 67
R Phylogenesis 73

Botswana 88
PN 28 **SC** 06645
B Africa 67

Bottle Feeding 73
PN 79 **SC** 06650
B Feeding Practices 73

Boundaries (Psychological) 97
PN 0 **SC** 06660
SN Psychological barriers that separate or divide, and, in some cases, protect the integrity of individuals or groups.
R ↓ Group Dynamics 67
Intergroup Dynamics 73
↓ Interpersonal Interaction 67
Personal Space 73
↓ Personality Processes 67
Territoriality 67

Boundary Violations (Sexual)
Use Professional Client Sexual Relations

Bourgeois
Use Middle Class

Bowel Disorders
Use Colon Disorders

Boys
Use Human Males

Brachial Plexus
Use Spinal Nerves

Bradycardia 73
PN 97 **SC** 06730
B Arrhythmias (Heart) 73

Braille 78
PN 115 **SC** 06737
B Reading 67
R Braille Instruction 73
Reading Education 73
Reading Materials 73
↓ Tactual Perception 67
↓ Visually Disabled 97

Braille Instruction 73
PN 46 **SC** 06740
B Curriculum 67
R Braille 78
Reading Education 73
↓ Visually Disabled 97

Brain 67
PN 4440 **SC** 06750
N ↓ Brain Stem 73
↓ Forebrain 85
↓ Hindbrain 97
↓ Mesencephalon 73
R Blood Brain Barrier 94
↓ Brain Disorders 67
Brain Size 73
Brain Weight 73
Cerebral Atrophy 94
↓ Cerebral Dominance 73
↓ Lateral Dominance 67
Left Brain 91
Ocular Dominance 73
Right Brain 91

Brain Ablation
Use Brain Lesions

Brain Concussion 73
PN 80 **SC** 06770
UF Concussion (Brain)
B Brain Damage 67
Head Injuries 73

Brain Damage [67]
PN 3689 **SC** 06780
B Brain Disorders [67]
N Brain Concussion [73]
Traumatic Brain Injury [97]
R ↓ Brain Damaged [73]
Cerebral Atrophy [94]
↓ Epilepsy [67]
Global Amnesia [97]
↓ Head Injuries [73]
↓ Mental Retardation [67]
↓ Neuropsychological Assessment [82]

Brain Damaged [73]
PN 3716 **SC** 06790
B Disabled [97]
N Minimally Brain Damaged [73]
R ↓ Brain Damage [67]
Congenitally Disabled [97]
Traumatic Brain Injury [97]

Brain Disorders [67]
PN 1626 **SC** 06800
B Central Nervous System Disorders [73]
N Acute Alcoholic Intoxication [73]
Anencephaly [73]
↓ Aphasia [67]
Athetosis [73]
↓ Brain Damage [67]
Brain Neoplasms [73]
Cerebral Palsy [67]
Cerebrovascular Accidents [73]
Chronic Alcoholic Intoxication [73]
Encephalitis [73]
↓ Encephalopathies [82]
↓ Epilepsy [67]
↓ Epileptic Seizures [73]
Hydrocephaly [73]
Microcephaly [73]
Minimal Brain Disorders [73]
↓ Organic Brain Syndromes [73]
Parkinsons Disease [73]
R ↓ Brain [67]
Cerebral Atrophy [94]
↓ Convulsions [67]
↓ Memory Disorders [73]
↓ Mental Disorders [67]
Rett Syndrome [94]

Brain Injury (Traumatic)
Use Traumatic Brain Injury

Brain Lesions [67]
PN 7407 **SC** 06830
SN Not defined prior to 1982. From 1982, limited to experimentally induced lesions and used primarily for animal populations.
UF Brain Ablation
Cerebral Lesions
Subcortical Lesions
B Lesions [67]
N Hypothalamus Lesions [73]
R Decerebration [73]
Decortication (Brain) [73]

Brain Mapping
Use Stereotaxic Atlas

Brain Maps
Use Stereotaxic Atlas

Brain Metabolism
Use Neurochemistry

Brain Neoplasms [73]
PN 318 **SC** 06860
B Brain Disorders [67]
Nervous System Neoplasms [73]

Brain Self Stimulation [85]
PN 365 **SC** 06864
UF Intracranial Self Stimulation
B Brain Stimulation [67]
Self Stimulation [67]

Brain Size [73]
PN 413 **SC** 06868
B Size [73]
R ↓ Brain [67]
Brain Weight [73]
Cerebral Atrophy [94]

Brain Stem [73]
PN 1051 **SC** 06870
B Brain [67]
N Locus Ceruleus [82]
Medulla Oblongata [73]
↓ Pons [73]
Reticular Formation [67]
R ↓ Hindbrain [97]

Brain Stimulation [67]
PN 1725 **SC** 06880
B Stereotaxic Techniques [73]
Stimulation [67]
N Brain Self Stimulation [85]
Chemical Brain Stimulation [73]
Electrical Brain Stimulation [73]
Spreading Depression [67]
R Physiological Arousal [67]

Brain Weight [73]
PN 123 **SC** 06882
R ↓ Brain [67]
Brain Size [73]
Cerebral Atrophy [94]

Brainstorming [82]
PN 65 **SC** 06883
SN Group problem-solving technique involving spontaneous contribution of ideas from all group members.
B Group Problem Solving [73]
R Choice Shift [94]
↓ Group Dynamics [67]

Brainwashing [82]
PN 24 **SC** 06884
SN Indoctrination of an individual or group by means of physical or psychological duress in order to alter their political, social, religious, or moral beliefs.
UF Thought Control
B Persuasive Communication [67]
R Attitude Change [67]
Coercion [94]
Propaganda [73]

Brand Names [78]
PN 507 **SC** 06885
B Names [85]
R ↓ Advertising [67]
Brand Preferences [94]
↓ Consumer Behavior [67]
↓ Consumer Research [73]
Marketing [73]
Retailing [91]

Brand Preferences [94]
PN 59 **SC** 06887
SN Includes loyalty to brand name products or product switching.
B Consumer Attitudes [73]
Preferences [67]
R ↓ Advertising [67]
Brand Names [78]
↓ Consumer Behavior [67]

Brand Preferences — (cont'd)
R ↓ Consumer Research [73]
Marketing [73]

Bravery
Use Courage

Brazil [73]
PN 682 **SC** 06900
B South America [67]

Breakthrough (Psychotherapeutic)
Use Psychotherapeutic Breakthrough

Breakup (Relationship)
Use Relationship Termination

Breast [73]
PN 185 **SC** 06920
B Anatomy [67]

Breast Cancer Screening
Use Cancer Screening

Breast Examination
Use Self Examination (Medical)

Breast Feeding [73]
PN 387 **SC** 06930
B Feeding Practices [73]
R Weaning [73]

Breast Neoplasms [73]
PN 713 **SC** 06940
UF Mammary Neoplasms
B Neoplasms [67]
R Mammography [94]
Mastectomy [73]

Breathing
Use Respiration

Breeding (Animal)
Use Animal Breeding

Brief Psychotherapy [67]
PN 1621 **SC** 06970
SN Short-term or time-limited methods of psychotherapy.
UF Short Term Psychotherapy
Time Limited Psychotherapy
B Psychotherapy [67]

Brief Reactive Psychosis
Use Acute Psychosis

Bright Light Therapy
Use Phototherapy

Brightness Constancy [85]
PN 18 **SC** 06975
SN The tendency to perceive the brightness of stimuli as stable despite objective changes in illumination.
B Brightness Perception [73]
Perceptual Constancy [85]

Brightness Contrast [85]
PN 138 **SC** 06977
B Visual Contrast [85]

Brightness Perception [73]
PN 1112 **SC** 06980
UF Luminance Threshold
B Visual Perception [67]
N Brightness Constancy [85]

Brightness Perception — (cont'd)
R ↓ Illumination [67]
Luminance [82]

Bromides [73]
PN 25 SC 06990
UF Lithium Bromide
B Drugs [67]
R Arecoline [73]
Neostigmine [73]
Scopolamine [73]

Bromocriptine [88]
PN 141 SC 06995
B Alkaloids [73]
Enzyme Inhibitors [85]
Ergot Derivatives [73]

Bronchi [73]
PN 8 SC 07000
B Respiratory System [73]

Bronchial Disorders [73]
PN 44 SC 07010
B Respiratory Tract Disorders [73]

Brothers [73]
PN 123 SC 07020
B Human Males [73]
Siblings [67]

Bruxism [85]
PN 26 SC 07035
SN Use NOCTURNAL TEETH GRINDING to access references from 73–84.
UF Teeth Grinding
N Nocturnal Teeth Grinding [73]
R Myofascial Pain [91]

Buddhism [73]
PN 165 SC 07040
B Religious Affiliation [73]
N Zen Buddhism [73]
R Buddhists [97]

Buddhists [97]
PN 0 SC 07045
B Religious Groups [97]
R ↓ Buddhism [73]

Budgerigars [73]
PN 50 SC 07050
B Birds [67]

Budgets [97]
PN 0 SC 07052
SN Use COSTS AND COST ANALYSIS to access references from 73–96.
B Costs and Cost Analysis [73]
R Cost Containment [91]
Economics [85]
Economy [73]
Funding [88]
Income (Economic) [73]
Money [67]

Bufotenine [73]
PN 15 SC 07060
B Amines [73]
Hallucinogenic Drugs [67]
Vasoconstrictor Drugs [73]

Bulgaria [82]
PN 45 SC 07075
B Europe [73]

Bulimia [85]
PN 2315 SC 07078
SN Disorder characterized primarily by binge eating and often accompanied by self-induced vomiting and/or misuse of laxatives.
B Eating Disorders [97]
R Anorexia Nervosa [73]
Binge Eating [91]
↓ Psychosomatic Disorders [67]

Bulls
Use Cattle

Bupropion [94]
PN 23 SC 07081
B Antidepressant Drugs [71]

Burma [91]
PN 2 SC 07083
B Southeast Asia [73]

Burnout
Use Occupational Stress

Burns [73]
PN 222 SC 07090
B Injuries [73]
R Electrical Injuries [73]
↓ Wounds [73]

Buses
Use Motor Vehicles

Bush Babies
Use Lemurs

Business [67]
PN 943 SC 07110
UF Commerce
Industry
Manufacturing
R Business Management [73]
Business Organizations [73]
Business Students [73]
Entrepreneurship [91]
↓ Management [67]
Ownership [85]
Retailing [91]
Self Employment [94]

Business and Industrial Personnel [67]
PN 4255 SC 07120
UF Businessmen
Industrial Personnel
B Personnel [67]
N Architects [73]
↓ Blue Collar Workers [73]
Industrial Psychologists [73]
Sales Personnel [73]
Secretarial Personnel [73]
↓ Service Personnel [91]
Skilled Industrial Workers [73]
↓ Technical Personnel [78]
↓ White Collar Workers [73]
R ↓ Aerospace Personnel [73]
↓ Agricultural Workers [73]
Engineers [67]
↓ Government Personnel [73]
↓ Nonprofessional Personnel [82]
↓ Professional Personnel [78]
Scientists [67]
Technical Service Personnel [73]

Business Education [73]
PN 274 SC 07123
B Curriculum [67]
R Business Management [73]

Business Education — (cont'd)
R Management Training [73]
↓ Personnel Management [73]
↓ Personnel Training [67]

Business Management [73]
PN 309 SC 07130
B Management [67]
R Business [67]
Business Education [73]
Entrepreneurship [91]
↓ Management Methods [73]
↓ Personnel Management [73]

Business Organizations [73]
PN 924 SC 07140
UF Companies
Corporations
B Organizations [67]
Private Sector [85]
R Business [67]

Business Students [73]
PN 500 SC 07150
B Students [67]
R Business [67]

Businessmen
Use Business and Industrial Personnel

Buspirone [91]
PN 292 SC 07165
B Minor Tranquilizers [73]
R Serotonin Agonists [88]

Butterflies [73]
PN 91 SC 07170
B Insects [67]
R Larvae [73]

Butyrylperazine
SN Term discontinued in 1997. Use BUTYRYLPERAZINE to access references from 73–96.
Use Phenothiazine Derivatives

Buying
Use Consumer Behavior

Cadres
Use Social Groups

Caffeine [73]
PN 887 SC 07210
B Alkaloids [73]
CNS Stimulating Drugs [73]
Diuretics [73]
Heart Rate Affecting Drugs [73]
Respiration Stimulating Drugs [73]
R ↓ Analeptic Drugs [73]

Cage Apparatus [73]
PN 51 SC 07220
B Apparatus [67]

Calcium [73]
PN 333 SC 07240
B Chemical Elements [73]
Metallic Elements [73]
N Calcium Ions [73]

Calcium Channel Blockers
Use Channel Blockers

Calcium Ions [73]
PN 70 SC 07260

Calcium Ions — (cont'd)
B Calcium [73]
Electrolytes [73]

Calculators
Use Digital Computers

Calculus
Use Mathematics

California F Scale [73]
PN 29 **SC** 07290
B Nonprojective Personality Measures [73]

California Psychological Inventory [67]
PN 262 **SC** 07300
B Personality Measures [67]

California Test of Mental Maturity [73]
PN 9 **SC** 07310
B Intelligence Measures [67]

California Test of Personality [73]
PN 14 **SC** 07320
B Nonprojective Personality Measures [73]

Calories [73]
PN 250 **SC** 07330
R Energy Expenditure [67]

Cambodia [88]
PN 8 **SC** 07340
B Southeast Asia [73]

Cameras [73]
PN 31 **SC** 07350
B Apparatus [67]

Cameroon [91]
PN 13 **SC** 07355
B Africa [67]

Campaigns (Political)
Use Political Campaigns

Camping [73]
PN 92 **SC** 07370
B Recreation [67]
R Summer Camps (Recreation) [73]
Vacationing [73]

Camps (Therapeutic)
Use Therapeutic Camps

Campuses [73]
PN 30 **SC** 07390
B School Facilities [73]

Canada [71]
PN 2673 **SC** 07400
B North America [73]

Canaries [73]
PN 40 **SC** 07410
B Birds [67]

Cancer Screening [97]
PN 0 **SC** 07415
UF Breast Cancer Screening
Prostate Cancer Screening
Skin Cancer Screening
B Health Screening [97]
R Health Promotion [91]
Mammography [94]
Physical Examination [88]
Self Examination (Medical) [88]

Cancers
Use Neoplasms

Candidates (Political)
Use Political Candidates

Canids [97]
PN 0 **SC** 07434
UF Coyotes
B Mammals [73]
N Dogs [67]
Foxes [73]
Wolves [73]

Cannabinoids [82]
PN 69 **SC** 07436
UF Nabilone
N Tetrahydrocannabinol [73]
R ↓ Cannabis [73]

Cannabis [73]
PN 277 **SC** 07440
UF Hemp (Cannabis)
B Drugs [67]
N Hashish [73]
Marihuana [71]
R Aphrodisiacs [73]
↓ Cannabinoids [82]
↓ Hallucinogenic Drugs [67]
↓ Narcotic Drugs [73]
Tetrahydrocannabinol [73]

Canonical Correlation
Use Multivariate Analysis

Capgras Syndrome [85]
PN 151 **SC** 07447
SN Clinical condition in which patient believes an acquaintance, a closely related person, or a close associate has been replaced by a double or an impostor.
B Psychosis [67]
Syndromes [73]
R Delusions [67]
↓ Symptoms [67]

Capillaries (Anatomy) [73]
PN 13 **SC** 07450
B Blood Vessels [73]

Capital Punishment [73]
PN 256 **SC** 07460
UF Death Penalty
Punishment (Capital)

Capitalism [73]
PN 108 **SC** 07470
B Political Economic Systems [73]
R Entrepreneurship [91]
Ownership [85]

Capsaicin [91]
PN 53 **SC** 07475
B Fatty Acids [73]

Captivity (Animal)
Use Animal Captivity

Captopril [91]
PN 26 **SC** 07477
B Antihypertensive Drugs [73]
Enzyme Inhibitors [85]
R Angiotensin [73]

Carbachol [73]
PN 186 **SC** 07480
B Cholinomimetic Drugs [73]

Carbamazepine [88]
PN 461 **SC** 07483
B Analgesic Drugs [73]
Anticonvulsive Drugs [73]

Carbidopa [88]
PN 22 **SC** 07485
SN Use DECARBOXYLASES to access references from 82-87.
B Decarboxylase Inhibitors [82]
R DOPA [73]

Carbohydrate Metabolism [73]
PN 72 **SC** 07490
B Metabolism [67]
N Glucose Metabolism [94]
R Acetaldehyde [82]
Guanosine [85]

Carbohydrates [73]
PN 330 **SC** 07510
N Deoxyglucose [91]
↓ Sugars [73]

Carbon [73]
PN 9 **SC** 07520

Carbon Dioxide [73]
PN 186 **SC** 07530
R Respiration [67]

Carbon Monoxide [73]
PN 129 **SC** 07540
R ↓ Poisons [73]

Carbon Monoxide Poisoning [73]
PN 44 **SC** 07550
UF Carboxyhemoglobinemia
B Toxic Disorders [73]

Carbonic Anhydrase
SN Term discontinued in 1997. Use CARBONIC ANHYDRASE to access references from 73–96.
Use Enzymes

Carboxyhemoglobinemia
Use Carbon Monoxide Poisoning

Carcinogens [73]
PN 13 **SC** 07580
R ↓ Drugs [67]
Pollution [73]
Tobacco Smoking [67]

Carcinomas
Use Neoplasms

Cardiac Arrest
Use Heart Disorders

Cardiac Disorders
Use Heart Disorders

Cardiac Rate
Use Heart Rate

Cardiac Surgery
Use Heart Surgery

Cardiography [73]
PN 13 **SC** 07620
B Medical Diagnosis [73]
N Electrocardiography [67]

Cardiology [73]
PN 29 **SC** 07630

Cardiology — (cont'd)
B Medical Sciences [67]
R ↓ Cardiovascular System [67]

Cardiotonic Drugs
SN Term discontinued in 1997. Use CARDIOTONIC DRUGS to access references from 85–96.
Use Drugs

Cardiovascular Disorders [67]
PN 1884 SC 07640
UF Circulatory Disorders
Coronary Disorders
Raynauds Disease
Vascular Disorders
B Physical Disorders [97]
N Aneurysms [73]
↓ Arteriosclerosis [73]
↓ Blood Pressure Disorders [73]
↓ Cerebrovascular Disorders [73]
Embolisms [73]
↓ Heart Disorders [73]
↓ Hemorrhage [73]
↓ Hypertension [73]
↓ Ischemia [73]
↓ Thromboses [73]
R ↓ Cardiovascular System [67]
Coronary Prone Behavior [82]
↓ Dyspnea [73]
↓ Heart Rate Affecting Drugs [73]

Cardiovascular Reactivity [94]
PN 281 SC 07645
SN Cardiovascular system responses to mental, physical, or environmental stress or other states due to intervention or natural occurrence.
R ↓ Blood Pressure [67]
↓ Cardiovascular System [67]
Heart Rate [67]
Physiological Arousal [67]
Physiological Correlates [67]
↓ Psychophysiology [67]
Stress Reactions [73]

Cardiovascular System [67]
PN 1589 SC 07650
B Anatomical Systems [73]
N ↓ Blood Vessels [73]
↓ Heart [67]
R Blood Brain Barrier [94]
Cardiology [73]
↓ Cardiovascular Disorders [67]
Cardiovascular Reactivity [94]
Spleen [73]

Career Aspirations
Use Occupational Aspirations

Career Change [78]
PN 375 SC 07666
UF Job Change
R Career Development [85]
Employment History [78]
Job Satisfaction [67]
Occupational Adjustment [73]
Occupational Aspirations [73]
Occupational Choice [67]
Occupational Mobility [73]
↓ Occupations [67]
Professional Development [82]

Career Choice
Use Occupational Choice

Career Counseling
Use Occupational Guidance

Career Development [85]
PN 1238 SC 07672
SN Formation of work identity or progression of career decisions and/or events as influenced by life or work experience, education, on-the-job training, or other factors.
UF Career Transitions
Management Development
B Development [67]
Personnel Management [73]
R Career Change [78]
Employment History [78]
↓ Management [67]
Occupational Choice [67]
↓ Occupations [67]
Personnel Placement [73]
Personnel Promotion [78]
↓ Personnel Training [67]
Professional Development [82]
Professional Identity [91]
Professional Specialization [91]

Career Education [78]
PN 607 SC 07675
SN Comprehensive educational programs focusing on individual career development beginning in childhood and continuing through the adult years.
UF Career Exploration
B Curriculum [67]
R Occupational Guidance [67]

Career Exploration
Use Career Education

Career Goals
Use Occupational Aspirations

Career Guidance
Use Occupational Guidance

Career Maturity
Use Vocational Maturity

Career Preference
Use Occupational Preference

Career Transitions
Use Career Development

Careers
Use Occupations

Caregiver Burden [94]
PN 224 SC 07713
SN Used primarily for family or nonprofessional caregivers and the stress or associated emotional responses experienced when caring for the mentally or physically disabled. Consider OCCUPATIONAL STRESS for professional caregivers, e.g., health care personnel.
R Caregivers [88]
Elder Care [94]
Home Care [85]
Homebound [88]
Respite Care [88]
↓ Stress [67]

Caregivers [88]
PN 1986 SC 07715
SN Family members, professionals, or paraprofessionals who provide care to the mentally or physically disabled.
UF Family Caregivers
R Caregiver Burden [94]
Elder Care [94]
↓ Health Care Services [78]
Home Care [85]
Home Care Personnel [97]

Caregivers — (cont'd)
R Quality of Care [88]
Respite Care [88]
↓ Treatment [67]

Carotid Arteries [73]
PN 94 SC 07720
B Arteries (Anatomy) [73]

Carp [73]
PN 39 SC 07740
B Fishes [67]
N Goldfish [73]

Cartoons (Humor) [73]
PN 192 SC 07780
B Humor [67]

Case History
Use Patient History

Case Law [85]
PN 730 SC 07787
SN Mandatory term applied to descriptions of specific legal cases. Limited to documents that describe or summarize court decisions. Not used for documents that discuss or describe the implications or effects of specific legal decisions. Consider LEGAL DECISIONS for discussions of the effects of specific court decisions.
R ↓ Adjudication [67]
↓ Laws [67]
Legal Decisions [91]
↓ Legal Processes [73]

Case Management [91]
PN 394 SC 07788
SN Evaluation of health and social service needs of individuals and development and delivery of service or treatment. Includes attention to justification and length of treatment, costs, and health insurance reimbursement.
B Management [67]
N Discharge Planning [94]
R Cost Containment [91]
↓ Health Care Administration [97]
Health Care Costs [94]
↓ Health Care Delivery [78]
↓ Health Insurance [73]
Health Service Needs [97]
Intake Interview [94]
Long Term Care [94]
↓ Managed Care [94]
Needs Assessment [85]
Outreach Programs [97]
Social Casework [67]
↓ Treatment [67]
↓ Treatment Duration [88]
↓ Treatment Planning [97]

Case Report [67]
PN 18177 SC 07790
SN Mandatory term applied to exploratory studies of single or multiple clinical cases. Not used for illustrative case examples.

Caseworkers
Use Social Workers

Caste System [73]
PN 195 SC 07810
B Social Structure [67]
Systems [67]

Castration [67]
PN 197 SC 07820
B Endocrine Gland Surgery [73]
Sterilization (Sex) [73]

Castration — (cont'd)
N Male Castration 73
Ovariectomy 73

Castration Anxiety 73
PN 114 SC 07830
B Anxiety Disorders 97
R ↓ Body Image Disturbances 73

Cat Learning 67
PN 115 SC 07840
SN Not defined prior to 1982. Use CAT LEARNING or CATS to access references from 67–81. From 1982 used for discussions of hypotheses or theories of learning in cats.
B Learning 67
R Cats 67

CAT Scan
Use Tomography

Catabolism 73
PN 16 SC 07850
SN Destructive metabolism involving release of energy (heat) and resulting in breakdown of complex materials within the organism.
B Metabolism 67

Catabolites
Use Metabolites

Catalepsy 73
PN 283 SC 07860
SN Condition of muscular semirigidity and trance-like postures. Cataleptic persons make no voluntary motor movements and may display waxy flexibility.
B Movement Disorders 85
Symptoms 67
R Autohypnosis 73
↓ Hysteria 67
↓ Schizophrenia 67
Suggestibility 67

Catamnesis
Use Posttreatment Followup

Cataplexy 73
PN 54 SC 07880
SN Temporary loss of muscle tone or weakness following extreme emotion.
B Movement Disorders 85
Muscular Disorders 73
Neuromuscular Disorders 73
R Narcolepsy 73

Cataracts 73
PN 51 SC 07890
B Eye Disorders 73

Catatonia 73
PN 280 SC 07900
SN Reaction characterized by muscular rigidity or stupor sometimes punctuated by sudden violent outbursts, panic, or hallucinations.
B Symptoms 67
R Catatonic Schizophrenia 73

Catatonic Schizophrenia 73
PN 97 SC 07910
B Schizophrenia 67
R Catatonia 73

Catecholamines 73
PN 1486 SC 07920
UF Monoamines (Brain)
B Neurotransmitters 85
Sympathomimetic Amines 73

Catecholamines — (cont'd)
N Dopamine 73
Epinephrine 67
Norepinephrine 73
R ↓ Adrenergic Drugs 73
↓ Decarboxylase Inhibitors 82
↓ Dopamine Antagonists 82
Methyldopa 73

Categorizing
Use Classification (Cognitive Process)

Catharsis 73
PN 163 SC 07940
SN Process of reliving painful experiences and feelings, and the associated emotional responses.
UF Abreaction
B Personality Processes 67
R ↓ Psychoanalysis 67

Catheterization 73
PN 63 SC 07950
B Physical Treatment Methods 73

Cathexis 73
PN 89 SC 07960
SN Psychoanalytic term designating the attachment of intense emotions to a particular object, person, or oneself.
B Personality Processes 67

Cathode Ray Tubes
Use Video Display Units

Catholicism (Roman)
Use Roman Catholicism

Catholics 97
PN 0 SC 07975
B Christians 97
R Roman Catholicism 73

Cats 67
PN 6063 SC 07980
B Felids 97
R Cat Learning 67

Cattell Culture Fair Intell Test
Use Culture Fair Intelligence Test

Cattell Infant Intelligence Scale
Use Infant Intelligence Scale

Cattle 73
PN 356 SC 08010
UF Bulls
Cows
B Mammals 73

Caucasians
SN Term discontinued in 1982. Use CAUCASIANS to access references from 73–81.
Use Whites

Cauda Equina
Use Spinal Nerves

Caudate Nucleus 73
PN 671 SC 08040
B Basal Ganglia 73
R Nucleus Accumbens 82

Causal Analysis 94
PN 50 SC 08045
SN Systematic analysis of causal relationships among variables.

Causal Analysis — (cont'd)
B Analysis 67
Methodology 67
R Attribution 73
↓ Experimentation 67
Path Analysis 91
↓ Statistical Regression 85
Structural Equation Modeling 94

Celiac Plexus
Use Autonomic Ganglia

Celibacy
Use Sexual Abstinence

Cell Nucleus 73
PN 12 SC 08070
R ↓ Cells (Biology) 73

Cells (Biology) 73
PN 339 SC 08080
B Anatomy 67
N ↓ Blood Cells 73
↓ Chromosomes 73
Cones (Eye) 73
Connective Tissue Cells 73
Epithelial Cells 73
↓ Neurons 73
Sperm 73
R Absorption (Physiological) 73
Cell Nucleus 73
Cytology 73
Cytoplasm 73
↓ Physiology 67

Censorship 78
PN 37 SC 08086
R ↓ Civil Rights 78
↓ Communication 67
↓ Communications Media 73
Freedom 78
Information 67
↓ Laws 67
↓ Social Issues 91

Centering 91
PN 2 SC 08088
SN Focusing of attention and concentration on a particular stimulus or on the whole of the present environment and circumstances. Used primarily in, but not limited to, therapeutic settings.
R ↓ Consciousness States 71
Meditation 73
↓ Psychotherapeutic Techniques 67
↓ Self Management 85

Central America 73
PN 229 SC 08090
N Belize 88
Costa Rica 88
El Salvador 88
Guatemala 82
Honduras 88
Nicaragua 88
Panama 88
R Latin America 88

Central Nervous System 67
PN 1584 SC 08100
B Nervous System 67
N Extrapyramidal Tracts 73
Meninges 73
Neural Analyzers 73
↓ Neural Pathways 82
↓ Spinal Cord 73
R ↓ Central Nervous System Disorders 73

Central Nervous System Disorders 73
PN 462 SC 08110
B Nervous System Disorders 67
N ↓ Brain Disorders 67
↓ Chorea 73
Dysarthria 73
↓ Meningitis 73
↓ Myelitis 73
Neurosyphilis 73
Progressive Supranuclear Palsy 97
R ↓ Central Nervous System 67
Hemiplegia 78
Hypothermia 73
↓ Paralysis 73
Paraplegia 78
Quadriplegia 85
↓ Spinal Cord Injuries 73

Central Nervous System Drugs
Use CNS Affecting Drugs

Central Tendency Measures 73
PN 20 SC 08130
B Statistical Analysis 67
Statistical Measurement 73
N Mean 73
Median 73
R ↓ Population (Statistics) 73
T Test 73
↓ Variability Measurement 73

Central Vision
Use Foveal Vision

CER (Conditioning)
Use Conditioned Emotional Responses

Cerebellar Cortex
Use Cerebellum

Cerebellar Nuclei
Use Cerebellum

Cerebellopontile Angle
Use Cerebellum

Cerebellum 73
PN 834 SC 08180
UF Cerebellar Cortex
Cerebellar Nuclei
Cerebellopontile Angle
B Hindbrain 97
N Purkinje Cells 94

Cerebral Aqueduct
Use Cerebral Ventricles

Cerebral Arteriosclerosis 73
PN 37 SC 08210
B Arteriosclerosis 73
Cerebrovascular Disorders 73
R Cerebrovascular Accidents 73
↓ Senile Dementia 73

Cerebral Atrophy 94
PN 78 SC 08215
UF Atrophy (Cerebral)
Cortical Atrophy
R ↓ Brain 67
↓ Brain Damage 67
↓ Brain Disorders 67
Brain Size 73
Brain Weight 73
↓ Cerebral Cortex 67
↓ Cerebral Dominance 73

Cerebral Blood Flow 94
PN 231 SC 08217
B Blood Flow 73
R Blood Circulation 73
↓ Blood Pressure 67
↓ Cerebral Cortex 67

Cerebral Cortex 67
PN 3771 SC 08220
UF Cortex (Cerebral)
B Telencephalon 73
N Cerebral Ventricles 73
Corpus Callosum 73
↓ Frontal Lobe 73
Left Brain 91
↓ Limbic System 73
↓ Occipital Lobe 73
↓ Parietal Lobe 73
Right Brain 91
↓ Temporal Lobe 73
R Cerebral Atrophy 94
Cerebral Blood Flow 94
Interhemispheric Interaction 85

Cerebral Dominance 73
PN 4204 SC 08230
SN The control of lower brain centers by the cerebrum or cerebral cortex. Compare LATERAL DOMINANCE.
B Dominance 67
N ↓ Lateral Dominance 67
R ↓ Brain 67
Cerebral Atrophy 94
Interhemispheric Interaction 85
Left Brain 91
Right Brain 91

Cerebral Hemorrhage 73
PN 149 SC 08250
B Cerebrovascular Disorders 73
Hemorrhage 73
R Cerebrovascular Accidents 73

Cerebral Ischemia 73
PN 209 SC 08260
B Cerebrovascular Disorders 73
Ischemia 73
R Cerebrovascular Accidents 73

Cerebral Lesions
Use Brain Lesions

Cerebral Palsy 67
PN 786 SC 08280
B Brain Disorders 67
Paralysis 73
R Athetosis 73

Cerebral Vascular Disorders
Use Cerebrovascular Disorders

Cerebral Ventricles 73
PN 574 SC 08310
UF Cerebral Aqueduct
Choroid Plexus
Ependyma
Ventricles (Cerebral)
B Cerebral Cortex 67

Cerebrospinal Fluid 73
PN 1143 SC 08320
UF Spinal Fluid
B Body Fluids 73
R Blood Brain Barrier 94

Cerebrovascular Accidents 73
PN 1561 SC 08330

Cerebrovascular Accidents — (cont'd)
UF Apoplexy
Stroke (Cerebrum)
B Brain Disorders 67
Cerebrovascular Disorders 73
R Cerebral Arteriosclerosis 73
Cerebral Hemorrhage 73
Cerebral Ischemia 73
Coma 73

Cerebrovascular Disorders 73
PN 310 SC 08340
UF Cerebral Vascular Disorders
B Cardiovascular Disorders 67
N Cerebral Arteriosclerosis 73
Cerebral Hemorrhage 73
Cerebral Ischemia 73
Cerebrovascular Accidents 73
R Coma 73
↓ Hypertension 73
Multi Infarct Dementia 91
↓ Nervous System Disorders 67
↓ Vascular Dementia 97

Certification (Professional)
Use Professional Certification

Certification Examinations
Use Professional Examinations

Certified Public Accountants
Use Accountants

Cervical Plexus
Use Spinal Nerves

Cervical Sprain Syndrome
Use Whiplash

Cervix 73
PN 90 SC 08390
B Uterus 73

Chance (Fortune) 73
PN 194 SC 08420
SN The possibility of a favorable or unfavorable outcome in an uncertain situation.
UF Luck
B Probability 67
N ↓ Statistical Probability 67
R Uncertainty 91

Change (Organizational)
Use Organizational Change

Change (Social)
Use Social Change

Channel Blockers 91
PN 202 SC 08450
UF Calcium Channel Blockers
B Drugs 67
R ↓ Vasodilator Drugs 73
Verapamil 91

Chaos Theory 97
PN 0 SC 09455
B Theories 67
R ↓ Mathematical Modeling 73
Predictability (Measurement) 73
↓ Prediction 67
↓ Probability 67
↓ Stochastic Modeling 73
Uncertainty 91

Chaplains 73
PN 42 SC 08460
SN Clergy officially attached to a branch of the military, hospital, institution, court, or university.
B Clergy 73
R Lay Religious Personnel 73
↓ Military Personnel 67
Ministers (Religion) 73
Priests 73
Rabbis 73

Character
Use Personality

Character
Use Personality Development

Character
Use Personality Disorders

Character Formation
Use Personality Development

Charisma 88
PN 72 SC 08515
B Personality Traits 67
R Leadership Qualities 97
Leadership Style 73

Charitable Behavior 73
PN 408 SC 08520
SN Generous or spontaneous goodness as manifested in actions for the benefit of others, especially of the needy, poor, or helpless.
B Interpersonal Interaction 67
Prosocial Behavior 82
R Altruism 73
Assistance (Social Behavior) 73
Sharing (Social Behavior) 78
Tissue Donation 91

Cheating 73
PN 246 SC 08530
B Deception 67
R Dishonesty 73
Fraud 94
Test Taking 85

Chemical Brain Stimulation 73
PN 932 SC 08540
B Brain Stimulation 67
Stereotaxic Techniques 73

Chemical Elements 73
PN 180 SC 08550
UF Nonmetallic Elements
B Chemicals 91
N ↓ Calcium 73
R ↓ Electrolytes 73
Food Additives 78

Chemicals 91
PN 129 SC 08555
SN May include compounds.
N ↓ Chemical Elements 73
R ↓ Hazardous Materials 91

Chemistry 67
PN 300 SC 08560
SN Study of the atomic composition of substances, elements, and their reactions, and the formation, decomposition, and properties of molecules. Used for the scientific discipline or the chemical processes themselves.
B Sciences 67
N ↓ Biochemistry 67

Chemoreceptors 73
PN 288 SC 08570
B Neural Receptors 73
Sensory Neurons 73
R Olfactory Mucosa 73
Taste Buds 73
Vomeronasal Sense 82

Chemotherapy
Use Drug Therapy

Chess 73
PN 96 SC 08590
B Games 67

Chest
Use Thorax

Chewing Tobacco
Use Smokeless Tobacco

Chi Square Test 73
PN 143 SC 08620
B Nonparametric Statistical Tests 67
R Statistical Significance 73

Chicanos
Use Mexican Americans

Chickens 67
PN 1612 SC 08630
B Birds 67

Child Abuse 71
PN 5637 SC 08650
SN Abuse of children or adolescents in a family, institutional, or other setting.
B Crime 67
Family Violence 82
N Battered Child Syndrome 73
R Abandonment 97
↓ Abuse Reporting 97
Anatomically Detailed Dolls 91
Child Abuse Reporting 97
Child Neglect 88
Child Welfare 88
Emotional Abuse 91
Failure to Thrive 88
Munchausen Syndrome by Proxy 97
Patient Abuse 91
Pedophilia 73
Physical Abuse 91
↓ Sexual Abuse 88

Child Abuse Reporting 97
PN 0 SC 08652
SN Reporting of physical abuse, emotional abuse, sexual abuse, verbal abuse, or child neglect by the victim or other individuals.
B Abuse Reporting 97
R ↓ Child Abuse 71
Child Neglect 88
Child Welfare 88

Child Advocacy
Use Advocacy

Child Attitudes 88
PN 936 SC 08658
SN Attitudes of, not toward, children.
B Attitudes 67
R ↓ Children 67

Child Behavior Checklist 94
PN 28 SC 08659
B Nonprojective Personality Measures 73

Child Care 91
PN 308 SC 08660
SN Care of children of any age in any setting.
UF Babysitting
N Child Day Care 73
Child Self Care 88
R ↓ Childrearing Practices 67
Foster Care 78

Child Care Workers 78
PN 660 SC 08663
SN Mental health, educational, or social services personnel providing day care or residential care for children.
R Child Day Care 73
Day Care Centers 73
↓ Nonprofessional Personnel 82
↓ Service Personnel 91

Child Custody 82
PN 776 SC 08665
SN Legal guardianship of a child.
B Legal Processes 73
R Child Support 88
Child Visitation 88
Divorce 73
Guardianship 88
Joint Custody 88
↓ Living Arrangements 91
Mediation 88
↓ Parental Absence 73
Protective Services 97

Child Day Care 73
PN 1157 SC 08670
SN Day care that provides for a child's physical needs and often his/her developmental or educational needs. Kinds of day care include day care centers and school-based programs.
UF Day Care (Child)
B Child Care 91
R Child Care Workers 78
Child Self Care 88
Child Welfare 88
Day Care Centers 73
Quality of Care 88

Child Discipline 73
PN 574 SC 08680
UF Discipline (Child)
B Childrearing Practices 67
Family Relations 67
N Parental Permissiveness 73
R ↓ Parent Child Relations 67
Parental Role 73

Child Guidance Clinics 73
PN 215 SC 08690
SN Facilities which exist for the diagnosis and treatment of behavioral and emotional disorders in childhood.
UF Child Psychiatric Clinics
B Clinics 67
R ↓ Community Facilities 73
Community Mental Health Centers 73
↓ Mental Health Programs 73
↓ Mental Health Services 78
Psychiatric Clinics 73

Child Molestation
Use Pedophilia

Child Neglect 88
PN 536 SC 08695
SN Failure of parents or caretakers to provide basic care and emotional support necessary for normal development.
B Antisocial Behavior 71
R Abandonment 97

Child Neglect — (cont'd)
R ↓ Child Abuse [71]
Child Abuse Reporting [97]
Child Welfare [88]
Emotional Abuse [91]
Failure to Thrive [88]
Munchausen Syndrome by Proxy [97]

Child Psychiatric Clinics
Use Child Guidance Clinics

Child Psychiatry [67]
PN 1298 **SC** 08710
SN Branch of psychiatry devoted to the study and treatment of behavioral, mental, and emotional disorders of children. Use a more specific term if possible.
B Psychiatry [67]
R Orthopsychiatry [73]

Child Psychology [67]
PN 348 **SC** 08720
SN Branch of developmental psychology devoted to the study of behavior, adjustment, and development and the treatment of behavioral, mental, and emotional disorders of children. Use a more specific term if possible.
B Developmental Psychology [73]

Child Psychotherapy [67]
PN 1661 **SC** 08730
B Psychotherapy [67]
N Play Therapy [73]
R Adolescent Psychotherapy [94]

Child Self Care [88]
PN 56 **SC** 08733
SN Responsibility for personal care without adult supervision usually before or after the school day. Primarily used for children under age 14.
UF Latchkey Children
B Child Care [91]
R Child Day Care [73]
Child Welfare [88]
Self Care Skills [78]

Child Support [88]
PN 39 **SC** 08735
SN Legal obligation of parents or guardians to contribute to the economic maintenance of their children including provision of education, clothing, and food.
R Child Custody [82]
Divorce [73]
Joint Custody [88]
↓ Marital Separation [73]

Child Visitation [88]
PN 97 **SC** 08737
SN The right of or court-granted permission to parents, grandparents, or guardians to visit children.
UF Visitation Rights
B Legal Processes [73]
R Child Custody [82]

Child Welfare [88]
PN 405 **SC** 08738
R ↓ Adoption (Child) [67]
Advocacy [85]
↓ Child Abuse [71]
Child Abuse Reporting [97]
Child Day Care [73]
Child Neglect [88]
Child Self Care [88]
Foster Care [78]
Protective Services [97]

Child Welfare — (cont'd)
R Social Casework [67]
↓ Social Services [82]

Childbirth
Use Birth

Childbirth (Natural)
Use Natural Childbirth

Childbirth Training [78]
PN 161 **SC** 08746
B Prenatal Care [91]
R ↓ Birth [67]
Labor (Childbirth) [73]
Natural Childbirth [78]
↓ Obstetrics [78]
↓ Pregnancy [67]

Childhood [84]
PN 71706 **SC** 08750
SN Mandatory age identifier used for ages 0–12. Where appropriate, more specific index terms (e.g., INFANTS, PRESCHOOL AGE CHILDREN) are used in addition to this age identifier. The other two age identifiers are ADOLESCENCE and ADULTHOOD.
R ↓ Children [67]
↓ Infants [67]
Neonates [67]

Childhood Development [67]
PN 5678 **SC** 08760
SN Process of physical, cognitive, personality, and psychosocial growth occurring from birth through age 12. Use a more specific term if possible.
B Human Development [67]
N ↓ Early Childhood Development [73]
R Adolescent Development [73]
↓ Children [67]
↓ Developmental Age Groups [73]
↓ Developmental Stages [73]
↓ Motor Development [73]
Object Relations [82]
↓ Perceptual Development [73]
↓ Physical Development [73]
Preschool Age Children [67]
↓ Psychogenesis [73]
↓ Psychomotor Development [73]
↓ School Age Children [73]
Separation Individuation [82]
Transitional Objects [85]

Childhood Memories
Use Early Memories

Childhood Neurosis [73]
PN 128 **SC** 08770
UF Infantile Neurosis
B Neurosis [67]

Childhood Play Behavior [78]
PN 2234 **SC** 08777
UF Play Behavior (Childhood)
B Behavior [67]
R Anatomically Detailed Dolls [91]
Childhood Play Development [73]
Childrens Recreational Games [73]
Doll Play [73]
↓ Games [67]
↓ Recreation [67]
Role Playing [67]
Toy Selection [73]
↓ Toys [73]

Childhood Play Development [73]
PN 564 **SC** 08780

Childhood Play Development — (cont'd)
UF Play Development (Childhood)
B Psychosocial Development [73]
R Childhood Play Behavior [78]
Childrens Recreational Games [73]
Emotional Development [73]

Childhood Psychosis [67]
PN 545 **SC** 08790
UF Infantile Psychosis
B Psychosis [67]
N Childhood Schizophrenia [67]
Early Infantile Autism [73]
Symbiotic Infantile Psychosis [73]
R Autistic Children [73]
↓ Emotionally Disturbed [73]

Childhood Schizophrenia [67]
PN 603 **SC** 08800
B Childhood Psychosis [67]
Schizophrenia [67]
R Early Infantile Autism [73]
Symbiotic Infantile Psychosis [73]

Childlessness [82]
PN 133 **SC** 08805
SN State of having no children.
B Family Structure [73]
Parenthood Status [85]
R Delayed Parenthood [85]
Family Planning Attitudes [73]

Childrearing Attitudes [73]
PN 896 **SC** 08810
B Attitudes [67]
R ↓ Family Relations [67]
↓ Parental Attitudes [73]

Childrearing Practices [67]
PN 3632 **SC** 08820
SN Limited to human populations.
B Family Relations [67]
N ↓ Child Discipline [73]
Toilet Training [73]
Weaning [73]
R ↓ Child Care [91]
Father Child Relations [73]
↓ Feeding Practices [73]
Mother Child Relations [67]
↓ Parent Child Relations [67]
Parent Training [78]
↓ Parental Attitudes [73]
↓ Parental Characteristics [94]
Parental Role [73]
Parenting Skills [97]
↓ Sociocultural Factors [67]

Children [67]
PN 20362 **SC** 08830
SN Ages 0–12 years. Used in noneducational contexts. Application of terms designating age is mandatory for ages 0–17.
UF Youth (Children)
B Developmental Age Groups [73]
N ↓ Infants [67]
Only Children [82]
Preschool Age Children [67]
↓ School Age Children [73]
R Adopted Children [73]
Autistic Children [73]
Child Attitudes [88]
Childhood [84]
↓ Childhood Development [67]
↓ Elementary School Students [67]
Foster Children [73]
Illegitimate Children [73]
Intermediate School Students [73]
Junior High School Students [71]

Children — (cont'd)
R Kindergarten Students [73]
Nursery School Students [73]
Predelinquent Youth [78]
Primary School Students [73]
Stepchildren [73]

Childrens Apperception Test [73]
PN 25 **SC** 08840
B Projective Personality Measures [73]

Childrens Manifest Anxiety Scale [73]
PN 25 **SC** 08850
B Nonprojective Personality Measures [73]

Childrens Personality Questionnaire [73]
PN 15 **SC** 08860
B Nonprojective Personality Measures [73]

Childrens Recreational Games [73]
PN 51 **SC** 08870
B Games [67]
Recreation [67]
R Childhood Play Behavior [78]
Childhood Play Development [73]
↓ Toys [73]

Chile [82]
PN 119 **SC** 08878
B South America [67]

Chimpanzees [73]
PN 598 **SC** 08890
B Mammals [73]
Primates (Nonhuman) [73]
R Bonobos [97]

China
Use Peoples Republic of China

Chinchillas [73]
PN 64 **SC** 08900
B Mammals [73]
Rodents [73]

Chinese Cultural Groups [97]
PN 0 **SC** 08902
SN Populations of Chinese descent residing in countries other than the country of their origin. For Chinese residing in their own country use the appropriate country name. Use ASIANS to access references from 82–96.
B Asians [82]

Chiroptera
Use Bats

Chloral Hydrate [73]
PN 25 **SC** 08910
B Anticonvulsive Drugs [73]
Hypnotic Drugs [73]
Sedatives [73]

Chloralose
SN Term discontinued in 1997. Use CHLORALOSE to access references from 73–96.
Use Hypnotic Drugs

Chlordiazepoxide [73]
PN 747 **SC** 08930
UF Librium
B Amines [73]
Benzodiazepines [78]
Minor Tranquilizers [73]

Chloride Ions [73]
PN 48 **SC** 08940
B Electrolytes [73]

Chlorimipramine [73]
PN 630 **SC** 08950
UF Clomipramine
B Amines [73]
Serotonin Reuptake Inhibitors [97]
Tricyclic Antidepressant Drugs [97]

Chlorisondamine
SN Term discontinued in 1997. Use CHLORISONDAMINE to access references from 73–96.
Use Amines

Chloroform [73]
PN 8 **SC** 08970
B General Anesthetics [73]

Chlorophenylpiperazine
Use Piperazines

Chlorpromazine [67]
PN 1324 **SC** 08990
UF Thorazine
B Amines [73]
Antiemetic Drugs [73]
Antihypertensive Drugs [73]
CNS Depressant Drugs [73]
Phenothiazine Derivatives [73]
Sedatives [73]

Chlorprothixene [73]
PN 21 **SC** 09000
B Amines [73]
Antiemetic Drugs [73]
Antihistaminic Drugs [73]
Antispasmodic Drugs [73]
Minor Tranquilizers [73]
Phenothiazine Derivatives [73]

Choice Behavior [67]
PN 4387 **SC** 09010
SN Motivational or judgmental processes involved in the decision or tendency to select one alternative over another or others. Also used for the choices themselves. Used for human or animal populations.
B Behavior [67]
Decision Making [67]
R Classification (Cognitive Process) [67]
Freedom [78]
Human Mate Selection [88]
Psychological Reactance [78]
Therapist Selection [94]
Uncertainty [91]
Volition [88]

Choice Shift [94]
PN 6 **SC** 09013
SN In social psychology, the changes or shifts in choices made by groups during decision making processes that may differ from choices made by each group member acting on their own.
UF Risky Shift
B Group Decision Making [78]
R Brainstorming [82]
Group Discussion [67]
↓ Group Dynamics [67]
↓ Group Problem Solving [73]
↓ Risk Taking [67]

Cholecystokinin [82]
PN 517 **SC** 09015
SN Hormone secreted by upper intestinal mucosa on contact with gastric contents, it stimulates contraction of the gallbladder. Also, a neurotransmitter.
UF Pancreozymin
B Hormones [67]
Neurotransmitters [85]
Peptides [73]

Cholesterol [73]
PN 275 **SC** 09020
B Steroids [73]

Choline [73]
PN 277 **SC** 09030
UF Choline Chloride
B Vitamins [73]
N Lecithin [91]
R Acetylcholine [73]
Cholinesterase [73]
Succinylcholine [73]

Choline Chloride
Use Choline

Cholinergic Blocking Drugs [73]
PN 596 **SC** 09050
UF Anticholinergic Drugs
Cholinolytic Drugs
Parasympatholytic Drugs
B Drugs [67]
N Atropine [73]
Benactyzine [73]
Levodopa [73]
Nicotine [73]
Orphenadrine [73]
Scopolamine [73]
Trihexyphenidyl [73]
R ↓ Antiemetic Drugs [73]
↓ Antispasmodic Drugs [73]
Cholinergic Nerves [73]
Cholinesterase [73]
↓ Cholinomimetic Drugs [73]
↓ Hallucinogenic Drugs [67]
↓ Parasympathetic Nervous System [73]
↓ Phenothiazine Derivatives [73]

Cholinergic Drugs [73]
PN 367 **SC** 09060
UF Muscarinic Drugs
B Drugs [67]
N Acetylcholine [73]
Physostigmine [73]
Pilocarpine [73]
R ↓ Cholinomimetic Drugs [73]

Cholinergic Nerves [73]
PN 492 **SC** 09070
UF Nerves (Cholinergic)
B Autonomic Nervous System [67]
R Acetylcholine [73]
↓ Cholinergic Blocking Drugs [73]
↓ Cholinomimetic Drugs [73]

Cholinesterase [73]
PN 77 **SC** 09080
B Esterases [73]
R Acetylcholinesterase [73]
↓ Choline [73]
↓ Cholinergic Blocking Drugs [73]
↓ Cholinesterase Inhibitors [73]

Cholinesterase Inhibitors [73]
PN 245 **SC** 09090
UF Anticholinesterase Drugs
B Enzyme Inhibitors [85]
N Galanthamine [73]

Cholinesterase Inhibitors — (cont'd)
N Neostigmine 73
Physostigmine 73
R Cholinesterase 73
↓ Cholinomimetic Drugs 73

Cholinolytic Drugs
Use Cholinergic Blocking Drugs

Cholinomimetic Drugs 73
PN 106 SC 09100
UF Parasympathomimetic Drugs
B Drugs 67
N Acetylcholine 73
Arecoline 73
Carbachol 73
Neostigmine 73
Physostigmine 73
Pilocarpine 73
R ↓ Analeptic Drugs 73
↓ Cholinergic Blocking Drugs 73
↓ Cholinergic Drugs 73
Cholinergic Nerves 73
↓ Cholinesterase Inhibitors 73
↓ Parasympathetic Nervous System 73

Chorda Tympani Nerve
Use Facial Nerve

Chorea 73
PN 42 SC 09120
B Central Nervous System Disorders 73
Movement Disorders 85
N Huntingtons Disease 73
R ↓ Infectious Disorders 73

Choroid
Use Eye (Anatomy)

Choroid Plexus
Use Cerebral Ventricles

Christianity 73
PN 1124 SC 09150
B Religious Affiliation 73
N ↓ Protestantism 73
Roman Catholicism 73
R Bible 73
↓ Christians 97

Christians 97
PN 0 SC 09152
B Religious Groups 97
N Catholics 97
Protestants 97
R ↓ Christianity 73

Chromaticity 97
PN 0 SC 09155
SN The collective aspects of a color stimulus determined by its hue (dominant wavelength of light) and its saturation (purity).
N Color Saturation 97
Hue 73
R Achromatic Color 73
↓ Color 67
↓ Color Perception 67
Luminance 82

Chromosome Disorders 73
PN 230 SC 09160
UF Karyotype Disorders
Mosaicism
B Genetic Disorders 73
N ↓ Autosome Disorders 73
Deletion (Chromosome) 73
↓ Sex Chromosome Disorders 73

Chromosome Disorders — (cont'd)
N Translocation (Chromosome) 73
↓ Trisomy 73
R ↓ Chromosomes 73

Chromosomes 73
PN 208 SC 09170
B Cells (Biology) 73
N Autosomes 73
Sex Chromosomes 73
R ↓ Chromosome Disorders 73
Genes 73
Genetic Linkage 94
↓ Genetics 67
Mutations 73

Chronic Alcoholic Intoxication 73
PN 39 SC 09180
B Alcohol Intoxication 73
Brain Disorders 67
Chronic Illness 91
R Toxic Encephalopathies 73

Chronic Fatigue Syndrome 97
PN 0 SC 09181
SN Syndrome thought to be caused by a viral organism resulting in chronic fatigue, fever, pain, sore throat, and, in some cases, depression.
B Chronic Illness 91
Syndromes 73
R ↓ Encephalopathies 82
Epstein Barr Viral Disorder 94
Fatigue 67
↓ Muscular Disorders 73
↓ Viral Disorders 73

Chronic Illness 91
PN 592 SC 09183
SN An illness or disorder that persists for a prolonged period of time. Used in conjunction with other specific terms where appropriate.
N Chronic Alcoholic Intoxication 73
Chronic Fatigue Syndrome 97
↓ Chronic Mental Illness 97
Chronic Pain 85
R Chronicity (Disorders) 82
↓ Disorders 67
↓ Mental Disorders 67
↓ Physical Disorders 97
Severity (Disorders) 82

Chronic Mental Illness 97
PN 0 SC 09184
SN A mental illness that persists for a prolonged period of time. Use a more specific term if possible.
UF Persistent Mental Illness
B Chronic Illness 91
Mental Disorders 67
N Chronic Psychosis 73
R Chronicity (Disorders) 82
Prognosis 73
Severity (Disorders) 82
↓ Treatment Resistant Disorders 94

Chronic Pain 85
PN 1477 SC 09185
B Chronic Illness 91
Pain 67
R Back Pain 82
Myofascial Pain 91
Somatoform Pain Disorder 97

Chronic Psychosis 73
PN 104 SC 09190
B Chronic Mental Illness 97
Psychosis 67

Chronic Schizophrenia
SN Term discontinued in 1988. Use CHRONIC SCHIZOPHRENIA to access references from 67-87.
Use Schizophrenia

Chronicity (Disorders) 82
PN 1293 SC 09203
SN Used only when chronicity itself is a factor, variable, or major focus of the research. Used in conjunction with other specific terms where appropriate.
R ↓ Chronic Illness 91
↓ Chronic Mental Illness 97
↓ Disorders 67
↓ Mental Disorders 67
↓ Physical Disorders 97
Severity (Disorders) 82

Churches
Use Religious Buildings

Cichlids 73
PN 201 SC 09210
B Fishes 67

Cigarette Smoking
Use Tobacco Smoking

Cimetidine 85
PN 33 SC 09225
B Antihistaminic Drugs 73

Circadian Rhythms (Animal)
Use Animal Circadian Rhythms

Circadian Rhythms (Human)
Use Human Biological Rhythms

Circulation (Blood)
Use Blood Circulation

Circulatory Disorders
Use Cardiovascular Disorders

Circumcision
Use Birth Rites AND Surgery

Cirrhosis (Liver) 73
PN 70 SC 09260
B Liver Disorders 73
R Jaundice 73

Citalopram 97
PN 0 SC 09265
B Antidepressant Drugs 71
Serotonin Reuptake Inhibitors 97

Cities
Use Urban Environments

Citizenship 73
PN 72 SC 09280
SN Formal status or social quality of being a member of a community, country, or some other political designation.
R Immigration 73
↓ Laws 67
↓ Political Attitudes 73

Civil Law 94
PN 28 SC 09284
B Law (Government) 73
R ↓ Civil Rights 78
Disability Laws 94
↓ Law Enforcement 78
↓ Legal Processes 73

Civil Rights [78]
PN 1026 **SC** 09288
SN Rights of personal liberty and equality guaranteed to citizens by constitution and legislation.
B Human Rights [78]
N ↓ Client Rights [88]
Equal Education [78]
R Advocacy [85]
Affirmative Action [85]
Age Discrimination [94]
Censorship [78]
Civil Law [94]
Civil Rights Movement [73]
Democracy [73]
Disability Discrimination [97]
Disability Laws [94]
Empowerment [91]
Freedom [78]
Informed Consent [85]
↓ Justice [73]
↓ Laws [67]
↓ Legal Processes [73]
Race and Ethnic Discrimination [94]
Sex Discrimination [78]
↓ Social Discrimination [82]
Social Equality [73]
↓ Social Integration [82]
↓ Social Issues [91]
↓ Social Movements [67]

Civil Rights Movement [73]
PN 105 **SC** 09290
SN Social and political effort to gain the constitutional rights of citizens, especially by minority groups whose rights have been denied. See SOCIAL MOVEMENTS for more specific terms.
B Social Movements [67]
R ↓ Activist Movements [73]
↓ Civil Rights [78]

Civil Servants
Use Government Personnel

Clairvoyance [73]
PN 96 **SC** 09310
B Extrasensory Perception [67]
N Precognition [73]

Class Attitudes
Use Socioeconomic Class Attitudes

Classical Conditioning [67]
PN 3201 **SC** 09330
SN Learned behavior or the experimental paradigm or procedure used to develop and evoke classically conditioned responses.
UF Conditioning (Classical)
Pavlovian Conditioning
Respondent Conditioning
B Conditioning [67]
N Conditioned Emotional Responses [67]
↓ Conditioned Responses [67]
Eyelid Conditioning [73]
Higher Order Conditioning [97]
Unconditioned Responses [73]
R Conditioned Stimulus [73]
Learning Theory [67]
Orienting Responses [67]
Pavlov (Ivan) [91]
Unconditioned Stimulus [73]

Classification (Cognitive Process) [67]
PN 5352 **SC** 09370
UF Categorizing
Sorting (Cognition)
B Cognitive Processes [67]
R Choice Behavior [67]

Classification Systems
Use Taxonomies

Classmates [73]
PN 34 **SC** 09400
B Students [67]

Classroom Behavior [73]
PN 3184 **SC** 09405
B Behavior [67]
R Classroom Behavior Modification [73]
Classroom Discipline [73]
Classroom Environment [73]

Classroom Behavior Modification [73]
PN 1857 **SC** 09410
B Behavior Modification [73]
R Classroom Behavior [73]
Classroom Discipline [73]
↓ Education [67]

Classroom Discipline [73]
PN 928 **SC** 09420
UF Discipline (Classroom)
R Classroom Behavior [73]
Classroom Behavior Modification [73]
↓ Education [67]
School Suspension [73]
Teacher Student Interaction [73]

Classroom Environment [73]
PN 2332 **SC** 09430
SN Physical, social, emotional, psychological, or intellectual characteristics of a classroom, especially as they contribute to the learning process. Includes classroom climate and class size.
B Academic Environment [73]
R Classroom Behavior [73]
Classrooms [67]
↓ School Environment [73]

Classroom Instruction
Use Teaching

Classroom Teachers
Use Teachers

Classrooms [67]
PN 556 **SC** 09460
B School Facilities [73]
R Classroom Environment [73]

Claustrophobia [73]
PN 50 **SC** 09470
B Phobias [67]

Cleft Palate [67]
PN 106 **SC** 09480
B Congenital Disorders [73]
Neonatal Disorders [73]
R ↓ Speech Disorders [67]

Clergy [73]
PN 332 **SC** 09490
B Religious Personnel [73]
N Chaplains [73]
Ministers (Religion) [73]
Priests [73]
Rabbis [73]
R Evangelists [73]
Lay Religious Personnel [73]
Missionaries [73]
↓ Religious Groups [97]

Clerical Personnel [73]
PN 459 **SC** 09500

Clerical Personnel — (cont'd)
UF Keypunch Operators
Typists
B White Collar Workers [73]
R Secretarial Personnel [73]

Clerical Secretarial Skills [73]
PN 190 **SC** 09510
UF Secretarial Skills
B Employee Skills [73]
R Proofreading [88]
Typing [91]
Word Processing [91]

Client Abuse
Use Patient Abuse

Client Attitudes [82]
PN 3516 **SC** 09527
SN Attitudes of clients that may affect compliance with a particular treatment modality, or preferences for a particular type of treatment. May include attitudes toward health care professionals.
UF Patient Attitudes
B Attitudes [67]
Client Characteristics [73]
N Client Satisfaction [94]
R Clients [73]
Therapist Selection [94]
Treatment Compliance [82]

Client Centered Therapy [67]
PN 559 **SC** 09530
UF Nondirective Therapy
Person Centered Psychotherapy
Rogerian Therapy
B Psychotherapy [67]
R ↓ Humanistic Psychology [85]
↓ Psychotherapeutic Techniques [67]
Rogers (Carl) [91]

Client Characteristics [73]
PN 7474 **SC** 09540
SN Physical, psychological, emotional, and other traits of individual clients or patients influencing the outcome of the therapeutic process.
UF Patient Characteristics
N ↓ Client Attitudes [82]
Health Behavior [82]
Illness Behavior [82]
Patient Violence [94]
R Client Participation [97]
Client Treatment Matching [97]
Clients [73]
Cross Cultural Treatment [94]
Patient History [73]
Patient Selection [97]
↓ Treatment Planning [97]

Client Compliance
Use Treatment Compliance

Client Counselor Interaction
Use Psychotherapeutic Processes

Client Dropouts
Use Treatment Dropouts

Client Education [85]
PN 1047 **SC** 09555
SN Informing or instructing patients or clients on the specifics of their disorder and/or its treatment. For client educational level use EDUCATIONAL BACKGROUND.
UF Patient Education
Pretraining (Therapy)
B Education [67]

Client Education — (cont'd)
R ↓ Health Education 73
Health Knowledge 94
Health Promotion 91
Psychoeducation 94
↓ Therapeutic Processes 78
Treatment Compliance 82

Client Participation 97
PN 0 SC 09556
UF Patient Participation
B Participation 73
R ↓ Client Characteristics 73
↓ Client Rights 88
Clients 73
↓ Patients 67
Treatment Compliance 82

Client Records 97
PN 0 SC 57455
UF Patient Records
B Medical Records 78
R Patient History 73
Privileged Communication 73

Client Rights 88
PN 470 SC 09557
SN Right of patient or client to be fully informed of benefits or risks of treatment procedures and to make informed decisions to accept or reject treatment.
UF Patient Rights
B Civil Rights 78
N Right to Treatment 97
R Advance Directives 94
Client Participation 97
Clients 73
Empowerment 91
Guardianship 88
↓ Human Rights 78
Informed Consent 85
Involuntary Treatment 94
Life Sustaining Treatment 97
Quality of Care 88
↓ Treatment 67
Treatment Compliance 82
Treatment Refusal 94
Treatment Withholding 88

Client Satisfaction 94
PN 170 SC 09558
UF Patient Satisfaction
B Client Attitudes 82
Satisfaction 73
R Clients 73

Client Transfer 97
PN 0 SC 57465
SN Transfer of client or patient care within or between treatment settings, therapists, or other health care providers.
UF Patient Transfer
R ↓ Facility Discharge 88
↓ Hospital Discharge 73
Patient Selection 97
Professional Referral 73
Psychiatric Hospital Discharge 78
↓ Treatment 67
Treatment Refusal 94
Treatment Termination 82

Client Treatment Matching 97
PN 0 SC 57470
SN Treatment selection based on matching the client's characteristics and needs with appropriate treatment modalities.
UF Patient Treatment Matching
Treatment Client Matching
R ↓ Client Characteristics 73

Client Treatment Matching — (cont'd)
R Clinical Judgment (Not Diagnosis) 73
Patient Selection 97
↓ Treatment 67
↓ Treatment Outcomes 82
↓ Treatment Planning 97

Client Violence
Use Patient Violence

Clients 73
PN 863 SC 09560
SN Persons receiving psychotherapy, counseling, or other mental health or social service. Consider also PATIENTS or one of its narrower terms.
UF Counselees
R ↓ Client Attitudes 82
↓ Client Characteristics 73
Client Participation 97
↓ Client Rights 88
Client Satisfaction 94
Patient Selection 97

Climacteric Depression
Use Involutional Depression

Climacteric Paranoia
Use Involutional Paranoid Psychosis

Climate (Meteorological)
Use Atmospheric Conditions

Climate (Organizational)
Use Organizational Climate

Climax (Sexual)
Use Orgasm

Clinical Judgment (Med Diagnosis)
Use Medical Diagnosis

Clinical Judgment (Not Diagnosis) 73
PN 2341 SC 09620
SN Analysis, evaluation, or prediction of disordered or abnormal behavior, symptoms, or other aspects of psychological functioning. Includes assessing the appropriateness of a particular treatment and the degree or likelihood of clinical improvement.
B Judgment 67
R Anatomically Detailed Dolls 91
Client Treatment Matching 97
↓ Diagnosis 67
Geriatric Assessment 97
Intake Interview 94
↓ Measurement 67
Prognosis 73
↓ Psychiatric Evaluation 97
↓ Psychodiagnosis 67
↓ Psychodiagnostic Typologies 67
↓ Psychological Assessment 97
↓ Treatment Planning 97

Clinical Judgment (Psychodiagnosis)
Use Psychodiagnosis

Clinical Markers
Use Biological Markers

Clinical Methods Training 73
PN 1662 SC 09640

Clinical Methods Training — (cont'd)
SN Instruction and skills training in methods for management and treatment of mental and behavior disorders. Includes training of populations such as parents, teachers, clergy, and administrators as well as mental health or medical personnel.
UF Training (Clinical Methods)
B Education 67
N ↓ Clinical Psychology Grad Training 73
Clinical Psychology Internship 73
↓ Community Mental Health Training 73
Psychiatric Training 73
Psychoanalytic Training 73
Psychotherapy Training 73
R Counselor Education 73
Microcounseling 78
Personal Therapy 91
Practicum Supervision 78
Theoretical Orientation 82

Clinical Psychologists 73
PN 831 SC 09650
B Mental Health Personnel 67
Psychologists 67
R Clinicians 73
Hypnotherapists 73
↓ Psychotherapists 73

Clinical Psychology 67
PN 1324 SC 09660
B Applied Psychology 73
Psychology 67
N Medical Psychology 73

Clinical Psychology Grad Training 73
PN 742 SC 09670
UF Training (Clinical Psychology Grad)
B Clinical Methods Training 73
Graduate Psychology Education 67
Postgraduate Training 73
N Clinical Psychology Internship 73
R Practicum Supervision 78

Clinical Psychology Internship 73
PN 219 SC 09680
B Clinical Methods Training 73
Clinical Psychology Grad Training 73
Postgraduate Training 73
R Practicum Supervision 78

Clinical Supervision
Use Professional Supervision

Clinicians 73
PN 405 SC 09690
B Professional Personnel 78
R Clinical Psychologists 73
Counseling Psychologists 88
↓ Medical Personnel 67
↓ Mental Health Personnel 67
↓ Physicians 67
Psychiatrists 67
↓ Therapists 67

Clinics 67
PN 652 SC 09700
B Treatment Facilities 73
N Child Guidance Clinics 73
Psychiatric Clinics 73
Walk In Clinics 73
R Community Mental Health Centers 73
↓ Crisis Intervention Services 73
↓ Hospitals 67
↓ Treatment 67

Cliques
Use Social Groups

Clomipramine
Use Chlorimipramine

Clonazepam [91]
PN 98 **SC** 09735
B Anticonvulsive Drugs [73]
Benzodiazepines [78]
Minor Tranquilizers [73]

Clonidine [73]
PN 791 **SC** 09740
B Antihypertensive Drugs [73]
CNS Stimulating Drugs [73]

Closed Circuit Television [73]
PN 58 **SC** 09750
B Television [67]

Closedmindedness
Use Openmindedness

Closure (Perceptual)
Use Perceptual Closure

Clothing [67]
PN 604 **SC** 09770
SN Use CLOTHING FASHIONS to access references prior to 1991.
B Fads and Fashions [73]
R ↓ Physical Appearance [82]

Clozapine [91]
PN 639 **SC** 09775
B Neuroleptic Drugs [73]
Sedatives [73]

Cloze Testing [73]
PN 241 **SC** 09780
SN Tests or procedures assessing comprehension (e.g., reading or listening) in which the person being tested is required to provide missing components.
B Testing Methods [67]
R Sentence Completion Tests [91]

Clubs (Social Organizations) [73]
PN 63 **SC** 09790
B Recreation [67]

Cluster Analysis [73]
PN 839 **SC** 09800
UF Clustering
B Statistical Analysis [67]

Clustering
Use Cluster Analysis

CNS Affecting Drugs [73]
PN 143 **SC** 09840
UF Central Nervous System Drugs
B Drugs [67]
N ↓ CNS Depressant Drugs [73]
↓ CNS Stimulating Drugs [73]
R ↓ Heart Rate Affecting Drugs [73]

CNS Depressant Drug Antagonists
Use Analeptic Drugs

CNS Depressant Drugs [73]
PN 77 **SC** 09860
B CNS Affecting Drugs [73]
N Amobarbital [73]
Barbital [73]
Chlorpromazine [67]
Glutethimide [73]
Haloperidol [73]
Scopolamine [73]

CNS Depressant Drugs — (cont'd)
R ↓ Analgesic Drugs [73]
↓ Anesthetic Drugs [73]
↓ Anticonvulsive Drugs [73]
↓ Barbiturates [67]
↓ Dopamine Antagonists [82]
Flurazepam [82]
↓ Hypnotic Drugs [73]
↓ Muscle Relaxing Drugs [73]
↓ Narcotic Drugs [73]
↓ Sedatives [73]

CNS Stimulating Drugs [73]
PN 578 **SC** 09870
UF Stimulants of CNS
B CNS Affecting Drugs [73]
N ↓ Amphetamine [67]
↓ Analeptic Drugs [73]
Caffeine [73]
Clonidine [73]
Dextroamphetamine [73]
Ephedrine [73]
Methamphetamine [73]
Methylphenidate [73]
Pemoline [78]
Pentylenetetrazol [73]
Pipradrol [73]
Piracetam [82]
R ↓ Antidepressant Drugs [71]
↓ Emetic Drugs [73]
↓ Heart Rate Affecting Drugs [73]
Smokeless Tobacco [94]

Coaches [88]
PN 199 **SC** 09880
SN Use TEACHERS to access references from 73-87.
R Athletic Training [91]
↓ Sports [67]

Coagulation (Blood)
Use Blood Coagulation

Coalition Formation [73]
PN 203 **SC** 09910
SN Temporary alliance of distinct parties, persons, or states for joint action.
B Social Processes [67]
R ↓ Social Movements [67]

Coast Guard Personnel [88]
PN 14 **SC** 00915
B Military Personnel [67]

Cobalt [73]
PN 16 **SC** 09920
B Metallic Elements [73]

Cocaine [73]
PN 2443 **SC** 09930
B Alkaloids [73]
Amines [73]
Local Anesthetics [73]

Cochlea [73]
PN 434 **SC** 09940
UF Organ of Corti
B Labyrinth (Anatomy) [73]
R Cochlear Implants [94]

Cochlear Implants [94]
PN 37 **SC** 09945
B Hearing Aids [73]
Prostheses [73]
Surgery [71]
R ↓ Aurally Disabled [97]
Cochlea [73]
↓ Deaf [67]

Cochlear Implants — (cont'd)
R Hearing Disorders [82]
Partially Hearing Impaired [73]

Cochran Q Test [73]
PN 4 **SC** 09950
UF Q Test
B Nonparametric Statistical Tests [67]

Cockroaches [73]
PN 141 **SC** 09960
B Insects [67]
R Larvae [73]

Code Switching [88]
PN 55 **SC** 09965
SN Alternating use of languages, dialects, or language styles in speech.
UF Language Alternation
B Oral Communication [85]
R Bilingualism [73]
Sociolinguistics [85]

Codeine [73]
PN 59 **SC** 09970
UF Codeine Sulfate
Methylmorphine
B Alkaloids [73]
Analgesic Drugs [73]
Hypnotic Drugs [73]
Opiates [73]

Codeine Sulfate
Use Codeine

Codependency [91]
PN 112 **SC** 09985
R ↓ Alcohol Abuse [88]
Dependency (Personality) [67]
Dependent Personality [94]
↓ Drug Abuse [73]
Dysfunctional Family [91]
↓ Emotional Adjustment [73]
Enabling [97]
↓ Family [67]
↓ Family Relations [67]
↓ Interpersonal Interaction [67]
↓ Marital Relations [67]
↓ Parent Child Relations [67]
↓ Personality Traits [67]

Coeds
Use College Students

Coeducation [73]
PN 101 **SC** 10000
SN Education of male and female students at the same institution.
R ↓ Education [67]

Coercion [94]
PN 57 **SC** 10020
B Aggressive Behavior [67]
Social Influences [67]
R Abuse of Power [97]
Authority [67]
Brainwashing [82]
↓ Dominance [67]
Obedience [73]
↓ Persuasive Communication [67]
↓ Power [67]
↓ Punishment [67]
↓ Resistance [97]
Threat [67]
Torture [88]
↓ Violence [73]

Coffee
Use Beverages (Nonalcoholic)

Cognition 67
PN 2803 **SC** 10040
SN Act or process of knowing which includes awareness and judgment, perceiving, reasoning, and conceiving.
R ↓ Cognitive Development 73
↓ Cognitive Processes 67
Intuition 73
Metacognition 91
Need for Cognition 97

Cognition Enhancing Drugs
Use Nootropic Drugs

Cognitions 85
PN 1530 **SC** 10045
SN The content of cognitive or thinking processes.
UF Thought Content
N ↓ Expectations 67
Irrational Beliefs 82
R ↓ Attitudes 67
Concepts 67
Mind 91
Schema 88

Cognitive Ability 73
PN 8495 **SC** 10050
SN Level of functioning in intellectual tasks.
UF Cognitive Functioning
Intellectual Functioning
B Ability 67
N Mathematical Ability 73
Reading Ability 73
↓ Spatial Ability 82
Verbal Ability 67
R Cognitive Assessment 97
Cognitive Processing Speed 97
Metacognition 91

Cognitive Assessment 97
PN 0 **SC** 10053
SN Used only for references that focus on the assessment process or the particular assessment itself.
UF Assessment (Cognitive)
B Psychological Assessment 97
R ↓ Cognitive Ability 73
↓ Cognitive Processes 67
Intelligence 67
↓ Intelligence Measures 67
Intelligence Quotient 67
↓ Neuropsychological Assessment 82
↓ Psychiatric Evaluation 97

Cognitive Behavior Therapy
Use Cognitive Therapy

Cognitive Complexity 73
PN 812 **SC** 10060
SN Conceptual, behavioral, or perceptual dimensions of thinking style that characterize an individual's differentiation or processing of stimuli.
UF Complexity (Cognitive)
B Cognitive Style 67

Cognitive Contiguity 73
PN 37 **SC** 10070
SN View of memory organization which holds that events that are experienced together tend to become associated with each other in memory.
UF Contiguity (Cognitive)
B Associative Processes 67

Cognitive Development 73
PN 10332 **SC** 10080
SN Acquisition of conscious thought, reasoning, symbol manipulation, and problem solving abilities beginning in infancy and following an orderly sequence. Compare INTELLECTUAL DEVELOPMENT.
B Psychogenesis 73
N ↓ Intellectual Development 73
↓ Language Development 67
↓ Perceptual Development 73
R Cognition 67
↓ Concept Formation 67
Conservation (Concept) 73
Constructivism 94
Egocentrism 78
Object Permanence 85
Piaget (Jean) 67
↓ Speech Development 73

Cognitive Discrimination 73
PN 924 **SC** 10090
SN Ability to distinguish between examples vs nonexamples of a concept, based on the presence or absence of its defining attributes.
UF Discrimination (Cognitive)
B Cognitive Processes 67
Concept Formation 67
Discrimination 67
R ↓ Lexical Access 88
Lexical Decision 88
Stroop Effect 88
Visual Search 82

Cognitive Dissonance 67
PN 1086 **SC** 10100
SN Psychological conflict resulting from incongruous beliefs or attitudes held simultaneously, or from inconsistency between belief and behavior.
UF Dissonance (Cognitive)
R ↓ Cognitive Processes 67
Psychological Reactance 78

Cognitive Functioning
Use Cognitive Ability

Cognitive Generalization 67
PN 577 **SC** 10110
SN Ability to evaluate the equivalence of an example of a concept or object across different contexts or modalities.
UF Generalization (Cognitive)
B Cognitive Processes 67
Concept Formation 67
R ↓ Associative Processes 67
Semantic Generalization 73

Cognitive Hypothesis Testing 82
PN 287 **SC** 10112
SN Problem-solving behavior in which the individual derives a set of rules (hypotheses) that are then sampled and tested until the one rule is discovered that consistently results in correct responding to the problem. Use HYPOTHESIS TESTING or other appropriate terms to access references prior to 1982.
UF Hypothesis Testing (Cognitive)
Rule Learning
B Learning 67
Problem Solving 67
R ↓ Concept Formation 67
↓ Reasoning 67

Cognitive Load
Use Human Channel Capacity

Cognitive Maps 82
PN 622 **SC** 10117

Cognitive Maps — (cont'd)
SN Internal or symbolic representations of social or physical environments, means-end relationships, or spatial relationships.
B Cognitive Processes 67
R Direction Perception 97
Schema 88
Spatial Imagery 82
↓ Spatial Memory 88
Spatial Organization 73
Spatial Orientation (Perception) 73

Cognitive Mediation 67
PN 1030 **SC** 10120
SN Intervention of cognitive processes between observable stimuli and responses, resulting in a change in subsequent behavior.
UF Mediation (Cognitive)
B Cognitive Processes 67
R Naming 88

Cognitive Processes 67
PN 17648 **SC** 10130
SN Mental processes involved in the acquisition, processing, and utilization of knowledge or information.
UF Human Information Processes
Information Processes (Human)
N ↓ Associative Processes 67
Classification (Cognitive Process) 67
Cognitive Discrimination 73
Cognitive Generalization 67
Cognitive Maps 82
Cognitive Mediation 67
↓ Comprehension 67
Concentration 82
↓ Concept Formation 67
↓ Decision Making 67
↓ Fantasy 97
↓ Ideation 73
Imagination 67
Intuition 73
Mental Rotation 91
Metacognition 91
Naming 88
↓ Problem Solving 67
Schema 88
Semantic Generalization 73
Social Cognition 94
↓ Thinking 67
Transposition (Cognition) 73
R ↓ Artificial Intelligence 82
Cognition 67
Cognitive Assessment 97
Cognitive Dissonance 67
Cognitive Processing Speed 97
Cognitive Psychology 85
↓ Conflict Resolution 82
Connectionism 94
Declarative Knowledge 97
Generation Effect (Learning) 91
Human Information Storage 73
↓ Learning 67
↓ Learning Strategies 91
↓ Memory 67
Mind 91
Procedural Knowledge 97
Questioning 82
Reality Testing 73
↓ Spatial Ability 82
↓ Strategies 67
Word Associations 67

Cognitive Processing Speed 97
PN 0 **SC** 10133
UF Information Processing Speed
R ↓ Cognitive Ability 73
↓ Cognitive Processes 67
↓ Cognitive Style 67

Cognitive Processing Speed — (cont'd)
R Conceptual Tempo [85]
Human Channel Capacity [73]
Reaction Time [67]
Response Latency [67]

Cognitive Psychology [85]
PN 811 SC 10135
SN Branch of psychology concerned with aspects of behavior as they relate to mental processes.
B Psychology [67]
R ↓ Cognitive Processes [67]
Connectionism [94]

Cognitive Rehabilitation [85]
PN 398 SC 10136
SN Procedures used to restore or enhance the cognitive functioning level of individuals with mental disability, injury, or disease (e.g., brain damaged stroke patients).
B Neuropsychological Rehabilitation [97]
Rehabilitation [67]
R Memory Training [94]

Cognitive Restructuring [85]
PN 249 SC 10137
SN Cognitive technique for altering self-defeating thought patterns by first identifying and analyzing negative self-statements and then developing adaptive self-statements.
B Cognitive Techniques [85]
R ↓ Behavior Modification [73]
Cognitive Therapy [82]

Cognitive Style [67]
PN 4646 SC 10140
SN Preferred or habitual style of learning or thinking.
UF Learning Style
B Personality Traits [67]
N Cognitive Complexity [73]
Conceptual Tempo [85]
Field Dependence [73]
Impulsiveness [73]
Reflectiveness [97]
R Cognitive Processing Speed [97]
↓ Learning Strategies [91]
Neurolinguistic Programing [88]
Perceptual Style [73]
↓ Personality [67]
Schema [88]

Cognitive Techniques [85]
PN 680 SC 10142
SN Methods directed at producing change in thought patterns that may result in changes in affect and behavior.
B Treatment [67]
N Cognitive Restructuring [85]
Cognitive Therapy [82]
Self Instructional Training [85]
R Anxiety Management [97]
Stress Management [85]

Cognitive Therapy [82]
PN 2913 SC 10144
SN Directive therapy based on the belief that the way one perceives and structures the world determines one's feelings and behavior. Treatment aims at altering cognitive schema and hence permitting the patient to change his/her distorted self-view and worldview.
UF Cognitive Behavior Therapy
B Cognitive Techniques [85]
R Anxiety Management [97]
↓ Behavior Modification [73]
Cognitive Restructuring [85]
↓ Psychotherapy [67]

Cognitive Therapy — (cont'd)
R Rational Emotive Therapy [78]
Self Instructional Training [85]
↓ Self Management [85]

Cohabitation [73]
PN 204 SC 10150
SN Primarily, but not exclusively, used for unmarried couples living together.
B Living Arrangements [91]
R Couples [82]
↓ Family [67]
Living Alone [94]
Roommates [73]

Cohesion (Group)
Use Group Cohesion

Cohort Analysis [88]
PN 195 SC 10165
SN Analysis of the effects attributed to being a member of a group sharing a particular characteristic, experience, or event. Use AGE DIFFERENCES for effects attributable to normal biological, cognitive, or psychosocial maturation.
B Analysis [67]
Experimental Design [67]
Methodology [67]
R Age Differences [67]
Generation Gap [73]

Coitus
Use Sexual Intercourse (Human)

Coitus (Animal)
Use Animal Mating Behavior

Cold Effects [73]
PN 547 SC 10200
B Temperature Effects [67]

Colitis [73]
PN 34 SC 10220
B Colon Disorders [73]
N Ulcerative Colitis [73]
R Gastrointestinal Ulcers [67]
Irritable Bowel Syndrome [91]

Coll Ent Exam Bd Scholastic Apt Test [73]
PN 264 SC 10230
UF Preliminary Scholastic Aptitude Test
SAT
Scholastic Aptitude Test
B Aptitude Measures [67]
Entrance Examinations [73]

Collaboration
Use Cooperation

Collective Behavior [67]
PN 1843 SC 10250
SN Behaviors which characterize groups or individuals acting in groups, usually working toward or achieving a specific goal. Used for human or animal populations.
B Interpersonal Interaction [67]
N Riots [73]
R Contagion [88]
Entrapment Games [73]
↓ Group Dynamics [67]
Group Participation [73]
Mass Hysteria [73]
Social Demonstrations [73]
↓ Sociometry [91]

Collective Unconscious [97]
PN 0 SC 10255

Collective Unconscious — (cont'd)
SN Genetically determined part of the unconscious shared by all members of a species or race of people. Consider JUNGIAN PSYCHOLOGY to access references prior to 1997.
B Jungian Psychology [73]
N Archetypes [91]
R Analytical Psychotherapy [73]
Jung (Carl) [73]

College Academic Achievement [67]
PN 4574 SC 10260
B Academic Achievement [67]

College Athletes [94]
PN 87 SC 10270
B Athletes [73]
College Students [67]
R Athletic Participation [73]
Athletic Performance [91]
Athletic Training [91]
↓ Sports [67]
Teams [88]

College Degrees
Use Educational Degrees

College Dropouts [73]
PN 402 SC 10290
B School Dropouts [67]

College Education
Use Undergraduate Education

College Environment [73]
PN 840 SC 10300
SN Social or emotional climate or physical setting of a college or university.
B School Environment [73]
R ↓ Colleges [67]
Community Colleges [78]

College Graduates [82]
PN 236 SC 10304
R ↓ College Students [67]
Educational Degrees [73]
School Graduation [91]
School to Work Transition [94]

College Major
Use Academic Specialization

College Students [67]
PN 22850 SC 10320
SN Students attending an institution of higher education.
UF Coeds
Undergraduates
B Students [67]
N College Athletes [94]
Community College Students [73]
Education Students [82]
Junior College Students [73]
Nursing Students [73]
ROTC Students [73]
R ↓ Adolescents [67]
College Graduates [82]
Graduate Students [67]
Postgraduate Students [73]
Preservice Teachers [82]
Reentry Students [85]
Young Adults [73]

College Teachers [73]
PN 2921 SC 10330
UF Professors
B Teachers [67]

Colleges [67]
PN 2098 **SC** 10350
UF Junior Colleges
Universities
B Schools [67]
N Community Colleges [78]
R College Environment [73]
↓ Higher Education [73]
Military Schools [73]

Colombia [82]
PN 127 **SC** 10360
B South America [67]

Colon Disorders [73]
PN 168 **SC** 10370
UF Bowel Disorders
B Gastrointestinal Disorders [73]
N ↓ Colitis [73]
Constipation [73]
Diarrhea [73]
Fecal Incontinence [73]
Irritable Bowel Syndrome [91]

Color [67]
PN 2091 **SC** 10380
SN Property of matter or light sources that corresponds to the relative reflectance or absorption of incident light and the wavelength of the incident light or light source. Color is described perceptually by the dimensions of hue, lightness, brightness, and saturation. Compare HUE.
N Achromatic Color [73]
Eye Color [91]
Hue [73]
R ↓ Chromaticity [97]
Color Saturation [97]
↓ Pigments [73]
↓ Visual Stimulation [73]

Color Blindness [73]
PN 214 **SC** 10390
B Eye Disorders [73]
R ↓ Color Perception [67]
↓ Genetic Disorders [73]

Color Constancy [85]
PN 55 **SC** 10395
SN The tendency to perceive hue, brightness, and saturation as stable despite objective changes in context and illumination.
B Color Perception [67]
Perceptual Constancy [85]

Color Contrast [85]
PN 74 **SC** 10397
B Color Perception [67]
Visual Contrast [85]

Color Perception [67]
PN 2726 **SC** 10400
UF Spectral Sensitivity
B Visual Perception [67]
N Color Constancy [85]
Color Contrast [85]
R ↓ Chromaticity [97]
Color Blindness [73]
Color Saturation [97]
Prismatic Stimulation [73]

Color Pyramid Test
SN Term discontinued in 1997. Use COLOR PYRAMID TEST to access references from 73–96.
Use Projective Personality Measures

Color Saturation [97]
PN 0 **SC** 10420

Color Saturation — (cont'd)
SN The degree of purity or richness of a color.
UF Saturation (Color)
B Chromaticity [97]
R Achromatic Color [73]
↓ Color [67]
↓ Color Perception [67]
Hue [73]
Luminance [82]

Colostomy [73]
PN 34 **SC** 10430
B Surgery [71]

Columbia Mental Maturity Scale [73]
PN 14 **SC** 10440
B Intelligence Measures [67]

Coma [73]
PN 221 **SC** 10450
B Symptoms [67]
R Cerebrovascular Accidents [73]
↓ Cerebrovascular Disorders [73]
↓ Consciousness Disturbances [73]
↓ Epileptic Seizures [73]
↓ Injuries [73]
Insulin Shock Therapy [73]

Combat Experience [91]
PN 255 **SC** 10452
SN Direct participation in war.
R ↓ Experiences (Events) [73]
↓ Military Personnel [67]
Posttraumatic Stress Disorder [85]
↓ War [67]

Comfort (Physical)
Use Physical Comfort

Commerce
Use Business

Commercials
Use Television Advertising

Commissioned Officers [73]
PN 190 **SC** 10470
SN Military officers who have received a formal certificate granting rank and authority and who thereby hold a position of command.
UF Military Officers
Officers (Commissioned)
B Military Personnel [67]
R ↓ Management Personnel [73]
Volunteer Military Personnel [73]

Commissurotomy [85]
PN 153 **SC** 10475
UF Split Brain
B Neurosurgery [73]
R Corpus Callosum [73]

Commitment [85]
PN 682 **SC** 10478
SN The process or extent of devoting one's efforts or resources to an activity, task, or interpersonal relationship.
N Organizational Commitment [91]
R ↓ Involvement [73]
↓ Motivation [67]

Commitment (Outpatient)
Use Outpatient Commitment

Commitment (Psychiatric) [73]
PN 916 **SC** 10480

Commitment (Psychiatric) — (cont'd)
B Hospitalization [67]
Legal Processes [73]
N Outpatient Commitment [91]
R Court Referrals [94]
Guardianship [88]
Health Care Seeking Behavior [97]
↓ Institutional Release [78]
Involuntary Treatment [94]
↓ Psychiatric Hospital Admission [73]
Psychiatric Hospital Discharge [78]
↓ Psychiatric Hospitalization [73]
Right to Treatment [97]
Self Referral [91]

Commonwealth of Independent States [97]
PN 0 **SC** 10490
SN Independent states or republics formed after the collapse of the former Union of Soviet Socialist Republics (USSR) in 1991.
R ↓ Asia [73]
↓ Europe [73]
Union of Soviet Socialist Republics [67]

Communes [73]
PN 88 **SC** 10510
B Communities [67]
N Kibbutz [73]

Communicable Diseases
Use Infectious Disorders

Communication [67]
PN 2908 **SC** 10570
SN Conceptually broad array term referring to the transmission of verbal or nonverbal information. Use a more specific term if possible.
N ↓ Animal Communication [67]
↓ Augmentative Communication [94]
↓ Interpersonal Communication [73]
↓ Nonverbal Communication [71]
↓ Persuasive Communication [67]
↓ Scientific Communication [73]
↓ Verbal Communication [67]
R Censorship [78]
↓ Communication Skills [73]
Communication Skills Training [82]
↓ Communication Systems [73]
Communication Theory [73]
↓ Communications Media [73]
↓ Content Analysis [78]
Emotional Content [73]
Information [67]
Messages [73]
Privileged Communication [73]
Rhetoric [91]
Symbolism [67]
↓ Vocalization [67]
↓ Voice [73]

Communication (Privileged)
Use Privileged Communication

Communication (Professional)
Use Scientific Communication

Communication Apprehension
Use Speech Anxiety

Communication Disorders [82]
PN 376 **SC** 10533
SN Impaired ability to communicate usually due to speech, language, or hearing disorders.
N Hearing Disorders [82]
↓ Language Disorders [82]
↓ Speech Disorders [67]
R ↓ Augmentative Communication [94]
↓ Aurally Disabled [97]

Communication Disorders — (cont'd)
R ↓ Communication Skills [73]
Communication Skills Training [82]
Developmental Disabilities [82]
↓ Mental Disorders [67]
↓ Physical Disorders [97]
Speech Anxiety [85]
Speech Disabled [97]
Speech Therapy [67]

Communication Skills [73]
PN 2166 SC 10540
SN Individual ability or competency in any type of communication. Limited to human populations.
UF Communicative Competence
B Ability [67]
N Language Proficiency [88]
Rhetoric [91]
Writing Skills [85]
R ↓ Communication [67]
↓ Communication Disorders [82]
Communication Skills Training [82]
Pragmatics [85]
Social Cognition [94]
↓ Verbal Communication [67]

Communication Skills Training [82]
PN 940 SC 10542
SN Instruction, usually group oriented, to increase quality and capability of interpersonal communication.
B Education [67]
R Assertiveness Training [78]
↓ Behavior Modification [73]
↓ Communication [67]
↓ Communication Disorders [82]
↓ Communication Skills [73]
Human Relations Training [78]
Sensitivity Training [73]
↓ Skill Learning [73]
Social Skills Training [82]

Communication Systems [73]
PN 355 SC 10550
SN Organized scheme for transmitting and receiving information.
B Systems [67]
N Telephone Systems [73]
R ↓ Automated Information Processing [73]
↓ Communication [67]
Information Systems [91]

Communication Theory [73]
PN 209 SC 10560
B Theories [67]
R ↓ Communication [67]
Cybernetics [67]
Information Theory [67]

Communications Media [73]
PN 374 SC 10580
UF Media (Communications)
N ↓ Audiovisual Communications Media [73]
↓ Mass Media [67]
↓ Telecommunications Media [73]
R Censorship [78]
↓ Communication [67]

Communicative Competence
Use Communication Skills

Communism [73]
PN 429 SC 10590
UF Marxism
B Political Economic Systems [73]

Communities [67]
PN 1605 SC 10600

Communities — (cont'd)
B Social Environments [73]
N ↓ Communes [73]
Neighborhoods [73]
Retirement Communities [97]
R Community Development [97]

Community Attitudes [73]
PN 862 SC 10620
SN Attitudes which characterize a group of individuals living in close proximity and organized into a social structure, however tenuous.
B Attitudes [67]
R Public Opinion [73]

Community College Students [73]
PN 1075 SC 10627
SN Students attending public postsecondary institutions offering 2-year degree programs and transfer components. Mandatory term in educational contexts.
B College Students [67]
R Junior College Students [73]

Community Colleges [78]
PN 336 SC 10630
B Colleges [67]
R College Environment [73]
↓ Community Facilities [73]

Community Development [97]
PN 0 SC 10635
UF Rural Development
Urban Development
B Development [67]
R ↓ Communities [67]
↓ Community Services [67]
Rural Environments [67]
↓ Urban Environments [67]
Urban Planning [73]

Community Facilities [73]
PN 456 SC 10640
N Community Mental Health Centers [73]
↓ Housing [73]
Public Transportation [73]
Shopping Centers [73]
Suicide Prevention Centers [73]
R Child Guidance Clinics [73]
Community Colleges [78]
↓ Community Services [67]
Day Care Centers [73]
Group Homes [82]
Halfway Houses [73]
↓ Libraries [82]
↓ Recreation Areas [73]
↓ Rehabilitation Centers [73]
Religious Buildings [73]
↓ Schools [67]
Sheltered Workshops [67]
Shelters [91]
Urban Planning [73]

Community Mental Health [73]
PN 419 SC 10647
SN General psychological well-being or adjustment of persons in a given area.
B Mental Health [67]
R Community Mental Health Centers [73]
Community Mental Health Services [78]
↓ Community Mental Health Training [73]
Community Psychiatry [73]
Community Psychology [73]
Deinstitutionalization [82]
↓ Mental Health Programs [73]

Community Mental Health Centers [73]
PN 1475 SC 10650

Community Mental Health Centers — (cont'd)
UF Mental Health Centers (Community)
B Community Facilities [73]
Treatment Facilities [73]
R Child Guidance Clinics [73]
↓ Clinics [67]
Community Mental Health [73]
Community Mental Health Services [78]
↓ Crisis Intervention Services [73]
Day Care Centers [73]
Hot Line Services [73]
↓ Mental Health Programs [73]
↓ Mental Health Services [78]
Psychiatric Clinics [73]
Suicide Prevention Centers [73]

Community Mental Health Services [78]
PN 2254 SC 10656
B Community Services [67]
Mental Health Services [78]
R Community Mental Health [73]
Community Mental Health Centers [73]
Community Psychiatry [73]
Community Psychology [73]
Deinstitutionalization [82]
Group Homes [82]
↓ Mental Health [67]
↓ Mental Health Programs [73]
Outreach Programs [97]
Supported Employment [94]

Community Mental Health Training [73]
PN 239 SC 10660
UF Mental Health Training (Community)
Training (Community Mental Health)
B Clinical Methods Training [73]
N Mental Health Inservice Training [73]
R Community Mental Health [73]
↓ Mental Health Programs [73]

Community Psychiatry [73]
PN 248 SC 10670
SN Branch of psychiatry concerned with the provision and delivery of community health care needs such as diagnosis; treatment; primary, secondary, and tertiary prevention; rehabilitation; and aftercare. Such services are usually delivered at community mental health centers.
B Psychiatry [67]
R Community Mental Health [73]
Community Mental Health Services [78]
Community Psychology [73]
↓ Mental Health [67]
↓ Mental Health Programs [73]

Community Psychology [73]
PN 515 SC 10680
SN Branch of psychology that emphasizes the analysis of social processes and interactions and design of social interventions within groups and the community.
B Applied Psychology [73]
R Community Mental Health [73]
Community Mental Health Services [78]
Community Psychiatry [73]
↓ Mental Health Programs [73]

Community Services [67]
PN 4124 SC 10690
B Social Services [82]
N Community Mental Health Services [78]
Community Welfare Services [73]
↓ Crisis Intervention Services [73]
Home Visiting Programs [73]
Public Health Services [73]
R Alcoholics Anonymous [73]
Community Development [97]
↓ Community Facilities [73]

Community Services — (cont'd)
R ↓ Health Care Services [78]
Independent Living Programs [91]
Integrated Services [97]
↓ Mental Health Programs [73]
↓ Mental Health Services [78]
Outreach Programs [97]
↓ Self Help Techniques [82]
Shelters [91]
↓ Support Groups [91]

Community Welfare Services [73]
PN 121 SC 10700
UF Public Welfare Services
B Community Services [67]
R Welfare Services (Government) [73]

Commuting (Travel) [85]
PN 45 SC 10705
R Geographical Mobility [78]
↓ Transportation [73]
Traveling [73]

Comorbidity [91]
PN 1173 SC 10707
SN Coexistence of two or more physical and/or mental disorders.
R ↓ Diagnosis [67]
Differential Diagnosis [67]
↓ Disorders [67]
Dual Diagnosis [91]
↓ Mental Disorders [67]
↓ Physical Disorders [97]
Psychopathology [67]

Companies
Use Business Organizations

Comparative Psychiatry
Use Transcultural Psychiatry

Comparative Psychology [67]
PN 912 SC 10720
SN Branch of psychology devoted to the study of behavioral differences between organisms of different species. Prior to 1982, also used for comparative studies. From 1982, limited to the scientific discipline. Use SPECIES DIFFERENCES for comparative studies.
B Psychology [67]

Compatibility (Interpersonal)
Use Interpersonal Compatibility

Compensation (Defense Mechanism) [73]
PN 33 SC 10740
SN Defense mechanism of covering up or making up for conscious or unconscious insecurity or feelings of failure.
B Defense Mechanisms [67]

Compensatory Education [73]
PN 184 SC 10745
SN Education designed to enhance intellectual and social skills of disadvantaged students, and to compensate for environmental, experiential, cultural, or economic deficits. Compare REMEDIAL EDUCATION.
B Curriculum [67]
R ↓ Educational Programs [73]
Project Follow Through [73]
Project Head Start [73]
↓ Remedial Education [85]
Upward Bound [73]

Competence [82]
PN 2045 SC 10747

Competence — (cont'd)
SN Possession of sufficient skills, knowledge, or qualities as required in a given situation.
N Professional Competence [97]
R ↓ Ability [67]
Accountability [88]
↓ Achievement [67]
Competency to Stand Trial [85]
Minimum Competency Tests [85]
↓ Performance [67]
Social Skills [78]

Competence (Social)
Use Social Skills

Competency to Stand Trial [85]
PN 243 SC 10749
B Legal Processes [73]
R ↓ Competence [82]
Criminal Responsibility [91]
Forensic Evaluation [94]
Mentally Ill Offenders [85]

Competition [67]
PN 2572 SC 10750
SN Used for human and animal populations.
B Social Behavior [67]
R Rivalry [73]

Complexity (Cognitive)
Use Cognitive Complexity

Complexity (Stimulus)
Use Stimulus Complexity

Complexity (Task)
Use Task Complexity

Compliance [73]
PN 1338 SC 10810
SN Limited to human populations.
B Social Behavior [67]
N Treatment Compliance [82]
R Obedience [73]
↓ Resistance [97]

Comprehension [67]
PN 2532 SC 10820
SN Knowledge or understanding of communications, objects, events, or situations as relates to their meaning, significance, relationships, or general principles.
UF Understanding
B Cognitive Processes [67]
N Number Comprehension [73]
↓ Verbal Comprehension [85]
R Intuition [73]
↓ Meaning [67]
Meaningfulness [67]
Metacognition [91]

Comprehension Tests [73]
PN 42 SC 10830
B Measurement [67]

Compressed Speech [73]
PN 136 SC 10840
B Speech Processing (Mechanical) [73]

Compulsions [73]
PN 394 SC 10850
N Compulsive Repetition [73]
R Obsessions [67]
Obsessive Compulsive Neurosis [73]
Obsessive Compulsive Personality [73]
Perfectionism [88]

Compulsive Gambling
Use Pathological Gambling

Compulsive Neurosis
Use Obsessive Compulsive Neurosis

Compulsive Personality Disorder
Use Obsessive Compulsive Personality

Compulsive Repetition [73]
PN 87 SC 10890
UF Repetition (Compulsive)
B Compulsions [73]

Compulsivity (Sexual)
Use Sexual Addiction

Computer Applications [73]
PN 3953 SC 10900
SN Application of computers, computer technology, or software to any area.
N ↓ Artificial Intelligence [82]
Computer Assisted Design [97]
Computer Assisted Diagnosis [73]
Computer Assisted Instruction [73]
Computer Assisted Testing [88]
↓ Computer Simulation [73]
Hypermedia [97]
Hypertext [97]
R Automated Speech Recognition [94]
Computer Searching [91]
↓ Computers [67]
Databases [91]
Decision Support Systems [97]
Information Systems [91]
Microcomputers [85]
Virtual Reality [97]
Word Processing [91]

Computer Assisted Design [97]
PN 0 SC 10905
SN Use of a computer system to design a product so that it can be displayed, manipulated, and revised or modified quickly and easily.
B Computer Applications [73]
R ↓ Architecture [73]
↓ Computer Simulation [73]
↓ Computer Software [67]
↓ Computers [67]
↓ Environmental Planning [82]
Human Factors Engineering [73]
Human Machine Systems Design [97]
Product Design [97]

Computer Assisted Diagnosis [73]
PN 915 SC 10910
B Computer Applications [73]
Diagnosis [67]
R Magnetic Resonance Imaging [94]
↓ Medical Diagnosis [73]
↓ Psychodiagnosis [67]
↓ Tomography [88]

Computer Assisted Instruction [73]
PN 3344 SC 10920
SN Use of computers to present instructional materials to students and to assess performance. Compare TEACHING MACHINES.
UF Instruction (Computer Assisted)
B Computer Applications [73]
Teaching Methods [67]
R Individualized Instruction [73]
Programed Instruction [67]
Teaching Machines [73]

Computer Assisted Testing [88]
PN 490 SC 10921

Computer Assisted Testing — (cont'd)
SN Use of computers in test construction or administration, usually in an educational or employment setting. Not used for diagnosis.
B Computer Applications 73
Testing 67
R Adaptive Testing 85

Computer Attitudes 88
PN 519 **SC** 10922
B Attitudes 67
R ↓ Computers 67

Computer Conferencing
Use Teleconferencing

Computer Games 88
PN 224 **SC** 10923
UF Video Games
B Computers 67
Games 67
R ↓ Computer Simulation 73
↓ Recreation 67
Simulation Games 73
↓ Toys 73

Computer Literacy 91
PN 70 **SC** 10924
B Literacy 73
R Computer Searching 91
Computer Training 94
↓ Computers 67

Computer Peripheral Devices 85
PN 96 **SC** 10925
SN Devices used for entering (e.g., keyboards) or displaying (e.g., printers, CRTs) data and programs in computer memory.
B Apparatus 67
N Video Display Units 85
R ↓ Computers 67
Human Computer Interaction 97
Human Machine Systems 97
Keyboards 85
↓ Visual Displays 73

Computer Programing 94
PN 86 **SC** 10928
UF Programing (Computer)
R Algorithms 73
↓ Computer Programing Languages 73
↓ Computer Software 67
↓ Computers 67
↓ Data Processing 67
Systems Analysis 73

Computer Programing Languages 73
PN 587 **SC** 10930
UF FORTRAN
Programing Languages (Computer)
N Virtual Reality 97
R Computer Programing 94
Computer Training 94
↓ Computers 67
↓ Data Processing 67

Computer Programs
Use Computer Software

Computer Searching 91
PN 78 **SC** 10945
SN Use of computerized interactive communication system to access and retrieve information.
UF Online Searching
B Automated Information Retrieval 73
R ↓ Computer Applications 73
Computer Literacy 91
↓ Computers 67

Computer Searching — (cont'd)
R Databases 91
Human Machine Systems 97
Information 67
Information Exchange 73
Information Seeking 73
Information Services 88

Computer Simulation 73
PN 1299 **SC** 10950
B Computer Applications 73
Simulation 67
N Neural Networks 91
Virtual Reality 97
R Computer Assisted Design 97
Computer Games 88
Decision Support Systems 97
Simulation Games 73

Computer Software 67
PN 3164 **SC** 10960
UF Computer Programs
N Decision Support Systems 97
Word Processing 91
R Computer Assisted Design 97
Computer Programing 94
↓ Computers 67
↓ Data Processing 67
Databases 91
Hypermedia 97
Hypertext 97
↓ Systems 67

Computer Training 94
PN 51 **SC** 10963
B Curriculum 67
R Computer Literacy 91
↓ Computer Programing Languages 73

Computerized Databases
Use Databases

Computers 67
PN 2442 **SC** 10970
B Apparatus 67
N Analog Computers 73
Computer Games 88
Digital Computers 73
Microcomputers 85
R ↓ Artificial Intelligence 82
Automated Information Coding 73
↓ Automated Information Processing 73
↓ Automated Information Retrieval 73
Automated Information Storage 73
Automation 67
↓ Computer Applications 73
Computer Assisted Design 97
Computer Attitudes 88
Computer Literacy 91
↓ Computer Peripheral Devices 85
Computer Programing 94
↓ Computer Programing Languages 73
Computer Searching 91
↓ Computer Software 67
Cybernetics 67
↓ Data Processing 67
Databases 91
↓ Expert Systems 91
Human Computer Interaction 97
Robotics 85
↓ Systems 67

Concentration 82
PN 219 **SC** 10977
SN Cognitive effort directed to one object or area of study.
B Cognitive Processes 67
Sustained Attention 97

Concentration — (cont'd)
R ↓ Attention 67
Distraction 78
Selective Attention 73

Concentration Camps 73
PN 302 **SC** 10980
R Holocaust 88
Prisons 67

Concept Formation 67
PN 3178 **SC** 11000
SN Developmental or learning process involving identification of common properties of objects, events, or qualities, usually represented by words or symbols, and generalization of those properties to all appropriate objects, events, or qualities. Use CONCEPT FORMATION or CONCEPT LEARNING to access references prior to 1982.
UF Concept Learning
Conceptualization
B Cognitive Processes 67
N Cognitive Discrimination 73
Cognitive Generalization 67
R ↓ Cognitive Development 73
Cognitive Hypothesis Testing 82
Concepts 67
Conservation (Concept) 73
↓ Discrimination Learning 82
Egocentrism 78
↓ Generalization (Learning) 82
↓ Learning 67

Concept Learning
SN Term discontinued in 1982. Use CONCEPT LEARNING or CONCEPT FORMATION to access references prior to 1982.
Use Concept Formation

Concept Validity
Use Construct Validity

Concepts 67
PN 1559 **SC** 11030
SN Generic ideas or categories derived from common properties of objects, events, or qualities, usually represented by words or symbols.
R ↓ Cognitions 85
↓ Concept Formation 67
Information 67
↓ Mathematics (Concepts) 67
↓ Terminology 91

Conceptual Imagery 73
PN 298 **SC** 11040
SN Mental representation of concepts or conceptual relationships.
UF Imagery (Conceptual)
B Imagery 67
R Imagination 67
Schema 88

Conceptual Tempo 85
PN 42 **SC** 11045
SN The dimension of cognitive style often measured by response latency or the time required to solve a problem.
B Cognitive Style 67
R Attention Span 73
Cognitive Processing Speed 97
Impulsiveness 73
Perceptual Style 73
Reaction Time 67
Reflectiveness 97

Conceptualization
Use Concept Formation

Concurrent Reinforcement Schedules [88]
PN 118 **SC** 11057
SN Simultaneous use of two or more reinforcement schedules.
B Reinforcement Schedules [67]

Concurrent Validity [88]
PN 736 **SC** 11058
SN Internal consistency of different parts of a test battery or the correlation between the results of two or more measures or tests presumably taken at the same time.
B Statistical Validity [73]
R Construct Validity [82]
Predictive Validity [73]
Test Validity [73]

Concussion (Brain)
Use Brain Concussion

Conditioned Emotional Responses [67]
PN 497 **SC** 11070
UF CER (Conditioning)
B Classical Conditioning [67]
Conditioned Responses [67]
Emotional Responses [67]
Operant Conditioning [67]

Conditioned Inhibition
Use Conditioned Suppression

Conditioned Place Preference
Use Place Conditioning

Conditioned Reflex
Use Conditioned Responses

Conditioned Responses [67]
PN 2849 **SC** 11090
UF Conditioned Reflex
B Classical Conditioning [67]
Operant Conditioning [67]
Responses [67]
N Conditioned Emotional Responses [67]
Conditioned Suppression [73]

Conditioned Stimulus [73]
PN 1803 **SC** 11100
SN In classical conditioning, that stimulus (e.g., a light) that acquires the capacity to elicit a conditioned response (e.g., salivation) as a result of that stimulus having been paired consistently with an unconditioned stimulus (e.g., food). In operant conditioning, those stimuli (S+,S-) which differentially signal the presence or absence of reinforcement. Compare CUES.
UF Discriminative Stimulus
B Conditioning [67]
R ↓ Classical Conditioning [67]
↓ Latent Inhibition [97]
↓ Operant Conditioning [67]
Preconditioning [94]
Secondary Reinforcement [67]
↓ Stimulation [67]

Conditioned Suppression [73]
PN 813 **SC** 11110
SN Learned behavior or the conditioning procedure in which the pairing of a neutral stimulus with an aversive stimulus, presented during the performance of a positively-reinforced behavior, results in a decrease of that behavior.
UF Conditioned Inhibition
Suppression (Conditioned)
B Conditioned Responses [67]
R Prepulse Inhibition [97]

Conditioning [67]
PN 2551 **SC** 11120
B Learning [67]
N Autoshaping [78]
↓ Aversion Conditioning [82]
↓ Classical Conditioning [67]
Conditioned Stimulus [73]
Counterconditioning [73]
↓ Operant Conditioning [67]
Place Conditioning [91]
Preconditioning [94]
Unconditioned Stimulus [73]
R ↓ Biofeedback [73]
↓ Latent Inhibition [97]
Primary Reinforcement [73]
↓ Reinforcement [67]
Spontaneous Recovery (Learning) [73]
↓ Stimulation [67]

Conditioning (Avoidance)
Use Avoidance Conditioning

Conditioning (Classical)
Use Classical Conditioning

Conditioning (Escape)
Use Escape Conditioning

Conditioning (Eyelid)
Use Eyelid Conditioning

Conditioning (Operant)
Use Operant Conditioning

Conditioning (Verbal)
Use Verbal Learning

Condoms [91]
PN 325 **SC** 11185
B Contraceptive Devices [73]
R AIDS Prevention [94]
↓ Birth Control [71]
↓ Family Planning [73]
↓ Prevention [73]
↓ Venereal Diseases [73]

Conduct Disorder [91]
PN 453 **SC** 11187
SN Repetitive and persistent aggressive or nonaggressive behavior in which basic rights of others or social norms are violated. Self esteem is generally low, and an inability to develop social relationships and lack of concern for others may or may not be present. Consider using BEHAVIOR DISORDERS prior to 1991.
R ↓ Aggressive Behavior [67]
↓ Behavior Disorders [71]
↓ Behavior Problems [67]
Explosive Personality [73]
Impulse Control Disorders [97]
↓ Mental Disorders [67]
Oppositional Defiant Disorder [97]

Cones (Eye) [73]
PN 425 **SC** 11190
B Cells (Biology) [73]
Photoreceptors [73]
Retina [67]
R Fovea [82]

Confabulation [73]
PN 36 **SC** 11200
SN Giving untruthful answers to questions about situations or events that are not recalled due to loss of memory. Confabulation is not a conscious attempt to deceive.
B Thought Disturbances [73]
R ↓ Deception [67]

Confabulation — (cont'd)
R False Memory [97]
Korsakoffs Psychosis [73]

Conference Proceedings
SN Term discontinued in 1982. Prior to 1982 this term was not defined and was used interchangeably with PROFESSIONAL MEETINGS AND SYMPOSIA.
Use Professional Meetings and Symposia

Confession (Religion) [73]
PN 9 **SC** 11220
B Religious Practices [73]

Confidence (Self)
Use Self Confidence

Confidence Limits (Statistics) [73]
PN 127 **SC** 11230
B Statistical Analysis [67]
R Effect Size (Statistical) [85]
↓ Hypothesis Testing [73]
Predictability (Measurement) [73]
↓ Statistical Measurement [73]
↓ Statistical Sample Parameters [73]
Statistical Significance [73]
↓ Statistical Tests [73]

Confidentiality of Information
Use Privileged Communication

Confirmatory Factor Analysis
Use Factor Analysis

Conflict [67]
PN 3318 **SC** 11250
SN Hostile encounter or antagonistic state or action.
B Aggressive Behavior [67]
Interpersonal Interaction [67]
N Arguments [73]
Riots [73]
↓ Violence [73]
↓ War [67]

Conflict Resolution [82]
PN 1360 **SC** 11255
SN Process of reducing or removing antagonisms among individuals, groups, organizations, or political entities.
N Mediation [88]
R ↓ Cognitive Processes [67]
Forgiveness [88]
↓ Negotiation [73]
↓ Social Interaction [67]

Conformity (Personality) [67]
PN 1123 **SC** 11270
B Personality Traits [67]
Social Behavior [67]
R Nonconformity (Personality) [73]
Openness to Experience [97]

Confusion (Mental)
Use Mental Confusion

Congenital Disorders [73]
PN 521 **SC** 11290
N Cleft Palate [67]
↓ Drug Induced Congenital Disorders [73]
Hermaphroditism [73]
Microcephaly [73]
Prader Willi Syndrome [91]
Spina Bifida [78]
R Congenitally Disabled [97]
Cystic Fibrosis [85]

Congenital Disorders — (cont'd)
R Deaf Blind [91]
Developmental Disabilities [82]
↓ Genetic Disorders [73]
Hydrocephaly [73]
↓ Mental Disorders [67]
Myotonia [73]
↓ Neonatal Disorders [73]
↓ Physical Disorders [97]
Prenatal Diagnosis [88]
↓ Syphilis [73]
Teratogens [88]

Congenitally Disabled [97]
PN 0 SC 11295
SN Use CONGENITALLY HANDICAPPED to access references from 73-96.
UF Congenitally Handicapped
B Disabled [97]
R Adventitiously Disabled [97]
↓ Brain Damaged [73]
↓ Congenital Disorders [73]

Congenitally Handicapped
SN Term discontinued in 1997. Use CONGENITALLY HANDICAPPED to access references from 73-96.
Use Congenitally Disabled

Congo [91]
PN 3 SC 11305
B Africa [67]

Conjoint Measurement [94]
PN 10 SC 11307
SN Statistical measurement of a variable that is composed of two or more components which affect the variable being measured.
B Statistical Measurement [73]
R ↓ Experimental Design [67]
Psychometrics [67]
↓ Statistical Analysis [67]

Conjoint Therapy [73]
PN 297 SC 11310
SN Type of marriage or family therapy in which partners or family members are seen in joint sessions.
UF Triadic Therapy
B Family Therapy [67]
Marriage Counseling [73]
R Couples Therapy [94]
↓ Group Psychotherapy [67]
↓ Psychotherapeutic Techniques [67]

Connectionism [94]
PN 112 SC 11315
SN Theoretical principles that characterize all learning and behavior as connected to the stimulus-response paradigm and that neural linkages, whether inherited or acquired, bond these behaviors.
R ↓ Associative Processes [67]
↓ Cognitive Processes [67]
Cognitive Psychology [85]
↓ Learning [67]
Learning Theory [67]
Neural Networks [91]

Connective Tissue Cells [73]
PN 9 SC 11320
B Cells (Biology) [73]
R ↓ Connective Tissues [73]

Connective Tissues [73]
PN 14 SC 11330
B Tissues (Body) [73]
N Bones [73]
R Connective Tissue Cells [73]

Connotations [73]
PN 186 SC 11340
B Associative Processes [67]
R Analogy [91]
↓ Figurative Language [85]
Semantic Generalization [73]
Word Meaning [73]

Consanguineous Marriage [73]
PN 29 SC 11350
B Endogamous Marriage [73]

Conscience [67]
PN 94 SC 11360
SN Cognitive and affective processes which govern the individual's standards of behavior, performance and morality.
B Psychoanalytic Personality Factors [73]
Superego [73]

Conscientiousness [97]
PN 0 SC 11365
SN Extent to which an individual is purposeful, well-organized, strong-willed, and determined.
B Personality Traits [67]
R Perfectionism [88]
Persistence [73]
↓ Responsibility [73]
Self Monitoring (Personality) [85]

Conscious (Personality Factor) [73]
PN 190 SC 11370
SN That portion of personal mental functioning which is known to the individual or is observable by introspection. Use CONSCIOUS (PERSONALITY FACTORS) prior to 1988.
B Psychoanalytic Personality Factors [73]

Consciousness Disturbances [73]
PN 112 SC 11380
N Delirium [73]
↓ Hypnosis [67]
Place Disorientation [73]
↓ Sleep Disorders [73]
Sleep Talking [73]
Suggestibility [67]
Time Disorientation [73]
R Coma [73]
↓ Consciousness States [71]
↓ Mental Disorders [67]
↓ Sleep [67]

Consciousness Raising Groups [78]
PN 103 SC 11387
SN Disciplined interaction of a small group of people whose exchange of feelings and experiences results in an increased awareness of social issues such as discriminatory social practices and stereotyped thinking.
B Human Potential Movement [82]
R ↓ Encounter Group Therapy [73]
↓ Group Dynamics [67]
↓ Group Psychotherapy [67]
Sensitivity Training [73]

Consciousness States [71]
PN 1701 SC 11390
SN Conceptually broad term referring to variations in the degree and type of mental awareness. Use a more specific term if possible.
UF Deja Vu
N ↓ Awareness [67]
Wakefulness [73]
R Centering [91]
↓ Consciousness Disturbances [73]
Mind [91]
Physiological Arousal [67]
↓ Sleep [67]

Conservation (Concept) [73]
PN 1139 SC 11400
SN Knowledge of constancy of size, volume, or amount in spite of changed distance or shape; used as measure of cognitive development.
R ↓ Cognitive Development [73]
↓ Concept Formation [67]
Object Permanence [85]
↓ Perceptual Development [73]
Piaget (Jean) [67]

Conservation (Ecological Behavior) [78]
PN 436 SC 11403
B Behavior [67]
R Ecology [73]
Environmental Attitudes [78]
Environmental Education [94]

Conservatism [73]
PN 363 SC 11405
UF Traditionalism
B Personality Traits [67]
R Political Conservatism [73]

Conservatism (Political)
Use Political Conservatism

Conservatorship
Use Guardianship

Consistency (Measurement) [73]
PN 173 SC 11420
B Statistical Analysis [67]
R Error of Measurement [85]
↓ Prediction Errors [73]
Statistical Reliability [73]
↓ Statistical Validity [73]

Consonants [73]
PN 693 SC 11430
B Letters (Alphabet) [73]
Phonemes [73]
R Syllables [73]
Words (Phonetic Units) [67]

Constant Time Delay [97]
PN 0 SC 11435
SN Instruction involving a prompting technique in which dependence on the prompting is faded by a fixed time delay between the presentation of a target stimulus and the delivery of the controlling prompt.
B Prompting [97]
R ↓ Behavior Modification [73]
↓ Learning Strategies [91]
Task Analysis [67]
↓ Teaching Methods [67]

Constipation [73]
PN 44 SC 11440
B Colon Disorders [73]

Construct Validity [82]
PN 2197 SC 11445
SN Extent to which a test can be said to measure a theoretical construct or trait.
UF Concept Validity
R Concurrent Validity [88]
Factor Structure [85]
Factorial Validity [73]
↓ Hypothesis Testing [73]
↓ Measurement [67]
↓ Statistical Correlation [67]
↓ Statistical Validity [73]
Test Validity [73]
↓ Theories [67]

Constructionism
Use Constructivism

Constructivism 94
PN 155 **SC** 11448
SN Theoretical perspective that characterizes perceptual experience and reality as constructed by the mind in the observation of the effects of independent actions on objects.
UF Constructionism
B Theories 67
R ↓ Cognitive Development 73
↓ Learning 67
↓ Perception 67
Phenomenology 67
Piaget (Jean) 67

Consultation (Professional)
Use Professional Consultation

Consultation Liaison Psychiatry 91
PN 218 **SC** 11465
B Professional Consultation 73
Psychiatry 67

Consumer Attitudes 73
PN 2096 **SC** 11470
SN Attitudes of, not toward, consumers.
B Attitudes 67
N Brand Preferences 94
Consumer Satisfaction 94
R ↓ Consumer Research 73
Consumer Surveys 73
Public Relations 73
↓ Quality of Services 97

Consumer Behavior 67
PN 3282 **SC** 11480
UF Buying
B Behavior 67
N Shopping 97
R Brand Names 78
Brand Preferences 94
↓ Consumer Research 73
Consumer Satisfaction 94
Consumer Surveys 73
Retailing 91
Shopping Centers 73

Consumer Fraud
Use Fraud

Consumer Product Design
Use Product Design

Consumer Protection 73
PN 96 **SC** 11490
R Accountability 88
↓ Laws 67
↓ Legal Processes 73
Product Design 97
Warning Labels 97
↓ Warnings 97

Consumer Psychology 73
PN 109 **SC** 11500
SN Subdiscipline in psychology that has as its emphasis the behavioral and psychological aspects of consumer behavior.
B Applied Psychology 73

Consumer Research 73
PN 882 **SC** 11510
SN Marketing and advertising research assessing consumer needs, competition, and methods of sale for a product.
B Experimentation 67
N Consumer Surveys 73

Consumer Research — (cont'd)
R ↓ Advertising 67
Brand Names 78
Brand Preferences 94
↓ Consumer Attitudes 73
↓ Consumer Behavior 67
Consumer Satisfaction 94
Mail Surveys 94
Marketing 73
Product Design 97
Telephone Surveys 94

Consumer Satisfaction 94
PN 59 **SC** 11515
UF Customer Satisfaction
B Consumer Attitudes 73
Satisfaction 73
R ↓ Consumer Behavior 67
↓ Consumer Research 73
Consumer Surveys 73
Quality Control 88
↓ Quality of Services 97

Consumer Surveys 73
PN 194 **SC** 11520
SN Surveys assessing consumer needs, product usage, and effectiveness of marketing and advertising.
B Consumer Research 73
Surveys 67
R ↓ Consumer Attitudes 73
↓ Consumer Behavior 67
Consumer Satisfaction 94
Mail Surveys 94
Product Design 97
Telephone Surveys 94

Contact Lenses 73
PN 32 **SC** 11540
B Optical Aids 73

Contagion 88
PN 59 **SC** 11544
SN Transmission of behavior, attitudes, or emotions to other persons through suggestions, verbal communication, imitation, or gestures. Not used for infectious disorders.
B Social Behavior 67
R ↓ Collective Behavior 67
Mass Hysteria 73

Content Analysis 78
PN 1329 **SC** 11548
SN Systematic, objective, quantitative or qualitative description of the manifest or latent content of communications.
B Analysis 67
Methodology 67
N Discourse Analysis 97
R ↓ Communication 67

Content Analysis (Test) 67
PN 169 **SC** 11550
SN Systematic examination of a test, primarily to determine whether the test items constitute an adequate sample of the domain or subject matter to be tested.
B Analysis 67
Test Construction 73
Testing 67

Contextual Associations 67
PN 3255 **SC** 11560
SN In learning and memory, associations made to environmental or internal conditions during learning or memorization. In perception and communication, environmental conditions that affect such aspects as perceptual accuracy, comprehension, or meaning.

Contextual Associations — (cont'd)
UF Associations (Contextual)
B Associative Processes 67
R Place Conditioning 91
↓ Priming 88
Semantic Priming 94
Word Frequency 73
Word Meaning 73

Contiguity (Cognitive)
Use Cognitive Contiguity

Contingency Management 73
PN 831 **SC** 11580
SN Behavior modification technique in which the stimuli and reinforcers that control a given behavior are manipulated to increase the likelihood of occurrence of the desired behavior.
B Behavior Modification 73
N Token Economy Programs 73
R Noncontingent Reinforcement 88

Contingent Negative Variation 82
PN 192 **SC** 11583
SN Cortical evoked potential of slow negativity recorded in the period between stimulus-presentation and responses and which is associated with states of attention or expectancy.
UF Readiness Potential
B Cortical Evoked Potentials 73

Continuing Education 85
PN 242 **SC** 11590
SN Formal or informal courses, educational programs or services, usually at the postsecondary level, designed to advance or update adult learning for personal, academic, or occupational and professional purposes.
B Adult Education 73
N ↓ Inservice Training 85
R Adult Learning 97
↓ Higher Education 73
Individualized Instruction 73
Professional Development 82
Reentry Students 85

Continuous Reinforcement
Use Reinforcement Schedules

Contour
Use Form and Shape Perception

Contour Perception
Use Form and Shape Perception

Contraception
Use Birth Control

Contraceptive Devices 73
PN 148 **SC** 11630
B Birth Control 71
N Condoms 91
Diaphragms (Birth Control) 73
Intrauterine Devices 73
Oral Contraceptives 73

Contribution (Professional)
Use Professional Criticism

Control (Emotional)
Use Emotional Control

Control (Locus of)
Use Internal External Locus of Control

Control (Self)
Use Self Control

Control (Social)
Use Social Control

Control Groups
Use Experiment Controls

Controls (Instrument)
Use Instrument Controls

Convergent Thinking
Use Inductive Deductive Reasoning

Conversation 73
PN 1900 **SC** 11710
B Interpersonal Communication 73
Verbal Communication 67
R Listening (Interpersonal) 97

Conversion Hysteria
Use Conversion Neurosis

Conversion Neurosis 73
PN 345 **SC** 11730
UF Conversion Hysteria
Hysterical Neurosis (Conversion)
B Psychosomatic Disorders 67
N Hysterical Anesthesia 73
Hysterical Paralysis 73
Hysterical Vision Disturbances 73
Pseudocyesis 73
R ↓ Defense Mechanisms 67
Hypochondriasis 73
↓ Hysteria 67
Hysterical Personality 73
Somatization 94
Somatoform Pain Disorder 97

Conviction (Criminal)
Use Criminal Conviction

Convulsions 67
PN 1807 **SC** 11750
UF Seizures
B Nervous System Disorders 67
Symptoms 67
N Audiogenic Seizures 78
R ↓ Anticonvulsive Drugs 73
↓ Brain Disorders 67
↓ Epileptic Seizures 73
Experimental Epilepsy 78
Hydrocephaly 73
↓ Spasms 73

Cooperating Teachers 78
PN 100 **SC** 11756
SN Experienced elementary or secondary teachers employed to supervise student teachers or teacher interns in schools which, although not integral parts of teacher education institutions, provide experiences for the student teachers and teacher interns.
UF Supervising Teachers
B Teachers 67
R Practicum Supervision 78
Student Teachers 73
Student Teaching 73
↓ Teacher Education 67

Cooperation 67
PN 2858 **SC** 11760
SN Used for human or animal populations.
UF Collaboration
B Interpersonal Interaction 67
Prosocial Behavior 82
R Agreeableness 97
Cooperative Learning 94

Cooperative Education 82
PN 83 **SC** 11765
SN Combined complementary work and study experience or program coordinated by a teacher and designed by the school and the employer to achieve some occupational goal. Not to be confused with work study programs which serve as means for financial assistance.
B Vocational Education 73
R Curricular Field Experience 82
↓ Educational Programs 73
↓ Experiential Learning 97

Cooperative Learning 94
PN 159 **SC** 11766
SN Learning in small groups where cooperation among group members determines rewards and performance.
B Learning 67
R Cooperation 67
Group Instruction 73
Individualized Instruction 73
Peer Tutoring 73
School Learning 67
↓ Teaching 67
↓ Teaching Methods 67
Teams 88

Cooperative Therapy
Use Cotherapy

Coordination (Motor)
Use Motor Coordination

Coordination (Perceptual Motor)
Use Perceptual Motor Coordination

Coping Behavior 67
PN 9498 **SC** 11790
SN Use of conscious or unconscious strategies or mechanisms in adapting to stress, various disorders, or environmental demands.
B Behavior 67
R Adaptability (Personality) 73
Adjustment Disorders 94
Anosognosia 94
↓ Emotional Adjustment 73
↓ Emotional Control 73
Hardiness 97
↓ Helplessness 97
Illness Behavior 82

Copper 73
PN 68 **SC** 11800
B Metallic Elements 73

Copulation
Use Sexual Intercourse (Human)

Copulation (Animal)
Use Animal Mating Behavior

Cornea 73
PN 39 **SC** 11830
B Eye (Anatomy) 67

Coronary Disorders
Use Cardiovascular Disorders

Coronary Heart Disease
Use Heart Disorders

Coronary Prone Behavior 82
PN 1782 **SC** 11855

Coronary Prone Behavior — (cont'd)
SN Constellation of behaviors or attitudes constituting a risk factor for coronary heart disease. Traits can include ambition, competitiveness, sense of time urgency, devotion to work over relaxation, positive attitude toward pressure, aggressiveness, impatience, need for recognition, and tendency toward hostility.
UF Type A Personality
Type B Personality
B Behavior 67
R At Risk Populations 85
↓ Cardiovascular Disorders 67
Illness Behavior 82
↓ Personality 67
↓ Personality Traits 67
Predisposition 73
Stress Reactions 73
Susceptibility (Disorders) 73

Coronary Thromboses 73
PN 5 **SC** 11860
B Heart Disorders 73
Thromboses 73
R Myocardial Infarctions 73

Coronary Vessels
Use Arteries (Anatomy)

Corporal Punishment
Use Punishment

Corporations
Use Business Organizations

Corpus Callosum 73
PN 479 **SC** 11900
B Cerebral Cortex 67
Neural Pathways 82
R Commissurotomy 85
Interhemispheric Interaction 85
Left Brain 91
Right Brain 91

Corpus Striatum
Use Basal Ganglia

Correctional Institutions 73
PN 822 **SC** 11910
UF Institutions (Correctional)
N Prisons 67
Reformatories 73
R Halfway Houses 73
Incarceration 73
Institution Visitation 73
Institutional Schools 78
Maximum Security Facilities 85
Penology 73

Corrective Lenses
Use Optical Aids

Correlation (Statistical)
Use Statistical Correlation

Cortex (Auditory)
Use Auditory Cortex

Cortex (Cerebral)
Use Cerebral Cortex

Cortex (Motor)
Use Motor Cortex

Cortex (Somatosensory)
Use Somatosensory Cortex

Cortex (Visual)
Use Visual Cortex

Cortical Atrophy
Use Cerebral Atrophy

Cortical Evoked Potentials 73
PN 1322 **SC** 11980
B Electrical Activity 67
Evoked Potentials 67
N Contingent Negative Variation 82
R Auditory Evoked Potentials 73
Olfactory Evoked Potentials 73
Somatosensory Evoked Potentials 73
Visual Evoked Potentials 73

Corticoids
Use Corticosteroids

Corticosteroids 73
PN 371 **SC** 12000
UF Adrenal Cortex Steroids
Corticoids
B Steroids 73
N Aldosterone 73
Corticosterone 73
Cortisone 73
Deoxycorticosterone 73
Hydrocortisone 73
Prednisolone 73
R ↓ Adrenal Cortex Hormones 73

Corticosterone 73
PN 834 **SC** 12010
B Adrenal Cortex Hormones 73
Corticosteroids 73

Corticotropin 73
PN 1085 **SC** 12020
UF ACTH (Hormone)
Adrenocorticotropin
B Pituitary Hormones 73
R Corticotropin Releasing Factor 94

Corticotropin Releasing Factor 94
PN 87 **SC** 12025
UF ACTH Releasing Factor
B Hormones 67
Peptides 73
R Corticotropin 73

Cortisol
Use Hydrocortisone

Cortisone 73
PN 29 **SC** 12040
B Adrenal Cortex Hormones 73
Corticosteroids 73

Cost Containment 91
PN 46 **SC** 12041
SN Policies or procedures to restrain or control expenses in any setting.
R Budgets 97
↓ Case Management 91
↓ Costs and Cost Analysis 73
Diagnosis Related Groups 88
Economics 85
Fee for Service 94
Health Care Costs 94
↓ Health Care Services 78
Health Maintenance Organizations 82
↓ Managed Care 94
Money 67
↓ Professional Fees 78
Resource Allocation 97
↓ Treatment 67

Cost Effectiveness
Use Costs and Cost Analysis

Costa Rica 88
PN 25 **SC** 12043
B Central America 73

Costs and Cost Analysis 73
PN 2581 **SC** 12045
SN Applied to any subject and includes prices, expenses, or payments; also attachment of dollar estimates to the costs of an operation and its alternatives.
UF Cost Effectiveness
Price
B Analysis 67
N Budgets 97
Health Care Costs 94
R Cost Containment 91
Economics 85
Economy 73
Funding 88
Money 67
↓ Professional Fees 78
Resource Allocation 97
Risk Management 97

Cotherapy 82
PN 143 **SC** 12047
SN Psychotherapeutic process in which a client or a group of clients are treated by more than one therapist. Use CONJOINT THERAPY to access references from 73-81.
UF Cooperative Therapy
Multiple Therapy
B Psychotherapeutic Techniques 67
R Psychiatric Training 73
↓ Psychotherapy 67
Psychotherapy Training 73

Counselees
Use Clients

Counseling 67
PN 6095 **SC** 12080
SN Conceptually broad array term referring to a form of helping process which involves giving advice and information, in order to assist individuals or groups in coping with their problems. Use a more specific term if possible.
N Educational Counseling 67
Genetic Counseling 78
Group Counseling 73
↓ Marriage Counseling 73
Microcounseling 78
Occupational Guidance 67
Pastoral Counseling 67
Peer Counseling 78
Premarital Counseling 73
↓ Psychotherapeutic Counseling 73
Rehabilitation Counseling 78
School Counseling 82
R Counseling Psychology 73
↓ Counselors 67
Employee Assistance Programs 85
↓ Family Therapy 67
Feminist Therapy 94
↓ Health Care Services 78
↓ Mental Health Services 78
Social Casework 67
Student Personnel Services 78
↓ Support Groups 91
↓ Treatment 67

Counseling (Group)
Use Group Counseling

Counseling Psychologists 88
PN 116 **SC** 12065

Counseling Psychologists — (cont'd)
B Psychologists 67
R Clinicians 73
Counseling Psychology 73

Counseling Psychology 73
PN 686 **SC** 12070
B Applied Psychology 73
R ↓ Counseling 67
Counseling Psychologists 88

Counselor Attitudes 73
PN 899 **SC** 12090
SN Attitudes of, not toward, counselors.
B Attitudes 67
Counselor Characteristics 73
R Counselor Role 73
↓ Counselors 67
↓ Health Personnel Attitudes 85
Psychologist Attitudes 91

Counselor Characteristics 73
PN 2341 **SC** 12100
UF Counselor Effectiveness
Counselor Personality
N Counselor Attitudes 73
R ↓ Counselors 67

Counselor Client Interaction
Use Psychotherapeutic Processes

Counselor Education 73
PN 2791 **SC** 12120
B Education 67
R ↓ Clinical Methods Training 73
Counselor Trainees 73
Microcounseling 78
Practicum Supervision 78
↓ Psychology Education 78
Psychotherapy Training 73
Rehabilitation Education 97

Counselor Effectiveness
Use Counselor Characteristics

Counselor Personality
Use Counselor Characteristics

Counselor Role 73
PN 859 **SC** 12150
UF Role (Counselor)
B Roles 67
R Counselor Attitudes 73
↓ Counselors 67
Therapist Role 78

Counselor Trainees 73
PN 1461 **SC** 12160
R Counselor Education 73
↓ Counselors 67
Therapist Trainees 73

Counselors 67
PN 2379 **SC** 12170
B Professional Personnel 78
N Rehabilitation Counselors 78
School Counselors 73
Vocational Counselors 73
R ↓ Counseling 67
Counselor Attitudes 73
↓ Counselor Characteristics 73
Counselor Role 73
Counselor Trainees 73
↓ Health Personnel 94
↓ Mental Health Personnel 67
↓ Psychologists 67
↓ Social Workers 73

Counselors — (cont'd)
R Sociologists [73]
↓ Therapists [67]

Counterconditioning [73]
PN 76 **SC** 12180
SN Technique used to extinguish a response to a certain stimulus by conditioning an alternative, often incompatible response to that stimulus.
B Conditioning [67]
R ↓ Aversion Therapy [73]
↓ Behavior Modification [73]
↓ Behavior Therapy [67]
Reciprocal Inhibition Therapy [73]

Countertransference [73]
PN 1520 **SC** 12190
SN Conscious or unconscious emotional reaction of the therapist to the patient which may interfere with the treatment.
B Psychotherapeutic Processes [67]
R Enactments [97]
Negative Therapeutic Reaction [97]
Professional Client Sexual Relations [94]
Psychotherapeutic Transference [67]

Countries [67]
PN 1931 **SC** 12195
SN Applies to cross-national studies when individual countries are not mentioned or are too numerous to list.
N Developed Countries [85]
Developing Countries [85]
R Geography [73]

County Agricultural Agents
Use Agricultural Extension Workers

Couples [82]
PN 1499 **SC** 12205
SN Two individuals in an intimate relationship.
R Cohabitation [73]
Dyads [73]
↓ Family [67]
Romance [97]
Significant Others [91]
Social Dating [73]
↓ Spouses [73]

Couples Therapy [94]
PN 63 **SC** 12207
SN Used specifically for unmarried couples. Use MARRIAGE COUNSELING for married couples.
R Conjoint Therapy [73]
↓ Marriage Counseling [73]
↓ Psychotherapy [67]
Sex Therapy [78]

Courage [73]
PN 43 **SC** 12210
UF Bravery
B Personality Traits [67]

Course Evaluation [78]
PN 366 **SC** 12215
SN Procedures, materials, or the process involved in the assessment of quality or effectiveness of an academic or vocational course or program by its students or participants. Evaluation may include content, structure, or method of material presentation.
B Evaluation [67]
R ↓ Curriculum [67]
Educational Program Evaluation [73]
Educational Quality [97]
Teacher Effectiveness Evaluation [78]
↓ Teaching [67]

Course Objectives
Use Educational Objectives

Course of Illness
Use Disease Course

Court Ordered Treatment
Use Court Referrals

Court Referrals [94]
PN 39 **SC** 12219
SN Court ordered assessment, treatment, consultation, or other services for defendants, plaintiffs, or criminals.
UF Court Ordered Treatment
B Adjudication [67]
R ↓ Commitment (Psychiatric) [73]
↓ Criminal Justice [91]
↓ Criminals [67]
Defendants [85]
Forensic Evaluation [94]
Insanity Defense [85]
Involuntary Treatment [94]
Mediation [88]
Mentally Ill Offenders [85]
Probation [73]
Professional Referral [73]
↓ Treatment [67]

Courts
Use Adjudication

Courtship (Animal)
Use Animal Courtship Behavior

Courtship (Human)
Use Human Courtship

Courtship Displays (Animal)
Use Animal Courtship Displays

Cousins [73]
PN 13 **SC** 12260
B Family Members [73]

Covert Sensitization [88]
PN 19 **SC** 12265
SN Form of aversion conditioning in which noxious mental images, thoughts, or feelings are associated with undesirable behavior by verbal cues. Frequently used in therapeutic settings.
B Aversion Conditioning [82]
Aversion Therapy [73]
R Aversive Stimulation [73]

Cows
Use Cattle

Coyotes
Use Canids

Crabs [73]
PN 224 **SC** 12300
B Crustacea [73]

Crafts [73]
PN 31 **SC** 12310
UF Handicrafts
B Art [67]

Cramps (Muscle)
Use Muscular Disorders

Cranial Nerves [73]
PN 100 **SC** 12330

Cranial Nerves — (cont'd)
UF Accessory Nerve
Glossopharyngeal Nerve
Hypoglossal Nerve
Nerve (Accessory)
Nerves (Cranial)
Oculomotor Nerve
Trochlear Nerve
B Peripheral Nervous System [73]
N Abducens Nerve [73]
Acoustic Nerve [73]
Facial Nerve [73]
Olfactory Nerve [73]
Optic Nerve [73]
Trigeminal Nerve [73]
Vagus Nerve [73]

Cranial Spinal Cord [73]
PN 3 **SC** 12340
B Spinal Cord [73]

Craving [97]
PN 0 **SC** 12350
R ↓ Addiction [73]
↓ Appetite [73]
↓ Drug Abuse [73]
↓ Drug Usage [71]
↓ Eating [67]
↓ Emotional States [73]
Food [78]
↓ Needs [67]

Crayfish [73]
PN 86 **SC** 12360
B Crustacea [73]

Creative Arts Therapy [94]
PN 35 **SC** 12365
SN Therapeutic use of the arts in medicine, mental health, or education.
B Treatment [67]
N Art Therapy [73]
Dance Therapy [73]
Music Therapy [73]
Poetry Therapy [94]
Recreation Therapy [73]
R Movement Therapy [97]
↓ Psychotherapeutic Techniques [67]

Creative Writing [94]
PN 35 **SC** 12370
SN Use LITERATURE to access references from 73-93.
UF Writing (Creative)
B Written Communication [85]
R ↓ Literature [67]
Narratives [97]
Poetry [73]
↓ Prose [73]
Rhetoric [91]
Storytelling [88]

Creativity [67]
PN 6131 **SC** 12380
SN Ability to perceive new relationships, and to derive new ideas and solve problems by pursuing nontraditional patterns of thinking. Compare DIVERGENT THINKING.
UF Innovativeness
Originality
B Personality Traits [67]
R ↓ Ability [67]
↓ Artistic Ability [73]
Divergent Thinking [73]
Gifted [67]
Intelligence [67]
Openness to Experience [97]

Creativity Measurement [73]
PN 359 SC 12390
B Measurement [67]

Credibility [73]
PN 639 SC 12400
R ↓ Interpersonal Communication [73]
Reputation [97]
↓ Social Perception [67]

Creutzfeldt Jakob Syndrome [94]
PN 11 SC 12410
B Encephalopathies [82]
Presenile Dementia [73]
Syndromes [73]
Viral Disorders [73]

Cri du Chat Syndrome
Use Crying Cat Syndrome

Crib Death
Use Sudden Infant Death

Crime [67]
PN 3555 SC 12430
UF Felonies
Misdemeanors
B Antisocial Behavior [71]
Social Issues [91]
N Arson [85]
↓ Child Abuse [71]
Driving Under The Influence [88]
Drug Distribution [97]
Kidnapping [88]
↓ Sex Offenses [82]
↓ Theft [73]
Vandalism [78]
R ↓ Behavior Disorders [71]
↓ Behavior Problems [67]
Crime Prevention [85]
↓ Crime Victims [82]
↓ Criminal Justice [91]
Criminal Responsibility [91]
↓ Criminals [67]
Fraud [94]
Informants [88]
↓ Perpetrators [88]
Self Defense [85]
Terrorism [82]
Victimization [73]

Crime Prevention [85]
PN 254 SC 12432
SN Measures aimed at deterring the occurrence of crime or delinquent behavior.
B Prevention [73]
R ↓ Crime [67]
↓ Criminal Justice [91]
Juvenile Delinquency [67]
↓ Law Enforcement [78]

Crime Victims [82]
PN 842 SC 12434
SN Individuals subjected to and adversely affected by criminal activity. Use VICTIMIZATION to access references from 73-81.
N Hostages [88]
R ↓ Crime [67]
Self Defense [85]
Victimization [73]

Criminal Conviction [73]
PN 306 SC 12440
SN Declaration made by a court finding a person guilty and responsible for a criminal offense.
UF Conviction (Criminal)
B Criminal Justice [91]
R ↓ Adjudication [67]

Criminal Conviction — (cont'd)
R ↓ Criminals [67]
Legal Decisions [91]

Criminal Interrogation
Use Legal Interrogation

Criminal Justice [91]
PN 189 SC 12445
SN Used for the system, discipline, or the actual process itself.
B Justice [73]
Legal Processes [73]
N Criminal Conviction [73]
R ↓ Adjudication [67]
Court Referrals [94]
↓ Crime [67]
Crime Prevention [85]
Criminal Law [73]
Forensic Psychiatry [73]
Forensic Psychology [85]
↓ Law Enforcement [78]
Legal Decisions [91]
Penology [73]

Criminal Law [73]
PN 240 SC 12450
B Law (Government) [73]
R ↓ Criminal Justice [91]

Criminal Responsibility [91]
PN 112 SC 12453
SN State of mind that permits one to be held accountable for criminal acts.
B Responsibility [73]
R Accountability [88]
↓ Adjudication [67]
Competency to Stand Trial [85]
↓ Crime [67]
↓ Criminals [67]
Defendants [85]
Insanity Defense [85]
↓ Perpetrators [88]

Criminally Insane
Use Mentally Ill Offenders

Criminals [67]
PN 2787 SC 12460
UF Offenders (Adult)
B Perpetrators [88]
N Female Criminals [73]
Male Criminals [73]
Mentally Ill Offenders [85]
R Antisocial Personality [73]
Court Referrals [94]
↓ Crime [67]
Criminal Conviction [73]
Criminal Responsibility [91]
Defendants [85]
Forensic Evaluation [94]
↓ Juvenile Delinquents [73]
↓ Prisoners [67]
Recidivism [73]

Criminology [73]
PN 217 SC 12470
R Penology [73]

Crises [71]
PN 683 SC 12490
N Family Crises [73]
Identity Crisis [73]
Organizational Crises [73]
R ↓ Crisis Intervention [73]
↓ Crisis Intervention Services [73]
↓ Disasters [73]

Crises — (cont'd)
R ↓ Experiences (Events) [73]
↓ Stress [67]

Crisis (Reactions to)
Use Stress Reactions

Crisis Intervention [73]
PN 923 SC 12510
SN Brief therapeutic approach which is ameliorative rather than curative of acute psychiatric emergencies. Used in such contexts as emergency rooms of psychiatric or general hospitals, or in the home or place of crisis occurrence, this treatment approach focuses on interpersonal and intrapsychic factors and environmental modification of behavior.
B Treatment [67]
N Suicide Prevention [73]
R ↓ Crises [71]
↓ Crisis Intervention Services [73]

Crisis Intervention Services [73]
PN 411 SC 12520
SN Community organizations, programs, or mental health personnel which provide crisis care.
B Community Services [67]
Mental Health Programs [73]
Treatment [67]
N Hot Line Services [73]
Suicide Prevention Centers [73]
R ↓ Clinics [67]
Community Mental Health Centers [73]
↓ Crises [71]
↓ Crisis Intervention [73]
Emergency Services [73]
↓ Treatment Facilities [73]
Walk In Clinics [73]

Criterion Referenced Tests [82]
PN 234 SC 12525
SN Tests in which scores are measured against explicitly stated objectives rather than a group norm.
UF Mastery Tests
Objective Referenced Tests
B Measurement [67]
R ↓ Achievement Measures [67]
Performance Tests [73]

Critical Flicker Fusion Threshold [67]
PN 350 SC 12530
UF Flicker Fusion Frequency
B Visual Thresholds [73]
R ↓ Perceptual Measures [73]

Critical Period [88]
PN 29 SC 12533
R ↓ Development [67]
Imprinting [67]

Critical Scores
Use Cutting Scores

Criticism [73]
PN 207 SC 12540
B Social Behavior [67]
Social Influences [67]
R Social Approval [67]

Criticism (Professional)
Use Professional Criticism

Crocodilians [73]
PN 21 SC 12570
UF Alligators
B Reptiles [67]

Cross Cultural Communication [97]
PN 0 **SC** 12580
UF Intercultural Communication
Interethnic Communication
B Interpersonal Communication [73]
R Bilingualism [73]
Cross Cultural Differences [67]
Cross Cultural Psychology [97]
Cross Cultural Treatment [94]
Cultural Assimilation [73]
Cultural Sensitivity [94]
Multicultural Education [88]
Multiculturalism [97]
Racial and Ethnic Differences [82]
Racial and Ethnic Relations [82]

Cross Cultural Differences [67]
PN 9424 **SC** 12590
UF Cultural Differences
B Sociocultural Factors [67]
R Cross Cultural Communication [97]
Cross Cultural Psychology [97]
Cross Cultural Treatment [94]
Cultural Sensitivity [94]
Ethnology [67]
Multiculturalism [97]
Racial and Ethnic Differences [82]

Cross Cultural Psychology [97]
PN 0 **SC** 12591
SN Branch of psychology that studies members of various cultural groups and their specific cultural experiences resulting in similarities and differences in human behavior.
B Psychology [67]
R Cross Cultural Communication [97]
Cross Cultural Differences [67]
Cultural Assimilation [73]
↓ Culture (Anthropological) [67]
↓ Ethnic Groups [73]
Ethnocentrism [73]
Ethnology [67]
↓ Ethnospecific Disorders [73]
Racial and Ethnic Differences [82]
↓ Sociocultural Factors [67]
Transcultural Psychiatry [73]

Cross Cultural Treatment [94]
PN 96 **SC** 12593
SN Treatment, in any context, where the racial, ethnic, or cultural background of the patient or client is different from that of the health care provider, e.g., therapist, counselor, or physician. Used primarily when the cultural or racial aspects of the treatment paradigm are the major focus.
B Treatment [67]
R ↓ Client Characteristics [73]
Cross Cultural Communication [97]
Cross Cultural Differences [67]
Cultural Sensitivity [94]
Racial and Ethnic Differences [82]
↓ Therapist Characteristics [73]
Transcultural Psychiatry [73]

Cross Disciplinary Research
Use Interdisciplinary Research

Crossed Eyes
Use Strabismus

Crowding [78]
PN 417 **SC** 12610
SN Conditions of high population density for a given area. Used for animal or human populations.
R Environmental Stress [73]
Overpopulation [73]
Personal Space [73]
Social Density [78]

CRT
Use Video Display Units

Cruelty [73]
PN 35 **SC** 12620
B Antisocial Behavior [71]
Personality Traits [67]
R ↓ Aggressive Behavior [67]

Crustacea [73]
PN 248 **SC** 12630
B Arthropoda [73]
N Crabs [73]
Crayfish [73]

Crying [73]
PN 401 **SC** 12640
B Vocalization [67]
Voice [73]
R Infant Vocalization [73]

Crying Cat Syndrome [73]
PN 17 **SC** 12650
UF Cri du Chat Syndrome
B Autosome Disorders [73]
Mental Retardation [67]
Neonatal Disorders [73]
Syndromes [73]

Cuba [73]
PN 151 **SC** 12670
B West Indies [73]

Cuban Americans
Use Hispanics

Cued Recall [94]
PN 61 **SC** 12678
B Recall (Learning) [67]
R Cues [67]
Forgetting [73]
Free Recall [73]
↓ Memory [67]
↓ Prompting [97]

Cues [67]
PN 6344 **SC** 12680
SN Internal or external verbal or nonverbal signals which influence learning, performance, or behavior. Cues are often only obscure secondary stimuli which, though not fully detected, serve to facilitate learning, performance, or behavior. Compare CONDITIONED STIMULUS.
R ↓ Associative Processes [67]
Cued Recall [94]
Isolation Effect [73]
↓ Memory [67]
Mnemonic Learning [73]
↓ Priming [88]
↓ Prompting [97]
Semantic Priming [94]

Cultism [73]
PN 370 **SC** 12690
R Ethnology [67]
Myths [67]
Occultism [78]
↓ Religious Beliefs [73]
Religious Experiences [97]
Shamanism [73]
↓ Sociocultural Factors [67]

Cultural Assimilation [73]
PN 1342 **SC** 12700

Cultural Assimilation — (cont'd)
SN Contact of at least two autonomous cultural groups resulting in change in one or the other, or both groups. Includes the process of a minority group giving up its own cultural traits and absorbing those of a dominant society. Use CULTURAL ASSIMILATION or ACCULTURATION to access references from 73–81.
UF Acculturation
Assimilation (Cultural)
B Culture Change [67]
R Cross Cultural Communication [97]
Cross Cultural Psychology [97]
Cultural Sensitivity [94]
Multiculturalism [97]

Cultural Deprivation [73]
PN 192 **SC** 12710
SN Inability of individuals to participate in their society's cultural achievements because of poverty, social discrimination, or other disadvantage. Consider also SOCIAL DEPRIVATION.
UF Culturally Disadvantaged
B Deprivation [67]
Sociocultural Factors [67]
R Disadvantaged [67]
Multiculturalism [97]
Poverty Areas [73]
↓ Social Deprivation [73]
↓ Social Environments [73]

Cultural Differences
Use Cross Cultural Differences

Cultural Factors
Use Sociocultural Factors

Cultural Familial Mental Retardation
Use Psychosocial Mental Retardation

Cultural Pluralism
Use Multiculturalism

Cultural Psychiatry
Use Transcultural Psychiatry

Cultural Sensitivity [94]
PN 251 **SC** 12728
SN Awareness and appreciation of the values, norms, and beliefs unique to a particular cultural, minority, ethnic, or racial group.
UF Ethnic Sensitivity
R Cross Cultural Communication [97]
Cross Cultural Differences [67]
Cross Cultural Treatment [94]
Cultural Assimilation [73]
↓ Culture (Anthropological) [67]
↓ Ethnic Groups [73]
Ethnic Identity [73]
Ethnic Values [73]
Minority Groups [67]
Multicultural Education [88]
Multiculturalism [97]
↓ Racial and Ethnic Attitudes [82]
Racial and Ethnic Differences [82]
Racial and Ethnic Relations [82]
Sensitivity Training [73]
↓ Sociocultural Factors [67]

Cultural Test Bias [73]
PN 653 **SC** 12730
SN Any significant differential performance on tests by different populations (e.g., Hispanics vs Blacks) as a result of test characteristics that are sensitive to cultural, subcultural, racial, or ethnic factors but which are irrelevant to the variable or construct being measured.
UF Test Bias (Cultural)
B Test Bias [85]

Cultural Test Bias — (cont'd)
R Response Bias [67]
Test Interpretation [85]

Culturally Disadvantaged
Use Cultural Deprivation

Culture (Anthropological) [67]
PN 3511 SC 12750
N ↓ Society [67]
Subculture (Anthropological) [73]
R Cross Cultural Psychology [97]
Cultural Sensitivity [94]
Ethnology [67]
↓ Family Structure [73]
Multiculturalism [97]
↓ Sociocultural Factors [67]

Culture Change [67]
PN 348 SC 12760
SN Modification in behavior, values, customs, or artifacts over time or as the result of migration to a different cultural environment.
B Sociocultural Factors [67]
N Cultural Assimilation [73]
R Culture Shock [73]
Ethnology [67]
Multiculturalism [97]

Culture Fair Intelligence Test [73]
PN 29 SC 12770
UF Cattell Culture Fair Intell Test
B Intelligence Measures [67]

Culture Shock [73]
PN 137 SC 12780
SN Social, psychological, or emotional difficulties in adapting to a new culture or similar difficulties in adapting to one's own culture as the result of rapid social or cultural changes.
R ↓ Culture Change [67]
Ethnology [67]

Curare [73]
PN 26 SC 12790
B Muscle Relaxing Drugs [73]
R ↓ Alkaloids [73]
Tubocurarine [73]

Curiosity [67]
PN 261 SC 12800
UF Inquisitiveness
B Personality Traits [67]
R ↓ Exploratory Behavior [67]
Openness to Experience [97]
Questioning [82]

Curricular Field Experience [82]
PN 248 SC 12805
SN Organizationally or institutionally supervised educational activities, restricted primarily to high school and college, usually undertaken outside the classroom or campus in order to promote practical experience in a specific discipline.
UF Field Instruction
Field Work (Educational)
B Experiential Learning [97]
R Cooperative Education [82]
↓ Curriculum [67]
Educational Field Trips [73]
↓ Educational Programs [73]
↓ Practice [67]

Curriculum [67]
PN 5371 SC 12810
SN Set of courses constituting a framework for education in a given subject area.

Curriculum — (cont'd)
B Education [67]
N Affective Education [82]
Art Education [73]
Braille Instruction [73]
Business Education [73]
Career Education [78]
Compensatory Education [73]
Computer Training [94]
Driver Education [73]
Foreign Language Education [73]
↓ Health Education [73]
Home Economics [85]
↓ Language Arts Education [73]
Mathematics Education [73]
Music Education [73]
Physical Education [67]
↓ Psychology Education [78]
Science Education [73]
Social Studies Education [78]
↓ Vocational Education [73]
R Course Evaluation [78]
Curricular Field Experience [82]
Curriculum Based Assessment [94]
Curriculum Development [73]
Educational Objectives [78]
Educational Program Accreditation [94]
Home Schooling [94]
↓ Nontraditional Education [82]

Curriculum Based Assessment [94]
PN 31 SC 12815
B Educational Measurement [67]
R ↓ Curriculum [67]

Curriculum Development [73]
PN 1763 SC 12820
SN Initiating, designing, implementing, and testing of activities designed to create new curricula or to change existing ones.
B Development [67]
R ↓ Curriculum [67]
Educational Program Planning [73]
↓ Program Development [91]

Cursive Writing [73]
PN 45 SC 12830
UF Writing (Cursive)
B Handwriting [67]
R Orthography [73]

Cushings Syndrome [73]
PN 60 SC 12840
B Adrenal Gland Disorders [73]
Metabolism Disorders [73]
Syndromes [73]

Customer Satisfaction
Use Consumer Satisfaction

Cutaneous Receptive Fields [85]
PN 33 SC 12845
SN The area of skin being supplied by specific peripheral nerves and localized synaptic distribution in the CNS.
UF Dermatomes
B Receptive Fields [85]

Cutaneous Sense [67]
PN 1169 SC 12850
SN Any of the senses, such as pressure, pain, warmth, cold, and touch, whose receptors lie within or beneath the skin or in the mucous membrane.
UF Haptic Perception
B Somesthetic Perception [67]
N ↓ Tactual Perception [67]

Cutting Scores [85]
PN 67 SC 12855
SN Points at which a continuum of scores may be divided into groups for such purposes as pass/fail decisions or test interpretations.
UF Critical Scores
B Scoring (Testing) [73]
Test Scores [67]
R Score Equating [85]
Test Interpretation [85]

Cybernetics [67]
PN 356 SC 12860
SN Study of control and communication between humans, machines, animals, and organizations and the parallels between information processing machines and human or animal intellectual or brain function.
R ↓ Artificial Intelligence [82]
Communication Theory [73]
↓ Computers [67]
↓ Expert Systems [91]
Human Machine Systems [97]
Robotics [85]

Cyclic Adenosine Monophosphate [78]
PN 178 SC 12875
B Nucleotides [78]
R Guanosine [85]

Cycloheximide [73]
PN 147 SC 12880
B Antibiotics [73]

Cyclothymic Disorder
Use Cyclothymic Personality

Cyclothymic Personality [73]
PN 89 SC 12890
SN Affective disorder characterized by alternating and recurring periods of depression and elation, similar to manic depressive disorder but of a less severe nature.
UF Cyclothymic Disorder
B Manic Depression [73]
R Hypomania [73]

Cynicism [73]
PN 74 SC 12900
B Personality Traits [67]
R Agreeableness [97]
Fatalism [73]
Hopelessness [88]
Negativism [73]
Pessimism [73]

Cyprus [91]
PN 6 SC 12905
R Middle East [78]

Cysteine [73]
PN 9 SC 12910
B Amino Acids [73]

Cystic Fibrosis [85]
PN 180 SC 12915
B Digestive System Disorders [73]
Lung Disorders [73]
Metabolism Disorders [73]
R ↓ Congenital Disorders [73]

Cytochrome Oxidase [73]
PN 27 SC 12920
B Oxidases [73]

Cytology [73]
PN 68 SC 12930
R ↓ Cells (Biology) [73]

Cytoplasm [73]
PN 14 SC 12940
R ↓ Cells (Biology) [73]

Czechoslovakia [73]
PN 384 SC 12950
B Europe [73]

Daily Activities [94]
PN 102 SC 12955
SN Daily patterns of behavior that are not reflective of functional ability. Compare ACTIVITIES OF DAILY LIVING.
R Activities of Daily Living [91]
Activity Level [82]
↓ Disabled [97]
Hobbies [73]
↓ Interests [67]
Leisure Time [73]
↓ Lifestyle [78]
↓ Recreation [67]
Self Care Skills [78]

Daily Biological Rhythms (Animal)
Use Animal Circadian Rhythms

Dance [73]
PN 214 SC 12970
UF Ballet
B Arts [73]
Recreation [67]
R Dance Therapy [73]

Dance Therapy [73]
PN 193 SC 12980
B Creative Arts Therapy [94]
R Dance [73]
Movement Therapy [97]
Recreation Therapy [73]

Dangerousness [88]
PN 340 SC 12985
R Patient Violence [94]
↓ Violence [73]

Dark Adaptation [73]
PN 351 SC 12990
UF Adaptation (Dark)
B Sensory Adaptation [67]
Visual Perception [67]
R Light Adaptation [82]
↓ Perceptual Measures [73]
↓ Visual Thresholds [73]

Darwinism [73]
PN 143 SC 13000
SN Biological theory of evolution formulated by C. Darwin, including the fundamental tenet of natural selection as the operating principle of organic change.
B Theories [67]
N Natural Selection [97]
R Theory of Evolution [67]

Data Collection [82]
PN 819 SC 13005
SN Systematic accumulation, generation, or assembly of information. Compare EXPERIMENTAL METHODS.
B Methodology [67]
R ↓ Data Processing [67]
Information [67]
↓ Medical Records [78]
↓ Sampling (Experimental) [73]
Statistical Data [82]
↓ Statistical Measurement [73]
↓ Surveys [67]

Data Pooling
Use Meta Analysis

Data Processing [67]
PN 231 SC 13020
N Word Processing [91]
R ↓ Automated Information Processing [73]
Computer Programing [94]
↓ Computer Programing Languages [73]
↓ Computer Software [67]
↓ Computers [67]
Data Collection [82]
↓ Expert Systems [91]
Information [67]
Information Systems [91]
↓ Medical Records [78]

Databases [91]
PN 159 SC 13024
SN Collection of computerized data stored in a computer or on magnetic tape or disks from which information can be accessed and retrieved.
UF Computerized Databases
Online Databases
R ↓ Automated Information Retrieval [73]
Automated Information Storage [73]
↓ Computer Applications [73]
Computer Searching [91]
↓ Computer Software [67]
↓ Computers [67]
Decision Support Systems [97]
↓ Expert Systems [91]
Human Machine Systems [97]
Information [67]
Information Exchange [73]
Information Services [88]
Information Systems [91]

Date Rape
Use Acquaintance Rape

Dating (Social)
Use Social Dating

Daughters [73]
PN 992 SC 13040
B Family Members [73]
Human Females [73]
Offspring [88]

Day Camps (Recreation)
Use Summer Camps (Recreation)

Day Care (Child)
Use Child Day Care

Day Care (Treatment)
Use Partial Hospitalization

Day Care Centers [73]
PN 459 SC 13070
SN Facilities for day care of individuals of any age.
R Adult Day Care [97]
Child Care Workers [78]
Child Day Care [73]
↓ Community Facilities [73]
Community Mental Health Centers [73]

Day Hospital
Use Partial Hospitalization

Daydreaming [73]
PN 224 SC 13080
R ↓ Fantasy [97]
Fantasy (Defense Mechanism) [67]

DDT (Insecticide) [73]
PN 4 SC 13090
B Insecticides [73]

Deaf [67]
PN 3895 SC 13100
SN Profoundly or severely hearing impaired. Consider also PARTIALLY HEARING IMPAIRED for severely hearing impaired.
B Aurally Disabled [97]
N Deaf Blind [91]
R Cochlear Implants [94]
Hearing Disorders [82]
Lipreading [73]
Partially Hearing Impaired [73]

Deaf Blind [91]
PN 53 SC 13103
B Blind [67]
Deaf [67]
Multiply Disabled [97]
R ↓ Congenital Disorders [73]
Developmental Disabilities [82]

Deanol
SN Term discontinued in 1997. Use DEANOL to access references from 82–96.
Use Antidepressant Drugs

Death and Dying [67]
PN 4235 SC 13110
UF Dying
Mortality
N Euthanasia [73]
R Advance Directives [94]
Assisted Suicide [97]
Death Anxiety [78]
Death Attitudes [73]
Death Education [82]
Death Rites [73]
Grief [73]
Mortality Rate [73]
Near Death Experiences [85]
Palliative Care [91]
Psychological Autopsy [88]
Sudden Infant Death [82]
↓ Suicide [67]
Terminal Cancer [73]
Terminally Ill Patients [73]
Treatment Withholding [88]

Death Anxiety [78]
PN 682 SC 13115
B Anxiety Disorders [97]
R ↓ Death and Dying [67]
Death Attitudes [73]

Death Attitudes [73]
PN 1277 SC 13120
B Attitudes [67]
R ↓ Death and Dying [67]
Death Anxiety [78]
Euthanasia [73]
↓ Religious Beliefs [73]

Death Education [82]
PN 218 SC 13124
SN Education in the process of death and dying. Applies to patients or students of any age including helping professionals.
UF Thanatology
B Education [67]
R ↓ Death and Dying [67]
↓ Treatment [67]

Death Instinct [88]
PN 116 SC 13127

Death Instinct — (cont'd)
UF Thanatos
B Psychoanalytic Personality Factors [73]
R Self Preservation [97]
Unconscious (Personality Factor) [67]

Death Penalty
Use Capital Punishment

Death Rate
Use Mortality Rate

Death Rites [73]
PN 91 SC 13150
UF Funerals
B Rites of Passage [73]
R ↓ Death and Dying [67]

Debates [97]
PN 0 SC 13153
UF Political Debates
Presidential Debates
R Arguments [73]
Group Discussion [67]
↓ Persuasive Communication [67]
Political Campaigns [73]
Political Candidates [73]
Political Elections [73]
↓ Political Processes [73]
Public Speaking [73]
Rhetoric [91]

Debriefing (Experimental) [91]
PN 11 SC 13154
SN At the conclusion of an experiment, the process that removes any deception and discloses the facts to subjects participating in the research by giving full details of the research purpose and procedures.
UF Disclosure (Experimental)
R ↓ Experimental Design [67]
Experimental Ethics [78]
↓ Experimental Subjects [85]
↓ Experimentation [67]
Informed Consent [85]

Decarboxylase Inhibitors [82]
PN 44 SC 13157
B Enzyme Inhibitors [85]
N Carbidopa [88]
R ↓ Antitremor Drugs [73]
↓ Catecholamines [73]
↓ Dopamine Antagonists [82]
↓ Enzymes [73]
↓ Serotonin Antagonists [73]

Decarboxylases [73]
PN 65 SC 13160
B Enzymes [73]

Decentralization [78]
PN 40 SC 13166
SN Process of distributing or allocating administrative control over organizational functions to authorities that are more local.
R Educational Administration [67]
Hospital Administration [78]
↓ Organizational Change [73]
Organizational Development [73]
Organizational Objectives [73]
Organizational Structure [67]

Deception [67]
PN 1272 SC 13170
UF Lying
N Cheating [73]
Faking [73]
Fraud [94]

Deception — (cont'd)
N Malingering [73]
R Confabulation [73]
Dishonesty [73]
Secrecy [94]
Sincerity [73]

Decerebration [73]
PN 107 SC 13180
SN Elimination of cerebral functioning by transecting the brain stem or by cutting off the cerebral blood supply.
B Neurosurgery [73]
R ↓ Brain Lesions [67]

Decision Making [67]
PN 8185 SC 13190
SN Cognitive process involving evaluation of the incentives, goals, and outcomes of alternative actions.
B Cognitive Processes [67]
N Choice Behavior [67]
↓ Group Decision Making [78]
Management Decision Making [73]
R Decision Support Systems [97]
↓ Expert Systems [91]
↓ Judgment [67]
↓ Problem Solving [67]
Risk Analysis [91]
Uncertainty [91]
Volition [88]

Decision Support Systems [97]
PN 0 SC 13193
SN Computer-based planning and decision making systems that provide data on the outcomes or results of alternative decision choices.
B Computer Software [67]
Expert Systems [91]
R ↓ Artificial Intelligence [82]
↓ Computer Applications [73]
↓ Computer Simulation [73]
Databases [91]
↓ Decision Making [67]
Information Systems [91]

Declarative Knowledge [97]
PN 0 SC 13194
SN Knowledge about "how" and "what" things are, which can be modified due to new experiences or internal thought processes. Compare PROCEDURAL KNOWLEDGE.
UF Factual Knowledge
R ↓ Cognitive Processes [67]
Divergent Thinking [73]
Information [67]
↓ Knowledge Level [78]
↓ Memory [67]
Metacognition [91]
↓ Problem Solving [67]
Procedural Knowledge [97]
↓ Reasoning [67]

Decoding
Use Human Information Storage

Decompression Effects [73]
PN 24 SC 13200
R Acceleration Effects [73]
↓ Gravitational Effects [67]
Physiological Stress [67]
Spaceflight [67]
Underwater Effects [73]

Decortication (Brain) [73]
PN 113 SC 13210
SN Functional deactivation or physical removal of all or portions of the cortical substance of the brain. Primarily used for experimental contexts.

Decortication (Brain) — (cont'd)
B Neurosurgery [73]
R ↓ Brain Lesions [67]

Deductive Reasoning
Use Inductive Deductive Reasoning

Deer [73]
PN 155 SC 13230
B Mammals [73]

Defecation [67]
PN 191 SC 13240
B Excretion [67]

Defendants [85]
PN 295 SC 13245
SN Persons who are being sued or prosecuted in a court of law.
R Court Referrals [94]
Criminal Responsibility [91]
↓ Criminals [67]
↓ Law (Government) [73]

Defense Mechanisms [67]
PN 2160 SC 13250
SN Any intrapsychic strategies that serve to provide relief from emotional conflict or frustration or from unreasonable or undesirable thoughts which lead to anxiety, distress, or depression.
B Personality Processes [67]
N Compensation (Defense Mechanism) [73]
Denial [73]
Displacement (Defense Mechanism) [73]
Fantasy (Defense Mechanism) [67]
Grandiosity [94]
Identification (Defense Mechanism) [73]
Intellectualization [73]
Introjection [73]
Isolation (Defense Mechanism) [73]
Projection (Defense Mechanism) [67]
Projective Identification [94]
Rationalization [73]
Reaction Formation [73]
Regression (Defense Mechanism) [67]
Repression (Defense Mechanism) [67]
Sublimation [73]
Suppression (Defense Mechanism) [73]
Withdrawal (Defense Mechanism) [73]
R ↓ Conversion Neurosis [73]
Externalization [73]
↓ Internalization [97]
↓ Mental Disorders [67]
↓ Personality Disorders [67]
Psychopathology [67]

Defensive Behavior (Animal)
Use Animal Defensive Behavior

Defensiveness [67]
PN 372 SC 13260
B Personality Traits [67]

Deformity
Use Physical Disfigurement

Degrees (Educational)
Use Educational Degrees

Dehydration [88]
PN 35 SC 13285
SN State of excessively reduced body water or water deficit.
R Homeostasis [73]
Water Deprivation [67]
Water Intake [67]

Dehydrogenases 73
PN 66 **SC** 13290
B Enzymes 73
N Alcohol Dehydrogenases 73
Lactate Dehydrogenase 73

Deinstitutionalization 82
PN 989 **SC** 13293
SN Programs emphasizing out-of-hospital treatment and community residence of clients, usually chronic psychiatric or handicapped patients, including those who may never have been hospitalized or who may or may not have experienced normal community life.
B Mental Health Programs 73
R Community Mental Health 73
Community Mental Health Services 78
Discharge Planning 94
Habilitation 91
↓ Homeless 88
Homeless Mentally Ill 97
↓ Institutional Release 78
↓ Mainstreaming 91
Partial Hospitalization 85
↓ Rehabilitation 67
Right to Treatment 97

Deja Vu
Use Consciousness States

Delay of Gratification 78
PN 197 **SC** 13297
SN Voluntary postponement of need satisfaction or fulfillment of desires.
R Impulse Control Disorders 97
↓ Motivation 67
↓ Reinforcement 67
Reinforcement Delay 85
↓ Rewards 67

Delayed Alternation 94
PN 12 **SC** 13298
SN Alternation of rewards, usually in maze learning, with a delay between successive trials, forcing experimental subject to also alternate responses in order to receive the reward.
B Operant Conditioning 67
R ↓ Learning 67
Reinforcement Delay 85
Response Variability 73
↓ Rewards 67
Spontaneous Alternation 82

Delayed Auditory Feedback 73
PN 109 **SC** 13300
B Auditory Feedback 73
Delayed Feedback 73

Delayed Development 73
PN 1382 **SC** 13310
SN Delays in any or all areas including cognitive, social, language, sensory, and emotional development.
B Development 67
N Failure to Thrive 88
Language Delay 88
Retarded Speech Development 73
R ↓ Developmental Age Groups 73
Developmental Disabilities 82
↓ Human Development 67
↓ Physical Development 73
↓ Psychogenesis 73

Delayed Feedback 73
PN 126 **SC** 13320
B Feedback 67
Perceptual Stimulation 73
N Delayed Auditory Feedback 73

Delayed Parenthood 85
PN 33 **SC** 13325
SN Voluntary decision to postpone parenthood, usually for reasons involving personal development or career interests.
R Childlessness 82
↓ Family Planning 73
Family Planning Attitudes 73
Parental Role 73

Delayed Reinforcement
Use Reinforcement Delay

Delayed Speech
Use Retarded Speech Development

Deletion (Chromosome) 73
PN 6 **SC** 13340
B Chromosome Disorders 73

Delinquency (Juvenile)
Use Juvenile Delinquency

Delirium 73
PN 481 **SC** 13360
B Consciousness Disturbances 73
Symptoms 67
R Hyperthermia 73

Delirium Tremens 73
PN 105 **SC** 13370
SN Acute alcoholic, psychotic condition characterized by intense tremors, anxiety, hallucinations, and delusions.
B Alcoholic Hallucinosis 73
Syndromes 73

Delta Rhythm 73
PN 66 **SC** 13380
SN Electrically measured impulses or waves of high amplitude and low frequency (1-3 cycles per second) observable in the electroencephalogram during sleep stages 3 and 4 (moderate to deep sleep).
B Electrical Activity 67
Electroencephalography 67

Delusions 67
PN 1267 **SC** 13390
SN False personal beliefs held contrary to reality, despite contradictory evidence and common sense.
B Thought Disturbances 73
R Capgras Syndrome 85
Erotomania 97
Grandiosity 94

Dementia 85
PN 3292 **SC** 13395
B Mental Disorders 67
Organic Brain Syndromes 73
N AIDS Dementia Complex 97
↓ Presenile Dementia 73
↓ Senile Dementia 73
↓ Vascular Dementia 97
R Pseudodementia 85

Dementia (Multi Infarct)
Use Multi Infarct Dementia

Dementia (Presenile)
Use Presenile Dementia

Dementia (Senile)
Use Senile Dementia

Dementia Paralytica
Use General Paresis

Dementia Praecox
Use Schizophrenia

Democracy 73
PN 120 **SC** 13440
B Political Economic Systems 73
R ↓ Civil Rights 78

Democratic Party
Use Political Parties

Demographic Characteristics 67
PN 10939 **SC** 13460
UF Population Characteristics
R Biographical Data 78
↓ Population 73
Psychosocial Factors 88

Demonic Possession
Use Spirit Possession

Demonstrations (Social)
Use Social Demonstrations

Dendrites 73
PN 150 **SC** 13490
B Neurons 73

Denial 73
PN 558 **SC** 13500
SN Exclusion from conscious awareness of unpleasant realities, which would produce anxiety if acknowledged.
B Defense Mechanisms 67
R Anosognosia 94

Denmark 73
PN 500 **SC** 13510
B Scandinavia 78

Density (Social)
Use Social Density

Dental Education 73
PN 56 **SC** 13520
B Graduate Education 73

Dental Students 73
PN 100 **SC** 13530
B Students 67
R Graduate Students 67

Dental Surgery 73
PN 67 **SC** 13540
B Dental Treatment 73
Surgery 71

Dental Treatment 73
PN 485 **SC** 13550
B Physical Treatment Methods 73
N Dental Surgery 73

Dentist Patient Interaction
Use Therapeutic Processes

Dentistry 73
PN 79 **SC** 13560
B Medical Sciences 67

Dentists 73
PN 135 **SC** 13570
B Medical Personnel 67

Deoxycorticosterone [73]
PN 24 **SC** 13580
B Adrenal Cortex Hormones [73]
Corticosteroids [73]

Deoxyglucose [91]
PN 34 **SC** 13585
B Carbohydrates [73]

Deoxyribonucleic Acid [73]
PN 189 **SC** 13590
UF DNA (Deoxyribonucleic Acid)
B Nucleic Acids [73]

Dependency (Drug)
Use Drug Dependency

Dependency (Personality) [67]
PN 1691 **SC** 13620
SN Lack of self-reliance, reflecting need for security, love, and protection from others.
B Personality Traits [67]
R Abandonment [97]
Attachment Behavior [85]
Codependency [91]
Dependent Personality [94]
Enabling [97]

Dependent Personality [94]
PN 9 **SC** 13625
SN Personality disorder characterized by pervasive patterns of dependent, passive, and submissive behavior.
B Personality Disorders [67]
R Codependency [91]
Dependency (Personality) [67]

Dependent Variables [73]
PN 73 **SC** 13630
SN Statistical or experimental parameters whose values change as a consequence of changes in one or more other independent variables.
B Statistical Variables [73]

Depersonalization [73]
PN 183 **SC** 13640
SN State in which an individual perceives or experiences a sensation of unreality concerning himself or his environment; seen in disorders such as schizophrenia, affective disorders, organic mental disorders, and personality disorders.
B Symptoms [67]
R Alienation [71]
↓ Dissociative Patterns [73]

Depression (Emotion) [67]
PN 13581 **SC** 13650
SN Mild depression that is not considered clinical depression. Prior to 1988, also used for major depression in clinical populations. For clinical depression, use MAJOR DEPRESSION.
B Emotional States [73]
R ↓ Major Depression [88]
Sadness [73]
↓ Separation Reactions [97]

Depressive Reaction (Neurotic)
Use Neurotic Depressive Reaction

Deprivation [67]
PN 1050 **SC** 13680
SN Removal, denial, or lack of something needed or desired.
N Cultural Deprivation [73]
Food Deprivation [67]
REM Dream Deprivation [73]
Sleep Deprivation [67]

Deprivation — (cont'd)
N ↓ Stimulus Deprivation [73]
Water Deprivation [67]
R Environmental Stress [73]
↓ Motivation [67]
Physiological Stress [67]
Psychological Stress [73]
↓ Stress [67]

Depth Perception [67]
PN 1455 **SC** 13690
B Spatial Perception [67]
N Stereoscopic Vision [73]
R Eye Convergence [82]
Linear Perspective [82]
Motion Parallax [97]
Ocular Accommodation [82]

Depth Psychology [73]
PN 88 **SC** 13700
SN Any of the psychological theories which study the unconscious processes of the personality.
B Psychology [67]

Dermatitis [73]
PN 63 **SC** 13710
B Skin Disorders [73]
N Eczema [73]
Neurodermatitis [73]
R Allergic Skin Disorders [73]
↓ Infectious Disorders [73]
↓ Toxic Disorders [73]

Dermatomes
Use Cutaneous Receptive Fields

Desegregation
Use Social Integration

Desensitization (Systematic)
Use Systematic Desensitization Therapy

Desertion
Use Abandonment

Design (Experimental)
Use Experimental Design

Design (Man Machine Systems)
Use Human Machine Systems Design

Desipramine [73]
PN 720 **SC** 13760
B Tricyclic Antidepressant Drugs [97]

Desirability (Social)
Use Social Desirability

Desires
Use Motivation

Detection (Signal)
Use Signal Detection (Perception)

Detention (Legal)
Use Legal Detention

Determinism [97]
PN 0 **SC** 13815
SN A doctrine that assumes events or objects have antecedent causes that determine their nature.
B Philosophies [67]
R Epistemology [73]
Idealism [73]

Determinism — (cont'd)
R Positivism [73]
Volition [88]

Detoxification [73]
PN 494 **SC** 13820
B Alcohol Rehabilitation [82]
Drug Rehabilitation [73]
R Alcohol Withdrawal [94]
↓ Drug Abstinence [94]
↓ Drug Therapy [67]
↓ Drug Withdrawal [73]
Sobriety [88]

Developed Countries [85]
PN 102 **SC** 13823
B Countries [67]

Developing Countries [85]
PN 428 **SC** 13825
UF Third World Countries
Underdeveloped Countries
B Countries [67]

Development [67]
PN 1428 **SC** 13830
UF Growth
Ontogeny
N Animal Development [78]
Career Development [85]
Community Development [97]
Curriculum Development [73]
↓ Delayed Development [73]
↓ Human Development [67]
Organizational Development [73]
↓ Physical Development [73]
Precocious Development [73]
Professional Development [82]
↓ Program Development [91]
↓ Psychogenesis [73]
R Age Differences [67]
Critical Period [88]
↓ Developmental Age Groups [73]
↓ Developmental Stages [73]
Sex Linked Developmental Differences [73]

Developmental Age Groups [73]
PN 171 **SC** 13840
SN Groups defined by a chronological age span, and characterized by certain physical, behavioral, psychological, and social attributes. Use AGE DIFFERENCES for age comparisons within or between groups.
N ↓ Adolescents [67]
↓ Adults [67]
↓ Children [67]
R Adolescent Development [73]
Adult Development [78]
Age Differences [67]
↓ Aging [91]
↓ Childhood Development [67]
↓ Delayed Development [73]
↓ Development [67]
↓ Developmental Stages [73]
Emotional Development [73]
↓ Human Development [67]
Mental Age [73]
↓ Motor Development [73]
↓ Physical Development [73]
Precocious Development [73]
↓ Psychogenesis [73]

Developmental Differences
SN Term discontinued in 1982. Use DEVELOPMENTAL DIFFERENCES or AGE DIFFERENCES to access references from 73–81.
Use Age Differences

Developmental Disabilities 82
PN 1912 SC 13853
SN As encompassed in federal legislation for educational assistance to handicapped children, includes disabilities originating before age 18 that constitute substantial barriers to normal functioning. Use a more specific term if possible.
R ↓ Autism 67
↓ Communication Disorders 82
↓ Congenital Disorders 73
Deaf Blind 91
↓ Delayed Development 73
↓ Disabled 97
↓ Genetic Disorders 73
↓ Human Development 67
↓ Learning Disorders 67
↓ Mental Retardation 67
↓ Nervous System Disorders 67

Developmental Measures 94
PN 30 SC 13857
N Bayley Scales of Infant Development 94

Developmental Psychology 73
PN 757 SC 13860
B Psychology 67
N Adolescent Psychology 73
Child Psychology 67
Gerontology 67
R ↓ Human Development 67

Developmental Stages 73
PN 1441 SC 13870
SN Phases in an individual's development characterized by certain physical, behavioral, mental, or social attributes, e.g., the latency stage of psychosexual development or the sensorimotor intelligence stage of cognitive development.
N Menopause 73
↓ Prenatal Developmental Stages 73
Puberty 73
R Adolescent Development 73
Adult Development 78
↓ Aging 91
↓ Childhood Development 67
↓ Development 67
↓ Developmental Age Groups 73
Erikson (Erik) 91
↓ Human Development 67
Object Permanence 85
↓ Perceptual Development 73
↓ Physical Development 73
Piaget (Jean) 67
↓ Psychogenesis 73
↓ Rites of Passage 73

Deviant Behavior
Use Antisocial Behavior

Deviation IQ
Use Standard Scores

Deviations (Sexual)
Use Sexual Deviations

Devices (Experimental)
Use Apparatus

Dexamethasone 85
PN 625 SC 13905
SN A synthetic analogue of cortisol.
B Glucocorticoids 82
R Dexamethasone Suppression Test 88

Dexamethasone Suppression Test 88
PN 575 SC 13907

Dexamethasone Suppression Test — (cont'd)
SN Laboratory analysis of hypersecretion of cortisol and the body's failure to suppress cortisol after the administration of dexamethasone. Used primarily for diagnosis of major depressive disorders.
B Medical Diagnosis 73
R Dexamethasone 85

Dexamphetamine
Use Dextroamphetamine

Dexedrine
Use Dextroamphetamine

Dexterity (Physical)
Use Physical Dexterity

Dextroamphetamine 73
PN 1529 SC 13940
UF Amphetamine (d-)
Dexamphetamine
Dexedrine
B Adrenergic Drugs 73
Amphetamine 67
Appetite Depressing Drugs 73
CNS Stimulating Drugs 73
Sympathomimetic Amines 73

Diabetes 73
PN 983 SC 13950
B Endocrine Disorders 73
Metabolism Disorders 73
N Diabetes Insipidus 73
Diabetes Mellitus 73

Diabetes Insipidus 73
PN 85 SC 13960
B Diabetes 73
R ↓ Genetic Disorders 73

Diabetes Mellitus 73
PN 580 SC 13970
B Diabetes 73

Diacetylmorphine
Use Heroin

Diagnosis 67
PN 4887 SC 13990
N Computer Assisted Diagnosis 73
Differential Diagnosis 67
Educational Diagnosis 78
Galvanic Skin Response 67
↓ Medical Diagnosis 73
↓ Psychodiagnosis 67
R Autopsy 73
Clinical Judgment (Not Diagnosis) 73
Comorbidity 91
Diagnosis Related Groups 88
↓ Disorders 67
Dual Diagnosis 91
General Health Questionnaire 91
Geriatric Assessment 97
Intake Interview 94
International Class of Diseases 97
Labeling 78
↓ Measurement 67
↓ Mental Disorders 67
Misdiagnosis 97
↓ Neuropsychological Assessment 82
Pain Measurement 97
Patient History 73
↓ Physical Disorders 97
Prognosis 73
Research Diagnostic Criteria 94
↓ Screening 82

Diagnosis — (cont'd)
R Severity (Disorders) 82
Symptom Checklists 91

Diagnosis Related Groups 88
PN 58 SC 13985
UF DRGs
R Cost Containment 91
↓ Diagnosis 67
Health Care Costs 94
↓ Health Insurance 73
Misdiagnosis 97
↓ Professional Fees 78

Diagnostic and Statistical Manual 94
PN 316 SC 13988
SN Used when the current Diagnostic and Statistical Manual or its revisions is the primary focus of the reference. Use PSYCHODIAGNOSTIC TYPOLOGIES to access references prior to 1994. Not used for specific psychodiagnostic categories.
UF DSM
B Psychodiagnostic Typologies 67
R International Class of Diseases 97
↓ Mental Disorders 67
↓ Psychodiagnosis 67
Research Diagnostic Criteria 94

Diagnostic Interview Schedule 91
PN 53 SC 13900
B Psychodiagnostic Interview 73
R ↓ Psychodiagnostic Typologies 67
↓ Screening 82

Dialect 73
PN 252 SC 14000
SN A variety of language characteristic of a geographical region or ethnic, occupational, socioeconomic, or other group.
B Language 67
N Nonstandard English 73
R Ethnolinguistics 73

Dialectics 73
PN 219 SC 14010
SN Intellectual investigation through deductive reasoning and juxtaposition of opposing or contradictory ideas.
R ↓ Reasoning 67

Dialysis 73
PN 160 SC 14020
B Physical Treatment Methods 73
N Hemodialysis 73

Diaphragm (Anatomy) 73
PN 15 SC 14030
B Muscles 67
Respiratory System 73
R Thorax 73

Diaphragms (Birth Control) 73
PN 9 SC 14040
B Contraceptive Devices 73

Diarrhea 73
PN 55 SC 14050
B Colon Disorders 73
R Fecal Incontinence 73

Diastolic Pressure 73
PN 186 SC 14060
B Blood Pressure 67

Diazepam 73
PN 1597 SC 14070

Diazepam — (cont'd)
UF Valium
B Benzodiazepines [78]
Minor Tranquilizers [73]
Muscle Relaxing Drugs [73]

Dichoptic Stimulation [82]
PN 96 SC 14075
SN Simultaneous presentation of different stimuli to each eye independently.
B Visual Stimulation [73]

Dichotic Stimulation [82]
PN 621 SC 14077
SN Simultaneous presentation of different sounds to the two ears.
B Auditory Stimulation [67]

Dictionary [73]
PN 13 SC 14090
SN Mandatory term used as a document type identifier.
R Glossary [73]

Dieldrin
SN Term discontinued in 1997. Use DIELDRIN to access references from 73-96.
Use Insecticides

Diencephalon [73]
PN 240 SC 14110
B Forebrain [85]
N ↓ Hypothalamus [67]
Optic Chiasm [73]
↓ Thalamus [67]

Dietary Restraint [94]
PN 57 SC 14112
R ↓ Appetite [73]
Diets [78]
↓ Eating [67]
↓ Food Intake [67]

Diets [78]
PN 2222 SC 14114
SN Food and drink regularly consumed or prescribed for a special reason. Used for human or animal populations.
R Dietary Restraint [94]
↓ Drinking Behavior [78]
↓ Eating [67]
Food [78]
Food Additives [78]
Food Allergies [73]
Food Deprivation [67]
Food Preferences [73]
Health Behavior [82]
Nutrition [73]
↓ Nutritional Deficiencies [73]
Obesity [73]
↓ Underweight [73]
Weight Control [85]

Differential Aptitude Tests [73]
PN 36 SC 14150
B Aptitude Measures [67]

Differential Diagnosis [67]
PN 3660 SC 14160
SN Diagnosis aimed at distinguishing between physical and/or mental disorders of similar character by comparison of symptoms.
B Diagnosis [67]
R Comorbidity [91]
Dual Diagnosis [91]
Educational Diagnosis [78]
↓ Medical Diagnosis [73]
↓ Psychodiagnosis [67]

Differential Limen
Use Thresholds

Differential Personality Inventory
SN Term discontinued in 1997. Use DIFFERENTIAL PERSONALITY INVENTORY to access references from 73-96.
Use Nonprojective Personality Measures

Differential Reinforcement [73]
PN 751 SC 14190
SN Selective reinforcement of one response in a defined category (response class) of responses to the exclusion of any other members (responses) of that category. Has application in treatment as well as in experimental contexts.
B Reinforcement [67]
R ↓ Discrimination Learning [82]
Omission Training [85]

Difficulty Level (Test) [73]
PN 254 SC 14200
UF Test Difficulty
B Test Construction [73]
Testing [67]
R Item Response Theory [85]

Digestion [73]
PN 70 SC 14210
B Physiology [67]
R ↓ Digestive System [67]
Salivation [73]
Swallowing [88]

Digestive System [67]
PN 367 SC 14220
B Anatomical Systems [73]
N Esophagus [73]
↓ Gastrointestinal System [73]
Liver [73]
Mouth (Anatomy) [67]
Pharynx [73]
Teeth (Anatomy) [73]
↓ Tongue [73]
R Digestion [73]
↓ Digestive System Disorders [73]
Salivary Glands [73]

Digestive System Disorders [73]
PN 72 SC 14230
B Physical Disorders [97]
N Cystic Fibrosis [85]
↓ Gastrointestinal Disorders [73]
Jaundice [73]
↓ Liver Disorders [73]
R ↓ Digestive System [67]
↓ Infectious Disorders [73]
↓ Neoplasms [67]
↓ Symptoms [67]
↓ Toxic Disorders [73]

Digit Span Testing [73]
PN 199 SC 14240
SN Test of immediate recall involving presentation of a random series of numerals which the subject repeats after the series has been presented.
B Measurement [67]

Digital Computers [73]
PN 151 SC 14250
SN Electronic or electromechanical machines that operate directly on binary digits when executing programs and manipulating data (e.g., calculators).
UF Calculators
B Computers [67]

Digits (Mathematics)
Use Numbers (Numerals)

Dihydroergotamine [73]
PN 23 SC 14270
B Adrenergic Blocking Drugs [73]
Analgesic Drugs [73]
Ergot Derivatives [73]
Vasoconstrictor Drugs [73]

Dihydroxyphenylacetic Acid [91]
PN 79 SC 14273
UF DOPAC
B Acids [73]
Dopamine Metabolites [82]

Dihydroxytryptamine [91]
PN 30 SC 14275
B Serotonin Antagonists [73]

Dilantin
Use Diphenylhydantoin

Dilation (Pupil)
Use Pupil Dilation

Diphenhydramine [73]
PN 46 SC 14310
UF Benadryl
B Amines [73]
Antihistaminic Drugs [73]
Antitremor Drugs [73]

Diphenylhydantoin [73]
PN 163 SC 14320
UF Dilantin
Diphenylhydantoin Sodium
Phenytoin
B Anticonvulsive Drugs [73]

Diphenylhydantoin Sodium
Use Diphenylhydantoin

Diptera [73]
PN 220 SC 14350
UF Flies
B Insects [67]
N Drosophila [73]
R Larvae [73]

Directed Discussion Method [73]
PN 98 SC 14360
B Teaching Methods [67]
R Lecture Method [73]

Directed Reverie Therapy [78]
PN 208 SC 14364
SN Waking dream technique in psychotherapy used especially in brief therapy and group therapy.
UF Guided Daydreams
Guided Fantasy
B Psychotherapeutic Techniques [67]
Psychotherapy [67]
R Dream Analysis [73]

Direction Perception [97]
PN 0 SC 14365
B Spatial Perception [67]
R Cognitive Maps [82]
↓ Motion Perception [67]
↓ Perceptual Localization [67]
↓ Spatial Memory [88]
Spatial Organization [73]

Disability Discrimination [97]
PN 0 SC 57480

Disability Discrimination — (cont'd)
B Social Discrimination [82]
R Affirmative Action [85]
↓ Civil Rights [78]
Disability Laws [94]
↓ Disabled [97]
↓ Disabled (Attitudes Toward) [97]
↓ Disorders [67]
↓ Mental Disorders [67]
Mental Illness (Attitudes Toward) [67]
↓ Physical Illness (Attitudes Toward) [85]
↓ Prejudice [67]
Sensory Disabilities (Attit Toward) [97]
Stereotyped Attitudes [67]

Disability Evaluation [88]
PN 72 **SC** 14367
SN Evaluation of one's ability to work in order to determine the need for insurance or health benefits.
R ↓ Employee Benefits [73]
↓ Insurance [73]
Social Security [88]

Disability Laws [94]
PN 46 **SC** 57410
SN Rules declared by federal or state governments and enacted by legislative bodies that affect populations with mental or physical disabilities or disorders. Used for the laws themselves, or the interpretation or application of the laws.
B Laws [67]
R Civil Law [94]
↓ Civil Rights [78]
Disability Discrimination [97]
↓ Disabled [97]
Disabled Personnel [97]

Disability Management [91]
PN 18 **SC** 14368
SN Process of returning an impaired or disabled worker to the workplace. Includes evaluation, assessment, early intervention, and rehabilitation.
B Management [67]
R Disabled Personnel [97]
Employee Assistance Programs [85]
↓ Prevention [73]
↓ Rehabilitation [67]
Vocational Evaluation [91]
↓ Vocational Rehabilitation [67]

Disabled [97]
PN 0 **SC** 14376
SN Use HANDICAPPED to access references prior to 1997.
UF Exceptional Children (Handicapped)
Handicapped
N Adventitiously Disabled [97]
↓ Brain Damaged [73]
Congenitally Disabled [97]
Disabled Personnel [97]
↓ Emotionally Disturbed [73]
↓ Mentally Retarded [67]
↓ Multiply Disabled [97]
↓ Physically Disabled [97]
↓ Sensorially Disabled [97]
Slow Learners [73]
Speech Disabled [97]
R Activities of Daily Living [91]
Adaptive Behavior [91]
Daily Activities [94]
Developmental Disabilities [82]
Disability Discrimination [97]
Disability Laws [94]
Homebound [88]
↓ Learning Disabilities [73]
Physical Mobility [94]
Special Needs [94]

Disabled (Attitudes Toward) [97]
PN 0 **SC** 14373
SN Use HANDICAPPED (ATTITUDES TOWARD) to access references from 73–96.
UF Handicapped (Attitudes Toward)
B Attitudes [67]
N Mental Illness (Attitudes Toward) [67]
Mental Retardation (Attit Toward) [73]
Physical Disabilities (Attit Toward) [97]
Sensory Disabilities (Attit Toward) [97]
R Disability Discrimination [97]
↓ Physical Illness (Attitudes Toward) [85]

Disabled Personnel [97]
PN 0 **SC** 14369
SN Employees with physical or mental disabilities or injuries resulting from work-related activities.
B Disabled [97]
Personnel [67]
R Disability Laws [94]
Disability Management [91]
Impaired Professionals [85]
Supported Employment [94]
↓ Working Conditions [73]
Workmens Compensation Insurance [73]

Disadvantaged [67]
PN 2878 **SC** 14370
SN Individuals deprived of equal access to society's resources, especially as regards education, culture, and employment.
UF Economically Disadvantaged
Socially Disadvantaged
Underprivileged
R Cultural Deprivation [73]
↓ Homeless [88]
Poverty [73]
↓ Social Class [67]
↓ Social Deprivation [73]
↓ Socioeconomic Status [67]

Disappointment [73]
PN 23 **SC** 14380
B Emotional States [73]
R Dissatisfaction [73]
↓ Separation Reactions [97]

Disasters [73]
PN 383 **SC** 14390
N Natural Disasters [73]
R ↓ Accidents [67]
↓ Crises [71]
↓ Stress [67]

Discharge Planning [94]
PN 14 **SC** 14395
B Case Management [91]
Treatment Planning [97]
R Aftercare [73]
Deinstitutionalization [82]
↓ Facility Discharge [88]
↓ Hospital Discharge [73]
↓ Institutional Release [78]
Posttreatment Followup [73]
Psychiatric Hospital Discharge [78]
Treatment Termination [82]

Discipline (Child)
Use Child Discipline

Discipline (Classroom)
Use Classroom Discipline

Disclosure (Experimental)
Use Debriefing (Experimental)

Disclosure (Self)
Use Self Disclosure

Discourse Analysis [97]
PN 0 **SC** 14425
SN Analysis of written and spoken language.
B Content Analysis [78]
R ↓ Grammar [67]
↓ Language [67]
↓ Linguistics [73]
Morphology (Language) [73]
Pragmatics [85]
Rhetoric [91]
↓ Semantics [67]
↓ Syntax [71]
Text Structure [82]
↓ Verbal Communication [67]

Discovery Teaching Method [73]
PN 115 **SC** 14430
SN Unstructured or guided instruction which encourages independent exploration or discovery.
B Teaching Methods [67]
R ↓ Experiential Learning [97]
Montessori Method [73]
Nondirected Discussion Method [73]
Open Classroom Method [73]

Discrimination [67]
PN 2450 **SC** 14450
SN Conceptually broad array term referring to the general process of differentiation between qualities, entities, or people. Use a more specific term if possible.
N Cognitive Discrimination [73]
Drug Discrimination [85]
↓ Perceptual Discrimination [73]
↓ Social Discrimination [82]
Stimulus Discrimination [73]
R ↓ Discrimination Learning [82]
↓ Perception [67]

Discrimination (Cognitive)
Use Cognitive Discrimination

Discrimination (Social)
Use Social Discrimination

Discrimination Learning [82]
PN 2057 **SC** 14445
SN Learning paradigm in which responses to one stimulus (S+) are reinforced while responses to another stimulus (S-) are either not reinforced or are punished. Also, the learned discriminative responses themselves.
UF Discriminative Learning
B Learning [67]
Operant Conditioning [67]
N Drug Discrimination [85]
Matching to Sample [94]
Nonreversal Shift Learning [73]
Reversal Shift Learning [67]
R ↓ Concept Formation [67]
Differential Reinforcement [73]
↓ Discrimination [67]
Extinction (Learning) [67]
Fading (Conditioning) [82]
↓ Generalization (Learning) [82]
Kinship Recognition [88]
Stimulus Control [67]
Stimulus Discrimination [73]

Discriminative Learning
Use Discrimination Learning

Discriminative Stimulus
Use Conditioned Stimulus

Discussion (Group)
Use Group Discussion

Disease Course [91]
PN 951 **SC** 14470
SN Stages or progression of physical or mental disorders. Compare PROGNOSIS.
UF Course of Illness
Disorder Course
R ↓ Disorders [67]
↓ Mental Disorders [67]
↓ Physical Disorders [97]
Prognosis [73]

Diseases (Venereal)
Use Venereal Diseases

Disgust [94]
PN 9 **SC** 14495
B Emotional States [73]
R ↓ Aversion [67]

Dishonesty [73]
PN 65 **SC** 14500
B Personality Traits [67]
R Cheating [73]
↓ Deception [67]
Fraud [94]
Sincerity [73]

Dislike
Use Aversion

Disorder Course
Use Disease Course

Disorders [67]
PN 6676 **SC** 14520
SN Conceptually broad array term referring primarily to physical illness. Also used when particular disorders are not specified. Use a more specific term if possible. For general discussions of health impairment consider also the term HEALTH.
N ↓ Mental Disorders [67]
↓ Physical Disorders [97]
R ↓ Chronic Illness [91]
Chronicity (Disorders) [82]
Comorbidity [91]
↓ Diagnosis [67]
Disability Discrimination [97]
Disease Course [91]
Etiology [67]
Health Complaints [97]
Health Impaired [73]
Illness Behavior [82]
↓ Injuries [73]
International Class of Diseases [97]
Onset (Disorders) [73]
Predisposition [73]
Premorbidity [78]
Prenatal Exposure [91]
Prognosis [73]
Recovery (Disorders) [73]
Relapse (Disorders) [73]
↓ Remission (Disorders) [73]
Severity (Disorders) [82]
Special Needs [94]
Susceptibility (Disorders) [73]
↓ Symptoms [67]
↓ Syndromes [73]

Disorientation (Place)
Use Place Disorientation

Disorientation (Time)
Use Time Disorientation

Displacement (Defense Mechanism) [73]
PN 42 **SC** 14550
B Defense Mechanisms [67]

Displays [67]
PN 328 **SC** 14560
SN Physical arrangements of stimuli to form a desired pattern; temporal, spatial, or otherwise.
N Auditory Displays [73]
Graphical Displays [85]
Tactual Displays [73]
↓ Visual Displays [73]
R ↓ Instrument Controls [85]

Disposition
Use Personality

Disruptive Behavior
Use Behavior Problems

Dissatisfaction [73]
PN 89 **SC** 14590
B Emotional States [73]
R Disappointment [73]
Frustration [67]
↓ Satisfaction [73]

Dissociative Identity Disorder [97]
PN 0 **SC** 14595
SN Use MULTIPLE PERSONALITY to access references from 73–96.
UF Multiple Personality
Split Personality
R ↓ Dissociative Patterns [73]

Dissociative Neurosis
SN Term discontinued in 1997. Use DISSOCIATIVE NEUROSIS to access references from 73–96.
Use Dissociative Patterns

Dissociative Patterns [73]
PN 566 **SC** 14610
SN Neurotic reactions involving repression and alteration of normal integrative functions of identity, consciousness, or motor behavior. Aspects of personality and memory become separate entities and function independently of the rest of the mental processes.
UF Dissociative Neurosis
Hysterical Neurosis (Dissociation)
B Mental Disorders [67]
N ↓ Amnesia [67]
Fugue Reaction [73]
R Depersonalization [73]
Dissociative Identity Disorder [97]
↓ Hysteria [67]
Hysterical Personality [73]
↓ Personality Disorders [67]
Sleepwalking [73]
Spirit Possession [97]

Dissonance (Cognitive)
Use Cognitive Dissonance

Distance Discrimination
Use Distance Perception

Distance Perception [73]
PN 661 **SC** 14640
UF Distance Discrimination
B Spatial Perception [67]
N Apparent Distance [73]
Motion Parallax [97]
R Eye Convergence [82]
Linear Perspective [82]

Distortion (Perceptual)
Use Perceptual Distortion

Distractibility [73]
PN 286 **SC** 14660
B Symptoms [67]
R Attention Deficit Disorder [85]
Distraction [78]

Distraction [78]
PN 831 **SC** 14663
SN Process or potential cause of interruption of attention.
R ↓ Attention [67]
Attention Span [73]
Concentration [82]
Distractibility [73]
Divided Attention [73]
Selective Attention [73]

Distress [73]
PN 2258 **SC** 14670
SN Negative emotional state characterized by physical and/or emotional discomfort, pain, or anguish. Compare STRESS.
UF Anguish
B Emotional States [73]
R Agitation [91]
↓ Separation Reactions [97]
↓ Stress [67]
Suffering [73]

Distress Calls (Animal)
Use Animal Distress Calls

Distributed Practice [73]
PN 137 **SC** 14690
SN Practice schedule in which relatively short periods of practice are spaced with intermittent rest or periods of activity unrelated to the practiced task. Compare MASSED PRACTICE.
B Learning Schedules [67]
Practice [67]

Distribution (Frequency)
Use Frequency Distribution

Distributive Justice
Use Justice

Distrust
Use Suspicion

Disulfiram [78]
PN 133 **SC** 14725
UF Antabuse
B Emetic Drugs [73]

Diuresis [73]
PN 18 **SC** 14730
SN Increased flow of urine.
B Urination [67]
R ↓ Diuretics [73]

Diuretics [73]
PN 92 **SC** 14740
B Drugs [67]
N Acetazolamide [73]
Caffeine [73]
Theophylline [73]
R ↓ Antihypertensive Drugs [73]
Diuresis [73]
Probenecid [82]
↓ Urination [67]

Diurnal Variations
Use Human Biological Rhythms

Divergent Thinking 73
PN 502 **SC** 14760
SN Component of intelligence which is manifested in the ability to generate a wide variety of original ideas or solutions to a particular problem. Compare CREATIVITY.
B Thinking 67
R ↓ Abstraction 67
Creativity 67
Declarative Knowledge 97
↓ Inductive Deductive Reasoning 73
Intelligence 67
Procedural Knowledge 97

Divided Attention 73
PN 423 **SC** 14765
SN Simultaneous attending to two or more stimuli or through two or more perceptual modalities. Compare SELECTIVE ATTENTION.
B Attention 67
R Distraction 78
Selective Attention 73

Division of Labor 88
PN 157 **SC** 14767
N Animal Division of Labor 73
R Economics 85
Household Management 85
↓ Occupations 67
Sex Roles 67
Work Load 82

Division of Labor (Animal)
Use Animal Division of Labor

Divorce 73
PN 2717 **SC** 14780
B Marital Separation 73
R Child Custody 82
Child Support 88
Divorced Persons 73
↓ Family 67
Joint Custody 88
Mediation 88
Remarriage 85

Divorced Persons 73
PN 572 **SC** 14790
R Divorce 73
↓ Family 67
↓ Marital Separation 73
↓ Marital Status 73
↓ Parental Absence 73

Dizygotic Twins
Use Heterozygotic Twins

Dizziness
Use Vertigo

DNA (Deoxyribonucleic Acid)
Use Deoxyribonucleic Acid

Doctors
Use Physicians

Dogmatism 78
PN 490 **SC** 14830
B Personality Traits 67
R Authoritarianism 67
Openmindedness 78
Relativism 97

Dogs 67
PN 1789 **SC** 14840
B Canids 97

Doll Play 73
PN 83 **SC** 14850
B Recreation 67
R Anatomically Detailed Dolls 91
Childhood Play Behavior 78

Dolphins 73
PN 107 **SC** 14860
B Whales 85
R Porpoises 73

Domestic Service Personnel 73
PN 22 **SC** 14870
UF Maids
B Service Personnel 91
R ↓ Nonprofessional Personnel 82

Domestic Violence
Use Family Violence

Domestication (Animal)
Use Animal Domestication

Dominance 67
PN 734 **SC** 14900
SN Conceptually broad array term referring to relative positions of objects, persons, things, or processes. Use a more specific term if possible.
N Animal Dominance 73
↓ Cerebral Dominance 73
Dominance Hierarchy 73
Genetic Dominance 73
R Abuse of Power 97
Authoritarianism 67
Authority 67
Coercion 94
Emotional Superiority 73
Obedience 73
↓ Power 67
↓ Status 67

Dominance (Animal)
Use Animal Dominance

Dominance Hierarchy 73
PN 650 **SC** 14890
SN Social structure of a group as it relates to the relative social rank or dominance status of its members. Used for human or animal populations.
B Dominance 67
R Animal Dominance 73
↓ Social Behavior 67
↓ Social Structure 67

Domination
Use Authoritarianism

Dominican Republic 73
PN 18 **SC** 14920
B West Indies 73
R Hispaniola 73

DOPA 73
PN 69 **SC** 14940
B Amino Acids 73
R Carbidopa 88
Dopamine 73
Levodopa 73
Methyldopa 73

DOPAC
Use Dihydroxyphenylacetic Acid

Dopamine 73
PN 3826 **SC** 14950
B Catecholamines 73
R DOPA 73

Dopamine — (cont'd)
R ↓ Dopamine Metabolites 82
↓ Heart Rate Affecting Drugs 73
Homovanillic Acid 78
Levodopa 73
Methyldopa 73
Methylphenyltetrahydropyridine 94

Dopamine Agonists 85
PN 639 **SC** 14951
B Drugs 67
N ↓ Amphetamine 67
Apomorphine 73
Morphine 73
Quinpirole 94

Dopamine Antagonists 82
PN 722 **SC** 14952
B Amine Oxidase Inhibitors 73
N Sulpiride 73
R ↓ Catecholamines 73
↓ CNS Depressant Drugs 73
↓ Decarboxylase Inhibitors 82
↓ Narcotic Drugs 73
↓ Tranquilizing Drugs 67

Dopamine Metabolites 82
PN 198 **SC** 14955
SN Molecules generated from the metabolism of dopamine.
B Metabolites 73
N Dihydroxyphenylacetic Acid 91
Homovanillic Acid 78
R Acetaldehyde 82
Dopamine 73
↓ Metabolism 67

Dormitories 73
PN 383 **SC** 14960
UF Residence Halls
B Housing 73
School Facilities 73

Dorsal Horns 85
PN 87 **SC** 14965
SN Longitudinal columns of gray matter (i.e., neuronal cell bodies) in the posterior spinal cord mainly serving sensory mechanisms.
B Spinal Cord 73
R ↓ Afferent Pathways 82
Dorsal Roots 73

Dorsal Roots 73
PN 69 **SC** 14970
B Spinal Cord 73
R Dorsal Horns 85

Double Bind Interaction 73
PN 86 **SC** 14990
SN Simultaneous communication of conflicting messages in which the response to either message evokes rejection or disapproval.
B Interpersonal Communication 73
R Dysfunctional Family 91
Schizophrenogenic Family 67
Schizophrenogenic Mothers 73

Doubt 73
PN 36 **SC** 15000
B Emotional States 73
R Mental Confusion 73
Suspicion 73
Uncertainty 91

Doves 73
PN 147 **SC** 15010
B Birds 67

Downs Syndrome [67]
PN 1728 **SC** 15020
UF Mongolism
B Autosome Disorders [73]
Mental Retardation [67]
Neonatal Disorders [73]
Syndromes [73]
R Trainable Mentally Retarded [73]
Trisomy 21 [73]

Doxepin [94]
PN 10 **SC** 15025
SN Use ANTIDEPRESSANT DRUGS or TRANQUILIZING DRUGS to access references from 73-93.
B Tranquilizing Drugs [67]
Tricyclic Antidepressant Drugs [97]

Draftees [73]
PN 50 **SC** 15030
SN Military personnel conscripted for service.
B Enlisted Military Personnel [73]
R Army Personnel [67]
Navy Personnel [67]

Drama [73]
PN 637 **SC** 15040
B Theatre [73]
R ↓ Literature [67]
Motion Pictures (Entertainment) [73]
Writers [91]

Draw A Man Test
SN Prior to 1988, use Goodenough Harris Draw A Person Test.
Use Human Figures Drawing

Drawing [67]
PN 2071 **SC** 15050
B Art [67]

Dream Analysis [73]
PN 920 **SC** 15060
UF Dream Interpretation
B Psychoanalysis [67]
Psychotherapeutic Techniques [67]
R Directed Reverie Therapy [78]
↓ Dreaming [67]
↓ Parapsychology [67]

Dream Content [73]
PN 850 **SC** 15070
R ↓ Dreaming [67]
Nightmares [73]
↓ Sleep [67]

Dream Interpretation
Use Dream Analysis

Dream Recall [73]
PN 233 **SC** 15090
R ↓ Dreaming [67]
Lucid Dreaming [94]

Dreaming [67]
PN 1207 **SC** 15100
N Lucid Dreaming [94]
Nightmares [73]
REM Dreams [73]
R Dream Analysis [73]
Dream Content [73]
Dream Recall [73]
↓ Sleep [67]

DRGs
Use Diagnosis Related Groups

Drinking (Alcohol)
Use Alcohol Drinking Patterns

Drinking Attitudes
Use Alcohol Drinking Attitudes

Drinking Behavior [78]
PN 105 **SC** 15127
B Behavior [67]
N ↓ Alcohol Drinking Patterns [67]
Animal Drinking Behavior [73]
Water Intake [67]
R ↓ Alcoholic Beverages [73]
Beverages (Nonalcoholic) [78]
Diets [78]
Driving Under The Influence [88]
↓ Fluid Intake [85]
Sucking [78]
Thirst [67]

Drinking Behavior (Animal)
Use Animal Drinking Behavior

Drive
Use Motivation

Driver Education [73]
PN 148 **SC** 15150
B Curriculum [67]
R Drivers [73]

Driver Safety
Use Highway Safety

Drivers [73]
PN 811 **SC** 15170
R Automobiles [73]
Driver Education [73]
↓ Driving Behavior [67]
Highway Safety [73]
Motor Traffic Accidents [73]
↓ Motor Vehicles [82]

Driving Behavior [67]
PN 1775 **SC** 15180
SN Manner in which one operates a motor vehicle.
B Behavior [67]
N Driving Under The Influence [88]
R Drivers [73]
Highway Safety [73]
Motor Traffic Accidents [73]
Pedestrian Accidents [73]
Safety Belts [73]

Driving Under The Influence [88]
PN 504 **SC** 15185
UF Drunk Driving
B Crime [67]
Driving Behavior [67]
R ↓ Accidents [67]
↓ Alcohol Intoxication [73]
Blood Alcohol Concentration [94]
↓ Drinking Behavior [78]
↓ Drug Usage [71]
Highway Safety [73]

Dropouts [73]
PN 237 **SC** 15190
N Potential Dropouts [73]
↓ School Dropouts [67]
Treatment Dropouts [78]
R ↓ Education [67]
Experimental Attrition [94]
↓ School Enrollment [73]

Drosophila [73]
PN 477 **SC** 15200
UF Fruit Fly
B Diptera [73]
R Larvae [73]

Drowsiness
Use Sleep Onset

Drug Abstinence [94]
PN 102 **SC** 15215
SN Voluntary or involuntary abstinence from drugs. For alcohol abstinence, use SOBRIETY.
UF Abstinence (Drugs)
N Sobriety [88]
R Detoxification [73]
↓ Drug Abuse [73]
↓ Drug Rehabilitation [73]
↓ Drug Usage [71]
↓ Drug Withdrawal [73]
Recovery (Disorders) [73]
Smoking Cessation [88]

Drug Abuse [73]
PN 7140 **SC** 15220
UF Substance Abuse
B Behavior Disorders [71]
Drug Usage [71]
N ↓ Alcohol Abuse [88]
↓ Drug Dependency [73]
↓ Inhalant Abuse [85]
Polydrug Abuse [94]
R ↓ Addiction [73]
Codependency [91]
Craving [97]
↓ Drug Abstinence [94]
Drug Abuse Liability [94]
Drug Abuse Prevention [94]
↓ Drug Addiction [67]
Drug Distribution [97]
↓ Drug Legalization [97]
Drug Overdoses [78]
Drug Usage Screening [88]
↓ Drugs [67]
Intravenous Drug Usage [94]
Needle Sharing [94]
↓ Social Issues [91]

Drug Abuse Liability [94]
PN 45 **SC** 15225
SN Properties of any psychoactive drug or substance which lead to self administration and potentiality for abuse, dependence, and addiction.
UF Abuse Potential (Drugs)
R ↓ Alcohol Abuse [88]
↓ Drug Abuse [73]
↓ Drug Addiction [67]
↓ Drug Dependency [73]
↓ Pharmacology [73]
Psychopharmacology [67]

Drug Abuse Prevention [94]
PN 206 **SC** 15227
UF Substance Abuse Prevention
B Prevention [73]
R ↓ Drug Abuse [73]
Drug Education [73]
Early Intervention [82]
Preventive Medicine [73]
Primary Mental Health Prevention [73]

Drug Addiction [67]
PN 3290 **SC** 15230
SN Physical and emotional dependence on a chemical substance. Compare DRUG DEPENDENCY.
B Addiction [73]
Drug Dependency [73]
Side Effects (Drug) [73]

Drug Addiction — (cont'd)
N Heroin Addiction [73]
R ↓ Drug Abuse [73]
Drug Abuse Liability [94]
Drug Overdoses [78]
↓ Drug Withdrawal [73]
Intravenous Drug Usage [94]
Methadone Maintenance [78]
Polydrug Abuse [94]

Drug Administration Methods [73]
PN 1327 SC 15240
SN Techniques, procedures, and routes (e.g., oral, intravenous) of administration of drugs (in experimental or therapeutic contexts) including dosage forms (e.g., liquids, tablets), frequency, and duration of drug administration. Used only when methodological aspects of administering drugs are discussed.
N ↓ Injections [73]
R ↓ Drug Dosages [73]
↓ Drugs [67]

Drug Adverse Reactions
SN Term discontinued in 1982. Use DRUG ADVERSE REACTIONS or SIDE EFFECTS (DRUG) to access references from 73–81.
Use Side Effects (Drug)

Drug Allergies [73]
PN 13 SC 15260
B Allergic Disorders [73]
Side Effects (Drug) [73]
R Drug Sensitivity [73]

Drug Dependency [73]
PN 2404 SC 15270
SN Psychological craving for or habituation to the use of a chemical substance which may or may not be accompanied by physical dependency. Used for animal or human populations. Compare DRUG ADDICTION.
UF Dependency (Drug)
B Drug Abuse [73]
Side Effects (Drug) [73]
N ↓ Drug Addiction [67]
R Drug Abuse Liability [94]
Drug Usage Screening [88]
Polydrug Abuse [94]

Drug Discrimination [85]
PN 740 SC 15272
SN A discrimination learning paradigm used to study psychopharmacological and neuropharmacological phenomena. Also, the organism's ability to discriminate the presence, absence, or other qualitative aspects of a chemical substance.
B Discrimination [67]
Discrimination Learning [82]
R ↓ Drugs [67]

Drug Dissociation
Use State Dependent Learning

Drug Distribution [97]
PN 0 SC 15277
B Crime [67]
R ↓ Drug Abuse [73]
↓ Drug Laws [73]
↓ Drug Legalization [97]
↓ Drug Usage [71]

Drug Dosages [73]
PN 3474 SC 15280
N Drug Overdoses [78]
R Bioavailability [91]
↓ Drug Administration Methods [73]
↓ Drugs [67]

Drug Education [73]
PN 1248 SC 15290
UF Alcohol Education
B Health Education [73]
R Drug Abuse Prevention [94]
↓ Drugs [67]

Drug Effects
SN Term discontinued in 1982. Prior to 1982, a mandatory term applied to all studies involving any use of chemical substances administered for nontreatment purposes to human or animal subjects. From 1982, use DRUGS, specific drug classes or names, or terms referring to the chemical substance introduced for nontreatment purposes.
Use Drugs

Drug Induced Congenital Disorders [73]
PN 69 SC 15310
B Congenital Disorders [73]
Toxic Disorders [73]
N Fetal Alcohol Syndrome [85]
R Thalidomide [73]

Drug Induced Hallucinations [73]
PN 41 SC 15320
B Hallucinations [67]
R Psychedelic Experiences [73]

Drug Interactions [82]
PN 2589 SC 15325
SN Chemical and/or pharmacological reactions of drugs in combination, including agonistic and antagonistic interactions. Use DRUG POTENTIATION or DRUG SYNERGISM to access references from 73–81.
UF Drug Potentiation
Drug Synergism
Potentiation (Drugs)
R ↓ Drugs [67]
↓ Neurotoxins [82]
Polydrug Abuse [94]

Drug Laws [73]
PN 238 SC 15330
B Laws [67]
N ↓ Marihuana Laws [73]
R Drug Distribution [97]
↓ Drug Legalization [97]
↓ Drugs [67]

Drug Legalization [97]
PN 0 SC 15333
N Marihuana Legalization [73]
R ↓ Drug Abuse [73]
Drug Distribution [97]
↓ Drug Laws [73]
↓ Drug Usage [71]

Drug Overdoses [78]
PN 237 SC 15335
B Drug Dosages [73]
R ↓ Drug Abuse [73]
↓ Drug Addiction [67]
↓ Drug Therapy [67]
↓ Drug Usage [71]

Drug Potentiation
SN Term discontinued in 1982. Use DRUG POTENTIATION or DRUG SYNERGISM to access references from 73–81.
Use Drug Interactions

Drug Rehabilitation [73]
PN 5810 SC 15350
UF Rehabilitation (Drug)
B Rehabilitation [67]

Drug Rehabilitation — (cont'd)
N ↓ Alcohol Rehabilitation [82]
Detoxification [73]
R ↓ Drug Abstinence [94]
Drug Usage Screening [88]
↓ Drugs [67]
Employee Assistance Programs [85]
Methadone Maintenance [78]
↓ Psychosocial Rehabilitation [73]
Rehabilitation Counseling [78]
Smoking Cessation [88]
Sobriety [88]
↓ Twelve Step Programs [97]

Drug Sensitivity [73]
PN 928 SC 15360
SN Behavioral or physical sensitivity, resistance, or reactivity to a particular chemical substance.
UF Sensitivity (Drugs)
B Side Effects (Drug) [73]
R Drug Allergies [73]
Drug Tolerance [73]

Drug Synergism
SN Use DRUG SYNERGISM or DRUG POTENTIATION to access references from 73–81.
Use Drug Interactions

Drug Testing
Use Drug Usage Screening

Drug Therapy [67]
PN 29193 SC 15380
SN Mandatory term applied to studies dealing with any aspect of drug therapy in clinical contexts.
UF Chemotherapy
Medication
Pharmacotherapy
Therapy (Drug)
B Organic Therapies [73]
N Hormone Therapy [94]
↓ Narcoanalysis [73]
R Bioavailability [91]
Detoxification [73]
Drug Overdoses [78]
↓ Drugs [67]
Maintenance Therapy [97]
Neuroleptic Malignant Syndrome [88]
↓ Outpatient Treatment [67]
Prescribing (Drugs) [91]
Prescription Drugs [91]
Self Medication [91]
↓ Side Effects (Drug) [73]
Sleep Treatment [73]
Tardive Dyskinesia [88]
Treatment Resistant Depression [94]

Drug Tolerance [73]
PN 1601 SC 15390
SN Condition in which, after repeated administration, a drug produces a decreased effect and must be administered in larger doses to produce the effect of the original dose.
UF Tolerance (Drug)
R Drug Sensitivity [73]
↓ Drugs [67]
↓ Side Effects (Drug) [73]

Drug Usage [71]
PN 4291 SC 15400
SN Act, amount, or mode of using any type of drug. Applies only to humans and should be used when neither abuse nor addiction are the subject matter, regardless of the legality of the particular drug.
N ↓ Alcohol Drinking Patterns [67]
↓ Drug Abuse [73]
Intravenous Drug Usage [94]

Drug Usage — (cont'd)
N Marihuana Usage [73]
Tobacco Smoking [67]
R ↓ Addiction [73]
Craving [97]
Driving Under The Influence [88]
↓ Drug Abstinence [94]
Drug Distribution [97]
↓ Drug Legalization [97]
Drug Overdoses [78]
Drug Usage Screening [88]
↓ Drugs [67]
Needle Sharing [94]

Drug Usage Attitudes [73]
PN 948 SC 15410
B Attitudes [67]
N Alcohol Drinking Attitudes [73]
R Health Attitudes [85]
Marihuana Legalization [73]

Drug Usage Screening [88]
PN 203 SC 15415
SN Procedures used to measure or detect prevalence of drug use through analysis of blood, urine, or other body fluids. Not used for measuring the clinical efficacy of therapeutic drugs.
UF Drug Testing
B Screening [82]
R Blood Alcohol Concentration [94]
↓ Drug Abuse [73]
↓ Drug Dependency [73]
↓ Drug Rehabilitation [73]
↓ Drug Usage [71]
↓ Drugs [67]
↓ Health Screening [97]
↓ Medical Diagnosis [73]
Physical Examination [88]
Urinalysis [73]

Drug Withdrawal [73]
PN 2079 SC 15420
SN Processes and symptomatic effects resulting from abstinence from a chemical agent or medication. Used for human or animal populations. Use DRUG WITHDRAWAL or DRUG WITHDRAWAL EFFECTS to access references from 73–81.
UF Drug Withdrawal Effects
Withdrawal (Drug)
N Alcohol Withdrawal [94]
Nicotine Withdrawal [97]
R Detoxification [73]
↓ Drug Abstinence [94]
↓ Drug Addiction [67]

Drug Withdrawal Effects
SN Term discontinued in 1982. Use DRUG WITHDRAWAL EFFECTS or DRUG WITHDRAWAL to access references from 73–81.
Use Drug Withdrawal

Drugs [67]
PN 4387 SC 15440
SN Conceptually broad array term referring to any substance other than food administered for experimental or treatment purposes. Use specific drug classes or names if possible.
UF Cardiotonic Drugs
Drug Effects
Narcoanalytic Drugs
Psychoactive Drugs
Psychotropic Drugs
N ↓ Adrenergic Blocking Drugs [73]
↓ Adrenergic Drugs [73]
↓ Alcohols [67]
↓ Alkaloids [73]
↓ Amines [73]
↓ Analgesic Drugs [73]

Drugs — (cont'd)
N ↓ Anesthetic Drugs [73]
↓ Anti Inflammatory Drugs [82]
Antiandrogens [82]
↓ Antibiotics [73]
↓ Anticoagulant Drugs [73]
↓ Anticonvulsive Drugs [73]
↓ Antidepressant Drugs [71]
↓ Antiemetic Drugs [73]
Antiestrogens [82]
↓ Antihistaminic Drugs [73]
↓ Antihypertensive Drugs [73]
Antineoplastic Drugs [82]
↓ Antispasmodic Drugs [73]
↓ Antitremor Drugs [73]
↓ Antitubercular Drugs [73]
↓ Antiviral Drugs [94]
↓ Appetite Depressing Drugs [73]
↓ Barbiturates [67]
↓ Benzodiazepines [78]
Bromides [73]
↓ Cannabis [73]
Channel Blockers [91]
↓ Cholinergic Blocking Drugs [73]
↓ Cholinergic Drugs [73]
↓ Cholinomimetic Drugs [73]
↓ CNS Affecting Drugs [73]
↓ Diuretics [73]
↓ Dopamine Agonists [85]
↓ Emetic Drugs [73]
↓ Enzyme Inhibitors [85]
↓ Enzymes [73]
↓ Ergot Derivatives [73]
↓ Ganglion Blocking Drugs [73]
↓ Hallucinogenic Drugs [67]
↓ Heart Rate Affecting Drugs [73]
↓ Hypnotic Drugs [73]
↓ Muscle Relaxing Drugs [73]
↓ Narcotic Agonists [88]
↓ Narcotic Antagonists [73]
↓ Narcotic Drugs [73]
Nonprescription Drugs [91]
↓ Nootropic Drugs [91]
Prescription Drugs [91]
↓ Psychedelic Drugs [73]
↓ Psychotomimetic Drugs [73]
↓ Respiration Stimulating Drugs [73]
↓ Sedatives [73]
Serotonin Agonists [88]
↓ Serotonin Antagonists [73]
↓ Steroids [73]
↓ Sympatholytic Drugs [73]
↓ Sympathomimetic Drugs [73]
↓ Tranquilizing Drugs [67]
↓ Vasoconstrictor Drugs [73]
↓ Vasodilator Drugs [73]
R ↓ Acids [73]
Antibodies [73]
Bioavailability [91]
Carcinogens [73]
↓ Drug Abuse [73]
↓ Drug Administration Methods [73]
Drug Discrimination [85]
↓ Drug Dosages [73]
Drug Education [73]
Drug Interactions [82]
↓ Drug Laws [73]
↓ Drug Rehabilitation [73]
↓ Drug Therapy [67]
Drug Tolerance [73]
↓ Drug Usage [71]
Drug Usage Screening [88]
↓ Hormones [67]
↓ Insecticides [73]
↓ Peptides [73]
Placebo [73]
Prenatal Exposure [91]
Prescribing (Drugs) [91]
↓ Proteins [73]

Drugs — (cont'd)
R Self Medication [91]
↓ Side Effects (Drug) [73]
Teratogens [88]
Toxicity [73]
↓ Vitamins [73]

Drunk Driving
Use Driving Under The Influence

Drunkenness
Use Alcohol Intoxication

DSM
Use Diagnostic and Statistical Manual

Dual Careers [82]
PN 514 SC 15455
SN Situation in which both partners or spouses in a family pursue careers.
R ↓ Family [67]
↓ Family Structure [73]
Family Work Relationship [97]
Working Women [78]

Dual Diagnosis [91]
PN 269 SC 15457
SN Diagnosis based on the coexistence of two or more DSM-III-R disorders.
R Comorbidity [91]
↓ Diagnosis [67]
Differential Diagnosis [67]
↓ Psychodiagnostic Typologies [67]

Dualism [73]
PN 377 SC 15460
SN Theory viewing mind and body as two separate and irreducible entities.
UF Mind Body
B Philosophies [67]
R Mind [91]

Duchennes Disease
Use Muscular Disorders

Ducks [73]
PN 280 SC 15480
B Birds [67]

Duodenum
Use Intestines

Duration (Response)
Use Response Duration

Duration (Stimulus)
Use Stimulus Duration

Dwarfism (Pituitary)
Use Hypopituitarism

Dyads [73]
PN 1605 SC 15540
B Social Groups [73]
R Couples [82]

Dying
Use Death and Dying

Dying Patients
Use Terminally Ill Patients

Dynamics (Group)
Use Group Dynamics

Dynorphins 85
PN 88 **SC** 15575
B Endogenous Opiates 85
Pituitary Hormones 73

Dysarthria 73
PN 177 **SC** 15580
SN Articulation disorder resulting from central nervous system disease, especially brain damage.
B Articulation Disorders 73
Central Nervous System Disorders 73
R Muscular Dystrophy 73
↓ Paralysis 73

Dyscalculia
Use Acalculia

Dysfunctional Family 91
PN 209 **SC** 15590
SN A family system in which relationships or communication are impaired.
R Codependency 91
Double Bind Interaction 73
↓ Family 67
↓ Family Relations 67
↓ Family Structure 73
Marital Conflict 73
Schizophrenogenic Family 67

Dyskinesia 73
PN 626 **SC** 15600
B Movement Disorders 85
Symptoms 67
N Tardive Dyskinesia 88
R ↓ Neuromuscular Disorders 73

Dyslexia 73
PN 1511 **SC** 15610
SN Reading disorder involving an inability to understand what is read. Less severe than alexia.
B Alexia 82
Learning Disabilities 73
Reading Disabilities 67
R Educational Diagnosis 78
↓ Reading 67

Dysmenorrhea 73
PN 91 **SC** 15620
SN Difficult and painful menstruation.
B Menstrual Disorders 73

Dysmetria
Use Ataxia

Dysmorphophobia 73
PN 73 **SC** 15640
SN Obsessive fear or delusional conviction that one is physically deformed or otherwise abnormal.
UF Atypical Somatoform Disorder
B Psychosomatic Disorders 67

Dyspareunia 73
PN 31 **SC** 15650
B Sexual Function Disturbances 73
Sexual Intercourse (Human) 73
R Frigidity 73
Vaginismus 73

Dysphasia 78
PN 142 **SC** 15655
SN Impairment of language comprehension, formulation, or use due to brain damage. Used only for partial impairments.
B Aphasia 67
N ↓ Alexia 82

Dysphonia 73
PN 165 **SC** 15660
SN Any speech disorder involving problems of voice quality, pitch, or intensity.
UF Voice Disorders
B Speech Disorders 67

Dysphoria
SN Use DEPRESSION (EMOTION) to access references from 73-87.
Use Major Depression

Dyspnea 73
PN 45 **SC** 15680
SN Difficulty in breathing which may or may not have an organic cause.
B Respiratory Distress 73
Respiratory Tract Disorders 73
Symptoms 67
N Asthma 67
R ↓ Cardiovascular Disorders 67
↓ Lung Disorders 73
↓ Psychosomatic Disorders 67

Dyspraxia
Use Movement Disorders

Dysthymia
SN Use DEPRESSION (EMOTION) to access references from 73-87.
Use Dysthymic Disorder

Dysthymic Disorder 88
PN 426 **SC** 15693
SN Chronic affective disorder characterized by either relatively mild depressive symptoms or marked loss of pleasure in usual activities. Consider DEPRESSION (EMOTION) to access references prior to 1988.
UF Dysthymia
B Major Depression 88
R Anhedonia 85

Dystonia
Use Muscular Disorders

Dystrophy (Muscular)
Use Muscular Dystrophy

Eagerness
Use Enthusiasm

Ear (Anatomy) 67
PN 439 **SC** 15720
B Sense Organs 73
N External Ear 73
↓ Labyrinth (Anatomy) 73
Middle Ear 73
↓ Vestibular Apparatus 67
R ↓ Ear Disorders 73

Ear Canal
Use External Ear

Ear Disorders 73
PN 210 **SC** 15740
SN Disorders of the external, middle, or inner ear. Use HEARING DISORDERS for pathology involving auditory neural pathways beyond the inner ear.
UF Otosclerosis
B Sense Organ Disorders 73
N ↓ Labyrinth Disorders 73
Tinnitus 73
R ↓ Auditory Perception 67
↓ Aurally Disabled 97
↓ Ear (Anatomy) 67

Ear Disorders — (cont'd)
R Hearing Disorders 82
↓ Sensorially Disabled 97

Ear Ossicles
Use Middle Ear

Early Childhood
Use Preschool Age Children

Early Childhood Development 73
PN 1127 **SC** 15770
SN Process of physical, cognitive, personality, and psychosocial growth occurring from birth through age 5. Use a more specific term if possible.
B Childhood Development 67
N ↓ Infant Development 73
R Early Experience 67
Early Memories 85
↓ Physical Development 73
↓ Psychogenesis 73

Early Experience 67
PN 4989 **SC** 15780
SN Any occurrences early in an individual's life. Used for human or animal populations.
B Experiences (Events) 73
R Age Regression (Hypnotic) 88
Anniversary Events 94
Autobiographical Memory 94
↓ Early Childhood Development 73
Early Memories 85
Enactments 97
Life Review 91

Early Infantile Autism 73
PN 432 **SC** 15790
B Autism 67
Childhood Psychosis 67
R Autistic Children 73
Childhood Schizophrenia 67
Symbiotic Infantile Psychosis 73

Early Intervention 82
PN 1450 **SC** 15793
SN Action taken utilizing medical, family, school, social, or mental health resources and aimed at infants and children at risk for, or in the early stages of mental, physical, learning, or other disorders.
R Drug Abuse Prevention 94
↓ Prenatal Care 91
↓ Prevention 73
Primary Mental Health Prevention 73
Special Education 67
Special Needs 94
↓ Treatment 67

Early Memories 85
PN 371 **SC** 15796
SN Memories of events that occurred early in an individual's life.
UF Childhood Memories
B Memory 67
R Age Regression (Hypnotic) 88
Anniversary Events 94
Autobiographical Memory 94
↓ Early Childhood Development 73
Early Experience 67
False Memory 97
Life Review 91
Reminiscence 85
Repressed Memory 97

Earthworms 73
PN 25 **SC** 15800
B Worms 67

East Africa 88
PN 10 SC 15805
B Africa 67

East German Democratic Republic
SN Term discontinued in 1982. Use EAST GERMAN DEMOCRATIC REPUBLIC to access references from 67-81.
Use East Germany

East Germany 82
PN 160 SC 15812
SN Use EAST GERMAN DEMOCRATIC REPUBLIC to access references from 67-81.
UF East German Democratic Republic
B Germany 88

Eastern Europe 88
PN 46 SC 15815
B Europe 73

Eating 67
PN 1413 SC 15820
SN Use EATING or EATING PATTERNS to access references prior to 1982. Limited to human populations.
UF Eating Patterns
B Food Intake 67
N Binge Eating 91
R ↓ Appetite 73
Craving 97
Dietary Restraint 94
Diets 78
Eating Attitudes 94
Food 78

Eating Attitudes 94
PN 61 SC 15823
B Attitudes 67
R ↓ Appetite 73
↓ Eating 67
Food Preferences 73
Obesity (Attitudes Toward) 97

Eating Disorders 97
PN 0 SC 15825
SN Use APPETITE DISORDERS to access references from 73-96.
UF Appetite Disorders
B Mental Disorders 67
N Anorexia Nervosa 73
Bulimia 85
Hyperphagia 73
Obesity 73
R Aphagia 73
↓ Appetite 73
Binge Eating 91
Nausea 73
↓ Nutritional Deficiencies 73
↓ Physical Disorders 97
↓ Symptoms 67
↓ Underweight 73

Eating Patterns
SN Term discontinued in 1982. Use EATING PATTERNS or EATING to access references prior to 1982.
Use Eating

Echinodermata 73
PN 32 SC 15840
UF Starfish
B Invertebrates 73

Echoencephalography 73
PN 8 SC 15850
B Encephalography 73
Medical Diagnosis 73

Echolalia 73
PN 86 SC 15870
B Language Disorders 82
R Gilles de la Tourette Disorder 73

Echolocation 73
PN 121 SC 15880
R ↓ Animal Ethology 67
↓ Animal Vocalizations 73

Eclectic Psychology
Use Theoretical Orientation

Eclectic Psychotherapy 94
PN 8 SC 15887
B Psychotherapy 67
R Interdisciplinary Treatment Approach 73
Multimodal Treatment Approach 91

Ecological Factors 73
PN 597 SC 15890
SN Elements involved in relations between organisms and their natural environments.
N Pollution 73
Topography 73
R Behavioral Ecology 97
Ecological Psychology 94
Ecology 73
↓ Environmental Effects 73

Ecological Psychology 94
PN 16 SC 15895
SN Branch of psychology that studies the frequency or nature of psychological processes or behavior as they occur in natural settings. Compare ENVIRONMENTAL PSYCHOLOGY.
B Psychology 67
R Behavioral Ecology 97
↓ Ecological Factors 73
Environmental Psychology 82

Ecology 73
PN 471 SC 15900
R Behavioral Ecology 97
Conservation (Ecological Behavior) 78
↓ Ecological Factors 73
↓ Environment 67
Environmental Attitudes 78
Environmental Education 94
Pollution 73

Economically Disadvantaged
Use Disadvantaged

Economics 85
PN 1271 SC 15915
SN Social science dealing with the production, distribution, and consumption of goods and services. Used for the discipline or economic factors themselves.
B Social Sciences 67
R Budgets 97
Cost Containment 91
↓ Costs and Cost Analysis 73
↓ Division of Labor 88
Economy 73
Health Care Costs 94
Money 67
↓ Political Economic Systems 73
Resource Allocation 97

Economy 73
PN 622 SC 15920
R Budgets 97
↓ Costs and Cost Analysis 73
Economics 85
Money 67

Economy — (cont'd)
R ↓ Political Economic Systems 73
Taxation 85

ECS Therapy
Use Electroconvulsive Shock Therapy

Ecstasy (Drug)
Use Methylenedioxymethamphetamine

ECT (Therapy)
Use Electroconvulsive Shock Therapy

Ecuador 88
PN 22 SC 15945
B South America 67

Eczema 73
PN 34 SC 15950
B Dermatitis 73
R Allergic Skin Disorders 73

Educable Mentally Retarded 73
PN 3150 SC 15960
SN IQ 50-70.
UF Mildly Mentally Retarded
B Mentally Retarded 67
R Slow Learners 73

Education 67
PN 5876 SC 16000
SN Conceptually broad array term referring to the process of imparting or obtaining knowledge, skills, and values. Use a more specific term if possible.
UF Educational Process
Training
N ↓ Adult Education 73
Bilingual Education 78
Client Education 85
↓ Clinical Methods Training 73
Communication Skills Training 82
Counselor Education 73
↓ Curriculum 67
Death Education 82
Elementary Education 73
↓ Family Life Education 97
↓ Higher Education 73
Middle School Education 85
Multicultural Education 88
↓ Nontraditional Education 82
Nursing Education 73
Paraprofessional Education 73
Parent Training 78
↓ Personnel Training 67
Preschool Education 73
Private School Education 73
Public School Education 73
Religious Education 73
↓ Remedial Education 85
Secondary Education 73
Social Work Education 73
Special Education 67
↓ Teacher Education 67
R Ability Grouping 73
↓ Academic Achievement 67
Academic Aptitude 73
Accreditation (Education Personnel) 73
Athletic Training 91
Boards of Education 78
Classroom Behavior Modification 73
Classroom Discipline 73
Coeducation 73
↓ Dropouts 73
Educational Administration 67
Educational Aspirations 73
↓ Educational Background 67
Educational Counseling 67

Education — (cont'd)
R Educational Degrees 73
Educational Diagnosis 78
Educational Financial Assistance 73
Educational Incentives 73
↓ Educational Laboratories 73
↓ Educational Measurement 67
Educational Objectives 78
↓ Educational Personnel 73
Educational Placement 78
Educational Program Accreditation 94
↓ Educational Programs 73
↓ Educational Psychology 67
Educational Quality 97
Educational Reform 97
Educational Television 67
Environmental Education 94
Equal Education 78
↓ Extracurricular Activities 73
Grade Level 94
Home Schooling 94
Mainstreaming (Educational) 78
Psychoeducation 94
Questioning 82
School Adjustment 67
School Attendance 73
School Counseling 82
↓ School Dropouts 67
↓ School Enrollment 73
↓ School Environment 73
↓ School Facilities 73
School Graduation 91
School Integration 82
School Learning 67
School Readiness 73
School to Work Transition 94
School Transition 97
School Truancy 73
↓ Schools 67
Student Admission Criteria 73
Student Attitudes 67
↓ Student Characteristics 82
Student Personnel Services 78
Student Records 78
↓ Students 67
Study Habits 73
↓ Teacher Characteristics 73
Teacher Student Interaction 73
Teacher Tenure 73
↓ Teaching 67
↓ Teaching Methods 67
Theories of Education 73

Education Students 82
PN 354 SC 15995
SN Students enrolled in a school or department of education.
B College Students 67
R Preservice Teachers 82
Student Teachers 73
↓ Teacher Education 67

Educational Administration 67
PN 1992 SC 16010
UF School Administration
School Organization
B Management 67
R Boards of Education 78
Decentralization 78
↓ Education 67
Educational Reform 97

Educational Administrators
Use School Administrators

Educational Aspirations 73
PN 843 SC 16020
SN Personal desire for achievement in a certain educational field or to a certain level or degree.

Educational Aspirations — (cont'd)
B Aspirations 67
R Academic Specialization 73
↓ Education 67
Educational Objectives 78

Educational Attainment Level 97
PN 0 SC 16025
SN Completion of a course of study or reaching a specific educational level.
UF Attainment Level (Education)
B Educational Background 67
R ↓ Academic Achievement 67
Educational Degrees 73
School Graduation 91
School to Work Transition 94

Educational Audiovisual Aids 73
PN 224 SC 16030
UF Audiovisual Aids (Educational)
B Audiovisual Communications Media 73
Instructional Media 67
N Motion Pictures (Educational) 73
R ↓ Audiovisual Instruction 73
Educational Television 67
Film Strips 67
Televised Instruction 73
Videotape Instruction 73

Educational Background 67
PN 3594 SC 16040
N Educational Attainment Level 97
Parent Educational Background 73
R Biographical Data 78
↓ Education 67
School Leavers 88

Educational Background (Parents)
Use Parent Educational Background

Educational Counseling 67
PN 2446 SC 16060
SN Assistance offered to school or college students on school program planning, course selection, or academic specialization. Compare SCHOOL COUNSELING.
UF Educational Guidance
Guidance (Educational)
B Counseling 67
R ↓ Education 67
Occupational Guidance 67
Student Personnel Services 78

Educational Degrees 73
PN 585 SC 16070
UF College Degrees
Degrees (Educational)
Graduate Degrees
High School Diplomas
Undergraduate Degrees
R College Graduates 82
↓ Education 67
Educational Attainment Level 97
Educational Program Accreditation 94
High School Graduates 78
↓ Higher Education 73
School Graduation 91

Educational Diagnosis 78
PN 2391 SC 16075
SN Identification of cognitive, perceptual, emotional, and other factors which influence academic performance or school adjustment, usually for such purposes as placement of students in curricula or programs suited to their needs, and referral.
B Diagnosis 67
R Differential Diagnosis 67
Dyslexia 73

Educational Diagnosis — (cont'd)
R ↓ Education 67
↓ Educational Measurement 67
Educational Placement 78
↓ Learning Disabilities 73
↓ Learning Disorders 67
↓ Psychodiagnosis 67
Psychological Report 88
↓ Reading Disabilities 67
Woodcock Johnson Psychoed Battery 94

Educational Environment
Use School Environment

Educational Field Trips 73
PN 55 SC 16080
UF Field Trips (Educational)
B Teaching Methods 67
R Curricular Field Experience 82
↓ Experiential Learning 97

Educational Financial Assistance 73
PN 132 SC 16090
UF Financial Assistance (Educational)
Scholarships
School Federal Aid
School Financial Assistance
Stipends
R ↓ Education 67
Funding 88
Student Personnel Services 78

Educational Guidance
Use Educational Counseling

Educational Incentives 73
PN 106 SC 16120
SN Any type of incentive used or experienced in a school, classroom, or other educational context.
B Incentives 67
Motivation 67
R ↓ Education 67

Educational Inequality
Use Equal Education

Educational Laboratories 73
PN 139 SC 16130
UF Laboratories (Educational)
B School Facilities 73
N Language Laboratories 73
R ↓ Education 67

Educational Measurement 67
PN 4106 SC 16140
SN Practices, procedures, methods, and tests used in the assessment of student characteristics or performance, such as academic achievement and school adjustment.
B Testing 67
N Curriculum Based Assessment 94
↓ Entrance Examinations 73
Grading (Educational) 73
Minimum Competency Tests 85
R ↓ Education 67
Educational Diagnosis 78
↓ Screening 82

Educational Objectives 78
PN 1057 SC 16145
SN Specific educational goals toward which one's efforts are directed, or goals proposed or established by educational authorities.
UF Course Objectives
Instructional Objectives
B Goals 67
R ↓ Curriculum 67

Educational Objectives — (cont'd)
R ↓ Educational [67]
Educational Aspirations [73]
Educational Quality [97]
Educational Reform [97]
Mastery Learning [85]

Educational Personnel [73]
PN 1825 SC 16150
UF Faculty
B Professional Personnel [78]
N ↓ School Administrators [73]
School Counselors [73]
School Nurses [73]
Teacher Aides [73]
↓ Teachers [67]
R ↓ Education [67]
↓ Educational Psychologists [73]
↓ Mental Health Personnel [67]
Missionaries [73]
Professional Supervision [88]
Speech Therapists [73]
↓ Volunteer Personnel [73]

Educational Placement [78]
PN 1480 SC 16155
SN Assignment of students to classes, programs, or schools according to their abilities and readiness.
UF Placement (Educational)
R Ability Grouping [73]
↓ Education [67]
Educational Diagnosis [78]
Grade Level [94]
↓ Mainstreaming [91]
Mainstreaming (Educational) [78]
Remedial Reading [73]
↓ Screening [82]
Special Education [67]

Educational Process
Use Education

Educational Program Accreditation [94]
PN 35 SC 16165
SN Recognition and approval of educational programs or institution's maintenance of standards to qualify graduates for professional practice or admission to higher or more specialized educational institutions.
UF Accreditation (Educational Programs)
School Accreditation
R ↓ Curriculum [67]
↓ Education [67]
Educational Degrees [73]
↓ Educational Programs [73]
Educational Quality [97]
↓ Graduate Psychology Education [67]
↓ Higher Education [73]
↓ Psychology Education [78]

Educational Program Evaluation [73]
PN 2094 SC 16170
SN Techniques, materials, or process of determining the worth or effectiveness of an educational program in relation to its goals or other criteria.
UF Program Evaluation (Educational)
B Program Evaluation [85]
R Behavioral Assessment [82]
Course Evaluation [78]
↓ Educational Programs [73]
Educational Quality [97]

Educational Program Planning [73]
PN 897 SC 16180
UF Program Planning (Educational)
B Program Development [91]

Educational Program Planning — (cont'd)
R Curriculum Development [73]
↓ Educational Programs [73]

Educational Programs [73]
PN 4839 SC 16190
UF Work Study Programs
N Foreign Study [73]
Literacy Programs [97]
Project Follow Through [73]
Project Head Start [73]
Special Education [67]
Upward Bound [73]
R Compensatory Education [73]
Cooperative Education [82]
Curricular Field Experience [82]
↓ Education [67]
Educational Program Accreditation [94]
Educational Program Evaluation [73]
Educational Program Planning [73]
Educational Reform [97]
Multicultural Education [88]
↓ Nontraditional Education [82]
↓ Program Development [91]

Educational Psychologists [73]
PN 301 SC 16200
SN Psychologists conducting research and formulating policies in areas of diagnosis and measurement, school adjustment, school learning, and special education.
B Psychologists [67]
N School Psychologists [73]
R ↓ Educational Personnel [73]

Educational Psychology [67]
PN 1158 SC 16210
SN Branch of psychology that emphasizes the application of psychological theories and research findings to educational processes, especially in the areas of learning and motivation.
B Applied Psychology [73]
N School Psychology [73]
R ↓ Education [67]

Educational Quality [97]
PN 0 SC 16205
UF Quality of Education
R Accreditation (Education Personnel) [73]
Course Evaluation [78]
↓ Education [67]
Educational Objectives [78]
Educational Program Accreditation [94]
Educational Program Evaluation [73]
Educational Reform [97]
Equal Education [78]
Teacher Effectiveness Evaluation [78]

Educational Reform [97]
PN 0 SC 16217
R ↓ Education [67]
Educational Administration [67]
Educational Objectives [78]
↓ Educational Programs [73]
Educational Quality [97]
↓ Policy Making [88]

Educational Supervision
Use Professional Supervision

Educational Television [67]
PN 155 SC 16220
B Television [67]
R ↓ Education [67]
↓ Educational Audiovisual Aids [73]
Televised Instruction [73]

Educational Theory
Use Theories of Education

Educational Therapy [97]
PN 0 SC 16225
SN Use SCHOOL COUNSELING to access references from 82–96.
R Art Therapy [73]
Music Therapy [73]
Psychoeducation [94]
↓ Psychotherapy [67]
↓ Remedial Education [85]
School Counseling [82]
Special Education [67]
↓ Teaching Methods [67]

Educational Toys [73]
PN 20 SC 16230
B Toys [73]

Edwards Personal Preference Schedule [67]
PN 107 SC 16240
B Nonprojective Personality Measures [73]

Edwards Personality Inventory [73]
PN 6 SC 16250
B Nonprojective Personality Measures [73]

Edwards Social Desirability Scale [73]
PN 11 SC 16260
B Nonprojective Personality Measures [73]

EEG (Electrophysiology)
Use Electroencephalography

Effect Size (Statistical) [85]
PN 118 SC 16272
SN A statistical estimate that represents the magnitude of a statistically significant result.
UF Magnitude of Effect (Statistical)
B Statistical Analysis [67]
R Confidence Limits (Statistics) [73]
Statistical Significance [73]

Efferent Pathways [82]
PN 291 SC 16275
SN Collections of fibers that typically carry neural impulses away from central nervous system connections toward muscular and glandular innervations.
UF Motor Pathways
B Neural Pathways [82]
Parasympathetic Nervous System [73]
N Extrapyramidal Tracts [73]
Pyramidal Tracts [73]
R ↓ Afferent Pathways [82]
Motor Neurons [73]
↓ Motor Processes [67]

Efficacy Expectations
Use Self Efficacy

Efficiency (Employee)
Use Employee Efficiency

Effort
Use Energy Expenditure

Egalitarianism [85]
PN 40 SC 16287
B Personality Traits [67]
R Authoritarianism [67]
↓ Equity (Social) [78]
Resource Allocation [97]

Ego 67
PN 3153 **SC** 16290
B Psychoanalytic Personality Factors 73
R ↓ Ego Development 91
Ego Identity 91

Ego Development 91
PN 282 **SC** 16294
SN Gradual emergence development of a part of the id into the ego or an awareness of a child that he or she is a real distinct and separate entity.
B Personality Development 67
N Ego Identity 91
R Ego 67
↓ Psychoanalytic Theory 67

Ego Identity 91
PN 151 **SC** 16297
SN The experience of the self as a recognizable entity resulting from one's ego ideal, behavior and social roles, and adjustments to reality.
B Ego Development 91
R Ego 67
Erikson (Erik) 91
↓ Personality Development 67
↓ Self Concept 67

Egocentrism 78
PN 547 **SC** 16300
SN Self-centered preoccupation or concern regarding one's own needs, wishes, desires, or preferences and usually accompanied by a disregard for the concerns of others. Also, in cognitive development, the inclination to believe that others maintain the same experiential perspective as oneself. Use EGOCENTRISM to access references to role taking or perspective taking from 78–81.
R Agreeableness 97
↓ Cognitive Development 73
↓ Concept Formation 67
Narcissism 67
↓ Personality 67
↓ Personality Traits 67
Role Taking 82

Egotism 73
PN 118 **SC** 16310
B Personality Traits 67
R Emotional Superiority 73
Grandiosity 94

Egypt 82
PN 166 **SC** 16315
SN Use UNITED ARAB REPUBLIC to access references from 73–81.
UF United Arab Republic
B Africa 67
R Middle East 78

Eidetic Imagery 73
PN 91 **SC** 16320
SN Clear and detailed memory for objects or events perceived, usually visually.
UF Photographic Memory
B Memory 67
R Episodic Memory 88
↓ Spatial Memory 88
↓ Visual Memory 94

Ejaculation
Use Male Orgasm

EKG (Electrophysiology)
Use Electrocardiography

El Salvador 88
PN 22 **SC** 16345
B Central America 73

Elavil
Use Amitriptyline

Elbow (Anatomy) 73
PN 54 **SC** 16360
B Joints (Anatomy) 73
R Arm (Anatomy) 73

Elder Abuse 88
PN 97 **SC** 16363
SN Abuse or neglect of elderly persons in a family, institutional, or other setting.
B Antisocial Behavior 71
R ↓ Abuse Reporting 97
↓ Aged 73
Emotional Abuse 91
↓ Family Violence 82
Patient Abuse 91
Physical Abuse 91
↓ Sexual Abuse 88

Elder Care 94
PN 73 **SC** 16364
SN Informal or formal support systems or programs for the care of the elderly or assistance to the families who have responsibilities for their care.
R Adult Day Care 97
↓ Aged 73
Caregiver Burden 94
Caregivers 88
Employee Assistance Programs 85
↓ Employee Benefits 73
Home Care 85
Home Care Personnel 97
Home Visiting Programs 73
Homebound 88
Protective Services 97

Elected Government Officials
Use Government Personnel

Elections (Political)
Use Political Elections

Elective Abortion
Use Induced Abortion

Elective Mutism 73
PN 158 **SC** 16390
B Mental Disorders 67
Mutism 73

Electra Complex 73
PN 5 **SC** 16400
B Psychoanalytic Personality Factors 73

Electric Fishes 73
PN 83 **SC** 16410
B Fishes 67

Electrical Activity 67
PN 6847 **SC** 16420
SN Electrically measured responses or response patterns, usually of individual units (i.e., cells) or groups of cells, in any part of the nervous system. Includes neural or neuron impulses; neural depolarization or hyperpolarization; spike, resting, action, generator, graded, presynaptic, or postsynaptic potentials. Compare ELECTROPHYSIOLOGY.
B Electrophysiology 73
N Alpha Rhythm 73
↓ Cortical Evoked Potentials 73

Electrical Activity — (cont'd)
N Delta Rhythm 73
↓ Evoked Potentials 67
Kindling 85
Postactivation Potentials 85
Theta Rhythm 73
R Electrocardiography 67
↓ Electroencephalography 67

Electrical Brain Stimulation 73
PN 2998 **SC** 16430
B Brain Stimulation 67
Electrical Stimulation 73
Electrophysiology 73
Stereotaxic Techniques 73
R ↓ Evoked Potentials 67
Kindling 85
Postactivation Potentials 85
↓ Self Stimulation 67

Electrical Injuries 73
PN 14 **SC** 16440
B Injuries 73
R Burns 73
Shock 67
↓ Wounds 73

Electrical Stimulation 73
PN 1484 **SC** 16460
B Stimulation 67
N Electrical Brain Stimulation 73
↓ Electroconvulsive Shock 67
R Experimental Epilepsy 78
Shock 67

Electro Oculography 73
PN 127 **SC** 16470
UF EOG (Electrophysiology)
B Electrophysiology 73
Medical Diagnosis 73
Ophthalmologic Examination 73
R Electroretinography 67

Electrocardiography 67
PN 278 **SC** 16480
UF EKG (Electrophysiology)
B Cardiography 73
Electrophysiology 73
R ↓ Electrical Activity 67

Electroconvulsive Shock 67
PN 791 **SC** 16490
B Electrical Stimulation 73
N Electroconvulsive Shock Therapy 67
R Shock 67

Electroconvulsive Shock Therapy 67
PN 1951 **SC** 16500
UF ECS Therapy
ECT (Therapy)
Electroshock Therapy
B Electroconvulsive Shock 67
Shock Therapy 73

Electrodermal Response
Use Galvanic Skin Response

Electrodes 67
PN 244 **SC** 16520
B Apparatus 67
R ↓ Stimulators (Apparatus) 73

Electroencephalography 67
PN 7126 **SC** 16530

Electroencephalography — (cont'd)
SN Method of graphically recording the electrical activity (potentials) of the brain by means of intracranial electrodes or electrodes applied to the scalp. Used both for the method as well as the resulting electroencephalogram or the electrophysiological activity itself.
UF EEG (Electrophysiology)
B Electrophysiology 73
Encephalography 73
Medical Diagnosis 73
N Alpha Rhythm 73
Delta Rhythm 73
Theta Rhythm 73
R ↓ Electrical Activity 67
Magnetoencephalography 85
Rheoencephalography 73

Electrolytes 73
PN 192 **SC** 16540
UF Ions
N Calcium Ions 73
Chloride Ions 73
Magnesium Ions 73
Potassium Ions 73
Sodium Ions 73
Zinc 85
R ↓ Chemical Elements 73

Electromyography 67
PN 2100 **SC** 16550
UF EMG (Electrophysiology)
B Electrophysiology 73
Medical Diagnosis 73

Electronystagmography 73
PN 9 **SC** 16560
B Electrophysiology 73
Medical Diagnosis 73

Electrophysiology 73
PN 1312 **SC** 16570
SN Branch of physiology concerned with the study of electrical phenomena within the living organism (i.e., nerve and muscle tissue). Used for the scientific discipline or the electrophysiological processes themselves. Compare ELECTRICAL ACTIVITY.
B Physiology 67
N ↓ Electrical Activity 67
Electrical Brain Stimulation 73
Electro Oculography 73
Electrocardiography 67
↓ Electroencephalography 67
Electromyography 67
Electronystagmography 73
Electroplethysmography 73
Electroretinography 67
Galvanic Skin Response 67
↓ Skin Electrical Properties 73
Skin Potential 73
R ↓ Medical Diagnosis 73

Electroplethysmography 73
PN 6 **SC** 16580
B Electrophysiology 73
Medical Diagnosis 73
Plethysmography 73

Electroretinography 67
PN 162 **SC** 16590
B Electrophysiology 73
Medical Diagnosis 73
Ophthalmologic Examination 73
R Electro Oculography 73

Electroshock Therapy
Use Electroconvulsive Shock Therapy

Electrosleep Treatment 78
PN 15 **SC** 16605
SN Therapeutic application of a low intensity, intermittent electrical current to the skull, often producing a state of relaxation, but not necessarily sleep.
B Organic Therapies 73
R ↓ Shock Therapy 73
Sleep Treatment 73

Elementarism
Use Reductionism

Elementary Education 73
PN 711 **SC** 16620
B Education 67
R Elementary Schools 73

Elementary School Students 67
PN 24756 **SC** 16630
SN Students in grades 1-6. Mandatory term in educational contexts.
B Students 67
N Intermediate School Students 73
Primary School Students 73
R ↓ Children 67
Grade Level 94
Middle School Students 85
Preadolescents 88
↓ School Age Children 73

Elementary School Teachers 73
PN 4207 **SC** 16640
B Teachers 67

Elementary Schools 73
PN 640 **SC** 16650
UF Grammar Schools
Primary Schools
B Schools 67
R Elementary Education 73

Elephants 73
PN 34 **SC** 16660
B Mammals 73

Elimination (Excretion)
Use Excretion

Ellis (Albert) 91
PN 6 **SC** 16680
SN Identifies biographical or autobiographical studies and discussions of Ellis's works.
R ↓ Psychologists 67
Rational Emotive Therapy 78
Self Talk 88

Embarrassment 73
PN 150 **SC** 16690
B Emotional States 73
R Shame 94

Embedded Figures Testing 67
PN 166 **SC** 16700
B Nonprojective Personality Measures 73

Embolisms 73
PN 22 **SC** 16710
B Cardiovascular Disorders 67
R ↓ Thromboses 73

Embryo 73
PN 150 **SC** 16720
B Prenatal Developmental Stages 73

EMDR
Use Eye Movement Desensitization Therapy

Emergency Services 73
PN 899 **SC** 16730
R ↓ Crisis Intervention Services 73
Natural Disasters 73

Emetic Drugs 73
PN 71 **SC** 16740
UF Vomit Inducing Drugs
B Drugs 67
N Apomorphine 73
Disulfiram 78
R ↓ CNS Stimulating Drugs 73
↓ Narcotic Drugs 73
Vomiting 73

EMG (Electrophysiology)
Use Electromyography

Emotional Abuse 91
PN 153 **SC** 16755
UF Psychological Abuse
B Antisocial Behavior 71
R ↓ Child Abuse 71
Child Neglect 88
Elder Abuse 88
Erotomania 97
Partner Abuse 91
Patient Abuse 91
Physical Abuse 91

Emotional Adjustment 73
PN 5892 **SC** 16760
SN Personal acceptance, adaptation, and relation to one's inner self and environment.
UF Emotional Maladjustment
Maladjustment (Emotional)
Personal Adjustment
Psychological Adjustment
B Adjustment 67
N ↓ Emotional Control 73
Identity Crisis 73
R Adjustment Disorders 94
Codependency 91
Coping Behavior 67
↓ Emotionally Disturbed 73
↓ Emotions 67
Hardiness 97
↓ Mental Disorders 67
↓ Mental Health 67
↓ Personality 67
Psychopathology 67

Emotional Content 73
PN 1058 **SC** 16765
SN Emotional themes, substance, form, or characteristics of feelings, especially as they are portrayed in various forms of communication (e.g., reading material, motion pictures) or as manifested in specific situations.
R ↓ Communication 67
↓ Emotions 67

Emotional Control 73
PN 179 **SC** 16770
SN Directing or governing one's own or another's emotions. Not to be confused with EMOTIONAL MATURITY which involves the exhibition of emotional behavior appropriate to one's age.
UF Control (Emotional)
Emotional Restraint
B Emotional Adjustment 73
N Anger Control 97
R Coping Behavior 67
Internal External Locus of Control 67
Self Control 73
Social Control 88
Tantrums 73

Emotional Development 73
PN 1485 **SC** 16780
B Psychogenesis 73
R Attachment Behavior 85
Childhood Play Development 73
↓ Developmental Age Groups 73
↓ Emotions 67
Object Relations 82
↓ Personality Development 67
↓ Physical Development 73
Psychosexual Development 82
↓ Psychosocial Development 73

Emotional Expressiveness
Use Emotionality (Personality)

Emotional Immaturity 73
PN 40 **SC** 16800
SN Tendency to exhibit emotional reactions considered inappropriate for one's age.
UF Immaturity (Emotional)
B Personality Traits 67
R Emotional Maturity 73

Emotional Inferiority 73
PN 44 **SC** 16810
SN Conscious or unconscious feelings of insecurity, insignificance, and inadequacy and of being unable to cope with life's demands.
UF Inferiority (Emotional)
B Personality Traits 67
R Neuroticism 73

Emotional Insecurity
Use Emotional Security

Emotional Instability 73
PN 84 **SC** 16830
SN Tendency to display unpredictable and rapidly changing emotions or moods.
UF Instability (Emotional)
B Personality Traits 67
R Emotional Stability 73
Neuroticism 73

Emotional Maladjustment
Use Emotional Adjustment

Emotional Maturity 73
PN 365 **SC** 16850
SN Attainment of a level of emotional development and exhibition of emotional patterns commonly associated with persons of a specific age level. Not to be confused with EMOTIONAL CONTROL which involves the suppression or control of direction of one's emotions.
UF Maturity (Emotional)
B Personality Traits 67
R Emotional Immaturity 73

Emotional Needs
Use Psychological Needs

Emotional Responses 67
PN 4741 **SC** 16860
SN From 1982, limited to human populations. Use ANIMAL EMOTIONALITY for nonhuman subjects.
B Responses 67
N Conditioned Emotional Responses 67
R Animal Emotionality 78
↓ Emotions 67
Laughter 78
Stranger Reactions 88

Emotional Restraint
Use Emotional Control

Emotional Security 73
PN 275 **SC** 16880
SN Possession of inner resources enabling one to cope with unfamiliar or threatening situations, especially as engendered through early nurturance.
UF Emotional Insecurity
Insecurity (Emotional)
Security (Emotional)
B Personality Traits 67
R Emotional Stability 73

Emotional Stability 73
PN 266 **SC** 16890
SN Resistance to affective disruption or tendency toward evenness of feelings.
UF Stability (Emotional)
B Personality Traits 67
R Emotional Instability 73
Emotional Security 73
Hardiness 97
Neuroticism 73

Emotional States 73
PN 6451 **SC** 16900
UF Moods
B Emotions 67
N Affection 73
Alienation 71
Ambivalence 73
↓ Anger 67
↓ Anxiety 67
Apathy 73
↓ Aversion 67
Boredom 73
Depression (Emotion) 67
Disappointment 73
Disgust 94
Dissatisfaction 73
Distress 73
Doubt 73
Embarrassment 73
Emotional Trauma 67
Enthusiasm 73
Euphoria 73
↓ Fear 67
Frustration 67
Grief 73
Guilt 67
Happiness 73
↓ Helplessness 97
Homesickness 94
Hope 91
Hopelessness 88
Jealousy 73
Loneliness 73
Love 73
↓ Mania 67
Mental Confusion 73
Optimism 73
Pessimism 73
Pleasure 73
Pride 73
Restlessness 73
Sadness 73
Shame 94
Suffering 73
Suspicion 73
Sympathy 73
R Abandonment 97
Craving 97
↓ Emotionally Disturbed 73
Irritability 88
Learned Helplessness 78
Morale 78
↓ Personality 67

Emotional Superiority 73
PN 21 **SC** 16910

Emotional Superiority — (cont'd)
SN Feeling that one is better than others in ability, virtue, or worth.
UF Superiority (Emotional)
B Personality Traits 67
R ↓ Dominance 67
Egotism 73
Grandiosity 94

Emotional Trauma 67
PN 1485 **SC** 16920
UF Trauma (Emotional)
B Emotional States 73
R Adjustment Disorders 94
False Memory 97
Posttraumatic Stress Disorder 85
Repressed Memory 97
↓ Separation Reactions 97

Emotionality (Animal)
Use Animal Emotionality

Emotionality (Personality) 73
PN 947 **SC** 16930
SN Personality trait characteristic of a person who tends to react strongly or excessively to emotional situations.
UF Emotional Expressiveness
B Personality Traits 67
R ↓ Emotions 67
Neuroticism 73

Emotionally Disturbed 73
PN 3417 **SC** 16940
B Disabled 97
N Autistic Children 73
R Acting Out 67
↓ Childhood Psychosis 67
↓ Emotional Adjustment 73
↓ Emotional States 73
↓ Emotions 67

Emotions 67
PN 5454 **SC** 16960
SN Conceptually broad array term referring to the affective aspects of human consciousness. Use a more specific term if possible. Use ANIMAL EMOTIONALITY for nonhuman subjects.
UF Feelings
N ↓ Emotional States 73
R ↓ Emotional Adjustment 73
Emotional Content 73
Emotional Development 73
↓ Emotional Responses 67
Emotionality (Personality) 73
↓ Emotionally Disturbed 73
Expressed Emotion 91
Human Nature 97
Morale 78
↓ Personality 67

Empathy 67
PN 2764 **SC** 16970
B Personality Traits 67
R Agreeableness 97

Emphysema (Pulmonary)
Use Pulmonary Emphysema

Empirical Methods 73
PN 615 **SC** 16990
SN Scientific methodology based on experimentation, systematic observation, or measurement, rather than theoretical formulation.
B Methodology 67
N ↓ Experimental Methods 67
Observation Methods 67

Empirical Methods — (cont'd)
R Behavioral Assessment 82
Positivism (Philosophy) 97

Employability 73
PN 413 SC 17000
SN Potential usefulness of an individual as judged on the basis of job skills, functional literacy, emotional or social maturity, intellectual development, or personal values (e.g., personal responsibility).
R ↓ Employee Skills 73
↓ Employment Status 82
↓ Personnel 67
Supported Employment 94
Vocational Evaluation 91

Employee Absenteeism 73
PN 620 SC 17010
UF Absenteeism (Employee)
R ↓ Personnel 67

Employee Assistance Programs 85
PN 747 SC 17015
SN Programs or services provided by the employer to help employees with personal or other matters, including retirement planning or alcohol rehabilitation.
B Employee Benefits 73
R ↓ Counseling 67
Disability Management 91
↓ Drug Rehabilitation 73
Elder Care 94
↓ Program Development 91
↓ Support Groups 91

Employee Attitudes 67
PN 3636 SC 17020
SN Attitudes of, not toward, employees.
B Attitudes 67
Employee Characteristics 88
N Job Satisfaction 67
R Employee Motivation 73
Job Involvement 78
↓ Job Performance 67
Organizational Commitment 91
Work (Attitudes Toward) 73

Employee Benefits 73
PN 262 SC 17030
SN Benefits provided by an employer that may be voluntary or mandated by federal or state law.
N Bonuses 73
Employee Assistance Programs 85
↓ Employee Health Insurance 73
Employee Leave Benefits 73
Employee Pension Plans 73
Workmens Compensation Insurance 73
R Disability Evaluation 88
Elder Care 94
↓ Personnel 67
Salaries 73

Employee Characteristics 88
PN 604 SC 17035
N ↓ Employee Attitudes 67
Employee Efficiency 73
Employee Motivation 73
Employee Productivity 73
↓ Employee Skills 73
Job Experience Level 73
Job Knowledge 97
R Organizational Commitment 91
↓ Personnel 67
Professional Competence 97
Professional Identity 91

Employee Efficiency 73
PN 117 SC 17040

Employee Efficiency — (cont'd)
UF Efficiency (Employee)
B Employee Characteristics 88
Job Performance 67

Employee Health Insurance 73
PN 32 SC 17050
B Employee Benefits 73
Health Insurance 73
N Workmens Compensation Insurance 73

Employee Interaction 88
PN 809 SC 17055
SN Dynamics of interpersonal interactions between employees.
B Interpersonal Interaction 67
Organizational Behavior 78
N Supervisor Employee Interaction 97
R ↓ Personnel 67

Employee Leave Benefits 73
PN 49 SC 17060
UF Annual Leave
Sick Leave
Vacation Benefits
B Employee Benefits 73

Employee Motivation 73
PN 1365 SC 17080
B Employee Characteristics 88
Motivation 67
R ↓ Employee Attitudes 67
Job Involvement 78

Employee Pension Plans 73
PN 15 SC 17090
UF Pension Plans (Employee)
B Employee Benefits 73

Employee Productivity 73
PN 962 SC 17110
UF Productivity (Employee)
B Employee Characteristics 88
Job Performance 67

Employee Selection
Use Personnel Selection

Employee Skills 73
PN 365 SC 17130
B Ability 67
Employee Characteristics 88
N Clerical Secretarial Skills 73
R Employability 73
Job Knowledge 97
Professional Competence 97
Supported Employment 94
Vocational Evaluation 91

Employee Supervisor Interaction
Use Supervisor Employee Interaction

Employee Termination
Use Personnel Termination

Employee Turnover 73
PN 953 SC 17140
UF Personnel Turnover
Turnover
R Employment History 78
Job Security 78
↓ Occupational Tenure 73
↓ Personnel 67

Employees
Use Personnel

Employer Attitudes 73
PN 345 SC 17160
SN Attitudes of, not toward, employers.
B Attitudes 67
R Organizational Commitment 91
↓ Personnel 67
Work (Attitudes Toward) 73

Employment
Use Employment Status

Employment Discrimination 94
PN 38 SC 17173
SN Prejudiced and differential treatment of employees or job applicants based on factors other than performance or qualifications.
UF Job Discrimination
B Social Discrimination 82
R Affirmative Action 85
Age Discrimination 94
Job Applicant Screening 73
↓ Personnel Evaluation 73
↓ Personnel Management 73
↓ Personnel Selection 67
↓ Prejudice 67
Race and Ethnic Discrimination 94
Racism 73
Sex Discrimination 78
Sexism 88

Employment History 78
PN 331 SC 17174
SN Past record of an individual's working life, including periods of unemployment.
R Career Change 78
Career Development 85
Employee Turnover 73
↓ Employment Status 82
Job Experience Level 73
Occupational Mobility 73
Occupational Success 78
↓ Occupational Tenure 73
↓ Occupations 67
↓ Personnel 67
Personnel Promotion 78
Personnel Termination 73
Professional Development 82
Retirement 73
Unemployment 67

Employment Interviews
Use Job Applicant Interviews

Employment Processes
Use Personnel Recruitment

Employment Status 82
PN 2157 SC 17196
SN Condition of employment including full- or part-time, temporary or permanent, and unemployment. Use OCCUPATIONS to access references from 67–81.
UF Employment
N Self Employment 94
Unemployment 67
R Employability 73
Employment History 78
Job Applicants 85
↓ Occupational Tenure 73
Reemployment 91
Retirement 73
Supported Employment 94
Working Women 78

Employment Tests 73
PN 311 SC 17200
SN Tests used in personnel selection to measure the suitability of an applicant for a given occupation.

Employment Tests — (cont'd)
B Measurement 67
R Job Applicant Screening 73

Empowerment 91
PN 405 **SC** 17203
SN Promotion or attainment of autonomy and freedom of choice for individuals or groups.
R Advocacy 85
Assertiveness 73
↓ Civil Rights 78
↓ Client Rights 88
↓ Helplessness 97
Independence (Personality) 73
↓ Involvement 73
↓ Power 67
Self Determination 94

Empty Nest 91
PN 10 **SC** 17205
SN Home environment after children have reached maturity and left home. Also, includes the concept of adult children returning to the home.
UF Return to Home
R Adult Offspring 85
↓ Family 67
↓ Family Relations 67
Family Size 73
↓ Family Structure 73
Home Environment 73
Intergenerational Relations 88
↓ Living Arrangements 91
↓ Parent Child Relations 67

Enabling 97
PN 0 **SC** 17207
B Social Influences 67
R Codependency 91
Dependency (Personality) 67
↓ Social Reinforcement 67

Enactments 97
PN 0 **SC** 17209
SN Regressive or defensive interactions between a therapist and client or interaction between two or more people that reenacts past experiences or emotional conflicts of one or more of the persons involved.
UF Reenactments
R Acting Out 67
Age Regression (Hypnotic) 88
Countertransference 73
Early Experience 67
↓ Interpersonal Interaction 67
Projective Identification 94
↓ Psychotherapeutic Processes 67
Psychotherapeutic Transference 67
Reminiscence 85

Encephalitis 73
PN 203 **SC** 17210
B Brain Disorders 67
Viral Disorders 73
R Encephalomyelitis 73
↓ Infectious Disorders 73

Encephalography 73
PN 12 **SC** 17220
B Medical Diagnosis 73
N Echoencephalography 73
↓ Electroencephalography 67
Pneumoencephalography 73
Rheoencephalography 73
R ↓ Roentgenography 73

Encephalography (Air)
Use Pneumoencephalography

Encephalomyelitis 73
PN 26 **SC** 17240
B Myelitis 73
R Encephalitis 73
↓ Infectious Disorders 73

Encephalopathies 82
PN 234 **SC** 17247
SN Degenerative diseases of the brain.
B Brain Disorders 67
N Creutzfeldt Jakob Syndrome 94
Toxic Encephalopathies 73
Wernickes Syndrome 73
R Chronic Fatigue Syndrome 97
Thyrotoxicosis 73

Encoding
Use Human Information Storage

Encopresis
Use Fecal Incontinence

Encounter Group Therapy 73
PN 243 **SC** 17270
SN Goal-oriented unstructured groups whose members seek heightened self-awareness and fulfillment of their human potential. The group leader (not necessarily a clinically trained therapist) participates freely in the group activity. Techniques used include role playing, sensory awareness, and physical contact.
B Group Psychotherapy 67
Human Potential Movement 82
N Marathon Group Therapy 73
R Consciousness Raising Groups 78
Human Relations Training 78
Sensitivity Training 73

Encouragement 73
PN 109 **SC** 17290
B Social Interaction 67
R ↓ Social Reinforcement 67

Endocrine Disorders 73
PN 130 **SC** 17300
B Physical Disorders 97
N ↓ Adrenal Gland Disorders 73
↓ Diabetes 73
Endocrine Neoplasms 73
↓ Endocrine Sexual Disorders 73
Parathyroid Disorders 73
↓ Pituitary Disorders 73
↓ Thyroid Disorders 73
R ↓ Endocrine System 73
Hypothermia 73
Migraine Headache 73
↓ Psychosomatic Disorders 67
↓ Secretion (Gland) 73

Endocrine Gland Secretion 73
PN 88 **SC** 17310
B Secretion (Gland) 73
N Adrenal Gland Secretion 73
R ↓ Endocrine Glands 73

Endocrine Gland Surgery 73
PN 5 **SC** 17320
B Surgery 71
N Adrenalectomy 73
↓ Castration 67
Hypophysectomy 73
Pinealectomy 73
Thyroidectomy 73

Endocrine Glands 73
PN 32 **SC** 17330
B Endocrine System 73
Glands 67

Endocrine Glands — (cont'd)
N ↓ Adrenal Glands 73
↓ Gonads 73
Parathyroid Glands 73
Pineal Body 73
↓ Pituitary Gland 73
Thyroid Gland 73
R ↓ Endocrine Gland Secretion 73
↓ Hormones 67
Pancreas 73

Endocrine Neoplasms 73
PN 15 **SC** 17340
B Endocrine Disorders 73
Neoplasms 67

Endocrine Sexual Disorders 73
PN 34 **SC** 17350
UF Ovary Disorders
Testes Disorders
B Endocrine Disorders 73
Genital Disorders 67
N ↓ Hypogonadism 73
Testicular Feminization Syndrome 73
R ↓ Adrenal Gland Disorders 73
↓ Gynecological Disorders 73
Hermaphroditism 73
↓ Infertility 73
↓ Male Genital Disorders 73
↓ Pituitary Disorders 73
↓ Thyroid Disorders 73

Endocrine System 73
PN 166 **SC** 17360
B Anatomical Systems 73
N ↓ Endocrine Glands 73
R ↓ Endocrine Disorders 73
Pancreas 73

Endocrinology 73
PN 136 **SC** 17370
SN Scientific discipline dealing with the study of endocrine glands and internal secretions.
B Medical Sciences 67
N Neuroendocrinology 85
R Psychoneuroimmunology 91

Endogamous Marriage 73
PN 17 **SC** 17380
B Marriage 67
N Consanguineous Marriage 73

Endogenous Depression 78
PN 1119 **SC** 17384
B Major Depression 88

Endogenous Opiates 85
PN 284 **SC** 17385
UF Opioids (Endogenous)
B Opiates 73
Peptides 73
N Dynorphins 85
↓ Endorphins 82

Endorphins 82
PN 697 **SC** 17386
SN Endogenous morphine-like brain polypeptides that can bind to opiate receptors.
B Endogenous Opiates 85
Neurotransmitters 85
Proteins 73
N Enkephalins 82
R Analgesia 82

Endurance 73
PN 70 **SC** 17390
SN Ability to withstand hardship, adversity, or stress. Used for human or animal populations.

Endurance — (cont'd)
N Physical Endurance 73
Psychological Endurance 73
R ↓ Stress 67

Energy Expenditure 67
PN 1119 **SC** 17400
SN Expenditure of mental or physical effort.
UF Effort
R Calories 73
Metabolic Rates 73

Engineering Psychology 67
PN 477 **SC** 17410
SN Branch of applied psychology that emphasizes the study of machine design, the relationship between humans and machines, and the effects of machines on human behavior. Use a more specific term if possible.
B Applied Psychology 73
R Human Factors Engineering 73

Engineers 67
PN 556 **SC** 17420
B Professional Personnel 78
R ↓ Aerospace Personnel 73
↓ Business and Industrial Personnel 67
Scientists 67

England 73
PN 1419 **SC** 17430
B Great Britain 71

English as Second Language 97
PN 0 **SC** 17450
UF ESL
R Bilingual Education 78
Bilingualism 73
Foreign Language Education 73
Foreign Languages 73
↓ Language 67
↓ Language Arts Education 73
Language Proficiency 88
↓ Multilingualism 73

Enjoyment
Use Pleasure

Enkephalins 82
PN 405 **SC** 17475
SN Endogenous morphine-like brain polypeptides closely related to endorphins.
B Endorphins 82
R Analgesia 82
↓ Peptides 73

Enlisted Military Personnel 73
PN 207 **SC** 17480
SN Military personnel ranking below commissioned officers.
B Military Personnel 67
N Draftees 73
Noncommissioned Officers 73
R Volunteer Military Personnel 73

Enlistment (Military)
Use Military Enlistment

Enrollment (School)
Use School Enrollment

Enteropeptidase
Use Kinases

Enthusiasm 73
PN 35 **SC** 17530

Enthusiasm — (cont'd)
UF Eagerness
B Emotional States 73
R Morale 78
↓ Motivation 67

Entrance Examinations 73
PN 131 **SC** 17540
B Educational Measurement 67
N Coll Ent Exam Bd Scholastic Apt Test 73
R Student Admission Criteria 73

Entrapment Games 73
PN 14 **SC** 17550
B Games 67
R ↓ Collective Behavior 67
Game Theory 67
Non Zero Sum Games 73
Prisoners Dilemma Game 73

Entrepreneurship 91
PN 111 **SC** 17555
SN Initiation, organization, management, and assumption of the attendant risks of a business or enterprise.
R Business 67
Business Management 73
Capitalism 73
↓ Leadership 67
↓ Management 67
Ownership 85
↓ Private Sector 85
Self Employment 94

Enuresis
Use Urinary Incontinence

Environment 67
PN 4519 **SC** 17570
SN Totality of physical, social, psychological, or cultural conditions surrounding an organism.
N ↓ Facility Environment 88
↓ Social Environments 73
R ↓ Architecture 73
Ecology 73
Environmental Adaptation 73
Environmental Attitudes 78
Environmental Education 94
↓ Environmental Planning 82
Environmental Stress 73
Geography 73
↓ Hazardous Materials 91
Nature Nurture 94
Person Environment Fit 91
Physical Comfort 82
Urban Planning 73

Environmental Adaptation 73
PN 362 **SC** 17590
SN Physiological or biological adaptation to conditions in the physical environment. For psychological, social, or emotional adaptation use ADJUSTMENT or one of its related terms.
UF Adaptation (Environmental)
B Adaptation 67
R ↓ Environment 67
Person Environment Fit 91

Environmental Attitudes 78
PN 892 **SC** 17594
SN Perceptions of or beliefs regarding the physical environment, including factors affecting its quality (e.g., overpopulation, pollution).
B Attitudes 67
R Conservation (Ecological Behavior) 78
Ecology 73
↓ Environment 67
Environmental Education 94

Environmental Design
Use Environmental Planning

Environmental Education 94
PN 37 **SC** 17598
SN Used for educational and noneducational settings.
R Conservation (Ecological Behavior) 78
Ecology 73
↓ Education 67
↓ Environment 67
Environmental Attitudes 78
Pollution 73

Environmental Effects 73
PN 817 **SC** 17600
N Altitude Effects 73
Atmospheric Conditions 73
↓ Gravitational Effects 67
Noise Effects 73
Seasonal Variations 73
↓ Temperature Effects 67
Underwater Effects 73
R ↓ Ecological Factors 73
Environmental Stress 73
Lunar Synodic Cycle 73
Physiological Stress 67

Environmental Planning 82
PN 335 **SC** 17607
SN Planning and design of environment with goals of efficient human-environment interaction and minimal ecological disruption.
UF Environmental Design
N Interior Design 82
Urban Planning 73
R ↓ Architecture 73
Computer Assisted Design 97
↓ Environment 67
Person Environment Fit 91
↓ Recreation Areas 73

Environmental Psychology 82
PN 285 **SC** 17609
SN Branch of psychology that studies the relationship between environmental variables and behavior, including manipulation of one by the other.
B Applied Psychology 73
R Behavioral Ecology 97
Ecological Psychology 94

Environmental Stress 73
PN 503 **SC** 17610
SN Naturally occurring or experimentally manipulated qualities of the physical environment which result in strain or disequilibrium. Consider also other specific terms (e.g., CROWDING, NOISE EFFECTS).
B Stress 67
R Crowding 78
↓ Deprivation 67
↓ Environment 67
↓ Environmental Effects 73
Overpopulation 73
Physiological Stress 67
Thermal Acclimatization 73

Environmental Therapy
Use Milieu Therapy

Envy
Use Jealousy

Enzyme Inhibitors 85
PN 156 **SC** 17625
SN Any agent that slows or otherwise disrupts the activity of an enzyme, such as antienzymes or enzyme antibodies.

Enzyme Inhibitors — (cont'd)
B Drugs 67
N Acetazolamide 73
↓ Amine Oxidase Inhibitors 73
Bromocriptine 88
Captopril 91
↓ Cholinesterase Inhibitors 73
↓ Decarboxylase Inhibitors 82
Hydroxylase Inhibitors 85
↓ Monoamine Oxidase Inhibitors 73
Theophylline 73
R ↓ Enzymes 73

Enzymes 73
PN 673 SC 17630
UF Aldolases
Carbonic Anhydrase
B Drugs 67
N Decarboxylases 73
↓ Dehydrogenases 73
↓ Esterases 73
Hydroxylases 73
Isozymes 73
Kinases 82
↓ Oxidases 73
Phosphatases 73
Phosphorylases 73
Proteinases 73
↓ Transferases 73
R ↓ Anti Inflammatory Drugs 82
↓ Decarboxylase Inhibitors 82
↓ Enzyme Inhibitors 85
↓ Proteins 73

EOG (Electrophysiology)
Use Electro Oculography

Ependyma
Use Cerebral Ventricles

Ephedrine 73
PN 29 SC 17660
B Adrenergic Drugs 73
Alcohols 67
Alkaloids 73
CNS Stimulating Drugs 73
Sympathomimetic Amines 73
Vasoconstrictor Drugs 73
R ↓ Local Anesthetics 73

Epidemiology 73
PN 5328 SC 17670
SN Study of the occurrence, distribution, and containment of disease or mental disorders. Used for the scientific discipline as a whole or for specific epidemiological factors or findings (e.g., disease incidence or prevalence statistics).
B Medical Sciences 67

Epilepsy 67
PN 3375 SC 17680
B Brain Disorders 67
N ↓ Epileptic Seizures 73
Experimental Epilepsy 78
Grand Mal Epilepsy 73
Petit Mal Epilepsy 73
R ↓ Anticonvulsive Drugs 73
Aura 73
↓ Brain Damage 67
Fugue Reaction 73

Epileptic Seizures 73
PN 587 SC 17690
B Brain Disorders 67
Epilepsy 67
N Experimental Epilepsy 78
R Coma 73
↓ Convulsions 67

Epinephrine 67
PN 745 SC 17700
UF Adrenaline
B Adrenergic Drugs 73
Catecholamines 73
Heart Rate Affecting Drugs 73
Hormones 67
R Vasoconstriction 73
Vasodilation 73

Episcopalians
Use Protestants

Episodic Memory 88
PN 160 SC 17705
B Memory 67
R Eidetic Imagery 73

Epistemology 73
PN 786 SC 17710
SN Philosophical study of knowledge, including its origin, nature, and limits.
B Philosophies 67
R Determinism 97
Hermeneutics 91
Metaphysics 73
Positivism (Philosophy) 97
Relativism 97

Epithelial Cells 73
PN 10 SC 17720
B Cells (Biology) 73
R Skin (Anatomy) 67

Epithelium
Use Skin (Anatomy)

Epstein Barr Viral Disorder 94
PN 9 SC 17740
B Infectious Disorders 73
Viral Disorders 73
R Chronic Fatigue Syndrome 97

Equal Education 78
PN 128 SC 17745
SN Provision of comparable educational opportunities to all individuals irrespective of race, national origin, religion, sex, socioeconomic status, or ability.
UF Educational Inequality
B Civil Rights 78
R ↓ Education 67
Educational Quality 97
School Integration 82
Social Equality 73

Equality (Social)
Use Social Equality

Equilibrium 73
PN 334 SC 17760
SN Maintenance of postural balance. For physiological equilibrium consider HOMEOSTASIS.
UF Balance (Motor Processes)
R ↓ Perceptual Motor Processes 67
Spatial Orientation (Perception) 73

Equimax Rotation 73
PN 2 SC 17770
B Orthogonal Rotation 73

Equipment
Use Apparatus

Equity (Payment) 78
PN 493 SC 17784
SN In society, group, or other interpersonal situations, the process of equal allocation of economic resources, rewards, or payoffs.
B Equity (Social) 78
R ↓ Justice 73
Money 67
Resource Allocation 97
Salaries 73
↓ Social Behavior 67
↓ Social Processes 67

Equity (Social) 78
PN 492 SC 17786
SN In society, group, or other interpersonal situations, the maintenance of relationships in which the proportions of each member's societal and cultural contributions or benefits are approximately equal.
N Equity (Payment) 78
R Egalitarianism 85
↓ Justice 73
Resource Allocation 97
↓ Social Behavior 67
↓ Social Processes 67

Erection (Penis) 73
PN 402 SC 17790
B Psychosexual Behavior 67
R Impotence 73

Ergonomics
Use Human Factors Engineering

Ergot Derivatives 73
PN 138 SC 17810
B Drugs 67
N Bromocriptine 88
Dihydroergotamine 73
R ↓ Adrenergic Blocking Drugs 73
↓ Alkaloids 73
Lysergic Acid Diethylamide 67
Tyramine 73

Erikson (Erik) 91
PN 33 SC 17815
SN Identifies biographical or autobiographical studies and discussions of Erikson's works.
R ↓ Developmental Stages 73
Ego Identity 91
↓ Neopsychoanalytic School 73
↓ Psychoanalysis 67
↓ Psychoanalytic Theory 67
↓ Psychologists 67
↓ Psychosocial Development 73

Eroticism 73
PN 391 SC 17820
B Sexual Arousal 78
R Autoeroticism 97
Inhibited Sexual Desire 97

Erotomania 97
PN 0 SC 17823
R ↓ Antisocial Behavior 71
Attachment Behavior 85
Delusions 67
Emotional Abuse 91
Grandiosity 94
Hypersexuality 73
Love 73
Obsessions 67
Partner Abuse 91
↓ Psychosexual Behavior 67
Sexual Fantasy 97
Victimization 73

Errata [91]
PN 786 **SC** 17825
SN Mandatory term applied to corrections of errors in the text, abstract, or data of previously published material. Also used as a document type identifier.
R ↓ Errors [67]
Retraction of Publication [91]
↓ Scientific Communication [73]

Error Analysis [73]
PN 554 **SC** 17830
SN Collection, classification and/or analysis of mistakes, especially in task or test performance.
B Analysis [67]
R ↓ Errors [67]
Human Machine Systems [97]

Error of Measurement [85]
PN 205 **SC** 17835
SN Observed differences in obtained scores or measures due to chance variance.
UF Error Variance
Standard Error of Measurement
B Errors [67]
Statistical Analysis [67]
R Consistency (Measurement) [73]
Least Squares [85]
↓ Scoring (Testing) [73]
Standard Deviation [73]
↓ Statistical Estimation [85]
↓ Statistical Measurement [73]
↓ Test Bias [85]
Test Reliability [73]
↓ Test Scores [67]

Error Variance
Use Error of Measurement

Errors [67]
PN 2075 **SC** 17840
SN Inappropriate, inaccurate, or incorrect responses or performance. Also, factual errors or other informational inaccuracies and performance errors on the part of others to which a subject reacts.
UF Mistakes
N Error of Measurement [85]
↓ Prediction Errors [73]
↓ Refraction Errors [73]
R Errata [91]
Error Analysis [73]
Halo Effect [82]
Proofreading [88]

Erythroblastosis Fetalis
Use Rh Incompatibility

Erythrocytes [73]
PN 305 **SC** 17860
UF Red Blood Cells
B Blood Cells [73]
R Blood Groups [73]

Escape
Use Avoidance

Escape Behavior (Animal)
Use Animal Escape Behavior

Escape Conditioning [73]
PN 409 **SC** 17890
SN Learned behavior or the operant conditioning procedure in which the subject learns a specific behavior that results in the termination of an ongoing aversive stimulus. Consider also NEGATIVE REINFORCEMENT. Compare AVOIDANCE CONDITIONING.

Escape Conditioning — (cont'd)
UF Conditioning (Escape)
B Operant Conditioning [67]

Eserine
Use Physostigmine

Eskimos [73]
PN 197 **SC** 17910
SN Native populations of northern Canada, Greenland, Alaska, and eastern Siberia.
B Ethnic Groups [73]
R Alaska Natives [97]
Minority Groups [67]

ESL
Use English as Second Language

Esophagus [73]
PN 87 **SC** 17920
B Digestive System [67]

ESP (Parapsychology)
Use Extrasensory Perception

Essay Testing [73]
PN 61 **SC** 17940
B Testing Methods [67]

Essential Hypertension [73]
PN 300 **SC** 17950
B Hypertension [73]

Esterases [73]
PN 31 **SC** 17970
B Enzymes [73]
N Acetylcholinesterase [73]
Cholinesterase [73]
R Hydroxylases [73]
Phosphatases [73]

Estimation [67]
PN 1261 **SC** 17980
SN Subjective judgment or inference about the character, quality, or nature of a person, process, or thing which may or may not involve the inspection or availability of data or pertinent information.
N ↓ Statistical Estimation [85]
Time Estimation [67]
R ↓ Expectations [67]
↓ Prediction [67]

Estradiol [73]
PN 976 **SC** 18000
B Estrogens [73]

Estrogen Antagonists
Use Antiestrogens

Estrogen Replacement Therapy
Use Hormone Therapy

Estrogens [73]
PN 678 **SC** 18010
B Sex Hormones [73]
N Estradiol [73]
Estrone [73]
R Antiandrogens [82]
Antiestrogens [82]

Estrone [73]
PN 10 **SC** 18020
B Estrogens [73]

Estrus [73]
PN 529 **SC** 18030

Estrus — (cont'd)
R ↓ Animal Biological Rhythms [73]
Animal Sexual Receptivity [73]
↓ Menstrual Cycle [73]
↓ Menstruation [73]

Ethanal
Use Acetaldehyde

Ethanol [73]
PN 3469 **SC** 18040
UF Alcohol (Grain)
Ethyl Alcohol
B Alcohols [67]
R Fetal Alcohol Syndrome [85]

Ether (Anesthetic) [73]
PN 42 **SC** 18050
UF Ethyl Ether (Anesthetic)
B General Anesthetics [73]

Ethics [67]
PN 1071 **SC** 18060
SN For ethics in social or cultural situations, consider MORALITY.
N Experimental Ethics [78]
Professional Ethics [73]
R Euthanasia [73]
Integrity [97]
Morality [67]
↓ Religious Beliefs [73]
↓ Social Influences [67]
↓ Values [67]

Ethiopia [82]
PN 53 **SC** 18064
B Africa [67]

Ethnic Differences
Use Racial and Ethnic Differences

Ethnic Discrimination
Use Race and Ethnic Discrimination

Ethnic Disorders
Use Ethnospecific Disorders

Ethnic Groups [73]
PN 2959 **SC** 18080
N Alaska Natives [97]
American Indians [67]
Anglos [88]
Arabs [88]
↓ Asians [82]
Eskimos [73]
Gypsies [73]
↓ Hispanics [82]
R Blacks [82]
Cross Cultural Psychology [97]
Cultural Sensitivity [94]
Ethnic Values [73]
Ethnology [67]
↓ Ethnospecific Disorders [73]
Jews [97]
Minority Groups [67]
Multiculturalism [97]
↓ Racial and Ethnic Attitudes [82]
Racial and Ethnic Differences [82]
Tribes [73]
Whites [82]

Ethnic Identity [73]
PN 1368 **SC** 18090
SN Feelings, ties, or associations that an individual experiences as a member of a particular ethnic group.

Ethnic Identity — (cont'd)
B Sociocultural Factors 67
R Cultural Sensitivity 94
Ingroup Outgroup 97
Reference Groups 94
↓ Self Concept 67
↓ Social Identity 88

Ethnic Sensitivity
Use Cultural Sensitivity

Ethnic Values 73
PN 256 SC 18100
B Social Influences 67
Sociocultural Factors 67
Values 67
R Cultural Sensitivity 94
↓ Ethnic Groups 73

Ethnocentrism 73
PN 195 SC 18110
SN Exaggerated tendency to identify with one's own ethnic group, or the inclination to judge others in terms of standards and values of one's own group.
B Racial and Ethnic Attitudes 82
R Cross Cultural Psychology 97
↓ Social Identity 88

Ethnography 73
PN 466 SC 18120
SN Descriptive study of cultures and societies. Used for the scientific discipline or the descriptive analyses themselves. Consider also ETHNOLOGY.
R Anthropology 67
Ethnology 67
Folk Psychology 97
Kinship Structure 73
Race (Anthropological) 73
↓ Rites of Passage 73
↓ Sociocultural Factors 67

Ethnolinguistics 73
PN 162 SC 18130
SN A part of anthropological linguistics concerned with the interrelation between a language and the cultural behavior of those who speak it.
B Linguistics 73
R ↓ Dialect 73
Ethnology 67
Metalinguistics 94
Psycholinguistics 67
Slang 73
Sociolinguistics 85

Ethnology 67
PN 1538 SC 18140
SN Conceptually broad array term referring to the study of the origin, distribution, characteristics, and relations of the cultures or ethnic groups of the world. Also, a branch of anthropology dealing with the comparative or analytical study of human culture or societies. Use a more specific term if possible. Consider also ETHNOGRAPHY.
R Animism 73
Anthropology 67
Cross Cultural Differences 67
Cross Cultural Psychology 97
Cultism 73
↓ Culture (Anthropological) 67
↓ Culture Change 67
Culture Shock 73
↓ Ethnic Groups 73
Ethnography 73
Ethnolinguistics 73
↓ Ethnospecific Disorders 73
Folk Medicine 73

Ethnology — (cont'd)
R Folk Psychology 97
Folklore 91
Kinship 85
Kinship Structure 73
Myths 67
Race (Anthropological) 73
↓ Racial and Ethnic Attitudes 82
Racial and Ethnic Differences 82
Racial and Ethnic Relations 82
Shamanism 73
↓ Sociocultural Factors 67
Taboos 73
Transcultural Psychiatry 73
Witchcraft 73

Ethnospecific Disorders 73
PN 35 SC 18150
UF Ethnic Disorders
N Koro 94
Sickle Cell Disease 94
R Cross Cultural Psychology 97
↓ Ethnic Groups 73
Ethnology 67
↓ Mental Disorders 67
↓ Personality Disorders 67
↓ Physical Disorders 97
Transcultural Psychiatry 73

Ethology (Animal)
Use Animal Ethology

Ethyl Alcohol
Use Ethanol

Ethyl Ether (Anesthetic)
Use Ether (Anesthetic)

Ethylaldehyde
Use Acetaldehyde

Etiology 67
PN 7254 SC 18190
SN Study of the causes and origins of psychological or physical conditions. Used for the science itself or the specific etiological findings and processes.
UF Aetiology
Pathogenesis
R ↓ Disorders 67
↓ Mental Disorders 67
Patient History 73
↓ Physical Disorders 97

Etymology 73
PN 57 SC 18200
SN Branch of linguistic science which traces the origin of words and morphemes to their earliest determinable base in a given language group and describes historical changes in words. Used for the discipline or specific etymological aspects of given words.
UF Word Origins
B Linguistics 73
R Words (Phonetic Units) 67

Eugenics 73
PN 35 SC 18210
SN Applied science or the biosocial movement which advocates the use of practices aimed at improving the genetic composition of a population. Usually refers to human populations. Compare ANIMAL BREEDING, ANIMAL DOMESTICATION, and SELECTIVE BREEDING.
B Genetic Engineering 94
Genetics 67
Sciences 67
R ↓ Family Planning 73

Eugenics — (cont'd)
R Genetic Counseling 78
Reproductive Technology 88
Selective Breeding 73
↓ Sterilization (Sex) 73

Euphoria 73
PN 108 SC 18230
B Emotional States 73
R Happiness 73
Pleasure 73

Europe 73
PN 629 SC 18240
N Austria 73
Belgium 73
Bulgaria 82
Czechoslovakia 73
Eastern Europe 88
Finland 73
France 67
↓ Germany 88
Greece 73
Hungary 73
Iceland 82
↓ Ireland 73
Italy 67
Liechtenstein 91
Netherlands 73
Poland 73
Portugal 82
Romania 82
↓ Scandinavia 78
Spain 73
Switzerland 73
Union of Soviet Socialist Republics 67
↓ United Kingdom 73
Western Europe 88
Yugoslavia 73
R Commonwealth of Independent States 97

Eustachian Tube
Use Middle Ear

Euthanasia 73
PN 231 SC 18255
UF Mercy Killing
B Death and Dying 67
R Advance Directives 94
Assisted Suicide 97
Death Attitudes 73
↓ Ethics 67
Professional Ethics 73
↓ Treatment 67
Treatment Withholding 88

Evaluation 67
PN 3557 SC 18260
SN Conceptually broad term referring to the appraisal of the characteristics, significance, importance, or relative value of a person, organization, or thing.
N Course Evaluation 78
Forensic Evaluation 94
Geriatric Assessment 97
Needs Assessment 85
Peer Evaluation 82
↓ Personnel Evaluation 73
↓ Program Evaluation 85
↓ Psychiatric Evaluation 97
Self Evaluation 67
Treatment Effectiveness Evaluation 73
Vocational Evaluation 91
R Intake Interview 94
↓ Measurement 67
↓ Psychological Assessment 97
Psychological Report 88

Evaluation (Psychiatric)
Use Psychiatric Evaluation

Evaluation (Treatment Effectiveness)
Use Treatment Effectiveness Evaluation

Evangelists [73]
PN 48 **SC** 18320
B Religious Personnel [73]
R ↓ Clergy [73]
Lay Religious Personnel [73]
Missionaries [73]

Evidence (Legal)
Use Legal Evidence

Evoked Potentials [67]
PN 2385 **SC** 18330
B Electrical Activity [67]
N Auditory Evoked Potentials [73]
↓ Cortical Evoked Potentials [73]
Olfactory Evoked Potentials [73]
Somatosensory Evoked Potentials [73]
Visual Evoked Potentials [73]
R Electrical Brain Stimulation [73]
Sensory Gating [91]

Evolution (Theory of)
Use Theory of Evolution

Exceptional Children (Gifted)
Use Gifted

Exceptional Children (Handicapped)
Use Disabled

Excitation (Physiological)
Use Physiological Arousal

Excretion [67]
PN 578 **SC** 18370
UF Elimination (Excretion)
B Physiology [67]
N Defecation [67]
↓ Urination [67]

Executives
Use Top Level Managers

Exercise [73]
PN 2469 **SC** 18390
UF Physical Exercise
B Motor Processes [67]
N Aerobic Exercise [88]
Weightlifting [94]
Yoga [73]
R Health Behavior [82]
Movement Therapy [97]
Physical Fitness [73]
Weight Control [85]

Exhaustion
Use Fatigue

Exhibitionism [73]
PN 168 **SC** 18420
B Sexual Deviations [67]
R Voyeurism [73]

Existential Therapy [73]
PN 137 **SC** 18430

Existential Therapy — (cont'd)
SN Form of psychotherapy that deals with the here and now of the patient's total situation rather than with his/her past; it emphasizes emotional experiences rather than rational thinking, and stresses a person's responsibility for his/her own existence.
B Psychotherapy [67]
R Logotherapy [73]

Existentialism [67]
PN 717 **SC** 18440
SN Philosophy based on the analysis of the individual's existence in the world which holds that human existence cannot be completely described in scientific terms. Existentialism also stresses the freedom and responsibility of the individual as well as the uniqueness of religious and ethical experiences and the analysis of subjective phenomena such as anxiety, guilt, and suffering.
B Philosophies [67]
R Relativism [97]
↓ Religious Beliefs [73]

Exogamous Marriage [73]
PN 70 **SC** 18450
UF Interethnic Marriage
Intermarriage
B Marriage [67]
N Interfaith Marriage [73]
Interracial Marriage [73]

Expectant Fathers [85]
PN 76 **SC** 18455
B Expectant Parents [85]
R ↓ Fathers [67]

Expectant Mothers [85]
PN 205 **SC** 18456
B Expectant Parents [85]
R ↓ Mothers [67]

Expectant Parents [85]
PN 66 **SC** 18457
N Expectant Fathers [85]
Expectant Mothers [85]
R ↓ Parents [67]

Expectations [67]
PN 8089 **SC** 18460
SN Anticipation of future behavior or events. Also refers to investigations of the effects of that anticipation on behavior.
B Cognitions [85]
N Experimenter Expectations [73]
Parental Expectations [97]
Role Expectations [73]
Teacher Expectations [78]
R ↓ Estimation [67]
Future [91]
Halo Effect [82]
Hope [91]
Self Efficacy [85]
Self Fulfilling Prophecies [97]

Experience (Practice)
Use Practice

Experience Level [88]
PN 1516 **SC** 18495
SN Amount of practical knowledge, skill, or practice as a result of direct participation in a particular activity.
UF Expertise
N Job Experience Level [73]
R ↓ Knowledge Level [78]

Experience Level (Job)
Use Job Experience Level

Experiences (Events) [73]
PN 1953 **SC** 18510
SN Perceptual, emotional, and/or cognitive consequences associated with specific events or contexts. Compare LIFE EXPERIENCES.
N Anniversary Events [94]
Early Experience [67]
Life Experiences [73]
Vicarious Experiences [73]
R Combat Experience [91]
↓ Crises [71]
Familiarity [67]
Homesickness [94]
Near Death Experiences [85]
↓ Practice [67]

Experiences (Life)
Use Life Experiences

Experiential Learning [97]
PN 0 **SC** 18517
B Learning [67]
Teaching Methods [67]
N Curricular Field Experience [82]
R Apprenticeship [73]
Cooperative Education [82]
Discovery Teaching Method [73]
Educational Field Trips [73]
On the Job Training [73]
School Learning [67]

Experiential Psychotherapy [73]
PN 114 **SC** 18520
SN Psychotherapeutic approach, having some roots in existentialism, that emphasizes the concrete, lived, and felt experience of the client.
B Psychotherapy [67]

Experiment Controls [73]
PN 214 **SC** 18530
UF Control Groups
R ↓ Experimental Design [67]
↓ Experimental Subjects [85]
↓ Experimentation [67]
↓ Methodology [67]

Experiment Volunteers [73]
PN 312 **SC** 18540
UF Volunteers (Experiment)
B Experimental Subjects [85]
R Biased Sampling [73]
↓ Experimental Design [67]
Informed Consent [85]
Random Sampling [73]

Experimental Apparatus
Use Apparatus

Experimental Attrition [94]
PN 9 **SC** 18555
SN Reduction in the number of experimental subjects over time as a result of resignation or other factors.
UF Research Dropouts
R ↓ Dropouts [73]
↓ Experimental Subjects [85]
↓ Experimentation [67]

Experimental Design [67]
PN 3164 **SC** 18560
SN General procedural plan for conducting an experiment or other research study in view of the specific data desired. This may include identification of the independent and dependent variables; selection of subjects and their assignment to specific experimental conditions/treatments; the sequence of experimental conditions/treatments; and a method of analysis. Consider also EXPERIMENTAL METHODS.

Experimental Design — (cont'd)
UF Design (Experimental)
Research Design
N Between Groups Design 85
Cohort Analysis 88
Followup Studies 73
↓ Hypothesis Testing 73
↓ Longitudinal Studies 73
Repeated Measures 85
R Animal Models 88
Conjoint Measurement 94
Debriefing (Experimental) 91
Experiment Controls 73
Experiment Volunteers 73
↓ Experimental Methods 67
↓ Experimentation 67
↓ Methodology 67
↓ Population (Statistics) 73
Psychometrics 67
↓ Sampling (Experimental) 73
↓ Statistical Analysis 67
↓ Statistical Variables 73
↓ Test Construction 73

Experimental Epilepsy 78
PN 158 SC 18564
SN Paroxysmal transient disruption of normal electrical activity in the brain induced by chemical, electrical, or physical stimulation of the brain or by repetitive sensory stimulation.
B Epilepsy 67
Epileptic Seizures 73
R ↓ Convulsions 67
↓ Electrical Stimulation 73
Kindling 85

Experimental Ethics 78
PN 573 SC 18566
B Ethics 67
R Animal Welfare 85
Debriefing (Experimental) 91
↓ Experimentation 67
Fraud 94
Informed Consent 85
Professional Ethics 73

Experimental Instructions 67
PN 2592 SC 18570
SN Directions given to a subject participating in an experiment.
UF Instructions (Experimental)
R ↓ Experimentation 67
↓ Methodology 67

Experimental Laboratories 73
PN 273 SC 18580
UF Laboratories (Experimental)
R ↓ Experimentation 67
↓ Methodology 67

Experimental Methods 67
PN 3855 SC 18590
SN System of scientific investigation, usually based on a design and carried out under controlled conditions with the aim of testing a hypothesis, in which one or more variables is manipulated.
UF Scientific Methods
B Empirical Methods 73
N ↓ Stimulus Presentation Methods 73
R ↓ Experimental Design 67

Experimental Neurosis 73
PN 52 SC 18600

Experimental Neurosis — (cont'd)
SN Acute neurotic-like state produced experimentally by requiring discrimination or problem solving responses which are beyond the subject's ability or level of learning. Such states are induced by the repeated delivery of aversive stimulation following failure.
B Neurosis 67
R Experimental Psychosis 73
Learned Helplessness 78

Experimental Psychologists 73
PN 36 SC 18610
B Psychologists 67

Experimental Psychology 67
PN 519 SC 18620
B Psychology 67
R ↓ Experimentation 67

Experimental Psychosis 73
PN 13 SC 18630
SN Experimentally induced psychotic-like state or condition usually achieved through drug administration. Not to be confused with inadvertent induction of psychotic conditions resulting from toxic side effects in drug therapy. Compare TOXIC PSYCHOSES.
B Psychosis 67
R Experimental Neurosis 73
↓ Hallucinogenic Drugs 67
↓ Psychotomimetic Drugs 73

Experimental Replication 73
PN 3076 SC 18640
SN Mandatory term applied to replications of original research findings using same or different subjects or variations in procedure and instrumentation.
UF Replication (Experimental)
R ↓ Experimentation 67
↓ Methodology 67

Experimental Subjects 85
PN 459 SC 18645
SN Any individual who is, knowingly or unknowingly, a member of an experiment or research population. Used only when methodological or procedural aspects are discussed regarding research subjects. Used primarily for human populations.
UF Research Subjects
N Experiment Volunteers 73
R Debriefing (Experimental) 91
Experiment Controls 73
Experimental Attrition 94
↓ Experimentation 67

Experimentation 67
PN 12037 SC 18650
SN Conceptually broad array term referring to any or all aspects of scientific research. Use a more specific term if possible.
UF Investigation
Research
N ↓ Consumer Research 73
Interdisciplinary Research 85
R Animal Models 88
Causal Analysis 94
Debriefing (Experimental) 91
Experiment Controls 73
Experimental Attrition 94
↓ Experimental Design 67
Experimental Ethics 78
Experimental Instructions 67
Experimental Laboratories 73
Experimental Psychology 67
Experimental Replication 73
↓ Experimental Subjects 85
Experimenters 73

Experimentation — (cont'd)
R ↓ Measurement 67
↓ Methodology 67
↓ Population (Statistics) 73
Privileged Communication 73
Psychometrics 67
Psychophysics 67
↓ Sampling (Experimental) 73
↓ Statistical Analysis 67
↓ Statistical Correlation 67
Statistical Reliability 73
↓ Statistical Validity 73
↓ Statistical Variables 73
↓ Theories 67

Experimenter Bias 67
PN 417 SC 18660
SN Potential and unintentional influence on experimental outcomes caused by the experimenter.
UF Bias (Experimenter)
R Experimenter Expectations 73
Experimenters 73
Halo Effect 82

Experimenter Expectations 73
PN 136 SC 18670
SN Results from experimentation which are anticipated or desired by the researcher in order to confirm a hypothesis and which may serve as a potential factor in experimenter bias.
B Expectations 67
R Experimenter Bias 67
Experimenters 73

Experimenters 73
PN 320 SC 18680
R ↓ Experimentation 67
Experimenter Bias 67
Experimenter Expectations 73

Expert Systems 91
PN 443 SC 18685
UF Knowledge Based Systems
B Artificial Intelligence 82
Systems 67
N Decision Support Systems 97
R ↓ Automated Information Processing 73
Automated Speech Recognition 94
↓ Computers 67
Cybernetics 67
↓ Data Processing 67
Databases 91
↓ Decision Making 67
Human Machine Systems 97
Information Systems 91
↓ Problem Solving 67
Robotics 85

Expert Testimony 73
PN 784 SC 18690
SN Legal testimony by persons who by virtue of their training, skills, or expertise are qualified to give evidence concerning some scientific, technical, or professional matter.
UF Testimony (Expert)
B Legal Testimony 82
R Forensic Evaluation 94
Forensic Psychiatry 73
Forensic Psychology 85

Expertise
Use Experience Level

Explicit Memory 97
PN 0 SC 18695
B Memory 67

Exploratory Behavior [67]
PN 588 **SC** 18700
SN Locomotor activity or perceptual processes involved in investigating and/or orienting oneself to an environment. From 1973, limited to human populations. From 1973, use ANIMAL EXPLORATORY BEHAVIOR to access references to nonhumans.
B Behavior [67]
N Animal Exploratory Behavior [73]
R Curiosity [67]
Information Seeking [73]
↓ Motivation [67]

Explosive Personality [73]
PN 24 **SC** 18710
SN Disorder characterized by discrete episodes of loss of control of aggressive impulses that may result in serious assault or destruction of property.
UF Intermittent Explosive Personality
B Mental Disorders [67]
R Anger Control [97]
↓ Antisocial Behavior [71]
Conduct Disorder [91]
Impulse Control Disorders [97]
↓ Personality Disorders [67]

Exposure Therapy [97]
PN 0 **SC** 18715
B Behavior Therapy [67]
N Implosive Therapy [73]
Systematic Desensitization Therapy [73]

Exposure Time (Stimulus)
Use Stimulus Duration

Expressed Emotion [91]
PN 178 **SC** 18725
SN Frequency and quality of negative emotions, e.g., anger or hostility, expressed by family members or significant others, that often lead to a high relapse rate, especially in schizophrenic patients.
R ↓ Emotions [67]
Relapse (Disorders) [73]
↓ Schizophrenia [67]

Expressions (Facial)
Use Facial Expressions

Expressive Psychotherapy [73]
PN 45 **SC** 18740
SN Psychotherapeutic method used to promote more effective personality functioning through uninhibited expression of feelings and open discussion of personal problems.
B Psychotherapy [67]
R Supportive Psychotherapy [97]

Expulsion (School)
Use School Expulsion

Extended Family [73]
PN 141 **SC** 18760
B Family [67]
Family Structure [73]

Extension Workers (Agricultural)
Use Agricultural Extension Workers

External Ear [73]
PN 47 **SC** 18780
UF Ear Canal
B Ear (Anatomy) [67]

External Rewards [73]
PN 286 **SC** 18790

External Rewards — (cont'd)
SN Tangible or overtly identifiable rewards given in return for service or attainment which may act as reinforcement for the activity rewarded. Compare PRIMARY REINFORCEMENT.
UF Extrinsic Rewards
B Rewards [67]
R Extrinsic Motivation [73]
Internal External Locus of Control [67]

Externalization [73]
PN 90 **SC** 18800
B Personality Processes [67]
R ↓ Defense Mechanisms [67]
↓ Internalization [97]
↓ Personality Development [67]

Extinction (Learning) [67]
PN 3081 **SC** 18810
SN Learned behavior or the experimental paradigm involving withholding reinforcement for a conditioned response and resulting in a gradual reduction and eventual elimination of responding or a return to a rate of responding comparable to levels prior to conditioning. Term may be used in either classical (Pavlovian) or operant (instrumental) conditioning contexts.
B Learning [67]
R ↓ Discrimination Learning [82]
↓ Reinforcement [67]

Extracurricular Activities [73]
PN 389 **SC** 18820
N Fraternity Membership [73]
School Club Membership [73]
Sorority Membership [73]
R Athletic Participation [73]
Athletic Training [91]
↓ Education [67]

Extradimensional Shift Learning
Use Nonreversal Shift Learning

Extramarital Intercourse [73]
PN 168 **SC** 18830
UF Adultery
Affairs (Sexual)
Mate Swapping
B Psychosexual Behavior [67]
Sexual Intercourse (Human) [73]
R ↓ Marital Relations [67]
Monogamy [97]
Promiscuity [73]

Extrapyramidal Symptoms [94]
PN 61 **SC** 18835
B Symptoms [67]
R ↓ Basal Ganglia [73]
Extrapyramidal Tracts [73]
↓ Nervous System Disorders [67]

Extrapyramidal Tracts [73]
PN 103 **SC** 18840
B Central Nervous System [67]
Efferent Pathways [82]
Spinal Cord [73]
R Extrapyramidal Symptoms [94]

Extrasensory Perception [67]
PN 555 **SC** 18850
UF ESP (Parapsychology)
B Parapsychological Phenomena [73]
Perception [67]
N ↓ Clairvoyance [73]
Psychokinesis [73]
R Telepathy [73]

Extraversion [67]
PN 2210 **SC** 18854
SN Personality trait which reflects the extent to which an individual likes people and prefers large gatherings; is assertive, active and talkative; enjoys excitement and stimulation; and tends to have a cheerful disposition.
B Personality Traits [67]
R Assertiveness [73]
Five Factor Personality Model [97]
Gregariousness [73]
Introversion [67]
Sensation Seeking [78]
Sociability [73]

Extrinsic Motivation [73]
PN 342 **SC** 18860
SN Need or desire arising from outside the individual which causes action toward some goal.
B Motivation [67]
R External Rewards [73]
↓ Goals [67]
Internal External Locus of Control [67]
↓ Needs [67]

Extrinsic Rewards
Use External Rewards

Eye (Anatomy) [67]
PN 973 **SC** 18890
UF Choroid
Sclera
B Sense Organs [73]
N Cornea [73]
Eye Color [91]
Fovea [82]
Iris (Eye) [73]
Lens (Eye) [73]
Pupil (Eye) [73]
↓ Retina [67]
R ↓ Eye Disorders [73]
↓ Eye Movements [67]
Ocular Dominance [73]
Pupil Dilation [73]
Retinal Image [73]
↓ Visual Perception [67]

Eye Accommodation
Use Ocular Accommodation

Eye Color [91]
PN 14 **SC** 18895
B Color [67]
Eye (Anatomy) [67]
R Iris (Eye) [73]
↓ Pigments [73]

Eye Contact [73]
PN 544 **SC** 18900
SN Form of nonverbal communication in which two individuals meet each other's glance.
B Interpersonal Communication [73]
Nonverbal Communication [71]
R ↓ Social Reinforcement [67]

Eye Convergence [82]
PN 144 **SC** 18902
SN Turning the eyes toward or away from each other when fixating on distal objects.
UF Vergence Movements
B Eye Movements [67]
R ↓ Depth Perception [67]
↓ Distance Perception [73]
Strabismus [73]

Eye Disorders [73]
PN 281 **SC** 18910

Eye Disorders — (cont'd)
SN Diseases or defects of the eye. Use VISION DISORDERS for other pathology involving visual neural pathways.
B Vision Disorders [82]
N Amblyopia [73]
Cataracts [73]
Color Blindness [73]
Glaucoma [73]
Hemianopia [73]
Nystagmus [73]
↓ Refraction Errors [73]
Strabismus [73]
Tunnel Vision [73]
R Albinism [73]
↓ Eye (Anatomy) [67]
Hysterical Vision Disturbances [73]
Ocular Dominance [73]
↓ Sensorially Disabled [97]
↓ Visual Perception [67]

Eye Dominance
Use Ocular Dominance

Eye Examination
Use Ophthalmologic Examination

Eye Fixation [82]
PN 756 **SC** 18924
SN Orienting one's eye(s) toward and stabilizing one's gaze on a specified visual stimulus.
UF Gazing
Ocular Fixation
Visual Fixation
B Visual Perception [67]
R Visual Field [67]

Eye Movement Desensitization Therapy [97]
PN 0 **SC** 18927
SN Treatment methodology used in the reduction of the emotional impact of trauma-based symptomatology associated with anxiety, nightmares, flashbacks, or intrusive thought processes.
UF EMDR
B Psychotherapy [67]
R ↓ Behavior Therapy [67]
↓ Eye Movements [67]

Eye Movements [67]
PN 4155 **SC** 18930
UF Oculomotor Response
Saccadic Eye Movements
N Eye Convergence [82]
Nystagmus [73]
Rapid Eye Movement [71]
R ↓ Eye (Anatomy) [67]
Eye Movement Desensitization Therapy [97]
REM Dreams [73]
REM Sleep [73]
Visual Search [82]

Eyeblink Reflex [73]
PN 397 **SC** 18940
UF Blink Reflex
B Reflexes [71]
R Startle Reflex [67]

Eyelid Conditioning [73]
PN 492 **SC** 18950
SN Conditioned eye blinking or the classical conditioning paradigm resulting in conditioned eye blinking.
UF Conditioning (Eyelid)
B Classical Conditioning [67]

Eyewitnesses
Use Witnesses

Eysenck Personality Inventory [73]
PN 385 **SC** 18960
B Nonprojective Personality Measures [73]

F Test [73]
PN 75 **SC** 18970
B Parametric Statistical Tests [73]
R ↓ Variability Measurement [73]

Face (Anatomy) [73]
PN 386 **SC** 18980
B Anatomy [67]
R Facial Features [73]
Head (Anatomy) [73]

Face Perception [85]
PN 1143 **SC** 18985
SN Used for human or animal populations.
UF Face Recognition
B Visual Perception [67]
R ↓ Facial Expressions [67]
Facial Features [73]
Prosopagnosia [94]
↓ Social Perception [67]

Face Recognition
Use Face Perception

Facial Expressions [67]
PN 1565 **SC** 18990
UF Expressions (Facial)
B Nonverbal Communication [71]
N Grimaces [73]
Smiles [73]
R Face Perception [85]
Facial Features [73]

Facial Features [73]
PN 576 **SC** 18993
R Face (Anatomy) [73]
Face Perception [85]
↓ Facial Expressions [67]
↓ Physical Appearance [82]
Physical Attractiveness [73]

Facial Muscles [73]
PN 211 **SC** 19000
B Muscles [67]

Facial Nerve [73]
PN 94 **SC** 19010
UF Chorda Tympani Nerve
Nerve (Facial)
B Cranial Nerves [73]

Facilitated Communication
Use Augmentative Communication

Facilitation (Social)
Use Social Facilitation

Facility Admission [88]
PN 80 **SC** 19024
UF Facility Readmission
N ↓ Hospital Admission [73]
R ↓ Facility Discharge [88]
↓ Institutionalization [67]
↓ Treatment Facilities [73]

Facility Discharge [88]
PN 47 **SC** 19026
N ↓ Hospital Discharge [73]
R Client Transfer [97]
Discharge Planning [94]

Facility Discharge — (cont'd)
R ↓ Facility Admission [88]
↓ Institutionalization [67]
↓ Treatment Facilities [73]

Facility Environment [88]
PN 252 **SC** 19028
B Environment [67]
N Hospital Environment [82]
R ↓ Treatment Facilities [73]

Facility Readmission
Use Facility Admission

Factitious Disorders [88]
PN 190 **SC** 19035
UF Ganser Syndrome
B Mental Disorders [67]
N Munchausen Syndrome [94]
R Malingering [73]
Pseudodementia [85]

Factor Analysis [67]
PN 4369 **SC** 19040
SN Use FACTOR ANALYSIS to access references to the factor structure of psychometric measures from 67-84.
UF Confirmatory Factor Analysis
B Multivariate Analysis [82]
N Item Analysis (Statistical) [73]
↓ Statistical Rotation [73]
R Factor Structure [85]
Goodness of Fit [88]
Path Analysis [91]
↓ Statistical Correlation [67]
Statistical Significance [73]
Structural Equation Modeling [94]

Factor Structure [85]
PN 2570 **SC** 19045
SN The internal correlational structure of a set of variables said to measure a given construct. Use FACTOR ANALYSIS to access references prior to 1985.
R Construct Validity [82]
↓ Factor Analysis [67]
Factorial Validity [73]
↓ Statistical Rotation [73]
Structural Equation Modeling [94]

Factorial Validity [73]
PN 404 **SC** 19050
SN Degree of correlation of an assessment instrument or its individual items with the factors derived from factor analysis of another instrument or group of instruments. The proportion of total variance in the test scores that are accounted for by a specific factor can be used as an index of the construct validity of the instrument for that particular factor.
B Statistical Validity [73]
R Construct Validity [82]
Factor Structure [85]
Test Validity [73]

Factory Environments
Use Working Conditions

Factual Knowledge
Use Declarative Knowledge

Faculty
Use Educational Personnel

Fading (Conditioning) [82]
PN 119 **SC** 19087

Fading (Conditioning) — (cont'd)
SN Gradual attenuation of dissimilarity of stimuli dimensions contingent on the subject's mastery of difference between those stimuli. The fading technique is used to facilitate errorless discrimination learning.
B Behavior Modification 73
Operant Conditioning 67
R ↓ Discrimination Learning 82
Stimulus Attenuation 73
Stimulus Discrimination 73

Fads and Fashions 73
PN 58 **SC** 19090
N Clothing 67
R Social Change 67
Trends 91

Failure 67
PN 1387 **SC** 19100
N Academic Failure 78
R Academic Underachievement 67
↓ Achievement 67

Failure to Thrive 88
PN 93 **SC** 19105
SN Growth disorder of infants and children due to nutritional and/or emotional deprivation and resulting in loss of weight and delayed physical, emotional and social development.
UF Reactive Attachment Disorder
B Delayed Development 73
R ↓ Child Abuse 71
Child Neglect 88
↓ Nutritional Deficiencies 73

Fainting
Use Syncope

Fairbairnian Theory
Use Object Relations

Fairy Tales
Use Folklore

Faith Healing 73
PN 254 **SC** 19120
UF Psychic Healing
B Alternative Medicine 97
Religious Practices 73
R Folk Medicine 73
Shamanism 73
Witchcraft 73

Faking 73
PN 335 **SC** 19130
B Deception 67
R ↓ Behavior Disorders 71

False Memory 97
PN 0 **SC** 19135
UF Pseudomemory
B Memory 67
R Age Regression (Hypnotic) 88
↓ Amnesia 67
Confabulation 73
Early Memories 85
Emotional Trauma 67
↓ Hypnosis 67
↓ Hypnotherapy 73
Repressed Memory 97
Suggestibility 67

False Pregnancy
Use Pseudocyesis

Fame 85
PN 40 **SC** 19145
R Reputation 97
↓ Social Perception 67
↓ Status 67

Familial Idiocy (Amaurotic)
Use Amaurotic Familial Idiocy

Familiarity 67
PN 3032 **SC** 19160
SN Knowledge of, or close acquaintance with, an object, stimulus, person, environment, situation or act.
R ↓ Experiences (Events) 73
↓ Practice 67
Stranger Reactions 88

Family 67
PN 3863 **SC** 19300
SN Conceptually broad array term. Use a more specific term if possible.
N Biological Family 88
Extended Family 73
Family of Origin 91
Interethnic Family 88
Interracial Family 88
Nuclear Family 73
Schizophrenogenic Family 67
Stepfamily 91
R Codependency 91
Cohabitation 73
Couples 82
Divorce 73
Divorced Persons 73
Dual Careers 82
Dysfunctional Family 91
Empty Nest 91
↓ Family Background 73
Family Crises 73
↓ Family Life Education 97
↓ Family Members 73
↓ Family Planning 73
↓ Family Relations 67
Family Resemblance 91
↓ Family Structure 73
Kinship 85
↓ Living Arrangements 91
↓ Marital Separation 73
↓ Marital Status 73
↓ Marriage 67
Transgenerational Patterns 91
Widowers 73
Widows 73
Working Women 78

Family Background 73
PN 2808 **SC** 19170
UF Background (Family)
N Family Socioeconomic Level 73
Parent Educational Background 73
Parental Occupation 73
R Biographical Data 78
↓ Family 67
Family of Origin 91
↓ Marital Status 73

Family Caregivers
Use Caregivers

Family Counseling
Use Family Therapy

Family Crises 73
PN 312 **SC** 19190
B Crises 71
R ↓ Family 67
↓ Stress 67

Family Life
Use Family Relations

Family Life Education 97
PN 0 **SC** 19203
UF Marriage and Family Education
B Education 67
N Parent Training 78
Sex Education 73
R ↓ Family 67
↓ Family Relations 67
↓ Family Therapy 67
Household Management 85

Family Medicine 88
PN 174 **SC** 19205
B Medical Sciences 67
R Family Physicians 73
General Practitioners 73

Family Members 73
PN 4915 **SC** 19210
N Adopted Children 73
Adult Offspring 85
↓ Ancestors 73
Biological Family 88
Cousins 73
Daughters 73
Foster Children 73
Grandchildren 73
Grandparents 73
Illegitimate Children 73
Inlaws 97
Orphans 73
↓ Parents 67
↓ Siblings 67
Sons 73
↓ Spouses 73
Stepchildren 73
R ↓ Family 67
Family of Origin 91
Family Resemblance 91
↓ Offspring 88
Only Children 82
Significant Others 91

Family of Origin 91
PN 190 **SC** 19215
SN Family in which an individual was raised. Compare BIOLOGICAL FAMILY.
B Family 67
R Biological Family 88
↓ Family Background 73
↓ Family Members 73
↓ Family Structure 73
Stepfamily 91

Family Physicians 73
PN 604 **SC** 19220
B Physicians 67
R Family Medicine 88
General Practitioners 73

Family Planning 73
PN 447 **SC** 19230
N ↓ Birth Control 71
R Condoms 91
Delayed Parenthood 85
Eugenics 73
↓ Family 67
Fertility Enhancement 73
Induced Abortion 71
↓ Sterilization (Sex) 73

Family Planning Attitudes 73
PN 723 **SC** 19240
UF Birth Control Attitudes
B Attitudes 67

Family Planning Attitudes — (cont'd)
R Childlessness 82
Delayed Parenthood 85
↓ Family Relations 67

Family Relations 67
PN 12195 SC 19250
SN Dynamics of interpersonal interaction and developmental processes taking place between and among members of a biological or socially defined family unit. See FAMILY MEMBERS for references to biological relatives in a family.
UF Family Life
N ↓ Child Discipline 73
↓ Childrearing Practices 67
↓ Marital Relations 67
↓ Parent Child Relations 67
Parental Role 73
Sibling Relations 73
R Childrearing Attitudes 73
Codependency 91
Dysfunctional Family 91
Empty Nest 91
↓ Family 67
↓ Family Life Education 97
Family Planning Attitudes 73
↓ Family Violence 82
Family Work Relationship 97
Intergenerational Relations 88
Marriage Attitudes 73
Social Support Networks 82
Transgenerational Patterns 91

Family Resemblance 91
PN 22 SC 19255
R Assortative Mating 91
↓ Family 67
↓ Family Members 73
↓ Genetics 67
Transgenerational Patterns 91
↓ Twins 67

Family Size 73
PN 727 SC 19260
B Family Structure 73
Size 73
R Empty Nest 91
↓ Parenthood Status 85

Family Socioeconomic Level 73
PN 591 SC 19270
B Family Background 73
Socioeconomic Status 67
R Parent Educational Background 73
Parental Occupation 73

Family Structure 73
PN 2087 SC 19280
N Birth Order 67
Childlessness 82
Extended Family 73
Family Size 73
Matriarchy 73
Monogamy 97
Nuclear Family 73
↓ Parental Absence 73
Patriarchy 73
Polygamy 73
Schizophrenogenic Family 67
Stepfamily 91
R ↓ Culture (Anthropological) 67
Dual Careers 82
Dysfunctional Family 91
Empty Nest 91
↓ Family 67
Family of Origin 91
Homosexual Parents 94
Kinship Structure 73
Living Alone 94

Family Structure — (cont'd)
R ↓ Living Arrangements 91
Only Children 82
↓ Parenthood Status 85
↓ Single Parents 78
↓ Sociocultural Factors 67
Stepchildren 73
Stepparents 73

Family Therapy 67
PN 7147 SC 19290
UF Family Counseling
B Psychotherapeutic Counseling 73
N Conjoint Therapy 73
R ↓ Counseling 67
↓ Family Life Education 97
Social Casework 67

Family Violence 82
PN 1352 SC 19294
SN Injurious or abusive behavior in family or other domestic interpersonal situations.
UF Domestic Violence
B Violence 73
N ↓ Child Abuse 71
R Battered Females 88
Elder Abuse 88
↓ Family Relations 67
Marital Conflict 73
Partner Abuse 91
Physical Abuse 91
↓ Sexual Abuse 88
Shelters 91

Family Work Relationship 97
PN 0 SC 19297
UF Job Family Relationship
Work Family Relationship
R Dual Careers 82
↓ Family Relations 67
Role Conflicts 73
Work (Attitudes Toward) 73
↓ Working Conditions 73
Working Women 78

Fans (Sports)
Use Sports Spectators

Fantasies (Thought Disturbances) 67
PN 437 SC 19310
SN Thinking that severely distorts reality.
B Thought Disturbances 73
R ↓ Fantasy 97
Magical Thinking 73

Fantasy 97
PN 0 SC 19315
SN Use IMAGINATION to access references from 82–96.
B Cognitive Processes 67
N Sexual Fantasy 97
R Daydreaming 73
Fantasies (Thought Disturbances) 67
Fantasy (Defense Mechanism) 67
↓ Ideation 73
Imagination 67
Magical Thinking 73

Fantasy (Defense Mechanism) 67
PN 683 SC 19320
SN Daydreaming dominated by unconscious material and primary processes for the purpose of wish fulfillment or to alleviate social isolation.
B Defense Mechanisms 67
R Daydreaming 73
↓ Fantasy 97
Sexual Fantasy 97

Farmers
Use Agricultural Workers

Fascism 73
PN 211 SC 19342
UF Nazism
B Political Economic Systems 73
R Holocaust 88

Fat Metabolism
Use Lipid Metabolism

Fatalism 73
PN 45 SC 19360
B Philosophies 67
R Cynicism 73
Nihilism 73
Pessimism 73

Father Absence 73
PN 475 SC 19370
SN From 1982, limited to human populations. For animals consider ANIMAL PARENTAL BEHAVIOR.
B Parental Absence 73
R Matriarchy 73

Father Child Communication 85
PN 45 SC 19375
SN Verbal or nonverbal communication between father and child.
B Parent Child Communication 73
R Father Child Relations 73

Father Child Relations 73
PN 1419 SC 19380
SN From 1982, limited to human populations. For animals consider ANIMAL PARENTAL BEHAVIOR.
B Parent Child Relations 67
R ↓ Childrearing Practices 67
Father Child Communication 85
↓ Parental Attitudes 73
Parental Permissiveness 73
Parental Role 73

Fathers 67
PN 2326 SC 19390
SN From 1982, limited to human populations. For animals consider ANIMAL PARENTAL BEHAVIOR.
B Human Males 73
Parents 67
N Adolescent Fathers 85
Single Fathers 94
R Expectant Fathers 85

Fatigue 67
PN 1095 SC 19400
UF Exhaustion
Tiredness
B Symptoms 67
R Chronic Fatigue Syndrome 97
Hypersomnia 94

Fatty Acids 73
PN 252 SC 19410
B Acids 73
Lipids 73
N Capsaicin 91
↓ Phosphatides 73
R Prostaglandins 82

Fear 67
PN 3606 SC 19420
B Emotional States 73
N Fear of Success 78
Panic 73

Fear — (cont'd)
R Alarm Responses [73]
↓ Anxiety [67]
Neophobia [85]
↓ Phobias [67]
Shame [94]
Social Anxiety [85]
Stranger Reactions [88]

Fear of Public Speaking
Use Speech Anxiety

Fear of Strangers
Use Stranger Reactions

Fear of Success [78]
PN 352 **SC** 19424
SN Need to inhibit maximum utilization of one's abilities in achievement situations due to expected negative consequences.
B Fear [67]
Motivation [67]
R ↓ Achievement Motivation [67]
↓ Anxiety [67]
↓ Anxiety Disorders [97]
Self Handicapping Strategy [88]

Fear Survey Schedule [73]
PN 40 **SC** 19430
B Nonprojective Personality Measures [73]

Fecal Incontinence [73]
PN 250 **SC** 19440
UF Encopresis
Incontinence (Fecal)
B Colon Disorders [73]
R ↓ Behavior Disorders [71]
Diarrhea [73]
↓ Symptoms [67]

Fee for Service [94]
PN 12 **SC** 19450
SN Payment for health related services in which the health care provider is reimbursed for services by the client or health insurance carrier.
B Health Insurance [73]
Professional Fees [78]
R Cost Containment [91]
↓ Health Care Delivery [78]
↓ Health Care Services [78]
Health Maintenance Organizations [82]
↓ Managed Care [94]

Feedback [67]
PN 5285 **SC** 19460
SN General concept denoting the return of information that may regulate or control subsequent behavior, cognition, perception, or performance. Use a more specific term if possible.
N ↓ Biofeedback [73]
↓ Delayed Feedback [73]
Knowledge of Results [67]
↓ Sensory Feedback [73]
R ↓ Learning [67]
↓ Reinforcement [67]
↓ Stimulation [67]

Feeding Behavior (Animal)
Use Animal Feeding Behavior

Feeding Practices [73]
PN 217 **SC** 19480
SN Limited to human populations.
UF Mealtimes
N Bottle Feeding [73]
Breast Feeding [73]
Weaning [73]
R ↓ Childrearing Practices [67]

Feelings
Use Emotions

Feet (Anatomy) [73]
PN 128 **SC** 19500
UF Heels (Anatomy)
Toes (Anatomy)
B Anatomy [67]
Musculoskeletal System [73]
R Ankle [73]
Leg (Anatomy) [73]

Felids [97]
PN 0 **SC** 19505
UF Lions
Tigers
B Mammals [73]
N Cats [67]

Felonies
Use Crime

Female Animals [73]
PN 2893 **SC** 19520
B Animals [67]

Female Criminals [73]
PN 271 **SC** 19530
B Criminals [67]
Human Females [73]

Female Delinquents [73]
PN 266 **SC** 19540
B Human Females [73]
Juvenile Delinquents [73]
R Male Delinquents [73]

Female Genitalia [73]
PN 184 **SC** 19550
SN Used for both human and animal populations.
UF Genitalia (Female)
B Urogenital System [73]
N Ovaries [73]
↓ Uterus [73]
Vagina [73]

Female Orgasm [73]
PN 246 **SC** 19560
SN Used for both human and animal populations.
B Orgasm [73]
R Frigidity [73]
Masturbation [73]
↓ Sexual Intercourse (Human) [73]

Females (Human)
Use Human Females

Femininity [67]
PN 1590 **SC** 19580
B Personality Traits [67]
R Androgyny [82]
Gender Identity [85]
Masculinity [67]
Sex Roles [67]

Feminism [78]
PN 1451 **SC** 19585
R Feminist Therapy [94]
↓ Sex Role Attitudes [78]
Womens Liberation Movement [73]

Feminist Therapy [94]
PN 18 **SC** 19587

Feminist Therapy — (cont'd)
SN An approach to psychotherapy, counseling, or consultation based on the assumptions and tenets of feminism.
B Psychotherapy [67]
R ↓ Counseling [67]
Feminism [78]

Feminization Syndrome (Testicular)
Use Testicular Feminization Syndrome

Femoral Nerve
Use Spinal Nerves

Fenfluramine [73]
PN 383 **SC** 19610
B Appetite Depressing Drugs [73]
Sympathomimetic Drugs [73]

Fentanyl [85]
PN 80 **SC** 19613
SN Synthetic opiate frequently used illicitly.
B Opiates [73]

Fertility [88]
PN 153 **SC** 19618
SN The quality or state of being capable of breeding or reproducing. Used for human and animal populations.
B Sexual Reproduction [73]
R Birth Rate [82]
Fertility Enhancement [73]
↓ Infertility [73]

Fertility Enhancement [73]
PN 20 **SC** 19620
R ↓ Family Planning [73]
Fertility [88]
↓ Hormones [67]
Oral Contraceptives [73]

Fertilization [73]
PN 68 **SC** 19630
R ↓ Pregnancy [67]
Reproductive Technology [88]
↓ Sexual Reproduction [73]

Fetal Alcohol Syndrome [85]
PN 168 **SC** 19635
B Drug Induced Congenital Disorders [73]
Syndromes [73]
R ↓ Alcoholism [67]
Ethanol [73]
↓ Mental Retardation [67]
↓ Prenatal Development [73]

Fetal Exposure
Use Prenatal Exposure

Fetishism [73]
PN 148 **SC** 19640
UF Sexual Fetishism
B Sexual Deviations [67]
R Sexual Masochism [73]
Sexual Sadism [73]
Transvestism [73]

Fetus [67]
PN 555 **SC** 19650
B Prenatal Developmental Stages [73]

Fever
Use Hyperthermia

Fibrillation (Heart) [73]
PN 15 **SC** 19680

Fibrillation (Heart) — (cont'd)
UF Atrial Fibrillation
Auricular Fibrillation
Ventricular Fibrillation
B Arrhythmias (Heart) [73]

Fibromyalgia Syndrome
Use Muscular Disorders

Fiction
Use Literature

Field Dependence [73]
PN 1887 **SC** 19710
SN Aspect of cognitive style as seen in relative lack of autonomy from external referents, the inability to overcome embedding contexts, or the reliance on visual rather than gravitational cues in perception of the upright. Used also for reciprocal concept of field independence.
B Cognitive Style [67]

Field Instruction
Use Curricular Field Experience

Field Trips (Educational)
Use Educational Field Trips

Field Work (Educational)
Use Curricular Field Experience

Fighting
Use Aggressive Behavior

Figurative Language [85]
PN 177 **SC** 19736
SN Verbal expressions that signify one concept by using words that would normally be used to signify some other concept as a result of a conceptual analogy or qualitative similarity between the concepts.
UF Figures of Speech
Simile
B Language [67]
N Metaphor [82]
R Analogy [91]
Connotations [73]
Symbolism [67]
↓ Verbal Meaning [73]

Figure Ground Discrimination [73]
PN 589 **SC** 19740
SN Discrimination of a portion of a visual configuration as a coherent figure distinct from the background.
B Perceptual Discrimination [73]
R Form and Shape Perception [67]
Pattern Discrimination [67]
↓ Spatial Perception [67]

Figures of Speech
Use Figurative Language

Fiji [91]
PN 5 **SC** 19747
B South Pacific [78]

Film Strips [67]
PN 526 **SC** 19750
SN Strips of film for still projection. Not used as a document type identifier.
B Audiovisual Communications Media [73]
R ↓ Educational Audiovisual Aids [73]

Filtered Noise [73]
PN 30 **SC** 19760
B Auditory Stimulation [67]

Filtered Speech [73]
PN 34 **SC** 19770
B Speech Processing (Mechanical) [73]

Financial Assistance (Educational)
Use Educational Financial Assistance

Fine Motor Skill Learning [73]
PN 114 **SC** 19790
B Perceptual Motor Learning [67]
Skill Learning [73]

Finger Tapping [73]
PN 251 **SC** 19800
B Motor Performance [73]

Fingers (Anatomy) [73]
PN 330 **SC** 19820
B Musculoskeletal System [73]
N Thumb [73]
R Hand (Anatomy) [67]

Fingerspelling [73]
PN 61 **SC** 19830
B Manual Communication [78]
R Sign Language [73]

Finland [73]
PN 542 **SC** 19840
B Europe [73]
R ↓ Scandinavia [78]

Fire Fighters [91]
PN 65 **SC** 19845
R Fire Prevention [73]
↓ Government Personnel [73]
↓ Paramedical Personnel [73]
↓ Volunteer Personnel [73]

Fire Prevention [73]
PN 34 **SC** 19850
B Prevention [73]
R Fire Fighters [91]
↓ Safety [67]

Firearms
Use Weapons

Firesetting
Use Arson

FIRO-B
Use Fund Interper Rela Orientat Beh Ques

Fishes [67]
PN 1696 **SC** 19870
B Vertebrates [73]
N Bass (Fish) [73]
↓ Carp [73]
Cichlids [73]
Electric Fishes [73]
Salmon [73]
Sticklebacks [73]
R Larvae [73]

Five Factor Personality Model [97]
PN 0 **SC** 19875
SN A model of personality dimensions that encompass five broad factors: neuroticism, extraversion, openness to experience, agreeableness, and conscientiousness.
UF Big Five Personality Model
B Personality Theory [67]
R Extraversion [67]
NEO Personality Inventory [97]
Neuroticism [73]
Openness to Experience [97]

Five Factor Personality Model — (cont'd)
R ↓ Personality [67]
↓ Personality Development [67]
↓ Personality Traits [67]

Fixed Interval Reinforcement [73]
PN 673 **SC** 19880
UF Interval Reinforcement
B Reinforcement Schedules [67]

Fixed Ratio Reinforcement [73]
PN 684 **SC** 19890
UF Ratio Reinforcement
B Reinforcement Schedules [67]

Flashbacks
Use Hallucinations

Flexibility (Personality)
Use Adaptability (Personality)

Flexion Reflex [73]
PN 118 **SC** 19910
B Reflexes [71]

Flextime
Use Work Scheduling

Flicker Fusion Frequency
Use Critical Flicker Fusion Threshold

Flies
Use Diptera

Flight Attendants
Use Aerospace Personnel

Flight Instrumentation [73]
PN 114 **SC** 19930
UF Instrumentation (Flight)
B Aviation [67]
Instrument Controls [85]

Flight Simulation [73]
PN 473 **SC** 19940
B Simulation [67]
R Acceleration Effects [73]
↓ Gravitational Effects [67]

Flooding Therapy
Use Implosive Therapy

Fluency
Use Verbal Fluency

Fluid Intake [85]
PN 670 **SC** 19965
SN Ingestion of liquids or solutions. Frequently used as an objective measure of physiological or motivational state or learning. Used for human or animal populations.
N Water Intake [67]
R ↓ Drinking Behavior [78]
Thirst [67]

Fluoxetine [91]
PN 823 **SC** 19967
UF Prozac
B Antidepressant Drugs [71]
Serotonin Reuptake Inhibitors [97]

Fluphenazine [73]
PN 414 **SC** 19970
UF Prolixin
B Antiemetic Drugs [73]
Phenothiazine Derivatives [73]

Flurazepam [82]
PN 87 SC 19974
SN Organic heterocyclic compound, used as a benzodiazepine tranquilizer and a nonbarbiturate sedative.
B Benzodiazepines [78]
Hypnotic Drugs [73]
Sedatives [73]
R ↓ CNS Depressant Drugs [73]

Fluvoxamine [94]
PN 97 SC 19975
B Antidepressant Drugs [71]
Serotonin Reuptake Inhibitors [97]

Focusing (Visual)
Use Ocular Accommodation

Folic Acid [73]
PN 74 SC 19980
B Amino Acids [73]

Folie A Deux [73]
PN 74 SC 19990
UF Shared Paranoid Disorder
B Paranoia (Psychosis) [67]
R Involutional Paranoid Psychosis [73]
Paranoid Schizophrenia [67]

Folk Medicine [73]
PN 368 SC 20000
B Alternative Medicine [97]
R Ethnology [67]
Faith Healing [73]
↓ Medical Sciences [67]
Shamanism [73]
Transcultural Psychiatry [73]

Folk Psychology [97]
PN 0 SC 20005
SN Branch of psychology that deals with legends, beliefs, folklore, and customs of a race or people, especially primitive societies.
B Psychology [67]
R Anthropology [67]
Ethnography [73]
Ethnology [67]
Folklore [91]
Social Psychology [67]
Transcultural Psychiatry [73]

Folklore [91]
PN 118 SC 20010
SN Use MYTHS to access references from 73-90.
UF Fairy Tales
Folktales
R Ethnology [67]
Folk Psychology [97]
↓ Literature [67]
Myths [67]
Storytelling [88]

Folktales
SN Use MYTHS to access references from 73-90.
Use Folklore

Follicle Stimulating Hormone [91]
PN 14 SC 20025
B Gonadotropic Hormones [73]

Followup (Posttreatment)
Use Posttreatment Followup

Followup Studies [73]
PN 9697 SC 20040
SN Mandatory term applied to studies of an individual or group followed and reexamined to assess and compare present findings with the original observations or measurements. Differentiate from POSTTREATMENT FOLLOWUP which is used in the context of aftercare.
UF Studies (Followup)
B Experimental Design [67]
R ↓ Longitudinal Studies [73]

Food [78]
PN 923 SC 20045
R Craving [97]
Diets [78]
↓ Eating [67]
Food Additives [78]
Food Allergies [73]
↓ Food Intake [67]
Food Preferences [73]
Nutrition [73]

Food Additives [78]
PN 103 SC 20047
R ↓ Chemical Elements [73]
Diets [78]
Food [78]
Nutrition [73]

Food Allergies [73]
PN 48 SC 20050
B Allergic Disorders [73]
R Diets [78]
Food [78]

Food Deprivation [67]
PN 1737 SC 20060
SN Absence of ad libitum food access. In experimental settings, food deprivation is used to achieve a definable level of motivation within the organism.
B Deprivation [67]
Stimulus Deprivation [73]
R Diets [78]
Hunger [67]
↓ Nutritional Deficiencies [73]
Starvation [73]

Food Intake [67]
PN 5205 SC 20070
SN Ingestion of food. Frequently used as an objective measure of physiological or motivational state or learning. Used for human or animal populations.
N ↓ Eating [67]
R Animal Feeding Behavior [73]
Dietary Restraint [94]
Food [78]
Sucking [78]
Weight Control [85]

Food Preferences [73]
PN 1307 SC 20080
B Preferences [67]
R Diets [78]
Eating Attitudes [94]
Food [78]

Football [73]
PN 172 SC 20090
B Recreation [67]
Sports [67]

Foraging (Animal)
Use Animal Foraging Behavior

Forced Choice (Testing Method) [67]
PN 177 SC 20100
SN Assessment method requiring a choice between equally unlikely or undesirable alternatives, designed to reduce the effects of social desirability on the selection of test answers.
UF True False Tests
B Testing Methods [67]

Forebrain [85]
PN 407 SC 20105
UF Prosencephalon
B Brain [67]
N ↓ Diencephalon [73]
Nucleus Basalis Magnocellularis [94]
↓ Telencephalon [73]

Foreign Language Education [73]
PN 668 SC 20110
SN Curriculum, teaching methods, and educational programs used in the instruction of a language that is not native to the learner.
UF Immersion Programs
Second Language Education
B Curriculum [67]
R English as Second Language [97]

Foreign Language Learning [67]
PN 1485 SC 20120
B Learning [67]
R Bilingual Education [78]
Foreign Languages [73]
↓ Language Development [67]
Language Laboratories [73]
Language Proficiency [88]

Foreign Language Translation [73]
PN 1675 SC 20130
SN Rendering from one language to another. Use with foreign language test translations. Not used as a document type identifier.
R Foreign Languages [73]

Foreign Languages [73]
PN 974 SC 20140
SN Second or nonnative languages.
B Language [67]
R Bilingual Education [78]
English as Second Language [97]
Foreign Language Learning [67]
Foreign Language Translation [73]

Foreign Nationals [85]
PN 69 SC 20145
SN Persons living in a country other than their own, generally with intent to return to their home country.
N Foreign Students [73]
Foreign Workers [85]
R Immigration [73]

Foreign Organizations [73]
PN 21 SC 20150
SN Organizations located in or originating from a foreign country.
B Organizations [67]
R International Organizations [73]

Foreign Policy Making [73]
PN 129 SC 20160
UF Policy Making (Foreign)
B Government Policy Making [73]
R Government [67]
International Relations [67]
Peace [88]
↓ War [67]

Foreign Students [73]
PN 709 SC 20168

Foreign Students — (cont'd)
SN Persons attending school or a training program in a country other than their own, generally with intent to return to their home country.
B Foreign Nationals 85
Students 67
R Foreign Study 73

Foreign Study 73
PN 88 **SC** 20170
SN Pursuit of an educational program in a country other than one's own, generally with intent to return to the home country.
B Educational Programs 73
R Foreign Students 73

Foreign Workers 85
PN 88 **SC** 20175
SN Persons employed in a country other than their own, generally with intent to return to their home country.
UF Guest Workers
B Foreign Nationals 85
R Migrant Farm Workers 73

Foremen (Industrial)
Use Industrial Foremen

Forensic Evaluation 94
PN 82 **SC** 20185
B Evaluation 67
Legal Processes 73
Psychiatric Evaluation 97
R Competency to Stand Trial 85
Court Referrals 94
↓ Criminals 67
Expert Testimony 73
Forensic Psychiatry 73
Forensic Psychology 85
Insanity Defense 85
Mentally Ill Offenders 85
↓ Psychodiagnosis 67
↓ Psychological Assessment 97
Psychological Report 88

Forensic Psychiatry 73
PN 691 **SC** 20190
SN Branch of psychiatry devoted to legal issues relating to disordered behavior and mental disorders, including legal responsibility, competency to stand trial, and commitment issues.
B Psychiatry 67
R ↓ Criminal Justice 91
Expert Testimony 73
Forensic Evaluation 94
Forensic Psychology 85
Insanity Defense 85

Forensic Psychology 85
PN 343 **SC** 20195
UF Legal Psychology
B Psychology 67
R ↓ Criminal Justice 91
Expert Testimony 73
Forensic Evaluation 94
Forensic Psychiatry 73
Psychological Autopsy 88

Forgetting 73
PN 570 **SC** 20200
SN Inability to recall, recollect, or reproduce previously learned material, behavior, or experience. Compare AMNESIA and MEMORY DECAY.
R ↓ Amnesia 67
Cued Recall 94
Free Recall 73
Fugue Reaction 73
↓ Interference (Learning) 67
↓ Latent Inhibition 97

Forgetting — (cont'd)
R ↓ Learning 67
↓ Memory 67
Memory Decay 73
Memory Training 94
Reminiscence 85
↓ Retention 67
Serial Recall 94
Suppression (Defense Mechanism) 73

Forgiveness 88
PN 70 **SC** 20205
R ↓ Conflict Resolution 82
↓ Religious Beliefs 73
↓ Social Interaction 67

Form and Shape Perception 67
PN 3253 **SC** 20210
SN Perception of the physical form or shape of objects through any of the senses, usually haptic or visual.
UF Contour
Contour Perception
Form Perception
Shape Perception
B Perception 67
R Figure Ground Discrimination 73
Motion Parallax 97
Object Recognition 97
Pattern Discrimination 67

Form Classes (Language) 73
PN 293 **SC** 20220
UF Words (Form Classes)
B Language 67
Syntax 71
N Adjectives 73
Adverbs 73
Nouns 73
Pronouns 73
Verbs 73

Form Perception
Use Form and Shape Perception

Fornix 82
PN 143 **SC** 20234
SN Arched white fiber tract extending from the hippocampal formation to the septum, anterior nucleus of the thalamus, and mammillary body.
UF Hippocampal Commissure
Trigonum Cerebrale
B Limbic System 73
Neural Pathways 82
R Medial Forebrain Bundle 82
Septal Nuclei 82

FORTRAN
Use Computer Programing Languages

Forward Masking
Use Masking

Foster Care 78
PN 804 **SC** 20245
SN Family care provided by persons other than the natural or adoptive parents.
UF Foster Homes
R ↓ Child Care 91
Child Welfare 88
Foster Children 73
Foster Parents 73
Protective Services 97

Foster Children 73
PN 267 **SC** 20250

Foster Children — (cont'd)
B Family Members 73
R ↓ Children 67
Foster Care 78

Foster Homes
Use Foster Care

Foster Parents 73
PN 253 **SC** 20260
B Parents 67
R Foster Care 78
Surrogate Parents (Humans) 73

Fovea 82
PN 137 **SC** 20265
SN Centrally located and depressed portion of the retina containing only cone photoreceptors.
B Eye (Anatomy) 67
R Cones (Eye) 73
Foveal Vision 88
Visual Field 67

Foveal Vision 88
PN 169 **SC** 20267
UF Central Vision
B Visual Perception 67
R Fovea 82

Fowl
Use Birds

Foxes 73
PN 55 **SC** 20290
B Canids 97

Fragile X Syndrome 94
PN 29 **SC** 20295
B Sex Linked Hereditary Disorders 73
Syndromes 73
R ↓ Mental Retardation 67
↓ Sex Chromosome Disorders 73

Fragmentation (Schizophrenia) 73
PN 6 **SC** 20300
UF Loosening of Associations
B Thought Disturbances 73
R ↓ Schizophrenia 67

Frail
Use Health Impaired

France 67
PN 1580 **SC** 20310
B Europe 73

Franck Drawing Completion Test 73
PN 4 **SC** 20320
B Projective Personality Measures 73
Projective Techniques 67

Frankness
Use Honesty

Fraternal Twins
Use Heterozygotic Twins

Fraternity Membership 73
PN 101 **SC** 20340
SN Belonging to a club traditionally restricted to males. Used also for fraternity organizations.
B Extracurricular Activities 73

Fraud 94
PN 15 **SC** 20345

Fraud — (cont'd)
UF Consumer Fraud
B Deception 67
R Cheating 73
↓ Crime 67
Dishonesty 73
Experimental Ethics 78
Retraction of Publication 91

Free Association 94
PN 20 SC 20347
SN Spontaneous association of ideas or mental images restricted by consciousness. Primarily used in, but not restricted to, psychoanalysis or Jungian analysis as a method to gain access to the organization and content of a patient's mind.
UF Association (Free)
R ↓ Jungian Psychology 73
↓ Psychoanalysis 67
↓ Psychoanalytic Theory 67
↓ Psychotherapeutic Techniques 67
Unconscious (Personality Factor) 67

Free Recall 73
PN 1624 SC 20350
SN Method of measuring the retention of learned material in which a subject is asked to recall as much of the material as possible, in any order, without the aid of external cues. Compare SERIAL ANTICIPATION (LEARNING) and RECONSTRUCTION (LEARNING).
B Recall (Learning) 67
R Cued Recall 94
Forgetting 73
↓ Memory 67
Serial Recall 94

Free Will
Use Volition

Freedom 78
PN 291 SC 20354
R Censorship 78
Choice Behavior 67
↓ Civil Rights 78
↓ Justice 73
↓ Political Processes 73
Psychological Reactance 78
Volition 88

Frequency (Pitch)
Use Pitch (Frequency)

Frequency (Response)
Use Response Frequency

Frequency (Stimulus)
Use Stimulus Frequency

Frequency Distribution 73
PN 265 SC 20380
UF Distribution (Frequency)
B Statistical Analysis 67
Statistical Measurement 73
N Normal Distribution 73
Skewed Distribution 73
R Standard Deviation 73

Freud (Sigmund) 67
PN 2230 SC 20390
SN Identifies biographical or autobiographical studies and discussions of Freud's works.
R Freudian Psychoanalytic School 73
↓ Neopsychoanalytic School 73
↓ Psychoanalysis 67
↓ Psychoanalytic Theory 67
↓ Psychologists 67

Freudian Psychoanalytic School 73
PN 370 SC 20400
UF Psychoanalytic School (Freudian)
B History of Psychology 67
Psychoanalytic Theory 67
R Freud (Sigmund) 67
Metapsychology 94
↓ Neopsychoanalytic School 73
Psychoanalytic Interpretation 67

Friendship 67
PN 1847 SC 20410
B Interpersonal Interaction 67
R Interpersonal Compatibility 73
Peer Pressure 94
↓ Peer Relations 67
↓ Relationship Termination 97
Significant Others 91
Social Dating 73
Social Support Networks 82

Frigidity 73
PN 49 SC 20420
B Sexual Function Disturbances 73
R Dyspareunia 73
Female Orgasm 73
Impotence 73
↓ Orgasm 73
↓ Symptoms 67
Vaginismus 73

Frogs 67
PN 735 SC 20430
B Amphibia 73
R Larvae 73

Frontal Lobe 73
PN 1921 SC 20440
B Cerebral Cortex 67
N Gyrus Cinguli 73
Motor Cortex 73
Prefrontal Cortex 94

Frostig Development Test Vis Percept 73
PN 34 SC 20450
B Intelligence Measures 67

Fruit Fly
Use Drosophila

Frustration 67
PN 1117 SC 20470
B Emotional States 73
R Dissatisfaction 73
Mental Confusion 73

Fugue Reaction 73
PN 18 SC 20480
SN Dissociative reaction characterized by extensive amnesia and a sudden change in one's lifestyle. Upon recovery, prefugue events are remembered but those that occurred during the fugue are forgotten.
B Amnesia 67
Dissociative Patterns 73
R ↓ Epilepsy 67
Forgetting 73

Fulfillment
Use Satisfaction

Functional Knowledge
Use Procedural Knowledge

Functionalism 73
PN 89 SC 20500

Functionalism — (cont'd)
SN Doctrine or system of psychology which holds (contrary to structural psychology) that mental processes are the proper subject matter of psychology and that an essential feature of all psychological processes is the part they play in the adaptive functions of an organism.
B History of Psychology 67
R James (William) 91

Fund Interper Rela Orientat Beh Ques 73
PN 51 SC 20510
UF FIRO-B
B Nonprojective Personality Measures 73

Fundamentalism 73
PN 108 SC 20520
B Protestantism 73

Funding 88
PN 323 SC 20524
R Budgets 97
↓ Costs and Cost Analysis 73
Educational Financial Assistance 73
↓ Government Policy Making 73
↓ Government Programs 73
Money 67
Resource Allocation 97

Funerals
Use Death Rites

Furniture 85
PN 21 SC 20527
R Human Factors Engineering 73
Interior Design 82
Physical Comfort 82

Future 91
PN 183 SC 20528
R ↓ Expectations 67
↓ History 73
↓ Prediction 67
Social Change 67
↓ Time 67
Trends 91

Fuzzy Set Theory 91
PN 81 SC 20529
B Statistical Analysis 67
Theories 67
R ↓ Mathematical Modeling 73
↓ Psychophysical Measurement 67
↓ Statistical Probability 67

GABA Agonists
Use Gamma Aminobutyric Acid Agonists

GABA Antagonists
Use Gamma Aminobutyric Acid Antagonists

Galanin
Use Peptides

Galanthamine 73
PN 13 SC 20530
B Amines 73
Cholinesterase Inhibitors 73

Galvanic Skin Response 67
PN 1725 SC 20550
SN Means of assessing sympathetic nervous system activity (i.e., arousal) by measuring onset of palmar sweat gland response.
UF Electrodermal Response
GSR (Electrophysiology)
Psychogalvanic Reflex

Galvanic Skin Response — (cont'd)
B Diagnosis [67]
Electrophysiology [73]
Medical Diagnosis [73]
R Skin Potential [73]
↓ Skin Resistance [73]

Gamblers Anonymous
Use Twelve Step Programs

Gambling [73]
PN 427 SC 20560
B Recreation [67]
Risk Taking [67]
Social Behavior [67]
N Pathological Gambling [88]
R ↓ Games [67]
Risk Analysis [91]

Game Theory [67]
PN 355 SC 20570
SN Mathematical theory which attempts to analyze and model the decision making process involved in gain-loss situations.
B Theories [67]
R Entrapment Games [73]
↓ Games [67]
Non Zero Sum Games [73]
Prisoners Dilemma Game [73]
Risk Analysis [91]
↓ Simulation [67]

Games [67]
PN 1594 SC 20580
N Chess [73]
Childrens Recreational Games [73]
Computer Games [88]
Entrapment Games [73]
Non Zero Sum Games [73]
Prisoners Dilemma Game [73]
Simulation Games [73]
R Childhood Play Behavior [78]
↓ Gambling [73]
Game Theory [67]
↓ Recreation [67]
↓ Toys [73]

Gamma Aminobutyric Acid [78]
PN 796 SC 20585
B Amino Acids [73]
Neurotransmitters [85]
R ↓ Gamma Aminobutyric Acid Agonists [85]
↓ Gamma Aminobutyric Acid Antagonists [85]

Gamma Aminobutyric Acid Agonists [85]
PN 229 SC 20587
UF GABA Agonists
N Muscimol [94]
R Gamma Aminobutyric Acid [78]

Gamma Aminobutyric Acid Antagonists [85]
PN 199 SC 20589
UF GABA Antagonists
B Alkaloids [73]
N Bicuculline [94]
Picrotoxin [73]
R Gamma Aminobutyric Acid [78]

Gamma Globulin [73]
PN 9 SC 20590
B Immunoglobulins [73]
R Antibodies [73]

Ganglia [73]
PN 188 SC 20600
B Nervous System [67]
N Autonomic Ganglia [73]

Ganglia — (cont'd)
N ↓ Basal Ganglia [73]
Spinal Ganglia [73]

Ganglion Blocking Drugs [73]
PN 11 SC 20610
B Drugs [67]
N Hexamethonium [73]
Mecamylamine [73]
Nicotine [73]
R ↓ Antihypertensive Drugs [73]

Ganglion Cells (Retina) [85]
PN 109 SC 20615
UF Retinal Ganglion Cells
B Neurons [73]
Retina [67]

Gangs (Juvenile)
Use Juvenile Gangs

Ganser Syndrome
Use Factitious Disorders

Gastrointestinal Disorders [73]
PN 374 SC 20630
B Digestive System Disorders [73]
N ↓ Colon Disorders [73]
Gastrointestinal Ulcers [67]
Vomiting [73]
R Influenza [73]
↓ Neoplasms [67]
↓ Psychosomatic Disorders [67]
↓ Toxic Disorders [73]

Gastrointestinal System [73]
PN 220 SC 20640
B Digestive System [67]
N Intestines [73]
Stomach [73]
R Pancreas [73]

Gastrointestinal Ulcers [67]
PN 477 SC 20650
UF Peptic Ulcers
Ulcers (Gastrointestinal)
B Gastrointestinal Disorders [73]
R ↓ Colitis [73]

Gastropods
Use Mollusca

Gates MacGinitie Reading Tests [73]
PN 15 SC 20670
UF Gates Reading Readiness Tests
Gates Reading Test
B Reading Measures [73]

Gates Reading Readiness Tests
Use Gates MacGinitie Reading Tests

Gates Reading Test
Use Gates MacGinitie Reading Tests

Gating (Sensory)
Use Sensory Gating

Gaussian Distribution
Use Normal Distribution

Gay Liberation Movement
Use Homosexual Liberation Movement

Gay Males
Use Male Homosexuality

Gay Parents
Use Homosexual Parents

Gazing
Use Eye Fixation

Geese [73]
PN 87 SC 20710
B Birds [67]

Gender Differences
Use Human Sex Differences

Gender Identity [85]
PN 531 SC 20717
SN Inner conviction that one is male or female or inner sense of being masculine or feminine.
UF Sexual Identity (Gender)
R Androgyny [82]
Femininity [67]
Gender Identity Disorder [97]
Masculinity [67]
↓ Personality [67]
Psychosexual Development [82]
↓ Self Concept [67]
Sex Roles [67]
↓ Sexual Orientation [97]
Transsexualism [73]

Gender Identity Disorder [97]
PN 0 SC 20719
SN Consider GENDER IDENTITY to access references from 85–96.
B Mental Disorders [67]
R Gender Identity [85]
Hermaphroditism [73]
↓ Sexual Orientation [97]
Transsexualism [73]
Transvestism [73]

Gender Role Attitudes
Use Sex Role Attitudes

Gender Roles
Use Sex Roles

General Anesthetics [73]
PN 54 SC 20720
B Anesthetic Drugs [73]
N Chloroform [73]
Ether (Anesthetic) [73]
Methohexital [73]
Thiopental [73]

General Aptitude Test Battery [73]
PN 46 SC 20730
B Aptitude Measures [67]

General Health Questionnaire [91]
PN 74 SC 20740
B Personality Measures [67]
Questionnaires [67]
R ↓ Diagnosis [67]
↓ Health [73]
↓ Screening Tests [82]

General Paresis [73]
PN 30 SC 20750
UF Dementia Paralytica
Paresis (General)
B Paralysis [73]
R Neurosyphilis [73]
↓ Syphilis [73]

General Practitioners [73]
PN 536 SC 20760

General Practitioners — (cont'd)
B Physicians [67]
R Family Medicine [88]
Family Physicians [73]

Generalization (Cognitive)
Use Cognitive Generalization

Generalization (Learning) [82]
PN 1091 **SC** 20775
SN Responding in a similar manner to different stimuli that have some common property as the result of a conditioned or learned similarity. Also known as secondary generalization. Also includes generalization of any learned behavior to a new context or setting. Compare TRANSFER (LEARNING) or STIMULUS GENERALIZATION.
B Learning [67]
N Response Generalization [73]
Stimulus Generalization [67]
R ↓ Concept Formation [67]
↓ Discrimination Learning [82]
↓ Transfer (Learning) [67]

Generalization (Response)
Use Response Generalization

Generalization (Semantic)
Use Semantic Generalization

Generalization (Stimulus)
Use Stimulus Generalization

Generalized Anxiety Disorder
Use Anxiety Disorders

Generation Effect (Learning) [91]
PN 44 **SC** 20802
SN In learning or memory contexts, the effect of generating a stimuli oneself rather than having it presented by external sources.
B Learning [67]
R ↓ Cognitive Processes [67]
↓ Memory [67]

Generation Gap [73]
PN 148 **SC** 20805
SN Differences in values, morals, attitudes, and behavior of young adults and older adults in contemporary society.
R Age Differences [67]
Cohort Analysis [88]
Intergenerational Relations [88]
↓ Parent Child Relations [67]
Transgenerational Patterns [91]

Generators (Apparatus) [73]
PN 30 **SC** 20810
B Apparatus [67]

Genes [73]
PN 393 **SC** 20820
R ↓ Chromosomes [73]
Genetic Linkage [94]
↓ Genetics [67]

Genetic Counseling [78]
PN 172 **SC** 20826
SN Presentation and discussion, usually with prospective parents, of factors involved in potential inheritance of disorders.
B Counseling [67]
R Eugenics [73]
↓ Genetic Disorders [73]
↓ Genetic Engineering [94]
↓ Genetics [67]

Genetic Disorders [73]
PN 421 **SC** 20830
UF Hereditary Disorders
B Physical Disorders [97]
N Albinism [73]
Amaurotic Familial Idiocy [73]
↓ Chromosome Disorders [73]
Huntingtons Disease [73]
Phenylketonuria [73]
Porphyria [73]
Rh Incompatibility [73]
↓ Sex Linked Hereditary Disorders [73]
Sickle Cell Disease [94]
R Alopecia [73]
Anemia [73]
Behavioral Genetics [94]
Color Blindness [73]
↓ Congenital Disorders [73]
Developmental Disabilities [82]
Diabetes Insipidus [73]
Genetic Counseling [78]
↓ Genetic Engineering [94]
↓ Genetics [67]
Hypopituitarism [73]
Mutations [73]
Picks Disease [73]
Prenatal Diagnosis [88]
↓ Refraction Errors [73]

Genetic Dominance [73]
PN 42 **SC** 20840
B Dominance [67]
R Behavioral Genetics [94]
Genetic Recessiveness [73]
↓ Genetics [67]

Genetic Engineering [94]
PN 7 **SC** 20845
N Eugenics [73]
R Genetic Counseling [78]
↓ Genetic Disorders [73]
Genetic Linkage [94]
↓ Genetics [67]
Population Genetics [73]
Reproductive Technology [88]
Selective Breeding [73]

Genetic Linkage [94]
PN 76 **SC** 20847
SN Linkage of genes at different loci on the same chromosome and analysis of how genes are inherited together.
UF Linkage Analysis
R ↓ Chromosomes [73]
Genes [73]
↓ Genetic Engineering [94]
↓ Genetics [67]
Genotypes [73]

Genetic Recessiveness [73]
PN 27 **SC** 20850
UF Recessiveness (Genetic)
R Behavioral Genetics [94]
Genetic Dominance [73]
↓ Genetics [67]

Genetics [67]
PN 7904 **SC** 20860
SN Conceptually broad array term referring both to the science of heredity and the biological process of transmission of characteristics from progenitor to offspring.
UF Heredity
N Behavioral Genetics [94]
Eugenics [73]
Population Genetics [73]
R ↓ Animal Breeding [73]
Animal Mate Selection [82]
Animal Strain Differences [82]

Genetics — (cont'd)
R Assortative Mating [91]
Blood Groups [73]
↓ Chromosomes [73]
Family Resemblance [91]
Genes [73]
Genetic Counseling [78]
↓ Genetic Disorders [73]
Genetic Dominance [73]
↓ Genetic Engineering [94]
Genetic Linkage [94]
Genetic Recessiveness [73]
Genotypes [73]
Hybrids (Biology) [73]
Instinctive Behavior [82]
Mutations [73]
Natural Selection [97]
Nature Nurture [94]
↓ Nucleic Acids [73]
Phenotypes [73]
Predisposition [73]
Reproductive Technology [88]
Selective Breeding [73]
↓ Sexual Reproduction [73]
Species Differences [82]
Translocation (Chromosome) [73]
↓ Twins [67]

Geniculate Bodies (Thalamus) [73]
PN 373 **SC** 20870
B Thalamus [67]
R Visual Receptive Fields [82]

Genital Disorders [67]
PN 142 **SC** 20880
UF Sex Differentiation Disorders
Sexual Disorders (Physiological)
B Urogenital Disorders [73]
N ↓ Endocrine Sexual Disorders [73]
↓ Gynecological Disorders [73]
Hermaphroditism [73]
↓ Infertility [73]
↓ Male Genital Disorders [73]
R Sex [67]

Genital Herpes
Use Herpes Genitalis

Genitalia (Female)
Use Female Genitalia

Genitalia (Male)
Use Male Genitalia

Geniuses
Use Gifted

Genocide [88]
PN 19 **SC** 20915
SN Deliberate and systematic destruction of a racial, political, or cultural group.
B Homicide [67]
N Holocaust [88]

Genotypes [73]
PN 369 **SC** 20920
R Genetic Linkage [94]
↓ Genetics [67]
Phenotypes [73]

Genuineness
Use Sincerity

Geographic Regions
Use Geography

Geographical Mobility 78
PN 318 **SC** 20924
SN Capacity or facility of individuals to move from one geographic region to another. Includes job- or study-related commuting.
UF Mobility (Geographical)
R Commuting (Travel) 85
↓ Human Migration 73

Geography 73
PN 619 **SC** 20925
SN Science dealing with the description of the topographical features of the earth and the distribution of life on earth. Also, geographic areas or their features.
UF Geographic Regions
Physical Divisions (Geographic)
Physical Geography
Political Divisions (Geographic)
B Sciences 67
R ↓ Countries 67
↓ Environment 67

Geomagnetism
Use Magnetism

Geometry
Use Mathematics

Gerbils 73
PN 558 **SC** 20940
B Rodents 73

Geriatric Assessment 97
PN 0 **SC** 20945
B Evaluation 67
R Activities of Daily Living 91
Clinical Judgment (Not Diagnosis) 73
↓ Diagnosis 67
Geriatric Patients 73
Geriatric Psychiatry 97
Geriatrics 67
Gerontology 67
↓ Measurement 67
Needs Assessment 85
↓ Psychiatric Evaluation 97
↓ Psychological Assessment 97
↓ Screening 82

Geriatric Patients 73
PN 2590 **SC** 20950
SN Older persons suffering from mental or physical diseases and disabilities and under some form of treatment.
B Patients 67
R ↓ Aged 73
Geriatric Assessment 97

Geriatric Psychiatry 97
PN 0 **SC** 20955
B Psychiatry 67
R ↓ Aging 91
Geriatric Assessment 97
Geriatric Psychotherapy 73
Geriatrics 67
Gerontology 67

Geriatric Psychotherapy 73
PN 146 **SC** 20960
B Psychotherapy 67
R ↓ Aging 91
Animal Assisted Therapy 94
Geriatric Psychiatry 97
Geriatrics 67
Gerontology 67
Physiological Aging 67

Geriatrics 67
PN 1096 **SC** 20970
SN Medical subdiscipline which deals with the problems of old age and aging. Use GERIATRICS or GERONTOLOGY to access references on the aged (elderly) from 67–72.
B Medical Sciences 67
R ↓ Aged 73
Aged (Attitudes Toward) 78
↓ Aging 91
Geriatric Assessment 97
Geriatric Psychiatry 97
Geriatric Psychotherapy 73
Gerontology 67
Physiological Aging 67

German Measles
Use Rubella

Germany 88
PN 467 **SC** 20995
SN Used for articles about Germany prior to 1945 or when East Germany or West Germany is not specified. Use a more specific term if possible.
B Europe 73
N East Germany 82
West Germany 82

Gerontology 67
PN 917 **SC** 21000
SN Scientific study of old age and the phenomena associated with old age. Use GERONTOLOGY or GERIATRICS to access references to the aged (elderly) from 67–72.
B Developmental Psychology 73
R ↓ Aged 73
Aged (Attitudes Toward) 78
↓ Aging 91
Geriatric Assessment 97
Geriatric Psychiatry 97
Geriatric Psychotherapy 73
Geriatrics 67
Life Review 91

Gestalt Psychology 67
PN 503 **SC** 21010
SN School of psychology concerned with the study of the individual's perception of and response to configurational wholes.
B History of Psychology 67

Gestalt Therapy 73
PN 548 **SC** 21020
SN Type of psychotherapy which emphasizes treatment of the individual as a whole and focuses on sensory awareness of present experience.
B Human Potential Movement 82
Psychotherapy 67

Gestation
Use Pregnancy

Gestures 73
PN 527 **SC** 21040
B Nonverbal Communication 71
R Body Language 73

Ghana 88
PN 37 **SC** 21045
B Africa 67

Ghettoes 73
PN 89 **SC** 21050
UF Urban Ghettoes
B Urban Environments 67
R Poverty Areas 73

Gifted 67
PN 3691 **SC** 21060
UF Exceptional Children (Gifted)
Geniuses
Intellectually Gifted
Talented
R ↓ Ability 67
Creativity 67
Idiot Savants 73
Intelligence 67

Gilles de la Tourette Disorder 73
PN 690 **SC** 21070
UF Tourette Syndrome
B Neuromuscular Disorders 73
R Echolalia 73

Gipsies
Use Gypsies

Girls
Use Human Females

Glands 67
PN 646 **SC** 21080
N ↓ Endocrine Glands 73
Mammary Glands 73
Pancreas 73
Salivary Glands 73
R Pheromones 73

Glaucoma 73
PN 34 **SC** 21090
B Eye Disorders 73

Global Amnesia 97
PN 0 **SC** 21095
SN Use AMNESIA to access references from 67–96.
B Amnesia 67
R ↓ Brain Damage 67

Globulins 73
PN 50 **SC** 21100
UF Glycoproteins
B Proteins 73
N Antibodies 73
↓ Immunoglobulins 73

Globus Pallidus 73
PN 182 **SC** 21110
B Basal Ganglia 73

Glossary 73
PN 12 **SC** 21120
SN Mandatory term used as a document type identifier. Compare PSYCHOLOGICAL TERMINOLOGY.
R Dictionary 73

Glossolalia 73
PN 38 **SC** 21130
SN Unintelligible speech occurring in hypnotic or mediumistic trances, religious experiences, or some mental disorders.
R ↓ Mental Disorders 67
↓ Religious Practices 73

Glossopharyngeal Nerve
Use Cranial Nerves

Glucagon 73
PN 52 **SC** 21150
B Hormones 67

Glucocorticoids 82
PN 238 **SC** 21155

Glucocorticoids — (cont'd)
SN Any steroid-like compound capable of significantly influencing intermediary metabolism. Glucocorticoids are also clinically useful anti-inflammatory agents.
B Adrenal Cortex Hormones [73]
Anti Inflammatory Drugs [82]
N Dexamethasone [85]

Glucose [73]
PN 945 **SC** 21160
B Sugars [73]
N Blood Sugar [73]
R Glucose Metabolism [94]
Glycogen [73]

Glucose Metabolism [94]
PN 103 **SC** 21165
B Carbohydrate Metabolism [73]
R ↓ Glucose [73]
↓ Neurochemistry [73]

Glue Sniffing [73]
PN 54 **SC** 21170
B Inhalant Abuse [85]

Glutamic Acid [73]
PN 348 **SC** 21180
B Amino Acids [73]
Neurotransmitters [85]
R Kainic Acid [88]

Glutamine [73]
PN 52 **SC** 21190
B Amino Acids [73]

Glutethimide [73]
PN 14 **SC** 21210
B CNS Depressant Drugs [73]
Hypnotic Drugs [73]
Sedatives [73]

Glycine [73]
PN 101 **SC** 21220
B Amino Acids [73]
Neurotransmitters [85]

Glycogen [73]
PN 40 **SC** 21230
R ↓ Glucose [73]

Glycoproteins
Use Globulins

Goal Setting [97]
PN 0 **SC** 21237
R ↓ Aspirations [67]
↓ Goals [67]
↓ Motivation [67]

Goals [67]
PN 2723 **SC** 21240
SN Aims toward which an individual or a group aspire or toward which effort is directed. Use a more specific term if possible.
UF Objectives
N Educational Objectives [78]
Organizational Objectives [73]
R ↓ Aspirations [67]
Extrinsic Motivation [73]
Goal Setting [97]
↓ Incentives [67]
Intention [88]
Intrinsic Motivation [73]
↓ Motivation [67]
↓ Needs [67]

Goats [73]
PN 110 **SC** 21250
B Mammals [73]

God Concepts [73]
PN 242 **SC** 21260
B Religious Beliefs [73]

Goiters [73]
PN 17 **SC** 21270
B Thyroid Disorders [73]
R Hyperthyroidism [73]
Hypothyroidism [73]

Goldfish [73]
PN 434 **SC** 21280
B Carp [73]

Goldstein Scheerer Object Sort Test [73]
PN 4 **SC** 21290
B Nonprojective Personality Measures [73]

Gonadotropic Hormones [73]
PN 253 **SC** 21300
UF Gonadotropin
B Hormones [67]
N Follicle Stimulating Hormone [91]
Luteinizing Hormone [78]
Prolactin [73]
R ↓ Pituitary Hormones [73]
↓ Sex Hormones [73]

Gonadotropin
Use Gonadotropic Hormones

Gonads [73]
PN 86 **SC** 21320
B Endocrine Glands [73]
Urogenital System [73]
N Ovaries [73]
Testes [73]

Gonorrhea [73]
PN 20 **SC** 21330
B Bacterial Disorders [73]
Venereal Diseases [73]

Goodenough Harris Draw A Person Test [67]
PN 120 **SC** 21340
B Intelligence Measures [67]
R Human Figures Drawing [73]

Goodness of Fit [88]
PN 117 **SC** 21350
B Statistical Analysis [67]
R ↓ Factor Analysis [67]
↓ Mathematical Modeling [73]
Maximum Likelihood [85]
Statistical Significance [73]

Gorillas [73]
PN 156 **SC** 21370
B Primates (Nonhuman) [73]

Gossip [82]
PN 41 **SC** 21375
SN Idle personal talk or communication of unsubstantiated information.
UF Rumors
B Interpersonal Communication [73]
R Messages [73]

Gough Adjective Check List [73]
PN 23 **SC** 21380
B Nonprojective Personality Measures [73]

Government [67]
PN 591 **SC** 21390
UF Government Bureaucracy
B Public Sector [85]
R Autonomy (Government) [73]
Foreign Policy Making [73]
Government Agencies [73]
↓ Government Personnel [73]
↓ Government Policy Making [73]
↓ Government Programs [73]
Gun Control Laws [73]
Job Corps [73]
↓ Law (Government) [73]
↓ Law Enforcement [78]
↓ Laws [67]
↓ Legal Processes [73]
Legislative Processes [73]
↓ Marihuana Laws [73]
Marihuana Legalization [73]
Peace Corps [73]
↓ Political Economic Systems [73]
↓ Politics [67]
Project Follow Through [73]
Project Head Start [73]
Taxation [85]
Upward Bound [73]
Volunteers in Service to America [73]
Welfare Services (Government) [73]

Government Agencies [73]
PN 399 **SC** 21400
B Organizations [67]
Public Sector [85]
R Government [67]

Government Bureaucracy
Use Government

Government Personnel [73]
PN 1028 **SC** 21420
UF Civil Servants
Elected Government Officials
B Personnel [67]
N Agricultural Extension Workers [73]
↓ Law Enforcement Personnel [73]
↓ Military Personnel [67]
Police Personnel [73]
Public Health Service Nurses [73]
R ↓ Business and Industrial Personnel [67]
Fire Fighters [91]
Government [67]

Government Policy Making [73]
PN 2215 **SC** 21430
UF Policy Making (Government)
Public Policy
B Policy Making [88]
N Foreign Policy Making [73]
↓ Laws [67]
Legislative Processes [73]
R Advocacy [85]
Funding [88]
Government [67]
Health Care Policy [94]
↓ Legal Processes [73]
↓ War [67]

Government Programs [73]
PN 782 **SC** 21440
UF Programs (Government)
N Job Corps [73]
Medicaid [94]
Medicare [88]
Peace Corps [73]
Project Follow Through [73]
Project Head Start [73]
Social Security [88]
Upward Bound [73]

Government Programs — (cont'd)
N Volunteers in Service to America 73
Welfare Services (Government) 73
R Funding 88
Government 67
↓ Program Development 91
Shelters 91
↓ Social Services 82

Grade Level 94
PN 96 **SC** 21445
UF Academic Grade Level
R Ability Grouping 73
Age Differences 67
↓ Education 67
Educational Placement 78
↓ Elementary School Students 67
High School Students 67
Junior High School Students 71
Kindergarten Students 73
School Transition 97
Special Education Students 73
Transfer Students 73

Gradepoint Average
Use Academic Achievement

Grading (Educational) 73
PN 510 **SC** 21460
SN Rating of achievement level by means of established scales or standards. Consider also SCORING (TESTING) or TEST SCORES.
B Educational Measurement 67
R ↓ Scoring (Testing) 73

Graduate Degrees
Use Educational Degrees

Graduate Education 73
PN 417 **SC** 21480
B Higher Education 73
N Dental Education 73
↓ Graduate Psychology Education 67
↓ Medical Education 73
Rehabilitation Education 97

Graduate Psychology Education 67
PN 2211 **SC** 21490
UF Training (Graduate Psychology)
B Graduate Education 73
Psychology Education 78
N ↓ Clinical Psychology Grad Training 73
R Educational Program Accreditation 94

Graduate Record Examination 73
PN 98 **SC** 21500
B Aptitude Measures 67

Graduate Schools 73
PN 45 **SC** 21510
B Schools 67
R ↓ Higher Education 73
School Graduation 91

Graduate Students 67
PN 2609 **SC** 21520
SN Students pursuing academic studies past the college level. Mandatory term in educational contexts.
B Students 67
R ↓ College Students 67
Dental Students 73
Law Students 78
Medical Students 67
Postgraduate Students 73
Young Adults 73

Graduation (School)
Use School Graduation

Grammar 67
PN 1585 **SC** 21530
SN Science of the structure of language including universal grammar, descriptive and prescriptive grammar, and the rules and principles of syntax, phonology, and semantics applied in verbal communication. Compare SYNTAX.
B Linguistics 73
N Morphology (Language) 73
↓ Phonology 73
↓ Semantics 67
↓ Syntax 71
Transformational Generative Grammar 73
R Discourse Analysis 97
↓ Language 67
↓ Verbal Communication 67
Words (Phonetic Units) 67

Grammar Schools
Use Elementary Schools

Grand Mal Epilepsy 73
PN 25 **SC** 21550
B Epilepsy 67

Grandchildren 73
PN 141 **SC** 21560
B Family Members 73

Grandiosity 94
PN 8 **SC** 21565
B Defense Mechanisms 67
R Delusions 67
Egotism 73
Emotional Superiority 73
Erotomania 97
Narcissism 67
Omnipotence 94

Grandparents 73
PN 383 **SC** 21570
B Ancestors 73
Family Members 73

Graphical Displays 85
PN 503 **SC** 21575
SN Pictorial rendering of data (e.g., bar graphs, continuous line graphs, and data plots). Consider VISUAL DISPLAYS to access references from 73-84.
B Displays 67
R Statistical Data 82
↓ Statistical Measurement 73

Graphology
Use Handwriting

Grasping 97
PN 0 **SC** 21585
B Motor Processes 67

Grasshoppers 73
PN 76 **SC** 21590
B Insects 67
R Larvae 73

Gravitational Effects 67
PN 139 **SC** 21600
B Environmental Effects 73
N Weightlessness 67
R Acceleration Effects 73
Altitude Effects 73
↓ Aviation 67
Decompression Effects 73
Flight Simulation 73

Gravitational Effects — (cont'd)
R Spaceflight 67
Underwater Effects 73

Great Britain 71
PN 1183 **SC** 21620
B United Kingdom 73
N England 73
Scotland 73
Wales 73
R Northern Ireland 73

Great Grandparents
Use Ancestors

Greece 73
PN 277 **SC** 21650
B Europe 73
R Middle East 78

Gregariousness 73
PN 16 **SC** 21660
B Personality Traits 67
R Extraversion 67
Sociability 73

Grief 73
PN 2559 **SC** 21680
UF Bereavement
Mourning
B Emotional States 73
R ↓ Death and Dying 67
↓ Separation Reactions 97
Suffering 73

Grimaces 73
PN 9 **SC** 21690
B Facial Expressions 67

Grooming Behavior (Animal)
Use Animal Grooming Behavior

Gross Motor Skill Learning 73
PN 151 **SC** 21700
B Perceptual Motor Learning 67
Skill Learning 73

Ground Transportation 73
PN 80 **SC** 21710
B Transportation 73
N ↓ Motor Vehicles 82
Railroad Trains 73
R Highway Safety 73

Group Cohesion 73
PN 696 **SC** 21730
SN Mutual bonds formed among the members of a group as a consequence of their combined efforts toward a common goal or purpose.
UF Cohesion (Group)
B Group Dynamics 67
R Group Development 97

Group Counseling 73
PN 2711 **SC** 21740
UF Counseling (Group)
B Counseling 67
R ↓ Self Help Techniques 82
↓ Support Groups 91
↓ Twelve Step Programs 97

Group Decision Making 78
PN 961 **SC** 21745
SN Process of arriving at a decision or judgment by a group.

Group Decision Making — (cont'd)
B Decision Making [67]
N Choice Shift [94]
R Management Decision Making [73]

Group Development [97]
PN 0 **SC** 21747
SN Used in treatment and nontreatment settings.
B Group Dynamics [67]
R Group Cohesion [73]
Group Participation [73]
↓ Group Psychotherapy [67]
Group Size [67]
Group Structure [67]

Group Discussion [67]
PN 1672 **SC** 21750
UF Discussion (Group)
B Group Dynamics [67]
Interpersonal Communication [73]
R Choice Shift [94]
Debates [97]

Group Dynamics [67]
PN 5235 **SC** 21760
UF Dynamics (Group)
N Group Cohesion [73]
Group Development [97]
Group Discussion [67]
Group Participation [73]
Group Performance [67]
Group Size [67]
Group Structure [67]
Intergroup Dynamics [73]
R Boundaries (Psychological) [97]
Brainstorming [82]
Choice Shift [94]
↓ Collective Behavior [67]
Consciousness Raising Groups [78]
Group Instruction [73]
↓ Group Problem Solving [73]
↓ Group Psychotherapy [67]
Human Relations Training [78]
Ingroup Outgroup [97]
↓ Organizational Behavior [78]
Peer Pressure [94]
Reference Groups [94]
Sensitivity Training [73]
↓ Sociometry [91]
Teams [88]

Group Health Plans
Use Health Maintenance Organizations

Group Homes [82]
PN 503 **SC** 21767
SN Housing for groups of patients, children, or others who need or desire emotional and physical support.
B Housing [73]
R ↓ Community Facilities [73]
Community Mental Health Services [78]
↓ Residential Care Institutions [73]
Retirement Communities [97]
Shelters [91]

Group Instruction [73]
PN 679 **SC** 21770
B Teaching Methods [67]
R Cooperative Learning [94]
↓ Group Dynamics [67]

Group Participation [73]
PN 1169 **SC** 21780
SN Involvement in a group's purpose or activities.

Group Participation — (cont'd)
B Group Dynamics [67]
Interpersonal Interaction [67]
Participation [73]
R ↓ Collective Behavior [67]
Group Development [97]

Group Performance [67]
PN 1105 **SC** 21790
SN Process and effectiveness of a group in accomplishing an intended goal.
B Group Dynamics [67]
Interpersonal Interaction [67]
Performance [67]

Group Problem Solving [73]
PN 1034 **SC** 21800
SN Dynamics of group interaction during the process of analyzing, defining, and attaining the solution to a problem.
B Problem Solving [67]
N Brainstorming [82]
R Choice Shift [94]
↓ Group Dynamics [67]

Group Psychotherapy [67]
PN 6886 **SC** 21810
UF Group Therapy
B Psychotherapy [67]
N ↓ Encounter Group Therapy [73]
Therapeutic Community [67]
R Conjoint Therapy [73]
Consciousness Raising Groups [78]
Group Development [97]
↓ Group Dynamics [67]
↓ Human Potential Movement [82]
Psychodrama [67]
Sensitivity Training [73]
↓ Support Groups [91]
Transactional Analysis [73]
↓ Twelve Step Programs [97]

Group Size [67]
PN 1177 **SC** 21820
UF Size (Group)
B Group Dynamics [67]
Size [73]
R Group Development [97]

Group Structure [67]
PN 849 **SC** 21830
SN Patterns of organization, behavior, and communication of a group that determine the interpersonal relations of its members.
B Group Dynamics [67]
R Group Development [97]

Group Testing [73]
PN 189 **SC** 21840
B Measurement [67]
R Test Administration [73]

Group Therapy
Use Group Psychotherapy

Groups (Organizations)
Use Organizations

Groups (Social)
Use Social Groups

Grown Children
Use Adult Offspring

Growth
Use Development

Growth Centers
Use Human Potential Movement

Growth Hormone
Use Somatotropin

Growth Hormone Inhibitor
Use Somatostatin

GSR (Electrophysiology)
Use Galvanic Skin Response

Guanethidine [73]
PN 33 **SC** 21930
B Amines [73]
Antihypertensive Drugs [73]
R Norepinephrine [73]

Guanosine [85]
PN 40 **SC** 21929
R ↓ Carbohydrate Metabolism [73]
Cyclic Adenosine Monophosphate [78]
↓ Nucleic Acids [73]

Guardianship [88]
PN 75 **SC** 21932
SN Court appointment of an individual to act as a guardian or conservator and to legally act and speak in the interest of a minor or a physically or mentally disabled adult.
UF Conservatorship
B Legal Processes [73]
R Child Custody [82]
↓ Client Rights [88]
↓ Commitment (Psychiatric) [73]
Informed Consent [85]
Protective Services [97]

Guatemala [82]
PN 56 **SC** 21931
B Central America [73]

Guessing [73]
PN 180 **SC** 21933
SN Responding to questions or test items on the basis of little or no knowledge of the correct answer.
R Intuition [73]
Questioning [82]
↓ Strategies [67]
Test Taking [85]

Guest Workers
Use Foreign Workers

Guidance (Educational)
Use Educational Counseling

Guidance (Occupational)
Use Occupational Guidance

Guidance Counseling
Use School Counseling

Guided Daydreams
Use Directed Reverie Therapy

Guided Fantasy
Use Directed Reverie Therapy

Guilford Zimmerman Temperament Surv [73]
PN 19 **SC** 21960
B Nonprojective Personality Measures [73]

Guilt 67
PN 1323 SC 21970
B Emotional States 73
R ↓ Anxiety 67
↓ Anxiety Disorders 97
Blame 94
Shame 94

Guinea 91
PN 0 SC 21975
B Africa 67

Guinea Pigs 67
PN 721 SC 21980
B Rodents 73

Gulls
Use Sea Gulls

Gun Control Laws 73
PN 51 SC 22000
B Laws 67
R Government 67
Weapons 78

Gustatory Perception
Use Taste Perception

Guyana 88
PN 7 SC 22020
B South America 67

Gymnastic Therapy
Use Recreation Therapy

Gynecological Disorders 73
PN 111 SC 22040
B Genital Disorders 67
Urogenital Disorders 73
N ↓ Menstrual Disorders 73
R ↓ Endocrine Sexual Disorders 73
Hermaphroditism 73
↓ Hypogonadism 73
↓ Infertility 73
Pseudocyesis 73
Sterility 73

Gynecologists 73
PN 38 SC 22050
B Physicians 67
R Obstetricians 78
Surgeons 73

Gynecology 78
PN 98 SC 22053
SN Medical specialty dealing with the female endocrine system, reproductive physiology, and diseases of the genital tract. Used for the medical specialty or the specific gynecological issues or findings.
B Medical Sciences 67
R ↓ Obstetrics 78

Gypsies 73
PN 32 SC 22055
SN Nomadic populations of Indian descent living chiefly in Europe and the U.S.
UF Gipsies
B Ethnic Groups 73
R ↓ Human Migration 73
Minority Groups 67

Gyrus Cinguli 73
PN 130 SC 22060
B Frontal Lobe 73
Limbic System 73

Habilitation 91
PN 47 SC 22065
SN Establishment, not restoration, of fundamental capabilities, knowledge, experiences, and attitudes before or along with the usual rehabilitation procedures as a means of increasing patient awareness and developing their potential . Used primarily for physically or mentally disabled populations. Compare REHABILITATION.
R Activities of Daily Living 91
Deinstitutionalization 82
Independent Living Programs 91
↓ Mainstreaming 91
↓ Rehabilitation 67
↓ Skill Learning 73

Habitat Selection
Use Territoriality

Habitats (Animal)
Use Animal Environments

Habits 67
PN 264 SC 22080
UF Mannerisms
N Hair Pulling 73
Nail Biting 73
Thumbsucking 73
Tobacco Smoking 67
R ↓ Learning 67

Habituation 67
PN 1904 SC 22090
SN Progressive attenuation of a response elicited by repetitive stimulation.
R ↓ Sensory Adaptation 67

Hair 73
PN 154 SC 22100
B Anatomy 67
R Alopecia 73
Scalp (Anatomy) 73
Skin (Anatomy) 67

Hair Loss
Use Alopecia

Hair Pulling 73
PN 181 SC 22120
UF Trichotillomania
B Habits 67
R ↓ Behavior Disorders 71
↓ Self Destructive Behavior 85

Haiti 73
PN 20 SC 22130
B West Indies 73
R Hispaniola 73

Halcion
Use Triazolam

Halfway Houses 73
PN 208 SC 22140
SN Facilities for psychiatric, drug, or alcohol rehabilitation patients or mentally retarded individuals who no longer need hospitalization or institutionalization, but who are not yet fully prepared to return to their communities.
B Residential Care Institutions 73
Treatment Facilities 73
R ↓ Community Facilities 73
↓ Correctional Institutions 73
↓ Psychiatric Hospital Programs 67
Psychiatric Hospitals 67

Hallucinations 67
PN 744 SC 22150

Hallucinations — (cont'd)
SN Perceptions through any sense modality in the absence of an appropriate stimulus. (Usually indicative of abnormality but may be experienced occasionally by normal persons).
UF Flashbacks
B Perceptual Disturbances 73
N Auditory Hallucinations 73
Drug Induced Hallucinations 73
Hypnagogic Hallucinations 73
Visual Hallucinations 73
R ↓ Hallucinogenic Drugs 67
↓ Hallucinosis 73
Near Death Experiences 85

Hallucinogenic Drugs 67
PN 357 SC 22160
B Drugs 67
N Bufotenine 73
Lysergic Acid Diethylamide 67
Mescaline 73
Peyote 73
Phencyclidine 82
Psilocybin 73
R ↓ Cannabis 73
↓ Cholinergic Blocking Drugs 73
Experimental Psychosis 73
↓ Hallucinations 67
↓ Psychedelic Drugs 73
↓ Psychotomimetic Drugs 73
Tetrahydrocannabinol 73

Hallucinosis 73
PN 29 SC 22170
SN Mental disorder characterized by hallucinations occurring in a normal state of consciousness and attributable to specific organic factors.
B Psychosis 67
N ↓ Alcoholic Hallucinosis 73
R ↓ Hallucinations 67

Halo Effect 82
PN 114 SC 22177
SN Tendency to rate individuals too high or too low on the basis of one outstanding trait or an erroneous overall impression. Often the source of error in rating scales.
R ↓ Errors 67
↓ Expectations 67
Experimenter Bias 67
Rating 67
↓ Social Perception 67

Haloperidol 73
PN 2288 SC 22180
B CNS Depressant Drugs 73
Sedatives 73
Tranquilizing Drugs 67

Halstead Reitan Neuropsych Battery 91
PN 51 SC 22184
SN Use NEUROPSYCHOLOGICAL ASSESSMENT to access references from 82-90.
B Neuropsychological Assessment 82

Hamsters 73
PN 1097 SC 22190
B Rodents 73

Hand (Anatomy) 67
PN 671 SC 22200
B Anatomy 67
Musculoskeletal System 73
R Arm (Anatomy) 73
↓ Fingers (Anatomy) 73
Palm (Anatomy) 73
Wrist 73

Handedness 78
PN 1871 **SC** 22210
SN Learned or spontaneous differential dexterity with and tendency to use one hand rather than the other.
B Lateral Dominance 67

Handicapped
SN Term discontinued in 1997. Use HANDICAPPED to access references prior to 1997.
Use Disabled

Handicapped (Attitudes Toward)
SN Term discontinued in 1997. Use HANDICAPPED (ATTITUDES TOWARD) to access references from 73-96.
Use Disabled (Attitudes Toward)

Handicrafts
Use Crafts

Handwriting 67
PN 726 **SC** 22250
UF Graphology
Writing (Handwriting)
B Verbal Communication 67
Written Language 67
N Cursive Writing 73
Handwriting Legibility 73
Printing (Handwriting) 73

Handwriting Legibility 73
PN 45 **SC** 22260
UF Legibility (Handwriting)
B Handwriting 67
Legibility 78

Happiness 73
PN 610 **SC** 22270
UF Joy
B Emotional States 73
R Euphoria 73
Pleasure 73

Haptic Perception
Use Cutaneous Sense

Harassment (Sexual)
Use Sexual Harassment

Hardiness 97
PN 0 **SC** 22285
SN Use PSYCHOLOGICAL ENDURANCE to access references from 91-96.
UF Resilience (Psychological)
B Personality Traits 67
R Adaptability (Personality) 73
Coping Behavior 67
↓ Emotional Adjustment 73
Emotional Stability 73
Psychological Endurance 73
Psychological Stress 73

Hashish 73
PN 64 **SC** 22290
B Cannabis 73
R Marihuana 71
Tetrahydrocannabinol 73

Hate 73
PN 90 **SC** 22300
B Aversion 67
R ↓ Anger 67
Hostility 67

Hawaii 73
PN 177 **SC** 22310
B United States 67

Hay Fever 73
PN 12 **SC** 22320
B Allergic Disorders 73
Respiratory Tract Disorders 73
R ↓ Psychosomatic Disorders 67

Hazardous Materials 91
PN 91 **SC** 22325
UF Asbestos
Toxic Waste
N ↓ Insecticides 73
↓ Poisons 73
Teratogens 88
R ↓ Accidents 67
↓ Chemicals 91
↓ Environment 67
Occupational Exposure 88
Pollution 73
↓ Safety 67
Toxicity 73

Hazards 73
PN 151 **SC** 22330
R ↓ Accidents 67
Risk Perception 97
↓ Safety 67
↓ Safety Devices 73
Warning Labels 97
↓ Warnings 97

Head (Anatomy) 73
PN 370 **SC** 22340
B Anatomy 67
R Face (Anatomy) 73
Scalp (Anatomy) 73
Skin (Anatomy) 67

Head Banging 73
PN 44 **SC** 22350
B Self Destructive Behavior 85

Head Injuries 73
PN 1753 **SC** 22360
B Injuries 73
N Brain Concussion 73
R ↓ Brain Damage 67
Traumatic Brain Injury 97
Whiplash 97
↓ Wounds 73

Head Start
Use Project Head Start

Headache 73
PN 749 **SC** 22380
B Pain 67
Symptoms 67
N Migraine Headache 73
Muscle Contraction Headache 73
R ↓ Psychosomatic Disorders 67

Health 73
PN 5050 **SC** 22390
UF Wellness
N Holistic Health 85
↓ Mental Health 67
Public Health 88
R General Health Questionnaire 91
Health Attitudes 85
Health Behavior 82
Health Complaints 97
Health Knowledge 94
Hygiene 94
Preventive Medicine 73

Health — (cont'd)
R Public Health Services 73
Well Being 94

Health Attitudes 85
PN 1865 **SC** 22391
UF Health Locus of Control
B Attitudes 67
R ↓ Drug Usage Attitudes 73
↓ Health 73
Health Behavior 82
Health Knowledge 94
Health Promotion 91
Lifestyle Changes 97
Obesity (Attitudes Toward) 97
↓ Physical Illness (Attitudes Toward) 85

Health Behavior 82
PN 2447 **SC** 22392
SN Individual lifestyle and behavior which may or may not enhance or maintain good health.
B Behavior 67
Client Characteristics 73
R Aerobic Exercise 88
AIDS Prevention 94
Diets 78
↓ Exercise 73
↓ Health 73
Health Attitudes 85
Health Knowledge 94
Health Promotion 91
Holistic Health 85
Hygiene 94
↓ Lifestyle 78
Lifestyle Changes 97
↓ Prenatal Care 91
Preventive Medicine 73
Self Examination (Medical) 88
Self Referral 91
Weight Control 85

Health Care Administration 97
PN 0 **SC** 57485
B Management 67
N Hospital Administration 78
R ↓ Case Management 91
↓ Health Care Delivery 78
Health Care Policy 94
↓ Health Care Services 78
↓ Mental Health Programs 73
↓ Mental Health Services 78
↓ Treatment Facilities 73

Health Care Costs 94
PN 197 **SC** 22393
UF Medical Care Costs
Mental Health Care Costs
B Costs and Cost Analysis 73
R ↓ Case Management 91
Cost Containment 91
Diagnosis Related Groups 88
Economics 85
↓ Health Care Delivery 78
↓ Health Care Services 78
Health Care Utilization 85
↓ Health Insurance 73
Health Maintenance Organizations 82
↓ Managed Care 94
↓ Mental Health Services 78
↓ Professional Fees 78
↓ Treatment 67

Health Care Delivery 78
PN 3478 **SC** 22394
SN Practices, policies, or referral processes that contribute to making mental and/or medical health care personnel, services, or facilities available to persons in need of such care.

Health Care Delivery — (cont'd)
N Home Care [85]
Hospice [82]
↓ Managed Care [94]
R ↓ Case Management [91]
Fee for Service [94]
↓ Health Care Administration [97]
Health Care Costs [94]
Health Care Policy [94]
↓ Health Care Services [78]
Health Care Utilization [85]
Health Maintenance Organizations [82]
Health Service Needs [97]
↓ Mental Health Programs [73]
↓ Mental Health Services [78]
Needs Assessment [85]
Outreach Programs [97]
Palliative Care [91]
↓ Prevention [73]
Primary Health Care [88]
Private Practice [78]
Quality of Care [88]
↓ Quality of Services [97]
↓ Treatment [67]
↓ Treatment Planning [97]

Health Care Policy [94]
PN 188 SC 57415
UF Mental Health Care Policy
B Policy Making [88]
R ↓ Government Policy Making [73]
↓ Health Care Administration [97]
↓ Health Care Delivery [78]
↓ Health Care Services [78]
↓ Health Insurance [73]
Medicaid [94]
Medicare [88]
↓ Mental Health Services [78]

Health Care Professionals
SN Use MEDICAL PERSONNEL or MENTAL HEALTH PERSONNEL to access references prior to 1994.
Use Health Personnel

Health Care Psychology [85]
PN 329 SC 22398
UF Behavioral Health
Behavioral Medicine
Health Psychology
N Medical Psychology [73]
R Interdisciplinary Treatment Approach [73]
Psychosomatic Medicine [78]

Health Care Seeking Behavior [97]
PN 0 SC 22399
SN Consider HELP SEEKING BEHAVIOR or HEALTH CARE UTILIZATION to access references from 78-84 and 85-96 respectively.
UF Treatment Seeking Behavior
B Help Seeking Behavior [78]
R ↓ Commitment (Psychiatric) [73]
↓ Health Care Services [78]
Health Care Utilization [85]
Health Service Needs [97]
↓ Hospital Admission [73]
↓ Mental Health Services [78]
Self Referral [91]
↓ Treatment [67]

Health Care Services [78]
PN 2190 SC 22396
B Treatment [67]
N Long Term Care [94]
↓ Mental Health Services [78]
Palliative Care [91]
Primary Health Care [88]
R Caregivers [88]
↓ Community Services [67]

Health Care Services — (cont'd)
R Cost Containment [91]
↓ Counseling [67]
Fee for Service [94]
↓ Health Care Administration [97]
Health Care Costs [94]
↓ Health Care Delivery [78]
Health Care Policy [94]
Health Care Seeking Behavior [97]
Health Care Utilization [85]
Health Maintenance Organizations [82]
Health Service Needs [97]
Integrated Services [97]
↓ Managed Care [94]
↓ Mental Health Programs [73]
Outreach Programs [97]
↓ Prenatal Care [91]
↓ Prevention [73]
Quality of Care [88]
↓ Quality of Services [97]
↓ Rehabilitation [67]
Self Referral [91]
Social Casework [67]
↓ Social Services [82]

Health Care Utilization [85]
PN 2398 SC 22397
SN Processes involved in or factors affecting usage of professional or nonprofessional health services or programs. Use HEALTH CARE SEEKING BEHAVIOR for factors involved in seeking treatment. Use HELP SEEKING BEHAVIOR to access references from 78-84.
UF Assistance Seeking (Professional)
Health Service Utilization
Utilization (Health Care)
R Health Care Costs [94]
↓ Health Care Delivery [78]
Health Care Seeking Behavior [97]
↓ Health Care Services [78]
↓ Help Seeking Behavior [78]
Self Referral [91]

Health Complaints [97]
PN 0 SC 22402
R ↓ Disorders [67]
↓ Health [73]
Symptom Checklists [91]
↓ Symptoms [67]

Health Education [73]
PN 2464 SC 22400
SN Instruction or programs in school, institutional, or community settings which present material about factors affecting health behavior and attitudes.
B Curriculum [67]
N Drug Education [73]
Sex Education [73]
R AIDS Prevention [94]
Client Education [85]
Health Knowledge [94]
Health Promotion [91]
↓ Prenatal Care [91]
↓ Prevention [73]
Psychoeducation [94]

Health Impaired [73]
PN 338 SC 22410
UF Frail
B Physically Disabled [97]
R ↓ Disorders [67]
Homebound [88]

Health Insurance [73]
PN 552 SC 22420
B Insurance [73]
N ↓ Employee Health Insurance [73]
Fee for Service [94]

Health Insurance — (cont'd)
N Health Maintenance Organizations [82]
Medicaid [94]
Medicare [88]
R ↓ Case Management [91]
Diagnosis Related Groups [88]
Health Care Costs [94]
Health Care Policy [94]
↓ Hospitalization [67]
↓ Managed Care [94]

Health Knowledge [94]
PN 249 SC 22421
SN Knowledge or understanding of illness, health, or mental health and health related issues.
B Knowledge Level [78]
R Client Education [85]
↓ Health [73]
Health Attitudes [85]
Health Behavior [82]
↓ Health Education [73]
Health Promotion [91]
Mental Illness (Attitudes Toward) [67]
↓ Physical Illness (Attitudes Toward) [85]

Health Locus of Control
Use Health Attitudes

Health Maintenance Organizations [82]
PN 241 SC 22425
SN Organizations providing comprehensive, coordinated medical services to voluntarily enrolled members on a prepaid basis.
UF Group Health Plans
HMO
B Health Insurance [73]
Managed Care [94]
Organizations [67]
R Cost Containment [91]
Fee for Service [94]
Health Care Costs [94]
↓ Health Care Delivery [78]
↓ Health Care Services [78]
Health Promotion [91]
Preventive Medicine [73]

Health Personnel [94]
PN 254 SC 57420
SN Personnel working in a medical or mental health profession. Used for unspecified health care professionals or when both medical and mental health professionals are discussed. Use a more specific term if possible. Consider MEDICAL PERSONNEL OR MENTAL HEALTH PERSONNEL to access references prior to 1994.
UF Health Care Professionals
B Professional Personnel [78]
N ↓ Medical Personnel [67]
↓ Mental Health Personnel [67]
R ↓ Counselors [67]
Home Care Personnel [97]
↓ Social Workers [73]
↓ Therapists [67]

Health Personnel Attitudes [85]
PN 2389 SC 22426
SN Attitudes of persons working in health or medical professions.
B Attitudes [67]
N ↓ Therapist Attitudes [78]
R Counselor Attitudes [73]
Psychologist Attitudes [91]

Health Promotion [91]
PN 649 SC 22423

Health Promotion — (cont'd)
SN Education or other types of interventions used to improve and encourage both physical and mental health. Consider using HEALTH EDUCATION to access references from 73-90.
R AIDS Prevention 94
Cancer Screening 97
Client Education 85
Health Attitudes 85
Health Behavior 82
↓ Health Education 73
Health Knowledge 94
Health Maintenance Organizations 82
↓ Health Screening 97
Lifestyle Changes 97
↓ Prevention 73
Preventive Medicine 73
Public Health 88
↓ Screening 82

Health Psychology
Use Health Care Psychology

Health Screening 97
PN 0 **SC** 22431
SN Consider PHYSICAL EXAMINATION to access references from 88–96.
B Screening 82
N Cancer Screening 97
HIV Testing 97
Physical Examination 88
R Drug Usage Screening 88
Health Promotion 91
Mammography 94
↓ Medical Diagnosis 73
Preventive Medicine 73
Public Health 88

Health Service Needs 97
PN 0 **SC** 22432
UF Mental Health Service Needs
B Needs 67
R ↓ Case Management 91
↓ Health Care Delivery 78
Health Care Seeking Behavior 97
↓ Health Care Services 78
Intake Interview 94
↓ Mental Health Services 78
Needs Assessment 85

Health Service Utilization
Use Health Care Utilization

Hearing Acuity
Use Auditory Acuity

Hearing Aids 73
PN 385 **SC** 22430
B Medical Therapeutic Devices 73
N Cochlear Implants 94

Hearing Disorders 82
PN 756 **SC** 22435
SN Disorders involving the hearing mechanisms, specifically the sensorineural pathways.
UF Sensorineural Hearing Loss
B Communication Disorders 82
R ↓ Aurally Disabled 97
Cochlear Implants 94
↓ Deaf 67
↓ Ear Disorders 73
↓ Sensorially Disabled 97

Hearing Impaired (Partially)
Use Partially Hearing Impaired

Hearing Measures
Use Speech and Hearing Measures

Heart 67
PN 392 **SC** 22460
B Cardiovascular System 67
N Heart Auricles 73
Heart Valves 73
Heart Ventricles 73
Myocardium 73
R ↓ Blood 67
Vagus Nerve 73

Heart Attacks
Use Heart Disorders

Heart Auricles 73
PN 9 **SC** 22470
UF Atria (Heart)
Auricles (Heart)
B Heart 67

Heart Beat
Use Heart Rate

Heart Disorders 73
PN 1049 **SC** 22480
UF Cardiac Arrest
Cardiac Disorders
Coronary Heart Disease
Heart Attacks
B Cardiovascular Disorders 67
N Angina Pectoris 73
↓ Arrhythmias (Heart) 73
Coronary Thromboses 73
Myocardial Infarctions 73
R Rheumatic Fever 73

Heart Rate 67
PN 5111 **SC** 22490
UF Cardiac Rate
Heart Beat
Heartbeat
R Cardiovascular Reactivity 94

Heart Rate Affecting Drugs 73
PN 50 **SC** 22500
B Drugs 67
N Caffeine 73
Epinephrine 67
Theophylline 73
Verapamil 91
R ↓ Analeptic Drugs 73
↓ Antihypertensive Drugs 73
↓ Cardiovascular Disorders 67
↓ CNS Affecting Drugs 73
↓ CNS Stimulating Drugs 73
Dopamine 73
↓ Muscle Relaxing Drugs 73
↓ Vasoconstrictor Drugs 73
↓ Vasodilator Drugs 73

Heart Surgery 73
PN 335 **SC** 22510
UF Cardiac Surgery
B Surgery 71
R Organ Transplantation 73

Heart Transplants
Use Organ Transplantation

Heart Valves 73
PN 40 **SC** 22530
UF Valves (Heart)
B Heart 67

Heart Ventricles 73
PN 28 **SC** 22540
UF Ventricles (Heart)
B Heart 67

Heartbeat
Use Heart Rate

Heat Effects 73
PN 463 **SC** 22560
B Temperature Effects 67

Hebephrenic Schizophrenia 73
PN 106 **SC** 22570
UF Schizophrenia (Disorganized Type)
B Schizophrenia 67

Hedonism 73
PN 65 **SC** 22580
R ↓ Attitudes 67
↓ Philosophies 67

Heels (Anatomy)
Use Feet (Anatomy)

Height (Body)
Use Body Height

Helicopters 73
PN 50 **SC** 22610
B Aircraft 73

Helium 73
PN 25 **SC** 22620

Help Seeking Behavior 78
PN 1165 **SC** 22624
SN Searching for or requesting help from others through formal or informal mechanisms. From 78-84 used primarily for the seeking or utilization of professional care or services. From 1997, use HEALTH CARE SEEKING BEHAVIOR to access references on help seeking in a treatment context.
B Social Behavior 67
N Health Care Seeking Behavior 97
R Assistance (Social Behavior) 73
Health Care Utilization 85
Self Referral 91

Helping Behavior
Use Assistance (Social Behavior)

Helplessness 97
PN 0 **SC** 22627
B Emotional States 73
N Learned Helplessness 78
R Coping Behavior 67
Empowerment 91
Hopelessness 88
Internal External Locus of Control 67
↓ Power 67
Self Control 73
Self Determination 94
Self Efficacy 85

Helplessness (Learned)
Use Learned Helplessness

Hematologic Disorders
Use Blood and Lymphatic Disorders

Hematoma 73
PN 40 **SC** 22640
B Hemorrhage 73
Symptoms 67
R ↓ Injuries 73

Hemianopia 73
PN 75 **SC** 22650

Hemianopia — (cont'd)
UF Hemiopia
B Eye Disorders [73]
R ↓ Nervous System Disorders [67]

Hemiopia
Use Hemianopia

Hemiplegia [78]
PN 178 SC 22675
SN Paralysis of one side of the body resulting from disease or injury to the brain or spinal cord.
B Paralysis [73]
R ↓ Central Nervous System Disorders [73]
↓ Injuries [73]
↓ Musculoskeletal Disorders [73]
Paraplegia [78]
↓ Physically Disabled [97]
Quadriplegia [85]
↓ Spinal Cord Injuries [73]

Hemispherectomy [73]
PN 84 SC 22680
B Neurosurgery [73]

Hemispheric Specialization
SN Use CEREBRAL DOMINANCE to access references from 73-90.
Use Lateral Dominance

Hemodialysis [73]
PN 430 SC 22690
B Dialysis [73]
R Blood Transfusion [73]

Hemoglobin [73]
PN 61 SC 22700
B Blood Proteins [73]
Pigments [73]

Hemophilia [73]
PN 159 SC 22710
B Blood and Lymphatic Disorders [73]
Sex Linked Hereditary Disorders [73]

Hemorrhage [73]
PN 46 SC 22720
B Cardiovascular Disorders [67]
Symptoms [67]
N Cerebral Hemorrhage [73]
Hematoma [73]

Hemp (Cannabis)
Use Cannabis

Henmon Nelson Tests Mental Ability
SN Term discontinued in 1997. Use HENMON NELSON TESTS MENTAL ABILITY to access references from 73–96.
Use Intelligence Measures

Heparin [73]
PN 9 SC 22750
B Acids [73]
Anticoagulant Drugs [73]

Hepatic Disorders
Use Liver Disorders

Hepatitis [73]
PN 78 SC 22770
B Liver Disorders [73]
N Toxic Hepatitis [73]
R ↓ Infectious Disorders [73]
Jaundice [73]

Hereditary Disorders
Use Genetic Disorders

Heredity
Use Genetics

Hermaphroditism [73]
PN 59 SC 22800
UF Intersexuality
Pseudohermaphroditism
B Congenital Disorders [73]
Genital Disorders [67]
R ↓ Endocrine Sexual Disorders [73]
Gender Identity Disorder [97]
↓ Gynecological Disorders [73]
↓ Male Genital Disorders [73]
Sterility [73]
Testicular Feminization Syndrome [73]

Hermeneutics [91]
PN 126 SC 22805
B Philosophies [67]
R Epistemology [73]
Metaphysics [73]
Phenomenology [67]
Positivism (Philosophy) [97]
Rhetoric [91]
↓ Semiotics [85]

Heroin [73]
PN 340 SC 22810
UF Diacetylmorphine
B Alkaloids [73]
Analgesic Drugs [73]
Opiates [73]
Sedatives [73]
R Heroin Addiction [73]

Heroin Addiction [73]
PN 1072 SC 22820
B Drug Addiction [67]
R Heroin [73]
Methadone Maintenance [78]

Herpes Genitalis [88]
PN 50 SC 22825
UF Genital Herpes
B Venereal Diseases [73]
Viral Disorders [73]

Herpes Simplex [73]
PN 143 SC 22830
B Skin Disorders [73]
Viral Disorders [73]

Heterogeneity of Variance
Use Variance Homogeneity

Heterosexual Interaction
Use Male Female Relations

Heterosexuality [73]
PN 736 SC 22840
B Psychosexual Behavior [67]
Sexual Orientation [97]
R Lesbianism [73]
Male Female Relations [88]
Male Homosexuality [73]
Sex Linked Developmental Differences [73]
Sexual Development [73]

Heterozygotic Twins [73]
PN 514 SC 22850
UF Dizygotic Twins
Fraternal Twins
B Twins [67]

Heuristic Modeling [73]
PN 201 SC 22860
B Simulation [67]
R ↓ Mathematical Modeling [73]

Hexamethonium [73]
PN 24 SC 22870
B Antihypertensive Drugs [73]
Ganglion Blocking Drugs [73]

Hexobarbital [73]
PN 26 SC 22880
B Anesthetic Drugs [73]
Barbiturates [67]
Hypnotic Drugs [73]
Sedatives [73]

Hibernation [73]
PN 65 SC 22890
B Animal Ethology [67]
R ↓ Animal Biological Rhythms [73]

Hidden Figures Test [73]
PN 15 SC 22900
B Intelligence Measures [67]

High Risk Populations
Use At Risk Populations

High Sch Personality Questionnaire [73]
PN 31 SC 22910
B Nonprojective Personality Measures [73]

High School Diplomas
Use Educational Degrees

High School Equivalency
Use Adult Education

High School Graduates [78]
PN 217 SC 22924
R ↓ Adolescents [67]
Educational Degrees [73]
High School Students [67]
School Graduation [91]
School to Work Transition [94]

High School Students [67]
PN 14165 SC 22930
SN Students in grades 9–12. Mandatory term in educational contexts.
B Students [67]
R ↓ Adolescents [67]
Grade Level [94]
High School Graduates [78]
Reentry Students [85]

High School Teachers [73]
PN 2025 SC 22940
B Teachers [67]

High Schools [73]
PN 619 SC 22950
B Schools [67]
R Military Schools [73]
Secondary Education [73]

Higher Education [73]
PN 934 SC 22960
SN College or university education beyond the successful completion of high school or grammar school, or the attainment of an approved equivalent.
B Education [67]
N ↓ Graduate Education [73]
↓ Postgraduate Training [73]
Undergraduate Education [78]

Higher Education — (cont'd)
R ↓ Colleges 67
↓ Continuing Education 85
Educational Degrees 73
Educational Program Accreditation 94
Graduate Schools 73
Professional Specialization 91
School Graduation 91

Higher Order Conditioning 97
PN 0 SC 22970
SN A classical conditioning method in which the original conditioned stimulus is used as the unconditioned stimulus in a new experimental setting.
UF Second Order Conditioning
B Classical Conditioning 67

Highway Safety 73
PN 571 SC 22980
UF Automobile Safety
Driver Safety
B Safety 67
R Drivers 73
↓ Driving Behavior 67
Driving Under The Influence 88
↓ Ground Transportation 73
Motor Traffic Accidents 73
↓ Transportation Accidents 73

Hindbrain 97
PN 0 SC 22985
UF Rhombencephalon
B Brain 67
N ↓ Cerebellum 73
Medulla Oblongata 73
↓ Pons 73
R ↓ Brain Stem 73
Raphe Nuclei 82

Hinduism 73
PN 210 SC 22990
B Religious Affiliation 73
R Hindus 97

Hindus 97
PN 0 SC 22995
B Religious Groups 97
R Hinduism 73

Hippies
Use Subculture (Anthropological)

Hippocampal Commissure
Use Fornix

Hippocampus 67
PN 3546 SC 23010
B Limbic System 73
R Medial Forebrain Bundle 82
Septal Nuclei 82

Hips 73
PN 66 SC 23020
B Musculoskeletal System 73

Hiring
Use Personnel Selection

Hispanics 82
PN 2849 SC 23035
SN Populations of Spanish, Portuguese, or Latin American descent residing in countries other than the country of their origin. (For those residing in their own country use the appropriate country name). Use SPANISH AMERICANS to access references from 78–81.

Hispanics — (cont'd)
UF Cuban Americans
Latinos
Puerto Rican Americans
Spanish Americans
B Ethnic Groups 73
N Mexican Americans 73
R Minority Groups 67

Hispaniola 73
PN 3 SC 23040
B West Indies 73
R Dominican Republic 73
Haiti 73

Histamine 73
PN 145 SC 23050
B Amines 73
Neurotransmitters 85
R ↓ Antihistaminic Drugs 73
Histidine 73

Histidine 73
PN 28 SC 23060
B Amino Acids 73
R Histamine 73

Histology 73
PN 81 SC 23070
SN Branch of anatomy dealing with the structure of cells, tissues, and organs in relation to their functions. Used for the scientific discipline or the organic structure itself.
R Morphology 73
↓ Physiology 67
↓ Tissues (Body) 73

History 73
PN 4398 SC 23075
SN Recording and/or explanation of previous events, experiences, trends, and treatments.
N ↓ History of Psychology 67
R Future 91
Psychohistory 78
Trends 91

History of Psychology 67
PN 4648 SC 23080
B History 73
N Associationism 73
Behaviorism 67
Freudian Psychoanalytic School 73
Functionalism 73
Gestalt Psychology 67
↓ Neopsychoanalytic School 73
Structuralism 73
R Phenomenology 67
↓ Psychology 67
↓ Theories 67

Histrionic Personality Disorder
Use Hysterical Personality

HIV
Use Human Immunodeficiency Virus

HIV Testing 97
PN 0 SC 23084
UF AIDS Testing
B Health Screening 97
Medical Diagnosis 73
R Acquired Immune Deficiency Syndrome 88
AIDS Prevention 94
↓ Human Immunodeficiency Virus 91

HMO
Use Health Maintenance Organizations

Hoarding Behavior (Animal)
Use Animal Hoarding Behavior

Hobbies 73
PN 29 SC 23100
SN Use RECREATION to access references from 73-88.
R Daily Activities 94
↓ Interests 67
Leisure Time 73
↓ Recreation 67

Hoffmanns Reflex 73
PN 35 SC 23110
SN Flexing of the thumb and some other finger resulting from a sudden tapping of the nail of the index, middle, or ring finger. Also known as digital reflex, finger flexion reflex, snapping reflex, H reflex, or Hoffmann's (H) response.
B Reflexes 71

Holidays 88
PN 39 SC 23113
SN Days marked by general suspension of work in commemoration or celebration of an event.
R Leisure Time 73
↓ Recreation 67
Vacationing 73

Holistic Health 85
PN 301 SC 23115
SN Personal practices or medical or psychological diagnosis and treatment based on the concept that humans are composed of body, mind, and spirit. An observed disorder or dysfunction in one component implies the need for treatment of the whole organism to restore health.
UF Wholistic Health
B Health 73
R ↓ Alternative Medicine 97
Biopsychosocial Approach 91
Health Behavior 82
↓ Lifestyle 78
Meditation 73
↓ Physical Treatment Methods 73
Preventive Medicine 73
↓ Psychotherapy 67

Holocaust 88
PN 109 SC 23117
SN Nazi persecution and genocide of Jews and others in Europe between 1933 and 1945.
B Genocide 88
R AntiSemitism 73
Concentration Camps 73
Fascism 73
Holocaust Survivors 88
Jews 97
Judaism 67

Holocaust Survivors 88
PN 189 SC 23118
B Survivors 94
R Holocaust 88
Jews 97

Holtzman Inkblot Technique 67
PN 133 SC 23120
B Projective Personality Measures 73
Projective Techniques 67

Homatropine
SN Term discontinued in 1997. Use HOMATROPINE to access references from 73–96.
Use Alkaloids

Home Accidents [73]
PN 37 SC 23140
B Accidents [67]

Home Birth
Use Midwifery

Home Care [85]
PN 773 SC 23145
SN Health and personal care provided in the home environment, usually by family members.
B Health Care Delivery [78]
R Adult Day Care [97]
Caregiver Burden [94]
Caregivers [88]
Elder Care [94]
Home Care Personnel [97]
Home Visiting Programs [73]
Homebound [88]
Hospice [82]
Long Term Care [94]
↓ Outpatient Treatment [67]
Quality of Care [88]
Respite Care [88]

Home Care Personnel [97]
PN 0 SC 23146
SN Personnel providing personal care, nursing services, medical treatment, or followup care to patients in their homes.
UF Home Health Aides
B Paraprofessional Personnel [73]
R Caregivers [88]
Elder Care [94]
↓ Health Personnel [94]
Home Care [85]
Home Visiting Programs [73]
↓ Paramedical Personnel [73]

Home Economics [85]
PN 44 SC 23147
B Curriculum [67]
R Household Management [85]

Home Environment [73]
PN 3191 SC 23150
B Social Environments [73]
R Empty Nest [91]
Living Alone [94]
↓ Living Arrangements [91]

Home Health Aides
Use Home Care Personnel

Home Reared Mentally Retarded [73]
PN 40 SC 23160
B Mentally Retarded [67]
R Institutionalized Mentally Retarded [73]

Home Schooling [94]
PN 10 SC 23165
SN Provision of compulsory education in the home.
B Nontraditional Education [82]
R ↓ Curriculum [67]
↓ Education [67]
↓ Teaching Methods [67]

Home Visiting Programs [73]
PN 422 SC 23170
SN Planned educational, health, or counseling procedures or activities that take place in the home.
B Community Services [67]
Mental Health Programs [73]
R Adult Day Care [97]
Elder Care [94]
Home Care [85]

Home Visiting Programs — (cont'd)
R Home Care Personnel [97]
Homebound [88]
↓ Program Development [91]

Homebound [88]
PN 24 SC 23173
SN Individuals restricted to place of residence for health or disability reasons.
R ↓ Aged [73]
Caregiver Burden [94]
↓ Disabled [97]
Elder Care [94]
Health Impaired [73]
Home Care [85]
Home Visiting Programs [73]

Homeless [88]
PN 944 SC 23174
B Social Issues [91]
N Homeless Mentally Ill [97]
R Deinstitutionalization [82]
Disadvantaged [67]
Poverty [73]
Shelters [91]
↓ Social Deprivation [73]

Homeless Mentally Ill [97]
PN 0 SC 23171
UF Mentally Ill Homeless
B Homeless [88]
R Deinstitutionalization [82]
↓ Mental Disorders [67]
Psychopathology [67]

Homemaking
Use Household Management

Homeostasis [73]
PN 196 SC 23180
SN Tendency of an organism to maintain a state of physiological equilibrium and the processes by which such a stable internal environment is maintained.
UF Autoregulation
B Physiology [67]
R Dehydration [88]
Instinctive Behavior [82]

Homesickness [94]
PN 7 SC 23183
B Emotional States [73]
R ↓ Experiences (Events) [73]
Life Experiences [73]
Loneliness [73]
Reminiscence [85]
Sadness [73]
↓ Separation Reactions [97]

Homework [88]
PN 126 SC 23185
SN Assignment given to students or clients to be completed outside regular classroom period or therapeutic setting.
R Note Taking [91]
↓ Psychotherapeutic Techniques [67]
Study Habits [73]

Homicide [67]
PN 1308 SC 23190
UF Murder
B Behavior Disorders [71]
N ↓ Genocide [88]
Infanticide [78]

Homing (Animal)
Use Animal Homing

Homographs [73]
PN 59 SC 23200
SN Words identical in spelling but different in derivation, pronunciation, and meaning.
B Vocabulary [67]
R Homonyms [73]
Orthography [73]
Words (Phonetic Units) [67]

Homonyms [73]
PN 60 SC 23210
B Semantics [67]
Vocabulary [67]
R Homographs [73]
Words (Phonetic Units) [67]

Homophobia
Use Homosexuality (Attitudes Toward)

Homosexual Liberation Movement [73]
PN 36 SC 23220
UF Gay Liberation Movement
B Social Movements [67]
R ↓ Activist Movements [73]

Homosexual Parents [94]
PN 14 SC 23225
UF Gay Parents
Lesbian Parents
B Parents [67]
R ↓ Family Structure [73]
Lesbianism [73]
Male Homosexuality [73]
Significant Others [91]

Homosexuality [67]
PN 1331 SC 23230
B Psychosexual Behavior [67]
Sexual Orientation [97]
N Bisexuality [73]
Lesbianism [73]
Male Homosexuality [73]
R Homosexuality (Attitudes Toward) [82]
Transsexualism [73]
Transvestism [73]

Homosexuality (Attitudes Toward) [82]
PN 579 SC 23233
SN Attitudes regarding sexual contact between persons of the same sex.
UF Homophobia
B Attitudes [67]
R ↓ Homosexuality [67]
↓ Sexual Orientation [97]

Homovanillic Acid [78]
PN 483 SC 23235
SN Excretion product of dopamine metabolism.
B Acids [73]
Dopamine Metabolites [82]
R Dopamine [73]

Honduras [88]
PN 7 SC 23237
B Central America [73]

Honesty [73]
PN 232 SC 23240
UF Frankness
B Personality Traits [67]
R Integrity [97]

Hong Kong [78]
PN 500 SC 23245
B Asia [73]

Hope [91]
PN 81 **SC** 23247
B Emotional States [73]
R ↓ Expectations [67]
Hopelessness [88]
Optimism [73]
Positivism [73]
Trust (Social Behavior) [67]

Hopelessness [88]
PN 279 **SC** 23250
SN Feeling that one's physical, emotional, or social state is beyond improvement.
B Emotional States [73]
R Apathy [73]
Cynicism [73]
↓ Helplessness [97]
Hope [91]
Pessimism [73]

Hormone Therapy [94]
PN 51 **SC** 23255
UF Estrogen Replacement Therapy
B Drug Therapy [67]
R ↓ Hormones [67]

Hormones [67]
PN 2246 **SC** 23260
N ↓ Adrenal Cortex Hormones [73]
↓ Adrenal Medulla Hormones [73]
Cholecystokinin [82]
Corticotropin Releasing Factor [94]
Epinephrine [67]
Glucagon [73]
↓ Gonadotropic Hormones [73]
Insulin [73]
Melatonin [73]
Parathyroid Hormone [73]
↓ Pituitary Hormones [73]
↓ Progestational Hormones [85]
↓ Sex Hormones [73]
↓ Thyroid Hormones [73]
R ↓ Anti Inflammatory Drugs [82]
Antineoplastic Drugs [82]
↓ Drugs [67]
↓ Endocrine Glands [73]
Fertility Enhancement [73]
Hormone Therapy [94]
Pheromones [73]
Prostaglandins [82]
↓ Steroids [73]

Horses [73]
PN 161 **SC** 23270
B Mammals [73]

Hospice [82]
PN 406 **SC** 23275
SN Supportive palliative care of terminally ill patients usually in their own home by a treatment team and family members; sometimes involves residential care.
B Health Care Delivery [78]
R Home Care [85]
Palliative Care [91]
Terminally Ill Patients [73]

Hospital Accreditation [73]
PN 16 **SC** 23280
SN Recognition of a hospital as maintaining standards set by a government agency.
R ↓ Hospitals [67]

Hospital Addiction Syndrome
Use Munchausen Syndrome

Hospital Administration [78]
PN 242 **SC** 23286

Hospital Administration — (cont'd)
B Health Care Administration [97]
R Decentralization [78]
↓ Hospitals [67]
↓ Medical Records [78]

Hospital Admission [73]
PN 296 **SC** 23290
UF Admission (Hospital)
Readmission (Hospital)
B Facility Admission [88]
Hospitalization [67]
N ↓ Psychiatric Hospital Admission [73]
R Health Care Seeking Behavior [97]
↓ Hospital Discharge [73]
↓ Institutional Release [78]
↓ Psychiatric Hospitalization [73]

Hospital Attendants
Use Attendants (Institutions)

Hospital Discharge [73]
PN 365 **SC** 23303
B Facility Discharge [88]
Hospitalization [67]
Institutional Release [78]
N Psychiatric Hospital Discharge [78]
R Client Transfer [97]
Discharge Planning [94]
↓ Hospital Admission [73]
↓ Psychiatric Hospital Admission [73]
Psychiatric Hospital Readmission [73]
↓ Psychiatric Hospitalization [73]
Treatment Termination [82]

Hospital Environment [82]
PN 625 **SC** 23304
SN Physical, organizational, or psychological characteristics of a hospital, and their potential impact on hospital staff and patients.
B Facility Environment [88]
R ↓ Hospitals [67]
Intensive Care [88]

Hospital Programs [78]
PN 1251 **SC** 23306
SN Organized plans for care, including psychiatric treatment, or training in general medical hospital settings.
N ↓ Psychiatric Hospital Programs [67]
R Intensive Care [88]
Partial Hospitalization [85]
↓ Program Development [91]
Psychiatric Units [91]

Hospital Psychiatric Units
Use Psychiatric Units

Hospital Staff
Use Medical Personnel

Hospitalization [67]
PN 1260 **SC** 23320
B Institutionalization [67]
N ↓ Commitment (Psychiatric) [73]
↓ Hospital Admission [73]
↓ Hospital Discharge [73]
↓ Psychiatric Hospitalization [73]
R ↓ Health Insurance [73]
Long Term Care [94]
Patient Seclusion [94]
Psychiatric Units [91]

Hospitalized Patients [73]
PN 4022 **SC** 23330
B Patients [67]

Hospitals [67]
PN 1527 **SC** 23340
UF Infirmaries
B Residential Care Institutions [73]
Treatment Facilities [73]
N Psychiatric Hospitals [67]
Sanatoriums [73]
R ↓ Clinics [67]
Hospital Accreditation [73]
Hospital Administration [78]
Hospital Environment [82]
Intensive Care [88]
Maximum Security Facilities [85]
Nursing Homes [73]
Psychiatric Clinics [73]
Psychiatric Units [91]

Hostages [88]
PN 35 **SC** 23347
SN Use CRIME VICTIMS to access references from 82-87.
B Crime Victims [82]
R Kidnapping [88]
Prisoners of War [73]
Terrorism [82]

Hostility [67]
PN 1759 **SC** 23350
UF Antagonism
Resentment
B Anger [67]
R Hate [73]
Retaliation [91]

Hot Line Services [73]
PN 308 **SC** 23360
SN Telephone information, counseling, and crisis intervention services.
UF Telephone Hot Lines
B Crisis Intervention Services [73]
Mental Health Programs [73]
R Community Mental Health Centers [73]
Information Services [88]
Suicide Prevention Centers [73]

Household Management [85]
PN 368 **SC** 23365
SN Activities carried out for the regular maintenance of home and personal belongings.
UF Homemaking
Housework
B Management [67]
R ↓ Division of Labor [88]
↓ Family Life Education [97]
Home Economics [85]
Housewives [73]

Household Structure
Use Living Arrangements

Housewives [73]
PN 364 **SC** 23370
B Wives [73]
R Household Management [85]

Housework
Use Household Management

Housing [73]
PN 981 **SC** 23380
B Community Facilities [73]
N Dormitories [73]
Group Homes [82]
Retirement Communities [97]
Shelters [91]
R ↓ Living Arrangements [91]
↓ Social Programs [73]

Hue [73]
PN 246 **SC** 23390
SN One of the perceived dimensions of color corresponding to the wavelength of the light. Compare COLOR.
B Chromaticity [97]
Color [67]
R Color Saturation [97]

Human Animal Interaction
Use Interspecies Interaction

Human Biological Rhythms [73]
PN 1745 **SC** 23400
SN Periodic variations in human physiological and psychological functions. Use BIOLOGICAL RHYTHMS to access references from 67-72.
UF Circadian Rhythms (Human)
Diurnal Variations
B Biological Rhythms [67]

Human Channel Capacity [73]
PN 802 **SC** 23410
SN Number of signals or information volume which can be processed simultaneously.
UF Cognitive Load
Mental Load
R ↓ Attention [67]
Cognitive Processing Speed [97]
Human Information Storage [73]
Work Load [82]

Human Computer Interaction [97]
PN 0 **SC** 23415
SN Consider MAN MACHINE SYSTEMS to access references from 73-96.
R ↓ Computer Peripheral Devices [85]
↓ Computers [67]
Human Factors Engineering [73]
Human Machine Systems [97]
Human Machine Systems Design [97]
Keyboards [85]

Human Courtship [73]
PN 166 **SC** 23420
UF Courtship (Human)
B Psychosexual Behavior [67]
N Social Dating [73]
R Acquaintance Rape [91]
Human Mate Selection [88]
Male Female Relations [88]
Monogamy [97]
↓ Relationship Termination [97]
Romance [97]

Human Development [67]
PN 1057 **SC** 23430
SN Conceptually broad array term. Use a more specific term if possible.
UF Maturation
B Development [67]
N Adolescent Development [73]
Adult Development [78]
↓ Childhood Development [67]
R Age Differences [67]
↓ Aging [91]
↓ Delayed Development [73]
↓ Developmental Age Groups [73]
Developmental Disabilities [82]
↓ Developmental Psychology [73]
↓ Developmental Stages [73]
Life Expectancy [82]
Nature Nurture [94]
↓ Physical Development [73]
↓ Psychogenesis [73]

Human Factors Engineering [73]
PN 1465 **SC** 23440
UF Ergonomics
R Computer Assisted Design [97]
Engineering Psychology [67]
Furniture [85]
Human Computer Interaction [97]
Human Machine Systems [97]
↓ Instrument Controls [85]
Quality Control [88]
↓ Working Conditions [73]

Human Females [73]
PN 18057 **SC** 23450
SN Used for all-female populations when sex is pertinent to the focus of the study. For comparison of sexes use HUMAN SEX DIFFERENCES.
UF Females (Human)
Girls
Women
N Battered Females [88]
Daughters [73]
Female Criminals [73]
Female Delinquents [73]
↓ Mothers [67]
Sisters [73]
Widows [73]
↓ Wives [73]
Working Women [78]
R ↓ Human Sex Differences [67]
Sex Linked Developmental Differences [73]

Human Figures Drawing [73]
PN 518 **SC** 23460
SN Projective measures or techniques designed to yield information from drawings of human figures and responses to questions about the drawings.
UF Draw A Man Test
B Projective Personality Measures [73]
R Goodenough Harris Draw A Person Test [67]
Mirror Image [91]

Human Immunodeficiency Virus [91]
PN 2486 **SC** 23465
UF HIV
B Immunologic Disorders [73]
Viral Disorders [73]
N Acquired Immune Deficiency Syndrome [88]
R AIDS (Attitudes Toward) [97]
AIDS Dementia Complex [97]
AIDS Prevention [94]
HIV Testing [97]
↓ Venereal Diseases [73]
Zidovudine [94]

Human Information Processes
Use Cognitive Processes

Human Information Storage [73]
PN 5335 **SC** 23480
SN Process of information perception, encoding, or storage, and retrieval of material from memory.
UF Decoding
Encoding
Information Storage (Human)
R ↓ Cognitive Processes [67]
Human Channel Capacity [73]
Information [67]
↓ Lexical Access [88]
Lexical Decision [88]
↓ Memory [67]
Word Recognition [88]

Human Machine Systems [97]
PN 0 **SC** 23485
SN Systems based on the human engineering concept that views human operators and the machines they operate as functionally integrated parts of a larger goal-oriented system. Use MAN MACHINE SYSTEMS to access references from 73-96.
UF Man Machine Systems
B Systems [67]
R ↓ Artificial Intelligence [82]
↓ Computer Peripheral Devices [85]
Computer Searching [91]
Cybernetics [67]
Databases [91]
Error Analysis [73]
↓ Expert Systems [91]
Human Computer Interaction [97]
Human Factors Engineering [73]
Human Machine Systems Design [97]
Systems Analysis [73]
Virtual Reality [97]

Human Machine Systems Design [97]
PN 0 **SC** 23487
SN Use MAN MACHINE SYSTEMS DESIGN to access references from 73-96.
UF Design (Man Machine Systems)
Man Machine Systems Design
R Computer Assisted Design [97]
Human Computer Interaction [97]
Human Machine Systems [97]
↓ Instrument Controls [85]
↓ Systems [67]
Systems Analysis [73]

Human Males [73]
PN 5956 **SC** 23490
SN Used for all-male populations when sex is pertinent to the focus of the study. For comparison of sexes use HUMAN SEX DIFFERENCES.
UF Boys
Males (Human)
Men
N Brothers [73]
↓ Fathers [67]
Husbands [73]
Male Criminals [73]
Male Delinquents [73]
Sons [73]
Widowers [73]
R ↓ Human Sex Differences [67]
Sex Linked Developmental Differences [73]

Human Mate Selection [88]
PN 157 **SC** 23495
UF Mate Selection
R Assortative Mating [91]
Choice Behavior [67]
↓ Human Courtship [73]
Interpersonal Attraction [67]
Interpersonal Compatibility [73]
↓ Psychosexual Behavior [67]
Romance [97]

Human Migration [73]
PN 836 **SC** 23500
SN Movement of residence from one place to another. Includes nomadism; labor or seasonal migration; patterns of rural, urban, or suburban migration; or voluntary or forced relocation.
UF Migration (Human)
Population Shifts
B Social Processes [67]
N Refugees [88]
R Geographical Mobility [78]
Gypsies [73]
Immigration [73]
Migrant Farm Workers [73]

Human Nature [97]
PN 0 SC 23502
R ↓ Behavior [67]
↓ Emotions [67]
Instinctive Behavior [82]
Mind [91]
↓ Personality [67]

Human Potential Movement [82]
PN 171 SC 23504
SN Movement aimed at the enhancement of personal psychological growth. Formats used include Gestalt therapy, sensory awakening, sensory awareness, meditation, encounter groups, transactional analysis, assertiveness training, and humanistic psychology.
UF Growth Centers
Personal Growth Techniques
N Assertiveness Training [78]
Consciousness Raising Groups [78]
↓ Encounter Group Therapy [73]
Gestalt Therapy [73]
Human Relations Training [78]
Sensitivity Training [73]
Transactional Analysis [73]
R ↓ Group Psychotherapy [67]
Humanism [73]
↓ Humanistic Psychology [85]
Maslow (Abraham Harold) [91]
Meditation [73]
Self Actualization [73]

Human Relations Training [78]
PN 447 SC 23506
SN Techniques aimed at promoting awareness of feelings and needs of others in order to facilitate positive interpersonal interactions.
UF T Groups
B Human Potential Movement [82]
R Assertiveness Training [78]
Communication Skills Training [82]
↓ Encounter Group Therapy [73]
↓ Group Dynamics [67]
Marathon Group Therapy [73]
Parent Training [78]
↓ Personnel Training [67]
Sensitivity Training [73]
Social Skills Training [82]

Human Resources
Use Personnel Management

Human Rights [78]
PN 323 SC 23508
SN Fundamental rights of every human being to life, freedom, and equality. Often used for freedom from arbitrary governmental interference.
B Social Issues [91]
N ↓ Civil Rights [78]
R ↓ Client Rights [88]
Social Equality [73]
↓ Social Movements [67]
↓ Social Processes [67]
Treatment Withholding [88]

Human Sex Differences [67]
PN 33226 SC 23510
UF Gender Differences
Sex Differences (Human)
N Sex Linked Developmental Differences [73]
R Androgyny [82]
↓ Human Females [73]
↓ Human Males [73]
Sex [67]
Sex Recognition [97]

Humanism [73]
PN 581 SC 23520

Humanism — (cont'd)
SN Philosophy that asserts an individual's capacity for self-realization through reason and often rejects the supernatural.
B Philosophies [67]
R ↓ Human Potential Movement [82]
↓ Humanistic Psychology [85]

Humanistic Education
Use Affective Education

Humanistic Psychology [85]
PN 292 SC 23527
SN School of psychology emphasizing a holistic approach including self-actualization, creativity, and free choice.
B Psychology [67]
N Transpersonal Psychology [88]
R Client Centered Therapy [67]
↓ Human Potential Movement [82]
Humanism [73]
Maslow (Abraham Harold) [91]
Neurolinguistic Programing [88]
Rogers (Carl) [91]
Self Psychology [88]

Humor [67]
PN 1201 SC 23540
N Cartoons (Humor) [73]
Jokes [73]
R Laughter [78]

Hungary [73]
PN 217 SC 23550
B Europe [73]

Hunger [67]
PN 385 SC 23560
SN Need or desire for food. May also be defined operationally in experimental settings as the duration of food deprivation or the organism's percentage of normal body weight following food deprivation. Compare APPETITE.
B Appetite [73]
Motivation [67]
R Animal Feeding Behavior [73]
Food Deprivation [67]
Starvation [73]

Huntingtons Chorea
SN Term discontinued in 1997. Use HUNTINGTONS CHOREA to access references from 73–96.
Use Huntingtons Disease

Huntingtons Disease [73]
PN 498 SC 23570
SN Use HUNTINGTONS CHOREA to access references from 73–96.
UF Huntingtons Chorea
B Chorea [73]
Genetic Disorders [73]

Husbands [73]
PN 1024 SC 23590
B Human Males [73]
Spouses [73]

Hybrids (Biology) [73]
PN 76 SC 23600
R ↓ Genetics [67]

Hydralazine [73]
PN 8 SC 23620
B Antihypertensive Drugs [73]
Sympatholytic Drugs [73]

Hydrocephaly [73]
PN 208 SC 23630
B Brain Disorders [67]
R ↓ Congenital Disorders [73]
↓ Convulsions [67]
↓ Infectious Disorders [73]
↓ Mental Retardation [67]
↓ Neonatal Disorders [73]

Hydrocortisone [73]
PN 1545 SC 23640
UF Cortisol
B Adrenal Cortex Hormones [73]
Corticosteroids [73]
R ↓ Anti Inflammatory Drugs [82]

Hydrogen [73]
PN 11 SC 23650

Hydroxydopamine (6-) [78]
PN 577 SC 23656
UF Oxidopamine
B Adrenergic Blocking Drugs [73]

Hydroxyindoleacetic Acid (5-) [85]
PN 325 SC 23658
SN Major metabolic product of serotonin.
B Acids [73]
Serotonin Metabolites [78]

Hydroxylamine [73]
PN 1 SC 23660
B Amines [73]

Hydroxylase Inhibitors [85]
PN 17 SC 23665
B Enzyme Inhibitors [85]
R Hydroxylases [73]

Hydroxylases [73]
PN 228 SC 23670
B Enzymes [73]
R ↓ Esterases [73]
Hydroxylase Inhibitors [85]
Phosphatases [73]

Hydroxytryptamine (5-)
Use Serotonin

Hydroxytryptophan (5-) [91]
PN 46 SC 23685
B Tryptophan [73]

Hydroxyzine [73]
PN 21 SC 23690
B Minor Tranquilizers [73]
R ↓ Antihistaminic Drugs [73]

Hygiene [94]
PN 17 SC 23700
SN Use HEALTH to access references from 73–93.
R Activities of Daily Living [91]
↓ Health [73]
Health Behavior [82]
Self Care Skills [78]

Hyoscine
Use Scopolamine

Hyoscyamine (dl-)
Use Atropine

Hyperactivity
Use Hyperkinesis

Hypercholesterolemia
Use Metabolism Disorders

Hyperglycemia [85]
PN 32 **SC** 23745
B Metabolism Disorders [73]
Symptoms [67]

Hyperkinesis [73]
PN 3297 **SC** 23760
SN Excessive and usually inappropriate motor activity accompanied by poor attention span and restlessness. Consider also ATTENTION DEFICIT DISORDER.
UF Hyperactivity
B Nervous System Disorders [67]
Symptoms [67]
R Ataxia [73]
Attention Deficit Disorder [85]
Minimal Brain Disorders [73]
↓ Neuromuscular Disorders [73]
Oppositional Defiant Disorder [97]
Restlessness [73]

Hypermedia [97]
PN 0 **SC** 23780
SN Computerized multimedia that contain images, video clips, and sounds in addition to or instead of text, and include highlighted elements that, when selected by the user, instruct the computer program to retrieve one or more of the computerized media.
B Computer Applications [73]
R ↓ Computer Software [67]
Hypertext [97]

Hyperparathyroidism
Use Parathyroid Disorders

Hyperphagia [73]
PN 239 **SC** 23800
UF Polyphagia
B Eating Disorders [97]
Symptoms [67]
R Obesity [73]
↓ Psychosomatic Disorders [67]

Hypersensitivity (Immunologic)
Use Immunologic Disorders

Hypersexuality [73]
PN 45 **SC** 23820
UF Nymphomania
B Psychosexual Behavior [67]
R Erotomania [97]
Promiscuity [73]
Sex Drive [73]
Sexual Addiction [97]

Hypersomnia [94]
PN 7 **SC** 23825
SN Excessive sleepiness.
B Sleep Disorders [73]
R Fatigue [67]
Narcolepsy [73]
↓ Symptoms [67]

Hypertension [73]
PN 1492 **SC** 23830
B Blood Pressure Disorders [73]
Cardiovascular Disorders [67]
N Essential Hypertension [73]
R ↓ Antihypertensive Drugs [73]
↓ Cerebrovascular Disorders [73]

Hypertext [97]
PN 0 **SC** 23835

Hypertext — (cont'd)
SN Computer-readable text that contains highlighted words or phrases that when selected by the user, instruct the computer program to retrieve one or more similar documents.
B Computer Applications [73]
R ↓ Computer Software [67]
Hypermedia [97]

Hyperthermia [73]
PN 203 **SC** 23840
UF Fever
B Symptoms [67]
R Delirium [73]
Thermoregulation (Body) [73]

Hyperthyroidism [73]
PN 113 **SC** 23850
B Thyroid Disorders [73]
R Goiters [73]
Tachycardia [73]
Thyrotoxicosis [73]
↓ Underweight [73]

Hyperventilation [73]
PN 201 **SC** 23860
B Respiratory Distress [73]
Respiratory Tract Disorders [73]
Symptoms [67]
R ↓ Psychosomatic Disorders [67]

Hypnagogic Hallucinations [73]
PN 23 **SC** 23870
SN False sensory perceptions without actual appropriate stimuli, occurring while falling asleep.
B Hallucinations [67]
R ↓ Sleep Disorders [73]

Hypnoanalysis
Use Hypnotherapy

Hypnosis [67]
PN 2854 **SC** 23890
SN Trance-like state induced by effective suggestion and characterized by increased suggestibility to the hypnotist. For hypnosis used in treatment, use HYPNOTHERAPY.
B Consciousness Disturbances [73]
N Age Regression (Hypnotic) [88]
Autohypnosis [73]
R False Memory [97]
↓ Hypnotherapy [73]
Posthypnotic Suggestions [94]

Hypnotherapists [73]
PN 27 **SC** 23900
SN Persons conducting treatment by means of hypnosis.
B Hypnotists [73]
Psychotherapists [73]
R Clinical Psychologists [73]
Psychiatrists [67]
Psychoanalysts [73]

Hypnotherapy [73]
PN 2049 **SC** 23910
SN Use of hypnosis in treatment.
UF Hypnoanalysis
B Psychotherapy [67]
N Age Regression (Hypnotic) [88]
R ↓ Alternative Medicine [97]
False Memory [97]
↓ Hypnosis [67]
Posthypnotic Suggestions [94]
Progressive Relaxation Therapy [78]
↓ Psychoanalysis [67]
↓ Relaxation Therapy [78]

Hypnotic Drugs [73]
PN 496 **SC** 23920
UF Chloralose
Sleep Inducing Drugs
B Drugs [67]
N Amobarbital [73]
Apomorphine [73]
Barbital [73]
Chloral Hydrate [73]
Codeine [73]
Flurazepam [82]
Glutethimide [73]
Hexobarbital [73]
Meprobamate [73]
Methaqualone [73]
Nitrazepam [78]
Pentobarbital [73]
Phenobarbital [73]
Secobarbital [73]
Thalidomide [73]
Thiopental [73]
Triazolam [88]
R ↓ Analgesic Drugs [73]
↓ Anesthetic Drugs [73]
↓ Anticonvulsive Drugs [73]
↓ Antiemetic Drugs [73]
↓ Antihistaminic Drugs [73]
↓ Antihypertensive Drugs [73]
↓ Barbiturates [67]
↓ Benzodiazepines [78]
↓ CNS Depressant Drugs [73]
↓ Narcotic Drugs [73]
↓ Sedatives [73]

Hypnotic Susceptibility [73]
PN 1220 **SC** 23930
SN Personal characteristic or state of being receptive to hypnosis.
UF Susceptibility (Hypnotic)
B Personality Traits [67]
R Openness to Experience [97]
Posthypnotic Suggestions [94]

Hypnotists [73]
PN 27 **SC** 23940
SN Persons conducting scientific experiments by means of hypnosis.
B Personnel [67]
N Hypnotherapists [73]

Hypoactive Sexual Desire Disorder
Use Inhibited Sexual Desire

Hypochondriasis [73]
PN 413 **SC** 23950
B Psychosomatic Disorders [67]
R ↓ Anxiety Disorders [97]
↓ Conversion Neurosis [73]
Somatization [94]
Somatoform Pain Disorder [97]

Hypogastric Plexus
Use Autonomic Ganglia

Hypoglossal Nerve
Use Cranial Nerves

Hypoglycemia [73]
PN 171 **SC** 23980
B Metabolism Disorders [73]
Symptoms [67]

Hypogonadism [73]
PN 30 **SC** 24000
B Endocrine Sexual Disorders [73]
N Klinefelters Syndrome [73]
Turners Syndrome [73]
R ↓ Gynecological Disorders [73]

Hypogonadism — (cont'd)
R Hypopituitarism [73]
↓ Male Genital Disorders [73]
Sterility [73]

Hypomania [73]
PN 146 SC 24010
B Mania [67]
R Cyclothymic Personality [73]

Hyponatremia [97]
PN 0 SC 24015
SN Abnormally low blood sodium level.
B Metabolism Disorders [73]
R Polydipsia [82]
↓ Sodium [73]
↓ Toxic Disorders [73]

Hypoparathyroidism
Use Parathyroid Disorders

Hypophysectomy [73]
PN 118 SC 24030
UF Pituitary Gland Surgery
B Endocrine Gland Surgery [73]

Hypophysis Disorders
Use Pituitary Disorders

Hypopituitarism [73]
PN 54 SC 24050
UF Dwarfism (Pituitary)
Pituitary Dwarfism
B Pituitary Disorders [73]
R ↓ Genetic Disorders [73]
↓ Hypogonadism [73]

Hypotension [73]
PN 91 SC 24060
B Blood Pressure Disorders [73]

Hypothalamo Hypophyseal System [73]
PN 303 SC 24070
B Hypothalamus [67]
Pituitary Gland [73]
R Hypothalamo Pituitary Adrenal System [97]
↓ Pituitary Hormones [73]

Hypothalamo Pituitary Adrenal System [97]
PN 0 SC 24075
B Adrenal Glands [73]
Hypothalamus [67]
Pituitary Gland [73]
R Hypothalamo Hypophyseal System [73]

Hypothalamus [67]
PN 3674 SC 24080
UF Mammillary Bodies (Hypothalamic)
B Diencephalon [73]
N Hypothalamo Hypophyseal System [73]
Hypothalamo Pituitary Adrenal System [97]
Preoptic Area [94]
R Medial Forebrain Bundle [82]

Hypothalamus Lesions [73]
PN 849 SC 24090
SN Not defined prior to 1982. From 1982, limited to experimentally induced lesions and used primarily for animal populations.
B Brain Lesions [67]

Hypothermia [73]
PN 369 SC 24100
B Symptoms [67]
R ↓ Body Temperature [73]
↓ Central Nervous System Disorders [73]

Hypothermia — (cont'd)
R ↓ Endocrine Disorders [73]
Thermoregulation (Body) [73]

Hypothesis Testing [73]
PN 614 SC 24110
SN Application of statistical tests to determine whether a research hypothesis should be accepted or rejected. From 1982, limited to discussions of statistical procedures. Use HYPOTHESIS TESTING or other appropriate terms to access references to COGNITIVE HYPOTHESIS TESTING prior to 1982.
B Experimental Design [67]
N Null Hypothesis Testing [73]
R Confidence Limits (Statistics) [73]
Construct Validity [82]
Predictability (Measurement) [73]
↓ Prediction Errors [73]
↓ Probability [67]
↓ Statistical Analysis [67]
Statistical Power [91]
Statistical Significance [73]
↓ Theories [67]
Theory Formulation [73]
Theory Verification [73]

Hypothesis Testing (Cognitive)
Use Cognitive Hypothesis Testing

Hypothyroidism [73]
PN 187 SC 24120
UF Myxedema
B Thyroid Disorders [73]
R Goiters [73]
↓ Infertility [73]
↓ Metabolism Disorders [73]
Thyrotropin [73]
Thyroxine [73]

Hypoxia
Use Anoxia

Hysterectomy [73]
PN 162 SC 24150
B Sterilization (Sex) [73]
Surgery [71]
R Ovariectomy [73]

Hysteria [67]
PN 764 SC 24160
B Mental Disorders [67]
N Mass Hysteria [73]
R Catalepsy [73]
↓ Conversion Neurosis [73]
↓ Dissociative Patterns [73]
Hysterical Personality [73]
Suggestibility [67]

Hysterical Anesthesia [73]
PN 2 SC 24170
B Anesthesia (Feeling) [73]
Conversion Neurosis [73]

Hysterical Blindness
Use Hysterical Vision Disturbances

Hysterical Neurosis (Conversion)
Use Conversion Neurosis

Hysterical Neurosis (Dissociation)
Use Dissociative Patterns

Hysterical Paralysis [73]
PN 23 SC 24220
UF Paralysis (Hysterical)
B Conversion Neurosis [73]

Hysterical Personality [73]
PN 215 SC 24230
SN Personality disorder characterized by emotional instability, excitability, overreaction, self-dramatization, self-centeredness, and over-dependence on others.
UF Histrionic Personality Disorder
B Personality Disorders [67]
R ↓ Conversion Neurosis [73]
↓ Dissociative Patterns [73]
↓ Hysteria [67]

Hysterical Vision Disturbances [73]
PN 21 SC 24240
UF Hysterical Blindness
Vision Disturbances (Hysterical)
B Conversion Neurosis [73]
R ↓ Eye Disorders [73]

Iatrogenic Effects
Use Side Effects (Treatment)

Ibotenic Acid [91]
PN 46 SC 24245
B Insecticides [73]
Neurotoxins [82]
N Muscimol [94]

ICD
Use International Class of Diseases

Iceland [82]
PN 70 SC 24247
B Europe [73]
R ↓ Scandinavia [78]

Iconic Memory [85]
PN 62 SC 24248
SN Brief sensory memory, usually lasting only fractions of a second.
B Short Term Memory [67]

Id [73]
PN 57 SC 24250
B Psychoanalytic Personality Factors [73]
R Unconscious (Personality Factor) [67]

Ideal Self
Use Self Concept

Idealism [73]
PN 86 SC 24260
B Philosophies [67]
R Determinism [97]

Ideation [73]
PN 235 SC 24270
SN Process of idea or image formation.
B Cognitive Processes [67]
N Imagination [67]
Suicidal Ideation [91]
R ↓ Fantasy [97]

Identical Twins
Use Monozygotic Twins

Identification (Defense Mechanism) [73]
PN 596 SC 24290
B Defense Mechanisms [67]
R Introjection [73]
Projective Identification [94]

Identity (Personal)
Use Self Concept

Identity (Professional)
Use Professional Identity

Identity Crisis 73
PN 241 SC 24320
B Crises 71
Emotional Adjustment 73
R ↓ Personality Development 67
↓ Self Concept 67
↓ Stress 67

Idiocy (Amaurotic Familial)
Use Amaurotic Familial Idiocy

Idiot Savants 73
PN 65 SC 24350
B Mentally Retarded 67
R Gifted 67

Ileum
Use Intestines

Illegitimate Children 73
PN 33 SC 24380
B Family Members 73
R ↓ Children 67

Illinois Test Psycholinguist Abil 73
PN 169 SC 24390
B Intelligence Measures 67

Illiteracy
Use Literacy

Illness (Physical)
Use Physical Disorders

Illness Behavior 82
PN 869 SC 24415
SN Adaptive or nonadaptive behaviors exhibited by an individual during the course of an illness or dysfunction.
B Behavior 67
Client Characteristics 73
R Anosognosia 94
Coping Behavior 67
Coronary Prone Behavior 82
↓ Disorders 67
↓ Physical Disorders 97
↓ Physical Illness (Attitudes Toward) 85
↓ Psychosomatic Disorders 67
Recovery (Disorders) 73
Somatization 94
Treatment Compliance 82

Illumination 67
PN 3930 SC 24420
SN Visible portion of the electromagnetic radiation spectrum but may include ultraviolet and infrared light. May also refer more generally to ambient light. Compare LUMINANCE.
UF Light
Photic Threshold
B Visual Stimulation 73
N Photopic Stimulation 73
Scotopic Stimulation 73
R ↓ Brightness Perception 73
Light Adaptation 82
↓ Light Refraction 82
Luminance 82

Illumination Therapy
Use Phototherapy

Illusion (Autokinetic)
Use Autokinetic Illusion

Illusions (Perception) 67
PN 2197 SC 24440

Illusions (Perception) — (cont'd)
SN Misperception or alteration of reality in subjective perception.
UF Optical Illusions
B Perception 67
N Mueller Lyer Illusion 88
↓ Perceptual Aftereffect 67
Spatial Distortion 73
R ↓ Perceptual Distortion 82
↓ Perceptual Disturbances 73

Image (Retinal)
Use Retinal Image

Imagery 67
PN 4913 SC 24470
UF Visualization
B Abstraction 67
N Conceptual Imagery 73
Spatial Imagery 82
R Archetypes 91
Imagination 67

Imagery (Conceptual)
Use Conceptual Imagery

Imagination 67
PN 1547 SC 24490
SN Process of forming mental images of objects, qualities, situations, or relationships, which are not immediately apparent to the senses.
B Cognitive Processes 67
Ideation 73
R Conceptual Imagery 73
↓ Fantasy 97
↓ Imagery 67
Magical Thinking 73
Vicarious Experiences 73

Imaginativeness
Use Openness to Experience

Imipramine 73
PN 1569 SC 24520
UF Tofranil
B Amines 73
Tricyclic Antidepressant Drugs 97

Imitation (Learning) 67
PN 3212 SC 24530
SN Mimicking by human or animal subjects to learn a model's behavior or responses.
UF Modeling Behavior
B Social Learning 73
R Observational Learning 73
Role Models 82

Immaturity (Emotional)
Use Emotional Immaturity

Immersion Programs
Use Foreign Language Education

Immigrants
Use Immigration

Immigration 73
PN 1533 SC 24560
SN Permanent resettlement in a country other than the country of one's origin.
UF Immigrants
B Social Processes 67
R Citizenship 73
↓ Foreign Nationals 85
↓ Human Migration 73
Refugees 88

Immunization 73
PN 129 SC 24570
UF Vaccination
B Physical Treatment Methods 73
R Antibodies 73

Immunogens
Use Antigens

Immunoglobulins 73
PN 179 SC 24580
B Blood Proteins 73
Globulins 73
N Gamma Globulin 73
R Antibodies 73
Antigens 82
↓ Immunologic Disorders 73
Immunoreactivity 94
Interferons 94

Immunologic Disorders 73
PN 339 SC 24590
UF Autoimmune Disorders
Hypersensitivity (Immunologic)
B Physical Disorders 97
N ↓ Allergic Disorders 73
Anaphylactic Shock 73
↓ Human Immunodeficiency Virus 91
Rh Incompatibility 73
R Asthma 67
↓ Immunoglobulins 73

Immunology 73
PN 1235 SC 24600
SN Medical science dealing with the study of immunity. Used for the scientific discipline or the immunological processes themselves.
UF Immunopathology
B Medical Sciences 67
N Psychoneuroimmunology 91
R Immunoreactivity 94

Immunopathology
Use Immunology

Immunoreactivity 94
PN 235 SC 24613
SN Use IMMUNOLOGY to access references from 73-93.
R ↓ Immunoglobulins 73
↓ Immunology 73
Interleukins 94

Impaired Professionals 85
PN 186 SC 24615
SN Professional personnel who are physically or psychologically disordered to the extent that such disorders interfere with the performance of professional duties or conflict with professional standards. Does not include handicaps that do not interfere with professional performance.
R Disabled Personnel 97
↓ Medical Personnel 67
↓ Mental Health Personnel 67
Personal Therapy 91
Professional Ethics 73
Professional Liability 85
↓ Professional Personnel 78
↓ Professional Standards 73

Implosive Therapy 73
PN 342 SC 24620
SN Behavioral therapy involving flooding the client with anxiety through intense or prolonged real-life or imagined exposure to feared objects or situations, thereby demonstrating that they cause no harm. The aim is gradual extinction of anxiety or phobic responses.

Implosive Therapy — (cont'd)
UF Flooding Therapy
B Behavior Therapy 67
Exposure Therapy 97

Impotence 73
PN 388 SC 24630
B Sexual Function Disturbances 73
R Erection (Penis) 73
Frigidity 73
↓ Male Orgasm 73
↓ Orgasm 73
Premature Ejaculation 73

Impression Formation 78
PN 1009 SC 24634
SN Process by which an individual transforms various perceptions and observations about another person or group into an overall impression or set of attitudes toward or about that person or group.
B Social Perception 67
R ↓ Attitudes 67
Attribution 73
Impression Management 78

Impression Management 78
PN 438 SC 24636
SN Techniques of image cultivation or impression formation designed to obtain good evaluations of one's self and to win approval from others. Used for both individuals and groups.
UF Ingratiation
R Impression Formation 78
Self Monitoring (Personality) 85
↓ Social Behavior 67
↓ Social Perception 67
Uncertainty 91

Imprinting 67
PN 370 SC 24640
SN Rapid learning process that takes place during early critical periods of development in social animals. Establishes the basis for patterns of social behavior. Used for both human and animal populations.
B Animal Ethology 67
Social Learning 73
R Critical Period 88
Species Recognition 85

Impulse Control Disorders 97
PN 0 SC 24645
SN A mental disorder characterized by an intense need to gratify one's immediate desires and failure to resist the impulse or temptation.
B Mental Disorders 67
R ↓ Antisocial Behavior 71
Conduct Disorder 91
Delay of Gratification 78
Explosive Personality 73
Impulsiveness 73
Kleptomania 73
Pathological Gambling 88
Pyromania 73
Self Control 73
↓ Sexual Deviations 67

Impulsiveness 73
PN 1492 SC 24650
B Cognitive Style 67
R Attention Deficit Disorder 85
Conceptual Tempo 85
Impulse Control Disorders 97
Kleptomania 73
Pathological Gambling 88
Pyromania 73
Reflectiveness 97

In Vitro Fertilization
Use Reproductive Technology

Inadequate Personality 73
PN 3 SC 24660
SN Inadequate responses to physical, social, and emotional demands; general ineptness and instability, despite absence of actual physical or mental deficit.
B Personality Disorders 67

Incarceration 73
PN 606 SC 24670
B Institutionalization 67
Law Enforcement 78
R ↓ Correctional Institutions 73
Institution Visitation 73
↓ Institutional Release 78

Incentives 67
PN 980 SC 24680
SN Events or objects which increase or induce drives or determination. Popularly described as one's expectation of reward. May be used for human or animal populations. Compare REWARDS and REINFORCEMENT.
B Motivation 67
N Educational Incentives 73
Monetary Incentives 73
R ↓ Goals 67
↓ Needs 67
↓ Rewards 67
Temptation 73

Incest 73
PN 1307 SC 24690
B Sexual Abuse 88
Sexual Deviations 67
Sexual Intercourse (Human) 73
R Pedophilia 73
↓ Perpetrators 88
↓ Sex Offenses 82

Incidental Learning 67
PN 688 SC 24700
SN Learning which takes place without the intent to learn or in the absence of formal instructions. From 1982, limited to human populations. Use LATENT LEARNING for animal populations.
B Learning 67
N Latent Learning 73

Income (Economic) 73
PN 344 SC 24710
SN Monetary gain (such as wages, interest, dividends, profits) received by individuals or nations within a given period for labor or services rendered or from capital resources.
R Budgets 97
↓ Income Level 73
Poverty 73
Salaries 73
↓ Socioeconomic Status 67
Taxation 85

Income Level 73
PN 789 SC 24720
SN Total amount of monetary gain received within a given period that is associated with socioeconomic status.
B Socioeconomic Status 67
N Lower Income Level 73
Middle Income Level 73
Upper Income Level 73
R Income (Economic) 73
Salaries 73
↓ Social Class 67

Incompatibility (Rh)
Use Rh Incompatibility

Incomplete Man Test 73
PN 2 SC 24750
B Projective Techniques 67

Incontinence (Fecal)
Use Fecal Incontinence

Incontinence (Urinary)
Use Urinary Incontinence

Incorporation (Psychological)
Use Internalization

Incubators (Apparatus) 73
PN 6 SC 24780
B Apparatus 67

Independence (Personality) 73
PN 1266 SC 24790
UF Autonomy (Personality)
B Personality Traits 67
R Empowerment 91
Internal External Locus of Control 67
↓ Resistance 97
Self Determination 94

Independent Living
Use Self Care Skills

Independent Living Programs 91
PN 82 SC 24798
SN Community-based programs or services to assist disabled individuals to perform all or most of their daily functions, thus increasing self sufficiency and self determination and eliminating a need to depend on others.
R Activities of Daily Living 91
↓ Community Services 67
Habilitation 91
↓ Mainstreaming 91
↓ Program Development 91
↓ Rehabilitation 67
Self Care Skills 78
Supported Employment 94

Independent Party (Political)
Use Political Parties

Independent Study
Use Individualized Instruction

Independent Variables 73
PN 83 SC 24810
SN Statistical or experimental parameters that are manipulated in an attempt to analyze their relative effect on specified dependent variables.
B Statistical Variables 73

India 67
PN 2921 SC 24820
B Asia 73

Indians (American)
Use American Indians

Indifference
Use Apathy

Individual Counseling
Use Individual Psychotherapy

Individual Differences 67
PN 4460 SC 24860

Individual Differences — (cont'd)
SN Any specific characteristic or quantitative difference in a quality or trait that can serve to distinguish one individual from another. Used for both human and animal populations.
R ↓ Personality [67]
Personality Correlates [67]
↓ Personality Theory [67]

Individual Problem Solving
Use Problem Solving

Individual Psychology [73]
PN 732 **SC** 24880
SN Theory and practice of Adlerian psychology, stressing the unique wholeness of the individual and viewing the striving to overcome and master obstacles as the primary motivating force.
B Neopsychoanalytic School [73]
R Adler (Alfred) [67]
Adlerian Psychotherapy [97]

Individual Psychotherapy [73]
PN 1051 **SC** 24890
SN Psychotherapy occurring on a one-on-one basis as compared to a group setting or environment. Use ADLERIAN PSYCHOTHERAPY to access references on Adlerian individual psychotherapy.
UF Individual Counseling
Individual Therapy
Psychotherapy (Individual)
B Psychotherapy [67]

Individual Psychotherapy (Adlerian)
Use Adlerian Psychotherapy

Individual Testing [73]
PN 72 **SC** 24900
B Measurement [67]
R Test Administration [73]

Individual Therapy
Use Individual Psychotherapy

Individualism
Use Individuality

Individuality [73]
PN 498 **SC** 24930
UF Individualism
B Personality Traits [67]
R Nonconformity (Personality) [73]
Self Determination [94]

Individualized Instruction [73]
PN 1712 **SC** 24940
SN Instruction adapted to individual needs or instruction in which a student works alone or only with a teacher. Also, self-initiated study with or without formal academic guidance or involvement.
UF Independent Study
Instruction (Individualized)
Self Directed Learning
Self Instruction
B Teaching Methods [67]
R Computer Assisted Instruction [73]
↓ Continuing Education [85]
Cooperative Learning [94]
↓ Learning [67]
Open Classroom Method [73]
Programed Instruction [67]
↓ Tutoring [73]

Indonesia [82]
PN 148 **SC** 24945
B Southeast Asia [73]

Induced Abortion [71]
PN 850 **SC** 24950
UF Abortion (Induced)
Elective Abortion
Therapeutic Abortion
B Surgery [71]
R Abortion Laws [73]
↓ Birth Control [71]
↓ Family Planning [73]
Spontaneous Abortion [71]

Inductive Deductive Reasoning [73]
PN 828 **SC** 24960
UF Convergent Thinking
Deductive Reasoning
Syllogistic Reasoning
B Reasoning [67]
N Inference [73]
R Divergent Thinking [73]
Logical Thinking [67]
↓ Problem Solving [67]

Industrial Accidents [73]
PN 395 **SC** 24970
B Accidents [67]
R Occupational Exposure [88]
Occupational Safety [73]
Work Related Illnesses [94]

Industrial Arts Education
Use Vocational Education

Industrial Foremen [73]
PN 52 **SC** 24980
UF Foremen (Industrial)
B Blue Collar Workers [73]
R ↓ Management Personnel [73]

Industrial Personnel
Use Business and Industrial Personnel

Industrial Psychologists [73]
PN 85 **SC** 25000
B Business and Industrial Personnel [67]
Psychologists [67]
R Social Psychologists [73]

Industrial Psychology [67]
PN 872 **SC** 25010
UF Organizational Psychology
B Applied Psychology [73]

Industrial Safety
Use Occupational Safety

Industrialization [73]
PN 356 **SC** 25030
B Social Processes [67]
R ↓ Technology [73]
Urbanization [73]

Industry
Use Business

Infancy
Use Infants

Infant Development [73]
PN 2083 **SC** 25060
B Early Childhood Development [73]
N Neonatal Development [73]
R ↓ Physical Development [73]
↓ Psychogenesis [73]

Infant Intelligence Scale [73]
PN 3 **SC** 25070

Infant Intelligence Scale — (cont'd)
UF Cattell Infant Intelligence Scale
B Intelligence Measures [67]

Infant Vocalization [73]
PN 476 **SC** 25080
UF Babbling
Vocalization (Infant)
B Voice [73]
R Crying [73]

Infanticide [78]
PN 220 **SC** 25085
UF Neonaticide
B Homicide [67]

Infantile Neurosis
Use Childhood Neurosis

Infantile Paralysis
Use Poliomyelitis

Infantile Psychosis
Use Childhood Psychosis

Infantilism [73]
PN 12 **SC** 25120
R ↓ Mental Disorders [67]

Infants [67]
PN 12814 **SC** 25130
SN Ages 2-23 months. Application of terms designating age is mandatory for ages 0-17 years.
UF Babies
Infancy
B Children [67]
N Neonates [67]
R Childhood [84]

Infants (Animal) [78]
PN 4293 **SC** 25134
UF Neonates (Animal)
B Animals [67]

Infarctions (Myocardial)
Use Myocardial Infarctions

Infections
Use Infectious Disorders

Infectious Disorders [73]
PN 216 **SC** 25160
UF Communicable Diseases
Infections
Neuroinfections
B Physical Disorders [97]
N ↓ Bacterial Disorders [73]
Epstein Barr Viral Disorder [94]
↓ Parasitic Disorders [73]
↓ Venereal Diseases [73]
↓ Viral Disorders [73]
R ↓ Arthritis [73]
↓ Chorea [73]
↓ Dermatitis [73]
↓ Digestive System Disorders [73]
Encephalitis [73]
Encephalomyelitis [73]
↓ Hepatitis [73]
Hydrocephaly [73]
Jaundice [73]
↓ Liver Disorders [73]
↓ Myelitis [73]

Inference [73]
PN 1640 **SC** 25180

Inference — (cont'd)
B Inductive Deductive Reasoning [73]
R Analogy [91]
Attribution [73]

Inferior Colliculus [73]
PN 151 SC 25190
B Mesencephalon [73]

Inferiority (Emotional)
Use Emotional Inferiority

Infertility [73]
PN 362 SC 25210
B Genital Disorders [67]
N Sterility [73]
R ↓ Endocrine Sexual Disorders [73]
Fertility [88]
↓ Gynecological Disorders [73]
Hypothyroidism [73]
Klinefelters Syndrome [73]
↓ Male Genital Disorders [73]
↓ Venereal Diseases [73]

Infirmaries
Use Hospitals

Inflection [73]
PN 340 SC 25230
SN A grammatically functional change in the pitch or loudness of the voice. Also, the syntactic change in words to designate such factors as case, gender, or tense.
B Prosody [91]
R ↓ Phonology [73]
↓ Speech Characteristics [73]
↓ Syntax [71]

Influence (Interpersonal)
Use Interpersonal Influences

Influences (Social)
Use Social Influences

Influenza [73]
PN 75 SC 25260
B Viral Disorders [73]
R ↓ Gastrointestinal Disorders [73]
↓ Nervous System Disorders [67]
↓ Respiratory Tract Disorders [73]

Informants [88]
PN 28 SC 25270
SN Persons who provide information against another person who is suspected of committing a violation.
UF Whistleblowing
R ↓ Abuse Reporting [97]
↓ Crime [67]
Labor Management Relations [67]
↓ Organizational Behavior [78]
↓ Social Behavior [67]

Information [67]
PN 3691 SC 25360
SN Conceptually broad array term referring to a body of knowledge. Use a more specific term if possible. Differentiate from KNOWLEDGE LEVEL which is the amount of information acquired or received by an individual or group.
R ↓ Automated Information Processing [73]
Censorship [78]
↓ Communication [67]
Computer Searching [91]
Concepts [67]
Data Collection [82]
↓ Data Processing [67]
Databases [91]

Information — (cont'd)
R Declarative Knowledge [97]
Human Information Storage [73]
Information Exchange [73]
Information Seeking [73]
Information Services [88]
↓ Information Specialists [88]
Information Systems [91]
Information Theory [67]
↓ Knowledge Level [78]
↓ Libraries [82]
Messages [73]
Privileged Communication [73]
Procedural Knowledge [97]

Information (Messages)
Use Messages

Information Exchange [73]
PN 547 SC 25290
SN Interchange of information between humans or humans and machines.
R Computer Searching [91]
Databases [91]
Information [67]
Information Seeking [73]
↓ Scientific Communication [73]

Information Processes (Human)
Use Cognitive Processes

Information Processing (Automated)
Use Automated Information Processing

Information Processing Speed
Use Cognitive Processing Speed

Information Retrieval (Automated)
Use Automated Information Retrieval

Information Seeking [73]
PN 1003 SC 25330
R Computer Searching [91]
↓ Exploratory Behavior [67]
Information [67]
Information Exchange [73]
Questioning [82]

Information Services [88]
PN 71 SC 25335
R ↓ Automated Information Retrieval [73]
Computer Searching [91]
Databases [91]
Hot Line Services [73]
Information [67]
Information Systems [91]
↓ Libraries [82]

Information Specialists [88]
PN 10 SC 25338
B Professional Personnel [78]
N Librarians [88]
R Information [67]

Information Storage (Human)
Use Human Information Storage

Information Systems [91]
PN 235 SC 25345
SN Collection, organization, and storage of data or the operational functions used to process information.
UF Management Information Systems
B Systems [67]
R ↓ Automated Information Processing [73]
↓ Automated Information Retrieval [73]
Automated Information Storage [73]

Information Systems — (cont'd)
R ↓ Communication Systems [73]
↓ Computer Applications [73]
↓ Data Processing [67]
Databases [91]
Decision Support Systems [97]
↓ Expert Systems [91]
Information [67]
Information Services [88]
Word Processing [91]

Information Theory [67]
PN 462 SC 25350
SN Branch of science which deals statistically with the transmission of information and its measurable characteristics. Used for the scientific discipline or for application of information theory to specific areas of investigation.
B Theories [67]
R Communication Theory [73]
Information [67]
↓ Stochastic Modeling [73]

Informed Consent [85]
PN 500 SC 25363
SN Process of making rational decisions regarding one's treatment or participation in experimental procedures.
R ↓ Civil Rights [78]
↓ Client Rights [88]
Debriefing (Experimental) [91]
Experiment Volunteers [73]
Experimental Ethics [78]
Guardianship [88]
Involuntary Treatment [94]
↓ Legal Processes [73]
Professional Ethics [73]
Treatment Compliance [82]
Treatment Refusal [94]
Treatment Withholding [88]

Ingratiation
Use Impression Management

Ingroup Outgroup [97]
PN 0 SC 25366
UF Outgroup Ingroup
B Social Groups [73]
R Ethnic Identity [73]
↓ Group Dynamics [67]
Intergroup Dynamics [73]
Self Perception [67]
↓ Social Identity [88]
↓ Social Networks [94]
↓ Social Perception [67]

Inhalant Abuse [85]
PN 146 SC 25367
SN Inhalation of vapors from volatile chemical substances (such as aerosol sprays, solvents, and anesthetics) in order to produce mind-altering effects.
UF Solvent Abuse
B Drug Abuse [73]
N Glue Sniffing [73]
R ↓ Solvents [82]

Inhibited Sexual Desire [97]
PN 0 SC 25370
SN Lack of sexual interest or feelings.
UF Hypoactive Sexual Desire Disorder
B Sexual Function Disturbances [73]
R Eroticism [73]
Libido [73]
Sex Drive [73]
↓ Sexual Arousal [78]

Inhibition (Personality) [73]
PN 455 **SC** 25380
B Personality Processes [67]

Inhibition (Proactive)
Use Proactive Inhibition

Inhibition (Retroactive)
Use Retroactive Inhibition

Initial Teaching Alphabet [73]
PN 16 **SC** 25410
B Alphabets [73]
R ↓ Language Arts Education [73]
↓ Reading [67]
Reading Education [73]
↓ Teaching Methods [67]

Initiation Rites [73]
PN 48 **SC** 25420
B Rites of Passage [73]

Initiative [73]
PN 65 **SC** 25430
B Personality Traits [67]

Injections [73]
PN 129 **SC** 25440
B Drug Administration Methods [73]
N Intramuscular Injections [73]
Intraperitoneal Injections [73]
Intravenous Injections [73]
Subcutaneous Injections [73]

Injuries [73]
PN 1108 **SC** 25450
UF Physical Trauma
Trauma (Physical)
N Birth Injuries [73]
Burns [73]
Electrical Injuries [73]
↓ Head Injuries [73]
↓ Spinal Cord Injuries [73]
↓ Wounds [73]
R ↓ Accidents [67]
Coma [73]
↓ Disorders [67]
Hematoma [73]
Hemiplegia [78]
Paraplegia [78]
Physical Disfigurement [78]
↓ Physical Disorders [97]
Quadriplegia [85]
↓ Safety [67]
Shock [67]

Injuries (Birth)
Use Birth Injuries

Inlaws [97]
PN 0 **SC** 25465
B Family Members [73]
R ↓ Parents [67]
↓ Spouses [73]

Inmates (Prison)
Use Prisoners

Innate Behavior (Animal)
Use Instinctive Behavior

Inner City
Use Urban Environments

Inner Ear
Use Labyrinth (Anatomy)

Inner Speech
Use Self Talk

Innovativeness
Use Creativity

Inquisitiveness
Use Curiosity

Insanity
Use Mental Disorders

Insanity Defense [85]
PN 441 **SC** 25525
SN Legal defense designed to invoke an exemption from criminal responsibility on the basis of a mental disorder at the time of the alleged criminal offense.
B Legal Processes [73]
R Court Referrals [94]
Criminal Responsibility [91]
Forensic Evaluation [94]
Forensic Psychiatry [73]
↓ Mental Disorders [67]
Mentally Ill Offenders [85]

Insecticides [73]
PN 147 **SC** 25530
UF Dieldrin
Pesticides
B Hazardous Materials [91]
N DDT (Insecticide) [73]
↓ Ibotenic Acid [91]
Parathion [73]
R ↓ Drugs [67]
↓ Insects [67]
↓ Neurotoxins [82]
Nicotine [73]
↓ Poisons [73]

Insects [67]
PN 1070 **SC** 25540
B Arthropoda [73]
N Ants [73]
Bees [73]
Beetles [73]
Butterflies [73]
Cockroaches [73]
↓ Diptera [73]
Grasshoppers [73]
Larvae [73]
Mantis [73]
Moths [73]
Wasps [82]
R ↓ Insecticides [73]

Insecurity (Emotional)
Use Emotional Security

Insensitivity (Personality)
Use Sensitivity (Personality)

Inservice Teacher Education [73]
PN 1376 **SC** 25570
SN Course or program designed to provide teachers with growth in job-related competencies or skills. Usually school sponsored.
B Inservice Training [85]
Teacher Education [67]
R On the Job Training [73]
Professional Development [82]

Inservice Training [85]
PN 268 **SC** 25575
B Continuing Education [85]
Personnel Training [67]
N Inservice Teacher Education [73]

Inservice Training — (cont'd)
N Mental Health Inservice Training [73]
R On the Job Training [73]
Professional Development [82]

Inservice Training (Mental Health)
Use Mental Health Inservice Training

Insight [73]
PN 233 **SC** 25590
B Personality Processes [67]
R Intuition [73]
Perceptiveness (Personality) [73]

Insight (Psychotherapeutic Process) [73]
PN 160 **SC** 25600
B Psychotherapeutic Processes [67]

Insight Therapy [73]
PN 148 **SC** 25610
SN Psychotherapeutic method which seeks to uncover the causes of the client's conflicts through conscious awareness (i.e., insight) into unconscious dynamics of feelings, responses, and behavior.
B Psychotherapy [67]

Insomnia [73]
PN 853 **SC** 25620
UF Sleeplessness
B Sleep Disorders [73]
Symptoms [67]

Instability (Emotional)
Use Emotional Instability

Instinctive Behavior [82]
PN 258 **SC** 25638
SN Stereotyped, unlearned, largely stimulus-bound, adaptive behavior limited in its expression by the inherent properties of the nervous system and genetic factors. Used for human or animal populations. Use ANIMAL INSTINCTIVE BEHAVIOR or ANIMAL INNATE BEHAVIOR to access references to nonhuman populations from 67–81 and 73–81 respectively.
UF Animal Innate Behavior
Animal Instinctive Behavior
Innate Behavior (Animal)
B Behavior [67]
R ↓ Animal Defensive Behavior [82]
Animal Distress Calls [73]
↓ Animal Ethology [67]
Animal Exploratory Behavior [73]
Animal Homing [91]
Animal Motivation [67]
Animal Predatory Behavior [78]
↓ Animal Sexual Behavior [85]
Attack Behavior [73]
↓ Genetics [67]
Homeostasis [73]
Human Nature [97]
↓ Motivation [67]
Neophobia [85]
↓ Nervous System [67]
↓ Physiology [67]
↓ Reflexes [71]
Self Preservation [97]
Species Recognition [85]
Spontaneous Alternation [82]
Stereotyped Behavior [73]

Institution Visitation [73]
PN 94 **SC** 25650
SN Visiting a patient or convict in an institution (e.g., hospital, prison, or nursing home) by someone from outside the institution (e.g., friends or family).

Institution Visitation — (cont'd)
UF Visitation (Institution)
R ↓ Correctional Institutions 73
Incarceration 73
↓ Residential Care Institutions 73

Institutional Release 78
PN 137 SC 25664
SN Discharge or release of an individual from any type of correctional or therapeutic residential facility.
B Institutionalization 67
N ↓ Hospital Discharge 73
R ↓ Commitment (Psychiatric) 73
Deinstitutionalization 82
Discharge Planning 94
↓ Hospital Admission 73
Incarceration 73
↓ Psychiatric Hospital Admission 73
↓ Psychiatric Hospitalization 73

Institutional Schools 78
PN 204 SC 25666
SN Schools that are part of larger residential institutions such as hospitals or prisons.
B Schools 67
R Boarding Schools 88
↓ Correctional Institutions 73
↓ Residential Care Institutions 73
↓ Treatment Facilities 73

Institutionalization 67
PN 1626 SC 25670
N ↓ Hospitalization 67
Incarceration 73
↓ Institutional Release 78
R ↓ Facility Admission 88
↓ Facility Discharge 88
Orphanages 73

Institutionalized Mentally Retarded 73
PN 1265 SC 25680
B Mentally Retarded 67
R Home Reared Mentally Retarded 73
↓ Residential Care Institutions 73

Institutions (Correctional)
Use Correctional Institutions

Institutions (Residential Care)
Use Residential Care Institutions

Instruction
Use Teaching

Instruction (Computer Assisted)
Use Computer Assisted Instruction

Instruction (Individualized)
Use Individualized Instruction

Instruction (Programed)
Use Programed Instruction

Instructional Media 67
PN 1049 SC 25740
SN Formats or technologies for conveyance of didactic content, including print, film, computers, phonographic records and magnetic tape.
B Teaching 67
N Advance Organizers 85
↓ Educational Audiovisual Aids 73
Reading Materials 73
Teaching Machines 73
↓ Textbooks 78

Instructional Objectives
Use Educational Objectives

Instructions (Experimental)
Use Experimental Instructions

Instructors
Use Teachers

Instrument Controls 85
PN 64 SC 25765
SN May include knobs, handles, levers, latches, dials, switches, buttons, and any other mechanism used to control the operation of machines and instruments. Consider VISUAL DISPLAYS to access references from 73-84.
UF Controls (Instrument)
N Flight Instrumentation 73
R ↓ Displays 67
Human Factors Engineering 73
Human Machine Systems Design 97
Keyboards 85

Instrumental Conditioning
Use Operant Conditioning

Instrumental Learning
Use Operant Conditioning

Instrumentality 91
PN 45 SC 25785
R ↓ Motivation 67
↓ Personality Traits 67
Self Efficacy 85

Instrumentation (Flight)
Use Flight Instrumentation

Insulin 73
PN 533 SC 25800
B Hormones 67
R Insulin Shock Therapy 73

Insulin Shock Therapy 73
PN 32 SC 25820
B Shock Therapy 73
R Coma 73
Insulin 73

Insurance 73
PN 102 SC 25830
N ↓ Health Insurance 73
Life Insurance 73
Social Security 88
R Disability Evaluation 88
Risk Management 97

Insurance Agents
Use Sales Personnel

Intake Interview 94
PN 24 SC 25845
SN Initial evaluation, assessment, or screening of clients or patients to determine needs and appropriate health, mental health, rehabilitation, or other services.
B Interviews 67
R ↓ Case Management 91
Clinical Judgment (Not Diagnosis) 73
↓ Diagnosis 67
↓ Evaluation 67
Health Service Needs 97
Needs Assessment 85
↓ Psychiatric Evaluation 97
↓ Psychodiagnostic Interview 73
↓ Screening 82

Integrated Services 97
PN 0 SC 25847
SN Collaboration and cooperation among social service, education, health, or community service providers.
UF Interagency Services
R ↓ Community Services 67
↓ Health Care Services 78
Interdisciplinary Treatment Approach 73
↓ Mental Health Programs 73
↓ Mental Health Services 78
Multimodal Treatment Approach 91
Public Health Services 73
↓ Social Programs 73
↓ Social Services 82

Integration (Racial)
Use Social Integration

Integrity 97
PN 0 SC 25855
B Personality Traits 67
R ↓ Ethics 67
Honesty 73
Morality 67
↓ Values 67

Intellectual Development 73
PN 1142 SC 25860
SN Acquisition of factual knowledge. Consider COGNITIVE DEVELOPMENT for acquisition of reasoning, thought, and problem solving abilities.
B Cognitive Development 73
N ↓ Language Development 67
R Intelligence 67

Intellectual Functioning
Use Cognitive Ability

Intellectualism 73
PN 12 SC 25870
SN Doctrine which attempts to explain emotion and volition in terms of cognitive processes.
B Philosophies 67

Intellectualization 73
PN 12 SC 25880
SN Defense mechanism in which distressful emotional content of a painful situation is avoided by focusing on intellectual (cognitive) aspects of the situation or by engaging in abstract thinking.
B Defense Mechanisms 67
R Isolation (Defense Mechanism) 73

Intellectually Gifted
Use Gifted

Intelligence 67
PN 6186 SC 25900
SN General ability to think, reason, learn, apply knowledge, or deal effectively with the environment. Consider also INTELLIGENCE QUOTIENT.
R ↓ Ability 67
↓ Artificial Intelligence 82
Cognitive Assessment 97
Creativity 67
Divergent Thinking 73
Gifted 67
↓ Intellectual Development 73
Intelligence Quotient 67
Mental Age 73
↓ Reasoning 67
↓ Thinking 67
Wisdom 94

Intelligence Age
Use Mental Age

Intelligence Measures [67]
PN 3554 **SC** 25910
UF Henmon Nelson Tests Mental Ability
Leiter Adult Intelligence Scale
Temporal Spatial Concept Scale
Tests (Intelligence)
Vane Kindergarten Test
B Measurement [67]
N Benton Revised Visual Retention Test [73]
California Test of Mental Maturity [73]
Columbia Mental Maturity Scale [73]
Culture Fair Intelligence Test [73]
Frostig Development Test Vis Percept [73]
Goodenough Harris Draw A Person Test [67]
Hidden Figures Test [73]
Illinois Test Psycholinguist Abil [73]
Infant Intelligence Scale [73]
Kaufman Assessment Battery Children [88]
Kohs Block Design Test [73]
Lorge Thorndike Intelligence Test [73]
Lowenfeld Mosaic Test [73]
Miller Analogies Test [73]
Peabody Picture Vocabulary Test [73]
Porteus Maze Test [73]
Raven Coloured Progressive Matrices [73]
Raven Progressive Matrices [78]
Remote Associates Test [73]
Slosson Intelligence Test for Child [73]
Stanford Binet Intelligence Scale [67]
Wechsler Adult Intelligence Scale [67]
Wechsler Bellevue Intelligence Scale [67]
Wechsler Intelligence Scale Children [67]
Wechsler Preschool Primary Scale [88]
R Bayley Scales of Infant Development [94]
Cognitive Assessment [97]

Intelligence Quotient [67]
PN 2953 **SC** 25920
SN Relative intelligence of an individual expressed as a score on a standardized test of intelligence. Consider also INTELLIGENCE.
B Test Scores [67]
R Cognitive Assessment [97]
Intelligence [67]
Mental Age [73]

Intensity (Stimulus)
Use Stimulus Intensity

Intensive Care [88]
PN 175 **SC** 25942
R Hospital Environment [82]
↓ Hospital Programs [78]
↓ Hospitals [67]

Intention [88]
PN 1063 **SC** 25945
SN Determination to act in a certain manner.
R ↓ Goals [67]
↓ Motivation [67]
Planned Behavior [97]

Intentional Learning [73]
PN 269 **SC** 25950
SN Purposive or motivated learning.
B Learning [67]

Interaction (Interpersonal)
Use Interpersonal Interaction

Interaction (Social)
Use Social Interaction

Interaction Analysis (Statistics) [73]
PN 93 **SC** 25990
B Statistical Analysis [67]
R Interaction Variance [73]

Interaction Variance [73]
PN 12 **SC** 26000
B Variability Measurement [73]
R Interaction Analysis (Statistics) [73]

Interagency Services
Use Integrated Services

Intercourse (Sexual)
Use Sexual Intercourse (Human)

Intercultural Communication
Use Cross Cultural Communication

Interdisciplinary Research [85]
PN 182 **SC** 26025
SN Any research effort coordinated or executed by members of two or more specialties, disciplines, or theoretical orientations.
UF Cross Disciplinary Research
Multidisciplinary Research
B Experimentation [67]
R Interdisciplinary Treatment Approach [73]

Interdisciplinary Treatment Approach [73]
PN 1899 **SC** 26030
SN Combination of two or more disciplines in the prevention, diagnosis, treatment, or rehabilitation of mental or physical disorders.
UF Multidisciplinary Treatment Approach
B Treatment [67]
R Biopsychosocial Approach [91]
Eclectic Psychotherapy [94]
↓ Health Care Psychology [85]
Integrated Services [97]
Interdisciplinary Research [85]
Multimodal Treatment Approach [91]
Partial Hospitalization [85]
Teams [88]

Interest Inventories [73]
PN 441 **SC** 26040
B Inventories [67]

Interest Patterns
SN Term discontinued in 1982. Use INTEREST PATTERNS or INTERESTS to access references prior to 1982.
Use Interests

Interests [67]
PN 1031 **SC** 26080
SN Use INTERESTS or INTEREST PATTERNS to access references prior to 1982.
UF Interest Patterns
N Occupational Interests [67]
R Daily Activities [94]
Hobbies [73]

Interethnic Communication
Use Cross Cultural Communication

Interethnic Family [88]
PN 15 **SC** 26070
B Family [67]
R Interracial Adoption [94]
Interracial Family [88]
Racial and Ethnic Differences [82]

Interethnic Marriage
Use Exogamous Marriage

Interfaith Marriage [73]
PN 30 **SC** 26090
B Exogamous Marriage [73]

Interference (Learning) [67]
PN 2807 **SC** 26100
SN Inhibition of learning due to negative transfer effects of competing memories, thoughts, or learned behavior. Effects include slower learning and poorer memory.
B Learning [67]
N ↓ Latent Inhibition [97]
Proactive Inhibition [73]
Retroactive Inhibition [73]
R Forgetting [73]
↓ Memory [67]
↓ Retention [67]
Stroop Effect [88]

Interferons [94]
PN 21 **SC** 26103
B Proteins [73]
R Antineoplastic Drugs [82]
↓ Immunoglobulins [73]

Intergenerational Relations [88]
PN 525 **SC** 26105
SN Contact between related or nonrelated persons of different generational age groups.
R Empty Nest [91]
↓ Family Relations [67]
Generation Gap [73]
Transgenerational Patterns [91]

Intergenerational Transmission
Use Transgenerational Patterns

Intergroup Dynamics [73]
PN 663 **SC** 26110
B Group Dynamics [67]
R Boundaries (Psychological) [97]
Ingroup Outgroup [97]

Interhemispheric Interaction [85]
PN 401 **SC** 26112
SN Any neurophysiological, electrophysiological, or neurochemical exchange occurring between the cerebral hemispheres.
UF Interhemispheric Transfer
R ↓ Cerebral Cortex [67]
↓ Cerebral Dominance [73]
Corpus Callosum [73]
Left Brain [91]
Right Brain [91]

Interhemispheric Transfer
Use Interhemispheric Interaction

Interior Design [82]
PN 190 **SC** 26115
SN Practice or resultant product of planning and implementing the design of architectural interiors and furnishings.
B Architecture [73]
Environmental Planning [82]
R Aesthetic Preferences [73]
Aesthetics [67]
Furniture [85]

Interleukins [94]
PN 78 **SC** 26117
SN Compounds produced by lymphocytes that regulate immune system functioning and individual cell mediated immunity.
R Antigens [82]
Biological Markers [91]
Immunoreactivity [94]
Lymphocytes [73]

Intermarriage
Use Exogamous Marriage

Intermediate School Students [73]
PN 56 SC 26130
SN Includes the middle and/or upper elementary school grades, usually grades 4, 5, and 6. Use ELEMENTARY SCHOOL STUDENTS unless specific reference is made to population as intermediate school students. Use of a student term is mandatory in educational contexts.
B Elementary School Students [67]
R ↓ Children [67]
Preadolescents [88]
↓ School Age Children [73]

Intermittent Explosive Personality
Use Explosive Personality

Intermittent Reinforcement
Use Reinforcement Schedules

Internal Consistency
Use Test Reliability

Internal External Locus of Control [67]
PN 8383 SC 26150
UF Control (Locus of)
Locus of Control
B Personality Traits [67]
R Attribution [73]
↓ Emotional Control [73]
External Rewards [73]
Extrinsic Motivation [73]
↓ Helplessness [97]
Independence (Personality) [73]
Internal Rewards [73]
Intrinsic Motivation [73]
Self Control [73]
Self Determination [94]

Internal Rewards [73]
PN 106 SC 26160
SN Satisfaction of a personal value or intrinsic criteria of behavior through action or attainment. Compare SECONDARY REINFORCEMENT.
UF Intrinsic Rewards
B Rewards [67]
R Internal External Locus of Control [67]
Intrinsic Motivation [73]

Internalization [97]
PN 0 SC 26165
UF Incorporation (Psychological)
B Personality Processes [67]
N Introjection [73]
R ↓ Defense Mechanisms [67]
Externalization [73]
Object Permanence [85]
Object Relations [82]
↓ Personality Development [67]
↓ Psychotherapeutic Processes [67]

International Class of Diseases [97]
PN 0 SC 26167
SN Used when the International Classification of Diseases or its revisions is the primary focus of the reference. Consider PSYCHODIAGNOSTIC TYPOLOGIES to access references prior to 1997. Not used for specific psychodiagnostic categories.
UF ICD
B Psychodiagnostic Typologies [67]
R ↓ Diagnosis [67]
Diagnostic and Statistical Manual [94]
↓ Disorders [67]
↓ Mental Disorders [67]
↓ Psychodiagnosis [67]
Research Diagnostic Criteria [94]

International Organizations [73]
PN 161 SC 26170

International Organizations — (cont'd)
B Organizations [67]
R Foreign Organizations [73]

International Relations [67]
PN 665 SC 26180
R Foreign Policy Making [73]
Peace [88]

Internists [73]
PN 99 SC 26190
B Physicians [67]

Internship (Medical)
Use Medical Internship

Interobserver Reliability
Use Interrater Reliability

Interocular Transfer [85]
PN 70 SC 26207
SN Any neurophysiological, electrophysiological, or perceptual interaction between the two eyes.
B Visual Perception [67]
R Ocular Dominance [73]
↓ Perceptual Aftereffect [67]
↓ Sensory Adaptation [67]

Interpersonal Attraction [67]
PN 2463 SC 26210
UF Attraction (Interpersonal)
B Interpersonal Interaction [67]
R Human Mate Selection [88]
Likability [88]
Physical Attractiveness [73]

Interpersonal Communication [73]
PN 5113 SC 26220
B Communication [67]
Interpersonal Interaction [67]
N Arguments [73]
Body Language [73]
Conversation [73]
Cross Cultural Communication [97]
Double Bind Interaction [73]
Eye Contact [73]
Gossip [82]
Group Discussion [67]
Interviewing [73]
↓ Interviews [67]
Job Applicant Interviews [73]
Listening (Interpersonal) [97]
↓ Negotiation [73]
↓ Parent Child Communication [73]
R Credibility [73]
Neurolinguistic Programing [88]
Pragmatics [85]
↓ Scientific Communication [73]
Self Disclosure [73]
Self Reference [94]
Speech Anxiety [85]

Interpersonal Compatibility [73]
PN 345 SC 26230
UF Compatibility (Interpersonal)
B Interpersonal Interaction [67]
R Friendship [67]
Human Mate Selection [88]

Interpersonal Competence
Use Social Skills

Interpersonal Distance
Use Personal Space

Interpersonal Influences [67]
PN 3049 SC 26240

Interpersonal Influences — (cont'd)
SN Effect one individual has on another with or without apparent intention or direct exercise of command.
UF Influence (Interpersonal)
B Interpersonal Interaction [67]
Social Influences [67]
N Peer Pressure [94]
R ↓ Persuasive Communication [67]
Reference Groups [94]
Suggestibility [67]

Interpersonal Interaction [67]
PN 12030 SC 26250
UF Interaction (Interpersonal)
Rapport
B Social Interaction [67]
N Assistance (Social Behavior) [73]
Charitable Behavior [73]
↓ Collective Behavior [67]
↓ Conflict [67]
Cooperation [67]
↓ Employee Interaction [88]
Friendship [67]
Group Participation [73]
Group Performance [67]
Interpersonal Attraction [67]
↓ Interpersonal Communication [73]
Interpersonal Compatibility [73]
↓ Interpersonal Influences [67]
Male Female Relations [88]
↓ Participation [73]
↓ Peer Relations [67]
Persecution [73]
Rivalry [73]
Social Dating [73]
Stranger Reactions [88]
R Affection [73]
Boundaries (Psychological) [97]
Codependency [91]
Enactments [97]
Intimacy [73]
Mentor [85]
Mirroring [97]
Popularity [88]
Retaliation [91]
Social Cognition [94]
↓ Social Networks [94]

Interpersonal Perception
Use Social Perception

Interpersonal Psychotherapy [97]
PN 0 SC 26263
SN Technique formulated by H. S. Sullivan based on the study of the patient's interpersonal relationships both within and outside of the psychotherapeutic situation.
B Psychotherapy [67]
R ↓ Psychotherapeutic Techniques [67]

Interracial Adoption [94]
PN 8 SC 26265
UF Transracial Adoption
B Adoption (Child) [67]
R Adopted Children [73]
↓ Adoptees [85]
Adoptive Parents [73]
Interethnic Family [88]
Interracial Family [88]

Interracial Family [88]
PN 23 SC 26270
B Family [67]
R Interethnic Family [88]
Interracial Adoption [94]
Interracial Marriage [73]
Interracial Offspring [88]

Interracial Family — (cont'd)
R Racial and Ethnic Differences [82]
Racial and Ethnic Relations [82]

Interracial Marriage [73]
PN 90 SC 26280
UF Miscegenous Marriage
B Exogamous Marriage [73]
R Interracial Family [88]
Interracial Offspring [88]
Racial and Ethnic Relations [82]

Interracial Offspring [88]
PN 33 SC 26282
UF Biracial Children
B Offspring [88]
R Interracial Family [88]
Interracial Marriage [73]
Racial and Ethnic Differences [82]
Racial and Ethnic Relations [82]

Interrater Reliability [82]
PN 1162 SC 26284
SN Statistically measured correspondence between judgments by observers of a common event.
UF Interobserver Reliability
R Observation Methods [67]
Rating [67]
Statistical Reliability [73]
Test Reliability [73]

Interresponse Time [73]
PN 245 SC 26290
SN Interval between successive responses.
B Response Parameters [73]
Time [67]
R Response Frequency [73]

Intersensory Integration
Use Sensory Integration

Intersensory Processes [78]
PN 792 SC 26295
B Perception [67]
N Sensory Integration [91]
R Perceptual Motor Development [91]
↓ Perceptual Motor Processes [67]

Intersexuality
Use Hermaphroditism

Interspecies Interaction [91]
PN 278 SC 26297
SN Social behavior involving members of two or more animal species, including humans and animals.
UF Animal Human Interaction
Human Animal Interaction
B Social Behavior [67]
R Animal Assisted Therapy [94]
↓ Animal Social Behavior [67]
↓ Animals [67]
Biological Symbiosis [73]
Pets [82]
Species Differences [82]

Interstimulus Interval [67]
PN 2014 SC 26300
SN In conditioning contexts, the temporal interval separating the conditioned stimulus and unconditioned stimulus or the temporal interval between the elements of a multiple component (i.e., compound) stimulus.
B Stimulus Intervals [73]
R Reinforcement Delay [85]

Intertrial Interval [73]
PN 912 SC 26310
SN Temporal interval between successive discrete trials in conditioning or learning contexts.
B Stimulus Intervals [73]

Interval Reinforcement
Use Fixed Interval Reinforcement OR Variable Interval Reinforcement

Interviewers [88]
PN 79 SC 26330
R Interviewing [73]
↓ Interviews [67]

Interviewing [73]
PN 942 SC 26340
SN Used for the methods, techniques, principles, and practice of interviewing.
B Interpersonal Communication [73]
R Interviewers [88]
↓ Interviews [67]
Legal Interrogation [94]
Microcounseling [78]
Questioning [82]

Interviews [67]
PN 1888 SC 26350
B Interpersonal Communication [73]
N Intake Interview [94]
Job Applicant Interviews [73]
↓ Psychodiagnostic Interview [73]
R Interviewers [88]
Interviewing [73]
↓ Measurement [67]
Questioning [82]

Intestines [73]
PN 126 SC 26360
UF Duodenum
Ileum
B Gastrointestinal System [73]
R Absorption (Physiological) [73]

Intimacy [73]
PN 1614 SC 26370
R Affection [73]
Attachment Behavior [85]
↓ Interpersonal Interaction [67]
Love [73]
Physical Contact [82]
Romance [97]

Intoxication
Use Toxic Disorders

Intoxication (Alcohol)
Use Alcohol Intoxication

Intra Aural Muscle Reflex
Use Acoustic Reflex

Intracranial Self Stimulation
Use Brain Self Stimulation

Intramuscular Injections [73]
PN 31 SC 26400
B Injections [73]

Intraperitoneal Injections [73]
PN 44 SC 26410
B Injections [73]

Intrauterine Devices [73]
PN 21 SC 26420
B Contraceptive Devices [73]

Intravenous Drug Usage [94]
PN 263 SC 26425
UF IV Drug Usage
B Drug Usage [71]
R ↓ Drug Abuse [73]
↓ Drug Addiction [67]
Intravenous Injections [73]
Needle Sharing [94]

Intravenous Injections [73]
PN 373 SC 26430
B Injections [73]
R Intravenous Drug Usage [94]
Needle Sharing [94]

Intrinsic Motivation [73]
PN 978 SC 26440
SN Need or desire which arises from within the individual and causes action toward some goal.
B Motivation [67]
R ↓ Goals [67]
Internal External Locus of Control [67]
Internal Rewards [73]
Need for Cognition [97]
↓ Needs [67]

Intrinsic Rewards
Use Internal Rewards

Introjection [73]
PN 76 SC 26460
B Defense Mechanisms [67]
Internalization [97]
R Identification (Defense Mechanism) [73]

Introspection [73]
PN 161 SC 26470
B Personality Processes [67]
R Reflectiveness [97]
Self Monitoring (Personality) [85]
Self Perception [67]

Introversion [67]
PN 1029 SC 26480
B Personality Traits [67]
R Extraversion [67]

Intuition [73]
PN 345 SC 26485
B Cognitive Processes [67]
R Cognition [67]
↓ Comprehension [67]
Guessing [73]
Insight [73]

Inventories [67]
PN 2814 SC 26490
B Measurement [67]
N Biographical Inventories [73]
Interest Inventories [73]

Invertebrates [73]
PN 149 SC 26540
B Animals [67]
N ↓ Arthropoda [73]
Echinodermata [73]
↓ Mollusca [73]
↓ Worms [67]
R ↓ Vertebrates [73]

Investigation
Use Experimentation

Involuntary Treatment [94]
PN 42 SC 26555
B Treatment [67]
R ↓ Client Rights [88]

Involuntary Treatment — (cont'd)
R ↓ Commitment (Psychiatric) 73
Court Referrals 94
Informed Consent 85
Right to Treatment 97
Treatment Compliance 82
Treatment Dropouts 78
Treatment Refusal 94

Involutional Depression 73
PN 59 SC 26560
UF Climacteric Depression
B Affective Psychosis 73
Major Depression 88

Involutional Paranoid Psychosis 73
PN 7 SC 26570
UF Climacteric Paranoia
B Paranoia (Psychosis) 67
R Folie A Deux 73
Paranoid Schizophrenia 67

Involvement 73
PN 1422 SC 26575
B Social Behavior 67
N Job Involvement 78
R ↓ Commitment 85
Empowerment 91
↓ Participation 73

Ions
Use Electrolytes

Iowa Tests of Basic Skills 73
PN 44 SC 26590
B Achievement Measures 67

Iproniazid 73
PN 16 SC 26600
B Amine Oxidase Inhibitors 73
Antidepressant Drugs 71
Antihypertensive Drugs 73
Antitubercular Drugs 73
Monoamine Oxidase Inhibitors 73

Iran 73
PN 238 SC 26610
B Asia 73
R Middle East 78

Iraq 88
PN 12 SC 26615
B Asia 73
R Middle East 78

Ireland 73
PN 304 SC 26620
B Europe 73
N Northern Ireland 73

Iris (Eye) 73
PN 49 SC 26630
B Eye (Anatomy) 67
R Eye Color 91

Iron 73
PN 81 SC 26640
B Metallic Elements 73

Irradiation
Use Radiation

Irrational Beliefs 82
PN 455 SC 26654
SN Erroneous or distorted convictions or ideas firmly held despite objective and obvious contradictory proof or evidence.

Irrational Beliefs — (cont'd)
B Cognitions 85
R ↓ Attitudes 67
Superstitions 73

Irritability 88
PN 102 SC 26658
SN Used for human or animal populations.
B Personality Traits 67
R ↓ Emotional States 73

Irritable Bowel Syndrome 91
PN 62 SC 26659
SN Functional disorder of the colon that is generally psychosomatic.
B Colon Disorders 73
R ↓ Colitis 73
↓ Psychosomatic Disorders 67
↓ Syndromes 73

Ischemia 73
PN 173 SC 26660
B Cardiovascular Disorders 67
N Cerebral Ischemia 73
R Anoxia 73

Islam 73
PN 275 SC 26670
B Religious Affiliation 73
R Muslims 97

Isocarboxazid 73
PN 32 SC 26680
B Amine Oxidase Inhibitors 73
Antidepressant Drugs 71
Monoamine Oxidase Inhibitors 73

Isoenzymes
Use Isozymes

Isolation (Defense Mechanism) 73
PN 130 SC 26700
SN Unconscious separation of an unacceptable impulse, idea, or act from its original memory source, removing the emotional charge associated with the original memory.
B Defense Mechanisms 67
R Intellectualization 73

Isolation (Social)
Use Social Isolation

Isolation Effect 73
PN 204 SC 26720
SN Facilitating effect of isolation of distinctive features of an item (e.g., type face, color) in learning. Prior to 1982 the term was not defined and was used inconsistently.
B Associative Processes 67
R Cues 67
Stimulus Salience 73
↓ Verbal Learning 67

Isoniazid 73
PN 21 SC 26730
B Antitubercular Drugs 73

Isoproterenol 73
PN 122 SC 26740
B Alcohols 67
Sympathomimetic Drugs 73

Isozymes 73
PN 23 SC 26750
UF Isoenzymes
B Enzymes 73

Israel 67
PN 1955 SC 26760
B Asia 73
R Middle East 78

Italy 67
PN 963 SC 26780
B Europe 73

Itching
Use Pruritus

Item Analysis (Statistical) 73
PN 648 SC 26800
SN Quantitative analysis of a test item, especially regarding its difficulty level and validity.
B Factor Analysis 67
R Adaptive Testing 85
Item Response Theory 85
Statistical Weighting 85
Test Items 73

Item Analysis (Test) 67
PN 1151 SC 26810
SN Qualitative analysis of a test item, especially regarding its content and form.
B Analysis 67
Test Construction 73
Testing 67
R Item Content (Test) 73
Test Items 73

Item Bias
Use Test Bias

Item Content (Test) 73
PN 356 SC 26820
SN Topics or subject matter covered in test questions, units, or tasks.
B Test Construction 73
Testing 67
R Item Analysis (Test) 67
Test Forms 88
Test Items 73

Item Response Theory 85
PN 664 SC 26825
SN A statistical approach in psychological measurement. Also known as item characteristic curve theory.
UF Latent Trait Theory
Logistic Models
Rasch Model
B Testing 67
Theories 67
R Difficulty Level (Test) 73
Item Analysis (Statistical) 73
Psychometrics 67
↓ Test Scores 67

IV Drug Usage
Use Intravenous Drug Usage

Ivory Coast 88
PN 14 SC 26830
B Africa 67

Jails
Use Prisons

Jamaica 73
PN 122 SC 26850
B West Indies 73

James (William) 91
PN 63 SC 26855

James (William) — (cont'd)
SN Identifies biographical or autobiographical studies and discussions of James's works.
R Functionalism 73
↓ Psychologists 67

Japan 67
PN 2354 **SC** 26860
B Asia 73

Japanese Cultural Groups 97
PN 0 **SC** 26865
SN Populations of Japanese descent residing in countries other than the country of their origin. For Japanese residing in their own country use the appropriate country name. Use ASIANS to access references from 82–96.
B Asians 82

Jaundice 73
PN 25 **SC** 26870
B Digestive System Disorders 73
Liver Disorders 73
R Cirrhosis (Liver) 73
↓ Hepatitis 73
↓ Infectious Disorders 73

Jaw 73
PN 163 **SC** 26880
UF Mandibula
Maxilla
B Musculoskeletal System 73
R Bones 73

Jealousy 73
PN 334 **SC** 26890
UF Envy
B Emotional States 73
R ↓ Anger 67
↓ Anxiety 67

Jews 97
PN 0 **SC** 26900
SN Use JUDAISM to access references prior to 73–96.
B Religious Groups 97
R AntiSemitism 73
↓ Ethnic Groups 73
Holocaust 88
Holocaust Survivors 88
Judaism 67
Minority Groups 67

Job Analysis 67
PN 1373 **SC** 26910
SN Analysis specifying job duties, responsibilities, and technical components.
B Analysis 67
Personnel Management 73
R ↓ Job Characteristics 85
Task Analysis 67
Work Load 82

Job Applicant Attitudes 73
PN 137 **SC** 26920
SN Attitudes of, not toward, job applicants.
B Attitudes 67
R Job Applicants 85
Job Search 85
Occupational Attitudes 73
↓ Personnel 67

Job Applicant Interviews 73
PN 543 **SC** 26930
UF Employment Interviews
B Interpersonal Communication 73
Interviews 67
Personnel Selection 67

Job Applicant Interviews — (cont'd)
R Job Search 85
↓ Personnel Evaluation 73
↓ Personnel Recruitment 73

Job Applicant Screening 73
PN 487 **SC** 26940
UF Testing (Job Applicants)
B Personnel Selection 67
Screening 82
R Employment Discrimination 94
Employment Tests 73
Job Search 85
↓ Personnel Evaluation 73
↓ Personnel Recruitment 73

Job Applicants 85
PN 319 **SC** 26953
SN Persons seeking employment.
R ↓ Employment Status 82
Job Applicant Attitudes 73
Job Search 85
↓ Personnel 67

Job Change
Use Career Change

Job Characteristics 85
PN 1431 **SC** 26957
SN Responsibilities or tasks that characterize a specific job.
N Work Load 82
R Job Analysis 67
↓ Occupations 67
Quality of Work Life 88

Job Corps 73
PN 30 **SC** 26960
SN U.S. Government program of vocational and psychosocial training and counseling for disadvantaged adolescents and adults.
B Government Programs 73
R Government 67

Job Discrimination
Use Employment Discrimination

Job Enrichment 73
PN 92 **SC** 26980
SN Formal or informal programs or techniques used to enhance the quality of a job or to further challenge the employee.
B Working Conditions 73
R Job Experience Level 73
Job Satisfaction 67
Occupational Guidance 67
Occupational Mobility 73
↓ Personnel Training 67

Job Experience Level 73
PN 1611 **SC** 26990
UF Experience Level (Job)
B Employee Characteristics 88
Experience Level 88
R Employment History 78
Job Enrichment 73
Job Knowledge 97
Occupational Status 78

Job Family Relationship
Use Family Work Relationship

Job Involvement 78
PN 896 **SC** 26994
B Involvement 73
R ↓ Employee Attitudes 67
Employee Motivation 73
↓ Job Performance 67

Job Involvement — (cont'd)
R Job Satisfaction 67
Organizational Commitment 91
Participative Management 88
Work (Attitudes Toward) 73

Job Knowledge 97
PN 0 **SC** 26996
B Employee Characteristics 88
Knowledge Level 78
R ↓ Employee Skills 73
Job Experience Level 73
↓ Job Performance 67

Job Mobility
Use Occupational Mobility

Job Performance 67
PN 6054 **SC** 27010
B Performance 67
N Employee Efficiency 73
Employee Productivity 73
R ↓ Employee Attitudes 67
Job Involvement 78
Job Knowledge 97
Organizational Commitment 91
↓ Personnel 67
↓ Personnel Evaluation 73
Personnel Promotion 78
Work Load 82

Job Promotion
Use Personnel Promotion

Job Reentry
Use Reemployment

Job Satisfaction 67
PN 6693 **SC** 27040
SN Positive attitudes toward one's work when tangible and/or intangible rewards fulfill expectations.
UF Work Satisfaction
B Employee Attitudes 67
Satisfaction 73
R Career Change 78
Job Enrichment 73
Job Involvement 78
Organizational Commitment 91
Quality of Work Life 88
Role Satisfaction 94

Job Search 85
PN 242 **SC** 27043
SN Process of seeking employment. For consideration of career alternatives use CAREER EDUCATION.
R Job Applicant Attitudes 73
Job Applicant Interviews 73
Job Applicant Screening 73
Job Applicants 85
Reemployment 91
Unemployment 67

Job Security 78
PN 88 **SC** 27045
SN Probable assurance of continued employment.
R Employee Turnover 73
↓ Occupational Tenure 73
Personnel Termination 73
Retirement 73
Unemployment 67

Job Selection
Use Occupational Choice

Job Status
Use Occupational Status

Job Training
Use Personnel Training

Jobs
Use Occupations

Joint Custody [88]
PN 48 **SC** 27065
R Child Custody [82]
Child Support [88]
Divorce [73]

Joint Disorders [73]
PN 59 **SC** 27070
B Musculoskeletal Disorders [73]
N ↓ Arthritis [73]
R ↓ Joints (Anatomy) [73]

Joints (Anatomy) [73]
PN 102 **SC** 27080
B Musculoskeletal System [73]
N Ankle [73]
Elbow (Anatomy) [73]
Knee [73]
Shoulder (Anatomy) [73]
Wrist [73]
R ↓ Joint Disorders [73]

Jokes [73]
PN 165 **SC** 27090
B Humor [67]

Jordan [88]
PN 62 **SC** 27095
B Asia [73]
R Middle East [78]

Journalists [73]
PN 72 **SC** 27100
B Professional Personnel [78]
R ↓ News Media [97]

Joy
Use Happiness

Judaism [67]
PN 1190 **SC** 27130
B Religious Affiliation [73]
R AntiSemitism [73]
Bible [73]
Holocaust [88]
Jews [97]
Rabbis [73]

Judges [85]
PN 179 **SC** 27135
B Legal Personnel [85]

Judgment [67]
PN 3689 **SC** 27140
SN Mental act of comparing or evaluating choices within a given set of values frequently with the purpose of choosing a course of action.
N Clinical Judgment (Not Diagnosis) [73]
Probability Judgment [78]
R ↓ Decision Making [67]
Judgment Disturbances [73]
Uncertainty [91]
Wisdom [94]

Judgment Disturbances [73]
PN 6 **SC** 27150

Judgment Disturbances — (cont'd)
SN Maladaptive judgment resulting from wish-fulfilling, impulsive decisions based on need for immediate infantile gratification.
B Thought Disturbances [73]
R ↓ Judgment [67]

Judo [73]
PN 30 **SC** 27160
B Recreation [67]
Sports [67]
R Martial Arts [85]

Jumping [73]
PN 92 **SC** 27170
B Motor Performance [73]
Motor Processes [67]

Jung (Carl) [73]
PN 386 **SC** 27180
SN Identifies biographical or autobiographical studies and discussions of Jung's works.
R Analytical Psychotherapy [73]
Archetypes [91]
↓ Collective Unconscious [97]
↓ Jungian Psychology [73]
↓ Psychologists [67]

Jungian Psychology [73]
PN 1261 **SC** 27190
SN Analytical psychology characterized by theories of the collective unconscious, the archetype, the complex, and psychological types.
UF Analytic Psychology
B Neopsychoanalytic School [73]
N ↓ Collective Unconscious [97]
R Analytical Psychotherapy [73]
Archetypes [91]
Free Association [94]
Jung (Carl) [73]

Jungian Psychotherapy
Use Analytical Psychotherapy

Junior College Students [73]
PN 185 **SC** 27200
SN Students in 2-year colleges. Mandatory term in educational contexts.
B College Students [67]
R Community College Students [73]

Junior Colleges
Use Colleges

Junior High School Students [71]
PN 8419 **SC** 27220
SN Students in 7th and 8th grade. Sometimes includes students in 9th grade. Mandatory term in educational contexts.
B Students [67]
R ↓ Adolescents [67]
↓ Children [67]
Grade Level [94]
Middle School Students [85]

Junior High School Teachers [73]
PN 1215 **SC** 27230
B Teachers [67]

Junior High Schools [73]
PN 241 **SC** 27240
B Schools [67]
R Secondary Education [73]

Juries [85]
PN 513 **SC** 27245

Juries — (cont'd)
SN Bodies of persons sworn to give a verdict in a court of law. Also used for mock and simulated juries. Use ADJUDICATION to access references from 73-84.
R ↓ Adjudication [67]
Jury Selection [94]
↓ Legal Personnel [85]

Jury Selection [94]
PN 7 **SC** 27252
SN Use JURIES to access references from 85-93.
R ↓ Adjudication [67]
Juries [85]

Justice [73]
PN 757 **SC** 27260
SN Used for the impartial and fair settlement of conflict and differences, or the designation of rewards or punishment.
UF Distributive Justice
N ↓ Criminal Justice [91]
R ↓ Civil Rights [78]
Equity (Payment) [78]
↓ Equity (Social) [78]
Freedom [78]
↓ Law (Government) [73]
↓ Law Enforcement [78]
Morality [67]
Reward Allocation [88]
Social Equality [73]
↓ Social Issues [91]

Juvenile Court
Use Adjudication

Juvenile Delinquency [67]
PN 2482 **SC** 27280
UF Delinquency (Juvenile)
B Antisocial Behavior [71]
Behavior Disorders [71]
R Antisocial Personality [73]
Crime Prevention [85]
↓ Juvenile Delinquents [73]
Predelinquent Youth [78]

Juvenile Delinquents [73]
PN 2402 **SC** 27290
SN Youths characterized by antisocial behavior which is subject to legal sanctions.
UF Offenders (Juvenile)
N Female Delinquents [73]
Male Delinquents [73]
R ↓ Adolescents [67]
↓ Criminals [67]
Juvenile Delinquency [67]
Juvenile Gangs [73]
Preadolescents [88]
Predelinquent Youth [78]

Juvenile Gangs [73]
PN 134 **SC** 27300
UF Gangs (Juvenile)
R ↓ Juvenile Delinquents [73]

Kainic Acid [88]
PN 92 **SC** 27305
B Acids [73]
R Glutamic Acid [73]
↓ Neurotoxins [82]

Kangaroos [73]
PN 14 **SC** 27310
B Marsupials [73]

Karate
Use Martial Arts

Karyotype Disorders
Use Chromosome Disorders

Kaufman Assessment Battery Children 88
PN 131 **SC** 27324
B Intelligence Measures 67

Kenya 82
PN 156 **SC** 27326
B Africa 67

Ketamine 97
PN 0 **SC** 27327
B Anesthetic Drugs 73

Keyboards 85
PN 58 **SC** 27328
B Apparatus 67
R ↓ Computer Peripheral Devices 85
Human Computer Interaction 97
↓ Instrument Controls 85
Typing 91

Keypunch Operators
Use Clerical Personnel

Kibbutz 73
PN 290 **SC** 27340
B Communes 73

Kidnapping 88
PN 39 **SC** 27345
B Crime 67
R Hostages 88

Kidney Diseases 88
PN 220 **SC** 27347
UF Renal Diseases
B Urogenital Disorders 73

Kidney Transplants
Use Organ Transplantation

Kidneys 73
PN 213 **SC** 27360
B Urogenital System 73

Kinases 82
PN 99 **SC** 27366
SN Enzymes that catalyze the conversion of proenzymes to active enzymes or the transfer of phosphate groups to form triphosphates (ATP).
UF Enteropeptidase
B Enzymes 73

Kindergarten Students 73
PN 2647 **SC** 27370
SN Students in kindergarten. Mandatory term in educational contexts.
B Students 67
R ↓ Children 67
Grade Level 94
Preschool Age Children 67
↓ Preschool Students 82

Kindergartens 73
PN 180 **SC** 27380
B Schools 67

Kindling 85
PN 178 **SC** 27385
SN Afterdischarges and generalized convulsions produced by repeated brain stimulation, usually electrical. Often used as an experimental model of epilepsy.

Kindling — (cont'd)
B Electrical Activity 67
R Electrical Brain Stimulation 73
Experimental Epilepsy 78

Kinesthetic Perception 67
PN 885 **SC** 27390
SN Sensory modality involving awareness of body movement, position, and posture, and movement of body parts, such as muscles, tendons, and joints. Used for human or animal populations.
B Somesthetic Perception 67
R Spatial Orientation (Perception) 73

Kinship 85
PN 311 **SC** 27395
SN The state of being related such as by birth, common ancestry, or marriage. Used for human or animal populations.
R Ethnology 67
↓ Family 67
Kinship Recognition 88
Kinship Structure 73

Kinship Recognition 88
PN 205 **SC** 27399
R ↓ Discrimination Learning 82
Kinship 85
Species Recognition 85

Kinship Structure 73
PN 156 **SC** 27400
R Ethnography 73
Ethnology 67
↓ Family Structure 73
Kinship 85
↓ Sociocultural Factors 67

Kirton Adaption Innovation Inven 97
PN 0 **SC** 27410
B Personality Measures 67

Kleptomania 73
PN 35 **SC** 27420
R Impulse Control Disorders 97
Impulsiveness 73
↓ Personality Disorders 67

Klinefelters Syndrome 73
PN 64 **SC** 27430
B Hypogonadism 73
Male Genital Disorders 73
Neonatal Disorders 73
Sex Chromosome Disorders 73
Syndromes 73
R ↓ Infertility 73
↓ Mental Retardation 67

Knee 73
PN 53 **SC** 27440
B Joints (Anatomy) 73
R Leg (Anatomy) 73

Knowledge Based Systems
Use Expert Systems

Knowledge Level 78
PN 6207 **SC** 27446
SN Range of received or acquired information, understanding, or awareness. Limited to human populations.
N Health Knowledge 94
Job Knowledge 97
R Declarative Knowledge 97
↓ Experience Level 88
Information 67

Knowledge Level — (cont'd)
R Procedural Knowledge 97
Wisdom 94

Knowledge of Results 67
PN 489 **SC** 27450
B Feedback 67

Kohlberg (Lawrence) 91
PN 15 **SC** 27455
SN Identifies biographical or autobiographical studies and discussions of Kohlberg's works.
R Moral Development 73
↓ Psychologists 67

Kohs Block Design Test 73
PN 24 **SC** 27460
UF Block Design Test (Kohs)
B Intelligence Measures 67

Kolmogorov Smirnov Test 73
PN 3 **SC** 27470
B Nonparametric Statistical Tests 67

Korea 73
PN 227 **SC** 27480
SN Used for historical articles or when North Korea or South Korea is not specified. Term discontinued from 82–87, but reinstated in 1988. Use North Korea or South Korea from 82–87.
B Asia 73
N North Korea 82
South Korea 82

Korean Cultural Groups 97
PN 0 **SC** 27483
SN Populations of Korean descent residing in countries other than the country of their origin. For Koreans residing in their own country use the appropriate country name. Use ASIANS to access references prior to 82–96.
B Asians 82

Koro 94
PN 12 **SC** 27485
SN A mental disorder characterized by fear or delusions of the shrinkage of the penis, labia, or breasts into the abdomen or chest. Observed primarily in Southern Chinese and some African cultures.
B Body Image Disturbances 73
Ethnospecific Disorders 73
Mental Disorders 67

Korsakoffs Psychosis 73
PN 374 **SC** 27490
B Alcoholic Hallucinosis 73
Alcoholism 67
R Confabulation 73

Kuder Occupational Interest Survey 73
PN 39 **SC** 27510
B Occupational Interest Measures 73

Kuder Preference Record 73
PN 18 **SC** 27520
B Preference Measures 73

Kupfer Detre Self Rating Scale
SN Term discontinued in 1997. Use KUPFER DETRE SELF RATING SCALE to access references from 73–96.
Use Nonprojective Personality Measures

Kuwait 91
PN 41 **SC** 27545
R Middle East 78

Kwashiorkor 73
PN 8 SC 27550
B Protein Deficiency Disorders 73

L Dopa
Use Levodopa

Labeling 78
PN 999 SC 27565
SN In social or therapeutic settings, designating the condition of an individual or group by a simplistic word or phrase which may serve to indicate status, stigma, or other characteristics.
R ↓ Attitudes 67
↓ Diagnosis 67
↓ Names 85
↓ Psychodiagnostic Typologies 67
↓ Social Perception 67
Stigma 91

Labor (Childbirth) 73
PN 282 SC 27570
R ↓ Birth 67
Childbirth Training 78
Midwifery 85
Obstetrical Complications 78

Labor Management Relations 67
PN 468 SC 27580
UF Labor Relations
B Personnel Management 73
R Informants 88
Labor Unions 73
↓ Management 67
Mediation 88
↓ Organizational Behavior 78
Strikes 73
Supervisor Employee Interaction 97

Labor Relations
Use Labor Management Relations

Labor Union Members 73
PN 166 SC 27600
R ↓ Personnel 67

Labor Unions 73
PN 296 SC 27610
B Organizations 67
R Labor Management Relations 67

Laboratories (Educational)
Use Educational Laboratories

Laboratories (Experimental)
Use Experimental Laboratories

Laborers (Construct and Indust)
Use Blue Collar Workers

Laborers (Farm)
Use Agricultural Workers

Labyrinth (Anatomy) 73
PN 87 SC 27660
SN The bony structure of the inner ear that houses the membranous labyrinth (i.e., the cochlea, vestibule, semicircular canals, utricle, and saccule). May also refer to these latter membranous structures.
UF Inner Ear
B Ear (Anatomy) 67
N Cochlea 73
R ↓ Vestibular Apparatus 67

Labyrinth (Apparatus)
Use Mazes

Labyrinth Disorders 73
PN 22 SC 27680
B Ear Disorders 73
N Menieres Disease 73
Motion Sickness 73
R ↓ Somesthetic Perception 67
Vertigo 73

Lactate Dehydrogenase 73
PN 16 SC 27690
B Dehydrogenases 73

Lactation 73
PN 436 SC 27700
B Secretion (Gland) 73
R Postnatal Period 73

Lactic Acid 91
PN 39 SC 27720
UF Sodium Lactate
B Acids 73

Landscapes
Use Topography

Language 67
PN 4953 SC 27740
N ↓ Dialect 73
↓ Figurative Language 85
Foreign Languages 73
↓ Form Classes (Language) 73
Phrases 73
Profanity 91
Rhetoric 91
Sentences 67
Sign Language 73
Spelling 73
↓ Vocabulary 67
↓ Written Language 67
R Bilingualism 73
Discourse Analysis 97
English as Second Language 97
↓ Grammar 67
↓ Language Development 67
↓ Linguistics 73
↓ Literacy 73
Metalinguistics 94
Monolingualism 73
↓ Multilingualism 73
Neurolinguistics 91
Symbolism 67
↓ Verbal Communication 67

Language Alternation
Use Code Switching

Language Arts Education 73
PN 1568 SC 27750
SN Education in subjects aimed at development of comprehension and use of written and oral language.
B Curriculum 67
N Phonics 73
Reading Education 73
Spelling 73
R English as Second Language 97
Initial Teaching Alphabet 73
↓ Literacy 73
Literacy Programs 97

Language Delay 88
PN 161 SC 27755
B Delayed Development 73
Language Development 67
R ↓ Language Disorders 82
Retarded Speech Development 73

Language Development 67
PN 7228 SC 27760
SN Acquisition of the rules governing the structure of language (e.g., syntax) and meaning. Use SPEECH DEVELOPMENT for acquisition of speech sound production. Compare VERBAL LEARNING.
B Cognitive Development 73
Intellectual Development 73
N Language Delay 88
R Foreign Language Learning 67
↓ Language 67
↓ Language Disorders 82
Metalinguistics 94
Reading Development 97
↓ Speech Development 73
↓ Verbal Communication 67
Vygotsky (Lev) 91

Language Disorders 82
PN 1555 SC 27763
SN Disorders, usually due to cognitive or neurological dysfunction, resulting in problems in symbolization or in delays in language and speech development.
B Communication Disorders 82
N ↓ Aphasia 67
Echolalia 73
↓ Mutism 73
R Language Delay 88
↓ Language Development 67
Neurolinguistics 91
Speech Disabled 97
↓ Speech Disorders 67

Language Laboratories 73
PN 6 SC 27770
B Educational Laboratories 73
R Foreign Language Learning 67
Learning Centers (Educational) 73

Language Proficiency 88
PN 375 SC 27773
SN Accuracy and fluency of verbal communication in a second language learning or bilingual context. Includes concept of Limited English Proficiency, which is knowledge of English without sufficient proficiency to communicate or participate in an English-speaking society. Consider VERBAL FLUENCY for other contexts.
UF Limited English Proficiency
B Communication Skills 73
Verbal Communication 67
R Bilingualism 73
English as Second Language 97
Foreign Language Learning 67
Verbal Ability 67
Verbal Fluency 73

Laos 88
PN 2 SC 27775
B Southeast Asia 73

Larvae 73
PN 199 SC 27780
B Insects 67
R Ants 73
Bees 73
Beetles 73
Butterflies 73
Cockroaches 73
↓ Diptera 73
Drosophila 73
↓ Fishes 67
Frogs 67
Grasshoppers 73
Mantis 73
Moths 73
Salamanders 73

Larvae — (cont'd)
R Toads 73
Wasps 82

Laryngeal Disorders 73
PN 82 SC 27790
B Respiratory Tract Disorders 73

Larynx 73
PN 121 SC 27800
B Respiratory System 73
N Vocal Cords 73

Laser Irradiation 73
PN 19 SC 27810
B Radiation 67

Latchkey Children
Use Child Self Care

Latency (Response)
Use Response Latency

Latent Inhibition 97
PN 0 SC 27825
B Interference (Learning) 67
N Proactive Inhibition 73
Retroactive Inhibition 73
R Conditioned Stimulus 73
↓ Conditioning 67
Forgetting 73
↓ Memory 67
Prepulse Inhibition 97

Latent Learning 73
PN 90 SC 27830
SN Learning that is not immediately manifested in performance but which remains dormant until activated by some contingency. From 1982, limited to animal populations. Use INCIDENTAL LEARNING for human populations.
B Incidental Learning 67

Latent Trait Theory
Use Item Response Theory

Lateral Dominance 67
PN 4662 SC 27840
SN The tendency for the right or left hemisphere to be dominant over the other for most functions, leading to a differential primacy, functional asymmetry, or preference for one side of the body. Compare CEREBRAL DOMINANCE.
UF Hemispheric Specialization
B Cerebral Dominance 73
N Handedness 78
Ocular Dominance 73
R ↓ Brain 67
Left Brain 91
Right Brain 91

Latin America 88
PN 103 SC 27843
R ↓ Central America 73
Mexico 73
↓ South America 67
↓ West Indies 73

Latinos
Use Hispanics

Laughter 78
PN 174 SC 27855
B Vocalization 67
R ↓ Emotional Responses 67
↓ Humor 67

Laughter — (cont'd)
R ↓ Nonverbal Communication 71
Smiles 73

Law (Government) 73
PN 114 SC 27860
SN Science and philosophy of law as sanctioned by governmental authority. For specific laws or statutes, use LAWS.
N Civil Law 94
Criminal Law 73
R Defendants 85
Government 67
↓ Justice 73
↓ Law Enforcement 78
↓ Laws 67
Political Psychology 97

Law Enforcement 78
PN 394 SC 27865
B Legal Processes 73
N ↓ Adjudication 67
Incarceration 73
Legal Arrest 73
Legal Detention 73
R Civil Law 94
Crime Prevention 85
↓ Criminal Justice 91
Government 67
↓ Justice 73
↓ Law (Government) 73
↓ Laws 67
↓ Legal Evidence 91
Legal Interrogation 94
Parole 73
Probation 73

Law Enforcement Personnel 73
PN 276 SC 27870
B Government Personnel 73
Legal Personnel 85
N Parole Officers 73
Police Personnel 73
Prison Personnel 73
Probation Officers 73
R Attorneys 73
↓ Social Workers 73

Law Students 78
PN 134 SC 27875
B Students 67
R Attorneys 73
Graduate Students 67

Laws 67
PN 3174 SC 27880
SN Rules of conduct made obligatory by some legal or controlling authority; includes statutes enacted by a legislative body.
B Government Policy Making 73
N Abortion Laws 73
Disability Laws 94
↓ Drug Laws 73
Gun Control Laws 73
R ↓ Abuse Reporting 97
Case Law 85
Censorship 78
Citizenship 73
↓ Civil Rights 78
Consumer Protection 73
Government 67
↓ Law (Government) 73
↓ Law Enforcement 78
Legal Decisions 91
↓ Legal Processes 73
Legislative Processes 73

Lawyers
Use Attorneys

Lay Religious Personnel 73
PN 58 SC 27900
SN Participants or members of a religious group or organization who perform various functional and ceremonial tasks not requiring a member of the clergy.
B Religious Personnel 73
R Chaplains 73
↓ Clergy 73
Evangelists 73
Missionaries 73

Lead (Metal) 73
PN 139 SC 27910
B Metallic Elements 73

Lead Poisoning 73
PN 251 SC 27920
B Toxic Disorders 73
R Pica 73

Leadership 67
PN 3780 SC 27930
B Social Behavior 67
N Leadership Qualities 97
Leadership Style 73
R Abuse of Power 97
Authority 67
Entrepreneurship 91
↓ Management 67

Leadership Qualities 97
PN 0 SC 27935
B Leadership 67
R Charisma 88
Leadership Style 73
↓ Management 67
↓ Personality Traits 67

Leadership Style 73
PN 2041 SC 27940
B Leadership 67
Social Behavior 67
R Charisma 88
Leadership Qualities 97

Learned Helplessness 78
PN 1263 SC 27945
SN Learned expectation that one's responses are independent of reward and, hence, do not predict or control the occurrence of rewards. Learned helplessness derives from a history, experimentally induced or naturally occurring, of having received punishment/aversive stimulation regardless of responses made. Such circumstances result in an impaired ability to learn. Used for human or animal populations.
UF Helplessness (Learned)
B Helplessness 97
R Attribution 73
↓ Emotional States 73
Experimental Neurosis 73

Learning 67
PN 9629 SC 28030
SN Conceptually broad array term referring to the process of acquiring knowledge, skills, or behaviors by instruction, study, or experience. Use a more specific term if possible. Used for both human and animal populations.
N Adult Learning 97
Cat Learning 67
Cognitive Hypothesis Testing 82
↓ Conditioning 67
Cooperative Learning 94
↓ Discrimination Learning 82

Learning — (cont'd)
N ↓ Experiential Learning 97
Extinction (Learning) 67
Foreign Language Learning 67
↓ Generalization (Learning) 82
Generation Effect (Learning) 91
↓ Incidental Learning 67
Intentional Learning 73
↓ Interference (Learning) 67
Mastery Learning 85
Maze Learning 67
Mnemonic Learning 73
Nonverbal Learning 73
Observational Learning 73
Overlearning 67
↓ Perceptual Motor Learning 67
Probability Learning 67
Rat Learning 67
Relearning 73
School Learning 67
Sequential Learning 73
↓ Serial Learning 67
↓ Skill Learning 73
↓ Social Learning 73
Spatial Learning 94
Spontaneous Recovery (Learning) 73
State Dependent Learning 82
↓ Transfer (Learning) 67
Trial and Error Learning 73
↓ Verbal Learning 67
R ↓ Cognitive Processes 67
↓ Concept Formation 67
Connectionism 94
Constructivism 94
Delayed Alternation 94
↓ Feedback 67
Forgetting 73
↓ Habits 67
Individualized Instruction 73
Learning Ability 73
↓ Learning Disorders 67
Learning Rate 73
↓ Learning Schedules 67
↓ Learning Strategies 91
Learning Theory 67
↓ Memory 67
Metacognition 91
Primacy Effect 73
↓ Prompting 97
Recency Effect 73
↓ Reinforcement 67
↓ Retention 67
↓ Serial Position Effect 82
Spontaneous Alternation 82
↓ Strategies 67
Time On Task 88

Learning Ability 73
PN 732 **SC** 27960
SN Capacity to acquire a behavior, skill, or knowledge from experience, formal instruction, or conditioning. Used for animal or human populations.
B Ability 67
R ↓ Learning 67

Learning Centers (Educational) 73
PN 58 **SC** 27970
B School Facilities 73
R Language Laboratories 73

Learning Disabilities 73
PN 9521 **SC** 27980

Learning Disabilities — (cont'd)
SN According to U.S. federal legislation, disabilities involved in understanding or using language, manifested in impaired listening, thinking, talking, reading, writing, or arithmetic skills. Includes perceptual handicaps, brain injury, minimal brain dysfunction, and developmental aphasia. Compare LEARNING DISORDERS.
B Learning Disorders 67
N Dyslexia 73
R Acalculia 73
Agraphia 73
↓ Aphasia 67
↓ Disabled 97
Educational Diagnosis 78
Minimally Brain Damaged 73
↓ Perceptual Disturbances 73

Learning Disorders 67
PN 1086 **SC** 27990
SN According to U.S. federal legislation, learning problems that are due to visual, hearing, or motor handicaps, mental retardation, emotional disturbance or environmental, cultural, or economic disadvantage. Compare LEARNING DISABILITIES.
N ↓ Learning Disabilities 73
↓ Reading Disabilities 67
R Developmental Disabilities 82
Educational Diagnosis 78
↓ Learning 67
↓ Mental Disorders 67
↓ Physical Disorders 97

Learning Rate 73
PN 513 **SC** 28000
R ↓ Learning 67
↓ Serial Position Effect 82

Learning Schedules 67
PN 87 **SC** 28010
UF Schedules (Learning)
N Distributed Practice 73
Massed Practice 73
R ↓ Learning 67

Learning Strategies 91
PN 758 **SC** 28013
SN Techniques, methods, or tactics used for learning. Limited to human populations.
UF Strategies (Learning)
B Strategies 67
N Mnemonic Learning 73
Observational Learning 73
↓ Social Learning 73
Trial and Error Learning 73
R Advance Organizers 85
↓ Cognitive Processes 67
↓ Cognitive Style 67
Constant Time Delay 97
↓ Learning 67
Memory Training 94
Metacognition 91
Note Taking 91
↓ Prompting 97
Study Habits 73
Time Management 94

Learning Style
Use Cognitive Style

Learning Theory 67
PN 1356 **SC** 28020
B Theories 67
R ↓ Classical Conditioning 67
Connectionism 94
↓ Learning 67
↓ Operant Conditioning 67

Learys Interpersonal Check List 73
PN 9 **SC** 28040
SN Use LEARYS INTERPERSONAL CHECK LIST or LEARY INTERPERSONAL CHECK LIST to access references from 73–77.
B Nonprojective Personality Measures 73

Least Preferred Coworker Scale 73
PN 59 **SC** 28050
B Preference Measures 73

Least Squares 85
PN 126 **SC** 28055
SN Method of estimating the curve-of-best-fit or regression line of a set of points representing statistical data.
B Statistical Estimation 85
R Error of Measurement 85
↓ Statistical Regression 85

Lebanon 88
PN 41 **SC** 28057
B Asia 73
R Middle East 78

Lecithin 91
PN 8 **SC** 28058
B Choline 73
Phosphatides 73

Lecture Method 73
PN 551 **SC** 28060
B Teaching Methods 67
R Directed Discussion Method 73

Left Brain 91
PN 109 **SC** 28070
SN Used only when the left hemisphere of the brain is the focus of the document.
B Cerebral Cortex 67
R ↓ Brain 67
↓ Cerebral Dominance 73
Corpus Callosum 73
Interhemispheric Interaction 85
↓ Lateral Dominance 67
Ocular Dominance 73
Right Brain 91

Leg (Anatomy) 73
PN 168 **SC** 28080
B Musculoskeletal System 73
R Ankle 73
Feet (Anatomy) 73
Knee 73
Thigh 73

Legal Arrest 73
PN 322 **SC** 28090
SN Taking custody, under legal authority, of a person for the purpose of holding or detaining him/her to answer criminal charges or civil demands.
UF Arrest (Law)
B Law Enforcement 78

Legal Decisions 91
PN 154 **SC** 28095
SN Used for discussions of the implications or the effects of specific judicial decisions. Not used for the actual process of judicial decision making. Consider CASE LAW for descriptions, not discussions, of laws resulting from court decisions.
R ↓ Adjudication 67
Case Law 85
Criminal Conviction 73
↓ Criminal Justice 91
↓ Laws 67
↓ Legal Processes 73
Legislative Processes 73

Legal Detention 73
PN 66 **SC** 28100
SN Being detained (e.g., in jail) by law enforcers for having committed or for being suspected of having committed a crime, especially immediately prior to a legal court disposition.
UF Detention (Legal)
B Law Enforcement 78
R Legal Interrogation 94

Legal Evidence 91
PN 83 **SC** 28103
SN Testimony, records, documents, objects, and diagrams submitted to a court during a hearing or trial.
UF Evidence (Legal)
B Legal Processes 73
N ↓ Legal Testimony 82
R ↓ Adjudication 67
↓ Law Enforcement 78
Legal Interrogation 94
Witnesses 85

Legal Interrogation 94
PN 20 **SC** 28104
UF Criminal Interrogation
Police Interrogation
B Legal Processes 73
R Interviewing 73
↓ Law Enforcement 78
Legal Detention 73
↓ Legal Evidence 91
↓ Legal Testimony 82
Polygraphs 73
Questioning 82
Witnesses 85

Legal Liability (Professional)
Use Professional Liability

Legal Personnel 85
PN 91 **SC** 28107
UF Paralegal Personnel
B Professional Personnel 78
N Attorneys 73
Judges 85
↓ Law Enforcement Personnel 73
R Juries 85

Legal Processes 73
PN 3466 **SC** 28110
SN Broad concept encompassing psychological and behavioral aspects of the law—its formation, enforcement, impact, and implications. Also includes reference to the legal justice system and legislative processes as they relate to psychology.
N ↓ Adoption (Child) 67
Child Custody 82
Child Visitation 88
↓ Commitment (Psychiatric) 73
Competency to Stand Trial 85
↓ Criminal Justice 91
Forensic Evaluation 94
Guardianship 88
Insanity Defense 85
↓ Law Enforcement 78
↓ Legal Evidence 91
Legal Interrogation 94
↓ Legal Testimony 82
Legislative Processes 73
Parole 73
Probation 73
R Advance Directives 94
Case Law 85
Civil Law 94
↓ Civil Rights 78
Consumer Protection 73
Government 67

Legal Processes — (cont'd)
R ↓ Government Policy Making 73
Informed Consent 85
↓ Laws 67
Legal Decisions 91
Professional Liability 85
Protective Services 97
Risk Management 97
↓ Social Issues 91

Legal Psychology
Use Forensic Psychology

Legal Testimony 82
PN 407 **SC** 28115
SN Evidence presented by a witness under oath or affirmation (as distinguished from evidence derived from other sources) either orally or written as deposition or affidavit.
B Legal Evidence 91
Legal Processes 73
N Expert Testimony 73
R Legal Interrogation 94
Witnesses 85

Legalization (Marihuana)
Use Marihuana Legalization

Legibility 78
PN 41 **SC** 28127
N Handwriting Legibility 73
R Readability 78
↓ Written Language 67

Legibility (Handwriting)
Use Handwriting Legibility

Legislative Processes 73
PN 415 **SC** 28140
B Government Policy Making 73
Legal Processes 73
R Advocacy 85
Government 67
↓ Laws 67
Legal Decisions 91

Leisure Time 73
PN 1310 **SC** 28150
R Daily Activities 94
Hobbies 73
Holidays 88
↓ Recreation 67
Relaxation 73

Leiter Adult Intelligence Scale
SN Term discontinued in 1997. Use LEITER ADULT INTELLIGENCE SCALE to access references from 73–96.
Use Intelligence Measures

Lemniscal System 85
PN 11 **SC** 28165
SN Long ascending sensory neural pathways projecting to the diencephalon. This system includes the medial lemniscus, lateral lemniscus, spinothalamic tracts, and secondary trigeminal projections.
B Afferent Pathways 82
N Spinothalamic Tracts 73
R Reticular Formation 67

Lemurs 73
PN 210 **SC** 28170
UF Bush Babies
B Mammals 73

Length of Stay
Use Treatment Duration

Lens (Eye) 73
PN 50 **SC** 28180
B Eye (Anatomy) 67
R ↓ Light Refraction 82
Ocular Accommodation 82

Lesbian Parents
Use Homosexual Parents

Lesbianism 73
PN 1093 **SC** 28190
B Homosexuality 67
R Bisexuality 73
Heterosexuality 73
Homosexual Parents 94
Male Homosexuality 73

Lesions 67
PN 2079 **SC** 28200
SN Not defined prior to 1982. From 1982, limited to experimentally induced lesions and used primarily for animal populations.
UF Ablation
Sectioning (Lesion)
N ↓ Brain Lesions 67
Neural Lesions 73
R ↓ Surgery 71

Lesson Plans 73
PN 103 **SC** 28220
B Teaching Methods 67

Letters (Alphabet) 73
PN 1441 **SC** 28230
B Alphabets 73
N Consonants 73
Vowels 73

Leucine 73
PN 45 **SC** 28240
B Amino Acids 73

Leucocytes 73
PN 222 **SC** 28250
UF Leukocytes
White Blood Cells
B Blood Cells 73
N Lymphocytes 73

Leukemias 73
PN 255 **SC** 28260
B Blood and Lymphatic Disorders 73
Neoplasms 67

Leukocytes
Use Leucocytes

Leukotomy
Use Psychosurgery

Levodopa 73
PN 558 **SC** 28290
UF L Dopa
B Antitremor Drugs 73
Cholinergic Blocking Drugs 73
R DOPA 73
Dopamine 73

Lexical Access 88
PN 516 **SC** 29293
N Lexical Decision 88
R Cognitive Discrimination 73
Human Information Storage 73
Semantic Memory 88
↓ Verbal Memory 94
Word Meaning 73
Words (Phonetic Units) 67

Lexical Decision [88]
PN 705 **SC** 29296
B Lexical Access [88]
R Cognitive Discrimination [73]
Human Information Storage [73]
Semantic Memory [88]
↓ Verbal Memory [94]
Word Meaning [73]
Words (Phonetic Units) [67]

Liberalism [73]
PN 120 **SC** 28298
B Personality Traits [67]
R Political Liberalism [73]

Liberalism (Political)
Use Political Liberalism

Liberia [91]
PN 1 **SC** 28305
B Africa [67]

Libido [73]
PN 131 **SC** 28310
B Psychoanalytic Personality Factors [73]
R Inhibited Sexual Desire [97]
Sex Drive [73]

Librarians [88]
PN 31 **SC** 28314
B Information Specialists [88]
R ↓ Professional Personnel [78]

Libraries [82]
PN 73 **SC** 28317
N School Libraries [73]
R ↓ Community Facilities [73]
Information [67]
Information Services [88]

Libraries (School)
Use School Libraries

Librium
Use Chlordiazepoxide

Libya [88]
PN 10 **SC** 28335
B Africa [67]
R Middle East [78]

Licensing (Professional)
Use Professional Licensing

Licensure Examinations
Use Professional Examinations

Licking [88]
PN 100 **SC** 28345
SN Used for human or animal populations.
UF Animal Licking Behavior
B Animal Ethology [67]
Motor Processes [67]
R Animal Drinking Behavior [73]
Animal Grooming Behavior [78]
Animal Maternal Behavior [73]

Lidocaine [73]
PN 119 **SC** 28350
UF Xylocaine
B Local Anesthetics [73]

Liechtenstein [91]
PN 1 **SC** 28353
B Europe [73]

Life Change
Use Life Experiences

Life Expectancy [82]
PN 213 **SC** 28352
SN Anticipated number of years of life for an individual, based on statistical probability. Use AGED and PHYSIOLOGICAL AGING together to access references from 73–81. Used for both human and animal populations.
UF Life Span
Longevity
R ↓ Aging [91]
↓ Human Development [67]
Physiological Aging [67]

Life Experiences [73]
PN 4329 **SC** 28355
SN Specific events which are commonly considered noteworthy or memorable (e.g., college graduation, wedding) or are considered unusual or otherwise significant (e.g., life change due to illness). Compare EXPERIENCES (EVENTS).
UF Experiences (Life)
Life Change
B Experiences (Events) [73]
R Age Regression (Hypnotic) [88]
Anniversary Events [94]
Autobiographical Memory [94]
Biographical Data [78]
Homesickness [94]
Life Review [91]
Life Satisfaction [85]

Life Insurance [73]
PN 17 **SC** 28360
B Insurance [73]

Life Review [91]
PN 84 **SC** 28361
SN Reflection on and return to past life experiences in order to think about and reintegrate them into present life circumstances. Usually performed in a treatment or intervention setting. Not limited to elderly populations. Consider using REMINISCENCE to access references from 85-90.
R Anniversary Events [94]
Autobiographical Memory [94]
Early Experience [67]
Early Memories [85]
Gerontology [67]
Life Experiences [73]
Narratives [97]
Reminiscence [85]
↓ Treatment [67]

Life Satisfaction [85]
PN 1349 **SC** 28362
B Satisfaction [73]
R Life Experiences [73]
Lifestyle Changes [97]
↓ Quality of Life [85]
Role Satisfaction [94]
Well Being [94]

Life Span
Use Life Expectancy

Life Sustaining Treatment [97]
PN 0 **SC** 28368
B Treatment [67]
R Advance Directives [94]
Assisted Suicide [97]
↓ Client Rights [88]
Medical Treatment (General) [73]
Palliative Care [91]
Terminally Ill Patients [73]

Life Sustaining Treatment — (cont'd)
R Treatment Refusal [94]
Treatment Withholding [88]

Lifesaving
Use Artificial Respiration

Lifestyle [78]
PN 1642 **SC** 28375
SN Typical way of life or manner of living characteristic of an individual or group .
N Lifestyle Changes [97]
R Daily Activities [94]
Health Behavior [82]
Holistic Health [85]
↓ Personality [67]
↓ Personality Processes [67]
↓ Quality of Life [85]

Lifestyle Changes [97]
PN 0 **SC** 28380
B Lifestyle [78]
R Behavior Change [73]
Health Attitudes [85]
Health Behavior [82]
Health Promotion [91]
Life Satisfaction [85]
↓ Quality of Life [85]
Well Being [94]

Light
Use Illumination

Light Adaptation [82]
PN 163 **SC** 28393
SN Change in the general level of sensitivity of the photoreceptors as a result of exposure to light.
UF Adaptation (Light)
B Sensory Adaptation [67]
R Dark Adaptation [73]
↓ Illumination [67]
↓ Visual Thresholds [73]

Light Refraction [82]
PN 25 **SC** 28395
SN Deflection of light from a straight path when passing obliquely through the interface of two media that have different densities.
N ↓ Refraction Errors [73]
R ↓ Illumination [67]
Lens (Eye) [73]

Likability [88]
PN 77 **SC** 28387
B Personality Traits [67]
R Agreeableness [97]
Interpersonal Attraction [67]
Peer Pressure [94]
Social Approval [67]
↓ Social Perception [67]

Likert Scales [94]
PN 8 **SC** 28388
B Rating Scales [67]
R Attitude Measurement [73]
↓ Attitude Measures [67]
Self Report [82]
Semantic Differential [67]
↓ Surveys [67]

Liking
Use Affection

Limbic System [73]
PN 820 **SC** 28410
B Cerebral Cortex [67]
Neural Pathways [82]

Limbic System — (cont'd)
N Amygdaloid Body 73
Fornix 82
Gyrus Cinguli 73
Hippocampus 67
Medial Forebrain Bundle 82
Olfactory Bulb 73
Septal Nuclei 82
R Nucleus Accumbens 82
Raphe Nuclei 82

Limen
Use Thresholds

Limited English Proficiency
Use Language Proficiency

Linear Perspective 82
PN 87 **SC** 28427
SN Apparent convergence of parallel contours that are projected into the plane of sight of the observer.
UF Visual Perspective
B Vision 67
R ↓ Depth Perception 67
↓ Distance Perception 73
↓ Size Discrimination 67
↓ Visual Stimulation 73

Linear Regression 73
PN 247 **SC** 28430
B Statistical Correlation 67
Statistical Regression 85
R Multiple Regression 82

Linguistics 73
PN 1526 **SC** 28450
N Ethnolinguistics 73
Etymology 73
↓ Grammar 67
Metalinguistics 94
Neurolinguistics 91
Orthography 73
Psycholinguistics 67
Sociolinguistics 85
R Discourse Analysis 97
↓ Language 67
Pragmatics 85
↓ Prosody 91
↓ Semiotics 85
↓ Verbal Communication 67

Linkage Analysis
Use Genetic Linkage

Lions
Use Felids

Lipid Metabolism 73
PN 97 **SC** 28460
UF Fat Metabolism
B Metabolism 67
R ↓ Lipids 73

Lipid Metabolism Disorders 73
PN 27 **SC** 28470
B Metabolism Disorders 73
N Amaurotic Familial Idiocy 73

Lipids 73
PN 419 **SC** 28480
N ↓ Fatty Acids 73
R Lipid Metabolism 73
↓ Steroids 73

Lipoproteins 73
PN 56 **SC** 28490
R ↓ Proteins 73

Lipreading 73
PN 234 **SC** 28500
UF Speechreading
R ↓ Deaf 67
Speech Perception 67
↓ Visual Perception 67

Lips (Face) 73
PN 90 **SC** 28510
R Mouth (Anatomy) 67

Liquor 73
PN 25 **SC** 28520
B Alcoholic Beverages 73

Listening
Use Auditory Perception

Listening (Interpersonal) 97
PN 0 **SC** 28535
B Interpersonal Communication 73
R ↓ Attention 67
↓ Auditory Perception 67
Conversation 73
Listening Comprehension 73
Social Skills 78

Listening Comprehension 73
PN 1191 **SC** 28540
B Verbal Comprehension 85
R Listening (Interpersonal) 97

Literacy 73
PN 911 **SC** 28550
UF Illiteracy
N Computer Literacy 91
R ↓ Language 67
↓ Language Arts Education 73
Literacy Programs 97
Reading Development 97
Reading Education 73
↓ Reading Skills 73
Writing Skills 85

Literacy Programs 97
PN 0 **SC** 28555
B Educational Programs 73
R ↓ Adult Education 73
↓ Language Arts Education 73
↓ Literacy 73
Reading Education 73
↓ Reading Skills 73
↓ Social Services 82
Writing Skills 85

Literature 67
PN 3754 **SC** 28560
UF Fiction
B Arts 73
N Poetry 73
↓ Prose 73
R Creative Writing 94
Drama 73
Folklore 91
Metaphor 82
Myths 67
Narratives 97
Postmodernism 97
↓ Religious Literature 73
Writers 91

Literature Review 67
PN 17177 **SC** 28580

Literature Review — (cont'd)
SN Mandatory term applied to surveys of previously published material. Limited to documents that are entirely or primarily literature reviews. Also used as a document type identifier.
UF Review (of Literature)
R Bibliography 67
Meta Analysis 85

Lithium 73
PN 2408 **SC** 28590
SN Used for documents that do not specify the type of lithium used, e.g., carbonate, chloride or bromide. Use a more specific term if possible.
B Metallic Elements 73
N Lithium Carbonate 73
R ↓ Antidepressant Drugs 71
↓ Tricyclic Antidepressant Drugs 97

Lithium Bromide
SN Term discontinued in 1997. Use LITHIUM BROMIDE to access references from 73-96.
Use Bromides

Lithium Carbonate 73
PN 663 **SC** 28610
B Antidepressant Drugs 71
Lithium 73

Litter Size 85
PN 74 **SC** 28615
SN Used for animal populations only.
B Size 73
R ↓ Animal Breeding 73

Liver 73
PN 234 **SC** 28620
B Digestive System 67

Liver Disorders 73
PN 136 **SC** 28630
UF Hepatic Disorders
B Digestive System Disorders 73
N Cirrhosis (Liver) 73
↓ Hepatitis 73
Jaundice 73
R ↓ Infectious Disorders 73
↓ Neoplasms 67
↓ Toxic Disorders 73

Living Alone 94
PN 10 **SC** 28633
SN Use LIVING ARRANGEMENTS to access references from 91-93.
B Living Arrangements 91
R Cohabitation 73
↓ Family Structure 73
Home Environment 73
↓ Marital Status 73
Single Persons 73

Living Arrangements 91
PN 308 **SC** 28635
UF Household Structure
N Cohabitation 73
Living Alone 94
R Child Custody 82
Empty Nest 91
↓ Family 67
↓ Family Structure 73
Home Environment 73
↓ Housing 73
↓ Marital Status 73
Retirement Communities 97
Roommates 73
Shelters 91

Living Wills
Use Advance Directives

Lizards 73
PN 316 **SC** 28640
B Reptiles 67

Lobotomy
Use Psychosurgery

Local Anesthetics 73
PN 55 **SC** 28660
B Anesthetic Drugs 73
N Cocaine 73
Lidocaine 73
Quinine 73
R Ephedrine 73
Methoxamine 73

Localization (Perceptual)
Use Perceptual Localization

Localization (Sound)
Use Auditory Localization

Locus Ceruleus 82
PN 282 **SC** 28687
SN Pigmented nucleus in the brain stem that synthesizes norepinephrine.
B Brain Stem 73
R Reticular Formation 67

Locus of Control
Use Internal External Locus of Control

Logic (Philosophy) 73
PN 188 **SC** 28700
B Philosophies 67

Logical Thinking 67
PN 1128 **SC** 28710
UF Ratiocination
B Thinking 67
R Analogy 91
↓ Inductive Deductive Reasoning 73

Logistic Models
Use Item Response Theory

Logotherapy 73
PN 230 **SC** 28720
SN Existential analysis based on spiritual values and emphasizing search for the meaning of human existence.
B Psychotherapy 67
R Existential Therapy 73

Loneliness 73
PN 912 **SC** 28730
B Emotional States 73
R Abandonment 97
Homesickness 94

Long Term Care 94
PN 82 **SC** 28735
SN Delivery of health or mental health services over a prolonged or extended period. Care can be in an institutional setting or in the community, e.g., at home, and delivered by health care professionals, family, or friends.
B Health Care Services 78
Treatment Duration 88
R Adult Day Care 97
↓ Case Management 91
Home Care 85
↓ Hospitalization 67
↓ Mental Health Services 78

Long Term Care — (cont'd)
R Nursing Homes 73
Palliative Care 91

Long Term Memory 73
PN 1234 **SC** 28740
SN Retention of events or learned material for relatively long periods, presumed to be based on permanent encoding and storage of information transferred from short term memory. Consider also RETENTION.
B Memory 67

Long Term Potentiation
Use Postactivation Potentials

Longevity
Use Life Expectancy

Longitudinal Studies 73
PN 9423 **SC** 28760
SN Mandatory term applied to observations or measurements of the same individual or group over an extended period.
UF Studies (Longitudinal)
B Experimental Design 67
N Prospective Studies 97
R Followup Studies 73
Retrospective Studies 97

Loosening of Associations
Use Fragmentation (Schizophrenia)

Lorazepam 88
PN 211 **SC** 28765
B Benzodiazepines 78
Minor Tranquilizers 73

Lordosis (Animal)
Use Animal Sexual Receptivity

Lorge Thorndike Intelligence Test 73
PN 14 **SC** 28770
B Intelligence Measures 67

Loudness 67
PN 344 **SC** 28780
UF Sound Pressure Level
B Auditory Stimulation 67
N Noise Levels (Work Areas) 73

Loudness Discrimination 73
PN 143 **SC** 28790
B Loudness Perception 73

Loudness Perception 73
PN 249 **SC** 28800
B Auditory Perception 67
N Loudness Discrimination 73

Love 73
PN 928 **SC** 28830
B Emotional States 73
R Affection 73
Attachment Behavior 85
Erotomania 97
Intimacy 73
Romance 97

Low Birth Weight
Use Birth Weight

Lowenfeld Mosaic Test 73
PN 9 **SC** 28840
B Intelligence Measures 67

Lower Class 73
PN 755 **SC** 28850
B Social Class 67
Socioeconomic Status 67

Lower Class Attitudes 73
PN 48 **SC** 28860
SN Attitudes of, not toward, the lower class.
B Socioeconomic Class Attitudes 73

Lower Income Level 73
PN 1037 **SC** 28870
B Income Level 73
R Poverty 73

Loxapine 82
PN 35 **SC** 28875
SN Organic heterocyclic compound used as a tranquilizing agent.
UF Oxilapine
B Minor Tranquilizers 73

Loyalty 73
PN 122 **SC** 28880
B Personality Traits 67

LSD (Drug)
Use Lysergic Acid Diethylamide

Lucid Dreaming 94
PN 14 **SC** 28893
B Dreaming 67
R Dream Recall 73
REM Dreams 73
REM Sleep 73
↓ Sleep 67

Luck
Use Chance (Fortune)

Lumbar Spinal Cord 73
PN 78 **SC** 28900
B Spinal Cord 73

Lumbrosacral Plexus
Use Spinal Nerves

Luminance 82
PN 817 **SC** 28930
SN Product of multiplying the physical intensity of a light wave by the spectral sensitivity of the typical observer's visual system for that specific wavelength. Compare ILLUMINATION.
R ↓ Brightness Perception 73
↓ Chromaticity 97
Color Saturation 97
↓ Illumination 67
Stimulus Intensity 67
↓ Visual Thresholds 73

Luminance Threshold
Use Brightness Perception AND Visual Thresholds

Lunar Synodic Cycle 73
PN 95 **SC** 28950
SN Successive phases of the moon reflecting its motion around the earth.
R ↓ Biological Rhythms 67
↓ Environmental Effects 73

Lung 73
PN 54 **SC** 28960
B Respiratory System 73

Lung Disorders 73
PN 201 **SC** 28970

Lung Disorders — (cont'd)
UF Pulmonary Disorders
B Respiratory Tract Disorders [73]
N Cystic Fibrosis [85]
Pneumonia [73]
Pulmonary Emphysema [73]
Pulmonary Tuberculosis [73]
R ↓ Dyspnea [73]

Lupus [73]
PN 141 SC 28980
B Skin Disorders [73]
R ↓ Tuberculosis [73]

Luria Nebraska Neuropsych Battery [91]
PN 49 SC 28982
SN Use NEUROPSYCHOLOGICAL ASSESSMENT to access references from 82-90.
B Neuropsychological Assessment [82]

Luteinizing Hormone [78]
PN 378 SC 28985
B Gonadotropic Hormones [73]
R ↓ Pituitary Hormones [73]
↓ Sex Hormones [73]

Lutherans
Use Protestants

Lying
Use Deception

Lymphatic Disorders
Use Blood and Lymphatic Disorders

Lymphocytes [73]
PN 405 SC 29060
B Leucocytes [73]
R Interleukins [94]

Lysergic Acid Diethylamide [67]
PN 748 SC 29070
UF LSD (Drug)
B Acids [73]
Amine Oxidase Inhibitors [73]
Hallucinogenic Drugs [67]
Psychedelic Drugs [73]
Psychotomimetic Drugs [73]
Serotonin Antagonists [73]
R ↓ Ergot Derivatives [73]

Machiavellianism [73]
PN 313 SC 29087
SN Extent to which an individual feels that any means, however unscrupulous, can justifiably be used to achieve power.
B Personality Traits [67]

Madagascar [91]
PN 4 SC 29088
R ↓ Africa [67]

Magazines [73]
PN 265 SC 29090
B Printed Communications Media [73]

Magical Thinking [73]
PN 82 SC 29100
SN Belief that one's utterances, thoughts, or behavior can have a controlling influence on specific events or prevent their occurrence by means that operate beyond the normal laws of cause and effect.
B Thinking [67]
Thought Disturbances [73]
R Fantasies (Thought Disturbances) [67]
↓ Fantasy [97]

Magical Thinking — (cont'd)
R Imagination [67]
Omnipotence [94]

Magnesium [73]
PN 129 SC 29110
B Metallic Elements [73]
N Magnesium Ions [73]

Magnesium Ions [73]
PN 11 SC 29120
B Electrolytes [73]
Magnesium [73]

Magnet Schools
Use Nontraditional Education

Magnetic Resonance Imaging [94]
PN 133 SC 29133
UF MRI
B Tomography [88]
R Computer Assisted Diagnosis [73]
Magnetoencephalography [85]

Magnetism [85]
PN 227 SC 29135
UF Geomagnetism
R Magnetoencephalography [85]
Physics [73]

Magnetoencephalography [85]
PN 71 SC 29136
R ↓ Electroencephalography [67]
Magnetic Resonance Imaging [94]
Magnetism [85]

Magnitude Estimation [91]
PN 76 SC 29138
SN Unidimensional scaling method in statistics and psychophysics for quantitative judgment and ratio estimation.
B Psychophysical Measurement [67]
Statistical Estimation [85]
R Scaling (Testing) [67]

Magnitude of Effect (Statistical)
Use Effect Size (Statistical)

Maids
Use Domestic Service Personnel

Mail Surveys [94]
PN 31 SC 29141
B Surveys [67]
R ↓ Consumer Research [73]
Consumer Surveys [73]
↓ Methodology [67]
↓ Questionnaires [67]
Telephone Surveys [94]

Mainstreaming [91]
PN 63 SC 29144
SN Integration or transition into society of individuals who have been considered for institutionalization or other type of isolation, but are now considered able to learn from education or community involvement.
N Mainstreaming (Educational) [78]
R Deinstitutionalization [82]
Educational Placement [78]
Habilitation [91]
Independent Living Programs [91]
↓ Rehabilitation [67]
School to Work Transition [94]
↓ Social Integration [82]
Special Education [67]
Special Needs [94]

Mainstreaming (Educational) [78]
PN 2131 SC 29145
SN Integration of students with special education needs into classes or schools with regular students.
B Mainstreaming [91]
R ↓ Education [67]
Educational Placement [78]
School Integration [82]
Special Education [67]

Maintenance Therapy [97]
PN 0 SC 29142
SN Treatment or therapy that is designed to maintain patients in a stable condition and to promote either gradual healing or to prevent the relapse of a disorder or condition. Used primarily, but not exclusively, in drug therapy settings.
R Aftercare [73]
↓ Drug Therapy [67]
Methadone Maintenance [78]
↓ Outpatient Treatment [67]
Relapse Prevention [94]
↓ Treatment Duration [88]

Major Depression [88]
PN 14799 SC 29143
SN Affective disorder marked by dysphoric mood, inactivity, lack of interest, insomnia, feelings of worthlessness, diminished ability to think, and thoughts of suicide. Consider DEPRESSION (EMOTION) to access references prior to 1988. Use DEPRESSION (EMOTION) for nonclinical depression.
UF Agitated Depression
Dysphoria
Melancholia
Psychotic Depressive Reaction
Unipolar Depression
B Affective Disturbances [67]
N Anaclitic Depression [73]
Dysthymic Disorder [88]
Endogenous Depression [78]
Involutional Depression [73]
Neurotic Depressive Reaction [73]
Postpartum Depression [73]
Reactive Depression [73]
Recurrent Depression [94]
Treatment Resistant Depression [94]
R Depression (Emotion) [67]
↓ Manic Depression [73]
Pseudodementia [85]
Seasonal Affective Disorder [91]

Major Tranquilizers
Use Neuroleptic Drugs

Maladjustment (Emotional)
Use Emotional Adjustment

Maladjustment (Social)
Use Social Adjustment

Malaria [73]
PN 29 SC 29180
B Blood and Lymphatic Disorders [73]
Parasitic Disorders [73]
R ↓ Nervous System Disorders [67]

Malawi [91]
PN 14 SC 29183
B Africa [67]

Malaysia [82]
PN 140 SC 29184
B Southeast Asia [73]

Male Animals 73
PN 2893 **SC** 29190
B Animals 67

Male Castration 73
PN 637 **SC** 29200
SN Used for both human and animal populations.
B Castration 67

Male Criminals 73
PN 693 **SC** 29210
B Criminals 67
Human Males 73

Male Delinquents 73
PN 909 **SC** 29220
B Human Males 73
Juvenile Delinquents 73
R Female Delinquents 73

Male Female Relations 88
PN 668 **SC** 29225
SN Relationships or interactions between the sexes. Limited to human populations.
UF Heterosexual Interaction
B Interpersonal Interaction 67
R Heterosexuality 73
↓ Human Courtship 73
↓ Marital Relations 67
↓ Relationship Termination 97
Social Dating 73
Social Skills 78

Male Genital Disorders 73
PN 29 **SC** 29230
B Genital Disorders 67
N Klinefelters Syndrome 73
Testicular Feminization Syndrome 73
R ↓ Endocrine Sexual Disorders 73
Hermaphroditism 73
↓ Hypogonadism 73
↓ Infertility 73
Sterility 73

Male Genitalia 73
PN 114 **SC** 29240
SN Used for both human and animal populations.
UF Genitalia (Male)
B Urogenital System 73
N Penis 73
Prostate 73
Testes 73

Male Homosexuality 73
PN 2011 **SC** 29250
UF Gay Males
B Homosexuality 67
R Bisexuality 73
Heterosexuality 73
Homosexual Parents 94
Lesbianism 73

Male Orgasm 73
PN 231 **SC** 29260
SN Used for both human and animal populations.
UF Ejaculation
B Orgasm 73
N Nocturnal Emission 73
Premature Ejaculation 73
R Impotence 73
Masturbation 73
↓ Sexual Intercourse (Human) 73

Males (Human)
Use Human Males

Mali 91
PN 4 **SC** 29275
B Africa 67

Malignant Neoplasms
Use Neoplasms

Malingering 73
PN 309 **SC** 29290
SN Feigning or exaggerating illness or symptoms usually in order to escape work, evoke sympathy, or gain compensation.
B Deception 67
R ↓ Factitious Disorders 88
↓ Mental Disorders 67
Munchausen Syndrome 94
↓ Physical Disorders 97
↓ Psychosomatic Disorders 67

Malnutrition
Use Nutritional Deficiencies

Malpractice
Use Professional Liability

Mammals 73
PN 1008 **SC** 29310
B Vertebrates 73
N Bats 73
↓ Canids 97
Cattle 73
Chimpanzees 73
Chinchillas 73
Deer 73
Elephants 73
↓ Felids 97
Goats 73
Horses 73
Lemurs 73
↓ Marsupials 73
↓ Primates (Nonhuman) 73
Rabbits 67
↓ Rodents 73
Seals (Animal) 73
Sheep 73
↓ Whales 85

Mammary Glands 73
PN 13 **SC** 29320
B Glands 67

Mammary Neoplasms
Use Breast Neoplasms

Mammillary Bodies (Hypothalamic)
Use Hypothalamus

Mammography 94
PN 47 **SC** 29345
B Roentgenography 73
R Breast Neoplasms 73
Cancer Screening 97
↓ Health Screening 97
↓ Medical Diagnosis 73
Physical Examination 88
Preventive Medicine 73

Man Machine Systems
SN Term discontinued in 1997. Use MAN MACHINE SYSTEMS to access references from 73–96.
Use Human Machine Systems

Man Machine Systems Design
SN Term discontinued in 1997. Use MAN MACHINE SYSTEMS DESIGN to access references from 73–96.
Use Human Machine Systems Design

Managed Care 94
PN 122 **SC** 29365
SN Competitive prepaid plan of health care delivery to contain costs and provide access to quality health care. Use CASE MANAGEMENT to access references from 91-93.
B Health Care Delivery 78
N Health Maintenance Organizations 82
R ↓ Case Management 91
Cost Containment 91
Fee for Service 94
Health Care Costs 94
↓ Health Care Services 78
↓ Health Insurance 73
Quality of Care 88
↓ Treatment Planning 97

Management 67
PN 1413 **SC** 29420
SN Conceptually broad array term referring to the process of manipulation of human or material resources to accomplish given goals. Use a more specific term if possible.
N Business Management 73
↓ Case Management 91
Disability Management 91
Educational Administration 67
↓ Health Care Administration 97
Household Management 85
↓ Personnel Management 73
Risk Management 97
↓ Self Management 85
Stress Management 85
Time Management 94
R Accountability 88
Business 67
Career Development 85
Entrepreneurship 91
Labor Management Relations 67
↓ Leadership 67
Leadership Qualities 97
Management Decision Making 73
↓ Management Methods 73
↓ Management Personnel 73
Management Planning 73
Management Training 73

Management Decision Making 73
PN 1072 **SC** 29370
B Decision Making 67
R ↓ Group Decision Making 78
↓ Management 67
↓ Management Methods 73
Management Planning 73
Participative Management 88

Management Development
Use Career Development

Management Information Systems
Use Information Systems

Management Methods 73
PN 2311 **SC** 29380
N Participative Management 88
R Business Management 73
↓ Management 67
Management Decision Making 73
Management Planning 73
Supervisor Employee Interaction 97
Teams 88
Work Scheduling 73

Management Personnel [73]
PN 5783 **SC** 29390
UF Administrators
Supervisors
B White Collar Workers [73]
N Middle Level Managers [73]
Top Level Managers [73]
R Commissioned Officers [73]
Industrial Foremen [73]
↓ Management [67]
↓ School Administrators [73]
Supervisor Employee Interaction [97]

Management Planning [73]
PN 263 **SC** 29400
UF Planning (Management)
R ↓ Management [67]
Management Decision Making [73]
↓ Management Methods [73]
Marketing [73]

Management Training [73]
PN 1044 **SC** 29410
B Personnel Training [67]
R Business Education [73]
↓ Management [67]
Wilderness Experience [91]

Manager Employee Interaction
Use Supervisor Employee Interaction

Mandibula
Use Jaw

Mania [67]
PN 1376 **SC** 29450
B Affective Disturbances [67]
Emotional States [73]
N Hypomania [73]
R ↓ Manic Depression [73]

Manic Depression [73]
PN 3258 **SC** 29457
UF Bipolar Affective Disorder
Bipolar Mood Disorder
Manic Depressive Psychosis
B Affective Disturbances [67]
N Cyclothymic Personality [73]
R ↓ Affective Psychosis [73]
↓ Major Depression [88]
↓ Mania [67]

Manic Depressive Psychosis
SN Term discontinued in 1988. Use MANIC DEPRESSIVE PSYCHOSIS to access references from 67-87.
Use Manic Depression

Mann Whitney U Test [73]
PN 16 **SC** 29470
B Nonparametric Statistical Tests [67]

Mannerisms
Use Habits

Manpower
SN Use PERSONNEL to access references from 67–81.
Use Personnel Supply

Mantis [73]
PN 19 **SC** 29500
UF Praying Mantis
B Insects [67]
R Larvae [73]

Manual Communication [78]
PN 116 **SC** 29505
SN Form of communication used by the deaf in which sign language and finger spelling are substituted for speech. Also, an unsystematic or informal method of communication with gestures.
B Augmentative Communication [94]
Nonverbal Communication [71]
Verbal Communication [67]
N Fingerspelling [73]
Sign Language [73]

Manufacturing
Use Business

Maprotiline [82]
PN 174 **SC** 29527
B Tricyclic Antidepressant Drugs [97]

Marathon Group Therapy [73]
PN 133 **SC** 29540
SN Encounter group that meets for extended sessions and that aims to develop the ability to express oneself emotionally and to initiate intimate interpersonal interactions.
B Encounter Group Therapy [73]
R Human Relations Training [78]
Sensitivity Training [73]

Marihuana [71]
PN 571 **SC** 29550
UF Marijuana
B Cannabis [73]
R Hashish [73]
↓ Marihuana Laws [73]
Marihuana Usage [73]
Tetrahydrocannabinol [73]

Marihuana Laws [73]
PN 21 **SC** 29560
B Drug Laws [73]
N Marihuana Legalization [73]
R Government [67]
Marihuana [71]
Marihuana Usage [73]

Marihuana Legalization [73]
PN 32 **SC** 29570
UF Legalization (Marihuana)
B Drug Legalization [97]
Marihuana Laws [73]
R ↓ Drug Usage Attitudes [73]
Government [67]

Marihuana Usage [73]
PN 931 **SC** 29580
B Drug Usage [71]
R Marihuana [71]
↓ Marihuana Laws [73]

Marijuana
Use Marihuana

Marine Personnel [73]
PN 168 **SC** 29600
B Military Personnel [67]

Marital Adjustment
Use Marital Relations

Marital Conflict [73]
PN 930 **SC** 29620
B Marital Relations [67]
R Dysfunctional Family [91]
↓ Family Violence [82]
↓ Relationship Termination [97]

Marital Fidelity
Use Monogamy

Marital Relations [67]
PN 5474 **SC** 29640
UF Marital Adjustment
B Family Relations [67]
N Marital Conflict [73]
Marital Satisfaction [88]
R Codependency [91]
Extramarital Intercourse [73]
Male Female Relations [88]
Postpartum Depression [73]
↓ Relationship Termination [97]
Romance [97]

Marital Satisfaction [88]
PN 763 **SC** 29645
B Marital Relations [67]
Satisfaction [73]
R ↓ Relationship Termination [97]
Role Satisfaction [94]

Marital Separation [73]
PN 629 **SC** 29650
UF Separation (Marital)
B Relationship Termination [97]
N Divorce [73]
R Child Support [88]
Divorced Persons [73]
↓ Family [67]
↓ Marital Status [73]
↓ Parental Absence [73]

Marital Status [73]
PN 1457 **SC** 29660
N Never Married [94]
R Divorced Persons [73]
↓ Family [67]
↓ Family Background [73]
Living Alone [94]
↓ Living Arrangements [91]
↓ Marital Separation [73]
↓ Marriage [67]
Remarriage [85]
↓ Single Parents [78]
Single Persons [73]
Widowers [73]
Widows [73]

Marital Therapy
Use Marriage Counseling

Marketing [73]
PN 1455 **SC** 29670
R ↓ Advertising [67]
Brand Names [78]
Brand Preferences [94]
↓ Consumer Research [73]
Management Planning [73]
Product Design [97]
↓ Quality of Services [97]
Retailing [91]

Markov Chains [73]
PN 165 **SC** 29680
SN Statistical model representing conditional and sequential probabilities to determine the future values of a random variable.
B Simulation [67]
Stochastic Modeling [73]

Marlowe Crowne Soc Desirabil Scale [73]
PN 44 **SC** 29690
B Nonprojective Personality Measures [73]

Marriage [67]
PN 1287 **SC** 29700

Marriage — (cont'd)
N ↓ Endogamous Marriage [73]
↓ Exogamous Marriage [73]
Monogamy [97]
Polygamy [73]
Remarriage [85]
R ↓ Family [67]
↓ Marital Status [73]
Marriage Rites [73]
Romance [97]

Marriage and Family Education
Use Family Life Education

Marriage Attitudes [73]
PN 555 SC 29710
SN General attitudes toward marriage and divorce, or attitudes toward a specific marital relationship.
B Attitudes [67]
R ↓ Family Relations [67]

Marriage Counseling [73]
PN 2120 SC 29720
UF Marital Therapy
Marriage Therapy
B Counseling [67]
N Conjoint Therapy [73]
R Couples Therapy [94]
↓ Psychotherapeutic Counseling [73]
↓ Psychotherapy [67]
Sex Therapy [78]

Marriage Rites [73]
PN 34 SC 29730
B Rites of Passage [73]
R ↓ Marriage [67]

Marriage Therapy
Use Marriage Counseling

Married Couples
Use Spouses

Marsupials [73]
PN 30 SC 29760
B Mammals [73]
N Kangaroos [73]
Opossums [73]

Martial Arts [85]
PN 75 SC 29765
UF Karate
B Recreation [67]
Sports [67]
R Judo [73]
Meditation [73]
Self Defense [85]

Marxism
Use Communism

Masculinity [67]
PN 1507 SC 29780
B Personality Traits [67]
R Androgyny [82]
Femininity [67]
Gender Identity [85]
Sex Roles [67]

Masking [67]
PN 546 SC 29790
SN Changes in perceptual sensitivity to a stimulus due to the presence of a second stimulus in close temporal proximity.
UF Backward Masking
Forward Masking

Masking — (cont'd)
N Auditory Masking [73]
Visual Masking [73]
R ↓ Perceptual Stimulation [73]

Maslow (Abraham Harold) [91]
PN 24 SC 29795
SN Identifies biographical or autobiographical studies and discussions of Maslow's works.
R ↓ Human Potential Movement [82]
↓ Humanistic Psychology [85]
↓ Psychologists [67]
Self Actualization [73]

Masochism [73]
PN 188 SC 29800
SN Pleasure derived from being physically or psychologically abused.
B Sadomasochism [73]
N Sexual Masochism [73]
R Masochistic Personality [73]
↓ Sadism [73]
↓ Self Destructive Behavior [85]

Masochistic Personality [73]
PN 46 SC 29810
SN Personality marked by self-destructiveness or self-defeating behavior, a conscious or unconscious need to suffer, and seeking out opportunities for suffering or self-injury.
B Sadomasochistic Personality [73]
R ↓ Masochism [73]
↓ Self Destructive Behavior [85]
Sexual Masochism [73]

Mass Hysteria [73]
PN 47 SC 29820
B Hysteria [67]
R ↓ Collective Behavior [67]
Contagion [88]

Mass Media [67]
PN 1120 SC 29830
B Communications Media [73]
N ↓ Motion Pictures [73]
↓ News Media [97]
↓ Printed Communications Media [73]
Radio [73]
↓ Television [67]
R ↓ Advertising [67]

Massed Practice [73]
PN 147 SC 29840
SN Practice schedule with trials that are closely spaced and continuous over a long period. Compare DISTRIBUTED PRACTICE.
B Learning Schedules [67]
Practice [67]

Mastectomy [73]
PN 197 SC 29850
B Amputation [73]
R Breast Neoplasms [73]

Mastery Learning [85]
PN 158 SC 29855
SN Educational approach involving specification of educational objectives and success criteria and individual pacing in attaining them.
B Learning [67]
R Educational Objectives [78]
School Learning [67]
Sequential Learning [73]
↓ Teaching Methods [67]

Mastery Tests
Use Criterion Referenced Tests

Masticatory Muscles [73]
PN 31 SC 29860
B Muscles [67]

Masturbation [73]
PN 260 SC 29870
B Psychosexual Behavior [67]
R Autoeroticism [97]
Female Orgasm [73]
↓ Male Orgasm [73]

Matching Test
Use Matching to Sample

Matching to Sample [94]
PN 111 SC 29873
UF Matching Test
B Discrimination Learning [82]
R ↓ Memory [67]
↓ Recognition (Learning) [67]

Mate Selection
Use Animal Mate Selection OR Human Mate Selection

Mate Swapping
Use Extramarital Intercourse

Materialism [73]
PN 127 SC 29890
B Philosophies [67]

Maternal Behavior (Animal)
Use Animal Maternal Behavior

Maternal Behavior (Human)
Use Mother Child Relations

Maternal Investment
Use Parental Investment

Mates (Humans)
Use Spouses

Mathematical Ability [73]
PN 1312 SC 29930
UF Numerical Ability
B Cognitive Ability [73]
Nonverbal Ability [88]
R ↓ Mathematics (Concepts) [67]
Mathematics Anxiety [85]

Mathematical Modeling [73]
PN 3092 SC 29940
SN Use of mathematical formulas or equations to analyze or systematize data for description in quantitative terms.
B Simulation [67]
N Structural Equation Modeling [94]
R Chaos Theory [97]
Fuzzy Set Theory [91]
Goodness of Fit [88]
Heuristic Modeling [73]
↓ Stochastic Modeling [73]

Mathematical Psychology [73]
PN 54 SC 29950
SN Discipline that attempts to systematize the data of psychology by means of mathematical and statistical models and applications.
B Psychology [67]

Mathematicians [73]
PN 22 SC 29960
B Professional Personnel [78]
R Physicists [73]
Scientists [67]

Mathematics [82]
PN 592 SC 29965
SN Science of numbers and the operations performed on them. Compare MATHEMATICS (CONCEPTS).
UF Algebra
Arithmetic
Calculus
Geometry
B Sciences [67]
N Statistics [82]
R Mathematics Anxiety [85]

Mathematics (Concepts) [67]
PN 1990 SC 29970
SN Specific principles that are cognitively internalized or are to be learned concerning numbers, their relations, and mathematical operations performed on them. Compare MATHEMATICS.
N Algorithms [73]
Number Systems [73]
Numbers (Numerals) [67]
R Concepts [67]
Mathematical Ability [73]
Mathematics Achievement [73]
Mathematics Education [73]
↓ Statistical Analysis [67]

Mathematics Achievement [73]
PN 3106 SC 29980
B Academic Achievement [67]
R ↓ Mathematics (Concepts) [67]
Mathematics Anxiety [85]
Mathematics Education [73]
Science Achievement [97]

Mathematics Anxiety [85]
PN 182 SC 29985
SN Fear or tension associated with the study or performance of arithmetic and mathematical tasks.
B Anxiety [67]
R ↓ Anxiety Disorders [97]
Mathematical Ability [73]
↓ Mathematics [82]
Mathematics Achievement [73]

Mathematics Education [73]
PN 2554 SC 29990
B Curriculum [67]
R ↓ Mathematics (Concepts) [67]
Mathematics Achievement [73]
Science Achievement [97]

Mating Behavior (Animal)
Use Animal Mating Behavior

Matriarchy [73]
PN 18 SC 30010
B Family Structure [73]
R Father Absence [73]
Patriarchy [73]
↓ Sex Role Attitudes [78]
Sex Roles [67]

Matriculation
Use School Enrollment

Maturation
Use Human Development

Maturity (Emotional)
Use Emotional Maturity

Maturity (Physical)
Use Physical Maturity

Maturity (Vocational)
Use Vocational Maturity

Maudsley Personality Inventory [73]
PN 14 SC 30060
B Nonprojective Personality Measures [73]

Mauritius [91]
PN 1 SC 30065
R ↓ Africa [67]

Maxilla
Use Jaw

Maximum Likelihood [85]
PN 197 SC 30075
SN Method of estimating population parameters from sample data by selecting parameter values that maximize the likelihood of the occurrence of the observed sample results.
B Statistical Estimation [85]
R Goodness of Fit [88]

Maximum Security Facilities [85]
PN 66 SC 30077
R ↓ Correctional Institutions [73]
↓ Hospitals [67]

Maze Learning [67]
PN 1859 SC 30080
SN Learning the correct route through a maze to obtain reinforcement. Used for human or animal populations.
B Learning [67]
R Spatial Learning [94]

Maze Pathways [73]
PN 104 SC 30090
SN Used when specifically referring to pathway choice, discrimination, or spatial organization of pathway. Used for human or animal populations. When comparing types of mazes, use MAZES.
UF Runways (Maze)
B Mazes [67]

Mazes [67]
PN 158 SC 30110
SN System of pathways consisting of a number of blind alleys and one or more correct paths leading to a goal/reinforcement. Used to study learning and motivation in humans and animals.
UF Labyrinth (Apparatus)
B Apparatus [67]
N Maze Pathways [73]
T Mazes [73]

MCPP
Use Piperazines

MDMA
Use Methylenedioxymethamphetamine

Mealtimes
Use Feeding Practices

Mean [73]
PN 188 SC 30160
B Central Tendency Measures [73]
R Standard Scores [85]

Meaning [67]
PN 1726 SC 30170
SN Generally refers to the significance, sense, connotation, or denotation conveyed by any form of information.
N Nonverbal Meaning [73]
↓ Verbal Meaning [73]

Meaning — (cont'd)
R ↓ Comprehension [67]
Meaningfulness [67]

Meaningfulness [67]
PN 1077 SC 30180
R ↓ Comprehension [67]
↓ Meaning [67]

Measles [73]
PN 8 SC 30190
B Viral Disorders [73]
R Rubella [73]

Measurement [67]
PN 12275 SC 30200
SN Conceptually broad array term referring to the process and tools used in psychological assessment of human subjects. Use specific test names or procedures if possible. For other types of measurement that do not involve psychological tests, consider METHODOLOGY, EVALUATION, or other appropriate terms.
UF Assessment
Tests
N ↓ Achievement Measures [67]
↓ Aptitude Measures [67]
Attitude Measurement [73]
↓ Attitude Measures [67]
Body Sway Testing [73]
Comprehension Tests [73]
Creativity Measurement [73]
Criterion Referenced Tests [82]
Digit Span Testing [73]
Employment Tests [73]
Group Testing [73]
Individual Testing [73]
↓ Intelligence Measures [67]
↓ Inventories [67]
Multidimensional Scaling [82]
Needs Assessment [85]
↓ Occupational Interest Measures [73]
Pain Measurement [97]
↓ Perceptual Measures [73]
Performance Tests [73]
↓ Personality Measures [67]
Posttesting [73]
↓ Preference Measures [73]
Pretesting [73]
Professional Examinations [94]
Profiles (Measurement) [73]
Projective Testing Technique [73]
↓ Psychiatric Evaluation [97]
↓ Psychological Assessment [97]
Psychometrics [67]
↓ Questionnaires [67]
↓ Rating Scales [67]
↓ Reading Measures [73]
↓ Retention Measures [73]
↓ Screening [82]
↓ Screening Tests [82]
↓ Selection Tests [73]
↓ Sensorimotor Measures [73]
Sociometric Tests [67]
↓ Speech and Hearing Measures [73]
Standardized Tests [85]
↓ Statistical Measurement [73]
Subtests [73]
↓ Surveys [67]
Symptom Checklists [91]
↓ Testing [67]
Verbal Tests [73]
R Clinical Judgment (Not Diagnosis) [73]
Construct Validity [82]
↓ Diagnosis [67]
↓ Evaluation [67]
↓ Experimentation [67]
Geriatric Assessment [97]
↓ Interviews [67]

Measurement — (cont'd)
R ↓ Methodology 67
Piagetian Tasks 73
↓ Prediction Errors 73
Response Bias 67
Semantic Differential 67
Sociograms 73
↓ Statistical Analysis 67
↓ Test Construction 73
Test Norms 73
↓ Test Scores 67
↓ Testing Methods 67
Testwiseness 78

Mecamylamine 73
PN 85 **SC** 30220
B Amines 73
Antihypertensive Drugs 73
Ganglion Blocking Drugs 73

Mechanical Aptitude 73
PN 62 **SC** 30230
B Nonverbal Ability 88

Mechanoreceptors 73
PN 140 **SC** 30250
B Neural Receptors 73
Sensory Neurons 73

Media (Communications)
Use Communications Media

Medial Forebrain Bundle 82
PN 118 **SC** 30286
SN Complex group of nerve fibers arising from basal olfactory regions, the periamygdaloid region, and the septal nuclei passing to, and through, the lateral preoptic and hypothalamic regions. This bundle provides the chief pathway for reciprocal connections between the hypothalamus and the biogenic amine systems of the brain stem.
B Limbic System 73
R Amygdaloid Body 73
Fornix 82
Hippocampus 67
↓ Hypothalamus 67
Septal Nuclei 82

Median 73
PN 15 **SC** 30290
B Central Tendency Measures 73

Median Nerve
Use Spinal Nerves

Mediated Responses 67
PN 57 **SC** 30310
SN Intervening or anticipatory responses aroused by stimuli and subsequently responsible for the initiation of behavior.
B Responses 67

Mediation 88
PN 529 **SC** 30315
SN Intervention by independent and impartial third party or parties to promote reconciliation, settlement, or compromise between conflicting parties.
B Conflict Resolution 82
R Child Custody 82
Court Referrals 94
Divorce 73
Labor Management Relations 67
↓ Negotiation 73

Mediation (Cognitive)
Use Cognitive Mediation

Medicaid 94
PN 26 **SC** 30323
SN U.S. Government health care program for impoverished citizens administered by most local public assistance offices. Compare MEDICARE.
B Government Programs 73
Health Insurance 73
R Health Care Policy 94
Medicare 88
Social Security 88
Welfare Services (Government) 73

Medical Care Costs
Use Health Care Costs

Medical Diagnosis 73
PN 2264 **SC** 30330
SN Diagnosis of mental or physical disorders through use of medical methods or tests. Compare PSYCHODIAGNOSIS.
UF Clinical Judgment (Med Diagnosis)
B Diagnosis 67
N Biopsy 73
↓ Cardiography 73
Dexamethasone Suppression Test 88
Echoencephalography 73
Electro Oculography 73
↓ Electroencephalography 67
Electromyography 67
Electronystagmography 73
Electroplethysmography 73
Electroretinography 67
↓ Encephalography 73
Galvanic Skin Response 67
HIV Testing 97
↓ Ophthalmologic Examination 73
↓ Plethysmography 73
Pneumoencephalography 73
Prenatal Diagnosis 88
Rheoencephalography 73
↓ Roentgenography 73
↓ Tomography 88
Urinalysis 73
R Autopsy 73
Biological Markers 91
Computer Assisted Diagnosis 73
Differential Diagnosis 67
Drug Usage Screening 88
↓ Electrophysiology 73
↓ Health Screening 97
Mammography 94
Patient History 73
Physical Examination 88
Prognosis 73
Psychological Report 88

Medical Education 73
PN 1940 **SC** 30340
B Graduate Education 73
N Medical Internship 73
Medical Residency 73
Psychiatric Training 73
R Nursing Education 73

Medical History
Use Patient History

Medical Internship 73
PN 95 **SC** 30350
UF Internship (Medical)
B Medical Education 73
Postgraduate Training 73

Medical Model 78
PN 397 **SC** 30355

Medical Model — (cont'd)
SN Conceptual approach to disorders originally applied to the study and treatment of physical illness. Also known as the disease or faulty mechanism model.
B Models 67

Medical Patients 73
PN 2489 **SC** 30360
B Patients 67

Medical Personnel 67
PN 2051 **SC** 30370
UF Hospital Staff
B Health Personnel 94
N Dentists 73
Military Medical Personnel 73
↓ Nurses 67
Optometrists 73
↓ Paramedical Personnel 73
Pharmacists 91
Physical Therapists 73
↓ Physicians 67
↓ Psychiatric Hospital Staff 73
R Clinicians 73
Impaired Professionals 85
↓ Medical Sciences 67
↓ Mental Health Personnel 67
Scientists 67

Medical Personnel Supply 73
PN 19 **SC** 30380
SN Manpower needs and availability of medical personnel.
B Personnel Supply 73

Medical Psychology 73
PN 176 **SC** 30390
SN Subspecialty of clinical psychology concerned with physical health and illness.
B Clinical Psychology 67
Health Care Psychology 85
R ↓ Medical Sciences 67

Medical Records 78
PN 365 **SC** 30395
SN Use MEDICAL RECORDS KEEPING to access references from 78–96.
N Client Records 97
R Data Collection 82
↓ Data Processing 67
Hospital Administration 78
Patient History 73
↓ Treatment 67

Medical Regimen Compliance
Use Treatment Compliance

Medical Residency 73
PN 1053 **SC** 30400
SN Required hospital training in a medical specialty for a graduate and licensed physician.
UF Psychiatric Residency
Residency (Medical)
B Medical Education 73
Postgraduate Training 73

Medical Sciences 67
PN 1402 **SC** 30410
UF Medicine (Science of)
B Sciences 67
N Anesthesiology 73
Cardiology 73
Dentistry 73
↓ Endocrinology 73
Epidemiology 73
Family Medicine 88
Geriatrics 67

Medical Sciences — (cont'd)
N Gynecology [78]
↓ Immunology [73]
Neurology [67]
↓ Obstetrics [78]
Ophthalmology [73]
↓ Pathology [73]
Pediatrics [73]
↓ Psychiatry [67]
Psychosomatic Medicine [78]
Radiology [73]
↓ Surgery [71]
Veterinary Medicine [73]
R Folk Medicine [73]
↓ Medical Personnel [67]
Medical Psychology [73]
↓ Neurosciences [73]
↓ Paramedical Sciences [73]

Medical Students [67]
PN 2290 SC 30420
B Students [67]
R Graduate Students [67]

Medical Therapeutic Devices [73]
PN 289 SC 30430
SN Equipment designed for rehabilitation or treatment of abnormal or undesirable conditions.
UF Therapeutic Devices (Medical)
N Artificial Pacemakers [73]
↓ Hearing Aids [73]
↓ Optical Aids [73]
↓ Prostheses [73]
R ↓ Augmentative Communication [94]
Mobility Aids [78]

Medical Treatment (General) [73]
PN 1188 SC 30440
SN Use for medical treatment as a broad topic.
B Treatment [67]
R ↓ Alternative Medicine [97]
Life Sustaining Treatment [97]
↓ Physical Treatment Methods [73]

Medicare [88]
PN 92 SC 30445
SN U.S. Government health care program for the aged administered through the Social Security Administration or the US Health Care Financing Administration. Compare MEDICAID.
B Government Programs [73]
Health Insurance [73]
R Health Care Policy [94]
Medicaid [94]
Social Security [88]

Medication
Use Drug Therapy

Medicine (Science of)
Use Medical Sciences

Medics
SN Term discontinued in 1997. Use MEDICS to access references from 73–96.
Use Paramedical Personnel

Meditation [73]
PN 942 SC 30480
SN Family of contemplative techniques all of which involve a conscious attempt to focus one's attention in a nonanalytical way and to refrain from ruminating, discursive thought. Sometimes, considered a spiritual or religious practice.
B Religious Practices [73]
R ↓ Alternative Medicine [97]
Centering [91]
Holistic Health [85]

Meditation — (cont'd)
R ↓ Human Potential Movement [82]
Martial Arts [85]
Prayer [73]
↓ Relaxation Therapy [78]

Medulla Oblongata [73]
PN 326 SC 30490
B Brain Stem [73]
Hindbrain [97]

Melancholia
SN Use DEPRESSION (EMOTION) to access references from 73-87.
Use Major Depression

Melancholy
Use Sadness

Melanin [73]
PN 25 SC 30530
B Pigments [73]
R Melanocyte Stimulating Hormone [85]
Melatonin [73]
↓ Tyrosine [73]

Melanocyte Stimulating Hormone [85]
PN 67 SC 30535
UF Melanotropin
B Peptides [73]
Pituitary Hormones [73]
R Melanin [73]
Melatonin [73]

Melanotropin
Use Melanocyte Stimulating Hormone

Melatonin [73]
PN 364 SC 30540
B Hormones [67]
R Melanin [73]
Melanocyte Stimulating Hormone [85]
Pineal Body [73]

Mellaril
Use Thioridazine

Membranes [73]
PN 145 SC 30560
B Tissues (Body) [73]
N Meninges [73]
↓ Nasal Mucosa [73]
Nictitating Membrane [73]

Memory [67]
PN 15627 SC 30570
N Autobiographical Memory [94]
Early Memories [85]
Eidetic Imagery [73]
Episodic Memory [88]
Explicit Memory [97]
False Memory [97]
Long Term Memory [73]
Memory Decay [73]
Memory Trace [73]
Reminiscence [85]
Repressed Memory [97]
↓ Short Term Memory [67]
↓ Spatial Memory [88]
Spontaneous Recovery (Learning) [73]
↓ Verbal Memory [94]
↓ Visual Memory [94]
R ↓ Amnesia [67]
↓ Cognitive Processes [67]
Cued Recall [94]
Cues [67]
Declarative Knowledge [97]

Memory — (cont'd)
R Forgetting [73]
Free Recall [73]
Generation Effect (Learning) [91]
Human Information Storage [73]
↓ Interference (Learning) [67]
↓ Latent Inhibition [97]
↓ Learning [67]
Matching to Sample [94]
↓ Memory Disorders [73]
Memory Training [94]
Metacognition [91]
Note Taking [91]
Procedural Knowledge [97]
↓ Prompting [97]
↓ Recall (Learning) [67]
Relearning [73]
↓ Retention [67]
Rote Learning [73]
Serial Recall [94]

Memory Decay [73]
PN 139 SC 30580
SN Fading of memory traces over time. Compare FORGETTING and AMNESIA.
B Memory [67]
R Forgetting [73]
Memory Training [94]

Memory Disorders [73]
PN 703 SC 30590
B Thought Disturbances [73]
N ↓ Amnesia [67]
R ↓ Brain Disorders [67]
↓ Memory [67]
Memory Training [94]
↓ Mental Disorders [67]
↓ Physical Disorders [97]

Memory Enhancing Drugs
Use Nootropic Drugs

Memory for Designs Test [73]
PN 29 SC 30610
B Nonprojective Personality Measures [73]
R ↓ Neuropsychological Assessment [82]

Memory Trace [73]
PN 289 SC 30620
SN Hypothetical change in nerve cells or brain activity that accompanies the storage of information.
B Memory [67]

Memory Training [94]
PN 34 SC 30623
R Cognitive Rehabilitation [85]
Forgetting [73]
↓ Learning Strategies [91]
↓ Memory [67]
Memory Decay [73]
↓ Memory Disorders [73]
Mnemonic Learning [73]
↓ Neuropsychological Rehabilitation [97]
↓ Practice [67]
↓ Recall (Learning) [67]
↓ Recognition (Learning) [67]
↓ Retention [67]

Men
Use Human Males

Menarche [73]
PN 136 SC 30630
B Menstruation [73]
R Puberty [73]

Menieres Disease 73
PN 35 **SC** 30640
B Labyrinth Disorders 73
Syndromes 73
R Vertigo 73

Meninges 73
PN 18 **SC** 30650
B Central Nervous System Membranes 73

Meningitis 73
PN 35 **SC** 30660
B Central Nervous System Disorders 73
N Bacterial Meningitis 73

Meningomyelocele
Use Spina Bifida

Menopause 73
PN 340 **SC** 30670
B Developmental Stages 73
R ↓ Menstrual Cycle 73

Menstrual Cycle 73
PN 800 **SC** 30680
N ↓ Menstruation 73
Ovulation 73
Premenstrual Tension 73
R Estrus 73
Menopause 73

Menstrual Disorders 73
PN 120 **SC** 30690
B Gynecological Disorders 73
N Amenorrhea 73
Dysmenorrhea 73
R Premenstrual Tension 73

Menstruation 73
PN 217 **SC** 30700
B Menstrual Cycle 73
N Menarche 73
R Estrus 73

Mental Age 73
PN 225 **SC** 30710
SN Intelligence level expressed in units of chronological age and determined by comparison with other individuals of the same age using intelligence test scores.
UF Intelligence Age
R ↓ Developmental Age Groups 73
Intelligence 67
Intelligence Quotient 67

Mental Confusion 73
PN 277 **SC** 30720
UF Confusion (Mental)
B Emotional States 73
R Doubt 73
Frustration 67
↓ Thought Disturbances 73
Wandering Behavior 91

Mental Deficiency
Use Mental Retardation

Mental Disorders 67
PN 15864 **SC** 30740
SN Conceptually broad array term referring to all forms of psychopathology. Use a more specific term if possible.
UF Insanity
Mental Illness
Nervous Breakdown
Psychiatric Disorders
B Disorders 67

Mental Disorders — (cont'd)
N Adjustment Disorders 94
Alexithymia 82
↓ Anxiety Disorders 97
↓ Autism 67
Borderline States 78
↓ Chronic Mental Illness 97
↓ Dementia 85
↓ Dissociative Patterns 73
↓ Eating Disorders 97
Elective Mutism 73
Explosive Personality 73
↓ Factitious Disorders 88
Gender Identity Disorder 97
↓ Hysteria 67
Impulse Control Disorders 97
Koro 94
↓ Neurosis 67
↓ Personality Disorders 67
Pseudodementia 85
↓ Psychosis 67
↓ Sexual Deviations 67
R Adaptive Behavior 91
Attention Deficit Disorder 85
↓ Behavior Disorders 71
↓ Brain Disorders 67
↓ Chronic Illness 91
Chronicity (Disorders) 82
↓ Communication Disorders 82
Comorbidity 91
Conduct Disorder 91
↓ Congenital Disorders 73
↓ Consciousness Disturbances 73
↓ Defense Mechanisms 67
↓ Diagnosis 67
Diagnostic and Statistical Manual 94
Disability Discrimination 97
Disease Course 91
↓ Emotional Adjustment 73
↓ Ethnospecific Disorders 73
Etiology 67
Glossolalia 73
Homeless Mentally Ill 97
Infantilism 73
Insanity Defense 85
International Class of Diseases 97
↓ Learning Disorders 67
Malingering 73
↓ Memory Disorders 73
Mental Illness (Attitudes Toward) 67
↓ Mental Retardation 67
Mentally Ill Offenders 85
Microcephaly 73
Narcissism 67
Onset (Disorders) 73
↓ Organic Brain Syndromes 73
↓ Perceptual Disturbances 73
↓ Personality Processes 67
↓ Physical Disorders 97
Porphyria 73
Predisposition 73
Premorbidity 78
Prognosis 73
Psychiatric Patients 67
Psychiatric Symptoms 97
↓ Psychodiagnosis 67
↓ Psychological Assessment 97
Psychopathology 67
Recovery (Disorders) 73
Relapse (Disorders) 73
↓ Remission (Disorders) 73
Research Diagnostic Criteria 94
Rett Syndrome 94
↓ Sadomasochism 73
Schizophrenogenic Family 67
Severity (Disorders) 82
↓ Sexual Function Disturbances 73
↓ Sleep Disorders 73
Special Needs 94

Mental Disorders — (cont'd)
R ↓ Suicide 67
Susceptibility (Disorders) 73
↓ Symptoms 67
↓ Syndromes 73
↓ Thought Disturbances 73
↓ Toxic Disorders 73
↓ Treatment Resistant Disorders 94
Work Related Illnesses 94

Mental Health 67
PN 5832 **SC** 30750
B Health 73
N Community Mental Health 73
R Community Mental Health Services 78
Community Psychiatry 73
↓ Emotional Adjustment 73
↓ Mental Health Personnel 67
↓ Mental Health Programs 73
↓ Mental Health Services 78
Primary Mental Health Prevention 73
Well Being 94

Mental Health Care Costs
Use Health Care Costs

Mental Health Care Policy
Use Health Care Policy

Mental Health Centers (Community)
Use Community Mental Health Centers

Mental Health Consultation
SN Term discontinued in 1982. Use MENTAL HEALTH CONSULTATION or PROFESSIONAL CONSULTATION to access references prior to 1982.
Use Professional Consultation

Mental Health Inservice Training 73
PN 375 **SC** 30780
UF Inservice Training (Mental Health)
Training (Mental Health Inservice)
B Community Mental Health Training 73
Inservice Training 85
R ↓ Mental Health Programs 73
Professional Development 82

Mental Health Personnel 67
PN 3919 **SC** 30790
B Health Personnel 94
N Clinical Psychologists 73
↓ Psychiatric Hospital Staff 73
Psychiatric Nurses 73
Psychiatric Social Workers 73
Psychiatrists 67
↓ Psychotherapists 73
School Psychologists 73
R Clinicians 73
↓ Counselors 67
↓ Educational Personnel 73
Impaired Professionals 85
↓ Medical Personnel 67
↓ Mental Health 67
Mental Health Personnel Supply 73
Occupational Therapists 73
↓ Paraprofessional Personnel 73
Personal Therapy 91
Professional Supervision 88
↓ Psychologists 67
↓ Social Workers 73
↓ Therapists 67

Mental Health Personnel Supply 73
PN 90 **SC** 30800
B Personnel Supply 73
R ↓ Mental Health Personnel 67

Mental Health Program Evaluation 73
PN 889 **SC** 30810
SN Methodology or procedures for assessment of any mental health program in relation to previously established goals or other criteria. Also used for the formal evaluations themselves. For effectiveness of particular treatment modes, use the specific type of treatment (e.g., DRUG THERAPY). For efficacy of treatment for a particular disorder, use the specific disorder (e.g., MANIA).
UF Program Evaluation (Mental Health)
B Program Evaluation 85
R Behavioral Assessment 82
↓ Mental Health Programs 73
Psychotherapeutic Outcomes 73
↓ Treatment 67
Treatment Effectiveness Evaluation 73
↓ Treatment Outcomes 82

Mental Health Programs 73
PN 1471 **SC** 30820
SN Programs for the maintenance of mental health.
UF Programs (Mental Health)
N ↓ Crisis Intervention Services 73
Deinstitutionalization 82
Home Visiting Programs 73
Hot Line Services 73
Suicide Prevention Centers 73
R Child Guidance Clinics 73
Community Mental Health 73
Community Mental Health Centers 73
Community Mental Health Services 78
↓ Community Mental Health Training 73
Community Psychiatry 73
Community Psychology 73
↓ Community Services 67
↓ Health Care Administration 97
↓ Health Care Delivery 78
↓ Health Care Services 78
Integrated Services 97
↓ Mental Health 67
Mental Health Inservice Training 73
Mental Health Program Evaluation 73
↓ Mental Health Services 78
Outreach Programs 97
Partial Hospitalization 85
Primary Mental Health Prevention 73
↓ Program Development 91
Psychiatric Clinics 73
Public Health Services 73

Mental Health Service Needs
Use Health Service Needs

Mental Health Services 78
PN 3937 **SC** 30825
SN Services available for maintenance of mental health and treatment of mental disorders.
B Health Care Services 78
N Community Mental Health Services 78
R Child Guidance Clinics 73
Community Mental Health Centers 73
↓ Community Services 67
↓ Counseling 67
↓ Health Care Administration 97
Health Care Costs 94
↓ Health Care Delivery 78
Health Care Policy 94
Health Care Seeking Behavior 97
Health Service Needs 97
Integrated Services 97
Long Term Care 94
↓ Mental Health 67
↓ Mental Health Programs 73
Outreach Programs 97
↓ Prevention 73
↓ Psychiatric Hospital Programs 67
Quality of Care 88

Mental Health Services — (cont'd)
R ↓ Quality of Services 97
School Counseling 82
Social Casework 67
↓ Social Services 82
Student Personnel Services 78
↓ Support Groups 91
↓ Twelve Step Programs 97

Mental Health Training (Community)
Use Community Mental Health Training

Mental Hospitals
Use Psychiatric Hospitals

Mental Illness
Use Mental Disorders

Mental Illness (Attitudes Toward) 67
PN 1167 **SC** 30860
B Disabled (Attitudes Toward) 97
R Disability Discrimination 97
Health Knowledge 94
↓ Mental Disorders 67

Mental Load
Use Human Channel Capacity

Mental Retardation 67
PN 4824 **SC** 30870
SN Impaired intellectual (IQ below 70) and adaptive functioning manifested during the developmental period. Use for the concept or disorder itself, and use MENTALLY RETARDED, or a more specific term, for mentally retarded populations.
UF Amentia
Mental Deficiency
Oligophrenia
Retardation (Mental)
N Amaurotic Familial Idiocy 73
Anencephaly 73
Borderline Mental Retardation 73
Crying Cat Syndrome 73
Downs Syndrome 67
Psychosocial Mental Retardation 73
R Adaptive Behavior 91
↓ Brain Damage 67
Developmental Disabilities 82
Fetal Alcohol Syndrome 85
Fragile X Syndrome 94
Hydrocephaly 73
Klinefelters Syndrome 73
↓ Mental Disorders 67
Mental Retardation (Attit Toward) 73
↓ Mentally Retarded 67
Microcephaly 73
Phenylketonuria 73
Prader Willi Syndrome 91
Rett Syndrome 94

Mental Retardation (Attit Toward) 73
PN 538 **SC** 30880
B Disabled (Attitudes Toward) 97
R ↓ Mental Retardation 67

Mental Rotation 91
PN 125 **SC** 30883
B Cognitive Processes 67
R Mirror Image 91
↓ Spatial Ability 82
Spatial Imagery 82
Spatial Organization 73
↓ Spatial Perception 67

Mentally Ill Homeless
Use Homeless Mentally Ill

Mentally Ill Offenders 85
PN 788 **SC** 30885
UF Criminally Insane
B Criminals 67
R Competency to Stand Trial 85
Court Referrals 94
Forensic Evaluation 94
Insanity Defense 85
↓ Mental Disorders 67

Mentally Retarded 67
PN 8122 **SC** 30890
SN Persons exhibiting impaired intellectual (IQ below 70) and adaptive functioning manifested during the developmental period. Use for populations of mentally retarded persons. Use a more specific term if possible. Use MENTAL RETARDATION for discussions of the concept or the disorder itself.
UF Retarded (Mentally)
B Disabled 97
N Educable Mentally Retarded 73
Home Reared Mentally Retarded 73
Idiot Savants 73
Institutionalized Mentally Retarded 73
Profoundly Mentally Retarded 73
Severely Mentally Retarded 73
Trainable Mentally Retarded 73
R Adaptive Behavior 91
↓ Mental Retardation 67
Slow Learners 73

Mentor 85
PN 376 **SC** 30895
SN An individual who befriends and facilitates the development of a less experienced individual, especially within a profession, business, trade, or academic environment.
R Adult Development 78
Apprenticeship 73
↓ Interpersonal Interaction 67
Occupational Aspirations 73
Occupational Guidance 67
Peer Counseling 78
Professional Development 82
Significant Others 91
↓ Social Influences 67
Supervisor Employee Interaction 97
Vocational Counselors 73

Meperidine 73
PN 55 **SC** 30900
B Amines 73
Analgesic Drugs 73
Antispasmodic Drugs 73
Narcotic Drugs 73
Sedatives 73

Mephenesin
SN Term discontinued in 1997. Use MEPHENESIN to access references from 73-96.
Use Muscle Relaxing Drugs

Meprobamate 73
PN 53 **SC** 30920
B Hypnotic Drugs 73
Muscle Relaxing Drugs 73
Sedatives 73
Tranquilizing Drugs 67

Mercury (Metal) 73
PN 49 **SC** 30930
B Metallic Elements 73

Mercury Poisoning 73
PN 67 **SC** 30940
B Toxic Disorders 73

Mercy Killing
Use Euthanasia

Mescaline 73
PN 108 **SC** 30950
B Alkaloids 73
Hallucinogenic Drugs 67
Psychotomimetic Drugs 73
R Peyote 73

Mesencephalon 73
PN 1455 **SC** 30960
UF Midbrain
Red Nucleus
B Brain 67
N Inferior Colliculus 73
Optic Lobe 73
Substantia Nigra 94
Superior Colliculus 73
↓ Tegmentum 91

Mesoridazine 73
PN 35 **SC** 30970
B Phenothiazine Derivatives 73

Messages 73
PN 928 **SC** 30980
SN Informational content of communications transmitted between persons or systems.
UF Information (Messages)
R ↓ Communication 67
Gossip 82
Information 67

Meta Analysis 85
PN 1523 **SC** 30985
SN Statistical analysis of a large collection of results from individual studies for the purpose of integrating findings. Also used as a document type identifier.
UF Data Pooling
B Methodology 67
Statistical Analysis 67
R Literature Review 67

Metabolic Rates 73
PN 135 **SC** 30990
R Energy Expenditure 67
↓ Metabolism 67
↓ Physiology 67

Metabolism 67
PN 2029 **SC** 31000
SN Biochemical changes in the cells, digestive system, and body tissues by which energy is provided, new material is incorporated, and substances, such as drugs, are disposed.
B Physiology 67
N Anabolism 73
Basal Metabolism 73
Biosynthesis 73
↓ Carbohydrate Metabolism 73
Catabolism 73
Lipid Metabolism 73
↓ Metabolites 73
Protein Metabolism 73
R Bioavailability 91
↓ Dopamine Metabolites 82
Metabolic Rates 73
↓ Metabolism Disorders 73
↓ Norepinephrine Metabolites 82
Thermoregulation (Body) 73

Metabolism Disorders 73
PN 321 **SC** 31020
UF Hypercholesterolemia
B Physical Disorders 97
N Cushings Syndrome 73

Metabolism Disorders — (cont'd)
N Cystic Fibrosis 85
↓ Diabetes 73
Hyperglycemia 85
Hypoglycemia 73
Hyponatremia 97
↓ Lipid Metabolism Disorders 73
Phenylketonuria 73
Porphyria 73
R Hypothyroidism 73
↓ Metabolism 67
↓ Nutritional Deficiencies 73

Metabolites 73
PN 675 **SC** 31030
SN Biochemical products of metabolism.
UF Anabolites
Catabolites
B Metabolism 67
N ↓ Dopamine Metabolites 82
↓ Norepinephrine Metabolites 82
↓ Serotonin Metabolites 78

Metacognition 91
PN 501 **SC** 31040
SN Awareness, monitoring, and knowledge of one's own cognitive processes and activities including memory and comprehension.
UF Metamemory
B Cognitive Processes 67
R ↓ Awareness 67
Cognition 67
↓ Cognitive Ability 73
↓ Comprehension 67
Declarative Knowledge 97
↓ Learning 67
↓ Learning Strategies 91
↓ Memory 67
Metalinguistics 94
Procedural Knowledge 97
School Learning 67

Metalinguistics 94
PN 19 **SC** 31045
SN Branch of linguistics concerned with how language is used, the role of language in culture, and the use of particular linguistic forms.
B Linguistics 73
R Ethnolinguistics 73
↓ Language 67
↓ Language Development 67
Metacognition 91
Pragmatics 85
Psycholinguistics 67
Sociolinguistics 85
Verbal Ability 67
↓ Verbal Communication 67

Metallic Elements 73
PN 277 **SC** 31050
B Metals 91
N Aluminum 94
Barium 73
↓ Calcium 73
Cobalt 73
Copper 73
Iron 73
Lead (Metal) 73
↓ Lithium 73
↓ Magnesium 73
Mercury (Metal) 73
↓ Potassium 73
↓ Sodium 73
Zinc 85

Metals 91
PN 22 **SC** 31052
SN May include alloys.
N ↓ Metallic Elements 73

Metamemory
Use Metacognition

Metaphor 82
PN 972 **SC** 31057
SN Figures of speech used to suggest an analogy between one kind of object or idea and another.
B Figurative Language 85
R Analogy 91
↓ Literature 67
Myths 67
↓ Semantics 67
Symbolism 67

Metaphysics 73
PN 142 **SC** 31060
SN Branch of philosophy concerned with the fundamental nature of things and existence.
B Philosophies 67
R Epistemology 73
Hermeneutics 91
Reality 73
Relativism 97

Metapsychology 94
PN 28 **SC** 31070
B Psychology 67
R Freudian Psychoanalytic School 73
Object Relations 82
↓ Psychoanalytic Theory 67

Methadone 73
PN 543 **SC** 31080
B Analgesic Drugs 73
Narcotic Drugs 73
R Methadone Maintenance 78

Methadone Maintenance 78
PN 960 **SC** 31083
SN Rehabilitation of heroin addicts by substituting methadone for heroin, enabling the addict to lead a relatively normal life. Methadone maintenance does not actually treat the addiction.
R ↓ Drug Addiction 67
↓ Drug Rehabilitation 73
Heroin Addiction 73
Maintenance Therapy 97
Methadone 73

Methamphetamine 73
PN 338 **SC** 31090
UF Methedrine
B Amphetamine 67
CNS Stimulating Drugs 73
Vasoconstrictor Drugs 73
R Methylenedioxymethamphetamine 91

Methanol 73
PN 24 **SC** 31100
UF Methyl Alcohol
B Alcohols 67

Methaqualone 73
PN 44 **SC** 31110
UF Quaalude
B Hypnotic Drugs 73
Sedatives 73

Methedrine
Use Methamphetamine

Methionine 73
PN 98 **SC** 31130
B Amino Acids 73

Methodists
Use Protestants

Methodology 67
PN 9969 **SC** 31140
SN Conceptually broad array term that refers generally to strategies, techniques, or procedures used in applied, descriptive, or empirical studies. Compare EXPERIMENTAL METHODS.
UF Research Methods
N Causal Analysis 94
Cohort Analysis 88
↓ Content Analysis 78
Data Collection 82
↓ Empirical Methods 73
Meta Analysis 85
Self Report 82
R Experiment Controls 73
↓ Experimental Design 67
Experimental Instructions 67
Experimental Laboratories 73
Experimental Replication 73
↓ Experimentation 67
Mail Surveys 94
↓ Measurement 67
↓ Surveys 67
Telephone Surveys 94
Theory Formulation 73
Theory Verification 73

Methohexital 73
PN 36 **SC** 31150
B Barbiturates 67
General Anesthetics 73

Methoxamine 73
PN 20 **SC** 31160
B Adrenergic Drugs 73
Alcohols 67
Sympathomimetic Amines 73
Vasoconstrictor Drugs 73
R ↓ Local Anesthetics 73

Methoxyhydroxyphenylglycol (3,4) 91
PN 92 **SC** 31165
UF MHPG
B Norepinephrine Metabolites 82

Methyl Alcohol
Use Methanol

Methylatropine
Use Atropine

Methyldiphenylhydramine
Use Orphenadrine

Methyldopa 73
PN 50 **SC** 31190
B Antihypertensive Drugs 73
R ↓ Catecholamines 73
DOPA 73
Dopamine 73

Methylenedioxymethamphetamine 91
PN 67 **SC** 31195
UF Ecstasy (Drug)
MDMA
R Methamphetamine 73

Methylmorphine
Use Codeine

Methylphenidate 73
PN 916 **SC** 31210
UF Ritalin
B Amines 73
Antidepressant Drugs 71
CNS Stimulating Drugs 73
R ↓ Analeptic Drugs 73

Methylphenyltetrahydropyridine 94
PN 9 **SC** 31213
UF MPTP
B Neurotoxins 82
R Dopamine 73

Methysergide
Use Serotonin Antagonists

Metrazole
Use Pentylenetetrazol

Metronomes 73
PN 16 **SC** 31230
B Apparatus 67

Metropolitan Readiness Tests 78
PN 25 **SC** 31240
SN Use METROPOLITAN READING READINESS TEST to access references from 73–77.
B Reading Measures 73

Mexican Americans 73
PN 2300 **SC** 31250
SN Populations of Mexican descent residing permanently in the U.S.
UF Chicanos
B Hispanics 82

Mexico 73
PN 774 **SC** 31260
B North America 73
R Latin America 88

MHPG
Use Methoxyhydroxyphenylglycol (3,4)

Mianserin 82
PN 241 **SC** 31266
SN Organic heterocyclic compound having antiserotonin properties and used as an antihistamine.
B Antidepressant Drugs 71
Antihistaminic Drugs 73
Serotonin Antagonists 73

Mice 73
PN 8713 **SC** 31270
B Rodents 73

Microcephaly 73
PN 44 **SC** 31280
SN Smallness of the head produced by incomplete development of the brain often associated with below normal mental and cognitive development.
B Brain Disorders 67
Congenital Disorders 73
R ↓ Mental Disorders 67
↓ Mental Retardation 67
↓ Neonatal Disorders 73

Microcomputers 85
PN 799 **SC** 31282
UF Personal Computers
B Computers 67
R ↓ Computer Applications 73

Microcounseling 78
PN 89 **SC** 31284
SN Short-term technique for teaching basic interviewing skills using role playing, videotape analysis, and feedback in prepracticum training.
B Counseling 67
R ↓ Clinical Methods Training 73
Counselor Education 73
Interviewing 73
Paraprofessional Education 73

Microorganisms 85
PN 34 **SC** 31287
SN Single-celled microscopic or ultramicroscopic organisms.
UF Bacteria
Single Cell Organisms
N Protozoa 73

Microscopes 73
PN 5 **SC** 31290
B Apparatus 67

Micturition
Use Urination

Midazolam 91
PN 114 **SC** 31303
B Benzodiazepines 78
Minor Tranquilizers 73

Midbrain
Use Mesencephalon

Middle Aged 73
PN 2138 **SC** 31310
SN Ages 40–59. Applied only if age is important to the research focus.
B Adults 67
R Adult Development 78
↓ Aging 91

Middle Class 73
PN 610 **SC** 31320
UF Bourgeois
B Social Class 67

Middle Class Attitudes 73
PN 44 **SC** 31330
SN Attitudes of, not toward, the middle class.
B Socioeconomic Class Attitudes 73

Middle Ear 73
PN 114 **SC** 31340
UF Ear Ossicles
Eustachian Tube
Tympanic Membrane
B Ear (Anatomy) 67

Middle East 78
PN 354 **SC** 31344
B Asia 73
R ↓ Africa 67
Cyprus 91
Egypt 82
Greece 73
Iran 73
Iraq 88
Israel 67
Jordan 88
Kuwait 91
Lebanon 88
Libya 88
Saudi Arabia 85
Syria 88
Turkey 73
Yemen 91

Middle Income Level 73
PN 80 **SC** 31350
B Income Level 73

Middle Level Managers 73
PN 467 **SC** 31360
SN Second-line managers or supervisors primarily responsible for daily work flow and production in a business or industrial organization.
B Management Personnel 73
R Top Level Managers 73

Middle School Education 85
PN 124 **SC** 31364
SN Education for grades six through eight (sometimes five through eight) using methods and materials specifically focusing on the needs and characteristics of early adolescents.
B Education 67

Middle School Students 85
PN 761 **SC** 31367
SN Students in 6th, 7th, and 8th grades. Sometimes may include students in 5th grade. Use ELEMENTARY SCHOOL STUDENTS or JUNIOR HIGH SCHOOL STUDENTS, as appropriate, unless specific reference is made to the population as middle school students. Application of a student term is mandatory in educational contexts.
R ↓ Elementary School Students 67
Junior High School Students 71
Preadolescents 88

Midwifery 85
PN 42 **SC** 31368
UF Home Birth
B Obstetrics 78
R ↓ Birth 67
Labor (Childbirth) 73

Migraine Headache 73
PN 883 **SC** 31370
B Headache 73
R ↓ Endocrine Disorders 73
Nausea 73
↓ Psychosomatic Disorders 67

Migrant Farm Workers 73
PN 75 **SC** 31380
B Agricultural Workers 73
R Foreign Workers 85
↓ Human Migration 73

Migration (Human)
Use Human Migration

Migratory Behavior (Animal) 73
PN 469 **SC** 31400
UF Animal Navigation
B Animal Ethology 67
R Animal Homing 91

Mildly Mentally Retarded
Use Educable Mentally Retarded

Milieu Therapy 88
PN 104 **SC** 31420
SN Modification or manipulation of patient's personal life circumstances or environment through controlled and stimulatory environments. Treatment setting can be a hospital, therapeutic community or home. Use THERAPEUTIC COMMUNITY to access references from 73-87.
UF Environmental Therapy
Socioenvironmental Therapy
B Treatment 67
R Sociotherapy 73
Therapeutic Community 67

Militancy 73
PN 51 **SC** 31430
B Social Behavior 67

Military Enlistment 73
PN 219 **SC** 31440
UF Enlistment (Military)
R Military Recruitment 73

Military Medical Personnel 73
PN 121 **SC** 31450

Military Medical Personnel — (cont'd)
B Medical Personnel 67
Military Personnel 67

Military Officers
Use Commissioned Officers

Military Personnel 67
PN 2233 **SC** 31470
UF Servicemen
B Government Personnel 73
N Air Force Personnel 67
Army Personnel 67
Coast Guard Personnel 88
Commissioned Officers 73
↓ Enlisted Military Personnel 73
Marine Personnel 73
Military Medical Personnel 73
Military Psychologists 97
National Guardsmen 73
Navy Personnel 67
ROTC Students 73
Volunteer Military Personnel 73
R Astronauts 73
Chaplains 73
Combat Experience 91
Military Veterans 73

Military Psychologists 97
PN 0 **SC** 31475
B Military Personnel 67
Psychologists 67
R Military Psychology 67

Military Psychology 67
PN 385 **SC** 31480
B Applied Psychology 73
R Military Psychologists 97

Military Recruitment 73
PN 203 **SC** 31490
UF Recruitment (Military)
B Personnel Recruitment 73
R Military Enlistment 73

Military Schools 73
PN 138 **SC** 31500
B Schools 67
R ↓ Colleges 67
High Schools 73

Military Training 73
PN 1119 **SC** 31510
B Personnel Training 67

Military Veterans 73
PN 1754 **SC** 31520
UF Veterans (Military)
R ↓ Military Personnel 67
↓ Personnel 67

Miller Analogies Test 73
PN 12 **SC** 31530
B Intelligence Measures 67

Millon Clinical Multiaxial Inventory 88
PN 218 **SC** 31540
B Nonprojective Personality Measures 73

Mind 91
PN 326 **SC** 31550
SN Conceptually broad term referring to the organized totality of conscious and unconscious mental processes or psychic activities of an individual.
R ↓ Cognitions 85
↓ Cognitive Processes 67

Mind — (cont'd)
R ↓ Consciousness States 71
Dualism 73
Human Nature 97
↓ Perception 67
Unconscious (Personality Factor) 67

Mind Body
Use Dualism

Mini Mental State Examination 94
PN 51 **SC** 31548
B Neuropsychological Assessment 82

Minimal Brain Disorders 73
PN 382 **SC** 31560
B Brain Disorders 67
R Attention Deficit Disorder 85
Hyperkinesis 73
Minimally Brain Damaged 73

Minimally Brain Damaged 73
PN 96 **SC** 31580
B Brain Damaged 73
R ↓ Learning Disabilities 73
Minimal Brain Disorders 73

Minimum Competency Tests 85
PN 86 **SC** 31585
UF Basic Skills Testing
B Educational Measurement 67
R ↓ Competence 82

Ministers (Religion) 73
PN 394 **SC** 31590
UF Pastors
B Clergy 73
R Chaplains 73
Missionaries 73

Minks 73
PN 27 **SC** 31600
B Rodents 73

Minn Multiphasic Personality Inven 67
PN 3402 **SC** 31610
UF MMPI
B Nonprojective Personality Measures 73

Minnesota Teacher Attitude Inventory
SN Term discontinued in 1997. Use MINNESOTA TEACHER ATTITUDE INVENTORY to access references from 73–96.
Use Attitude Measures

Minor Tranquilizers 73
PN 171 **SC** 31630
B Tranquilizing Drugs 67
N Alprazolam 88
Buspirone 91
Chlordiazepoxide 73
Chlorprothixene 73
Clonazepam 91
Diazepam 73
Hydroxyzine 73
Lorazepam 88
Loxapine 82
Midazolam 91
Oxazepam 78
R ↓ Benzodiazepines 78
↓ Neurosis 67

Minority Group Discrimination
SN Term discontinued in 1982. Use RACIAL DISCRIMINATION to access references from 73-81 and MINORITY GROUP DISCRIMINATION to access references from 78-81. Use SOCIAL DISCRIMINATION to access references from 82-93.
Use Race and Ethnic Discrimination

Minority Groups 67
PN 1721 **SC** 31640
SN Includes ethnic and linguistic minority groups and in/out social groups.
B Social Groups 73
R Affirmative Action 85
Alaska Natives 97
American Indians 67
Arabs 88
↓ Asians 82
Blacks 82
Cultural Sensitivity 94
Eskimos 73
↓ Ethnic Groups 73
Gypsies 73
↓ Hispanics 82
Jews 97
Multiculturalism 97
Race and Ethnic Discrimination 94
↓ Social Identity 88

Mirror Image 91
PN 88 **SC** 31645
R Human Figures Drawing 73
Mental Rotation 91
↓ Perceptual Discrimination 73
Self Perception 67
↓ Visual Perception 67

Mirroring 97
PN 0 **SC** 31647
SN Reflecting or emulating another person's behavior or other qualities in interactional or psychotherapeutic contexts. Also a technique in psychodrama.
B Psychotherapeutic Techniques 67
R ↓ Interpersonal Interaction 67
Psychodrama 67
↓ Psychotherapeutic Processes 67
Self Psychology 88

Misanthropy 73
PN 16 **SC** 31650
UF Misogyny
B Personality Traits 67

Misarticulation
Use Articulation Disorders

Misbehavior
Use Behavior Problems

Miscarriage
Use Spontaneous Abortion

Miscegenous Marriage
Use Interracial Marriage

Misconduct
Use Behavior Problems

Misdemeanors
Use Crime

Misdiagnosis 97
PN 0 **SC** 31705
R ↓ Diagnosis 67
Diagnosis Related Groups 88
Patient History 73

Misdiagnosis — (cont'd)
R Professional Liability 85
↓ Psychodiagnostic Typologies 67
↓ Screening 82

Misogyny
Use Misanthropy

Missionaries 73
PN 101 **SC** 31720
B Religious Personnel 73
R ↓ Clergy 73
↓ Educational Personnel 73
Evangelists 73
Lay Religious Personnel 73
Ministers (Religion) 73
Nuns 73
Priests 73

Mistakes
Use Errors

MMPI
Use Minn Multiphasic Personality Inven

Mnemonic Learning 73
PN 694 **SC** 31750
SN Use of artificial ways (e.g., imagery) to facilitate learning, memory, recognition, and recall of material learned.
B Learning 67
Learning Strategies 91
R Cues 67
Memory Training 94
Note Taking 91

Mobility (Geographical)
Use Geographical Mobility

Mobility (Occupational)
Use Occupational Mobility

Mobility (Social)
Use Social Mobility

Mobility Aids 78
PN 141 **SC** 31774
UF Seeing Eye Dogs
Tactual Maps
Wheelchairs
R ↓ Medical Therapeutic Devices 73
Physical Mobility 94

Moclobemide 97
PN 0 **SC** 31780
B Antidepressant Drugs 71
Monoamine Oxidase Inhibitors 73

Modeling
Use Simulation

Modeling Behavior
Use Imitation (Learning)

Models 67
PN 15543 **SC** 31805
SN Quantitative or descriptive representations of how systems function, or criteria used for comparison purposes. Not to be used for role models.
N Animal Models 88
Medical Model 78

Moderately Mentally Retarded
Use Trainable Mentally Retarded

Modern Language Aptitude Test 73
PN 4 **SC** 31820
B Aptitude Measures 67

Molindone 82
PN 32 **SC** 31833
SN Organic heterocyclic indole having antiserotonin properties and used as an antidepressant, sedative, and tranquilizer.
B Antidepressant Drugs 71
Neuroleptic Drugs 73
Sedatives 73
Serotonin Antagonists 73

Mollusca 73
PN 288 **SC** 31840
UF Gastropods
B Invertebrates 73
N Octopus 73
Snails 73

Monetary Incentives 73
PN 442 **SC** 31850
SN Money expected or promised in return for service or attainment which may encourage the continued occurrence of the activity being rewarded.
B Incentives 67
Motivation 67
R Monetary Rewards 73
↓ Needs 67

Monetary Rewards 73
PN 376 **SC** 31860
SN Money given in return for service or attainment which may act as reinforcement for the activity being rewarded.
B Rewards 67
R Monetary Incentives 73

Money 67
PN 993 **SC** 31870
R Budgets 97
Cost Containment 91
↓ Costs and Cost Analysis 73
Economics 85
Economy 73
Equity (Payment) 78
Funding 88
↓ Professional Fees 78
Resource Allocation 97

Mongolism
Use Downs Syndrome

Monitoring 73
PN 541 **SC** 31890
SN Systematic observation or recording of events, processes, or individuals.
B Attention 67
N Self Monitoring 82
Vigilance 67
R Selective Attention 73
↓ Tracking 67

Monkeys 67
PN 8291 **SC** 31900
B Primates (Nonhuman) 73

Monoamine Oxidase Inhibitors 73
PN 727 **SC** 31920
B Enzyme Inhibitors 85
N Iproniazid 73
Isocarboxazid 73
Moclobemide 97
Nialamide 73
Pargyline 73
Phenelzine 73

Monoamine Oxidase Inhibitors — (cont'd)
N Pheniprazine 73
Tranylcypromine 73
R ↓ Amine Oxidase Inhibitors 73
↓ Antidepressant Drugs 71
Monoamine Oxidases 73
↓ Tricyclic Antidepressant Drugs 97

Monoamine Oxidases 73
PN 506 SC 31930
B Oxidases 73
R ↓ Monoamine Oxidase Inhibitors 73

Monoamines (Brain)
Use Catecholamines

Monocular Vision 73
PN 594 SC 31940
B Visual Perception 67
R Motion Parallax 97

Monogamy 97
PN 0 SC 31945
SN Used for human or animal populations.
UF Marital Fidelity
B Family Structure 73
Marriage 67
Psychosexual Behavior 67
R Extramarital Intercourse 73
↓ Human Courtship 73
Polygamy 73

Monolingualism 73
PN 107 SC 31950
R ↓ Language 67

Monotony 78
PN 50 SC 31955
SN Quality of task or stimulation characterized by tedious or wearisome sameness and uniformity.
R Boredom 73

Monozygotic Twins 73
PN 785 SC 31960
UF Identical Twins
B Twins 67

Montessori Method 73
PN 63 SC 31970
SN Method of early childhood education developed by M. Montessori, stressing individual instruction and guidance and emphasizing practical life activities.
B Teaching Methods 67
R Discovery Teaching Method 73
Open Classroom Method 73

Mood Disorders
Use Affective Disturbances

Moodiness 73
PN 7 SC 31980
B Personality Traits 67

Moods
Use Emotional States

Mooney Problem Check List 73
PN 10 SC 32000
B Nonprojective Personality Measures 73

Moral Development 73
PN 2529 SC 32006
SN Process of acquiring ethical judgment.
B Psychogenesis 73
R Kohlberg (Lawrence) 91

Moral Development — (cont'd)
R Morality 67
↓ Personality Development 67
↓ Psychosocial Development 73

Morale 78
PN 490 SC 32008
SN Prevailing spirit or attitude of an individual or group characterized by self confidence and motivation and sense of purpose.
R ↓ Emotional States 73
↓ Emotions 67
Enthusiasm 73

Morality 67
PN 1915 SC 32010
SN Subjective or objective standards of right or wrong, based on societal norms or ethical principles. Use MORALITY or MORALS to access references prior to 1982.
UF Morals
R ↓ Ethics 67
Integrity 97
↓ Justice 73
Moral Development 73
Personal Values 73
↓ Religious Beliefs 73
Reputation 97
Shame 94
Social Values 73
↓ Values 67

Morals
SN Term discontinued in 1982. Use MORALS or MORALITY to access references prior to 1982.
Use Morality

Mores
Use Values

Morita Therapy 94
PN 12 SC 32035
B Psychotherapeutic Techniques 67

Morocco 88
PN 26 SC 32040
B Africa 67

Morphemes 73
PN 164 SC 32050
SN Minimum meaningful linguistic units that contain no smaller meaningful units.
R Morphology (Language) 73
Phonetics 67

Morphine 73
PN 2756 SC 32060
B Alkaloids 73
Analgesic Drugs 73
Dopamine Agonists 85
Opiates 73

Morphology 73
PN 612 SC 32070
SN Branch of biology that deals with the structure and form of plants and animals. Used for the scientific discipline or the morphological structure itself.
R ↓ Anatomy 67
Histology 73
↓ Physiology 67

Morphology (Language) 73
PN 283 SC 32080

Morphology (Language) — (cont'd)
SN Study of morphemes, including both their phonology and semantics. Used for the linguistic discipline or the specific morphological principles or characteristics of words. Compare MORPHEMES.
B Grammar 67
R Discourse Analysis 97
Morphemes 73
↓ Phonology 73
↓ Prosody 91
↓ Semantics 67
↓ Syntax 71
Words (Phonetic Units) 67

Mortality
Use Death and Dying

Mortality Rate 73
PN 1131 SC 32100
UF Death Rate
R ↓ Death and Dying 67
↓ Population 73

Mosaicism
Use Chromosome Disorders

Moslems
Use Muslims

Mother Absence 73
PN 225 SC 32120
SN From 1982, limited to human populations. For animals use ANIMAL MATERNAL DEPRIVATION.
B Parental Absence 73
R Patriarchy 73

Mother Child Communication 85
PN 645 SC 32125
SN Verbal or nonverbal communication between mother and child.
B Parent Child Communication 73
R Mother Child Relations 67

Mother Child Relations 67
PN 6612 SC 32130
SN From 1982, limited to human populations. For animals consider ANIMAL MATERNAL BEHAVIOR.
UF Maternal Behavior (Human)
B Parent Child Relations 67
R ↓ Childrearing Practices 67
Mother Child Communication 85
↓ Parental Attitudes 73
Parental Permissiveness 73
Parental Role 73
Postpartum Depression 73
Schizophrenogenic Mothers 73
Separation Individuation 82
Symbiotic Infantile Psychosis 73

Mothers 67
PN 9472 SC 32140
SN From 1982, limited to human populations. For animals consider ANIMAL MATERNAL BEHAVIOR.
B Human Females 73
Parents 67
N Adolescent Mothers 85
Schizophrenogenic Mothers 73
Single Mothers 94
Unwed Mothers 73
R Expectant Mothers 85

Moths 73
PN 97 SC 32150

Moths — (cont'd)
B Insects 67
R Larvae 73

Motion Parallax 97
PN 0 SC 32155
SN Monocular distance cues for motion perception based on observer movements and the resultant movements of objects in the visual field.
B Distance Perception 73
Motion Perception 67
R ↓ Depth Perception 67
Form and Shape Perception 67
Monocular Vision 73

Motion Perception 67
PN 3247 SC 32160
UF Movement Perception
B Spatial Perception 67
N ↓ Apparent Movement 67
Motion Parallax 97
R Direction Perception 97

Motion Pictures 73
PN 276 SC 32170
SN Use a more specific term if possible. Not used as a document type identifier.
B Audiovisual Communications Media 73
Mass Media 67
N Motion Pictures (Educational) 73
Motion Pictures (Entertainment) 73

Motion Pictures (Educational) 73
PN 138 SC 32180
SN Films produced for educational purposes. Not used as a document type identifier.
B Educational Audiovisual Aids 73
Motion Pictures 73

Motion Pictures (Entertainment) 73
PN 552 SC 32190
SN Not used as a document type identifier.
UF Movies
B Motion Pictures 73
R Drama 73
Photographic Art 73

Motion Sickness 73
PN 257 SC 32200
B Labyrinth Disorders 73

Motivation 67
PN 8858 SC 32210
UF Desires
Drive
N ↓ Achievement Motivation 67
Affiliation Motivation 67
Animal Motivation 67
Educational Incentives 73
Employee Motivation 73
Extrinsic Motivation 73
Fear of Success 78
Hunger 67
↓ Incentives 67
Intrinsic Motivation 73
Monetary Incentives 73
Procrastination 85
Sex Drive 73
Temptation 73
Thirst 67
R Activity Level 82
↓ Aspirations 67
↓ Commitment 85
Delay of Gratification 78
↓ Deprivation 67
Enthusiasm 73
↓ Exploratory Behavior 67
Goal Setting 97

Motivation — (cont'd)
R ↓ Goals 67
Instinctive Behavior 82
Instrumentality 91
Intention 88
Motivation Training 73
↓ Needs 67
Persistence 73
Planned Behavior 97
↓ Reinforcement 67
Satiation 67

Motivation Training 73
PN 88 SC 32220
UF Training (Motivation)
R ↓ Motivation 67

Motor Coordination 73
PN 750 SC 32230
UF Coordination (Motor)
B Motor Processes 67
R ↓ Motor Performance 73
Motor Skills 73
↓ Perceptual Motor Coordination 73
↓ Physical Agility 73

Motor Cortex 73
PN 495 SC 32240
UF Cortex (Motor)
B Frontal Lobe 73

Motor Development 73
PN 1296 SC 32250
B Physical Development 73
N Perceptual Motor Development 91
↓ Psychomotor Development 73
R Animal Development 78
↓ Childhood Development 67
↓ Developmental Age Groups 73
↓ Motor Processes 67
Physical Mobility 94

Motor Disorders
Use Nervous System Disorders

Motor Evoked Potentials
Use Somatosensory Evoked Potentials

Motor Neurons 73
PN 432 SC 32290
B Neurons 73
R ↓ Efferent Pathways 82

Motor Pathways
Use Efferent Pathways

Motor Performance 73
PN 4134 SC 32300
B Motor Processes 67
Performance 67
N Finger Tapping 73
Jumping 73
Running 73
Walking 73
R Motor Coordination 73

Motor Processes 67
PN 8227 SC 32310
N Activity Level 82
Animal Locomotion 82
↓ Exercise 73
Grasping 97
Jumping 73
Licking 88
Motor Coordination 73
↓ Motor Performance 73
Motor Skills 73

Motor Processes — (cont'd)
N ↓ Physical Agility 73
Physical Mobility 94
Rotational Behavior 94
Sucking 78
Swallowing 88
Swimming 73
Tonic Immobility 78
Tool Use 91
Wandering Behavior 91
R ↓ Efferent Pathways 82
↓ Motor Development 73
Muscle Tone 85
↓ Perceptual Motor Processes 67
Physical Restraint 82
Posture 73

Motor Skill Learning
Use Perceptual Motor Learning

Motor Skills 73
PN 932 SC 32330
B Motor Processes 67
Nonverbal Ability 88
R Motor Coordination 73
↓ Tracking 67

Motor Traffic Accidents 73
PN 942 SC 32340
UF Automobile Accidents
Traffic Accidents (Motor)
B Transportation Accidents 73
R Drivers 73
↓ Driving Behavior 67
Highway Safety 73
Pedestrian Accidents 73

Motor Vehicles 82
PN 132 SC 32350
SN Automotive vehicles not operated on rails.
UF Buses
Motorcycles
Trucks
B Ground Transportation 73
N Automobiles 73
R Drivers 73

Motorcycles
Use Motor Vehicles

Mourning
Use Grief

Mouse Killing
Use Muricide

Mouth (Anatomy) 67
PN 294 SC 32370
B Digestive System 67
R Lips (Face) 73
Salivary Glands 73
Teeth (Anatomy) 73
↓ Tongue 73

Movement Disorders 85
PN 271 SC 32375
SN Physically- or psychologically-based abnormalities in motor processes relating primarily to posture, coordination, or locomotion.
UF Dyspraxia
B Nervous System Disorders 67
N Apraxia 73
Ataxia 73
Athetosis 73
Catalepsy 73
Cataplexy 73
↓ Chorea 73
↓ Dyskinesia 73

Movement Disorders — (cont'd)
N Myasthenia Gravis 73
Myoclonia 73
↓ Paralysis 73
↓ Spasms 73
Tics 73
Torticollis 73
Tremor 73
R ↓ Muscular Disorders 73
↓ Musculoskeletal Disorders 73
↓ Neuromuscular Disorders 73
↓ Symptoms 67

Movement Perception
Use Motion Perception

Movement Therapy 97
PN 0 **SC** 32385
SN Therapeutic technique utilizing bodily movements and rhythmic exercises used to improve psychological and/or physical functioning of patients or clients.
B Treatment 67
R Art Therapy 73
↓ Creative Arts Therapy 94
Dance Therapy 73
↓ Exercise 73
Music Therapy 73
Recreation Therapy 73

Movies
Use Motion Pictures (Entertainment)

Mozambique 88
PN 7 **SC** 32430
B Africa 67

MPTP
Use Methylphenyltetrahydropyridine

MRI
Use Magnetic Resonance Imaging

Mucus 73
PN 20 **SC** 32440
B Body Fluids 73

Mueller Lyer Illusion 88
PN 61 **SC** 32439
B Illusions (Perception) 67

Multi Infarct Dementia 91
PN 194 **SC** 32442
UF Dementia (Multi Infarct)
B Vascular Dementia 97
R ↓ Cerebrovascular Disorders 73

Multicultural Education 88
PN 144 **SC** 32441
SN Educational program involving two or more ethnic or cultural groups designed to help participants define their own ethnic or cultural identity and to appreciate that of others. The primary purposes are to reduce prejudice and stereotyping, and to promote cultural pluralism.
B Education 67
R Bilingual Education 78
Cross Cultural Communication 97
Cultural Sensitivity 94
↓ Educational Programs 73
Multiculturalism 97

Multiculturalism 97
PN 0 **SC** 57500
UF Cultural Pluralism
R Cross Cultural Communication 97
Cross Cultural Differences 67
Cultural Assimilation 73

Multiculturalism — (cont'd)
R Cultural Deprivation 73
Cultural Sensitivity 94
↓ Culture (Anthropological) 67
↓ Culture Change 67
↓ Ethnic Groups 73
Minority Groups 67
Multicultural Education 88
↓ Racial and Ethnic Attitudes 82
Racial and Ethnic Differences 82
Racial and Ethnic Relations 82
↓ Sociocultural Factors 67

Multidimensional Scaling 82
PN 469 **SC** 32443
SN Set of psychological data analysis techniques that represent perceived stimuli in multidimensional spatial or pictorial configurations.
B Measurement 67
R ↓ Analysis 67
↓ Rating Scales 67
Scaling (Testing) 67

Multidisciplinary Research
Use Interdisciplinary Research

Multidisciplinary Treatment Approach
Use Interdisciplinary Treatment Approach

Multidrug Abuse
Use Polydrug Abuse

Multilingualism 73
PN 62 **SC** 32450
N Bilingualism 73
R Bilingual Education 78
English as Second Language 97
↓ Language 67

Multimodal Treatment Approach 91
PN 182 **SC** 32455
SN Use of different therapeutic techniques based on the theoretical principles from one medical or psychological specialty or discipline. Compare INTERDISCIPLINARY TREATMENT APPROACH.
B Treatment 67
R Eclectic Psychotherapy 94
Integrated Services 97
Interdisciplinary Treatment Approach 73

Multiple Births 73
PN 23 **SC** 32460
SN Birth of more than one child at the same time to the same parents. Also used to refer to the children themselves. Use a more specific term if possible. Limited to human populations.
B Siblings 67
N Triplets 73
↓ Twins 67

Multiple Choice (Testing Method) 73
PN 553 **SC** 32470
B Testing Methods 67

Multiple Personality
SN Term discontinued in 1997. Use MULTIPLE PERSONALITY to access references from 73–96.
Use Dissociative Identity Disorder

Multiple Regression 82
PN 219 **SC** 32485
SN Method of analyzing the collective and separate influences of two or more independent variables on the variation of a criterion variable.
B Multivariate Analysis 82
Statistical Regression 85
R Analysis of Covariance 73

Multiple Regression — (cont'd)
R Analysis of Variance 67
Linear Regression 73
Nonlinear Regression 73
Path Analysis 91
↓ Statistical Correlation 67

Multiple Sclerosis 73
PN 712 **SC** 32490
B Sclerosis (Nervous System) 73
R ↓ Myelitis 73

Multiple Therapy
Use Cotherapy

Multiply Disabled 97
PN 0 **SC** 32509
SN Use MULTIPLY HANDICAPPED to access references from 73–96.
UF Multiply Handicapped
B Disabled 97
N Deaf Blind 91

Multiply Handicapped
SN Term discontinued in 1997. Use MULTIPLY HANDICAPPED to access references from 73–96.
Use Multiply Disabled

Multivariate Analysis 82
PN 640 **SC** 32513
SN Any statistical technique designed to measure the influence of many independent variables acting simultaneously on more than one dependent variable.
UF Canonical Correlation
B Statistical Analysis 67
N ↓ Factor Analysis 67
Multiple Regression 82
Path Analysis 91
R Analysis of Covariance 73
Analysis of Variance 67
↓ Statistical Correlation 67
↓ Statistical Regression 85

Munchausen Syndrome 94
PN 23 **SC** 32517
SN A disorder characterized by plausible presentations of physical symptoms or an acute illness that are under the individual's control, and often resulting in multiple, unnecessary hospitalizations. Use FACTITIOUS DISORDERS to access references from 88-93.
UF Hospital Addiction Syndrome
B Factitious Disorders 88
R Malingering 73
Munchausen Syndrome by Proxy 97
↓ Psychosomatic Disorders 67

Munchausen Syndrome by Proxy 97
PN 0 **SC** 32519
SN A phenomenon in which symptoms of an acute illness are fabricated by an individual other than the patient (e.g., a caregiver or parent) resulting in habitual seeking of medical care.
R ↓ Child Abuse 71
Child Neglect 88
Munchausen Syndrome 94

Murder
Use Homicide

Muricide 88
PN 33 **SC** 32523
UF Mouse Killing
B Animal Aggressive Behavior 73

Muscarinic Drugs
Use Cholinergic Drugs

Muscimol 94
PN 23 **SC** 32525
SN Use GAMMA AMINOBUTYRIC ACID AGONISTS to access references from 85-93.
UF Pantherine
B Gamma Aminobutyric Acid Agonists 85
Ibotenic Acid 91

Muscle Contraction Headache 73
PN 405 **SC** 32530
UF Tension Headache
B Headache 73

Muscle Contractions 73
PN 497 **SC** 32540
UF Rigidity (Muscles)
R Muscle Relaxation 73
Muscle Tone 85
↓ Muscles 67
Parkinsonism 94
↓ Reflexes 71

Muscle Cramps
Use Muscular Disorders

Muscle Relaxation 73
PN 398 **SC** 32557
R Muscle Contractions 73
↓ Muscles 67
Progressive Relaxation Therapy 78
Relaxation 73
↓ Relaxation Therapy 78

Muscle Relaxation Therapy
Use Relaxation Therapy

Muscle Relaxing Drugs 73
PN 140 **SC** 32560
UF Mephenesin
Neuromuscular Blocking Drugs
B Drugs 67
N Baclofen 91
Curare 73
Diazepam 73
Meprobamate 73
Orphenadrine 73
Papaverine 73
Succinylcholine 73
Theophylline 73
Tubocurarine 73
R ↓ Anesthetic Drugs 73
↓ Anticonvulsive Drugs 73
↓ Antihypertensive Drugs 73
↓ Antispasmodic Drugs 73
↓ Benzodiazepines 78
↓ CNS Depressant Drugs 73
↓ Heart Rate Affecting Drugs 73
↓ Tranquilizing Drugs 67
Vasodilation 73

Muscle Spasms 73
PN 55 **SC** 32570
B Spasms 73
R ↓ Muscles 67

Muscle Tone 85
PN 47 **SC** 32575
R ↓ Motor Processes 67
Muscle Contractions 73
↓ Reflexes 71

Muscles 67
PN 1377 **SC** 32580

Muscles — (cont'd)
B Musculoskeletal System 73
N Abdominal Wall 73
Diaphragm (Anatomy) 73
Facial Muscles 73
Masticatory Muscles 73
Oculomotor Muscles 73
R Muscle Contractions 73
Muscle Relaxation 73
Muscle Spasms 73
↓ Tissues (Body) 73

Muscular Atrophy 73
PN 22 **SC** 32590
UF Atrophy (Muscular)
B Muscular Disorders 73

Muscular Disorders 73
PN 389 **SC** 32600
UF Cramps (Muscle)
Duchennes Disease
Dystonia
Fibromyalgia Syndrome
Muscle Cramps
B Musculoskeletal Disorders 73
N Cataplexy 73
Muscular Atrophy 73
Muscular Dystrophy 73
Myasthenia Gravis 73
Myoclonia 73
Myofascial Pain 91
Myotonia 73
Torticollis 73
R Chronic Fatigue Syndrome 97
↓ Movement Disorders 85
↓ Neuromuscular Disorders 73

Muscular Dystrophy 73
PN 107 **SC** 32610
UF Dystrophy (Muscular)
B Muscular Disorders 73
Neuromuscular Disorders 73
R Dysarthria 73
↓ Peripheral Nerve Disorders 73

Musculocutaneous Nerve
Use Spinal Nerves

Musculoskeletal Disorders 73
PN 223 **SC** 32630
UF Skeletomuscular Disorders
Temporomandibular Joint Syndrome
B Physical Disorders 97
N ↓ Bone Disorders 73
↓ Joint Disorders 73
↓ Muscular Disorders 73
R Hemiplegia 78
↓ Movement Disorders 85
↓ Musculoskeletal System 73
↓ Neuromuscular Disorders 73
↓ Paralysis 73
Paraplegia 78
Poliomyelitis 73
Quadriplegia 85
↓ Tuberculosis 73

Musculoskeletal System 73
PN 53 **SC** 32640
B Anatomical Systems 73
N Arm (Anatomy) 73
Bones 73
Feet (Anatomy) 73
↓ Fingers (Anatomy) 73
Hand (Anatomy) 67
Hips 73
Jaw 73
↓ Joints (Anatomy) 73
Leg (Anatomy) 73

Musculoskeletal System — (cont'd)
N ↓ Muscles 67
Skull 73
Spinal Column 73
Tendons 73
Thorax 73
R ↓ Musculoskeletal Disorders 73
↓ Nose 73

Music 67
PN 3029 **SC** 32650
UF Songs
B Arts 73
N Musical Instruments 73
Rock Music 91
R Music Perception 97
Musicians 91
↓ Rhythm 91
Singing 97
Tempo 97

Music Education 73
PN 776 **SC** 32660
B Curriculum 67

Music Perception 97
PN 0 **SC** 32665
B Auditory Perception 67
R ↓ Music 67
Musical Ability 73
↓ Pitch Perception 73
↓ Rhythm 91
Singing 97
Tempo 97

Music Therapy 73
PN 714 **SC** 32670
B Creative Arts Therapy 94
R Educational Therapy 97
Movement Therapy 97
Recreation Therapy 73

Musical Ability 73
PN 580 **SC** 32680
B Artistic Ability 73
R Music Perception 97

Musical Instruments 73
PN 139 **SC** 32690
UF Piano
B Music 67

Musicians 91
PN 185 **SC** 32695
B Artists 73
R ↓ Music 67

Muslims 97
PN 0 **SC** 32700
SN Use ISLAM to access references prior to 1997.
UF Moslems
B Religious Groups 97
R Islam 73

Mutations 73
PN 258 **SC** 32710
SN Individual, strain, or species genetic variation resulting from an abrupt or unusual change in gene structure. Also, an externally induced or naturally occurring change in gene characteristics that is propagated in subsequent divisions of the cell.
R ↓ Chromosomes 73
↓ Genetic Disorders 73
↓ Genetics 67
Translocation (Chromosome) 73

Mutilation (Self)
Use Self Mutilation

Mutism 73
PN 180 **SC** 32730
B Language Disorders 82
N Elective Mutism 73

Mutual Storytelling Technique 73
PN 41 **SC** 32740
UF Storytelling Technique
B Psychotherapeutic Techniques 67

Myasthenia 73
PN 8 **SC** 32750
SN Anomaly of the muscles, resulting in muscular debility, weakness, lack of tone, fatigue, or exhaustion.
B Asthenia 73

Myasthenia Gravis 73
PN 44 **SC** 32760
B Movement Disorders 85
Muscular Disorders 73
Neuromuscular Disorders 73
Peripheral Nerve Disorders 73

Myelin Sheath 73
PN 56 **SC** 32780
B Nerve Tissues 73

Myelitis 73
PN 6 **SC** 32790
B Central Nervous System Disorders 73
N Encephalomyelitis 73
Poliomyelitis 73
R ↓ Infectious Disorders 73
Multiple Sclerosis 73

Myelomeningocele
Use Spina Bifida

Myenteric Plexus
Use Autonomic Ganglia

Myers Briggs Type Indicator 73
PN 251 **SC** 32810
B Nonprojective Personality Measures 73

Myocardial Infarctions 73
PN 709 **SC** 32820
UF Infarctions (Myocardial)
B Heart Disorders 73
R Angina Pectoris 73
Coronary Thromboses 73

Myocardium 73
PN 15 **SC** 32830
B Heart 67

Myoclonia 73
PN 136 **SC** 32840
B Movement Disorders 85
Muscular Disorders 73

Myofascial Pain 91
PN 30 **SC** 32845
B Muscular Disorders 73
Pain 67
R ↓ Bruxism 85
Chronic Pain 85
↓ Psychosomatic Disorders 67
↓ Syndromes 73

Myopia 73
PN 99 **SC** 32850

Myopia — (cont'd)
UF Nearsightedness
B Refraction Errors 73

Myotonia 73
PN 29 **SC** 32860
B Muscular Disorders 73
R ↓ Congenital Disorders 73

Mysticism 67
PN 305 **SC** 32870
UF Visions (Mysticism)
B Philosophies 67
R Occultism 78
↓ Parapsychology 67
↓ Religious Beliefs 73
Religious Experiences 97
↓ Religious Practices 73
Witchcraft 73

Myths 67
PN 876 **SC** 32890
R Animism 73
Archetypes 91
Cultism 73
Ethnology 67
Folklore 91
↓ Literature 67
Metaphor 82
Storytelling 88
Transcultural Psychiatry 73

Myxedema
Use Hypothyroidism

N-Methyl-D-Aspartate 94
PN 337 **SC** 32905
UF NMDA
B Aspartic Acid 73

Nabilone
Use Cannabinoids

NAch
Use Achievement Motivation

Nail Biting 73
PN 61 **SC** 32920
B Habits 67

Nalorphine 73
PN 42 **SC** 32940
B Narcotic Antagonists 73

Naloxone 78
PN 1541 **SC** 32944
B Narcotic Antagonists 73

Naltrexone 88
PN 359 **SC** 32945
B Narcotic Antagonists 73

Names 85
PN 258 **SC** 32947
N Brand Names 78
R Labeling 78
Nouns 73

Naming 88
PN 638 **SC** 32948
SN Process of identifying an object or concept with a word or phrase.
B Cognitive Processes 67
R Cognitive Mediation 67
Object Recognition 97

Napping 94
PN 17 **SC** 32949
B Sleep 67
R Sleep Onset 73
Sleep Wake Cycle 85

Narcissism 67
PN 1123 **SC** 32950
SN Self-love in which all sources of pleasure are unrealistically believed to emanate from within oneself, resulting in a false sense of omnipotence, and in which the libido is no longer attached to external love objects, but is redirected to one's self.
B Personality Traits 67
R Autoeroticism 97
Egocentrism 78
Grandiosity 94
↓ Mental Disorders 67
Narcissistic Personality 73
Selfishness 73

Narcissistic Personality 73
PN 587 **SC** 32960
SN Personality disorder characterized by excessive self-love, egocentrism, grandiosity, exhibitionism, excessive needs for attention, and sensitivity to criticism.
B Personality Disorders 67
R Antisocial Personality 73
Narcissism 67

Narcoanalysis 73
PN 18 **SC** 32970
SN Sleep-like state induced by medication or hypnosis and used in the treatment of mental disorders.
B Drug Therapy 67
Organic Therapies 73
N Sleep Treatment 73

Narcoanalytic Drugs
SN Term discontinued in 1997. Use NARCOANALYTIC DRUGS to access references from 73–96.
Use Drugs

Narcolepsy 73
PN 252 **SC** 32990
UF Paroxysmal Sleep
B Sleep Disorders 73
R Cataplexy 73
Hypersomnia 94

Narcosis 73
PN 66 **SC** 33000
B Toxic Disorders 73
R ↓ Narcotic Drugs 73

Narcotic Agonists 88
PN 414 **SC** 32995
UF Opiate Agonists
B Drugs 67
N Pentazocine 91
R ↓ Narcotic Drugs 73

Narcotic Antagonists 73
PN 702 **SC** 33010
UF Opiate Antagonists
Opioid Antagonists
B Drugs 67
N Nalorphine 73
Naloxone 78
Naltrexone 88
R ↓ Narcotic Drugs 73

Narcotic Drugs 73
PN 415 **SC** 33020

Narcotic Drugs — (cont'd)
B Drugs [67]
N Apomorphine [73]
Atropine [73]
Meperidine [73]
Methadone [73]
↓ Opiates [73]
R ↓ Analgesic Drugs [73]
↓ Anesthetic Drugs [73]
↓ Anticonvulsive Drugs [73]
↓ Cannabis [73]
↓ CNS Depressant Drugs [73]
↓ Dopamine Antagonists [82]
↓ Emetic Drugs [73]
↓ Hypnotic Drugs [73]
Narcosis [73]
↓ Narcotic Agonists [88]
↓ Narcotic Antagonists [73]
↓ Tranquilizing Drugs [67]

Narcotics Anonymous
Use Twelve Step Programs

Narratives [97]
PN 0 **SC** 33025
SN Construction or reconstruction of an event or story. Not a document type identifier.
B Verbal Communication [67]
R ↓ Biography [67]
Creative Writing [94]
Life Review [91]
↓ Literature [67]
Storytelling [88]

Nasal Mucosa [73]
PN 33 **SC** 33030
B Membranes [73]
Nose [73]
N Olfactory Mucosa [73]

National Guardsmen [73]
PN 35 **SC** 33040
B Military Personnel [67]
R Air Force Personnel [67]
Army Personnel [67]
Volunteer Military Personnel [73]
↓ Volunteer Personnel [73]

Nationalism [67]
PN 140 **SC** 33050
B Political Attitudes [73]

Native Americans
Use American Indians

Natural Childbirth [78]
PN 35 **SC** 33056
UF Childbirth (Natural)
B Birth [67]
R Childbirth Training [78]

Natural Disasters [73]
PN 388 **SC** 33060
SN Calamity caused by natural forces resulting in substantial damage, loss, and distress.
B Disasters [73]
R Emergency Services [73]
↓ Stress [67]

Natural Family
Use Biological Family

Natural Selection [97]
PN 0 **SC** 33073

Natural Selection — (cont'd)
SN Natural evolutionary process that results in the survival of organisms best suited to changing living conditions through the perpetuation of desirable genetic qualities and the elimination of undesirable ones. Consider DARWINISM to access references from 73–96.
B Darwinism [73]
R ↓ Genetics [67]
Theory of Evolution [67]

Nature Nurture [94]
PN 65 **SC** 33075
SN Debatable issue concerning the controversial role of genetics or heredity versus environment or experience in normal or abnormal developmental processes.
R Behavioral Genetics [94]
↓ Environment [67]
↓ Genetics [67]
↓ Human Development [67]
Predisposition [73]
↓ Psychogenesis [73]

Nausea [73]
PN 170 **SC** 33080
B Symptoms [67]
R ↓ Antiemetic Drugs [73]
↓ Eating Disorders [97]
Migraine Headache [73]
Vomiting [73]

Navigators (Aircraft)
Use Aerospace Personnel

Navy Personnel [67]
PN 954 **SC** 33100
B Military Personnel [67]
R Draftees [73]

Nazism
Use Fascism

Near Death Experiences [85]
PN 206 **SC** 33105
SN Psychological and sensory phenomena reported by persons who were near clinical death.
B Parapsychological Phenomena [73]
R ↓ Death and Dying [67]
↓ Experiences (Events) [73]
↓ Hallucinations [67]
Out of Body Experiences [88]

Nearsightedness
Use Myopia

Neck (Anatomy) [73]
PN 117 **SC** 33120
B Anatomy [67]

Need Achievement
Use Achievement Motivation

Need for Affiliation
Use Affiliation Motivation

Need for Approval [97]
PN 0 **SC** 33160
B Personality Traits [67]
R ↓ Needs [67]
Social Acceptance [67]
Social Approval [67]
Social Desirability [67]

Need for Cognition [97]
PN 0 **SC** 33167

Need for Cognition — (cont'd)
B Personality Traits [67]
R Cognition [67]
Intrinsic Motivation [73]
↓ Needs [67]

Need Satisfaction [73]
PN 508 **SC** 33170
B Satisfaction [73]
R ↓ Needs [67]
Psychological Needs [97]

Needle Sharing [94]
PN 47 **SC** 33175
R ↓ Drug Abuse [73]
↓ Drug Usage [71]
Intravenous Drug Usage [94]
Intravenous Injections [73]
Sharing (Social Behavior) [78]

Needs [67]
PN 2954 **SC** 33180
N Health Service Needs [97]
Psychological Needs [97]
R ↓ Achievement Motivation [67]
Affiliation Motivation [67]
Craving [97]
Extrinsic Motivation [73]
↓ Goals [67]
↓ Incentives [67]
Intrinsic Motivation [73]
Monetary Incentives [73]
↓ Motivation [67]
Need for Approval [97]
Need for Cognition [97]
Need Satisfaction [73]
Needs Assessment [85]
Nurturance [85]
Special Needs [94]

Needs Assessment [85]
PN 866 **SC** 33185
SN Systematic identification of needs of an individual or a group.
B Evaluation [67]
Measurement [67]
R ↓ Case Management [91]
Geriatric Assessment [97]
↓ Health Care Delivery [78]
Health Service Needs [97]
Intake Interview [94]
↓ Needs [67]
↓ Psychological Assessment [97]
Psychological Needs [97]
Special Needs [94]
↓ Surveys [67]
↓ Treatment Planning [97]

Negative and Positive Symptoms
Use Positive and Negative Symptoms

Negative Reinforcement [73]
PN 319 **SC** 33200
SN A stimulus or stimulus situation that, when withdrawn or discontinued following a response, increases the probability of occurrence of that response. Consider also ESCAPE CONDITIONING.
B Reinforcement [67]

Negative Therapeutic Reaction [97]
PN 0 **SC** 33205
SN In psychoanalysis, after a period of successful and constructive treatment, the worsening of a patient's symptoms and neurotic behavior.
B Psychotherapeutic Processes [67]
R Countertransference [73]
↓ Psychoanalysis [67]

Negative Therapeutic Reaction — (cont'd)
R Psychotherapeutic Resistance [73]
Psychotherapeutic Transference [67]

Negative Transfer [73]
PN 185 **SC** 33210
SN Previous learning or practice that hinders the acquisition of new material or skills as the result of dissimilar characteristics of the prior and current learning situation.
B Transfer (Learning) [67]

Negativism [73]
PN 173 **SC** 33220
SN State of mind or behavior characterized by extreme skepticism and persistent opposition or resistance to outside suggestions or advice.
B Personality Traits [67]
R Cynicism [73]
Pessimism [73]

Negotiation [73]
PN 775 **SC** 33230
B Interpersonal Communication [73]
N Bargaining [73]
R ↓ Conflict Resolution [82]
Mediation [88]

Negroes
SN Term discontinued in 1982. Use NEGROES to access references from 67–81.
Use Blacks

Neighborhoods [73]
PN 515 **SC** 33260
B Communities [67]

Nembutal
Use Pentobarbital

NEO Personality Inventory [97]
PN 0 **SC** 33275
B Personality Measures [67]
R Five Factor Personality Model [97]

NeoFreudian School
Use Neopsychoanalytic School

Neologisms [73]
PN 28 **SC** 33290
B Vocabulary [67]
R Words (Phonetic Units) [67]

Neonatal Development [73]
PN 501 **SC** 33320
SN Process of physical, cognitive, personality, and psychosocial growth occurring during the first month of life. Use a more specific term if possible.
B Infant Development [73]
R ↓ Physical Development [73]
↓ Psychogenesis [73]

Neonatal Disorders [73]
PN 89 **SC** 33330
B Physical Disorders [97]
N Amaurotic Familial Idiocy [73]
Anencephaly [73]
Cleft Palate [67]
Crying Cat Syndrome [73]
Downs Syndrome [67]
Klinefelters Syndrome [73]
Phenylketonuria [73]
Turners Syndrome [73]
R ↓ Apnea [73]
Birth Injuries [73]
↓ Congenital Disorders [73]
Hydrocephaly [73]

Neonatal Disorders — (cont'd)
R Microcephaly [73]
Rh Incompatibility [73]
Sleep Apnea [91]

Neonates [67]
PN 2886 **SC** 33360
SN Ages 0 through 1 month. Application of terms designating age is mandatory for ages 0–17 years.
UF Newborn Infants
B Infants [67]
R Birth Weight [85]
Childhood [84]

Neonates (Animal)
Use Infants (Animal)

Neonaticide
Use Infanticide

Neophobia [85]
PN 101 **SC** 33368
SN Fearful or cautious exploration or reaction to novel objects, situations, or stimuli. Usually examined in subhuman species.
R Animal Exploratory Behavior [73]
Avoidance [67]
↓ Fear [67]
Instinctive Behavior [82]
Stimulus Novelty [73]

Neoplasms [67]
PN 3366 **SC** 33370
UF Cancers
Carcinomas
Malignant Neoplasms
Sarcomas
Tumors
B Physical Disorders [97]
N Benign Neoplasms [73]
Breast Neoplasms [73]
Endocrine Neoplasms [73]
Leukemias [73]
↓ Nervous System Neoplasms [73]
Terminal Cancer [73]
R Antineoplastic Drugs [82]
↓ Digestive System Disorders [73]
↓ Gastrointestinal Disorders [73]
↓ Liver Disorders [73]

Neopsychoanalytic School [73]
PN 32 **SC** 33380
SN School of psychoanalysis originating with Jung and Adler which differs from Freudian psychoanalysis in emphasizing the importance of social and cultural factors in development of an individual's personality.
UF NeoFreudian School
B History of Psychology [67]
N Individual Psychology [73]
↓ Jungian Psychology [73]
R Erikson (Erik) [91]
Freud (Sigmund) [67]
Freudian Psychoanalytic School [73]
↓ Psychoanalytic Theory [67]

Neostigmine [73]
PN 38 **SC** 33390
UF Proserine
B Cholinesterase Inhibitors [73]
Cholinomimetic Drugs [73]
R Bromides [73]

Nepal [91]
PN 27 **SC** 33395
B Asia [73]

Nerve (Abducens)
Use Abducens Nerve

Nerve (Accessory)
Use Cranial Nerves

Nerve (Acoustic)
Use Acoustic Nerve

Nerve (Facial)
Use Facial Nerve

Nerve Cells
Use Neurons

Nerve Endings [73]
PN 32 **SC** 33450
B Nervous System [67]
N ↓ Neural Receptors [73]
Proprioceptors [73]
Synapses [73]
Thermoreceptors [73]

Nerve Growth Factor [94]
PN 42 **SC** 33455
SN Polypeptide proteins that stimulate growth and development of peripheral, sympathetic, and sensory neurons.
B Peptides [73]
R ↓ Amino Acids [73]
↓ Nervous System [67]
Neural Development [85]
↓ Neurons [73]

Nerve Tissues [73]
PN 71 **SC** 33460
B Nervous System [67]
Tissues (Body) [73]
N Myelin Sheath [73]
R ↓ Neurons [73]

Nerves (Adrenergic)
Use Adrenergic Nerves

Nerves (Cholinergic)
Use Cholinergic Nerves

Nerves (Cranial)
Use Cranial Nerves

Nerves (Peripheral)
Use Peripheral Nervous System

Nerves (Spinal)
Use Spinal Nerves

Nervous Breakdown
Use Mental Disorders

Nervous System [67]
PN 509 **SC** 33530
B Anatomical Systems [73]
N ↓ Central Nervous System [67]
↓ Ganglia [73]
↓ Nerve Endings [73]
↓ Nerve Tissues [73]
↓ Neurons [73]
↓ Peripheral Nervous System [73]
↓ Receptive Fields [85]
R Afferent Stimulation [73]
Instinctive Behavior [82]
Nerve Growth Factor [94]
↓ Nervous System Disorders [67]
Neural Development [85]
Neural Networks [91]

Nervous System — (cont'd)
R Neural Plasticity [94]
↓ Stereotaxic Techniques [73]

Nervous System Disorders [67]
PN 3767 SC 33540
UF Motor Disorders
Neuroinfections
Neurological Disorders
Neuropathy
B Physical Disorders [97]
N Autonomic Nervous System Disorders [73]
↓ Central Nervous System Disorders [73]
↓ Convulsions [67]
Hyperkinesis [73]
↓ Movement Disorders [85]
↓ Nervous System Neoplasms [73]
↓ Neuromuscular Disorders [73]
↓ Peripheral Nerve Disorders [73]
↓ Sclerosis (Nervous System) [73]
R ↓ Cerebrovascular Disorders [73]
Developmental Disabilities [82]
Extrapyramidal Symptoms [94]
Hemianopia [73]
Influenza [73]
Malaria [73]
↓ Nervous System [67]
Nystagmus [73]
Parkinsonism [94]
↓ Symptoms [67]
↓ Tuberculosis [73]

Nervous System Neoplasms [73]
PN 16 SC 33550
B Neoplasms [67]
Nervous System Disorders [67]
N Brain Neoplasms [73]

Nervous System Plasticity
Use Neural Plasticity

Nervousness [73]
PN 47 SC 33560
B Personality Traits [67]

Nest Building [73]
PN 463 SC 33570
B Animal Ethology [67]
R ↓ Animal Mating Behavior [67]

Netherlands [73]
PN 899 SC 33580
B Europe [73]

Netherlands Antilles [88]
PN 2 SC 33590
B West Indies [73]

Networks (Social)
Use Social Networks

Neural Analyzers [73]
PN 20 SC 33600
SN The peripheral sensory receptors or nerve endings (e.g., visual analyzer, acoustic analyzer) that select and transform stimuli and their associated projections and terminations in the central nervous system where synthesis of the transformations occurs.
B Central Nervous System [67]

Neural Development [85]
PN 976 SC 33605
SN Functional and morphological development of central and peripheral nervous systems and supportive tissue.
UF Neural Regeneration
Reinnervation

Neural Development — (cont'd)
B Physical Development [73]
R Animal Development [78]
Nerve Growth Factor [94]
↓ Nervous System [67]
Neural Plasticity [94]
Neural Transplantation [85]

Neural Lesions [73]
PN 796 SC 33610
SN Not defined prior to 1982. From 1982, limited to experimentally induced neural lesions and used primarily for animal populations.
B Lesions [67]

Neural Networks [91]
PN 1003 SC 33612
SN Computer simulation that duplicates the neural structure and cognitive processes of the human or animal brain.
B Artificial Intelligence [82]
Computer Simulation [73]
R Connectionism [94]
↓ Nervous System [67]
Neuroanatomy [67]

Neural Pathways [82]
PN 656 SC 33615
SN Collections of central or peripheral neural fibers having a common neurological function and serving to connect neuroanatomical systems such as sensory or motor mechanisms or central nervous system nuclei.
B Central Nervous System [67]
Peripheral Nervous System [73]
N ↓ Afferent Pathways [82]
Corpus Callosum [73]
↓ Efferent Pathways [82]
Fornix [82]
↓ Limbic System [73]
Optic Chiasm [73]
Optic Tract [82]
Reticular Formation [67]

Neural Plasticity [94]
PN 118 SC 33617
SN Change in reactivity of the nervous system and its components as a result of constant successive activations.
UF Nervous System Plasticity
R ↓ Nervous System [67]
Neural Development [85]
Postactivation Potentials [85]
↓ Receptive Fields [85]

Neural Receptors [73]
PN 3011 SC 33620
UF Receptors (Neural)
B Nerve Endings [73]
N Baroreceptors [73]
Chemoreceptors [73]
Mechanoreceptors [73]
Nociceptors [85]
↓ Photoreceptors [73]
Proprioceptors [73]
Thermoreceptors [73]
R Receptor Binding [85]

Neural Regeneration
Use Neural Development

Neural Transplantation [85]
PN 243 SC 33628
R Neural Development [85]
Organ Transplantation [73]
Tissue Donation [91]

Neuralgia [73]
PN 41 SC 33630

Neuralgia — (cont'd)
B Pain [67]
Peripheral Nerve Disorders [73]
N Trigeminal Neuralgia [73]

Neurasthenic Neurosis [73]
PN 96 SC 33640
B Neurosis [67]
R ↓ Asthenia [73]

Neuroanatomy [67]
PN 1941 SC 33660
SN Branch of neurology concerned with the anatomy of the nervous system. Used for the scientific discipline or the anatomical structures themselves.
B Neurosciences [73]
R ↓ Anatomy [67]
Neural Networks [91]

Neurobiology [73]
PN 517 SC 33670
SN Biology of the nervous system. Used for the scientific discipline or the neurobiological processes themselves.
B Biology [67]
Neurosciences [73]
R Biological Psychiatry [94]

Neurochemistry [73]
PN 6591 SC 33680
SN Chemical makeup and metabolism of nervous tissue. Used for the scientific discipline or the neurochemical processes themselves.
UF Brain Metabolism
B Biochemistry [67]
Neurosciences [73]
N Neuroendocrinology [85]
Receptor Binding [85]
R Blood Brain Barrier [94]
Glucose Metabolism [94]

Neurodermatitis [73]
PN 27 SC 33690
B Dermatitis [73]
Psychosomatic Disorders [67]
R Allergic Skin Disorders [73]

Neuroendocrinology [85]
PN 553 SC 33695
SN Study of the biological, chemical, and physical relations between the nervous system and endocrine glands. Used for the scientific discipline or neuroendocrinological processes themselves.
B Endocrinology [73]
Neurochemistry [73]
Neurophysiology [73]

Neuroinfections
Use Infectious Disorders AND Nervous System Disorders

Neurokinins [97]
PN 0 SC 33705
B Amino Acids [73]
Anti Inflammatory Drugs [82]
Neurotransmitters [85]
Peptides [73]
N Substance P [85]

Neuroleptic Drugs [73]
PN 3934 SC 33710
SN Use NEUROLEPTIC DRUGS, ANTIPSYCHOTIC DRUGS, ANTISCHIZOPHRENIC DRUGS, or the specific tranquilizing drugs, neuroleptic drugs, or other appropriate drug classes to access references from 73–81.

Neuroleptic Drugs — (cont'd)
UF Antipsychotic Drugs
Antischizophrenic Drugs
Major Tranquilizers
B Tranquilizing Drugs 67
N Clozapine 91
Molindone 82
Nialamide 73
Reserpine 67
Risperidone 97
Spiroperidol 91
Sulpiride 73
Tetrabenazine 73
R Neuroleptic Malignant Syndrome 88
Prostaglandins 82
Tardive Dyskinesia 88

Neuroleptic Malignant Syndrome 88
PN 268 SC 33715
B Syndromes 73
Toxic Disorders 73
R ↓ Drug Therapy 67
↓ Neuroleptic Drugs 73
↓ Side Effects (Drug) 73

Neurolinguistic Programing 88
PN 60 SC 33718
SN R. Bandler's model of techniques and strategies for interpersonal communication based on elements of transformational grammar and preferred sensory representations for learning and self expression. Also, self intervention method in humanistic psychology aimed at personal growth and human potential.
R ↓ Cognitive Style 67
↓ Humanistic Psychology 85
↓ Interpersonal Communication 73
Neurolinguistics 91
Perceptual Style 73

Neurolinguistics 91
PN 31 SC 33719
SN Study of the neurological mechanisms involved in the development, acquisition, and use of language. Used for the scientific discipline or the neurolinguistic processes themselves.
B Linguistics 73
R ↓ Language 67
↓ Language Disorders 82
Neurolinguistic Programing 88
Psycholinguistics 67
↓ Verbal Communication 67

Neurological Disorders
Use Nervous System Disorders

Neurologists 73
PN 58 SC 33730
UF Neuropathologists
B Physicians 67
R Surgeons 73

Neurology 67
PN 4986 SC 33740
SN Scientific discipline dealing with the anatomy, physiology, and organic diseases of the nervous system. Used for the scientific discipline or the neurological findings themselves.
B Medical Sciences 67
Neurosciences 73
R Neuropathology 73
↓ Neurosurgery 73

Neuromuscular Blocking Drugs
Use Muscle Relaxing Drugs

Neuromuscular Disorders 73
PN 146 SC 33760

Neuromuscular Disorders — (cont'd)
B Nervous System Disorders 67
N Cataplexy 73
Gilles de la Tourette Disorder 73
Muscular Dystrophy 73
Myasthenia Gravis 73
↓ Paralysis 73
Parkinsons Disease 73
R ↓ Dyskinesia 73
Hyperkinesis 73
↓ Movement Disorders 85
↓ Muscular Disorders 73
↓ Musculoskeletal Disorders 73
↓ Sclerosis (Nervous System) 73
↓ Spinal Cord Injuries 73

Neurons 73
PN 2629 SC 33770
UF Nerve Cells
B Cells (Biology) 73
Nervous System 67
N Axons 73
Dendrites 73
Ganglion Cells (Retina) 85
Motor Neurons 73
Purkinje Cells 94
↓ Sensory Neurons 73
R Nerve Growth Factor 94
↓ Nerve Tissues 73
Visual Receptive Fields 82

Neuropathologists
Use Neurologists

Neuropathology 73
PN 1301 SC 33790
SN Branch of medicine dealing with morphological and other aspects of nervous system disorders. Used for the scientific discipline or the neuropathological findings themselves.
B Neurosciences 73
Pathology 73
R Neurology 67

Neuropathy
Use Nervous System Disorders

Neuropeptides
Use Peptides

Neurophysiology 73
PN 2822 SC 33810
SN Physiology of the nervous system. Used for the scientific discipline or the neurophysiological processes themselves.
B Neurosciences 73
Physiology 67
N Neuroendocrinology 85
Receptor Binding 85

Neuropsychiatrists
Use Psychiatrists

Neuropsychiatry 73
PN 404 SC 33830
SN Medical specialty that combines psychiatry and neurology. Used for the scientific discipline or the neuropsychiatric findings themselves.
B Neurosciences 73
Psychiatry 67
R Biological Psychiatry 94

Neuropsychological Assessment 82
PN 2695 SC 33835
SN Use of tests, including intelligence, motor, and lateralization measures, to diagnose brain damage or other neurological dysfunction.

Neuropsychological Assessment — (cont'd)
B Psychological Assessment 97
N Halstead Reitan Neuropsych Battery 91
Luria Nebraska Neuropsych Battery 91
Mini Mental State Examination 94
Wechsler Memory Scale 88
Wisconsin Card Sorting Test 94
R Bender Gestalt Test 67
Benton Revised Visual Retention Test 73
Body Sway Testing 73
↓ Brain Damage 67
Cognitive Assessment 97
↓ Diagnosis 67
Memory for Designs Test 73
↓ Neuropsychological Rehabilitation 97
↓ Testing 67
Traumatic Brain Injury 97

Neuropsychological Rehabilitation 97
PN 0 SC 33837
B Rehabilitation 67
N Cognitive Rehabilitation 85
R Memory Training 94
↓ Neuropsychological Assessment 82

Neuropsychology 73
PN 3150 SC 33840
SN Branch of clinical psychology emphasizing the relationship between brain and behavior, including the diagnosis of brain pathology using cognitive or psychological tests. Used for the discipline or the neuropsychological functions themselves.
B Neurosciences 73
Physiological Psychology 67
R Psychoneuroimmunology 91

Neurosciences 73
PN 156 SC 33850
SN Scientific disciplines concerned with the development, structure, function, chemistry, and pathology of the nervous system.
B Sciences 67
N Neuroanatomy 67
Neurobiology 73
↓ Neurochemistry 73
Neurology 67
Neuropathology 73
↓ Neurophysiology 73
Neuropsychiatry 73
Neuropsychology 73
R ↓ Medical Sciences 67

Neurosis 67
PN 4300 SC 33860
UF Psychoneurosis
B Mental Disorders 67
N ↓ Affective Disturbances 67
Childhood Neurosis 73
Experimental Neurosis 73
Neurasthenic Neurosis 73
Neurotic Depressive Reaction 73
Occupational Neurosis 73
Traumatic Neurosis 73
R Anhedonia 85
Borderline States 78
↓ Minor Tranquilizers 73

Neurosurgeons
Use Surgeons

Neurosurgery 73
PN 525 SC 33890
B Surgery 71
N Commissurotomy 85
Decerebration 73
Decortication (Brain) 73
Hemispherectomy 73
↓ Psychosurgery 73

Neurosurgery — (cont'd)
N Pyramidotomy [73]
Sympathectomy [73]
Tractotomy [73]
Vagotomy [73]
R Neurology [67]

Neurosyphilis [73]
PN 29 SC 33900
B Central Nervous System Disorders [73]
Syphilis [73]
R General Paresis [73]

Neurotensin [85]
PN 115 SC 33905
B Neurotransmitters [85]
Peptides [73]

Neurotic Depressive Reaction [73]
PN 325 SC 33910
SN Major depressive episode including some interference in social and occupational functioning.
UF Depressive Reaction (Neurotic)
B Major Depression [88]
Neurosis [67]
R Reactive Depression [73]

Neuroticism [73]
PN 1422 SC 33915
SN Personality trait that contrasts adjustment or emotional stability with maladjustment. Experience of anxiety, anger, disgust, sadness, embarrassment, and a variety of other negative emotions.
B Personality Traits [67]
R Emotional Inferiority [73]
Emotional Instability [73]
Emotional Stability [73]
Emotionality (Personality) [73]
Five Factor Personality Model [97]

Neurotoxins [82]
PN 792 SC 33920
SN Bacterial, chemical, or pharmacological substances that are destructive to nerve tissue.
B Poisons [73]
N ↓ Ibotenic Acid [91]
Methylphenyltetrahydropyridine [94]
R Antibodies [73]
Drug Interactions [82]
↓ Insecticides [73]
Kainic Acid [88]
↓ Toxic Disorders [73]
Toxicity [73]

Neurotransmitters [85]
PN 515 SC 33924
SN Chemical substances, synthesized and released by nerve cells, or glandular hormones that excite or inhibit other nerve, muscle, or gland cells by producing a brief alteration in the postsynaptic membrane of the receiving cell. Use a more specific term if possible.
N Acetylcholine [73]
↓ Aspartic Acid [73]
↓ Catecholamines [73]
Cholecystokinin [82]
↓ Endorphins [82]
Gamma Aminobutyric Acid [78]
Glutamic Acid [73]
Glycine [73]
Histamine [73]
↓ Neurokinins [97]
Neurotensin [85]
Serotonin [73]
Substance P [85]
R ↓ Amino Acids [73]
↓ Peptides [73]

Neutrality (Psychotherapeutic)
Use Psychotherapeutic Neutrality

Never Married [94]
PN 16 SC 33926
B Marital Status [73]
R ↓ Single Parents [78]
Single Persons [73]
Unwed Mothers [73]

New Guinea
SN Term discontinued in 1982. Use NEW GUINEA to access references from 73–81.
Use Papua New Guinea

New Zealand [73]
PN 639 SC 33930
R ↓ South Pacific [78]

Newborn Infants
Use Neonates

News Media [97]
PN 0 SC 33945
B Mass Media [67]
N Newspapers [73]
R Journalists [73]
Radio [73]
↓ Television [67]

Newsletters (Professional)
Use Scientific Communication

Newspapers [73]
PN 348 SC 33960
B News Media [97]
Printed Communications Media [73]

Niacin
Use Nicotinic Acid

Niacinamide
Use Nicotinamide

Nialamide [73]
PN 40 SC 33990
B Amine Oxidase Inhibitors [73]
Antidepressant Drugs [71]
Monoamine Oxidase Inhibitors [73]
Neuroleptic Drugs [73]

Nicaragua [88]
PN 19 SC 33995
B Central America [73]

Nicotinamide [73]
PN 26 SC 34000
UF Niacinamide
Nicotinic Acid Amide
B Vitamins [73]
R Nicotinic Acid [73]
Pellagra [73]

Nicotine [73]
PN 1314 SC 34010
UF Tobacco (Drug)
B Alkaloids [73]
Cholinergic Blocking Drugs [73]
Ganglion Blocking Drugs [73]
R ↓ Insecticides [73]
Nicotine Withdrawal [97]
Smokeless Tobacco [94]
Tobacco Smoking [67]

Nicotine Withdrawal [97]
PN 0 SC 34015

Nicotine Withdrawal — (cont'd)
B Drug Withdrawal [73]
R Nicotine [73]
Smokeless Tobacco [94]
Smoking Cessation [88]
Tobacco Smoking [67]

Nicotinic Acid [73]
PN 60 SC 34020
UF Niacin
B Acids [73]
Vasodilator Drugs [73]
Vitamins [73]
R Nicotinamide [73]

Nicotinic Acid Amide
Use Nicotinamide

Nictitating Membrane [73]
PN 274 SC 34040
SN Fold of transparent or semitransparent mucous membrane present in many vertebrates that can be drawn over the eye like a third eyelid. This membrane cleans and moistens the cornea without occluding light.
B Membranes [73]

Niger [91]
PN 5 SC 34043
B Africa [67]

Nigeria [82]
PN 706 SC 34045
B Africa [67]

Night Terrors
Use Sleep Disorders

Nightmares [73]
PN 219 SC 34050
B Dreaming [67]
R Dream Content [73]

Nihilism [73]
PN 10 SC 34060
B Philosophies [67]
R Fatalism [73]
Pessimism [73]

Nitrazepam [78]
PN 51 SC 34066
B Anticonvulsive Drugs [73]
Benzodiazepines [78]
Hypnotic Drugs [73]
Sedatives [73]

Nitrogen [73]
PN 115 SC 34070

NMDA
Use N-Methyl-D-Aspartate

Nociception
Use Pain Perception

Nociceptors [85]
PN 100 SC 34080
UF Pain Receptors
B Neural Receptors [73]
Sensory Neurons [73]

Nocturnal Behavior (Animal)
Use Animal Nocturnal Behavior

Nocturnal Emission [73]
PN 6 **SC** 34100
B Male Orgasm [73]

Nocturnal Teeth Grinding [73]
PN 43 **SC** 34110
SN Use NOCTURNAL TEETH GRINDING to access references to BRUXISM from 73–84.
B Bruxism [85]
R ↓ Sleep [67]

Noise (Sound)
Use Auditory Stimulation

Noise Effects [73]
PN 1234 **SC** 34150
SN Behavioral, physiological, or psychological effects of environmental or experimentally manipulated noise on an organism.
B Environmental Effects [73]
R Acoustics [97]
Pollution [73]

Noise Levels (Work Areas) [73]
PN 232 **SC** 34160
B Loudness [67]
Working Conditions [73]

Nomenclature (Psychological)
Use Psychological Terminology

Nomifensine [82]
PN 121 **SC** 34175
SN Organic heterocyclic compound used as an antiparkinson agent and antidepressive agent.
B Antidepressant Drugs [71]
Antitremor Drugs [73]

Non Zero Sum Games [73]
PN 32 **SC** 34180
SN Quantitative games in which all players may win points as opposed to zero sum games in which points won by one player must be lost by another or others.
B Games [67]
R Entrapment Games [73]
Game Theory [67]
Prisoners Dilemma Game [73]

Noncommissioned Officers [73]
PN 37 **SC** 34200
SN Subordinate military officers (e.g., sergeants) appointed from enlisted personnel.
UF Officers (Noncommissioned)
B Enlisted Military Personnel [73]

Nonconformity (Personality) [73]
PN 59 **SC** 34210
B Personality Traits [67]
R Conformity (Personality) [67]
Individuality [73]

Noncontingent Reinforcement [88]
PN 39 **SC** 34215
SN Presentation of reinforcement (punishment or positive rewards) independently of behavior.
B Reinforcement [67]
R Autoshaping [78]
↓ Contingency Management [73]

Nondirected Discussion Method [73]
PN 14 **SC** 34220
SN Teaching method which encourages students' spontaneity and restricts the leader's role to that of a moderator.
B Teaching Methods [67]
R Discovery Teaching Method [73]

Nondirective Therapy
Use Client Centered Therapy

Nongraded Schools [73]
PN 11 **SC** 34250
SN Schools that group students according to such characteristics as academic achievement, mental and physical ability, or emotional development, rather than by age or grade level.
B Schools [67]

Nonlinear Regression [73]
PN 48 **SC** 34260
B Statistical Correlation [67]
Statistical Regression [85]
R Multiple Regression [82]

Nonmetallic Elements
SN Term discontinued in 1997. Use NONMETALLIC ELEMENTS to access references from 73–96.
Use Chemical Elements

Nonparametric Statistical Tests [67]
PN 283 **SC** 34280
B Statistical Tests [73]
N Chi Square Test [73]
Cochran Q Test [73]
Kolmogorov Smirnov Test [73]
Mann Whitney U Test [73]
Sign Test [73]
Wilcoxon Sign Rank Test [73]

Nonprescription Drugs [91]
PN 51 **SC** 34285
SN Drugs or medication sold legally without prescription.
UF Over The Counter Drugs
B Drugs [67]
R Prescription Drugs [91]
Self Medication [91]

Nonprofessional Personnel [82]
PN 95 **SC** 34290
SN Conceptually broad array term. Use a more specific term if possible. Use PARAPROFESSIONAL PERSONNEL to access references from 73–81.
B Personnel [67]
N ↓ Agricultural Workers [73]
R ↓ Business and Industrial Personnel [67]
Child Care Workers [78]
Domestic Service Personnel [73]
↓ Paraprofessional Personnel [73]
↓ Professional Personnel [78]
↓ Service Personnel [91]
Technical Service Personnel [73]

Nonprofit Organizations [73]
PN 102 **SC** 34300
B Organizations [67]

Nonprojective Personality Measures [73]
PN 1121 **SC** 34304
SN Direct assessment of personality traits through scoring of a subject's responses to questions on structured, standardized tests. Use a more specific term if possible.
UF Authoritarianism Rebellion Scale
Differential Personality Inventory
Kupfer Detre Self Rating Scale
White Betz A B Scale
B Personality Measures [67]
N Bannister Repertory Grid [73]
Barrett Lennard Relationship Invent [73]
Barron Welsh Art Scale [73]
Beck Depression Inventory [88]
Bem Sex Role Inventory [88]
California F Scale [73]

Nonprojective Personality Measures — (cont'd)
N California Test of Personality [73]
Child Behavior Checklist [94]
Childrens Manifest Anxiety Scale [73]
Childrens Personality Questionnaire [73]
Edwards Personal Preference Schedule [67]
Edwards Personality Inventory [73]
Edwards Social Desirability Scale [73]
Embedded Figures Testing [67]
Eysenck Personality Inventory [73]
Fear Survey Schedule [73]
Fund Interper Rela Orientat Beh Ques [73]
Goldstein Scheerer Object Sort Test [73]
Gough Adjective Check List [73]
Guilford Zimmerman Temperament Surv [73]
High Sch Personality Questionnaire [73]
Learys Interpersonal Check List [73]
Marlowe Crowne Soc Desirabil Scale [73]
Maudsley Personality Inventory [73]
Memory for Designs Test [73]
Millon Clinical Multiaxial Inventory [88]
Minn Multiphasic Personality Inven [67]
Mooney Problem Check List [73]
Myers Briggs Type Indicator [73]
Omnibus Personality Inventory [73]
Personal Orientation Inventory [73]
Psychological Screening Inventory [73]
Repression Sensitization Scale [73]
Rod and Frame Test [73]
Rokeach Dogmatism Scale [73]
Rotter Intern Extern Locus Cont Scal [73]
Sixteen Personality Factors Question [73]
State Trait Anxiety Inventory [73]
Taylor Manifest Anxiety Scale [73]
Tennessee Self Concept Scale [73]
Vineland Social Maturity Scale [73]
Welsh Figure Preference Test [73]
Zungs Self Rating Depression Scale [73]

Nonrapid Eye Movement Sleep
Use NREM Sleep

NonREM Sleep
Use NREM Sleep

Nonreversal Shift Learning [73]
PN 38 **SC** 34330
SN Experimental technique used for the demonstration of mediating processes in concept formation that assesses the ability to shift dimensions in stimulus discrimination tasks, as, for example, from size to color.
UF Extradimensional Shift Learning
B Discrimination Learning [82]

Nonsense Syllable Learning [67]
PN 160 **SC** 34340
SN Verbal learning paradigm in which collections or lists of letters, which have no obvious meaning (e.g., XAB, GZL), are used as stimulus items. Also, the actual acquisition, retention, and retrieval of such stimulus items.
B Verbal Learning [67]

Nonstandard English [73]
PN 244 **SC** 34350
B Dialect [73]
R Slang [73]

Nontraditional Careers [85]
PN 278 **SC** 34352
SN Occupations in which certain groups (usually males or females) have traditionally been underrepresented.

Nontraditional Careers — (cont'd)
B Occupations 67
R Occupational Choice 67
Sex Roles 67

Nontraditional Education 82
PN 317 SC 34355
SN Alternative educational programs within or without the formal educational system that provide flexible and innovative teaching, curriculum, grading, or degree requirements.
UF Alternative Schools
Magnet Schools
Open Universities
B Education 67
N Home Schooling 94
R ↓ Curriculum 67
↓ Educational Programs 73
↓ Teaching Methods 67

Nonverbal Ability 88
PN 160 SC 34357
SN Ability in nonlanguage areas such as spatial relations, mathematics, or music.
B Ability 67
N ↓ Artistic Ability 73
Mathematical Ability 73
Mechanical Aptitude 73
Motor Skills 73
↓ Spatial Ability 82
R Academic Aptitude 73
↓ Nonverbal Communication 71

Nonverbal Communication 71
PN 2696 SC 34360
B Communication 67
N Body Language 73
Eye Contact 73
↓ Facial Expressions 67
Gestures 73
↓ Manual Communication 78
R Laughter 78
↓ Nonverbal Ability 88

Nonverbal Learning 73
PN 125 SC 34370
SN Acquisition, retention, and retrieval of knowledge or skills that do not involve verbally presented information or language, such as perceptual responses or motor activities.
B Learning 67

Nonverbal Meaning 73
PN 47 SC 34380
B Meaning 67

Nonverbal Reinforcement 73
PN 30 SC 34390
B Social Reinforcement 67

Nonviolence 91
PN 9 SC 34393
B Social Interaction 67
R Pacifism 73
↓ Political Attitudes 73
↓ Violence 73

Nootropic Drugs 91
PN 149 SC 34395
UF Cognition Enhancing Drugs
Memory Enhancing Drugs
B Drugs 67
N Piracetam 82

Noradrenaline
Use Norepinephrine

Norepinephrine 73
PN 2413 SC 34410
UF Noradrenaline
B Adrenal Medulla Hormones 73
Catecholamines 73
Vasoconstrictor Drugs 73
R Guanethidine 73
↓ Norepinephrine Metabolites 82

Norepinephrine Metabolites 82
PN 285 SC 34413
SN Molecules generated from the metabolism of norepinephrine.
B Metabolites 73
N Methoxyhydroxyphenylglycol (3,4) 91
R ↓ Metabolism 67
Norepinephrine 73

Normal Distribution 73
PN 103 SC 34420
UF Gaussian Distribution
B Frequency Distribution 73
R ↓ Statistical Sample Parameters 73

Normalization (Test)
Use Test Standardization

Norms (Social)
Use Social Norms

Norms (Statistical)
Use Statistical Norms

Norms (Test)
Use Test Norms

North America 73
PN 134 SC 34460
N Canada 71
Mexico 73
↓ United States 67

North Korea 82
PN 10 SC 34465
SN Use KOREA to access references from 73–81.
B Korea 73

North Vietnam
SN Term discontinued in 1982. Use NORTH VIETNAM to access references from 73–81.
Use Vietnam

Northern Ireland 73
PN 159 SC 34480
B Ireland 73
R ↓ Great Britain 71

Nortriptyline 94
PN 45 SC 34485
SN Use ANTIDEPRESSANT DRUGS to access references from 78-93.
B Tricyclic Antidepressant Drugs 97

Norway 73
PN 467 SC 34490
B Scandinavia 78

Norway Rats 73
PN 107 SC 34500
B Rats 67

Nose 73
PN 54 SC 34510
B Respiratory System 73
N ↓ Nasal Mucosa 73
R ↓ Musculoskeletal System 73

Note Taking 91
PN 47 SC 34515
R Homework 88
↓ Learning Strategies 91
↓ Memory 67
Mnemonic Learning 73
↓ Strategies 67
Study Habits 73
↓ Written Communication 85

Nouns 73
PN 489 SC 34520
B Form Classes (Language) 73
R ↓ Names 85

Novel Stimuli
Use Stimulus Novelty

Novelty Seeking
Use Sensation Seeking

Novocaine
SN Term discontinued in 1982. Use NOVOCAINE to access references from 73–81.
Use Procaine

NREM Sleep 73
PN 513 SC 34550
UF Nonrapid Eye Movement Sleep
NonREM Sleep
Slow Wave Sleep
B Sleep 67

Nuclear Family 73
PN 143 SC 34560
B Family 67
Family Structure 73

Nuclear Technology 85
PN 278 SC 34565
B Technology 73

Nuclear War 85
PN 427 SC 34567
B War 67

Nucleic Acids 73
PN 59 SC 34570
B Acids 73
N Adenosine 73
Deoxyribonucleic Acid 73
↓ Nucleotides 78
Ribonucleic Acid 73
R ↓ Genetics 67
Guanosine 85

Nucleotides 78
PN 109 SC 34573
B Nucleic Acids 73
N Cyclic Adenosine Monophosphate 78

Nucleus Accumbens 82
PN 745 SC 34574
SN One of the largest nuclei in the septal region lying anteriorly and medially to the junction of the caudate nucleus and putamen and laterally to the septal nuclei.
R Caudate Nucleus 73
↓ Limbic System 73
Septal Nuclei 82

Nucleus Basalis Magnocellularis 94
PN 40 SC 57425
B Forebrain 85
R ↓ Basal Ganglia 73

Nudity 73
PN 37 **SC** 34575
R Obscenity 78
↓ Physical Appearance 82
Pornography 73

Null Hypothesis Testing 73
PN 114 **SC** 34580
SN Application of statistical tests to determine whether a null hypothesis should be accepted or rejected. Limited to discussions of statistical procedures.
B Hypothesis Testing 73

Number Comprehension 73
PN 263 **SC** 34590
SN Knowledge or understanding of the meaning, significance, and relationships symbolized by numerals.
B Comprehension 67

Number Systems 73
PN 37 **SC** 34600
B Mathematics (Concepts) 67
Systems 67
R Numbers (Numerals) 67

Numbers (Numerals) 67
PN 815 **SC** 34610
SN Symbol of a member of an abstract mathematical system which is subject to rules of succession, addition, and multiplication.
UF Digits (Mathematics)
B Mathematics (Concepts) 67
Written Language 67
R Number Systems 73
Numerosity Perception 67

Numerical Ability
Use Mathematical Ability

Numerosity Perception 67
PN 313 **SC** 34630
SN Perception of quantities in stimulus sets in visual, auditory, or other perceptual modes.
B Perception 67
R Numbers (Numerals) 67

Nuns 73
PN 109 **SC** 34640
B Religious Personnel 73
R Missionaries 73

Nurse Patient Interaction
Use Therapeutic Processes

Nursery School Students 73
PN 356 **SC** 34650
SN Students attending a nursery school, usually ages 2, 3, and 4. Mandatory term in educational contexts.
B Preschool Students 82
R ↓ Children 67
Preschool Age Children 67

Nursery Schools 73
PN 105 **SC** 34660
B Schools 67

Nurses 67
PN 3940 **SC** 34670
B Medical Personnel 67
N Psychiatric Nurses 73
Public Health Service Nurses 73
School Nurses 73

Nursing 73
PN 1601 **SC** 34680
B Paramedical Sciences 73

Nursing Education 73
PN 929 **SC** 34690
B Education 67
R ↓ Medical Education 73

Nursing Homes 73
PN 1914 **SC** 34700
SN Establishments where maintenance and personal or nursing care are provided for persons (as the aged or chronically ill) who are unable to care for themselves.
B Residential Care Institutions 73
Treatment Facilities 73
R ↓ Hospitals 67
Long Term Care 94
Psychiatric Units 91
Retirement Communities 97
Sanatoriums 73

Nursing Students 73
PN 1254 **SC** 34710
B College Students 67

Nurturance 85
PN 144 **SC** 34714
SN Need, tendency, or process of providing care and support to others. For animal populations, use ANIMAL MATERNAL BEHAVIOR or ANIMAL PARENTAL BEHAVIOR.
B Personality Traits 67
Social Behavior 67
R ↓ Needs 67
↓ Parent Child Relations 67

Nutrition 73
PN 1128 **SC** 34720
R Beverages (Nonalcoholic) 78
Diets 78
Food 78
Food Additives 78
↓ Nutritional Deficiencies 73
↓ Physiology 67

Nutritional Deficiencies 73
PN 753 **SC** 34730
UF Malnutrition
B Physical Disorders 97
N ↓ Protein Deficiency Disorders 73
Starvation 73
↓ Vitamin Deficiency Disorders 73
R ↓ Alcoholic Psychosis 73
↓ Alcoholism 67
Anorexia Nervosa 73
Diets 78
↓ Eating Disorders 97
Failure to Thrive 88
Food Deprivation 67
↓ Metabolism Disorders 73
Nutrition 73
↓ Underweight 73

Nymphomania
Use Hypersexuality

Nystagmus 73
PN 484 **SC** 34760
SN Eye movement reflex stabilizing the retinal image of a visual stimulus to compensate for head or stimulus movement. Also, eye movement defects resulting from neurological, muscular, or genetic disorders.
UF Optokinetic Nystagmus
Vestibular Nystagmus
B Eye Disorders 73
Eye Movements 67

Nystagmus — (cont'd)
B Reflexes 71
R ↓ Nervous System Disorders 67

Obedience 73
PN 215 **SC** 34770
SN Limited to human populations.
UF Submissiveness
B Personality Traits 67
R Coercion 94
↓ Compliance 73
↓ Dominance 67
↓ Resistance 97

Obesity 73
PN 2798 **SC** 34780
UF Overweight
B Body Weight 67
Eating Disorders 97
Symptoms 67
R Diets 78
Hyperphagia 73
Obesity (Attitudes Toward) 97
↓ Psychosomatic Disorders 67

Obesity (Attitudes Toward) 97
PN 0 **SC** 34783
B Attitudes 67
R ↓ Body Weight 67
Eating Attitudes 94
Health Attitudes 85
Obesity 73
Weight Control 85

Obituary 67
PN 226 **SC** 34785
SN Mandatory term used as a document type identifier.

Object Permanence 85
PN 130 **SC** 34788
SN Knowledge of the continued existence of an object even when it is not directly perceived.
R ↓ Cognitive Development 73
Conservation (Concept) 73
↓ Developmental Stages 73
↓ Internalization 97
↓ Perceptual Constancy 85

Object Recognition 97
PN 0 **SC** 34789
B Perception 67
Recognition (Learning) 67
R Form and Shape Perception 67
Naming 88
↓ Perceptual Discrimination 73

Object Relations 82
PN 1790 **SC** 34786
SN Psychoanalytic description of emotional attachments formed with other persons, as opposed to interest and love for oneself; individual's mode of relation to others and self.
UF Fairbairnian Theory
Winnicottian Theory
R Anaclitic Depression 73
Attachment Behavior 85
↓ Childhood Development 67
Emotional Development 73
↓ Internalization 97
Metapsychology 94
↓ Psychoanalytic Theory 67
↓ Psychosocial Development 73
Self Psychology 88
Separation Individuation 82
Transitional Objects 85

Objective Referenced Tests
Use Criterion Referenced Tests

Objectives
Use Goals

Objectives (Organizational)
Use Organizational Objectives

Objectivity [73]
PN 350 **SC** 34810
B Personality Traits [67]
R Subjectivity [94]

Oblique Rotation [73]
PN 54 **SC** 34820
B Statistical Rotation [73]

Obscenity [78]
PN 66 **SC** 34826
R Nudity [73]
Pornography [73]
Profanity [91]

Observation Methods [67]
PN 2085 **SC** 34830
SN In research, any techniques used in the intentional examination of persons or processes in natural or manipulated settings for the purpose of obtaining facts or reporting conclusions.
B Empirical Methods [73]
R Interrater Reliability [82]
Self Monitoring [82]

Observational Learning [73]
PN 639 **SC** 34840
SN Learning by observation of others by human or animal subjects or learning by visualization of behavior without actually performing an act and experiencing its consequences. Compare SOCIAL LEARNING.
B Learning [67]
Learning Strategies [91]
R Imitation (Learning) [67]
↓ Social Learning [73]

Observers [73]
PN 445 **SC** 34850
SN Individuals who examine, record, or rate specified events, behaviors, or processes in experimental, social, or therapeutic situations.
R ↓ Audiences [67]

Obsessions [67]
PN 515 **SC** 34860
B Thought Disturbances [73]
R ↓ Compulsions [73]
Erotomania [97]
Obsessive Compulsive Neurosis [73]
Obsessive Compulsive Personality [73]

Obsessive Compulsive Disorder
Use Obsessive Compulsive Neurosis

Obsessive Compulsive Neurosis [73]
PN 1958 **SC** 34870
SN Disorder characterized by recurrent obsessions or compulsions that may interfere with the individual's daily functioning or serve as a source of distress.
UF Compulsive Neurosis
Obsessive Compulsive Disorder
Obsessive Neurosis
B Anxiety Disorders [97]
R ↓ Compulsions [73]
Obsessions [67]
Obsessive Compulsive Personality [73]

Obsessive Compulsive Personality [73]
PN 194 **SC** 34880
SN Personality disorder characterized by perfectionism, indecisiveness, excessive devotion to work, inability to express warm emotions, and insistence that things be done in accord with one's own preferences.
UF Anankastic Personality
Compulsive Personality Disorder
B Personality Disorders [67]
R ↓ Compulsions [73]
Obsessions [67]
Obsessive Compulsive Neurosis [73]

Obsessive Neurosis
Use Obsessive Compulsive Neurosis

Obstetrical Complications [78]
PN 387 **SC** 34895
R ↓ Birth [67]
Birth Injuries [73]
Labor (Childbirth) [73]
↓ Obstetrics [78]
Postsurgical Complications [73]
↓ Pregnancy [67]
Premature Birth [73]

Obstetricians [78]
PN 38 **SC** 34900
B Physicians [67]
R Gynecologists [73]
Surgeons [73]

Obstetrics [78]
PN 123 **SC** 34910
SN Use OBSTETRICS GYNECOLOGY to access references from 73–77.
B Medical Sciences [67]
N Midwifery [85]
R Childbirth Training [78]
Gynecology [78]
Obstetrical Complications [78]
↓ Prenatal Care [91]

Obturator Nerve
Use Spinal Nerves

Occipital Lobe [73]
PN 355 **SC** 34930
B Cerebral Cortex [67]
N Visual Cortex [67]

Occultism [78]
PN 85 **SC** 34935
R Cultism [73]
Mysticism [67]
↓ Parapsychological Phenomena [73]
↓ Parapsychology [67]
↓ Religious Beliefs [73]
Spirit Possession [97]
Witchcraft [73]

Occupation (Parental)
Use Parental Occupation

Occupational Adjustment [73]
PN 943 **SC** 34950
SN Personal adaptation to one's vocation.
UF Vocational Adjustment
B Adjustment [67]
R Adjustment Disorders [94]
Career Change [78]
Occupational Neurosis [73]
↓ Occupations [67]
School to Work Transition [94]
Work Adjustment Training [91]

Occupational Aspirations [73]
PN 1716 **SC** 34960
UF Career Aspirations
Career Goals
Vocational Aspirations
B Aspirations [67]
R Career Change [78]
Mentor [85]
↓ Occupations [67]
Professional Development [82]

Occupational Attitudes [73]
PN 1595 **SC** 34970
SN Attitudes toward specific occupations or careers.
B Attitudes [67]
R Job Applicant Attitudes [73]
↓ Occupations [67]
Vocational Maturity [78]
Work (Attitudes Toward) [73]

Occupational Choice [67]
PN 3169 **SC** 34980
UF Career Choice
Job Selection
Vocational Choice
R Career Change [78]
Career Development [85]
Nontraditional Careers [85]
Occupational Preference [73]
↓ Occupations [67]
Professional Specialization [91]
Reemployment [91]
Vocational Maturity [78]

Occupational Exposure [88]
PN 241 **SC** 34985
SN Exposure to conditions, substances, or apparatus in the workplace that may be harmful to health.
R ↓ Hazardous Materials [91]
Industrial Accidents [73]
Occupational Safety [73]
↓ Occupations [67]
Work Related Illnesses [94]
↓ Working Conditions [73]

Occupational Guidance [67]
PN 3562 **SC** 34990
SN Assistance in career selection or development; assessment of interests, abilities, or aptitude; compilation of occupational and economic information; and referral to placement services.
UF Career Counseling
Career Guidance
Guidance (Occupational)
Vocational Counseling
Vocational Guidance
B Counseling [67]
R Assessment Centers [82]
Career Education [78]
Educational Counseling [67]
Job Enrichment [73]
Mentor [85]
Occupational Success Prediction [73]
↓ Occupations [67]
Student Personnel Services [78]
Vocational Counselors [73]

Occupational Interest Measures [73]
PN 577 **SC** 35000
B Measurement [67]
N Kuder Occupational Interest Survey [73]
Strong Vocational Interest Blank [67]

Occupational Interests [67]
PN 1481 **SC** 35010
UF Vocational Interests
B Interests [67]

Occupational Interests — (cont'd)
R ↓ Occupations 67
Vocational Maturity 78

Occupational Mobility 73
PN 443 SC 35020
SN The capacity or actual tendency toward upward progression in occupational status or occupational attainment.
UF Job Mobility
Mobility (Occupational)
Vocational Mobility
R Career Change 78
Employment History 78
Job Enrichment 73
↓ Occupational Tenure 73
↓ Occupations 67

Occupational Neurosis 73
PN 18 SC 35030
SN Neurotic disorder developed as a consequence of occupational stress, inappropriate occupational choice, overwork, job dissatisfaction, or other job-related stress.
B Neurosis 67
R Occupational Adjustment 73
Occupational Stress 73

Occupational Preference 73
PN 866 SC 35040
UF Career Preference
Vocational Preference
B Preferences 67
R Occupational Choice 67
↓ Occupations 67
Professional Specialization 91
Vocational Maturity 78

Occupational Safety 73
PN 431 SC 35050
UF Industrial Safety
B Safety 67
Working Conditions 73
R Industrial Accidents 73
Occupational Exposure 88
↓ Occupations 67
Work Related Illnesses 94

Occupational Status 78
PN 1380 SC 35056
SN Occupational rank or position achieved by employee, usually based on abilities or competence. Also, social prestige attributed to specific occupations.
UF Job Status
Prestige (Occupational)
B Status 67
R Job Experience Level 73
↓ Occupational Tenure 73
↓ Occupations 67
Personnel Promotion 78

Occupational Stress 73
PN 4540 SC 35060
UF Burnout
B Stress 67
R Occupational Neurosis 73
↓ Occupations 67
Quality of Work Life 88
Work Related Illnesses 94

Occupational Success 78
PN 775 SC 35067
B Achievement 67
R Employment History 78
Occupational Success Prediction 73
↓ Occupations 67
Personnel Promotion 78

Occupational Success Prediction 73
PN 647 SC 35070
B Personnel Evaluation 73
Prediction 67
R Occupational Guidance 67
Occupational Success 78

Occupational Tenure 73
PN 362 SC 35080
UF Tenure (Occupational)
N Teacher Tenure 73
R Employee Turnover 73
Employment History 78
↓ Employment Status 82
Job Security 78
Occupational Mobility 73
Occupational Status 78
↓ Occupations 67
Personnel Termination 73

Occupational Therapists 73
PN 372 SC 35090
B Therapists 67
R ↓ Mental Health Personnel 67
↓ Paraprofessional Personnel 73
↓ Psychiatric Hospital Staff 73

Occupational Therapy 67
PN 1417 SC 35100
SN Method of treatment for physical or mental disorders that involves engagement of patients in useful or creative activities or work as a means of improving functional skills in the areas of work, daily living, or vocational activities.
B Rehabilitation 67
R Physical Therapy 73

Occupations 67
PN 3468 SC 35110
SN Conceptually broad array term referring to work specialties as defined by duties and required skills. Use OCCUPATIONS to access references on employment status from 67-81. Use a more specific term if possible.
UF Careers
Jobs
Vocations
N Nontraditional Careers 85
R Career Change 78
Career Development 85
↓ Division of Labor 88
Employment History 78
↓ Job Characteristics 85
Occupational Adjustment 73
Occupational Aspirations 73
Occupational Attitudes 73
Occupational Choice 67
Occupational Exposure 88
Occupational Guidance 67
Occupational Interests 67
Occupational Mobility 73
Occupational Preference 73
Occupational Safety 73
Occupational Status 78
Occupational Stress 73
Occupational Success 78
↓ Occupational Tenure 73
↓ Personnel 67
↓ Professional Personnel 78
↓ Vocational Education 73
Vocational Maturity 78
Working Women 78

Octopus 73
PN 37 SC 35120
B Mollusca 73

Ocular Accommodation 82
PN 200 SC 35127

Ocular Accommodation — (cont'd)
SN Process of focusing an image on the retina by means of a flattening or bulging of the lens.
UF Eye Accommodation
Focusing (Visual)
B Reflexes 71
R ↓ Depth Perception 67
Lens (Eye) 73
↓ Refraction Errors 73

Ocular Dominance 73
PN 224 SC 35130
UF Eye Dominance
B Lateral Dominance 67
R ↓ Brain 67
↓ Eye (Anatomy) 67
↓ Eye Disorders 73
Interocular Transfer 85
Left Brain 91
Right Brain 91

Ocular Fixation
Use Eye Fixation

Oculomotor Muscles 73
PN 96 SC 35140
B Muscles 67

Oculomotor Nerve
Use Cranial Nerves

Oculomotor Response
Use Eye Movements

Odor Aversion Conditioning
Use Aversion Conditioning

Odor Discrimination 73
PN 644 SC 35170
B Olfactory Perception 67
Perceptual Discrimination 73
R Olfactory Thresholds 73

Oedipal Complex 73
PN 648 SC 35180
B Psychoanalytic Personality Factors 73

Offenders (Adult)
Use Criminals

Offenders (Juvenile)
Use Juvenile Delinquents

Office Environment
Use Working Conditions

Officers (Commissioned)
Use Commissioned Officers

Officers (Noncommissioned)
Use Noncommissioned Officers

Offspring 88
PN 899 SC 35230
SN Used specifically for children, regardless of age, whose parents had significant experiences or conditions, e.g., alcoholism, fame, or political persecution. Not used as an age identifier. Limited to human populations.
N Adult Offspring 85
Daughters 73
Interracial Offspring 88
Sons 73
R ↓ Family Members 73

Old Age
Use Aged

Olfactory Bulb 73
PN 521 **SC** 35247
B Limbic System 73

Olfactory Evoked Potentials 73
PN 44 **SC** 35250
B Evoked Potentials 67
R ↓ Cortical Evoked Potentials 73

Olfactory Impairment
Use Anosmia

Olfactory Mucosa 73
PN 50 **SC** 35260
B Nasal Mucosa 73
R Chemoreceptors 73

Olfactory Nerve 73
PN 101 **SC** 35270
B Cranial Nerves 73

Olfactory Perception 67
PN 1668 **SC** 35280
UF Smell Perception
B Perception 67
N Odor Discrimination 73
Olfactory Thresholds 73
R Anosmia 73
Taste Perception 67
Vomeronasal Sense 82

Olfactory Stimulation 78
PN 704 **SC** 35285
B Perceptual Stimulation 73

Olfactory Thresholds 73
PN 125 **SC** 35290
B Olfactory Perception 67
Thresholds 67
R Odor Discrimination 73
↓ Perceptual Measures 73

Oligophrenia
Use Mental Retardation

Oligophrenia (Phenylpyruvic)
Use Phenylketonuria

Omission Training 85
PN 11 **SC** 35315
SN Removal of positive reinforcement upon occurrence of undesirable behavior. Has applications in both therapeutic and experimental contexts.
B Behavior Modification 73
Operant Conditioning 67
R Differential Reinforcement 73
Time Out 85

Omnibus Personality Inventory 73
PN 11 **SC** 35320
B Nonprojective Personality Measures 73

Omnipotence 94
PN 3 **SC** 35325
B Personality Traits 67
R Authority 67
Grandiosity 94
Magical Thinking 73
↓ Power 67

On the Job Training 73
PN 144 **SC** 35330

On the Job Training — (cont'd)
B Personnel Training 67
R ↓ Experiential Learning 97
Inservice Teacher Education 73
↓ Inservice Training 85

Online Databases
Use Databases

Online Searching
Use Computer Searching

Only Children 82
PN 64 **SC** 35335
SN Children having no siblings.
B Children 67
R ↓ Family Members 73
↓ Family Structure 73

Onomatopoeia and Images Test
SN Term discontinued in 1997. Use ONOMATOPOEIA and IMAGES TEST to access references from 73–96.
Use Projective Personality Measures

Onset (Disorders) 73
PN 1725 **SC** 35350
SN Beginning or first appearance of a mental or physical disorder.
R ↓ Disorders 67
↓ Mental Disorders 67
↓ Physical Disorders 97
Premorbidity 78

Ontogeny
Use Development

Open Classroom Method 73
PN 359 **SC** 35370
SN Approach to teaching and learning emphasizing the student's right to make decisions and viewing the teacher as a facilitator of learning rather than a transmitter of knowledge. May include grouping of students across grades, independent study, individualized rates of progression, open-plan schools without interior walls, or unstructured time and curricula.
B Teaching Methods 67
R Discovery Teaching Method 73
Individualized Instruction 73
Montessori Method 73
Team Teaching Method 73

Open Field Behavior (Animal)
Use Animal Open Field Behavior

Open Universities
Use Nontraditional Education

Openmindedness 78
PN 141 **SC** 35376
SN Willingness to consider new and unconventional ideas, and readiness to reexamine social, political, and religious values.
UF Closedmindedness
B Personality Traits 67
R Agreeableness 97
Authoritarianism 67
Dogmatism 78

Openness to Experience 97
PN 0 **SC** 35378
SN A broad experiential trait manifested in active imagination, aesthetic sensitivity, attentiveness to inner feelings, preference for variety, intellectual curiosity, and independence of judgment.

Openness to Experience — (cont'd)
UF Imaginativeness
B Personality Traits 67
R Adaptability (Personality) 73
Conformity (Personality) 67
Creativity 67
Curiosity 67
Five Factor Personality Model 97
Hypnotic Susceptibility 73
Rigidity (Personality) 67
↓ Tolerance 73

Operant Conditioning 67
PN 6071 **SC** 35380
SN Learned behavior or the experimental paradigm in which reinforcers (positive or negative) or punishers immediately and contingently follow the performance of some behavior, the frequency of which changes as a direct consequence of such contingent reinforcement.
UF Conditioning (Operant)
Instrumental Conditioning
Instrumental Learning
B Conditioning 67
N Avoidance Conditioning 67
Conditioned Emotional Responses 67
↓ Conditioned Responses 67
Delayed Alternation 94
↓ Discrimination Learning 82
Escape Conditioning 73
Fading (Conditioning) 82
Omission Training 85
Time Out 85
R ↓ Adjunctive Behavior 82
↓ Behavior Modification 73
Conditioned Stimulus 73
Learning Theory 67
Polydipsia 82
↓ Reinforcement 67
↓ Self Stimulation 67
Skinner (Burrhus Frederic) 91
Unconditioned Stimulus 73

Operation (Surgery)
Use Surgery

Ophidiophobia 73
PN 248 **SC** 35400
SN Fear of snakes.
UF Snake Phobia
B Phobias 67

Ophthalmologic Examination 73
PN 53 **SC** 35410
UF Eye Examination
B Medical Diagnosis 73
N Electro Oculography 73
Electroretinography 67

Ophthalmology 73
PN 33 **SC** 35420
B Medical Sciences 67
R Optometry 73

Opiate Agonists
Use Narcotic Agonists

Opiate Antagonists
Use Narcotic Antagonists

Opiates 73
PN 1668 **SC** 35430
UF Opioids
Opium Alkaloids
Opium Derivatives
B Narcotic Drugs 73
N Codeine 73
↓ Endogenous Opiates 85

Opiates — (cont'd)
N Fentanyl [85]
Heroin [73]
Morphine [73]
Papaverine [73]

Opinion (Public)
Use Public Opinion

Opinion Attitude and Interest Survey
SN Term discontinued in 1997. Use OPINION ATTITUDE and INTEREST SURVEY to access references from 73-96.
Use Attitude Measures

Opinion Change
Use Attitude Change

Opinion Questionnaires
Use Attitude Measures

Opinion Surveys
Use Attitude Measures

Opinions
Use Attitudes

Opioid Antagonists
Use Narcotic Antagonists

Opioids
Use Opiates

Opioids (Endogenous)
Use Endogenous Opiates

Opium Alkaloids
Use Alkaloids AND Opiates

Opium Derivatives
Use Opiates

Opossums [73]
PN 62 **SC** 35530
B Marsupials [73]

Oppositional Defiant Disorder [97]
PN 0 **SC** 35535
SN A psychopathological disorder, usually beginning in childhood, consisting of negativism, disobedience, and hostile behavior toward authority figures.
R Attention Deficit Disorder [85]
↓ Behavior Disorders [71]
Conduct Disorder [91]
Hyperkinesis [73]

Optic Chiasm [73]
PN 63 **SC** 35540
B Diencephalon [73]
Neural Pathways [82]
R Optic Nerve [73]

Optic Lobe [73]
PN 115 **SC** 35550
B Mesencephalon [73]

Optic Nerve [73]
PN 192 **SC** 35560
B Cranial Nerves [73]
R Optic Chiasm [73]

Optic Tract [82]
PN 65 **SC** 35563

Optic Tract — (cont'd)
SN Portion of the optic pathway that extends posteriorly from the optic chiasm in two nerve fiber bundles to synapse near the superior colliculi and in the lateral geniculate body of the thalamus.
B Neural Pathways [82]

Optical Aids [73]
PN 126 **SC** 35565
UF Corrective Lenses
B Medical Therapeutic Devices [73]
N Contact Lenses [73]

Optical Illusions
Use Illusions (Perception)

Optimism [73]
PN 365 **SC** 35580
SN Attitude characterized by a positive and cheerful disposition and inclination to anticipate the most favorable outcome of events or actions.
B Emotional States [73]
Personality Traits [67]
R Hope [91]
Pessimism [73]
Positivism [73]

Optokinetic Nystagmus
Use Nystagmus

Optometrists [73]
PN 26 **SC** 35590
B Medical Personnel [67]

Optometry [73]
PN 105 **SC** 35600
B Paramedical Sciences [73]
R Ophthalmology [73]

Oral Communication [85]
PN 2414 **SC** 35610
SN Expression of information in oral form. Use VERBAL COMMUNICATION to access references from 67-84.
UF Speech
Verbalization
B Verbal Communication [67]
N Code Switching [88]
Oral Reading [73]
Public Speaking [73]
Self Talk [88]
Singing [97]
↓ Speech Characteristics [73]
R Rhetoric [91]
Verbal Ability [67]
Verbal Fluency [73]
↓ Vocalization [67]
↓ Voice [73]

Oral Contraceptives [73]
PN 222 **SC** 35620
B Contraceptive Devices [73]
R Fertility Enhancement [73]

Oral Reading [73]
PN 897 **SC** 35630
SN Reading aloud by individuals or groups or the condition of being read to by others.
UF Reading Aloud
B Oral Communication [85]
Reading [67]

Organ Donation
Use Tissue Donation

Organ of Corti
Use Cochlea

Organ Transplantation [73]
PN 497 **SC** 35660
UF Heart Transplants
Kidney Transplants
Renal Transplantation
Transplants (Organ)
B Surgery [71]
R Heart Surgery [73]
Neural Transplantation [85]
Tissue Donation [91]

Organic Brain Syndromes [73]
PN 625 **SC** 35670
B Brain Disorders [67]
Syndromes [73]
N ↓ Alcoholic Psychosis [73]
Alzheimers Disease [73]
↓ Dementia [85]
Toxic Psychoses [73]
R ↓ Mental Disorders [67]
Postpartum Depression [73]

Organic Therapies [73]
PN 75 **SC** 35680
SN Somatic treatment methods used in psychiatry. Compare PHYSICAL TREATMENT METHODS.
B Treatment [67]
N ↓ Drug Therapy [67]
Electrosleep Treatment [78]
↓ Narcoanalysis [73]
Phototherapy [91]
↓ Psychosurgery [73]
↓ Shock Therapy [73]
Vitamin Therapy [78]
R ↓ Alternative Medicine [97]
↓ Psychotherapy [67]

Organizational Behavior [78]
PN 3385 **SC** 35695
SN Behavior of organizations and of individuals within organizational settings.
B Social Behavior [67]
N ↓ Employee Interaction [88]
Organizational Effectiveness [85]
R ↓ Group Dynamics [67]
Informants [88]
Labor Management Relations [67]
↓ Organizational Characteristics [97]
Organizational Commitment [91]
Organizational Structure [67]
↓ Organizations [67]
↓ Sociometry [91]

Organizational Change [73]
PN 1412 **SC** 35700
UF Change (Organizational)
N Organizational Merger [73]
R Decentralization [78]
Organizational Climate [73]
Organizational Crises [73]
Organizational Development [73]

Organizational Characteristics [97]
PN 0 **SC** 35705
N Organizational Climate [73]
Organizational Structure [67]
R ↓ Organizational Behavior [78]
Organizational Commitment [91]
Organizational Objectives [73]
Quality of Work Life [88]

Organizational Climate [73]
PN 2266 **SC** 35710
SN Social or environmental characteristics of an organization which affect the behavior or performance of its members.
UF Climate (Organizational)
B Organizational Characteristics [97]

Organizational Climate — (cont'd)
R ↓ Organizational Change 73
Organizational Crises 73
Organizational Structure 67
Quality of Work Life 88
↓ Working Conditions 73

Organizational Commitment 91
PN 490 SC 35715
SN Commitment of organizations and of individuals within organizational settings.
B Commitment 85
R ↓ Employee Attitudes 67
↓ Employee Characteristics 88
Employer Attitudes 73
Job Involvement 78
↓ Job Performance 67
Job Satisfaction 67
↓ Organizational Behavior 78
↓ Organizational Characteristics 97
Organizational Effectiveness 85
Organizational Objectives 73

Organizational Crises 73
PN 104 SC 35720
B Crises 71
R ↓ Organizational Change 73
Organizational Climate 73
↓ Stress 67

Organizational Development 73
PN 1213 SC 35730
SN Application of behavioral, management, or other techniques to organizations in order to integrate individuals' or members' needs with organizational goals and objectives.
B Development 67
R Decentralization 78
↓ Organizational Change 73
Organizational Objectives 73
Organizational Structure 67

Organizational Effectiveness 85
PN 509 SC 35735
SN Measure of the ability of an organization to meet the needs of its environment, including personnel needs.
UF Organizational Performance
B Organizational Behavior 78
R Organizational Commitment 91
Organizational Objectives 73
Quality Control 88

Organizational Goals
Use Organizational Objectives

Organizational Merger 73
PN 72 SC 35750
B Organizational Change 73
R Organizational Structure 67

Organizational Objectives 73
PN 452 SC 35760
UF Objectives (Organizational)
Organizational Goals
B Goals 67
R Decentralization 78
↓ Organizational Characteristics 97
Organizational Commitment 91
Organizational Development 73
Organizational Effectiveness 85
Quality Control 88

Organizational Performance
Use Organizational Effectiveness

Organizational Policy Making
Use Policy Making

Organizational Psychology
Use Industrial Psychology

Organizational Structure 67
PN 2577 SC 35770
B Organizational Characteristics 97
R Decentralization 78
↓ Organizational Behavior 78
Organizational Climate 73
Organizational Development 73
Organizational Merger 73
↓ Organizations 67

Organizations 67
PN 1325 SC 35780
UF Agencies (Groups)
Associations (Groups)
Groups (Organizations)
N Business Organizations 73
Foreign Organizations 73
Government Agencies 73
Health Maintenance Organizations 82
International Organizations 73
Labor Unions 73
Nonprofit Organizations 73
Professional Organizations 73
Religious Organizations 91
R ↓ Organizational Behavior 78
Organizational Structure 67

Orgasm 73
PN 58 SC 35790
UF Climax (Sexual)
B Psychosexual Behavior 67
N Female Orgasm 73
↓ Male Orgasm 73
R Frigidity 73
Impotence 73
Sexual Satisfaction 94

Orientals
Use Asians

Orientation (Perceptual)
Use Perceptual Orientation

Orientation (Spatial)
Use Spatial Orientation (Perception)

Orienting Reflex 67
PN 885 SC 35820
SN Innate physiological responses, such as pupil dilation, galvanic skin response, and EEG activity, to novel stimuli.
B Reflexes 71
Sensory Adaptation 67

Orienting Responses 67
PN 946 SC 35830
SN Behavioral reactions in an organism, such as arrest of movement or head turning, to novel stimuli; behavioral correlate of orienting reflex.
B Responses 67
Sensory Adaptation 67
R ↓ Classical Conditioning 67

Originality
Use Creativity

Orphanages 73
PN 39 SC 35850
B Residential Care Institutions 73
R ↓ Institutionalization 67
Orphans 73

Orphans 73
PN 82 SC 35860

Orphans — (cont'd)
B Family Members 73
R Orphanages 73

Orphenadrine 73
PN 13 SC 35870
UF Methyldiphenylhydramine
B Amines 73
Antihistaminic Drugs 73
Antispasmodic Drugs 73
Antitremor Drugs 73
Cholinergic Blocking Drugs 73
Muscle Relaxing Drugs 73

Orthogonal Rotation 73
PN 80 SC 35880
B Statistical Rotation 73
N Equimax Rotation 73
Quartimax Rotation 73
Varimax Rotation 73

Orthography 73
PN 573 SC 35890
SN Art and formal rules of writing and spelling according to accepted usage. Also used to refer to the representation of the sounds of a language by written symbols.
B Linguistics 73
R ↓ Alphabets 73
Cursive Writing 73
Homographs 73
Proofreading 88
Spelling 73
↓ Written Language 67

Orthopedically Handicapped
Use Physically Disabled

Orthopsychiatry 73
PN 15 SC 35910
SN Interdisciplinary approach combining psychiatry, psychology, pediatrics, and other related fields for prevention and early treatment of mental disorders, particularly in children and adolescents.
B Psychiatry 67
R Child Psychiatry 67

Oscilloscopes 73
PN 23 SC 35920
B Apparatus 67

Osteoporosis 91
PN 27 SC 35930
B Bone Disorders 73

Otosclerosis
SN Term discontinued in 1997. Use OTOSCLEROSIS to access references from 73–96.
Use Ear Disorders

Out of Body Experiences 88
PN 38 SC 35945
B Parapsychological Phenomena 73
R Near Death Experiences 85

Outcomes (Psychotherapeutic)
Use Psychotherapeutic Outcomes

Outcomes (Treatment)
Use Treatment Outcomes

Outgroup Ingroup
Use Ingroup Outgroup

Outpatient Commitment [91]
PN 18 **SC** 35957
SN Legally mandated psychiatric or psychological treatment on an outpatient basis.
UF Commitment (Outpatient)
B Commitment (Psychiatric) [73]
Outpatient Treatment [67]
R Aftercare [73]
Partial Hospitalization [85]

Outpatient Psychiatric Clinics
Use Psychiatric Clinics

Outpatient Treatment [67]
PN 2012 **SC** 35970
SN Treatment in private practice, clinic, or hospital for ambulatory, non-hospitalized patients. Compare PARTIAL HOSPITALIZATION.
UF Ambulatory Care
B Treatment [67]
N Outpatient Commitment [91]
R Aftercare [73]
↓ Drug Therapy [67]
Home Care [85]
Maintenance Therapy [97]
Outpatients [73]
Psychiatric Clinics [73]

Outpatients [73]
PN 1120 **SC** 35980
B Patients [67]
R ↓ Outpatient Treatment [67]

Outreach Programs [97]
PN 0 **SC** 35983
B Social Programs [73]
Social Services [82]
R ↓ Case Management [91]
Community Mental Health Services [78]
↓ Community Services [67]
↓ Health Care Delivery [78]
↓ Health Care Services [78]
↓ Mental Health Programs [73]
↓ Mental Health Services [78]
Social Casework [67]
↓ Support Groups [91]

Outward Bound
Use Wilderness Experience

Ovariectomy [73]
PN 774 **SC** 35990
B Castration [67]
R Hysterectomy [73]

Ovaries [73]
PN 88 **SC** 36000
B Female Genitalia [73]
Gonads [73]

Ovary Disorders
Use Endocrine Sexual Disorders

Over The Counter Drugs
Use Nonprescription Drugs

Overachievement (Academic)
Use Academic Overachievement

Overcorrection [85]
PN 41 **SC** 36025
SN Therapeutic technique involving restitution and/or intensive practice of appropriate behavior following the occurrence of disruptive or inappropriate behavior.

Overcorrection — (cont'd)
B Behavior Modification [73]
R Overlearning [67]
↓ Practice [67]

Overlearning [67]
PN 209 **SC** 36030
SN Learning in which practice continues beyond the point of mastery of the material or task.
B Learning [67]
R Overcorrection [85]

Overpopulation [73]
PN 174 **SC** 36040
B Population [73]
R ↓ Birth Control [71]
Crowding [78]
Environmental Stress [73]
Social Density [78]

Overweight
Use Obesity

Ovulation [73]
PN 106 **SC** 36060
B Menstrual Cycle [73]

Owls [97]
PN 0 **SC** 36063
R ↓ Birds [67]

Ownership [85]
PN 210 **SC** 36065
UF Possession
Property
R Business [67]
Capitalism [73]
Entrepreneurship [91]
↓ Private Sector [85]
Self Employment [94]

Oxazepam [78]
PN 99 **SC** 36075
B Anticonvulsive Drugs [73]
Benzodiazepines [78]
Minor Tranquilizers [73]

Oxidases [73]
PN 22 **SC** 36080
B Enzymes [73]
N Cytochrome Oxidase [73]
Monoamine Oxidases [73]

Oxidopamine
Use Hydroxydopamine (6-)

Oxilapine
Use Loxapine

Oxygen [73]
PN 206 **SC** 36090

Oxygenation [73]
PN 53 **SC** 36100
B Physiology [67]

Oxytocin [73]
PN 244 **SC** 36120
B Pituitary Hormones [73]

Pacemakers (Artificial)
Use Artificial Pacemakers

Pacific Islands [88]
PN 39 **SC** 36135
N ↓ South Pacific [78]

Pacifism [73]
PN 23 **SC** 36140
B Philosophies [67]
R Nonviolence [91]

Pain [67]
PN 3211 **SC** 36150
UF Aches
B Symptoms [67]
N Aphagia [73]
Back Pain [82]
Chronic Pain [85]
↓ Headache [73]
Myofascial Pain [91]
↓ Neuralgia [73]
Somatoform Pain Disorder [97]
R ↓ Analgesic Drugs [73]
Pain Management [94]
Pain Measurement [97]
↓ Pain Perception [73]
Pain Thresholds [73]
↓ Physical Disorders [97]
↓ Spasms [73]
Suffering [73]

Pain (Psychogenic)
Use Somatoform Pain Disorder

Pain Management [94]
PN 198 **SC** 36165
B Treatment [67]
R Analgesia [82]
↓ Analgesic Drugs [73]
↓ Pain [67]
Pain Measurement [97]
↓ Pain Perception [73]
Pain Thresholds [73]
Palliative Care [91]
↓ Physical Treatment Methods [73]
Somatoform Pain Disorder [97]

Pain Measurement [97]
PN 0 **SC** 36167
SN Tests, scales, or other techniques used to assess or evaluate pain in human or animal populations. Used only when the methodology is the focus of the reference.
B Measurement [67]
R Analgesia [82]
↓ Diagnosis [67]
↓ Pain [67]
Pain Management [94]
↓ Pain Perception [73]
Pain Thresholds [73]
↓ Perceptual Measures [73]

Pain Perception [73]
PN 2274 **SC** 36170
UF Nociception
B Somesthetic Perception [67]
N Analgesia [82]
Pain Thresholds [73]
R ↓ Pain [67]
Pain Management [94]
Pain Measurement [97]

Pain Receptors
Use Nociceptors

Pain Relieving Drugs
Use Analgesic Drugs

Pain Thresholds [73]
PN 704 **SC** 36190
B Pain Perception [73]
Thresholds [67]
R ↓ Pain [67]
Pain Management [94]

Pain Thresholds — (cont'd)
R Pain Measurement [97]
↓ Perceptual Measures [73]

Painting (Art) [73]
PN 402 SC 36200
B Art [67]

Paired Associate Learning [67]
PN 2693 SC 36210
B Verbal Learning [67]
R Word Associations [67]

Pakistan [82]
PN 93 SC 36215
SN Use WEST PAKISTAN to access references from 73–81.
B Asia [73]

Palestinians
Use Arabs

Palliative Care [91]
PN 147 SC 36219
B Health Care Services [78]
R Advance Directives [94]
Assisted Suicide [97]
↓ Death and Dying [67]
↓ Health Care Delivery [78]
Hospice [82]
Life Sustaining Treatment [97]
Long Term Care [94]
Pain Management [94]
Terminally Ill Patients [73]

Palm (Anatomy) [73]
PN 30 SC 36220
B Anatomy [67]
R Hand (Anatomy) [67]

Palsy
Use Paralysis

Panama [88]
PN 8 SC 36235
B Central America [73]

Pancreas [73]
PN 73 SC 36240
B Glands [67]
R ↓ Endocrine Glands [73]
↓ Endocrine System [73]
↓ Gastrointestinal System [73]

Pancreozymin
Use Cholecystokinin

Panic [73]
PN 708 SC 36260
SN Prior to 1988, also used for PANIC DISORDER.
B Fear [67]
R ↓ Anxiety [67]
Panic Disorder [88]

Panic Disorder [88]
PN 2177 SC 36265
SN Consider PANIC to access references from 73–87.
B Anxiety Disorders [97]
R ↓ Anxiety [67]
Panic [73]

Pantherine
Use Muscimol

Papaverine [73]
PN 31 SC 36270
B Alkaloids [73]
Analgesic Drugs [73]
Antispasmodic Drugs [73]
Muscle Relaxing Drugs [73]
Opiates [73]

Papua New Guinea [82]
PN 153 SC 36273
SN Use NEW GUINEA to access references from 73–81.
UF New Guinea

Parachlorophenylalanine [78]
PN 170 SC 36275
B Phenylalanine [73]
Serotonin Antagonists [73]

Paradigmatic Techniques
Use Paradoxical Techniques

Paradoxical Sleep
Use REM Sleep

Paradoxical Techniques [82]
PN 342 SC 36282
SN Techniques designed to disrupt dysfunctional behavior patterns through systematically encouraging them, thus allaying anticipatory anxiety, creating resistance to the symptomatic behavior, or enabling clients to achieve voluntary control over this behavior.
UF Paradigmatic Techniques
Reframing
Symptom Prescription
B Psychotherapeutic Techniques [67]
R ↓ Behavior Therapy [67]
↓ Psychotherapy [67]

Paragraphs [73]
PN 63 SC 36300
B Written Language [67]

Paraguay [88]
PN 8 SC 36303
B South America [67]

Paraldehyde
SN Term discontinued in 1997. Use PARALDEHYDE or PARALYDEHYDE to access references from 73–81.
Use Anticonvulsive Drugs

Paralegal Personnel
Use Legal Personnel

Paralysis [73]
PN 237 SC 36320
UF Palsy
B Movement Disorders [85]
Neuromuscular Disorders [73]
N Cerebral Palsy [67]
General Paresis [73]
Hemiplegia [78]
Paraplegia [78]
Parkinsons Disease [73]
Quadriplegia [85]
R ↓ Central Nervous System Disorders [73]
Dysarthria [73]
↓ Musculoskeletal Disorders [73]
↓ Peripheral Nerve Disorders [73]
Poliomyelitis [73]
↓ Sclerosis (Nervous System) [73]
↓ Spinal Cord Injuries [73]

Paralysis (Hysterical)
Use Hysterical Paralysis

Paralysis (Infantile)
Use Poliomyelitis

Paralysis Agitans
Use Parkinsons Disease

Paramedical Personnel [73]
PN 205 SC 36360
UF Medics
B Medical Personnel [67]
Paraprofessional Personnel [73]
N Attendants (Institutions) [73]
Psychiatric Aides [73]
R Fire Fighters [91]
Home Care Personnel [97]
↓ Paramedical Sciences [73]
↓ Psychiatric Hospital Staff [73]

Paramedical Sciences [73]
PN 5 SC 36370
N Audiology [73]
Nursing [73]
Optometry [73]
↓ Pharmacology [73]
Physical Therapy [73]
R ↓ Medical Sciences [67]
↓ Paramedical Personnel [73]

Parameter Estimation
Use Statistical Estimation

Parameters (Response)
Use Response Parameters

Parameters (Stimulus)
Use Stimulus Parameters

Parametric Statistical Tests [73]
PN 81 SC 36400
B Statistical Tests [73]
N F Test [73]
T Test [73]

Paranoia [88]
PN 85 SC 36410
SN Mild paranoia in nonpsychotic persons.
B Personality Traits [67]
R Paranoid Personality [73]

Paranoia (Psychosis) [67]
PN 745 SC 36420
SN Gradual development of an elaborate and complex delusional system, usually involving persecutory or grandiose delusions with few other signs of personality or thought disturbance.
UF Acute Paranoid Disorder
Atypical Paranoid Disorder
Paranoid Disorder
B Psychosis [67]
N Folie A Deux [73]
Involutional Paranoid Psychosis [73]
R Paranoid Personality [73]
Paranoid Schizophrenia [67]

Paranoid Disorder
Use Paranoia (Psychosis)

Paranoid Personality [73]
PN 125 SC 36430
SN Nonpsychotic personality disorder marked by hypersensitivity, jealousy, and unwarranted suspicion with tendency to blame others for one's shortcomings.
UF Paranoid Personality Disorder
B Personality Disorders [67]
R Paranoia [88]

Paranoid Personality — (cont'd)
R ↓ Paranoia (Psychosis) 67
Paranoid Schizophrenia 67

Paranoid Personality Disorder
Use Paranoid Personality

Paranoid Schizophrenia 67
PN 1044 **SC** 36440
SN Type of schizophrenia characterized by grandiosity, suspiciousness, and delusions of persecution, often with hallucinations.
B Schizophrenia 67
R Folie A Deux 73
Involutional Paranoid Psychosis 73
↓ Paranoia (Psychosis) 67
Paranoid Personality 73
↓ Psychosis 67

Paraphilias
Use Sexual Deviations

Paraplegia 78
PN 123 **SC** 36446
SN Paralysis of the lower limbs and trunk.
B Paralysis 73
R ↓ Central Nervous System Disorders 73
Hemiplegia 78
↓ Injuries 73
↓ Musculoskeletal Disorders 73
↓ Physically Disabled 97
Quadriplegia 85
↓ Spinal Cord Injuries 73

Paraprofessional Education 73
PN 570 **SC** 36450
SN Training or education of aides, such as paramedical and paralegal personnel, who assist professional persons.
B Education 67
R Microcounseling 78

Paraprofessional Personnel 73
PN 1031 **SC** 36460
SN Persons with minimal or special training in a profession working as aides or assistants to professionals. Use PARAPROFESSIONAL PERSONNEL to access references to nonprofessional personnel from 73–81.
B Personnel 67
N Home Care Personnel 97
↓ Paramedical Personnel 73
Teacher Aides 73
R ↓ Mental Health Personnel 67
↓ Nonprofessional Personnel 82
Occupational Therapists 73
↓ Professional Personnel 78
Volunteer Civilian Personnel 73
↓ Volunteer Personnel 73

Parapsychological Phenomena 73
PN 916 **SC** 36470
B Parapsychology 67
N ↓ Extrasensory Perception 67
Near Death Experiences 85
Out of Body Experiences 88
Telepathy 73
R Occultism 78
Religious Experiences 97
Spirit Possession 97
Superstitions 73

Parapsychology 67
PN 865 **SC** 36480
N ↓ Parapsychological Phenomena 73
R Astrology 73
Dream Analysis 73
Mysticism 67

Parapsychology — (cont'd)
R Occultism 78
Witchcraft 73

Parasitic Disorders 73
PN 73 **SC** 36490
B Infectious Disorders 73
N Malaria 73

Parasitism
Use Biological Symbiosis

Parasuicide
Use Attempted Suicide

Parasympathetic Nervous System 73
PN 44 **SC** 36500
B Autonomic Nervous System 67
N ↓ Efferent Pathways 82
Vagus Nerve 73
R ↓ Cholinergic Blocking Drugs 73
↓ Cholinomimetic Drugs 73

Parasympatholytic Drugs
Use Cholinergic Blocking Drugs

Parasympathomimetic Drugs
Use Cholinomimetic Drugs

Parathion 73
PN 8 **SC** 36530
B Insecticides 73

Parathyroid Disorders 73
PN 40 **SC** 36540
UF Hyperparathyroidism
Hypoparathyroidism
B Endocrine Disorders 73

Parathyroid Glands 73
PN 7 **SC** 36550
B Endocrine Glands 73
R Parathyroid Hormone 73

Parathyroid Hormone 73
PN 12 **SC** 36560
B Hormones 67
R Parathyroid Glands 73

Parent Attitude Research Instrument 73
PN 6 **SC** 36570
B Attitude Measures 67

Parent Child Communication 73
PN 1250 **SC** 36580
SN From 1982, limited to human populations. For animals consider ANIMAL PARENTAL BEHAVIOR or ANIMAL MATERNAL BEHAVIOR.
B Interpersonal Communication 73
N Father Child Communication 85
Mother Child Communication 85
R ↓ Parent Child Relations 67
↓ Parental Characteristics 94

Parent Child Relations 67
PN 7309 **SC** 36590
SN From 1982, limited to human populations. For animals consider ANIMAL PARENTAL BEHAVIOR or ANIMAL MATERNAL BEHAVIOR.
UF Parental Influence
B Family Relations 67
N Father Child Relations 73
Mother Child Relations 67
↓ Parental Attitudes 73
Parental Permissiveness 73
R Attachment Behavior 85
↓ Child Discipline 73

Parent Child Relations — (cont'd)
R ↓ Childrearing Practices 67
Codependency 91
Empty Nest 91
Generation Gap 73
Nurturance 85
↓ Parent Child Communication 73
Parent School Relationship 82
Parent Training 78
↓ Parental Characteristics 94
Parental Expectations 97
Parental Investment 97
Parental Role 73
Parenting Skills 97
Transgenerational Patterns 91

Parent Educational Background 73
PN 621 **SC** 36600
UF Educational Background (Parents)
B Educational Background 67
Family Background 73
Parental Characteristics 94
R Family Socioeconomic Level 73
Parental Occupation 73

Parent Effectiveness Training
Use Parent Training

Parent School Relationship 82
PN 798 **SC** 36605
SN Interaction between parents and school and/or educational personnel, such as parent-teacher conferences.
UF PTA
R ↓ Parent Child Relations 67
Parent Training 78
↓ Teacher Attitudes 67

Parent Training 78
PN 2326 **SC** 36606
SN Educational materials, information, or instruction for parents.
UF Parent Effectiveness Training
B Education 67
Family Life Education 97
R ↓ Childrearing Practices 67
Human Relations Training 78
↓ Parent Child Relations 67
Parent School Relationship 82
Parental Role 73
Parenting Skills 97

Parental Absence 73
PN 382 **SC** 36610
SN From 1982, limited to human populations. For animals consider ANIMAL PARENTAL BEHAVIOR or ANIMAL MATERNAL BEHAVIOR.
B Family Structure 73
N Father Absence 73
Mother Absence 73
R Anaclitic Depression 73
Child Custody 82
Divorced Persons 73
↓ Marital Separation 73
↓ Parental Characteristics 94
↓ Single Parents 78
Widowers 73
Widows 73

Parental Attitudes 73
PN 5584 **SC** 36620
SN Attitudes of, not toward, parents.
B Attitudes 67
Parent Child Relations 67
Parental Characteristics 94
N Parental Expectations 97
R Childrearing Attitudes 73
↓ Childrearing Practices 67
Father Child Relations 73

Parental Attitudes — (cont'd)
R Mother Child Relations 67
Parental Permissiveness 73
Parental Role 73

Parental Authoritarianism
Use Parental Permissiveness

Parental Behavior (Animal)
Use Animal Parental Behavior

Parental Characteristics 94
PN 397 **SC** 36637
N Parent Educational Background 73
↓ Parental Attitudes 73
Parental Occupation 73
Parental Permissiveness 73
Parental Role 73
Parenting Skills 97
R ↓ Childrearing Practices 67
↓ Parent Child Communication 73
↓ Parent Child Relations 67
↓ Parental Absence 73
Parental Investment 97
↓ Parents 67

Parental Expectations 97
PN 0 **SC** 36639
SN Expectations or aspirations for a level of behavior, achievement, or performance (e.g., in school, life or career) that parents have for their children.
B Expectations 67
Parental Attitudes 73
R ↓ Parent Child Relations 67
Parental Investment 97
Parental Role 73
↓ Parents 67

Parental Influence
Use Parent Child Relations

Parental Investment 97
PN 0 **SC** 36645
SN Parental provision of resources and/or care to offspring. Used for both human and animal populations.
UF Maternal Investment
Paternal Investment
R ↓ Animal Parental Behavior 82
↓ Parent Child Relations 67
↓ Parental Characteristics 94
Parental Expectations 97

Parental Occupation 73
PN 325 **SC** 36650
UF Occupation (Parental)
B Family Background 73
Parental Characteristics 94
R Family Socioeconomic Level 73
Parent Educational Background 73

Parental Permissiveness 73
PN 258 **SC** 36660
UF Authoritarianism (Parental)
Parental Authoritarianism
Permissiveness (Parental)
B Child Discipline 73
Parent Child Relations 67
Parental Characteristics 94
R Father Child Relations 73
Mother Child Relations 67
↓ Parental Attitudes 73
Parental Role 73

Parental Role 73
PN 1679 **SC** 36670
SN Descriptions, perceptions, and attitudes about the social, psychological, behavioral, or emotional role of parents.
B Family Relations 67
Parental Characteristics 94
Roles 67
R ↓ Child Discipline 73
↓ Childrearing Practices 67
Delayed Parenthood 85
Father Child Relations 73
Mother Child Relations 67
↓ Parent Child Relations 67
Parent Training 78
↓ Parental Attitudes 73
Parental Expectations 97
Parental Permissiveness 73

Parenthood Status 85
PN 503 **SC** 36675
SN State of having or not having children, or, the number of children one has.
N Childlessness 82
R Family Size 73
↓ Family Structure 73

Parenting Skills 97
PN 0 **SC** 36677
B Parental Characteristics 94
R ↓ Childrearing Practices 67
↓ Parent Child Relations 67
Parent Training 78

Parents 67
PN 8275 **SC** 36680
SN From 1982, limited to human populations. For animals consider ANIMAL PARENTAL BEHAVIOR or ANIMAL MATERNAL BEHAVIOR.
B Ancestors 73
Family Members 73
N Adoptive Parents 73
↓ Fathers 67
Foster Parents 73
Homosexual Parents 94
↓ Mothers 67
↓ Single Parents 78
Stepparents 73
Surrogate Parents (Humans) 73
R ↓ Expectant Parents 85
Inlaws 97
↓ Parental Characteristics 94
Parental Expectations 97
↓ Spouses 73

Paresis (General)
Use General Paresis

Pargyline 73
PN 78 **SC** 36700
B Antihypertensive Drugs 73
Monoamine Oxidase Inhibitors 73

Parietal Lobe 73
PN 620 **SC** 36710
B Cerebral Cortex 67
N Somatosensory Cortex 73

Parkinsonism 94
PN 60 **SC** 36715
SN Clinical state, usually drug induced, characterized by tremors, muscle rigidity, postural reflex dysfunction, and akinesia. Compare PARKINSONS DISEASE.
R Apraxia 73
Muscle Contractions 73
↓ Nervous System Disorders 67
Parkinsons Disease 73
↓ Reflexes 71
↓ Symptoms 67
Tremor 73

Parkinsons Disease 73
PN 1718 **SC** 36720
SN A disease characterized as a progressive motor disability manifested by tremors, shaking, muscular rigidity, and lack of postural reflexes.
UF Paralysis Agitans
B Brain Disorders 67
Neuromuscular Disorders 73
Paralysis 73
R Amantadine 78
↓ Antitremor Drugs 73
Parkinsonism 94
Tremor 73

Parks (Recreational)
Use Recreation Areas

Parochial School Education
Use Private School Education

Parole 73
PN 215 **SC** 36750
SN Conditional release of a prisoner serving an indeterminate or unexpired sentence.
UF Parolees
B Legal Processes 73
R ↓ Law Enforcement 78
Probation 73

Parole Officers 73
PN 39 **SC** 36760
B Law Enforcement Personnel 73
R Probation Officers 73

Parolees
Use Parole

Paroxetine 94
PN 121 **SC** 36770
B Antidepressant Drugs 71
Serotonin Reuptake Inhibitors 97

Paroxysmal Sleep
Use Narcolepsy

Partial Hospitalization 85
PN 802 **SC** 36775
SN Ambulatory treatment program of intensive, multidisciplinary care. Involves stabilization, rehabilitation, and/or maintenance of patients through more comprehensive treatment than is possible in an outpatient setting. Compare OUTPATIENT TREATMENT.
UF Day Care (Treatment)
Day Hospital
B Treatment 67
R Aftercare 73
Deinstitutionalization 82
↓ Hospital Programs 78
Interdisciplinary Treatment Approach 73
↓ Mental Health Programs 73
Outpatient Commitment 91
↓ Rehabilitation 67

Partial Reinforcement
Use Reinforcement Schedules

Partially Hearing Impaired 73
PN 2239 **SC** 36790
UF Hearing Impaired (Partially)
B Aurally Disabled 97
R Cochlear Implants 94
↓ Deaf 67

Partially Sighted 73
PN 106 SC 36800
B Visually Disabled 97

Participation 73
PN 1587 SC 36810
SN Taking part in an activity. Use a more specific term if possible.
B Interpersonal Interaction 67
N Athletic Participation 73
Client Participation 97
Group Participation 73
Participative Management 88
R ↓ Involvement 73

Participative Management 88
PN 275 SC 36820
SN Management technique permitting nonmanagement personnel to be involved in the governance, management, or policy-making processes of an institution or organization.
UF Quality Circles
B Management Methods 73
Participation 73
R Job Involvement 78
Management Decision Making 73
Quality Control 88

Partner Abuse 91
PN 387 SC 36825
SN Includes married and unmarried persons.
UF Spouse Abuse
B Antisocial Behavior 71
R ↓ Abuse Reporting 97
Battered Females 88
Emotional Abuse 91
Erotomania 97
↓ Family Violence 82
Physical Abuse 91
↓ Sexual Abuse 88
↓ Violence 73

Parturition
Use Birth

Passive Aggressive Personality 73
PN 29 SC 36850
B Personality Disorders 67

Passive Avoidance
Use Avoidance Conditioning

Passiveness 73
PN 177 SC 36870
B Personality Traits 67

Pastoral Counseling 67
PN 912 SC 36880
SN Provision of counseling by religious personnel.
B Counseling 67
R ↓ Psychotherapy 67

Pastors
Use Ministers (Religion)

Paternal Investment
Use Parental Investment

Path Analysis 91
PN 37 SC 36895
SN Quantification of the causal relationships that exists among variables.
B Multivariate Analysis 82
R Causal Analysis 94
↓ Factor Analysis 67
Multiple Regression 82

Pathogenesis
Use Etiology

Pathological Gambling 88
PN 283 SC 36905
UF Compulsive Gambling
B Gambling 73
R ↓ Addiction 73
↓ Behavior Disorders 71
Impulse Control Disorders 97
Impulsiveness 73

Pathologists 73
PN 8 SC 36920
B Physicians 67
R Surgeons 73

Pathology 73
PN 218 SC 36930
B Medical Sciences 67
N Neuropathology 73
Psychopathology 67

Patient Abuse 91
PN 38 SC 36935
UF Client Abuse
B Antisocial Behavior 71
R ↓ Child Abuse 71
Elder Abuse 88
Emotional Abuse 91
Patient Violence 94
↓ Patients 67
Physical Abuse 91
Professional Client Sexual Relations 94
Professional Liability 85
↓ Professional Standards 73
↓ Sexual Abuse 88
↓ Therapeutic Processes 78
↓ Treatment 67

Patient Attitudes
Use Client Attitudes

Patient Care Planning
Use Treatment Planning

Patient Characteristics
Use Client Characteristics

Patient Dropouts
Use Treatment Dropouts

Patient Education
Use Client Education

Patient History 73
PN 1687 SC 36955
UF Case History
Medical History
Psychiatric History
R Biographical Data 78
↓ Client Characteristics 73
Client Records 97
↓ Diagnosis 67
Etiology 67
↓ Medical Diagnosis 73
↓ Medical Records 78
Misdiagnosis 97
Premorbidity 78
Prognosis 73
↓ Psychodiagnosis 67
↓ Treatment 67

Patient Participation
Use Client Participation

Patient Records
Use Client Records

Patient Rights
Use Client Rights

Patient Satisfaction
Use Client Satisfaction

Patient Seclusion 94
PN 26 SC 36959
UF Seclusion (Patient)
B Social Isolation 67
R ↓ Hospitalization 67
Patient Violence 94
↓ Patients 67
↓ Psychiatric Hospitalization 73
Psychiatric Hospitals 67
Psychiatric Units 91

Patient Selection 97
PN 0 SC 57505
SN Selection of patients or clients for participation in research studies or for specific treatment modalities.
R ↓ Client Characteristics 73
Client Transfer 97
Client Treatment Matching 97
Clients 73
↓ Patients 67
Therapist Selection 94

Patient Therapist Interaction
Use Psychotherapeutic Processes

Patient Therapist Sexual Relations
Use Professional Client Sexual Relations

Patient Transfer
Use Client Transfer

Patient Treatment Matching
Use Client Treatment Matching

Patient Violence 94
PN 76 SC 36965
SN Violence or behavioral disruptions by psychiatric or medical patients directed toward other patients, institutional staff, or themselves.
UF Client Violence
B Client Characteristics 73
Violence 73
R Dangerousness 88
Patient Abuse 91
Patient Seclusion 94
↓ Patients 67
Physical Restraint 82
↓ Therapeutic Processes 78

Patients 67
PN 1195 SC 36970
SN Persons under medical care. Use a more specific term if possible. Consider also CLIENTS.
N Geriatric Patients 73
Hospitalized Patients 73
Medical Patients 73
Outpatients 73
Psychiatric Patients 67
Surgical Patients 73
Terminally Ill Patients 73
R Client Participation 97
Patient Abuse 91
Patient Seclusion 94
Patient Selection 97
Patient Violence 94

Patriarchy [73]
PN 66 **SC** 36980
B Family Structure [73]
R Matriarchy [73]
Mother Absence [73]
↓ Sex Role Attitudes [78]
Sex Roles [67]

Pattern Discrimination [67]
PN 2674 **SC** 37000
SN Distinguishing temporal, spatial, or pictorial/symbolic regularities (patterns) of visual, auditory, or other types of stimuli. Includes the concept of pattern perception.
B Perceptual Discrimination [73]
R ↓ Auditory Perception [67]
Figure Ground Discrimination [73]
Form and Shape Perception [67]
Perceptual Closure [73]
↓ Rhythm [91]
Texture Perception [82]
Visual Acuity [82]
Visual Search [82]

Pavlov (Ivan) [91]
PN 21 **SC** 37005
SN Identifies biographical or autobiographical studies and discussions of Pavlov's works.
R ↓ Classical Conditioning [67]
↓ Psychologists [67]

Pavlovian Conditioning
Use Classical Conditioning

Pay
Use Salaries

PCP
Use Phencyclidine

Peabody Picture Vocabulary Test [73]
PN 271 **SC** 37030
B Intelligence Measures [67]

Peace [88]
PN 150 **SC** 37038
B Social Interaction [67]
Social Issues [91]
R Foreign Policy Making [73]
International Relations [67]
↓ Social Movements [67]
↓ War [67]

Peace Corps [73]
PN 20 **SC** 37040
B Government Programs [73]
R Government [67]

Pearson Prod Moment Correl Coeff
Use Statistical Correlation

Pecking Order
Use Animal Dominance

Pederasty
Use Pedophilia

Pedestrian Accidents [73]
PN 60 **SC** 37090
B Accidents [67]
R ↓ Driving Behavior [67]
Motor Traffic Accidents [73]
Pedestrians [73]

Pedestrians [73]
PN 122 **SC** 37100
R Pedestrian Accidents [73]

Pediatricians [73]
PN 322 **SC** 37110
B Physicians [67]

Pediatrics [73]
PN 691 **SC** 37120
B Medical Sciences [67]

Pedophilia [73]
PN 331 **SC** 37130
UF Child Molestation
Pederasty
B Sexual Deviations [67]
R Bisexuality [73]
↓ Child Abuse [71]
Incest [73]
↓ Sex Offenses [82]
↓ Sexual Abuse [88]

Peer Counseling [78]
PN 465 **SC** 37135
SN Supervised performance of limited counselor functions by a person of approximately the same age or status as the counselee.
B Counseling [67]
R Mentor [85]
↓ Peer Relations [67]
Peer Tutoring [73]
Peers [78]

Peer Evaluation [82]
PN 614 **SC** 37137
SN Appraisal by one's peers.
UF Peer Review
B Evaluation [67]
R ↓ Peer Relations [67]
↓ Personnel Evaluation [73]
Professional Competence [97]
↓ Professional Fees [78]
↓ Professional Standards [73]

Peer Pressure [94]
PN 39 **SC** 37138
B Interpersonal Influences [67]
Peer Relations [67]
R Friendship [67]
↓ Group Dynamics [67]
Likability [88]
Peers [78]
↓ Persuasive Communication [67]
Social Acceptance [67]
Social Approval [67]
Temptation [73]

Peer Relations [67]
PN 4989 **SC** 37140
B Interpersonal Interaction [67]
N Peer Pressure [94]
R Friendship [67]
Peer Counseling [78]
Peer Evaluation [82]
Peers [78]
Reference Groups [94]
↓ Relationship Termination [97]
↓ Sociometry [91]

Peer Review
Use Peer Evaluation

Peer Tutoring [73]
PN 610 **SC** 37150
SN Teaching method in which students provide individual instruction for other students, not necessarily of the same age or grade level.
B Tutoring [73]
R Cooperative Learning [94]
Peer Counseling [78]
Peers [78]

Peers [78]
PN 979 **SC** 37154
R Peer Counseling [78]
Peer Pressure [94]
↓ Peer Relations [67]
Peer Tutoring [73]
Significant Others [91]

Pellagra [73]
PN 9 **SC** 37160
B Vitamin Deficiency Disorders [73]
R Nicotinamide [73]

Pemoline [78]
PN 55 **SC** 37175
B CNS Stimulating Drugs [73]

Penguins [73]
PN 42 **SC** 37180
B Birds [67]

Penicillins [73]
PN 58 **SC** 37190
B Antibiotics [73]

Penis [73]
PN 216 **SC** 37200
B Male Genitalia [73]

Penis Envy [73]
PN 60 **SC** 37210
R ↓ Psychoanalytic Personality Factors [73]

Penitentiaries
Use Prisons

Penology [73]
PN 160 **SC** 37230
R ↓ Correctional Institutions [73]
↓ Criminal Justice [91]
Criminology [73]

Pension Plans (Employee)
Use Employee Pension Plans

Pentazocine [91]
PN 21 **SC** 37245
B Analgesic Drugs [73]
Narcotic Agonists [88]

Pentobarbital [73]
PN 624 **SC** 37250
UF Nembutal
Sodium Pentobarbital
B Anesthetic Drugs [73]
Anticonvulsive Drugs [73]
Barbiturates [67]
Hypnotic Drugs [73]
Sedatives [73]

Pentothal
Use Thiopental

Pentylenetetrazol [73]
PN 213 **SC** 37270
UF Metrazole
Pentylenetetrazole
B CNS Stimulating Drugs [73]
R ↓ Analeptic Drugs [73]

Pentylenetetrazole
Use Pentylenetetrazol

Peoples Republic of China [73]
PN 963 **SC** 37290

Peoples Republic of China — (cont'd)
UF China
B Asia [73]
N Tibet [91]

Peptic Ulcers
Use Gastrointestinal Ulcers

Peptides [73]
PN 1674 SC 37330
UF Galanin
Neuropeptides
N Angiotensin [73]
Bombesin [88]
Cholecystokinin [82]
Corticotropin Releasing Factor [94]
↓ Endogenous Opiates [85]
Melanocyte Stimulating Hormone [85]
Nerve Growth Factor [94]
↓ Neurokinins [97]
Neurotensin [85]
Somatostatin [91]
Substance P [85]
R ↓ Drugs [67]
Enkephalins [82]
↓ Neurotransmitters [85]
↓ Proteins [73]

Perception [67]
PN 3780 SC 37350
SN Conceptually broad array term referring to the process of obtaining cognitive or sensory information about the environment. Use a more specific term if possible.
UF Sensation
N ↓ Auditory Perception [67]
↓ Extrasensory Perception [67]
Form and Shape Perception [67]
↓ Illusions (Perception) [67]
↓ Intersensory Processes [78]
Numerosity Perception [67]
Object Recognition [97]
↓ Olfactory Perception [67]
Perceptual Closure [73]
↓ Perceptual Constancy [85]
↓ Perceptual Discrimination [73]
↓ Perceptual Distortion [82]
↓ Perceptual Localization [67]
↓ Perceptual Motor Learning [67]
↓ Perceptual Motor Processes [67]
↓ Perceptual Orientation [73]
Perceptual Style [73]
Risk Perception [97]
Role Perception [73]
Self Perception [67]
Sensory Gating [91]
↓ Social Perception [67]
↓ Somesthetic Perception [67]
↓ Spatial Perception [67]
Subliminal Perception [73]
Taste Perception [67]
↓ Time Perception [67]
↓ Visual Perception [67]
R Apperception [73]
↓ Attention [67]
Constructivism [94]
↓ Discrimination [67]
Mind [91]
↓ Perceptual Development [73]
↓ Perceptual Disturbances [73]
↓ Perceptual Measures [73]
↓ Perceptual Stimulation [73]
↓ Priming [88]
↓ Rhythm [91]
Sensory Neglect [94]
Signal Detection (Perception) [67]

Perceptiveness (Personality) [73]
PN 15 SC 37360
SN Demonstrating insight or sympathetic understanding or keen powers of observation.
B Personality Traits [67]
R Insight [73]
Sensitivity (Personality) [67]
↓ Social Perception [67]

Perceptual Aftereffect [67]
PN 1006 SC 37370
SN Subjective perceptual alterations resulting from prolonged exposure to preceding sensory stimulation.
UF Aftereffect (Perceptual)
B Illusions (Perception) [67]
N Afterimage [67]
R Interocular Transfer [85]

Perceptual Closure [73]
PN 98 SC 37380
SN Perception of units which together form a closed unit or whole, being organized together and perceived as a whole.
UF Closure (Perceptual)
Perceptual Fill
B Perception [67]
R Pattern Discrimination [67]

Perceptual Constancy [85]
PN 55 SC 37385
SN Stable perception of a stimulus in any sensory modality despite changes in its objective properties.
B Perception [67]
N Brightness Constancy [85]
Color Constancy [85]
Size Constancy [85]
R Object Permanence [85]

Perceptual Development [73]
PN 2337 SC 37390
SN The acquisition of sensory skills or abilities in the natural course of physical and psychological maturation.
B Cognitive Development [73]
N Perceptual Motor Development [91]
R ↓ Childhood Development [67]
Conservation (Concept) [73]
↓ Developmental Stages [73]
↓ Perception [67]
↓ Physical Development [73]
↓ Psychomotor Development [73]

Perceptual Discrimination [73]
PN 721 SC 37400
B Discrimination [67]
Perception [67]
N Auditory Acuity [88]
Auditory Discrimination [67]
Figure Ground Discrimination [73]
Odor Discrimination [73]
Pattern Discrimination [67]
Visual Discrimination [67]
R Mirror Image [91]
Object Recognition [97]
Stroop Effect [88]

Perceptual Distortion [82]
PN 103 SC 37410
SN Lack of correspondence between the common perception of a stimulus and the perception by an individual. Perceptual distortion does not involve hallucinatory or illusory components, but rather is a function of individual differences.
UF Distortion (Perceptual)
B Perception [67]
N Spatial Distortion [73]
R ↓ Illusions (Perception) [67]

Perceptual Distortion — (cont'd)
R ↓ Perceptual Disturbances [73]
Sensory Neglect [94]

Perceptual Disturbances [73]
PN 385 SC 37420
N ↓ Agnosia [73]
↓ Hallucinations [67]
R ↓ Aphasia [67]
↓ Illusions (Perception) [67]
↓ Learning Disabilities [73]
↓ Mental Disorders [67]
↓ Perception [67]
↓ Perceptual Distortion [82]
Sensory Neglect [94]

Perceptual Fill
Use Perceptual Closure

Perceptual Localization [67]
PN 640 SC 37440
SN Discrimination of the physical displacement or spatial location of a stimulus in any sensory modality.
UF Localization (Perceptual)
B Perception [67]
N Auditory Localization [73]
R Direction Perception [97]
↓ Tracking [67]

Perceptual Measures [73]
PN 563 SC 37450
B Measurement [67]
N Rod and Frame Test [73]
Stroop Color Word Test [73]
R ↓ Audiometry [67]
Auditory Thresholds [73]
Bone Conduction Audiometry [73]
Critical Flicker Fusion Threshold [67]
Dark Adaptation [73]
Olfactory Thresholds [73]
Pain Measurement [97]
Pain Thresholds [73]
↓ Perception [67]
↓ Psychophysical Measurement [67]
↓ Sensorimotor Measures [73]
↓ Speech and Hearing Measures [73]
↓ Thresholds [67]
Vibrotactile Thresholds [73]
↓ Visual Thresholds [73]

Perceptual Motor Coordination [73]
PN 787 SC 37460
UF Coordination (Perceptual Motor)
B Perceptual Motor Processes [67]
N Physical Dexterity [73]
R Motor Coordination [73]
Perceptual Motor Development [91]

Perceptual Motor Development [91]
PN 99 SC 37470
SN Use MOTOR DEVELOPMENT and PERCEPTUAL DEVELOPMENT to access references from 73-90.
UF Sensorimotor Development
B Motor Development [73]
Perceptual Development [73]
R Animal Development [78]
↓ Intersensory Processes [78]
↓ Perceptual Motor Coordination [73]
↓ Perceptual Motor Learning [67]
↓ Perceptual Motor Processes [67]
↓ Psychomotor Development [73]

Perceptual Motor Learning [67]
PN 1368 SC 37480
UF Motor Skill Learning
B Learning [67]

Perceptual Motor Learning — (cont'd)
B Perception 67
N Fine Motor Skill Learning 73
Gross Motor Skill Learning 73
R Perceptual Motor Development 91
↓ Skill Learning 73
↓ Tracking 67

Perceptual Motor Measures
Use Sensorimotor Measures

Perceptual Motor Processes 67
PN 4278 SC 37490
UF Psychomotor Processes
Sensorimotor Processes
B Perception 67
N ↓ Perceptual Motor Coordination 73
Sensory Integration 91
↓ Tracking 67
R Equilibrium 73
↓ Intersensory Processes 78
↓ Motor Processes 67
Perceptual Motor Development 91

Perceptual Neglect
Use Sensory Neglect

Perceptual Orientation 73
PN 767 SC 37500
SN Awareness of one's position in time and space.
UF Orientation (Perceptual)
B Perception 67
N Spatial Orientation (Perception) 73
R Time Perspective 78

Perceptual Stimulation 73
PN 343 SC 37510
B Stimulation 67
N ↓ Auditory Stimulation 67
↓ Delayed Feedback 73
Olfactory Stimulation 78
↓ Sensory Feedback 73
↓ Somesthetic Stimulation 73
Taste Stimulation 67
↓ Visual Stimulation 73
R Afferent Stimulation 73
↓ Masking 67
↓ Perception 67
Sensory Gating 91

Perceptual Style 73
PN 455 SC 37520
SN Manner in which sensory information or stimuli are organized meaningfully by an individual.
B Perception 67
R ↓ Cognitive Style 67
Conceptual Tempo 85
Neurolinguistic Programing 88
Schema 88

Perfectionism 88
PN 105 SC 37523
B Personality Traits 67
R ↓ Compulsions 73
Conscientiousness 97

Performance 67
PN 3695 SC 37525
SN Conceptually broad term, having application across broad disciplines and subject matter contexts in which execution or accomplishment of a specified task or objective is of concern. Use terms describing specific activity or performance when possible.
N Athletic Performance 91
Group Performance 67

Performance — (cont'd)
N ↓ Job Performance 67
↓ Motor Performance 73
R ↓ Ability 67
↓ Achievement 67
↓ Competence 82
Performance Anxiety 94

Performance Anxiety 94
PN 20 SC 37527
B Anxiety 67
R ↓ Anxiety Disorders 97
↓ Performance 67

Performance Tests 73
PN 547 SC 37530
SN Tests requiring nonverbal responses, for example, the manipulation of objects or the performance of motor skills.
B Measurement 67
R Criterion Referenced Tests 82

Performing Arts
Use Arts

Periaqueductal Gray 85
PN 193 SC 37550
SN Mesencephalic cells in the gray area surrounding the cerebral aqueduct important for visceral and limbic mechanisms.
B Tegmentum 91

Perinatal Period 94
PN 46 SC 37555
SN Usually the period just preceding or just following birth. Compare NEONATAL PERIOD. Used for both human and animal populations.
R ↓ Birth 67
Postnatal Period 73
↓ Pregnancy 67
↓ Prenatal Development 73

Peripheral Nerve Disorders 73
PN 72 SC 37560
B Nervous System Disorders 67
N Myasthenia Gravis 73
↓ Neuralgia 73
R Muscular Dystrophy 73
↓ Paralysis 73
↓ Peripheral Nervous System 73

Peripheral Nervous System 73
PN 267 SC 37570
SN Anatomical systems of structures outside the brain and spinal cord composed of neural tissue. Use PERIPHERAL NERVES to access references from 73-93.
UF Nerves (Peripheral)
B Nervous System 67
N ↓ Autonomic Nervous System 67
↓ Cranial Nerves 73
↓ Neural Pathways 82
Spinal Nerves 73
R Autonomic Ganglia 73
↓ Peripheral Nerve Disorders 73

Peripheral Vision 88
PN 208 SC 37580
B Visual Perception 67
R Visual Field 67

Permissiveness (Parental)
Use Parental Permissiveness

Perpetrators 88
PN 1095 SC 37595
N ↓ Criminals 67
R ↓ Crime 67

Perpetrators — (cont'd)
R Criminal Responsibility 91
Incest 73
Victimization 73

Perphenazine 73
PN 115 SC 37600
B Antiemetic Drugs 73
Phenothiazine Derivatives 73

Persecution 73
PN 83 SC 37610
B Antisocial Behavior 71
Interpersonal Interaction 67
R Torture 88
Victimization 73

Perseverance
Use Persistence

Perseveration 67
PN 158 SC 37630
SN Persistent repetition of a response to different and perhaps inappropriate stimuli which may be due to a refusal or an inability to interrupt one's behavior or to change from one task to another. Also, pathological repetition of thoughts, acts, or verbalizations.
B Thought Disturbances 73

Persistence 73
PN 770 SC 37640
SN Maintenance of particular behavior despite effort, opposition, or cessation of initiating stimulus. Used for human or animal populations.
UF Perseverance
B Personality Traits 67
R Conscientiousness 97
↓ Motivation 67

Persistent Mental Illness
Use Chronic Mental Illness

Person Centered Psychotherapy
Use Client Centered Therapy

Person Environment Fit 91
PN 144 SC 37645
SN Compatibility between individuals and their surroundings.
R ↓ Adjustment 67
↓ Environment 67
Environmental Adaptation 73
↓ Environmental Planning 82
↓ Personality 67
↓ Systems 67
↓ Working Conditions 73

Personal Adjustment
Use Emotional Adjustment

Personal Computers
Use Microcomputers

Personal Construct Theory
Use Personality Theory

Personal Defense
Use Self Defense

Personal Growth Techniques
Use Human Potential Movement

Personal Orientation Inventory 73
PN 115 SC 37670
B Nonprojective Personality Measures 73

Personal Space [73]
PN 1042 **SC** 37680
SN Minimal spatial distance preferred by an individual in his/her relations with others.
UF Interpersonal Distance
R Boundaries (Psychological) [97]
Crowding [78]
Physical Contact [82]
↓ Social Behavior [67]
Social Density [78]

Personal Therapy [91]
PN 47 **SC** 37685
SN Therapy for professionals working in the mental health field, for example, psychologists, psychiatrists, or social workers.
B Treatment [67]
R ↓ Clinical Methods Training [73]
Impaired Professionals [85]
↓ Mental Health Personnel [67]
↓ Professional Consultation [73]
Professional Supervision [88]
Psychoanalytic Training [73]
Self Analysis [94]

Personal Values [73]
PN 1914 **SC** 37690
SN Set of ideals that an individual deems worthwhile and that influence his/her behavior.
B Values [67]
R Anomie [78]
Morality [67]

Personality [67]
PN 7385 **SC** 37870
SN Conceptually broad array term referring to the totality of an individual's behavioral or emotional characteristics. Use a more specific term if possible.
UF Character
Disposition
Temperament
N ↓ Personality Traits [67]
↓ Psychoanalytic Personality Factors [73]
R ↓ Cognitive Style [67]
Coronary Prone Behavior [82]
Egocentrism [78]
↓ Emotional Adjustment [73]
↓ Emotional States [73]
↓ Emotions [67]
Five Factor Personality Model [97]
Gender Identity [85]
Human Nature [97]
Individual Differences [67]
↓ Lifestyle [78]
Person Environment Fit [91]
Personality Change [67]
Personality Correlates [67]
↓ Personality Development [67]
↓ Personality Disorders [67]
↓ Personality Processes [67]
↓ Personality Theory [67]
Predisposition [73]
Psychodynamics [73]
Self Actualization [73]
↓ Self Concept [67]
Self Disclosure [73]
Self Evaluation [67]
Self Monitoring (Personality) [85]
Self Perception [67]
Somatotypes [73]
Teacher Personality [73]

Personality Assessment
Use Personality Measures

Personality Change [67]
PN 1064 **SC** 37720

Personality Change — (cont'd)
SN Process or fact of change associated either with development and maturity, or as the result of stress, illness, treatment, or other factors.
B Personality Processes [67]
R Behavior Change [73]
↓ Personality [67]
↓ Personality Development [67]

Personality Correlates [67]
PN 3921 **SC** 37740
SN Description of numerous or unspecified personality traits which bear a mutual or reciprocal relationship to a particular phenomenon or behavior.
R Individual Differences [67]
↓ Personality [67]

Personality Development [67]
PN 4024 **SC** 37750
UF Character Development
Character Formation
B Psychosocial Development [73]
N ↓ Ego Development [91]
Separation Individuation [82]
R Ego Identity [91]
Emotional Development [73]
Externalization [73]
Five Factor Personality Model [97]
Identity Crisis [73]
↓ Internalization [97]
Moral Development [73]
↓ Personality [67]
Personality Change [67]
↓ Personality Theory [67]

Personality Disorders [67]
PN 2328 **SC** 37760
UF Asthenic Personality
Character Disorders
B Mental Disorders [67]
N Antisocial Personality [73]
Aspergers Syndrome [91]
Avoidant Personality [94]
Dependent Personality [94]
Hysterical Personality [73]
Inadequate Personality [73]
Narcissistic Personality [73]
Obsessive Compulsive Personality [73]
Paranoid Personality [73]
Passive Aggressive Personality [73]
↓ Sadomasochistic Personality [73]
Schizoid Personality [73]
Schizotypal Personality [91]
R Borderline States [78]
↓ Defense Mechanisms [67]
↓ Dissociative Patterns [73]
↓ Ethnospecific Disorders [73]
Explosive Personality [73]
Kleptomania [73]
↓ Personality [67]
↓ Personality Processes [67]
↓ Personality Theory [67]
Pyromania [73]

Personality Factors
Use Personality Traits

Personality Factors (Psychoanalytic)
Use Psychoanalytic Personality Factors

Personality Measures [67]
PN 7006 **SC** 37790
UF Personality Assessment
Personality Tests
Tests (Personality)
B Measurement [67]
N California Psychological Inventory [67]

Personality Measures — (cont'd)
N General Health Questionnaire [91]
Kirton Adaption Innovation Inven [97]
NEO Personality Inventory [97]
↓ Nonprojective Personality Measures [73]
↓ Projective Personality Measures [73]
Rokeach Dogmatism Scale [73]
Sensation Seeking Scale [73]
Sentence Completion Tests [91]

Personality Processes [67]
PN 1143 **SC** 37800
SN Conceptually broad array term referring to the interaction among personality structures (e.g., ego, id) or pattern of characteristic tendencies, often but not exclusively from a psychoanalytic perspective. Use a more specific term if possible.
N Catharsis [73]
Cathexis [73]
↓ Defense Mechanisms [67]
Externalization [73]
Inhibition (Personality) [73]
Insight [73]
↓ Internalization [97]
Introspection [73]
Personality Change [67]
R Boundaries (Psychological) [97]
↓ Lifestyle [78]
↓ Mental Disorders [67]
↓ Personality [67]
↓ Personality Disorders [67]
↓ Psychoanalytic Personality Factors [73]
↓ Psychoanalytic Theory [67]
Reality Testing [73]

Personality Tests
Use Personality Measures

Personality Theory [67]
PN 1973 **SC** 37850
UF Personal Construct Theory
B Theories [67]
N Five Factor Personality Model [97]
R Individual Differences [67]
↓ Personality [67]
↓ Personality Development [67]
↓ Personality Disorders [67]
Self Perception [67]
Self Psychology [88]

Personality Traits [67]
PN 15839 **SC** 37860
UF Personality Factors
B Personality [67]
N Adaptability (Personality) [73]
Aggressiveness [73]
Agreeableness [97]
Altruism [73]
Androgyny [82]
Assertiveness [73]
Authoritarianism [67]
Charisma [88]
↓ Cognitive Style [67]
Conformity (Personality) [67]
Conscientiousness [97]
Conservatism [73]
Courage [73]
Creativity [67]
Cruelty [73]
Curiosity [67]
Cynicism [73]
Defensiveness [67]
Dependency (Personality) [67]
Dishonesty [73]
Dogmatism [78]
Egalitarianism [85]
Egotism [73]
Emotional Immaturity [73]
Emotional Inferiority [73]

Personality Traits — (cont'd)
N Emotional Instability 73
Emotional Maturity 73
Emotional Security 73
Emotional Stability 73
Emotional Superiority 73
Emotionality (Personality) 73
Empathy 67
Extraversion 67
Femininity 67
Gregariousness 73
Hardiness 97
Honesty 73
Hypnotic Susceptibility 73
Independence (Personality) 73
Individuality 73
Initiative 73
Integrity 97
Internal External Locus of Control 67
Introversion 67
Irritability 88
Liberalism 73
Likability 88
Loyalty 73
Machiavellianism 73
Masculinity 67
Misanthropy 73
Moodiness 73
Narcissism 67
Need for Approval 97
Need for Cognition 97
Negativism 73
Nervousness 73
Neuroticism 73
Nonconformity (Personality) 73
Nurturance 85
Obedience 73
Objectivity 73
Omnipotence 94
Openmindedness 78
Openness to Experience 97
Optimism 73
Paranoia 88
Passiveness 73
Perceptiveness (Personality) 73
Perfectionism 88
Persistence 73
Pessimism 73
Positivism 73
Psychoticism 78
Repression Sensitization 73
Rigidity (Personality) 67
↓ Risk Taking 67
Self Control 73
Selfishness 73
Sensation Seeking 78
Sensitivity (Personality) 67
Seriousness 73
Sexuality 73
Sincerity 73
Sociability 73
Subjectivity 94
Suggestibility 67
Timidity 73
↓ Tolerance 73
R Codependency 91
Coronary Prone Behavior 82
Egocentrism 78
Five Factor Personality Model 97
Instrumentality 91
Leadership Qualities 97

Personnel 67
PN 2738 SC 37980
SN Conceptually broad array term referring to the body of persons employed by a given organization or associated with a particular occupation. Use a more specific term if possible.

Personnel — (cont'd)
UF Employees
Workers
N ↓ Artists 73
↓ Business and Industrial Personnel 67
Disabled Personnel 97
↓ Government Personnel 73
↓ Hypnotists 73
↓ Nonprofessional Personnel 82
↓ Paraprofessional Personnel 73
↓ Professional Personnel 78
↓ Religious Personnel 73
↓ Social Workers 73
↓ Volunteer Personnel 73
R Affirmative Action 85
Employability 73
Employee Absenteeism 73
↓ Employee Benefits 73
↓ Employee Characteristics 88
↓ Employee Interaction 88
Employee Turnover 73
Employer Attitudes 73
Employment History 78
Job Applicant Attitudes 73
Job Applicants 85
↓ Job Performance 67
Labor Union Members 73
Military Veterans 73
↓ Occupations 67
↓ Personnel Management 73
↓ Personnel Supply 73
↓ Personnel Training 67
Reemployment 91
Retirement 73
Teams 88
Unemployment 67
Work (Attitudes Toward) 73
↓ Working Conditions 73
Working Women 78

Personnel Development
Use Personnel Training

Personnel Evaluation 73
PN 2173 SC 37900
B Evaluation 67
Personnel Management 73
N Occupational Success Prediction 73
Teacher Effectiveness Evaluation 78
R Assessment Centers 82
Employment Discrimination 94
Job Applicant Interviews 73
Job Applicant Screening 73
↓ Job Performance 67
Peer Evaluation 82
Personnel Promotion 78
↓ Personnel Selection 67
Professional Competence 97

Personnel Management 73
PN 848 SC 37910
UF Human Resources
B Management 67
N Career Development 85
Job Analysis 67
Labor Management Relations 67
↓ Personnel Evaluation 73
Personnel Placement 73
Personnel Promotion 78
↓ Personnel Recruitment 73
↓ Personnel Selection 67
Personnel Termination 73
R Affirmative Action 85
Business Education 73
Business Management 73
Employment Discrimination 94
↓ Personnel 67
Resource Allocation 97

Personnel Management — (cont'd)
R Supervisor Employee Interaction 97
Supported Employment 94

Personnel Placement 73
PN 253 SC 37920
UF Placement (Personnel)
B Personnel Management 73
R Assessment Centers 82
Career Development 85

Personnel Promotion 78
PN 289 SC 37925
UF Job Promotion
B Personnel Management 73
R Assessment Centers 82
Career Development 85
Employment History 78
↓ Job Performance 67
Occupational Status 78
Occupational Success 78
↓ Personnel Evaluation 73

Personnel Recruitment 73
PN 302 SC 37930
UF Employment Processes
Recruitment (Personnel)
B Personnel Management 73
N Military Recruitment 73
Teacher Recruitment 73
R Affirmative Action 85
Job Applicant Interviews 73
Job Applicant Screening 73

Personnel Selection 67
PN 2526 SC 37940
UF Employee Selection
Hiring
Selection (Personnel)
B Personnel Management 73
N Job Applicant Interviews 73
Job Applicant Screening 73
R Affirmative Action 85
Assessment Centers 82
Employment Discrimination 94
↓ Personnel Evaluation 73
↓ Screening 82

Personnel Supply 73
PN 97 SC 37950
SN Availability of manpower or human resources required for an occupation or service in order to meet demands.
UF Manpower
N Medical Personnel Supply 73
Mental Health Personnel Supply 73
R ↓ Personnel 67

Personnel Termination 73
PN 289 SC 37960
UF Employee Termination
B Personnel Management 73
R Employment History 78
Job Security 78
↓ Occupational Tenure 73
Retirement 73
Unemployment 67

Personnel Training 67
PN 2736 SC 37970
UF Job Training
Personnel Development
Training (Personnel)
B Education 67
N Apprenticeship 73
↓ Inservice Training 85
Management Training 73
Military Training 73

Personnel Training — (cont'd)
N On the Job Training 73
R Business Education 73
Career Development 85
Human Relations Training 78
Job Enrichment 73
↓ Personnel 67
Sensitivity Training 73

Personnel Turnover
Use Employee Turnover

Perspective Taking
Use Role Taking

Perspiration
Use Sweat

Persuasion Therapy 73
PN 10 SC 38000
SN Limited directive therapy in which the client is encouraged to follow the therapist's advice to deal with current crises.
B Psychotherapy 67

Persuasive Communication 67
PN 1933 SC 38010
SN Communication, in written or oral form, aimed at influencing others to accept a position, belief, or course of action.
B Communication 67
N Brainwashing 82
R Coercion 94
Debates 97
↓ Interpersonal Influences 67
Peer Pressure 94
Propaganda 73
Rhetoric 91

Peru 88
PN 61 SC 38015
B South America 67

Perversions (Sexual)
Use Sexual Deviations

Pessimism 73
PN 232 SC 38020
SN Attitude characterized by a gloomy and desperate temperament and inclination to emphasize and expect the worst possible outcome of events and actions.
B Emotional States 73
Personality Traits 67
R Cynicism 73
Fatalism 73
Hopelessness 88
Negativism 73
Nihilism 73
Optimism 73

Pesticides
Use Insecticides

Pet Therapy
Use Animal Assisted Therapy

Petit Mal Epilepsy 73
PN 39 SC 38030
B Epilepsy 67

Pets 82
PN 315 SC 38035
SN Domesticated animals kept primarily for pleasure rather than utility.
R Animal Assisted Therapy 94
Animal Domestication 78

Pets — (cont'd)
R ↓ Animals 67
Interspecies Interaction 91

Peyote 73
PN 5 SC 38050
B Alkaloids 73
Hallucinogenic Drugs 67
Psychotomimetic Drugs 73
R Mescaline 73

Phantom Limbs 73
PN 85 SC 38060
B Body Image Disturbances 73
R ↓ Amputation 73

Pharmacists 91
PN 37 SC 38065
B Medical Personnel 67

Pharmacology 73
PN 735 SC 38070
B Paramedical Sciences 73
N Psychopharmacology 67
R Bioavailability 91
Drug Abuse Liability 94

Pharmacotherapy
Use Drug Therapy

Pharyngeal Disorders 73
PN 15 SC 38090
B Respiratory Tract Disorders 73

Pharynx 73
PN 31 SC 38100
B Digestive System 67
Respiratory System 73

Phenaglycodol
SN Term discontinued in 1997. Use PHENAGLYCODOL to access references from 73-96.
Use Sedatives

Phencyclidine 82
PN 518 SC 38125
SN Piperadine having hallucinogenic, anesthetic, and analgesic properties.
UF PCP
B Analgesic Drugs 73
Anesthetic Drugs 73
Hallucinogenic Drugs 67

Phenelzine 73
PN 258 SC 38130
B Antidepressant Drugs 71
Monoamine Oxidase Inhibitors 73

Phenethylamines 85
PN 96 SC 38135
UF Phenylethylamines
B Amines 73
R ↓ Amphetamine 67

Pheniprazine 73
PN 6 SC 38140
B Antidepressant Drugs 71
Antihypertensive Drugs 73
Monoamine Oxidase Inhibitors 73

Phenmetrazine 73
PN 14 SC 38150
B Appetite Depressing Drugs 73
Sympathomimetic Amines 73

Phenobarbital 73
PN 283 SC 38160
B Anticonvulsive Drugs 73
Barbiturates 67
Hypnotic Drugs 73
Sedatives 73

Phenomenology 67
PN 1214 SC 38180
B Philosophies 67
R Constructivism 94
Hermeneutics 91
↓ History of Psychology 67

Phenothiazine Derivatives 73
PN 209 SC 38190
UF Butyrylperazine
Triflupromazine
B Tranquilizing Drugs 67
N Chlorpromazine 67
Chlorprothixene 73
Fluphenazine 73
Mesoridazine 73
Perphenazine 73
Prochlorperazine 73
Promazine 73
Thioridazine 73
Trifluoperazine 73
R ↓ Cholinergic Blocking Drugs 73

Phenotypes 73
PN 311 SC 38200
R Assortative Mating 91
↓ Genetics 67
Genotypes 73

Phenoxybenzamine 73
PN 69 SC 38210
B Adrenergic Blocking Drugs 73
Amines 73
Antihypertensive Drugs 73

Phenylalanine 73
PN 133 SC 38220
B Alanines 73
N Parachlorophenylalanine 78

Phenylethylamines
Use Phenethylamines

Phenylketonuria 73
PN 148 SC 38230
UF Oligophrenia (Phenylpyruvic)
PKU (Hereditary Disorder)
B Genetic Disorders 73
Metabolism Disorders 73
Neonatal Disorders 73
R ↓ Mental Retardation 67

Phenytoin
Use Diphenylhydantoin

Pheromones 73
PN 659 SC 38240
SN Chemical substances released by an organism that may influence the behavior of other organisms of the same species in characteristic ways.
R ↓ Animal Mating Behavior 67
Animal Scent Marking 85
↓ Glands 67
↓ Hormones 67

Phi Coefficient 73
PN 20 SC 38250
B Statistical Correlation 67

Philippines 73
PN 336 SC 38260
B Southeast Asia 73

Philosophies 67
PN 3100 SC 38270
N Animism 73
Asceticism 73
Determinism 97
Dualism 73
Epistemology 73
Existentialism 67
Fatalism 73
Hermeneutics 91
Humanism 73
Idealism 73
Intellectualism 73
Logic (Philosophy) 73
Materialism 73
Metaphysics 73
Mysticism 67
Nihilism 73
Pacifism 73
Phenomenology 67
Positivism (Philosophy) 97
Postmodernism 97
Pragmatism 73
Realism (Philosophy) 73
Reductionism 73
Relativism 97
R Hedonism 73

Philosophy of Life
Use World View

Phobias 67
PN 2001 SC 38280
SN Disorders characterized by persistent, unrealistic, intense fear of an object, activity, or situation.
UF Arachnophobia
Phobic Neurosis
Spider Phobia
B Anxiety Disorders 97
N Acrophobia 73
Agoraphobia 73
Claustrophobia 73
Ophidiophobia 73
School Phobia 73
Social Phobia 85
R ↓ Anxiety 67
↓ Fear 67

Phobic Neurosis
SN Term discontinued in 1988. Use PHOBIC NEUROSIS to access references from 73-87.
Use Phobias

Phonemes 73
PN 854 SC 38300
SN Members of the set of the smallest units of speech that serve to distinguish one utterance from another, as the p of pat and the f of fat. Used both for the concept of phonemes as well as the discipline of phonemics. Compare PHONOLOGY.
B Phonology 73
N Consonants 73
R Phonetics 67
↓ Prosody 91
Vowels 73

Phonetics 67
PN 894 SC 38310
SN Science, study, analysis, and classification of sounds including their production in speech, transmission and perception. Used for the linguistic discipline or the specific phonetic characteristics of utterances themselves.

Phonetics — (cont'd)
B Phonology 73
R Articulation (Speech) 67
Morphemes 73
↓ Phonemes 73
Syllables 73

Phonics 73
PN 169 SC 38320
SN Science of sound. Also, a method of teaching beginners to read and pronounce words by hearing the phonetic value of letters, letter groups, and especially syllables.
B Language Arts Education 73
R Reading Education 73

Phonology 73
PN 1370 SC 38330
SN Study of the ways in which speech sounds (phonemes) and phonetic features form systems and patterns at a given point in time or from a historical perspective. Used for the linguistic discipline or the specific phonological processes or factors themselves. Compare PHONEMES.
B Grammar 67
N ↓ Phonemes 73
Phonetics 67
↓ Prosody 91
Syllables 73
Vowels 73
R Inflection 73
Morphology (Language) 73
↓ Semantics 67
↓ Syntax 71

Phosphatases 73
PN 85 SC 38340
B Enzymes 73
R ↓ Esterases 73
Hydroxylases 73

Phosphatides 73
PN 174 SC 38350
UF Phospholipids
B Fatty Acids 73
N Lecithin 91

Phospholipids
Use Phosphatides

Phosphorus 73
PN 48 SC 38370

Phosphorylases 73
PN 14 SC 38380
B Enzymes 73

Photic Threshold
Use Illumination AND Visual Thresholds

Photographic Art 73
PN 31 SC 38400
B Art 67
R Motion Pictures (Entertainment) 73

Photographic Memory
Use Eidetic Imagery

Photographs 67
PN 644 SC 38410
SN Use for photographs as stimuli. Not used as a document type identifier.
B Audiovisual Communications Media 73
R Pictorial Stimuli 78

Photopic Stimulation 73
PN 189 SC 38420

Photopic Stimulation — (cont'd)
SN Presentation of light at intensity levels characteristic of daylight illumination, activating cone photoreceptors in the retina.
B Illumination 67
R Scotopic Stimulation 73

Photoreceptors 73
PN 300 SC 38430
B Neural Receptors 73
Sensory Neurons 73
N Cones (Eye) 73
Rods (Eye) 73
R Visual Receptive Fields 82

Phototherapy 91
PN 168 SC 38435
UF Bright Light Therapy
Illumination Therapy
B Organic Therapies 73
R ↓ Alternative Medicine 97
↓ Psychotherapy 67
Seasonal Affective Disorder 91

Phrases 73
PN 115 SC 38440
SN Groups of words that function as an element in grammatical structure.
B Language 67
R ↓ Syntax 71

Phrenic Nerve
Use Spinal Nerves

Phylogenesis 73
PN 133 SC 38460
R ↓ Biology 67
Botany 73

Physical Abuse 91
PN 593 SC 38465
B Antisocial Behavior 71
R ↓ Abuse Reporting 97
Battered Child Syndrome 73
Battered Females 88
↓ Child Abuse 71
Elder Abuse 88
Emotional Abuse 91
↓ Family Violence 82
Partner Abuse 91
Patient Abuse 91
↓ Sexual Abuse 88
↓ Violence 73

Physical Agility 73
PN 59 SC 38470
UF Agility (Physical)
B Motor Processes 67
N Physical Dexterity 73
R Motor Coordination 73
Physical Mobility 94

Physical Appearance 82
PN 365 SC 38473
SN Externally visible characteristics or features of a person.
N Physique 67
R Clothing 67
Facial Features 73
Nudity 73
Physical Attractiveness 73
Somatotypes 73

Physical Attractiveness 73
PN 1293 SC 38475
R Facial Features 73
Interpersonal Attraction 67
↓ Physical Appearance 82

Physical Comfort 82
PN 117 **SC** 38477
SN Perceived degree of physical well-being in response to internal or environmental conditions.
UF Comfort (Physical)
R ↓ Environment 67
Furniture 85
↓ Satisfaction 73

Physical Contact 82
PN 561 **SC** 38478
SN Bodily contact. Used for human or animal populations.
UF Touching
B Social Interaction 67
R Affection 73
↓ Animal Social Behavior 67
Intimacy 73
Personal Space 73
↓ Tactual Perception 67

Physical Development 73
PN 1415 **SC** 38480
UF Physical Growth
B Development 67
N ↓ Motor Development 73
Neural Development 85
↓ Prenatal Development 73
Sexual Development 73
R Adolescent Development 73
Age Differences 67
Aging (Attitudes Toward) 85
Animal Development 78
↓ Childhood Development 67
↓ Delayed Development 73
↓ Developmental Age Groups 73
↓ Developmental Stages 73
↓ Early Childhood Development 73
Emotional Development 73
↓ Human Development 67
↓ Infant Development 73
Neonatal Development 73
↓ Perceptual Development 73
Physical Maturity 73
Precocious Development 73
↓ Psychogenesis 73
Sex Linked Developmental Differences 73

Physical Dexterity 73
PN 134 **SC** 38490
UF Dexterity (Physical)
B Perceptual Motor Coordination 73
Physical Agility 73
R Physical Mobility 94

Physical Disabilities (Attit Toward) 97
PN 0 **SC** 38491
SN Use PHYSICAL HANDICAPS (ATTIT TOWARD) to access references from 73-96.
UF Physical Handicaps (Attit Toward)
B Disabled (Attitudes Toward) 97
R ↓ Physically Disabled 97

Physical Disfigurement 78
PN 123 **SC** 38492
UF Deformity
R ↓ Injuries 73
↓ Physical Disorders 97
↓ Physically Disabled 97

Physical Disorders 97
PN 0 **SC** 38493
SN Consider DISORDERS to access references prior to 1997.
UF Illness (Physical)
Physical Illness
B Disorders 67
N ↓ Blood and Lymphatic Disorders 73
↓ Cardiovascular Disorders 67

Physical Disorders — (cont'd)
N ↓ Digestive System Disorders 73
↓ Endocrine Disorders 73
↓ Genetic Disorders 73
↓ Immunologic Disorders 73
↓ Infectious Disorders 73
↓ Metabolism Disorders 73
↓ Musculoskeletal Disorders 73
↓ Neonatal Disorders 73
↓ Neoplasms 67
↓ Nervous System Disorders 67
↓ Nutritional Deficiencies 73
↓ Respiratory Tract Disorders 73
↓ Sense Organ Disorders 73
↓ Skin Disorders 73
↓ Toxic Disorders 73
↓ Urogenital Disorders 73
↓ Vision Disorders 82
R ↓ Anesthesia (Feeling) 73
Back Pain 82
↓ Chronic Illness 91
Chronicity (Disorders) 82
↓ Communication Disorders 82
Comorbidity 91
↓ Congenital Disorders 73
↓ Diagnosis 67
Disease Course 91
↓ Eating Disorders 97
↓ Ethnospecific Disorders 73
Etiology 67
Illness Behavior 82
↓ Injuries 73
↓ Learning Disorders 67
Malingering 73
↓ Memory Disorders 73
↓ Mental Disorders 67
Onset (Disorders) 73
↓ Pain 67
Physical Disfigurement 78
Predisposition 73
Premorbidity 78
Prenatal Exposure 91
Prognosis 73
Recovery (Disorders) 73
Relapse (Disorders) 73
↓ Remission (Disorders) 73
Rett Syndrome 94
Severity (Disorders) 82
↓ Sexual Function Disturbances 73
↓ Sleep Disorders 73
Special Needs 94
Susceptibility (Disorders) 73
↓ Symptoms 67
↓ Syndromes 73
↓ Treatment Resistant Disorders 94
Work Related Illnesses 94

Physical Divisions (Geographic)
Use Geography

Physical Education 67
PN 1264 **SC** 38500
B Curriculum 67

Physical Endurance 73
PN 214 **SC** 38510
B Endurance 73
R Physical Fitness 73
Physical Strength 73
Physiological Stress 67

Physical Examination 88
PN 212 **SC** 38515
SN Examination or screening of an individual's overall physical health.
B Health Screening 97
R Cancer Screening 97
Drug Usage Screening 88
Mammography 94

Physical Examination — (cont'd)
R ↓ Medical Diagnosis 73
Preventive Medicine 73
Self Examination (Medical) 88

Physical Exercise
Use Exercise

Physical Fitness 73
PN 870 **SC** 38530
R Aerobic Exercise 88
↓ Exercise 73
Physical Endurance 73
Physical Strength 73

Physical Geography
Use Geography

Physical Growth
Use Physical Development

Physical Handicaps (Attit Toward)
SN Term discontinued in 1997. Use PHYSICAL HANDICAPS (ATTIT TOWARD) to access references from 73-96.
Use Physical Disabilities (Attit Toward)

Physical Illness
Use Physical Disorders

Physical Illness (Attitudes Toward) 85
PN 904 **SC** 38557
SN Attitudes toward one's own or other's physical illness.
N AIDS (Attitudes Toward) 97
R Disability Discrimination 97
↓ Disabled (Attitudes Toward) 97
Health Attitudes 85
Health Knowledge 94
Illness Behavior 82

Physical Maturity 73
PN 79 **SC** 38560
SN Attainment of a stage of physical development commonly associated with persons of a given age level.
UF Maturity (Physical)
R ↓ Physical Development 73

Physical Mobility 94
PN 38 **SC** 38563
SN Ability to move within one's environment. May be used for mobility problems associated with aging or handicapping conditions. Used for human populations only.
B Motor Processes 67
R Activities of Daily Living 91
Activity Level 82
↓ Disabled 97
Mobility Aids 78
↓ Motor Development 73
↓ Physical Agility 73
Physical Dexterity 73

Physical Restraint 82
PN 650 **SC** 38566
SN Use of any physical means to restrict the movement of a client or subject, human or animal.
UF Restraint (Physical)
R ↓ Motor Processes 67
Patient Violence 94
↓ Physical Treatment Methods 73
↓ Treatment 67

Physical Strength 73
PN 315 **SC** 38570

Physical Strength — (cont'd)
UF Strength (Physical)
R Physical Endurance 73
Physical Fitness 73

Physical Therapists 73
PN 82 SC 38580
B Medical Personnel 67
Therapists 67

Physical Therapy 73
PN 305 SC 38590
SN Treatment of disorder or injury by physical means, such as light, heat, cold, water, electricity, or by mechanical apparatus or kinesitherapy.
UF Physiotherapy
B Paramedical Sciences 73
Rehabilitation 67
R Occupational Therapy 67

Physical Trauma
Use Injuries

Physical Treatment Methods 73
PN 432 SC 38610
SN Medical, dental, and surgical methods for treatment of disorder or injury. Use a more specific term if possible. Compare ORGANIC THERAPIES.
UF Treatment Methods (Physical)
B Treatment 67
N Acupuncture 73
Artificial Respiration 73
Blood Transfusion 73
Catheterization 73
↓ Dental Treatment 73
↓ Dialysis 73
Immunization 73
Radiation Therapy 73
↓ Surgery 71
R ↓ Alternative Medicine 97
Holistic Health 85
Medical Treatment (General) 73
Pain Management 94
Physical Restraint 82

Physically Disabled 97
PN 0 SC 38615
SN Use PHYSICALLY HANDICAPPED to access references prior to 1997.
UF Orthopedically Handicapped
Physically Handicapped
B Disabled 97
N Amputees 73
Health Impaired 73
R Hemiplegia 78
Paraplegia 78
Physical Disabilities (Attit Toward) 97
Physical Disfigurement 78
Quadriplegia 85

Physically Handicapped
SN Term discontinued in 1997. Use PHYSICALLY HANDICAPPED to access references prior to 1997.
Use Physically Disabled

Physician Patient Interaction
Use Therapeutic Processes

Physicians 67
PN 3540 SC 38640
UF Doctors
B Medical Personnel 67
N Family Physicians 73
General Practitioners 73
Gynecologists 73

Physicians — (cont'd)
N Internists 73
Neurologists 73
Obstetricians 78
Pathologists 73
Pediatricians 73
Psychiatrists 67
Surgeons 73
R Clinicians 73

Physicists 73
PN 17 SC 38650
B Professional Personnel 78
R ↓ Aerospace Personnel 73
Mathematicians 73
Scientists 67

Physics 73
PN 488 SC 38660
B Sciences 67
R Magnetism 85
Relativism 97

Physiological Aging 67
PN 2630 SC 38670
SN Biological changes which occur in an organism with the passage of time.
UF Aging (Physiological)
B Aging 91
R Adult Development 78
↓ Aged 73
Aged (Attitudes Toward) 78
Aging (Attitudes Toward) 85
Geriatric Psychotherapy 73
Geriatrics 67
Life Expectancy 82
↓ Physiology 67
↓ Senile Dementia 73

Physiological Arousal 67
PN 3157 SC 38680
SN Condition of alertness and readiness to respond as evidenced by physiological signs such as heart rate or blood pressure.
UF Arousal (Physiological)
Excitation (Physiological)
R ↓ Brain Stimulation 67
Cardiovascular Reactivity 94
↓ Consciousness States 71
Physiological Stress 67
↓ Physiology 67
↓ Sexual Arousal 78

Physiological Correlates 67
PN 5361 SC 38690
SN Numerous or unspecified physiological processes which accompany a particular psychological or physical action, state, or characteristic.
R Biological Markers 91
Cardiovascular Reactivity 94
Physiological Stress 67
↓ Physiology 67
↓ Symptoms 67

Physiological Psychology 67
PN 455 SC 38700
SN Branch of psychology concerned with the physiological correlates of cognitive, emotional, and behavioral processes. Use PHYSIOLOGY, PSYCHOPHYSIOLOGY, or a more specific term for the specific physiological processes themselves.
B Psychology 67
N Neuropsychology 73
R ↓ Psychophysiology 67

Physiological Stress 67
PN 1485 SC 38710

Physiological Stress — (cont'd)
B Stress 67
R Acceleration Effects 73
Decompression Effects 73
↓ Deprivation 67
↓ Environmental Effects 73
Environmental Stress 73
Physical Endurance 73
Physiological Arousal 67
Physiological Correlates 67
↓ Physiology 67
Pollution 73
Thermal Acclimatization 73

Physiology 67
PN 1347 SC 38720
SN Conceptually broad array term referring both to a branch of biological science and the functions and processes of living organisms. Use a more specific term if possible.
N Absorption (Physiological) 73
↓ Appetite 73
↓ Body Temperature 73
Digestion 73
↓ Electrophysiology 73
↓ Excretion 67
Homeostasis 73
↓ Metabolism 67
↓ Neurophysiology 73
Oxygenation 73
↓ Psychophysiology 67
↓ Reflexes 71
↓ Secretion (Gland) 73
↓ Sexual Reproduction 73
Thermal Acclimatization 73
R ↓ Anatomy 67
↓ Biochemistry 67
↓ Body Fluids 73
↓ Cells (Biology) 73
Histology 73
Instinctive Behavior 82
Metabolic Rates 73
Morphology 73
Nutrition 73
Physiological Aging 67
Physiological Arousal 67
Physiological Correlates 67
Physiological Stress 67

Physiotherapy
Use Physical Therapy

Physique 67
PN 431 SC 38740
SN Overall body structure and appearance, including size, musculature, and posture. Limited primarily to human populations. Consider also BODY SIZE or SOMATOTYPES.
B Physical Appearance 82
R Body Height 73
↓ Body Size 85
↓ Body Weight 67
Posture 73
Somatotypes 73

Physostigmine 73
PN 487 SC 38750
UF Eserine
B Alkaloids 73
Amines 73
Cholinergic Drugs 73
Cholinesterase Inhibitors 73
Cholinomimetic Drugs 73

Piaget (Jean) 67
PN 859 SC 38755
SN Identifies biographical or autobiographical studies and discussions of Piaget's works.

Piaget (Jean) — (cont'd)
R ↓ Cognitive Development [73]
Conservation (Concept) [73]
Constructivism [94]
↓ Developmental Stages [73]
Piagetian Tasks [73]
↓ Psychologists [67]

Piagetian Tasks [73]
PN 707 SC 38757
SN In measurement context, tasks used to assess children's cognitive abilities, based on Piaget's theory of cognitive development.
R ↓ Measurement [67]
Piaget (Jean) [67]

Piano
Use Musical Instruments

Pica [73]
PN 82 SC 38770
R ↓ Adjunctive Behavior [82]
Lead Poisoning [73]
Toxicomania [73]

Picketing
Use Social Demonstrations

Picks Disease [73]
PN 74 SC 38790
B Presenile Dementia [73]
R Alzheimers Disease [73]
↓ Genetic Disorders [73]

Picrotoxin [73]
PN 182 SC 38800
B Analeptic Drugs [73]
Gamma Aminobutyric Acid Antagonists [85]

Pictorial Stimuli [78]
PN 2691 SC 38805
SN Drawings, pictures, or other visual stimuli not composed of letters or digits.
R Photographs [67]
↓ Stimulus Presentation Methods [73]
↓ Visual Displays [73]
↓ Visual Stimulation [73]

Pigeons [67]
PN 4266 SC 38810
B Birds [67]

Pigments [73]
PN 237 SC 38820
N Hemoglobin [73]
Melanin [73]
Rhodopsin [85]
R Animal Coloration [85]
↓ Color [67]
Eye Color [91]

Pigs [73]
PN 431 SC 38830
B Vertebrates [73]

Pilocarpine [73]
PN 122 SC 38840
B Alkaloids [73]
Cholinergic Drugs [73]
Cholinomimetic Drugs [73]

Pilots (Aircraft)
Use Aircraft Pilots

Pimozide [73]
PN 410 SC 38860
B Tranquilizing Drugs [67]

Pineal Body [73]
PN 193 SC 38870
B Endocrine Glands [73]
R Melatonin [73]

Pinealectomy [73]
PN 59 SC 38880
B Endocrine Gland Surgery [73]

Piperazines [94]
PN 32 SC 38885
UF Chlorophenylpiperazine
MCPP
N Trazodone [88]

Pipradrol [73]
PN 14 SC 38890
B Antidepressant Drugs [71]
CNS Stimulating Drugs [73]

Piracetam [82]
PN 130 SC 38900
B Antiemetic Drugs [73]
CNS Stimulating Drugs [73]
Nootropic Drugs [91]

Pitch (Frequency) [67]
PN 1672 SC 38910
SN Perceived changes in auditory stimuli that are a function of the sound's frequency usually measured in hertz. Also, in linguistics, a phonetic element marking the fundamental frequency of a component of speech.
UF Frequency (Pitch)
Tone (Frequency)
B Auditory Stimulation [67]
N Speech Pitch [73]
Ultrasound [73]

Pitch Discrimination [73]
PN 451 SC 38920
B Pitch Perception [73]

Pitch Perception [73]
PN 311 SC 38930
B Auditory Perception [67]
N Pitch Discrimination [73]
R Music Perception [97]

Pituitary Disorders [73]
PN 33 SC 38940
UF Hypophysis Disorders
B Endocrine Disorders [73]
N Hypopituitarism [73]
R ↓ Adrenal Gland Disorders [73]
↓ Endocrine Sexual Disorders [73]
↓ Thyroid Disorders [73]

Pituitary Dwarfism
Use Hypopituitarism

Pituitary Gland [73]
PN 297 SC 38960
B Endocrine Glands [73]
N Hypothalamo Hypophyseal System [73]
Hypothalamo Pituitary Adrenal System [97]

Pituitary Gland Surgery
Use Hypophysectomy

Pituitary Hormones [73]
PN 221 SC 38980
B Hormones [67]
N Corticotropin [73]
Dynorphins [85]
Melanocyte Stimulating Hormone [85]
Oxytocin [73]

Pituitary Hormones — (cont'd)
N Somatotropin [73]
Thyrotropin [73]
Vasopressin [73]
R ↓ Gonadotropic Hormones [73]
Hypothalamo Hypophyseal System [73]
Luteinizing Hormone [78]

PKU (Hereditary Disorder)
Use Phenylketonuria

Place Conditioning [91]
PN 229 SC 39005
SN Learned behavior or the conditioning procedure in which a stimulus is paired with an environment, location, or physical position.
UF Conditioned Place Preference
B Conditioning [67]
R ↓ Animal Environments [67]
Contextual Associations [67]

Place Disorientation [73]
PN 37 SC 39010
SN Impaired awareness of place, often characteristic of organic mental disorders.
UF Disorientation (Place)
B Consciousness Disturbances [73]
R Wandering Behavior [91]

Placebo [73]
PN 681 SC 39020
SN Any effect of therapeutic intervention that cannot be attributed to the specific action of a drug or the treatment. Also, the specific substance used as a control in experiments testing the effect of a particular drug. Term is used selectively for studies of the placebo effect or other methodological issues.
R ↓ Drugs [67]

Placement (Educational)
Use Educational Placement

Placement (Personnel)
Use Personnel Placement

Placenta [73]
PN 41 SC 39040
R ↓ Pregnancy [67]
↓ Uterus [73]

Planarians [73]
PN 26 SC 39060
B Worms [67]

Planned Behavior [97]
PN 0 SC 39065
SN Based on I. Ajzen's theory that behavioral intentions are determined by one's perceived control over the behavior, attitude toward the behavior, and subjective norms.
R ↓ Attitudes [67]
↓ Behavior [67]
Intention [88]
↓ Motivation [67]

Planning (Management)
Use Management Planning

Plasma (Blood)
Use Blood Plasma

Plastic Surgery [73]
PN 89 SC 39090
B Surgery [71]

Platelets (Blood)
Use Blood Platelets

Play
Use Recreation

Play (Animal)
Use Animal Play

Play Behavior (Childhood)
Use Childhood Play Behavior

Play Development (Childhood)
Use Childhood Play Development

Play Therapy 73
PN 514 **SC** 39150
B Child Psychotherapy 67

Playgrounds 73
PN 83 **SC** 39160
B Recreation Areas 73
R ↓ School Facilities 73

Pleasure 73
PN 466 **SC** 39170
UF Enjoyment
B Emotional States 73
R Anhedonia 85
Euphoria 73
Happiness 73

Plethysmography 73
PN 52 **SC** 39180
B Medical Diagnosis 73
N Electroplethysmography 73

PMS
Use Premenstrual Tension

Pneumoencephalography 73
PN 27 **SC** 39190
UF Air Encephalography
Encephalography (Air)
B Encephalography 73
Medical Diagnosis 73
Roentgenography 73

Pneumonia 73
PN 26 **SC** 39200
B Lung Disorders 73
R ↓ Bacterial Disorders 73
↓ Viral Disorders 73

Poetry 73
PN 663 **SC** 39210
B Literature 67
R Creative Writing 94

Poetry Therapy 94
PN 5 **SC** 39215
B Creative Arts Therapy 94
R Bibliotherapy 73
↓ Psychotherapeutic Techniques 67

Point Biserial Correlation 73
PN 18 **SC** 39220
B Statistical Correlation 67

Poisoning
Use Toxic Disorders

Poisons 73
PN 318 **SC** 39240
UF Toxins
B Hazardous Materials 91

Poisons — (cont'd)
N ↓ Neurotoxins 82
R Carbon Monoxide 73
↓ Insecticides 73
Prenatal Exposure 91
Teratogens 88

Poisson Distribution
Use Skewed Distribution

Poland 73
PN 460 **SC** 39260
B Europe 73

Police Interrogation
Use Legal Interrogation

Police Personnel 73
PN 1750 **SC** 39270
B Government Personnel 73
Law Enforcement Personnel 73

Policy Making 88
PN 882 **SC** 39278
UF Organizational Policy Making
N ↓ Government Policy Making 73
Health Care Policy 94
R Educational Reform 97

Policy Making (Foreign)
Use Foreign Policy Making

Policy Making (Government)
Use Government Policy Making

Poliomyelitis 73
PN 35 **SC** 39300
UF Infantile Paralysis
Paralysis (Infantile)
B Myelitis 73
Viral Disorders 73
R ↓ Musculoskeletal Disorders 73
↓ Paralysis 73
↓ Respiratory Tract Disorders 73

Political Assassination 73
PN 49 **SC** 39320
UF Assassination (Political)

Political Attitudes 73
PN 1904 **SC** 39330
B Attitudes 67
Politics 67
N Nationalism 67
Political Conservatism 73
Political Liberalism 73
Political Radicalism 73
R Citizenship 73
Nonviolence 91
Political Socialization 88
Voting Behavior 73

Political Campaigns 73
PN 164 **SC** 39340
UF Campaigns (Political)
B Political Processes 73
R Debates 97
Political Candidates 73
Political Elections 73
Political Issues 73
Political Parties 73
Politicians 78

Political Candidates 73
PN 297 **SC** 39350
UF Candidates (Political)
B Politics 67

Political Candidates — (cont'd)
R Debates 97
Political Campaigns 73
Political Elections 73
Politicians 78

Political Conservatism 73
PN 223 **SC** 39360
UF Conservatism (Political)
B Political Attitudes 73
R Conservatism 73

Political Debates
Use Debates

Political Divisions (Geographic)
Use Geography

Political Economic Systems 73
PN 206 **SC** 39370
B Systems 67
N Capitalism 73
Communism 73
Democracy 73
Fascism 73
Socialism 73
Totalitarianism 73
R Economics 85
Economy 73
Government 67
Political Psychology 97

Political Elections 73
PN 249 **SC** 39380
UF Elections (Political)
B Political Processes 73
R Debates 97
Political Campaigns 73
Political Candidates 73
Political Parties 73
Politicians 78
Voting Behavior 73

Political Involvement
Use Political Participation

Political Issues 73
PN 285 **SC** 39390
B Politics 67
R Political Campaigns 73
↓ Social Issues 91
Voting Behavior 73

Political Liberalism 73
PN 165 **SC** 39400
UF Liberalism (Political)
B Political Attitudes 73
R Liberalism 73

Political Participation 88
PN 161 **SC** 39405
UF Political Involvement
B Politics 67
N Voting Behavior 73
R Political Psychology 97
Social Demonstrations 73
↓ Social Movements 67

Political Parties 73
PN 225 **SC** 39410
UF Democratic Party
Independent Party (Political)
Republican Party
B Politics 67
R Political Campaigns 73
Political Elections 73

Political Processes 73
PN 664 SC 39420
B Politics 67
N Political Campaigns 73
Political Elections 73
Voting Behavior 73
R Debates 97
Freedom 78
Political Psychology 97
Political Revolution 73
↓ Social Processes 67

Political Psychology 97
PN 0 SC 39425
B Applied Psychology 73
R ↓ Law (Government) 73
↓ Political Economic Systems 73
↓ Political Participation 88
↓ Political Processes 73
↓ Politics 67
Public Opinion 73
Voting Behavior 73

Political Radicalism 73
PN 118 SC 39430
UF Radicalism (Political)
B Political Attitudes 73

Political Refugees
Use Refugees

Political Revolution 73
PN 100 SC 39440
UF Revolutions (Political)
B Radical Movements 73
R ↓ Political Processes 73
Terrorism 82

Political Socialization 88
PN 56 SC 39443
SN Transmission of political norms through social agents, e.g., school, parents, peers, or mass media.
B Socialization 67
R ↓ Political Attitudes 73

Politicians 78
PN 513 SC 39445
R Political Campaigns 73
Political Candidates 73
Political Elections 73
↓ Politics 67

Politics 67
PN 1382 SC 39450
N ↓ Political Attitudes 73
Political Candidates 73
Political Issues 73
↓ Political Participation 88
Political Parties 73
↓ Political Processes 73
R Government 67
Political Psychology 97
Politicians 78

Pollution 73
PN 253 SC 39460
B Ecological Factors 73
R Atmospheric Conditions 73
Carcinogens 73
Ecology 73
Environmental Education 94
↓ Hazardous Materials 91
Noise Effects 73
Physiological Stress 67
↓ Temperature Effects 67

Polydipsia 82
PN 309 SC 39465
SN Noncontingent excessive drinking behavior usually produced and maintained by operant schedules of reinforcement involving food as a reinforcer. Also used for disordered human populations.
B Adjunctive Behavior 82
R Animal Drinking Behavior 73
Hyponatremia 97
↓ Operant Conditioning 67

Polydrug Abuse 94
PN 50 SC 39467
UF Multidrug Abuse
B Drug Abuse 73
R ↓ Alcohol Abuse 88
↓ Drug Addiction 67
↓ Drug Dependency 73
Drug Interactions 82

Polygamy 73
PN 58 SC 39470
SN Used for human or animal populations.
B Family Structure 73
Marriage 67
R Monogamy 97

Polygraphs 73
PN 187 SC 39480
B Apparatus 67
R Legal Interrogation 94

Polyphagia
Use Hyperphagia

Pons 73
PN 458 SC 39510
B Brain Stem 73
Hindbrain 97
N Raphe Nuclei 82

Popularity 88
PN 189 SC 39520
SN Use SOCIAL APPROVAL to access references from 73-87.
R ↓ Interpersonal Interaction 67
Reputation 97
Social Acceptance 67
Social Approval 67
↓ Social Influences 67
↓ Social Perception 67

Population 73
PN 299 SC 39530
SN Total number of organisms (human or animal) inhabiting a given locality.
N Overpopulation 73
↓ Population (Statistics) 73
R Birth Rate 82
Demographic Characteristics 67
Mortality Rate 73
Social Density 78

Population (Statistics) 73
PN 637 SC 39540
SN All the objects or people of a given class.
B Population 73
N ↓ Statistical Samples 73
R ↓ Central Tendency Measures 73
↓ Experimental Design 67
↓ Experimentation 67
↓ Sampling (Experimental) 73
↓ Statistical Analysis 67
Statistical Reliability 73
↓ Statistical Variables 73

Population Characteristics
Use Demographic Characteristics

Population Control
Use Birth Control

Population Density
Use Social Density

Population Genetics 73
PN 97 SC 39570
SN Study of the genetic composition of human or animal populations; gene interactions and alterations that promote population changes and evolution.
B Genetics 67
R Assortative Mating 91
Behavioral Genetics 94
↓ Genetic Engineering 94

Population Shifts
Use Human Migration

Pornography 73
PN 299 SC 39580
UF X Rated Materials
R Nudity 73
Obscenity 78
↓ Psychosexual Behavior 67
Sex 67
↓ Sex Offenses 82
↓ Sexual Deviations 67

Porphyria 73
PN 30 SC 39590
B Blood and Lymphatic Disorders 73
Genetic Disorders 73
Metabolism Disorders 73
R ↓ Mental Disorders 67

Porpoises 73
PN 7 SC 39600
B Whales 85
R Dolphins 73

Porteus Maze Test 73
PN 19 SC 39610
B Intelligence Measures 67

Portugal 82
PN 106 SC 39613
B Europe 73

Positive and Negative Symptoms 97
PN 0 SC 39618
UF Negative and Positive Symptoms
B Symptoms 67
R ↓ Schizophrenia 67

Positive Reinforcement 73
PN 789 SC 39620
SN Presentation of a positive reinforcer contingent on the performance of some behavior. Also, the positively reinforcing object or event itself which, when made to follow the performance of some behavior, results in an increase in the frequency of occurrence of that behavior. Compare REWARDS.
B Reinforcement 67
N Praise 73

Positive Transfer 73
PN 165 SC 39630
SN Previous learning or practice which aids the acquisition of new material or skills as the result of common characteristics shared by the prior and current learning situation.
B Transfer (Learning) 67

Positivism [73]
PN 120 **SC** 39640
SN Personal quality or state of being positive or confident. Compare OPTIMISM.
B Personality Traits [67]
R Determinism [97]
Hope [91]
Optimism [73]

Positivism (Philosophy) [97]
PN 0 **SC** 39642
SN Philosophical view that scientific knowledge comes only from direct observation and application of empirical methods.
B Philosophies [67]
R Behaviorism [67]
↓ Empirical Methods [73]
Epistemology [73]
Hermeneutics [91]
Reductionism [73]

Positron Emission Tomography
Use Tomography

Possession
Use Ownership

Postactivation Potentials [85]
PN 241 **SC** 39650
SN Enhancement of synaptic and cellular responses induced by brief high frequency electrical stimulation.
UF Long Term Potentiation
Short Term Potentiation
B Electrical Activity [67]
R Electrical Brain Stimulation [73]
Neural Plasticity [94]

Postganglionic Autonomic Fibers
Use Autonomic Ganglia

Postgraduate Students [73]
PN 98 **SC** 39684
SN Students involved in study or research after having completed a master's or doctoral degree. Such students are not necessarily pursuing a degree. Mandatory term in educational contexts.
B Students [67]
R ↓ College Students [67]
Graduate Students [67]
Young Adults [73]

Postgraduate Training [73]
PN 162 **SC** 39685
SN Studies or research beyond master's or doctoral degree.
B Higher Education [73]
N ↓ Clinical Psychology Grad Training [73]
Clinical Psychology Internship [73]
Medical Internship [73]
Medical Residency [73]
R Professional Specialization [91]

Posthypnotic Suggestions [94]
PN 19 **SC** 39687
R ↓ Hypnosis [67]
↓ Hypnotherapy [73]
Hypnotic Susceptibility [73]
↓ Relaxation Therapy [78]
Suggestibility [67]

Postmodernism [97]
PN 0 **SC** 39689
B Philosophies [67]
R ↓ Arts [73]
↓ Literature [67]

Postnatal Dysphoria
Use Postpartum Depression

Postnatal Period [73]
PN 1215 **SC** 39690
R Lactation [73]
Perinatal Period [94]
Postpartum Depression [73]
↓ Pregnancy [67]

Postpartum Depression [73]
PN 493 **SC** 39700
UF Postnatal Dysphoria
Postpartum Psychosis
B Major Depression [88]
R ↓ Acute Psychosis [73]
Acute Schizophrenia [73]
Attachment Behavior [85]
↓ Marital Relations [67]
Mother Child Relations [67]
↓ Organic Brain Syndromes [73]
Postnatal Period [73]

Postpartum Psychosis
Use Postpartum Depression

Postsurgical Complications [73]
PN 136 **SC** 39710
UF Surgical Complications
R Obstetrical Complications [78]
Recovery (Disorders) [73]
Relapse (Disorders) [73]
↓ Surgery [71]
↓ Treatment Outcomes [82]

Posttesting [73]
PN 84 **SC** 39720
SN Measurement performed after experimental manipulation, treatment, or program intervention. Comparison of pretest and posttest scores gives a measure of effectiveness of independent variables such as treatments or programs.
B Measurement [67]
R Repeated Measures [85]
↓ Testing Methods [67]

Posttraumatic Stress Disorder [85]
PN 2058 **SC** 39727
SN Acute, chronic, or delayed reactions to traumatic events such as military combat, assault, or natural disaster. Use TRAUMATIC NEUROSIS or STRESS REACTIONS to access references from 1973–1984.
B Anxiety Disorders [97]
R Adjustment Disorders [94]
Combat Experience [91]
Emotional Trauma [67]
Stress Reactions [73]
Traumatic Neurosis [73]

Posttreatment Followup [73]
PN 719 **SC** 39730
SN Periodic check-ups of patients. Usually part of a comprehensive aftercare treatment. Differentiate from FOLLOWUP STUDIES which is a mandatory term identifying a type of methodology used in research.
UF Catamnesis
Followup (Posttreatment)
R Aftercare [73]
Discharge Planning [94]
↓ Treatment [67]
↓ Treatment Planning [97]

Posture [73]
PN 915 **SC** 39740
R Body Language [73]
↓ Motor Processes [67]
Physique [67]

Potassium [73]
PN 166 **SC** 39750
B Metallic Elements [73]
N Potassium Ions [73]

Potassium Ions [73]
PN 44 **SC** 39770
B Electrolytes [73]
Potassium [73]

Potential (Achievement)
Use Achievement Potential

Potential Dropouts [73]
PN 120 **SC** 39790
B Dropouts [73]

Potentiation (Drugs)
Use Drug Interactions

Poverty [73]
PN 581 **SC** 39820
B Social Issues [91]
R Disadvantaged [67]
↓ Homeless [88]
Income (Economic) [73]
Lower Income Level [73]
↓ Socioeconomic Status [67]

Poverty Areas [73]
PN 76 **SC** 39830
UF Slums
B Social Environments [73]
R Cultural Deprivation [73]
Ghettoes [73]

Power [67]
PN 2573 **SC** 39840
SN Social control an individual has over others.
B Social Influences [67]
N Abuse of Power [97]
R Authority [67]
Coercion [94]
↓ Dominance [67]
Empowerment [91]
↓ Helplessness [97]
Omnipotence [94]

Practical Knowledge
Use Procedural Knowledge

Practice [67]
PN 3518 **SC** 39850
SN Use PRACTICE or PRACTICE EFFECTS to access references prior to 1982.
UF Experience (Practice)
Practice Effects
Rehearsal
N Distributed Practice [73]
Massed Practice [73]
R Curricular Field Experience [82]
↓ Experiences (Events) [73]
Familiarity [67]
Memory Training [94]
Overcorrection [85]
Test Coaching [97]

Practice Effects
SN Term discontinued in 1982. Use PRACTICE EFFECTS or PRACTICE to access references prior to 1982.
Use Practice

Practicum Supervision [78]
PN 697 **SC** 39865
SN Supervision of students involved in practical application of learned material.

Practicum Supervision — (cont'd)
R ↓ Clinical Methods Training 73
↓ Clinical Psychology Grad Training 73
Clinical Psychology Internship 73
Cooperating Teachers 78
Counselor Education 73
↓ Teacher Education 67

Prader Willi Syndrome 91
PN 36 SC 39867
B Congenital Disorders 73
Syndromes 73
R ↓ Mental Retardation 67

Pragmatics 85
PN 422 SC 39868
SN Study of the rules governing the use of language in context. Also used for the actual social interaction aspects of communication.
B Semiotics 85
Verbal Communication 67
R ↓ Communication Skills 73
Discourse Analysis 97
↓ Interpersonal Communication 73
↓ Linguistics 73
Metalinguistics 94

Pragmatism 73
PN 38 SC 39870
B Philosophies 67

Praise 73
PN 461 SC 39880
B Positive Reinforcement 73
Verbal Reinforcement 73

Prayer 73
PN 81 SC 39890
B Religious Practices 73
R Meditation 73

Praying Mantis
Use Mantis

Preadolescents 88
PN 182 SC 39905
SN Ages 10-12 years. Use SCHOOL AGE CHILDREN or ADOLESCENTS, as appropriate, unless specific reference is made to the population as preadolescents. Used in noneducational contexts. Application of terms designating age is mandatory for ages 0-17.
B School Age Children 73
R Adolescence 84
↓ Adolescents 67
↓ Elementary School Students 67
Intermediate School Students 73
↓ Juvenile Delinquents 73
Middle School Students 85
Predelinquent Youth 78

Precocious Development 73
PN 64 SC 39910
B Development 67
R ↓ Developmental Age Groups 73
↓ Physical Development 73
↓ Psychogenesis 73

Precognition 73
PN 101 SC 39920
B Clairvoyance 73

Preconditioning 94
PN 6 SC 39923
SN Presentation of two stimuli in a consecutive manner without reinforcement to determine if subject will respond to both stimuli in a conditioning paradigm.

Preconditioning — (cont'd)
UF Sensory Preconditioning
B Conditioning 67
R Conditioned Stimulus 73

Predatory Behavior (Animal)
Use Animal Predatory Behavior

Predelinquent Youth 78
PN 67 SC 39927
SN Children considered at risk for developing delinquent behavior because their sociocultural and family backgrounds and early behavior patterns parallel those of juvenile delinquents.
R ↓ Adolescents 67
↓ Children 67
Juvenile Delinquency 67
↓ Juvenile Delinquents 73
Preadolescents 88
↓ School Age Children 73

Predictability (Measurement) 73
PN 139 SC 39930
SN Statistical procedures used to forecast the value of the criterion variables (such as behavior, performance, or outcomes) on the basis of selected predictor variables.
B Statistical Analysis 67
Statistical Measurement 73
R Chaos Theory 97
Confidence Limits (Statistics) 73
↓ Hypothesis Testing 73
↓ Prediction 67
↓ Prediction Errors 73
↓ Probability 67
↓ Statistical Estimation 85

Prediction 67
PN 6148 SC 39940
N Academic Achievement Prediction 67
Occupational Success Prediction 73
R Chaos Theory 97
↓ Estimation 67
Future 91
Predictability (Measurement) 73
↓ Prediction Errors 73
Predictive Validity 73
Prognosis 73
Self Fulfilling Prophecies 97

Prediction Errors 73
PN 59 SC 39950
B Errors 67
N Type I Errors 73
Type II Errors 73
R Consistency (Measurement) 73
↓ Hypothesis Testing 73
↓ Measurement 67
Predictability (Measurement) 73
↓ Prediction 67
↓ Statistical Analysis 67
Statistical Power 91
Statistical Reliability 73
↓ Statistical Validity 73
↓ Statistical Variables 73

Predictive Validity 73
PN 2729 SC 39960
SN Usually expressed as a correlation coefficient, predictive validity is the extent to which test scores, grades, assessment methods, scoring techniques, and other variables can be used to reliably predict future behavior or performance.
B Statistical Validity 73
R Concurrent Validity 88
↓ Prediction 67
Test Validity 73

Predisposition 73
PN 1966 SC 39970
SN Proneness toward disorders or propensity toward certain behaviors due to physical, psychological, social, or situational factors. Consider also SUSCEPTIBILITY (DISORDERS).
R At Risk Populations 85
Biological Markers 91
Coronary Prone Behavior 82
↓ Disorders 67
↓ Genetics 67
↓ Mental Disorders 67
Nature Nurture 94
↓ Personality 67
↓ Physical Disorders 97
Premorbidity 78
Response Bias 67
Susceptibility (Disorders) 73

Prednisolone 73
PN 29 SC 39980
B Adrenal Cortex Hormones 73
Corticosteroids 73

Preference Measures 73
PN 650 SC 39990
B Measurement 67
N Kuder Preference Record 73
Least Preferred Coworker Scale 73
R ↓ Attitude Measures 67
↓ Preferences 67

Preferences 67
PN 5214 SC 39995
N Aesthetic Preferences 73
Brand Preferences 94
Food Preferences 73
Occupational Preference 73
R ↓ Preference Measures 73
Preferred Rewards 73

Preferred Rewards 73
PN 127 SC 40030
B Rewards 67
R ↓ Preferences 67

Prefrontal Cortex 94
PN 181 SC 40035
B Frontal Lobe 73

Preganglionic Autonomic Fibers
Use Autonomic Ganglia

Pregnancy 67
PN 3608 SC 40050
UF Gestation
N Adolescent Pregnancy 88
R ↓ Birth 67
Childbirth Training 78
Fertilization 73
Obstetrical Complications 78
Perinatal Period 94
Placenta 73
Postnatal Period 73
↓ Prenatal Care 91
Reproductive Technology 88
↓ Sexual Reproduction 73
Sexual Risk Taking 97

Pregnancy (False)
Use Pseudocyesis

Prejudice 67
PN 1141 SC 40070
B Social Influences 67
N ↓ Religious Prejudices 73
R Age Discrimination 94
AntiSemitism 73

Prejudice — (cont'd)
R ↓ Attitudes 67
Disability Discrimination 97
Employment Discrimination 94
Race and Ethnic Discrimination 94
↓ Racial and Ethnic Attitudes 82
Racial and Ethnic Relations 82
Racism 73
Sex Discrimination 78
Sexism 88
Stigma 91

Preliminary Scholastic Aptitude Test
Use Coll Ent Exam Bd Scholastic Apt Test

Premarital Counseling 73
PN 125 **SC** 40090
B Counseling 67
R ↓ Psychotherapeutic Counseling 73

Premarital Intercourse 73
PN 245 **SC** 40100
B Sexual Intercourse (Human) 73
R ↓ Birth Control 71
Promiscuity 73
Social Dating 73
Unwed Mothers 73
Virginity 73

Premature Birth 73
PN 1097 **SC** 40110
B Birth 67
R Birth Weight 85
Obstetrical Complications 78

Premature Ejaculation 73
PN 107 **SC** 40120
B Male Orgasm 73
Sexual Function Disturbances 73
R Impotence 73

Premenstrual Syndrome
Use Premenstrual Tension

Premenstrual Tension 73
PN 705 **SC** 40130
SN Physiological, emotional, and mental stress related to the period of time immediately preceding menstruation.
UF PMS
Premenstrual Syndrome
B Menstrual Cycle 73
R ↓ Menstrual Disorders 73
↓ Psychosomatic Disorders 67

Premorbidity 78
PN 481 **SC** 40135
SN Condition of an individual before onset of illness or disorder.
R At Risk Populations 85
↓ Disorders 67
↓ Mental Disorders 67
Onset (Disorders) 73
Patient History 73
↓ Physical Disorders 97
Predisposition 73
Susceptibility (Disorders) 73

Prenatal Care 91
PN 148 **SC** 40137
SN Medical, health, and educational services provided or obtained during pregnancy. Includes maternal health behavior affecting prenatal development.
N Childbirth Training 78
R Early Intervention 82
Health Behavior 82
↓ Health Care Services 78

Prenatal Care — (cont'd)
R ↓ Health Education 73
↓ Obstetrics 78
↓ Pregnancy 67
↓ Prenatal Development 73
Prenatal Diagnosis 88
↓ Prevention 73
Preventive Medicine 73

Prenatal Development 73
PN 1733 **SC** 40140
SN Development of an organism prior to birth. Used for human or animal populations.
B Physical Development 73
N ↓ Prenatal Developmental Stages 73
R Animal Development 78
Fetal Alcohol Syndrome 85
Perinatal Period 94
↓ Prenatal Care 91
Prenatal Diagnosis 88
Prenatal Exposure 91
↓ Psychogenesis 73
Teratogens 88

Prenatal Developmental Stages 73
PN 28 **SC** 40150
B Developmental Stages 73
Prenatal Development 73
N Embryo 73
Fetus 67

Prenatal Diagnosis 88
PN 96 **SC** 40152
SN Techniques or procedures used to detect or identify specific abnormalities or characteristics of the fetus.
UF Amniocentesis
B Medical Diagnosis 73
R ↓ Congenital Disorders 73
↓ Genetic Disorders 73
↓ Prenatal Care 91
↓ Prenatal Development 73
Reproductive Technology 88

Prenatal Exposure 91
PN 754 **SC** 40156
SN Exposure to chemicals or other environmental factors prior to birth. Used for human and animal populations.
UF Fetal Exposure
R ↓ Alcoholic Beverages 73
↓ Disorders 67
↓ Drugs 67
↓ Physical Disorders 97
↓ Poisons 73
↓ Prenatal Development 73
Teratogens 88
Thalidomide 73
Tobacco Smoking 67

Preoptic Area 94
PN 68 **SC** 40158
SN Consider HYPOTHALAMUS to access references prior to 1994.
B Hypothalamus 67

Prepulse Inhibition 97
PN 0 **SC** 40159
SN Markedly reduced startle response resulting from a weaker stimulus preceding a stronger startle-inducing stimulus.
R Conditioned Suppression 73
↓ Latent Inhibition 97
Sensory Gating 91
Startle Reflex 67

Presbyterians
Use Protestants

Preschool Age Children 67
PN 30188 **SC** 40160
SN Ages 2-5 years. Used in noneducational contexts. Application of terms designating age is mandatory for ages 0-17.
UF Early Childhood
B Children 67
R ↓ Childhood Development 67
Kindergarten Students 73
Nursery School Students 73
↓ Preschool Students 82

Preschool Education 73
PN 1203 **SC** 40170
B Education 67
R Project Head Start 73

Preschool Students 82
PN 1856 **SC** 40173
SN Students from infancy to entrance in kindergarten or 1st grade. Mandatory term in educational contexts.
B Students 67
N Nursery School Students 73
R Kindergarten Students 73
Preschool Age Children 67

Preschool Teachers 85
PN 337 **SC** 40176
B Teachers 67

Prescribing (Drugs) 91
PN 216 **SC** 40177
R ↓ Drug Therapy 67
↓ Drugs 67
↓ Treatment 67

Prescription Drugs 91
PN 70 **SC** 40178
B Drugs 67
R ↓ Drug Therapy 67
Nonprescription Drugs 91
Self Medication 91

Presenile Dementia 73
PN 176 **SC** 40180
UF Dementia (Presenile)
B Dementia 85
N Alzheimers Disease 73
Creutzfeldt Jakob Syndrome 94
Picks Disease 73
R ↓ Senile Dementia 73

Preservice Teachers 82
PN 501 **SC** 40205
SN Education students or graduates prior to employment as teachers.
B Teachers 67
R ↓ College Students 67
Education Students 82
Student Teachers 73
↓ Teacher Education 67

Presidential Debates
Use Debates

Pressoreceptors
Use Baroreceptors

Pressors (Drugs)
Use Vasoconstrictor Drugs

Pressure Sensation 73
PN 51 **SC** 40270
R ↓ Somesthetic Perception 67

Prestige (Occupational)
Use Occupational Status

Pretesting [73]
PN 129 **SC** 40280
SN Running preliminary trials to establish a baseline. Comparison of pretest and posttest scores gives a measure of effectiveness of independent variables such as treatments or programs.
B Measurement [67]
R Repeated Measures [85]
↓ Testing Methods [67]

Pretraining (Therapy)
Use Client Education

Prevention [73]
PN 4424 **SC** 40290
SN Conceptually broad array term referring to any process that acts to deter undesirable occurrences. Use a more specific term if possible.
N Accident Prevention [73]
AIDS Prevention [94]
Crime Prevention [85]
Drug Abuse Prevention [94]
Fire Prevention [73]
Preventive Medicine [73]
Primary Mental Health Prevention [73]
Relapse Prevention [94]
Suicide Prevention [73]
R Condoms [91]
Disability Management [91]
Early Intervention [82]
↓ Health Care Delivery [78]
↓ Health Care Services [78]
↓ Health Education [73]
Health Promotion [91]
↓ Mental Health Services [78]
↓ Prenatal Care [91]
Risk Management [97]
Risk Perception [97]
↓ Safety [67]
Suicide Prevention Centers [73]
↓ Treatment [67]

Preventive Medicine [73]
PN 345 **SC** 40300
B Prevention [73]
Treatment [67]
R ↓ Alternative Medicine [97]
Drug Abuse Prevention [94]
↓ Health [73]
Health Behavior [82]
Health Maintenance Organizations [82]
Health Promotion [91]
↓ Health Screening [97]
Holistic Health [85]
Mammography [94]
Physical Examination [88]
↓ Prenatal Care [91]
Relapse Prevention [94]

Price
Use Costs and Cost Analysis

Pride [73]
PN 70 **SC** 40310
B Emotional States [73]

Priests [73]
PN 161 **SC** 40320
B Clergy [73]
R Chaplains [73]
Missionaries [73]

Primacy Effect [73]
PN 185 **SC** 40328

Primacy Effect — (cont'd)
SN Component of the serial position effect which is manifested by a greater ease in learning items that occur at the beginning of a series rather than those toward the middle. Compare RECENCY EFFECT.
B Serial Position Effect [82]
R ↓ Learning [67]
Recency Effect [73]

Primal Therapy [78]
PN 45 **SC** 40329
SN Combination of intensive individual therapy and group psychotherapy with emphasis on experiencing and expression of blocked traumatic events or feelings (primals) and their integration into total life functioning.
B Psychotherapy [67]
R ↓ Psychotherapeutic Techniques [67]

Primary Health Care [88]
PN 580 **SC** 40331
SN Health care provided by a medical professional with whom a patient has initial contact when entering the health care system and by whom a patient may be referred to a specialist.
B Health Care Services [78]
R ↓ Health Care Delivery [78]

Primary Mental Health Prevention [73]
PN 1019 **SC** 40330
SN Mental health programs designed to prevent onset or occurrence of mental illness in high risk or target populations.
B Prevention [73]
R Drug Abuse Prevention [94]
Early Intervention [82]
↓ Mental Health [67]
↓ Mental Health Programs [73]
Relapse Prevention [94]

Primary Reinforcement [73]
PN 51 **SC** 40340
SN Presentation of a primary reinforcer. Also, objects or events which do not require prior pairing with other reinforcers in order to maintain reinforcing properties. Also known as unconditioned reinforcers or unconditioned stimuli. Compare EXTERNAL REWARDS.
B Reinforcement [67]
R ↓ Conditioning [67]
Unconditioned Stimulus [73]

Primary School Students [73]
PN 271 **SC** 40350
SN Students in kindergarten through 3rd grade. Use ELEMENTARY SCHOOL STUDENTS or KINDERGARTEN STUDENTS unless specific reference is made to population as primary school students. Use of a student term is mandatory in educational contexts.
B Elementary School Students [67]
R ↓ Children [67]
↓ School Age Children [73]

Primary Schools
Use Elementary Schools

Primates (Nonhuman) [73]
PN 818 **SC** 40370
UF Apes
B Mammals [73]
N Baboons [73]
Bonobos [97]
Chimpanzees [73]
Gorillas [73]
Monkeys [67]

Primidone [73]
PN 15 **SC** 40380
B Anticonvulsive Drugs [73]
R ↓ Barbiturates [67]

Priming [88]
PN 962 **SC** 40385
N Semantic Priming [94]
R Contextual Associations [67]
Cues [67]
↓ Perception [67]
↓ Prompting [97]
↓ Semantics [67]

Printed Communications Media [73]
PN 312 **SC** 40390
B Mass Media [67]
N ↓ Books [73]
Magazines [73]
Newspapers [73]

Printing (Handwriting) [73]
PN 39 **SC** 40400
B Handwriting [67]

Prismatic Stimulation [73]
PN 168 **SC** 40410
SN Visual stimulation technique in which special lenses are used to spatially distort or invert visual images or the visual field. Also includes prisms that differentially refract light of different wavelengths to produce an array or spectrum of colors.
B Visual Stimulation [73]
R ↓ Color Perception [67]
Spatial Distortion [73]

Prison Personnel [73]
PN 375 **SC** 40420
B Law Enforcement Personnel [73]
R Attendants (Institutions) [73]

Prisoners [67]
PN 2781 **SC** 40430
UF Inmates (Prison)
N Prisoners of War [73]
R ↓ Criminals [67]

Prisoners Dilemma Game [73]
PN 306 **SC** 40440
SN Nonzero-sum game in which individual outcomes are determined by joint actions of two players. Incentives for both cooperation and competition exist, and no communication is permitted between the two players.
B Games [67]
R Entrapment Games [73]
Game Theory [67]
Non Zero Sum Games [73]

Prisoners of War [73]
PN 123 **SC** 40450
B Prisoners [67]
R Hostages [88]

Prisons [67]
PN 865 **SC** 40460
UF Jails
Penitentiaries
B Correctional Institutions [73]
R Concentration Camps [73]
Reformatories [73]

Privacy [73]
PN 339 **SC** 40467
R Privileged Communication [73]
Secrecy [94]
↓ Social Behavior [67]

Private Practice 78
PN 343 SC 40469
SN Employment of professional personnel in independent for-profit practices (as opposed to public offices or nonprofit settings) in which there is direct contact with clients and payment for services rendered. Private practitioners may function in individual practices, partnerships, or incorporated business settings.
R ↓ Health Care Delivery 78

Private School Education 73
PN 429 SC 40470
SN Schools or formal education in schools supported and administered by organizations not affiliated with the government.
UF Parochial School Education
B Education 67
R Religious Education 73

Private Sector 85
PN 230 SC 40475
SN Any type of non-government organization, service, or sphere of involvement.
N Business Organizations 73
R Entrepreneurship 91
Ownership 85

Privileged Communication 73
PN 588 SC 40480
SN Confidential communication between doctors, lawyers, or therapists and their clients which, by legal sanction, may not be revealed to others. Also, any documents or recorded statements of such communication which can be legally withheld from public inspection.
UF Communication (Privileged)
Confidentiality of Information
R ↓ Abuse Reporting 97
Anonymity 73
Client Records 97
↓ Communication 67
↓ Experimentation 67
Information 67
Privacy 73

Proactive Inhibition 73
PN 675 SC 40490
SN The theory that previous learning of material can interfere with the retention of newly-learned material. Also, the actual proactive interference itself.
UF Inhibition (Proactive)
B Interference (Learning) 67
Latent Inhibition 97

Probability 67
PN 1441 SC 40500
SN The likelihood of the chance occurrence of specific events. May include the mathematical study of probability theory.
N ↓ Chance (Fortune) 73
Response Probability 73
↓ Statistical Probability 67
R Chaos Theory 97
↓ Hypothesis Testing 73
Predictability (Measurement) 73
Probability Judgment 78
Probability Learning 67

Probability Judgment 78
PN 643 SC 40505
SN Process of ascertaining or estimating the degree of likelihood that certain specified conditions or events have, can, or will occur.
B Judgment 67
R ↓ Probability 67
Probability Learning 67

Probability Learning 67
PN 552 SC 40510
SN Experimental paradigm in which subjects are asked to guess or estimate whether an experimentally controlled event will occur or choose which of various alternative events will occur. As learning occurs, the proportion of correct responses tends to approach the actual probability proportion of event occurrences. Used for the experimental paradigm or task as well as the learned behavior itself.
B Learning 67
R ↓ Probability 67
Probability Judgment 78

Probation 73
PN 334 SC 40520
SN Period of suspended sentence of a convicted offender following good behavior and during which the offender is not incarcerated but is under the supervision of a probation officer.
B Legal Processes 73
R Court Referrals 94
↓ Law Enforcement 78
Parole 73

Probation Officers 73
PN 166 SC 40530
B Law Enforcement Personnel 73
R Parole Officers 73

Probenecid 82
PN 15 SC 40535
SN Agent that promotes the urinary excretion of uric acid.
R ↓ Diuretics 73

Problem Drinking
SN Term discontinued in 1988. Use PROBLEM DRINKING to access references from 73-87.
Use Alcohol Abuse

Problem Solving 67
PN 8323 SC 40550
SN Process of determining a correct sequence of alternatives leading to a desired goal or to successful completion or performance of a task.
UF Individual Problem Solving
B Cognitive Processes 67
N Anagram Problem Solving 73
Cognitive Hypothesis Testing 82
↓ Group Problem Solving 73
R ↓ Decision Making 67
Declarative Knowledge 97
↓ Expert Systems 91
↓ Inductive Deductive Reasoning 73
↓ Reasoning 67

Procaine 82
PN 47 SC 40560
SN Use NOVOCAINE to access references from 73–81.
UF Novocaine
B Analgesic Drugs 73
Anesthetic Drugs 73

Procedural Knowledge 97
PN 0 SC 40565
SN Knowledge regarding how to do things. Compare DECLARATIVE KNOWLEDGE.
UF Functional Knowledge
Practical Knowledge
R ↓ Cognitive Processes 67
Declarative Knowledge 97
Divergent Thinking 73
Information 67
↓ Knowledge Level 78
↓ Memory 67

Procedural Knowledge — (cont'd)
R Metacognition 91
↓ Reasoning 67

Process Psychosis 73
PN 65 SC 40570
UF Process Schizophrenia
B Psychosis 67

Process Schizophrenia
Use Process Psychosis AND Schizophrenia

Prochlorperazine 73
PN 15 SC 40640
B Antiemetic Drugs 73
Phenothiazine Derivatives 73

Procrastination 85
PN 103 SC 40645
SN Habitual, often counterproductive postponing. Use STUDY HABITS to access references in educational contexts from 73-84.
B Motivation 67

Product Design 97
PN 0 SC 40647
SN Process of conceptualizing, planning, researching, developing, and field testing products or goods.
UF Consumer Product Design
R ↓ Advertising 67
Computer Assisted Design 97
Consumer Protection 73
↓ Consumer Research 73
Consumer Surveys 73
Marketing 73

Productivity (Employee)
Use Employee Productivity

Profanity 91
PN 9 SC 40655
B Language 67
R Obscenity 78

Professional Certification 73
PN 532 SC 40660
SN In general, certification constitutes permission to use a particular professional title contingent on fulfilling requisite educational and training programs.
UF Certification (Professional)
N Accreditation (Education Personnel) 73
R Professional Development 82
Professional Examinations 94
↓ Professional Licensing 73
↓ Professional Personnel 78

Professional Client Sexual Relations 94
PN 76 SC 40665
SN Sexual relations, intimacy, or affectionate behavior between a professional (e.g., therapist, lawyer, religious personnel, or educator) and their clients or patients.
UF Boundary Violations (Sexual)
Patient Therapist Sexual Relations
Sexual Boundary Violations
Therapist Patient Sexual Relations
R Countertransference 73
Patient Abuse 91
Professional Ethics 73
↓ Professional Standards 73
↓ Psychosexual Behavior 67
↓ Psychotherapeutic Processes 67
Psychotherapeutic Transference 67
↓ Sexual Abuse 88
Sexual Harassment 85
↓ Therapeutic Processes 78

Professional Communication
Use Scientific Communication

Professional Competence [97]
PN 0 **SC** 40675
B Competence [82]
R ↓ Employee Characteristics [88]
↓ Employee Skills [73]
Peer Evaluation [82]
↓ Personnel Evaluation [73]
Professional Development [82]
Professional Liability [85]
↓ Professional Standards [73]

Professional Consultation [73]
PN 2597 **SC** 40680
SN Advisory services offered by specialists in a particular field which may be client or colleague oriented or focus on policy setting, planning, and programs of an organization. Use PROFESSIONAL CONSULTATION or MENTAL HEALTH CONSULTATION to access references prior to 1982.
UF Consultation (Professional)
Mental Health Consultation
N Consultation Liaison Psychiatry [91]
R Personal Therapy [91]
↓ Professional Personnel [78]
Professional Supervision [88]

Professional Contribution
SN Prior to 1982 this term was not defined and was used inconsistently.
Use Professional Criticism

Professional Criticism [67]
PN 18461 **SC** 40700
SN Mandatory term applied to evaluative comments on previously published work.
UF Contribution (Professional)
Criticism (Professional)
Professional Contribution

Professional Criticism Reply [73]
PN 6196 **SC** 40710
SN Mandatory term applied to replies to comments on previously published work.
UF Rebuttal
Reply (to Professional Criticism)

Professional Development [82]
PN 1235 **SC** 40715
SN Participation in activities which promote professional career development.
B Development [67]
R Career Change [78]
Career Development [85]
↓ Continuing Education [85]
Employment History [78]
Inservice Teacher Education [73]
↓ Inservice Training [85]
Mental Health Inservice Training [73]
Mentor [85]
Occupational Aspirations [73]
↓ Professional Certification [73]
Professional Competence [97]
Professional Identity [91]
↓ Professional Personnel [78]
Professional Specialization [91]
↓ Professional Standards [73]

Professional Ethics [73]
PN 3244 **SC** 40720
SN Moral principles of conducting professional research or practices.
B Ethics [67]
R ↓ Abuse Reporting [97]
Assisted Suicide [97]
Euthanasia [73]
Experimental Ethics [78]

Professional Ethics — (cont'd)
R Impaired Professionals [85]
Informed Consent [85]
Professional Client Sexual Relations [94]
Professional Liability [85]
↓ Professional Personnel [78]
↓ Professional Standards [73]

Professional Examinations [94]
PN 25 **SC** 40723
SN Required examinations for licensure or certification in order to practice a profession.
UF Certification Examinations
Licensure Examinations
State Board Examinations
B Measurement [67]
R Accreditation (Education Personnel) [73]
↓ Professional Certification [73]
↓ Professional Licensing [73]

Professional Fees [78]
PN 280 **SC** 40724
N Fee for Service [94]
R Cost Containment [91]
↓ Costs and Cost Analysis [73]
Diagnosis Related Groups [88]
Health Care Costs [94]
Money [67]
Peer Evaluation [82]
↓ Professional Personnel [78]
Salaries [73]

Professional Identity [91]
PN 206 **SC** 40725
SN Concept of self and role within a professional domain.
UF Identity (Professional)
B Social Identity [88]
R Career Development [85]
↓ Employee Characteristics [88]
Professional Development [82]
↓ Professional Personnel [78]
Role Perception [73]
↓ Self Concept [67]

Professional Liability [85]
PN 505 **SC** 40727
SN Legal liabilities relating to the conduct of one's profession.
UF Legal Liability (Professional)
Malpractice
B Professional Standards [73]
R Accountability [88]
Impaired Professionals [85]
↓ Legal Processes [73]
Misdiagnosis [97]
Patient Abuse [91]
Professional Competence [97]
Professional Ethics [73]
↓ Responsibility [73]
Risk Management [97]

Professional Licensing [73]
PN 371 **SC** 40730
SN Permission from an authority (e.g., government review board) to use a particular professional title as well as to practice the profession. Professional licensing laws also specify what activities constitute the legal or legitimate practice of the profession. One does not necessarily need to be certified (professionally) in order to be licensed.
UF Licensing (Professional)
N Accreditation (Education Personnel) [73]
R ↓ Professional Certification [73]
Professional Examinations [94]
↓ Professional Personnel [78]

Professional Meetings and Symposia [67]
PN 18305 **SC** 40740
SN Mandatory term applied to documents relating information presented at a meeting or convention. Consider also CONFERENCE PROCEEDINGS to access references prior to 1982. For behavioral aspects of meetings (attendance, communication, or participation) consider PROFESSIONAL DEVELOPMENT or SCIENTIFIC COMMUNICATION.
UF Conference Proceedings
Symposia
B Scientific Communication [73]

Professional Newsletters
Use Scientific Communication

Professional Organizations [73]
PN 1437 **SC** 40760
B Organizations [67]
R ↓ Professional Personnel [78]

Professional Orientation
Use Theoretical Orientation

Professional Personnel [78]
PN 1366 **SC** 40765
SN Conceptually broad array term referring to members of professions requiring prolonged and specialized training. Use a more specific term if possible.
B Personnel [67]
N ↓ Aerospace Personnel [73]
Anthropologists [73]
Clinicians [73]
↓ Counselors [67]
↓ Educational Personnel [73]
Engineers [67]
↓ Health Personnel [94]
↓ Information Specialists [88]
Journalists [73]
↓ Legal Personnel [85]
Mathematicians [73]
Physicists [73]
↓ Psychologists [67]
Scientists [67]
Sociologists [73]
↓ Therapists [67]
R ↓ Business and Industrial Personnel [67]
Impaired Professionals [85]
Librarians [88]
↓ Nonprofessional Personnel [82]
↓ Occupations [67]
↓ Paraprofessional Personnel [73]
↓ Professional Certification [73]
↓ Professional Consultation [73]
Professional Development [82]
Professional Ethics [73]
↓ Professional Fees [78]
Professional Identity [91]
↓ Professional Licensing [73]
Professional Organizations [73]
Professional Referral [73]
Professional Specialization [91]
↓ Professional Standards [73]
Professional Supervision [88]
↓ Religious Personnel [73]

Professional Referral [73]
PN 1279 **SC** 40770
SN Act of directing a client to a professional or agency for assessment, treatment, or consultation.
UF Referral (Professional)
R Client Transfer [97]
Court Referrals [94]
↓ Professional Personnel [78]
Self Referral [91]

Professional Specialization [91]
PN 195 **SC** 40775
SN Training in or choice of a speciality within a profession.
UF Specialization (Professional)
R Academic Specialization [73]
Career Development [85]
↓ Higher Education [73]
Occupational Choice [67]
Occupational Preference [73]
↓ Postgraduate Training [73]
Professional Development [82]
↓ Professional Personnel [78]

Professional Standards [73]
PN 1680 **SC** 40780
SN Minimally acceptable levels of quality professional care or services maintained in order to promote the welfare of those who make use of such services.
UF Standards (Professional)
N Professional Liability [85]
R Accountability [88]
Impaired Professionals [85]
Patient Abuse [91]
Peer Evaluation [82]
Professional Client Sexual Relations [94]
Professional Competence [97]
Professional Development [82]
Professional Ethics [73]
↓ Professional Personnel [78]
↓ Quality of Services [97]

Professional Supervision [88]
PN 903 **SC** 40785
SN Processes or techniques of supervision of fully trained educational or mental health personnel.
UF Clinical Supervision
Educational Supervision
Supervision (Professional)
R ↓ Educational Personnel [73]
↓ Mental Health Personnel [67]
Personal Therapy [91]
↓ Professional Consultation [73]
↓ Professional Personnel [78]

Professors
Use College Teachers

Profiles (Measurement) [73]
PN 1133 **SC** 40800
SN Usually a composite of scores obtained through psychological testing utilizing instruments which yield separate measures and which comprises a picture or profile of the individual's characteristics across several areas.
B Measurement [67]

Profoundly Mentally Retarded [73]
PN 1220 **SC** 40810
SN IQ below 20.
B Mentally Retarded [67]

Progestational Hormones [85]
PN 57 **SC** 40815
UF Progestins
B Hormones [67]
N Progesterone [73]

Progesterone [73]
PN 754 **SC** 40820
B Progestational Hormones [85]
Sex Hormones [73]
Steroids [73]

Progestins
Use Progestational Hormones

Prognosis [73]
PN 1979 **SC** 40830
SN Prediction of the course, duration, and outcome of a disorder. Compare DISEASE COURSE.
R Biological Markers [91]
↓ Chronic Mental Illness [97]
Clinical Judgment (Not Diagnosis) [73]
↓ Diagnosis [67]
Disease Course [91]
↓ Disorders [67]
↓ Medical Diagnosis [73]
↓ Mental Disorders [67]
Patient History [73]
↓ Physical Disorders [97]
↓ Prediction [67]
↓ Psychodiagnosis [67]
Severity (Disorders) [82]
↓ Treatment [67]

Program Development [91]
PN 496 **SC** 40832
SN Formulation and/or implementation of programs in any setting.
UF Program Planning
B Development [67]
N Educational Program Planning [73]
R Curriculum Development [73]
↓ Educational Programs [73]
Employee Assistance Programs [85]
↓ Government Programs [73]
Home Visiting Programs [73]
↓ Hospital Programs [78]
Independent Living Programs [91]
↓ Mental Health Programs [73]
↓ Program Evaluation [85]
↓ Psychiatric Hospital Programs [67]
↓ Social Programs [73]

Program Evaluation [85]
PN 945 **SC** 40835
SN Assessment of programs in any setting.
B Evaluation [67]
N Educational Program Evaluation [73]
Mental Health Program Evaluation [73]
R ↓ Program Development [91]

Program Evaluation (Educational)
Use Educational Program Evaluation

Program Evaluation (Mental Health)
Use Mental Health Program Evaluation

Program Planning
Use Program Development

Program Planning (Educational)
Use Educational Program Planning

Programed Instruction [67]
PN 943 **SC** 40870
UF Instruction (Programed)
B Teaching Methods [67]
R Computer Assisted Instruction [73]
Individualized Instruction [73]
Programed Textbooks [73]
↓ Prompting [97]
Teaching Machines [73]

Programed Textbooks [73]
PN 40 **SC** 40900
SN Textbooks prepared for use with programed instruction. Not used as a document type identifier.
B Textbooks [78]
R Programed Instruction [67]

Programing (Computer)
SN Use COMPUTER SOFTWARE to access references from 73-93.
Use Computer Programing

Programing Languages (Computer)
Use Computer Programing Languages

Programs (Government)
Use Government Programs

Programs (Mental Health)
Use Mental Health Programs

Progressive Relaxation Therapy [78]
PN 511 **SC** 40945
SN Therapeutic procedures which teach clients to tense and relax muscle groups, focusing on the sensations involved in relaxation. This method provides clients with practice in recognizing the sensation of tension which will serve as a cue to produce a state of muscle relaxation.
B Relaxation Therapy [78]
R ↓ Hypnotherapy [73]
Muscle Relaxation [73]
Systematic Desensitization Therapy [73]

Progressive Supranuclear Palsy [97]
PN 0 **SC** 40947
SN A progressive neurological disorder characterized by ophthalmoplegia, dystonia, memory impairment, personality disorders, and dementia. Etiology is unknown.
B Central Nervous System Disorders [73]
R ↓ Basal Ganglia [73]
↓ Senile Dementia [73]

Project Follow Through [73]
PN 34 **SC** 40950
SN U.S. Government educational program for disadvantaged elementary school students to supplement Project Head Start and encourage academic and psychosocial growth.
B Educational Programs [73]
Government Programs [73]
R Compensatory Education [73]
Government [67]

Project Head Start [73]
PN 335 **SC** 40960
SN U.S. Government program for disadvantaged 3-5 yr olds aimed at improving children's educational potential by encouraging their psychosocial development and by providing economic assistance to their families.
UF Head Start
B Educational Programs [73]
Government Programs [73]
R Compensatory Education [73]
Government [67]
Preschool Education [73]
School Readiness [73]

Projection (Defense Mechanism) [67]
PN 359 **SC** 40970
B Defense Mechanisms [67]
R Projective Identification [94]

Projective Identification [94]
PN 52 **SC** 40975
B Defense Mechanisms [67]
R Enactments [97]
Identification (Defense Mechanism) [73]
Projection (Defense Mechanism) [67]

Projective Personality Measures [73]
PN 740 **SC** 40980

Projective Personality Measures — (cont'd)
SN Tests which derive an indirect and global assessment of personality through the analysis of meaning or structure freely imposed by the subject upon unstructured or ambiguous materials. Use a more specific term if possible. (Compare NONPROJECTIVE PERSONALITY MEASURES.).
UF Blacky Pictures Test
Color Pyramid Test
Onomatopoeia and Images Test
B Personality Measures 67
Projective Techniques 67
N Bender Gestalt Test 67
Childrens Apperception Test 73
Franck Drawing Completion Test 73
Holtzman Inkblot Technique 67
Human Figures Drawing 73
Rorschach Test 67
Rosenzweig Picture Frustration Study 67
Rotter Incomplete Sentences Blank 73
Sentence Completion Tests 91
Szondi Test 73
Thematic Apperception Test 67
Zulliger Z Test 73
R Psychoanalytic Interpretation 67

Projective Techniques 67
PN 1480 **SC** 40990
SN Utilization of ambiguous or unstructured stimuli designed to elicit responses which are believed to reveal an individual's attitudes, defense modes or motivations, and personality structure. Also, the specific tests or techniques themselves. Use a more specific term if possible.
UF Projective Tests
N Franck Drawing Completion Test 73
Holtzman Inkblot Technique 67
Incomplete Man Test 73
↓ Projective Personality Measures 73
R Psychoanalytic Interpretation 67

Projective Testing Technique 73
PN 321 **SC** 41000
SN Administration, construction, scoring, and interpretation of projective tests.
B Measurement 67

Projective Tests
Use Projective Techniques

Prolactin 73
PN 1106 **SC** 41020
B Gonadotropic Hormones 73

Proline 82
PN 15 **SC** 41027
B Amino Acids 73

Prolixin
Use Fluphenazine

Promazine 73
PN 23 **SC** 41040
B Phenothiazine Derivatives 73

Promethazine 73
PN 28 **SC** 41050
B Antiemetic Drugs 73
Antihistaminic Drugs 73
Sedatives 73

Promiscuity 73
PN 68 **SC** 41060
UF Sexual Delinquency
B Psychosexual Behavior 67
R Extramarital Intercourse 73
Hypersexuality 73

Promiscuity — (cont'd)
R Premarital Intercourse 73
Prostitution 73
Sexual Addiction 97

Prompting 97
PN 0 **SC** 41065
N Constant Time Delay 97
R ↓ Behavior Modification 73
Cued Recall 94
Cues 67
↓ Learning 67
↓ Learning Strategies 91
↓ Memory 67
↓ Priming 88
Programed Instruction 67
↓ Teaching Methods 67

Pronouns 73
PN 241 **SC** 41070
B Form Classes (Language) 73

Pronunciation 73
PN 379 **SC** 41080
B Speech Characteristics 73
R Articulation (Speech) 67

Proofreading 88
PN 40 **SC** 41085
R Clerical Secretarial Skills 73
↓ Errors 67
Orthography 73
↓ Reading 67
Verbal Ability 67
↓ Written Communication 85

Propaganda 73
PN 51 **SC** 41090
B Social Influences 67
R Brainwashing 82
↓ Persuasive Communication 67

Property
Use Ownership

Propranolol 73
PN 519 **SC** 41100
B Adrenergic Blocking Drugs 73
Alcohols 67

Proprioceptors 73
PN 110 **SC** 41110
B Nerve Endings 73
Neural Receptors 73
Sensory Neurons 73

Prose 73
PN 836 **SC** 41120
B Literature 67
N ↓ Biography 67
R Creative Writing 94
Text Structure 82

Prosencephalon
Use Forebrain

Proserine
Use Neostigmine

Prosocial Behavior 82
PN 722 **SC** 41133
SN Positive social behavior generally concerned with promotion of the welfare of others. Limited to human populations.
B Social Behavior 67
N Altruism 73
Assistance (Social Behavior) 73

Prosocial Behavior — (cont'd)
N Charitable Behavior 73
Cooperation 67
Sharing (Social Behavior) 78
Trust (Social Behavior) 67
R ↓ Antisocial Behavior 71

Prosody 91
PN 124 **SC** 41134
SN Physical characteristics of speech that indicate linguistic features such as stress, intonation, intensity, and duration of speech sounds. Use INFLECTION to access references from 88-90.
B Phonology 73
N Inflection 73
R ↓ Linguistics 73
Morphology (Language) 73
↓ Phonemes 73
Sentence Structure 73
↓ Speech Characteristics 73

Prosopagnosia 94
PN 24 **SC** 41135
SN A visual agnosia usually due to brain damage and characterized by an inability to recognize familiar faces, and in some cases, one's own face.
B Agnosia 73
R Face Perception 85

Prospective Studies 97
PN 0 **SC** 41137
SN Mandatory term applied to studies of observations of the same person or group over an extended period of time, usually to generate prognostic data or incidence rates related to a particular disorder, event, or behavior.
B Longitudinal Studies 73
R Retrospective Studies 97

Prostaglandins 82
PN 143 **SC** 41136
SN Physiologically potent compounds of ubiquitous occurrence formed from essential fatty acids and affecting the nervous system, female reproductive organs, and metabolism.
R ↓ Anti Inflammatory Drugs 82
↓ Fatty Acids 73
↓ Hormones 67
↓ Neuroleptic Drugs 73
↓ Sympathomimetic Drugs 73

Prostate 73
PN 44 **SC** 41140
B Male Genitalia 73

Prostate Cancer Screening
Use Cancer Screening

Prostheses 73
PN 211 **SC** 41150
UF Artificial Limbs
B Medical Therapeutic Devices 73
N Cochlear Implants 94
R ↓ Amputation 73

Prostitution 73
PN 326 **SC** 41160
B Psychosexual Behavior 67
R Promiscuity 73

Protective Services 97
PN 0 **SC** 41170
B Social Services 82
R Child Custody 82
Child Welfare 88
Elder Care 94
Foster Care 78

Protective Services — (cont'd)
R Guardianship 88
↓ Legal Processes 73
Shelters 91
Social Casework 67

Protein Deficiency Disorders 73
PN 37 SC 41180
B Nutritional Deficiencies 73
N Kwashiorkor 73

Protein Metabolism 73
PN 149 SC 41190
B Metabolism 67

Protein Sensitization
Use Anaphylactic Shock

Proteinases 73
PN 11 SC 41210
B Enzymes 73

Proteins 73
PN 1104 SC 41220
N ↓ Blood Proteins 73
↓ Endorphins 82
↓ Globulins 73
Interferons 94
R ↓ Amino Acids 73
↓ Drugs 67
↓ Enzymes 73
Lipoproteins 73
↓ Peptides 73

Protest (Student)
Use Student Activism

Protestantism 73
PN 403 SC 41250
B Christianity 73
N Fundamentalism 73
R Protestants 97

Protestants 97
PN 0 SC 41253
UF Baptists
Episcopalians
Lutherans
Methodists
Presbyterians
B Christians 97
R ↓ Protestantism 73

Protozoa 73
PN 19 SC 41255
B Microorganisms 85

Prozac
Use Fluoxetine

Pruritus 73
PN 34 SC 41260
UF Itching
B Skin Disorders 73
Symptoms 67
R Scratching 73

Pseudocyesis 73
PN 61 SC 41270
UF False Pregnancy
Pregnancy (False)
Pseudopregnancy
B Conversion Neurosis 73
R ↓ Gynecological Disorders 73

Pseudodementia 85
PN 76 SC 41280

Pseudodementia — (cont'd)
SN Dementia-like disorder in the absence of organic brain disease.
B Mental Disorders 67
R ↓ Dementia 85
↓ Factitious Disorders 88
↓ Major Depression 88

Pseudohermaphroditism
Use Hermaphroditism

Pseudomemory
Use False Memory

Pseudopregnancy
Use Pseudocyesis

Pseudopsychopathic Schizophrenia
SN Term discontinued in 1988. Use PSEUDOPSYCHOPATHIC SCHIZOPHRENIA to access references from 73-87.
Use Schizophrenia

Psilocybin 73
PN 29 SC 41310
B Hallucinogenic Drugs 67

Psychedelic Drugs 73
PN 78 SC 41320
B Drugs 67
N Lysergic Acid Diethylamide 67
R ↓ Hallucinogenic Drugs 67
↓ Psychotomimetic Drugs 73

Psychedelic Experiences 73
PN 35 SC 41330
R Drug Induced Hallucinations 73

Psychiatric Aides 73
PN 80 SC 41340
B Paramedical Personnel 73
Psychiatric Hospital Staff 73

Psychiatric Classifications (Taxon)
Use Psychodiagnostic Typologies

Psychiatric Clinics 73
PN 431 SC 41370
UF Outpatient Psychiatric Clinics
B Clinics 67
R Child Guidance Clinics 73
Community Mental Health Centers 73
↓ Hospitals 67
↓ Mental Health Programs 73
↓ Outpatient Treatment 67
Walk In Clinics 73

Psychiatric Disorders
Use Mental Disorders

Psychiatric Evaluation 97
PN 0 SC 41385
UF Evaluation (Psychiatric)
B Evaluation 67
Measurement 67
N Forensic Evaluation 94
R Clinical Judgment (Not Diagnosis) 73
Cognitive Assessment 97
Geriatric Assessment 97
Intake Interview 94
↓ Psychodiagnosis 67
↓ Psychodiagnostic Interview 73
↓ Psychological Assessment 97
Psychological Report 88
↓ Screening 82
↓ Screening Tests 82

Psychiatric History
Use Patient History

Psychiatric Hospital Admission 73
PN 811 SC 41390
UF Admission (Psychiatric Hospital)
B Hospital Admission 73
Psychiatric Hospitalization 73
N Psychiatric Hospital Readmission 73
R ↓ Commitment (Psychiatric) 73
↓ Hospital Discharge 73
↓ Institutional Release 78
Psychiatric Hospital Discharge 78

Psychiatric Hospital Discharge 78
PN 566 SC 41395
B Hospital Discharge 73
Psychiatric Hospitalization 73
R Client Transfer 97
↓ Commitment (Psychiatric) 73
Discharge Planning 94
↓ Psychiatric Hospital Admission 73
Psychiatric Hospital Readmission 73
Treatment Termination 82

Psychiatric Hospital Programs 67
PN 1537 SC 41400
SN Organized plans for care or training in psychiatric hospitals.
B Hospital Programs 78
N Therapeutic Community 67
R Halfway Houses 73
↓ Mental Health Services 78
↓ Program Development 91
Token Economy Programs 73

Psychiatric Hospital Readmission 73
PN 492 SC 41410
UF Readmission (Psychiatric Hospital)
B Psychiatric Hospital Admission 73
Psychiatric Hospitalization 73
R ↓ Hospital Discharge 73
Psychiatric Hospital Discharge 78

Psychiatric Hospital Staff 73
PN 654 SC 41420
B Medical Personnel 67
Mental Health Personnel 67
N Psychiatric Aides 73
R Attendants (Institutions) 73
Occupational Therapists 73
↓ Paramedical Personnel 73
Psychiatric Nurses 73
Psychiatrists 67

Psychiatric Hospitalization 73
PN 3259 SC 41430
B Hospitalization 67
N ↓ Psychiatric Hospital Admission 73
Psychiatric Hospital Discharge 78
Psychiatric Hospital Readmission 73
R ↓ Commitment (Psychiatric) 73
↓ Hospital Admission 73
↓ Hospital Discharge 73
↓ Institutional Release 78
Patient Seclusion 94

Psychiatric Hospitals 67
PN 3039 SC 41440
UF Asylums
Mental Hospitals
State Hospitals
B Hospitals 67
R Halfway Houses 73
Patient Seclusion 94
Psychiatric Units 91
Sanatoriums 73

Psychiatric Nurses 73
PN 601 SC 41450
B Mental Health Personnel 67
Nurses 67
R ↓ Psychiatric Hospital Staff 73

Psychiatric Patients 67
PN 16146 SC 41460
B Patients 67
R ↓ Mental Disorders 67
Psychiatric Symptoms 97
Psychopathology 67

Psychiatric Patients
Use Psychological Report

Psychiatric Patients
Use Medical Residency AND Psychiatric Training

Psychiatric Social Workers 73
PN 49 SC 41470
B Mental Health Personnel 67
Social Workers 73

Psychiatric Symptoms 97
PN 0 SC 41475
UF Psychotic Symptoms
B Symptoms 67
R ↓ Mental Disorders 67
Psychiatric Patients 67
Psychopathology 67
Symptom Checklists 91
Symptom Remission 73

Psychiatric Training 73
PN 1334 SC 41480
UF Psychiatric Residency
Training (Psychiatric)
B Clinical Methods Training 73
Medical Education 73
R Cotherapy 82
Psychoanalytic Training 73
Psychotherapy Training 73

Psychiatric Units 91
PN 250 SC 41485
SN Units in a general hospital or inpatient care facility specializing in psychiatric care of acutely disturbed patients.
UF Hospital Psychiatric Units
R ↓ Hospital Programs 78
↓ Hospitalization 67
↓ Hospitals 67
Nursing Homes 73
Patient Seclusion 94
Psychiatric Hospitals 67
↓ Residential Care Institutions 73

Psychiatrists 67
PN 3186 SC 41490
UF Neuropsychiatrists
B Mental Health Personnel 67
Physicians 67
R Clinicians 73
Hypnotherapists 73
↓ Psychiatric Hospital Staff 73
Psychoanalysts 73
↓ Psychologists 67
↓ Psychotherapists 73

Psychiatry 67
PN 5083 SC 41500
B Medical Sciences 67
N Adolescent Psychiatry 85
Biological Psychiatry 94
Child Psychiatry 67
Community Psychiatry 73

Psychiatry — (cont'd)
N Consultation Liaison Psychiatry 91
Forensic Psychiatry 73
Geriatric Psychiatry 97
Neuropsychiatry 73
Orthopsychiatry 73
Social Psychiatry 67
Transcultural Psychiatry 73
R ↓ Psychology 67
↓ Treatment 67

Psychic Healing
Use Faith Healing

Psychoactive Drugs
Use Drugs

Psychoanalysis 67
PN 11253 SC 41520
UF Psychoanalytic Therapy
B Psychotherapy 67
N Adlerian Psychotherapy 97
Dream Analysis 73
Self Analysis 94
R Catharsis 73
Erikson (Erik) 91
Free Association 94
Freud (Sigmund) 67
↓ Hypnotherapy 73
Negative Therapeutic Reaction 97
↓ Psychoanalytic Theory 67
Psychotherapeutic Neutrality 97
↓ Psychotherapeutic Processes 67
Transactional Analysis 73

Psychoanalysts 73
PN 1271 SC 41530
UF Analysts
B Psychotherapists 73
R Hypnotherapists 73
Psychiatrists 67

Psychoanalytic Interpretation 67
PN 4366 SC 41540
SN Description or formulation of the meaning or significance of any particular event, condition, or process (e.g., patient's productions, art, literature, or historical biographies) from a psychoanalytic perspective.
B Theoretical Interpretation 88
R Freudian Psychoanalytic School 73
↓ Projective Personality Measures 73
↓ Projective Techniques 67
↓ Psychoanalytic Theory 67
Psychohistory 78

Psychoanalytic Personality Factors 73
PN 384 SC 41550
UF Personality Factors (Psychoanalytic)
B Personality 67
N Conscience 67
Conscious (Personality Factor) 73
Death Instinct 88
Ego 67
Electra Complex 73
Id 73
Libido 73
Oedipal Complex 73
Subconscious 73
↓ Superego 73
Unconscious (Personality Factor) 67
R Penis Envy 73
↓ Personality Processes 67

Psychoanalytic School (Freudian)
Use Freudian Psychoanalytic School

Psychoanalytic Theory 67
PN 7470 SC 41570
B Theories 67
N Freudian Psychoanalytic School 73
R ↓ Ego Development 91
Erikson (Erik) 91
Free Association 94
Freud (Sigmund) 67
Metapsychology 94
↓ Neopsychoanalytic School 73
Object Relations 82
↓ Personality Processes 67
↓ Psychoanalysis 67
Psychoanalytic Interpretation 67
Self Psychology 88

Psychoanalytic Therapy
Use Psychoanalysis

Psychoanalytic Training 73
PN 466 SC 41590
UF Training (Psychoanalytic)
B Clinical Methods Training 73
R Personal Therapy 91
Psychiatric Training 73
Psychotherapy Training 73
Self Analysis 94

Psychobiology 82
PN 327 SC 41595
SN Scientific discipline emphasizing the holistic functioning of the individual in the environment in relation to normal or abnormal behavior.
B Sciences 67
R Behavioral Genetics 94
Biological Psychiatry 94
↓ Biology 67
Biopsychosocial Approach 91
↓ Psychology 67

Psychodiagnosis 67
PN 11360 SC 41600
SN Diagnosis of mental disorders through the use of psychological methods or tests. Compare MEDICAL DIAGNOSIS.
UF Clinical Judgment (Psychodiagnosis)
B Diagnosis 67
N ↓ Psychodiagnostic Interview 73
R Clinical Judgment (Not Diagnosis) 73
Computer Assisted Diagnosis 73
Diagnostic and Statistical Manual 94
Differential Diagnosis 67
Educational Diagnosis 78
Forensic Evaluation 94
International Class of Diseases 97
↓ Mental Disorders 67
Patient History 73
Prognosis 73
↓ Psychiatric Evaluation 97
↓ Psychodiagnostic Typologies 67
↓ Psychological Assessment 97
Psychological Report 88
Research Diagnostic Criteria 94

Psychodiagnostic Interview 73
PN 1233 SC 41630
B Interviews 67
Psychodiagnosis 67
N Diagnostic Interview Schedule 91
R Intake Interview 94
↓ Psychiatric Evaluation 97
↓ Psychological Assessment 97

Psychodiagnostic Typologies 67
PN 4292 SC 41640
SN Systematic classification of mental, cognitive, emotional, or behavioral disorders.
UF Psychiatric Classifications (Taxon)
Typologies (Psychodiagnostic)

Psychodiagnostic Typologies — (cont'd)
N Diagnostic and Statistical Manual 94
International Class of Diseases 97
Research Diagnostic Criteria 94
R Clinical Judgment (Not Diagnosis) 73
Diagnostic Interview Schedule 91
Dual Diagnosis 91
Labeling 78
Misdiagnosis 97
↓ Psychodiagnosis 67
Taxonomies 73

Psychodrama 67
PN 606 SC 41650
SN Projective technique and method of group psychotherapy in which personality make-up, interpersonal relations, conflicts, and emotional problems are explored through dramatization of meaningful situations.
B Psychotherapeutic Techniques 67
Psychotherapy 67
R ↓ Group Psychotherapy 67
Mirroring 97
Role Playing 67

Psychodynamics 73
PN 4252 SC 41660
SN Human behavior and emotions in terms of conscious and unconscious motivations.
UF Psychological Correlates
R ↓ Personality 67
Psychosocial Factors 88
↓ Social Behavior 67
↓ Social Interaction 67

Psychoeducation 94
PN 128 SC 41665
R Client Education 85
↓ Education 67
Educational Therapy 97
↓ Health Education 73
↓ Treatment 67

Psychogalvanic Reflex
Use Galvanic Skin Response

Psychogenesis 73
PN 546 SC 41670
SN Development of mental functions, traits, or states.
UF Psychological Development
B Development 67
N ↓ Cognitive Development 73
Emotional Development 73
Moral Development 73
↓ Psychosocial Development 73
R Adolescent Development 73
Adult Development 78
Age Differences 67
↓ Childhood Development 67
↓ Delayed Development 73
↓ Developmental Age Groups 73
↓ Developmental Stages 73
↓ Early Childhood Development 73
↓ Human Development 67
↓ Infant Development 73
Nature Nurture 94
Neonatal Development 73
↓ Physical Development 73
Precocious Development 73
↓ Prenatal Development 73
Sex Linked Developmental Differences 73
Sexual Development 73

Psychogenic Pain
SN Term discontinued in 1997. Use PSYCHOGENIC PAIN to access references from 73–96.
Use Somatoform Pain Disorder

Psychohistory 78
PN 756 SC 41685
SN Psychological, often psychoanalytical, interpretation of historical events and personalities. Includes psychobiographies, historical group fantasies and processes, studies of childhood from an historical perspective and historical psychodynamics.
R ↓ Biography 67
↓ History 73
Psychoanalytic Interpretation 67

Psychoimmunology
Use Psychoneuroimmunology

Psychokinesis 73
PN 173 SC 41690
UF Telekinesis
B Extrasensory Perception 67

Psycholinguistics 67
PN 1407 SC 41700
SN Discipline that combines the techniques of linguistics and psychology in the study of the relationship of language and behavior and cognitive processes. Used for the discipline as well as specific psycholinguistic processes themselves.
B Linguistics 73
R Ethnolinguistics 73
Metalinguistics 94
Neurolinguistics 91
Vygotsky (Lev) 91

Psychological Abuse
Use Emotional Abuse

Psychological Adjustment
Use Emotional Adjustment

Psychological Assessment 97
PN 0 SC 41706
SN Assessment of a patient/client by interviews, observations, or psychological tests to evaluate personality, adjustment, abilities, interests, cognitive functioning or functioning in other areas of life. Used for references that focus on the assessment process or the assessment itself.
UF Assessment (Psychological)
B Measurement 67
N Behavioral Assessment 82
Cognitive Assessment 97
↓ Neuropsychological Assessment 82
R Clinical Judgment (Not Diagnosis) 73
↓ Evaluation 67
Forensic Evaluation 94
Geriatric Assessment 97
↓ Mental Disorders 67
Needs Assessment 85
↓ Psychiatric Evaluation 97
↓ Psychodiagnosis 67
↓ Psychodiagnostic Interview 73
Psychological Report 88
Psychopathology 67

Psychological Autopsy 88
PN 40 SC 41705
SN Psychological profile developed after an individual's death by examination of personal letters or by interviewing acquaintances and relatives. Such autopsies are usually done following suicidal deaths and suspicious cases of death.
R Autopsy 73
↓ Death and Dying 67
Forensic Psychology 85
↓ Suicide 67

Psychological Correlates
Use Psychodynamics

Psychological Development
Use Psychogenesis

Psychological Endurance 73
PN 282 SC 41710
B Endurance 73
R Hardiness 97
Psychological Stress 73
Stress Reactions 73

Psychological Interpretation
Use Theoretical Interpretation

Psychological Needs 97
PN 0 SC 41715
UF Emotional Needs
B Needs 67
R Need Satisfaction 73
Needs Assessment 85

Psychological Reactance 78
PN 189 SC 41716
SN Decrease in the attractiveness of an activity, behavior, or attitude as a result of having been forced or induced by external sources to engage in the activity or behavior, or to maintain the attitude. Such reactions may appear as emotional dissatisfaction, involvement and performance decrements, or negative attitude.
UF Reactance
R Choice Behavior 67
Cognitive Dissonance 67
Freedom 78

Psychological Report 88
PN 49 SC 41718
UF Psychiatric Report
R Educational Diagnosis 78
↓ Evaluation 67
Forensic Evaluation 94
↓ Medical Diagnosis 73
↓ Psychiatric Evaluation 97
↓ Psychodiagnosis 67
↓ Psychological Assessment 97

Psychological Screening Inventory 73
PN 30 SC 41720
B Nonprojective Personality Measures 73
Screening Tests 82
Selection Tests 73

Psychological Stress 73
PN 2696 SC 41730
B Stress 67
R ↓ Deprivation 67
Hardiness 97
Psychological Endurance 73

Psychological Terminology 73
PN 1009 SC 41740
SN Definitions, analysis, evaluation, or review of individual terms or nomenclature in the field of psychology. Compare GLOSSARY.
UF Nomenclature (Psychological)
Terminology (Psychological)
B Terminology 91
R ↓ Scientific Communication 73

Psychological Testing
Use Psychometrics

Psychologist Attitudes 91
PN 186 SC 41747
SN Attitudes of, not toward, psychologists.
B Attitudes 67
R Counselor Attitudes 73
↓ Health Personnel Attitudes 85

Psychologist Attitudes — (cont'd)
R ↓ Psychologists 67
↓ Therapist Attitudes 78

Psychologists 67
PN 4320 SC 41750
B Professional Personnel 78
N Clinical Psychologists 73
Counseling Psychologists 88
↓ Educational Psychologists 73
Experimental Psychologists 73
Industrial Psychologists 73
Military Psychologists 97
Social Psychologists 73
R Adler (Alfred) 67
↓ Counselors 67
Ellis (Albert) 91
Erikson (Erik) 91
Freud (Sigmund) 67
James (William) 91
Jung (Carl) 73
Kohlberg (Lawrence) 91
Maslow (Abraham Harold) 91
↓ Mental Health Personnel 67
Pavlov (Ivan) 91
Piaget (Jean) 67
Psychiatrists 67
Psychologist Attitudes 91
↓ Psychotherapists 73
Rogers (Carl) 91
Scientists 67
Skinner (Burrhus Frederic) 91
↓ Social Workers 73
Vygotsky (Lev) 91
Watson (John Broadus) 91

Psychology 67
PN 5775 SC 41760
B Behavioral Sciences 97
N ↓ Applied Psychology 73
↓ Clinical Psychology 67
Cognitive Psychology 85
Comparative Psychology 67
Cross Cultural Psychology 97
Depth Psychology 73
↓ Developmental Psychology 73
Ecological Psychology 94
Experimental Psychology 67
Folk Psychology 97
Forensic Psychology 85
↓ Humanistic Psychology 85
Mathematical Psychology 73
Metapsychology 94
↓ Physiological Psychology 67
Self Psychology 88
R ↓ History of Psychology 67
↓ Psychiatry 67
Psychobiology 82
↓ Psychophysiology 67

Psychology Education 78
PN 1854 SC 41765
B Curriculum 67
N ↓ Graduate Psychology Education 67
R Counselor Education 73
Educational Program Accreditation 94
Theoretical Orientation 82

Psychometrics 67
PN 2008 SC 41770
SN Subdiscipline within psychology dealing with the development and application of statistical techniques to the analysis of psychological data. Also, psychological measurement in which numerical estimates are obtained of a specific aspect of performance.
UF Psychological Testing
B Measurement 67
R Conjoint Measurement 94

Psychometrics — (cont'd)
R ↓ Experimental Design 67
↓ Experimentation 67
Item Response Theory 85
Psychophysics 67
↓ Statistical Analysis 67
Test Interpretation 85
↓ Testing 67

Psychomotor Development 73
PN 284 SC 41780
B Motor Development 73
N ↓ Speech Development 73
R ↓ Childhood Development 67
↓ Perceptual Development 73
Perceptual Motor Development 91

Psychomotor Processes
Use Perceptual Motor Processes

Psychoneuroimmunology 91
PN 170 SC 41795
SN Study of the interrelationship among immune responses, psychological processes, and the nervous system. Used for the scientific discipline or the psychoneuroimmunologic processes themselves.
UF Psychoimmunology
B Immunology 73
Psychophysiology 67
R ↓ Endocrinology 73
Neuropsychology 73

Psychoneurosis
Use Neurosis

Psychopath
Use Antisocial Personality

Psychopathology 67
PN 6565 SC 41820
SN Study of mental disorders, emotional problems, or maladaptive behaviors. Used for the scientific discipline or for unspecified dysfunctions.
B Pathology 73
R ↓ Antisocial Behavior 71
Comorbidity 91
↓ Defense Mechanisms 67
↓ Emotional Adjustment 73
Homeless Mentally Ill 97
↓ Mental Disorders 67
Psychiatric Patients 67
Psychiatric Symptoms 97
↓ Psychological Assessment 97

Psychopathy
SN Term discontinued in 1997. Use PSYCHOPATHY to access references from 73–96.
Use Antisocial Personality

Psychopharmacology 67
PN 1210 SC 41840
B Pharmacology 73
R Drug Abuse Liability 94

Psychophysical Measurement 67
PN 1396 SC 41850
SN Techniques or methodology used to assess perceptual sensitivities and functions of any sensory modality as related to the parameters of stimulation.
N Magnitude Estimation 91
R Fuzzy Set Theory 91
↓ Perceptual Measures 73
Signal Detection (Perception) 67
Threshold Determination 73

Psychophysics 67
PN 710 SC 41860
R ↓ Experimentation 67
Psychometrics 67

Psychophysiologic Disorders
Use Psychosomatic Disorders

Psychophysiology 67
PN 1766 SC 41880
SN Study of the physiological correlates of mental, somatic, and behavioral processes.
B Physiology 67
N Psychoneuroimmunology 91
R Cardiovascular Reactivity 94
↓ Physiological Psychology 67
↓ Psychology 67

Psychosexual Behavior 67
PN 6218 SC 41890
SN Human sexual behavior which includes both mental and somatic aspects of sexuality.
UF Sexual Behavior
B Behavior 67
N Bisexuality 73
Erection (Penis) 73
Extramarital Intercourse 73
Heterosexuality 73
↓ Homosexuality 67
↓ Human Courtship 73
Hypersexuality 73
Masturbation 73
Monogamy 97
↓ Orgasm 73
Promiscuity 73
Prostitution 73
Seduction 94
Sex Roles 67
Sexual Abstinence 73
↓ Sexual Arousal 78
↓ Sexual Deviations 67
↓ Sexual Function Disturbances 73
↓ Sexual Intercourse (Human) 73
Sexual Risk Taking 97
Transsexualism 73
Transvestism 73
Virginity 73
R Affection 73
Assortative Mating 91
Autoeroticism 97
Erotomania 97
Human Mate Selection 88
Pornography 73
Professional Client Sexual Relations 94
Psychosexual Development 82
Romance 97
Sex 67
Sex Linked Developmental Differences 73
Sexual Addiction 97
Sexual Attitudes 73
Sexual Development 73
Sexual Fantasy 97
↓ Sexual Orientation 97
Sexual Satisfaction 94

Psychosexual Development 82
PN 856 SC 41895
SN Psychological maturation and development of sexual identity, desires, beliefs, and attitudes throughout the life cycle.
B Psychosocial Development 73
R Emotional Development 73
Gender Identity 85
↓ Psychosexual Behavior 67
Sex 67
Sexual Attitudes 73
Sexual Development 73
Sexuality 73

Psychosis 67
PN 5983 **SC** 41910
B Mental Disorders 67
N ↓ Acute Psychosis 73
↓ Affective Psychosis 73
↓ Alcoholic Psychosis 73
Capgras Syndrome 85
↓ Childhood Psychosis 67
Chronic Psychosis 73
Experimental Psychosis 73
↓ Hallucinosis 73
↓ Paranoia (Psychosis) 67
Process Psychosis 73
Reactive Psychosis 73
↓ Schizophrenia 67
Senile Psychosis 73
Toxic Psychoses 73
R Borderline States 78
Paranoid Schizophrenia 67

Psychosocial Development 73
PN 4391 **SC** 41920
SN Process of psychological and social maturation occurring at any time during the life cycle.
UF Social Development
B Psychogenesis 73
N Childhood Play Development 73
↓ Personality Development 67
Psychosexual Development 82
R Aging (Attitudes Toward) 85
Emotional Development 73
Erikson (Erik) 91
Moral Development 73
Object Relations 82

Psychosocial Factors 88
PN 4339 **SC** 41925
R Demographic Characteristics 67
Psychodynamics 73
↓ Social Influences 67
↓ Sociocultural Factors 67

Psychosocial Mental Retardation 73
PN 45 **SC** 41930
SN Reversible mental retardation due to environmental and/or social factors with no organic etiological component.
UF Cultural Familial Mental Retardation
B Mental Retardation 67
R Borderline Mental Retardation 73

Psychosocial Readjustment 73
PN 827 **SC** 41940
SN Attainment of attitudes and skills which will facilitate an individual's reintegration or functioning in society, usually following traumatic or unusual personal experiences. Use also PSYCHOSOCIAL RESOCIALIZATION to access references from 73–81.
UF Psychosocial Resocialization
Readjustment (Psychosocial)
Resocialization (Psychosocial)
R ↓ Psychosocial Rehabilitation 73
↓ Treatment 67

Psychosocial Rehabilitation 73
PN 1239 **SC** 41950
SN Programs, techniques, or processes of treatment by which individuals, institutionalized or otherwise removed from normal community life (e.g., prisoners), acquire psychological and social skills and attitudes which facilitate community reentry.
UF Rehabilitation (Psychosocial)
B Rehabilitation 67
N Therapeutic Social Clubs 73
↓ Vocational Rehabilitation 67
R ↓ Drug Rehabilitation 73
Psychosocial Readjustment 73
Rehabilitation Counseling 78

Psychosocial Resocialization
SN Term discontinued in 1982. Use PSYCHOSOCIAL RESOCIALIZATION or PSYCHOSOCIAL READJUSTMENT to access references from 73–81.
Use Psychosocial Readjustment

Psychosomatic Disorders 67
PN 3746 **SC** 41970
SN Disorders characterized by bodily symptoms caused by psychological factors.
UF Psychophysiologic Disorders
Somatization Disorder
N ↓ Conversion Neurosis 73
Dysmorphophobia 73
Hypochondriasis 73
Neurodermatitis 73
Somatoform Pain Disorder 97
R Anorexia Nervosa 73
Asthma 67
Bulimia 85
↓ Dyspnea 73
↓ Endocrine Disorders 73
↓ Gastrointestinal Disorders 73
Hay Fever 73
↓ Headache 73
Hyperphagia 73
Hyperventilation 73
Illness Behavior 82
Irritable Bowel Syndrome 91
Malingering 73
Migraine Headache 73
Munchausen Syndrome 94
Myofascial Pain 91
Obesity 73
Premenstrual Tension 73
Psychosomatic Medicine 78
↓ Sexual Function Disturbances 73
↓ Skin Disorders 73
Somatization 94
↓ Symptoms 67
↓ Urinary Function Disorders 73
↓ Urogenital Disorders 73

Psychosomatic Medicine 78
PN 365 **SC** 41975
SN Medical specialty dealing with the diagnosis and treatment of psychosomatic disorders.
B Medical Sciences 67
R ↓ Health Care Psychology 85
↓ Psychosomatic Disorders 67

Psychosurgery 73
PN 195 **SC** 41980
UF Leukotomy
Lobotomy
B Neurosurgery 73
Organic Therapies 73
N Thalamotomy 73
R Sympathectomy 73
Tractotomy 73

Psychotherapeutic Breakthrough 73
PN 9 **SC** 41990
UF Breakthrough (Psychotherapeutic)
B Psychotherapeutic Processes 67

Psychotherapeutic Counseling 73
PN 586 **SC** 42000
B Counseling 67
Psychotherapy 67
N ↓ Family Therapy 67
R ↓ Marriage Counseling 73
Premarital Counseling 73

Psychotherapeutic Methods
Use Psychotherapeutic Techniques

Psychotherapeutic Neutrality 97
PN 0 **SC** 42025
UF Neutrality (Psychotherapeutic)
R ↓ Psychoanalysis 67
↓ Psychotherapeutic Processes 67
↓ Psychotherapeutic Techniques 67

Psychotherapeutic Outcomes 73
PN 2111 **SC** 42030
SN Limited to treatment results that are a direct function of specific characteristics of clients or therapists or a function of unique or specifically-described circumstances of the treatment itself.
UF Outcomes (Psychotherapeutic)
B Treatment Outcomes 82
R Mental Health Program Evaluation 73
Treatment Dropouts 78
Treatment Effectiveness Evaluation 73

Psychotherapeutic Processes 67
PN 10971 **SC** 42040
SN Experiential, attitudinal, emotional, or behavioral phenomena occurring during the course of psychotherapy. Applies to the client or psychotherapist individually or to their interaction.
UF Client Counselor Interaction
Counselor Client Interaction
Patient Therapist Interaction
Therapist Patient Interaction
B Therapeutic Processes 78
N Countertransference 73
Insight (Psychotherapeutic Process) 73
Negative Therapeutic Reaction 97
Psychotherapeutic Breakthrough 73
Psychotherapeutic Resistance 73
Psychotherapeutic Transference 67
Therapeutic Alliance 94
R Enactments 97
↓ Internalization 97
Mirroring 97
Professional Client Sexual Relations 94
↓ Psychoanalysis 67
Psychotherapeutic Neutrality 97
↓ Psychotherapy 67
↓ Treatment Outcomes 82

Psychotherapeutic Resistance 73
PN 567 **SC** 42050
SN Conscious or unconscious defensive attempts by the client to prevent repressed material from coming to consciousness.
UF Resistance (Psychotherapeutic)
B Psychotherapeutic Processes 67
Resistance 97
R Negative Therapeutic Reaction 97
Treatment Refusal 94

Psychotherapeutic Techniques 67
PN 7504 **SC** 42060
UF Psychotherapeutic Methods
Therapeutic Techniques (Psychother)
B Treatment 67
N Animal Assisted Therapy 94
Autogenic Training 73
Cotherapy 82
Directed Reverie Therapy 78
Dream Analysis 73
Mirroring 97
Morita Therapy 94
Mutual Storytelling Technique 73
Paradoxical Techniques 82
Psychodrama 67
R Age Regression (Hypnotic) 88
Centering 91
Client Centered Therapy 67
Conjoint Therapy 73
↓ Creative Arts Therapy 94
Free Association 94
Homework 88

Psychotherapeutic Techniques — (cont'd)
R Interpersonal Psychotherapy 97
Poetry Therapy 94
Primal Therapy 78
Psychotherapeutic Neutrality 97
↓ Psychotherapy 67
Rational Emotive Therapy 78
Reality Therapy 73
↓ Relaxation Therapy 78
Role Playing 67
↓ Self Help Techniques 82
Self Talk 88
↓ Twelve Step Programs 97
Wilderness Experience 91

Psychotherapeutic Transference 67
PN 1963 SC 42070
SN Unconscious projection of feelings, thoughts, and wishes to the therapist that were originally associated with important figures from the client's past.
UF Transference (Psychotherapeutic)
B Psychotherapeutic Processes 67
R Countertransference 73
Enactments 97
Negative Therapeutic Reaction 97
Professional Client Sexual Relations 94
Therapeutic Alliance 94

Psychotherapist Attitudes 73
PN 504 SC 42080
SN Attitudes of, not toward, psychotherapists.
B Therapist Attitudes 78
R ↓ Psychotherapists 73
Therapist Role 78

Psychotherapist Trainees
Use Therapist Trainees

Psychotherapists 73
PN 2240 SC 42100
B Mental Health Personnel 67
Therapists 67
N Hypnotherapists 73
Psychoanalysts 73
R Clinical Psychologists 73
Psychiatrists 67
↓ Psychologists 67
Psychotherapist Attitudes 73

Psychotherapy 67
PN 11580 SC 42110
UF Reconstructive Psychotherapy
B Treatment 67
N Adlerian Psychotherapy 97
Adolescent Psychotherapy 94
Analytical Psychotherapy 73
Autogenic Training 73
↓ Behavior Therapy 67
Brief Psychotherapy 67
↓ Child Psychotherapy 67
Client Centered Therapy 67
Directed Reverie Therapy 78
Eclectic Psychotherapy 94
Existential Therapy 73
Experiential Psychotherapy 73
Expressive Psychotherapy 73
Eye Movement Desensitization Therapy 97
Feminist Therapy 94
Geriatric Psychotherapy 73
Gestalt Therapy 73
↓ Group Psychotherapy 67
↓ Hypnotherapy 73
Individual Psychotherapy 73
Insight Therapy 73
Interpersonal Psychotherapy 97
Logotherapy 73

Psychotherapy — (cont'd)
N Persuasion Therapy 73
Primal Therapy 78
↓ Psychoanalysis 67
Psychodrama 67
↓ Psychotherapeutic Counseling 73
Rational Emotive Therapy 78
Reality Therapy 73
Relationship Therapy 73
Supportive Psychotherapy 97
Transactional Analysis 73
R Cognitive Therapy 82
Cotherapy 82
Couples Therapy 94
Educational Therapy 97
Holistic Health 85
↓ Marriage Counseling 73
↓ Organic Therapies 73
Paradoxical Techniques 82
Pastoral Counseling 67
Phototherapy 91
↓ Psychotherapeutic Processes 67
↓ Psychotherapeutic Techniques 67
Recreation Therapy 73
Spontaneous Remission 73
Theoretical Orientation 82

Psychotherapy (Individual)
Use Individual Psychotherapy

Psychotherapy Training 73
PN 966 SC 42120
UF Training (Psychotherapy)
B Clinical Methods Training 73
R Cotherapy 82
Counselor Education 73
Psychiatric Training 73
Psychoanalytic Training 73

Psychotic Depressive Reaction
SN Term discontinued in 1988. Use PSYCHOTIC DEPRESSIVE REACTION to access references from 73-87.
Use Major Depression

Psychotic Episode (Acute)
Use Acute Psychosis

Psychotic Symptoms
Use Psychiatric Symptoms

Psychoticism 78
PN 364 SC 42145
B Personality Traits 67

Psychotomimetic Drugs 73
PN 42 SC 42150
B Drugs 67
N Lysergic Acid Diethylamide 67
Mescaline 73
Peyote 73
R Experimental Psychosis 73
↓ Hallucinogenic Drugs 67
↓ Psychedelic Drugs 73

Psychotropic Drugs
Use Drugs

PTA
Use Parent School Relationship

Puberty 73
PN 370 SC 42160
B Developmental Stages 73
R Menarche 73

Pubescence
Use Sexual Development

Public Attitudes
Use Public Opinion

Public Health 88
PN 181 SC 42185
B Health 73
R Health Promotion 91
↓ Health Screening 97
Public Health Services 73

Public Health Service Nurses 73
PN 80 SC 42190
B Government Personnel 73
Nurses 67
R Public Health Services 73

Public Health Services 73
PN 437 SC 42200
B Community Services 67
R ↓ Health 73
Integrated Services 97
↓ Mental Health Programs 73
Public Health 88
Public Health Service Nurses 73

Public Opinion 73
PN 1166 SC 42210
UF Opinion (Public)
Public Attitudes
B Attitudes 67
R Community Attitudes 73
Political Psychology 97
Public Relations 73

Public Policy
Use Government Policy Making

Public Relations 73
PN 97 SC 42220
SN The business of attempting to influence or persuade individuals or the public to have an understanding or concern for, or positive disposition toward a particular person, organization, idea, policy, practice, or activity.
R ↓ Advertising 67
↓ Consumer Attitudes 73
Public Opinion 73

Public School Education 73
PN 827 SC 42230
SN Education in free tax-supported schools controlled by a local governmental authority.
B Education 67

Public Sector 85
PN 331 SC 42235
SN Any type of government-related or public organization, service, or sphere of involvement.
N Government 67
Government Agencies 73

Public Speaking 73
PN 428 SC 42240
SN Formal or informal speech in a group or public setting.
B Oral Communication 85
R Debates 97
Speech Anxiety 85

Public Transportation 73
PN 78 SC 42250
B Community Facilities 73
Transportation 73
R Air Transportation 73
Railroad Trains 73

Public Welfare Services
Use Community Welfare Services

Puerto Rican Americans
Use Hispanics

Puerto Rico [73]
PN 292 **SC** 42270
B West Indies [73]

Pulmonary Disorders
Use Lung Disorders

Pulmonary Emphysema [73]
PN 23 **SC** 42290
UF Emphysema (Pulmonary)
B Lung Disorders [73]

Pulmonary Tuberculosis [73]
PN 12 **SC** 42300
B Bacterial Disorders [73]
Lung Disorders [73]
Tuberculosis [73]

Pulse (Arterial)
Use Arterial Pulse

Punishment [67]
PN 2307 **SC** 42320
SN Presentation of a punisher contingent on the performance of some behavior. Also, the punishing event or object itself which, when following the performance of some behavior, results in a reduction in the occurrence or frequency of that behavior. Compare AVERSIVE STIMULATION. Used for both human and animal populations.
UF Corporal Punishment
B Reinforcement [67]
N Response Cost [97]
R Coercion [94]
Threat [67]

Punishment (Capital)
Use Capital Punishment

Pupil (Eye) [73]
PN 100 **SC** 42340
B Eye (Anatomy) [67]

Pupil Dilation [73]
PN 245 **SC** 42360
UF Dilation (Pupil)
R ↓ Eye (Anatomy) [67]

Purdue Perceptual Motor Survey [73]
PN 7 **SC** 42380
B Sensorimotor Measures [73]

Purkinje Cells [94]
PN 20 **SC** 42385
B Cerebellum [73]
Neurons [73]

Puromycin [73]
PN 34 **SC** 42390
B Amines [73]
Antibiotics [73]

Putamen [85]
PN 104 **SC** 42405
SN The largest and most lateral part of the basal ganglia which, together with the caudate nucleus and globus pallidus, forms the corpus striatum.
B Basal Ganglia [73]

Pygmalion Effect
Use Self Fulfilling Prophecies

Pygmy Chimpanzees
Use Bonobos

Pyramidal Tracts [73]
PN 82 **SC** 42410
B Efferent Pathways [82]
Spinal Cord [73]

Pyramidotomy [73]
PN 9 **SC** 42420
B Neurosurgery [73]
R Tractotomy [73]

Pyromania [73]
PN 24 **SC** 42430
R Impulse Control Disorders [97]
Impulsiveness [73]
↓ Personality Disorders [67]

Q Sort Testing Technique [67]
PN 128 **SC** 42440
B Testing Methods [67]

Q Test
Use Cochran Q Test

Quaalude
Use Methaqualone

Quadriplegia [85]
PN 79 **SC** 42470
SN Paralysis of both arms and both legs.
B Paralysis [73]
R ↓ Central Nervous System Disorders [73]
Hemiplegia [78]
↓ Injuries [73]
↓ Musculoskeletal Disorders [73]
Paraplegia [78]
↓ Physically Disabled [97]
↓ Spinal Cord Injuries [73]

Quails [73]
PN 273 **SC** 42480
B Birds [67]

Quality Circles
Use Participative Management

Quality Control [88]
PN 144 **SC** 42483
SN Efforts or techniques directed at the detection of imperfections or shortcomings in products or services.
R Accountability [88]
Consumer Satisfaction [94]
Human Factors Engineering [73]
Organizational Effectiveness [85]
Organizational Objectives [73]
Participative Management [88]
↓ Quality of Services [97]

Quality of Care [88]
PN 621 **SC** 42484
SN Quality of medical or mental health care.
B Quality of Services [97]
R Accountability [88]
Caregivers [88]
Child Day Care [73]
↓ Client Rights [88]
↓ Health Care Delivery [78]
↓ Health Care Services [78]
Home Care [85]
↓ Managed Care [94]

Quality of Care — (cont'd)
R ↓ Mental Health Services [78]
↓ Treatment [67]

Quality of Education
Use Educational Quality

Quality of Life [85]
PN 1565 **SC** 42485
N Quality of Work Life [88]
R Life Satisfaction [85]
↓ Lifestyle [78]
Lifestyle Changes [97]
Well Being [94]

Quality of Services [97]
PN 0 **SC** 57510
SN Used for health care and non-health care services. Consider QUALITY of CARE for health care services.
UF Service Quality
N Quality of Care [88]
R ↓ Advertising [67]
↓ Consumer Attitudes [73]
Consumer Satisfaction [94]
↓ Health Care Delivery [78]
↓ Health Care Services [78]
Marketing [73]
↓ Mental Health Services [78]
↓ Professional Standards [73]
Quality Control [88]
Retailing [91]

Quality of Work Life [88]
PN 141 **SC** 42487
SN Includes aspects such as salary, benefits, safety, and efficiency, as well as variety and challenge, responsibility, contribution, and recognition.
B Quality of Life [85]
R ↓ Job Characteristics [85]
Job Satisfaction [67]
Occupational Stress [73]
↓ Organizational Characteristics [97]
Organizational Climate [73]
↓ Working Conditions [73]

Quartimax Rotation [73]
PN 3 **SC** 42490
B Orthogonal Rotation [73]

Questioning [82]
PN 1013 **SC** 42495
R ↓ Cognitive Processes [67]
Curiosity [67]
↓ Education [67]
Guessing [73]
Information Seeking [73]
Interviewing [73]
↓ Interviews [67]
Legal Interrogation [94]
↓ Teaching Methods [67]

Questionnaires [67]
PN 3772 **SC** 42500
B Measurement [67]
N General Health Questionnaire [91]
R Mail Surveys [94]
↓ Surveys [67]
Telephone Surveys [94]

Quinidine
SN Term discontinued in 1997. Use QUINIDINE to access references from 73–96.
Use Alkaloids

Quinine [73]
PN 129 **SC** 42560

Quinine — (cont'd)
B Alkaloids [73]
Analgesic Drugs [73]
Local Anesthetics [73]

Quinpirole [94]
PN 33 SC 42570
B Antihypertensive Drugs [73]
Dopamine Agonists [85]

Rabbis [73]
PN 33 SC 42580
B Clergy [73]
R Chaplains [73]
Judaism [67]

Rabbits [67]
PN 2482 SC 42590
B Mammals [73]

Race (Anthropological) [73]
PN 199 SC 42600
R ↓ Asians [82]
Blacks [82]
Ethnography [73]
Ethnology [67]
↓ Racial and Ethnic Attitudes [82]
Racial and Ethnic Differences [82]
↓ Sociocultural Factors [67]
Whites [82]

Race and Ethnic Discrimination [94]
PN 61 SC 42605
SN Use SOCIAL DISCRIMINATION to access references from 82-93. Use MINORITY GROUP DISCRIMINATION to access references from 78-81 and RACIAL DISCRIMINATION to access references from 73-81.
UF Ethnic Discrimination
Minority Group Discrimination
Racial Discrimination
B Social Discrimination [82]
R Affirmative Action [85]
↓ Civil Rights [78]
Employment Discrimination [94]
Minority Groups [67]
↓ Prejudice [67]
↓ Racial and Ethnic Attitudes [82]
Racial and Ethnic Differences [82]
Racism [73]
Stereotyped Attitudes [67]

Race Attitudes
SN Term discontinued in 1982. Use RACE ATTITUDES to access references from 73–81.
Use Racial and Ethnic Attitudes

Race Relations
SN Term discontinued in 1982. Use RACE RELATIONS to access references from 78–81.
Use Racial and Ethnic Relations

Racial and Ethnic Attitudes [82]
PN 1054 SC 42617
SN Attitudes about race or ethnicity or toward members of a given racial or ethnic group. Use RACE ATTITUDES to access references from 73–81.
UF Race Attitudes
B Attitudes [67]
N AntiSemitism [73]
Ethnocentrism [73]
Racism [73]
R Cultural Sensitivity [94]
↓ Ethnic Groups [73]
Ethnology [67]
Multiculturalism [97]
↓ Prejudice [67]

Racial and Ethnic Attitudes — (cont'd)
R Race (Anthropological) [73]
Race and Ethnic Discrimination [94]
Racial and Ethnic Relations [82]
Stereotyped Attitudes [67]

Racial and Ethnic Differences [82]
PN 6141 SC 42618
SN Differences between two or more racial or ethnic groups. Use RACIAL DIFFERENCES to access references from 73–81. Use CROSS CULTURAL DIFFERENCES for cultural comparisons.
UF Ethnic Differences
Racial Differences
R Cross Cultural Communication [97]
Cross Cultural Differences [67]
Cross Cultural Psychology [97]
Cross Cultural Treatment [94]
Cultural Sensitivity [94]
↓ Ethnic Groups [73]
Ethnology [67]
Interethnic Family [88]
Interracial Family [88]
Interracial Offspring [88]
Multiculturalism [97]
Race (Anthropological) [73]
Race and Ethnic Discrimination [94]
Racism [73]

Racial and Ethnic Relations [82]
PN 482 SC 42619
SN Contact and interaction between and among different racial and ethnic groups. Use RACE RELATIONS to access references from 78–81.
UF Race Relations
B Social Behavior [67]
R Cross Cultural Communication [97]
Cultural Sensitivity [94]
Ethnology [67]
Interracial Family [88]
Interracial Marriage [73]
Interracial Offspring [88]
Multiculturalism [97]
↓ Prejudice [67]
↓ Racial and Ethnic Attitudes [82]
School Integration [82]
↓ Social Discrimination [82]
Social Equality [73]
↓ Social Integration [82]

Racial Differences
SN Term discontinued in 1982. Use RACIAL DIFFERENCES to access references from 73–81.
Use Racial and Ethnic Differences

Racial Discrimination
SN Term discontinued in 1982. Use RACIAL DISCRIMINATION to access references from 73-81 and MINORITY GROUP DISCRIMINATION to access references from 78-81. Use SOCIAL DISCRIMINATION to access references from 82-93.
Use Race and Ethnic Discrimination

Racial Integration
SN Term discontinued in 1982. Use RACIAL INTEGRATION to access references from 67–81.
Use Social Integration

Racial Segregation (Schools)
Use School Integration

Racism [73]
PN 464 SC 42660
SN Belief that racial differences produce inherent superiority of a particular race.
B Racial and Ethnic Attitudes [82]
R AntiSemitism [73]
Employment Discrimination [94]

Racism — (cont'd)
R ↓ Prejudice [67]
Race and Ethnic Discrimination [94]
Racial and Ethnic Differences [82]
↓ Social Discrimination [82]
↓ Social Issues [91]

Radial Nerve
Use Spinal Nerves

Radiation [67]
PN 496 SC 42680
UF Irradiation
N Laser Irradiation [73]
R Radiation Therapy [73]
↓ Roentgenography [73]

Radiation Therapy [73]
PN 146 SC 42690
UF X Ray Therapy
B Physical Treatment Methods [73]
R ↓ Radiation [67]

Radical Movements [73]
PN 60 SC 42700
N Political Revolution [73]
R ↓ Social Movements [67]
Terrorism [82]

Radicalism (Political)
Use Political Radicalism

Radio [73]
PN 231 SC 42730
B Audiovisual Communications Media [73]
Mass Media [67]
Telecommunications Media [73]
R ↓ News Media [97]

Radiography
Use Roentgenography

Radiology [73]
PN 37 SC 42740
B Medical Sciences [67]

Rage
Use Anger

Railroad Trains [73]
PN 103 SC 42760
UF Trains (Railroad)
B Ground Transportation [73]
R Public Transportation [73]

Random Sampling [73]
PN 129 SC 42780
B Sampling (Experimental) [73]
R Experiment Volunteers [73]

Rank Difference Correlation [73]
PN 21 SC 42790
UF Spearman Rho
B Statistical Correlation [67]

Rank Order Correlation [73]
PN 90 SC 42800
B Statistical Correlation [67]

Rape [73]
PN 1504 SC 42810
B Sexual Abuse [88]
Sexual Intercourse (Human) [73]
N Acquaintance Rape [91]

Raphe Nuclei [82]
PN 304 **SC** 42815
SN Serotonin synthesizing neurons in and near the median plane of the brain stem lying dorsally in the pons. These nuclei are sometimes grouped with the reticular formation and are thought to function as part of the limbic system.
B Pons [73]
R ↓ Hindbrain [97]
↓ Limbic System [73]
Reticular Formation [67]

Rapid Eye Movement [71]
PN 275 **SC** 42820
UF REM
B Eye Movements [67]
R REM Dream Deprivation [73]
REM Dreams [73]
REM Sleep [73]

Rapid Eye Movement Dreams
Use REM Dreams

Rapid Eye Movement Sleep
Use REM Sleep

Rapid Heart Rate
Use Tachycardia

Rapport
SN Use INTERPERSONAL ATTRACTION to access references from 73-90.
Use Interpersonal Interaction

Rasch Model
Use Item Response Theory

Rat Learning [67]
PN 1858 **SC** 42860
SN Not defined prior to 1982. Use RAT LEARNING or RATS to access references from 67–81. From 1982 used for discussions of hypotheses or theories of learning in rats.
B Learning [67]

Rating [67]
PN 1595 **SC** 42880
SN Measurement technique involving relative evaluation or estimate of characteristics or qualities of a person, process, or thing. Used when rating as a technique is the object of interest.
B Testing [67]
R Halo Effect [82]
Interrater Reliability [82]

Rating Scales [67]
PN 6451 **SC** 42890
B Measurement [67]
N Likert Scales [94]
R Multidimensional Scaling [82]

Ratio Reinforcement
Use Fixed Ratio Reinforcement OR Variable Ratio Reinforcement

Ratiocination
Use Logical Thinking

Rational Emotive Therapy [78]
PN 695 **SC** 42915
SN A therapy developed by Albert Ellis that stresses cognitive, philosophic, and value-oriented aspects of personality and views the goal of treatment as the client's development of rational as opposed to irrational beliefs about his/her problem.
B Psychotherapy [67]
R ↓ Behavior Therapy [67]

Rational Emotive Therapy — (cont'd)
R Cognitive Therapy [82]
Ellis (Albert) [91]
↓ Psychotherapeutic Techniques [67]

Rationalization [73]
PN 60 **SC** 42920
B Defense Mechanisms [67]

Rats [67]
PN 47283 **SC** 42930
UF Albino Rats
White Rats
B Rodents [73]
N Norway Rats [73]

Rauwolfia
SN Term discontinued in 1997. Use RAUWOLFIA to access references from 73–96.
Use Alkaloids

Raven Coloured Progressive Matrices [73]
PN 99 **SC** 42950
B Intelligence Measures [67]

Raven Progressive Matrices [78]
PN 160 **SC** 42960
SN Use RAVENS PROGRESSIVE MATRICES to access references from 73–77.
B Intelligence Measures [67]

Raynauds Disease
Use Cardiovascular Disorders

RDC
Use Research Diagnostic Criteria

Reactance
Use Psychological Reactance

Reaction Formation [73]
PN 17 **SC** 42990
SN Defense mechanism that leads to the formation of behaviors and attitudes opposite to the repressed anxiety-inducing behavior or feelings.
B Defense Mechanisms [67]

Reaction Time [67]
PN 6869 **SC** 43000
SN Minimal time interval between the onset of a stimulus and the beginning of a subject's response to that stimulus. Compare RESPONSE LATENCY.
UF Response Lag
Response Speed
Response Time
RT (Response)
Speed (Response)
B Response Parameters [73]
R Cognitive Processing Speed [97]
Conceptual Tempo [85]

Reactive Attachment Disorder
Use Failure to Thrive

Reactive Depression [73]
PN 242 **SC** 43020
B Major Depression [88]
R Neurotic Depressive Reaction [73]

Reactive Psychosis [73]
PN 183 **SC** 43030
UF Reactive Schizophrenia
Traumatic Psychosis
B Psychosis [67]

Reactive Schizophrenia
Use Reactive Psychosis AND Schizophrenia

Readability [78]
PN 368 **SC** 43045
SN Textual difficulty or other qualitative aspects of reading material that facilitate comprehension. May include clarity of graphic displays.
B Written Language [67]
R ↓ Legibility [78]
↓ Reading [67]
Reading Comprehension [73]
Reading Materials [73]

Readaptation
Use Adaptation

Readiness Potential
Use Contingent Negative Variation

Reading [67]
PN 2745 **SC** 43080
N Braille [78]
Oral Reading [73]
Remedial Reading [73]
Silent Reading [73]
R Dyslexia [73]
Initial Teaching Alphabet [73]
Proofreading [88]
Readability [78]
Reading Ability [73]
Reading Achievement [73]
Reading Comprehension [73]
Reading Development [97]
↓ Reading Disabilities [67]
Reading Education [73]
Reading Materials [73]
Reading Readiness [73]
↓ Reading Skills [73]
Reading Speed [73]
Sight Vocabulary [73]

Reading Ability [73]
PN 2750 **SC** 43090
SN Perceptual and intellectual capacity or efficiency in reading.
B Cognitive Ability [73]
R Academic Aptitude [73]
↓ Reading [67]
Reading Development [97]
↓ Reading Skills [73]

Reading Achievement [73]
PN 3179 **SC** 43100
B Academic Achievement [67]
R ↓ Reading [67]

Reading Aloud
Use Oral Reading

Reading Comprehension [73]
PN 4245 **SC** 43110
B Reading Skills [73]
Verbal Comprehension [85]
R Readability [78]
↓ Reading [67]

Reading Development [97]
PN 0 **SC** 43115
R ↓ Language Development [67]
↓ Literacy [73]
↓ Reading [67]
Reading Ability [73]
Reading Readiness [73]
↓ Reading Skills [73]

Reading Disabilities 67
PN 2388 SC 43120
B Learning Disorders 67
N Dyslexia 73
R ↓ Alexia 82
Educational Diagnosis 78
↓ Reading 67

Reading Education 73
PN 3224 SC 43130
B Language Arts Education 73
R Braille 78
Braille Instruction 73
Initial Teaching Alphabet 73
↓ Literacy 73
Literacy Programs 97
Phonics 73
↓ Reading 67
Remedial Reading 73

Reading Materials 73
PN 1045 SC 43140
UF Basal Readers
B Instructional Media 67
R ↓ Books 73
Braille 78
Readability 78
↓ Reading 67
Text Structure 82
↓ Textbooks 78

Reading Measures 73
PN 604 SC 43150
B Measurement 67
N Gates MacGinitie Reading Tests 73
Metropolitan Readiness Tests 78

Reading Readiness 73
PN 379 SC 43160
SN Developmental level at which language skills; cognitive, perceptual and motor abilities; experience; and interest combine to enable a child to profit from specific reading activities. Compare SCHOOL READINESS.
R ↓ Reading 67
Reading Development 97

Reading Skills 73
PN 1435 SC 43170
SN Proficiency in reading developed through practice and influenced by ability. Includes word recognition, pronunciation, and comprehension.
B Ability 67
N Reading Comprehension 73
Reading Speed 73
R ↓ Literacy 73
Literacy Programs 97
↓ Reading 67
Reading Ability 73
Reading Development 97
Sight Vocabulary 73
Word Recognition 88

Reading Speed 73
PN 565 SC 43180
B Reading Skills 73
R ↓ Reading 67

Readjustment (Psychosocial)
Use Psychosocial Readjustment

Readmission (Hospital)
Use Hospital Admission

Readmission (Psychiatric Hospital)
Use Psychiatric Hospital Readmission

Realism (Philosophy) 73
PN 64 SC 43220
B Philosophies 67

Reality 73
PN 686 SC 43230
R Metaphysics 73
Reality Testing 73
Reality Therapy 73

Reality Testing 73
PN 150 SC 43240
SN Cognitive process of evaluation and judgment for differentiation between objective perceptions originating outside of the self and subjective stimuli or fantasies.
R ↓ Cognitive Processes 67
↓ Personality Processes 67
Reality 73

Reality Therapy 73
PN 307 SC 43250
SN Method of psychotherapeutic treatment based on assumption of client's personal responsibility for his/her behavior. Therapist actively guides client to accurate self-perception for fulfillment of needs of self-worth and respect for others.
B Psychotherapy 67
R ↓ Psychotherapeutic Techniques 67
Reality 73

Reasoning 67
PN 2565 SC 43260
B Thinking 67
N ↓ Inductive Deductive Reasoning 73
R Analogy 91
Cognitive Hypothesis Testing 82
Declarative Knowledge 97
Dialectics 73
Intelligence 67
↓ Problem Solving 67
Procedural Knowledge 97

Rebuttal
Use Professional Criticism Reply

Recall (Learning) 67
PN 8817 SC 43290
B Retention 67
N Cued Recall 94
Free Recall 73
Serial Recall 94
R ↓ Memory 67
Memory Training 94
Reminiscence 85

Recency Effect 73
PN 289 SC 43298
SN Component of the serial position effect which is manifested by a greater ease in learning items which occur at the end of a series rather than those toward the middle.
B Serial Position Effect 82
R ↓ Learning 67
Primacy Effect 73

Receptive Fields 85
PN 70 SC 43299
SN Spatially discrete patterns of peripheral and central neuronal innervation of sensory mechanisms.
B Nervous System 67
N Cutaneous Receptive Fields 85
Visual Receptive Fields 82
R ↓ Afferent Pathways 82
Neural Plasticity 94
Sensory Neglect 94
↓ Sensory Neurons 73

Receptor Binding 85
PN 1784 SC 43297
SN Affinity processes occurring between chemical substances and specific cellular sites in the body (e.g., blood platelet or neural receptor binding of an adrenergic drug.) Consider also NEURAL RECEPTORS.
B Neurochemistry 73
Neurophysiology 73
R ↓ Neural Receptors 73

Receptors (Neural)
Use Neural Receptors

Recessiveness (Genetic)
Use Genetic Recessiveness

Recidivism 73
PN 969 SC 43320
SN Repetition or recurrence of previous condition or behavior pattern (e.g., behavior disorder or criminal or delinquent behavior), especially when recurrence leads to recommitment or a second conviction.
B Antisocial Behavior 71
R ↓ Criminals 67

Reciprocal Inhibition Therapy 73
PN 65 SC 43330
SN Form of behavior therapy which seeks to evoke one response in order to bring about a suppression or decrease in the strength of a simultaneous response. Used to weaken unadaptive habits, particularly anxiety responses.
B Behavior Therapy 67
R Counterconditioning 73
Systematic Desensitization Therapy 73

Reciprocity 73
PN 652 SC 43340
B Social Behavior 67
R Retaliation 91

Recognition (Learning) 67
PN 5942 SC 43350
B Retention 67
N Object Recognition 97
R Matching to Sample 94
Memory Training 94
Word Recognition 88

Reconstruction (Learning) 73
PN 127 SC 43360
SN Recalling memorized items in the order in which they were originally presented. Compare FREE RECALL.
B Retention 67

Reconstructive Psychotherapy
Use Psychotherapy

Recorders (Tape)
Use Tape Recorders

Recovery (Disorders) 73
PN 1662 SC 43390
R ↓ Disorders 67
↓ Drug Abstinence 94
Illness Behavior 82
↓ Mental Disorders 67
↓ Physical Disorders 97
Postsurgical Complications 73
Relapse Prevention 94
↓ Remission (Disorders) 73
Sobriety 88
↓ Treatment Outcomes 82

Recreation 67
PN 1589 **SC** 43400
UF Play
N Athletic Participation 73
Baseball 73
Basketball 73
Camping 73
Childrens Recreational Games 73
Clubs (Social Organizations) 73
Dance 73
Doll Play 73
Football 73
↓ Gambling 73
Judo 73
Martial Arts 85
Soccer 94
Summer Camps (Recreation) 73
Swimming 73
Television Viewing 73
Tennis 73
Traveling 73
Vacationing 73
Weightlifting 94
R Childhood Play Behavior 78
Computer Games 88
Daily Activities 94
↓ Games 67
Hobbies 73
Holidays 88
Leisure Time 73
Relaxation 73
↓ Sports 67
↓ Toys 73
Wilderness Experience 91

Recreation Areas 73
PN 232 **SC** 43410
UF Parks (Recreational)
N Playgrounds 73
R ↓ Community Facilities 73
↓ Environmental Planning 82
Urban Planning 73

Recreation Therapy 73
PN 266 **SC** 43420
UF Activity Therapy
Gymnastic Therapy
B Creative Arts Therapy 94
R Art Therapy 73
Dance Therapy 73
Movement Therapy 97
Music Therapy 73
↓ Psychotherapy 67
Therapeutic Camps 78

Recreational Day Camps
Use Summer Camps (Recreation)

Recruitment (Military)
Use Military Recruitment

Recruitment (Personnel)
Use Personnel Recruitment

Recruitment (Teachers)
Use Teacher Recruitment

Recurrence (Disorders)
Use Relapse (Disorders)

Recurrent Depression 94
PN 30 **SC** 43465
B Major Depression 88
R Relapse (Disorders) 73
Seasonal Affective Disorder 91

Red Blood Cells
Use Erythrocytes

Red Nucleus
Use Mesencephalon

Reductionism 73
PN 85 **SC** 43480
UF Atomism
Elementarism
B Philosophies 67
R Positivism (Philosophy) 97

Reemployment 91
PN 67 **SC** 43485
SN Returning to work following a period of absence, e.g., unemployment or retirement.
UF Job Reentry
Return to Work
R ↓ Employment Status 82
Job Search 85
Occupational Choice 67
↓ Personnel 67
Retirement 73
Unemployment 67

Reenactments
Use Enactments

Reentry Students 85
PN 270 **SC** 43495
SN Persons reentering school or an educational program after an extended absence; for example, middle-aged adults enrolled in undergraduate programs.
B Students 67
R ↓ Adult Education 73
Adult Learning 97
↓ College Students 67
↓ Continuing Education 85
High School Students 67
↓ School Dropouts 67

Reference Groups 94
PN 28 **SC** 43497
SN Social groups used as sources for personal and behavioral identification, motivation, and evaluation of one's own status.
B Social Groups 73
R Ethnic Identity 73
↓ Group Dynamics 67
↓ Interpersonal Influences 67
↓ Peer Relations 67
↓ Self Concept 67
↓ Social Identity 88
↓ Social Influences 67
Social Support Networks 82
↓ Socialization 67

Referral (Professional)
Use Professional Referral

Referral (Self)
Use Self Referral

Reflectiveness 97
PN 0 **SC** 43505
SN Use IMPULSIVENESS to access references from 85-96.
B Cognitive Style 67
R Conceptual Tempo 85
Impulsiveness 73
Introspection 73
Reminiscence 85
Self Monitoring (Personality) 85
Self Perception 67

Reflexes 71
PN 1239 **SC** 43530
SN Simple automatic involuntary neuromuscular responses to stimuli.
UF Unconditioned Reflex
B Physiology 67
N Achilles Tendon Reflex 73
Acoustic Reflex 73
Babinski Reflex 73
Eyeblink Reflex 73
Flexion Reflex 73
Hoffmanns Reflex 73
Nystagmus 73
Ocular Accommodation 82
Orienting Reflex 67
Startle Reflex 67
Yawning 88
R Instinctive Behavior 82
Muscle Contractions 73
Muscle Tone 85
Parkinsonism 94

Reformatories 73
PN 47 **SC** 43540
SN Specific type of correctional institution to which young or first offenders are committed for training and reformation.
B Correctional Institutions 73
R Prisons 67

Refraction Errors 73
PN 79 **SC** 43550
B Errors 67
Eye Disorders 73
Light Refraction 82
N Myopia 73
R Amblyopia 73
↓ Genetic Disorders 73
Ocular Accommodation 82

Reframing
Use Paradoxical Techniques

Refugees 88
PN 440 **SC** 43555
SN Uprooted, homeless, voluntary or involuntary migrants who flee their native country, usually to escape danger or persecution because of their race, religion, or political views, and who no longer possess protection of their former government. Use HUMAN MIGRATION to access references from 82-87.
UF Political Refugees
B Human Migration 73
R Immigration 73
↓ Social Processes 67

Refusal (Treatment)
Use Treatment Refusal

Regression (Defense Mechanism) 67
PN 384 **SC** 43560
B Defense Mechanisms 67

Regression Analysis
Use Statistical Regression

Regression Artifact
Use Statistical Regression

Rehabilitation 67
PN 3981 **SC** 43580
SN Treatment designed to restore or bring a client to a condition of health or useful and constructive activity. Used for populations including sensory handicapped, retarded, delinquent, criminal, or disordered. Use a more specific term if possible.

Rehabilitation — (cont'd)
B Treatment [67]
N Cognitive Rehabilitation [85]
↓ Drug Rehabilitation [73]
↓ Neuropsychological Rehabilitation [97]
Occupational Therapy [67]
Physical Therapy [73]
↓ Psychosocial Rehabilitation [73]
R Activities of Daily Living [91]
Adaptive Behavior [91]
Animal Assisted Therapy [94]
Deinstitutionalization [82]
Disability Management [91]
Habilitation [91]
↓ Health Care Services [78]
Independent Living Programs [91]
↓ Mainstreaming [91]
Partial Hospitalization [85]
↓ Rehabilitation Centers [73]
Rehabilitation Counseling [78]
Self Care Skills [78]
↓ Support Groups [91]
↓ Twelve Step Programs [97]
Wilderness Experience [91]

Rehabilitation (Drug)
Use Drug Rehabilitation

Rehabilitation (Psychosocial)
Use Psychosocial Rehabilitation

Rehabilitation (Vocational)
Use Vocational Rehabilitation

Rehabilitation Centers [73]
PN 206 SC 43620
N Sheltered Workshops [67]
R ↓ Community Facilities [73]
↓ Rehabilitation [67]

Rehabilitation Counseling [78]
PN 448 SC 43624
B Counseling [67]
R ↓ Alcohol Rehabilitation [82]
↓ Drug Rehabilitation [73]
↓ Psychosocial Rehabilitation [73]
↓ Rehabilitation [67]
Rehabilitation Education [97]
↓ Vocational Rehabilitation [67]
Work Adjustment Training [91]

Rehabilitation Counselors [78]
PN 515 SC 43626
B Counselors [67]
R Rehabilitation Education [97]
↓ Social Workers [73]

Rehabilitation Education [97]
PN 0 SC 43627
SN Graduate education to train students in rehabilitation processes or counseling in such areas as drug rehabilitation, vocational rehabilitation, or occupational rehabilitation.
B Graduate Education [73]
R Counselor Education [73]
Rehabilitation Counseling [78]
Rehabilitation Counselors [78]

Rehearsal
Use Practice

Reinforcement [67]
PN 5791 SC 43630

Reinforcement — (cont'd)
SN Presentation of a reinforcer contingent on the performance of some behavior. Also, the reinforcing event or object itself (i.e., the reinforcer) which, when made to follow the performance of some behavior, results in a change in the frequency of occurrence of that behavior. Compare REWARDS and INCENTIVES.
N Differential Reinforcement [73]
Negative Reinforcement [73]
Noncontingent Reinforcement [88]
↓ Positive Reinforcement [73]
Primary Reinforcement [73]
↓ Punishment [67]
Reinforcement Amounts [73]
↓ Reinforcement Schedules [67]
↓ Rewards [67]
Secondary Reinforcement [67]
Self Reinforcement [73]
↓ Social Reinforcement [67]
R Autoshaping [78]
Behavioral Contrast [78]
↓ Biofeedback [73]
↓ Conditioning [67]
Delay of Gratification [78]
Extinction (Learning) [67]
↓ Feedback [67]
↓ Learning [67]
↓ Motivation [67]
↓ Operant Conditioning [67]
↓ Self Stimulation [67]
Vicarious Experiences [73]

Reinforcement (Vicarious)
Use Vicarious Experiences

Reinforcement Amounts [73]
PN 911 SC 43640
B Reinforcement [67]
R Reinforcement Delay [85]

Reinforcement Delay [85]
PN 226 SC 43645
SN Time delay between the occurrence of a conditioned response and the administration of reinforcement in an operant conditioning paradigm. Consider INTERSTIMULUS INTERVAL for classical conditioning studies.
UF Delayed Reinforcement
B Reinforcement Schedules [67]
R Delay of Gratification [78]
Delayed Alternation [94]
Interstimulus Interval [67]
Reinforcement Amounts [73]
↓ Stimulus Intervals [73]

Reinforcement Schedules [67]
PN 4581 SC 43650
UF Continuous Reinforcement
Intermittent Reinforcement
Partial Reinforcement
Schedules (Reinforcement)
B Reinforcement [67]
N Concurrent Reinforcement Schedules [88]
Fixed Interval Reinforcement [73]
Fixed Ratio Reinforcement [73]
Reinforcement Delay [85]
Variable Interval Reinforcement [73]
Variable Ratio Reinforcement [73]

Reinnervation
Use Neural Development

Rejection (Social)
Use Social Acceptance

Relapse (Disorders) [73]
PN 1460 SC 43660

Relapse (Disorders) — (cont'd)
SN Recurrence of symptoms after apparent cure or period of improvement.
UF Recurrence (Disorders)
R ↓ Disorders [67]
Expressed Emotion [91]
↓ Mental Disorders [67]
↓ Physical Disorders [97]
Postsurgical Complications [73]
Recurrent Depression [94]
Relapse Prevention [94]
↓ Treatment Outcomes [82]

Relapse Prevention [94]
PN 82 SC 43670
B Prevention [73]
R Maintenance Therapy [97]
Preventive Medicine [73]
Primary Mental Health Prevention [73]
Recovery (Disorders) [73]
Relapse (Disorders) [73]
↓ Remission (Disorders) [73]
↓ Treatment [67]
↓ Treatment Outcomes [82]

Relationship Termination [97]
PN 0 SC 43680
SN Voluntary or involuntary ending of a relationship.
UF Breakup (Relationship)
N ↓ Marital Separation [73]
R Abandonment [97]
Friendship [67]
↓ Human Courtship [73]
Male Female Relations [88]
Marital Conflict [73]
↓ Marital Relations [67]
Marital Satisfaction [88]
↓ Peer Relations [67]
Romance [97]
Separation Anxiety [73]
↓ Separation Reactions [97]
Social Dating [73]

Relationship Therapy [73]
PN 21 SC 43690
SN Psychotherapeutic approach in which the relationship between the therapist and client serves as the basis for the therapy. The therapist provides a supportive setting in which the client can grow and develop and gradually reach differentiation from the therapist and come to perceive his/her own self as separate and distinct.
B Psychotherapy [67]

Relativism [97]
PN 0 SC 43694
B Philosophies [67]
R Dogmatism [78]
Epistemology [73]
Existentialism [67]
Metaphysics [73]
Physics [73]

Relaxation [73]
PN 792 SC 43697
SN Tranquil and restful state, activity, or pasttime of lessened muscle tension, stress, or attention.
R Leisure Time [73]
Muscle Relaxation [73]
↓ Recreation [67]
Yoga [73]

Relaxation Therapy [78]
PN 1894 SC 43700
SN Therapy emphasizing relaxation and teaching a person or patient how to relax in order to reduce psychological tensions.

Relaxation Therapy — (cont'd)
UF Muscle Relaxation Therapy
B Treatment 67
N Progressive Relaxation Therapy 78
R Anxiety Management 97
Autogenic Training 73
↓ Behavior Modification 73
↓ Hypnotherapy 73
Meditation 73
Muscle Relaxation 73
Posthypnotic Suggestions 94
↓ Psychotherapeutic Techniques 67
Systematic Desensitization Therapy 73

Relearning 73
PN 103 SC 43710
B Learning 67
R ↓ Memory 67

Reliability (Statistical)
SN Term discontinued in 1973. Use RELIABILITY (STATISTICAL) to access references from 67-72.
Use Statistical Reliability

Reliability (Test)
Use Test Reliability

Religion 67
PN 2390 SC 43740
SN Conceptually broad array term. Use a more specific term if possible.
UF Theology
R Asceticism 73
↓ Religious Beliefs 73
Religious Buildings 73
Religious Education 73
Religious Experiences 97
↓ Religious Literature 73
Religious Organizations 91
↓ Religious Personnel 73
↓ Religious Practices 73
↓ Religious Prejudices 73
Spirituality 88

Religiosity 73
PN 1246 SC 43750
SN Degree of one's religious involvement, devotion to religious beliefs, or adherence to religious observances.
B Religious Beliefs 73
R Spirituality 88

Religious Affiliation 73
PN 961 SC 43760
B Religious Beliefs 73
N ↓ Buddhism 73
↓ Christianity 73
Hinduism 73
Islam 73
Judaism 67
Shamanism 73
R ↓ Religious Groups 97
↓ Religious Practices 73

Religious Beliefs 73
PN 2564 SC 43770
UF Beliefs (Religion)
N Atheism 73
God Concepts 73
Religiosity 73
↓ Religious Affiliation 73
Sin 73
R Asceticism 73
↓ Attitudes 67
Bible 73
Cultism 73
Death Attitudes 73

Religious Beliefs — (cont'd)
R ↓ Ethics 67
Existentialism 67
Forgiveness 88
Morality 67
Mysticism 67
Occultism 78
Religion 67
Religious Education 73
Religious Experiences 97
↓ Religious Literature 73
↓ Religious Practices 73
↓ Religious Prejudices 73
Spirit Possession 97
Spirituality 88
Superstitions 73
Witchcraft 73

Religious Buildings 73
PN 27 SC 43780
UF Churches
R ↓ Architecture 73
↓ Community Facilities 73
Religion 67

Religious Education 73
PN 453 SC 43790
B Education 67
R Private School Education 73
Religion 67
↓ Religious Beliefs 73
↓ Religious Personnel 73
Seminaries 73

Religious Experiences 97
PN 0 SC 43795
R Cultism 73
Mysticism 67
↓ Parapsychological Phenomena 73
Religion 67
↓ Religious Beliefs 73
Spirituality 88

Religious Groups 97
PN 0 SC 43797
SN Groups and their members sharing common religious beliefs and belonging to the same religious affiliation.
N Buddhists 97
↓ Christians 97
Hindus 97
Jews 97
Muslims 97
R ↓ Clergy 73
↓ Religious Affiliation 73
Religious Organizations 91
↓ Religious Practices 73

Religious Literature 73
PN 91 SC 43800
N Bible 73
R ↓ Literature 67
Religion 67
↓ Religious Beliefs 73

Religious Occupations
Use Religious Personnel

Religious Organizations 91
PN 116 SC 43815
SN Any type of agency, organization, or institution operated by religious groups or persons. Includes, but not limited to, church, social service, educational, fraternal, recreational, missionary, or rehabilitation organizations.
B Organizations 67
R Religion 67
↓ Religious Groups 97

Religious Personnel 73
PN 220 SC 43820
UF Religious Occupations
B Personnel 67
N ↓ Clergy 73
Evangelists 73
Lay Religious Personnel 73
Missionaries 73
Nuns 73
Seminarians 73
R ↓ Professional Personnel 78
Religion 67
Religious Education 73
↓ Volunteer Personnel 73

Religious Practices 73
PN 783 SC 43830
UF Rites (Religion)
Rituals (Religion)
Worship
N Asceticism 73
Confession (Religion) 73
Faith Healing 73
Meditation 73
Prayer 73
Yoga 73
R Glossolalia 73
Mysticism 67
Religion 67
↓ Religious Affiliation 73
↓ Religious Beliefs 73
↓ Religious Groups 97

Religious Prejudices 73
PN 29 SC 43840
B Prejudice 67
N AntiSemitism 73
R Religion 67
↓ Religious Beliefs 73

REM
Use Rapid Eye Movement

REM Dream Deprivation 73
PN 19 SC 43860
B Deprivation 67
R Rapid Eye Movement 71

REM Dreams 73
PN 72 SC 43870
UF Rapid Eye Movement Dreams
B Dreaming 67
R ↓ Eye Movements 67
Lucid Dreaming 94
Rapid Eye Movement 71
REM Sleep 73

REM Sleep 73
PN 1515 SC 43880
UF Paradoxical Sleep
Rapid Eye Movement Sleep
B Sleep 67
R ↓ Eye Movements 67
Lucid Dreaming 94
Rapid Eye Movement 71
REM Dreams 73

Remarriage 85
PN 235 SC 43885
B Marriage 67
R Divorce 73
↓ Marital Status 73
Stepfamily 91

Remedial Education 85
PN 429 SC 43887

Remedial Education — (cont'd)
SN Specialized instruction designed to raise academic competence of students with below-normal achievement or learning difficulties. Compare COMPENSATORY EDUCATION.
B Education [67]
N Remedial Reading [73]
R Compensatory Education [73]
Educational Therapy [97]
Special Education [67]

Remedial Reading [73]
PN 706 **SC** 43890
SN Specialized instruction designed to correct faulty reading habits or to improve imperfectly learned reading skills.
B Reading [67]
Remedial Education [85]
R Educational Placement [78]
Reading Education [73]

Remembering
Use Retention

Reminiscence [85]
PN 387 **SC** 43905
SN Process of recalling past experiences.
B Memory [67]
R Anniversary Events [94]
Autobiographical Memory [94]
Early Memories [85]
Enactments [97]
Forgetting [73]
Homesickness [94]
Life Review [91]
↓ Recall (Learning) [67]
Reflectiveness [97]
↓ Retention [67]

Remission (Disorders) [73]
PN 386 **SC** 43910
SN Diminution or disappearance of symptoms.
N Spontaneous Remission [73]
Symptom Remission [73]
R ↓ Disorders [67]
↓ Mental Disorders [67]
↓ Physical Disorders [97]
Recovery (Disorders) [73]
Relapse Prevention [94]
↓ Treatment Outcomes [82]

Remote Associates Test [73]
PN 16 **SC** 43920
B Intelligence Measures [67]

Renal Diseases
Use Kidney Diseases

Renal Transplantation
Use Organ Transplantation

Repairmen
Use Technical Service Personnel

Repeated Measures [85]
PN 110 **SC** 43935
SN Experimental design in which the subjects serve in all experimental, treatment, or control conditions.
UF Within Subjects Design
B Experimental Design [67]
Testing [67]
R Posttesting [73]
Pretesting [73]

Repetition (Compulsive)
Use Compulsive Repetition

Replication (Experimental)
Use Experimental Replication

Reply (to Professional Criticism)
Use Professional Criticism Reply

Repressed Memory [97]
PN 0 **SC** 43955
B Memory [67]
R Age Regression (Hypnotic) [88]
↓ Amnesia [67]
Early Memories [85]
Emotional Trauma [67]
False Memory [97]
Repression (Defense Mechanism) [67]

Repression (Defense Mechanism) [67]
PN 548 **SC** 43960
B Defense Mechanisms [67]
R Repressed Memory [97]
Suppression (Defense Mechanism) [73]

Repression Sensitization [73]
PN 252 **SC** 43968
SN Personality continuum which characterizes individual's defensive response to threat, with avoidance (repression or denial) at one extreme and approach (worry or intellectualization) at the other.
UF Sensitization Repression
B Personality Traits [67]

Repression Sensitization Scale [73]
PN 28 **SC** 43970
B Nonprojective Personality Measures [73]

Reproductive Technology [88]
PN 163 **SC** 43975
UF Artificial Insemination
In Vitro Fertilization
Test Tube Babies
R Eugenics [73]
Fertilization [73]
↓ Genetic Engineering [94]
↓ Genetics [67]
↓ Pregnancy [67]
Prenatal Diagnosis [88]
Selective Breeding [73]
↓ Sexual Reproduction [73]

Reptiles [67]
PN 41 **SC** 43980
B Vertebrates [73]
N Crocodilians [73]
Lizards [73]
Snakes [73]
Turtles [73]

Republican Party
Use Political Parties

Reputation [97]
PN 0 **SC** 43995
R Credibility [73]
Fame [85]
Morality [67]
Popularity [88]
Social Approval [67]
Social Cognition [94]
↓ Social Perception [67]
↓ Status [67]

Research
Use Experimentation

Research Design
Use Experimental Design

Research Diagnostic Criteria [94]
PN 10 **SC** 44013
SN Used when the Research Diagnostic Criteria or its revisions are the focus of the reference. Use PSYCHODIAGNOSTIC TYPOLOGIES to access references prior to 1994. Not used for specific psychodiagnostic categories.
UF RDC
B Psychodiagnostic Typologies [67]
R ↓ Diagnosis [67]
Diagnostic and Statistical Manual [94]
International Class of Diseases [97]
↓ Mental Disorders [67]
↓ Psychodiagnosis [67]

Research Dropouts
Use Experimental Attrition

Research Methods
Use Methodology

Research Subjects
Use Experimental Subjects

Resentment
Use Hostility

Reserpine [67]
PN 298 **SC** 44040
UF Serpasil
B Alkaloids [73]
Antihypertensive Drugs [73]
Neuroleptic Drugs [73]
Sedatives [73]
Sympatholytic Drugs [73]

Residence Halls
Use Dormitories

Residency (Medical)
Use Medical Residency

Residential Care Attendants
Use Attendants (Institutions)

Residential Care Institutions [73]
PN 3279 **SC** 44080
SN Facilities where individuals or patients live and receive appropriate treatment or care.
UF Institutions (Residential Care)
N Halfway Houses [73]
↓ Hospitals [67]
Nursing Homes [73]
Orphanages [73]
R Group Homes [82]
Institution Visitation [73]
Institutional Schools [78]
Institutionalized Mentally Retarded [73]
Psychiatric Units [91]
Retirement Communities [97]
↓ Treatment Facilities [73]

Resilience (Psychological)
Use Hardiness

Resistance [97]
PN 0 **SC** 44087
N Psychotherapeutic Resistance [73]
R Assertiveness [73]
Avoidance [67]
Coercion [94]
↓ Compliance [73]
Independence (Personality) [73]
Obedience [73]
School Refusal [94]
Temptation [73]
Treatment Refusal [94]

Resistance (Psychotherapeutic)
Use Psychotherapeutic Resistance

Resocialization (Psychosocial)
Use Psychosocial Readjustment

Resonance
Use Vibration

Resource Allocation [97]
PN 0 **SC** 44125
UF Allocation of Resources
R Cost Containment [91]
↓ Costs and Cost Analysis [73]
Economics [85]
Egalitarianism [85]
Equity (Payment) [78]
↓ Equity (Social) [78]
Funding [88]
Money [67]
↓ Personnel Management [73]
Reward Allocation [88]

Resource Teachers [73]
PN 94 **SC** 44130
SN Teachers with special competencies who supplement regular curricula or programs or who assist other teachers in specified areas.
B Teachers [67]
R Special Education Teachers [73]

Respiration [67]
PN 2037 **SC** 44140
UF Breathing
R Artificial Respiration [73]
Carbon Dioxide [73]
↓ Respiration Stimulating Drugs [73]
↓ Respiratory Distress [73]
↓ Respiratory System [73]
↓ Respiratory Tract Disorders [73]
Yawning [88]

Respiration Stimulating Drugs [73]
PN 7 **SC** 44160
B Drugs [67]
N Caffeine [73]
R Respiration [67]

Respiratory Distress [73]
PN 73 **SC** 44170
B Symptoms [67]
N ↓ Apnea [73]
↓ Dyspnea [73]
Hyperventilation [73]
R Anoxia [73]
Respiration [67]

Respiratory System [73]
PN 60 **SC** 44180
B Anatomical Systems [73]
N Bronchi [73]
Diaphragm (Anatomy) [73]
↓ Larynx [73]
Lung [73]
↓ Nose [73]
Pharynx [73]
Thorax [73]
Trachea [73]
R Artificial Respiration [73]
Respiration [67]

Respiratory Tract Disorders [73]
PN 294 **SC** 44190
B Physical Disorders [97]
N ↓ Apnea [73]
Bronchial Disorders [73]
↓ Dyspnea [73]
Hay Fever [73]

Respiratory Tract Disorders — (cont'd)
N Hyperventilation [73]
Laryngeal Disorders [73]
↓ Lung Disorders [73]
Pharyngeal Disorders [73]
R Artificial Respiration [73]
Influenza [73]
Poliomyelitis [73]
Respiration [67]

Respite Care [88]
PN 110 **SC** 44195
SN Provision of care, relief, or support to caregivers of physically or mentally disabled persons.
R Caregiver Burden [94]
Caregivers [88]
Home Care [85]

Respondent Conditioning
Use Classical Conditioning

Response Amplitude [73]
PN 563 **SC** 44210
UF Amplitude (Response)
B Response Parameters [73]

Response Bias [67]
PN 1313 **SC** 44220
SN Tendency to respond with different styles or criteria as a result of motivational or physical influences. Response bias frequently serves as a source of measurement error in psychophysical, personality, and other types of measurement.
UF Bias (Response)
R Cultural Test Bias [73]
↓ Measurement [67]
Predisposition [73]
↓ Test Bias [85]
Test Taking [85]

Response Consistency
Use Response Variability

Response Cost [97]
PN 0 **SC** 44228
SN Punishment procedure in which positive reinforcer is lost when a specified behavior is performed.
B Behavior Therapy [67]
Punishment [67]
R Token Economy Programs [73]

Response Duration [73]
PN 342 **SC** 44230
UF Duration (Response)
B Response Parameters [73]

Response Frequency [73]
PN 1557 **SC** 44240
SN Number of responses measured during a fixed time period.
UF Frequency (Response)
Response Rate
B Response Parameters [73]
R Behavioral Contrast [78]
Interresponse Time [73]

Response Generalization [73]
PN 401 **SC** 44250
SN Learning phenomenon in which an emitted response is functionally identical to the originally-conditioned response but which, unlike the conditioned response, was never specifically conditioned. Compare GENERALIZATION (LEARNING) and STIMULUS GENERALIZATION.
UF Generalization (Response)
B Generalization (Learning) [82]
Response Parameters [73]

Response Lag
Use Reaction Time

Response Latency [67]
PN 1777 **SC** 44270
SN Duration of the interval between a stimulus and the onset of the elicited response. Compare REACTION TIME.
UF Latency (Response)
B Response Parameters [73]
R Behavioral Contrast [78]
Cognitive Processing Speed [97]

Response Parameters [73]
PN 864 **SC** 44280
UF Parameters (Response)
N Interresponse Time [73]
Reaction Time [67]
Response Amplitude [73]
Response Duration [73]
Response Frequency [73]
Response Generalization [73]
Response Latency [67]
Response Probability [73]
Response Set [67]
Response Variability [73]
R ↓ Responses [67]

Response Probability [73]
PN 178 **SC** 44290
B Probability [67]
Response Parameters [73]

Response Rate
Use Response Frequency

Response Set [67]
PN 566 **SC** 44300
SN Cognitive state of concentration or behavioral readiness to respond. Also, deliberate or inadvertent style or tendency to respond to test items in characteristic ways (e.g., with socially desirable answers) that detract from the validity of the obtained measures.
UF Set (Response)
B Response Parameters [73]

Response Speed
Use Reaction Time

Response Time
Use Reaction Time

Response Variability [73]
PN 446 **SC** 44330
UF Response Consistency
Variability (Response)
B Response Parameters [73]
R Delayed Alternation [94]
Spontaneous Alternation [82]

Responses [67]
PN 1893 **SC** 44340
N ↓ Conditioned Responses [67]
↓ Emotional Responses [67]
Mediated Responses [67]
Orienting Responses [67]
Unconditioned Responses [73]
R ↓ Response Parameters [73]

Responsibility [73]
PN 1850 **SC** 44345
B Social Behavior [67]
N Accountability [88]
Criminal Responsibility [91]
R Blame [94]
Conscientiousness [97]
Professional Liability [85]

Restlessness [73]
PN 133 **SC** 44350
B Emotional States [73]
Symptoms [67]
R Agitation [91]
Akathisia [91]
Hyperkinesis [73]

Restraint (Physical)
Use Physical Restraint

Restricted Environmental Stimulation
Use Stimulus Deprivation

Retail Stores
SN Use SHOPPING CENTERS to access references from 73-90.
Use Retailing

Retailing [91]
PN 181 **SC** 44362
UF Retail Stores
R ↓ Advertising [67]
Brand Names [78]
Business [67]
↓ Consumer Behavior [67]
Marketing [73]
↓ Quality of Services [97]
Sales Personnel [73]
Self Employment [94]
Shopping [97]
Shopping Centers [73]

Retaliation [91]
PN 33 **SC** 44364
SN Use RECIPROCITY to access references from 73-90.
UF Revenge
B Social Behavior [67]
R ↓ Aggressive Behavior [67]
Attack Behavior [73]
Hostility [67]
↓ Interpersonal Interaction [67]
Reciprocity [73]

Retardation (Mental)
Use Mental Retardation

Retarded (Mentally)
Use Mentally Retarded

Retarded Speech Development [73]
PN 118 **SC** 44390
SN Speech development that is below normal for a specific age level.
UF Delayed Speech
B Delayed Development [73]
Speech Development [73]
R Language Delay [88]
↓ Speech Disorders [67]

Retention [67]
PN 4127 **SC** 44400
SN Persistence of a learned act, information, or experience as measured by reproduction, recall, recognition, or relearning. Consider also LONG TERM MEMORY or SHORT TERM MEMORY. Used for both human and animal populations.
UF Remembering
N ↓ Recall (Learning) [67]
↓ Recognition (Learning) [67]
Reconstruction (Learning) [73]
R Forgetting [73]
↓ Interference (Learning) [67]
↓ Learning [67]
↓ Memory [67]
Memory Training [94]

Retention — (cont'd)
R Reminiscence [85]
↓ Retention Measures [73]

Retention (School)
Use School Retention

Retention Measures [73]
PN 110 **SC** 44410
B Measurement [67]
N Wechsler Memory Scale [88]
R ↓ Retention [67]

Reticular Formation [67]
PN 469 **SC** 44420
B Brain Stem [73]
Neural Pathways [82]
R ↓ Lemniscal System [85]
Locus Ceruleus [82]
Raphe Nuclei [82]

Retina [67]
PN 1237 **SC** 44430
B Eye (Anatomy) [67]
N Cones (Eye) [73]
Ganglion Cells (Retina) [85]
Rods (Eye) [73]
R Retinal Eccentricity [91]

Retinal Eccentricity [91]
PN 69 **SC** 44435
R ↓ Retina [67]
Retinal Image [73]
Spatial Organization [73]
↓ Visual Perception [67]
Visual Receptive Fields [82]
↓ Visual Thresholds [73]

Retinal Ganglion Cells
Use Ganglion Cells (Retina)

Retinal Image [73]
PN 445 **SC** 44450
UF Image (Retinal)
R ↓ Eye (Anatomy) [67]
Retinal Eccentricity [91]

Retinal Vessels
Use Arteries (Anatomy)

Retirement [73]
PN 967 **SC** 44470
R Employment History [78]
↓ Employment Status [82]
Job Security [78]
↓ Personnel [67]
Personnel Termination [73]
Reemployment [91]
Retirement Communities [97]
Unemployment [67]

Retirement Communities [97]
PN 0 **SC** 44473
B Communities [67]
Housing [73]
R Group Homes [82]
↓ Living Arrangements [91]
Nursing Homes [73]
↓ Residential Care Institutions [73]
Retirement [73]

Retraction of Publication [91]
PN 2 **SC** 44475

Retraction of Publication — (cont'd)
SN Mandatory term applied to notices from journals or authors that retract or recant previously published material because of scientific misconduct, error, unsubstantiated or fabricated data, or other reasons.
R Errata [91]
Fraud [94]
↓ Scientific Communication [73]

Retroactive Inhibition [73]
PN 495 **SC** 44480
SN The theory that learning new material can interfere with the retention of previously learned material. Also, the actual retroactive interference itself.
UF Inhibition (Retroactive)
B Interference (Learning) [67]
Latent Inhibition [97]

Retrospective Studies [97]
PN 0 **SC** 44481
SN Mandatory term applied to studies which involve collecting data about experiences or events that occurred in the past usually to study etiologic hypotheses or causative factors related to a disorder, behavior, or phenomenon.
R ↓ Longitudinal Studies [73]
Prospective Studies [97]

Rett Syndrome [94]
PN 25 **SC** 44482
B Syndromes [73]
R ↓ Brain Disorders [67]
↓ Mental Disorders [67]
↓ Mental Retardation [67]
↓ Physical Disorders [97]

Return to Home
Use Empty Nest

Return to Work
Use Reemployment

Revenge
Use Retaliation

Reversal Shift Learning [67]
PN 628 **SC** 44490
SN Experimental technique for demonstration of mediating processes in concept formation which assesses ability to learn to reverse responses in stimulus discrimination task, so that the subject is required to respond to a formerly negative stimulus and not to respond to the formerly positive discriminative stimulus.
B Discrimination Learning [82]

Review (of Literature)
SN Term discontinued in 1973. Use REVIEW (OF LITERATURE) to access references from 67-72.
Use Literature Review

Revolutions (Political)
Use Political Revolution

Reward Allocation [88]
PN 100 **SC** 44515
R ↓ Justice [73]
Resource Allocation [97]
↓ Rewards [67]
↓ Social Perception [67]

Rewards [67]
PN 2454 **SC** 44520

Rewards — (cont'd)
SN Events or objects subjectively deemed to be pleasant to a recipient. Compare INCENTIVES, REINFORCEMENT, and POSITIVE REINFORCEMENT.
B Reinforcement [67]
N External Rewards [73]
Internal Rewards [73]
Monetary Rewards [73]
Preferred Rewards [73]
R Delay of Gratification [78]
Delayed Alternation [94]
↓ Incentives [67]
Reward Allocation [88]

Rh Incompatibility [73]
PN 3 **SC** 44530
UF Erythroblastosis Fetalis
Incompatibility (Rh)
B Blood and Lymphatic Disorders [73]
Genetic Disorders [73]
Immunologic Disorders [73]
R ↓ Neonatal Disorders [73]

Rheoencephalography [73]
PN 18 **SC** 44540
B Encephalography [73]
Medical Diagnosis [73]
R ↓ Electroencephalography [67]

Rhetoric [91]
PN 129 **SC** 44545
B Communication Skills [73]
Language [67]
R ↓ Communication [67]
Creative Writing [94]
Debates [97]
Discourse Analysis [97]
Hermeneutics [91]
↓ Oral Communication [85]
↓ Persuasive Communication [67]
↓ Written Communication [85]

Rheumatic Fever [73]
PN 13 **SC** 44550
R ↓ Bacterial Disorders [73]
↓ Heart Disorders [73]
Rheumatoid Arthritis [73]

Rheumatism
Use Arthritis

Rheumatoid Arthritis [73]
PN 512 **SC** 44570
B Arthritis [73]
R Rheumatic Fever [73]

Rhodopsin [85]
PN 9 **SC** 44575
SN A red pigment localized in the outer segments of rod cells in the retina.
B Pigments [73]
R Rods (Eye) [73]

Rhombencephalon
Use Hindbrain

Rhythm [91]
PN 135 **SC** 44577
N Speech Rhythm [73]
R ↓ Auditory Perception [67]
↓ Music [67]
Music Perception [97]
Pattern Discrimination [67]
↓ Perception [67]
Speech Perception [67]
Tempo [97]

Rhythm Method [73]
PN 4 **SC** 44580
B Birth Control [71]

Ribonucleic Acid [73]
PN 260 **SC** 44600
UF RNA (Ribonucleic Acid)
B Nucleic Acids [73]

Right Brain [91]
PN 183 **SC** 44610
SN Used only when the right hemisphere of the brain is the focus of the document.
B Cerebral Cortex [67]
R ↓ Brain [67]
↓ Cerebral Dominance [73]
Corpus Callosum [73]
Interhemispheric Interaction [85]
↓ Lateral Dominance [67]
Left Brain [91]
Ocular Dominance [73]

Right to Treatment [97]
PN 0 **SC** 44615
B Client Rights [88]
R Advocacy [85]
↓ Commitment (Psychiatric) [73]
Deinstitutionalization [82]
Involuntary Treatment [94]
Self Referral [91]

Rigidity (Muscles)
Use Muscle Contractions

Rigidity (Personality) [67]
PN 216 **SC** 44620
B Personality Traits [67]
R Openness to Experience [97]

Riots [73]
PN 87 **SC** 44640
B Collective Behavior [67]
Conflict [67]
R ↓ Violence [73]

Risk Analysis [91]
PN 432 **SC** 44643
B Analysis [67]
R ↓ Decision Making [67]
↓ Gambling [73]
Game Theory [67]
Risk Management [97]
Risk Perception [97]
↓ Risk Taking [67]
↓ Statistical Probability [67]

Risk Management [97]
PN 0 **SC** 44644
SN Reducing and preventing loss, damage, harm, or danger to a business, group, or individual through safety and protective measures. Used for clinical and nonclinical environments.
B Management [67]
R Accident Prevention [73]
↓ Costs and Cost Analysis [73]
↓ Insurance [73]
↓ Legal Processes [73]
↓ Prevention [73]
Professional Liability [85]
Risk Analysis [91]
↓ Risk Taking [67]
↓ Safety [67]

Risk Perception [97]
PN 0 **SC** 44646
SN Awareness of, or attitudes toward, potential risk. Primarily used for risk associated with disease or behavior.

Risk Perception — (cont'd)
B Perception [67]
R Hazards [73]
↓ Prevention [73]
Risk Analysis [91]
↓ Risk Taking [67]
↓ Safety [67]
Sexual Risk Taking [97]

Risk Populations
Use At Risk Populations

Risk Taking [67]
PN 2941 **SC** 44650
B Personality Traits [67]
Social Behavior [67]
N ↓ Gambling [73]
Sexual Risk Taking [97]
R Choice Shift [94]
Risk Analysis [91]
Risk Management [97]
Risk Perception [97]

Risky Shift
Use Choice Shift

Risperidone [97]
PN 0 **SC** 44657
B Neuroleptic Drugs [73]

Ritalin
Use Methylphenidate

Ritanserin [97]
PN 0 **SC** 44665
B Serotonin Antagonists [73]

Rites (Nonreligious) [73]
PN 374 **SC** 44670
UF Rituals (Nonreligious)
R ↓ Rites of Passage [73]

Rites (Religion)
Use Religious Practices

Rites of Passage [73]
PN 85 **SC** 44690
B Sociocultural Factors [67]
N Birth Rites [73]
Death Rites [73]
Initiation Rites [73]
Marriage Rites [73]
R ↓ Developmental Stages [73]
Ethnography [73]
Rites (Nonreligious) [73]
Taboos [73]

Rituals (Nonreligious)
Use Rites (Nonreligious)

Rituals (Religion)
Use Religious Practices

Rivalry [73]
PN 31 **SC** 44720
B Interpersonal Interaction [67]
R Competition [67]

RNA (Ribonucleic Acid)
Use Ribonucleic Acid

Robbery
Use Theft

Robins 73
PN 43 SC 44750
B Birds 67

Robotics 85
PN 170 SC 44755
R ↓ Artificial Intelligence 82
↓ Computers 67
Cybernetics 67
↓ Expert Systems 91

Rock Music 91
PN 54 SC 44757
B Music 67

Rocking (Body)
Use Body Rocking

Rod and Frame Test 73
PN 118 SC 44770
B Nonprojective Personality Measures 73
Perceptual Measures 73

Rodents 73
PN 681 SC 44780
UF Voles
B Mammals 73
N Beavers 73
Chinchillas 73
Gerbils 73
Guinea Pigs 67
Hamsters 73
Mice 73
Minks 73
↓ Rats 67
Squirrels 73

Rods (Eye) 73
PN 223 SC 44790
B Photoreceptors 73
Retina 67
R Rhodopsin 85

Roentgenography 73
PN 126 SC 44800
UF Radiography
X Ray Diagnosis
B Medical Diagnosis 73
N Angiography 73
Mammography 94
Pneumoencephalography 73
R ↓ Encephalography 73
↓ Radiation 67
↓ Tomography 88

Rogerian Therapy
Use Client Centered Therapy

Rogers (Carl) 91
PN 42 SC 44805
SN Identifies biographical or autobiographical studies and discussions of Rogers's works.
R Client Centered Therapy 67
↓ Humanistic Psychology 85
↓ Psychologists 67

Rokeach Dogmatism Scale 73
PN 31 SC 44810
B Nonprojective Personality Measures 73
Personality Measures 67

Role (Counselor)
Use Counselor Role

Role Conflicts 73
PN 1630 SC 44830

Role Conflicts — (cont'd)
UF Role Strain
R Family Work Relationship 97
Role Satisfaction 94
↓ Roles 67

Role Expectations 73
PN 774 SC 44840
SN Functional patterns or types of behavior expected from an individual in a specific social or professional position or situation.
B Expectations 67
R Role Satisfaction 94
↓ Roles 67

Role Models 82
PN 314 SC 44845
SN Real or theoretical persons consciously or unconsciously perceived as being a standard for emulation in one or more of their roles.
R Imitation (Learning) 67
Role Perception 73
↓ Roles 67
Significant Others 91
↓ Social Influences 67

Role Perception 73
PN 1858 SC 44850
SN Views or understanding of one's own or others' function or behavior in particular situations.
B Perception 67
R Professional Identity 91
Role Models 82
Role Satisfaction 94
Role Taking 82
↓ Roles 67

Role Playing 67
PN 1237 SC 44860
SN Psychological or behavioral enactment of social roles other than one's own, typically seen in child's play, or used as an experimental, instructional, or psychotherapeutic technique. Compare ROLE TAKING.
R Childhood Play Behavior 78
Psychodrama 67
↓ Psychotherapeutic Techniques 67
Role Taking 82
↓ Roles 67

Role Satisfaction 94
PN 25 SC 44863
B Satisfaction 73
R Job Satisfaction 67
Life Satisfaction 85
Marital Satisfaction 88
Role Conflicts 73
Role Expectations 73
Role Perception 73
↓ Roles 67
↓ Self Concept 67

Role Strain
Use Role Conflicts

Role Taking 82
PN 465 SC 44865
SN Perceiving, understanding, or experiencing the social, emotional or physical aspects of a situation from a standpoint of another person or persons. Use EGOCENTRISM to access references from 78-81. Compare ROLE PLAYING.
UF Perspective Taking
R Egocentrism 78
Role Perception 73
Role Playing 67
↓ Roles 67
Symbolic Interactionism 88

Roles 67
PN 3744 SC 44870
N Counselor Role 73
Parental Role 73
Sex Roles 67
Therapist Role 78
R Role Conflicts 73
Role Expectations 73
Role Models 82
Role Perception 73
Role Playing 67
Role Satisfaction 94
Role Taking 82

Roman Catholicism 73
PN 644 SC 44880
UF Catholicism (Roman)
B Christianity 73
R Catholics 97

Romance 97
PN 0 SC 44883
R Affection 73
Couples 82
↓ Human Courtship 73
Human Mate Selection 88
Intimacy 73
Love 73
↓ Marital Relations 67
↓ Marriage 67
↓ Psychosexual Behavior 67
↓ Relationship Termination 97
Significant Others 91
Social Dating 73

Romania 82
PN 96 SC 44885
B Europe 73

Roommates 73
PN 100 SC 44890
SN Individuals residing in common abodes.
R Cohabitation 73
↓ Living Arrangements 91

Rorschach Test 67
PN 2051 SC 44900
B Projective Personality Measures 73

Rosenzweig Picture Frustration Study 67
PN 52 SC 44910
B Projective Personality Measures 73

Rotary Pursuit 67
PN 181 SC 44920
B Tracking 67
R ↓ Attention 67

Rotation Methods (Statistical)
Use Statistical Rotation

Rotational Behavior 94
PN 48 SC 44935
SN Used primarily for animal populations.
UF Body Rotation
B Motor Processes 67
R Activity Level 82
Stereotyped Behavior 73

ROTC Students 73
PN 66 SC 44940
B College Students 67
Military Personnel 67
R Volunteer Military Personnel 73
↓ Volunteer Personnel 73

Rote Learning [73]
PN 106 **SC** 44950
SN Verbatim memorization of information which requires no understanding.
R ↓ Memory [67]

Rotter Incomplete Sentences Blank [73]
PN 15 **SC** 44960
B Projective Personality Measures [73]

Rotter Intern Extern Locus Cont Scal [73]
PN 145 **SC** 44970
B Nonprojective Personality Measures [73]

RT (Response)
Use Reaction Time

Rubella [73]
PN 31 **SC** 45000
UF German Measles
B Viral Disorders [73]
R Measles [73]

Rule Learning
Use Cognitive Hypothesis Testing

Rumors
Use Gossip

Runaway Behavior [73]
PN 252 **SC** 45015
B Antisocial Behavior [71]
R Shelters [91]

Running [73]
PN 552 **SC** 45020
B Motor Performance [73]

Runways (Maze)
Use Maze Pathways

Rural Development
Use Community Development

Rural Environments [67]
PN 3474 **SC** 45040
B Social Environments [73]
R Community Development [97]

Rwanda [91]
PN 9 **SC** 45045
B Africa [67]

Saccadic Eye Movements
Use Eye Movements

Saccharin [73]
PN 360 **SC** 45050
R ↓ Sugars [73]

SAD
Use Seasonal Affective Disorder

Sadism [73]
PN 45 **SC** 45070
B Sadomasochism [73]
N Sexual Sadism [73]
R ↓ Masochism [73]

Sadness [73]
PN 246 **SC** 45090
UF Melancholy
B Emotional States [73]
R Depression (Emotion) [67]
Homesickness [94]
↓ Separation Reactions [97]

Sadomasochism [73]
PN 77 **SC** 45100
SN Derivation of pleasure from infliction of physical or mental pain on others and oneself, with presence of high degree of destructiveness.
N ↓ Masochism [73]
↓ Sadism [73]
R ↓ Mental Disorders [67]
↓ Sadomasochistic Personality [73]

Sadomasochistic Personality [73]
PN 4 **SC** 45110
B Personality Disorders [67]
N Masochistic Personality [73]
R ↓ Sadomasochism [73]

Safety [67]
PN 692 **SC** 45120
N ↓ Aviation Safety [73]
Highway Safety [73]
Occupational Safety [73]
Water Safety [73]
R Accident Prevention [73]
Accident Proneness [73]
↓ Accidents [67]
Fire Prevention [73]
↓ Hazardous Materials [91]
Hazards [73]
↓ Injuries [73]
↓ Prevention [73]
Risk Management [97]
Risk Perception [97]
↓ Safety Devices [73]
Warning Labels [97]
↓ Warnings [97]

Safety Belts [73]
PN 212 **SC** 45130
UF Seat Belts
B Safety Devices [73]
R ↓ Driving Behavior [67]
↓ Transportation Accidents [73]

Safety Devices [73]
PN 142 **SC** 45140
N Safety Belts [73]
R Hazards [73]
↓ Safety [67]
Warning Labels [97]
↓ Warnings [97]

Safety Warnings
Use Warnings

Saint Lucia [91]
PN 3 **SC** 45145
B West Indies [73]

Saint Vincent [91]
PN 4 **SC** 45147
B West Indies [73]

Salamanders [73]
PN 173 **SC** 45150
B Amphibia [73]
R Larvae [73]

Salaries [73]
PN 966 **SC** 45160
UF Pay
Wages
R Bonuses [73]
↓ Employee Benefits [73]
Equity (Payment) [78]
Income (Economic) [73]
↓ Income Level [73]
↓ Professional Fees [78]

Sales Personnel [73]
PN 671 **SC** 45170
UF Insurance Agents
B Business and Industrial Personnel [67]
White Collar Workers [73]
R Retailing [91]
↓ Service Personnel [91]

Salience (Stimulus)
Use Stimulus Salience

Saliva [73]
PN 224 **SC** 45200
B Body Fluids [73]
R Salivation [73]

Salivary Glands [73]
PN 34 **SC** 45210
B Glands [67]
R ↓ Digestive System [67]
Mouth (Anatomy) [67]

Salivation [73]
PN 176 **SC** 45220
B Secretion (Gland) [73]
R Digestion [73]
Saliva [73]

Salmon [73]
PN 59 **SC** 45230
B Fishes [67]

Saltiness
Use Taste Perception

Sample Size [97]
PN 0 **SC** 45245
B Statistical Sample Parameters [73]
R ↓ Sampling (Experimental) [73]

Sampling (Experimental) [73]
PN 529 **SC** 45250
SN Systematic selection of part of a larger population of individual responses, individuals, or groups for use in empirical study or research . Results about the entire population are then generalized from this smaller sample.
N Biased Sampling [73]
Random Sampling [73]
R Data Collection [82]
↓ Experimental Design [67]
↓ Experimentation [67]
↓ Population (Statistics) [73]
Sample Size [97]
↓ Statistical Analysis [67]
Statistical Power [91]
Statistical Reliability [73]
↓ Statistical Samples [73]
↓ Statistical Variables [73]

Sanatoriums [73]
PN 12 **SC** 45260
B Hospitals [67]
R Nursing Homes [73]
Psychiatric Hospitals [67]

Sarcomas
Use Neoplasms

SAT
Use Coll Ent Exam Bd Scholastic Apt Test

Satiation [67]
PN 685 **SC** 45280

Satiation — (cont'd)
SN Primarily limited to gratification or satisfaction of a physiologically-based motivation (e.g., need for food and water) but may also refer to gratification of a psychic goal or motivation. Consider also SATISFACTION or NEED SATISFACTION for the latter concept.
R ↓ Appetite 73
↓ Motivation 67

Satisfaction 73
PN 3548 **SC** 45290
UF Fulfillment
N Client Satisfaction 94
Consumer Satisfaction 94
Job Satisfaction 67
Life Satisfaction 85
Marital Satisfaction 88
Need Satisfaction 73
Role Satisfaction 94
Sexual Satisfaction 94
R Dissatisfaction 73
Physical Comfort 82

Saturation (Color)
Use Color Saturation

Saudi Arabia 85
PN 167 **SC** 45295
B Asia 73
R Middle East 78

Scaling (Testing) 67
PN 1183 **SC** 45360
B Testing 67
Testing Methods 67
R Magnitude Estimation 91
Multidimensional Scaling 82

Scalp (Anatomy) 73
PN 44 **SC** 45370
B Anatomy 67
R Hair 73
Head (Anatomy) 73
Skin (Anatomy) 67

Scalp Disorders
Use Skin Disorders

Scandinavia 78
PN 90 **SC** 45385
B Europe 73
N Denmark 73
Norway 73
Sweden 73
R Finland 73
Iceland 82

Scent Marking (Animal)
Use Animal Scent Marking

Schedules (Learning)
Use Learning Schedules

Schedules (Reinforcement)
Use Reinforcement Schedules

Scheduling (Work)
Use Work Scheduling

Schema 88
PN 973 **SC** 45425
SN Cognitive structure used for comprehension, perception, and interpretation of stimuli.
UF Scripts
B Cognitive Processes 67
R ↓ Cognitions 85

Schema — (cont'd)
R Cognitive Maps 82
↓ Cognitive Style 67
Conceptual Imagery 73
Perceptual Style 73
Social Cognition 94

Schizoaffective Disorder 94
PN 217 **SC** 45427
SN Presence of an affective disorder accompanied by schizophrenia-like symptomatology.
B Affective Disturbances 67
R ↓ Schizophrenia 67

Schizoid Personality 73
PN 333 **SC** 45430
SN Personality disorder characterized by alienation, shyness, oversensitivity, seclusiveness, egocentricity, avoidance of intimate relationships, autistic thinking, and withdrawal from and lack of response to the environment.
B Personality Disorders 67
R ↓ Schizophrenia 67
Schizotypal Personality 91

Schizophrenia 67
PN 20449 **SC** 45440
UF Chronic Schizophrenia
Dementia Praecox
Process Schizophrenia
Pseudopsychopathic Schizophrenia
Reactive Schizophrenia
Schizophrenia (Residual Type)
Simple Schizophrenia
B Psychosis 67
N Acute Schizophrenia 73
Catatonic Schizophrenia 73
Childhood Schizophrenia 67
Hebephrenic Schizophrenia 73
Paranoid Schizophrenia 67
Schizophreniform Disorder 94
Undifferentiated Schizophrenia 73
R Anhedonia 85
Catalepsy 73
Expressed Emotion 91
Fragmentation (Schizophrenia) 73
Positive and Negative Symptoms 97
Schizoaffective Disorder 94
Schizoid Personality 73
Schizotypal Personality 91

Schizophrenia (Disorganized Type)
Use Hebephrenic Schizophrenia

Schizophrenia (Residual Type)
Use Schizophrenia

Schizophreniform Disorder 94
PN 40 **SC** 45447
SN Use ACUTE SCHIZOPHRENIA to access references from 88-93.
B Schizophrenia 67

Schizophrenogenic Family 67
PN 268 **SC** 45450
B Family 67
Family Structure 73
R Double Bind Interaction 73
Dysfunctional Family 91
↓ Mental Disorders 67
Schizophrenogenic Mothers 73

Schizophrenogenic Mothers 73
PN 31 **SC** 45460
B Mothers 67
R Double Bind Interaction 73
Mother Child Relations 67
Schizophrenogenic Family 67

Schizotypal Personality 91
PN 146 **SC** 45465
SN Personality disorder characterized by eccentric thoughts and appearance, inappropriate affect and behavior, extreme social anxiety, and limited interpersonal interaction. Consider using SCHIZOID PERSONALITY to access references from 73-90.
B Personality Disorders 67
R Schizoid Personality 73
↓ Schizophrenia 67

Scholarships
Use Educational Financial Assistance

Scholastic Achievement
Use Academic Achievement

Scholastic Aptitude
Use Academic Aptitude

Scholastic Aptitude Test
Use Coll Ent Exam Bd Scholastic Apt Test

School Accreditation
Use Educational Program Accreditation

School Achievement
Use Academic Achievement

School Adjustment 67
PN 2953 **SC** 45510
SN Process of adjusting to school environment and to the role of a student.
UF Student Adjustment
B Adjustment 67
R Adjustment Disorders 94
↓ Education 67
School Transition 97

School Administration
Use Educational Administration

School Administrators 73
PN 2077 **SC** 45530
UF Administrators (School)
Educational Administrators
B Educational Personnel 73
N School Principals 73
School Superintendents 73
R Boards of Education 78
↓ Management Personnel 73

School Age Children 73
PN 52592 **SC** 45540
SN Ages 6–12 years. Used in noneducational contexts. Application of terms designating age is mandatory for ages 0–17.
B Children 67
N Preadolescents 88
R ↓ Childhood Development 67
↓ Elementary School Students 67
Intermediate School Students 73
Predelinquent Youth 78
Primary School Students 73

School and College Ability Test
SN Term discontinued in 1997. Use SCHOOL and COLLEGE ABILITY TEST to access references from 73–96.
Use Aptitude Measures

School Attendance 73
PN 954 **SC** 45560
SN Regular presence of students in school or classes or absenteeism due to factors other than truancy. Compare SCHOOL ENROLLMENT.

School Attendance — (cont'd)
UF Attendance (School)
R ↓ Education [67]
↓ School Enrollment [73]
School Refusal [94]
School Retention [94]
Student Attrition [91]

School Club Membership [73]
PN 20 SC 45570
B Extracurricular Activities [73]

School Counseling [82]
PN 2191 SC 45579
SN Counseling services provided by counselors or teacher counselors in order to help school, college, or university students cope with adjustment problems. Compare EDUCATIONAL COUNSELING.
UF Guidance Counseling
School Guidance
B Counseling [67]
R ↓ Education [67]
Educational Therapy [97]
↓ Mental Health Services [78]
School Counselors [73]
Student Personnel Services [78]

School Counselors [73]
PN 1449 SC 45580
B Counselors [67]
Educational Personnel [73]
R School Counseling [82]
School Psychologists [73]
Vocational Counselors [73]

School Dropouts [67]
PN 1029 SC 45590
B Dropouts [73]
N College Dropouts [73]
R ↓ Education [67]
Reentry Students [85]
School Refusal [94]
School Retention [94]
Student Attrition [91]

School Enrollment [73]
PN 378 SC 45600
SN Number of students registered to attend school, college or university. Also, the act of enrolling in school. Compare SCHOOL ATTENDANCE.
UF Enrollment (School)
Matriculation
N School Expulsion [73]
School Suspension [73]
Student Attrition [91]
R ↓ Dropouts [73]
↓ Education [67]
School Attendance [73]
School Retention [94]
School Truancy [73]

School Environment [73]
PN 2669 SC 45610
SN School characteristics, including overall social and physical atmosphere or school climate.
UF Educational Environment
B Academic Environment [73]
N College Environment [73]
R Classroom Environment [73]
↓ Education [67]
↓ School Facilities [73]
↓ Schools [67]

School Expulsion [73]
PN 33 SC 45620
UF Expulsion (School)
B School Enrollment [73]

School Expulsion — (cont'd)
R School Suspension [73]
Student Attrition [91]

School Facilities [73]
PN 101 SC 45630
N Campuses [73]
Classrooms [67]
Dormitories [73]
↓ Educational Laboratories [73]
Learning Centers (Educational) [73]
School Libraries [73]
R ↓ Education [67]
Playgrounds [73]
↓ School Environment [73]
↓ Schools [67]

School Federal Aid
Use Educational Financial Assistance

School Financial Assistance
Use Educational Financial Assistance

School Graduation [91]
PN 77 SC 45653
SN Completion of a course of study resulting in the award or acceptance of a diploma or degree.
UF Graduation (School)
R ↓ Academic Achievement [67]
College Graduates [82]
↓ Education [67]
Educational Attainment Level [97]
Educational Degrees [73]
Graduate Schools [73]
High School Graduates [78]
↓ Higher Education [73]
School to Work Transition [94]
School Transition [97]

School Guidance
Use School Counseling

School Integration [82]
PN 198 SC 45658
SN Incorporation of students of different racial, ethnic, or other types of groups into the same school. Use SCHOOL INTEGRATION (RACIAL) to access references from 73–81.
UF Racial Segregation (Schools)
School Integration (Racial)
B Social Integration [82]
R ↓ Activist Movements [73]
↓ Education [67]
Equal Education [78]
Mainstreaming (Educational) [78]
Racial and Ethnic Relations [82]

School Integration (Racial)
SN Term discontinued in 1982. Use SCHOOL INTEGRATION (RACIAL) to access references from 73–81.
Use School Integration

School Learning [67]
PN 3314 SC 45670
SN Learning in an academic environment. For educational performance use ACADEMIC ACHIEVEMENT or one of its narrower terms.
B Learning [67]
R ↓ Academic Achievement [67]
Cooperative Learning [94]
↓ Education [67]
↓ Experiential Learning [97]
Mastery Learning [85]
Metacognition [91]

School Leavers [88]
PN 56 SC 45675

School Leavers — (cont'd)
SN British term referring to persons who have recently left school, generally after the completion of a basic education program and satisfaction of government requirements.
R ↓ Educational Background [67]
School Retention [94]
Student Attrition [91]

School Libraries [73]
PN 86 SC 45680
UF Libraries (School)
B Libraries [82]
School Facilities [73]

School Nurses [73]
PN 56 SC 45690
B Educational Personnel [73]
Nurses [67]

School Organization
Use Educational Administration

School Phobia [73]
PN 215 SC 45710
B Phobias [67]
R School Refusal [94]
Separation Anxiety [73]
Student Attitudes [67]

School Principals [73]
PN 2140 SC 45720
B School Administrators [73]

School Psychologists [73]
PN 1433 SC 45730
SN Psychologists usually associated with elementary or secondary schools who provide counseling, testing, or diagnostic services to students, teachers, or parents.
B Educational Psychologists [73]
Mental Health Personnel [67]
R School Counselors [73]

School Psychology [73]
PN 876 SC 45740
SN Branch of psychology that emphasizes training and certification of school psychologists.
B Educational Psychology [67]

School Readiness [73]
PN 455 SC 45750
SN Developmental level at which a child is prepared to adjust to school and the student role. Compare READING READINESS.
R ↓ Education [67]
Project Head Start [73]

School Refusal [94]
PN 26 SC 45755
SN Unwillingness of students to attend school or classes.
R ↓ Resistance [97]
School Attendance [73]
↓ School Dropouts [67]
School Phobia [73]
School Truancy [73]
Separation Anxiety [73]
Student Attitudes [67]

School Retention [94]
PN 91 SC 45757
SN Retention of students in school or educational programs.
UF Retention (School)
R School Attendance [73]
↓ School Dropouts [67]
↓ School Enrollment [73]

School Retention — (cont'd)
R School Leavers 88
School Truancy 73
Student Attrition 91
↓ Students 67

School Superintendents 73
PN 381 SC 45760
SN Administrators who coordinate and direct the operations and activities of a school system at the district, city, or state level.
UF Superintendents (School)
B School Administrators 73

School Suspension 73
PN 119 SC 45770
SN Temporary, forced withdrawal of a student from school, usually for disciplinary reasons.
UF Suspension (School)
B School Enrollment 73
R Classroom Discipline 73
School Expulsion 73

School to Work Transition 94
PN 48 SC 45775
SN Transition following school graduation or termination and entry into the work force. Used for normal and disordered populations.
R College Graduates 82
↓ Education 67
Educational Attainment Level 97
High School Graduates 78
↓ Mainstreaming 91
Occupational Adjustment 73
School Graduation 91
↓ Vocational Rehabilitation 67

School Transition 97
PN 0 SC 45777
SN Movement or advancement from one grade, school, or program to the next.
R ↓ Academic Achievement 67
↓ Education 67
Grade Level 94
School Adjustment 67
School Graduation 91

School Truancy 73
PN 183 SC 45780
SN Student's deliberate, often chronic absence from school without an accepted medical or other justifiable reason.
B Truancy 73
R ↓ Education 67
↓ School Enrollment 73
School Refusal 94
School Retention 94

Schools 67
PN 1307 SC 45790
N Boarding Schools 88
↓ Colleges 67
Elementary Schools 73
Graduate Schools 73
High Schools 73
Institutional Schools 78
Junior High Schools 73
Kindergartens 73
Military Schools 73
Nongraded Schools 73
Nursery Schools 73
Seminaries 73
Technical Schools 73
R ↓ Community Facilities 73
↓ Education 67
↓ School Environment 73
↓ School Facilities 73

Sciatic Nerve
Use Spinal Nerves

Science Achievement 97
PN 0 SC 45815
B Academic Achievement 67
R Mathematics Achievement 73
Mathematics Education 73
Science Education 73

Science Education 73
PN 2672 SC 45820
B Curriculum 67
R Science Achievement 97

Sciences 67
PN 1393 SC 45825
N ↓ Biology 67
↓ Chemistry 67
Eugenics 73
Geography 73
↓ Mathematics 82
↓ Medical Sciences 67
↓ Neurosciences 73
Physics 73
Psychobiology 82
↓ Social Sciences 67
R ↓ Technology 73

Scientific Communication 73
PN 2715 SC 45830
SN Formal or informal communication among professionals.
UF Communication (Professional)
Newsletters (Professional)
Professional Communication
Professional Newsletters
B Communication 67
N Professional Meetings and Symposia 67
R Errata 91
Information Exchange 73
↓ Interpersonal Communication 73
Psychological Terminology 73
Retraction of Publication 91
↓ Terminology 91

Scientific Methods
Use Experimental Methods

Scientists 67
PN 933 SC 45850
SN Conceptually broad array term. Use a more specific term if possible.
B Professional Personnel 78
R ↓ Aerospace Personnel 73
Anthropologists 73
↓ Business and Industrial Personnel 67
Engineers 67
Mathematicians 73
↓ Medical Personnel 67
Physicists 73
↓ Psychologists 67
Sociologists 73

Sclera
Use Eye (Anatomy)

Sclerosis (Nervous System) 73
PN 128 SC 45870
B Nervous System Disorders 67
N Multiple Sclerosis 73
R ↓ Neuromuscular Disorders 73
↓ Paralysis 73

Scopolamine 73
PN 893 SC 45880
UF Hyoscine
Scopolamine Hydrobromide

Scopolamine — (cont'd)
B Alkaloids 73
Amines 73
Analgesic Drugs 73
Cholinergic Blocking Drugs 73
CNS Depressant Drugs 73
Sedatives 73
R Bromides 73

Scopolamine Hydrobromide
Use Scopolamine

Score Equating 85
PN 124 SC 45895
SN Techniques, procedures, or methods used to allow comparision of scores obtained from various editions of the same test or from different tests measuring the same trait.
UF Test Equating
R Cutting Scores 85
↓ Scoring (Testing) 73
Standard Scores 85

Scores (Test)
Use Test Scores

Scoring (Testing) 73
PN 1561 SC 45910
SN Assignment of numerical values or other types of codes, or the application of comments to test results in order to evaluate a test performance in reference to some established standard or other criterion. Compare GRADING (EDUCATIONAL) or TEST SCORES.
B Testing 67
N Cutting Scores 85
R Error of Measurement 85
Grading (Educational) 73
Score Equating 85
Standard Scores 85
Statistical Weighting 85
Test Interpretation 85
↓ Test Scores 67

Scotland 73
PN 384 SC 45920
B Great Britain 71

Scotopic Stimulation 73
PN 117 SC 45940
SN Presentation of light at intensity levels characteristic of nighttime illumination, activating rod photoreceptors in the retina.
B Illumination 67
R Photopic Stimulation 73

Scratching 73
PN 54 SC 45950
B Symptoms 67
R Pruritus 73

Screening 82
PN 1100 SC 45960
SN Preliminary use of testing procedures or instruments to identify individuals at risk for a particular problem, or in need of a more thorough evaluation, or to determine an individual's suitability for a specific treatment, education, or occupation.
B Measurement 67
N Drug Usage Screening 88
↓ Health Screening 97
Job Applicant Screening 73
R Biological Markers 91
↓ Diagnosis 67
Diagnostic Interview Schedule 91
↓ Educational Measurement 67
Educational Placement 78
Geriatric Assessment 97

Screening — (cont'd)
R Health Promotion 91
Intake Interview 94
Misdiagnosis 97
↓ Personnel Selection 67
↓ Psychiatric Evaluation 97
↓ Screening Tests 82
Symptom Checklists 91

Screening Tests 82
PN 1330 SC 45980
B Measurement 67
N Psychological Screening Inventory 73
R General Health Questionnaire 91
↓ Psychiatric Evaluation 97
↓ Screening 82

Scripts
Use Schema

Sculpturing 73
PN 46 SC 45990
B Art 67

Sea Gulls 73
PN 176 SC 46010
UF Gulls
B Birds 67

Seals (Animal) 73
PN 102 SC 46020
B Mammals 73

Seasonal Affective Disorder 91
PN 247 SC 46025
UF SAD
Winter Depression
B Affective Disturbances 67
R ↓ Major Depression 88
Phototherapy 91
Recurrent Depression 94

Seasonal Variations 73
PN 1082 SC 46030
SN Periodic changes in behavioral, psychological, or physiological responses in relation to seasonal changes. Used for human or animal populations.
B Environmental Effects 73
R ↓ Biological Rhythms 67
↓ Temperature Effects 67

Seat Belts
Use Safety Belts

Seclusion (Patient)
Use Patient Seclusion

Secobarbital 73
PN 49 SC 46040
UF Seconal
B Barbiturates 67
Hypnotic Drugs 73
Sedatives 73

Seconal
Use Secobarbital

Second Language Education
Use Foreign Language Education

Second Order Conditioning
Use Higher Order Conditioning

Secondary Education 73
PN 818 SC 46060

Secondary Education — (cont'd)
SN Education provided by comprehensive schools, grammar schools, junior high or high schools, typically for grades 7–12.
B Education 67
R High Schools 73
Junior High Schools 73

Secondary Reinforcement 67
PN 345 SC 46070
SN Presentation of a secondary reinforcer. Also, objects or events which acquire reinforcing properties only through having been consistently paired or associated with other reinforcers. Also known as conditioned reinforcers. Compare INTERNAL REWARDS.
UF Token Reinforcement
B Reinforcement 67
R Conditioned Stimulus 73

Secrecy 94
PN 21 SC 46075
R Anonymity 73
↓ Deception 67
Privacy 73
Self Disclosure 73

Secretarial Personnel 73
PN 137 SC 46080
B Business and Industrial Personnel 67
White Collar Workers 73
R Clerical Personnel 73

Secretarial Skills
Use Clerical Secretarial Skills

Secretion (Gland) 73
PN 123 SC 46100
B Physiology 67
N ↓ Endocrine Gland Secretion 73
Lactation 73
Salivation 73
Sweating 73
R ↓ Endocrine Disorders 73

Sectioning (Lesion)
Use Lesions

Security (Emotional)
Use Emotional Security

Sedatives 73
PN 362 SC 46130
UF Phenaglycodol
B Drugs 67
N Alprazolam 88
Amobarbital 73
Atropine 73
Barbital 73
Chloral Hydrate 73
Chlorpromazine 67
Clozapine 91
Flurazepam 82
Glutethimide 73
Haloperidol 73
Heroin 73
Hexobarbital 73
Meperidine 73
Meprobamate 73
Methaqualone 73
Molindone 82
Nitrazepam 78
Pentobarbital 73
Phenobarbital 73
Promethazine 73
Reserpine 67
Scopolamine 73
Secobarbital 73

Sedatives — (cont'd)
N Thalidomide 73
Thiopental 73
Triazolam 88
R ↓ Analgesic Drugs 73
↓ Anesthetic Drugs 73
↓ Anticonvulsive Drugs 73
↓ Antiemetic Drugs 73
↓ Antihistaminic Drugs 73
↓ Antihypertensive Drugs 73
↓ Barbiturates 67
↓ Benzodiazepines 78
↓ CNS Depressant Drugs 73
↓ Hypnotic Drugs 73
↓ Tranquilizing Drugs 67

Seduction 94
PN 28 SC 46133
B Psychosexual Behavior 67

Seeing Eye Dogs
Use Mobility Aids

Segregation (Racial)
Use Social Integration

Seizures
Use Convulsions

Selected Readings 73
PN 546 SC 46150
SN Mandatory term applied to collections of previously published material.

Selection (Personnel)
Use Personnel Selection

Selection (Therapist)
Use Therapist Selection

Selection Tests 73
PN 430 SC 46170
SN Tests developed to assess specific traits or skills with the purpose of screening or selecting individuals for occupational or educational placement.
B Measurement 67
N Psychological Screening Inventory 73

Selective Attention 73
PN 1598 SC 46175
SN Focusing of awareness on a limited range of stimuli. Compare DIVIDED ATTENTION.
B Attention 67
R Concentration 82
Distraction 78
Divided Attention 73
↓ Monitoring 73
Sensory Gating 91
Vigilance 67

Selective Breeding 73
PN 226 SC 46180
SN Systematic approach to the development of genotype-dependent differences in a physical or behavioral trait. Compare ANIMAL BREEDING, ANIMAL DOMESTICATION, and EUGENICS.
B Animal Breeding 73
R Animal Domestication 78
Eugenics 73
↓ Genetic Engineering 94
↓ Genetics 67
Reproductive Technology 88

Self Acceptance
Use Self Perception

Self Actualization [73]
PN 1960 **SC** 46190
SN According to A. Maslow's theory, the process of striving to fulfull one's talents, capacities, and potentialities for maximum self realization, ideally with integration of physical, social, intellectual, and emotional needs.
UF Actualization (Self)
Self Realization
R Affective Education [82]
↓ Human Potential Movement [82]
Maslow (Abraham Harold) [91]
↓ Personality [67]
Self Determination [94]
↓ Self Help Techniques [82]

Self Analysis [94]
PN 13 **SC** 46195
SN A psychotherapist's application of psychoanalytic principles to his or her personal feelings, drives, and behaviors.
B Psychoanalysis [67]
R Personal Therapy [91]
Psychoanalytic Training [73]

Self Assessment
Use Self Evaluation

Self Care Skills [78]
PN 1289 **SC** 46215
SN Skills such as personal hygiene, feeding, independent housekeeping, public transportation use, which are often taught in rehabilitation programs for persons with mental, physical, or emotional handicaps.
UF Independent Living
B Ability [67]
R Activities of Daily Living [91]
Adaptive Behavior [91]
Child Self Care [88]
Daily Activities [94]
Hygiene [94]
Independent Living Programs [91]
↓ Rehabilitation [67]
↓ Skill Learning [73]
Special Education [67]

Self Concept [67]
PN 13758 **SC** 46220
UF Ideal Self
Identity (Personal)
Self Image
N Academic Self Concept [97]
Self Confidence [94]
Self Esteem [73]
R Affective Education [82]
Ego Identity [91]
Ethnic Identity [73]
Gender Identity [85]
Identity Crisis [73]
↓ Personality [67]
Professional Identity [91]
Reference Groups [94]
Role Satisfaction [94]
Self Congruence [78]
Self Perception [67]
↓ Social Identity [88]
Symbolic Interactionism [88]

Self Confidence [94]
PN 103 **SC** 46230
SN Use SELF ESTEEM to access references from 73-93.
UF Confidence (Self)
B Self Concept [67]
R Academic Self Concept [97]
Self Efficacy [85]
Self Esteem [73]
Self Perception [67]

Self Congruence [78]
PN 190 **SC** 46235
SN State of harmony between actual and ideal selves, or congruence between experience, personality, and self-concept.
R ↓ Self Concept [67]

Self Consciousness
Use Self Perception

Self Control [73]
PN 2560 **SC** 46240
SN The ability to repress or the practice of repressing one's behavior, impulsive reactions, emotions, or desires.
UF Control (Self)
Willpower
B Personality Traits [67]
R Anger Control [97]
↓ Emotional Control [73]
↓ Helplessness [97]
Impulse Control Disorders [97]
Internal External Locus of Control [67]
Temptation [73]

Self Defeating Behavior [88]
PN 77 **SC** 46243
SN Behavior that blocks one's own goals and wishes, e.g., the tendency to compete so aggressively that one cannot hold a job.
B Behavior [67]
R ↓ Self Destructive Behavior [85]
Self Handicapping Strategy [88]

Self Defense [85]
PN 57 **SC** 46245
SN Protecting one's self or property against crime.
UF Personal Defense
R ↓ Crime [67]
↓ Crime Victims [82]
Martial Arts [85]
Self Preservation [97]
↓ Violence [73]

Self Destructive Behavior [85]
PN 633 **SC** 46244
B Behavior [67]
N Attempted Suicide [73]
Head Banging [73]
Self Inflicted Wounds [73]
Self Mutilation [73]
↓ Suicide [67]
R ↓ Behavior Disorders [71]
Hair Pulling [73]
↓ Masochism [73]
Masochistic Personality [73]
Self Defeating Behavior [88]

Self Determination [94]
PN 45 **SC** 46246
SN The power of individuals to determine their own destiny or actions.
R Empowerment [91]
↓ Helplessness [97]
Independence (Personality) [73]
Individuality [73]
Internal External Locus of Control [67]
Self Actualization [73]
↓ Self Management [85]
Volition [88]
World View [88]

Self Directed Learning
Use Individualized Instruction

Self Disclosure [73]
PN 2326 **SC** 46250

Self Disclosure — (cont'd)
UF Disclosure (Self)
R Anonymity [73]
↓ Interpersonal Communication [73]
↓ Personality [67]
Secrecy [94]

Self Efficacy [85]
PN 2111 **SC** 46255
SN Cognitive mechanism based on expectations or beliefs about one's ability to perform actions necessary to produce a given effect. Also, a theoretical component of behavior change in various therapeutic treatments.
UF Efficacy Expectations
R Academic Self Concept [97]
↓ Expectations [67]
↓ Helplessness [97]
Instrumentality [91]
Self Confidence [94]
Self Evaluation [67]
Self Fulfilling Prophecies [97]
Self Perception [67]

Self Employment [94]
PN 5 **SC** 46257
B Employment Status [82]
R Business [67]
Entrepreneurship [91]
Ownership [85]
Retailing [91]

Self Esteem [73]
PN 8178 **SC** 46260
UF Self Respect
B Self Concept [67]
R Self Confidence [94]
Self Perception [67]

Self Evaluation [67]
PN 3559 **SC** 46270
UF Self Assessment
B Evaluation [67]
R ↓ Personality [67]
Self Efficacy [85]
↓ Self Management [85]
Self Monitoring [82]
Self Report [82]
Social Comparison [85]

Self Examination (Medical) [88]
PN 161 **SC** 46273
SN Self examination for detection of medical conditions or disorders, e.g., breast or testicular cancer. Also used for self administration of medical diagnostic procedures.
UF Breast Examination
R Cancer Screening [97]
Health Behavior [82]
Physical Examination [88]

Self Fulfilling Prophecies [97]
PN 0 **SC** 46271
SN Expectations or predictions that turn out just as one prophesized. The fulfillment of expectations is usually due to behavior that optimizes the outcome.
UF Pygmalion Effect
R Attribution [73]
↓ Expectations [67]
↓ Prediction [67]
Self Efficacy [85]
Social Cognition [94]
↓ Social Perception [67]
Stereotyped Attitudes [67]

Self Handicapping Strategy [88]
PN 62 **SC** 46274

Self Handicapping Strategy — (cont'd)
SN Conscious or unconscious efforts to lessens one's chances of performing well at a task in which one is ego-involved and fears failure so that poor performance or lack of ability may be attributed to circumstance.
R Fear of Success [78]
Self Defeating Behavior [88]

Self Help Techniques [82]
PN 985 **SC** 46275
SN Techniques, materials, or processes designed to assist individuals in solving their own problems. Consider also SUPPORT GROUPS.
N ↓ Self Management [85]
R ↓ Behavior Modification [73]
↓ Community Services [67]
Group Counseling [73]
↓ Psychotherapeutic Techniques [67]
Self Actualization [73]
Self Monitoring [82]
Self Referral [91]
Social Support Networks [82]
↓ Support Groups [91]
↓ Treatment [67]
↓ Twelve Step Programs [97]

Self Hypnosis
Use Autohypnosis

Self Image
Use Self Concept

Self Inflicted Wounds [73]
PN 306 **SC** 46290
SN Any injury to body tissue (including bones) resulting from self directed physical violence. Compare SELF MUTILATION.
B Self Destructive Behavior [85]
Wounds [73]
R Self Mutilation [73]

Self Instruction
Use Individualized Instruction

Self Instructional Training [85]
PN 161 **SC** 46294
SN Cognitive technique for overcoming cognitive deficits in areas such as problem solving, verbal mediation, and information seeking. Overt verbalizations of thought processes are modeled for and imitated by the client. Covert self-verbalizations follow which result in the client gaining verbal control over behavior.
B Cognitive Techniques [85]
Self Management [85]
R Cognitive Therapy [82]

Self Management [85]
PN 718 **SC** 46295
SN Self-regulated modification and/or maintenance of behavior by self-governing of behavioral consequences. Used with disordered or normal populations of all ages.
B Behavior Modification [73]
Management [67]
Self Help Techniques [82]
N Self Instructional Training [85]
R Centering [91]
Cognitive Therapy [82]
Self Determination [94]
Self Evaluation [67]
Self Monitoring [82]
Self Reinforcement [73]
Time Management [94]

Self Medication [91]
PN 62 **SC** 46298

Self Medication — (cont'd)
R ↓ Drug Therapy [67]
↓ Drugs [67]
Nonprescription Drugs [91]
Prescription Drugs [91]

Self Monitoring [82]
PN 829 **SC** 46296
SN Systematic observation and recording of one's own behavior usually for the purpose of changing the behavior by means of behavior modification techniques.
UF Self Observation
B Monitoring [73]
R ↓ Behavior Modification [73]
Observation Methods [67]
Self Evaluation [67]
↓ Self Help Techniques [82]
↓ Self Management [85]
Self Report [82]

Self Monitoring (Personality) [85]
PN 308 **SC** 46297
SN The process of subjectively observing and comparing one's own behaviors and expressions with those of others in social interactions for the purpose of regulating and controlling one's own verbal and nonverbal behaviors.
R Conscientiousness [97]
Impression Management [78]
Introspection [73]
↓ Personality [67]
Reflectiveness [97]
Self Perception [67]
Social Comparison [85]
↓ Social Interaction [67]

Self Mutilation [73]
PN 511 **SC** 46300
SN Act of inflicting permanent physical damage to oneself, such as cutting off or destroying a limb or other part of the body. Compare SELF INFLICTED WOUNDS.
UF Autotomy
Mutilation (Self)
B Behavior Disorders [71]
Self Destructive Behavior [85]
R Self Inflicted Wounds [73]

Self Observation
Use Self Monitoring

Self Perception [67]
PN 8272 **SC** 46310
SN Physical and social awareness and perceptions of oneself.
UF Self Acceptance
Self Consciousness
B Perception [67]
R Academic Self Concept [97]
Aging (Attitudes Toward) [85]
Body Awareness [82]
Ingroup Outgroup [97]
Introspection [73]
Mirror Image [91]
↓ Personality [67]
↓ Personality Theory [67]
Reflectiveness [97]
↓ Self Concept [67]
Self Confidence [94]
Self Efficacy [85]
Self Esteem [73]
Self Monitoring (Personality) [85]
Self Reference [94]
Self Report [82]

Self Preservation [97]
PN 0 **SC** 46312

Self Preservation — (cont'd)
UF Survival Instinct
R Death Instinct [88]
Instinctive Behavior [82]
Self Defense [85]
Theory of Evolution [67]

Self Psychology [88]
PN 430 **SC** 46315
SN Psychological theory and approach to psychotherapy focusing on interpretation of behavior in reference to self. Includes the psychoanalytic concept of an individual's need to organize the psyche into a cohesive whole, the self.
B Psychology [67]
R ↓ Humanistic Psychology [85]
Mirroring [97]
Object Relations [82]
↓ Personality Theory [67]
↓ Psychoanalytic Theory [67]

Self Realization
Use Self Actualization

Self Reference [94]
PN 23 **SC** 46323
R ↓ Interpersonal Communication [73]
Self Perception [67]
↓ Social Perception [67]

Self Referral [91]
PN 37 **SC** 46325
SN Act of directing oneself to an agency, service, or professional for assessment, diagnosis, treatment, or consultation.
UF Referral (Self)
R ↓ Commitment (Psychiatric) [73]
Health Behavior [82]
Health Care Seeking Behavior [97]
↓ Health Care Services [78]
Health Care Utilization [85]
↓ Help Seeking Behavior [78]
Professional Referral [73]
Right to Treatment [97]
↓ Self Help Techniques [82]

Self Reinforcement [73]
PN 1150 **SC** 46330
SN Used for human and animal populations.
B Reinforcement [67]
R ↓ Self Management [85]
↓ Self Stimulation [67]

Self Report [82]
PN 2364 **SC** 46335
SN Method for obtaining information through the elicitation of overt verbal responses, oral or written, from the subject/client by the use of questions or directives. Used only when self-report is discussed in reference to methodological considerations.
B Methodology [67]
R Likert Scales [94]
Self Evaluation [67]
Self Monitoring [82]
Self Perception [67]

Self Respect
Use Self Esteem

Self Stimulation [67]
PN 1757 **SC** 46350
B Stimulation [67]
N Brain Self Stimulation [85]
R Electrical Brain Stimulation [73]
↓ Operant Conditioning [67]
↓ Reinforcement [67]
Self Reinforcement [73]

Self Talk [88]
PN 168 **SC** 46355
SN Vocalized or unvocalized speech that is directed to oneself or an imaginary recipient.
UF Inner Speech
B Oral Communication [85]
R Ellis (Albert) [91]
↓ Psychotherapeutic Techniques [67]
Subvocalization [73]

Selfishness [73]
PN 47 **SC** 46360
B Personality Traits [67]
R Narcissism [67]

Semantic Differential [67]
PN 824 **SC** 46370
SN Technique or test which uses subjective ratings of an idea, concept, or object by means of scaling opposite adjectives in order to study connotative meaning. Also used to assess interactions between people and situations and for attitude assessment.
R ↓ Attitude Measures [67]
Likert Scales [94]
↓ Measurement [67]

Semantic Generalization [73]
PN 144 **SC** 46380
SN Conditioning of a reaction to a nonverbal stimulus and subsequent generalization of the response to verbal signs representative of the original stimulus. The types include generalization from object to sign, from sign to sign, and from sign to object.
UF Generalization (Semantic)
B Cognitive Processes [67]
R Cognitive Generalization [67]
Connotations [73]

Semantic Memory [88]
PN 446 **SC** 46385
SN Organized knowledge about words, their meanings, and their relations.
B Verbal Memory [94]
R ↓ Lexical Access [88]
Lexical Decision [88]
Semantic Priming [94]
↓ Semantics [67]

Semantic Priming [94]
PN 96 **SC** 46387
B Priming [88]
R Contextual Associations [67]
Cues [67]
Semantic Memory [88]
↓ Semantics [67]

Semantics [67]
PN 3616 **SC** 46390
SN Linguistic science dealing with the relations between language symbols (words, expressions, phrases) and the objects or concepts to which they refer. Also includes the study of changes in the meanings of words. Used for the discipline or the specific semantic characteristics of linguistic symbols.
B Grammar [67]
N Antonyms [73]
Homonyms [73]
Synonyms [73]
R Discourse Analysis [97]
Metaphor [82]
Morphology (Language) [73]
↓ Phonology [73]
↓ Priming [88]
Semantic Memory [88]
Semantic Priming [94]
↓ Syntax [71]
↓ Verbal Meaning [73]

Semantics — (cont'd)
R ↓ Vocabulary [67]
Words (Phonetic Units) [67]

Semicircular Canals [73]
PN 37 **SC** 46400
B Vestibular Apparatus [67]

Seminarians [73]
PN 176 **SC** 46410
B Religious Personnel [73]
Students [67]

Seminaries [73]
PN 23 **SC** 46420
SN Institutions for training for ministry, priesthood, or rabbinate.
B Schools [67]
R Religious Education [73]

Semiotics [85]
PN 158 **SC** 46425
SN Analysis of signs and symbols, especially their syntactic, semantic, and pragmatic functions in language.
N Pragmatics [85]
R Hermeneutics [91]
↓ Linguistics [73]
Symbolism [67]

Senegal [88]
PN 18 **SC** 46427
B Africa [67]

Senescence
Use Aged

Senile Dementia [73]
PN 761 **SC** 46440
UF Dementia (Senile)
B Dementia [85]
Syndromes [73]
N Senile Psychosis [73]
R ↓ Aged [73]
Alzheimers Disease [73]
Cerebral Arteriosclerosis [73]
Physiological Aging [67]
↓ Presenile Dementia [73]
Progressive Supranuclear Palsy [97]

Senile Psychosis [73]
PN 15 **SC** 46450
B Psychosis [67]
Senile Dementia [73]

Senior Citizens
Use Aged

Sensation
Use Perception

Sensation Seeking [78]
PN 588 **SC** 46477
SN Need for novel experience or stimulation in order to reach optimal levels of arousal. Limited to human populations.
UF Novelty Seeking
Stimulation Seeking (Personality)
B Personality Traits [67]
R Extraversion [67]

Sensation Seeking Scale [73]
PN 65 **SC** 46480
B Personality Measures [67]

Sense Organ Disorders [73]
PN 19 **SC** 46490

Sense Organ Disorders — (cont'd)
B Physical Disorders [97]
N Anosmia [73]
↓ Ear Disorders [73]
↓ Vision Disorders [82]
R ↓ Anesthesia (Feeling) [73]
↓ Sense Organs [73]
↓ Sensorially Disabled [97]

Sense Organs [73]
PN 60 **SC** 46500
B Anatomy [67]
N ↓ Ear (Anatomy) [67]
↓ Eye (Anatomy) [67]
Taste Buds [73]
R ↓ Sense Organ Disorders [73]

Sensitivity (Drugs)
Use Drug Sensitivity

Sensitivity (Personality) [67]
PN 1064 **SC** 46520
UF Insensitivity (Personality)
B Personality Traits [67]
R Perceptiveness (Personality) [73]

Sensitivity Training [73]
PN 1052 **SC** 46530
SN Group training that focuses on interpersonal relations within the group and enhancement of self-confidence, self-perception, behavioral skills, and role flexibility.
B Human Potential Movement [82]
R Communication Skills Training [82]
Consciousness Raising Groups [78]
Cultural Sensitivity [94]
↓ Encounter Group Therapy [73]
↓ Group Dynamics [67]
↓ Group Psychotherapy [67]
Human Relations Training [78]
Marathon Group Therapy [73]
↓ Personnel Training [67]
Social Skills Training [82]

Sensitization (Protein)
Use Anaphylactic Shock

Sensitization Repression
Use Repression Sensitization

Sensorially Disabled [97]
PN 0 **SC** 46544
SN Use SENSORIALLY HANDICAPPED to access references from 94–96.
UF Sensorially Handicapped
B Disabled [97]
N ↓ Aurally Disabled [97]
↓ Visually Disabled [97]
R ↓ Ear Disorders [73]
↓ Eye Disorders [73]
Hearing Disorders [82]
↓ Sense Organ Disorders [73]
Sensory Disabilities (Attit Toward) [97]
↓ Vision Disorders [82]

Sensorially Handicapped
SN Term discontinued in 1997. Use SENSORIALLY HANDICAPPED to access references from 94–96.
Use Sensorially Disabled

Sensorimotor Development
Use Perceptual Motor Development

Sensorimotor Measures [73]
PN 203 **SC** 46550
UF Perceptual Motor Measures
B Measurement [67]

Sensorimotor Measures — (cont'd)
N Purdue Perceptual Motor Survey 73
R ↓ Perceptual Measures 73

Sensorimotor Processes
Use Perceptual Motor Processes

Sensorineural Hearing Loss
Use Hearing Disorders

Sensory Adaptation 67
PN 1750 **SC** 46560
SN Change in sensitivity of sensory systems or components as a result of ongoing or prolonged stimulation.
UF Adaptation (Sensory)
B Adaptation 67
Thresholds 67
N Dark Adaptation 73
Light Adaptation 82
Orienting Reflex 67
Orienting Responses 67
R Habituation 67
Interocular Transfer 85
Sensory Integration 91

Sensory Deprivation 67
PN 1046 **SC** 46570
SN Restriction of sensory or environmental stimulation through surgical or other techniques. Used primarily for animal populations. Consider STIMULUS DEPRIVATION for human populations.
B Stimulus Deprivation 73

Sensory Disabilities (Attit Toward) 97
PN 0 **SC** 46575
SN Use SENSORY HANDICAPS (ATTIT TOWARD) to access references from 73–96.
UF Sensory Handicaps (Attit Toward)
B Disabled (Attitudes Toward) 97
R ↓ Aurally Disabled 97
Disability Discrimination 97
↓ Sensorially Disabled 97
↓ Visually Disabled 97

Sensory Feedback 73
PN 302 **SC** 46580
SN Return of afferent neural signals or information from sensory receptors. Sensory feedback may function in the regulation of behavior in general but is especially important in the control of bodily movement. Use a more specific term if possible.
B Feedback 67
Perceptual Stimulation 73
N ↓ Auditory Feedback 73
Visual Feedback 73

Sensory Gating 91
PN 90 **SC** 46585
SN The internal process of blocking one or more sensory stimuli while attention is focused on another sensory stimuli or sensory channel.
UF Gating (Sensory)
B Perception 67
R ↓ Awareness 67
↓ Evoked Potentials 67
↓ Perceptual Stimulation 73
Prepulse Inhibition 97
Selective Attention 73

Sensory Handicaps (Attit Toward)
SN Term discontinued in 1997. Use SENSORY HANDICAPS (ATTIT TOWARD) to access references from 73–96.
Use Sensory Disabilities (Attit Toward)

Sensory Integration 91
PN 130 **SC** 46595
SN Neural processes of organizing sensory inputs from the environment and producing an adaptive response. In treatment, the environment's sensory input is manipulated to facilitate environmental interaction.
UF Intersensory Integration
B Intersensory Processes 78
Perceptual Motor Processes 67
R ↓ Sensory Adaptation 67
↓ Treatment 67

Sensory Neglect 94
PN 171 **SC** 46597
UF Perceptual Neglect
Spatial Neglect
Visual Neglect
R ↓ Perception 67
↓ Perceptual Distortion 82
↓ Perceptual Disturbances 73
↓ Receptive Fields 85

Sensory Neurons 73
PN 541 **SC** 46610
B Neurons 73
N Auditory Neurons 73
Baroreceptors 73
Chemoreceptors 73
Mechanoreceptors 73
Nociceptors 85
↓ Photoreceptors 73
Proprioceptors 73
Taste Buds 73
Thermoreceptors 73
R ↓ Afferent Pathways 82
↓ Receptive Fields 85

Sensory Pathways
Use Afferent Pathways

Sensory Preconditioning
Use Preconditioning

Sentence Completion Tests 91
PN 10 **SC** 46617
B Personality Measures 67
Projective Personality Measures 73
R Cloze Testing 73

Sentence Comprehension 73
PN 1458 **SC** 46620
B Verbal Comprehension 85

Sentence Structure 73
PN 1395 **SC** 46630
SN Specific characteristics of a sentence's construction, including such aspects as its syntax, length, and complexity. Compare SYNTAX.
R ↓ Prosody 91
↓ Syntax 71
Text Structure 82

Sentences 67
PN 1427 **SC** 46640
SN Grammatically and syntactically arranged words that constitute a grammatically complete and meaningful unit.
B Language 67

Sentencing
Use Adjudication

Separation (Marital)
Use Marital Separation

Separation Anxiety 73
PN 572 **SC** 46660

Separation Anxiety — (cont'd)
B Anxiety Disorders 97
Separation Reactions 97
R Abandonment 97
Attachment Behavior 85
↓ Relationship Termination 97
School Phobia 73
School Refusal 94
Stranger Reactions 88

Separation Individuation 82
PN 948 **SC** 46665
SN Normal process begun in infancy of disengagement from one's mother and development of a separate, individual identity. Limited to human populations.
B Personality Development 67
R Attachment Behavior 85
↓ Childhood Development 67
Mother Child Relations 67
Object Relations 82
Transitional Objects 85

Separation Reactions 97
PN 0 **SC** 46670
N Separation Anxiety 73
R Abandonment 97
Alienation 71
Anaclitic Depression 73
Apathy 73
Attachment Behavior 85
Depression (Emotion) 67
Disappointment 73
Distress 73
Emotional Trauma 67
Grief 73
Homesickness 94
↓ Relationship Termination 97
Sadness 73
Withdrawal (Defense Mechanism) 73

Septal Nuclei 82
PN 423 **SC** 46676
SN Subcallosal nuclei that form an integral part of the limbic system. These nuclei contribute to the medial forebrain bundle and have processes synapsing in the hippocampus.
UF Septum
B Limbic System 73
R Fornix 82
Hippocampus 67
Medial Forebrain Bundle 82
Nucleus Accumbens 82

Septum
Use Septal Nuclei

Sequential Learning 73
PN 255 **SC** 46690
SN Type of learning in which a particular task is completed before the next task is given. The learning of each subsequent task is dependent on the previous task completed.
B Learning 67
R Mastery Learning 85

Serial Anticipation (Learning) 73
PN 101 **SC** 46700
SN Learning paradigm which involves the initial presentation of a list of items or a series of events with a short interval between the items or elements in the series. Upon subsequent presentation of the list/series, the subject attempts to guess or anticipate the next item/element in the sequence. Thus, each item/element serves as a cue for the recall of the next. Compare FREE RECALL.

Serial Anticipation (Learning) — (cont'd)
UF Anticipation (Serial Learning)
B Serial Learning [67]
R ↓ Verbal Learning [67]

Serial Learning [67]
PN 1240 SC 46720
SN Learning, usually memorization, of items in a list according to a prescribed order.
B Learning [67]
N Serial Anticipation (Learning) [73]
R ↓ Serial Position Effect [82]
Serial Recall [94]
↓ Verbal Learning [67]

Serial Position Effect [82]
PN 192 SC 46724
SN Effect of the relative position of an item in a series on the rate of learning that item.
N Primacy Effect [73]
Recency Effect [73]
R ↓ Learning [67]
Learning Rate [73]
↓ Serial Learning [67]
Serial Recall [94]

Serial Recall [94]
PN 34 SC 46727
B Recall (Learning) [67]
R Forgetting [73]
Free Recall [73]
↓ Memory [67]
↓ Serial Learning [67]
↓ Serial Position Effect [82]

Seriousness [73]
PN 14 SC 46730
B Personality Traits [67]

Serotonin [73]
PN 3441 SC 46740
UF Hydroxytryptamine (5-)
B Amines [73]
Neurotransmitters [85]
Vasoconstrictor Drugs [73]
R ↓ Adrenergic Drugs [73]
Serotonin Agonists [88]
↓ Serotonin Antagonists [73]
↓ Serotonin Metabolites [78]
↓ Serotonin Precursors [78]

Serotonin Agonists [88]
PN 678 SC 46745
B Drugs [67]
R Buspirone [91]
Serotonin [73]
↓ Serotonin Antagonists [73]

Serotonin Antagonists [73]
PN 1390 SC 46750
UF Methysergide
B Drugs [67]
N Dihydroxytryptamine [91]
Lysergic Acid Diethylamide [67]
Mianserin [82]
Molindone [82]
Parachlorophenylalanine [78]
Ritanserin [97]
Tetrabenazine [73]
R ↓ Decarboxylase Inhibitors [82]
Serotonin [73]
Serotonin Agonists [88]
↓ Serotonin Precursors [78]
↓ Serotonin Reuptake Inhibitors [97]

Serotonin Metabolites [78]
PN 130 SC 46754

Serotonin Metabolites — (cont'd)
B Metabolites [73]
N Hydroxyindoleacetic Acid (5-) [85]
R Serotonin [73]
↓ Serotonin Precursors [78]

Serotonin Precursors [78]
PN 92 SC 46756
N ↓ Tryptophan [73]
R Serotonin [73]
↓ Serotonin Antagonists [73]
↓ Serotonin Metabolites [78]

Serotonin Reuptake Inhibitors [97]
PN 0 SC 46758
SN Consider using SEROTONIN ANTAGONISTS to access references from 73-96.
N Chlorimipramine [73]
Citalopram [97]
Fluoxetine [91]
Fluvoxamine [94]
Paroxetine [94]
Zimeldine [88]
R ↓ Serotonin Antagonists [73]

Serpasil
Use Reserpine

Sertraline [97]
PN 0 SC 46765
B Antidepressant Drugs [71]

Serum (Blood)
Use Blood Serum

Serum Albumin [73]
PN 27 SC 46780
B Blood Proteins [73]

Service Personnel [91]
PN 139 SC 46785
SN Employees who have direct contact with the public; generally nonprofessional and nonsales personnel. Includes hotel, airline, and restaurant personnel, but does not include health care personnel.
B Business and Industrial Personnel [67]
N Domestic Service Personnel [73]
Technical Service Personnel [73]
R Child Care Workers [78]
↓ Nonprofessional Personnel [82]
Sales Personnel [73]
↓ Technical Personnel [78]

Service Quality
Use Quality of Services

Servicemen
Use Military Personnel

Set (Response)
Use Response Set

Severely Mentally Retarded [73]
PN 1925 SC 46820
SN IQ 20-34.
B Mentally Retarded [67]

Severity (Disorders) [82]
PN 2133 SC 46824
SN Degree of severity of mental or physical disorder.
R ↓ Chronic Illness [91]
↓ Chronic Mental Illness [97]
Chronicity (Disorders) [82]
↓ Diagnosis [67]
↓ Disorders [67]

Severity (Disorders) — (cont'd)
R ↓ Mental Disorders [67]
↓ Physical Disorders [97]
Prognosis [73]

Sex [67]
PN 641 SC 46950
SN Conceptually broad array term referring to the structural, functional, or behavioral characteristics of males and females of a given species. Use a more specific term if possible. For comparisons of the sexes use HUMAN SEX DIFFERENCES or ANIMAL SEX DIFFERENCES.
R Animal Sex Differences [67]
↓ Animal Sexual Behavior [85]
↓ Genital Disorders [67]
↓ Human Sex Differences [67]
Pornography [73]
↓ Psychosexual Behavior [67]
Psychosexual Development [82]
Sex Change [88]
Sex Chromosomes [73]
Sex Discrimination [78]
Sex Drive [73]
Sex Education [73]
↓ Sex Hormones [73]
↓ Sex Offenses [82]
Sex Recognition [97]
↓ Sex Role Attitudes [78]
Sex Therapy [78]
Sexual Attitudes [73]
Sexual Development [73]
Sexual Harassment [85]
↓ Sexual Reproduction [73]
Sexuality [73]

Sex Change [88]
PN 57 SC 46828
UF Sexual Reassignment
B Surgery [71]
R Sex [67]
Transsexualism [73]

Sex Chromosome Disorders [73]
PN 144 SC 46830
B Chromosome Disorders [73]
N Klinefelters Syndrome [73]
R Fragile X Syndrome [94]
↓ Sex Linked Hereditary Disorders [73]

Sex Chromosomes [73]
PN 68 SC 46840
B Chromosomes [73]
R Sex [67]

Sex Differences (Animal)
Use Animal Sex Differences

Sex Differences (Human)
Use Human Sex Differences

Sex Differentiation Disorders
Use Genital Disorders

Sex Discrimination [78]
PN 704 SC 46875
SN Prejudiced and differential treatment on the basis of sex rather than on the basis of merit.
B Social Discrimination [82]
R Affirmative Action [85]
↓ Civil Rights [78]
Employment Discrimination [94]
↓ Prejudice [67]
Sex [67]
Sexism [88]
Stereotyped Attitudes [67]

Sex Drive 73
PN 172 **SC** 46880
B Motivation 67
R Hypersexuality 73
Inhibited Sexual Desire 97
Libido 73
Sex 67
↓ Sexual Arousal 78

Sex Education 73
PN 962 **SC** 46890
B Family Life Education 97
Health Education 73
R Sex 67

Sex Hormones 73
PN 388 **SC** 46900
B Hormones 67
N ↓ Androgens 73
↓ Estrogens 73
Progesterone 73
R ↓ Gonadotropic Hormones 73
Luteinizing Hormone 78
Sex 67

Sex Linked Developmental Differences 73
PN 1337 **SC** 46920
SN Differential variation between males and females in specified areas of development. Limited to human populations.
B Human Sex Differences 67
R Adolescent Development 73
↓ Development 67
Heterosexuality 73
↓ Human Females 73
↓ Human Males 73
↓ Physical Development 73
↓ Psychogenesis 73
↓ Psychosexual Behavior 67
Sexual Development 73

Sex Linked Hereditary Disorders 73
PN 123 **SC** 46930
SN Disorders occurring in either sex and which are transmitted by genes in the sex chromosomes.
B Genetic Disorders 73
N Fragile X Syndrome 94
Hemophilia 73
Testicular Feminization Syndrome 73
Turners Syndrome 73
R ↓ Sex Chromosome Disorders 73

Sex Offenses 82
PN 1119 **SC** 46933
B Crime 67
N ↓ Sexual Abuse 88
R Incest 73
Pedophilia 73
Pornography 73
Sex 67
↓ Sexual Deviations 67
Sexual Harassment 85

Sex Recognition 97
PN 0 **SC** 46934
R Animal Sex Differences 67
↓ Human Sex Differences 67
Sex 67

Sex Role Attitudes 78
PN 4626 **SC** 46935
SN Attitudes toward culturally- or socially-prescribed patterns of behavior for males and females.
UF Gender Role Attitudes
B Attitudes 67
N Sexism 88
R Feminism 78

Sex Role Attitudes — (cont'd)
R Matriarchy 73
Patriarchy 73
Sex 67
Sex Roles 67
Stereotyped Attitudes 67

Sex Roles 67
PN 7477 **SC** 46940
SN Behavioral patterns in a given society which are deemed appropriate to one sex or the other.
UF Gender Roles
B Psychosexual Behavior 67
Roles 67
R Androgyny 82
↓ Division of Labor 88
Femininity 67
Gender Identity 85
Masculinity 67
Matriarchy 73
Nontraditional Careers 85
Patriarchy 73
↓ Sex Role Attitudes 78
Social Norms 85
Stereotyped Behavior 73

Sex Therapy 78
PN 690 **SC** 46945
SN Treatment of specific sexual function disturbances or therapy aimed at improving sexual relationships.
B Treatment 67
R Couples Therapy 94
↓ Marriage Counseling 73
Sex 67

Sexism 88
PN 184 **SC** 46955
B Sex Role Attitudes 78
R Employment Discrimination 94
↓ Prejudice 67
Sex Discrimination 78

Sexual Abstinence 73
PN 57 **SC** 46960
UF Abstinence (Sexual)
Celibacy
B Psychosexual Behavior 67
R ↓ Birth Control 71
Virginity 73

Sexual Abuse 88
PN 2960 **SC** 46965
B Antisocial Behavior 71
Sex Offenses 82
N Incest 73
↓ Rape 73
R ↓ Abuse Reporting 97
Anatomically Detailed Dolls 91
↓ Child Abuse 71
Elder Abuse 88
↓ Family Violence 82
Partner Abuse 91
Patient Abuse 91
Pedophilia 73
Physical Abuse 91
Professional Client Sexual Relations 94
↓ Sexual Deviations 67
Sexual Harassment 85

Sexual Addiction 97
PN 0 **SC** 46967
UF Compulsivity (Sexual)
Sexual Compulsivity
B Addiction 73
R Hypersexuality 73
Promiscuity 73

Sexual Addiction — (cont'd)
R ↓ Psychosexual Behavior 67
↓ Sexual Deviations 67

Sexual Arousal 78
PN 795 **SC** 46970
SN Physiological and/or emotional state of sexual excitation.
UF Arousal (Sexual)
B Psychosexual Behavior 67
N Eroticism 73
R Inhibited Sexual Desire 97
Physiological Arousal 67
Sex Drive 73
Sexual Fantasy 97
Sexual Satisfaction 94

Sexual Attitudes 73
PN 2127 **SC** 46980
SN Opinions or beliefs about sexual development and behavior.
B Attitudes 67
R ↓ Psychosexual Behavior 67
Psychosexual Development 82
Sex 67
↓ Sexual Orientation 97
Sexual Risk Taking 97
Sexual Satisfaction 94

Sexual Behavior
Use Psychosexual Behavior

Sexual Boundary Violations
Use Professional Client Sexual Relations

Sexual Compulsivity
Use Sexual Addiction

Sexual Delinquency
Use Promiscuity

Sexual Development 73
PN 557 **SC** 47010
SN Prior to 1982 used for maturation of cognitive, emotional, and physical aspects of sexuality in humans or animals. From 1982 consider PSYCHOSEXUAL DEVELOPMENT for references on cognitive and emotional aspects.
UF Pubescence
B Physical Development 73
R Adolescent Development 73
Heterosexuality 73
↓ Psychogenesis 73
↓ Psychosexual Behavior 67
Psychosexual Development 82
Sex 67
Sex Linked Developmental Differences 73

Sexual Deviations 67
PN 996 **SC** 47020
SN Any type of sexual behavior which differs from social standards for such behavior in any given culture.
UF Deviations (Sexual)
Paraphilias
Perversions (Sexual)
B Mental Disorders 67
Psychosexual Behavior 67
N Exhibitionism 73
Fetishism 73
Incest 73
Pedophilia 73
Sexual Masochism 73
Sexual Sadism 73
Voyeurism 73
R ↓ Antisocial Behavior 71
Impulse Control Disorders 97
Pornography 73

Sexual Deviations — (cont'd)
R ↓ Sex Offenses [82]
↓ Sexual Abuse [88]
Sexual Addiction [97]

Sexual Disorders (Physiological)
Use Genital Disorders

Sexual Fantasy [97]
PN 0 **SC** 47035
B Fantasy [97]
R Erotomania [97]
Fantasy (Defense Mechanism) [67]
↓ Psychosexual Behavior [67]
↓ Sexual Arousal [78]
Sexuality [73]

Sexual Fetishism
Use Fetishism

Sexual Function Disturbances [73]
PN 1348 **SC** 47050
B Psychosexual Behavior [67]
N Dyspareunia [73]
Frigidity [73]
Impotence [73]
Inhibited Sexual Desire [97]
Premature Ejaculation [73]
Vaginismus [73]
R ↓ Mental Disorders [67]
↓ Physical Disorders [97]
↓ Psychosomatic Disorders [67]
↓ Urogenital Disorders [73]

Sexual Harassment [85]
PN 334 **SC** 47055
SN Physical or psychological sexual threats or attempts to willfully subject a person to involuntary sexual activity usually for the purpose of social control.
UF Harassment (Sexual)
R Professional Client Sexual Relations [94]
Sex [67]
↓ Sex Offenses [82]
↓ Sexual Abuse [88]
Victimization [73]

Sexual Identity (Gender)
Use Gender Identity

Sexual Intercourse (Human) [73]
PN 558 **SC** 47060
UF Coitus
Copulation
Intercourse (Sexual)
B Psychosexual Behavior [67]
N Dyspareunia [73]
Extramarital Intercourse [73]
Incest [73]
Premarital Intercourse [73]
↓ Rape [73]
R Female Orgasm [73]
↓ Male Orgasm [73]
↓ Sexual Reproduction [73]
Sexual Satisfaction [94]

Sexual Masochism [73]
PN 30 **SC** 47070
B Masochism [73]
Sexual Deviations [67]
R Fetishism [73]
Masochistic Personality [73]
Sexual Sadism [73]

Sexual Orientation [97]
PN 0 **SC** 47072
N Heterosexuality [73]
↓ Homosexuality [67]

Sexual Orientation — (cont'd)
R Gender Identity [85]
Gender Identity Disorder [97]
Homosexuality (Attitudes Toward) [82]
↓ Psychosexual Behavior [67]
Sexual Attitudes [73]

Sexual Reassignment
Use Sex Change

Sexual Receptivity (Animal)
Use Animal Sexual Receptivity

Sexual Reproduction [73]
PN 686 **SC** 47090
B Physiology [67]
N Fertility [88]
R ↓ Animal Breeding [73]
Animal Mate Selection [82]
↓ Animal Mating Behavior [67]
↓ Birth [67]
Fertilization [73]
↓ Genetics [67]
↓ Pregnancy [67]
Reproductive Technology [88]
Sex [67]
↓ Sexual Intercourse (Human) [73]
Sperm [73]

Sexual Risk Taking [97]
PN 0 **SC** 47095
B Psychosexual Behavior [67]
Risk Taking [67]
R AIDS Prevention [94]
↓ Pregnancy [67]
Risk Perception [97]
Sexual Attitudes [73]
↓ Venereal Diseases [73]

Sexual Sadism [73]
PN 30 **SC** 47100
B Sadism [73]
Sexual Deviations [67]
R Fetishism [73]
Sexual Masochism [73]

Sexual Satisfaction [94]
PN 33 **SC** 47110
B Satisfaction [73]
R ↓ Orgasm [73]
↓ Psychosexual Behavior [67]
↓ Sexual Arousal [78]
Sexual Attitudes [73]
↓ Sexual Intercourse (Human) [73]
Sexuality [73]

Sexuality [73]
PN 1403 **SC** 47120
B Personality Traits [67]
R Affection [73]
Psychosexual Development [82]
Sex [67]
Sexual Fantasy [97]
Sexual Satisfaction [94]

Sexually Transmitted Diseases
Use Venereal Diseases

Shamanism [73]
PN 155 **SC** 47130
B Religious Affiliation [73]
R Cultism [73]
Ethnology [67]
Faith Healing [73]
Folk Medicine [73]
Transcultural Psychiatry [73]

Shamanism — (cont'd)
R ↓ Treatment [67]
Witchcraft [73]

Shame [94]
PN 115 **SC** 47140
SN Use GUILT to access references from 73-93.
B Emotional States [73]
R ↓ Anxiety [67]
Blame [94]
Embarrassment [73]
↓ Fear [67]
Guilt [67]
Morality [67]

Shape Perception
Use Form and Shape Perception

Shared Paranoid Disorder
Use Folie A Deux

Sharing (Social Behavior) [78]
PN 290 **SC** 47155
B Prosocial Behavior [82]
R Altruism [73]
Charitable Behavior [73]
Needle Sharing [94]

Sheep [73]
PN 485 **SC** 47170
B Mammals [73]

Sheltered Workshops [67]
PN 317 **SC** 47180
SN Places which provide handicapped individuals with job training and work experience.
B Rehabilitation Centers [73]
R ↓ Community Facilities [73]
Supported Employment [94]

Shelters [91]
PN 115 **SC** 47185
B Housing [73]
R Battered Females [88]
↓ Community Facilities [73]
↓ Community Services [67]
↓ Family Violence [82]
↓ Government Programs [73]
Group Homes [82]
↓ Homeless [88]
↓ Living Arrangements [91]
Protective Services [97]
Runaway Behavior [73]
↓ Social Services [82]

Shifts (Workday)
Use Workday Shifts

Shock [67]
PN 2937 **SC** 47200
B Symptoms [67]
R Anaphylactic Shock [73]
Electrical Injuries [73]
↓ Electrical Stimulation [73]
↓ Electroconvulsive Shock [67]
↓ Injuries [73]
↓ Shock Therapy [73]
Shock Units [73]
Syncope [73]

Shock Therapy [73]
PN 40 **SC** 47210
B Organic Therapies [73]
N Electroconvulsive Shock Therapy [67]
Insulin Shock Therapy [73]
R ↓ Alternative Medicine [97]

Shock Therapy — (cont'd)
R ↓ Aversion Therapy 73
Electrosleep Treatment 78
Shock 67

Shock Units 73
PN 21 SC 47220
B Stimulators (Apparatus) 73
R Shock 67

Shoplifting 73
PN 110 SC 47230
B Theft 73

Shopping 97
PN 0 SC 47240
SN Use CONSUMER BEHAVIOR to access references prior to 1997.
B Consumer Behavior 67
R Retailing 91
Shopping Centers 73

Shopping Centers 73
PN 112 SC 47250
B Community Facilities 73
R ↓ Consumer Behavior 67
Retailing 91
Shopping 97

Short Term Memory 67
PN 4311 SC 47260
SN Retention of information for very brief periods, usually seconds; also referred to as working memory. Consider also RETENTION.
UF Working Memory
B Memory 67
N Iconic Memory 85

Short Term Potentiation
Use Postactivation Potentials

Short Term Psychotherapy
Use Brief Psychotherapy

Shoulder (Anatomy) 73
PN 48 SC 47290
B Joints (Anatomy) 73
R Arm (Anatomy) 73

Shuttle Box Grids
SN Term discontinued in 1997. Use SHUTTLE BOX GRIDS to access references from 73-96.
Use Shuttle Boxes

Shuttle Box Hurdles
SN Term discontinued in 1997. Use SHUTTLE BOX HURDLES to access references from 73-96.
Use Shuttle Boxes

Shuttle Boxes 73
PN 72 SC 47320
UF Shuttle Box Grids
Shuttle Box Hurdles
B Apparatus 67

Shyness
Use Timidity

Siamese Twins 73
PN 3 SC 47340
B Twins 67

Sibling Relations 73
PN 667 SC 47350
B Family Relations 67

Siblings 67
PN 1442 SC 47360
B Family Members 73
N Brothers 73
↓ Multiple Births 73
Sisters 73

Sick Leave
Use Employee Leave Benefits

Sickle Cell Disease 94
PN 48 SC 47380
B Blood and Lymphatic Disorders 73
Ethnospecific Disorders 73
Genetic Disorders 73
R Anemia 73

Side Effects (Drug) 73
PN 5478 SC 47390
SN Acute or chronic and often undesirable effects of drugs occurring in addition to the intended or therapeutic objective. Use DRUG ADVERSE REACTIONS or SIDE EFFECTS (DRUG) to access references from 73-81.
UF Drug Adverse Reactions
B Side Effects (Treatment) 88
N ↓ Drug Addiction 67
Drug Allergies 73
↓ Drug Dependency 73
Drug Sensitivity 73
R Akathisia 91
↓ Drug Therapy 67
Drug Tolerance 73
↓ Drugs 67
Neuroleptic Malignant Syndrome 88
Tardive Dyskinesia 88

Side Effects (Treatment) 88
PN 422 SC 47392
SN Acute or chronic and often undesirable effects of treatment other than drug therapy occurring in addition to the intended or therapeutic objective. For side effects of drug therapy use SIDE EFFECTS (DRUG).
UF Iatrogenic Effects
N ↓ Side Effects (Drug) 73
R ↓ Treatment 67
↓ Treatment Outcomes 82

Sierra Leone 88
PN 5 SC 47395
B Africa 67

Sight Vocabulary 73
PN 118 SC 47400
SN Words that one recognizes immediately while reading.
B Vocabulary 67
R ↓ Reading 67
↓ Reading Skills 73
Word Recognition 88

Sign Language 73
PN 812 SC 47410
SN System of hand gestures for communication in which the gestures function as words.
B Language 67
Manual Communication 78
R Fingerspelling 73

Sign Rank Test
Use Wilcoxon Sign Rank Test

Sign Test 73
PN 5 SC 47430
B Nonparametric Statistical Tests 67
R Statistical Significance 73

Signal Detection (Perception) 67
PN 2355 SC 47440
SN Psychophysical technique that permits the estimation of the bias of the observer as well as the detectability of the signal (i.e., stimulus) in any sensory modality. Compare THRESHOLDS.
UF Detection (Signal)
R ↓ Attention 67
↓ Perception 67
↓ Psychophysical Measurement 67
Threshold Determination 73
Visual Search 82

Signal Intensity
Use Stimulus Intensity

Significance (Statistical)
Use Statistical Significance

Significant Others 91
PN 170 SC 47465
SN Includes teachers, peers, family members, friends, and unmarried persons or couples.
R Couples 82
↓ Family Members 73
Friendship 67
Homosexual Parents 94
Mentor 85
Peers 78
Role Models 82
Romance 97
Social Support Networks 82
↓ Spouses 73

Silent Reading 73
PN 220 SC 47470
B Reading 67

Similarity (Stimulus)
Use Stimulus Similarity

Simile
Use Figurative Language

Simple Schizophrenia
SN Term discontinued in 1988. Use SIMPLE SCHIZOPHRENIA to access references from 73-87.
Use Schizophrenia

Simulation 67
PN 1949 SC 47510
UF Modeling
Simulators
N ↓ Computer Simulation 73
Flight Simulation 73
Heuristic Modeling 73
Markov Chains 73
↓ Mathematical Modeling 73
Simulation Games 73
↓ Stochastic Modeling 73
R Game Theory 67

Simulation Games 73
PN 399 SC 47520
B Games 67
Simulation 67
R Computer Games 88
↓ Computer Simulation 73

Simulators
Use Simulation

Sin 73
PN 53 SC 47540
B Religious Beliefs 73

Sincerity 73
PN 31 **SC** 47550
UF Genuineness
B Personality Traits 67
R ↓ Deception 67
Dishonesty 73

Singapore 91
PN 72 **SC** 47551
B Southeast Asia 73

Singing 97
PN 0 **SC** 47552
SN Use ANIMAL VOCALIZATIONS for singing in animal populations.
B Oral Communication 85
R ↓ Music 67
Music Perception 97
↓ Vocalization 67
↓ Voice 73

Single Cell Organisms
Use Microorganisms

Single Fathers 94
PN 5 **SC** 47554
SN Use SINGLE PARENTS to access references from 78-93.
B Fathers 67
Single Parents 78
R Single Persons 73

Single Mothers 94
PN 54 **SC** 47555
SN Use SINGLE PARENTS to access references from 78-93.
B Mothers 67
Single Parents 78
R Single Persons 73
Unwed Mothers 73
Working Women 78

Single Parents 78
PN 760 **SC** 47556
SN Parents rearing children alone.
B Parents 67
N Single Fathers 94
Single Mothers 94
R ↓ Family Structure 73
↓ Marital Status 73
Never Married 94
↓ Parental Absence 73
Single Persons 73
Unwed Mothers 73

Single Persons 73
PN 317 **SC** 47560
SN Persons who are not married.
R Living Alone 94
↓ Marital Status 73
Never Married 94
Single Fathers 94
Single Mothers 94
↓ Single Parents 78

Sisters 73
PN 96 **SC** 47570
B Human Females 73
Siblings 67

Sixteen Personality Factors Question 73
PN 355 **SC** 47590
B Nonprojective Personality Measures 73

Size 73
PN 667 **SC** 47610
SN Relative physical dimensions of objects or stimuli.

Size — (cont'd)
B Stimulus Parameters 67
N ↓ Body Size 85
Brain Size 73
Family Size 73
Group Size 67
Litter Size 85
Size Constancy 85
↓ Size Discrimination 67

Size (Apparent)
Use Apparent Size

Size (Group)
Use Group Size

Size Constancy 85
PN 23 **SC** 47635
SN The tendency for the perceived size of stimuli to remain constant despite objective changes in context and stimulus parameters.
B Perceptual Constancy 85
Size 73
R ↓ Size Discrimination 67

Size Discrimination 67
PN 836 **SC** 47640
B Size 73
Spatial Perception 67
N Apparent Size 73
R Linear Perspective 82
Size Constancy 85

Skeletomuscular Disorders
Use Musculoskeletal Disorders

Skewed Distribution 73
PN 59 **SC** 47680
UF Poisson Distribution
B Frequency Distribution 73

Skill Learning 73
PN 1535 **SC** 47690
B Learning 67
N Fine Motor Skill Learning 73
Gross Motor Skill Learning 73
R Communication Skills Training 82
Habilitation 91
↓ Perceptual Motor Learning 67
Self Care Skills 78
Social Skills Training 82

Skilled Industrial Workers 73
PN 204 **SC** 47700
SN Blue collar workers who perform skilled labor in an industrial setting.
B Blue Collar Workers 73
Business and Industrial Personnel 67

Skills
Use Ability

Skin (Anatomy) 67
PN 675 **SC** 47720
UF Epithelium
B Tissues (Body) 73
R Absorption (Physiological) 73
Epithelial Cells 73
Hair 73
Head (Anatomy) 73
Scalp (Anatomy) 73

Skin Cancer Screening
Use Cancer Screening

Skin Conduction
Use Skin Resistance

Skin Disorders 73
PN 316 **SC** 47740
UF Scalp Disorders
B Physical Disorders 97
N Allergic Skin Disorders 73
Alopecia 73
↓ Dermatitis 73
Herpes Simplex 73
Lupus 73
Pruritus 73
R Albinism 73
↓ Psychosomatic Disorders 67
Sweating 73
↓ Tuberculosis 73

Skin Electrical Properties 73
PN 69 **SC** 47750
SN General electrodermal characteristics and responses as measured on the skin surface. Use a more specific term if possible.
B Electrophysiology 73
N Skin Potential 73
↓ Skin Resistance 73

Skin Potential 73
PN 89 **SC** 47760
SN Degree of electrical charge of the skin.
B Electrophysiology 73
Skin Electrical Properties 73
R Galvanic Skin Response 67
↓ Skin Resistance 73

Skin Resistance 73
PN 1176 **SC** 47770
SN Resistance of the skin to the flow of electric current; reciprocal of skin conductance.
UF Skin Conduction
B Skin Electrical Properties 73
N Basal Skin Resistance 73
R Galvanic Skin Response 67
Skin Potential 73

Skin Temperature 73
PN 558 **SC** 47780
B Body Temperature 73

Skinner (Burrhus Frederic) 91
PN 93 **SC** 47785
SN Identifies biographical or autobiographical studies and discussions of Skinner's works.
R Behaviorism 67
↓ Operant Conditioning 67
↓ Psychologists 67
Skinner Boxes 73

Skinner Boxes 73
PN 17 **SC** 47790
B Apparatus 67
R Skinner (Burrhus Frederic) 91

Skull 73
PN 21 **SC** 47800
B Musculoskeletal System 73

Slang 73
PN 44 **SC** 47810
B Vocabulary 67
R Ethnolinguistics 73
Nonstandard English 73

Sleep 67
PN 4541 **SC** 47820
N Napping 94
NREM Sleep 73
REM Sleep 73
R ↓ Consciousness Disturbances 73
↓ Consciousness States 71
Dream Content 73

Sleep — (cont'd)
R ↓ Dreaming [67]
Lucid Dreaming [94]
Nocturnal Teeth Grinding [73]
Sleep Apnea [91]
Sleep Deprivation [67]
↓ Sleep Disorders [73]
Sleep Onset [73]
Sleep Talking [73]
Sleep Treatment [73]
Sleep Wake Cycle [85]

Sleep Apnea [91]
PN 74 SC 47825
SN Temporary absence of breathing or prolonged respiratory failure occurring during sleep.
B Apnea [73]
R ↓ Neonatal Disorders [73]
↓ Sleep [67]
Sudden Infant Death [82]

Sleep Deprivation [67]
PN 934 SC 47830
B Deprivation [67]
R ↓ Sleep [67]
↓ Sleep Disorders [73]

Sleep Disorders [73]
PN 1003 SC 47840
UF Night Terrors
B Consciousness Disturbances [73]
N Hypersomnia [94]
Insomnia [73]
Narcolepsy [73]
Sleepwalking [73]
R Hypnagogic Hallucinations [73]
↓ Mental Disorders [67]
↓ Physical Disorders [97]
↓ Sleep [67]
Sleep Deprivation [67]

Sleep Inducing Drugs
Use Hypnotic Drugs

Sleep Onset [73]
PN 495 SC 47860
UF Drowsiness
R Napping [94]
↓ Sleep [67]

Sleep Talking [73]
PN 10 SC 47870
B Consciousness Disturbances [73]
R ↓ Sleep [67]

Sleep Treatment [73]
PN 30 SC 47880
SN Prolonged sleep or rest used in the treatment of mental disorders. Such sleep may be induced by drugs, hypnosis, or other means. For sleep withdrawal therapy, which is the deprivation of sleep for therapeutic purposes, use SLEEP DEPRIVATION.
B Narcoanalysis [73]
R ↓ Drug Therapy [67]
Electrosleep Treatment [78]
↓ Sleep [67]

Sleep Wake Cycle [85]
PN 704 SC 47885
B Biological Rhythms [67]
R Napping [94]
↓ Sleep [67]
Wakefulness [73]

Sleeplessness
Use Insomnia

Sleepwalking [73]
PN 87 SC 47890
SN Use SLEEPWALKING or SOMNAMBULISM to access references from 73–81.
UF Somnambulism
B Sleep Disorders [73]
R ↓ Dissociative Patterns [73]

Slosson Intelligence Test for Child [73]
PN 65 SC 47900
B Intelligence Measures [67]

Slow Learners [73]
PN 179 SC 47910
UF Borderline Mentally Retarded
B Disabled [97]
R Educable Mentally Retarded [73]
↓ Mentally Retarded [67]

Slow Wave Sleep
Use NREM Sleep

Slums
Use Poverty Areas

Smell Perception
Use Olfactory Perception

Smiles [73]
PN 222 SC 47950
B Facial Expressions [67]
R Laughter [78]

Smokeless Tobacco [94]
PN 28 SC 47960
UF Chewing Tobacco
Snuff
Tobacco (Smokeless)
R ↓ CNS Stimulating Drugs [73]
Nicotine [73]
Nicotine Withdrawal [97]
Tobacco Smoking [67]

Smoking (Tobacco)
Use Tobacco Smoking

Smoking Cessation [88]
PN 1015 SC 47980
SN Used for cigarette smoking rehabilitation programs or stopping the habit of smoking. Use DRUG REHABILITATION and TOBACCO SMOKING to access references prior to 1988.
R ↓ Drug Abstinence [94]
↓ Drug Rehabilitation [73]
Nicotine Withdrawal [97]
Tobacco Smoking [67]

Snails [73]
PN 298 SC 47990
UF Aplysia
B Mollusca [73]

Snake Phobia
Use Ophidiophobia

Snakes [73]
PN 239 SC 48010
B Reptiles [67]

Snuff
Use Smokeless Tobacco

Sobriety [88]
PN 312 SC 48020
UF Alcohol Abstinence
B Drug Abstinence [94]
R Alcohol Drinking Attitudes [73]

Sobriety — (cont'd)
R ↓ Alcohol Rehabilitation [82]
Alcohol Withdrawal [94]
↓ Alcoholism [67]
Detoxification [73]
↓ Drug Rehabilitation [73]
Recovery (Disorders) [73]

Soccer [94]
PN 23 SC 48025
B Recreation [67]
Sports [67]

Sociability [73]
PN 294 SC 48030
B Personality Traits [67]
R Extraversion [67]
Gregariousness [73]

Social Acceptance [67]
PN 1363 SC 48040
SN Degree to which an individual is incorporated by others in their activities or is welcomed to interact with others informally. Limited to human populations.
UF Acceptance (Social)
Rejection (Social)
Social Rejection
B Social Behavior [67]
R Need for Approval [97]
Peer Pressure [94]
Popularity [88]
Social Approval [67]
Stigma [91]
↓ Tolerance [73]

Social Adaptation
Use Social Adjustment

Social Adjustment [73]
PN 4375 SC 48060
UF Adaptation (Social)
Maladjustment (Social)
Social Adaptation
Social Maladjustment
B Adjustment [67]
Social Behavior [67]
R Adjustment Disorders [94]

Social Anxiety [85]
PN 368 SC 48065
SN Apprehension or fear of social interaction or social situations in general. Compare SOCIAL PHOBIA.
B Anxiety [67]
R ↓ Anxiety Disorders [97]
Avoidant Personality [94]
↓ Fear [67]
↓ Social Interaction [67]
↓ Social Isolation [67]
Speech Anxiety [85]

Social Approval [67]
PN 1577 SC 48070
SN Favorable direct or indirect judgment by member or members of a given social group of another member or members, based on conduct, physical makeup, or other characteristics.
UF Approval (Social)
B Social Behavior [67]
Social Influences [67]
R Criticism [73]
Likability [88]
Need for Approval [97]
Peer Pressure [94]
Popularity [88]
Reputation [97]
Social Acceptance [67]

Social Approval — (cont'd)
R ↓ Social Reinforcement 67
Stigma 91

Social Behavior 67
PN 4050 SC 48080
B Behavior 67
N ↓ Aggressive Behavior 67
↓ Animal Social Behavior 67
Competition 67
↓ Compliance 73
Conformity (Personality) 67
Contagion 88
Criticism 73
↓ Gambling 73
↓ Help Seeking Behavior 78
Interspecies Interaction 91
↓ Involvement 73
↓ Leadership 67
Leadership Style 73
Militancy 73
Nurturance 85
↓ Organizational Behavior 78
↓ Prosocial Behavior 82
Racial and Ethnic Relations 82
Reciprocity 73
↓ Responsibility 73
Retaliation 91
↓ Risk Taking 67
Social Acceptance 67
Social Adjustment 73
Social Approval 67
Social Cognition 94
Social Demonstrations 73
Social Drinking 73
Social Facilitation 73
↓ Social Interaction 67
↓ Social Perception 67
↓ Social Reinforcement 67
Social Skills 78
R ↓ Antisocial Behavior 71
Dominance Hierarchy 73
Equity (Payment) 78
↓ Equity (Social) 78
Impression Management 78
Informants 88
Personal Space 73
Privacy 73
Psychodynamics 73
Social Change 67
↓ Social Influences 67

Social Casework 67
PN 3184 SC 48090
UF Social Work
B Treatment 67
R ↓ Case Management 91
Child Welfare 88
↓ Counseling 67
↓ Family Therapy 67
↓ Health Care Services 78
↓ Mental Health Services 78
Outreach Programs 97
Protective Services 97
↓ Social Services 82

Social Caseworkers
Use Social Workers

Social Change 67
PN 2793 SC 48110
UF Change (Social)
R ↓ Fads and Fashions 73
Future 91
↓ Social Behavior 67
↓ Social Influences 67
↓ Social Movements 67
↓ Social Processes 67

Social Change — (cont'd)
R ↓ Social Programs 73
Trends 91

Social Class 67
PN 1938 SC 48120
B Social Structure 67
Socioeconomic Status 67
N Lower Class 73
Middle Class 73
Upper Class 73
R Disadvantaged 67
↓ Income Level 73
↓ Socioeconomic Class Attitudes 73

Social Class Attitudes
Use Socioeconomic Class Attitudes

Social Clubs (Therapeutic)
Use Therapeutic Social Clubs

Social Cognition 94
PN 290 SC 48143
SN Cognitive processes and activity that accompany and mediate social interaction.
B Cognitive Processes 67
Social Behavior 67
R ↓ Communication Skills 73
↓ Interpersonal Interaction 67
Reputation 97
Schema 88
Self Fulfilling Prophecies 97
↓ Social Interaction 67
↓ Social Perception 67
Social Skills Training 82

Social Comparison 85
PN 499 SC 48145
SN Subjective evaluation of personal characteristics (e.g., ability level, personality traits, accomplishments) of oneself or another person in relation to the perceived characteristics of others.
B Social Perception 67
R Self Evaluation 67
Self Monitoring (Personality) 85
↓ Social Influences 67

Social Control 88
PN 211 SC 48148
SN Power of institutions, organizations, or laws of society to influence or regulate behavior or attitudes of groups or individuals. Consider POWER to access references that describe the control an individual has over other persons.
UF Control (Social)
B Social Processes 67
R ↓ Emotional Control 73
↓ Social Influences 67

Social Dating 73
PN 819 SC 48150
UF Dating (Social)
B Human Courtship 73
Interpersonal Interaction 67
R Acquaintance Rape 91
Couples 82
Friendship 67
Male Female Relations 88
Premarital Intercourse 73
↓ Relationship Termination 97
Romance 97

Social Demonstrations 73
PN 63 SC 48160
UF Demonstrations (Social)
Picketing
B Social Behavior 67
R ↓ Collective Behavior 67

Social Demonstrations — (cont'd)
R ↓ Political Participation 88
↓ Social Movements 67
Student Activism 73

Social Density 78
PN 397 SC 48165
SN Number of animals or humans per given space unit. For specifically high density conditions use CROWDING.
UF Density (Social)
Population Density
R Crowding 78
Overpopulation 73
Personal Space 73
↓ Population 73
↓ Social Environments 73

Social Deprivation 73
PN 221 SC 48170
SN Limited access to society's resources due to poverty, neglect, social discrimination, or other disadvantage. For a lack of social contact use SOCIAL ISOLATION. Consider also CULTURAL DEPRIVATION.
B Social Processes 67
Stimulus Deprivation 73
N ↓ Social Isolation 67
R Cultural Deprivation 73
Disadvantaged 67
↓ Homeless 88

Social Desirability 67
PN 1172 SC 48180
UF Desirability (Social)
B Social Influences 67
R Need for Approval 97

Social Development
Use Psychosocial Development

Social Discrimination 82
PN 568 SC 48185
SN Prejudiced and differential treatment based on religion, sex, race, ethnicity, disability, or other personal characteristics rather than on the basis of merit. Use RACIAL DISCRIMINATION to access references from 73-81 and MINORITY GROUP DISCRIMINATION to access references from 78-81. Use a more specific term if possible.
UF Discrimination (Social)
B Discrimination 67
Social Issues 91
N Age Discrimination 94
Disability Discrimination 97
Employment Discrimination 94
Race and Ethnic Discrimination 94
Sex Discrimination 78
R Affirmative Action 85
↓ Civil Rights 78
Racial and Ethnic Relations 82
Racism 73
↓ Social Integration 82
Stigma 91

Social Drinking 73
PN 377 SC 48190
SN Consumption of alcoholic beverages in social settings.
B Alcohol Drinking Patterns 67
Social Behavior 67

Social Environments 73
PN 1586 SC 48200
B Environment 67
N ↓ Academic Environment 73
↓ Animal Environments 67
↓ Communities 67
Home Environment 73

Social Environments — (cont'd)
N Poverty Areas [73]
Rural Environments [67]
Suburban Environments [67]
Towns [73]
↓ Urban Environments [67]
↓ Working Conditions [73]
R Cultural Deprivation [73]
Social Density [78]

Social Equality [73]
PN 494 SC 48210
UF Equality (Social)
B Social Issues [91]
R Affirmative Action [85]
↓ Civil Rights [78]
Equal Education [78]
↓ Human Rights [78]
↓ Justice [73]
Racial and Ethnic Relations [82]
↓ Social Integration [82]

Social Facilitation [73]
PN 370 SC 48220
UF Facilitation (Social)
B Social Behavior [67]
R ↓ Social Influences [67]

Social Groups [73]
PN 754 SC 48230
UF Cadres
Cliques
Groups (Social)
N Dyads [73]
Ingroup Outgroup [97]
Minority Groups [67]
Reference Groups [94]
R ↓ Social Networks [94]

Social Identity [88]
PN 571 SC 48235
SN An aspect of self image based on in-group preference or ethnocentrism and a perception of belonging to a social or cultural group.
N Professional Identity [91]
R Ethnic Identity [73]
Ethnocentrism [73]
Ingroup Outgroup [97]
Minority Groups [67]
Reference Groups [94]
↓ Self Concept [67]

Social Immobility
Use Social Mobility

Social Influences [67]
PN 3822 SC 48250
UF Influences (Social)
N Coercion [94]
Criticism [73]
Enabling [97]
Ethnic Values [73]
↓ Interpersonal Influences [67]
↓ Power [67]
↓ Prejudice [67]
Propaganda [73]
Social Approval [67]
Social Desirability [67]
Social Norms [85]
Social Values [73]
Superstitions [73]
Taboos [73]
R Authority [67]
↓ Ethics [67]
Mentor [85]
Popularity [88]
Psychosocial Factors [88]
Reference Groups [94]

Social Influences — (cont'd)
R Role Models [82]
↓ Social Behavior [67]
Social Change [67]
Social Comparison [85]
Social Control [88]
Social Facilitation [73]
↓ Social Movements [67]
↓ Social Reinforcement [67]

Social Integration [82]
PN 411 SC 48258
SN Process of uniting diverse groups (e.g., racial, ethnic, religious, or disabled) of a society or organization. Use RACIAL INTEGRATION to access references from 67-81.
UF Desegregation
Integration (Racial)
Racial Integration
Segregation (Racial)
B Social Issues [91]
Social Processes [67]
N School Integration [82]
R ↓ Activist Movements [73]
↓ Civil Rights [78]
↓ Mainstreaming [91]
Racial and Ethnic Relations [82]
↓ Social Discrimination [82]
Social Equality [73]

Social Interaction [67]
PN 4950 SC 48260
UF Interaction (Social)
B Social Behavior [67]
N Encouragement [73]
↓ Interpersonal Interaction [67]
Nonviolence [91]
Peace [88]
Physical Contact [82]
Victimization [73]
R ↓ Aggressive Behavior [67]
↓ Conflict Resolution [82]
Forgiveness [88]
Psychodynamics [73]
Self Monitoring (Personality) [85]
Social Anxiety [85]
Social Cognition [94]
↓ Social Networks [94]
Social Support Networks [82]
Symbolic Interactionism [88]

Social Isolation [67]
PN 2449 SC 48270
SN Voluntary or involuntary absence of contact with others. Used for human or animal populations.
UF Isolation (Social)
B Social Deprivation [73]
Stimulus Deprivation [73]
N Patient Seclusion [94]
R Animal Maternal Deprivation [88]
Social Anxiety [85]

Social Issues [91]
PN 245 SC 48275
SN Social concerns, including but not limited to problems or conditions perceived to have social causes, definitions, consequences or possible solutions.
UF Social Problems
N ↓ Crime [67]
↓ Homeless [88]
↓ Human Rights [78]
Peace [88]
Poverty [73]
↓ Social Discrimination [82]
Social Equality [73]
↓ Social Integration [82]
Unemployment [67]

Social Issues — (cont'd)
N ↓ War [67]
R Adolescent Pregnancy [88]
Censorship [78]
↓ Civil Rights [78]
↓ Drug Abuse [73]
↓ Justice [73]
↓ Legal Processes [73]
Political Issues [73]
Racism [73]
↓ Social Movements [67]
↓ Social Processes [67]
↓ Social Programs [73]

Social Learning [73]
PN 1008 SC 48280
B Learning [67]
Learning Strategies [91]
N Imitation (Learning) [67]
Imprinting [67]
R Observational Learning [73]
↓ Social Reinforcement [67]

Social Maladjustment
Use Social Adjustment

Social Mobility [67]
PN 308 SC 48300
SN Change in social status by an individual or a group.
UF Mobility (Social)
Social Immobility
Upward Mobility
B Social Processes [67]

Social Movements [67]
PN 760 SC 48310
N ↓ Activist Movements [73]
Black Power Movement [73]
Civil Rights Movement [73]
Homosexual Liberation Movement [73]
Womens Liberation Movement [73]
R ↓ Civil Rights [78]
Coalition Formation [73]
↓ Human Rights [78]
Peace [88]
↓ Political Participation [88]
↓ Radical Movements [73]
Social Change [67]
Social Demonstrations [73]
↓ Social Influences [67]
↓ Social Issues [91]
↓ Social Programs [73]

Social Networks [94]
PN 177 SC 48313
SN A formal or informal linkage, association, or network of individuals or groups that share common interests, contacts, knowledge, or resources. Compare SOCIAL SUPPORT NETWORKS and SUPPORT GROUPS.
UF Networks (Social)
N Social Support Networks [82]
R Ingroup Outgroup [97]
↓ Interpersonal Interaction [67]
↓ Social Groups [73]
↓ Social Interaction [67]
Sociograms [73]
↓ Sociometry [91]
↓ Support Groups [91]

Social Norms [85]
PN 660 SC 48315
SN Rules for social conduct, or standards which comprise a cultural definition of desirable or acceptable behavior. Also, patterns or traits seen as typical in the behavior of a social group.
UF Norms (Social)
B Social Influences [67]

Social Norms — (cont'd)
R Sex Roles 67
Social Values 73
Stereotyped Behavior 73

Social Perception 67
PN 13091 SC 48320
SN Awareness of social phenomena, including attitudes or behaviors of persons or groups, especially as they relate to one's self.
UF Interpersonal Perception
B Perception 67
Social Behavior 67
N Attribution 73
Impression Formation 78
Social Comparison 85
R Anonymity 73
Blame 94
Credibility 73
Face Perception 85
Fame 85
Halo Effect 82
Impression Management 78
Ingroup Outgroup 97
Labeling 78
Likability 88
Perceptiveness (Personality) 73
Popularity 88
Reputation 97
Reward Allocation 88
Self Fulfilling Prophecies 97
Self Reference 94
Social Cognition 94
Stigma 91
Stranger Reactions 88

Social Phobia 85
PN 449 SC 48325
SN Extreme apprehension or fear of social interaction or social situations in general. Compare SOCIAL ANXIETY.
B Phobias 67
R Avoidant Personality 94

Social Problems
Use Social Issues

Social Processes 67
PN 2102 SC 48330
N Anomie 78
Coalition Formation 73
↓ Human Migration 73
Immigration 73
Industrialization 73
Social Control 88
↓ Social Deprivation 73
↓ Social Integration 82
Social Mobility 67
↓ Socialization 67
↓ Status 67
Urbanization 73
R Equity (Payment) 78
↓ Equity (Social) 78
↓ Human Rights 78
↓ Political Processes 73
Refugees 88
Social Change 67
↓ Social Issues 91
↓ Sociocultural Factors 67
Trends 91

Social Programs 73
PN 314 SC 48340
N Outreach Programs 97
R ↓ Housing 73
Integrated Services 97
↓ Program Development 91
Social Change 67
↓ Social Issues 91

Social Programs — (cont'd)
R ↓ Social Movements 67
↓ Social Services 82

Social Psychiatry 67
PN 182 SC 48350
SN Branch of psychiatry concerned with the role of ecological, social, cultural, and economic factors in the etiology, incidence, and manifestations of mental disorders. Differentiate from COMMUNITY PSYCHIATRY, which emphasizes the practical and clinical applications of social psychiatry.
B Psychiatry 67
R Social Psychology 67

Social Psychologists 73
PN 63 SC 48360
B Psychologists 67
R Industrial Psychologists 73
Sociologists 73

Social Psychology 67
PN 2062 SC 48370
SN Branch of psychology concerned with the study of individuals in groups and the interpersonal interactions within and between groups.
B Applied Psychology 73
R Folk Psychology 97
Social Psychiatry 67

Social Reinforcement 67
PN 1300 SC 48380
B Reinforcement 67
Social Behavior 67
N Nonverbal Reinforcement 73
↓ Verbal Reinforcement 73
R Enabling 97
Encouragement 73
Eye Contact 73
Social Approval 67
↓ Social Influences 67
↓ Social Learning 73

Social Rejection
Use Social Acceptance

Social Sciences 67
PN 1346 SC 48390
SN Group of scientific disciplines which study social institutions, their functioning, and the interpersonal relationships and behavior of individuals of those institutions.
B Sciences 67
N Anthropology 67
↓ Behavioral Sciences 97
Economics 85
↓ Sociology 67
R Theoretical Orientation 82

Social Security 88
PN 48 SC 48392
SN Government program providing for economic security and social welfare of individuals or families upon retirement, death, or disability. Used for US and non-US programs.
B Government Programs 73
Insurance 73
R Disability Evaluation 88
Medicaid 94
Medicare 88

Social Services 82
PN 1552 SC 48393
SN Activities designed to promote social welfare, usually associated with government or a helping organization (e.g., a church).
N ↓ Community Services 67
Outreach Programs 97
Protective Services 97

Social Services — (cont'd)
R Child Welfare 88
↓ Government Programs 73
↓ Health Care Services 78
Integrated Services 97
Literacy Programs 97
↓ Mental Health Services 78
Shelters 91
Social Casework 67
↓ Social Programs 73
↓ Support Groups 91

Social Skills 78
PN 3497 SC 48395
UF Competence (Social)
Interpersonal Competence
B Ability 67
Social Behavior 67
R Adaptive Behavior 91
Affective Education 82
↓ Competence 82
Listening (Interpersonal) 97
Male Female Relations 88
Social Skills Training 82

Social Skills Training 82
PN 1632 SC 48397
SN Instruction, usually group oriented, to increase quality and capability of interpersonal interaction.
R Assertiveness Training 78
↓ Behavior Modification 73
Communication Skills Training 82
Human Relations Training 78
Sensitivity Training 73
↓ Skill Learning 73
Social Cognition 94
Social Skills 78

Social Stigma
Use Stigma

Social Stress 73
PN 513 SC 48400
B Stress 67

Social Structure 67
PN 1404 SC 48410
B Society 67
N Caste System 73
↓ Social Class 67
R Dominance Hierarchy 73
↓ Status 67

Social Studies Education 78
PN 442 SC 48415
SN Social sciences education in elementary, junior high, and high schools. Includes history, current events, and political science.
B Curriculum 67

Social Support Networks 82
PN 7062 SC 48417
SN Family members or friends who provide social, emotional, or psychological support or comfort to an individual. Consider also SUPPORT GROUPS.
B Social Networks 94
R Assistance (Social Behavior) 73
↓ Family Relations 67
Friendship 67
Reference Groups 94
↓ Self Help Techniques 82
Significant Others 91
↓ Social Interaction 67
↓ Support Groups 91

Social Values 73
PN 1397 SC 48420
B Social Influences 67
Values 67
R Anomie 78
Morality 67
Social Norms 85
↓ Society 67

Social Work
Use Social Casework

Social Work Education 73
PN 811 SC 48440
B Education 67

Social Workers 73
PN 2348 SC 48450
UF Caseworkers
Social Caseworkers
B Personnel 67
N Psychiatric Social Workers 73
R ↓ Counselors 67
↓ Health Personnel 94
↓ Law Enforcement Personnel 73
↓ Mental Health Personnel 67
↓ Psychologists 67
Rehabilitation Counselors 78
Sociologists 73
↓ Therapists 67
Vocational Counselors 73

Socialism 73
PN 204 SC 48460
B Political Economic Systems 73

Socialization 67
PN 2531 SC 48470
SN Process by which individuals acquire social skills and other characteristics necessary to function effectively in society or in a particular group.
B Social Processes 67
N Political Socialization 88
R Reference Groups 94

Socially Disadvantaged
Use Disadvantaged

Society 67
PN 764 SC 48490
B Culture (Anthropological) 67
N ↓ Social Structure 67
↓ Socioeconomic Status 67
R Social Values 73

Sociobiology 82
PN 314 SC 48495
SN Systematic study of the biological basis of all aspects of social behavior. Used for both human and animal populations.
B Biology 67
Sociology 67
R Behavioral Genetics 94

Sociocultural Factors 67
PN 5543 SC 48500
UF Cultural Factors
N Cross Cultural Differences 67
Cultural Deprivation 73
↓ Culture Change 67
Ethnic Identity 73
Ethnic Values 73
↓ Rites of Passage 73
R ↓ Childrearing Practices 67
Cross Cultural Psychology 97
Cultism 73
Cultural Sensitivity 94
↓ Culture (Anthropological) 67

Sociocultural Factors — (cont'd)
R Ethnography 73
Ethnology 67
↓ Family Structure 73
Kinship Structure 73
Multiculturalism 97
Psychosocial Factors 88
Race (Anthropological) 73
↓ Social Processes 67

Socioeconomic Class Attitudes 73
PN 179 SC 48510
SN Attitudes of, not toward, members of a particular socioeconomic class.
UF Class Attitudes
Social Class Attitudes
B Attitudes 67
N Lower Class Attitudes 73
Middle Class Attitudes 73
Upper Class Attitudes 73
R ↓ Social Class 67
↓ Socioeconomic Status 67

Socioeconomic Status 67
PN 6694 SC 48520
SN The combination of one's social class and income level. Includes socioeconomic differences between individuals or groups.
B Society 67
Status 67
N Family Socioeconomic Level 73
↓ Income Level 73
Lower Class 73
↓ Social Class 67
R Disadvantaged 67
Income (Economic) 73
Poverty 73
↓ Socioeconomic Class Attitudes 73

Socioenvironmental Therapy
Use Milieu Therapy

Sociograms 73
PN 49 SC 48530
SN Diagrams in which interactions between group members are analyzed on the basis of mutual attractions or antipathies.
B Sociometry 91
R ↓ Measurement 67
↓ Social Networks 94

Sociolinguistics 85
PN 210 SC 48535
SN The study of the sociological aspects of language, concerned with the part language plays in maintaining the social roles in a community.
B Linguistics 73
R Code Switching 88
Ethnolinguistics 73
Metalinguistics 94
↓ Sociology 67
Symbolic Interactionism 88

Sociologists 73
PN 66 SC 48540
B Professional Personnel 78
R Anthropologists 73
↓ Counselors 67
Scientists 67
Social Psychologists 73
↓ Social Workers 73

Sociology 67
PN 1169 SC 48550
B Social Sciences 67
N Sociobiology 82
R ↓ Behavioral Sciences 97
Sociolinguistics 85
Symbolic Interactionism 88

Sociometric Tests 67
PN 389 SC 48560
SN Tests or techniques used to identify preferences, likes, or dislikes of group members with respect to each other, as well as to identify various patterns of group structure or interaction.
B Measurement 67
Sociometry 91

Sociometry 91
PN 116 SC 48565
SN Used for the scientific discipline or the sociometric processes and properties themselves.
N Sociograms 73
Sociometric Tests 67
R ↓ Collective Behavior 67
↓ Group Dynamics 67
↓ Organizational Behavior 78
↓ Peer Relations 67
↓ Social Networks 94

Sociopath
Use Antisocial Personality

Sociopathology
Use Antisocial Behavior

Sociotherapy 73
PN 85 SC 48580
SN Any therapy in which the main emphasis is on socioenvironmental and interpersonal factors. Sometimes used to refer to a therapeutic community.
B Treatment 67
R Milieu Therapy 88
Therapeutic Community 67

Sodium 73
PN 764 SC 48590
B Metallic Elements 73
N Sodium Ions 73
R Hyponatremia 97

Sodium Ions 73
PN 64 SC 48610
B Electrolytes 73
Sodium 73

Sodium Lactate
Use Lactic Acid

Sodium Pentobarbital
Use Pentobarbital

Solvent Abuse
Use Inhalant Abuse

Solvents 82
PN 251 SC 48625
SN Substances that react chemically with a solid to bring it into solution. Also, liquids that dissolve another substance (solute) without any change in chemical composition.
N Toluene 91
R ↓ Acids 73
↓ Alcohols 67
↓ Inhalant Abuse 85

Somalia 91
PN 6 SC 48626
B Africa 67

Somatization 94
PN 125 SC 57430
SN Process of organically manifesting and expressing cognitive and emotional disturbances through bodily symptoms.

Somatization — (cont'd)
R ↓ Conversion Neurosis [73]
Hypochondriasis [73]
Illness Behavior [82]
↓ Psychosomatic Disorders [67]
Somatoform Pain Disorder [97]
↓ Symptoms [67]

Somatization Disorder
Use Psychosomatic Disorders

Somatoform Pain Disorder [97]
PN 0 SC 48629
SN Use PSYCHOGENIC PAIN to access references from 73–96.
UF Pain (Psychogenic)
Psychogenic Pain
B Pain [67]
Psychosomatic Disorders [67]
R Chronic Pain [85]
↓ Conversion Neurosis [73]
Hypochondriasis [73]
Pain Management [94]
Somatization [94]

Somatosensory Cortex [73]
PN 412 SC 48630
UF Cortex (Somatosensory)
B Parietal Lobe [73]

Somatosensory Evoked Potentials [73]
PN 560 SC 48640
UF Motor Evoked Potentials
B Evoked Potentials [67]
R ↓ Cortical Evoked Potentials [73]

Somatostatin [91]
PN 90 SC 48645
UF Growth Hormone Inhibitor
B Peptides [73]
R Somatotropin [73]

Somatotropin [73]
PN 607 SC 48650
UF Growth Hormone
B Pituitary Hormones [73]
R Somatostatin [91]

Somatotypes [73]
PN 146 SC 48660
SN Body types as derived from any of various classifications of body build and which usually imply a correlation with personality characteristics.
UF Body Types
R ↓ Personality [67]
↓ Physical Appearance [82]
Physique [67]

Somesthetic Perception [67]
PN 702 SC 48670
SN Awareness of a bodily condition or stimuli, including kinesthetic and cutaneous perception.
B Perception [67]
N ↓ Cutaneous Sense [67]
Kinesthetic Perception [67]
↓ Pain Perception [73]
Temperature Perception [73]
Weight Perception [67]
R Body Awareness [82]
↓ Labyrinth Disorders [73]
Pressure Sensation [73]

Somesthetic Stimulation [73]
PN 536 SC 48680
UF Vestibular Stimulation
B Perceptual Stimulation [73]

Somesthetic Stimulation — (cont'd)
N ↓ Tactual Stimulation [73]
R Weightlessness [67]

Somnambulism
SN Term discontinued in 1982. Use SOMNAMBULISM or SLEEPWALKING to access references from 73–81.
Use Sleepwalking

Sonar [73]
PN 28 SC 48700
B Apparatus [67]

Songs
Use Music

Sons [73]
PN 704 SC 48710
B Family Members [73]
Human Males [73]
Offspring [88]

Sorority Membership [73]
PN 80 SC 48720
SN Belonging to a club traditionally restricted to females. Used also for sorority organizations.
B Extracurricular Activities [73]

Sorting (Cognition)
Use Classification (Cognitive Process)

Sound
Use Auditory Stimulation

Sound Localization
Use Auditory Localization

Sound Pressure Level
Use Loudness

Sound Waves
Use Acoustics

Sourness
Use Taste Perception

South Africa [82]
PN 736 SC 48775
SN Use UNION OF SOUTH AFRICA to access references from 73–81.
UF Union of South Africa
B Africa [67]

South America [67]
PN 681 SC 48780
N Argentina [82]
Bolivia [88]
Brazil [73]
Chile [82]
Colombia [82]
Ecuador [88]
Guyana [88]
Paraguay [88]
Peru [88]
Surinam [91]
Uruguay [88]
Venezuela [73]
R Latin America [88]

South Korea [82]
PN 128 SC 48782
SN Use KOREA to access references from 73–81.
B Korea [73]

South Pacific [78]
PN 110 SC 48785
B Pacific Islands [88]
N American Samoa [91]
Fiji [91]
Tonga [91]
Western Samoa [91]
R Australia [73]
New Zealand [73]

South Vietnam
SN Term discontinued in 1982. Use SOUTH VIETNAM to access references from 73–81.
Use Vietnam

Southeast Asia [73]
PN 194 SC 48800
B Asia [73]
N Burma [91]
Cambodia [88]
Indonesia [82]
Laos [88]
Malaysia [82]
Philippines [73]
Singapore [91]
Thailand [73]
Vietnam [82]

Spacecraft [73]
PN 28 SC 48820
R Air Transportation [73]
Astronauts [73]

Spaceflight [67]
PN 180 SC 48830
B Aviation [67]
R Acceleration Effects [73]
Decompression Effects [73]
↓ Gravitational Effects [67]
Weightlessness [67]

Spain [73]
PN 706 SC 48840
B Europe [73]

Spanish Americans
SN Term discontinued in 1982. Use SPANISH AMERICANS to access references from 78–81.
Use Hispanics

Spasms [73]
PN 96 SC 48850
B Movement Disorders [85]
Symptoms [67]
N Muscle Spasms [73]
R ↓ Anticonvulsive Drugs [73]
↓ Antispasmodic Drugs [73]
↓ Convulsions [67]
↓ Pain [67]

Spatial Ability [82]
PN 1340 SC 48855
SN Potential or actual performance on tasks involving mental manipulation of objects or judgments of spatial relationships with respect to actual or imagined bodily orientation.
B Cognitive Ability [73]
Nonverbal Ability [88]
N ↓ Visuospatial Ability [97]
R ↓ Cognitive Processes [67]
Mental Rotation [91]
Spatial Imagery [82]
Spatial Learning [94]
Spatial Orientation (Perception) [73]

Spatial Discrimination
Use Spatial Perception

Spatial Distortion 73
PN 139 SC 48870
SN Alterations of an organism's normal spatial perception in any sensory modality. Distortions may be induced by such means as optical lenses, prisms, mirror displays or images, and left-right inversion of sound stimuli.
B Illusions (Perception) 67
Perceptual Distortion 82
Spatial Perception 67
R Prismatic Stimulation 73

Spatial Frequency 82
PN 1104 SC 48872
SN Number of alternating cycles (e.g., patterns of vertical stripes of light and dark light) occurring in a specified visual angle as, for example, in sine wave or square wave displays.
B Stimulus Parameters 67
R Temporal Frequency 85
↓ Visual Displays 73
↓ Visual Stimulation 73

Spatial Imagery 82
PN 267 SC 48875
SN Mental representation of spatial relationships.
B Imagery 67
R Cognitive Maps 82
Mental Rotation 91
↓ Spatial Ability 82
↓ Spatial Memory 88
Spatial Organization 73
Spatial Orientation (Perception) 73

Spatial Learning 94
PN 167 SC 48876
B Learning 67
R Maze Learning 67
↓ Spatial Ability 82
↓ Spatial Memory 88
↓ Spatial Perception 67

Spatial Memory 88
PN 716 SC 48877
B Memory 67
N Visuospatial Memory 97
R Cognitive Maps 82
Direction Perception 97
Eidetic Imagery 73
Spatial Imagery 82
Spatial Learning 94
↓ Visual Memory 94

Spatial Neglect
Use Sensory Neglect

Spatial Organization 73
PN 2064 SC 48880
SN Perception of spatial relationships. Also, the actual pattern or physical arrangement of objects or stimuli, including the dimensions of proximity, continuation, and relative position.
B Spatial Perception 67
R Cognitive Maps 82
Direction Perception 97
Mental Rotation 91
Retinal Eccentricity 91
Spatial Imagery 82

Spatial Orientation (Perception) 73
PN 2616 SC 48890
SN Ability to perceive or orient oneself or external stimuli in space with respect to environmentally or egocentrically defined reference points.
UF Orientation (Spatial)
B Perceptual Orientation 73
Spatial Perception 67
R Cognitive Maps 82

Spatial Orientation (Perception) — (cont'd)
R Equilibrium 73
Kinesthetic Perception 67
↓ Spatial Ability 82
Spatial Imagery 82

Spatial Perception 67
PN 3317 SC 48900
UF Spatial Discrimination
B Perception 67
N ↓ Depth Perception 67
Direction Perception 97
↓ Distance Perception 73
↓ Motion Perception 67
↓ Size Discrimination 67
Spatial Distortion 73
Spatial Organization 73
Spatial Orientation (Perception) 73
R Figure Ground Discrimination 73
Mental Rotation 91
Spatial Learning 94
Visual Acuity 82

Spearman Brown Test 73
PN 8 SC 48910
B Statistical Tests 73
R Statistical Reliability 73

Spearman Rho
Use Rank Difference Correlation

Special Education 67
PN 10682 SC 48930
SN Educational programs and services for students with disabilities or gifted students whose characteristics and educational needs differ from those who can be taught through standard methods and materials.
B Education 67
Educational Programs 73
R Ability Grouping 73
Adaptive Behavior 91
Early Intervention 82
Educational Placement 78
Educational Therapy 97
↓ Mainstreaming 91
Mainstreaming (Educational) 78
↓ Remedial Education 85
Self Care Skills 78
Special Needs 94

Special Education Students 73
PN 2688 SC 49010
B Students 67
R Grade Level 94

Special Education Teachers 73
PN 1720 SC 49020
B Teachers 67
R Resource Teachers 73

Special Needs 94
PN 118 SC 49025
SN Unspecified disorder, disability, or other problem that requires special services or intervention practices. Use a more specific term if possible.
R ↓ Disabled 97
↓ Disorders 67
Early Intervention 82
↓ Mainstreaming 91
↓ Mental Disorders 67
↓ Needs 67
Needs Assessment 85
↓ Physical Disorders 97
Special Education 67

Specialization (Academic)
Use Academic Specialization

Specialization (Professional)
Use Professional Specialization

Species Differences 82
PN 1209 SC 49035
SN Anatomical, physiological, and/or behavioral variations between members of different species. May be used for comparisons between human and animal populations. Consider COMPARATIVE PSYCHOLOGY to access references from 67–81. Compare ANIMAL STRAIN DIFFERENCES.
R ↓ Animals 67
↓ Genetics 67
Interspecies Interaction 91

Species Recognition 85
PN 246 SC 49037
SN Ability of members of a given species to identify and recognize other members of the same species.
B Animal Ethology 67
R Imprinting 67
Instinctive Behavior 82
Kinship Recognition 88

Spectral Sensitivity
Use Color Perception

Speech
Use Oral Communication

Speech and Hearing Measures 73
PN 472 SC 49060
SN Consider also AUDIOLOGY and AUDIOMETRY.
UF Hearing Measures
Speech Measures
B Measurement 67
N Wepman Test of Auditory Discrim 73
R ↓ Perceptual Measures 73

Speech Anxiety 85
PN 256 SC 49065
SN Anxiety or fear associated with actual or anticipated oral communication with others.
UF Communication Apprehension
Fear of Public Speaking
B Anxiety 67
R ↓ Anxiety Disorders 97
↓ Communication Disorders 82
↓ Interpersonal Communication 73
Public Speaking 73
Social Anxiety 85

Speech Characteristics 73
PN 2966 SC 49070
B Oral Communication 85
N Articulation (Speech) 67
Pronunciation 73
Speech Pauses 73
Speech Pitch 73
Speech Rate 73
Speech Rhythm 73
R Acoustics 97
Inflection 73
↓ Prosody 91

Speech Development 73
PN 1255 SC 49080
B Psychomotor Development 73
N Retarded Speech Development 73
R ↓ Cognitive Development 73
↓ Language Development 67

Speech Disabled [97]
PN 0 **SC** 49085
SN Use SPEECH HANDICAPPED to access references from 73-96.
UF Speech Handicapped
B Disabled [97]
R ↓ Communication Disorders [82]
↓ Language Disorders [82]
↓ Speech Disorders [67]

Speech Disorders [67]
PN 1675 **SC** 49090
B Communication Disorders [82]
N ↓ Articulation Disorders [73]
Dysphonia [73]
Stuttering [67]
R Apraxia [73]
↓ Augmentative Communication [94]
Cleft Palate [67]
↓ Language Disorders [82]
Retarded Speech Development [73]
Speech Disabled [97]

Speech Handicapped
SN Term discontinued in 1997. Use SPEECH HANDICAPPED to access references from 73-96.
Use Speech Disabled

Speech Measures
Use Speech and Hearing Measures

Speech Pauses [73]
PN 238 **SC** 49120
B Speech Characteristics [73]

Speech Perception [67]
PN 3631 **SC** 49130
B Auditory Perception [67]
R Automated Speech Recognition [94]
Lipreading [73]
↓ Rhythm [91]
Word Recognition [88]

Speech Pitch [73]
PN 225 **SC** 49140
B Pitch (Frequency) [67]
Speech Characteristics [73]

Speech Processing (Mechanical) [73]
PN 160 **SC** 49150
N Automated Speech Recognition [94]
Compressed Speech [73]
Filtered Speech [73]
Synthetic Speech [73]
R ↓ Auditory Stimulation [67]
↓ Verbal Communication [67]

Speech Rate [73]
PN 509 **SC** 49160
UF Accelerated Speech
B Speech Characteristics [73]
R Tempo [97]
Verbal Fluency [73]

Speech Rhythm [73]
PN 146 **SC** 49170
B Rhythm [91]
Speech Characteristics [73]
R Tempo [97]

Speech Therapists [73]
PN 274 **SC** 49180
B Therapists [67]
R ↓ Educational Personnel [73]

Speech Therapy [67]
PN 1647 **SC** 49190
B Treatment [67]
R ↓ Augmentative Communication [94]
↓ Communication Disorders [82]

Speechreading
Use Lipreading

Speed
Use Velocity

Speed (Response)
Use Reaction Time

Spelling [73]
PN 1229 **SC** 49220
SN Instruction, ability, or performance in the formation of words from letters according to accepted orthographic standards.
B Language [67]
Language Arts Education [73]
R Orthography [73]

Sperm [73]
PN 92 **SC** 49230
B Cells (Biology) [73]
R ↓ Sexual Reproduction [73]

Sperm Donation
Use Tissue Donation

Spider Phobia
Use Phobias

Spiders
Use Arachnida

Spina Bifida [78]
PN 215 **SC** 49245
SN Birth defect involving inadequate closure of the bony casement of the spinal cord, through which the spinal membranes, with or without spinal cord tissue, may protrude.
UF Meningomyelocele
Myelomeningocele
B Congenital Disorders [73]

Spinal Column [73]
PN 46 **SC** 49250
B Musculoskeletal System [73]
R Bones [73]
↓ Spinal Cord [73]

Spinal Cord [73]
PN 751 **SC** 49260
B Central Nervous System [67]
N Cranial Spinal Cord [73]
Dorsal Horns [85]
Dorsal Roots [73]
Extrapyramidal Tracts [73]
Lumbar Spinal Cord [73]
Pyramidal Tracts [73]
Spinothalamic Tracts [73]
Ventral Roots [73]
R Spinal Column [73]

Spinal Cord Injuries [73]
PN 486 **SC** 49270
B Injuries [73]
N Whiplash [97]
R ↓ Central Nervous System Disorders [73]
Hemiplegia [78]
↓ Neuromuscular Disorders [73]
↓ Paralysis [73]
Paraplegia [78]
Quadriplegia [85]

Spinal Fluid
Use Cerebrospinal Fluid

Spinal Ganglia [73]
PN 29 **SC** 49290
B Ganglia [73]

Spinal Nerves [73]
PN 235 **SC** 49300
UF Brachial Plexus
Cauda Equina
Cervical Plexus
Femoral Nerve
Lumbrosacral Plexus
Median Nerve
Musculocutaneous Nerve
Nerves (Spinal)
Obturator Nerve
Phrenic Nerve
Radial Nerve
Sciatic Nerve
Thoracic Nerves
Ulnar Nerve
B Peripheral Nervous System [73]

Spinothalamic Tracts [73]
PN 42 **SC** 49310
B Afferent Pathways [82]
Lemniscal System [85]
Spinal Cord [73]

Spiperone
Use Spiroperidol

Spirit Possession [97]
PN 0 **SC** 49314
UF Demonic Possession
R ↓ Dissociative Patterns [73]
Occultism [78]
↓ Parapsychological Phenomena [73]
↓ Religious Beliefs [73]

Spirituality [88]
PN 591 **SC** 49315
SN Degree of involvement or state of awareness or devotion to a higher being or life philosophy. Not always related to conventional religious beliefs.
R Religion [67]
Religiosity [73]
↓ Religious Beliefs [73]
Religious Experiences [97]

Spiroperidol [91]
PN 34 **SC** 49317
UF Spiperone
B Neuroleptic Drugs [73]

Spleen [73]
PN 42 **SC** 49320
R ↓ Cardiovascular System [67]

Split Brain
Use Commissurotomy

Split Personality
Use Dissociative Identity Disorder

Spontaneous Abortion [71]
PN 202 **SC** 49350
UF Abortion (Spontaneous)
Miscarriage
R Induced Abortion [71]

Spontaneous Alternation [82]
PN 137 **SC** 49352

Spontaneous Alternation — (cont'd)
SN Instinctive successive alternation of responses between alternatives in a situation involving discrete choices or exploration.
R Animal Exploratory Behavior [73]
Delayed Alternation [94]
Instinctive Behavior [82]
↓ Learning [67]
Response Variability [73]

Spontaneous Recovery (Learning) [73]
PN 62 **SC** 49357
SN Recurrence of a conditioned response following experimental extinction. The response is weaker than when originally conditioned and will extinguish rapidly if not reinforced.
B Learning [67]
Memory [67]
R ↓ Conditioning [67]

Spontaneous Remission [73]
PN 56 **SC** 49360
B Remission (Disorders) [73]
R ↓ Psychotherapy [67]
↓ Treatment [67]

Sport Performance
Use Athletic Performance

Sport Psychology [82]
PN 378 **SC** 49365
SN Branch of psychology that investigates and applies psychological and physiological principles relating to athletic activity. Also used for psychological processes and their manifestations in such activity.
B Applied Psychology [73]

Sport Training
Use Athletic Training

Sports [67]
PN 1768 **SC** 49370
N Baseball [73]
Basketball [73]
Football [73]
Judo [73]
Martial Arts [85]
Soccer [94]
Swimming [73]
Tennis [73]
Weightlifting [94]
R ↓ Athletes [73]
Athletic Participation [73]
Athletic Performance [91]
Athletic Training [91]
Coaches [88]
College Athletes [94]
↓ Recreation [67]
Sports Spectators [97]
Teams [88]
Wilderness Experience [91]

Sports Spectators [97]
PN 0 **SC** 49373
UF Fans (Sports)
B Audiences [67]
R ↓ Sports [67]

Spouse Abuse
Use Partner Abuse

Spouses [73]
PN 5071 **SC** 49380
SN Married persons.
UF Married Couples
Mates (Humans)
B Family Members [73]

Spouses — (cont'd)
N Husbands [73]
↓ Wives [73]
R Couples [82]
Inlaws [97]
↓ Parents [67]
Significant Others [91]

Spreading Depression [67]
PN 117 **SC** 49390
SN Cerebral cortex cellular depolarization and a depressed electrical activity in depolarized cortical areas resulting from application of intense localized electrical stimulation or local application of a chemical or localized trauma to the cerebral cortex.
B Brain Stimulation [67]

Squirrels [73]
PN 260 **SC** 49400
B Rodents [73]

Sri Lanka [88]
PN 52 **SC** 49410
B Asia [73]

Stability (Emotional)
Use Emotional Stability

Stage Plays
Use Theatre

Stammering
SN Term discontinued in 1982. Use STAMMERING or STUTTERING to access references from 73-81 and 67-81, respectively.
Use Stuttering

Standard Deviation [73]
PN 111 **SC** 49450
B Variability Measurement [73]
R Error of Measurement [85]
↓ Frequency Distribution [73]
Standard Scores [85]
Variance Homogeneity [85]

Standard Error of Measurement
Use Error of Measurement

Standard Scores [85]
PN 54 **SC** 49455
SN Test scores measuring the distance of individual scores from the mean of the normative group, expressed in terms of the standard deviation.
UF Deviation IQ
Stanines
Z Scores
B Test Scores [67]
R Mean [73]
Score Equating [85]
↓ Scoring (Testing) [73]
Standard Deviation [73]

Standardization (Test)
Use Test Standardization

Standardized Tests [85]
PN 304 **SC** 49465
SN Tests with established norms, administration and scoring procedures, and validity and reliability data.
B Measurement [67]
R Test Norms [73]
Test Standardization [73]

Standards (Professional)
Use Professional Standards

Stanford Achievement Test [73]
PN 51 **SC** 49480
B Achievement Measures [67]

Stanford Binet Intelligence Scale [67]
PN 314 **SC** 49490
B Intelligence Measures [67]

Stanines
Use Standard Scores

Stapedius Reflex
Use Acoustic Reflex

Starfish
Use Echinodermata

Startle Reflex [67]
PN 661 **SC** 49510
B Reflexes [71]
R Acoustic Reflex [73]
Alarm Responses [73]
Eyeblink Reflex [73]
Prepulse Inhibition [97]

Starvation [73]
PN 70 **SC** 49520
B Nutritional Deficiencies [73]
R Food Deprivation [67]
Hunger [67]

State Board Examinations
Use Professional Examinations

State Dependent Learning [82]
PN 87 **SC** 49525
SN Learning phenomenon wherein the transfer of a response that was learned in the context of specific internal or external cues is dependent on the constancy of the stimulus complex in the new situation to which the behavior is to transfer.
UF Drug Dissociation
B Learning [67]

State Hospitals
Use Psychiatric Hospitals

State Trait Anxiety Inventory [73]
PN 143 **SC** 49540
B Nonprojective Personality Measures [73]

Statistical Analysis [67]
PN 5801 **SC** 49550
SN Application of statistical procedures to the interpretation of numerical data.
B Analysis [67]
N ↓ Central Tendency Measures [73]
Cluster Analysis [73]
Confidence Limits (Statistics) [73]
Consistency (Measurement) [73]
Effect Size (Statistical) [85]
Error of Measurement [85]
↓ Frequency Distribution [73]
Fuzzy Set Theory [91]
Goodness of Fit [88]
Interaction Analysis (Statistics) [73]
Meta Analysis [85]
↓ Multivariate Analysis [82]
Predictability (Measurement) [73]
↓ Statistical Correlation [67]
Statistical Data [82]
↓ Statistical Estimation [85]
Statistical Norms [71]
↓ Statistical Probability [67]
↓ Statistical Regression [85]
Statistical Reliability [73]
Statistical Significance [73]

Statistical Analysis — (cont'd)
N ↓ Statistical Tests 73
↓ Statistical Validity 73
Statistical Weighting 85
Time Series 85
↓ Variability Measurement 73
R Conjoint Measurement 94
↓ Experimental Design 67
↓ Experimentation 67
↓ Hypothesis Testing 73
↓ Mathematics (Concepts) 67
↓ Measurement 67
↓ Population (Statistics) 73
↓ Prediction Errors 73
Psychometrics 67
↓ Sampling (Experimental) 73
↓ Statistical Measurement 73
↓ Statistical Variables 73
Uncertainty 91

Statistical Correlation 67
PN 2874 SC 49560
UF Correlation (Statistical)
Pearson Prod Moment Correl Coeff
B Statistical Analysis 67
N Linear Regression 73
Nonlinear Regression 73
Phi Coefficient 73
Point Biserial Correlation 73
Rank Difference Correlation 73
Rank Order Correlation 73
Tetrachoric Correlation 73
R Construct Validity 82
↓ Experimentation 67
↓ Factor Analysis 67
Multiple Regression 82
↓ Multivariate Analysis 82
Statistical Data 82
↓ Statistical Regression 85
Statistical Significance 73
↓ Statistical Validity 73
↓ Statistical Variables 73
↓ Variability Measurement 73

Statistical Data 82
PN 337 SC 49564
SN Sets of quantitative values that summarize, through mathematical operation, or express the parameters that represent a population or some other sample (e.g., response frequency).
B Statistical Analysis 67
R Data Collection 82
Graphical Displays 85
↓ Statistical Correlation 67
↓ Statistical Measurement 73
Statistical Tables 82
↓ Statistical Variables 73
Time Series 85

Statistical Estimation 85
PN 627 SC 49567
SN Any inferential mathematical derivation of an estimate of a parameter from one or more samples. Includes interval estimation.
UF Parameter Estimation
B Estimation 67
Statistical Analysis 67
N Least Squares 85
Magnitude Estimation 91
Maximum Likelihood 85
R Error of Measurement 85
Predictability (Measurement) 73

Statistical Measurement 73
PN 482 SC 49570
SN Process of or products derived from the collection or manipulation of statistical data in order to derive basic summarizing quantitative values which describe a set of measurements.

Statistical Measurement — (cont'd)
B Measurement 67
N ↓ Central Tendency Measures 73
Conjoint Measurement 94
↓ Frequency Distribution 73
Predictability (Measurement) 73
Statistical Norms 71
↓ Statistical Probability 67
↓ Variability Measurement 73
Variance Homogeneity 85
R Confidence Limits (Statistics) 73
Data Collection 82
Error of Measurement 85
Graphical Displays 85
↓ Statistical Analysis 67
Statistical Data 82
Statistical Significance 73
↓ Statistical Tests 73

Statistical Norms 71
PN 234 SC 49580
UF Norms (Statistical)
B Statistical Analysis 67
Statistical Measurement 73
R ↓ Statistical Sample Parameters 73

Statistical Power 91
PN 89 SC 49585
SN The ability of a statistic to reject a false hypothesis.
B Statistical Probability 67
R ↓ Hypothesis Testing 73
↓ Prediction Errors 73
↓ Sampling (Experimental) 73
Statistical Significance 73
↓ Statistical Tests 73
Type I Errors 73
Type II Errors 73

Statistical Probability 67
PN 735 SC 49590
UF Bayes Theorem
B Chance (Fortune) 73
Probability 67
Statistical Analysis 67
Statistical Measurement 73
N Binomial Distribution 73
Statistical Power 91
R Fuzzy Set Theory 91
Risk Analysis 91

Statistical Regression 85
PN 289 SC 49595
SN Statistical comparison of the frequency distributions of one variable while the other(s) are held constant for the purpose of discovering predictive and functional relationships between variables. Use ANALYSIS OF VARIANCE or more specific terms prior to 1985.
UF Regression Analysis
Regression Artifact
B Statistical Analysis 67
N Linear Regression 73
Multiple Regression 82
Nonlinear Regression 73
R Analysis of Variance 67
Causal Analysis 94
Least Squares 85
↓ Multivariate Analysis 82
↓ Statistical Correlation 67

Statistical Reliability 73
PN 1692 SC 49600
SN Use RELIABILITY (STATISTICAL) to access references from 67-72.
UF Reliability (Statistical)
B Statistical Analysis 67
R Consistency (Measurement) 73
↓ Experimentation 67

Statistical Reliability — (cont'd)
R Interrater Reliability 82
↓ Population (Statistics) 73
↓ Prediction Errors 73
↓ Sampling (Experimental) 73
Spearman Brown Test 73
↓ Statistical Validity 73

Statistical Rotation 73
PN 62 SC 49610
UF Rotation Methods (Statistical)
B Factor Analysis 67
N Oblique Rotation 73
↓ Orthogonal Rotation 73
R Factor Structure 85

Statistical Sample Parameters 73
PN 342 SC 49620
SN Quantities and qualities describing a statistical population.
B Statistical Samples 73
N Sample Size 97
R Binomial Distribution 73
Confidence Limits (Statistics) 73
Normal Distribution 73
Statistical Norms 71

Statistical Samples 73
PN 217 SC 49630
SN Portion of a population taken as representative of the whole population.
B Population (Statistics) 73
N ↓ Statistical Sample Parameters 73
R ↓ Sampling (Experimental) 73

Statistical Significance 73
PN 525 SC 49640
UF Significance (Statistical)
B Statistical Analysis 67
R Chi Square Test 73
Confidence Limits (Statistics) 73
Effect Size (Statistical) 85
↓ Factor Analysis 67
Goodness of Fit 88
↓ Hypothesis Testing 73
Sign Test 73
↓ Statistical Correlation 67
↓ Statistical Measurement 73
Statistical Power 91
↓ Statistical Tests 73
T Test 73

Statistical Tables 82
PN 95 SC 49647
SN Systematically organized displays of statistical values or distributions or summary data derived from statistical calculation. The table of critical values of the F distribution is an example of the first category, and a contingency table showing test score means as related to the variables of sex and age is an example of the second category.
R Statistical Data 82
↓ Statistical Variables 73

Statistical Tests 73
PN 460 SC 49650
SN Specific mathematical techniques used to analyze data in order to assess the probability that a set of results could have occurred by chance and hence to test for the probable correctness of empirical hypotheses.
UF Tests (Statistical)
B Statistical Analysis 67
N ↓ Nonparametric Statistical Tests 67
↓ Parametric Statistical Tests 73
Spearman Brown Test 73
R Confidence Limits (Statistics) 73
↓ Statistical Measurement 73

Statistical Tests — (cont'd)
R Statistical Power [91]
Statistical Significance [73]

Statistical Validity [73]
PN 2162 SC 49660
SN Use VALIDITY (STATISTICAL) to access references from 67–72.
UF Validity (Statistical)
B Statistical Analysis [67]
N Concurrent Validity [88]
Factorial Validity [73]
Predictive Validity [73]
R Consistency (Measurement) [73]
Construct Validity [82]
↓ Experimentation [67]
↓ Prediction Errors [73]
↓ Statistical Correlation [67]
Statistical Reliability [73]
↓ Statistical Variables [73]

Statistical Variables [73]
PN 645 SC 49670
N Dependent Variables [73]
Independent Variables [73]
R ↓ Experimental Design [67]
↓ Experimentation [67]
↓ Population (Statistics) [73]
↓ Prediction Errors [73]
↓ Sampling (Experimental) [73]
↓ Statistical Analysis [67]
↓ Statistical Correlation [67]
Statistical Data [82]
Statistical Tables [82]
↓ Statistical Validity [73]

Statistical Weighting [85]
PN 122 SC 49671
SN A coefficient or mathematical constant that determines the relative contribution of a statistic to a total numeric value. Also, the process of assigning such statistical weights.
UF Weight (Statistics)
B Statistical Analysis [67]
R Item Analysis (Statistical) [73]
↓ Scoring (Testing) [73]
Test Interpretation [85]
↓ Test Scores [67]

Statistics [82]
PN 294 SC 49672
SN Subdiscipline of mathematics that deals with the gathering and evaluation of numerical data for making inferences from the data. Also used as a document type identifier.
B Mathematics [82]

Status [67]
PN 1486 SC 49675
SN General term used to indicate relative social position or rank.
B Social Processes [67]
N Occupational Status [78]
↓ Socioeconomic Status [67]
R Authority [67]
↓ Dominance [67]
Fame [85]
Reputation [97]
↓ Social Structure [67]

Stealing
Use Theft

Stelazine
Use Trifluoperazine

Stellate Ganglion
Use Autonomic Ganglia

Stepchildren [73]
PN 163 SC 49720
B Family Members [73]
R ↓ Children [67]
↓ Family Structure [73]
Stepfamily [91]

Stepfamily [91]
PN 98 SC 49725
B Family [67]
Family Structure [73]
R Family of Origin [91]
Remarriage [85]
Stepchildren [73]
Stepparents [73]

Stepparents [73]
PN 321 SC 49730
B Parents [67]
R ↓ Family Structure [73]
Stepfamily [91]

Stereopsis
Use Stereoscopic Vision

Stereoscopic Presentation [73]
PN 114 SC 49750
SN Simultaneous presentation of separate two-dimensional pictures (taken from slightly different angles) to each eye of one subject, resulting in a perception of depth.
B Stimulus Presentation Methods [73]
Visual Stimulation [73]

Stereoscopic Vision [73]
PN 528 SC 49760
UF Stereopsis
B Depth Perception [67]
Visual Perception [67]

Stereotaxic Atlas [73]
PN 349 SC 49770
UF Brain Mapping
Brain Maps
R ↓ Stereotaxic Techniques [73]

Stereotaxic Techniques [73]
PN 119 SC 49780
SN Methods, procedures, or apparatus which permit precise spatial positioning of electrodes or other probes into the brain for experimental or surgical purposes.
B Surgery [71]
N ↓ Brain Stimulation [67]
Chemical Brain Stimulation [73]
Electrical Brain Stimulation [73]
R Afferent Stimulation [73]
↓ Nervous System [67]
Stereotaxic Atlas [73]

Stereotyped Attitudes [67]
PN 3628 SC 49790
B Attitudes [67]
R Age Discrimination [94]
Disability Discrimination [97]
Race and Ethnic Discrimination [94]
↓ Racial and Ethnic Attitudes [82]
Self Fulfilling Prophecies [97]
Sex Discrimination [78]
↓ Sex Role Attitudes [78]

Stereotyped Behavior [73]
PN 1693 SC 49795

Stereotyped Behavior — (cont'd)
SN Behavior or response that is consistently elicited or determined by a particular situation or motive. The behavior varies little in its topography and is little altered by its outcome. Also used for behavioral patterns in a given society deemed appropriate for one group or another. Used for animal or human populations.
B Behavior [67]
R ↓ Animal Ethology [67]
Instinctive Behavior [82]
Rotational Behavior [94]
Sex Roles [67]
Social Norms [85]
↓ Symptoms [67]

Sterility [73]
PN 41 SC 49810
B Infertility [73]
R ↓ Gynecological Disorders [73]
Hermaphroditism [73]
↓ Hypogonadism [73]
↓ Male Genital Disorders [73]
Testicular Feminization Syndrome [73]
Turners Syndrome [73]
↓ Venereal Diseases [73]

Sterilization (Sex) [73]
PN 90 SC 49820
N ↓ Castration [67]
Hysterectomy [73]
Tubal Ligation [73]
Vasectomy [73]
R ↓ Birth Control [71]
Eugenics [73]
↓ Family Planning [73]

Steroids [73]
PN 427 SC 49830
B Drugs [67]
N Cholesterol [73]
↓ Corticosteroids [73]
Progesterone [73]
R ↓ Anti Inflammatory Drugs [82]
Antiandrogens [82]
Antiestrogens [82]
Antineoplastic Drugs [82]
↓ Hormones [67]
↓ Lipids [73]

Sticklebacks [73]
PN 141 SC 49840
B Fishes [67]

Stigma [91]
PN 211 SC 49843
SN Perception of a distinguishing personal characteristic or condition, e.g., a physical or psychological disorder, race, or religion, which carries or is believed to carry a physical, psychological, or social disadvantage.
UF Social Stigma
R ↓ Attitudes [67]
Labeling [78]
↓ Prejudice [67]
Social Acceptance [67]
Social Approval [67]
↓ Social Discrimination [82]
↓ Social Perception [67]

Stimulants of CNS
Use CNS Stimulating Drugs

Stimulation [67]
PN 1116 SC 49850
N Afferent Stimulation [73]
Aversive Stimulation [73]
↓ Brain Stimulation [67]
↓ Electrical Stimulation [73]

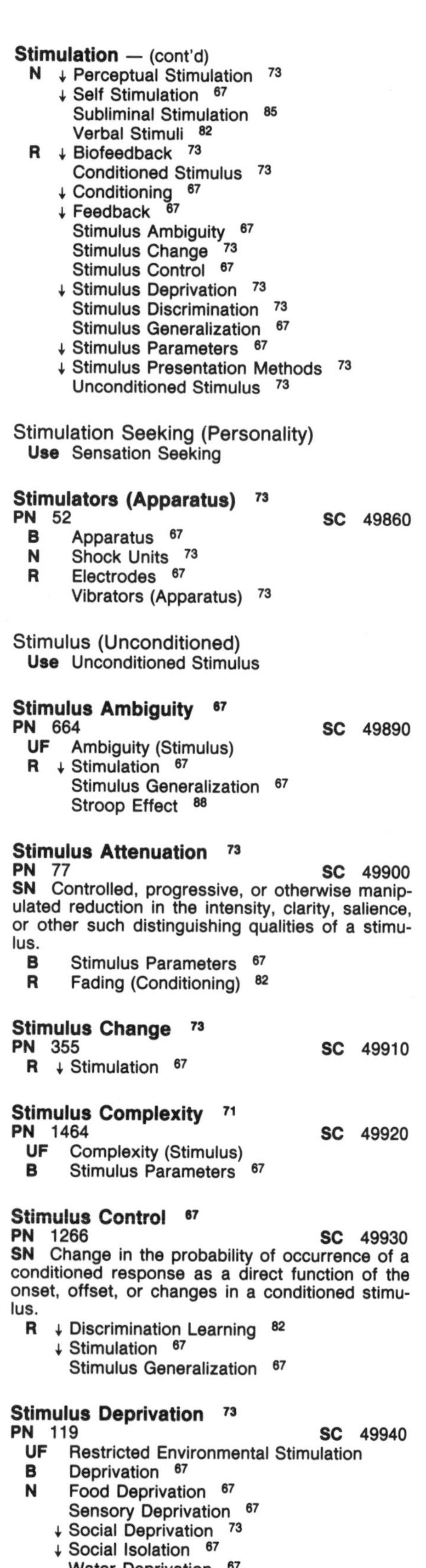

Stimulation — (cont'd)
N ↓ Perceptual Stimulation 73
↓ Self Stimulation 67
Subliminal Stimulation 85
Verbal Stimuli 82
R ↓ Biofeedback 73
Conditioned Stimulus 73
↓ Conditioning 67
↓ Feedback 67
Stimulus Ambiguity 67
Stimulus Change 73
Stimulus Control 67
↓ Stimulus Deprivation 73
Stimulus Discrimination 73
Stimulus Generalization 67
↓ Stimulus Parameters 67
↓ Stimulus Presentation Methods 73
Unconditioned Stimulus 73

Stimulation Seeking (Personality)
Use Sensation Seeking

Stimulators (Apparatus) 73
PN 52 **SC** 49860
B Apparatus 67
N Shock Units 73
R Electrodes 67
Vibrators (Apparatus) 73

Stimulus (Unconditioned)
Use Unconditioned Stimulus

Stimulus Ambiguity 67
PN 664 **SC** 49890
UF Ambiguity (Stimulus)
R ↓ Stimulation 67
Stimulus Generalization 67
Stroop Effect 88

Stimulus Attenuation 73
PN 77 **SC** 49900
SN Controlled, progressive, or otherwise manipulated reduction in the intensity, clarity, salience, or other such distinguishing qualities of a stimulus.
B Stimulus Parameters 67
R Fading (Conditioning) 82

Stimulus Change 73
PN 355 **SC** 49910
R ↓ Stimulation 67

Stimulus Complexity 71
PN 1464 **SC** 49920
UF Complexity (Stimulus)
B Stimulus Parameters 67

Stimulus Control 67
PN 1266 **SC** 49930
SN Change in the probability of occurrence of a conditioned response as a direct function of the onset, offset, or changes in a conditioned stimulus.
R ↓ Discrimination Learning 82
↓ Stimulation 67
Stimulus Generalization 67

Stimulus Deprivation 73
PN 119 **SC** 49940
UF Restricted Environmental Stimulation
B Deprivation 67
N Food Deprivation 67
Sensory Deprivation 67
↓ Social Deprivation 73
↓ Social Isolation 67
Water Deprivation 67
R ↓ Stimulation 67

Stimulus Discrimination 73
PN 1714 **SC** 49950
B Discrimination 67
R Behavioral Contrast 78
↓ Discrimination Learning 82
Fading (Conditioning) 82
↓ Stimulation 67
Stimulus Generalization 67

Stimulus Duration 73
PN 2179 **SC** 49960
UF Duration (Stimulus)
Exposure Time (Stimulus)
B Stimulus Parameters 67

Stimulus Frequency 73
PN 1046 **SC** 49980
SN Number of stimulus presentations within a given trial or per unit time.
UF Frequency (Stimulus)
B Stimulus Parameters 67
R Temporal Frequency 85

Stimulus Generalization 67
PN 701 **SC** 49990
SN Responding in a similar manner to different stimuli which have some common physical property. Also known as primary generalization. Compare GENERALIZATION (LEARNING) and RESPONSE GENERALIZATION.
UF Generalization (Stimulus)
B Generalization (Learning) 82
R ↓ Stimulation 67
Stimulus Ambiguity 67
Stimulus Control 67
Stimulus Discrimination 73

Stimulus Intensity 67
PN 2824 **SC** 50000
UF Intensity (Stimulus)
Signal Intensity
B Stimulus Parameters 67
R Luminance 82

Stimulus Intervals 73
PN 1038 **SC** 50010
SN Temporal intervals between stimuli presented in any sensory modality. Use INTERSTIMULUS INTERVAL in conditioning contexts.
B Stimulus Parameters 67
N Interstimulus Interval 67
Intertrial Interval 73
R Reinforcement Delay 85

Stimulus Novelty 73
PN 1493 **SC** 50020
SN New, unexpected, or unfamiliar quality of a stimulus.
UF Novel Stimuli
B Stimulus Parameters 67
R Neophobia 85

Stimulus Offset 85
PN 47 **SC** 50023
B Stimulus Parameters 67

Stimulus Onset 82
PN 326 **SC** 50025
B Stimulus Parameters 67

Stimulus Parameters 67
PN 4398 **SC** 50030
SN Applied when quantifiable or descriptive characteristics of stimuli in a study are emphasized. Use a more specific term if possible.
UF Parameters (Stimulus)
N ↓ Size 73
Spatial Frequency 82
Stimulus Attenuation 73

Stimulus Parameters — (cont'd)
N Stimulus Complexity 71
Stimulus Duration 73
Stimulus Frequency 73
Stimulus Intensity 67
↓ Stimulus Intervals 73
Stimulus Novelty 73
Stimulus Offset 85
Stimulus Onset 82
Stimulus Salience 73
Stimulus Similarity 67
Stimulus Variability 73
Temporal Frequency 85
R Acoustics 97
↓ Stimulation 67

Stimulus Pattern
Use Stimulus Variability

Stimulus Presentation Methods 73
PN 2141 **SC** 50050
SN Methodological, procedural, or technical aspects of stimulus presentation. Use a more specific term if possible, e.g., VISUAL STIMULATION for visual stimulus presentation.
B Experimental Methods 67
N Stereoscopic Presentation 73
Tachistoscopic Presentation 73
R Pictorial Stimuli 78
↓ Stimulation 67
Verbal Stimuli 82

Stimulus Salience 73
PN 716 **SC** 50060
SN Relative prominence or distinctiveness of a stimulus.
UF Salience (Stimulus)
B Stimulus Parameters 67
R Isolation Effect 73

Stimulus Similarity 67
PN 1862 **SC** 50070
SN Conceptual or physical resemblance of two or more stimuli.
UF Similarity (Stimulus)
B Stimulus Parameters 67

Stimulus Variability 73
PN 1242 **SC** 50080
UF Stimulus Pattern
Variability (Stimulus)
B Stimulus Parameters 67

Stipends
Use Educational Financial Assistance

Stochastic Modeling 73
PN 366 **SC** 50100
SN Statistical modeling for sequences of events whose probabilities are constantly changing.
B Simulation 67
N Markov Chains 73
R Chaos Theory 97
Information Theory 67
↓ Mathematical Modeling 73
Time Series 85

Stomach 73
PN 117 **SC** 50120
B Gastrointestinal System 73

Storytelling 88
PN 607 **SC** 50125
B Verbal Communication 67
R Creative Writing 94
Folklore 91
Myths 67
Narratives 97

Storytelling Technique
Use Mutual Storytelling Technique

Strabismus [73]
PN 136 **SC** 50140
UF Crossed Eyes
B Eye Disorders [73]
R Amblyopia [73]
Eye Convergence [82]

Strain Differences (Animal)
Use Animal Strain Differences

Stranger Reactions [88]
PN 135 **SC** 50148
SN Emotional or behavioral responses to unfamiliar persons. Used for all age groups.
UF Fear of Strangers
Xenophobia
B Interpersonal Interaction [67]
R Attachment Behavior [85]
↓ Emotional Responses [67]
Familiarity [67]
↓ Fear [67]
Separation Anxiety [73]
↓ Social Perception [67]

Strategies [67]
PN 3815 **SC** 50150
SN Methods, techniques, or tactics used in accomplishing a given goal or task.
N ↓ Learning Strategies [91]
R ↓ Cognitive Processes [67]
Guessing [73]
↓ Learning [67]
Note Taking [91]

Strategies (Learning)
Use Learning Strategies

Strength (Physical)
Use Physical Strength

Stress [67]
PN 12101 **SC** 50170
SN Refers to the emotional, psychological, or physical effects as well as the sources of agitation, strain, tension, or pressure. Compare DISTRESS. Used for both human and animal populations.
N Environmental Stress [73]
Occupational Stress [73]
Physiological Stress [67]
Psychological Stress [73]
Social Stress [73]
Stress Reactions [73]
R Adjustment Disorders [94]
↓ Adrenal Cortex Hormones [73]
↓ Anxiety [67]
Caregiver Burden [94]
↓ Crises [71]
↓ Deprivation [67]
↓ Disasters [73]
Distress [73]
↓ Endurance [73]
Family Crises [73]
Identity Crisis [73]
Natural Disasters [73]
Organizational Crises [73]
Stress Management [85]

Stress Management [85]
PN 980 **SC** 50175
SN Techniques or services designed to alleviate the effects and/or causes of stress.
B Management [67]
R Anxiety Management [97]
↓ Behavior Modification [73]

Stress Management — (cont'd)
R ↓ Cognitive Techniques [85]
↓ Stress [67]
↓ Treatment [67]

Stress Reactions [73]
PN 3261 **SC** 50180
SN Reactions to stressful events in everyday life or in experimental settings. Differentiate from POSTTRAUMATIC STRESS DISORDER which refers to reactions that seriously impair a person's functioning.
UF Crisis (Reactions to)
B Stress [67]
R Adjustment Disorders [94]
Cardiovascular Reactivity [94]
Coronary Prone Behavior [82]
Posttraumatic Stress Disorder [85]
Psychological Endurance [73]

Striate Cortex
Use Visual Cortex

Strikes [73]
PN 100 **SC** 50190
R Labor Management Relations [67]

Stroboscopic Movement
Use Apparent Movement

Stroke (Cerebrum)
Use Cerebrovascular Accidents

Strong Vocational Interest Blank [67]
PN 208 **SC** 50220
B Occupational Interest Measures [73]

Stroop Color Word Test [73]
PN 238 **SC** 50250
B Perceptual Measures [73]
R Stroop Effect [88]

Stroop Effect [88]
PN 190 **SC** 50255
SN Interference in information or perceptual processing due to presentation of stimuli that are contradictory in different dimensions as a measure of cognitive control, e.g., stimulus word "red" printed in the color green.
R Cognitive Discrimination [73]
↓ Interference (Learning) [67]
↓ Perceptual Discrimination [73]
Stimulus Ambiguity [67]
Stroop Color Word Test [73]

Structural Equation Modeling [94]
PN 103 **SC** 50257
B Mathematical Modeling [73]
R Causal Analysis [94]
↓ Factor Analysis [67]
Factor Structure [85]

Structuralism [73]
PN 125 **SC** 50260
B History of Psychology [67]

Structured Overview
Use Advance Organizers

Strychnine [73]
PN 106 **SC** 50270
B Alkaloids [73]
Analeptic Drugs [73]

Student Activism [73]
PN 209 **SC** 50280

Student Activism — (cont'd)
UF Activism (Student)
Protest (Student)
Student Protest
B Activist Movements [73]
R Social Demonstrations [73]

Student Adjustment
Use School Adjustment

Student Admission Criteria [73]
PN 599 **SC** 50290
UF Admission Criteria (Student)
R Academic Aptitude [73]
↓ Education [67]
↓ Entrance Examinations [73]

Student Attitudes [67]
PN 12095 **SC** 50300
SN Attitudes of, not toward, students.
B Attitudes [67]
Student Characteristics [82]
R ↓ Education [67]
School Phobia [73]
School Refusal [94]

Student Attrition [91]
PN 101 **SC** 50301
SN Reduction in students enrolled in school as a result of transfers or dropouts.
B School Enrollment [73]
R School Attendance [73]
↓ School Dropouts [67]
School Expulsion [73]
School Leavers [88]
School Retention [94]
↓ Students [67]

Student Characteristics [82]
PN 2566 **SC** 50303
SN Distinguishing traits or qualities of a student.
N Student Attitudes [67]
R ↓ Education [67]
↓ Students [67]

Student Personnel Services [78]
PN 1178 **SC** 50305
SN Services offered by schools, colleges, or universities related to health, housing, employment, or other student concerns.
R ↓ Counseling [67]
↓ Education [67]
Educational Counseling [67]
Educational Financial Assistance [73]
↓ Mental Health Services [78]
Occupational Guidance [67]
School Counseling [82]

Student Protest
Use Student Activism

Student Records [78]
PN 58 **SC** 50315
UF Academic Records
R ↓ Education [67]

Student Teachers [73]
PN 1153 **SC** 50320
SN Students engaged in practice teaching under the supervision of a cooperating master teacher as partial fulfillment of an education degree.
B Teachers [67]
R Cooperating Teachers [78]
Education Students [82]
Preservice Teachers [82]

Student Teaching [73]
PN 238 **SC** 50330

Student Teaching — (cont'd)
SN College students teaching under the supervision of a regular teacher in a real school situation. Part of the graduation requirement for education majors.
UF Teaching Internship
B Teacher Education [67]
R Cooperating Teachers [78]

Students [67]
PN 4629 **SC** 50340
SN Persons attending school. Application of a student term is mandatory in educational contexts. Use a more specific term if possible.
N Business Students [73]
Classmates [73]
↓ College Students [67]
Dental Students [73]
↓ Elementary School Students [67]
Foreign Students [73]
Graduate Students [67]
High School Students [67]
Junior High School Students [71]
Kindergarten Students [73]
Law Students [78]
Medical Students [67]
Postgraduate Students [73]
↓ Preschool Students [82]
Reentry Students [85]
Seminarians [73]
Special Education Students [73]
Transfer Students [73]
Vocational School Students [73]
R ↓ Education [67]
School Retention [94]
Student Attrition [91]
↓ Student Characteristics [82]

Students T Test
Use T Test

Studies (Followup)
Use Followup Studies

Studies (Longitudinal)
Use Longitudinal Studies

Study Habits [73]
PN 1400 **SC** 50380
UF Study Skills
R Advance Organizers [85]
↓ Education [67]
Homework [88]
↓ Learning Strategies [91]
Note Taking [91]
Test Taking [85]
Time Management [94]

Study Skills
Use Study Habits

Stuttering [67]
PN 1841 **SC** 50390
SN Use STUTTERING or STAMMERING to access references from 67–81 and 73–81, respectively.
UF Stammering
B Speech Disorders [67]

Subconscious [73]
PN 66 **SC** 50410
B Psychoanalytic Personality Factors [73]

Subcortical Lesions
Use Brain Lesions

Subculture (Anthropological) [73]
PN 388 **SC** 50430

Subculture (Anthropological) — (cont'd)
UF Hippies
B Culture (Anthropological) [67]

Subcutaneous Injections [73]
PN 30 **SC** 50440
B Injections [73]

Subjectivity [94]
PN 35 **SC** 50450
SN Use OBJECTIVITY to access references from 73-93.
B Personality Traits [67]
R Objectivity [73]

Sublimation [73]
PN 51 **SC** 50460
B Defense Mechanisms [67]

Subliminal Perception [73]
PN 257 **SC** 50470
SN Perceptual response to a stimulus that is below the threshold for conscious detection.
B Perception [67]
R Subliminal Stimulation [85]

Subliminal Stimulation [85]
PN 204 **SC** 50475
SN Below-threshold stimulation.
B Stimulation [67]
R Subliminal Perception [73]

Submarines [73]
PN 23 **SC** 50480
B Water Transportation [73]

Submissiveness
Use Obedience

Submucous Plexus
Use Autonomic Ganglia

Substance Abuse
Use Drug Abuse

Substance Abuse Prevention
Use Drug Abuse Prevention

Substance P [85]
PN 188 **SC** 50527
B Neurokinins [97]
Neurotransmitters [85]
Peptides [73]

Substantia Nigra [94]
PN 46 **SC** 50530
SN Use MESENCEPHALON to access references from 73-93.
B Mesencephalon [73]
R ↓ Basal Ganglia [73]

Subtests [73]
PN 1035 **SC** 50540
B Measurement [67]
R ↓ Testing Methods [67]

Suburban Environments [67]
PN 497 **SC** 50550
B Social Environments [73]

Subvocalization [73]
PN 87 **SC** 50555
SN Covert speech behavior which involves movement of the tongue, mouth, and larynx without producing audible sounds.
B Vocalization [67]
R Self Talk [88]

Success
Use Achievement

Successive Contrast
Use Afterimage

Succinylcholine [73]
PN 12 **SC** 50580
B Muscle Relaxing Drugs [73]
R ↓ Choline [73]

Sucking [78]
PN 294 **SC** 50585
B Motor Processes [67]
R Animal Drinking Behavior [73]
Animal Feeding Behavior [73]
↓ Drinking Behavior [78]
↓ Food Intake [67]
Weaning [73]

Sudan [88]
PN 21 **SC** 50586
B Africa [67]

Sudden Infant Death [82]
PN 100 **SC** 50587
SN Unexpected death of an apparently healthy infant during sleep.
UF Crib Death
R ↓ Apnea [73]
↓ Death and Dying [67]
Sleep Apnea [91]
↓ Syndromes [73]

Suffering [73]
PN 210 **SC** 50590
B Emotional States [73]
R Distress [73]
Grief [73]
↓ Pain [67]
Torture [88]

Suffocation
Use Anoxia

Sugars [73]
PN 657 **SC** 50600
B Carbohydrates [73]
N ↓ Glucose [73]
R Saccharin [73]

Suggestibility [67]
PN 443 **SC** 50610
B Consciousness Disturbances [73]
Personality Traits [67]
R Catalepsy [73]
False Memory [97]
↓ Hysteria [67]
↓ Interpersonal Influences [67]
Posthypnotic Suggestions [94]

Suicidal Ideation [91]
PN 448 **SC** 50605
SN Thoughts of or an unusual preoccupation with suicide.
B Ideation [73]
R Attempted Suicide [73]
↓ Suicide [67]

Suicide [67]
PN 5382 **SC** 50620
B Self Destructive Behavior [85]
N Assisted Suicide [97]
R Attempted Suicide [73]
↓ Death and Dying [67]
↓ Mental Disorders [67]
Psychological Autopsy [88]

Suicide — (cont'd)
R Suicidal Ideation [91]
Suicide Prevention [73]

Suicide (Attempted)
Use Attempted Suicide

Suicide Prevention [73]
PN 639 **SC** 50640
B Crisis Intervention [73]
Prevention [73]
R Attempted Suicide [73]
↓ Suicide [67]
Suicide Prevention Centers [73]

Suicide Prevention Centers [73]
PN 78 **SC** 50650
B Community Facilities [73]
Crisis Intervention Services [73]
Mental Health Programs [73]
R Community Mental Health Centers [73]
Hot Line Services [73]
↓ Prevention [73]
Suicide Prevention [73]

Sulpiride [73]
PN 305 **SC** 50660
B Antidepressant Drugs [71]
Antiemetic Drugs [73]
Dopamine Antagonists [82]
Neuroleptic Drugs [73]

Summer Camps (Recreation) [73]
PN 112 **SC** 50670
UF Day Camps (Recreation)
Recreational Day Camps
B Recreation [67]
R Camping [73]
Vacationing [73]

Superego [73]
PN 241 **SC** 50690
B Psychoanalytic Personality Factors [73]
N Conscience [67]

Superintendents (School)
Use School Superintendents

Superior Colliculus [73]
PN 462 **SC** 50700
B Mesencephalon [73]

Superiority (Emotional)
Use Emotional Superiority

Superstitions [73]
PN 121 **SC** 50720
B Social Influences [67]
R Astrology [73]
↓ Attitudes [67]
Irrational Beliefs [82]
↓ Parapsychological Phenomena [73]
↓ Religious Beliefs [73]
Taboos [73]

Supervising Teachers
Use Cooperating Teachers

Supervision (Professional)
Use Professional Supervision

Supervisor Employee Interaction [97]
PN 0 **SC** 50729
UF Employee Supervisor Interaction
Manager Employee Interaction
B Employee Interaction [88]

Supervisor Employee Interaction — (cont'd)
R Labor Management Relations [67]
↓ Management Methods [73]
↓ Management Personnel [73]
Mentor [85]
↓ Personnel Management [73]

Supervisors
Use Management Personnel

Support Groups [91]
PN 523 **SC** 50740
SN Groups, organizations, or institutions providing social and emotional support to an individual. Consider SOCIAL SUPPORT NETWORKS to access references from 82-90. Compare SOCIAL NETWORKS and SELF HELP TECHNIQUES.
N ↓ Twelve Step Programs [97]
R ↓ Community Services [67]
↓ Counseling [67]
Employee Assistance Programs [85]
Group Counseling [73]
↓ Group Psychotherapy [67]
↓ Mental Health Services [78]
Outreach Programs [97]
↓ Rehabilitation [67]
↓ Self Help Techniques [82]
↓ Social Networks [94]
↓ Social Services [82]
Social Support Networks [82]

Supported Employment [94]
PN 56 **SC** 50745
SN Competitive employment in an integrated setting for persons with disabilities who require ongoing support to perform their jobs.
B Vocational Rehabilitation [67]
R Community Mental Health Services [78]
Disabled Personnel [97]
Employability [73]
↓ Employee Skills [73]
↓ Employment Status [82]
Independent Living Programs [91]
↓ Personnel Management [73]
Sheltered Workshops [67]
Work Adjustment Training [91]

Supportive Psychotherapy [97]
PN 0 **SC** 50750
SN Psychotherapy aimed at supporting or reinforcing strengths and coping mechanisms, rather than interpreting or uncovering deeper psychological conflicts. May entail guidance, reassurance, advice, encouragement, and assistance. Use PSYCHOTHERAPY to access references from 73–96.
B Psychotherapy [67]
R Expressive Psychotherapy [73]

Suppression (Conditioned)
Use Conditioned Suppression

Suppression (Defense Mechanism) [73]
PN 47 **SC** 50770
B Defense Mechanisms [67]
R Forgetting [73]
Repression (Defense Mechanism) [67]

Surgeons [73]
PN 92 **SC** 50780
UF Neurosurgeons
B Physicians [67]
R Gynecologists [73]
Neurologists [73]
Obstetricians [78]
Pathologists [73]

Surgery [71]
PN 1422 **SC** 50790

Surgery — (cont'd)
UF Circumcision
Operation (Surgery)
B Medical Sciences [67]
Physical Treatment Methods [73]
N ↓ Amputation [73]
Cochlear Implants [94]
Colostomy [73]
Dental Surgery [73]
↓ Endocrine Gland Surgery [73]
Heart Surgery [73]
Hysterectomy [73]
Induced Abortion [71]
↓ Neurosurgery [73]
Organ Transplantation [73]
Plastic Surgery [73]
Sex Change [88]
↓ Stereotaxic Techniques [73]
Vasectomy [73]
R Afferent Stimulation [73]
Biopsy [73]
↓ Body Image Disturbances [73]
↓ Lesions [67]
Postsurgical Complications [73]

Surgical Complications
Use Postsurgical Complications

Surgical Patients [73]
PN 1152 **SC** 50810
B Patients [67]

Surinam [91]
PN 2 **SC** 50815
B South America [67]

Surrogate Parents (Humans) [73]
PN 87 **SC** 50820
B Parents [67]
R Foster Parents [73]

Surveys [67]
PN 1716 **SC** 50830
B Measurement [67]
N Consumer Surveys [73]
Mail Surveys [94]
Telephone Surveys [94]
R Data Collection [82]
Likert Scales [94]
↓ Methodology [67]
Needs Assessment [85]
↓ Questionnaires [67]

Survival Instinct
Use Self Preservation

Survivors [94]
PN 125 **SC** 50850
SN Family members, significant others, or individuals surviving traumatic life events. Not used as a general population type identifier.
N Holocaust Survivors [88]

Susceptibility (Disorders) [73]
PN 696 **SC** 50880
SN Vulnerability to mental or physical disorders due to genetic, immunologic, or other characteristics. Consider also PREDISPOSITION.
R At Risk Populations [85]
Biological Markers [91]
Coronary Prone Behavior [82]
↓ Disorders [67]
↓ Mental Disorders [67]
↓ Physical Disorders [97]
Predisposition [73]
Premorbidity [78]

Susceptibility (Hypnotic)
Use Hypnotic Susceptibility

Suspension (School)
Use School Suspension

Suspicion 73
PN 80 **SC** 50910
UF Distrust
B Emotional States 73
R Doubt 73
Uncertainty 91

Sustained Attention 97
PN 0 **SC** 50915
SN Focusing or attending to one or more stimuli over an extended period.
B Attention 67
N Attention Span 73
Concentration 82
Vigilance 67

Swallowing 88
PN 58 **SC** 50920
B Motor Processes 67
R Digestion 73

Swaziland 91
PN 7 **SC** 50925
B Africa 67

Sweat 73
PN 28 **SC** 50930
UF Perspiration
B Body Fluids 73
R Sweating 73

Sweating 73
PN 51 **SC** 50940
B Secretion (Gland) 73
R ↓ Skin Disorders 73
Sweat 73

Sweden 73
PN 1027 **SC** 50950
B Scandinavia 78

Sweetness
Use Taste Perception

Swimming 73
PN 478 **SC** 50970
B Motor Processes 67
Recreation 67
Sports 67

Switzerland 73
PN 251 **SC** 50980
B Europe 73

Syllables 73
PN 584 **SC** 50990
B Phonology 73
R Consonants 73
Phonetics 67
Vowels 73

Syllogistic Reasoning
Use Inductive Deductive Reasoning

Symbiosis (Biological)
Use Biological Symbiosis

Symbiotic Infantile Psychosis 73
PN 18 **SC** 51020

Symbiotic Infantile Psychosis — (cont'd)
B Childhood Psychosis 67
R Childhood Schizophrenia 67
Early Infantile Autism 73
Mother Child Relations 67

Symbolic Interactionism 88
PN 77 **SC** 51025
SN Sociological theory that assumes that self concept is created through interpretation of symbolic gestures, words, actions, and appearances expressed by others during social interaction.
R Role Taking 82
↓ Self Concept 67
↓ Social Interaction 67
Sociolinguistics 85
↓ Sociology 67

Symbolism 67
PN 1694 **SC** 51030
R ↓ Communication 67
↓ Figurative Language 85
↓ Language 67
Metaphor 82
↓ Semiotics 85

Sympathectomy 73
PN 41 **SC** 51050
B Neurosurgery 73
R ↓ Psychosurgery 73

Sympathetic Nervous System 73
PN 229 **SC** 51060
B Autonomic Nervous System 67
N Baroreceptors 73
R ↓ Adrenergic Blocking Drugs 73
↓ Adrenergic Drugs 73
↓ Sympatholytic Drugs 73
↓ Sympathomimetic Drugs 73

Sympatholytic Drugs 73
PN 21 **SC** 51080
UF Antiadrenergic Drugs
B Drugs 67
N Hydralazine 73
Reserpine 67
R ↓ Adrenergic Blocking Drugs 73
↓ Sympathetic Nervous System 73
↓ Sympathomimetic Drugs 73

Sympathomimetic Amines 73
PN 11 **SC** 51090
B Amines 73
Sympathomimetic Drugs 73
N ↓ Amphetamine 67
↓ Catecholamines 73
Dextroamphetamine 73
Ephedrine 73
Methoxamine 73
Phenmetrazine 73
Tyramine 73

Sympathomimetic Drugs 73
PN 89 **SC** 51100
B Drugs 67
N Fenfluramine 73
Isoproterenol 73
↓ Sympathomimetic Amines 73
R ↓ Adrenergic Drugs 73
Prostaglandins 82
↓ Sympathetic Nervous System 73
↓ Sympatholytic Drugs 73

Sympathy 73
PN 78 **SC** 51110
B Emotional States 73

Symposia
Use Professional Meetings and Symposia

Symptom Checklists 91
PN 102 **SC** 51124
B Measurement 67
R ↓ Diagnosis 67
Health Complaints 97
Psychiatric Symptoms 97
↓ Screening 82
↓ Symptoms 67

Symptom Prescription
Use Paradoxical Techniques

Symptom Remission 73
PN 51 **SC** 51130
B Remission (Disorders) 73
R Psychiatric Symptoms 97
↓ Symptoms 67

Symptoms 67
PN 9857 **SC** 51140
N Acting Out 67
Anhedonia 85
Anoxia 73
Aphagia 73
Apraxia 73
↓ Asthenia 73
Ataxia 73
Aura 73
Automatism 73
Body Rocking 73
Catalepsy 73
Catatonia 73
Coma 73
↓ Convulsions 67
Delirium 73
Depersonalization 73
Distractibility 73
↓ Dyskinesia 73
↓ Dyspnea 73
Extrapyramidal Symptoms 94
Fatigue 67
↓ Headache 73
Hematoma 73
↓ Hemorrhage 73
Hyperglycemia 85
Hyperkinesis 73
Hyperphagia 73
Hyperthermia 73
Hyperventilation 73
Hypoglycemia 73
Hypothermia 73
Insomnia 73
Nausea 73
Obesity 73
↓ Pain 67
Positive and Negative Symptoms 97
Pruritus 73
Psychiatric Symptoms 97
↓ Respiratory Distress 73
Restlessness 73
Scratching 73
Shock 67
↓ Spasms 73
Syncope 73
Tics 73
Tremor 73
↓ Underweight 73
Vertigo 73
Vomiting 73
R Akathisia 91
↓ Behavior Disorders 71
Binge Eating 91
Capgras Syndrome 85
↓ Digestive System Disorders 73
↓ Disorders 67

Symptoms — (cont'd)
R ↓ Eating Disorders [97]
Fecal Incontinence [73]
Frigidity [73]
Health Complaints [97]
Hypersomnia [94]
↓ Mental Disorders [67]
↓ Movement Disorders [85]
↓ Nervous System Disorders [67]
Parkinsonism [94]
↓ Physical Disorders [97]
Physiological Correlates [67]
↓ Psychosomatic Disorders [67]
Somatization [94]
Stereotyped Behavior [73]
Symptom Checklists [91]
Symptom Remission [73]
Urinary Incontinence [73]
Wandering Behavior [91]

Synapses [73]
PN 740 **SC** 51150
B Nerve Endings [73]

Syncope [73]
PN 56 **SC** 51160
UF Fainting
B Blood Pressure Disorders [73]
Symptoms [67]
R Shock [67]
Vertigo [73]

Syndromes [73]
PN 1960 **SC** 51170
N Acquired Immune Deficiency Syndrome [88]
Addisons Disease [73]
Aspergers Syndrome [91]
Battered Child Syndrome [73]
Capgras Syndrome [85]
Chronic Fatigue Syndrome [97]
Creutzfeldt Jakob Syndrome [94]
Crying Cat Syndrome [73]
Cushings Syndrome [73]
Delirium Tremens [73]
Downs Syndrome [67]
Fetal Alcohol Syndrome [85]
Fragile X Syndrome [94]
Klinefelters Syndrome [73]
Menieres Disease [73]
Neuroleptic Malignant Syndrome [88]
↓ Organic Brain Syndromes [73]
Prader Willi Syndrome [91]
Rett Syndrome [94]
↓ Senile Dementia [73]
Testicular Feminization Syndrome [73]
Turners Syndrome [73]
Wernickes Syndrome [73]
R ↓ Disorders [67]
Irritable Bowel Syndrome [91]
↓ Mental Disorders [67]
Myofascial Pain [91]
↓ Physical Disorders [97]
Sudden Infant Death [82]

Synonyms [73]
PN 95 **SC** 51190
B Semantics [67]
Vocabulary [67]
R Words (Phonetic Units) [67]

Syntax [71]
PN 2046 **SC** 51220

Syntax — (cont'd)
SN Study and rules of the relation of morphemes to one another as expressions of ideas and as structural components of sentences; the study and science of sentence construction; and, the actual grouping and specific combination and relationship of words in a sentence. Compare GRAMMAR and SENTENCE STRUCTURE.
B Grammar [67]
N ↓ Form Classes (Language) [73]
R Discourse Analysis [97]
Inflection [73]
Morphology (Language) [73]
↓ Phonology [73]
Phrases [73]
↓ Semantics [67]
Sentence Structure [73]
Transformational Generative Grammar [73]

Synthetic Speech [73]
PN 279 **SC** 51230
SN Sounds having similar characteristics and functional properties of natural speech but which are made by means other than natural vocalization mechanisms (e.g., computer-generated speech sounds).
B Speech Processing (Mechanical) [73]

Syphilis [73]
PN 36 **SC** 51240
B Venereal Diseases [73]
N Neurosyphilis [73]
R ↓ Congenital Disorders [73]
General Paresis [73]

Syria [88]
PN 3 **SC** 51245
B Asia [73]
R Middle East [78]

Systematic Desensitization Therapy [73]
PN 1481 **SC** 51250
UF Desensitization (Systematic)
B Behavior Therapy [67]
Exposure Therapy [97]
R Progressive Relaxation Therapy [78]
Reciprocal Inhibition Therapy [73]
↓ Relaxation Therapy [78]

Systems [67]
PN 584 **SC** 51270
SN Conceptually broad array term referring to interrelated elements acting as or constituting a unified whole. Use a more specific term if possible.
N ↓ Anatomical Systems [73]
Caste System [73]
↓ Communication Systems [73]
↓ Expert Systems [91]
Human Machine Systems [97]
Information Systems [91]
Number Systems [73]
↓ Political Economic Systems [73]
R ↓ Computer Software [67]
↓ Computers [67]
Human Machine Systems Design [97]
Person Environment Fit [91]
Systems Analysis [73]
Systems Theory [88]

Systems Analysis [73]
PN 447 **SC** 51260
B Analysis [67]
R Computer Programing [94]
Human Machine Systems [97]
Human Machine Systems Design [97]
↓ Systems [67]
Systems Theory [88]
Task Analysis [67]

Systems Theory [88]
PN 1319 **SC** 51265
SN Examination of organizations, structures, or procedures from a macroscopic perspective that integrates constituent parts into a whole.
B Theories [67]
R Biopsychosocial Approach [91]
↓ Systems [67]
Systems Analysis [73]

Systolic Pressure [73]
PN 255 **SC** 51280
B Blood Pressure [67]

Szondi Test [73]
PN 33 **SC** 51290
B Projective Personality Measures [73]

T Groups
Use Human Relations Training

T Mazes [73]
PN 42 **SC** 51310
B Mazes [67]

T Test [73]
PN 85 **SC** 51320
UF Students T Test
B Parametric Statistical Tests [73]
R ↓ Central Tendency Measures [73]
Statistical Significance [73]

Taboos [73]
PN 101 **SC** 51330
B Social Influences [67]
R Animism [73]
Ethnology [67]
↓ Rites of Passage [73]
Superstitions [73]
Transcultural Psychiatry [73]

Tachistoscopes [73]
PN 39 **SC** 51340
SN Apparatus used in experimental studies for presentation of visual stimuli for controlled stimulus intervals, intensities, and durations.
B Apparatus [67]

Tachistoscopic Presentation [73]
PN 428 **SC** 51350
B Stimulus Presentation Methods [73]
Visual Stimulation [73]

Tachycardia [73]
PN 62 **SC** 51360
UF Rapid Heart Rate
B Arrhythmias (Heart) [73]
R Hyperthyroidism [73]

Tactual Discrimination
Use Tactual Perception

Tactual Displays [73]
PN 80 **SC** 51380
SN Materials or apparatus designed to present information or patterns by means of touch or manipulation. Also, any information or patterns conveyed by such means.
B Displays [67]
Tactual Stimulation [73]

Tactual Maps
Use Mobility Aids

Tactual Perception [67]
PN 1538 **SC** 51390

Tactual Perception — (cont'd)
SN Awareness of the qualities or characteristics of objects, substances, or surfaces by means of touch.
UF Tactual Discrimination
Touch
B Cutaneous Sense [67]
N Texture Perception [82]
Vibrotactile Thresholds [73]
R ↓ Anesthesia (Feeling) [73]
Braille [78]
Physical Contact [82]

Tactual Stimulation [73]
PN 1054 **SC** 51400
SN Perceptual arousal or excitation of an organism by means of touch.
B Somesthetic Stimulation [73]
N Tactual Displays [73]

Tailored Testing
Use Adaptive Testing

Taiwan [73]
PN 520 **SC** 51410
B Asia [73]

Talent
Use Ability

Talented
Use Gifted

Tantrums [73]
PN 48 **SC** 51440
B Behavior Problems [67]
R ↓ Anger [67]
↓ Emotional Control [73]

Tanzania [82]
PN 52 **SC** 51445
B Africa [67]

Tape Recorders [73]
PN 76 **SC** 51450
UF Recorders (Tape)
B Apparatus [67]
N Videotape Recorders [73]

Tardive Dyskinesia [88]
PN 580 **SC** 51460
B Dyskinesia [73]
R ↓ Drug Therapy [67]
↓ Neuroleptic Drugs [73]
↓ Side Effects (Drug) [73]

Task Analysis [67]
PN 1118 **SC** 51470
B Analysis [67]
R Constant Time Delay [97]
Job Analysis [67]
Systems Analysis [73]
Task Complexity [73]

Task Complexity [73]
PN 3054 **SC** 51480
UF Complexity (Task)
Task Difficulty
R Task Analysis [67]

Task Difficulty
Use Task Complexity

Taste Aversion Conditioning
Use Aversion Conditioning

Taste Buds [73]
PN 157 **SC** 51500
B Sense Organs [73]
Sensory Neurons [73]
Tongue [73]
R Chemoreceptors [73]

Taste Discrimination
Use Taste Perception

Taste Perception [67]
PN 2608 **SC** 51520
UF Bitterness
Gustatory Perception
Saltiness
Sourness
Sweetness
Taste Discrimination
B Perception [67]
R ↓ Olfactory Perception [67]

Taste Stimulation [67]
PN 717 **SC** 51530
B Perceptual Stimulation [73]

Taurine [82]
PN 31 **SC** 51545
SN Suspected neurotransmitter or membrane stabilizer located in the posterior pituitary gland as well as other mammalian tissue.
B Acids [73]
R Bile [73]

Taxation [85]
PN 91 **SC** 51547
R Economy [73]
Government [67]
Income (Economic) [73]

Taxonomies [73]
PN 2144 **SC** 51550
UF Classification Systems
Typologies (General)
R ↓ Psychodiagnostic Typologies [67]

Tay Sachs Disease
Use Amaurotic Familial Idiocy

Taylor Manifest Anxiety Scale [73]
PN 20 **SC** 51570
SN Use MA SCALE (TEST) to access references from 67-72.
B Nonprojective Personality Measures [73]

Tea
Use Beverages (Nonalcoholic)

Teacher Accreditation
Use Accreditation (Education Personnel)

Teacher Aides [73]
PN 115 **SC** 51600
SN Paraprofessional school personnel who assist teachers in the instructional process or other classroom duties.
B Educational Personnel [73]
Paraprofessional Personnel [73]

Teacher Attitudes [67]
PN 7729 **SC** 51610
SN Attitudes of, not toward, teachers.
B Attitudes [67]
Teacher Characteristics [73]
N Teacher Expectations [78]
R Parent School Relationship [82]
Teacher Personality [73]
Teacher Student Interaction [73]

Teacher Characteristics [73]
PN 3779 **SC** 51615
UF Teacher Effectiveness
N ↓ Teacher Attitudes [67]
Teacher Personality [73]
R ↓ Education [67]
Teacher Effectiveness Evaluation [78]
Teacher Expectations [78]
Teacher Student Interaction [73]
↓ Teachers [67]
↓ Teaching [67]

Teacher Education [67]
PN 3256 **SC** 51620
UF Teacher Training
B Education [67]
N Inservice Teacher Education [73]
Student Teaching [73]
R Cooperating Teachers [78]
Education Students [82]
Practicum Supervision [78]
Preservice Teachers [82]

Teacher Effectiveness
Use Teacher Characteristics

Teacher Effectiveness Evaluation [78]
PN 1159 **SC** 51625
SN Techniques, materials, or the procedural aspects of judging teachers' performance by peers, students, or others based on stated criteria. Use PERSONNEL EVALUATION and TEACHERS (or a more specific term, e.g., COLLEGE TEACHERS) to access references from 73-77.
B Personnel Evaluation [73]
R Course Evaluation [78]
Educational Quality [97]
↓ Teacher Characteristics [73]

Teacher Expectations [78]
PN 636 **SC** 51627
B Expectations [67]
Teacher Attitudes [67]
R ↓ Teacher Characteristics [73]
Teacher Student Interaction [73]

Teacher Personality [73]
PN 460 **SC** 51630
B Teacher Characteristics [73]
R ↓ Personality [67]
↓ Teacher Attitudes [67]
Teacher Student Interaction [73]

Teacher Recruitment [73]
PN 25 **SC** 51640
SN Process of attracting candidates to the teaching profession or finding teachers to fill vacancies.
UF Recruitment (Teachers)
B Personnel Recruitment [73]

Teacher Student Interaction [73]
PN 3636 **SC** 51650
R Classroom Discipline [73]
↓ Education [67]
↓ Teacher Attitudes [67]
↓ Teacher Characteristics [73]
Teacher Expectations [78]
Teacher Personality [73]

Teacher Tenure [73]
PN 92 **SC** 51670
UF Tenure (Teacher)
B Occupational Tenure [73]
R ↓ Education [67]

Teacher Training
Use Teacher Education

Teachers [67]
PN 6088 SC 51690
UF Classroom Teachers
Instructors
Tutors
B Educational Personnel [73]
N College Teachers [73]
Cooperating Teachers [78]
Elementary School Teachers [73]
High School Teachers [73]
Junior High School Teachers [73]
Preschool Teachers [85]
Preservice Teachers [82]
Resource Teachers [73]
Special Education Teachers [73]
Student Teachers [73]
Vocational Education Teachers [88]
R ↓ Teacher Characteristics [73]

Teaching [67]
PN 2797 SC 51700
UF Classroom Instruction
Instruction
N ↓ Instructional Media [67]
↓ Teaching Methods [67]
R Bilingual Education [78]
Cooperative Learning [94]
Course Evaluation [78]
↓ Education [67]
↓ Teacher Characteristics [73]

Teaching Internship
Use Student Teaching

Teaching Machines [73]
PN 41 SC 51730
SN Mechanical, electronic, or electrically controlled apparatus for the presentation of programed instructional material or texts for independent, self-paced education. Compare COMPUTER ASSISTED INSTRUCTION.
B Instructional Media [67]
R Computer Assisted Instruction [73]
Programed Instruction [67]

Teaching Methods [67]
PN 14253 SC 51740
B Teaching [67]
N Advance Organizers [85]
↓ Audiovisual Instruction [73]
Computer Assisted Instruction [73]
Directed Discussion Method [73]
Discovery Teaching Method [73]
Educational Field Trips [73]
↓ Experiential Learning [97]
Group Instruction [73]
Individualized Instruction [73]
Lecture Method [73]
Lesson Plans [73]
Montessori Method [73]
Nondirected Discussion Method [73]
Open Classroom Method [73]
Programed Instruction [67]
Team Teaching Method [73]
↓ Tutoring [73]
R Constant Time Delay [97]
Cooperative Learning [94]
↓ Education [67]
Educational Therapy [97]
Home Schooling [94]
Initial Teaching Alphabet [73]
Mastery Learning [85]
↓ Nontraditional Education [82]
↓ Prompting [97]
Questioning [82]

Team Teaching Method [73]
PN 104 SC 51750
B Teaching Methods [67]
R Open Classroom Method [73]
Teams [88]

Teams [88]
PN 610 SC 51751
R Athletic Performance [91]
Athletic Training [91]
College Athletes [94]
Cooperative Learning [94]
↓ Group Dynamics [67]
Interdisciplinary Treatment Approach [73]
↓ Management Methods [73]
↓ Personnel [67]
↓ Sports [67]
Team Teaching Method [73]

Technical Education Teachers
Use Vocational Education Teachers

Technical Personnel [78]
PN 313 SC 51755
B Business and Industrial Personnel [67]
N Technical Service Personnel [73]
R ↓ Service Personnel [91]

Technical Schools [73]
PN 155 SC 51760
SN Schools that teach specific job skills, usually at the postsecondary level, often emphasizing underlying sciences and supporting mathematics as well as skills, methods, materials, and processes of a specialized field of technology.
UF Vocational Schools
B Schools [67]

Technical Service Personnel [73]
PN 115 SC 51770
UF Repairmen
B Service Personnel [91]
Technical Personnel [78]
R ↓ Blue Collar Workers [73]
↓ Business and Industrial Personnel [67]
↓ Nonprofessional Personnel [82]

Technology [73]
PN 1353 SC 51805
N Nuclear Technology [85]
R Industrialization [73]
↓ Sciences [67]

Teenage Fathers
Use Adolescent Fathers

Teenage Mothers
Use Adolescent Mothers

Teenage Pregnancy
Use Adolescent Pregnancy

Teenagers
Use Adolescents

Teeth (Anatomy) [73]
PN 173 SC 51820
B Digestive System [67]
R Mouth (Anatomy) [67]

Teeth Grinding
Use Bruxism

Tegmentum [91]
PN 155 SC 51835
UF Ventral Tegmental Area
B Mesencephalon [73]
N Periaqueductal Gray [85]

Telecommunications Media [73]
PN 167 SC 51840
B Communications Media [73]
N Radio [73]
Telephone Systems [73]
↓ Television [67]
Television Advertising [73]
R Teleconferencing [97]
Telemetry [73]

Teleconferencing [97]
PN 0 SC 51845
SN Communication between persons remote from one another by means of a telecommunication system with audio and/or visual links.
UF Computer Conferencing
R ↓ Telecommunications Media [73]
Telephone Systems [73]
↓ Television [67]

Telekinesis
Use Psychokinesis

Telemetry [73]
PN 40 SC 51860
SN Process of measuring and transmitting quantitative information and recording at a remote location.
R ↓ Telecommunications Media [73]

Telencephalon [73]
PN 332 SC 51870
B Forebrain [85]
N ↓ Basal Ganglia [73]
↓ Cerebral Cortex [67]

Telepathy [73]
PN 89 SC 51880
B Parapsychological Phenomena [73]
R ↓ Extrasensory Perception [67]

Telephone Hot Lines
Use Hot Line Services

Telephone Surveys [94]
PN 38 SC 51895
B Surveys [67]
R ↓ Consumer Research [73]
Consumer Surveys [73]
Mail Surveys [94]
↓ Methodology [67]
↓ Questionnaires [67]
Telephone Systems [73]

Telephone Systems [73]
PN 496 SC 51900
B Communication Systems [73]
Telecommunications Media [73]
R Teleconferencing [97]
Telephone Surveys [94]

Televised Instruction [73]
PN 161 SC 51910
B Audiovisual Instruction [73]
R ↓ Educational Audiovisual Aids [73]
Educational Television [67]

Television [67]
PN 1334 SC 51920
B Audiovisual Communications Media [73]
Mass Media [67]
Telecommunications Media [73]
N Closed Circuit Television [73]
Educational Television [67]
Television Advertising [73]
R ↓ Apparatus [67]
↓ News Media [97]

Television — (cont'd)
R Teleconferencing [97]
Video Display Units [85]

Television Advertising [73]
PN 578 SC 51930
UF Commercials
B Advertising [67]
Audiovisual Communications Media [73]
Telecommunications Media [73]
Television [67]

Television Viewing [73]
PN 1473 SC 51940
B Recreation [67]

Temperament
Use Personality

Temperature (Body)
Use Body Temperature

Temperature Effects [67]
PN 1149 SC 51990
UF Thermal Factors
B Environmental Effects [73]
N Cold Effects [73]
Heat Effects [73]
R Atmospheric Conditions [73]
Pollution [73]
Seasonal Variations [73]
Thermal Acclimatization [73]

Temperature Perception [73]
PN 302 SC 52000
B Somesthetic Perception [67]

Tempo [97]
PN 0 SC 52005
R ↓ Music [67]
Music Perception [97]
↓ Rhythm [91]
Speech Rate [73]
Speech Rhythm [73]
↓ Time Perception [67]

Temporal Frequency [85]
PN 343 SC 52015
SN Number of alternating cycles (e.g., patterns of vertical stripes of light and dark light) occurring during a specified time interval. Usually expressed in terms of cycles per second (Hz) as, for example, in sine or square wave visual displays.
B Stimulus Parameters [67]
R Spatial Frequency [82]
Stimulus Frequency [73]
↓ Visual Displays [73]
↓ Visual Stimulation [73]

Temporal Lobe [73]
PN 1317 SC 52010
B Cerebral Cortex [67]
N Auditory Cortex [67]

Temporal Spatial Concept Scale
SN Term discontinued in 1997. Use TEMPORAL SPATIAL CONCEPT SCALE to access references from 73-96.
Use Intelligence Measures

Temporomandibular Joint Syndrome
Use Musculoskeletal Disorders

Temptation [73]
PN 91 SC 52030

Temptation — (cont'd)
B Motivation [67]
R ↓ Incentives [67]
Peer Pressure [94]
↓ Resistance [97]
Self Control [73]

Tendons [73]
PN 11 SC 52050
B Musculoskeletal System [73]

Tennessee Self Concept Scale [73]
PN 45 SC 52060
B Nonprojective Personality Measures [73]

Tennis [73]
PN 151 SC 52070
B Recreation [67]
Sports [67]

Tension Headache
Use Muscle Contraction Headache

Tenure (Occupational)
Use Occupational Tenure

Tenure (Teacher)
Use Teacher Tenure

Teratogens [88]
PN 168 SC 52105
SN Drugs or other agents that cause developmental malformations.
B Hazardous Materials [91]
R ↓ Congenital Disorders [73]
↓ Drugs [67]
↓ Poisons [73]
↓ Prenatal Development [73]
Prenatal Exposure [91]
Thalidomide [73]
Toxicity [73]

Terminal Cancer [73]
PN 274 SC 52110
B Neoplasms [67]
R ↓ Death and Dying [67]
Terminally Ill Patients [73]

Terminally Ill Patients [73]
PN 1081 SC 52120
UF Dying Patients
B Patients [67]
R Advance Directives [94]
Assisted Suicide [97]
↓ Death and Dying [67]
Hospice [82]
Life Sustaining Treatment [97]
Palliative Care [91]
Terminal Cancer [73]

Terminology [91]
PN 176 SC 52125
SN Definitions, analysis, evaluation, or review of individual terms or nomenclature in any field.
N Psychological Terminology [73]
R Concepts [67]
↓ Scientific Communication [73]

Terminology (Psychological)
Use Psychological Terminology

Territoriality [67]
PN 1487 SC 52140
SN Behavioral patterns characteristic of defense or occupation of a territory. Used for both human and animal populations.

Territoriality — (cont'd)
UF Habitat Selection
B Animal Ethology [67]
R ↓ Animal Aggressive Behavior [73]
Animal Courtship Displays [73]
Animal Dominance [73]
Animal Homing [91]
Animal Scent Marking [85]
Boundaries (Psychological) [97]

Terrorism [82]
PN 141 SC 52150
SN Violence or threats of violence in order to achieve political, economic, or social goals.
B Antisocial Behavior [71]
R ↓ Crime [67]
Hostages [88]
Political Revolution [73]
↓ Radical Movements [73]
↓ Violence [73]

Test Administration [73]
PN 1483 SC 52180
SN Instructions, timing, preparation of test materials, testing conditions, mode of presentation, and other factors involved in the administration of tests.
UF Administration (Test)
B Testing [67]
R Group Testing [73]
Individual Testing [73]
↓ Testing Methods [67]

Test Anxiety [67]
PN 1709 SC 52190
SN Fear or tension in anticipation of formal examination frequently resulting in performance decrement and contributing to measurement error.
B Anxiety [67]
R ↓ Anxiety Disorders [97]
Test Taking [85]

Test Bias [85]
PN 271 SC 52196
SN Any significant differential performance on tests by different populations (e.g., males versus females) as a result of test characteristics which are irrelevant to the variable or construct being measured.
UF Item Bias
B Test Construction [73]
Testing [67]
N Cultural Test Bias [73]
R Error of Measurement [85]
Response Bias [67]

Test Bias (Cultural)
Use Cultural Test Bias

Test Coaching [97]
PN 0 SC 52205
R ↓ Practice [67]
Test Taking [85]
↓ Testing [67]
Testwiseness [78]
↓ Tutoring [73]

Test Construction [73]
PN 7917 SC 52210
SN Planning, selection, writing, editing, and statistical analysis of test items, and design of instructions for test administration and scoring.
N Content Analysis (Test) [67]
Difficulty Level (Test) [73]
Item Analysis (Test) [67]
Item Content (Test) [73]
↓ Test Bias [85]
Test Forms [88]
Test Items [73]

Test Construction — (cont'd)
N Test Reliability [73]
Test Standardization [73]
Test Validity [73]
R Adaptive Testing [85]
↓ Experimental Design [67]
↓ Measurement [67]

Test Difficulty
Use Difficulty Level (Test)

Test Equating
Use Score Equating

Test Forms [88]
PN 1118 **SC** 52214
SN Includes different versions or schedules of a test.
B Test Construction [73]
Testing [67]
R Item Content (Test) [73]

Test Interpretation [85]
PN 466 **SC** 52215
SN Judgment and explanation of the significance, meaning, application, or limitation of an assessment instrument and an obtained score or scores.
B Testing [67]
R Cultural Test Bias [73]
Cutting Scores [85]
Psychometrics [67]
↓ Scoring (Testing) [73]
Statistical Weighting [85]
↓ Test Scores [67]
Test Validity [73]

Test Items [73]
PN 919 **SC** 52220
B Test Construction [73]
Testing [67]
R Item Analysis (Statistical) [73]
Item Analysis (Test) [67]
Item Content (Test) [73]

Test Normalization
Use Test Standardization

Test Norms [73]
PN 1032 **SC** 52240
UF Norms (Test)
R ↓ Measurement [67]
Standardized Tests [85]

Test Reliability [73]
PN 8992 **SC** 52250
SN Consistency, dependability, and reproducibility of test scores, expressed as a reliability coefficient.
UF Internal Consistency
Reliability (Test)
B Test Construction [73]
Testing [67]
R Error of Measurement [85]
Interrater Reliability [82]
Test Standardization [73]

Test Scores [67]
PN 3365 **SC** 52260
SN Quantitative values or evaluations assigned to describe test performance of individuals. Compare SCORING (TESTING) and GRADING (EDUCATIONAL).
UF Scores (Test)
N Cutting Scores [85]
Intelligence Quotient [67]
Standard Scores [85]
R Error of Measurement [85]

Test Scores — (cont'd)
R Item Response Theory [85]
↓ Measurement [67]
↓ Scoring (Testing) [73]
Statistical Weighting [85]
Test Interpretation [85]

Test Standardization [73]
PN 644 **SC** 52270
UF Normalization (Test)
Standardization (Test)
Test Normalization
B Test Construction [73]
Testing [67]
R Standardized Tests [85]
Test Reliability [73]
Test Validity [73]

Test Taking [85]
PN 382 **SC** 52275
SN Strategies, attitudes, behaviors, or other factors associated with taking any type of test.
R Cheating [73]
Guessing [73]
Response Bias [67]
Study Habits [73]
Test Anxiety [67]
Test Coaching [97]
↓ Testing [67]
Testwiseness [78]

Test Tube Babies
Use Reproductive Technology

Test Validity [73]
PN 14331 **SC** 52280
SN Extent to which a test measures what it was designed to measure. Includes criterion-oriented and content validity.
UF Validity (Test)
B Test Construction [73]
Testing [67]
R Concurrent Validity [88]
Construct Validity [82]
Factorial Validity [73]
Predictive Validity [73]
Test Interpretation [85]
Test Standardization [73]

Testes [73]
PN 131 **SC** 52290
B Gonads [73]
Male Genitalia [73]

Testes Disorders
Use Endocrine Sexual Disorders

Testicular Feminization Syndrome [73]
PN 6 **SC** 52310
UF Feminization Syndrome (Testicular)
B Endocrine Sexual Disorders [73]
Male Genital Disorders [73]
Sex Linked Hereditary Disorders [73]
Syndromes [73]
R Hermaphroditism [73]
Sterility [73]

Testimony (Expert)
Use Expert Testimony

Testing [67]
PN 2915 **SC** 52330
SN Administration of tests, and analysis and interpretation of test scores in order to measure differences between individuals or between test performances of the same individual on different occasions.

Testing — (cont'd)
B Measurement [67]
N Computer Assisted Testing [88]
Content Analysis (Test) [67]
Difficulty Level (Test) [73]
↓ Educational Measurement [67]
Item Analysis (Test) [67]
Item Content (Test) [73]
Item Response Theory [85]
Rating [67]
Repeated Measures [85]
Scaling (Testing) [67]
↓ Scoring (Testing) [73]
Test Administration [73]
↓ Test Bias [85]
Test Forms [88]
Test Interpretation [85]
Test Items [73]
Test Reliability [73]
Test Standardization [73]
Test Validity [73]
R ↓ Neuropsychological Assessment [82]
Psychometrics [67]
Test Coaching [97]
Test Taking [85]
Testwiseness [78]

Testing (Job Applicants)
Use Job Applicant Screening

Testing Methods [67]
PN 1017 **SC** 52370
N Adaptive Testing [85]
Cloze Testing [73]
Essay Testing [73]
Forced Choice (Testing Method) [67]
Multiple Choice (Testing Method) [73]
Q Sort Testing Technique [67]
Scaling (Testing) [67]
R ↓ Measurement [67]
Posttesting [73]
Pretesting [73]
Subtests [73]
Test Administration [73]

Testosterone [73]
PN 1629 **SC** 52380
B Androgens [73]

Tests
Use Measurement

Tests (Achievement)
Use Achievement Measures

Tests (Aptitude)
Use Aptitude Measures

Tests (Intelligence)
Use Intelligence Measures

Tests (Personality)
Use Personality Measures

Tests (Statistical)
Use Statistical Tests

Testwiseness [78]
PN 102 **SC** 52415
SN High degree of sophistication in test-taking skills resulting in advantage over others with same knowledge or ability.
R ↓ Measurement [67]
Test Coaching [97]
Test Taking [85]
↓ Testing [67]

Tetrabenazine 73
PN 34 **SC** 52430
B Neuroleptic Drugs 73
Serotonin Antagonists 73

Tetrachoric Correlation 73
PN 10 **SC** 52450
B Statistical Correlation 67

Tetrahydrocannabinol 73
PN 566 **SC** 52470
B Alcohols 67
Cannabinoids 82
R ↓ Cannabis 73
↓ Hallucinogenic Drugs 67
Hashish 73
Marihuana 71

Text Structure 82
PN 1360 **SC** 52473
SN Arrangement of sentence or paragraph segments, concepts, or physical format of reading material.
R Discourse Analysis 97
↓ Prose 73
Reading Materials 73
Sentence Structure 73
↓ Verbal Communication 67

Textbooks 78
PN 675 **SC** 52475
SN Books focusing on principles of a specific subject and used as basis of instruction. Not used as a document type identifier. Use BOOK to access references that are in themselves textbooks. Use TEXTBOOKS when textbooks are the object of discussion or study (e.g., analyses of best format for textbook chapters).
B Books 73
Instructional Media 67
N Programed Textbooks 73
R Reading Materials 73

Texture Perception 82
PN 314 **SC** 52485
SN Perception of the surface characteristics (frequently patterned) or appearance of objects or substances, usually through the visual or haptic senses.
B Tactual Perception 67
Visual Perception 67
R Pattern Discrimination 67

Thailand 73
PN 323 **SC** 52490
B Southeast Asia 73

Thalamic Nuclei 73
PN 317 **SC** 52500
B Thalamus 67

Thalamotomy 73
PN 18 **SC** 52510
B Psychosurgery 73

Thalamus 67
PN 827 **SC** 52520
B Diencephalon 73
N Geniculate Bodies (Thalamus) 73
Thalamic Nuclei 73

Thalidomide 73
PN 11 **SC** 52530
B Amines 73
Hypnotic Drugs 73
Sedatives 73
R ↓ Drug Induced Congenital Disorders 73

Thalidomide — (cont'd)
R Prenatal Exposure 91
Teratogens 88

Thanatology
Use Death Education

Thanatos
Use Death Instinct

Theatre 73
PN 174 **SC** 52540
UF Stage Plays
B Arts 73
N Drama 73

Theft 73
PN 339 **SC** 52550
UF Robbery
Stealing
B Crime 67
N Shoplifting 73

Thematic Apperception Test 67
PN 439 **SC** 52560
B Projective Personality Measures 73

Theology
Use Religion

Theophylline 73
PN 78 **SC** 52580
B Alkaloids 73
Diuretics 73
Enzyme Inhibitors 85
Heart Rate Affecting Drugs 73
Muscle Relaxing Drugs 73
R ↓ Analeptic Drugs 73
Vasodilation 73

Theoretical Interpretation 88
PN 354 **SC** 52582
SN Description or analysis of any particular event, condition, or process from a specific psychological perspective. Usually used in conjunction with other index terms, e.g., humanistic psychology.
UF Psychological Interpretation
N Psychoanalytic Interpretation 67
R ↓ Theories 67

Theoretical Orientation 82
PN 2234 **SC** 52584
SN Adherence to a particular school of thought, theoretical movement, or practice in a scientific or other area of knowledge.
UF Eclectic Psychology
Professional Orientation
R ↓ Clinical Methods Training 73
↓ Psychology Education 78
↓ Psychotherapy 67
↓ Social Sciences 67
↓ Theories 67
↓ Therapist Characteristics 73

Theories 67
PN 13624 **SC** 52590
SN Conceptually broad array term referring to the systematic deductive derivation of secondary principles explaining observed phenomena. Use a more specific term if possible.
N Chaos Theory 97
Communication Theory 73
Constructivism 94
↓ Darwinism 73
Fuzzy Set Theory 91
Game Theory 67
Information Theory 67

Theories — (cont'd)
N Item Response Theory 85
Learning Theory 67
↓ Personality Theory 67
↓ Psychoanalytic Theory 67
Systems Theory 88
Theories of Education 73
Theory of Evolution 67
R Construct Validity 82
↓ Experimentation 67
↓ History of Psychology 67
↓ Hypothesis Testing 73
↓ Theoretical Interpretation 88
Theoretical Orientation 82
Theory Formulation 73
Theory Verification 73

Theories of Education 73
PN 486 **SC** 52587
SN Principles and supporting data concerning the educational process, with application for educational practice.
UF Educational Theory
B Theories 67
R ↓ Education 67

Theory Formulation 73
PN 821 **SC** 52600
SN Advancement of propositions and formulation of hypotheses concerning description, explanation, or interpretation of facts. Applies both to principles of theory formulation and presentation of new theories.
R ↓ Hypothesis Testing 73
↓ Methodology 67
↓ Theories 67
Theory Verification 73

Theory of Evolution 67
PN 1139 **SC** 52610
SN Theories explaining the origins of living organisms and the process by which they evolved into their present forms. For C. Darwin's theory of evolution, use DARWINISM.
UF Evolution (Theory of)
B Theories 67
R ↓ Darwinism 73
Natural Selection 97
Self Preservation 97

Theory Verification 73
PN 1309 **SC** 52620
SN Process of proving or disproving theoretical assumptions using empirical data. Applies both to principles of theory testing and their applications.
UF Verification (of Theories)
R ↓ Hypothesis Testing 73
↓ Methodology 67
↓ Theories 67
Theory Formulation 73

Therapeutic Abortion
Use Induced Abortion

Therapeutic Alliance 94
PN 105 **SC** 52633
UF Working Alliance
B Psychotherapeutic Processes 67
R Psychotherapeutic Transference 67
↓ Treatment 67

Therapeutic Camps 78
PN 114 **SC** 52635
SN Camps, usually for children, staffed by mental health personnel and offering treatment programs as well as outdoor activities fostering personal growth and accomplishment.

Therapeutic Camps — (cont'd)
UF Camps (Therapeutic)
B Treatment Facilities 73
R Recreation Therapy 73
Wilderness Experience 91

Therapeutic Community 67
PN 1149 SC 52640
SN Institutional or residential treatment setting emphasizing social and environmental factors in therapy and management and rehabilitation, usually of psychiatric or drug rehabilitation patients.
B Group Psychotherapy 67
Psychiatric Hospital Programs 67
R Milieu Therapy 88
Sociotherapy 73

Therapeutic Devices (Medical)
Use Medical Therapeutic Devices

Therapeutic Outcomes
Use Treatment Outcomes

Therapeutic Processes 78
PN 3328 SC 52655
SN Experiential, attitudinal, emotional, or behavioral phenomena occurring during the course of treatment. Applies to the patient or therapist (i.e., nurse, doctor, etc.) individually or to their interaction.
UF Dentist Patient Interaction
Nurse Patient Interaction
Physician Patient Interaction
N ↓ Psychotherapeutic Processes 67
R Client Education 85
Patient Abuse 91
Patient Violence 94
Professional Client Sexual Relations 94
Therapist Selection 94
↓ Treatment 67
↓ Treatment Outcomes 82
Treatment Termination 82

Therapeutic Social Clubs 73
PN 57 SC 52660
SN Associations of persons, usually patients or former patients, who engage in regular social activities stressing self-help and psychosocial rehabilitation.
UF Social Clubs (Therapeutic)
B Psychosocial Rehabilitation 73
R ↓ Treatment 67

Therapeutic Techniques (Psychother)
Use Psychotherapeutic Techniques

Therapist Attitudes 78
PN 839 SC 52680
SN Attitudes of, not toward, therapists.
B Health Personnel Attitudes 85
Therapist Characteristics 73
N Psychotherapist Attitudes 73
R Psychologist Attitudes 91
Therapist Role 78

Therapist Characteristics 73
PN 2580 SC 52690
SN Traits or qualities of therapists, including but not limited to effectiveness, experience level, and personality.
UF Therapist Effectiveness
Therapist Experience
Therapist Personality
N ↓ Therapist Attitudes 78
R Cross Cultural Treatment 94
Theoretical Orientation 82
Therapist Selection 94
↓ Therapists 67

Therapist Effectiveness
Use Therapist Characteristics

Therapist Experience
Use Therapist Characteristics

Therapist Patient Interaction
Use Psychotherapeutic Processes

Therapist Patient Sexual Relations
Use Professional Client Sexual Relations

Therapist Personality
Use Therapist Characteristics

Therapist Role 78
PN 639 SC 52735
B Roles 67
R Counselor Role 73
Psychotherapist Attitudes 73
↓ Therapist Attitudes 78

Therapist Selection 94
PN 1 SC 52737
SN Motivational and judgmental processes involved in the decision to choose a particular therapist or counselor.
UF Selection (Therapist)
R Choice Behavior 67
↓ Client Attitudes 82
Patient Selection 97
↓ Therapeutic Processes 78
↓ Therapist Characteristics 73
↓ Therapists 67
↓ Treatment 67

Therapist Trainees 73
PN 639 SC 52740
UF Psychotherapist Trainees
R Counselor Trainees 73
↓ Therapists 67

Therapists 67
PN 1247 SC 52750
SN Conceptually broad array term referring to persons trained in the treatment of problems including mental disorders and behavior disorders. Use a more specific term if possible.
B Professional Personnel 78
N Occupational Therapists 73
Physical Therapists 73
↓ Psychotherapists 73
Speech Therapists 73
R Clinicians 73
↓ Counselors 67
↓ Health Personnel 94
↓ Mental Health Personnel 67
↓ Social Workers 73
↓ Therapist Characteristics 73
Therapist Selection 94
Therapist Trainees 73

Therapy
Use Treatment

Therapy (Drug)
Use Drug Therapy

Thermal Acclimatization 73
PN 47 SC 52830
SN Adjustment to ambient temperature ranges that may be different from the organism's typical experience or that may be typical but cyclical in nature (e.g., seasonal changes in temperature). Compare THERMOREGULATION (BODY).
UF Acclimatization (Thermal)
B Adaptation 67
Physiology 67

Thermal Acclimatization — (cont'd)
R Atmospheric Conditions 73
Environmental Stress 73
Physiological Stress 67
↓ Temperature Effects 67
Thermoregulation (Body) 73

Thermal Factors
Use Temperature Effects

Thermoreceptors 73
PN 28 SC 52840
B Nerve Endings 73
Neural Receptors 73
Sensory Neurons 73

Thermoregulation (Body) 73
PN 487 SC 52850
SN Homeostatic behavioral or physiological responses that maintain body temperature within a viable range. Compare THERMAL ACCLIMATIZATION.
B Body Temperature 73
R Hyperthermia 73
Hypothermia 73
↓ Metabolism 67
Thermal Acclimatization 73

Theta Rhythm 73
PN 222 SC 52860
SN Electrically measured impulses or waves of low amplitude and a frequency of 4-7 cycles per second observable in the electroencephalogram during stage 1 sleep.
B Electrical Activity 67
Electroencephalography 67

Thigh 73
PN 3 SC 52870
B Anatomy 67
R Leg (Anatomy) 73

Thinking 67
PN 2957 SC 52880
SN Cognitive process involved in the manipulation of concepts and ideas.
B Cognitive Processes 67
N ↓ Abstraction 67
Autistic Thinking 73
Divergent Thinking 73
Logical Thinking 67
Magical Thinking 73
↓ Reasoning 67
R Intelligence 67

Thiopental 73
PN 26 SC 52890
UF Pentothal
B Barbiturates 67
General Anesthetics 73
Hypnotic Drugs 73
Sedatives 73

Thioridazine 73
PN 289 SC 52900
UF Mellaril
B Phenothiazine Derivatives 73

Thiothixene 73
PN 100 SC 52910
B Tranquilizing Drugs 67

Third World Countries
Use Developing Countries

Thirst 67
PN 238 SC 52920

Thirst — (cont'd)
B Motivation [67]
R Animal Drinking Behavior [73]
↓ Drinking Behavior [78]
↓ Fluid Intake [85]
Water Deprivation [67]

Thoracic Nerves
Use Spinal Nerves

Thorax [73]
PN 78 **SC** 52960
UF Chest
B Musculoskeletal System [73]
Respiratory System [73]
R Diaphragm (Anatomy) [73]

Thorazine
Use Chlorpromazine

Thought Content
Use Cognitions

Thought Control
Use Brainwashing

Thought Disturbances [73]
PN 770 **SC** 52980
SN Disturbances of thinking that affect thought content, language, and/or communication marked by delusions, incoherence, and profound loosening of associations.
N Autistic Thinking [73]
Confabulation [73]
Delusions [67]
Fantasies (Thought Disturbances) [67]
Fragmentation (Schizophrenia) [73]
Judgment Disturbances [73]
Magical Thinking [73]
↓ Memory Disorders [73]
Obsessions [67]
Perseveration [67]
R Mental Confusion [73]
↓ Mental Disorders [67]

Threat [67]
PN 1227 **SC** 52990
R Coercion [94]
↓ Punishment [67]
Threat Postures [73]

Threat Postures [73]
PN 83 **SC** 53000
B Animal Aggressive Behavior [73]
Animal Defensive Behavior [82]
R Animal Predatory Behavior [78]
Threat [67]

Threshold Determination [73]
PN 329 **SC** 53010
SN Methods and apparatus used in the measurement of both absolute and difference thresholds for any sensory modality.
R ↓ Psychophysical Measurement [67]
Signal Detection (Perception) [67]
↓ Thresholds [67]

Thresholds [67]
PN 1264 **SC** 53020
SN The minimal level (e.g., intensity) of stimulation, the minimal difference between any stimuli, or the minimal stimulus change that is perceptually detectable or to which a sensory receptor or other neuron will respond. Compare SIGNAL DETECTION (PERCEPTION).
UF Differential Limen
Limen
N Auditory Thresholds [73]

Thresholds — (cont'd)
N Olfactory Thresholds [73]
Pain Thresholds [73]
↓ Sensory Adaptation [67]
Vibrotactile Thresholds [73]
↓ Visual Thresholds [73]
R ↓ Perceptual Measures [73]
Threshold Determination [73]

Thromboses [73]
PN 21 **SC** 53040
B Cardiovascular Disorders [67]
N Coronary Thromboses [73]
R Embolisms [73]

Thumb [73]
PN 18 **SC** 53050
B Fingers (Anatomy) [73]

Thumbsucking [73]
PN 59 **SC** 53060
B Habits [67]
R ↓ Behavior Disorders [71]

Thymoleptic Drugs
Use Tranquilizing Drugs

Thyroid Disorders [73]
PN 118 **SC** 53090
B Endocrine Disorders [73]
N Goiters [73]
Hyperthyroidism [73]
Hypothyroidism [73]
Thyrotoxicosis [73]
R ↓ Endocrine Sexual Disorders [73]
↓ Pituitary Disorders [73]

Thyroid Extract
SN Term discontinued in 1997. Use THYROID EXTRACT to access references from 73–96.
Use Thyroid Hormones

Thyroid Gland [73]
PN 84 **SC** 53110
B Endocrine Glands [73]

Thyroid Hormones [73]
PN 216 **SC** 53120
UF Thyroid Extract
B Hormones [67]
N Thyroxine [73]
Triiodothyronine [73]

Thyroid Stimulating Hormone
Use Thyrotropin

Thyroidectomy [73]
PN 30 **SC** 53140
B Endocrine Gland Surgery [73]

Thyrotoxicosis [73]
PN 26 **SC** 53150
B Thyroid Disorders [73]
Toxic Disorders [73]
R ↓ Encephalopathies [82]
Hyperthyroidism [73]
Toxic Psychoses [73]

Thyrotropic Hormone
Use Thyrotropin

Thyrotropin [73]
PN 678 **SC** 53170
UF Thyroid Stimulating Hormone
Thyrotropic Hormone
B Pituitary Hormones [73]
R Hypothyroidism [73]

Thyroxine [73]
PN 186 **SC** 53180
B Thyroid Hormones [73]
R Hypothyroidism [73]

Tibet [91]
PN 3 **SC** 53185
B Peoples Republic of China [73]

Tic Doloureux
Use Trigeminal Neuralgia

Tics [73]
PN 259 **SC** 53200
B Movement Disorders [85]
Symptoms [67]

Tigers
Use Felids

Time [67]
PN 3549 **SC** 53210
SN Continuum in which events or experiences are expressed in terms of the past, the present, and the future. For effects of time-of-day or season consider also SEASONAL VARIATIONS and BIOLOGICAL RHYTHMS or their associated terms.
N Interresponse Time [73]
R Future [91]
Time Disorientation [73]
Time Management [94]
↓ Time Perception [67]
Time Perspective [78]
Trends [91]

Time Disorientation [73]
PN 70 **SC** 53230
UF Disorientation (Time)
B Consciousness Disturbances [73]
R ↓ Time [67]

Time Estimation [67]
PN 820 **SC** 53240
SN Estimation of duration or passage of time.
B Estimation [67]
Time Perception [67]
R Time Management [94]

Time Limited Psychotherapy
Use Brief Psychotherapy

Time Management [94]
PN 30 **SC** 51435
B Management [67]
R ↓ Learning Strategies [91]
↓ Self Management [85]
Study Habits [73]
↓ Time [67]
Time Estimation [67]
Time On Task [88]
↓ Time Perception [67]
Time Perspective [78]

Time On Task [88]
PN 306 **SC** 53244
SN Period of active involvement in a learning or production activity.
R ↓ Attention [67]
↓ Learning [67]
Time Management [94]

Time Out [85]
PN 124 **SC** 53245

Time Out — (cont'd)
SN Removal of the availability of gratification and reinforcement for any behavior following the occurrence of an undesired response. Has application in therapeutic, experimental, educational, and childrearing contexts.
B Behavior Modification [73]
Operant Conditioning [67]
R Omission Training [85]

Time Perception [67]
PN 1410 **SC** 53250
SN Perception of duration, simultaneity, or succession in the passage of time. Prior to the introduction of TIME PERSPECTIVE in 1978, TIME PERCEPTION was used for this concept also.
B Perception [67]
N Time Estimation [67]
R Tempo [97]
↓ Time [67]
Time Management [94]
Time Perspective [78]

Time Perspective [78]
PN 581 **SC** 53255
SN Mental representation of temporal relationships or the capacity to remember events in their actual chronology. Also, one's outlook on the past, present, and/or future in relation to subjective qualities of time passage. To access references prior to 1978 use TIME PERCEPTION.
R ↓ Perceptual Orientation [73]
↓ Time [67]
Time Management [94]
↓ Time Perception [67]

Time Series [85]
PN 202 **SC** 53257
SN A set of observational data ordered in time, typically with observations made at regular intervals.
B Statistical Analysis [67]
R Statistical Data [82]
↓ Stochastic Modeling [73]

Timers (Apparatus) [73]
PN 45 **SC** 53260
B Apparatus [67]

Timidity [73]
PN 331 **SC** 53270
UF Shyness
B Personality Traits [67]

Tinnitus [73]
PN 121 **SC** 53280
B Ear Disorders [73]

Tiredness
Use Fatigue

Tissue Donation [91]
PN 101 **SC** 53295
SN Donation of organs, blood, sperm, or other tissues for medical use.
UF Blood Donation
Organ Donation
Sperm Donation
R Blood Transfusion [73]
Charitable Behavior [73]
Neural Transplantation [85]
Organ Transplantation [73]

Tissues (Body) [73]
PN 98 **SC** 53300
B Anatomy [67]
N Bone Marrow [73]
↓ Connective Tissues [73]
↓ Membranes [73]

Tissues (Body) — (cont'd)
N ↓ Nerve Tissues [73]
Skin (Anatomy) [67]
R Histology [73]
↓ Muscles [67]

Toads [73]
PN 140 **SC** 53320
B Amphibia [73]
R Larvae [73]

Tobacco (Drug)
Use Nicotine

Tobacco (Smokeless)
Use Smokeless Tobacco

Tobacco Smoking [67]
PN 4593 **SC** 53340
UF Cigarette Smoking
Smoking (Tobacco)
B Drug Usage [71]
Habits [67]
R Carcinogens [73]
Nicotine [73]
Nicotine Withdrawal [97]
Prenatal Exposure [91]
Smokeless Tobacco [94]
Smoking Cessation [88]

Tobago
SN Term discontinued in 1982. Use TRINIDAD or TOBAGO to access references from 73-81.
Use Trinidad and Tobago

Toes (Anatomy)
Use Feet (Anatomy)

Tofranil
Use Imipramine

Toilet Training [73]
PN 94 **SC** 53400
B Childrearing Practices [67]

Token Economy Programs [73]
PN 626 **SC** 53410
SN Group treatment based on operant conditioning in which elements in a patient's environment are arranged so that reinforcement is made contingent on the patient's behavior. When the desired behavior occurs, a token is given which may be exchanged for a reinforcing agent (e.g., goods or services).
B Contingency Management [73]
R ↓ Psychiatric Hospital Programs [67]
Response Cost [97]

Token Reinforcement
Use Secondary Reinforcement

Tolerance [73]
PN 267 **SC** 53440
B Personality Traits [67]
N Tolerance for Ambiguity [67]
R Agreeableness [97]
Openness to Experience [97]
Social Acceptance [67]

Tolerance (Drug)
Use Drug Tolerance

Tolerance for Ambiguity [67]
PN 324 **SC** 53460
SN Willingness to accept situations having conflicting or multiple interpretations or outcomes.

Tolerance for Ambiguity — (cont'd)
UF Ambiguity (Tolerance)
B Tolerance [73]

Toluene [91]
PN 21 **SC** 53465
B Solvents [82]

Tomography [88]
PN 878 **SC** 53470
UF CAT Scan
Positron Emission Tomography
B Medical Diagnosis [73]
N Magnetic Resonance Imaging [94]
R Computer Assisted Diagnosis [73]
↓ Roentgenography [73]

Tone (Frequency)
Use Pitch (Frequency)

Tonga [91]
PN 1 **SC** 53485
B South Pacific [78]

Tongue [73]
PN 302 **SC** 53490
B Digestive System [67]
N Taste Buds [73]
R Mouth (Anatomy) [67]

Tonic Immobility [78]
PN 291 **SC** 53495
SN Adaptive escape or alarm response in certain species in which the animal adopts a motionless posture as if feigning death.
B Motor Processes [67]
R Alarm Responses [73]
↓ Animal Defensive Behavior [82]

Tool Use [91]
PN 66 **SC** 53497
SN Used for human or animal populations.
UF Animal Tool Use
B Motor Processes [67]
R ↓ Animal Ethology [67]

Top Level Managers [73]
PN 858 **SC** 53500
SN Executives in business or industry who are responsible for the major strategic and policy decisions.
UF Executives
B Management Personnel [73]
R Middle Level Managers [73]

Topography [73]
PN 78 **SC** 53510
UF Landscapes
B Ecological Factors [73]

Torticollis [73]
PN 65 **SC** 53520
UF Wryneck
B Movement Disorders [85]
Muscular Disorders [73]

Tortoises
Use Turtles

Torture [88]
PN 103 **SC** 53535
B Antisocial Behavior [71]
R ↓ Aggressive Behavior [67]
Coercion [94]
Persecution [73]
Suffering [73]

Torture — (cont'd)
R Victimization [73]
↓ Violence [73]

Totalitarianism [73]
PN 30 SC 53540
B Political Economic Systems [73]

Touch
Use Tactual Perception

Touching
Use Physical Contact

Tourette Syndrome
Use Gilles de la Tourette Disorder

Towns [73]
PN 52 SC 53560
B Social Environments [73]

Toxic Disorders [73]
PN 345 SC 53570
UF Intoxication
Poisoning
B Physical Disorders [97]
N Acute Alcoholic Intoxication [73]
Barbiturate Poisoning [73]
Carbon Monoxide Poisoning [73]
↓ Drug Induced Congenital Disorders [73]
Lead Poisoning [73]
Mercury Poisoning [73]
Narcosis [73]
Neuroleptic Malignant Syndrome [88]
Thyrotoxicosis [73]
Toxic Encephalopathies [73]
Toxic Hepatitis [73]
Toxic Psychoses [73]
R ↓ Alcohol Intoxication [73]
↓ Alcoholism [67]
↓ Dermatitis [73]
↓ Digestive System Disorders [73]
↓ Gastrointestinal Disorders [73]
Hyponatremia [97]
↓ Liver Disorders [73]
↓ Mental Disorders [67]
↓ Neurotoxins [82]
Toxicity [73]
Toxicomania [73]

Toxic Encephalopathies [73]
PN 70 SC 53580
B Encephalopathies [82]
Toxic Disorders [73]
R Acute Alcoholic Intoxication [73]
Chronic Alcoholic Intoxication [73]
Toxic Psychoses [73]

Toxic Hepatitis [73]
PN 5 SC 53590
B Hepatitis [73]
Toxic Disorders [73]

Toxic Psychoses [73]
PN 133 SC 53600
SN Psychotic states or conditions resulting from ingestion of toxic agents or by the presence of toxins within the body. Compare EXPERIMENTAL PSYCHOSIS.
B Organic Brain Syndromes [73]
Psychosis [67]
Toxic Disorders [73]
R ↓ Alcohol Intoxication [73]
↓ Alcoholic Psychosis [73]
Thyrotoxicosis [73]
Toxic Encephalopathies [73]

Toxic Waste
Use Hazardous Materials

Toxicity [73]
PN 677 SC 53610
R ↓ Drugs [67]
↓ Hazardous Materials [91]
↓ Neurotoxins [82]
Teratogens [88]
↓ Toxic Disorders [73]

Toxicomania [73]
PN 16 SC 53620
R Pica [73]
↓ Toxic Disorders [73]

Toxins
Use Poisons

Toy Selection [73]
PN 181 SC 53650
R Childhood Play Behavior [78]
↓ Toys [73]

Toys [73]
PN 341 SC 53660
N Anatomically Detailed Dolls [91]
Educational Toys [73]
R Childhood Play Behavior [78]
Childrens Recreational Games [73]
Computer Games [88]
↓ Games [67]
↓ Recreation [67]
Toy Selection [73]

Trachea [73]
PN 28 SC 53680
B Respiratory System [73]

Tracking [67]
PN 435 SC 53700
SN Following a moving stimulus or the contours (or shape) of a stationary target by means of direct physical contact or through any sensory modality. Used for human or animal populations.
B Perceptual Motor Processes [67]
N Rotary Pursuit [67]
Visual Tracking [73]
R ↓ Attention [67]
↓ Monitoring [73]
Motor Skills [73]
↓ Perceptual Localization [67]
↓ Perceptual Motor Learning [67]

Tractotomy [73]
PN 14 SC 53710
B Neurosurgery [73]
R ↓ Psychosurgery [73]
Pyramidotomy [73]

Traditionalism
Use Conservatism

Traffic Accidents (Motor)
Use Motor Traffic Accidents

Trainable Mentally Retarded [73]
PN 1584 SC 53760
SN IQ 35-49.
UF Moderately Mentally Retarded
B Mentally Retarded [67]
R Downs Syndrome [67]

Training
Use Education

Training (Athletic)
Use Athletic Training

Training (Clinical Methods)
Use Clinical Methods Training

Training (Clinical Psychology Grad)
Use Clinical Psychology Grad Training

Training (Community Mental Health)
Use Community Mental Health Training

Training (Graduate Psychology)
Use Graduate Psychology Education

Training (Mental Health Inservice)
Use Mental Health Inservice Training

Training (Motivation)
Use Motivation Training

Training (Personnel)
Use Personnel Training

Training (Psychiatric)
Use Psychiatric Training

Training (Psychoanalytic)
Use Psychoanalytic Training

Training (Psychotherapy)
Use Psychotherapy Training

Trains (Railroad)
Use Railroad Trains

Tranquilizing Drugs [67]
PN 1838 SC 53900
UF Antianxiety Drugs
Anxiety Reducing Drugs
Anxiolytic Drugs
Ataractic Drugs
Ataraxic Drugs
Thymoleptic Drugs
B Drugs [67]
N Amitriptyline [73]
Benactyzine [73]
Doxepin [94]
Haloperidol [73]
Meprobamate [73]
↓ Minor Tranquilizers [73]
↓ Neuroleptic Drugs [73]
↓ Phenothiazine Derivatives [73]
Pimozide [73]
Thiothixene [73]
R ↓ Anticonvulsive Drugs [73]
↓ Antiemetic Drugs [73]
↓ Antihypertensive Drugs [73]
↓ Benzodiazepines [78]
↓ Dopamine Antagonists [82]
↓ Muscle Relaxing Drugs [73]
↓ Narcotic Drugs [73]
↓ Sedatives [73]

Transactional Analysis [73]
PN 796 SC 53910
SN Type of psychotherapy developed by E. Berne based on the theory that all interactions between individuals reflect the inner relationships of the "Parent", "Adult", and "Child" ego states.
B Human Potential Movement [82]
Psychotherapy [67]
R ↓ Group Psychotherapy [67]
↓ Psychoanalysis [67]

Transaminases 73
PN 29 SC 53920
UF Aminotransferases
B Transferases 73

Transcultural Psychiatry 73
PN 282 SC 53930
SN Comparative study of mental illness and mental health among various societies or cultures, including epidemiology and symptomatology.
UF Comparative Psychiatry
Cultural Psychiatry
B Psychiatry 67
R ↓ Alternative Medicine 97
Cross Cultural Psychology 97
Cross Cultural Treatment 94
Ethnology 67
↓ Ethnospecific Disorders 73
Folk Medicine 73
Folk Psychology 97
Myths 67
Shamanism 73
Taboos 73

Transducers 73
PN 22 SC 53940
B Apparatus 67

Transfer (Learning) 67
PN 2531 SC 53950
SN Effect of previous learning on the acquisition of new material or skills as a function of the relative similarity between the prior and current learning situations. Compare GENERALIZATION (LEARNING).
B Learning 67
N Negative Transfer 73
Positive Transfer 73
R ↓ Generalization (Learning) 82

Transfer Students 73
PN 137 SC 53955
SN Students transferring from one school or educational program to another.
B Students 67
R Grade Level 94

Transferases 73
PN 225 SC 53960
B Enzymes 73
N Transaminases 73

Transference (Psychotherapeutic)
Use Psychotherapeutic Transference

Transformational Generative Grammar 73
PN 92 SC 53980
SN Transformational grammar relates the deep syntactic structures of a language to the surface structures by means of transformational rules. Generative grammar represents, through abstract formulas, all and only the grammatical utterances of a language.
B Grammar 67
R ↓ Syntax 71

Transfusion (Blood)
Use Blood Transfusion

Transgenerational Patterns 91
PN 149 SC 54005
SN Patterns of behavior, for example, pregnancy in adolescence, drug abuse, or child abuse, that appear in successive generations.
UF Intergenerational Transmission
R ↓ Family 67
↓ Family Relations 67
Family Resemblance 91

Transgenerational Patterns — (cont'd)
R Generation Gap 73
Intergenerational Relations 88
↓ Parent Child Relations 67
Trends 91

Transistors (Apparatus)
SN Term discontinued in 1997. Use TRANSISTORS (APPARATUS) to access references from 73-96.
Use Apparatus

Transitional Objects 85
PN 135 SC 54015
SN Psychoanalytic concept referring to any material object having a special value that serves an anxiety-reducing function. Such attachment is a normal phenomenon during transition from one phase to another in separation-individuation.
R ↓ Childhood Development 67
Object Relations 82
Separation Individuation 82

Translocation (Chromosome) 73
PN 23 SC 54020
B Chromosome Disorders 73
R ↓ Genetics 67
Mutations 73

Transpersonal Psychology 88
PN 102 SC 54025
SN Subdiscipline of humanistic psychology which studies higher states of consciousness and transcendental experiences.
B Humanistic Psychology 85

Transplants (Organ)
Use Organ Transplantation

Transportation 73
PN 105 SC 54040
N Air Transportation 73
↓ Ground Transportation 73
Public Transportation 73
↓ Water Transportation 73
R Commuting (Travel) 85
↓ Transportation Accidents 73

Transportation Accidents 73
PN 84 SC 54050
B Accidents 67
N Air Traffic Accidents 73
Motor Traffic Accidents 73
R Accident Prevention 73
Air Traffic Control 73
↓ Aviation Safety 73
Highway Safety 73
Safety Belts 73
↓ Transportation 73

Transposition (Cognition) 73
PN 43 SC 54060
SN Condition in learning in which subjects react to relationships between stimuli rather than to each stimulus itself.
B Cognitive Processes 67

Transracial Adoption
Use Interracial Adoption

Transsexualism 73
PN 525 SC 54070
B Psychosexual Behavior 67
R Bisexuality 73
Gender Identity 85
Gender Identity Disorder 97
↓ Homosexuality 67

Transsexualism — (cont'd)
R Sex Change 88
Transvestism 73

Transvestism 73
PN 159 SC 54080
B Psychosexual Behavior 67
R Bisexuality 73
Fetishism 73
Gender Identity Disorder 97
↓ Homosexuality 67
Transsexualism 73

Tranylcypromine 73
PN 152 SC 54090
B Antidepressant Drugs 71
Monoamine Oxidase Inhibitors 73

Trauma (Emotional)
Use Emotional Trauma

Trauma (Physical)
Use Injuries

Traumatic Brain Injury 97
PN 0 SC 54115
SN Brain injury resulting from an accident, surgery, or other trauma. Consider BRAIN DAMAGE or BRAIN DAMAGED to access references prior to 1997.
UF Brain Injury (Traumatic)
B Brain Damage 67
R ↓ Brain Damaged 73
↓ Head Injuries 73
↓ Neuropsychological Assessment 82

Traumatic Neurosis 73
PN 126 SC 54130
SN Use TRAUMATIC NEUROSIS or STRESS REACTIONS to access references to POSTTRAUMATIC STRESS DISORDER from 73-84.
B Neurosis 67
R Posttraumatic Stress Disorder 85

Traumatic Psychosis
Use Reactive Psychosis

Traveling 73
PN 202 SC 54150
B Recreation 67
R Commuting (Travel) 85
Vacationing 73

Trazodone 88
PN 155 SC 54152
B Antidepressant Drugs 71
Piperazines 94

Treatment 67
PN 12830 SC 54190
SN Conceptually broad array term referring to psychological or physical measures designed to ameliorate or cure an abnormal or undesirable condition. Use a more specific term if possible.
UF Therapy
N Aftercare 73
↓ Alternative Medicine 97
↓ Behavior Modification 73
Bibliotherapy 73
↓ Cognitive Techniques 85
↓ Creative Arts Therapy 94
↓ Crisis Intervention 73
↓ Crisis Intervention Services 73
Cross Cultural Treatment 94
↓ Health Care Services 78
Interdisciplinary Treatment Approach 73
Involuntary Treatment 94
Life Sustaining Treatment 97

Treatment — (cont'd)
N Medical Treatment (General) 73
Milieu Therapy 88
Movement Therapy 97
Multimodal Treatment Approach 91
↓ Organic Therapies 73
↓ Outpatient Treatment 67
Pain Management 94
Partial Hospitalization 85
Personal Therapy 91
↓ Physical Treatment Methods 73
Preventive Medicine 73
↓ Psychotherapeutic Techniques 67
↓ Psychotherapy 67
↓ Rehabilitation 67
↓ Relaxation Therapy 78
Sex Therapy 78
Social Casework 67
Sociotherapy 73
Speech Therapy 67
R Caregivers 88
↓ Case Management 91
↓ Client Rights 88
Client Transfer 97
Client Treatment Matching 97
↓ Clinics 67
Cost Containment 91
↓ Counseling 67
Court Referrals 94
Death Education 82
Early Intervention 82
Euthanasia 73
Health Care Costs 94
↓ Health Care Delivery 78
Health Care Seeking Behavior 97
Life Review 91
↓ Medical Records 78
Mental Health Program Evaluation 73
Patient Abuse 91
Patient History 73
Physical Restraint 82
Posttreatment Followup 73
Prescribing (Drugs) 91
↓ Prevention 73
Prognosis 73
↓ Psychiatry 67
Psychoeducation 94
Psychosocial Readjustment 73
Quality of Care 88
Relapse Prevention 94
↓ Self Help Techniques 82
Sensory Integration 91
Shamanism 73
↓ Side Effects (Treatment) 88
Spontaneous Remission 73
Stress Management 85
Therapeutic Alliance 94
↓ Therapeutic Processes 78
Therapeutic Social Clubs 73
Therapist Selection 94
Treatment Compliance 82
↓ Treatment Duration 88
Treatment Effectiveness Evaluation 73
↓ Treatment Facilities 73
↓ Treatment Outcomes 82
↓ Treatment Planning 97
↓ Treatment Resistant Disorders 94
Treatment Termination 82
Treatment Withholding 88
↓ Twelve Step Programs 97

Treatment Client Matching
Use Client Treatment Matching

Treatment Compliance 82
PN 2349 **SC** 54153
SN Adherence by a patient or client to professional advice or a systematic plan of treatment.
UF Client Compliance
Medical Regimen Compliance
B Compliance 73
R ↓ Client Attitudes 82
Client Education 85
Client Participation 97
↓ Client Rights 88
Illness Behavior 82
Informed Consent 85
Involuntary Treatment 94
↓ Treatment 67
Treatment Dropouts 78
↓ Treatment Duration 88
Treatment Refusal 94
Treatment Withholding 88

Treatment Dropouts 78
PN 893 **SC** 54155
SN Persons who drop out of treatment, or discontinuation of treatment without the consent of the person in charge of treatment or before scheduled termination. Compare TREATMENT TERMINATION.
UF Client Dropouts
Patient Dropouts
B Dropouts 73
R Involuntary Treatment 94
Psychotherapeutic Outcomes 73
Treatment Compliance 82
↓ Treatment Duration 88
↓ Treatment Outcomes 82
Treatment Refusal 94
Treatment Termination 82

Treatment Duration 88
PN 959 **SC** 54157
SN Length of hospital or institutional stay and length or number of treatment or therapy sessions. Used for any treatment modality.
UF Length of Stay
N Long Term Care 94
R ↓ Case Management 91
Maintenance Therapy 97
↓ Treatment 67
Treatment Compliance 82
Treatment Dropouts 78
↓ Treatment Outcomes 82
↓ Treatment Planning 97
Treatment Termination 82

Treatment Effectiveness Evaluation 73
PN 2900 **SC** 54160
SN Methodology or procedures for assessment of treatment success in relation to previously established goals or other criteria. Also used for formal evaluations themselves. For effectiveness of particular treatment modes, use the specific type of treatment (e.g., DRUG THERAPY). For efficacy of treatment for a particular disorder, use the specific disorder (e.g., MANIA) and the specific type of treatment.
UF Evaluation (Treatment Effectiveness)
B Evaluation 67
R Mental Health Program Evaluation 73
Psychotherapeutic Outcomes 73
↓ Treatment 67
↓ Treatment Outcomes 82

Treatment Facilities 73
PN 292 **SC** 54170
N ↓ Clinics 67
Community Mental Health Centers 73
Halfway Houses 73
↓ Hospitals 67
Nursing Homes 73
Therapeutic Camps 78
R ↓ Crisis Intervention Services 73
↓ Facility Admission 88
↓ Facility Discharge 88

Treatment Facilities — (cont'd)
R ↓ Facility Environment 88
↓ Health Care Administration 97
Institutional Schools 78
↓ Residential Care Institutions 73
↓ Treatment 67

Treatment Methods (Physical)
Use Physical Treatment Methods

Treatment Outcomes 82
PN 3361 **SC** 54185
SN Limited to treatment results that are a function of unique or specifically-described circumstances or characteristics (e.g., race) of the clients/patients, the treatment provider, or the treatment itself. For effectiveness of particular treatment modes, use the specific type of treatment (e.g., DRUG THERAPY). For efficacy of treatment for a particular disorder, use the specific disorder (e.g., MANIA) and the specific type of treatment.
UF Outcomes (Treatment)
Therapeutic Outcomes
N Psychotherapeutic Outcomes 73
R Client Treatment Matching 97
Mental Health Program Evaluation 73
Postsurgical Complications 73
↓ Psychotherapeutic Processes 67
Recovery (Disorders) 73
Relapse (Disorders) 73
Relapse Prevention 94
↓ Remission (Disorders) 73
↓ Side Effects (Treatment) 88
↓ Therapeutic Processes 78
↓ Treatment 67
Treatment Dropouts 78
↓ Treatment Duration 88
Treatment Effectiveness Evaluation 73
Treatment Termination 82

Treatment Planning 97
PN 0 **SC** 54189
UF Patient Care Planning
N Discharge Planning 94
R Aftercare 73
↓ Case Management 91
↓ Client Characteristics 73
Client Treatment Matching 97
Clinical Judgment (Not Diagnosis) 73
↓ Health Care Delivery 78
↓ Managed Care 94
Needs Assessment 85
Posttreatment Followup 73
↓ Treatment 67
↓ Treatment Duration 88

Treatment Refusal 94
PN 43 **SC** 54186
SN Patient or client refusal of or resistance to medical, psychological, or psychiatric treatment. Consider TREATMENT WITHHOLDING for life sustaining contexts.
UF Refusal (Treatment)
R Advance Directives 94
Assisted Suicide 97
↓ Client Rights 88
Client Transfer 97
Informed Consent 85
Involuntary Treatment 94
Life Sustaining Treatment 97
Psychotherapeutic Resistance 73
↓ Resistance 97
Treatment Compliance 82
Treatment Dropouts 78
Treatment Termination 82
Treatment Withholding 88

Treatment Resistant Depression 94
PN 93 **SC** 57440

Treatment Resistant Depression — (cont'd)
UF Tricyclic Resistant Depression
B Major Depression [88]
Treatment Resistant Disorders [94]
R ↓ Drug Therapy [67]

Treatment Resistant Disorders [94]
PN 170 SC 57445
SN Used for any disorder that is resistant to any type of psychological or medical treatment.
N Treatment Resistant Depression [94]
R ↓ Chronic Mental Illness [97]
↓ Mental Disorders [67]
↓ Physical Disorders [97]
↓ Treatment [67]

Treatment Seeking Behavior
Use Health Care Seeking Behavior

Treatment Termination [82]
PN 537 SC 54187
SN Completion of medical or psychological/behavioral treatment programs. Compare TREATMENT DROPOUTS.
R Client Transfer [97]
Discharge Planning [94]
↓ Hospital Discharge [73]
Psychiatric Hospital Discharge [78]
↓ Therapeutic Processes [78]
↓ Treatment [67]
Treatment Dropouts [78]
↓ Treatment Duration [88]
↓ Treatment Outcomes [82]
Treatment Refusal [94]
Treatment Withholding [88]

Treatment Withholding [88]
PN 126 SC 54188
SN Limiting or restricting medical treatment for seriously ill persons. Includes do-not-resuscitate orders. Compare TREATMENT TERMINATION.
R Advance Directives [94]
Assisted Suicide [97]
↓ Client Rights [88]
↓ Death and Dying [67]
Euthanasia [73]
↓ Human Rights [78]
Informed Consent [85]
Life Sustaining Treatment [97]
↓ Treatment [67]
Treatment Compliance [82]
Treatment Refusal [94]
Treatment Termination [82]

Tremor [73]
PN 202 SC 54200
B Movement Disorders [85]
Symptoms [67]
R ↓ Antitremor Drugs [73]
Parkinsonism [94]
Parkinsons Disease [73]

Trends [91]
PN 230 SC 54204
SN Used specifically for analysis of past, present, or future patterns in technology, economics, and social or developmental processes.
R ↓ Fads and Fashions [73]
Future [91]
↓ History [73]
Social Change [67]
↓ Social Processes [67]
↓ Time [67]
Transgenerational Patterns [91]

Triadic Therapy
Use Conjoint Therapy

Trial and Error Learning [73]
PN 55 SC 54210
B Learning [67]
Learning Strategies [91]

Triazolam [88]
PN 164 SC 54215
UF Halcion
B Hypnotic Drugs [73]
Sedatives [73]

Tribes [73]
PN 440 SC 54220
R Alaska Natives [97]
American Indians [67]
↓ Ethnic Groups [73]

Trichotillomania
Use Hair Pulling

Tricyclic Antidepressant Drugs [97]
PN 0 SC 54226
B Antidepressant Drugs [71]
N Amitriptyline [73]
Chlorimipramine [73]
Desipramine [73]
Doxepin [94]
Imipramine [73]
Maprotiline [82]
Nortriptyline [94]
R ↓ Adrenergic Blocking Drugs [73]
↓ Lithium [73]
↓ Monoamine Oxidase Inhibitors [73]

Tricyclic Resistant Depression
Use Treatment Resistant Depression

Trifluoperazine [73]
PN 113 SC 54230
UF Stelazine
B Phenothiazine Derivatives [73]

Triflupromazine
SN Term discontinued in 1997. Use TRIFLUPROMAZINE to access references from 73–96.
Use Phenothiazine Derivatives

Trigeminal Nerve [73]
PN 152 SC 54250
B Cranial Nerves [73]

Trigeminal Neuralgia [73]
PN 34 SC 54260
UF Tic Doloureux
B Neuralgia [73]

Trigonum Cerebrale
Use Fornix

Trihexyphenidyl [73]
PN 47 SC 54270
B Alcohols [67]
Amines [73]
Antispasmodic Drugs [73]
Antitremor Drugs [73]
Cholinergic Blocking Drugs [73]

Triiodothyronine [73]
PN 119 SC 54280
B Thyroid Hormones [73]

Trinidad
SN Term discontinued in 1982. Use TRINIDAD or TOBAGO to access references from 73–81.
Use Trinidad and Tobago

Trinidad and Tobago [82]
PN 34 SC 54300
SN Use TRINIDAD or TOBAGO to access references from 73–81.
UF Tobago
Trinidad
B West Indies [73]

Triplets [73]
PN 26 SC 54310
B Multiple Births [73]

Trisomy [73]
PN 48 SC 54320
B Chromosome Disorders [73]
N Trisomy 21 [73]

Trisomy 21 [73]
PN 50 SC 54340
B Autosome Disorders [73]
Trisomy [73]
R Downs Syndrome [67]

Trochlear Nerve
Use Cranial Nerves

Truancy [73]
PN 78 SC 54360
N School Truancy [73]

Trucks
Use Motor Vehicles

True False Tests
Use Forced Choice (Testing Method)

Trust (Social Behavior) [67]
PN 854 SC 54370
B Prosocial Behavior [82]
R Hope [91]

Tryptamine [73]
PN 99 SC 54380
B Amines [73]
Vasoconstrictor Drugs [73]

Tryptophan [73]
PN 785 SC 54390
B Amino Acids [73]
Serotonin Precursors [78]
N Hydroxytryptophan (5-) [91]

Tubal Ligation [73]
PN 42 SC 54400
B Birth Control [71]
Sterilization (Sex) [73]

Tuberculosis [73]
PN 74 SC 54410
B Bacterial Disorders [73]
N Pulmonary Tuberculosis [73]
R Addisons Disease [73]
↓ Antitubercular Drugs [73]
Lupus [73]
↓ Musculoskeletal Disorders [73]
↓ Nervous System Disorders [67]
↓ Skin Disorders [73]

Tubocurarine [73]
PN 14 SC 54420
B Alkaloids [73]
Muscle Relaxing Drugs [73]
R Curare [73]

Tumors
Use Neoplasms

Tunisia [91]
PN 4 **SC** 54435
B Africa [67]

Tunnel Vision [73]
PN 11 **SC** 54440
SN Disorder characterized by severe limitation or total lack of peripheral vision.
B Eye Disorders [73]
R ↓ Vision [67]

Turkey [73]
PN 199 **SC** 54450
B Asia [73]
R Middle East [78]

Turners Syndrome [73]
PN 95 **SC** 54460
B Hypogonadism [73]
Neonatal Disorders [73]
Sex Linked Hereditary Disorders [73]
Syndromes [73]
R Sterility [73]

Turnover
Use Employee Turnover

Turtles [73]
PN 166 **SC** 54480
UF Tortoises
B Reptiles [67]

Tutoring [73]
PN 503 **SC** 54490
B Teaching Methods [67]
N Peer Tutoring [73]
R Individualized Instruction [73]
Test Coaching [97]

Tutors
Use Teachers

Twelve Step Programs [97]
PN 0 **SC** 54505
UF Gamblers Anonymous
Narcotics Anonymous
B Support Groups [91]
N Alcoholics Anonymous [73]
R ↓ Drug Rehabilitation [73]
Group Counseling [73]
↓ Group Psychotherapy [67]
↓ Mental Health Services [78]
↓ Psychotherapeutic Techniques [67]
↓ Rehabilitation [67]
↓ Self Help Techniques [82]
↓ Treatment [67]

Twins [67]
PN 967 **SC** 54510
B Multiple Births [73]
N Heterozygotic Twins [73]
Monozygotic Twins [73]
Siamese Twins [73]
R Family Resemblance [91]
↓ Genetics [67]

Tympanic Membrane
Use Middle Ear

Type A Personality
Use Coronary Prone Behavior

Type B Personality
Use Coronary Prone Behavior

Type I Errors [73]
PN 215 **SC** 54530

Type I Errors — (cont'd)
B Prediction Errors [73]
R Statistical Power [91]

Type II Errors [73]
PN 64 **SC** 54540
B Prediction Errors [73]
R Statistical Power [91]

Typing [91]
PN 33 **SC** 54550
SN Use CLERICAL SECRETARIAL SKILLS to access references from 73-90.
R Clerical Secretarial Skills [73]
Keyboards [85]
Word Processing [91]

Typists
Use Clerical Personnel

Typologies (General)
Use Taxonomies

Typologies (Psychodiagnostic)
Use Psychodiagnostic Typologies

Tyramine [73]
PN 70 **SC** 54580
B Adrenergic Drugs [73]
Sympathomimetic Amines [73]
Vasoconstrictor Drugs [73]
R ↓ Ergot Derivatives [73]

Tyrosine [73]
PN 263 **SC** 54590
B Amino Acids [73]
N Alpha Methylparatyrosine [78]
R Melanin [73]

Uganda [88]
PN 27 **SC** 54600
B Africa [67]

Ulcerative Colitis [73]
PN 142 **SC** 54620
B Colitis [73]

Ulcers (Gastrointestinal)
Use Gastrointestinal Ulcers

Ulnar Nerve
Use Spinal Nerves

Ultrasound [73]
PN 263 **SC** 54650
SN Sound waves with frequencies above the range of human hearing.
B Pitch (Frequency) [67]

Uncertainty [91]
PN 334 **SC** 54655
SN May be used for uncertainty reduction processes; uncertainty in decision making, choice, or judgment; or in statistical contexts.
R ↓ Chance (Fortune) [73]
Chaos Theory [97]
Choice Behavior [67]
↓ Decision Making [67]
Doubt [73]
Impression Management [78]
↓ Judgment [67]
↓ Statistical Analysis [67]
Suspicion [73]

Unconditioned Reflex
Use Reflexes

Unconditioned Responses [73]
PN 96 **SC** 54680
B Classical Conditioning [67]
Responses [67]

Unconditioned Stimulus [73]
PN 1122 **SC** 54690
UF Stimulus (Unconditioned)
B Conditioning [67]
R ↓ Classical Conditioning [67]
↓ Operant Conditioning [67]
Primary Reinforcement [73]
↓ Stimulation [67]

Unconscious (Personality Factor) [67]
PN 879 **SC** 54700
B Psychoanalytic Personality Factors [73]
R Archetypes [91]
Death Instinct [88]
Free Association [94]
Id [73]
Mind [91]

Underachievement (Academic)
Use Academic Underachievement

Underdeveloped Countries
Use Developing Countries

Undergraduate Degrees
Use Educational Degrees

Undergraduate Education [78]
PN 648 **SC** 54725
UF College Education
B Higher Education [73]

Undergraduates
Use College Students

Underprivileged
Use Disadvantaged

Understanding
Use Comprehension

Underwater Effects [73]
PN 168 **SC** 54760
B Environmental Effects [73]
R Decompression Effects [73]
↓ Gravitational Effects [67]

Underweight [73]
PN 40 **SC** 54770
B Body Weight [67]
Symptoms [67]
N Anorexia Nervosa [73]
R Diets [78]
↓ Eating Disorders [97]
Hyperthyroidism [73]
↓ Nutritional Deficiencies [73]

Undifferentiated Schizophrenia [73]
PN 74 **SC** 54780
B Schizophrenia [67]

Unemployment [67]
PN 1081 **SC** 54790
B Employment Status [82]
Social Issues [91]
R Employment History [78]
Job Search [85]
Job Security [78]
↓ Personnel [67]
Personnel Termination [73]

Unemployment — (cont'd)
R Reemployment 91
Retirement 73

Union of South Africa
SN Term discontinued in 1982. Use UNION OF SOUTH AFRICA to access references from 73–81.
Use South Africa

Union of Soviet Socialist Republics 67
PN 2679 SC 54820
B Asia 73
Europe 73
R Commonwealth of Independent States 97

Unipolar Depression
SN Use DEPRESSION (EMOTION) to access references from 82-87.
Use Major Depression

United Arab Republic
SN Term discontinued in 1982. Use UNITED ARAB REPUBLIC to access references from 73–81.
Use Egypt

United Kingdom 73
PN 950 SC 54840
B Europe 73
N ↓ Great Britain 71

United States 67
PN 5308 SC 54850
B North America 73
N Alaska 73
Appalachia 73
Hawaii 73

Universities
Use Colleges

Unskilled Industrial Workers 73
PN 63 SC 54880
SN Blue collar workers who perform unskilled labor in an industrial setting.
B Blue Collar Workers 73

Unwed Mothers 73
PN 199 SC 54890
SN Consider also ADOLESCENT MOTHERS.
B Mothers 67
R Never Married 94
Premarital Intercourse 73
Single Mothers 94
↓ Single Parents 78

Upper Class 73
PN 113 SC 54900
B Social Class 67

Upper Class Attitudes 73
PN 8 SC 54910
SN Attitudes of, not toward, the upper class.
B Socioeconomic Class Attitudes 73

Upper Income Level 73
PN 55 SC 54920
B Income Level 73

Upward Bound 73
PN 38 SC 54930
SN U.S. Government educational and counseling program for disadvantaged high school and college students.
B Educational Programs 73
Government Programs 73

Upward Bound — (cont'd)
R Compensatory Education 73
Government 67

Upward Mobility
Use Social Mobility

Urban Development
Use Community Development

Urban Environments 67
PN 4719 SC 54940
UF Cities
Inner City
B Social Environments 73
N Ghettoes 73
R Community Development 97
Urban Planning 73

Urban Ghettoes
Use Ghettoes

Urban Planning 73
PN 145 SC 54960
B Environmental Planning 82
R ↓ Architecture 73
Community Development 97
↓ Community Facilities 73
↓ Environment 67
↓ Recreation Areas 73
↓ Urban Environments 67

Urbanization 73
PN 133 SC 54970
B Social Processes 67
R Industrialization 73

Uric Acid 73
PN 59 SC 55010
B Acids 73

Urinalysis 73
PN 168 SC 55020
B Medical Diagnosis 73
R Drug Usage Screening 88

Urinary Function Disorders 73
PN 99 SC 55040
B Urogenital Disorders 73
N Urinary Incontinence 73
R ↓ Psychosomatic Disorders 67

Urinary Incontinence 73
PN 677 SC 55050
UF Bedwetting
Enuresis
Incontinence (Urinary)
B Urinary Function Disorders 73
R ↓ Behavior Disorders 71
↓ Symptoms 67

Urination 67
PN 230 SC 55070
UF Micturition
B Excretion 67
N Diuresis 73
R ↓ Diuretics 73

Urine 73
PN 742 SC 55080
B Body Fluids 73

Urogenital Disorders 73
PN 224 SC 55090
B Physical Disorders 97
N ↓ Genital Disorders 67
↓ Gynecological Disorders 73

Urogenital Disorders — (cont'd)
N Kidney Diseases 88
↓ Urinary Function Disorders 73
R ↓ Psychosomatic Disorders 67
↓ Sexual Function Disturbances 73
↓ Urogenital System 73
↓ Venereal Diseases 73

Urogenital System 73
PN 43 SC 55100
B Anatomical Systems 73
N Bladder 73
↓ Female Genitalia 73
↓ Gonads 73
Kidneys 73
↓ Male Genitalia 73
R ↓ Urogenital Disorders 73

Uruguay 88
PN 9 SC 55105
B South America 67

Uterus 73
PN 50 SC 55110
B Female Genitalia 73
N Cervix 73
R Placenta 73

Utilization (Health Care)
Use Health Care Utilization

Vacation Benefits
Use Employee Leave Benefits

Vacationing 73
PN 96 SC 55130
B Recreation 67
R Camping 73
Holidays 88
Summer Camps (Recreation) 73
Traveling 73

Vaccination
Use Immunization

Vagina 73
PN 167 SC 55150
B Female Genitalia 73

Vaginismus 73
PN 51 SC 55160
B Sexual Function Disturbances 73
R Dyspareunia 73
Frigidity 73

Vagotomy 73
PN 130 SC 55170
B Neurosurgery 73

Vagus Nerve 73
PN 137 SC 55180
B Cranial Nerves 73
Parasympathetic Nervous System 73
R ↓ Heart 67

Validity (Statistical)
SN Use VALIDITY (STATISTICAL) to access references from 67–72.
Use Statistical Validity

Validity (Test)
Use Test Validity

Valium
Use Diazepam

Valproic Acid [91]
PN 154 **SC** 55215
B Anticonvulsive Drugs [73]

Values [67]
PN 4480 **SC** 55220
SN Qualities, principles or behaviors considered to be morally or intrinsically valuable or desirable. Use a more specific term if possible.
UF Mores
N Ethnic Values [73]
Personal Values [73]
Social Values [73]
R ↓ Ethics [67]
Integrity [97]
Morality [67]
World View [88]

Valves (Heart)
Use Heart Valves

Vandalism [78]
PN 77 **SC** 55235
SN Willful or malicious destruction or defacement of public or private property.
B Crime [67]

Vane Kindergarten Test
SN Term discontinued in 1997. Use VANE KINDERGARTEN TEST to access references from 73-96.
Use Intelligence Measures

Variability (Response)
Use Response Variability

Variability (Stimulus)
Use Stimulus Variability

Variability Measurement [73]
PN 200 **SC** 55270
B Statistical Analysis [67]
Statistical Measurement [73]
N Analysis of Covariance [73]
Analysis of Variance [67]
Interaction Variance [73]
Standard Deviation [73]
R ↓ Central Tendency Measures [73]
F Test [73]
↓ Statistical Correlation [67]

Variable Interval Reinforcement [73]
PN 600 **SC** 55280
UF Interval Reinforcement
B Reinforcement Schedules [67]

Variable Ratio Reinforcement [73]
PN 153 **SC** 55290
UF Ratio Reinforcement
B Reinforcement Schedules [67]

Variance Homogeneity [85]
PN 56 **SC** 55295
SN Extent to which the variance in two or more statistical samples is similar or different.
UF Heterogeneity of Variance
B Statistical Measurement [73]
R Analysis of Variance [67]
Standard Deviation [73]

Varimax Rotation [73]
PN 45 **SC** 55330
B Orthogonal Rotation [73]

Vascular Dementia [97]
PN 0 **SC** 55333

Vascular Dementia — (cont'd)
B Dementia [85]
N Multi Infarct Dementia [91]
R ↓ Cerebrovascular Disorders [73]

Vascular Disorders
Use Cardiovascular Disorders

Vasectomy [73]
PN 76 **SC** 55350
B Birth Control [71]
Sterilization (Sex) [73]
Surgery [71]

Vasoconstriction [73]
PN 83 **SC** 55360
R ↓ Blood Pressure Disorders [73]
Epinephrine [67]

Vasoconstrictor Drugs [73]
PN 22 **SC** 55370
UF Pressors (Drugs)
Vasopressor Drugs
B Drugs [67]
N ↓ Amphetamine [67]
Angiotensin [73]
Bufotenine [73]
Dihydroergotamine [73]
Ephedrine [73]
Methamphetamine [73]
Methoxamine [73]
Norepinephrine [73]
Serotonin [73]
Tryptamine [73]
Tyramine [73]
R ↓ Blood Pressure [67]
↓ Heart Rate Affecting Drugs [73]
↓ Vasodilator Drugs [73]
Vasopressin [73]

Vasodilation [73]
PN 57 **SC** 55380
R ↓ Blood Pressure Disorders [73]
Epinephrine [67]
↓ Muscle Relaxing Drugs [73]
Theophylline [73]

Vasodilator Drugs [73]
PN 165 **SC** 55390
B Drugs [67]
N Nicotinic Acid [73]
Verapamil [91]
R ↓ Antihypertensive Drugs [73]
↓ Blood Pressure [67]
Channel Blockers [91]
↓ Heart Rate Affecting Drugs [73]
↓ Vasoconstrictor Drugs [73]

Vasopressin [73]
PN 668 **SC** 55400
B Pituitary Hormones [73]
R ↓ Vasoconstrictor Drugs [73]

Vasopressor Drugs
Use Vasoconstrictor Drugs

Veins (Anatomy) [73]
PN 26 **SC** 55420
B Blood Vessels [73]

Velocity [73]
PN 759 **SC** 55430
UF Speed
R Vibration [67]

Venereal Diseases [73]
PN 270 **SC** 55440

Venereal Diseases — (cont'd)
UF Diseases (Venereal)
Sexually Transmitted Diseases
B Infectious Disorders [73]
N Gonorrhea [73]
Herpes Genitalis [88]
↓ Syphilis [73]
R Acquired Immune Deficiency Syndrome [88]
Condoms [91]
↓ Human Immunodeficiency Virus [91]
↓ Infertility [73]
Sexual Risk Taking [97]
Sterility [73]
↓ Urogenital Disorders [73]

Venezuela [73]
PN 97 **SC** 55450
B South America [67]

Ventral Roots [73]
PN 16 **SC** 55460
B Spinal Cord [73]

Ventral Tegmental Area
Use Tegmentum

Ventricles (Cerebral)
Use Cerebral Ventricles

Ventricles (Heart)
Use Heart Ventricles

Ventricular Fibrillation
Use Fibrillation (Heart)

Verapamil [91]
PN 52 **SC** 55495
B Heart Rate Affecting Drugs [73]
Vasodilator Drugs [73]
R Channel Blockers [91]

Verbal Ability [67]
PN 2354 **SC** 55500
B Cognitive Ability [73]
R Academic Aptitude [73]
Language Proficiency [88]
Metalinguistics [94]
↓ Oral Communication [85]
Proofreading [88]
↓ Verbal Communication [67]
↓ Verbal Memory [94]
Writing Skills [85]
↓ Written Communication [85]

Verbal Communication [67]
PN 8656 **SC** 55520
SN Communication through spoken or written language. Use narrower terms if possible.
B Communication [67]
N Articulation (Speech) [67]
Conversation [73]
↓ Handwriting [67]
Language Proficiency [88]
↓ Manual Communication [78]
Narratives [97]
↓ Oral Communication [85]
Pragmatics [85]
Storytelling [88]
↓ Written Communication [85]
R ↓ Communication Skills [73]
Discourse Analysis [97]
↓ Grammar [67]
↓ Language [67]
↓ Language Development [67]
↓ Linguistics [73]
Metalinguistics [94]

Verbal Communication — (cont'd)
R Neurolinguistics [91]
↓ Speech Processing (Mechanical) [73]
Text Structure [82]
Verbal Ability [67]
↓ Vocabulary [67]
↓ Vocalization [67]

Verbal Comprehension [85]
PN 749 SC 55525
B Comprehension [67]
N Listening Comprehension [73]
Reading Comprehension [73]
Sentence Comprehension [73]

Verbal Conditioning
Use Verbal Learning

Verbal Fluency [73]
PN 1209 SC 55540
SN Ability to produce and manipulate words in thought or speech.
UF Fluency
R Language Proficiency [88]
↓ Oral Communication [85]
Speech Rate [73]

Verbal Learning [67]
PN 3267 SC 55550
SN Acquisition, retention, and retrieval of verbal stimulus materials such as nonsense syllables, words, or sentences. Compare LANGUAGE DEVELOPMENT.
UF Conditioning (Verbal)
Verbal Conditioning
B Learning [67]
N Nonsense Syllable Learning [67]
Paired Associate Learning [67]
R Isolation Effect [73]
Serial Anticipation (Learning) [73]
↓ Serial Learning [67]
↓ Verbal Memory [94]

Verbal Meaning [73]
PN 622 SC 55560
SN Connotative or denotative meaning associated with any verbally informative unit (e.g., morpheme, word, sentence, or phrase).
B Meaning [67]
N Word Meaning [73]
R ↓ Figurative Language [85]
↓ Semantics [67]

Verbal Memory [94]
PN 161 SC 55565
B Memory [67]
N Semantic Memory [88]
R ↓ Lexical Access [88]
Lexical Decision [88]
Verbal Ability [67]
↓ Verbal Learning [67]

Verbal Reinforcement [73]
PN 699 SC 55570
B Social Reinforcement [67]
N Praise [73]

Verbal Stimuli [82]
PN 913 SC 55575
SN Aural or visual presentation of syllables or words or nonword letter combinations.
B Stimulation [67]
R ↓ Stimulus Presentation Methods [73]

Verbal Tests [73]
PN 122 SC 55580

Verbal Tests — (cont'd)
SN Tests designed to assess verbal ability or in which performance depends upon verbal ability.
B Measurement [67]

Verbalization
Use Oral Communication

Verbs [73]
PN 564 SC 55600
B Form Classes (Language) [73]

Verdict Determination
Use Adjudication

Vergence Movements
Use Eye Convergence

Verification (of Theories)
Use Theory Verification

Vernier Acuity
Use Visual Acuity

Vertebrates [73]
PN 158 SC 55620
B Animals [67]
N ↓ Amphibia [73]
↓ Birds [67]
↓ Fishes [67]
↓ Mammals [73]
Pigs [73]
↓ Reptiles [67]
R ↓ Invertebrates [73]

Vertigo [73]
PN 84 SC 55630
UF Dizziness
B Symptoms [67]
R ↓ Labyrinth Disorders [73]
Menieres Disease [73]
Syncope [73]

Very Old [88]
PN 4973 SC 55650
SN Ages 85 years or older.
B Aged [73]
R Aged (Attitudes Toward) [78]
↓ Aging [91]

Vestibular Apparatus [67]
PN 419 SC 55660
SN Major organ of equilibrium which acts as a sensory receptor that detects the position and changes in the position of the head in space.
B Ear (Anatomy) [67]
N Semicircular Canals [73]
R ↓ Labyrinth (Anatomy) [73]

Vestibular Nystagmus
Use Nystagmus

Vestibular Stimulation
Use Somesthetic Stimulation

Veterans (Military)
Use Military Veterans

Veterinary Medicine [73]
PN 38 SC 55680
B Medical Sciences [67]

Vibration [67]
PN 349 SC 55690
UF Resonance
R Velocity [73]

Vibrators (Apparatus) [73]
PN 16 SC 55700
B Apparatus [67]
R ↓ Stimulators (Apparatus) [73]

Vibrotactile Thresholds [73]
PN 265 SC 55710
SN The minimal level of vibratory stimulation, or the minimal difference between any such stimuli, or the minimal vibratory stimulus change that is tactually perceptible.
B Tactual Perception [67]
Thresholds [67]
R ↓ Perceptual Measures [73]

Vicarious Experiences [73]
PN 218 SC 55713
UF Reinforcement (Vicarious)
Vicarious Reinforcement
B Experiences (Events) [73]
R Imagination [67]
↓ Reinforcement [67]

Vicarious Reinforcement
Use Vicarious Experiences

Victimization [73]
PN 2954 SC 55716
SN Process or state of having been personally subjected to crime, deception, fraud, or other detrimental circumstances as a result of the deeds of others.
B Social Interaction [67]
R ↓ Crime [67]
↓ Crime Victims [82]
Erotomania [97]
↓ Perpetrators [88]
Persecution [73]
Sexual Harassment [85]
Torture [88]

Video Display Terminals
Use Video Display Units

Video Display Units [85]
PN 380 SC 55718
SN Electronic devices used to present information or stimulation through visual means. Use VISUAL DISPLAYS to access references from 73-84.
UF Cathode Ray Tubes
CRT
Video Display Terminals
B Computer Peripheral Devices [85]
Visual Displays [73]
R ↓ Television [67]
↓ Visual Stimulation [73]

Video Games
Use Computer Games

Videotape Instruction [73]
PN 506 SC 55720
SN Audiovisual teaching method which employs presentation of feedback as an aid to learning.
B Audiovisual Instruction [73]
R ↓ Educational Audiovisual Aids [73]

Videotape Recorders [73]
PN 69 SC 55730
SN Device for recording on magnetic tape and having varied applications (e.g., teaching aid, analysis of research data).
B Tape Recorders [73]

Videotapes [73]
PN 1170 SC 55740

Videotapes — (cont'd)
SN Audiovisual tape recordings used in both noneducational and educational settings. Not used as a document type identifier.
B Audiovisual Communications Media [73]

Vietnam [82]
PN 33 **SC** 55745
SN Use SOUTH VIETNAM or NORTH VIETNAM to access references from 73–81.
UF North Vietnam
South Vietnam
B Southeast Asia [73]

Vietnamese Cultural Groups [97]
PN 0 **SC** 57748
SN Populations of Vietnamese descent residing in countries other than the country of their origin. For Vietnamese residing in their own country use the appropriate country name. Use ASIANS to access references from 82–96.
B Asians [82]

Vigilance [67]
PN 1125 **SC** 55750
SN Intentional and conscious alertness characterized by a readiness to respond to environmental changes. Compare ATTENTION.
B Attention [67]
Monitoring [73]
Sustained Attention [97]
R Attention Span [73]
Selective Attention [73]

Vineland Social Maturity Scale [73]
PN 22 **SC** 55760
B Nonprojective Personality Measures [73]

Violence [73]
PN 3505 **SC** 55770
B Antisocial Behavior [71]
Conflict [67]
N ↓ Family Violence [82]
Patient Violence [94]
R Coercion [94]
Dangerousness [88]
Nonviolence [91]
Partner Abuse [91]
Physical Abuse [91]
Riots [73]
Self Defense [85]
Terrorism [82]
Torture [88]
↓ War [67]

Viral Disorders [73]
PN 256 **SC** 55780
B Infectious Disorders [73]
N Creutzfeldt Jakob Syndrome [94]
Encephalitis [73]
Epstein Barr Viral Disorder [94]
Herpes Genitalis [88]
Herpes Simplex [73]
↓ Human Immunodeficiency Virus [91]
Influenza [73]
Measles [73]
Poliomyelitis [73]
Rubella [73]
R Chronic Fatigue Syndrome [97]
Pneumonia [73]

Virgin Islands [73]
PN 24 **SC** 55800
B West Indies [73]

Virginity [73]
PN 57 **SC** 55810

Virginity — (cont'd)
B Psychosexual Behavior [67]
R Premarital Intercourse [73]
Sexual Abstinence [73]

Virtual Reality [97]
PN 0 **SC** 55815
B Computer Programing Languages [73]
Computer Simulation [73]
R ↓ Computer Applications [73]
Human Machine Systems [97]

Vision [67]
PN 2968 **SC** 55820
N Linear Perspective [82]
↓ Visual Perception [67]
R Tunnel Vision [73]
Visual Cortex [67]
Visual Evoked Potentials [73]
Visual Hallucinations [73]
Visual Tracking [73]
↓ Visually Disabled [97]

Vision Disorders [82]
PN 510 **SC** 55825
SN Disorders involving the visual system, including visual neural pathways.
B Physical Disorders [97]
Sense Organ Disorders [73]
N ↓ Eye Disorders [73]
R ↓ Blind [67]
↓ Sensorially Disabled [97]
↓ Visually Disabled [97]

Vision Disturbances (Hysterical)
Use Hysterical Vision Disturbances

Visions (Mysticism)
Use Mysticism

Visitation (Institution)
Use Institution Visitation

Visitation Rights
Use Child Visitation

VISTA Volunteers
Use Volunteers in Service to America

Visual Acuity [82]
PN 676 **SC** 55897
SN The ability or capacity of an observer to perceive fine detail. Consider VISUAL THRESHOLDS or VISUAL DISCRIMINATION to access references prior to 1982.
UF Vernier Acuity
B Visual Perception [67]
R Pattern Discrimination [67]
↓ Spatial Perception [67]

Visual Contrast [85]
PN 685 **SC** 55898
SN Perceived difference in color, brightness, or other qualities of two or more simultaneously or successively presented visual stimuli despite a lack of objective differences.
B Visual Perception [67]
N Brightness Contrast [85]
Color Contrast [85]

Visual Cortex [67]
PN 1772 **SC** 55900
UF Cortex (Visual)
Striate Cortex
B Occipital Lobe [73]
R ↓ Vision [67]
Visual Receptive Fields [82]

Visual Discrimination [67]
PN 5158 **SC** 55910
SN Ability to recognize quantitative or qualitative differences between visual shapes, forms, and patterns. Use VISUAL DISCRIMINATION or VISUAL THRESHOLDS to access references on visual acuity prior to 1982.
B Perceptual Discrimination [73]
Visual Perception [67]
R Visual Search [82]
Visual Tracking [73]

Visual Displays [73]
PN 2058 **SC** 55920
SN Presentation of visual information in the form of charts, graphs, maps, signs, symbols, or patterns. Prior to 1985, used for visual devices such as cathode-ray tubes or instrument panels. From 1985, consider also VIDEO DISPLAY UNITS, INSTRUMENT CONTROLS, or GRAPHICAL DISPLAYS.
B Displays [67]
Visual Stimulation [73]
N Video Display Units [85]
R ↓ Computer Peripheral Devices [85]
Pictorial Stimuli [78]
Spatial Frequency [82]
Temporal Frequency [85]

Visual Evoked Potentials [73]
PN 2044 **SC** 55930
B Evoked Potentials [67]
R ↓ Cortical Evoked Potentials [73]
↓ Vision [67]

Visual Feedback [73]
PN 358 **SC** 55940
SN Return of information on specified behavioral functions or parameters by means of visual stimulation. Such stimulation may serve to regulate or control subsequent behavior, cognition, perception, or performance.
B Sensory Feedback [73]
Visual Stimulation [73]

Visual Field [67]
PN 2607 **SC** 55950
B Visual Perception [67]
R Eye Fixation [82]
Fovea [82]
Peripheral Vision [88]

Visual Fixation
Use Eye Fixation

Visual Hallucinations [73]
PN 188 **SC** 55960
B Hallucinations [67]
R ↓ Vision [67]

Visual Masking [73]
PN 775 **SC** 55970
SN Changes in perceptual sensitivity to a visual stimulus due to the presence of a second stimulus in close temporal proximity.
B Masking [67]
R ↓ Visual Stimulation [73]

Visual Memory [94]
PN 133 **SC** 55973
B Memory [67]
N Visuospatial Memory [97]
R Eidetic Imagery [73]
↓ Spatial Memory [88]
↓ Visual Perception [67]

Visual Neglect
Use Sensory Neglect

Visual Perception 67
PN 12115 SC 55980
B Perception 67
Vision 67
N Autokinetic Illusion 67
Binocular Vision 67
↓ Brightness Perception 73
↓ Color Perception 67
Dark Adaptation 73
Eye Fixation 82
Face Perception 85
Foveal Vision 88
Interocular Transfer 85
Monocular Vision 73
Peripheral Vision 88
Stereoscopic Vision 73
Texture Perception 82
Visual Acuity 82
↓ Visual Contrast 85
Visual Discrimination 67
Visual Field 67
↓ Visual Thresholds 73
↓ Visuospatial Ability 97
R ↓ Eye (Anatomy) 67
↓ Eye Disorders 73
Lipreading 73
Mirror Image 91
Retinal Eccentricity 91
↓ Visual Memory 94
Visual Receptive Fields 82
Visual Tracking 73

Visual Perspective
Use Linear Perspective

Visual Receptive Fields 82
PN 428 SC 55985
SN Area of the retina which, when stimulated, affects a specific ganglion cell or lateral geniculate body cell, with zones in each field responding in a complementary way to various properties of visual stimuli such as color or onset/offset. Also, those zones in visual cortex which respond in a complementary way to straight-edge orientation-specific stimuli.
B Receptive Fields 85
R Geniculate Bodies (Thalamus) 73
↓ Neurons 73
↓ Photoreceptors 73
Retinal Eccentricity 91
Visual Cortex 67
↓ Visual Perception 67

Visual Search 82
PN 863 SC 55987
SN Perceptual processes associated with detecting and/or locating specified visual targets which are usually not continuously visible. Compare VISUAL TRACKING.
R Cognitive Discrimination 73
↓ Eye Movements 67
Pattern Discrimination 67
Signal Detection (Perception) 67
Visual Discrimination 67
↓ Visual Thresholds 73

Visual Spatial Ability
Use Visuospatial Ability

Visual Spatial Memory
Use Visuospatial Memory

Visual Stimulation 73
PN 5828 SC 55990
B Perceptual Stimulation 73
N Dichoptic Stimulation 82
↓ Illumination 67
Prismatic Stimulation 73
Stereoscopic Presentation 73

Visual Stimulation — (cont'd)
N Tachistoscopic Presentation 73
↓ Visual Displays 73
Visual Feedback 73
R ↓ Color 67
Linear Perspective 82
Pictorial Stimuli 78
Spatial Frequency 82
Temporal Frequency 85
Video Display Units 85
Visual Masking 73

Visual Thresholds 73
PN 1829 SC 56000
SN The minimal level of stimulation, the minimal difference between any stimuli, or the minimal stimulus change that is visually detectable.
UF Luminance Threshold
Photic Threshold
B Thresholds 67
Visual Perception 67
N Critical Flicker Fusion Threshold 67
R Dark Adaptation 73
Light Adaptation 82
Luminance 82
↓ Perceptual Measures 73
Retinal Eccentricity 91
Visual Search 82

Visual Tracking 73
PN 858 SC 56010
SN Perceptual processes associated with following a specified visual target with the eyes along its path of movement. Usually involves a continuously visible target. Compare VISUAL SEARCH.
B Tracking 67
R ↓ Vision 67
Visual Discrimination 67
↓ Visual Perception 67

Visualization
Use Imagery

Visually Disabled 97
PN 0 SC 56017
SN Persons with varying degrees of vision loss, due to eye disorders or an organic defect in the sensorineural pathways. Use VISUALLY HANDICAPPED to access references prior to 1997.
UF Visually Handicapped
B Sensorially Disabled 97
N ↓ Blind 67
Partially Sighted 73
R Braille 78
Braille Instruction 73
Sensory Disabilities (Attit Toward) 97
↓ Vision 67
↓ Vision Disorders 82

Visually Handicapped
SN Term discontinued in 1997. Use VISUALLY HANDICAPPED to access references prior to 1997.
Use Visually Disabled

Visuospatial Ability 97
PN 0 SC 56025
UF Visual Spatial Ability
B Spatial Ability 82
Visual Perception 67
N Visuospatial Memory 97

Visuospatial Memory 97
PN 0 SC 56027
UF Visual Spatial Memory
B Spatial Memory 88
Visual Memory 94
Visuospatial Ability 97

Vitamin C
Use Ascorbic Acid

Vitamin Deficiency Disorders 73
PN 117 SC 56040
B Nutritional Deficiencies 73
N Pellagra 73
Wernickes Syndrome 73
R ↓ Vitamins 73

Vitamin Therapy 78
PN 199 SC 56045
B Alternative Medicine 97
Organic Therapies 73
R ↓ Vitamins 73

Vitamins 73
PN 330 SC 56050
N Ascorbic Acid 73
↓ Choline 73
Nicotinamide 73
Nicotinic Acid 73
R ↓ Drugs 67
↓ Vitamin Deficiency Disorders 73
Vitamin Therapy 78

Vocabulary 67
PN 1655 SC 56060
UF Words (Vocabulary)
B Language 67
N Anagrams 73
Antonyms 73
Homographs 73
Homonyms 73
Neologisms 73
Sight Vocabulary 73
Slang 73
Synonyms 73
R ↓ Semantics 67
↓ Verbal Communication 67

Vocal Cords 73
PN 34 SC 56070
B Larynx 73

Vocalization 67
PN 644 SC 56075
SN Production of sounds by means of vocal cord vibrations.
N ↓ Animal Vocalizations 73
Crying 73
Laughter 78
Subvocalization 73
↓ Voice 73
R ↓ Animal Communication 67
↓ Communication 67
↓ Oral Communication 85
Singing 97
↓ Verbal Communication 67

Vocalization (Infant)
Use Infant Vocalization

Vocalizations (Animal)
Use Animal Vocalizations

Vocational Adjustment
Use Occupational Adjustment

Vocational Aspirations
Use Occupational Aspirations

Vocational Choice
Use Occupational Choice

Vocational Counseling
Use Occupational Guidance

Vocational Counselors 73
PN 199 **SC** 56140
SN Persons engaged in career guidance, usually in social service, school, government agency, industrial, or employment center settings.
B Counselors 67
R Mentor 85
Occupational Guidance 67
School Counselors 73
↓ Social Workers 73

Vocational Education 73
PN 1333 **SC** 56150
SN Formal training in or out of school, designed to teach skills and knowledge required for occupational proficiency, especially for paraprofessional, trade, or clerical occupations.
UF Industrial Arts Education
B Curriculum 67
N Cooperative Education 82
R ↓ Occupations 67

Vocational Education Teachers 88
PN 36 **SC** 56155
UF Technical Education Teachers
B Teachers 67

Vocational Evaluation 91
PN 77 **SC** 56157
SN Assessment of vocational aptitude, job skills, and performance potential using simulated or real work experiences and measures. Used for disabled or disordered populations.
B Evaluation 67
Vocational Rehabilitation 67
R Disability Management 91
Employability 73
↓ Employee Skills 73
Work Adjustment Training 91

Vocational Guidance
Use Occupational Guidance

Vocational Interests
Use Occupational Interests

Vocational Maturity 78
PN 841 **SC** 56175
SN Ability to make age-appropriate vocational decisions and choices, usually predictive of good vocational adjustment.
UF Career Maturity
Maturity (Vocational)
R Occupational Attitudes 73
Occupational Choice 67
Occupational Interests 67
Occupational Preference 73
↓ Occupations 67

Vocational Mobility
Use Occupational Mobility

Vocational Preference
Use Occupational Preference

Vocational Rehabilitation 67
PN 2594 **SC** 56210
SN Planning and providing necessary services required for successful job placement and subsequent vocational adjustment of handicapped clients.
UF Rehabilitation (Vocational)
B Psychosocial Rehabilitation 73
N Supported Employment 94
Vocational Evaluation 91
Work Adjustment Training 91
R Disability Management 91

Vocational Rehabilitation — (cont'd)
R Rehabilitation Counseling 78
School to Work Transition 94

Vocational School Students 73
PN 318 **SC** 56220
B Students 67
R ↓ Adolescents 67

Vocational Schools
Use Technical Schools

Vocations
Use Occupations

Voice 73
PN 576 **SC** 56250
B Vocalization 67
N Crying 73
Infant Vocalization 73
R ↓ Communication 67
↓ Oral Communication 85
Singing 97

Voice Disorders
Use Dysphonia

Voles
Use Rodents

Volition 88
PN 215 **SC** 56257
SN Process of deciding on a course of action voluntarily or without direct external influence.
UF Free Will
R Choice Behavior 67
↓ Decision Making 67
Determinism 97
Freedom 78
Self Determination 94

Volt Meters
SN Term discontinued in 1997. Use VOLT METERS to access references from 73–96.
Use Apparatus

Volunteer Civilian Personnel 73
PN 115 **SC** 56280
SN Civilians rendering services free of charge on behalf of various social causes (e.g., mental health, community services, politics).
B Volunteer Personnel 73
R ↓ Paraprofessional Personnel 73

Volunteer Military Personnel 73
PN 27 **SC** 56290
B Military Personnel 67
Volunteer Personnel 73
R Commissioned Officers 73
↓ Enlisted Military Personnel 73
National Guardsmen 73
ROTC Students 73

Volunteer Personnel 73
PN 737 **SC** 56300
B Personnel 67
N Volunteer Civilian Personnel 73
Volunteer Military Personnel 73
R ↓ Educational Personnel 73
Fire Fighters 91
National Guardsmen 73
↓ Paraprofessional Personnel 73
↓ Religious Personnel 73
ROTC Students 73

Volunteers (Experiment)
Use Experiment Volunteers

Volunteers in Service to America 73
PN 1 **SC** 56320
SN National corps of volunteers whose mission is to address poverty and poverty-related human, social, and environmental problems in the USA. Part of ACTION, a U.S. Government agency.
UF VISTA Volunteers
B Government Programs 73
R Government 67

Vomeronasal Sense 82
PN 101 **SC** 56327
SN Perceptual system activated by chemical stimuli which trigger vomeronasal nerve activity.
R Chemoreceptors 73
↓ Olfactory Perception 67

Vomit Inducing Drugs
Use Emetic Drugs

Vomiting 73
PN 354 **SC** 56340
B Gastrointestinal Disorders 73
Symptoms 67
R ↓ Antiemetic Drugs 73
↓ Emetic Drugs 73
Nausea 73

Voting Behavior 73
PN 616 **SC** 56350
B Behavior 67
Political Participation 88
Political Processes 73
R ↓ Political Attitudes 73
Political Elections 73
Political Issues 73
Political Psychology 97

Vowels 73
PN 720 **SC** 56360
B Letters (Alphabet) 73
Phonology 73
R ↓ Phonemes 73
Syllables 73
Words (Phonetic Units) 67

Voyeurism 73
PN 36 **SC** 56370
B Sexual Deviations 67
R Exhibitionism 73

Vygotsky (Lev) 91
PN 84 **SC** 56375
SN Identifies biographical or autobiographical studies and discussions of Vygotsky's works. Sometimes spelled Vigotsky or Vygotski.
R ↓ Language Development 67
Psycholinguistics 67
↓ Psychologists 67

Wages
Use Salaries

Wakefulness 73
PN 846 **SC** 56410
B Consciousness States 71
R Sleep Wake Cycle 85

Wales 73
PN 237 **SC** 56420
B Great Britain 71

Walk In Clinics 73
PN 44 **SC** 56430

Walk In Clinics — (cont'd)
SN Facilities in hospitals or other community locations which typically provide immediate access to counseling and referral; are often staffed by volunteers and nondegreed counselors and focus on minority, indigent, or youthful populations.
B Clinics 67
R ↓ Crisis Intervention Services 73
Psychiatric Clinics 73

Walking 73
PN 390 **SC** 56440
B Motor Performance 73

Wandering Behavior 91
PN 22 **SC** 56450
SN Aimless activity usually resulting from a confused mental state.
B Behavior 67
Motor Processes 67
R Mental Confusion 73
Place Disorientation 73
↓ Symptoms 67

War 67
PN 1642 **SC** 56460
B Conflict 67
Social Issues 91
N Nuclear War 85
R Combat Experience 91
Foreign Policy Making 73
↓ Government Policy Making 73
Peace 88
↓ Violence 73

Warning Labels 97
PN 0 **SC** 56464
B Warnings 97
R Accident Prevention 73
↓ Accidents 67
Consumer Protection 73
Hazards 73
↓ Safety 67
↓ Safety Devices 73

Warning Signs
Use Warnings

Warnings 97
PN 0 **SC** 56470
UF Safety Warnings
Warning Signs
N Warning Labels 97
R Accident Prevention 73
↓ Accidents 67
Consumer Protection 73
Hazards 73
↓ Safety 67
↓ Safety Devices 73

Wasps 82
PN 172 **SC** 56475
SN Any of numerous social or solitary winged hymenopterous insects.
B Insects 67
R Larvae 73

Water Deprivation 67
PN 675 **SC** 56480
SN Absence of ad libitum water access. In experimental settings, water deprivation is used to achieve a definable level of motivation within the organism.
B Deprivation 67
Stimulus Deprivation 73
R Dehydration 88
Thirst 67

Water Intake 67
PN 1867 **SC** 56490
SN Ingestion of water. Frequently used as an objective measure of physiological or motivational state or learning. Used for human or animal populations.
B Drinking Behavior 78
Fluid Intake 85
R Animal Drinking Behavior 73
Dehydration 88

Water Safety 73
PN 125 **SC** 56500
SN Programs or activities for accident prevention in aquatic environments.
B Safety 67

Water Transportation 73
PN 151 **SC** 56510
B Transportation 73
N Submarines 73

Watson (John Broadus) 91
PN 2 **SC** 56515
SN Identifies biographical or autobiographical studies and discussions of Watson's works.
R Behaviorism 67
↓ Psychologists 67

Weaning 73
PN 178 **SC** 56520
SN Process of acclimating an infant or child to a substitute for the mother's milk. Used for human or animal populations.
B Childrearing Practices 67
Feeding Practices 73
R Breast Feeding 73
Sucking 78

Weapons 78
PN 272 **SC** 56525
UF Firearms
R Gun Control Laws 73

Weather
Use Atmospheric Conditions

Wechsler Adult Intelligence Scale 67
PN 1404 **SC** 56530
B Intelligence Measures 67

Wechsler Bellevue Intelligence Scale 67
PN 40 **SC** 56540
B Intelligence Measures 67

Wechsler Intelligence Scale Children 67
PN 1939 **SC** 56550
B Intelligence Measures 67

Wechsler Memory Scale 88
PN 111 **SC** 56553
B Neuropsychological Assessment 82
Retention Measures 73

Wechsler Preschool Primary Scale 88
PN 79 **SC** 56555
B Intelligence Measures 67

Weight (Body)
Use Body Weight

Weight (Statistics)
Use Statistical Weighting

Weight Control 85
PN 863 **SC** 56565
SN Deliberate regulation of one's weight through diet, exercise, or other means. Also, the relative weight change resulting from such regulation practices. Used for human populations only.
R Aerobic Exercise 88
↓ Body Weight 67
Diets 78
↓ Exercise 73
↓ Food Intake 67
Health Behavior 82
Obesity (Attitudes Toward) 97

Weight Perception 67
PN 193 **SC** 56570
SN Awareness of mass or weight.
B Somesthetic Perception 67

Weightlessness 67
PN 48 **SC** 56580
B Gravitational Effects 67
R ↓ Somesthetic Stimulation 73
Spaceflight 67

Weightlifting 94
PN 12 **SC** 56585
B Exercise 73
Recreation 67
Sports 67

Welfare Services (Government) 73
PN 453 **SC** 56600
B Government Programs 73
R Community Welfare Services 73
Government 67
Medicaid 94

Well Being 94
PN 531 **SC** 56603
R ↓ Adjustment 67
↓ Health 73
Life Satisfaction 85
Lifestyle Changes 97
↓ Mental Health 67
↓ Quality of Life 85

Wellness
Use Health

Welsh Figure Preference Test 73
PN 5 **SC** 56610
B Nonprojective Personality Measures 73

Wepman Test of Auditory Discrim 73
PN 7 **SC** 56620
B Speech and Hearing Measures 73

Wernickes Syndrome 73
PN 75 **SC** 56630
SN Use APHASIA for Wernicke's aphasia.
B Alcoholism 67
Encephalopathies 82
Syndromes 73
Vitamin Deficiency Disorders 73

West Africa 88
PN 23 **SC** 56635
B Africa 67

West German Federal Republic
SN Term discontinued in 1982. Use WEST GERMAN FEDERAL REPUBLIC to access references from 67–81.
Use West Germany

West Germany 82
PN 924 SC 56642
SN Use WEST GERMAN FEDERAL REPUBLIC to access references from 67-81.
UF West German Federal Republic
B Germany 88

West Indies 73
PN 143 SC 56650
N Bahama Islands 73
Barbados 91
Bermuda 91
Cuba 73
Dominican Republic 73
Haiti 73
Hispaniola 73
Jamaica 73
Netherlands Antilles 88
Puerto Rico 73
Saint Lucia 91
Saint Vincent 91
Trinidad and Tobago 82
Virgin Islands 73
R Latin America 88

Western Europe 88
PN 45 SC 56663
B Europe 73

Western Samoa 91
PN 6 SC 56664
B South Pacific 78

Whales 85
PN 31 SC 56665
B Mammals 73
N Dolphins 73
Porpoises 73

Wheelchairs
Use Mobility Aids

Whiplash 97
PN 0 SC 56669
SN Soft tissue injury of cervical spine due to sudden hyperextension or hyperflexion or hyperrotation of neck or limbs.
UF Cervical Sprain Syndrome
B Spinal Cord Injuries 73
R ↓ Head Injuries 73

Whistleblowing
Use Informants

White Betz A B Scale
SN Term discontinued in 1997. Use WHITE BETZ A B SCALE to access references from 73-96.
Use Nonprojective Personality Measures

White Blood Cells
Use Leucocytes

White Collar Workers 73
PN 361 SC 56690
SN Individuals employed in technical, professional, sales, administrative, or clerical positions.
B Business and Industrial Personnel 67
N Accountants 73
Clerical Personnel 73
↓ Management Personnel 73
Sales Personnel 73
Secretarial Personnel 73

White Noise 73
PN 297 SC 56700

White Noise — (cont'd)
SN Noise composed of random mixture of sounds of different wavelengths.
B Auditory Stimulation 67

White Rats
Use Rats

Whites 82
PN 4268 SC 56720
SN Populations of European, North African, or Southwest Asian descent. May also be used to refer to population groups in these areas when cultural or ethnic comparisons are studied. Use CAUCASIANS to access references from 73-81.
UF Caucasians
R Anglos 88
↓ Ethnic Groups 73
Race (Anthropological) 73

Wholistic Health
Use Holistic Health

Wide Range Achievement Test 73
PN 152 SC 56730
B Achievement Measures 67

Widowers 73
PN 266 SC 56740
B Human Males 73
R ↓ Family 67
↓ Marital Status 73
↓ Parental Absence 73

Widows 73
PN 634 SC 56750
B Human Females 73
R ↓ Family 67
↓ Marital Status 73
↓ Parental Absence 73

Wilcoxon Sign Rank Test 73
PN 13 SC 56760
UF Sign Rank Test
B Nonparametric Statistical Tests 67

Wilderness Experience 91
PN 64 SC 56763
SN Outdoor environment and activities used to promote experiential learning or to treat and rehabilitate individuals with physical, emotional, or behavioral problems.
UF Outward Bound
R Management Training 73
↓ Psychotherapeutic Techniques 67
↓ Recreation 67
↓ Rehabilitation 67
↓ Sports 67
Therapeutic Camps 78

Willpower
Use Self Control

Wilson Patterson Conservatism Scale 73
PN 15 SC 56780
B Attitude Measures 67

Wine 73
PN 37 SC 56810
B Alcoholic Beverages 73

Winnicottian Theory
Use Object Relations

Winter Depression
Use Seasonal Affective Disorder

Wisconsin Card Sorting Test 94
PN 41 SC 56835
B Neuropsychological Assessment 82

Wisdom 94
PN 18 SC 56837
R Intelligence 67
↓ Judgment 67
↓ Knowledge Level 78

Witchcraft 73
PN 107 SC 56840
R Ethnology 67
Faith Healing 73
Mysticism 67
Occultism 78
↓ Parapsychology 67
↓ Religious Beliefs 73
Shamanism 73

Withdrawal (Defense Mechanism) 73
PN 127 SC 56860
SN Psychoanalytic term describing the escape from or avoidance of emotionally or psychologically painful situations.
B Defense Mechanisms 67
R ↓ Separation Reactions 97

Withdrawal (Drug)
Use Drug Withdrawal

Within Subjects Design
Use Repeated Measures

Witnesses 85
PN 623 SC 56885
SN Persons giving evidence in a court of law or observing traumatic events in a nonlegal context. Also used for analog studies of eyewitness identification performance, perception of witness credibility, and other studies of witness characteristics having legal implications.
UF Eyewitnesses
R ↓ Legal Evidence 91
Legal Interrogation 94
↓ Legal Testimony 82

Wives 73
PN 1792 SC 56900
B Human Females 73
Spouses 73
N Housewives 73

Wolves 73
PN 101 SC 56910
B Canids 97

Women
Use Human Females

Womens Liberation Movement 73
PN 377 SC 56920
B Social Movements 67
R ↓ Activist Movements 73
Feminism 78

Woodcock Johnson Psychoed Battery 94
PN 13 SC 56925
B Achievement Measures 67
R Educational Diagnosis 78

Word Associations 67
PN 1684 SC 56930
UF Associations (Word)
R ↓ Associative Processes 67
↓ Cognitive Processes 67
Paired Associate Learning 67

Word Blindness
Use Alexia

Word Deafness
Use Aphasia

Word Frequency 73
PN 664 **SC** 56970
SN Statistical probability of the occurrence of a given word in a given natural language.
R Contextual Associations 67

Word Meaning 73
PN 1971 **SC** 56980
SN Connotative or denotative significance of a word.
B Verbal Meaning 73
R Connotations 73
Contextual Associations 67
↓ Lexical Access 88
Lexical Decision 88

Word Origins
Use Etymology

Word Processing 91
PN 100 **SC** 56993
SN Use of computer software to compose, edit, and produce text.
B Computer Software 67
Data Processing 67
R Clerical Secretarial Skills 73
↓ Computer Applications 73
Information Systems 91
Typing 91

Word Recognition 88
PN 1343 **SC** 56995
R ↓ Associative Processes 67
Human Information Storage 73
↓ Reading Skills 73
↓ Recognition (Learning) 67
Sight Vocabulary 73
Speech Perception 67
Words (Phonetic Units) 67

Words (Form Classes)
Use Form Classes (Language)

Words (Phonetic Units) 67
PN 4911 **SC** 57020
SN Spoken or written symbolic representation of an idea, frequently viewed as the smallest grammatically independent unit.
R Antonyms 73
Consonants 73
Etymology 73
↓ Grammar 67
Homographs 73
Homonyms 73
↓ Lexical Access 88
Lexical Decision 88
Morphology (Language) 73
Neologisms 73
↓ Semantics 67
Synonyms 73
Vowels 73
Word Recognition 88

Words (Vocabulary)
Use Vocabulary

Work (Attitudes Toward) 73
PN 2022 **SC** 57037
SN General work values. Use EMPLOYEE ATTITUDES for specific job situations and OCCUPATIONAL ATTITUDES for specific careers.

Work (Attitudes Toward) — (cont'd)
UF Work Ethic
B Attitudes 67
R ↓ Employee Attitudes 67
Employer Attitudes 73
Family Work Relationship 97
Job Involvement 78
Occupational Attitudes 73
↓ Personnel 67

Work Adjustment Training 91
PN 24 **SC** 57045
SN Training or programs to help disabled individuals increase work productivity, handle day to day demands of competitive employment, develop work tolerance, and to encourage interpersonal work relationships.
B Vocational Rehabilitation 67
R ↓ Adjustment 67
Occupational Adjustment 73
Rehabilitation Counseling 78
Supported Employment 94
Vocational Evaluation 91

Work Environments
Use Working Conditions

Work Ethic
Use Work (Attitudes Toward)

Work Family Relationship
Use Family Work Relationship

Work Load 82
PN 516 **SC** 57055
SN Amount of work or working time expected from, assigned to, or performed by an individual.
B Job Characteristics 85
R ↓ Division of Labor 88
Human Channel Capacity 73
Job Analysis 67
↓ Job Performance 67
Work Scheduling 73
↓ Working Conditions 73

Work Related Illnesses 94
PN 56 **SC** 57057
SN Includes both physical and mental illnesses, injuries, or disorders. Consider OCCUPATIONAL STRESS for work related stress.
R Industrial Accidents 73
↓ Mental Disorders 67
Occupational Exposure 88
Occupational Safety 73
Occupational Stress 73
↓ Physical Disorders 97
↓ Working Conditions 73
Workmens Compensation Insurance 73

Work Rest Cycles 73
PN 98 **SC** 57060
SN Strictly scheduled periods of working and resting based on observations that any increase in number of working hours beyond an optimal point diminishes production and efficiency.
B Working Conditions 73
R Work Scheduling 73

Work Satisfaction
Use Job Satisfaction

Work Scheduling 73
PN 293 **SC** 57070
SN Individual or organizational distribution of workload or work hours. Consider also WORKDAY SHIFTS.
UF Flextime
Scheduling (Work)

Work Scheduling — (cont'd)
R ↓ Management Methods 73
Work Load 82
Work Rest Cycles 73

Work Study Programs
Use Educational Programs

Work Week Length 73
PN 63 **SC** 57080
SN Actual number of hours or workdays an employee is required to work during a consecutive 7-day period.
B Working Conditions 73

Workday Shifts 73
PN 455 **SC** 57090
SN Regularly scheduled daily working hours or scheduled working shifts with core hours being in morning, evening, or late night/predawn. Consider also WORK SCHEDULING.
UF Shifts (Workday)
B Working Conditions 73

Workers
Use Personnel

Working Alliance
Use Therapeutic Alliance

Working Conditions 73
PN 3109 **SC** 57120
SN Factors which contribute to the global milieu of the workplace. Includes physical environment characteristics, job content and work load, and psychosocial factors such as personnel composition, norms, attitudes, motivation, and employee services.
UF Factory Environments
Office Environment
Work Environments
B Social Environments 73
N Job Enrichment 73
Noise Levels (Work Areas) 73
Occupational Safety 73
Work Rest Cycles 73
Work Week Length 73
Workday Shifts 73
Working Space 73
R Disabled Personnel 97
Family Work Relationship 97
Human Factors Engineering 73
Occupational Exposure 88
Organizational Climate 73
Person Environment Fit 91
↓ Personnel 67
Quality of Work Life 88
Work Load 82
Work Related Illnesses 94

Working Memory
Use Short Term Memory

Working Space 73
PN 64 **SC** 57130
SN Physical characteristics of job setting, including such factors as amount of space, noise level, or lighting conditions.
B Working Conditions 73

Working Women 78
PN 1925 **SC** 57135
B Human Females 73
R Dual Careers 82
↓ Employment Status 82
↓ Family 67
Family Work Relationship 97
↓ Occupations 67

Working Women — (cont'd)
R ↓ Personnel [67]
Single Mothers [94]

Workmens Compensation Insurance [73]
PN 139 SC 57140
SN Insurance that provides medical benefits for employees who are injured in work-related accidents and provides continued income during disability.
B Employee Benefits [73]
Employee Health Insurance [73]
R Disabled Personnel [97]
Work Related Illnesses [94]

World View [88]
PN 570 SC 57150
UF Philosophy of Life
R ↓ Attitudes [67]
Self Determination [94]
↓ Values [67]

Worms [67]
PN 90 SC 57160
B Invertebrates [73]
N Earthworms [73]
Planarians [73]

Worry
Use Anxiety

Worship
Use Religious Practices

Wounds [73]
PN 17 SC 57180
B Injuries [73]
N Self Inflicted Wounds [73]
R Burns [73]
Electrical Injuries [73]
↓ Head Injuries [73]

Wrist [73]
PN 77 SC 57190
B Joints (Anatomy) [73]
R Arm (Anatomy) [73]
Hand (Anatomy) [67]

Writers [91]
PN 229 SC 57195
UF Authors
B Artists [73]
R Drama [73]
↓ Literature [67]

Writing (Creative)
SN Use LITERATURE to access references from 73-93.
Use Creative Writing

Writing (Cursive)
Use Cursive Writing

Writing (Handwriting)
Use Handwriting

Writing Skills [85]
PN 1216 SC 57225
SN Proficiency in writing as developed through practice and influenced by ability.
B Communication Skills [73]
R ↓ Literacy [73]
Literacy Programs [97]
Verbal Ability [67]
↓ Written Communication [85]

Written Communication [85]
PN 2030 SC 57227
SN Expression of information in written form.
B Verbal Communication [67]
N Creative Writing [94]
R Note Taking [91]
Proofreading [88]
Rhetoric [91]
Verbal Ability [67]
Writing Skills [85]

Written Language [67]
PN 1312 SC 57230
SN System of signs and symbols used to convey information.
B Language [67]
N ↓ Alphabets [73]
↓ Handwriting [67]
Numbers (Numerals) [67]
Paragraphs [73]
Readability [78]
R ↓ Legibility [78]
Orthography [73]

Wryneck
Use Torticollis

X Rated Materials
Use Pornography

X Ray Diagnosis
Use Roentgenography

X Ray Therapy
Use Radiation Therapy

Xenophobia
Use Stranger Reactions

Xylocaine
Use Lidocaine

Yawning [88]
PN 95 SC 57300
B Reflexes [71]
R Respiration [67]

Yemen [91]
PN 7 SC 57305
R Middle East [78]

Yoga [73]
PN 202 SC 57310
B Exercise [73]
Religious Practices [73]
R Relaxation [73]

Yohimbine [88]
PN 163 SC 57315
B Adrenergic Blocking Drugs [73]

Young Adults [73]
PN 4411 SC 57320
SN Ages 18-29. Used in noneducational contexts. Applied only if age is important to the research focus.
UF Youth (Adults)
B Adults [67]
R ↓ Adolescents [67]
Adult Development [78]
↓ College Students [67]
Graduate Students [67]
Postgraduate Students [73]

Youth (Adolescents)
Use Adolescents

Youth (Adults)
Use Young Adults

Youth (Children)
Use Children

Yugoslavia [73]
PN 251 SC 57360
B Europe [73]

Z Scores
Use Standard Scores

Zaire [88]
PN 45 SC 57364
B Africa [67]

Zambia [82]
PN 46 SC 57365
B Africa [67]

Zen Buddhism [73]
PN 91 SC 57370
B Buddhism [73]

Zidovudine [94]
PN 16 SC 57371
UF Azidothymidine
AZT
B Antiviral Drugs [94]
R Acquired Immune Deficiency Syndrome [88]
↓ Human Immunodeficiency Virus [91]

Zimbabwe [88]
PN 80 SC 57372
B Africa [67]

Zimeldine [88]
PN 43 SC 57373
B Antidepressant Drugs [71]
Serotonin Reuptake Inhibitors [97]

Zinc [85]
PN 89 SC 57375
B Electrolytes [73]
Metallic Elements [73]

Zoo Environment
Use Animal Captivity

Zoology [73]
PN 18 SC 57380
B Biology [67]

Zulliger Z Test [73]
PN 11 SC 57390
B Projective Personality Measures [73]

Zungs Self Rating Depression Scale [73]
PN 61 SC 57400
B Nonprojective Personality Measures [73]

ROTATED ALPHABETICAL TERMS SECTION

ROTATED ALPHABETICAL TERMS SECTION

Abandonment
Abdomen
Abdominal Wall
Abducens Nerve
Ability
Ability Grouping
Ability Level
Ability Tests *USE Aptitude Measures*
Artistic **Ability**
Cognitive **Ability**
Henmon Nelson Tests Mental Ability *USE Intelligence Measures*
Illinois Test Psycholinguist **Abil**
Learning **Ability**
Mathematical **Ability**
Musical **Ability**
Nonverbal **Ability**
Numerical Ability *USE Mathematical Ability*
Reading **Ability**
School and College Ability Test *USE Aptitude Measures*
Spatial **Ability**
Verbal **Ability**
Visual Spatial Ability *USE Visuospatial Ability*
Visuospatial **Ability**
Ablation *USE Lesions*
Abortion Laws
Elective Abortion *USE Induced Abortion*
Induced **Abortion**
Spontaneous **Abortion**
Therapeutic Abortion *USE Induced Abortion*
Maslow **(Abraham** Harold)
Abreaction *USE Catharsis*
Father **Absence**
Mother **Absence**
Parental **Absence**
Employee **Absenteeism**
Absorption (Physiological)
Abstinence (Drugs) *USE Drug Abstinence*
Alcohol Abstinence *USE Sobriety*
Drug **Abstinence**
Sexual **Abstinence**
Abstraction
Abuse of Power
Abuse Potential (Drugs)
USE Drug Abuse Liability
Abuse Reporting
Alcohol **Abuse**
Child **Abuse**
Child **Abuse** Reporting
Client Abuse *USE Patient Abuse*
Drug **Abuse**
Drug **Abuse** Liability
Drug **Abuse** Prevention
Elder **Abuse**
Emotional **Abuse**
Inhalant **Abuse**
Multidrug Abuse *USE Polydrug Abuse*
Partner **Abuse**
Patient **Abuse**
Physical **Abuse**
Polydrug **Abuse**
Psychological Abuse *USE Emotional Abuse*
Sexual **Abuse**
Solvent Abuse *USE Inhalant Abuse*
Spouse Abuse *USE Partner Abuse*
Substance Abuse *USE Drug Abuse*
Substance Abuse Prevention
USE Drug Abuse Prevention
Academic Achievement
Academic Achievement Motivation
Academic Achievement Prediction
Academic Aptitude
Academic Environment
Academic Failure
Academic Grade Level *USE Grade Level*
Academic Overachievement
Academic Records *USE Student Records*
Academic Self Concept
Academic Specialization
Academic Underachievement

College **Academic** Achievement
Acalculia
Accelerated Speech *USE Speech Rate*
Acceleration Effects
Self Acceptance *USE Self Perception*
Social **Acceptance**
Lexical **Access**
Accessory Nerve *USE Cranial Nerves*
Accident Prevention
Accident Proneness
Accidents
Air Traffic **Accidents**
Automobile Accidents *USE Motor Traffic Accidents*
Cerebrovascular **Accidents**
Home **Accidents**
Industrial **Accidents**
Motor Traffic **Accidents**
Pedestrian **Accidents**
Transportation **Accidents**
Thermal **Acclimatization**
Eye Accommodation
USE Ocular Accommodation
Ocular **Accommodation**
Accomplishment *USE Achievement*
Accountability
Accountants
Accreditation (Education Personnel)
Accreditation (Educational Programs)
USE Educational Program Accreditation
Educational Program **Accreditation**
Hospital **Accreditation**
School Accreditation
USE Educational Program Accreditation
Teacher Accreditation
USE Accreditation (Education Personnel)
Acculturation *USE Cultural Assimilation*
Nucleus **Accumbens**
Acetaldehyde
Acetazolamide
Acetic Aldehyde *USE Acetaldehyde*
Acetylcholine
Acetylcholinesterase
Acetylsalicylic Acid *USE Aspirin*
Aches *USE Pain*
Achievement
Achievement Measures
Achievement Motivation
Achievement Potential
Academic **Achievement**
Academic **Achievement** Motivation
Academic **Achievement** Prediction
Attainment (Achievement) *USE Achievement*
College Academic **Achievement**
Mathematics **Achievement**
Need Achievement *USE Achievement Motivation*
Reading **Achievement**
Scholastic Achievement *USE Academic Achievement*
School Achievement *USE Academic Achievement*
Science **Achievement**
Stanford **Achievement** Test
Wide Range **Achievement** Test
Achilles Tendon Reflex
Achromatic Color
Acetylsalicylic Acid *USE Aspirin*
Ascorbic **Acid**
Aspartic **Acid**
Deoxyribonucleic **Acid**
Dihydroxyphenylacetic **Acid**
DNA (Deoxyribonucleic Acid) *USE Deoxyribonucleic Acid*
Folic **Acid**
Gamma Aminobutyric **Acid**
Gamma Aminobutyric **Acid** Agonists
Gamma Aminobutyric **Acid** Antagonists
Glutamic **Acid**
Homovanillic **Acid**
Hydroxyindoleacetic **Acid** (5-)
Ibotenic **Acid**
Kainic **Acid**
Lactic **Acid**

ROTATED ALPHABETICAL TERMS SECTION

Lysergic **Acid** Diethylamide
Nicotinic **Acid**
Nicotinic Acid Amide *USE Nicotinamide*
Ribonucleic **Acid**
RNA (Ribonucleic Acid) *USE Ribonucleic Acid*
Uric **Acid**
Valproic **Acid**
Acids
Amino **Acids**
Fatty **Acids**
Nucleic **Acids**
Acoustic Nerve
Acoustic Reflex
Acoustic Stimuli *USE Auditory Stimulation*
Acoustics
Acquaintance Rape
Acquired Immune Deficiency Syndrome
Acrophobia
ACTH (Hormone) *USE Corticotropin*
ACTH Releasing Factor
USE Corticotropin Releasing Factor
Acting Out
Affirmative **Action**
Active Avoidance
USE Avoidance Conditioning
Student **Activism**
Activist Movements
Activities of Daily Living
Daily **Activities**
Extracurricular **Activities**
Activity Level
Activity Therapy *USE Recreation Therapy*
Electrical **Activity**
Self **Actualization**
Auditory **Acuity**
Hearing Acuity *USE Auditory Acuity*
Vernier Acuity *USE Visual Acuity*
Visual **Acuity**
Acupuncture
Acute Alcoholic Intoxication
Acute Paranoid Disorder
USE Paranoia (Psychosis)
Acute Psychosis
Acute Psychotic Episode
USE Acute Psychosis
Acute Schizophrenia
Psychotic Episode (Acute) *USE Acute Psychosis*
Adaptability (Personality)
Adaptation
Dark **Adaptation**
Environmental **Adaptation**
Light **Adaptation**
Sensory **Adaptation**
Social Adaptation *USE Social Adjustment*
Kirton **Adaption** Innovation Inven
Adaptive Behavior
Adaptive Testing
Addiction
Drug **Addiction**
Heroin **Addiction**
Hospital Addiction Syndrome
USE Munchausen Syndrome
Sexual **Addiction**
Addisons Disease
Food **Additives**
Adenosine
Cyclic **Adenosine** Monophosphate
Gough **Adjective** Check List
Adjectives
Adjudication
Adjunctive Behavior
Adjustment
Adjustment Disorders
Emotional **Adjustment**
Marital Adjustment *USE Marital Relations*
Occupational **Adjustment**
Personal Adjustment *USE Emotional Adjustment*
Psychological Adjustment *USE Emotional Adjustment*
School **Adjustment**
Social **Adjustment**
Student Adjustment *USE School Adjustment*
Vocational Adjustment *USE Occupational Adjustment*
Work **Adjustment** Training
Adler (Alfred)
Adlerian Psychotherapy
Individual Psychotherapy (Adlerian) *USE Adlerian Psychotherapy*
Drug **Administration** Methods
Educational **Administration**
Health Care **Administration**
Hospital **Administration**
School Administration
USE Educational Administration
Test **Administration**
Administrators
USE Management Personnel
Educational Administrators *USE School Administrators*
School **Administrators**
Facility **Admission**
Hospital **Admission**
Psychiatric Hospital **Admission**
Student **Admission** Criteria
Adolescence
Adolescent Attitudes
Adolescent Development
Adolescent Fathers
Adolescent Mothers
Adolescent Pregnancy
Adolescent Psychiatry
Adolescent Psychology
Adolescent Psychotherapy
Adolescents
Adopted Children
Adoptees
Adoption (Child)
Interracial **Adoption**
Transracial Adoption *USE Interracial Adoption*
Adoptive Parents
Adrenal Cortex Hormones
Adrenal Cortex Steroids
USE Corticosteroids
Adrenal Gland Disorders
Adrenal Gland Secretion
Adrenal Glands
Adrenal Medulla Hormones
Hypothalamo Pituitary **Adrenal** System
Adrenalectomy
Adrenaline *USE Epinephrine*
Adrenergic Blocking Drugs
Adrenergic Drugs
Adrenergic Nerves
Adrenocorticotropin *USE Corticotropin*
Adrenolytic Drugs *USE Adrenergic Drugs*
Adult Attitudes
Adult Children *USE Adult Offspring*
Adult Day Care
Adult Development
Adult Education
Adult Learning
Adult Offspring
Leiter Adult Intelligence Scale
USE Intelligence Measures
Offenders (Adult) *USE Criminals*
Wechsler **Adult** Intelligence Scale
Adultery *USE Extramarital Intercourse*
Adulthood
Adults
Young **Adults**
Advance Directives
Advance Organizers
Adventitiously Disabled
Adventitiously Handicapped
USE Adventitiously Disabled
Adverbs
Drug Adverse Reactions
USE Side Effects (Drug)
Advertising
Television **Advertising**
Advocacy

ROTATED ALPHABETICAL TERMS SECTION

Child Advocacy *USE Advocacy*
Aerobic Exercise
Aerospace Personnel
Aesthetic Preferences
Aesthetics
Affairs (Sexual) *USE Extramarital Intercourse*
CNS **Affecting** Drugs
Heart Rate **Affecting** Drugs
Affection
Affective Disorders *USE Affective Disturbances*
Affective Disturbances
Affective Education
Affective Psychosis
Bipolar Affective Disorder *USE Manic Depression*
Seasonal **Affective** Disorder
Afferent Pathways
Afferent Stimulation
Afferentation *USE Afferent Stimulation*
Affiliation Motivation
Need for Affiliation *USE Affiliation Motivation*
Religious **Affiliation**
Affirmative Action
Afghanistan
Africa
East **Africa**
South **Africa**
West **Africa**
African Americans *USE Blacks*
Aftercare
Perceptual **Aftereffect**
Afterimage
Age Differences
Age Discrimination
Age Regression (Hypnotic)
Developmental **Age** Groups
Intelligence Age *USE Mental Age*
Mental **Age**
Old Age *USE Aged*
Preschool **Age** Children
School **Age** Children
Aged
Aged (Attitudes Toward)
Middle **Aged**
Agencies (Groups) *USE Organizations*
Government **Agencies**
Insurance Agents *USE Sales Personnel*
Aggressive Behavior
Animal **Aggressive** Behavior
Passive **Aggressive** Personality
Aggressiveness
Physical **Agility**
Aging
Aging (Attitudes Toward)
Physiological **Aging**
Paralysis Agitans *USE Parkinsons Disease*
Agitated Depression *USE Major Depression*
Agitation
Agnosia
Agonistic Behavior *USE Aggressive Behavior*
Benzodiazepine **Agonists**
Dopamine **Agonists**
GABA Agonists *USE Gamma Aminobutyric Acid Agonists*
Gamma Aminobutyric Acid **Agonists**
Narcotic **Agonists**
Opiate Agonists *USE Narcotic Agonists*
Serotonin **Agonists**
Agoraphobia
Agrammatism *USE Aphasia*
Agraphia
Agreeableness
Agricultural Extension Workers
Agricultural Workers
School Federal Aid *USE Educational Financial Assistance*
Home Health Aides *USE Home Care Personnel*
Psychiatric **Aides**
Teacher **Aides**
AIDS *USE Acquired Immune Deficiency Syndrome*
AIDS (Attitudes Toward)
AIDS Dementia Complex
AIDS Prevention
AIDS Testing *USE HIV Testing*
Educational Audiovisual **Aids**
Hearing **Aids**
Mobility **Aids**
Optical **Aids**
Air Encephalography *USE Pneumoencephalography*
Air Force Personnel
Air Traffic Accidents
Air Traffic Control
Air Transportation
Encephalography (Air) *USE Pneumoencephalography*
Aircraft
Aircraft Crew *USE Aerospace Personnel*
Aircraft Pilots
Navigators (Aircraft) *USE Aerospace Personnel*
Airplanes *USE Aircraft*
Akathisia
Akinesia *USE Apraxia*
Alanines
Alanon *USE Alcohol Rehabilitation*
Alarm Responses
Alaska
Alaska Natives
Alateen *USE Alcohol Rehabilitation*
Ellis **(Albert)**
Albinism
Serum **Albumin**
Alcohol Abstinence *USE Sobriety*
Alcohol Abuse
Alcohol Dehydrogenases
Alcohol Drinking Attitudes
Alcohol Drinking Patterns
Alcohol Education *USE Drug Education*
Alcohol (Grain) *USE Ethanol*
Alcohol Intoxication
Alcohol Rehabilitation
Alcohol Withdrawal
Blood **Alcohol** Concentration
Ethyl Alcohol *USE Ethanol*
Fetal **Alcohol** Syndrome
Methyl Alcohol *USE Methanol*
Alcoholic Beverages
Alcoholic Hallucinosis
Alcoholic Psychosis
Acute **Alcoholic** Intoxication
Chronic **Alcoholic** Intoxication
Alcoholics Anonymous
Alcoholism
Alcohols
Acetic Aldehyde *USE Acetaldehyde*
Aldolases *USE Enzymes*
Aldosterone
Alexia
Alexithymia
Adler **(Alfred)**
Algebra *USE Mathematics*
Algeria
Algorithms
Alienation
Alkaloids
Opium Alkaloids *USE Alkaloids AND Opiates*
Allergens *USE Antigens*
Allergic Disorders
Allergic Skin Disorders
Drug **Allergies**
Food **Allergies**
Therapeutic **Alliance**
Working Alliance *USE Therapeutic Alliance*
Alligators *USE Crocodilians*

Allocation of Resources
USE Resource Allocation
Resource **Allocation**
Reward **Allocation**
Allport Vernon Lindzey Study Values
USE Attitude Measures
Living **Alone**
Alopecia
Reading Aloud *USE Oral Reading*
Alpha Methylparatyrosine
Alpha Rhythm
Initial Teaching **Alphabet**
Letters **(Alphabet)**
Alphabets
Alprazolam
Delayed **Alternation**
Language Alternation *USE Code Switching*
Spontaneous **Alternation**
Alternative Medicine
Alternative Schools
USE Nontraditional Education
Altitude Effects
Altruism
Aluminum
Alzheimers Disease
Amantadine
Amaurotic Familial Idiocy
Stimulus **Ambiguity**
Tolerance for **Ambiguity**
Ambition *USE Aspirations*
Ambivalence
Amblyopia
Ambulatory Care
USE Outpatient Treatment
Amenorrhea
Amentia *USE Mental Retardation*
Central **America**
Latin **America**
North **America**
South **America**
Volunteers in Service to **America**
American Indians
American Samoa
African Americans *USE Blacks*
Cuban Americans *USE Hispanics*
Mexican **Americans**
Native Americans *USE American Indians*
Puerto Rican Americans *USE Hispanics*
Spanish Americans *USE Hispanics*
Nicotinic Acid Amide *USE Nicotinamide*
Amine Oxidase Inhibitors
Amines
Sympathomimetic **Amines**
Amino Acids
Gamma **Aminobutyric** Acid
Gamma **Aminobutyric** Acid Agonists
Gamma **Aminobutyric** Acid Antagonists
Aminotransferases *USE Transaminases*
Amitriptyline
Amnesia
Global **Amnesia**
Amniocentesis *USE Prenatal Diagnosis*
Amniotic Fluid
Amobarbital
Reinforcement **Amounts**
Amphetamine
Amphibia
Amplifiers (Apparatus)
Response **Amplitude**
Amputation
Amputees
Amygdaloid Body
Amytal *USE Amobarbital*
Anabolism
Anabolites *USE Metabolites*
Anaclitic Depression
Anagram Problem Solving
Anagrams
Analeptic Drugs
Analgesia
Analgesic Drugs
Analog Computers
Miller **Analogies** Test
Analogy
Analysis
Analysis of Covariance
Analysis of Variance
Behavior Analysis *USE Behavioral Assessment*
Causal **Analysis**
Cluster **Analysis**
Cohort **Analysis**
Confirmatory Factor Analysis *USE Factor Analysis*
Content **Analysis**
Content **Analysis** (Test)
Costs and Cost **Analysis**
Discourse **Analysis**
Dream **Analysis**
Error **Analysis**
Factor **Analysis**
Interaction **Analysis** (Statistics)
Item **Analysis** (Statistical)
Item **Analysis** (Test)
Job **Analysis**
Linkage Analysis *USE Genetic Linkage*
Meta **Analysis**
Multivariate **Analysis**
Path **Analysis**
Regression Analysis *USE Statistical Regression*
Risk **Analysis**
Self **Analysis**
Statistical **Analysis**
Systems **Analysis**
Task **Analysis**
Transactional **Analysis**
Analysts *USE Psychoanalysts*
Analytic Psychology
USE Jungian Psychology
Analytical Psychotherapy
Neural **Analyzers**
Anankastic Personality
USE Obsessive Compulsive Personality
Anaphylactic Shock
Anatomical Systems
Anatomically Detailed Dolls
Anatomy
Arm **(Anatomy)**
Arteries **(Anatomy)**
Back **(Anatomy)**
Capillaries **(Anatomy)**
Diaphragm **(Anatomy)**
Ear **(Anatomy)**
Elbow **(Anatomy)**
Eye **(Anatomy)**
Face **(Anatomy)**
Feet **(Anatomy)**
Fingers **(Anatomy)**
Hand **(Anatomy)**
Head **(Anatomy)**
Heels (Anatomy) *USE Feet (Anatomy)*
Joints **(Anatomy)**
Labyrinth **(Anatomy)**
Leg **(Anatomy)**
Mouth **(Anatomy)**
Neck **(Anatomy)**
Palm **(Anatomy)**
Scalp **(Anatomy)**
Shoulder **(Anatomy)**
Skin **(Anatomy)**
Teeth **(Anatomy)**
Toes (Anatomy) *USE Feet (Anatomy)*
Veins **(Anatomy)**
Ancestors
Androgen Antagonists
USE Antiandrogens
Androgens
Androgyny
Anemia
Anencephaly

ROTATED ALPHABETICAL TERMS SECTION

Anesthesia (Feeling)
Hysterical **Anesthesia**
Anesthesiology
Anesthetic Drugs
Ether **(Anesthetic)**
General **Anesthetics**
Local **Anesthetics**
Aneurysms
Anger
Anger Control
Angina Pectoris
Angiography
Angiotensin
Cerebellopontile Angle *USE Cerebellum*
Anglos
Angola
Angst *USE Anxiety*
Anguish *USE Distress*
Anhedonia
Carbonic Anhydrase *USE Enzymes*
Animal Aggressive Behavior
Animal Assisted Therapy
Animal Behavior *USE Animal Ethology*
Animal Biological Rhythms
Animal Breeding
Animal Captivity
Animal Circadian Rhythms
Animal Coloration
Animal Communication
Animal Courtship Behavior
Animal Courtship Displays
Animal Defensive Behavior
Animal Development
Animal Distress Calls
Animal Division of Labor
Animal Domestication
Animal Dominance
Animal Drinking Behavior
Animal Emotionality
Animal Environments
Animal Escape Behavior
Animal Ethology
Animal Exploratory Behavior
Animal Feeding Behavior
Animal Foraging Behavior
Animal Grooming Behavior
Animal Hoarding Behavior
Animal Homing
Animal Human Interaction
USE Interspecies Interaction
Animal Innate Behavior
USE Instinctive Behavior
Animal Licking Behavior *USE Licking*
Animal Locomotion
Animal Mate Selection
Animal Maternal Behavior
Animal Maternal Deprivation
Animal Mating Behavior
Animal Models
Animal Motivation
Animal Navigation
USE Migratory Behavior (Animal)
Animal Nocturnal Behavior
Animal Open Field Behavior
Animal Parental Behavior
Animal Paternal Behavior
Animal Play
Animal Predatory Behavior
Animal Rearing
Animal Scent Marking
Animal Sex Differences
Animal Sexual Behavior
Animal Sexual Receptivity
Animal Social Behavior
Animal Strain Differences
Animal Tool Use *USE Tool Use*
Animal Vocalizations
Animal Welfare
Captivity (Animal) *USE Animal Captivity*
Coitus (Animal) *USE Animal Mating Behavior*
Copulation (Animal) *USE Animal Mating Behavior*
Daily Biological Rhythms (Animal) *USE Animal Circadian Rhythms*
Emotionality (Animal) *USE Animal Emotionality*
Habitats (Animal) *USE Animal Environments*
Homing (Animal) *USE Animal Homing*
Human Animal Interaction
USE Interspecies Interaction
Infants **(Animal)**
Lordosis (Animal) *USE Animal Sexual Receptivity*
Migratory Behavior **(Animal)**
Neonates (Animal) *USE Infants (Animal)*
Seals **(Animal)**
Animals
Female **Animals**
Male **Animals**
Animism
Ankle
Anniversary Events
Anniversary Reactions
USE Anniversary Events
Annual Leave
USE Employee Leave Benefits
Annual Report
Anodynes *USE Analgesic Drugs*
Anomie
Anonymity
Alcoholics **Anonymous**
Gamblers Anonymous *USE Twelve Step Programs*
Narcotics Anonymous *USE Twelve Step Programs*
Anorexia Nervosa
Anorexigenic Drugs
USE Appetite Depressing Drugs
Anosmia
Anosognosia
ANOVA (Statistics)
USE Analysis of Variance
Anoxia
Antabuse *USE Disulfiram*
Antagonism *USE Hostility*
Androgen Antagonists *USE Antiandrogens*
Benzodiazepine **Antagonists**
Dopamine **Antagonists**
Estrogen Antagonists *USE Antiestrogens*
GABA Antagonists
USE Gamma Aminobutyric Acid Antagonists
Gamma Aminobutyric Acid **Antagonists**
Narcotic **Antagonists**
Opiate Antagonists *USE Narcotic Antagonists*
Opioid Antagonists *USE Narcotic Antagonists*
Serotonin **Antagonists**
Antarctica
Culture **(Anthropological)**
Race **(Anthropological)**
Subculture **(Anthropological)**
Anthropologists
Anthropology
Anti Inflammatory Drugs
Antiadrenergic Drugs
USE Sympatholytic Drugs
Antiandrogens
Antianxiety Drugs
USE Tranquilizing Drugs
Antibiotics
Antibodies
Anticholinergic Drugs
USE Cholinergic Blocking Drugs
Anticholinesterase Drugs
USE Cholinesterase Inhibitors
Serial **Anticipation** (Learning)
Anticoagulant Drugs
Anticonvulsive Drugs
Antidepressant Drugs
Tricyclic **Antidepressant** Drugs
Antiemetic Drugs
Antiepileptic Drugs
USE Anticonvulsive Drugs
Antiestrogens

ROTATED ALPHABETICAL TERMS SECTION

Antigens
Antihistaminic Drugs
Antihypertensive Drugs
Netherlands **Antilles**
Antinauseant Drugs
USE Antiemetic Drugs
Antineoplastic Drugs
Antiparkinsonian Drugs
USE Antitremor Drugs
Antipathy *USE Aversion*
Antipsychotic Drugs
USE Neuroleptic Drugs
Antipyretic Drugs
USE Anti Inflammatory Drugs
Antischizophrenic Drugs
USE Neuroleptic Drugs
AntiSemitism
Antisocial Behavior
Antisocial Personality
Antispasmodic Drugs
Antitremor Drugs
Antitubercular Drugs
Antiviral Drugs
Antonyms
Ants
Anxiety
Anxiety Disorders
Anxiety Management
Anxiety Neurosis *USE Anxiety Disorders*
Anxiety Reducing Drugs
USE Tranquilizing Drugs
Castration **Anxiety**
Childrens Manifest **Anxiety** Scale
Death **Anxiety**
Generalized Anxiety Disorder *USE Anxiety Disorders*
Mathematics **Anxiety**
Performance **Anxiety**
Separation **Anxiety**
Social **Anxiety**
Speech **Anxiety**
State Trait **Anxiety** Inventory
Taylor Manifest **Anxiety** Scale
Test **Anxiety**
Anxiolytic Drugs *USE Tranquilizing Drugs*
Anxiousness *USE Anxiety*
Aorta
Apathy
Apes *USE Primates (Nonhuman)*
Aphagia
Aphasia
Aphrodisiacs
Aplysia *USE Snails*
Apnea
Sleep **Apnea**
Apomorphine
Apoplexy *USE Cerebrovascular Accidents*
Appalachia
Apparatus
Amplifiers **(Apparatus)**
Cage **Apparatus**
Experimental Apparatus *USE Apparatus*
Generators **(Apparatus)**
Incubators **(Apparatus)**
Labyrinth (Apparatus) *USE Mazes*
Stimulators **(Apparatus)**
Timers **(Apparatus)**
Transistors (Apparatus) *USE Apparatus*
Vestibular **Apparatus**
Vibrators **(Apparatus)**
Apparent Distance
Apparent Movement
Apparent Size
Physical **Appearance**
Apperception
Childrens **Apperception** Test
Thematic **Apperception** Test
Appetite
Appetite Depressing Drugs
Appetite Disorders *USE Eating Disorders*

Job **Applicant** Attitudes
Job **Applicant** Interviews
Job **Applicant** Screening
Job **Applicants**
Computer **Applications**
Applied Psychology
Apprehension *USE Anxiety*
Communication Apprehension *USE Speech Anxiety*
Apprenticeship
Biopsychosocial **Approach**
Interdisciplinary Treatment **Approach**
Multidisciplinary Treatment Approach
USE Interdisciplinary Treatment Approach
Multimodal Treatment **Approach**
Need for **Approval**
Social **Approval**
Apraxia
Aptitude *USE Ability*
Aptitude Measures
Academic **Aptitude**
Coll Ent Exam Bd Scholastic **Apt** Test
Differential **Aptitude** Tests
General **Aptitude** Test Battery
Mechanical **Aptitude**
Modern Language **Aptitude** Test
Preliminary Scholastic Aptitude Test
USE Coll Ent Exam Bd Scholastic Apt Test
Scholastic Aptitude *USE Academic Aptitude*
Scholastic Aptitude Test
USE Coll Ent Exam Bd Scholastic Apt Test
Cerebral Aqueduct *USE Cerebral Ventricles*
United Arab Republic *USE Egypt*
Saudi **Arabia**
Arabs
Arachnida
Arachnophobia *USE Phobias*
Archetypes
Architects
Architecture
Arctic Regions
Preoptic **Area**
Ventral Tegmental Area *USE Tegmentum*
Noise Levels (Work **Areas)**
Poverty **Areas**
Recreation **Areas**
Arecoline
Argentina
Arguments
Arithmetic *USE Mathematics*
Arm (Anatomy)
Army General Classification Test
Army Personnel
Physiological **Arousal**
Sexual **Arousal**
Living **Arrangements**
Cardiac Arrest *USE Heart Disorders*
Legal **Arrest**
Arrhythmias (Heart)
Arson
Art
Art Education
Art Therapy
Barron Welsh **Art** Scale
Painting **(Art)**
Photographic **Art**
Arterial Pulse
Arteries (Anatomy)
Carotid **Arteries**
Arteriosclerosis
Cerebral **Arteriosclerosis**
Arthritis
Rheumatoid **Arthritis**
Arthropoda
Articulation Disorders
Articulation (Speech)

Artificial Insemination
USE Reproductive Technology
Artificial Intelligence
Artificial Limbs *USE Prostheses*
Artificial Pacemakers
Artificial Respiration
Artistic Ability
Artists
Arts
Creative **Arts** Therapy
Industrial Arts Education *USE Vocational Education*
Language **Arts** Education
Martial **Arts**
Performing Arts *USE Arts*
English **as** Second Language
Asbestos *USE Hazardous Materials*
Asceticism
Ascorbic Acid
Asia
Southeast **Asia**
Asians
Aspartic Acid
Aspergers Syndrome
Asphyxia *USE Anoxia*
Aspiration Level
Aspirations
Career Aspirations *USE Occupational Aspirations*
Educational **Aspirations**
Occupational **Aspirations**
Vocational Aspirations *USE Occupational Aspirations*
Aspirin
Political **Assassination**
Assertiveness
Assertiveness Training
Assessment *USE Measurement*
Assessment Centers
Assessment (Cognitive)
USE Cognitive Assessment
Assessment (Psychological)
USE Psychological Assessment
Behavioral **Assessment**
Cognitive **Assessment**
Curriculum Based **Assessment**
Geriatric **Assessment**
Kaufman **Assessment** Battery Children
Needs **Assessment**
Neuropsychological **Assessment**
Personality Assessment *USE Personality Measures*
Psychological **Assessment**
Self Assessment *USE Self Evaluation*
Cultural **Assimilation**
Assistance Seeking (Professional)
USE Health Care Utilization
Assistance (Social Behavior)
Educational Financial **Assistance**
Employee **Assistance** Programs
Assisted Suicide
Animal **Assisted** Therapy
Computer **Assisted** Design
Computer **Assisted** Diagnosis
Computer **Assisted** Instruction
Computer **Assisted** Testing
Paired **Associate** Learning
Remote **Associates** Test
Association (Free) *USE Free Association*
Free **Association**
Associationism
Contextual **Associations**
Loosening of Associations
USE Fragmentation (Schizophrenia)
Word **Associations**
Associative Processes
Assortative Mating
Assortive Mating *USE Assortative Mating*
Asthenia
Asthenic Personality
USE Personality Disorders
Asthma
Astrology
Astronauts
Asylums *USE Psychiatric Hospitals*
Ataractic Drugs *USE Tranquilizing Drugs*
Ataraxic Drugs *USE Tranquilizing Drugs*
Ataxia
Atheism
Atherosclerosis
Athetosis
Athletes
College **Athletes**
Athletic Participation
Athletic Performance
Athletic Training
Training (Athletic) *USE Athletic Training*
Stereotaxic **Atlas**
Atmospheric Conditions
Atomism *USE Reductionism*
Atria (Heart) *USE Heart Auricles*
Atrial Fibrillation *USE Fibrillation (Heart)*
Atrophy (Cerebral) *USE Cerebral Atrophy*
Cerebral **Atrophy**
Cortical Atrophy *USE Cerebral Atrophy*
Muscular **Atrophy**
Atropine
Attachment Behavior
Reactive Attachment Disorder
USE Failure to Thrive
Attack Behavior
Heart Attacks *USE Heart Disorders*
Attainment (Achievement)
USE Achievement
Attainment Level (Education)
USE Educational Attainment Level
Educational **Attainment** Level
Attempted Suicide
School **Attendance**
Attendants (Institutions)
Flight Attendants *USE Aerospace Personnel*
Hospital Attendants *USE Attendants (Institutions)*
Residential Care Attendants *USE Attendants (Institutions)*
Attention
Attention Deficit Disorder
Attention Span
Divided **Attention**
Selective **Attention**
Sustained **Attention**
Stimulus **Attenuation**
Attitude Change
Attitude Formation
Attitude Measurement
Attitude Measures
Attitude Similarity
Minnesota Teacher Attitude Inventory *USE Attitude Measures*
Opinion Attitude and Interest Survey
USE Attitude Measures
Parent **Attitude** Research Instrument
Attitudes
Adolescent **Attitudes**
Adult **Attitudes**
Aged **(Attitudes** Toward)
Aging **(Attitudes** Toward)
AIDS **(Attitudes** Toward)
Alcohol Drinking **Attitudes**
Birth Control Attitudes *USE Family Planning Attitudes*
Child **Attitudes**
Childrearing **Attitudes**
Client **Attitudes**
Community **Attitudes**
Computer **Attitudes**
Consumer **Attitudes**
Counselor **Attitudes**
Death **Attitudes**
Disabled **(Attitudes** Toward)
Drug Usage **Attitudes**
Eating **Attitudes**
Employee **Attitudes**
Employer **Attitudes**
Environmental **Attitudes**
Family Planning **Attitudes**

Gender Role Attitudes *USE Sex Role Attitudes*
Handicapped (Attitudes Toward)
USE Disabled (Attitudes Toward)
Health **Attitudes**
Health Personnel **Attitudes**
Homosexuality **(Attitudes** Toward)
Job Applicant **Attitudes**
Lower Class **Attitudes**
Marriage **Attitudes**
Mental Illness **(Attitudes** Toward)
Mental Retardation **(Attit** Toward)
Middle Class **Attitudes**
Obesity **(Attitudes** Toward)
Occupational **Attitudes**
Parental **Attitudes**
Patient Attitudes *USE Client Attitudes*
Physical Disabilities **(Attit** Toward)
Physical Handicaps (Attit Toward)
USE Physical Disabilities (Attit Toward)
Physical Illness **(Attitudes** Toward)
Political **Attitudes**
Psychologist **Attitudes**
Psychotherapist **Attitudes**
Public Attitudes *USE Public Opinion*
Race Attitudes *USE Racial and Ethnic Attitudes*
Racial and Ethnic **Attitudes**
Sensory Disabilities **(Attit** Toward)
Sensory Handicaps (Attit Toward)
USE Sensory Disabilities (Attit Toward)
Sex Role **Attitudes**
Sexual **Attitudes**
Social Class Attitudes
USE Socioeconomic Class Attitudes
Socioeconomic Class **Attitudes**
Stereotyped **Attitudes**
Student **Attitudes**
Teacher **Attitudes**
Therapist **Attitudes**
Upper Class **Attitudes**
Work **(Attitudes** Toward)
Attorneys
Interpersonal **Attraction**
Physical **Attractiveness**
Attribution
Experimental **Attrition**
Student **Attrition**
Atypical Paranoid Disorder
USE Paranoia (Psychosis)
Atypical Somatoform Disorder
USE Dysmorphophobia
Audiences
Audiogenic Seizures
Audiology
Audiometers
Audiometry
Bone Conduction **Audiometry**
Audiotapes
Audiovisual Communications Media
Audiovisual Instruction
Educational **Audiovisual** Aids
Auditory Acuity
Auditory Cortex
Auditory Discrimination
Auditory Displays
Auditory Evoked Potentials
Auditory Feedback
Auditory Hallucinations
Auditory Localization
Auditory Masking
Auditory Nerve *USE Acoustic Nerve*
Auditory Neurons
Auditory Perception
Auditory Stimulation
Auditory Thresholds
Delayed **Auditory** Feedback
Wepman Test of **Auditory** Discrim
Augmentative Communication
Aura
Intra Aural Muscle Reflex *USE Acoustic Reflex*

Aurally Disabled
Aurally Handicapped
USE Aurally Disabled
Heart **Auricles**
Australia
Austria
Authoritarianism
Authoritarianism (Parental)
USE Parental Permissiveness
Authoritarianism Rebellion Scale
USE Nonprojective Personality Measures
Parental Authoritarianism
USE Parental Permissiveness
Authority
Authors *USE Writers*
Autism
Early Infantile **Autism**
Autistic Children
Autistic Psychopathy
USE Aspergers Syndrome
Autistic Thinking
Autobiographical Memory
Autobiography
Autoeroticism
Autogenic Training
Autohypnosis
Autoimmune Disorders
USE Immunologic Disorders
Autokinetic Illusion
Automated Information Coding
Automated Information Processing
Automated Information Retrieval
Automated Information Storage
Automated Speech Recognition
Automatic Speaker Recognition
USE Automated Speech Recognition
Automation
Automatism
Automobile Accidents
USE Motor Traffic Accidents
Automobile Safety *USE Highway Safety*
Automobiles
Autonomic Ganglia
Autonomic Nervous System
Autonomic Nervous System Disorders
Postganglionic Autonomic Fibers *USE Autonomic Ganglia*
Preganglionic Autonomic Fibers *USE Autonomic Ganglia*
Autonomy (Government)
Autonomy (Personality)
USE Independence (Personality)
Autopsy
Psychological **Autopsy**
Autoregulation *USE Homeostasis*
Autoshaping
Autosome Disorders
Autosomes
Autotomy *USE Self Mutilation*
Gradepoint Average *USE Academic Achievement*
Aversion
Aversion Conditioning
Aversion Therapy
Odor Aversion Conditioning
USE Aversion Conditioning
Taste Aversion Conditioning
USE Aversion Conditioning
Aversive Stimulation
Aviation
Aviation Personnel
USE Aerospace Personnel
Aviation Safety
Aviators *USE Aircraft Pilots*
Avoidance
Avoidance Conditioning
Active Avoidance *USE Avoidance Conditioning*
Passive Avoidance *USE Avoidance Conditioning*
Avoidant Personality
Awareness
Body **Awareness**
Axons

ROTATED ALPHABETICAL TERMS SECTION

Azidothymidine *USE Zidovudine*
AZT *USE Zidovudine*
Babbling *USE Infant Vocalization*
Babies *USE Infants*
Bush Babies *USE Lemurs*
Test Tube Babies *USE Reproductive Technology*
Babinski Reflex
Baboons
Babysitting *USE Child Care*
Back (Anatomy)
Back Pain
Educational **Background**
Family **Background**
Parent Educational **Background**
Backward Masking *USE Masking*
Baclofen
Bacteria *USE Microorganisms*
Bacterial Disorders
Bacterial Meningitis
Bahama Islands
Balance (Motor Processes)
USE Equilibrium
Baldness *USE Alopecia*
Ballet *USE Dance*
Head **Banging**
Bangladesh
Bannister Repertory Grid
Baptists *USE Protestants*
Barbados
Barbital
Barbiturate Poisoning
Barbiturates
Bargaining
Barium
Barometric Pressure
USE Atmospheric Conditions
Baroreceptors
Epstein **Barr** Viral Disorder
Barrett Lennard Relationship Invent
Blood Brain **Barrier**
Barron Welsh Art Scale
Basal Ganglia
Basal Metabolism
Basal Readers *USE Reading Materials*
Basal Skin Resistance
Nucleus **Basalis** Magnocellularis
Baseball
Curriculum **Based** Assessment
Knowledge Based Systems *USE Expert Systems*
Basic Skills Testing
USE Minimum Competency Tests
Iowa Tests of **Basic** Skills
Basketball
Bass (Fish)
Bats
Battered Child Syndrome
Battered Females
General Aptitude Test **Battery**
Halstead Reitan Neuropsych **Battery**
Kaufman Assessment **Battery** Children
Luria Nebraska Neuropsych **Battery**
Woodcock Johnson Psychoed **Battery**
Bayes Theorem *USE Statistical Probability*
Bayley Scales of Infant Development
Heart Beat *USE Heart Rate*
Beavers
Beck Depression Inventory
Bedwetting *USE Urinary Incontinence*
Beer
Bees
Beetles
Fund Interper Rela Orientat **Beh** Ques
Behavior
Behavior Analysis
USE Behavioral Assessment
Behavior Change
Behavior Contracting
Behavior Disorders
Behavior Modification
Behavior Problems
Behavior Therapy
Adaptive **Behavior**
Adjunctive **Behavior**
Aggressive **Behavior**
Agonistic Behavior *USE Aggressive Behavior*
Animal Behavior *USE Animal Ethology*
Animal Aggressive **Behavior**
Animal Courtship **Behavior**
Animal Defensive **Behavior**
Animal Drinking **Behavior**
Animal Escape **Behavior**
Animal Exploratory **Behavior**
Animal Feeding **Behavior**
Animal Foraging **Behavior**
Animal Grooming **Behavior**
Animal Hoarding **Behavior**
Animal Innate Behavior *USE Instinctive Behavior*
Animal Licking Behavior *USE Licking*
Animal Maternal **Behavior**
Animal Mating **Behavior**
Animal Nocturnal **Behavior**
Animal Open Field **Behavior**
Animal Parental **Behavior**
Animal Paternal **Behavior**
Animal Predatory **Behavior**
Animal Sexual **Behavior**
Animal Social **Behavior**
Antisocial **Behavior**
Assistance (Social **Behavior)**
Attachment **Behavior**
Attack **Behavior**
Charitable **Behavior**
Child **Behavior** Checklist
Childhood Play **Behavior**
Choice **Behavior**
Classroom **Behavior**
Classroom **Behavior** Modification
Cognitive Behavior Therapy *USE Cognitive Therapy*
Collective **Behavior**
Conservation (Ecological **Behavior)**
Consumer **Behavior**
Coping **Behavior**
Coronary Prone **Behavior**
Deviant Behavior *USE Antisocial Behavior*
Disruptive Behavior *USE Behavior Problems*
Drinking **Behavior**
Driving **Behavior**
Exploratory **Behavior**
Health **Behavior**
Health Care Seeking **Behavior**
Help Seeking **Behavior**
Helping Behavior
USE Assistance (Social Behavior)
Illness **Behavior**
Instinctive **Behavior**
Maternal Behavior (Human)
USE Mother Child Relations
Migratory **Behavior** (Animal)
Modeling Behavior *USE Imitation (Learning)*
Organizational **Behavior**
Planned **Behavior**
Prosocial **Behavior**
Psychosexual **Behavior**
Rotational **Behavior**
Runaway **Behavior**
Self Defeating **Behavior**
Self Destructive **Behavior**
Sexual Behavior *USE Psychosexual Behavior*
Sharing (Social **Behavior)**
Social **Behavior**
Stereotyped **Behavior**
Treatment Seeking Behavior
USE Health Care Seeking Behavior
Trust (Social **Behavior)**
Voting **Behavior**
Wandering **Behavior**
Behavioral Assessment
Behavioral Contrast

ROTATED ALPHABETICAL TERMS SECTION

Behavioral Ecology
Behavioral Genetics
Behavioral Health
USE Health Care Psychology
Behavioral Medicine
USE Health Care Psychology
Behavioral Sciences
Behaviorism
Well **Being**
Belgium
Beliefs (Nonreligious) *USE Attitudes*
Irrational **Beliefs**
Religious **Beliefs**
Belize
Wechsler **Bellevue** Intelligence Scale
Safety **Belts**
Seat Belts *USE Safety Belts*
Bem Sex Role Inventory
Bemegride
Benactyzine
Benadryl *USE Diphenhydramine*
Bender Gestalt Test
Employee **Benefits**
Employee Leave **Benefits**
Vacation Benefits *USE Employee Leave Benefits*
Benign Neoplasms
Benin
Benton Revised Visual Retention Test
Benzedrine *USE Amphetamine*
Benzodiazepine Agonists
Benzodiazepine Antagonists
Benzodiazepines
Bereavement *USE Grief*
Bermuda
Beta Blockers
USE Adrenergic Blocking Drugs
Between Groups Design
White Betz A B Scale
USE Nonprojective Personality Measures
Beverages (Nonalcoholic)
Alcoholic **Beverages**
Cultural Test **Bias**
Experimenter **Bias**
Item Bias *USE Test Bias*
Response **Bias**
Test **Bias**
Biased Sampling
Bible
Bibliography
Bibliotherapy
Bicuculline
Spina **Bifida**
Big Five Personality Model
USE Five Factor Personality Model
Bile
Bilingual Education
Bilingualism
Double **Bind** Interaction
Receptor **Binding**
Stanford **Binet** Intelligence Scale
Binge Eating
Binocular Vision
Binomial Distribution
Bioavailability
Biochemical Markers
USE Biological Markers
Biochemistry
Bioequivalence *USE Bioavailability*
Biofeedback
Biofeedback Training
Biographical Data
Biographical Inventories
Biography
Biological Family
Biological Markers
Biological Psychiatry
Biological Rhythms
Biological Symbiosis
Animal **Biological** Rhythms
Daily Biological Rhythms (Animal)
USE Animal Circadian Rhythms
Human **Biological** Rhythms
Biology
Cells **(Biology)**
Hybrids **(Biology)**
Biopsy
Biopsychosocial Approach
Biopsychosocial Model
USE Biopsychosocial Approach
Biosynthesis
Bipolar Affective Disorder
USE Manic Depression
Bipolar Mood Disorder
USE Manic Depression
Biracial Children *USE Interracial Offspring*
Birds
Birth
Birth Control
Birth Control Attitudes
USE Family Planning Attitudes
Birth Injuries
Birth Order
Birth Parents *USE Biological Family*
Birth Rate
Birth Rites
Birth Trauma
Birth Weight
Diaphragms **(Birth** Control)
Home Birth *USE Midwifery*
Low Birth Weight *USE Birth Weight*
Premature **Birth**
Multiple **Births**
Point **Biserial** Correlation
Bisexuality
Nail **Biting**
Bitterness *USE Taste Perception*
Black Power Movement
Blackbirds
Blacks
Blacky Pictures Test
USE Projective Personality Measures
Bladder
Blame
Rotter Incomplete Sentences **Blank**
Strong Vocational Interest **Blank**
Blind
Deaf **Blind**
Color **Blindness**
Hysterical Blindness
USE Hysterical Vision Disturbances
Word Blindness *USE Alexia*
Blink Reflex *USE Eyeblink Reflex*
Kohs **Block** Design Test
Beta Blockers *USE Adrenergic Blocking Drugs*
Calcium Channel Blockers *USE Channel Blockers*
Channel **Blockers**
Adrenergic **Blocking** Drugs
Cholinergic **Blocking** Drugs
Ganglion **Blocking** Drugs
Neuromuscular Blocking Drugs
USE Muscle Relaxing Drugs
Blood
Blood Alcohol Concentration
Blood and Lymphatic Disorders
Blood Brain Barrier
Blood Cells
Blood Circulation
Blood Coagulation
Blood Donation *USE Tissue Donation*
Blood Flow
Blood Glucose *USE Blood Sugar*
Blood Groups
Blood Plasma
Blood Platelets
Blood Pressure
Blood Pressure Disorders
Blood Proteins
Blood Serum

ROTATED ALPHABETICAL TERMS SECTION

Blood Sugar
Blood Transfusion
Blood Vessels
Blood Volume
Cerebral **Blood** Flow
Red Blood Cells *USE Erythrocytes*
White Blood Cells *USE Leucocytes*
Blue Collar Workers
State Board Examinations
USE Professional Examinations
Boarding Schools
Boards of Education
Geniculate **Bodies** (Thalamus)
Mammillary Bodies (Hypothalamic)
USE Hypothalamus
Body Awareness
Body Fluids
Body Height
Body Image
Body Image Disturbances
Body Language
Body Rocking
Body Rotation *USE Rotational Behavior*
Body Size
Body Sway Testing
Body Temperature
Body Types *USE Somatotypes*
Body Weight
Amygdaloid **Body**
Mind Body *USE Dualism*
Out of **Body** Experiences
Pineal **Body**
Thermoregulation **(Body)**
Tissues **(Body)**
Bolivia
Bombesin
Bonding (Emotional)
USE Attachment Behavior
Bone Conduction Audiometry
Bone Disorders
Bone Marrow
Bones
Bonobos
Bonuses
Book
Books
Borderline Mental Retardation
Borderline Mentally Retarded
USE Slow Learners
Borderline States
Boredom
Botany
Botswana
Bottle Feeding
Outward Bound *USE Wilderness Experience*
Upward **Bound**
Boundaries (Psychological)
Boundary Violations (Sexual)
USE Professional Client Sexual Relations
Sexual Boundary Violations
USE Professional Client Sexual Relations
Bourgeois *USE Middle Class*
Bowel Disorders *USE Colon Disorders*
Irritable **Bowel** Syndrome
Shuttle Box Grids *USE Shuttle Boxes*
Shuttle Box Hurdles *USE Shuttle Boxes*
Shuttle **Boxes**
Skinner **Boxes**
Boys *USE Human Males*
Brachial Plexus *USE Spinal Nerves*
Bradycardia
Braille
Braille Instruction
Brain
Brain Concussion
Brain Damage
Brain Damaged
Brain Disorders
Brain Injury (Traumatic)
USE Traumatic Brain Injury
Brain Lesions
Brain Maps *USE Stereotaxic Atlas*
Brain Metabolism *USE Neurochemistry*
Brain Neoplasms
Brain Self Stimulation
Brain Size
Brain Stem
Brain Stimulation
Brain Weight
Blood **Brain** Barrier
Chemical **Brain** Stimulation
Decortication **(Brain)**
Electrical **Brain** Stimulation
Left **Brain**
Minimal **Brain** Disorders
Minimally **Brain** Damaged
Monoamines (Brain) *USE Catecholamines*
Organic **Brain** Syndromes
Right **Brain**
Split Brain *USE Commissurotomy*
Traumatic **Brain** Injury
Brainstorming
Brainwashing
Brand Names
Brand Preferences
Bravery *USE Courage*
Brazil
Nervous Breakdown *USE Mental Disorders*
Psychotherapeutic **Breakthrough**
Breakup (Relationship)
USE Relationship Termination
Breast
Breast Cancer Screening
USE Cancer Screening
Breast Examination
USE Self Examination (Medical)
Breast Feeding
Breast Neoplasms
Breathing *USE Respiration*
Animal **Breeding**
Selective **Breeding**
Brief Psychotherapy
Brief Reactive Psychosis
USE Acute Psychosis
Myers **Briggs** Type Indicator
Bright Light Therapy *USE Phototherapy*
Brightness Constancy
Brightness Contrast
Brightness Perception
Great **Britain**
Watson (John **Broadus)**
Lithium Bromide *USE Bromides*
Bromides
Bromocriptine
Bronchi
Bronchial Disorders
Brothers
Spearman **Brown** Test
Bruxism
Buddhism
Zen **Buddhism**
Buddhists
Budgerigars
Budgets
Taste **Buds**
Bufotenine
Nest **Building**
Religious **Buildings**
Olfactory **Bulb**
Bulgaria
Bulimia
Bulls *USE Cattle*
Medial Forebrain **Bundle**
Bupropion
Caregiver **Burden**
Burma
Burnout *USE Occupational Stress*

Burns
Skinner **(Burrhus** Frederic)
Buses *USE Motor Vehicles*
Bush Babies *USE Lemurs*
Business
Business and Industrial Personnel
Business Education
Business Management
Business Organizations
Business Students
Buspirone
Butterflies
Butyrylperazine
USE Phenothiazine Derivatives
Buying *USE Consumer Behavior*
Munchausen Syndrome **by** Proxy
Vitamin C *USE Ascorbic Acid*
Cadres *USE Social Groups*
Caffeine
Cage Apparatus
Calcium
Calcium Channel Blockers
USE Channel Blockers
Calcium Ions
Calculators *USE Digital Computers*
Calculus *USE Mathematics*
California F Scale
California Psychological Inventory
California Test of Mental Maturity
California Test of Personality
Corpus **Callosum**
Animal Distress **Calls**
Calories
Cambodia
Cameras
Cameroon
Political **Campaigns**
Camping
Concentration **Camps**
Recreational Day Camps *USE Summer Camps (Recreation)*
Summer **Camps** (Recreation)
Therapeutic **Camps**
Campuses
Canada
Ear Canal *USE External Ear*
Semicircular **Canals**
Canaries
Cancer Screening
Breast Cancer Screening *USE Cancer Screening*
Prostate Cancer Screening *USE Cancer Screening*
Skin Cancer Screening *USE Cancer Screening*
Terminal **Cancer**
Cancers *USE Neoplasms*
Political **Candidates**
Canids
Cannabinoids
Cannabis
Canonical Correlation
USE Multivariate Analysis
Human Channel **Capacity**
Capgras Syndrome
Capillaries (Anatomy)
Capital Punishment
Capitalism
Capsaicin
Captivity (Animal) *USE Animal Captivity*
Animal **Captivity**
Captopril
Carbachol
Carbamazepine
Carbidopa
Carbohydrate Metabolism
Carbohydrates
Carbon
Carbon Dioxide
Carbon Monoxide
Carbon Monoxide Poisoning
Lithium **Carbonate**
Carbonic Anhydrase *USE Enzymes*

Carboxyhemoglobinemia
USE Carbon Monoxide Poisoning
Carcinogens
Carcinomas *USE Neoplasms*
Wisconsin **Card** Sorting Test
Cardiac Arrest *USE Heart Disorders*
Cardiac Disorders *USE Heart Disorders*
Cardiac Rate *USE Heart Rate*
Cardiac Surgery *USE Heart Surgery*
Cardiography
Cardiology
Cardiotonic Drugs *USE Drugs*
Cardiovascular Disorders
Cardiovascular Reactivity
Cardiovascular System
Adult Day **Care**
Ambulatory Care *USE Outpatient Treatment*
Child **Care**
Child **Care** Workers
Child Day **Care**
Child Self **Care**
Day **Care** Centers
Day Care (Treatment)
USE Partial Hospitalization
Elder **Care**
Foster **Care**
Health **Care** Administration
Health **Care** Costs
Health **Care** Delivery
Health **Care** Policy
Health Care Professionals *USE Health Personnel*
Health **Care** Psychology
Health **Care** Seeking Behavior
Health **Care** Services
Health **Care** Utilization
Home **Care**
Home **Care** Personnel
Intensive **Care**
Long Term **Care**
Managed **Care**
Medical Care Costs *USE Health Care Costs*
Mental Health Care Costs *USE Health Care Costs*
Mental Health Care Policy *USE Health Care Policy*
Palliative **Care**
Patient Care Planning *USE Treatment Planning*
Prenatal **Care**
Primary Health **Care**
Quality of **Care**
Residential Care Attendants
USE Attendants (Institutions)
Residential **Care** Institutions
Respite **Care**
Self **Care** Skills
Career Aspirations
USE Occupational Aspirations
Career Change
Career Choice *USE Occupational Choice*
Career Counseling
USE Occupational Guidance
Career Development
Career Education
Career Exploration *USE Career Education*
Career Goals
USE Occupational Aspirations
Career Guidance
USE Occupational Guidance
Career Maturity *USE Vocational Maturity*
Career Preference
USE Occupational Preference
Career Transitions
USE Career Development
Careers *USE Occupations*
Dual **Careers**
Nontraditional **Careers**
Caregiver Burden
Caregivers
Family Caregivers *USE Caregivers*
Jung **(Carl)**
Rogers **(Carl)**

Carotid Arteries
Carp
Cartoons (Humor)
Case History *USE Patient History*
Case Law
Case Management
Case Report
Social **Casework**
Caseworkers *USE Social Workers*
Social Caseworkers *USE Social Workers*
Caste System
Castration
Castration Anxiety
Male **Castration**
Cat Learning
CAT Scan *USE Tomography*
Crying **Cat** Syndrome
Catabolism
Catabolites *USE Metabolites*
Catalepsy
Catamnesis *USE Posttreatment Followup*
Cataplexy
Cataracts
Catatonia
Catatonic Schizophrenia
Catecholamines
Categorizing
USE Classification (Cognitive Process)
Catharsis
Catheterization
Cathexis
Cathode Ray Tubes
USE Video Display Units
Roman **Catholicism**
Catholics
Cats
Cattell Culture Fair Intell Test
USE Culture Fair Intelligence Test
Cattell Infant Intelligence Scale
USE Infant Intelligence Scale
Cattle
Caucasians *USE Whites*
Cauda Equina *USE Spinal Nerves*
Caudate Nucleus
Causal Analysis
Celiac Plexus *USE Autonomic Ganglia*
Celibacy *USE Sexual Abstinence*
Cell Nucleus
Sickle **Cell** Disease
Single Cell Organisms *USE Microorganisms*
Cells (Biology)
Blood **Cells**
Connective Tissue **Cells**
Epithelial **Cells**
Ganglion **Cells** (Retina)
Nerve Cells *USE Neurons*
Purkinje **Cells**
Red Blood Cells *USE Erythrocytes*
White Blood Cells *USE Leucocytes*
Censorship
Client **Centered** Therapy
Person Centered Psychotherapy
USE Client Centered Therapy
Centering
Assessment **Centers**
Community Mental Health **Centers**
Day Care **Centers**
Growth Centers *USE Human Potential Movement*
Learning **Centers** (Educational)
Rehabilitation **Centers**
Shopping **Centers**
Suicide Prevention **Centers**
Central America
Central Nervous System
Central Nervous System Disorders
Central Nervous System Drugs
USE CNS Affecting Drugs
Central Tendency Measures
Central Vision *USE Foveal Vision*

CER (Conditioning)
USE Conditioned Emotional Responses
Cerebellopontile Angle *USE Cerebellum*
Cerebellum
Cerebral Aqueduct
USE Cerebral Ventricles
Cerebral Arteriosclerosis
Cerebral Atrophy
Cerebral Blood Flow
Cerebral Cortex
Cerebral Dominance
Cerebral Hemorrhage
Cerebral Ischemia
Cerebral Lesions *USE Brain Lesions*
Cerebral Palsy
Cerebral Vascular Disorders
USE Cerebrovascular Disorders
Cerebral Ventricles
Atrophy (Cerebral) *USE Cerebral Atrophy*
Trigonum Cerebrale *USE Fornix*
Cerebrospinal Fluid
Cerebrovascular Accidents
Cerebrovascular Disorders
Stroke (Cerebrum)
USE Cerebrovascular Accidents
Certification Examinations
USE Professional Examinations
Professional **Certification**
Locus **Ceruleus**
Cervical Plexus *USE Spinal Nerves*
Cervical Sprain Syndrome *USE Whiplash*
Cervix
Smoking **Cessation**
Markov **Chains**
Chance (Fortune)
Attitude **Change**
Behavior **Change**
Career **Change**
Culture **Change**
Job Change *USE Career Change*
Life Change *USE Life Experiences*
Opinion Change *USE Attitude Change*
Organizational **Change**
Personality **Change**
Sex **Change**
Social **Change**
Stimulus **Change**
Lifestyle **Changes**
Channel Blockers
Calcium Channel Blockers *USE Channel Blockers*
Human **Channel** Capacity
Chaos Theory
Chaplains
Character *USE Personality*
Client **Characteristics**
Counselor **Characteristics**
Demographic **Characteristics**
Employee **Characteristics**
Job **Characteristics**
Organizational **Characteristics**
Parental **Characteristics**
Patient Characteristics *USE Client Characteristics*
Population Characteristics
USE Demographic Characteristics
Speech **Characteristics**
Student **Characteristics**
Teacher **Characteristics**
Therapist **Characteristics**
Charisma
Charitable Behavior
Cri du Chat Syndrome
USE Crying Cat Syndrome
Cheating
Gough Adjective **Check** List
Learys Interpersonal **Check** List
Mooney Problem **Check** List
Child Behavior **Checklist**
Symptom **Checklists**
Chemical Brain Stimulation

Chemical Elements
Chemicals
Chemistry
Chemoreceptors
Chemotherapy *USE Drug Therapy*
Chess
Chest *USE Thorax*
Chewing Tobacco
USE Smokeless Tobacco
Chi Square Test
Optic **Chiasm**
Chicanos *USE Mexican Americans*
Chickens
Child Abuse
Child Abuse Reporting
Child Advocacy *USE Advocacy*
Child Attitudes
Child Behavior Checklist
Child Care
Child Care Workers
Child Custody
Child Day Care
Child Discipline
Child Guidance Clinics
Child Molestation *USE Pedophilia*
Child Neglect
Child Psychiatric Clinics
USE Child Guidance Clinics
Child Psychiatry
Child Psychology
Child Psychotherapy
Child Self Care
Child Support
Child Visitation
Child Welfare
Adoption **(Child)**
Battered **Child** Syndrome
Father **Child** Communication
Father **Child** Relations
Mother **Child** Communication
Mother **Child** Relations
Parent **Child** Communication
Parent **Child** Relations
Slosson Intelligence Test for **Child**
Childbirth *USE Birth*
Childbirth Training
Labor **(Childbirth)**
Natural **Childbirth**
Childhood
Childhood Development
Childhood Memories *USE Early Memories*
Childhood Neurosis
Childhood Play Behavior
Childhood Play Development
Childhood Psychosis
Childhood Schizophrenia
Early Childhood *USE Preschool Age Children*
Early **Childhood** Development
Childlessness
Childrearing Attitudes
Childrearing Practices
Children
Adopted **Children**
Adult Children *USE Adult Offspring*
Autistic **Children**
Biracial Children *USE Interracial Offspring*
Exceptional Children (Gifted) *USE Gifted*
Exceptional Children (Handicapped) *USE Disabled*
Foster **Children**
Grown Children *USE Adult Offspring*
Illegitimate **Children**
Kaufman Assessment Battery **Children**
Latchkey Children *USE Child Self Care*
Only **Children**
Preschool Age **Children**
School Age **Children**
Wechsler Intelligence Scale **Children**
Childrens Apperception Test
Childrens Manifest Anxiety Scale
Childrens Personality Questionnaire
Childrens Recreational Games
Chile
Chimpanzees
Pygmy Chimpanzees *USE Bonobos*
China *USE Peoples Republic of China*
Peoples Republic of **China**
Chinchillas
Chinese Cultural Groups
Chiroptera *USE Bats*
Chloral Hydrate
Chloralose *USE Hypnotic Drugs*
Chlordiazepoxide
Chloride Ions
Chlorimipramine
Chlorisondamine *USE Amines*
Chloroform
Chlorophenylpiperazine *USE Piperazines*
Chlorpromazine
Chlorprothixene
Choice Behavior
Choice Shift
Career Choice *USE Occupational Choice*
Forced **Choice** (Testing Method)
Multiple **Choice** (Testing Method)
Occupational **Choice**
Vocational Choice *USE Occupational Choice*
Cholecystokinin
Cholesterol
Choline
Cholinergic Blocking Drugs
Cholinergic Drugs
Cholinergic Nerves
Cholinesterase
Cholinesterase Inhibitors
Cholinolytic Drugs
USE Cholinergic Blocking Drugs
Cholinomimetic Drugs
Chorda Tympani Nerve *USE Facial Nerve*
Chorea
Huntingtons Chorea *USE Huntingtons Disease*
Choroid *USE Eye (Anatomy)*
Choroid Plexus *USE Cerebral Ventricles*
Christianity
Christians
Chromaticity
Chromosome Disorders
Deletion **(Chromosome)**
Sex **Chromosome** Disorders
Translocation **(Chromosome)**
Chromosomes
Sex **Chromosomes**
Chronic Alcoholic Intoxication
Chronic Fatigue Syndrome
Chronic Illness
Chronic Mental Illness
Chronic Pain
Chronic Psychosis
Chronic Schizophrenia
USE Schizophrenia
Chronicity (Disorders)
Churches *USE Religious Buildings*
Cichlids
Cigarette Smoking *USE Tobacco Smoking*
Cimetidine
Gyrus **Cinguli**
Circadian Rhythms (Human)
USE Human Biological Rhythms
Animal **Circadian** Rhythms
Quality Circles *USE Participative Management*
Closed **Circuit** Television
Blood **Circulation**
Circulatory Disorders
USE Cardiovascular Disorders
Circumcision *USE Birth Rites AND Surgery*
Cirrhosis (Liver)
Citalopram
Cities *USE Urban Environments*
Senior Citizens *USE Aged*

ROTATED ALPHABETICAL TERMS SECTION

Citizenship
Inner City *USE Urban Environments*
Civil Law
Civil Rights
Civil Rights Movement
Civil Servants *USE Government Personnel*
Volunteer **Civilian** Personnel
Clairvoyance
International **Class** of Diseases
Lower **Class**
Lower **Class** Attitudes
Middle **Class**
Middle **Class** Attitudes
Social **Class**
Social Class Attitudes
USE Socioeconomic Class Attitudes
Socioeconomic **Class** Attitudes
Upper **Class**
Upper **Class** Attitudes
Form **Classes** (Language)
Words (Form Classes) *USE Form Classes (Language)*
Classical Conditioning
Classification (Cognitive Process)
Classification Systems *USE Taxonomies*
Army General **Classification** Test
Psychiatric Classifications (Taxon)
USE Psychodiagnostic Typologies
Classmates
Classroom Behavior
Classroom Behavior Modification
Classroom Discipline
Classroom Environment
Classroom Instruction *USE Teaching*
Open **Classroom** Method
Classrooms
Claustrophobia
Cleft Palate
Clergy
Clerical Personnel
Clerical Secretarial Skills
Client Abuse *USE Patient Abuse*
Client Attitudes
Client Centered Therapy
Client Characteristics
Client Compliance
USE Treatment Compliance
Client Counselor Interaction
USE Psychotherapeutic Processes
Client Dropouts *USE Treatment Dropouts*
Client Education
Client Participation
Client Records
Client Rights
Client Satisfaction
Client Transfer
Client Treatment Matching
Client Violence *USE Patient Violence*
Counselor Client Interaction
USE Psychotherapeutic Processes
Professional **Client** Sexual Relations
Treatment Client Matching
USE Client Treatment Matching
Clients
Climacteric Depression
USE Involutional Depression
Climacteric Paranoia
USE Involutional Paranoid Psychosis
Climate (Meteorological)
USE Atmospheric Conditions
Organizational **Climate**
Climax (Sexual) *USE Orgasm*
Clinical Judgment (Med Diagnosis)
USE Medical Diagnosis
Clinical Judgment (Not Diagnosis)
Clinical Judgment (Psychodiagnosis)
USE Psychodiagnosis
Clinical Markers *USE Biological Markers*
Clinical Methods Training
Clinical Psychologists
Clinical Psychology
Clinical Psychology Grad Training
Clinical Psychology Internship
Clinical Supervision
USE Professional Supervision
Millon **Clinical** Multiaxial Inventory
Clinicians
Clinics
Child Guidance **Clinics**
Child Psychiatric Clinics *USE Child Guidance Clinics*
Outpatient Psychiatric Clinics *USE Psychiatric Clinics*
Psychiatric **Clinics**
Walk In **Clinics**
Cliques *USE Social Groups*
Clomipramine *USE Chlorimipramine*
Clonazepam
Clonidine
Closed Circuit Television
Closedmindedness *USE Openmindedness*
Perceptual **Closure**
Clothing
Clozapine
Cloze Testing
School **Club** Membership
Clubs (Social Organizations)
Therapeutic Social **Clubs**
Cluster Analysis
CNS Affecting Drugs
CNS Depressant Drugs
CNS Stimulating Drugs
Stimulants of CNS *USE CNS Stimulating Drugs*
Coaches
Test **Coaching**
Blood **Coagulation**
Coalition Formation
Coast Guard Personnel
Ivory **Coast**
Cobalt
Cocaine
Cochlea
Cochlear Implants
Cochran Q Test
Cockroaches
Code Switching
Codeine
Codependency
Automated Information **Coding**
Coeducation
Pearson Prod Moment Correl Coeff *USE Statistical Correlation*
Phi **Coefficient**
Coercion
Coffee *USE Beverages (Nonalcoholic)*
Cognition
Cognition Enhancing Drugs
USE Nootropic Drugs
Need for **Cognition**
Social **Cognition**
Sorting (Cognition)
USE Classification (Cognitive Process)
Transposition **(Cognition)**
Cognitions
Cognitive Ability
Cognitive Assessment
Cognitive Behavior Therapy
USE Cognitive Therapy
Cognitive Complexity
Cognitive Contiguity
Cognitive Development
Cognitive Discrimination
Cognitive Dissonance
Cognitive Functioning
USE Cognitive Ability
Cognitive Generalization
Cognitive Hypothesis Testing
Cognitive Load
USE Human Channel Capacity
Cognitive Maps
Cognitive Mediation
Cognitive Processes

ROTATED ALPHABETICAL TERMS SECTION

Cognitive Processing Speed
Cognitive Psychology
Cognitive Rehabilitation
Cognitive Restructuring
Cognitive Style
Cognitive Techniques
Cognitive Therapy
Assessment (Cognitive) *USE Cognitive Assessment*
Classification **(Cognitive** Process)
Hypothesis Testing (Cognitive) *USE Cognitive Hypothesis Testing*
Cohabitation
Group **Cohesion**
Cohort Analysis
Coitus *USE Sexual Intercourse (Human)*
Coitus (Animal) *USE Animal Mating Behavior*
Cold Effects
Colitis
Ulcerative **Colitis**
Collaboration *USE Cooperation*
Blue **Collar** Workers
White **Collar** Workers
Data **Collection**
Collective Behavior
Collective Unconscious
College Academic Achievement
College Athletes
College Degrees *USE Educational Degrees*
College Dropouts
College Education *USE Undergraduate Education*
Coll Ent Exam Bd Scholastic Apt Test
College Environment
College Graduates
College Major *USE Academic Specialization*
College Students
College Teachers
Community **College** Students
Junior **College** Students
School and College Ability Test *USE Aptitude Measures*
Colleges
Community **Colleges**
Junior Colleges *USE Colleges*
Inferior **Colliculus**
Superior **Colliculus**
Colombia
Colon Disorders
Color
Color Blindness
Color Constancy
Color Contrast
Color Perception
Color Pyramid Test *USE Projective Personality Measures*
Color Saturation
Achromatic **Color**
Eye **Color**
Saturation (Color) *USE Color Saturation*
Stroop **Color** Word Test
Animal **Coloration**
Colostomy
Raven **Coloured** Progressive Matrices
Columbia Mental Maturity Scale
Spinal **Column**
Coma
Combat Experience
Physical **Comfort**
Commerce *USE Business*
Commercials *USE Television Advertising*
Commissioned Officers
Hippocampal Commissure *USE Fornix*
Commissurotomy
Commitment
Commitment (Outpatient) *USE Outpatient Commitment*
Commitment (Psychiatric)
Organizational **Commitment**
Outpatient **Commitment**
Commonwealth of Independent States
Communes
Communicable Diseases *USE Infectious Disorders*
Communication
Communication Apprehension *USE Speech Anxiety*
Communication Disorders
Communication (Professional) *USE Scientific Communication*
Communication Skills
Communication Skills Training
Communication Systems
Communication Theory
Animal **Communication**
Augmentative **Communication**
Cross Cultural **Communication**
Facilitated Communication *USE Augmentative Communication*
Father Child **Communication**
Intercultural Communication *USE Cross Cultural Communication*
Interethnic Communication *USE Cross Cultural Communication*
Interpersonal **Communication**
Manual **Communication**
Mother Child **Communication**
Nonverbal **Communication**
Oral **Communication**
Parent Child **Communication**
Persuasive **Communication**
Privileged **Communication**
Professional Communication *USE Scientific Communication*
Scientific **Communication**
Verbal **Communication**
Written **Communication**
Communications Media
Audiovisual **Communications** Media
Printed **Communications** Media
Communicative Competence *USE Communication Skills*
Communism
Communities
Retirement **Communities**
Community Attitudes
Community College Students
Community Colleges
Community Development
Community Facilities
Community Mental Health
Community Mental Health Centers
Community Mental Health Services
Community Mental Health Training
Community Psychiatry
Community Psychology
Community Services
Community Welfare Services
Therapeutic **Community**
Commuting (Travel)
Comorbidity
Companies *USE Business Organizations*
Comparative Psychiatry *USE Transcultural Psychiatry*
Comparative Psychology
Social **Comparison**
Interpersonal **Compatibility**
Compensation (Defense Mechanism)
Workmens **Compensation** Insurance
Compensatory Education
Competence
Competence (Social) *USE Social Skills*
Communicative Competence *USE Communication Skills*
Interpersonal Competence *USE Social Skills*
Professional **Competence**
Competency to Stand Trial

ROTATED ALPHABETICAL TERMS SECTION

Minimum **Competency** Tests
Competition
Health **Complaints**
Franck Drawing **Completion** Test
Sentence **Completion** Tests
AIDS Dementia **Complex**
Electra **Complex**
Oedipal **Complex**
Cognitive **Complexity**
Stimulus **Complexity**
Task **Complexity**
Compliance
Client Compliance *USE Treatment Compliance*
Medical Regimen Compliance *USE Treatment Compliance*
Treatment **Compliance**
Obstetrical **Complications**
Postsurgical **Complications**
Surgical Complications
USE Postsurgical Complications
Comprehension
Comprehension Tests
Listening **Comprehension**
Number **Comprehension**
Reading **Comprehension**
Sentence **Comprehension**
Verbal **Comprehension**
Compressed Speech
Compulsions
Compulsive Gambling
USE Pathological Gambling
Compulsive Neurosis
USE Obsessive Compulsive Neurosis
Compulsive Personality Disorder
USE Obsessive Compulsive Personality
Compulsive Repetition
Obsessive Compulsive Disorder
USE Obsessive Compulsive Neurosis
Obsessive **Compulsive** Neurosis
Obsessive **Compulsive** Personality
Compulsivity (Sexual)
USE Sexual Addiction
Sexual Compulsivity *USE Sexual Addiction*
Computer Applications
Computer Assisted Design
Computer Assisted Diagnosis
Computer Assisted Instruction
Computer Assisted Testing
Computer Attitudes
Computer Conferencing
USE Teleconferencing
Computer Games
Computer Literacy
Computer Peripheral Devices
Computer Programing
Computer Programing Languages
Computer Programs
USE Computer Software
Computer Searching
Computer Simulation
Computer Software
Computer Training
Human **Computer** Interaction
Programing (Computer) *USE Computer Programing*
Computerized Databases *USE Databases*
Computers
Analog **Computers**
Digital **Computers**
Personal Computers *USE Microcomputers*
Concentration
Concentration Camps
Blood Alcohol **Concentration**
Concept Formation
Concept Learning
USE Concept Formation
Concept Validity *USE Construct Validity*
Academic Self **Concept**
Conservation **(Concept)**
Self **Concept**
Temporal Spatial Concept Scale *USE Intelligence Measures*

Tennessee Self **Concept** Scale
Concepts
God **Concepts**
Mathematics **(Concepts)**
Conceptual Imagery
Conceptual Tempo
Conceptualization
USE Concept Formation
Concurrent Reinforcement Schedules
Concurrent Validity
Brain **Concussion**
Conditioned Emotional Responses
Conditioned Inhibition
USE Conditioned Suppression
Conditioned Place Preference
USE Place Conditioning
Conditioned Reflex
USE Conditioned Responses
Conditioned Responses
Conditioned Stimulus
Conditioned Suppression
Conditioning
Conditioning (Verbal) *USE Verbal Learning*
Aversion **Conditioning**
Avoidance **Conditioning**
CER (Conditioning)
USE Conditioned Emotional Responses
Classical **Conditioning**
Escape **Conditioning**
Eyelid **Conditioning**
Fading **(Conditioning)**
Higher Order **Conditioning**
Instrumental Conditioning *USE Operant Conditioning*
Odor Aversion Conditioning *USE Aversion Conditioning*
Operant **Conditioning**
Pavlovian Conditioning *USE Classical Conditioning*
Place **Conditioning**
Respondent Conditioning *USE Classical Conditioning*
Second Order Conditioning
USE Higher Order Conditioning
Taste Aversion Conditioning *USE Aversion Conditioning*
Verbal Conditioning *USE Verbal Learning*
Atmospheric **Conditions**
Working **Conditions**
Condoms
Conduct Disorder
Bone **Conduction** Audiometry
Skin Conduction *USE Skin Resistance*
Cones (Eye)
Confabulation
Conference Proceedings
USE Professional Meetings and Symposia
Computer Conferencing *USE Teleconferencing*
Confession (Religion)
Confidence Limits (Statistics)
Confidence (Self) *USE Self Confidence*
Self **Confidence**
Confidentiality of Information
USE Privileged Communication
Confirmatory Factor Analysis
USE Factor Analysis
Conflict
Conflict Resolution
Marital **Conflict**
Role **Conflicts**
Conformity (Personality)
Mental **Confusion**
Congenital Disorders
Drug Induced **Congenital** Disorders
Congenitally Disabled
Congenitally Handicapped
USE Congenitally Disabled
Congo
Self **Congruence**
Conjoint Measurement
Conjoint Therapy
Connectionism
Connective Tissue Cells

ROTATED ALPHABETICAL TERMS SECTION

Connective Tissues
Connotations
Consanguineous Marriage
Conscience
Conscientiousness
Conscious (Personality Factor)
Consciousness Disturbances
Consciousness Raising Groups
Consciousness States
Self Consciousness *USE Self Perception*
Informed **Consent**
Conservation (Concept)
Conservation (Ecological Behavior)
Conservatism
Political **Conservatism**
Wilson Patterson **Conservatism** Scale
Conservatorship *USE Guardianship*
Consistency (Measurement)
Internal Consistency *USE Test Reliability*
Response Consistency *USE Response Variability*
Consonants
Brightness **Constancy**
Color **Constancy**
Perceptual **Constancy**
Size **Constancy**
Constant Time Delay
Constipation
Construct Validity
Laborers (Construct and Indust)
USE Blue Collar Workers
Personal Construct Theory *USE Personality Theory*
Test **Construction**
Constructionism *USE Constructivism*
Constructivism
Consultation Liaison Psychiatry
Mental Health Consultation
USE Professional Consultation
Professional **Consultation**
Consumer Attitudes
Consumer Behavior
Consumer Fraud *USE Fraud*
Consumer Product Design
USE Product Design
Consumer Protection
Consumer Psychology
Consumer Research
Consumer Satisfaction
Consumer Surveys
Contact Lenses
Eye **Contact**
Physical **Contact**
Contagion
Cost **Containment**
Content Analysis
Content Analysis (Test)
Dream **Content**
Emotional **Content**
Item **Content** (Test)
Thought Content *USE Cognitions*
Contextual Associations
Cognitive **Contiguity**
Contingency Management
Contingent Negative Variation
Continuing Education
Continuous Reinforcement
USE Reinforcement Schedules
Contour *USE Form and Shape Perception*
Contour Perception
USE Form and Shape Perception
Contraception *USE Birth Control*
Contraceptive Devices
Oral **Contraceptives**
Behavior **Contracting**
Muscle **Contraction** Headache
Muscle **Contractions**
Behavioral **Contrast**
Brightness **Contrast**
Color **Contrast**
Successive Contrast *USE Afterimage*
Visual **Contrast**
Control (Emotional)
USE Emotional Control
Control Groups *USE Experiment Controls*
Control (Locus of)
USE Internal External Locus of Control
Control (Self) *USE Self Control*
Control (Social) *USE Social Control*
Air Traffic **Control**
Anger **Control**
Birth **Control**
Birth Control Attitudes
USE Family Planning Attitudes
Diaphragms (Birth **Control)**
Emotional **Control**
Gun **Control** Laws
Health Locus of Control *USE Health Attitudes*
Impulse **Control** Disorders
Internal External Locus of **Control**
Population Control *USE Birth Control*
Quality **Control**
Rotter Intern Extern Locus **Cont** Scal
Self **Control**
Social **Control**
Stimulus **Control**
Thought Control *USE Brainwashing*
Weight **Control**
Experiment **Controls**
Instrument **Controls**
Eye **Convergence**
Convergent Thinking
USE Inductive Deductive Reasoning
Conversation
Conversion Hysteria
USE Conversion Neurosis
Conversion Neurosis
Criminal **Conviction**
Convulsions
Cooperating Teachers
Cooperation
Cooperative Education
Cooperative Learning
Cooperative Therapy *USE Cotherapy*
Motor **Coordination**
Perceptual Motor **Coordination**
Coping Behavior
Copper
Copulation
USE Sexual Intercourse (Human)
Copulation (Animal)
USE Animal Mating Behavior
Cranial Spinal **Cord**
Lumbar Spinal **Cord**
Spinal **Cord**
Spinal **Cord** Injuries
Vocal **Cords**
Cornea
Coronary Disorders
USE Cardiovascular Disorders
Coronary Heart Disease
USE Heart Disorders
Coronary Prone Behavior
Coronary Thromboses
Coronary Vessels *USE Arteries (Anatomy)*
Corporal Punishment *USE Punishment*
Corporations *USE Business Organizations*
Job **Corps**
Peace **Corps**
Corpus Callosum
Corpus Striatum *USE Basal Ganglia*
Correctional Institutions
Corrective Lenses *USE Optical Aids*
Pearson Prod Moment Correl Coeff *USE Statistical Correlation*
Personality **Correlates**
Physiological **Correlates**
Psychological Correlates *USE Psychodynamics*
Canonical Correlation *USE Multivariate Analysis*
Point Biserial **Correlation**
Rank Difference **Correlation**

Rank Order **Correlation**
Statistical **Correlation**
Tetrachoric **Correlation**
Adrenal **Cortex** Hormones
Adrenal Cortex Steroids *USE Corticosteroids*
Auditory **Cortex**
Cerebral **Cortex**
Motor **Cortex**
Prefrontal **Cortex**
Somatosensory **Cortex**
Striate Cortex *USE Visual Cortex*
Visual **Cortex**
Organ of Corti *USE Cochlea*
Cortical Atrophy *USE Cerebral Atrophy*
Cortical Evoked Potentials
Corticoids *USE Corticosteroids*
Corticosteroids
Corticosterone
Corticotropin
Corticotropin Releasing Factor
Cortisol *USE Hydrocortisone*
Cortisone
Cost Containment
Cost Effectiveness
USE Costs and Cost Analysis
Costs and **Cost** Analysis
Response **Cost**
Costa Rica
Costs and Cost Analysis
Health Care **Costs**
Medical Care Costs *USE Health Care Costs*
Mental Health Care Costs *USE Health Care Costs*
Cotherapy
Counselees *USE Clients*
Counseling
Counseling Psychologists
Counseling Psychology
Career Counseling *USE Occupational Guidance*
Educational **Counseling**
Family Counseling *USE Family Therapy*
Genetic **Counseling**
Group **Counseling**
Guidance Counseling *USE School Counseling*
Individual Counseling *USE Individual Psychotherapy*
Marriage **Counseling**
Pastoral **Counseling**
Peer **Counseling**
Premarital **Counseling**
Psychotherapeutic **Counseling**
Rehabilitation **Counseling**
School **Counseling**
Vocational Counseling *USE Occupational Guidance*
Counselor Attitudes
Counselor Characteristics
Counselor Client Interaction
USE Psychotherapeutic Processes
Counselor Education
Counselor Effectiveness
USE Counselor Characteristics
Counselor Personality
USE Counselor Characteristics
Counselor Role
Counselor Trainees
Client Counselor Interaction
USE Psychotherapeutic Processes
Counselors
Rehabilitation **Counselors**
School **Counselors**
Vocational **Counselors**
Over The Counter Drugs
USE Nonprescription Drugs
Counterconditioning
Countertransference
Countries
Developed **Countries**
Developing **Countries**
Third World Countries *USE Developing Countries*
Underdeveloped Countries *USE Developing Countries*
Couples

Couples Therapy
Married Couples *USE Spouses*
Courage
Course Evaluation
Course Objectives
USE Educational Objectives
Course of Illness *USE Disease Course*
Disease **Course**
Disorder Course *USE Disease Course*
Court Ordered Treatment
USE Court Referrals
Court Referrals
Juvenile Court *USE Adjudication*
Courts *USE Adjudication*
Animal **Courtship** Behavior
Animal **Courtship** Displays
Human **Courtship**
Cousins
Analysis of **Covariance**
Covert Sensitization
Least Preferred **Coworker** Scale
Cows *USE Cattle*
Coyotes *USE Canids*
Crabs
Crafts
Cramps (Muscle) *USE Muscular Disorders*
Muscle Cramps *USE Muscular Disorders*
Cranial Nerves
Cranial Spinal Cord
Craving
Crayfish
Creative Arts Therapy
Creative Writing
Writing (Creative) *USE Creative Writing*
Creativity
Creativity Measurement
Credibility
Creutzfeldt Jakob Syndrome
Aircraft Crew *USE Aerospace Personnel*
Cri du Chat Syndrome
USE Crying Cat Syndrome
Crib Death *USE Sudden Infant Death*
Crime
Crime Prevention
Crime Victims
Criminal Conviction
Criminal Interrogation
USE Legal Interrogation
Criminal Justice
Criminal Law
Criminal Responsibility
Criminally Insane
USE Mentally Ill Offenders
Criminals
Female **Criminals**
Male **Criminals**
Criminology
Crises
Family **Crises**
Organizational **Crises**
Crisis Intervention
Crisis Intervention Services
Crisis (Reactions to)
USE Stress Reactions
Identity **Crisis**
Research Diagnostic **Criteria**
Student Admission **Criteria**
Criterion Referenced Tests
Critical Flicker Fusion Threshold
Critical Period
Critical Scores *USE Cutting Scores*
Criticism
Professional **Criticism**
Professional **Criticism** Reply
Crocodilians
Cross Cultural Communication
Cross Cultural Differences
Cross Cultural Psychology
Cross Cultural Treatment

Cross Disciplinary Research
USE Interdisciplinary Research
Crossed Eyes *USE Strabismus*
Crowding
Marlowe **Crowne** Soc Desirabil Scale
CRT *USE Video Display Units*
Cruelty
Crustacea
Crying
Crying Cat Syndrome
Cuba
Cuban Americans *USE Hispanics*
Cued Recall
Cues
Cultism
Cultural Assimilation
Cultural Deprivation
Cultural Factors
USE Sociocultural Factors
Cultural Familial Mental Retardation
USE Psychosocial Mental Retardation
Cultural Pluralism *USE Multiculturalism*
Cultural Psychiatry
USE Transcultural Psychiatry
Cultural Sensitivity
Cultural Test Bias
Chinese **Cultural** Groups
Cross **Cultural** Communication
Cross **Cultural** Differences
Cross **Cultural** Psychology
Cross **Cultural** Treatment
Japanese **Cultural** Groups
Korean **Cultural** Groups
Vietnamese **Cultural** Groups
Culturally Disadvantaged
USE Cultural Deprivation
Culture (Anthropological)
Culture Change
Culture Fair Intelligence Test
Culture Shock
Cattell Culture Fair Intell Test
USE Culture Fair Intelligence Test
Curare
Curiosity
Curricular Field Experience
Curriculum
Curriculum Based Assessment
Curriculum Development
Cursive Writing
Cushings Syndrome
Child **Custody**
Joint **Custody**
Customer Satisfaction
USE Consumer Satisfaction
Cutaneous Receptive Fields
Cutaneous Sense
Cutting Scores
Cybernetics
Lunar Synodic **Cycle**
Menstrual **Cycle**
Sleep Wake **Cycle**
Work Rest **Cycles**
Cyclic Adenosine Monophosphate
Cycloheximide
Cyclothymic Disorder
USE Cyclothymic Personality
Cyclothymic Personality
Cynicism
Cyprus
Cysteine
Cystic Fibrosis
Cytochrome Oxidase
Cytology
Cytoplasm
Czechoslovakia
Daily Activities
Daily Biological Rhythms (Animal)
USE Animal Circadian Rhythms
Activities of **Daily** Living
Brain **Damage**
Brain **Damaged**
Minimally Brain **Damaged**
Dance
Dance Therapy
Dangerousness
Dark Adaptation
Darwinism
Data Collection
Data Pooling *USE Meta Analysis*
Data Processing
Biographical **Data**
Statistical **Data**
Databases
Computerized Databases *USE Databases*
Online Databases *USE Databases*
Date Rape *USE Acquaintance Rape*
Social **Dating**
Daughters
Day Care Centers
Day Care (Treatment)
USE Partial Hospitalization
Day Hospital *USE Partial Hospitalization*
Adult **Day** Care
Child **Day** Care
Recreational Day Camps
USE Summer Camps (Recreation)
Daydreaming
Guided Daydreams *USE Directed Reverie Therapy*
DDT (Insecticide)
Deaf
Deaf Blind
Word Deafness *USE Aphasia*
Deanol *USE Antidepressant Drugs*
Death and Dying
Death Anxiety
Death Attitudes
Death Education
Death Instinct
Death Penalty *USE Capital Punishment*
Death Rate *USE Mortality Rate*
Death Rites
Crib Death *USE Sudden Infant Death*
Near **Death** Experiences
Sudden Infant **Death**
Debates
Political Debates *USE Debates*
Presidential Debates *USE Debates*
Debriefing (Experimental)
Decarboxylase Inhibitors
Decarboxylases
Memory **Decay**
Decentralization
Deception
Decerebration
Decision Making
Decision Support Systems
Group **Decision** Making
Lexical **Decision**
Management **Decision** Making
Legal **Decisions**
Declarative Knowledge
Decoding
USE Human Information Storage
Decompression Effects
Decortication (Brain)
Inductive **Deductive** Reasoning
Deer
Self **Defeating** Behavior
Defecation
Defendants
Defense Mechanisms
Compensation **(Defense** Mechanism)
Displacement **(Defense** Mechanism)
Fantasy **(Defense** Mechanism)
Identification **(Defense** Mechanism)
Insanity **Defense**
Isolation **(Defense** Mechanism)
Projection **(Defense** Mechanism)

Regression **(Defense** Mechanism)
Repression **(Defense** Mechanism)
Self **Defense**
Suppression **(Defense** Mechanism)
Withdrawal **(Defense** Mechanism)
Animal **Defensive** Behavior
Defensiveness
Oppositional **Defiant** Disorder
Nutritional **Deficiencies**
Acquired Immune **Deficiency** Syndrome
Mental Deficiency *USE Mental Retardation*
Protein **Deficiency** Disorders
Vitamin **Deficiency** Disorders
Attention **Deficit** Disorder
Deformity *USE Physical Disfigurement*
College Degrees *USE Educational Degrees*
Educational **Degrees**
Graduate Degrees *USE Educational Degrees*
Undergraduate Degrees *USE Educational Degrees*
Dehydration
Lactate **Dehydrogenase**
Dehydrogenases
Alcohol **Dehydrogenases**
Deinstitutionalization
Deja Vu *USE Consciousness States*
Delay of Gratification
Constant Time **Delay**
Language **Delay**
Reinforcement **Delay**
Delayed Alternation
Delayed Auditory Feedback
Delayed Development
Delayed Feedback
Delayed Parenthood
Delayed Speech
USE Retarded Speech Development
Deletion (Chromosome)
Juvenile **Delinquency**
Sexual Delinquency *USE Promiscuity*
Female **Delinquents**
Juvenile **Delinquents**
Male **Delinquents**
Delirium
Delirium Tremens
Health Care **Delivery**
Delta Rhythm
Delusions
Dementia
Dementia (Multi Infarct)
USE Multi Infarct Dementia
Dementia Paralytica *USE General Paresis*
Dementia Praecox *USE Schizophrenia*
AIDS **Dementia** Complex
Multi Infarct **Dementia**
Presenile **Dementia**
Senile **Dementia**
Vascular **Dementia**
Democracy
Democratic Party *USE Political Parties*
East German Democratic Republic *USE East Germany*
Demographic Characteristics
Demonic Possession
USE Spirit Possession
Social **Demonstrations**
Dendrites
Denial
Denmark
Population Density *USE Social Density*
Social **Density**
Dental Education
Dental Students
Dental Surgery
Dental Treatment
Dentist Patient Interaction
USE Therapeutic Processes
Dentistry
Dentists
Deoxycorticosterone
Deoxyglucose

Deoxyribonucleic Acid
DNA (Deoxyribonucleic Acid)
USE Deoxyribonucleic Acid
Field **Dependence**
Dependency (Personality)
Drug **Dependency**
Dependent Personality
Dependent Variables
State **Dependent** Learning
Depersonalization
CNS **Depressant** Drugs
Appetite **Depressing** Drugs
Depression (Emotion)
Agitated Depression *USE Major Depression*
Anaclitic **Depression**
Beck **Depression** Inventory
Climacteric Depression *USE Involutional Depression*
Endogenous **Depression**
Involutional **Depression**
Major **Depression**
Manic **Depression**
Postpartum **Depression**
Reactive **Depression**
Recurrent **Depression**
Spreading **Depression**
Treatment Resistant **Depression**
Tricyclic Resistant Depression
USE Treatment Resistant Depression
Unipolar Depression *USE Major Depression*
Winter Depression
USE Seasonal Affective Disorder
Zungs Self Rating **Depression** Scale
Manic Depressive Psychosis
USE Manic Depression
Neurotic **Depressive** Reaction
Psychotic Depressive Reaction
USE Major Depression
Deprivation
Animal Maternal **Deprivation**
Cultural **Deprivation**
Food **Deprivation**
REM Dream **Deprivation**
Sensory **Deprivation**
Sleep **Deprivation**
Social **Deprivation**
Stimulus **Deprivation**
Water **Deprivation**
Depth Perception
Depth Psychology
Ergot **Derivatives**
Opium Derivatives *USE Opiates*
Phenothiazine **Derivatives**
Dermatitis
Dermatomes
USE Cutaneous Receptive Fields
Desegregation *USE Social Integration*
Eye Movement **Desensitization** Therapy
Systematic **Desensitization** Therapy
Desertion *USE Abandonment*
Between Groups **Design**
Computer Assisted **Design**
Consumer Product Design *USE Product Design*
Environmental Design *USE Environmental Planning*
Experimental **Design**
Human Machine Systems **Design**
Interior **Design**
Kohs Block **Design** Test
Man Machine Systems Design
USE Human Machine Systems Design
Product **Design**
Research Design *USE Experimental Design*
Within Subjects Design *USE Repeated Measures*
Memory for **Designs** Test
Desipramine
Edwards Social **Desirability** Scale
Marlowe Crowne Soc **Desirabil** Scale
Social **Desirability**
Hypoactive Sexual Desire Disorder
USE Inhibited Sexual Desire

Inhibited Sexual **Desire**
Desires *USE Motivation*
Self **Destructive** Behavior
Anatomically **Detailed** Dolls
Signal **Detection** (Perception)
Legal **Detention**
Self **Determination**
Threshold **Determination**
Verdict Determination *USE Adjudication*
Determinism
Detoxification
Kupfer Detre Self Rating Scale *USE Nonprojective Personality Measures*
Folie A **Deux**
Developed Countries
Developing Countries
Development
Adolescent **Development**
Adult **Development**
Animal **Development**
Bayley Scales of Infant **Development**
Career **Development**
Childhood **Development**
Childhood Play **Development**
Cognitive **Development**
Community **Development**
Curriculum **Development**
Delayed **Development**
Early Childhood **Development**
Ego **Development**
Emotional **Development**
Frostig **Development** Test Vis Percept
Group **Development**
Human **Development**
Infant **Development**
Intellectual **Development**
Language **Development**
Management Development *USE Career Development*
Moral **Development**
Motor **Development**
Neonatal **Development**
Neural **Development**
Organizational **Development**
Perceptual **Development**
Perceptual Motor **Development**
Personality **Development**
Personnel Development *USE Personnel Training*
Physical **Development**
Precocious **Development**
Prenatal **Development**
Professional **Development**
Program **Development**
Psychological Development *USE Psychogenesis*
Psychomotor **Development**
Psychosexual **Development**
Psychosocial **Development**
Reading **Development**
Retarded Speech **Development**
Rural Development *USE Community Development*
Sensorimotor Development *USE Perceptual Motor Development*
Sexual **Development**
Social Development *USE Psychosocial Development*
Speech **Development**
Urban Development *USE Community Development*
Developmental Age Groups
Developmental Differences *USE Age Differences*
Developmental Disabilities
Developmental Measures
Developmental Psychology
Developmental Stages
Prenatal **Developmental** Stages
Sex Linked **Developmental** Differences
Deviant Behavior *USE Antisocial Behavior*
Deviation IQ *USE Standard Scores*
Standard **Deviation**
Sexual **Deviations**
Devices (Experimental) *USE Apparatus*
Computer Peripheral **Devices**
Contraceptive **Devices**
Intrauterine **Devices**
Medical Therapeutic **Devices**
Safety **Devices**
Dexamethasone
Dexamethasone Suppression Test
Dexedrine *USE Dextroamphetamine*
Physical **Dexterity**
Dextroamphetamine
Diabetes
Diabetes Insipidus
Diabetes Mellitus
Diacetylmorphine *USE Heroin*
Diagnosis
Diagnosis Related Groups
Clinical Judgment (Med Diagnosis) *USE Medical Diagnosis*
Clinical Judgment (Not **Diagnosis)**
Computer Assisted **Diagnosis**
Differential **Diagnosis**
Dual **Diagnosis**
Educational **Diagnosis**
Medical **Diagnosis**
Prenatal **Diagnosis**
X Ray Diagnosis *USE Roentgenography*
Diagnostic and Statistical Manual
Diagnostic Interview Schedule
Research **Diagnostic** Criteria
Dialect
Dialectics
Dialysis
Diaphragm (Anatomy)
Diaphragms (Birth Control)
Diarrhea
Diastolic Pressure
Diazepam
Dichoptic Stimulation
Dichotic Stimulation
Dictionary
Dieldrin *USE Insecticides*
Diencephalon
Dietary Restraint
Lysergic Acid **Diethylamide**
Diets
Rank **Difference** Correlation
Age **Differences**
Animal Sex **Differences**
Animal Strain **Differences**
Cross Cultural **Differences**
Developmental Differences *USE Age Differences*
Gender Differences *USE Human Sex Differences*
Human Sex **Differences**
Individual **Differences**
Racial and Ethnic **Differences**
Sex Linked Developmental **Differences**
Species **Differences**
Differential Aptitude Tests
Differential Diagnosis
Differential Limen *USE Thresholds*
Differential Personality Inventory *USE Nonprojective Personality Measures*
Differential Reinforcement
Semantic **Differential**
Sex Differentiation Disorders *USE Genital Disorders*
Difficulty Level (Test)
Task Difficulty *USE Task Complexity*
Test Difficulty *USE Difficulty Level (Test)*
Digestion
Digestive System
Digestive System Disorders
Digit Span Testing
Digital Computers
Digits (Mathematics) *USE Numbers (Numerals)*
Dihydroergotamine

Dihydroxyphenylacetic Acid
Dihydroxytryptamine
Dilantin *USE Diphenylhydantoin*
Pupil **Dilation**
Prisoners **Dilemma** Game
Carbon **Dioxide**
Diphenhydramine
Diphenylhydantoin
High School Diplomas *USE Educational Degrees*
Diptera
Directed Discussion Method
Directed Reverie Therapy
Self Directed Learning
USE Individualized Instruction
Direction Perception
Advance **Directives**
Developmental **Disabilities**
Learning **Disabilities**
Physical **Disabilities** (Attit Toward)
Reading **Disabilities**
Sensory **Disabilities** (Attit Toward)
Disability Discrimination
Disability Evaluation
Disability Laws
Disability Management
Disabled
Disabled (Attitudes Toward)
Disabled Personnel
Adventitiously **Disabled**
Aurally **Disabled**
Congenitally **Disabled**
Multiply **Disabled**
Physically **Disabled**
Sensorially **Disabled**
Speech **Disabled**
Visually **Disabled**
Disadvantaged
Culturally Disadvantaged *USE Cultural Deprivation*
Economically Disadvantaged *USE Disadvantaged*
Socially Disadvantaged *USE Disadvantaged*
Disappointment
Disasters
Natural **Disasters**
Discharge Planning
Facility **Discharge**
Hospital **Discharge**
Psychiatric Hospital **Discharge**
Cross Disciplinary Research
USE Interdisciplinary Research
Child **Discipline**
Classroom **Discipline**
Disclosure (Experimental)
USE Debriefing (Experimental)
Disclosure (Self) *USE Self Disclosure*
Self **Disclosure**
Discourse Analysis
Discovery Teaching Method
Discrimination
Discrimination Learning
Discrimination (Social)
USE Social Discrimination
Age **Discrimination**
Auditory **Discrimination**
Cognitive **Discrimination**
Disability **Discrimination**
Distance Discrimination *USE Distance Perception*
Drug **Discrimination**
Employment **Discrimination**
Ethnic Discrimination
USE Race and Ethnic Discrimination
Figure Ground **Discrimination**
Job Discrimination
USE Employment Discrimination
Loudness **Discrimination**
Minority Group Discrimination
USE Race and Ethnic Discrimination
Odor **Discrimination**
Pattern **Discrimination**
Perceptual **Discrimination**
Pitch **Discrimination**
Race and Ethnic **Discrimination**
Racial Discrimination
USE Race and Ethnic Discrimination
Sex **Discrimination**
Size **Discrimination**
Social **Discrimination**
Spatial Discrimination *USE Spatial Perception*
Stimulus **Discrimination**
Tactual Discrimination *USE Tactual Perception*
Taste Discrimination *USE Taste Perception*
Visual **Discrimination**
Wepman Test of Auditory **Discrim**
Discriminative Stimulus
USE Conditioned Stimulus
Directed **Discussion** Method
Group **Discussion**
Nondirected **Discussion** Method
Disease Course
Addisons **Disease**
Alzheimers **Disease**
Coronary Heart Disease *USE Heart Disorders*
Duchennes Disease *USE Muscular Disorders*
Huntingtons **Disease**
Menieres **Disease**
Parkinsons **Disease**
Picks **Disease**
Raynauds Disease *USE Cardiovascular Disorders*
Sickle Cell **Disease**
Tay Sachs Disease *USE Amaurotic Familial Idiocy*
Communicable Diseases *USE Infectious Disorders*
International Class of **Diseases**
Kidney **Diseases**
Renal Diseases *USE Kidney Diseases*
Sexually Transmitted Diseases *USE Venereal Diseases*
Venereal **Diseases**
Physical **Disfigurement**
Disgust
Dishonesty
Dislike *USE Aversion*
Disorder Course *USE Disease Course*
Acute Paranoid Disorder *USE Paranoia (Psychosis)*
Attention Deficit **Disorder**
Atypical Paranoid Disorder *USE Paranoia (Psychosis)*
Atypical Somatoform Disorder *USE Dysmorphophobia*
Bipolar Affective Disorder *USE Manic Depression*
Bipolar Mood Disorder *USE Manic Depression*
Compulsive Personality Disorder
USE Obsessive Compulsive Personality
Conduct **Disorder**
Cyclothymic Disorder *USE Cyclothymic Personality*
Dissociative Identity **Disorder**
Dysthymic **Disorder**
Epstein Barr Viral **Disorder**
Gender Identity **Disorder**
Generalized Anxiety Disorder *USE Anxiety Disorders*
Gilles de la Tourette **Disorder**
Histrionic Personality Disorder *USE Hysterical Personality*
Hypoactive Sexual Desire Disorder *USE Inhibited Sexual Desire*
Obsessive Compulsive Disorder
USE Obsessive Compulsive Neurosis
Oppositional Defiant **Disorder**
Panic **Disorder**
Paranoid Disorder *USE Paranoia (Psychosis)*
PKU (Hereditary Disorder) *USE Phenylketonuria*
Posttraumatic Stress **Disorder**
Reactive Attachment Disorder *USE Failure to Thrive*
Schizoaffective **Disorder**
Schizophreniform **Disorder**
Seasonal Affective **Disorder**
Shared Paranoid Disorder *USE Folie A Deux*
Somatization Disorder *USE Psychosomatic Disorders*
Somatoform Pain **Disorder**
Disorders
Adjustment **Disorders**
Adrenal Gland **Disorders**
Affective Disorders *USE Affective Disturbances*
Allergic **Disorders**
Allergic Skin **Disorders**

Anxiety **Disorders**
Appetite Disorders *USE Eating Disorders*
Articulation **Disorders**
Autoimmune Disorders *USE Immunologic Disorders*
Autonomic Nervous System **Disorders**
Autosome **Disorders**
Bacterial **Disorders**
Behavior **Disorders**
Blood and Lymphatic **Disorders**
Blood Pressure **Disorders**
Bone **Disorders**
Bowel Disorders *USE Colon Disorders*
Brain **Disorders**
Bronchial **Disorders**
Cardiac Disorders *USE Heart Disorders*
Cardiovascular **Disorders**
Central Nervous System **Disorders**
Cerebral Vascular Disorders *USE Cerebrovascular Disorders*
Cerebrovascular **Disorders**
Chromosome **Disorders**
Chronicity **(Disorders)**
Circulatory Disorders *USE Cardiovascular Disorders*
Colon **Disorders**
Communication **Disorders**
Congenital **Disorders**
Coronary Disorders *USE Cardiovascular Disorders*
Digestive System **Disorders**
Drug Induced Congenital **Disorders**
Ear **Disorders**
Eating **Disorders**
Endocrine **Disorders**
Endocrine Sexual **Disorders**
Ethnic Disorders *USE Ethnospecific Disorders*
Ethnospecific **Disorders**
Eye **Disorders**
Factitious **Disorders**
Gastrointestinal **Disorders**
Genetic **Disorders**
Genital **Disorders**
Gynecological **Disorders**
Hearing **Disorders**
Heart **Disorders**
Hematologic Disorders
USE Blood and Lymphatic Disorders
Hepatic Disorders *USE Liver Disorders*
Hereditary Disorders *USE Genetic Disorders*
Hypophysis Disorders *USE Pituitary Disorders*
Immunologic **Disorders**
Impulse Control **Disorders**
Infectious **Disorders**
Joint **Disorders**
Karyotype Disorders *USE Chromosome Disorders*
Labyrinth **Disorders**
Language **Disorders**
Laryngeal **Disorders**
Learning **Disorders**
Lipid Metabolism **Disorders**
Liver **Disorders**
Lung **Disorders**
Male Genital **Disorders**
Memory **Disorders**
Menstrual **Disorders**
Mental **Disorders**
Metabolism **Disorders**
Minimal Brain **Disorders**
Mood Disorders *USE Affective Disturbances*
Motor Disorders *USE Nervous System Disorders*
Movement **Disorders**
Muscular **Disorders**
Musculoskeletal **Disorders**
Neonatal **Disorders**
Nervous System **Disorders**
Neurological Disorders *USE Nervous System Disorders*
Neuromuscular **Disorders**
Onset **(Disorders)**
Ovary Disorders
USE Endocrine Sexual Disorders
Parasitic **Disorders**
Parathyroid **Disorders**
Peripheral Nerve **Disorders**
Personality **Disorders**
Pharyngeal **Disorders**
Physical **Disorders**
Pituitary **Disorders**
Protein Deficiency **Disorders**
Psychiatric Disorders *USE Mental Disorders*
Psychophysiologic Disorders *USE Psychosomatic Disorders*
Psychosomatic **Disorders**
Pulmonary Disorders *USE Lung Disorders*
Recovery **(Disorders)**
Recurrence (Disorders) *USE Relapse (Disorders)*
Relapse **(Disorders)**
Remission **(Disorders)**
Respiratory Tract **Disorders**
Scalp Disorders *USE Skin Disorders*
Sense Organ **Disorders**
Severity **(Disorders)**
Sex Chromosome **Disorders**
Sex Differentiation Disorders *USE Genital Disorders*
Sex Linked Hereditary **Disorders**
Sexual Disorders (Physiological)
USE Genital Disorders
Skeletomuscular Disorders *USE Musculoskeletal Disorders*
Skin **Disorders**
Sleep **Disorders**
Speech **Disorders**
Susceptibility **(Disorders)**
Testes Disorders
USE Endocrine Sexual Disorders
Thyroid **Disorders**
Toxic **Disorders**
Treatment Resistant **Disorders**
Urinary Function **Disorders**
Urogenital **Disorders**
Vascular Disorders *USE Cardiovascular Disorders*
Viral **Disorders**
Vision **Disorders**
Vitamin Deficiency **Disorders**
Voice Disorders *USE Dysphonia*
Schizophrenia (Disorganized Type)
USE Hebephrenic Schizophrenia
Place **Disorientation**
Time **Disorientation**
Displacement (Defense Mechanism)
Video Display Terminals
USE Video Display Units
Video **Display** Units
Displays
Animal Courtship **Displays**
Auditory **Displays**
Graphical **Displays**
Tactual **Displays**
Visual **Displays**
Disposition *USE Personality*
Disruptive Behavior
USE Behavior Problems
Dissatisfaction
Drug Dissociation
USE State Dependent Learning
Hysterical Neurosis (Dissociation) *USE Dissociative Patterns*
Dissociative Identity Disorder
Dissociative Neurosis
USE Dissociative Patterns
Dissociative Patterns
Cognitive **Dissonance**
Distance Discrimination
USE Distance Perception
Distance Perception
Apparent **Distance**
Interpersonal Distance *USE Personal Space*
Perceptual **Distortion**
Spatial **Distortion**
Distractibility
Distraction
Distress
Animal **Distress** Calls
Respiratory **Distress**
Distributed Practice

Binomial **Distribution**
Drug **Distribution**
Frequency **Distribution**
Gaussian Distribution *USE Normal Distribution*
Normal **Distribution**
Poisson Distribution *USE Skewed Distribution*
Skewed **Distribution**
Distributive Justice *USE Justice*
Distrust *USE Suspicion*
Affective **Disturbances**
Body Image **Disturbances**
Consciousness **Disturbances**
Fantasies (Thought **Disturbances)**
Hysterical Vision **Disturbances**
Judgment **Disturbances**
Perceptual **Disturbances**
Sexual Function **Disturbances**
Thought **Disturbances**
Emotionally **Disturbed**
Disulfiram
Diuresis
Diuretics
Diurnal Variations
USE Human Biological Rhythms
Divergent Thinking
Divided Attention
Division of Labor
Animal **Division** of Labor
Physical Divisions (Geographic) *USE Geography*
Political Divisions (Geographic) *USE Geography*
Divorce
Divorced Persons
Dizygotic Twins *USE Heterozygotic Twins*
Dizziness *USE Vertigo*
DNA (Deoxyribonucleic Acid)
USE Deoxyribonucleic Acid
Doctors *USE Physicians*
Dogmatism
Rokeach **Dogmatism** Scale
Dogs
Seeing Eye Dogs *USE Mobility Aids*
Doll Play
Anatomically Detailed **Dolls**
Tic Doloureux *USE Trigeminal Neuralgia*
Dolphins
Domestic Service Personnel
Domestic Violence *USE Family Violence*
Animal **Domestication**
Dominance
Dominance Hierarchy
Animal **Dominance**
Cerebral **Dominance**
Eye Dominance *USE Ocular Dominance*
Genetic **Dominance**
Lateral **Dominance**
Ocular **Dominance**
Domination *USE Authoritarianism*
Dominican Republic
Blood Donation *USE Tissue Donation*
Organ Donation *USE Tissue Donation*
Sperm Donation *USE Tissue Donation*
Tissue **Donation**
DOPA
L Dopa *USE Levodopa*
DOPAC *USE Dihydroxyphenylacetic Acid*
Dopamine
Dopamine Agonists
Dopamine Antagonists
Dopamine Metabolites
Dormitories
Dorsal Horns
Dorsal Roots
Drug **Dosages**
Double Bind Interaction
Doubt
Doves
Downs Syndrome
Doxepin
Draftees
Drama
Draw A Man Test
USE Human Figures Drawing
Goodenough Harris **Draw** A Person Test
Drawing
Franck **Drawing** Completion Test
Human Figures **Drawing**
Dream Analysis
Dream Content
Dream Interpretation *USE Dream Analysis*
Dream Recall
REM **Dream** Deprivation
Dreaming
Lucid **Dreaming**
Rapid Eye Movement Dreams *USE REM Dreams*
REM **Dreams**
DRGs *USE Diagnosis Related Groups*
Drinking Behavior
Alcohol **Drinking** Attitudes
Alcohol **Drinking** Patterns
Animal **Drinking** Behavior
Problem Drinking *USE Alcohol Abuse*
Social **Drinking**
Drive *USE Motivation*
Sex **Drive**
Driver Education
Driver Safety *USE Highway Safety*
Drivers
Driving Behavior
Driving Under The Influence
Drunk Driving *USE Driving Under The Influence*
Dropouts
Client Dropouts *USE Treatment Dropouts*
College **Dropouts**
Patient Dropouts *USE Treatment Dropouts*
Potential **Dropouts**
Research Dropouts *USE Experimental Attrition*
School **Dropouts**
Treatment **Dropouts**
Drosophila
Drowsiness *USE Sleep Onset*
Drug Abstinence
Drug Abuse
Drug Abuse Liability
Drug Abuse Prevention
Drug Addiction
Drug Administration Methods
Drug Adverse Reactions
USE Side Effects (Drug)
Drug Allergies
Drug Dependency
Drug Discrimination
Drug Dissociation
USE State Dependent Learning
Drug Distribution
Drug Dosages
Drug Education
Drug Effects *USE Drugs*
Drug Induced Congenital Disorders
Drug Induced Hallucinations
Drug Interactions
Drug Laws
Drug Legalization
Drug Overdoses
Drug Potentiation *USE Drug Interactions*
Drug Rehabilitation
Drug Sensitivity
Drug Synergism *USE Drug Interactions*
Drug Testing *USE Drug Usage Screening*
Drug Therapy
Drug Tolerance
Drug Usage
Drug Usage Attitudes
Drug Usage Screening
Drug Withdrawal
Ecstasy (Drug)
USE Methylenedioxymethamphetamine
Intravenous **Drug** Usage
IV Drug Usage *USE Intravenous Drug Usage*

LSD (Drug) *USE Lysergic Acid Diethylamide*
Side Effects **(Drug)**
Tobacco (Drug) *USE Nicotine*
Withdrawal (Drug) *USE Drug Withdrawal*
Drugs
Abstinence (Drugs) *USE Drug Abstinence*
Abuse Potential (Drugs) *USE Drug Abuse Liability*
Adrenergic **Drugs**
Adrenergic Blocking **Drugs**
Adrenolytic Drugs *USE Adrenergic Drugs*
Analeptic **Drugs**
Analgesic **Drugs**
Anesthetic **Drugs**
Anorexigenic Drugs *USE Appetite Depressing Drugs*
Anti Inflammatory **Drugs**
Antiadrenergic Drugs *USE Sympatholytic Drugs*
Antianxiety Drugs *USE Tranquilizing Drugs*
Anticholinergic Drugs *USE Cholinergic Blocking Drugs*
Anticholinesterase Drugs *USE Cholinesterase Inhibitors*
Anticoagulant **Drugs**
Anticonvulsive **Drugs**
Antidepressant **Drugs**
Antiemetic **Drugs**
Antiepileptic Drugs *USE Anticonvulsive Drugs*
Antihistaminic **Drugs**
Antihypertensive **Drugs**
Antinauseant Drugs *USE Antiemetic Drugs*
Antineoplastic **Drugs**
Antiparkinsonian Drugs *USE Antitremor Drugs*
Antipsychotic Drugs *USE Neuroleptic Drugs*
Antipyretic Drugs *USE Anti Inflammatory Drugs*
Antischizophrenic Drugs *USE Neuroleptic Drugs*
Antispasmodic **Drugs**
Antitremor **Drugs**
Antitubercular **Drugs**
Antiviral **Drugs**
Anxiety Reducing Drugs *USE Tranquilizing Drugs*
Anxiolytic Drugs *USE Tranquilizing Drugs*
Appetite Depressing **Drugs**
Ataractic Drugs *USE Tranquilizing Drugs*
Ataraxic Drugs *USE Tranquilizing Drugs*
Cardiotonic Drugs *USE Drugs*
Central Nervous System Drugs *USE CNS Affecting Drugs*
Cholinergic **Drugs**
Cholinergic Blocking **Drugs**
Cholinolytic Drugs *USE Cholinergic Blocking Drugs*
Cholinomimetic **Drugs**
CNS Affecting **Drugs**
CNS Depressant **Drugs**
CNS Stimulating **Drugs**
Cognition Enhancing Drugs *USE Nootropic Drugs*
Emetic **Drugs**
Ganglion Blocking **Drugs**
Hallucinogenic **Drugs**
Heart Rate Affecting **Drugs**
Hypnotic **Drugs**
Memory Enhancing Drugs *USE Nootropic Drugs*
Muscarinic Drugs *USE Cholinergic Drugs*
Muscle Relaxing **Drugs**
Narcoanalytic Drugs *USE Drugs*
Narcotic **Drugs**
Neuroleptic **Drugs**
Neuromuscular Blocking Drugs *USE Muscle Relaxing Drugs*
Nonprescription **Drugs**
Nootropic **Drugs**
Over The Counter Drugs *USE Nonprescription Drugs*
Pain Relieving Drugs *USE Analgesic Drugs*
Parasympatholytic Drugs *USE Cholinergic Blocking Drugs*
Parasympathomimetic Drugs *USE Cholinomimetic Drugs*
Prescribing **(Drugs)**
Prescription **Drugs**
Pressors (Drugs) *USE Vasoconstrictor Drugs*
Psychedelic **Drugs**
Psychoactive Drugs *USE Drugs*
Psychotomimetic **Drugs**
Psychotropic Drugs *USE Drugs*
Respiration Stimulating **Drugs**
Sleep Inducing Drugs *USE Hypnotic Drugs*
Sympatholytic **Drugs**
Sympathomimetic **Drugs**
Thymoleptic Drugs *USE Tranquilizing Drugs*
Tranquilizing **Drugs**
Tricyclic Antidepressant **Drugs**
Vasoconstrictor **Drugs**
Vasodilator **Drugs**
Vasopressor Drugs *USE Vasoconstrictor Drugs*
Vomit Inducing Drugs *USE Emetic Drugs*
Drunk Driving *USE Driving Under The Influence*
Drunkenness *USE Alcohol Intoxication*
DSM *USE Diagnostic and Statistical Manual*
Cri du Chat Syndrome *USE Crying Cat Syndrome*
Dual Careers
Dual Diagnosis
Dualism
Duchennes Disease *USE Muscular Disorders*
Ducks
Duodenum *USE Intestines*
Response **Duration**
Stimulus **Duration**
Treatment **Duration**
Pituitary Dwarfism *USE Hypopituitarism*
Dyads
Dying Patients *USE Terminally Ill Patients*
Death and **Dying**
Group **Dynamics**
Intergroup **Dynamics**
Dynorphins
Dysarthria
Dyscalculia *USE Acalculia*
Dysfunctional Family
Dyskinesia
Tardive **Dyskinesia**
Dyslexia
Dysmenorrhea
Dysmetria *USE Ataxia*
Dysmorphophobia
Dyspareunia
Dysphasia
Dysphonia
Dysphoria *USE Major Depression*
Postnatal Dysphoria *USE Postpartum Depression*
Dyspnea
Dyspraxia *USE Movement Disorders*
Dysthymia *USE Dysthymic Disorder*
Dysthymic Disorder
Dystonia *USE Muscular Disorders*
Muscular **Dystrophy**
Eagerness *USE Enthusiasm*
Ear (Anatomy)
Ear Canal *USE External Ear*
Ear Disorders
Ear Ossicles *USE Middle Ear*
External **Ear**
Inner Ear *USE Labyrinth (Anatomy)*
Middle **Ear**
Early Childhood *USE Preschool Age Children*
Early Childhood Development
Early Experience
Early Infantile Autism
Early Intervention
Early Memories
Earthworms
East Africa
East German Democratic Republic *USE East Germany*
East Germany
Middle **East**
Eastern Europe
Eating
Eating Attitudes
Eating Disorders
Binge **Eating**
Retinal **Eccentricity**

Echinodermata
Echoencephalography
Echolalia
Echolocation
Eclectic Psychology
USE Theoretical Orientation
Eclectic Psychotherapy
Ecological Factors
Ecological Psychology
Conservation **(Ecological** Behavior)
Ecology
Behavioral **Ecology**
Income **(Economic)**
Political **Economic** Systems
Economically Disadvantaged
USE Disadvantaged
Economics
Home **Economics**
Economy
Token **Economy** Programs
ECS Therapy
USE Electroconvulsive Shock Therapy
Ecstasy (Drug)
USE Methylenedioxymethamphetamine
ECT (Therapy)
USE Electroconvulsive Shock Therapy
Ecuador
Eczema
Educable Mentally Retarded
Education
Education Students
Accreditation **(Education** Personnel)
Adult **Education**
Affective **Education**
Alcohol Education *USE Drug Education*
Art **Education**
Attainment Level (Education)
USE Educational Attainment Level
Bilingual **Education**
Boards of **Education**
Business **Education**
Career **Education**
Client **Education**
College Education *USE Undergraduate Education*
Compensatory **Education**
Continuing **Education**
Cooperative **Education**
Counselor **Education**
Death **Education**
Dental **Education**
Driver **Education**
Drug **Education**
Elementary **Education**
Environmental **Education**
Equal **Education**
Family Life **Education**
Foreign Language **Education**
Graduate **Education**
Graduate Psychology **Education**
Health **Education**
Higher **Education**
Humanistic Education *USE Affective Education*
Industrial Arts Education *USE Vocational Education*
Inservice Teacher **Education**
Language Arts **Education**
Marriage and Family Education *USE Family Life Education*
Mathematics **Education**
Medical **Education**
Middle School **Education**
Multicultural **Education**
Music **Education**
Nontraditional **Education**
Nursing **Education**
Paraprofessional **Education**
Parochial School Education *USE Private School Education*
Patient Education *USE Client Education*
Physical **Education**
Preschool **Education**
Private School **Education**
Psychology **Education**
Public School **Education**
Quality of Education *USE Educational Quality*
Reading **Education**
Rehabilitation **Education**
Religious **Education**
Remedial **Education**
Science **Education**
Second Language Education
USE Foreign Language Education
Secondary **Education**
Sex **Education**
Social Studies **Education**
Social Work **Education**
Special **Education**
Special **Education** Students
Special **Education** Teachers
Teacher **Education**
Technical Education Teachers
USE Vocational Education Teachers
Theories of **Education**
Undergraduate **Education**
Vocational **Education**
Vocational **Education** Teachers
Educational Administration
Educational Administrators
USE School Administrators
Educational Aspirations
Educational Attainment Level
Educational Audiovisual Aids
Educational Background
Educational Counseling
Educational Degrees
Educational Diagnosis
Educational Environment
USE School Environment
Educational Field Trips
Educational Financial Assistance
Educational Guidance
USE Educational Counseling
Educational Incentives
Educational Inequality
USE Equal Education
Educational Laboratories
Educational Measurement
Educational Objectives
Educational Personnel
Educational Placement
Educational Process *USE Education*
Educational Program Accreditation
Educational Program Evaluation
Educational Program Planning
Educational Programs
Educational Psychologists
Educational Psychology
Educational Quality
Educational Reform
Educational Supervision
USE Professional Supervision
Educational Television
Educational Theory
USE Theories of Education
Educational Therapy
Educational Toys
Accreditation (Educational Programs)
USE Educational Program Accreditation
Field Work (Educational)
USE Curricular Field Experience
Grading **(Educational)**
Guidance (Educational) *USE Educational Counseling*
Learning Centers **(Educational)**
Mainstreaming **(Educational)**
Motion Pictures **(Educational)**
Parent **Educational** Background
Edwards Personal Preference Schedule
Edwards Personality Inventory
Edwards Social Desirability Scale
EEG (Electrophysiology)
USE Electroencephalography

Effect Size (Statistical)
Generation **Effect** (Learning)
Halo **Effect**
Isolation **Effect**
Magnitude of Effect (Statistical)
USE Effect Size (Statistical)
Primacy **Effect**
Pygmalion Effect *USE Self Fulfilling Prophecies*
Recency **Effect**
Serial Position **Effect**
Stroop **Effect**
Cost Effectiveness
USE Costs and Cost Analysis
Counselor Effectiveness
USE Counselor Characteristics
Organizational **Effectiveness**
Parent Effectiveness Training
USE Parent Training
Teacher Effectiveness
USE Teacher Characteristics
Teacher **Effectiveness** Evaluation
Therapist Effectiveness
USE Therapist Characteristics
Treatment **Effectiveness** Evaluation
Acceleration **Effects**
Altitude **Effects**
Cold **Effects**
Decompression **Effects**
Drug Effects *USE Drugs*
Environmental **Effects**
Gravitational **Effects**
Heat **Effects**
Iatrogenic Effects *USE Side Effects (Treatment)*
Noise **Effects**
Side **Effects** (Drug)
Side **Effects** (Treatment)
Temperature **Effects**
Underwater **Effects**
Efferent Pathways
Efficacy Expectations *USE Self Efficacy*
Self **Efficacy**
Employee **Efficiency**
Effort *USE Energy Expenditure*
Egalitarianism
Ego
Ego Development
Ego Identity
Egocentrism
Egotism
Egypt
Eidetic Imagery
Ejaculation *USE Male Orgasm*
Premature **Ejaculation**
EKG (Electrophysiology)
USE Electrocardiography
El Salvador
Elavil *USE Amitriptyline*
Elbow (Anatomy)
Elder Abuse
Elder Care
Elected Government Officials
USE Government Personnel
Political **Elections**
Elective Abortion *USE Induced Abortion*
Elective Mutism
Electra Complex
Electric Fishes
Electrical Activity
Electrical Brain Stimulation
Electrical Injuries
Electrical Stimulation
Skin **Electrical** Properties
Electro Oculography
Electrocardiography
Electroconvulsive Shock
Electroconvulsive Shock Therapy
Electrodermal Response
USE Galvanic Skin Response
Electrodes

Electroencephalography
Electrolytes
Electromyography
Electronystagmography
Electrophysiology
EEG (Electrophysiology)
USE Electroencephalography
EKG (Electrophysiology)
USE Electrocardiography
EMG (Electrophysiology)
USE Electromyography
EOG (Electrophysiology)
USE Electro Oculography
GSR (Electrophysiology)
USE Galvanic Skin Response
Electroplethysmography
Electroretinography
Electroshock Therapy
USE Electroconvulsive Shock Therapy
Electrosleep Treatment
Elementarism *USE Reductionism*
Elementary Education
Elementary School Students
Elementary School Teachers
Elementary Schools
Chemical **Elements**
Metallic **Elements**
Nonmetallic Elements *USE Chemical Elements*
Elephants
Ellis (Albert)
Embarrassment
Embedded Figures Testing
Embolisms
Embryo
EMDR
USE Eye Movement Desensitization Therapy
Emergency Services
Emetic Drugs
EMG (Electrophysiology)
USE Electromyography
Nocturnal **Emission**
Positron Emission Tomography *USE Tomography*
Depression **(Emotion)**
Expressed **Emotion**
Emotional Abuse
Emotional Adjustment
Emotional Content
Emotional Control
Emotional Development
Emotional Expressiveness
USE Emotionality (Personality)
Emotional Immaturity
Emotional Inferiority
Emotional Insecurity
USE Emotional Security
Emotional Instability
Emotional Maladjustment
USE Emotional Adjustment
Emotional Maturity
Emotional Needs
USE Psychological Needs
Emotional Responses
Emotional Restraint
USE Emotional Control
Emotional Security
Emotional Stability
Emotional States
Emotional Superiority
Emotional Trauma
Bonding (Emotional) *USE Attachment Behavior*
Conditioned **Emotional** Responses
Control (Emotional) *USE Emotional Control*
Emotionality (Animal)
USE Animal Emotionality
Emotionality (Personality)
Animal **Emotionality**
Emotionally Disturbed
Emotions

Rational **Emotive** Therapy
Empathy
Pulmonary **Emphysema**
Empirical Methods
Employability
Employee Absenteeism
Employee Assistance Programs
Employee Attitudes
Employee Benefits
Employee Characteristics
Employee Efficiency
Employee Health Insurance
Employee Interaction
Employee Leave Benefits
Employee Motivation
Employee Pension Plans
Employee Productivity
Employee Selection
USE Personnel Selection
Employee Skills
Employee Supervisor Interaction
USE Supervisor Employee Interaction
Employee Termination
USE Personnel Termination
Employee Turnover
Manager Employee Interaction
USE Supervisor Employee Interaction
Supervisor **Employee** Interaction
Employees *USE Personnel*
Employer Attitudes
Employment *USE Employment Status*
Employment Discrimination
Employment History
Employment Interviews
USE Job Applicant Interviews
Employment Processes
USE Personnel Recruitment
Employment Status
Employment Tests
Self **Employment**
Supported **Employment**
Empowerment
Empty Nest
Enabling
Enactments
Encephalitis
Encephalography
Encephalography (Air)
USE Pneumoencephalography
Air Encephalography
USE Pneumoencephalography
Encephalomyelitis
Encephalopathies
Toxic **Encephalopathies**
Encoding
USE Human Information Storage
Encopresis *USE Fecal Incontinence*
Encounter Group Therapy
Encouragement
Nerve **Endings**
Endocrine Disorders
Endocrine Gland Secretion
Endocrine Gland Surgery
Endocrine Glands
Endocrine Neoplasms
Endocrine Sexual Disorders
Endocrine System
Endocrinology
Endogamous Marriage
Endogenous Depression
Endogenous Opiates
Endorphins
Endurance
Physical **Endurance**
Psychological **Endurance**
Energy Expenditure
Law **Enforcement**
Law **Enforcement** Personnel
Engineering Psychology
Genetic **Engineering**
Human Factors **Engineering**
Engineers
England
English as Second Language
Limited English Proficiency
USE Language Proficiency
Nonstandard **English**
Fertility **Enhancement**
Cognition Enhancing Drugs *USE Nootropic Drugs*
Memory Enhancing Drugs *USE Nootropic Drugs*
Enjoyment *USE Pleasure*
Enkephalins
Enlisted Military Personnel
Military **Enlistment**
Job **Enrichment**
School **Enrollment**
Enteropeptidase *USE Kinases*
Motion Pictures **(Entertainment)**
Enthusiasm
Entrance Examinations
Coll **Ent** Exam Bd Scholastic Apt Test
Entrapment Games
Entrepreneurship
Enuresis *USE Urinary Incontinence*
Environment
Academic **Environment**
Classroom **Environment**
College **Environment**
Educational Environment *USE School Environment*
Facility **Environment**
Home **Environment**
Hospital **Environment**
Office Environment *USE Working Conditions*
Person **Environment** Fit
School **Environment**
Zoo Environment *USE Animal Captivity*
Environmental Adaptation
Environmental Attitudes
Environmental Design
USE Environmental Planning
Environmental Education
Environmental Effects
Environmental Planning
Environmental Psychology
Environmental Stress
Environmental Therapy
USE Milieu Therapy
Restricted Environmental Stimulation
USE Stimulus Deprivation
Animal **Environments**
Factory Environments *USE Working Conditions*
Rural **Environments**
Social **Environments**
Suburban **Environments**
Urban **Environments**
Work Environments *USE Working Conditions*
Envy *USE Jealousy*
Penis **Envy**
Enzyme Inhibitors
Enzymes
EOG (Electrophysiology)
USE Electro Oculography
Ependyma *USE Cerebral Ventricles*
Ephedrine
Epidemiology
Epilepsy
Experimental **Epilepsy**
Grand Mal **Epilepsy**
Petit Mal **Epilepsy**
Epileptic Seizures
Epinephrine
Episcopalians *USE Protestants*
Acute Psychotic Episode *USE Acute Psychosis*
Psychotic Episode (Acute) *USE Acute Psychosis*
Episodic Memory
Epistemology
Epithelial Cells
Epithelium *USE Skin (Anatomy)*

Epstein Barr Viral Disorder
Equal Education
Social **Equality**
Score **Equating**
Test Equating *USE Score Equating*
Structural **Equation** Modeling
Equilibrium
Equimax Rotation
Cauda Equina *USE Spinal Nerves*
Equipment *USE Apparatus*
Equity (Payment)
Equity (Social)
High School Equivalency *USE Adult Education*
Erection (Penis)
Ergonomics
USE Human Factors Engineering
Ergot Derivatives
Erikson **(Erik)**
Erikson (Erik)
Eroticism
Erotomania
Errata
Error Analysis
Error of Measurement
Error Variance *USE Error of Measurement*
Standard Error of Measurement
USE Error of Measurement
Trial and **Error** Learning
Errors
Prediction **Errors**
Refraction **Errors**
Type I **Errors**
Type II **Errors**
Erythroblastosis Fetalis
USE Rh Incompatibility
Erythrocytes
Escape *USE Avoidance*
Escape Conditioning
Animal **Escape** Behavior
Eserine *USE Physostigmine*
Eskimos
ESL *USE English as Second Language*
Esophagus
ESP (Parapsychology)
USE Extrasensory Perception
Essay Testing
Essential Hypertension
Self **Esteem**
Esterases
Estimation
Magnitude **Estimation**
Parameter Estimation *USE Statistical Estimation*
Statistical **Estimation**
Time **Estimation**
Estradiol
Estrogen Antagonists *USE Antiestrogens*
Estrogen Replacement Therapy
USE Hormone Therapy
Estrogens
Estrone
Estrus
Ethanal *USE Acetaldehyde*
Ethanol
Ether (Anesthetic)
Work Ethic *USE Work (Attitudes Toward)*
Ethics
Experimental **Ethics**
Professional **Ethics**
Ethiopia
Ethnic Discrimination
USE Race and Ethnic Discrimination
Ethnic Disorders
USE Ethnospecific Disorders
Ethnic Groups
Ethnic Identity
Ethnic Sensitivity *USE Cultural Sensitivity*
Ethnic Values
Race and **Ethnic** Discrimination
Racial and **Ethnic** Attitudes
Racial and **Ethnic** Differences
Racial and **Ethnic** Relations
Ethnocentrism
Ethnography
Ethnolinguistics
Ethnology
Ethnospecific Disorders
Animal **Ethology**
Ethyl Alcohol *USE Ethanol*
Ethylaldehyde *USE Acetaldehyde*
Etiology
Etymology
Eugenics
Euphoria
Europe
Eastern **Europe**
Western **Europe**
Eustachian Tube *USE Middle Ear*
Euthanasia
Evaluation
Evaluation (Psychiatric)
USE Psychiatric Evaluation
Course **Evaluation**
Disability **Evaluation**
Educational Program **Evaluation**
Forensic **Evaluation**
Mental Health Program **Evaluation**
Peer **Evaluation**
Personnel **Evaluation**
Program **Evaluation**
Psychiatric **Evaluation**
Self **Evaluation**
Teacher Effectiveness **Evaluation**
Treatment Effectiveness **Evaluation**
Vocational **Evaluation**
Evangelists
Anniversary **Events**
Experiences **(Events)**
Evidence (Legal) *USE Legal Evidence*
Legal **Evidence**
Evoked Potentials
Auditory **Evoked** Potentials
Cortical **Evoked** Potentials
Motor Evoked Potentials
USE Somatosensory Evoked Potentials
Olfactory **Evoked** Potentials
Somatosensory **Evoked** Potentials
Visual **Evoked** Potentials
Theory of **Evolution**
Breast Examination
USE Self Examination (Medical)
Coll Ent **Exam** Bd Scholastic Apt Test
Eye Examination
USE Ophthalmologic Examination
Graduate Record **Examination**
Mini Mental State **Examination**
Ophthalmologic **Examination**
Physical **Examination**
Self **Examination** (Medical)
Certification Examinations
USE Professional Examinations
Entrance **Examinations**
Licensure Examinations
USE Professional Examinations
Professional **Examinations**
State Board Examinations
USE Professional Examinations
Exceptional Children (Gifted) *USE Gifted*
Exceptional Children (Handicapped)
USE Disabled
Information **Exchange**
Excitation (Physiological)
USE Physiological Arousal
Excretion
Executives *USE Top Level Managers*
Exercise
Aerobic **Exercise**
Physical Exercise *USE Exercise*
Exhaustion *USE Fatigue*

Exhibitionism
Existential Therapy
Existentialism
Exogamous Marriage
Life **Expectancy**
Expectant Fathers
Expectant Mothers
Expectant Parents
Expectations
Efficacy Expectations *USE Self Efficacy*
Experimenter **Expectations**
Parental **Expectations**
Role **Expectations**
Teacher **Expectations**
Energy **Expenditure**
Experience Level
Experience (Practice) *USE Practice*
Combat **Experience**
Curricular Field **Experience**
Early **Experience**
Job **Experience** Level
Openness to **Experience**
Therapist Experience *USE Therapist Characteristics*
Wilderness **Experience**
Experiences (Events)
Life **Experiences**
Near Death **Experiences**
Out of Body **Experiences**
Psychedelic **Experiences**
Religious **Experiences**
Vicarious **Experiences**
Experiential Learning
Experiential Psychotherapy
Experiment Controls
Experiment Volunteers
Experimental Apparatus *USE Apparatus*
Experimental Attrition
Experimental Design
Experimental Epilepsy
Experimental Ethics
Experimental Instructions
Experimental Laboratories
Experimental Methods
Experimental Neurosis
Experimental Psychologists
Experimental Psychology
Experimental Psychosis
Experimental Replication
Experimental Subjects
Debriefing **(Experimental)**
Devices (Experimental) *USE Apparatus*
Disclosure (Experimental)
USE Debriefing (Experimental)
Sampling **(Experimental)**
Experimentation
Experimenter Bias
Experimenter Expectations
Experimenters
Expert Systems
Expert Testimony
Expertise *USE Experience Level*
Explicit Memory
Career Exploration *USE Career Education*
Exploratory Behavior
Animal **Exploratory** Behavior
Explosive Personality
Intermittent Explosive Personality
USE Explosive Personality
Exposure Therapy
Exposure Time (Stimulus)
USE Stimulus Duration
Fetal Exposure *USE Prenatal Exposure*
Occupational **Exposure**
Prenatal **Exposure**
Expressed Emotion
Facial **Expressions**
Expressive Psychotherapy
Emotional Expressiveness
USE Emotionality (Personality)

School **Expulsion**
Extended Family
Agricultural **Extension** Workers
External Ear
External Rewards
Internal **External** Locus of Control
Rotter Intern **Extern** Locus Cont Scal
Externalization
Extinction (Learning)
Thyroid Extract *USE Thyroid Hormones*
Extracurricular Activities
Extradimensional Shift Learning
USE Nonreversal Shift Learning
Extramarital Intercourse
Extrapyramidal Symptoms
Extrapyramidal Tracts
Extrasensory Perception
Extraversion
Extrinsic Motivation
Extrinsic Rewards *USE External Rewards*
Eye Accommodation
USE Ocular Accommodation
Eye (Anatomy)
Eye Color
Eye Contact
Eye Convergence
Eye Disorders
Eye Dominance *USE Ocular Dominance*
Eye Examination
USE Ophthalmologic Examination
Eye Fixation
Eye Movement Desensitization Therapy
Eye Movements
Cones **(Eye)**
Iris **(Eye)**
Lens **(Eye)**
Nonrapid Eye Movement Sleep *USE NREM Sleep*
Pupil **(Eye)**
Rapid **Eye** Movement
Rapid Eye Movement Dreams
USE REM Dreams
Rapid Eye Movement Sleep *USE REM Sleep*
Rods **(Eye)**
Saccadic Eye Movements *USE Eye Movements*
Seeing Eye Dogs *USE Mobility Aids*
Eyeblink Reflex
Eyelid Conditioning
Crossed Eyes *USE Strabismus*
Eyewitnesses *USE Witnesses*
Eysenck Personality Inventory
F Test
California **F** Scale
Face (Anatomy)
Face Perception
Face Recognition *USE Face Perception*
Lips **(Face)**
Facial Expressions
Facial Features
Facial Muscles
Facial Nerve
Facilitated Communication
USE Augmentative Communication
Social **Facilitation**
Community **Facilities**
Maximum Security **Facilities**
School **Facilities**
Treatment **Facilities**
Facility Admission
Facility Discharge
Facility Environment
Facility Readmission
USE Facility Admission
Factitious Disorders
Factor Analysis
Factor Structure
ACTH Releasing Factor *USE Corticotropin Releasing Factor*
Confirmatory Factor Analysis *USE Factor Analysis*
Conscious (Personality **Factor)**
Corticotropin Releasing **Factor**

Five **Factor** Personality Model
Nerve Growth **Factor**
Unconscious (Personality **Factor)**
Factorial Validity
Cultural Factors *USE Sociocultural Factors*
Ecological **Factors**
Human **Factors** Engineering
Personality Factors *USE Personality Traits*
Psychoanalytic Personality **Factors**
Psychosocial **Factors**
Sixteen Personality **Factors** Question
Sociocultural **Factors**
Thermal Factors *USE Temperature Effects*
Factory Environments
USE Working Conditions
Factual Knowledge
USE Declarative Knowledge
Faculty *USE Educational Personnel*
Fading (Conditioning)
Fads and Fashions
Failure
Failure to Thrive
Academic **Failure**
Fainting *USE Syncope*
Cattell Culture Fair Intell Test
USE Culture Fair Intelligence Test
Culture **Fair** Intelligence Test
Fairbairnian Theory *USE Object Relations*
Fairy Tales *USE Folklore*
Faith Healing
Faking
False Memory
False Pregnancy *USE Pseudocyesis*
True False Tests
USE Forced Choice (Testing Method)
Fame
Amaurotic **Familial** Idiocy
Cultural Familial Mental Retardation
USE Psychosocial Mental Retardation
Familiarity
Family
Family Background
Family Caregivers *USE Caregivers*
Family Counseling *USE Family Therapy*
Family Crises
Family Life *USE Family Relations*
Family Life Education
Family Medicine
Family Members
Family of Origin
Family Physicians
Family Planning
Family Planning Attitudes
Family Relations
Family Resemblance
Family Size
Family Socioeconomic Level
Family Structure
Family Therapy
Family Violence
Family Work Relationship
Biological **Family**
Dysfunctional **Family**
Extended **Family**
Interethnic **Family**
Interracial **Family**
Job Family Relationship
USE Family Work Relationship
Marriage and Family Education
USE Family Life Education
Natural Family *USE Biological Family*
Nuclear **Family**
Schizophrenogenic **Family**
Work Family Relationship
USE Family Work Relationship
Fans (Sports) *USE Sports Spectators*
Fantasies (Thought Disturbances)
Fantasy
Fantasy (Defense Mechanism)
Guided Fantasy *USE Directed Reverie Therapy*
Sexual **Fantasy**
Laborers (Farm) *USE Agricultural Workers*
Migrant **Farm** Workers
Farmers *USE Agricultural Workers*
Fascism
Fads and **Fashions**
Fat Metabolism *USE Lipid Metabolism*
Fatalism
Father Absence
Father Child Communication
Father Child Relations
Fathers
Adolescent **Fathers**
Expectant **Fathers**
Single **Fathers**
Teenage Fathers *USE Adolescent Fathers*
Fatigue
Chronic **Fatigue** Syndrome
Fatty Acids
Fear
Fear of Public Speaking
USE Speech Anxiety
Fear of Strangers
USE Stranger Reactions
Fear of Success
Fear Survey Schedule
Facial **Features**
Fecal Incontinence
School Federal Aid
USE Educational Financial Assistance
West German Federal Republic *USE West Germany*
Fee for Service
Feedback
Auditory **Feedback**
Delayed **Feedback**
Delayed Auditory **Feedback**
Sensory **Feedback**
Visual **Feedback**
Feeding Practices
Animal **Feeding** Behavior
Bottle **Feeding**
Breast **Feeding**
Anesthesia **(Feeling)**
Feelings *USE Emotions*
Professional **Fees**
Feet (Anatomy)
Felids
Felonies *USE Crime*
Female Animals
Female Criminals
Female Delinquents
Female Genitalia
Female Orgasm
Male **Female** Relations
Battered **Females**
Human **Females**
Femininity
Feminism
Feminist Therapy
Testicular **Feminization** Syndrome
Femoral Nerve *USE Spinal Nerves*
Fenfluramine
Fentanyl
Fertility
Fertility Enhancement
Fertilization
In Vitro Fertilization
USE Reproductive Technology
Fetal Alcohol Syndrome
Fetal Exposure *USE Prenatal Exposure*
Erythroblastosis Fetalis *USE Rh Incompatibility*
Fetishism
Fetus
Fever *USE Hyperthermia*
Hay **Fever**
Rheumatic **Fever**
Postganglionic Autonomic Fibers *USE Autonomic Ganglia*
Preganglionic Autonomic Fibers *USE Autonomic Ganglia*

Fibrillation (Heart)
Atrial Fibrillation *USE Fibrillation (Heart)*
Fibromyalgia Syndrome *USE Muscular Disorders*
Cystic **Fibrosis**
Fiction *USE Literature*
Marital Fidelity *USE Monogamy*
Field Dependence
Field Instruction *USE Curricular Field Experience*
Field Work (Educational) *USE Curricular Field Experience*
Animal Open **Field** Behavior
Curricular **Field** Experience
Educational **Field** Trips
Visual **Field**
Cutaneous Receptive **Fields**
Receptive **Fields**
Visual Receptive **Fields**
Fire **Fighters**
Fighting *USE Aggressive Behavior*
Figurative Language
Figure Ground Discrimination
Welsh **Figure** Preference Test
Figures of Speech *USE Figurative Language*
Embedded **Figures** Testing
Hidden **Figures** Test
Human **Figures** Drawing
Fiji
Perceptual Fill *USE Perceptual Closure*
Film Strips
Filtered Noise
Filtered Speech
Educational **Financial** Assistance
Fine Motor Skill Learning
Finger Tapping
Fingers (Anatomy)
Fingerspelling
Finland
Fire Fighters
Fire Prevention
Firearms *USE Weapons*
Firesetting *USE Arson*
FIRO-B *USE Fund Interper Rela Orientat Beh Ques*
Bass **(Fish)**
Fishes
Electric **Fishes**
Goodness of **Fit**
Person Environment **Fit**
Physical **Fitness**
Five Factor Personality Model
Big Five Personality Model *USE Five Factor Personality Model*
Eye **Fixation**
Ocular Fixation *USE Eye Fixation*
Visual Fixation *USE Eye Fixation*
Fixed Interval Reinforcement
Fixed Ratio Reinforcement
Flashbacks *USE Hallucinations*
Flexibility (Personality) *USE Adaptability (Personality)*
Flexion Reflex
Flextime *USE Work Scheduling*
Critical **Flicker** Fusion Threshold
Flies *USE Diptera*
Flight Attendants *USE Aerospace Personnel*
Flight Instrumentation
Flight Simulation
Flooding Therapy *USE Implosive Therapy*
Blood **Flow**
Cerebral Blood **Flow**
Verbal **Fluency**
Fluid Intake
Amniotic **Fluid**
Cerebrospinal **Fluid**
Spinal Fluid *USE Cerebrospinal Fluid*
Body **Fluids**
Fluoxetine
Fluphenazine
Flurazepam
Fluvoxamine
Fruit Fly *USE Drosophila*
Focusing (Visual) *USE Ocular Accommodation*
Folic Acid
Folie A Deux
Folk Medicine
Folk Psychology
Folklore
Follicle Stimulating Hormone
Project **Follow** Through
Followup Studies
Posttreatment **Followup**
Food
Food Additives
Food Allergies
Food Deprivation
Food Intake
Food Preferences
Football
Animal **Foraging** Behavior
Air **Force** Personnel
Forced Choice (Testing Method)
Forebrain
Medial **Forebrain** Bundle
Foreign Language Education
Foreign Language Learning
Foreign Language Translation
Foreign Languages
Foreign Nationals
Foreign Organizations
Foreign Policy Making
Foreign Students
Foreign Study
Foreign Workers
Industrial **Foremen**
Forensic Evaluation
Forensic Psychiatry
Forensic Psychology
Forgetting
Forgiveness
Form and Shape Perception
Form Classes (Language)
Words (Form Classes) *USE Form Classes (Language)*
Attitude **Formation**
Coalition **Formation**
Concept **Formation**
Impression **Formation**
Reaction **Formation**
Reticular **Formation**
Test **Forms**
Theory **Formulation**
Fornix
FORTRAN *USE Computer Programing Languages*
Chance **(Fortune)**
Forward Masking *USE Masking*
Foster Care
Foster Children
Foster Homes *USE Foster Care*
Foster Parents
Fovea
Foveal Vision
Fowl *USE Birds*
Foxes
Fragile X Syndrome
Fragmentation (Schizophrenia)
Frail *USE Health Impaired*
Rod and **Frame** Test
France
Franck Drawing Completion Test
Frankness *USE Honesty*
Fraternal Twins *USE Heterozygotic Twins*

Fraternity Membership
Fraud
Consumer Fraud *USE Fraud*
Skinner (Burrhus **Frederic)**
Free Association
Free Recall
Free Will *USE Volition*
Association (Free) *USE Free Association*
Freedom
Frequency Distribution
Pitch **(Frequency)**
Response **Frequency**
Spatial **Frequency**
Stimulus **Frequency**
Temporal **Frequency**
Tone (Frequency) *USE Pitch (Frequency)*
Word **Frequency**
Freud (Sigmund)
Freudian Psychoanalytic School
Friendship
Frigidity
Frogs
Frontal Lobe
Frostig Development Test Vis Percept
Fruit Fly *USE Drosophila*
Frustration
Rosenzweig Picture **Frustration** Study
Fugue Reaction
Self **Fulfilling** Prophecies
Fulfillment *USE Satisfaction*
Sexual **Function** Disturbances
Urinary **Function** Disorders
Functional Knowledge *USE Procedural Knowledge*
Functionalism
Cognitive Functioning *USE Cognitive Ability*
Intellectual Functioning *USE Cognitive Ability*
Fund Interper Rela Orientat Beh Ques
Fundamentalism
Funding
Funerals *USE Death Rites*
Furniture
Critical Flicker **Fusion** Threshold
Future
Fuzzy Set Theory
GABA Agonists *USE Gamma Aminobutyric Acid Agonists*
GABA Antagonists *USE Gamma Aminobutyric Acid Antagonists*
Galanin *USE Peptides*
Galanthamine
Galvanic Skin Response
Gamblers Anonymous *USE Twelve Step Programs*
Gambling
Compulsive Gambling *USE Pathological Gambling*
Pathological **Gambling**
Game Theory
Prisoners Dilemma **Game**
Games
Childrens Recreational **Games**
Computer **Games**
Entrapment **Games**
Non Zero Sum **Games**
Simulation **Games**
Video Games *USE Computer Games*
Gamma Aminobutyric Acid
Gamma Aminobutyric Acid Agonists
Gamma Aminobutyric Acid Antagonists
Gamma Globulin
Ganglia
Autonomic **Ganglia**
Basal **Ganglia**
Spinal **Ganglia**
Ganglion Blocking Drugs
Ganglion Cells (Retina)
Stellate Ganglion *USE Autonomic Ganglia*
Juvenile **Gangs**
Ganser Syndrome *USE Factitious Disorders*
Generation **Gap**
Gastrointestinal Disorders
Gastrointestinal System
Gastrointestinal Ulcers
Gastropods *USE Mollusca*
Gates MacGinitie Reading Tests
Gating (Sensory) *USE Sensory Gating*
Sensory **Gating**
Gaussian Distribution *USE Normal Distribution*
Gay Liberation Movement *USE Homosexual Liberation Movement*
Gay Males *USE Male Homosexuality*
Gay Parents *USE Homosexual Parents*
Gazing *USE Eye Fixation*
Geese
Gender Differences *USE Human Sex Differences*
Gender Identity
Gender Identity Disorder
Gender Role Attitudes *USE Sex Role Attitudes*
Gender Roles *USE Sex Roles*
Sexual Identity (Gender) *USE Gender Identity*
General Anesthetics
General Aptitude Test Battery
General Health Questionnaire
General Paresis
General Practitioners
Army **General** Classification Test
Medical Treatment **(General)**
Typologies (General) *USE Taxonomies*
Generalization (Learning)
Cognitive **Generalization**
Response **Generalization**
Semantic **Generalization**
Stimulus **Generalization**
Generalized Anxiety Disorder *USE Anxiety Disorders*
Generation Effect (Learning)
Generation Gap
Transformational **Generative** Grammar
Generators (Apparatus)
Genes
Genetic Counseling
Genetic Disorders
Genetic Dominance
Genetic Engineering
Genetic Linkage
Genetic Recessiveness
Genetics
Behavioral **Genetics**
Population **Genetics**
Geniculate Bodies (Thalamus)
Genital Disorders
Genital Herpes *USE Herpes Genitalis*
Male **Genital** Disorders
Female **Genitalia**
Male **Genitalia**
Herpes **Genitalis**
Geniuses *USE Gifted*
Genocide
Genotypes
Genuineness *USE Sincerity*
Geographic Regions *USE Geography*
Physical Divisions (Geographic) *USE Geography*
Political Divisions (Geographic) *USE Geography*
Geographical Mobility
Geography
Geomagnetism *USE Magnetism*
Geometry *USE Mathematics*
Gerbils
Geriatric Assessment
Geriatric Patients
Geriatric Psychiatry
Geriatric Psychotherapy
Geriatrics

ROTATED ALPHABETICAL TERMS SECTION

German Measles *USE Rubella*
East German Democratic Republic *USE East Germany*
West German Federal Republic *USE West Germany*
Germany
East **Germany**
West **Germany**
Gerontology
Gestalt Psychology
Gestalt Therapy
Bender **Gestalt** Test
Gestation *USE Pregnancy*
Gestures
Ghana
Ghettoes
Gifted
Exceptional Children (Gifted) *USE Gifted*
Gilles de la Tourette Disorder
Gipsies *USE Gypsies*
Girls *USE Human Females*
Adrenal **Gland** Disorders
Adrenal **Gland** Secretion
Endocrine **Gland** Secretion
Endocrine **Gland** Surgery
Pituitary **Gland**
Pituitary Gland Surgery *USE Hypophysectomy*
Secretion **(Gland)**
Thyroid **Gland**
Glands
Adrenal **Glands**
Endocrine **Glands**
Mammary **Glands**
Parathyroid **Glands**
Salivary **Glands**
Glaucoma
Global Amnesia
Gamma **Globulin**
Globulins
Globus Pallidus
Glossary
Glossolalia
Glossopharyngeal Nerve *USE Cranial Nerves*
Glucagon
Glucocorticoids
Glucose
Glucose Metabolism
Blood Glucose *USE Blood Sugar*
Glue Sniffing
Glutamic Acid
Glutamine
Glutethimide
Glycine
Glycogen
Glycoproteins *USE Globulins*
Goal Setting
Goals
Career Goals *USE Occupational Aspirations*
Organizational Goals *USE Organizational Objectives*
Goats
God Concepts
Goiters
Goldfish
Goldstein Scheerer Object Sort Test
Gonadotropic Hormones
Gonads
Gonorrhea
Goodenough Harris Draw A Person Test
Goodness of Fit
Gorillas
Gossip
Gough Adjective Check List
Government
Government Agencies
Government Personnel
Government Policy Making
Government Programs
Autonomy **(Government)**

Elected Government Officials *USE Government Personnel*
Law **(Government)**
Welfare Services **(Government)**
Grade Level
Academic Grade Level *USE Grade Level*
Gradepoint Average *USE Academic Achievement*
Grading (Educational)
Graduate Degrees *USE Educational Degrees*
Graduate Education
Graduate Psychology Education
Graduate Record Examination
Graduate Schools
Graduate Students
Clinical Psychology **Grad** Training
College **Graduates**
High School **Graduates**
Graduation (School) *USE School Graduation*
School **Graduation**
Alcohol (Grain) *USE Ethanol*
Grammar
Grammar Schools *USE Elementary Schools*
Transformational Generative **Grammar**
Grand Mal Epilepsy
Grandchildren
Grandiosity
Grandparents
Great Grandparents *USE Ancestors*
Graphical Displays
Graphology *USE Handwriting*
Grasping
Grasshoppers
Delay of **Gratification**
Myasthenia **Gravis**
Gravitational Effects
Periaqueductal **Gray**
Great Britain
Great Grandparents *USE Ancestors*
Greece
Gregariousness
Bannister Repertory **Grid**
Shuttle Box Grids *USE Shuttle Boxes*
Grief
Grimaces
Nocturnal Teeth **Grinding**
Teeth Grinding *USE Bruxism*
Animal **Grooming** Behavior
Gross Motor Skill Learning
Ground Transportation
Figure **Ground** Discrimination
Group Cohesion
Group Counseling
Group Decision Making
Group Development
Group Discussion
Group Dynamics
Group Health Plans *USE Health Maintenance Organizations*
Group Homes
Group Instruction
Group Participation
Group Performance
Group Problem Solving
Group Psychotherapy
Group Size
Group Structure
Group Testing
Group Therapy *USE Group Psychotherapy*
Encounter **Group** Therapy
Marathon **Group** Therapy
Minority Group Discrimination *USE Race and Ethnic Discrimination*
Ability **Grouping**
Agencies (Groups) *USE Organizations*

Between **Groups** Design
Blood **Groups**
Chinese Cultural **Groups**
Consciousness Raising **Groups**
Control Groups *USE Experiment Controls*
Developmental Age **Groups**
Diagnosis Related **Groups**
Ethnic **Groups**
Japanese Cultural **Groups**
Korean Cultural **Groups**
Minority **Groups**
Reference **Groups**
Religious **Groups**
Social **Groups**
Support **Groups**
T Groups *USE Human Relations Training*
Vietnamese Cultural **Groups**
Grown Children *USE Adult Offspring*
Growth *USE Development*
Growth Centers
USE Human Potential Movement
Growth Hormone *USE Somatotropin*
Growth Hormone Inhibitor
USE Somatostatin
Nerve **Growth** Factor
Personal Growth Techniques
USE Human Potential Movement
Physical Growth *USE Physical Development*
GSR (Electrophysiology)
USE Galvanic Skin Response
Guanethidine
Guanosine
Coast **Guard** Personnel
Guardianship
National **Guardsmen**
Guatemala
Guessing
Guest Workers *USE Foreign Workers*
Guidance Counseling
USE School Counseling
Guidance (Educational)
USE Educational Counseling
Career Guidance *USE Occupational Guidance*
Child **Guidance** Clinics
Educational Guidance *USE Educational Counseling*
Occupational **Guidance**
School Guidance *USE School Counseling*
Vocational Guidance *USE Occupational Guidance*
Guided Daydreams
USE Directed Reverie Therapy
Guided Fantasy
USE Directed Reverie Therapy
Guilford Zimmerman Temperament Surv
Guilt
Guinea
Guinea Pigs
Papua New **Guinea**
Sea **Gulls**
Gun Control Laws
Gustatory Perception
USE Taste Perception
Guyana
Gymnastic Therapy
USE Recreation Therapy
Gynecological Disorders
Gynecologists
Gynecology
Gypsies
Gyrus Cinguli
Habilitation
Habitat Selection *USE Territoriality*
Habitats (Animal)
USE Animal Environments
Habits
Study **Habits**
Habituation
Hair
Hair Loss *USE Alopecia*
Hair Pulling
Haiti
Halcion *USE Triazolam*
Halfway Houses
Residence Halls *USE Dormitories*
Hallucinations
Auditory **Hallucinations**
Drug Induced **Hallucinations**
Hypnagogic **Hallucinations**
Visual **Hallucinations**
Hallucinogenic Drugs
Hallucinosis
Alcoholic **Hallucinosis**
Halo Effect
Haloperidol
Halstead Reitan Neuropsych Battery
Hamsters
Hand (Anatomy)
Handedness
Handicapped *USE Disabled*
Handicapped (Attitudes Toward)
USE Disabled (Attitudes Toward)
Adventitiously Handicapped *USE Adventitiously Disabled*
Aurally Handicapped *USE Aurally Disabled*
Congenitally Handicapped *USE Congenitally Disabled*
Exceptional Children (Handicapped) *USE Disabled*
Multiply Handicapped *USE Multiply Disabled*
Orthopedically Handicapped *USE Physically Disabled*
Physically Handicapped *USE Physically Disabled*
Sensorially Handicapped *USE Sensorially Disabled*
Speech Handicapped *USE Speech Disabled*
Visually Handicapped *USE Visually Disabled*
Self **Handicapping** Strategy
Physical Handicaps (Attit Toward)
USE Physical Disabilities (Attit Toward)
Sensory Handicaps (Attit Toward)
USE Sensory Disabilities (Attit Toward)
Handicrafts *USE Crafts*
Handwriting
Handwriting Legibility
Printing **(Handwriting)**
Happiness
Haptic Perception *USE Cutaneous Sense*
Harassment (Sexual)
USE Sexual Harassment
Sexual **Harassment**
Hardiness
Maslow (Abraham **Harold)**
Goodenough **Harris** Draw A Person Test
Hashish
Hate
Hawaii
Hay Fever
Hazardous Materials
Hazards
Head (Anatomy)
Head Banging
Head Injuries
Project **Head** Start
Headache
Migraine **Headache**
Muscle Contraction **Headache**
Tension Headache
USE Muscle Contraction Headache
Faith **Healing**
Psychic Healing *USE Faith Healing*
Health
Health Attitudes
Health Behavior
Health Care Administration
Health Care Costs
Health Care Delivery
Health Care Policy
Health Care Professionals
USE Health Personnel
Health Care Psychology
Health Care Seeking Behavior
Health Care Services
Health Care Utilization
Health Complaints

Health Education
Health Impaired
Health Insurance
Health Knowledge
Health Locus of Control
USE Health Attitudes
Health Maintenance Organizations
Health Personnel
Health Personnel Attitudes
Health Promotion
Health Screening
Health Service Needs
Health Service Utilization
USE Health Care Utilization
Behavioral Health *USE Health Care Psychology*
Community Mental **Health**
Community Mental **Health** Centers
Community Mental **Health** Services
Community Mental **Health** Training
Employee **Health** Insurance
General **Health** Questionnaire
Group Health Plans
USE Health Maintenance Organizations
Holistic **Health**
Home Health Aides *USE Home Care Personnel*
Mental **Health**
Mental Health Care Costs
USE Health Care Costs
Mental Health Care Policy
USE Health Care Policy
Mental Health Consultation
USE Professional Consultation
Mental **Health** Inservice Training
Mental **Health** Personnel
Mental **Health** Personnel Supply
Mental **Health** Program Evaluation
Mental **Health** Programs
Mental Health Service Needs
USE Health Service Needs
Mental **Health** Services
Primary **Health** Care
Primary Mental **Health** Prevention
Public **Health**
Public **Health** Service Nurses
Public **Health** Services
Wholistic Health *USE Holistic Health*
Hearing Acuity *USE Auditory Acuity*
Hearing Aids
Hearing Disorders
Partially **Hearing** Impaired
Sensorineural Hearing Loss *USE Hearing Disorders*
Speech and **Hearing** Measures
Heart
Heart Attacks *USE Heart Disorders*
Heart Auricles
Heart Beat *USE Heart Rate*
Heart Disorders
Heart Rate
Heart Rate Affecting Drugs
Heart Surgery
Heart Transplants
USE Organ Transplantation
Heart Valves
Heart Ventricles
Arrhythmias **(Heart)**
Atria (Heart) *USE Heart Auricles*
Coronary Heart Disease *USE Heart Disorders*
Fibrillation **(Heart)**
Rapid Heart Rate *USE Tachycardia*
Heartbeat *USE Heart Rate*
Heat Effects
Hebephrenic Schizophrenia
Hedonism
Heels (Anatomy) *USE Feet (Anatomy)*
Body **Height**
Helicopters
Helium
Help Seeking Behavior
Self **Help** Techniques

Helping Behavior
USE Assistance (Social Behavior)
Helplessness
Learned **Helplessness**
Hematologic Disorders
USE Blood and Lymphatic Disorders
Hematoma
Hemianopia
Hemiopia *USE Hemianopia*
Hemiplegia
Hemispherectomy
Hemispheric Specialization
USE Lateral Dominance
Hemodialysis
Hemoglobin
Hemophilia
Hemorrhage
Cerebral **Hemorrhage**
Henmon Nelson Tests Mental Ability
USE Intelligence Measures
Heparin
Hepatic Disorders *USE Liver Disorders*
Hepatitis
Toxic **Hepatitis**
Hereditary Disorders
USE Genetic Disorders
PKU (Hereditary Disorder)
USE Phenylketonuria
Sex Linked **Hereditary** Disorders
Heredity *USE Genetics*
Hermaphroditism
Hermeneutics
Heroin
Heroin Addiction
Herpes Genitalis
Herpes Simplex
Genital Herpes *USE Herpes Genitalis*
Heterogeneity of Variance
USE Variance Homogeneity
Heterosexual Interaction
USE Male Female Relations
Heterosexuality
Heterozygotic Twins
Heuristic Modeling
Hexamethonium
Hexobarbital
Hibernation
Hidden Figures Test
Dominance **Hierarchy**
High Risk Populations
USE At Risk Populations
High Sch Personality Questionnaire
High School Diplomas
USE Educational Degrees
High School Equivalency
USE Adult Education
High School Graduates
High School Students
High School Teachers
High Schools
Junior **High** School Students
Junior **High** School Teachers
Junior **High** Schools
Higher Education
Higher Order Conditioning
Highway Safety
Hindbrain
Hinduism
Hindus
Hippies *USE Subculture (Anthropological)*
Hippocampal Commissure *USE Fornix*
Hippocampus
Hips
Hiring *USE Personnel Selection*
Hispanics
Hispaniola
Histamine
Histidine
Histology

History
History of Psychology
Case History *USE Patient History*
Employment **History**
Medical History *USE Patient History*
Patient **History**
Psychiatric History *USE Patient History*
Histrionic Personality Disorder
USE Hysterical Personality
HIV *USE Human Immunodeficiency Virus*
HIV Testing
HMO
USE Health Maintenance Organizations
Animal **Hoarding** Behavior
Hobbies
Hoffmanns Reflex
Holidays
Holistic Health
Holocaust
Holocaust Survivors
Holtzman Inkblot Technique
Homatropine *USE Alkaloids*
Home Accidents
Home Birth *USE Midwifery*
Home Care
Home Care Personnel
Home Economics
Home Environment
Home Health Aides
USE Home Care Personnel
Home Reared Mentally Retarded
Home Schooling
Home Visiting Programs
Return to Home *USE Empty Nest*
Homebound
Homeless
Homeless Mentally Ill
Mentally Ill Homeless *USE Homeless Mentally Ill*
Homemaking
USE Household Management
Homeostasis
Foster Homes *USE Foster Care*
Group **Homes**
Nursing **Homes**
Homesickness
Homework
Homicide
Homing (Animal) *USE Animal Homing*
Animal **Homing**
Variance **Homogeneity**
Homographs
Homonyms
Homophobia
USE Homosexuality (Attitudes Toward)
Homosexual Liberation Movement
Homosexual Parents
Homosexuality
Homosexuality (Attitudes Toward)
Male **Homosexuality**
Homovanillic Acid
Honduras
Honesty
Hong Kong
Hope
Hopelessness
Hormone Therapy
ACTH (Hormone) *USE Corticotropin*
Follicle Stimulating **Hormone**
Growth Hormone *USE Somatotropin*
Growth Hormone Inhibitor *USE Somatostatin*
Luteinizing **Hormone**
Melanocyte Stimulating **Hormone**
Parathyroid **Hormone**
Thyroid Stimulating Hormone *USE Thyrotropin*
Thyrotropic Hormone *USE Thyrotropin*
Hormones
Adrenal Cortex **Hormones**
Adrenal Medulla **Hormones**
Gonadotropic **Hormones**
Pituitary **Hormones**
Progestational **Hormones**
Sex **Hormones**
Thyroid **Hormones**
Dorsal **Horns**
Horses
Hospice
Hospital Accreditation
Hospital Addiction Syndrome
USE Munchausen Syndrome
Hospital Administration
Hospital Admission
Hospital Attendants
USE Attendants (Institutions)
Hospital Discharge
Hospital Environment
Hospital Programs
Hospital Psychiatric Units
USE Psychiatric Units
Hospital Staff *USE Medical Personnel*
Day Hospital *USE Partial Hospitalization*
Psychiatric **Hospital** Admission
Psychiatric **Hospital** Discharge
Psychiatric **Hospital** Programs
Psychiatric **Hospital** Readmission
Psychiatric **Hospital** Staff
Readmission (Hospital) *USE Hospital Admission*
Hospitalization
Partial **Hospitalization**
Psychiatric **Hospitalization**
Hospitalized Patients
Hospitals
Mental Hospitals *USE Psychiatric Hospitals*
Psychiatric **Hospitals**
State Hospitals *USE Psychiatric Hospitals*
Hostages
Hostility
Hot Line Services
Telephone Hot Lines *USE Hot Line Services*
Household Management
Household Structure
USE Living Arrangements
Halfway **Houses**
Housewives
Housework *USE Household Management*
Housing
Hue
Human Animal Interaction
USE Interspecies Interaction
Human Biological Rhythms
Human Channel Capacity
Human Computer Interaction
Human Courtship
Human Development
Human Factors Engineering
Human Females
Human Figures Drawing
Human Immunodeficiency Virus
Human Information Processes
USE Cognitive Processes
Human Information Storage
Human Machine Systems
Human Machine Systems Design
Human Males
Human Mate Selection
Human Migration
Human Nature
Human Potential Movement
Human Relations Training
Human Resources
USE Personnel Management
Human Rights
Human Sex Differences
Animal Human Interaction
USE Interspecies Interaction
Circadian Rhythms (Human) *USE Human Biological Rhythms*
Maternal Behavior (Human) *USE Mother Child Relations*
Sexual Intercourse **(Human)**
Humanism

Humanistic Education
USE Affective Education
Humanistic Psychology
Mates (Humans) *USE Spouses*
Surrogate Parents **(Humans)**
Humor
Cartoons **(Humor)**
Hungary
Hunger
Huntingtons Chorea
USE Huntingtons Disease
Huntingtons Disease
Shuttle Box Hurdles *USE Shuttle Boxes*
Husbands
Hybrids (Biology)
Hydralazine
Chloral **Hydrate**
Hydrocephaly
Hydrocortisone
Hydrogen
Hydroxydopamine (6-)
Hydroxyindoleacetic Acid (5-)
Hydroxylamine
Hydroxylase Inhibitors
Hydroxylases
Hydroxytryptamine (5-) *USE Serotonin*
Hydroxytryptophan (5-)
Hydroxyzine
Hygiene
Hyoscine *USE Scopolamine*
Hyoscyamine (dl-) *USE Atropine*
Hyperactivity *USE Hyperkinesis*
Hypercholesterolemia
USE Metabolism Disorders
Hyperglycemia
Hyperkinesis
Hypermedia
Hyperparathyroidism
USE Parathyroid Disorders
Hyperphagia
Hypersexuality
Hypersomnia
Hypertension
Essential **Hypertension**
Hypertext
Hyperthermia
Hyperthyroidism
Hyperventilation
Hypnagogic Hallucinations
Hypnoanalysis *USE Hypnotherapy*
Hypnosis
Self Hypnosis *USE Autohypnosis*
Hypnotherapists
Hypnotherapy
Hypnotic Drugs
Hypnotic Susceptibility
Age Regression **(Hypnotic)**
Hypnotists
Hypoactive Sexual Desire Disorder
USE Inhibited Sexual Desire
Hypochondriasis
Hypogastric Plexus
USE Autonomic Ganglia
Hypoglossal Nerve *USE Cranial Nerves*
Hypoglycemia
Hypogonadism
Hypomania
Hyponatremia
Hypoparathyroidism
USE Parathyroid Disorders
Hypothalamo **Hypophyseal** System
Hypophysectomy
Hypophysis Disorders
USE Pituitary Disorders
Hypopituitarism
Hypotension
Mammillary Bodies (Hypothalamic) *USE Hypothalamus*
Hypothalamo Hypophyseal System
Hypothalamo Pituitary Adrenal System

Hypothalamus
Hypothalamus Lesions
Hypothermia
Hypothesis Testing
Hypothesis Testing (Cognitive)
USE Cognitive Hypothesis Testing
Cognitive **Hypothesis** Testing
Null **Hypothesis** Testing
Hypothyroidism
Hypoxia *USE Anoxia*
Hysterectomy
Hysteria
Conversion Hysteria *USE Conversion Neurosis*
Mass **Hysteria**
Hysterical Anesthesia
Hysterical Blindness
USE Hysterical Vision Disturbances
Hysterical Neurosis (Dissociation)
USE Dissociative Patterns
Hysterical Paralysis
Hysterical Personality
Hysterical Vision Disturbances
Iatrogenic Effects
USE Side Effects (Treatment)
Ibotenic Acid
ICD *USE International Class of Diseases*
Iceland
Iconic Memory
Id
Ideal Self *USE Self Concept*
Idealism
Ideation
Suicidal **Ideation**
Identical Twins *USE Monozygotic Twins*
Identification (Defense Mechanism)
Projective **Identification**
Identity Crisis
Identity (Personal) *USE Self Concept*
Identity (Professional)
USE Professional Identity
Dissociative **Identity** Disorder
Ego **Identity**
Ethnic **Identity**
Gender **Identity**
Gender **Identity** Disorder
Professional **Identity**
Sexual Identity (Gender) *USE Gender Identity*
Social **Identity**
Amaurotic Familial **Idiocy**
Idiot Savants
Ileum *USE Intestines*
Homeless Mentally **Ill**
Mentally Ill Homeless *USE Homeless Mentally Ill*
Mentally **Ill** Offenders
Terminally **Ill** Patients
Illegitimate Children
Illinois Test Psycholinguist Abil
Illiteracy *USE Literacy*
Illness Behavior
Chronic **Illness**
Chronic Mental **Illness**
Course of Illness *USE Disease Course*
Mental Illness *USE Mental Disorders*
Mental **Illness** (Attitudes Toward)
Persistent Mental Illness *USE Chronic Mental Illness*
Physical Illness *USE Physical Disorders*
Physical **Illness** (Attitudes Toward)
Work Related **Illnesses**
Illumination
Illumination Therapy *USE Phototherapy*
Autokinetic **Illusion**
Mueller Lyer **Illusion**
Illusions (Perception)
Optical Illusions *USE Illusions (Perception)*
Body **Image**
Body **Image** Disturbances
Mirror **Image**
Retinal **Image**
Self Image *USE Self Concept*

Imagery
Conceptual **Imagery**
Eidetic **Imagery**
Spatial **Imagery**
Onomatopoeia and Images Test
USE Projective Personality Measures
Imagination
Imaginativeness
USE Openness to Experience
Magnetic Resonance **Imaging**
Imipramine
Imitation (Learning)
Emotional **Immaturity**
Immersion Programs
USE Foreign Language Education
Immigrants *USE Immigration*
Immigration
Social Immobility *USE Social Mobility*
Tonic **Immobility**
Acquired **Immune** Deficiency Syndrome
Immunization
Human **Immunodeficiency** Virus
Immunogens *USE Antigens*
Immunoglobulins
Immunologic Disorders
Immunology
Immunopathology *USE Immunology*
Immunoreactivity
Impaired Professionals
Health **Impaired**
Partially Hearing **Impaired**
Olfactory Impairment *USE Anosmia*
Cochlear **Implants**
Implosive Therapy
Impotence
Impression Formation
Impression Management
Imprinting
Impulse Control Disorders
Impulsiveness
Inadequate Personality
Incarceration
Incentives
Educational **Incentives**
Monetary **Incentives**
Incest
Incidental Learning
Income (Economic)
Income Level
Lower **Income** Level
Middle **Income** Level
Upper **Income** Level
Rh **Incompatibility**
Incomplete Man Test
Rotter **Incomplete** Sentences Blank
Fecal **Incontinence**
Urinary **Incontinence**
Incorporation (Psychological)
USE Internalization
Incubators (Apparatus)
Independence (Personality)
Independent Living *USE Self Care Skills*
Independent Living Programs
Independent Party (Political)
USE Political Parties
Independent Study
USE Individualized Instruction
Independent Variables
Commonwealth of **Independent** States
India
American **Indians**
Myers Briggs Type **Indicator**
West **Indies**
Indifference *USE Apathy*
Individual Counseling
USE Individual Psychotherapy
Individual Differences
Individual Psychology
Individual Psychotherapy
Individual Psychotherapy (Adlerian)
USE Adlerian Psychotherapy
Individual Testing
Individual Therapy
USE Individual Psychotherapy
Psychotherapy (Individual) *USE Individual Psychotherapy*
Individualism *USE Individuality*
Individuality
Individualized Instruction
Separation **Individuation**
Indonesia
Induced Abortion
Drug **Induced** Congenital Disorders
Drug **Induced** Hallucinations
Sleep Inducing Drugs *USE Hypnotic Drugs*
Vomit Inducing Drugs *USE Emetic Drugs*
Inductive Deductive Reasoning
Laborers (Construct and Indust) *USE Blue Collar Workers*
Industrial Accidents
Industrial Arts Education
USE Vocational Education
Industrial Foremen
Industrial Psychologists
Industrial Psychology
Industrial Safety *USE Occupational Safety*
Business and **Industrial** Personnel
Skilled **Industrial** Workers
Unskilled **Industrial** Workers
Industrialization
Industry *USE Business*
Educational Inequality *USE Equal Education*
Infant Development
Infant Intelligence Scale
Infant Vocalization
Bayley Scales of **Infant** Development
Cattell Infant Intelligence Scale
USE Infant Intelligence Scale
Sudden **Infant** Death
Infanticide
Infantile Neurosis
USE Childhood Neurosis
Infantile Paralysis *USE Poliomyelitis*
Infantile Psychosis
USE Childhood Psychosis
Early **Infantile** Autism
Paralysis (Infantile) *USE Poliomyelitis*
Symbiotic **Infantile** Psychosis
Infantilism
Infants
Infants (Animal)
Newborn Infants *USE Neonates*
Dementia (Multi Infarct) *USE Multi Infarct Dementia*
Multi **Infarct** Dementia
Myocardial **Infarctions**
Infectious Disorders
Inference
Inferior Colliculus
Emotional **Inferiority**
Infertility
Infirmaries *USE Hospitals*
Anti **Inflammatory** Drugs
Inflection
Self **Inflicted** Wounds
Driving Under The **Influence**
Parental Influence *USE Parent Child Relations*
Interpersonal **Influences**
Social **Influences**
Influenza
Informants
Information
Information Exchange
Information (Messages) *USE Messages*
Information Processing Speed
USE Cognitive Processing Speed
Information Seeking
Information Services
Information Specialists
Information Systems
Information Theory

Automated **Information** Coding
Automated **Information** Processing
Automated **Information** Retrieval
Automated **Information** Storage
Confidentiality of Information
USE Privileged Communication
Human Information Processes
USE Cognitive Processes
Human **Information** Storage
Management Information Systems
USE Information Systems
Informed Consent
Ingratiation *USE Impression Management*
Ingroup Outgroup
Outgroup Ingroup *USE Ingroup Outgroup*
Inhalant Abuse
Inhibited Sexual Desire
Inhibition (Personality)
Conditioned Inhibition *USE Conditioned Suppression*
Latent **Inhibition**
Prepulse **Inhibition**
Proactive **Inhibition**
Reciprocal **Inhibition** Therapy
Retroactive **Inhibition**
Growth Hormone Inhibitor *USE Somatostatin*
Amine Oxidase **Inhibitors**
Cholinesterase **Inhibitors**
Decarboxylase **Inhibitors**
Enzyme **Inhibitors**
Hydroxylase **Inhibitors**
Monoamine Oxidase **Inhibitors**
Serotonin Reuptake **Inhibitors**
Initial Teaching Alphabet
Initiation Rites
Initiative
Injections
Intramuscular **Injections**
Intraperitoneal **Injections**
Intravenous **Injections**
Subcutaneous **Injections**
Injuries
Birth **Injuries**
Electrical **Injuries**
Head **Injuries**
Spinal Cord **Injuries**
Brain Injury (Traumatic)
USE Traumatic Brain Injury
Traumatic Brain **Injury**
Holtzman **Inkblot** Technique
Inlaws
Inmates (Prison) *USE Prisoners*
Animal Innate Behavior *USE Instinctive Behavior*
Inner City *USE Urban Environments*
Inner Ear *USE Labyrinth (Anatomy)*
Inner Speech *USE Self Talk*
Kirton Adaption **Innovation** Inven
Innovativeness *USE Creativity*
Inquisitiveness *USE Curiosity*
Criminally Insane *USE Mentally Ill Offenders*
Insanity *USE Mental Disorders*
Insanity Defense
DDT **(Insecticide)**
Insecticides
Insects
Emotional Insecurity *USE Emotional Security*
Artificial Insemination
USE Reproductive Technology
Insensitivity (Personality)
USE Sensitivity (Personality)
Inservice Teacher Education
Inservice Training
Mental Health **Inservice** Training
Insight
Insight (Psychotherapeutic Process)
Insight Therapy
Diabetes **Insipidus**
Insomnia
Emotional **Instability**
Death **Instinct**
Survival Instinct *USE Self Preservation*
Instinctive Behavior
Institution Visitation
Institutional Release
Institutional Schools
Institutionalization
Institutionalized Mentally Retarded
Attendants **(Institutions)**
Correctional **Institutions**
Residential Care **Institutions**
Instruction *USE Teaching*
Audiovisual **Instruction**
Braille **Instruction**
Classroom Instruction *USE Teaching*
Computer Assisted **Instruction**
Field Instruction
USE Curricular Field Experience
Group **Instruction**
Individualized **Instruction**
Programed **Instruction**
Self Instruction *USE Individualized Instruction*
Televised **Instruction**
Videotape **Instruction**
Instructional Media
Instructional Objectives
USE Educational Objectives
Self **Instructional** Training
Experimental **Instructions**
Instructors *USE Teachers*
Instrument Controls
Parent Attitude Research **Instrument**
Instrumental Conditioning
USE Operant Conditioning
Instrumental Learning
USE Operant Conditioning
Instrumentality
Flight **Instrumentation**
Musical **Instruments**
Insulin
Insulin Shock Therapy
Insurance
Insurance Agents *USE Sales Personnel*
Employee Health **Insurance**
Health **Insurance**
Life **Insurance**
Workmens Compensation **Insurance**
Intake Interview
Fluid **Intake**
Food **Intake**
Water **Intake**
Integrated Services
Intersensory Integration *USE Sensory Integration*
Racial Integration *USE Social Integration*
School **Integration**
Sensory **Integration**
Social **Integration**
Integrity
Cattell Culture Fair Intell Test
USE Culture Fair Intelligence Test
Intellectual Development
Intellectual Functioning
USE Cognitive Ability
Intellectualism
Intellectualization
Intelligence
Intelligence Age *USE Mental Age*
Intelligence Measures
Intelligence Quotient
Artificial **Intelligence**
Cattell Infant Intelligence Scale
USE Infant Intelligence Scale
Culture Fair **Intelligence** Test
Infant **Intelligence** Scale
Leiter Adult Intelligence Scale
USE Intelligence Measures
Lorge Thorndike **Intelligence** Test
Slosson **Intelligence** Test for Child
Stanford Binet **Intelligence** Scale
Wechsler **Intelligence** Scale Children

Wechsler Adult **Intelligence** Scale
Wechsler Bellevue **Intelligence** Scale
Signal Intensity *USE Stimulus Intensity*
Stimulus **Intensity**
Intensive Care
Intention
Intentional Learning
Interaction Analysis (Statistics)
Interaction Variance
Animal Human Interaction *USE Interspecies Interaction*
Client Counselor Interaction
USE Psychotherapeutic Processes
Counselor Client Interaction
USE Psychotherapeutic Processes
Dentist Patient Interaction *USE Therapeutic Processes*
Double Bind **Interaction**
Employee **Interaction**
Employee Supervisor Interaction
USE Supervisor Employee Interaction
Heterosexual Interaction *USE Male Female Relations*
Human Animal Interaction *USE Interspecies Interaction*
Human Computer **Interaction**
Interhemispheric **Interaction**
Interpersonal **Interaction**
Interspecies **Interaction**
Manager Employee Interaction
USE Supervisor Employee Interaction
Nurse Patient Interaction *USE Therapeutic Processes*
Patient Therapist Interaction
USE Psychotherapeutic Processes
Physician Patient Interaction *USE Therapeutic Processes*
Social **Interaction**
Supervisor Employee **Interaction**
Teacher Student **Interaction**
Therapist Patient Interaction
USE Psychotherapeutic Processes
Symbolic **Interactionism**
Drug **Interactions**
Interagency Services
USE Integrated Services
Extramarital **Intercourse**
Premarital **Intercourse**
Sexual **Intercourse** (Human)
Intercultural Communication
USE Cross Cultural Communication
Interdisciplinary Research
Interdisciplinary Treatment Approach
Interest Inventories
Kuder Occupational **Interest** Survey
Occupational **Interest** Measures
Opinion Attitude and Interest Survey *USE Attitude Measures*
Strong Vocational **Interest** Blank
Interests
Occupational **Interests**
Vocational Interests *USE Occupational Interests*
Interethnic Communication
USE Cross Cultural Communication
Interethnic Family
Interethnic Marriage
USE Exogamous Marriage
Interfaith Marriage
Interference (Learning)
Interferons
Intergenerational Relations
Intergenerational Transmission
USE Transgenerational Patterns
Intergroup Dynamics
Interhemispheric Interaction
Interhemispheric Transfer
USE Interhemispheric Interaction
Interior Design
Interleukins
Intermarriage *USE Exogamous Marriage*
Intermediate School Students
Intermittent Explosive Personality
USE Explosive Personality
Intermittent Reinforcement
USE Reinforcement Schedules
Internal Consistency *USE Test Reliability*

Internal External Locus of Control
Internal Rewards
Rotter **Intern** Extern Locus Cont Scal
Internalization
International Class of Diseases
International Organizations
International Relations
Internists
Clinical Psychology **Internship**
Medical **Internship**
Teaching Internship *USE Student Teaching*
Interobserver Reliability
USE Interrater Reliability
Interocular Transfer
Interpersonal Attraction
Interpersonal Communication
Interpersonal Compatibility
Interpersonal Competence
USE Social Skills
Interpersonal Distance
USE Personal Space
Interpersonal Influences
Interpersonal Interaction
Interpersonal Perception
USE Social Perception
Interpersonal Psychotherapy
Fund **Interper** Rela Orientat Beh Ques
Learys **Interpersonal** Check List
Listening **(Interpersonal)**
Dream Interpretation *USE Dream Analysis*
Psychoanalytic **Interpretation**
Psychological Interpretation
USE Theoretical Interpretation
Test **Interpretation**
Theoretical **Interpretation**
Interracial Adoption
Interracial Family
Interracial Marriage
Interracial Offspring
Interrater Reliability
Interresponse Time
Criminal Interrogation *USE Legal Interrogation*
Legal **Interrogation**
Police Interrogation *USE Legal Interrogation*
Intersensory Integration
USE Sensory Integration
Intersensory Processes
Intersexuality *USE Hermaphroditism*
Interspecies Interaction
Interstimulus Interval
Intertrial Interval
Interval Reinforcement
USE Fixed Interval Reinforcement OR Variable Interval Reinforcement
Fixed **Interval** Reinforcement
Interstimulus **Interval**
Intertrial **Interval**
Variable **Interval** Reinforcement
Stimulus **Intervals**
Crisis **Intervention**
Crisis **Intervention** Services
Early **Intervention**
Diagnostic **Interview** Schedule
Intake **Interview**
Psychodiagnostic **Interview**
Interviewers
Interviewing
Interviews
Employment Interviews *USE Job Applicant Interviews*
Job Applicant **Interviews**
Intestines
Intimacy
Acute Alcoholic **Intoxication**
Alcohol **Intoxication**
Chronic Alcoholic **Intoxication**
Intra Aural Muscle Reflex
USE Acoustic Reflex
Intracranial Self Stimulation
USE Brain Self Stimulation

Intramuscular Injections
Intraperitoneal Injections
Intrauterine Devices
Intravenous Drug Usage
Intravenous Injections
Intrinsic Motivation
Intrinsic Rewards *USE Internal Rewards*
Introjection
Introspection
Introversion
Intuition
Kirton Adaption Innovation **Inven**
Minn Multiphasic Personality **Inven**
Inventories
Biographical **Inventories**
Interest **Inventories**
Barrett Lennard Relationship **Invent**
Beck Depression **Inventory**
Bem Sex Role **Inventory**
California Psychological **Inventory**
Differential Personality Inventory
USE Nonprojective Personality Measures
Edwards Personality **Inventory**
Eysenck Personality **Inventory**
Maudsley Personality **Inventory**
Millon Clinical Multiaxial **Inventory**
Minnesota Teacher Attitude Inventory *USE Attitude Measures*
NEO Personality **Inventory**
Omnibus Personality **Inventory**
Personal Orientation **Inventory**
Psychological Screening **Inventory**
State Trait Anxiety **Inventory**
Invertebrates
Investigation *USE Experimentation*
Maternal Investment *USE Parental Investment*
Parental **Investment**
Paternal Investment *USE Parental Investment*
Involuntary Treatment
Involutional Depression
Involutional Paranoid Psychosis
Involvement
Job **Involvement**
Political Involvement *USE Political Participation*
Ions *USE Electrolytes*
Calcium **Ions**
Chloride **Ions**
Magnesium **Ions**
Potassium **Ions**
Sodium **Ions**
Iowa Tests of Basic Skills
Iproniazid
Deviation IQ *USE Standard Scores*
Iran
Iraq
Ireland
Northern **Ireland**
Iris (Eye)
Iron
Irradiation *USE Radiation*
Laser **Irradiation**
Irrational Beliefs
Irritability
Irritable Bowel Syndrome
Ischemia
Cerebral **Ischemia**
Islam
Bahama **Islands**
Pacific **Islands**
Virgin **Islands**
Isocarboxazid
Isoenzymes *USE Isozymes*
Isolation (Defense Mechanism)
Isolation Effect
Social **Isolation**
Isoniazid
Isoproterenol
Isozymes
Israel
Political **Issues**
Social **Issues**
Italy
Itching *USE Pruritus*
Item Analysis (Statistical)
Item Analysis (Test)
Item Bias *USE Test Bias*
Item Content (Test)
Item Response Theory
Test **Items**
IV Drug Usage
USE Intravenous Drug Usage
Pavlov **(Ivan)**
Ivory Coast
Jails *USE Prisons*
Creutzfeldt **Jakob** Syndrome
Jamaica
James (William)
Japan
Japanese Cultural Groups
Jaundice
Jaw
Jealousy
Piaget **(Jean)**
Jews
Job Analysis
Job Applicant Attitudes
Job Applicant Interviews
Job Applicant Screening
Job Applicants
Job Change *USE Career Change*
Job Characteristics
Job Corps
Job Discrimination
USE Employment Discrimination
Job Enrichment
Job Experience Level
Job Family Relationship
USE Family Work Relationship
Job Involvement
Job Knowledge
Job Mobility *USE Occupational Mobility*
Job Performance
Job Promotion *USE Personnel Promotion*
Job Reentry *USE Reemployment*
Job Satisfaction
Job Search
Job Security
Job Selection *USE Occupational Choice*
Job Status *USE Occupational Status*
Job Training *USE Personnel Training*
On the **Job** Training
Jobs *USE Occupations*
Watson **(John** Broadus)
Woodcock **Johnson** Psychoed Battery
Joint Custody
Joint Disorders
Temporomandibular Joint Syndrome
USE Musculoskeletal Disorders
Joints (Anatomy)
Jokes
Jordan
Journalists
Joy *USE Happiness*
Judaism
Judges
Judgment
Judgment Disturbances
Clinical Judgment (Med Diagnosis)
USE Medical Diagnosis
Clinical **Judgment** (Not Diagnosis)
Clinical Judgment (Psychodiagnosis)
USE Psychodiagnosis
Probability **Judgment**
Judo
Jumping
Jung (Carl)
Jungian Psychology
Jungian Psychotherapy
USE Analytical Psychotherapy

Junior College Students
Junior Colleges *USE Colleges*
Junior High School Students
Junior High School Teachers
Junior High Schools
Juries
Jury Selection
Justice
Criminal **Justice**
Distributive Justice *USE Justice*
Juvenile Court *USE Adjudication*
Juvenile Delinquency
Juvenile Delinquents
Juvenile Gangs
Offenders (Juvenile) *USE Juvenile Delinquents*
Kainic Acid
Kangaroos
Karate *USE Martial Arts*
Karyotype Disorders
USE Chromosome Disorders
Kaufman Assessment Battery Children
Kenya
Ketamine
Keyboards
Kibbutz
Kidnapping
Kidney Diseases
Kidney Transplants
USE Organ Transplantation
Kidneys
Mercy Killing *USE Euthanasia*
Mouse Killing *USE Muricide*
Kinases
Kindergarten Students
Vane Kindergarten Test
USE Intelligence Measures
Kindergartens
Kindling
Kinesthetic Perception
United **Kingdom**
Kinship
Kinship Recognition
Kinship Structure
Kirton Adaption Innovation Inven
Kleptomania
Klinefelters Syndrome
Knee
Knowledge Based Systems
USE Expert Systems
Knowledge Level
Knowledge of Results
Declarative **Knowledge**
Factual Knowledge *USE Declarative Knowledge*
Functional Knowledge *USE Procedural Knowledge*
Health **Knowledge**
Job **Knowledge**
Practical Knowledge *USE Procedural Knowledge*
Procedural **Knowledge**
Kohlberg (Lawrence)
Kohs Block Design Test
Kolmogorov Smirnov Test
Hong **Kong**
Korea
North **Korea**
South **Korea**
Korean Cultural Groups
Koro
Korsakoffs Psychosis
Kuder Occupational Interest Survey
Kuder Preference Record
Kupfer Detre Self Rating Scale
USE Nonprojective Personality Measures
Kuwait
Kwashiorkor
L Dopa *USE Levodopa*
Labeling
Warning **Labels**
Labor (Childbirth)
Labor Management Relations
Labor Union Members
Labor Unions
Animal Division of **Labor**
Division of **Labor**
Educational **Laboratories**
Experimental **Laboratories**
Language **Laboratories**
Laborers (Construct and Indust)
USE Blue Collar Workers
Laborers (Farm) *USE Agricultural Workers*
Labyrinth (Anatomy)
Labyrinth (Apparatus) *USE Mazes*
Labyrinth Disorders
Lactate Dehydrogenase
Sodium Lactate *USE Lactic Acid*
Lactation
Lactic Acid
Response Lag *USE Reaction Time*
Landscapes *USE Topography*
Language
Language Alternation
USE Code Switching
Language Arts Education
Language Delay
Language Development
Language Disorders
Language Laboratories
Language Proficiency
Body **Language**
English as Second **Language**
Figurative **Language**
Foreign **Language** Education
Foreign **Language** Learning
Foreign **Language** Translation
Form Classes **(Language)**
Modern **Language** Aptitude Test
Morphology **(Language)**
Second Language Education
USE Foreign Language Education
Sign **Language**
Written **Language**
Computer Programing **Languages**
Foreign **Languages**
Sri **Lanka**
Laos
Larvae
Laryngeal Disorders
Larynx
Laser Irradiation
Latchkey Children *USE Child Self Care*
Latency (Response)
USE Response Latency
Response **Latency**
Latent Inhibition
Latent Learning
Latent Trait Theory
USE Item Response Theory
Lateral Dominance
Latin America
Latinos *USE Hispanics*
Laughter
Law Enforcement
Law Enforcement Personnel
Law (Government)
Law Students
Case **Law**
Civil **Law**
Criminal **Law**
Kohlberg **(Lawrence)**
Laws
Abortion **Laws**
Disability **Laws**
Drug **Laws**
Gun Control **Laws**
Marihuana **Laws**
Lawyers *USE Attorneys*
Lay Religious Personnel
Lead (Metal)
Lead Poisoning

Leadership
Leadership Qualities
Leadership Style
Learned Helplessness
Slow **Learners**
Learning
Learning Ability
Learning Centers (Educational)
Learning Disabilities
Learning Disorders
Learning Rate
Learning Schedules
Learning Strategies
Learning Style *USE Cognitive Style*
Learning Theory
Adult **Learning**
Cat **Learning**
Concept Learning *USE Concept Formation*
Cooperative **Learning**
Discrimination **Learning**
Experiential **Learning**
Extinction **(Learning)**
Extradimensional Shift Learning *USE Nonreversal Shift Learning*
Fine Motor Skill **Learning**
Foreign Language **Learning**
Generalization **(Learning)**
Generation Effect **(Learning)**
Gross Motor Skill **Learning**
Imitation **(Learning)**
Incidental **Learning**
Instrumental Learning *USE Operant Conditioning*
Intentional **Learning**
Interference **(Learning)**
Latent **Learning**
Mastery **Learning**
Maze **Learning**
Mnemonic **Learning**
Motor Skill Learning *USE Perceptual Motor Learning*
Nonreversal Shift **Learning**
Nonsense Syllable **Learning**
Nonverbal **Learning**
Observational **Learning**
Paired Associate **Learning**
Perceptual Motor **Learning**
Probability **Learning**
Rat **Learning**
Recall **(Learning)**
Recognition **(Learning)**
Reconstruction **(Learning)**
Reversal Shift **Learning**
Rote **Learning**
Rule Learning
USE Cognitive Hypothesis Testing
School **Learning**
Self Directed Learning *USE Individualized Instruction*
Sequential **Learning**
Serial **Learning**
Serial Anticipation **(Learning)**
Skill **Learning**
Social **Learning**
Spatial **Learning**
Spontaneous Recovery **(Learning)**
State Dependent **Learning**
Strategies (Learning) *USE Learning Strategies*
Transfer **(Learning)**
Trial and Error **Learning**
Verbal **Learning**
Learys Interpersonal Check List
Least Preferred Coworker Scale
Least Squares
Annual Leave *USE Employee Leave Benefits*
Employee **Leave** Benefits
Sick Leave *USE Employee Leave Benefits*
School **Leavers**
Lebanon
Lecithin
Lecture Method
Left Brain
Leg (Anatomy)

Legal Arrest
Legal Decisions
Legal Detention
Legal Evidence
Legal Interrogation
Legal Personnel
Legal Processes
Legal Psychology
USE Forensic Psychology
Legal Testimony
Evidence (Legal) *USE Legal Evidence*
Drug **Legalization**
Marihuana **Legalization**
Legibility
Handwriting **Legibility**
Legislative Processes
Leisure Time
Leiter Adult Intelligence Scale
USE Intelligence Measures
Lemniscal System
Lemurs
Length of Stay *USE Treatment Duration*
Work Week **Length**
Barrett **Lennard** Relationship Invent
Lens (Eye)
Contact **Lenses**
Corrective Lenses *USE Optical Aids*
Sierra **Leone**
Lesbian Parents
USE Homosexual Parents
Lesbianism
Sectioning (Lesion) *USE Lesions*
Lesions
Brain **Lesions**
Cerebral Lesions *USE Brain Lesions*
Hypothalamus **Lesions**
Neural **Lesions**
Subcortical Lesions *USE Brain Lesions*
Lesson Plans
Letters (Alphabet)
Leucine
Leucocytes
Leukemias
Leukotomy *USE Psychosurgery*
Vygotsky **(Lev)**
Ability **Level**
Academic Grade Level *USE Grade Level*
Activity **Level**
Aspiration **Level**
Attainment Level (Education)
USE Educational Attainment Level
Difficulty **Level** (Test)
Educational Attainment **Level**
Experience **Level**
Family Socioeconomic **Level**
Grade **Level**
Income **Level**
Job Experience **Level**
Knowledge **Level**
Lower Income **Level**
Middle **Level** Managers
Middle Income **Level**
Sound Pressure Level *USE Loudness*
Top **Level** Managers
Upper Income **Level**
Noise **Levels** (Work Areas)
Levodopa
Lexical Access
Lexical Decision
Drug Abuse **Liability**
Professional **Liability**
Consultation **Liaison** Psychiatry
Liberalism
Political **Liberalism**
Gay Liberation Movement
USE Homosexual Liberation Movement
Homosexual **Liberation** Movement
Womens **Liberation** Movement
Liberia

Libido
Librarians
Libraries
School **Libraries**
Librium *USE Chlordiazepoxide*
Libya
Professional **Licensing**
Licensure Examinations
USE Professional Examinations
Licking
Animal Licking Behavior *USE Licking*
Lidocaine
Liechtenstein
Life Change *USE Life Experiences*
Life Expectancy
Life Experiences
Life Insurance
Life Review
Life Satisfaction
Life Span *USE Life Expectancy*
Life Sustaining Treatment
Family Life *USE Family Relations*
Family **Life** Education
Philosophy of Life *USE World View*
Quality of **Life**
Quality of Work **Life**
Lifesaving *USE Artificial Respiration*
Lifestyle
Lifestyle Changes
Tubal **Ligation**
Light *USE Illumination*
Light Adaptation
Light Refraction
Bright Light Therapy *USE Phototherapy*
Likability
Maximum **Likelihood**
Likert Scales
Liking *USE Affection*
Limbic System
Artificial Limbs *USE Prostheses*
Phantom **Limbs**
Limen *USE Thresholds*
Differential Limen *USE Thresholds*
Limited English Proficiency
USE Language Proficiency
Time Limited Psychotherapy
USE Brief Psychotherapy
Confidence **Limits** (Statistics)
Allport Vernon Lindzey Study Values
USE Attitude Measures
Hot **Line** Services
Linear Perspective
Linear Regression
Telephone Hot Lines *USE Hot Line Services*
Linguistics
Linkage Analysis *USE Genetic Linkage*
Genetic **Linkage**
Sex **Linked** Developmental Differences
Sex **Linked** Hereditary Disorders
Lions *USE Felids*
Lipid Metabolism
Lipid Metabolism Disorders
Lipids
Lipoproteins
Lipreading
Lips (Face)
Liquor
Gough Adjective Check **List**
Learys Interpersonal Check **List**
Mooney Problem Check **List**
Listening *USE Auditory Perception*
Listening Comprehension
Listening (Interpersonal)
Literacy
Literacy Programs
Computer **Literacy**
Literature
Literature Review
Religious **Literature**

Lithium
Lithium Bromide *USE Bromides*
Lithium Carbonate
Litter Size
Liver
Liver Disorders
Cirrhosis **(Liver)**
Living Alone
Living Arrangements
Living Wills *USE Advance Directives*
Activities of Daily **Living**
Independent Living *USE Self Care Skills*
Independent **Living** Programs
Lizards
Cognitive Load *USE Human Channel Capacity*
Mental Load *USE Human Channel Capacity*
Work **Load**
Frontal **Lobe**
Occipital **Lobe**
Optic **Lobe**
Parietal **Lobe**
Temporal **Lobe**
Lobotomy *USE Psychosurgery*
Local Anesthetics
Auditory **Localization**
Perceptual **Localization**
Sound Localization *USE Auditory Localization*
Animal **Locomotion**
Locus Ceruleus
Control (Locus of)
USE Internal External Locus of Control
Health Locus of Control *USE Health Attitudes*
Internal External **Locus** of Control
Rotter Intern Extern **Locus** Cont Scal
Logic (Philosophy)
Logical Thinking
Logistic Models
USE Item Response Theory
Logotherapy
Loneliness
Long Term Care
Long Term Memory
Long Term Potentiation
USE Postactivation Potentials
Longevity *USE Life Expectancy*
Longitudinal Studies
Loosening of Associations
USE Fragmentation (Schizophrenia)
Lorazepam
Lordosis (Animal)
USE Animal Sexual Receptivity
Lorge Thorndike Intelligence Test
Hair Loss *USE Alopecia*
Sensorineural Hearing Loss *USE Hearing Disorders*
Loudness
Loudness Discrimination
Loudness Perception
Love
Low Birth Weight *USE Birth Weight*
Lowenfeld Mosaic Test
Lower Class
Lower Class Attitudes
Lower Income Level
Loxapine
Loyalty
LSD (Drug)
USE Lysergic Acid Diethylamide
Saint **Lucia**
Lucid Dreaming
Luck *USE Chance (Fortune)*
Lumbar Spinal Cord
Lumbrosacral Plexus *USE Spinal Nerves*
Luminance
Luminance Threshold
USE Brightness Perception AND Visual Thresholds
Lunar Synodic Cycle
Lung
Lung Disorders

Lupus
Luria Nebraska Neuropsych Battery
Luteinizing Hormone
Lutherans *USE Protestants*
Mueller **Lyer** Illusion
Lying *USE Deception*
Blood and **Lymphatic** Disorders
Lymphocytes
Lysergic Acid Diethylamide
Gates **MacGinitie** Reading Tests
Machiavellianism
Human **Machine** Systems
Human **Machine** Systems Design
Man Machine Systems
USE Human Machine Systems
Man Machine Systems Design
USE Human Machine Systems Design
Teaching **Machines**
Madagascar
Magazines
Magical Thinking
Magnesium
Magnesium Ions
Magnet Schools
USE Nontraditional Education
Magnetic Resonance Imaging
Magnetism
Magnetoencephalography
Magnitude Estimation
Magnitude of Effect (Statistical)
USE Effect Size (Statistical)
Nucleus Basalis **Magnocellularis**
Maids *USE Domestic Service Personnel*
Mail Surveys
Mainstreaming
Mainstreaming (Educational)
Maintenance Therapy
Health **Maintenance** Organizations
Methadone **Maintenance**
Major Depression
Major Tranquilizers
USE Neuroleptic Drugs
College Major *USE Academic Specialization*
Decision **Making**
Foreign Policy **Making**
Government Policy **Making**
Group Decision **Making**
Management Decision **Making**
Organizational Policy Making *USE Policy Making*
Policy **Making**
Grand **Mal** Epilepsy
Petit **Mal** Epilepsy
Emotional Maladjustment *USE Emotional Adjustment*
Social Maladjustment *USE Social Adjustment*
Malaria
Malawi
Malaysia
Male Animals
Male Castration
Male Criminals
Male Delinquents
Male Female Relations
Male Genital Disorders
Male Genitalia
Male Homosexuality
Male Orgasm
Gay Males *USE Male Homosexuality*
Human **Males**
Mali
Malignant Neoplasms *USE Neoplasms*
Neuroleptic **Malignant** Syndrome
Malingering
Malnutrition *USE Nutritional Deficiencies*
Malpractice *USE Professional Liability*
Mammals
Mammary Glands
Mammary Neoplasms
USE Breast Neoplasms
Mammillary Bodies (Hypothalamic)
USE Hypothalamus
Mammography
Man Machine Systems
USE Human Machine Systems
Man Machine Systems Design
USE Human Machine Systems Design
Draw A Man Test *USE Human Figures Drawing*
Incomplete **Man** Test
Managed Care
Management
Management Decision Making
Management Development
USE Career Development
Management Information Systems
USE Information Systems
Management Methods
Management Personnel
Management Planning
Management Training
Anxiety **Management**
Business **Management**
Case **Management**
Contingency **Management**
Disability **Management**
Household **Management**
Impression **Management**
Labor **Management** Relations
Pain **Management**
Participative **Management**
Personnel **Management**
Risk **Management**
Self **Management**
Stress **Management**
Time **Management**
Manager Employee Interaction
USE Supervisor Employee Interaction
Middle Level **Managers**
Top Level **Managers**
Mandibula *USE Jaw*
Mania
Manic Depression
Manic Depressive Psychosis
USE Manic Depression
Childrens **Manifest** Anxiety Scale
Taylor **Manifest** Anxiety Scale
Mann Whitney U Test
Mannerisms *USE Habits*
Manpower *USE Personnel Supply*
Mantis
Praying Mantis *USE Mantis*
Manual Communication
Diagnostic and Statistical **Manual**
Manufacturing *USE Business*
Maprotiline
Brain Maps *USE Stereotaxic Atlas*
Cognitive **Maps**
Tactual Maps *USE Mobility Aids*
Marathon Group Therapy
Marihuana
Marihuana Laws
Marihuana Legalization
Marihuana Usage
Marine Personnel
Marital Adjustment *USE Marital Relations*
Marital Conflict
Marital Fidelity *USE Monogamy*
Marital Relations
Marital Satisfaction
Marital Separation
Marital Status
Marital Therapy *USE Marriage Counseling*
Biochemical Markers *USE Biological Markers*
Biological **Markers**
Clinical Markers *USE Biological Markers*
Marketing
Animal Scent **Marking**
Markov Chains
Marlowe Crowne Soc Desirabil Scale

Marriage
Marriage and Family Education *USE Family Life Education*
Marriage Attitudes
Marriage Counseling
Marriage Rites
Consanguineous **Marriage**
Endogamous **Marriage**
Exogamous **Marriage**
Interethnic Marriage *USE Exogamous Marriage*
Interfaith **Marriage**
Interracial **Marriage**
Miscegenous Marriage *USE Interracial Marriage*
Married Couples *USE Spouses*
Never **Married**
Bone **Marrow**
Marsupials
Martial Arts
Marxism *USE Communism*
Masculinity
Masking
Auditory **Masking**
Backward Masking *USE Masking*
Forward Masking *USE Masking*
Visual **Masking**
Maslow (Abraham Harold)
Masochism
Sexual **Masochism**
Masochistic Personality
Mass Hysteria
Mass Media
Massed Practice
Mastectomy
Mastery Learning
Mastery Tests *USE Criterion Referenced Tests*
Masticatory Muscles
Masturbation
Matching Test *USE Matching to Sample*
Matching to Sample
Client Treatment **Matching**
Patient Treatment Matching *USE Client Treatment Matching*
Treatment Client Matching *USE Client Treatment Matching*
Mate Selection *USE Animal Mate Selection OR Human Mate Selection*
Mate Swapping *USE Extramarital Intercourse*
Animal **Mate** Selection
Human **Mate** Selection
Materialism
Hazardous **Materials**
Reading **Materials**
X Rated Materials *USE Pornography*
Maternal Behavior (Human) *USE Mother Child Relations*
Maternal Investment *USE Parental Investment*
Animal **Maternal** Behavior
Animal **Maternal** Deprivation
Mates (Humans) *USE Spouses*
Mathematical Ability
Mathematical Modeling
Mathematical Psychology
Mathematicians
Mathematics
Mathematics Achievement
Mathematics Anxiety
Mathematics (Concepts)
Mathematics Education
Digits (Mathematics) *USE Numbers (Numerals)*
Animal **Mating** Behavior
Assortative **Mating**
Assortive Mating *USE Assortative Mating*
Matriarchy
Raven Coloured Progressive **Matrices**
Raven Progressive **Matrices**
Matriculation *USE School Enrollment*
Maturation *USE Human Development*

California Test of Mental **Maturity**
Career Maturity *USE Vocational Maturity*
Columbia Mental **Maturity** Scale
Emotional **Maturity**
Physical **Maturity**
Vineland Social **Maturity** Scale
Vocational **Maturity**
Maudsley Personality Inventory
Mauritius
Maxilla *USE Jaw*
Maximum Likelihood
Maximum Security Facilities
Maze Learning
Maze Pathways
Porteus **Maze** Test
Runways (Maze) *USE Maze Pathways*
Mazes
T **Mazes**
MCPP *USE Piperazines*
MDMA *USE Methylenedioxymethamphetamine*
Mealtimes *USE Feeding Practices*
Mean
Meaning
Nonverbal **Meaning**
Verbal **Meaning**
Word **Meaning**
Meaningfulness
Measles
German Measles *USE Rubella*
Measurement
Attitude **Measurement**
Conjoint **Measurement**
Consistency **(Measurement)**
Creativity **Measurement**
Educational **Measurement**
Error of **Measurement**
Pain **Measurement**
Predictability **(Measurement)**
Profiles **(Measurement)**
Psychophysical **Measurement**
Standard Error of Measurement *USE Error of Measurement*
Statistical **Measurement**
Variability **Measurement**
Achievement **Measures**
Aptitude **Measures**
Attitude **Measures**
Central Tendency **Measures**
Developmental **Measures**
Intelligence **Measures**
Nonprojective Personality **Measures**
Occupational Interest **Measures**
Perceptual **Measures**
Perceptual Motor Measures *USE Sensorimotor Measures*
Personality **Measures**
Preference **Measures**
Projective Personality **Measures**
Reading **Measures**
Repeated **Measures**
Retention **Measures**
Sensorimotor **Measures**
Speech and Hearing **Measures**
Mecamylamine
Mechanical Aptitude
Speech Processing **(Mechanical)**
Compensation (Defense **Mechanism)**
Displacement (Defense **Mechanism)**
Fantasy (Defense **Mechanism)**
Identification (Defense **Mechanism)**
Isolation (Defense **Mechanism)**
Projection (Defense **Mechanism)**
Regression (Defense **Mechanism)**
Repression (Defense **Mechanism)**
Suppression (Defense **Mechanism)**
Withdrawal (Defense **Mechanism)**
Defense **Mechanisms**
Mechanoreceptors
Clinical Judgment (Med Diagnosis) *USE Medical Diagnosis*
Audiovisual Communications **Media**

ROTATED ALPHABETICAL TERMS SECTION

Communications **Media**
Instructional **Media**
Mass **Media**
News **Media**
Printed Communications **Media**
Telecommunications **Media**
Medial Forebrain Bundle
Median
Median Nerve *USE Spinal Nerves*
Mediated Responses
Mediation
Cognitive **Mediation**
Medicaid
Medical Care Costs
USE Health Care Costs
Medical Diagnosis
Medical Education
Medical History *USE Patient History*
Medical Internship
Medical Model
Medical Patients
Medical Personnel
Medical Personnel Supply
Medical Psychology
Medical Records
Medical Regimen Compliance
USE Treatment Compliance
Medical Residency
Medical Sciences
Medical Students
Medical Therapeutic Devices
Medical Treatment (General)
Military **Medical** Personnel
Self Examination **(Medical)**
Medicare
Medication *USE Drug Therapy*
Self **Medication**
Medicine (Science of)
USE Medical Sciences
Alternative **Medicine**
Behavioral Medicine *USE Health Care Psychology*
Family **Medicine**
Folk **Medicine**
Preventive **Medicine**
Psychosomatic **Medicine**
Veterinary **Medicine**
Medics *USE Paramedical Personnel*
Meditation
Medulla Oblongata
Adrenal **Medulla** Hormones
Professional **Meetings** and Symposia
Melancholia *USE Major Depression*
Melancholy *USE Sadness*
Melanin
Melanocyte Stimulating Hormone
Melanotropin
USE Melanocyte Stimulating Hormone
Melatonin
Mellaril *USE Thioridazine*
Diabetes **Mellitus**
Family **Members**
Labor Union **Members**
Fraternity **Membership**
School Club **Membership**
Sorority **Membership**
Nictitating **Membrane**
Tympanic Membrane *USE Middle Ear*
Membranes
Childhood Memories *USE Early Memories*
Early **Memories**
Memory
Memory Decay
Memory Disorders
Memory Enhancing Drugs
USE Nootropic Drugs
Memory for Designs Test
Memory Trace
Memory Training
Autobiographical **Memory**
Episodic **Memory**
Explicit **Memory**
False **Memory**
Iconic **Memory**
Long Term **Memory**
Photographic Memory *USE Eidetic Imagery*
Repressed **Memory**
Semantic **Memory**
Short Term **Memory**
Spatial **Memory**
Verbal **Memory**
Visual **Memory**
Visual Spatial Memory *USE Visuospatial Memory*
Visuospatial **Memory**
Wechsler **Memory** Scale
Working Memory *USE Short Term Memory*
Men *USE Human Males*
Menarche
Menieres Disease
Meninges
Meningitis
Bacterial **Meningitis**
Meningomyelocele *USE Spina Bifida*
Menopause
Menstrual Cycle
Menstrual Disorders
Menstruation
Mental Age
Mental Confusion
Mental Deficiency
USE Mental Retardation
Mental Disorders
Mental Health
Mental Health Care Costs
USE Health Care Costs
Mental Health Care Policy
USE Health Care Policy
Mental Health Consultation
USE Professional Consultation
Mental Health Inservice Training
Mental Health Personnel
Mental Health Personnel Supply
Mental Health Program Evaluation
Mental Health Programs
Mental Health Service Needs
USE Health Service Needs
Mental Health Services
Mental Hospitals
USE Psychiatric Hospitals
Mental Illness *USE Mental Disorders*
Mental Illness (Attitudes Toward)
Mental Load
USE Human Channel Capacity
Mental Retardation
Mental Retardation (Attit Toward)
Mental Rotation
Borderline **Mental** Retardation
California Test of **Mental** Maturity
Chronic **Mental** Illness
Columbia **Mental** Maturity Scale
Community **Mental** Health
Community **Mental** Health Centers
Community **Mental** Health Services
Community **Mental** Health Training
Cultural Familial Mental Retardation
USE Psychosocial Mental Retardation
Henmon Nelson Tests Mental Ability *USE Intelligence Measures*
Mini **Mental** State Examination
Persistent Mental Illness *USE Chronic Mental Illness*
Primary **Mental** Health Prevention
Psychosocial **Mental** Retardation
Mentally Ill Homeless
USE Homeless Mentally Ill
Mentally Ill Offenders
Mentally Retarded
Borderline Mentally Retarded *USE Slow Learners*
Educable **Mentally** Retarded
Home Reared **Mentally** Retarded
Homeless **Mentally** Ill

Institutionalized **Mentally** Retarded
Mildly Mentally Retarded
USE Educable Mentally Retarded
Moderately Mentally Retarded
USE Trainable Mentally Retarded
Profoundly **Mentally** Retarded
Severely **Mentally** Retarded
Trainable **Mentally** Retarded
Mentor
Meperidine
Mephenesin *USE Muscle Relaxing Drugs*
Meprobamate
Mercury (Metal)
Mercury Poisoning
Mercy Killing *USE Euthanasia*
Organizational **Merger**
Mescaline
Mesencephalon
Mesoridazine
Messages
Information (Messages) *USE Messages*
Meta Analysis
Metabolic Rates
Metabolism
Metabolism Disorders
Basal **Metabolism**
Brain Metabolism *USE Neurochemistry*
Carbohydrate **Metabolism**
Fat Metabolism *USE Lipid Metabolism*
Glucose **Metabolism**
Lipid **Metabolism**
Lipid **Metabolism** Disorders
Protein **Metabolism**
Metabolites
Dopamine **Metabolites**
Norepinephrine **Metabolites**
Serotonin **Metabolites**
Metacognition
Lead **(Metal)**
Mercury **(Metal)**
Metalinguistics
Metallic Elements
Metals
Metamemory *USE Metacognition*
Metaphor
Metaphysics
Metapsychology
Climate (Meteorological)
USE Atmospheric Conditions
Volt Meters *USE Apparatus*
Methadone
Methadone Maintenance
Methamphetamine
Methanol
Methaqualone
Methedrine *USE Methamphetamine*
Methionine
Directed Discussion **Method**
Discovery Teaching **Method**
Forced Choice (Testing **Method)**
Lecture **Method**
Montessori **Method**
Multiple Choice (Testing **Method)**
Nondirected Discussion **Method**
Open Classroom **Method**
Rhythm **Method**
Team Teaching **Method**
Methodists *USE Protestants*
Methodology
Clinical **Methods** Training
Drug Administration **Methods**
Empirical **Methods**
Experimental **Methods**
Management **Methods**
Observation **Methods**
Physical Treatment **Methods**
Research Methods *USE Methodology*
Scientific Methods *USE Experimental Methods*
Stimulus Presentation **Methods**
Teaching **Methods**
Testing **Methods**
Methohexital
Methoxamine
Methoxyhydroxyphenylglycol (3,4)
Methyl Alcohol *USE Methanol*
Methylatropine *USE Atropine*
Methyldiphenylhydramine
USE Orphenadrine
Methyldopa
Methylenedioxymethamphetamine
Methylmorphine *USE Codeine*
Alpha **Methylparatyrosine**
Methylphenidate
Methylphenyltetrahydropyridine
Methysergide *USE Serotonin Antagonists*
Metrazole *USE Pentylenetetrazol*
Metronomes
Metropolitan Readiness Tests
Mexican Americans
Mexico
MHPG
USE Methoxyhydroxyphenylglycol (3,4)
Mianserin
Mice
Microcephaly
Microcomputers
Microcounseling
Microorganisms
Microscopes
Micturition *USE Urination*
Midazolam
Midbrain *USE Mesencephalon*
Middle Aged
Middle Class
Middle Class Attitudes
Middle Ear
Middle East
Middle Income Level
Middle Level Managers
Middle School Education
Middle School Students
Midwifery
Migraine Headache
Migrant Farm Workers
Human **Migration**
Migratory Behavior (Animal)
Mildly Mentally Retarded
USE Educable Mentally Retarded
Milieu Therapy
Militancy
Military Enlistment
Military Medical Personnel
Military Officers
USE Commissioned Officers
Military Personnel
Military Psychologists
Military Psychology
Military Recruitment
Military Schools
Military Training
Military Veterans
Enlisted **Military** Personnel
Volunteer **Military** Personnel
Miller Analogies Test
Millon Clinical Multiaxial Inventory
Mind
Mind Body *USE Dualism*
Mini Mental State Examination
Minimal Brain Disorders
Minimally Brain Damaged
Minimum Competency Tests
Ministers (Religion)
Minks
Minn Multiphasic Personality Inven
Minnesota Teacher Attitude Inventory
USE Attitude Measures
Minor Tranquilizers

Minority Group Discrimination
USE Race and Ethnic Discrimination
Minority Groups
Mirror Image
Mirroring
Misanthropy
Misarticulation *USE Articulation Disorders*
Misbehavior *USE Behavior Problems*
Miscarriage *USE Spontaneous Abortion*
Miscegenous Marriage
USE Interracial Marriage
Misconduct *USE Behavior Problems*
Misdemeanors *USE Crime*
Misdiagnosis
Misogyny *USE Misanthropy*
Missionaries
Mistakes *USE Errors*
MMPI
USE Minn Multiphasic Personality Inven
Mnemonic Learning
Mobility Aids
Geographical **Mobility**
Job Mobility *USE Occupational Mobility*
Occupational **Mobility**
Physical **Mobility**
Social **Mobility**
Upward Mobility *USE Social Mobility*
Vocational Mobility *USE Occupational Mobility*
Moclobemide
Big Five Personality Model *USE Five Factor Personality Model*
Biopsychosocial Model *USE Biopsychosocial Approach*
Five Factor Personality **Model**
Medical **Model**
Rasch Model *USE Item Response Theory*
Modeling *USE Simulation*
Modeling Behavior
USE Imitation (Learning)
Heuristic **Modeling**
Mathematical **Modeling**
Stochastic **Modeling**
Structural Equation **Modeling**
Models
Animal **Models**
Logistic Models *USE Item Response Theory*
Role **Models**
Moderately Mentally Retarded
USE Trainable Mentally Retarded
Modern Language Aptitude Test
Behavior **Modification**
Classroom Behavior **Modification**
Child Molestation *USE Pedophilia*
Molindone
Mollusca
Pearson Prod Moment Correl Coeff
USE Statistical Correlation
Monetary Incentives
Monetary Rewards
Money
Mongolism *USE Downs Syndrome*
Monitoring
Self **Monitoring**
Self **Monitoring** (Personality)
Monkeys
Monoamine Oxidase Inhibitors
Monoamine Oxidases
Monoamines (Brain) *USE Catecholamines*
Monocular Vision
Monogamy
Monolingualism
Cyclic Adenosine **Monophosphate**
Monotony
Carbon **Monoxide**
Carbon **Monoxide** Poisoning
Monozygotic Twins
Montessori Method
Mood Disorders
USE Affective Disturbances
Bipolar Mood Disorder *USE Manic Depression*
Moodiness

Moods *USE Emotional States*
Mooney Problem Check List
Moral Development
Morale
Morality
Morals *USE Morality*
Mores *USE Values*
Morita Therapy
Morocco
Morphemes
Morphine
Morphology
Morphology (Language)
Mortality *USE Death and Dying*
Mortality Rate
Lowenfeld **Mosaic** Test
Mosaicism *USE Chromosome Disorders*
Moslems *USE Muslims*
Mother Absence
Mother Child Communication
Mother Child Relations
Mothers
Adolescent **Mothers**
Expectant **Mothers**
Schizophrenogenic **Mothers**
Single **Mothers**
Teenage Mothers *USE Adolescent Mothers*
Unwed **Mothers**
Moths
Motion Parallax
Motion Perception
Motion Pictures
Motion Pictures (Educational)
Motion Pictures (Entertainment)
Motion Sickness
Motivation
Motivation Training
Academic Achievement **Motivation**
Achievement **Motivation**
Affiliation **Motivation**
Animal **Motivation**
Employee **Motivation**
Extrinsic **Motivation**
Intrinsic **Motivation**
Motor Coordination
Motor Cortex
Motor Development
Motor Disorders
USE Nervous System Disorders
Motor Evoked Potentials
USE Somatosensory Evoked Potentials
Motor Neurons
Motor Pathways *USE Efferent Pathways*
Motor Performance
Motor Processes
Motor Skill Learning
USE Perceptual Motor Learning
Motor Skills
Motor Traffic Accidents
Motor Vehicles
Balance (Motor Processes) *USE Equilibrium*
Fine **Motor** Skill Learning
Gross **Motor** Skill Learning
Perceptual **Motor** Coordination
Perceptual **Motor** Development
Perceptual **Motor** Learning
Perceptual Motor Measures
USE Sensorimotor Measures
Perceptual **Motor** Processes
Purdue Perceptual **Motor** Survey
Motorcycles *USE Motor Vehicles*
Mourning *USE Grief*
Mouse Killing *USE Muricide*
Mouth (Anatomy)
Movement Disorders
Movement Perception
USE Motion Perception
Movement Therapy
Apparent **Movement**

Black Power **Movement**
Civil Rights **Movement**
Eye **Movement** Desensitization Therapy
Gay Liberation Movement *USE Homosexual Liberation Movement*
Homosexual Liberation **Movement**
Human Potential **Movement**
Nonrapid Eye Movement Sleep *USE NREM Sleep*
Rapid Eye **Movement**
Rapid Eye Movement Dreams *USE REM Dreams*
Rapid Eye Movement Sleep *USE REM Sleep*
Stroboscopic Movement *USE Apparent Movement*
Womens Liberation **Movement**
Activist **Movements**
Eye **Movements**
Radical **Movements**
Saccadic Eye Movements *USE Eye Movements*
Social **Movements**
Vergence Movements *USE Eye Convergence*
Movies *USE Motion Pictures (Entertainment)*
Mozambique
MPTP *USE Methylphenyltetrahydropyridine*
MRI *USE Magnetic Resonance Imaging*
Nasal **Mucosa**
Olfactory **Mucosa**
Mucus
Mueller Lyer Illusion
Multi Infarct Dementia
Dementia (Multi Infarct) *USE Multi Infarct Dementia*
Millon Clinical **Multiaxial** Inventory
Multicultural Education
Multiculturalism
Multidimensional Scaling
Multidisciplinary Research *USE Interdisciplinary Research*
Multidisciplinary Treatment Approach *USE Interdisciplinary Treatment Approach*
Multidrug Abuse *USE Polydrug Abuse*
Multilingualism
Multimodal Treatment Approach
Minn **Multiphasic** Personality Inven
Multiple Births
Multiple Choice (Testing Method)
Multiple Personality *USE Dissociative Identity Disorder*
Multiple Regression
Multiple Sclerosis
Multiple Therapy *USE Cotherapy*
Multiply Disabled
Multiply Handicapped *USE Multiply Disabled*
Multivariate Analysis
Munchausen Syndrome
Munchausen Syndrome by Proxy
Murder *USE Homicide*
Muricide
Muscarinic Drugs *USE Cholinergic Drugs*
Muscimol
Muscle Contraction Headache
Muscle Contractions
Muscle Cramps *USE Muscular Disorders*
Muscle Relaxation
Muscle Relaxation Therapy *USE Relaxation Therapy*
Muscle Relaxing Drugs
Muscle Spasms
Muscle Tone
Cramps (Muscle) *USE Muscular Disorders*
Intra Aural Muscle Reflex *USE Acoustic Reflex*
Muscles
Facial **Muscles**
Masticatory **Muscles**
Oculomotor **Muscles**
Rigidity (Muscles) *USE Muscle Contractions*
Muscular Atrophy
Muscular Disorders
Muscular Dystrophy
Musculocutaneous Nerve *USE Spinal Nerves*
Musculoskeletal Disorders
Musculoskeletal System
Music
Music Education
Music Perception
Music Therapy
Rock **Music**
Musical Ability
Musical Instruments
Musicians
Muslims
Mutations
Self **Mutilation**
Mutism
Elective **Mutism**
Mutual Storytelling Technique
Myasthenia
Myasthenia Gravis
Myelin Sheath
Myelitis
Myelomeningocele *USE Spina Bifida*
Myenteric Plexus *USE Autonomic Ganglia*
Myers Briggs Type Indicator
Myocardial Infarctions
Myocardium
Myoclonia
Myofascial Pain
Myopia
Myotonia
Mysticism
Myths
Myxedema *USE Hypothyroidism*
Nabilone *USE Cannabinoids*
NAch *USE Achievement Motivation*
Nail Biting
Nalorphine
Naloxone
Naltrexone
Names
Brand **Names**
Naming
Napping
Narcissism
Narcissistic Personality
Narcoanalysis
Narcoanalytic Drugs *USE Drugs*
Narcolepsy
Narcosis
Narcotic Agonists
Narcotic Antagonists
Narcotic Drugs
Narcotics Anonymous *USE Twelve Step Programs*
Narratives
Nasal Mucosa
National Guardsmen
Nationalism
Foreign **Nationals**
Native Americans *USE American Indians*
Alaska **Natives**
Natural Childbirth
Natural Disasters
Natural Family *USE Biological Family*
Natural Selection
Nature Nurture
Human **Nature**
Nausea
Animal Navigation *USE Migratory Behavior (Animal)*
Navigators (Aircraft) *USE Aerospace Personnel*
Navy Personnel
Nazism *USE Fascism*
Near Death Experiences
Nearsightedness *USE Myopia*
Luria **Nebraska** Neuropsych Battery

Neck (Anatomy)
Need Achievement
USE Achievement Motivation
Need for Affiliation
USE Affiliation Motivation
Need for Approval
Need for Cognition
Need Satisfaction
Needle Sharing
Needs
Needs Assessment
Emotional Needs *USE Psychological Needs*
Health Service **Needs**
Mental Health Service Needs *USE Health Service Needs*
Psychological **Needs**
Special **Needs**
Negative and Positive Symptoms
USE Positive and Negative Symptoms
Negative Reinforcement
Negative Therapeutic Reaction
Negative Transfer
Contingent **Negative** Variation
Positive and **Negative** Symptoms
Negativism
Child **Neglect**
Perceptual Neglect *USE Sensory Neglect*
Sensory **Neglect**
Spatial Neglect *USE Sensory Neglect*
Visual Neglect *USE Sensory Neglect*
Negotiation
Negroes *USE Blacks*
Neighborhoods
Henmon Nelson Tests Mental Ability
USE Intelligence Measures
Nembutal *USE Pentobarbital*
NEO Personality Inventory
NeoFreudian School
USE Neopsychoanalytic School
Neologisms
Neonatal Development
Neonatal Disorders
Neonates
Neonates (Animal) *USE Infants (Animal)*
Neonaticide *USE Infanticide*
Neophobia
Neoplasms
Benign **Neoplasms**
Brain **Neoplasms**
Breast **Neoplasms**
Endocrine **Neoplasms**
Malignant Neoplasms *USE Neoplasms*
Mammary Neoplasms *USE Breast Neoplasms*
Nervous System **Neoplasms**
Neopsychoanalytic School
Neostigmine
Nepal
Nerve Cells *USE Neurons*
Nerve Endings
Nerve Growth Factor
Nerve Tissues
Abducens **Nerve**
Accessory Nerve *USE Cranial Nerves*
Acoustic **Nerve**
Auditory Nerve *USE Acoustic Nerve*
Chorda Tympani Nerve *USE Facial Nerve*
Facial **Nerve**
Femoral Nerve *USE Spinal Nerves*
Glossopharyngeal Nerve *USE Cranial Nerves*
Hypoglossal Nerve *USE Cranial Nerves*
Median Nerve *USE Spinal Nerves*
Musculocutaneous Nerve *USE Spinal Nerves*
Obturator Nerve *USE Spinal Nerves*
Oculomotor Nerve *USE Cranial Nerves*
Olfactory **Nerve**
Optic **Nerve**
Peripheral **Nerve** Disorders
Phrenic Nerve *USE Spinal Nerves*
Radial Nerve *USE Spinal Nerves*
Sciatic Nerve *USE Spinal Nerves*
Trigeminal **Nerve**
Trochlear Nerve *USE Cranial Nerves*
Ulnar Nerve *USE Spinal Nerves*
Vagus **Nerve**
Adrenergic **Nerves**
Cholinergic **Nerves**
Cranial **Nerves**
Spinal **Nerves**
Thoracic Nerves *USE Spinal Nerves*
Anorexia **Nervosa**
Nervous Breakdown
USE Mental Disorders
Nervous System
Nervous System Disorders
Nervous System Neoplasms
Nervous System Plasticity
USE Neural Plasticity
Autonomic **Nervous** System
Autonomic **Nervous** System Disorders
Central **Nervous** System
Central **Nervous** System Disorders
Central Nervous System Drugs
USE CNS Affecting Drugs
Parasympathetic **Nervous** System
Peripheral **Nervous** System
Sclerosis **(Nervous** System)
Sympathetic **Nervous** System
Nervousness
Nest Building
Empty **Nest**
Netherlands
Netherlands Antilles
Networks (Social) *USE Social Networks*
Neural **Networks**
Social **Networks**
Social Support **Networks**
Neural Analyzers
Neural Development
Neural Lesions
Neural Networks
Neural Pathways
Neural Plasticity
Neural Receptors
Neural Regeneration
USE Neural Development
Neural Transplantation
Neuralgia
Trigeminal **Neuralgia**
Neurasthenic Neurosis
Neuroanatomy
Neurobiology
Neurochemistry
Neurodermatitis
Neuroendocrinology
Neuroinfections *USE Infectious Disorders AND Nervous System Disorders*
Neurokinins
Neuroleptic Drugs
Neuroleptic Malignant Syndrome
Neurolinguistic Programing
Neurolinguistics
Neurological Disorders
USE Nervous System Disorders
Neurologists
Neurology
Neuromuscular Blocking Drugs
USE Muscle Relaxing Drugs
Neuromuscular Disorders
Neurons
Auditory **Neurons**
Motor **Neurons**
Sensory **Neurons**
Neuropathologists *USE Neurologists*
Neuropathology
Neuropathy
USE Nervous System Disorders
Neuropeptides *USE Peptides*
Neurophysiology
Halstead Reitan **Neuropsych** Battery

Luria Nebraska **Neuropsych** Battery
Neuropsychiatrists *USE Psychiatrists*
Neuropsychiatry
Neuropsychological Assessment
Neuropsychological Rehabilitation
Neuropsychology
Neurosciences
Neurosis
Anxiety Neurosis *USE Anxiety Disorders*
Childhood **Neurosis**
Compulsive Neurosis
USE Obsessive Compulsive Neurosis
Conversion **Neurosis**
Dissociative Neurosis *USE Dissociative Patterns*
Experimental **Neurosis**
Hysterical Neurosis (Dissociation)
USE Dissociative Patterns
Infantile Neurosis *USE Childhood Neurosis*
Neurasthenic **Neurosis**
Obsessive Neurosis
USE Obsessive Compulsive Neurosis
Obsessive Compulsive **Neurosis**
Occupational **Neurosis**
Phobic Neurosis *USE Phobias*
Traumatic **Neurosis**
Neurosurgeons *USE Surgeons*
Neurosurgery
Neurosyphilis
Neurotensin
Neurotic Depressive Reaction
Neuroticism
Neurotoxins
Neurotransmitters
Neutrality (Psychotherapeutic)
USE Psychotherapeutic Neutrality
Psychotherapeutic **Neutrality**
Never Married
New Zealand
Papua **New** Guinea
Newborn Infants *USE Neonates*
News Media
Professional Newsletters
USE Scientific Communication
Newspapers
Niacin *USE Nicotinic Acid*
Niacinamide *USE Nicotinamide*
Nialamide
Nicaragua
Nicotinamide
Nicotine
Nicotine Withdrawal
Nicotinic Acid
Nicotinic Acid Amide *USE Nicotinamide*
Nictitating Membrane
Niger
Nigeria
Night Terrors *USE Sleep Disorders*
Nightmares
Substantia **Nigra**
Nihilism
Nitrazepam
Nitrogen
NMDA *USE N-Methyl-D-Aspartate*
N-Methyl-D-Aspartate
Nociception *USE Pain Perception*
Nociceptors
Nocturnal Emission
Nocturnal Teeth Grinding
Animal **Nocturnal** Behavior
Noise Effects
Noise Levels (Work Areas)
Noise (Sound) *USE Auditory Stimulation*
Filtered **Noise**
White **Noise**
Nomenclature (Psychological)
USE Psychological Terminology
Nomifensine
Non Zero Sum Games
Beverages **(Nonalcoholic)**
Noncommissioned Officers
Nonconformity (Personality)
Noncontingent Reinforcement
Nondirected Discussion Method
Nondirective Therapy
USE Client Centered Therapy
Nongraded Schools
Primates **(Nonhuman)**
Nonlinear Regression
Nonmetallic Elements
USE Chemical Elements
Nonparametric Statistical Tests
Nonprescription Drugs
Nonprofessional Personnel
Nonprofit Organizations
Nonprojective Personality Measures
Nonrapid Eye Movement Sleep
USE NREM Sleep
Beliefs (Nonreligious) *USE Attitudes*
Rites **(Nonreligious)**
Rituals (Nonreligious) *USE Rites (Nonreligious)*
NonREM Sleep *USE NREM Sleep*
Nonreversal Shift Learning
Nonsense Syllable Learning
Nonstandard English
Nontraditional Careers
Nontraditional Education
Nonverbal Ability
Nonverbal Communication
Nonverbal Learning
Nonverbal Meaning
Nonverbal Reinforcement
Nonviolence
Nootropic Drugs
Noradrenaline *USE Norepinephrine*
Norepinephrine
Norepinephrine Metabolites
Normal Distribution
Test Normalization *USE Test Standardization*
Social **Norms**
Statistical **Norms**
Test **Norms**
North America
North Korea
North Vietnam *USE Vietnam*
Northern Ireland
Nortriptyline
Norway
Norway Rats
Nose
Note Taking
Nouns
Novelty Seeking *USE Sensation Seeking*
Stimulus **Novelty**
Novocaine *USE Procaine*
NREM Sleep
Nuclear Family
Nuclear Technology
Nuclear War
Raphe **Nuclei**
Septal **Nuclei**
Thalamic **Nuclei**
Nucleic Acids
Nucleotides
Nucleus Accumbens
Nucleus Basalis Magnocellularis
Caudate **Nucleus**
Cell **Nucleus**
Red Nucleus *USE Mesencephalon*
Nudity
Null Hypothesis Testing
Number Comprehension
Number Systems
Numbers (Numerals)
Numbers **(Numerals)**
Numerical Ability *USE Mathematical Ability*
Numerosity Perception
Nuns

Nurse Patient Interaction
USE Therapeutic Processes
Nursery School Students
Nursery Schools
Nurses
Psychiatric **Nurses**
Public Health Service **Nurses**
School **Nurses**
Nursing
Nursing Education
Nursing Homes
Nursing Students
Nurturance
Nature **Nurture**
Nutrition
Nutritional Deficiencies
Nymphomania *USE Hypersexuality*
Nystagmus
Optokinetic Nystagmus *USE Nystagmus*
Vestibular Nystagmus *USE Nystagmus*
Obedience
Obesity
Obesity (Attitudes Toward)
Obituary
Object Permanence
Object Recognition
Object Relations
Goldstein Scheerer **Object** Sort Test
Objective Referenced Tests
USE Criterion Referenced Tests
Objectives *USE Goals*
Course Objectives *USE Educational Objectives*
Educational **Objectives**
Instructional Objectives *USE Educational Objectives*
Organizational **Objectives**
Objectivity
Transitional **Objects**
Oblique Rotation
Medulla **Oblongata**
Obscenity
Observation Methods
Self Observation *USE Self Monitoring*
Observational Learning
Observers
Obsessions
Obsessive Compulsive Disorder
USE Obsessive Compulsive Neurosis
Obsessive Compulsive Neurosis
Obsessive Compulsive Personality
Obsessive Neurosis
USE Obsessive Compulsive Neurosis
Obstetrical Complications
Obstetricians
Obstetrics
Obturator Nerve *USE Spinal Nerves*
Occipital Lobe
Occultism
Parental **Occupation**
Occupational Adjustment
Occupational Aspirations
Occupational Attitudes
Occupational Choice
Occupational Exposure
Occupational Guidance
Occupational Interest Measures
Occupational Interests
Occupational Mobility
Occupational Neurosis
Occupational Preference
Occupational Safety
Occupational Status
Occupational Stress
Occupational Success
Occupational Success Prediction
Occupational Tenure
Occupational Therapists
Occupational Therapy
Kuder **Occupational** Interest Survey
Prestige (Occupational) *USE Occupational Status*
Occupations
Religious Occupations *USE Religious Personnel*
Octopus
Ocular Accommodation
Ocular Dominance
Ocular Fixation *USE Eye Fixation*
Electro **Oculography**
Oculomotor Muscles
Oculomotor Nerve *USE Cranial Nerves*
Oculomotor Response
USE Eye Movements
Odor Aversion Conditioning
USE Aversion Conditioning
Odor Discrimination
Oedipal Complex
Offenders (Adult) *USE Criminals*
Offenders (Juvenile)
USE Juvenile Delinquents
Mentally Ill **Offenders**
Sex **Offenses**
Office Environment
USE Working Conditions
Commissioned **Officers**
Military Officers *USE Commissioned Officers*
Noncommissioned **Officers**
Parole **Officers**
Probation **Officers**
Elected Government Officials *USE Government Personnel*
Stimulus **Offset**
Offspring
Adult **Offspring**
Interracial **Offspring**
Old Age *USE Aged*
Very **Old**
Olfactory Bulb
Olfactory Evoked Potentials
Olfactory Impairment *USE Anosmia*
Olfactory Mucosa
Olfactory Nerve
Olfactory Perception
Olfactory Stimulation
Olfactory Thresholds
Oligophrenia *USE Mental Retardation*
Oligophrenia (Phenylpyruvic)
USE Phenylketonuria
Omission Training
Omnibus Personality Inventory
Omnipotence
On the Job Training
Time **On** Task
Online Databases *USE Databases*
Online Searching
USE Computer Searching
Only Children
Onomatopoeia and Images Test
USE Projective Personality Measures
Onset (Disorders)
Sleep **Onset**
Stimulus **Onset**
Ontogeny *USE Development*
Open Classroom Method
Open Universities
USE Nontraditional Education
Animal **Open** Field Behavior
Openmindedness
Openness to Experience
Operant Conditioning
Operation (Surgery) *USE Surgery*
Ophidiophobia
Ophthalmologic Examination
Ophthalmology
Opiate Agonists *USE Narcotic Agonists*
Opiate Antagonists
USE Narcotic Antagonists
Opiates
Endogenous **Opiates**
Opinion Attitude and Interest Survey
USE Attitude Measures
Opinion Change *USE Attitude Change*

Opinion Questionnaires *USE Attitude Measures*
Opinion Surveys *USE Attitude Measures*
Public **Opinion**
Opinions *USE Attitudes*
Opioid Antagonists *USE Narcotic Antagonists*
Opioids *USE Opiates*
Opium Alkaloids *USE Alkaloids AND Opiates*
Opium Derivatives *USE Opiates*
Opossums
Oppositional Defiant Disorder
Optic Chiasm
Optic Lobe
Optic Nerve
Optic Tract
Optical Aids
Optical Illusions *USE Illusions (Perception)*
Optimism
Optokinetic Nystagmus *USE Nystagmus*
Optometrists
Optometry
Oral Communication
Oral Contraceptives
Oral Reading
Birth **Order**
Higher **Order** Conditioning
Pecking Order *USE Animal Dominance*
Rank **Order** Correlation
Second Order Conditioning *USE Higher Order Conditioning*
Court Ordered Treatment *USE Court Referrals*
Organ Donation *USE Tissue Donation*
Organ of Corti *USE Cochlea*
Organ Transplantation
Sense **Organ** Disorders
Organic Brain Syndromes
Organic Therapies
Single Cell Organisms *USE Microorganisms*
School Organization *USE Educational Administration*
Spatial **Organization**
Organizational Behavior
Organizational Change
Organizational Characteristics
Organizational Climate
Organizational Commitment
Organizational Crises
Organizational Development
Organizational Effectiveness
Organizational Goals *USE Organizational Objectives*
Organizational Merger
Organizational Objectives
Organizational Performance *USE Organizational Effectiveness*
Organizational Policy Making *USE Policy Making*
Organizational Psychology *USE Industrial Psychology*
Organizational Structure
Organizations
Business **Organizations**
Clubs (Social **Organizations)**
Foreign **Organizations**
Health Maintenance **Organizations**
International **Organizations**
Nonprofit **Organizations**
Professional **Organizations**
Religious **Organizations**
Advance **Organizers**
Sense **Organs**
Orgasm
Female **Orgasm**
Male **Orgasm**
Orientals *USE Asians*
Fund Interper Rela **Orientat** Beh Ques
Perceptual **Orientation**
Personal **Orientation** Inventory
Professional Orientation *USE Theoretical Orientation*
Sexual **Orientation**
Spatial **Orientation** (Perception)
Theoretical **Orientation**
Orienting Reflex
Orienting Responses
Family of **Origin**
Originality *USE Creativity*
Word Origins *USE Etymology*
Orphanages
Orphans
Orphenadrine
Orthogonal Rotation
Orthography
Orthopedically Handicapped *USE Physically Disabled*
Orthopsychiatry
Oscilloscopes
Ear Ossicles *USE Middle Ear*
Osteoporosis
Significant **Others**
Otosclerosis *USE Ear Disorders*
Out of Body Experiences
Acting **Out**
Time **Out**
Psychotherapeutic **Outcomes**
Therapeutic Outcomes *USE Treatment Outcomes*
Treatment **Outcomes**
Outgroup Ingroup *USE Ingroup Outgroup*
Ingroup **Outgroup**
Outpatient Commitment
Outpatient Psychiatric Clinics *USE Psychiatric Clinics*
Outpatient Treatment
Commitment (Outpatient) *USE Outpatient Commitment*
Outpatients
Outreach Programs
Outward Bound *USE Wilderness Experience*
Ovariectomy
Ovaries
Ovary Disorders *USE Endocrine Sexual Disorders*
Over The Counter Drugs *USE Nonprescription Drugs*
Academic **Overachievement**
Overcorrection
Drug **Overdoses**
Overlearning
Overpopulation
Structured Overview *USE Advance Organizers*
Overweight *USE Obesity*
Ovulation
Owls
Ownership
Oxazepam
Amine **Oxidase** Inhibitors
Cytochrome **Oxidase**
Monoamine **Oxidase** Inhibitors
Oxidases
Monoamine **Oxidases**
Oxidopamine *USE Hydroxydopamine (6-)*
Oxilapine *USE Loxapine*
Oxygen
Oxygenation
Oxytocin
Substance **P**
Artificial **Pacemakers**
Pacific Islands
South **Pacific**
Pacifism
Pain
Pain Management
Pain Measurement
Pain Perception
Pain Receptors *USE Nociceptors*
Pain Relieving Drugs *USE Analgesic Drugs*

Pain Thresholds
Back **Pain**
Chronic **Pain**
Myofascial **Pain**
Psychogenic Pain *USE Somatoform Pain Disorder*
Somatoform **Pain** Disorder
Painting (Art)
Paired Associate Learning
Pakistan
Cleft **Palate**
Palestinians *USE Arabs*
Palliative Care
Globus **Pallidus**
Palm (Anatomy)
Palsy *USE Paralysis*
Cerebral **Palsy**
Progressive Supranuclear **Palsy**
Panama
Pancreas
Pancreozymin *USE Cholecystokinin*
Panic
Panic Disorder
Pantherine *USE Muscimol*
Papaverine
Papua New Guinea
Parachlorophenylalanine
Paradigmatic Techniques *USE Paradoxical Techniques*
Paradoxical Sleep *USE REM Sleep*
Paradoxical Techniques
Paragraphs
Paraguay
Paraldehyde *USE Anticonvulsive Drugs*
Paralegal Personnel *USE Legal Personnel*
Motion **Parallax**
Paralysis
Paralysis Agitans *USE Parkinsons Disease*
Paralysis (Infantile) *USE Poliomyelitis*
Hysterical **Paralysis**
Infantile Paralysis *USE Poliomyelitis*
Dementia Paralytica *USE General Paresis*
Paramedical Personnel
Paramedical Sciences
Parameter Estimation *USE Statistical Estimation*
Response **Parameters**
Statistical Sample **Parameters**
Stimulus **Parameters**
Parametric Statistical Tests
Paranoia
Paranoia (Psychosis)
Climacteric Paranoia *USE Involutional Paranoid Psychosis*
Paranoid Disorder *USE Paranoia (Psychosis)*
Paranoid Personality
Paranoid Schizophrenia
Acute Paranoid Disorder *USE Paranoia (Psychosis)*
Atypical Paranoid Disorder *USE Paranoia (Psychosis)*
Involutional **Paranoid** Psychosis
Shared Paranoid Disorder *USE Folie A Deux*
Paraphilias *USE Sexual Deviations*
Paraplegia
Paraprofessional Education
Paraprofessional Personnel
Parapsychological Phenomena
Parapsychology
ESP (Parapsychology) *USE Extrasensory Perception*
Parasitic Disorders
Parasitism *USE Biological Symbiosis*
Parasuicide *USE Attempted Suicide*
Parasympathetic Nervous System
Parasympatholytic Drugs *USE Cholinergic Blocking Drugs*
Parasympathomimetic Drugs *USE Cholinomimetic Drugs*
Parathion
Parathyroid Disorders
Parathyroid Glands
Parathyroid Hormone
Parent Attitude Research Instrument
Parent Child Communication
Parent Child Relations
Parent Educational Background
Parent Effectiveness Training *USE Parent Training*
Parent School Relationship
Parent Training
Parental Absence
Parental Attitudes
Parental Authoritarianism *USE Parental Permissiveness*
Parental Characteristics
Parental Expectations
Parental Influence *USE Parent Child Relations*
Parental Investment
Parental Occupation
Parental Permissiveness
Parental Role
Animal **Parental** Behavior
Authoritarianism (Parental) *USE Parental Permissiveness*
Parenthood Status
Delayed **Parenthood**
Parenting Skills
Parents
Adoptive **Parents**
Birth Parents *USE Biological Family*
Expectant **Parents**
Foster **Parents**
Gay Parents *USE Homosexual Parents*
Homosexual **Parents**
Lesbian Parents *USE Homosexual Parents*
Single **Parents**
Surrogate **Parents** (Humans)
General **Paresis**
Pargyline
Parietal Lobe
Parkinsonism
Parkinsons Disease
Parks (Recreational) *USE Recreation Areas*
Parochial School Education *USE Private School Education*
Parole
Parole Officers
Parolees *USE Parole*
Paroxetine
Paroxysmal Sleep *USE Narcolepsy*
Partial Hospitalization
Partial Reinforcement *USE Reinforcement Schedules*
Partially Hearing Impaired
Partially Sighted
Participation
Athletic **Participation**
Client **Participation**
Group **Participation**
Patient Participation *USE Client Participation*
Political **Participation**
Participative Management
Political **Parties**
Partner Abuse
Parturition *USE Birth*
Democratic Party *USE Political Parties*
Independent Party (Political) *USE Political Parties*
Republican Party *USE Political Parties*
Rites of **Passage**
Passive Aggressive Personality
Passive Avoidance *USE Avoidance Conditioning*
Passiveness
Pastoral Counseling

Pastors *USE Ministers (Religion)*
Paternal Investment
USE Parental Investment
Animal **Paternal** Behavior
Path Analysis
Pathogenesis *USE Etiology*
Pathological Gambling
Pathologists
Pathology
Afferent **Pathways**
Efferent **Pathways**
Maze **Pathways**
Motor Pathways *USE Efferent Pathways*
Neural **Pathways**
Sensory Pathways *USE Afferent Pathways*
Patient Abuse
Patient Attitudes *USE Client Attitudes*
Patient Care Planning
USE Treatment Planning
Patient Characteristics
USE Client Characteristics
Patient Dropouts
USE Treatment Dropouts
Patient Education *USE Client Education*
Patient History
Patient Participation
USE Client Participation
Patient Records *USE Client Records*
Patient Rights *USE Client Rights*
Patient Satisfaction
USE Client Satisfaction
Patient Seclusion
Patient Selection
Patient Therapist Interaction
USE Psychotherapeutic Processes
Patient Therapist Sexual Relations
USE Professional Client Sexual Relations
Patient Transfer *USE Client Transfer*
Patient Treatment Matching
USE Client Treatment Matching
Patient Violence
Dentist Patient Interaction
USE Therapeutic Processes
Nurse Patient Interaction
USE Therapeutic Processes
Physician Patient Interaction
USE Therapeutic Processes
Seclusion (Patient) *USE Patient Seclusion*
Therapist Patient Interaction
USE Psychotherapeutic Processes
Therapist Patient Sexual Relations
USE Professional Client Sexual Relations
Patients
Dying Patients *USE Terminally Ill Patients*
Geriatric **Patients**
Hospitalized **Patients**
Medical **Patients**
Psychiatric **Patients**
Surgical **Patients**
Terminally Ill **Patients**
Patriarchy
Pattern Discrimination
Stimulus Pattern *USE Stimulus Variability*
Alcohol Drinking **Patterns**
Dissociative **Patterns**
Transgenerational **Patterns**
Wilson **Patterson** Conservatism Scale
Speech **Pauses**
Pavlov (Ivan)
Pavlovian Conditioning
USE Classical Conditioning
Pay *USE Salaries*
Equity **(Payment)**
PCP *USE Phencyclidine*
Peabody Picture Vocabulary Test
Peace
Peace Corps
Pearson Prod Moment Correl Coeff
USE Statistical Correlation
Pecking Order *USE Animal Dominance*
Angina **Pectoris**
Pederasty *USE Pedophilia*
Pedestrian Accidents
Pedestrians
Pediatricians
Pediatrics
Pedophilia
Peer Counseling
Peer Evaluation
Peer Pressure
Peer Relations
Peer Review *USE Peer Evaluation*
Peer Tutoring
Peers
Pellagra
Pemoline
Death Penalty *USE Capital Punishment*
Penguins
Penicillins
Penis
Penis Envy
Erection **(Penis)**
Penitentiaries *USE Prisons*
Penology
Employee **Pension** Plans
Pentazocine
Pentobarbital
Sodium Pentobarbital *USE Pentobarbital*
Pentothal *USE Thiopental*
Pentylenetetrazol
Peoples Republic of China
Peptic Ulcers *USE Gastrointestinal Ulcers*
Peptides
Perception
Auditory **Perception**
Brightness **Perception**
Color **Perception**
Contour Perception
USE Form and Shape Perception
Depth **Perception**
Direction **Perception**
Distance **Perception**
Extrasensory **Perception**
Face **Perception**
Form and Shape **Perception**
Frostig Development Test Vis **Percept**
Gustatory Perception *USE Taste Perception*
Haptic Perception *USE Cutaneous Sense*
Illusions **(Perception)**
Interpersonal Perception *USE Social Perception*
Kinesthetic **Perception**
Loudness **Perception**
Motion **Perception**
Movement Perception *USE Motion Perception*
Music **Perception**
Numerosity **Perception**
Olfactory **Perception**
Pain **Perception**
Pitch **Perception**
Risk **Perception**
Role **Perception**
Self **Perception**
Signal Detection **(Perception)**
Smell Perception *USE Olfactory Perception*
Social **Perception**
Somesthetic **Perception**
Spatial **Perception**
Spatial Orientation **(Perception)**
Speech **Perception**
Subliminal **Perception**
Tactual **Perception**
Taste **Perception**
Temperature **Perception**
Texture **Perception**
Time **Perception**
Visual **Perception**
Weight **Perception**
Perceptiveness (Personality)

Perceptual Aftereffect
Perceptual Closure
Perceptual Constancy
Perceptual Development
Perceptual Discrimination
Perceptual Distortion
Perceptual Disturbances
Perceptual Fill *USE Perceptual Closure*
Perceptual Localization
Perceptual Measures
Perceptual Motor Coordination
Perceptual Motor Development
Perceptual Motor Learning
Perceptual Motor Measures
USE Sensorimotor Measures
Perceptual Motor Processes
Perceptual Neglect *USE Sensory Neglect*
Perceptual Orientation
Perceptual Stimulation
Perceptual Style
Purdue **Perceptual** Motor Survey
Perfectionism
Performance
Performance Anxiety
Performance Tests
Athletic **Performance**
Group **Performance**
Job **Performance**
Motor **Performance**
Organizational Performance
USE Organizational Effectiveness
Sport Performance *USE Athletic Performance*
Performing Arts *USE Arts*
Periaqueductal Gray
Perinatal Period
Critical **Period**
Perinatal **Period**
Postnatal **Period**
Peripheral Nerve Disorders
Peripheral Nervous System
Peripheral Vision
Computer **Peripheral** Devices
Object **Permanence**
Parental **Permissiveness**
Perpetrators
Perphenazine
Persecution
Perseverance *USE Persistence*
Perseveration
Persistence
Persistent Mental Illness
USE Chronic Mental Illness
Person Centered Psychotherapy
USE Client Centered Therapy
Person Environment Fit
Goodenough Harris Draw A **Person** Test
Personal Adjustment
USE Emotional Adjustment
Personal Computers
USE Microcomputers
Personal Construct Theory
USE Personality Theory
Personal Growth Techniques
USE Human Potential Movement
Personal Orientation Inventory
Personal Space
Personal Therapy
Personal Values
Edwards **Personal** Preference Schedule
Identity (Personal) *USE Self Concept*
Personality
Personality Assessment
USE Personality Measures
Personality Change
Personality Correlates
Personality Development
Personality Disorders
Personality Factors
USE Personality Traits

Personality Measures
Personality Processes
Personality Theory
Personality Traits
Adaptability **(Personality)**
Anankastic Personality
USE Obsessive Compulsive Personality
Antisocial **Personality**
Asthenic Personality *USE Personality Disorders*
Autonomy (Personality)
USE Independence (Personality)
Avoidant **Personality**
Big Five Personality Model
USE Five Factor Personality Model
California Test of **Personality**
Childrens **Personality** Questionnaire
Compulsive Personality Disorder
USE Obsessive Compulsive Personality
Conformity **(Personality)**
Conscious **(Personality** Factor)
Counselor Personality *USE Counselor Characteristics*
Cyclothymic **Personality**
Dependency **(Personality)**
Dependent **Personality**
Differential Personality Inventory
USE Nonprojective Personality Measures
Edwards **Personality** Inventory
Emotionality **(Personality)**
Explosive **Personality**
Eysenck **Personality** Inventory
Five Factor **Personality** Model
Flexibility (Personality) *USE Adaptability (Personality)*
High Sch **Personality** Questionnaire
Histrionic Personality Disorder
USE Hysterical Personality
Hysterical **Personality**
Inadequate **Personality**
Independence **(Personality)**
Inhibition **(Personality)**
Insensitivity (Personality) *USE Sensitivity (Personality)*
Intermittent Explosive Personality *USE Explosive Personality*
Masochistic **Personality**
Maudsley **Personality** Inventory
Minn Multiphasic **Personality** Inven
Multiple Personality
USE Dissociative Identity Disorder
Narcissistic **Personality**
NEO **Personality** Inventory
Nonconformity **(Personality)**
Nonprojective **Personality** Measures
Obsessive Compulsive **Personality**
Omnibus **Personality** Inventory
Paranoid **Personality**
Passive Aggressive **Personality**
Perceptiveness **(Personality)**
Projective **Personality** Measures
Psychoanalytic **Personality** Factors
Rigidity **(Personality)**
Sadomasochistic **Personality**
Schizoid **Personality**
Schizotypal **Personality**
Self Monitoring **(Personality)**
Sensitivity **(Personality)**
Sixteen **Personality** Factors Question
Split Personality
USE Dissociative Identity Disorder
Stimulation Seeking (Personality) *USE Sensation Seeking*
Teacher **Personality**
Therapist Personality *USE Therapist Characteristics*
Type A Personality *USE Coronary Prone Behavior*
Type B Personality *USE Coronary Prone Behavior*
Unconscious **(Personality** Factor)
Personnel
Personnel Development
USE Personnel Training
Personnel Evaluation
Personnel Management
Personnel Placement
Personnel Promotion

Personnel Recruitment
Personnel Selection
Personnel Supply
Personnel Termination
Personnel Training
Personnel Turnover
USE Employee Turnover
Accreditation (Education **Personnel)**
Aerospace **Personnel**
Air Force **Personnel**
Army **Personnel**
Aviation Personnel *USE Aerospace Personnel*
Business and Industrial **Personnel**
Clerical **Personnel**
Coast Guard **Personnel**
Disabled **Personnel**
Domestic Service **Personnel**
Educational **Personnel**
Enlisted Military **Personnel**
Government **Personnel**
Health **Personnel**
Health **Personnel** Attitudes
Home Care **Personnel**
Law Enforcement **Personnel**
Lay Religious **Personnel**
Legal **Personnel**
Management **Personnel**
Marine **Personnel**
Medical **Personnel**
Medical **Personnel** Supply
Mental Health **Personnel**
Mental Health **Personnel** Supply
Military **Personnel**
Military Medical **Personnel**
Navy **Personnel**
Nonprofessional **Personnel**
Paralegal Personnel *USE Legal Personnel*
Paramedical **Personnel**
Paraprofessional **Personnel**
Police **Personnel**
Prison **Personnel**
Professional **Personnel**
Religious **Personnel**
Sales **Personnel**
Secretarial **Personnel**
Service **Personnel**
Student **Personnel** Services
Technical **Personnel**
Technical Service **Personnel**
Volunteer **Personnel**
Volunteer Civilian **Personnel**
Volunteer Military **Personnel**
Divorced **Persons**
Single **Persons**
Perspective Taking *USE Role Taking*
Linear **Perspective**
Time **Perspective**
Visual Perspective *USE Linear Perspective*
Perspiration *USE Sweat*
Persuasion Therapy
Persuasive Communication
Peru
Perversions (Sexual)
USE Sexual Deviations
Pessimism
Pesticides *USE Insecticides*
Pet Therapy
USE Animal Assisted Therapy
Petit Mal Epilepsy
Pets
Peyote
Phantom Limbs
Pharmacists
Pharmacology
Pharmacotherapy *USE Drug Therapy*
Pharyngeal Disorders
Pharynx
Phenaglycodol *USE Sedatives*
Phencyclidine
Phenelzine
Phenethylamines
Pheniprazine
Phenmetrazine
Phenobarbital
Parapsychological **Phenomena**
Phenomenology
Phenothiazine Derivatives
Phenotypes
Phenoxybenzamine
Phenylalanine
Phenylketonuria
Oligophrenia (Phenylpyruvic) *USE Phenylketonuria*
Phenytoin *USE Diphenylhydantoin*
Pheromones
Phi Coefficient
Philippines
Philosophies
Philosophy of Life *USE World View*
Logic **(Philosophy)**
Positivism **(Philosophy)**
Realism **(Philosophy)**
School **Phobia**
Snake Phobia *USE Ophidiophobia*
Social **Phobia**
Spider Phobia *USE Phobias*
Phobias
Phobic Neurosis *USE Phobias*
Phonemes
Words **(Phonetic** Units)
Phonetics
Phonics
Phonology
Phosphatases
Phosphatides
Phospholipids *USE Phosphatides*
Phosphorus
Phosphorylases
Photic Threshold *USE Illumination AND Visual Thresholds*
Photographic Art
Photographic Memory
USE Eidetic Imagery
Photographs
Photopic Stimulation
Photoreceptors
Phototherapy
Phrases
Phrenic Nerve *USE Spinal Nerves*
Phylogenesis
Physical Abuse
Physical Agility
Physical Appearance
Physical Attractiveness
Physical Comfort
Physical Contact
Physical Development
Physical Dexterity
Physical Disabilities (Attit Toward)
Physical Disfigurement
Physical Disorders
Physical Divisions (Geographic)
USE Geography
Physical Education
Physical Endurance
Physical Examination
Physical Exercise *USE Exercise*
Physical Fitness
Physical Growth
USE Physical Development
Physical Handicaps (Attit Toward)
USE Physical Disabilities (Attit Toward)
Physical Illness *USE Physical Disorders*
Physical Illness (Attitudes Toward)
Physical Maturity
Physical Mobility
Physical Restraint
Physical Strength
Physical Therapists

ROTATED ALPHABETICAL TERMS SECTION

Physical Therapy
Physical Trauma *USE Injuries*
Physical Treatment Methods
Physically Disabled
Physically Handicapped
USE Physically Disabled
Physician Patient Interaction
USE Therapeutic Processes
Physicians
Family **Physicians**
Physicists
Physics
Physiological Aging
Physiological Arousal
Physiological Correlates
Physiological Psychology
Physiological Stress
Absorption **(Physiological)**
Excitation (Physiological) *USE Physiological Arousal*
Sexual Disorders (Physiological) *USE Genital Disorders*
Physiology
Physiotherapy *USE Physical Therapy*
Physique
Physostigmine
Piaget (Jean)
Piagetian Tasks
Piano *USE Musical Instruments*
Pica
Picketing *USE Social Demonstrations*
Picks Disease
Picrotoxin
Pictorial Stimuli
Peabody **Picture** Vocabulary Test
Rosenzweig **Picture** Frustration Study
Blacky Pictures Test
USE Projective Personality Measures
Motion **Pictures**
Motion **Pictures** (Educational)
Motion **Pictures** (Entertainment)
Pigeons
Pigments
Pigs
Guinea **Pigs**
Pilocarpine
Aircraft **Pilots**
Pimozide
Pineal Body
Pinealectomy
Piperazines
Pipradrol
Piracetam
Pitch Discrimination
Pitch (Frequency)
Pitch Perception
Speech **Pitch**
Pituitary Disorders
Pituitary Dwarfism *USE Hypopituitarism*
Pituitary Gland
Pituitary Gland Surgery
USE Hypophysectomy
Pituitary Hormones
Hypothalamo **Pituitary** Adrenal System
PKU (Hereditary Disorder)
USE Phenylketonuria
Place Conditioning
Place Disorientation
Conditioned Place Preference *USE Place Conditioning*
Placebo
Educational **Placement**
Personnel **Placement**
Placenta
Planarians
Planned Behavior
Discharge **Planning**
Educational Program **Planning**
Environmental **Planning**
Family **Planning**
Family **Planning** Attitudes
Management **Planning**
Patient Care Planning *USE Treatment Planning*
Program Planning *USE Program Development*
Treatment **Planning**
Urban **Planning**
Employee Pension **Plans**
Group Health Plans
USE Health Maintenance Organizations
Lesson **Plans**
Blood **Plasma**
Plastic Surgery
Nervous System Plasticity *USE Neural Plasticity*
Neural **Plasticity**
Blood **Platelets**
Play *USE Recreation*
Play Therapy
Animal **Play**
Childhood **Play** Behavior
Childhood **Play** Development
Doll **Play**
Playgrounds
Role **Playing**
Stage Plays *USE Theatre*
Pleasure
Plethysmography
Brachial Plexus *USE Spinal Nerves*
Celiac Plexus *USE Autonomic Ganglia*
Cervical Plexus *USE Spinal Nerves*
Choroid Plexus *USE Cerebral Ventricles*
Hypogastric Plexus *USE Autonomic Ganglia*
Lumbrosacral Plexus *USE Spinal Nerves*
Myenteric Plexus *USE Autonomic Ganglia*
Submucous Plexus *USE Autonomic Ganglia*
Cultural Pluralism *USE Multiculturalism*
PMS *USE Premenstrual Tension*
Pneumoencephalography
Pneumonia
Poetry
Poetry Therapy
Point Biserial Correlation
Poisoning *USE Toxic Disorders*
Barbiturate **Poisoning**
Carbon Monoxide **Poisoning**
Lead **Poisoning**
Mercury **Poisoning**
Poisons
Poisson Distribution
USE Skewed Distribution
Poland
Police Interrogation
USE Legal Interrogation
Police Personnel
Policy Making
Foreign **Policy** Making
Government **Policy** Making
Health Care **Policy**
Mental Health Care Policy *USE Health Care Policy*
Organizational Policy Making *USE Policy Making*
Public Policy *USE Government Policy Making*
Poliomyelitis
Political Assassination
Political Attitudes
Political Campaigns
Political Candidates
Political Conservatism
Political Debates *USE Debates*
Political Divisions (Geographic)
USE Geography
Political Economic Systems
Political Elections
Political Involvement
USE Political Participation
Political Issues
Political Liberalism
Political Participation
Political Parties
Political Processes
Political Psychology
Political Radicalism
Political Refugees *USE Refugees*

Political Revolution
Political Socialization
Independent Party (Political) *USE Political Parties*
Politicians
Politics
Pollution
Polydipsia
Polydrug Abuse
Polygamy
Polygraphs
Polyphagia *USE Hyperphagia*
Pons
Data Pooling *USE Meta Analysis*
Popularity
Population
Population Characteristics *USE Demographic Characteristics*
Population Control *USE Birth Control*
Population Density *USE Social Density*
Population Genetics
Population Shifts *USE Human Migration*
Population (Statistics)
At Risk **Populations**
High Risk Populations *USE At Risk Populations*
Pornography
Porphyria
Porpoises
Porteus Maze Test
Portugal
Serial **Position** Effect
Positive and Negative Symptoms
Positive Reinforcement
Positive Transfer
Negative and Positive Symptoms *USE Positive and Negative Symptoms*
Positivism
Positivism (Philosophy)
Positron Emission Tomography *USE Tomography*
Possession *USE Ownership*
Demonic Possession *USE Spirit Possession*
Spirit **Possession**
Postactivation Potentials
Postganglionic Autonomic Fibers *USE Autonomic Ganglia*
Postgraduate Students
Postgraduate Training
Posthypnotic Suggestions
Postmodernism
Postnatal Dysphoria *USE Postpartum Depression*
Postnatal Period
Postpartum Depression
Postpartum Psychosis *USE Postpartum Depression*
Postsurgical Complications
Posttesting
Posttraumatic Stress Disorder
Posttreatment Followup
Posture
Threat **Postures**
Potassium
Potassium Ions
Potential Dropouts
Abuse Potential (Drugs) *USE Drug Abuse Liability*
Achievement **Potential**
Human **Potential** Movement
Readiness Potential *USE Contingent Negative Variation*
Skin **Potential**
Auditory Evoked **Potentials**
Cortical Evoked **Potentials**
Evoked **Potentials**
Motor Evoked Potentials *USE Somatosensory Evoked Potentials*
Olfactory Evoked **Potentials**
Postactivation **Potentials**
Somatosensory Evoked **Potentials**
Visual Evoked **Potentials**
Drug Potentiation *USE Drug Interactions*
Long Term Potentiation *USE Postactivation Potentials*
Short Term Potentiation *USE Postactivation Potentials*
Poverty
Poverty Areas
Power
Abuse of **Power**
Black **Power** Movement
Statistical **Power**
Practical Knowledge *USE Procedural Knowledge*
Practice
Distributed **Practice**
Experience (Practice) *USE Practice*
Massed **Practice**
Private **Practice**
Childrearing **Practices**
Feeding **Practices**
Religious **Practices**
Practicum Supervision
General **Practitioners**
Prader Willi Syndrome
Dementia Praecox *USE Schizophrenia*
Pragmatics
Pragmatism
Praise
Prayer
Praying Mantis *USE Mantis*
Preadolescents
Precocious Development
Precognition
Preconditioning
Sensory Preconditioning *USE Preconditioning*
Serotonin **Precursors**
Animal **Predatory** Behavior
Predelinquent Youth
Predictability (Measurement)
Prediction
Prediction Errors
Academic Achievement **Prediction**
Occupational Success **Prediction**
Predictive Validity
Predisposition
Prednisolone
Preference Measures
Career Preference *USE Occupational Preference*
Conditioned Place Preference *USE Place Conditioning*
Edwards Personal **Preference** Schedule
Kuder **Preference** Record
Occupational **Preference**
Vocational Preference *USE Occupational Preference*
Welsh Figure **Preference** Test
Preferences
Aesthetic **Preferences**
Brand **Preferences**
Food **Preferences**
Preferred Rewards
Least **Preferred** Coworker Scale
Prefrontal Cortex
Preganglionic Autonomic Fibers *USE Autonomic Ganglia*
Pregnancy
Adolescent **Pregnancy**
False Pregnancy *USE Pseudocyesis*
Teenage Pregnancy *USE Adolescent Pregnancy*
Prejudice
Religious **Prejudices**
Preliminary Scholastic Aptitude Test *USE Coll Ent Exam Bd Scholastic Apt Test*
Premarital Counseling
Premarital Intercourse
Premature Birth
Premature Ejaculation
Premenstrual Syndrome *USE Premenstrual Tension*
Premenstrual Tension
Premorbidity

Prenatal Care
Prenatal Development
Prenatal Developmental Stages
Prenatal Diagnosis
Prenatal Exposure
Preoptic Area
Prepulse Inhibition
Presbyterians *USE Protestants*
Preschool Age Children
Preschool Education
Preschool Students
Preschool Teachers
Wechsler **Preschool** Primary Scale
Prescribing (Drugs)
Prescription Drugs
Symptom Prescription *USE Paradoxical Techniques*
Presenile Dementia
Stereoscopic **Presentation**
Stimulus **Presentation** Methods
Tachistoscopic **Presentation**
Self **Preservation**
Preservice Teachers
Presidential Debates *USE Debates*
Pressoreceptors *USE Baroreceptors*
Pressors (Drugs)
USE Vasoconstrictor Drugs
Pressure Sensation
Barometric Pressure *USE Atmospheric Conditions*
Blood **Pressure**
Blood **Pressure** Disorders
Diastolic **Pressure**
Peer **Pressure**
Sound Pressure Level *USE Loudness*
Systolic **Pressure**
Prestige (Occupational)
USE Occupational Status
Pretesting
Pretraining (Therapy)
USE Client Education
Prevention
Accident **Prevention**
AIDS **Prevention**
Crime **Prevention**
Drug Abuse **Prevention**
Fire **Prevention**
Primary Mental Health **Prevention**
Relapse **Prevention**
Substance Abuse Prevention *USE Drug Abuse Prevention*
Suicide **Prevention**
Suicide **Prevention** Centers
Preventive Medicine
Price *USE Costs and Cost Analysis*
Pride
Priests
Primacy Effect
Primal Therapy
Primary Health Care
Primary Mental Health Prevention
Primary Reinforcement
Primary School Students
Primary Schools *USE Elementary Schools*
Wechsler Preschool **Primary** Scale
Primates (Nonhuman)
Primidone
Priming
Semantic **Priming**
School **Principals**
Printed Communications Media
Printing (Handwriting)
Prismatic Stimulation
Prison Personnel
Inmates (Prison) *USE Prisoners*
Prisoners
Prisoners Dilemma Game
Prisoners of War
Prisons
Privacy
Private Practice
Private School Education
Private Sector
Privileged Communication
Proactive Inhibition
Probability
Probability Judgment
Probability Learning
Response **Probability**
Statistical **Probability**
Probation
Probation Officers
Probenecid
Problem Drinking *USE Alcohol Abuse*
Problem Solving
Anagram **Problem** Solving
Group **Problem** Solving
Mooney **Problem** Check List
Behavior **Problems**
Social Problems *USE Social Issues*
Procaine
Procedural Knowledge
Conference Proceedings
USE Professional Meetings and Symposia
Process Psychosis
Process Schizophrenia
USE Process Psychosis AND Schizophrenia
Classification (Cognitive **Process)**
Educational Process *USE Education*
Insight (Psychotherapeutic **Process)**
Associative **Processes**
Balance (Motor Processes) *USE Equilibrium*
Cognitive **Processes**
Employment Processes *USE Personnel Recruitment*
Human Information Processes *USE Cognitive Processes*
Intersensory **Processes**
Legal **Processes**
Legislative **Processes**
Motor **Processes**
Perceptual Motor **Processes**
Personality **Processes**
Political **Processes**
Psychomotor Processes
USE Perceptual Motor Processes
Psychotherapeutic **Processes**
Sensorimotor Processes
USE Perceptual Motor Processes
Social **Processes**
Therapeutic **Processes**
Automated Information **Processing**
Cognitive **Processing** Speed
Data **Processing**
Information Processing Speed
USE Cognitive Processing Speed
Speech **Processing** (Mechanical)
Word **Processing**
Prochlorperazine
Procrastination
Pearson Prod Moment Correl Coeff
USE Statistical Correlation
Product Design
Consumer Product Design *USE Product Design*
Employee **Productivity**
Profanity
Professional Certification
Professional Client Sexual Relations
Professional Communication
USE Scientific Communication
Professional Competence
Professional Consultation
Professional Criticism
Professional Criticism Reply
Professional Development
Professional Ethics
Professional Examinations
Professional Fees
Professional Identity
Professional Liability
Professional Licensing

Professional Meetings and Symposia
Professional Newsletters
USE Scientific Communication
Professional Organizations
Professional Orientation
USE Theoretical Orientation
Professional Personnel
Professional Referral
Professional Specialization
Professional Standards
Professional Supervision
Assistance Seeking (Professional) *USE Health Care Utilization*
Communication (Professional)
USE Scientific Communication
Identity (Professional) *USE Professional Identity*
Specialization (Professional)
USE Professional Specialization
Health Care Professionals *USE Health Personnel*
Impaired **Professionals**
Professors *USE College Teachers*
Language **Proficiency**
Limited English Proficiency *USE Language Proficiency*
Profiles (Measurement)
Profoundly Mentally Retarded
Progestational Hormones
Progesterone
Progestins *USE Progestational Hormones*
Prognosis
Program Development
Program Evaluation
Program Planning
USE Program Development
Educational **Program** Accreditation
Educational **Program** Evaluation
Educational **Program** Planning
Mental Health **Program** Evaluation
Programed Instruction
Programed Textbooks
Programing (Computer)
USE Computer Programing
Computer **Programing**
Computer **Programing** Languages
Neurolinguistic **Programing**
Accreditation (Educational Programs)
USE Educational Program Accreditation
Computer Programs *USE Computer Software*
Educational **Programs**
Employee Assistance **Programs**
Government **Programs**
Home Visiting **Programs**
Hospital **Programs**
Immersion Programs
USE Foreign Language Education
Independent Living **Programs**
Literacy **Programs**
Mental Health **Programs**
Outreach **Programs**
Psychiatric Hospital **Programs**
Social **Programs**
Token Economy **Programs**
Twelve Step **Programs**
Work Study Programs *USE Educational Programs*
Progressive Relaxation Therapy
Progressive Supranuclear Palsy
Raven **Progressive** Matrices
Raven Coloured **Progressive** Matrices
Project Follow Through
Project Head Start
Projection (Defense Mechanism)
Projective Identification
Projective Personality Measures
Projective Techniques
Projective Testing Technique
Prolactin
Proline
Prolixin *USE Fluphenazine*
Promazine
Promethazine
Promiscuity

Health **Promotion**
Job Promotion *USE Personnel Promotion*
Personnel **Promotion**
Prompting
Coronary **Prone** Behavior
Accident **Proneness**
Pronouns
Pronunciation
Proofreading
Propaganda
Skin Electrical **Properties**
Property *USE Ownership*
Self Fulfilling **Prophecies**
Propranolol
Proprioceptors
Prose
Prosencephalon *USE Forebrain*
Proserine *USE Neostigmine*
Prosocial Behavior
Prosody
Prosopagnosia
Prospective Studies
Prostaglandins
Prostate
Prostate Cancer Screening
USE Cancer Screening
Prostheses
Prostitution
Consumer **Protection**
Protective Services
Protein Deficiency Disorders
Protein Metabolism
Protein Sensitization
USE Anaphylactic Shock
Sensitization (Protein) *USE Anaphylactic Shock*
Proteinases
Proteins
Blood **Proteins**
Protest (Student) *USE Student Activism*
Student Protest *USE Student Activism*
Protestantism
Protestants
Protozoa
Munchausen Syndrome by **Proxy**
Prozac *USE Fluoxetine*
Pruritus
Pseudocyesis
Pseudodementia
Pseudohermaphroditism
USE Hermaphroditism
Pseudomemory *USE False Memory*
Pseudopregnancy *USE Pseudocyesis*
Pseudopsychopathic Schizophrenia
USE Schizophrenia
Psilocybin
Psychedelic Drugs
Psychedelic Experiences
Psychiatric Aides
Psychiatric Classifications (Taxon)
USE Psychodiagnostic Typologies
Psychiatric Clinics
Psychiatric Disorders
USE Mental Disorders
Psychiatric Evaluation
Psychiatric History *USE Patient History*
Psychiatric Hospital Admission
Psychiatric Hospital Discharge
Psychiatric Hospital Programs
Psychiatric Hospital Readmission
Psychiatric Hospital Staff
Psychiatric Hospitalization
Psychiatric Hospitals
Psychiatric Nurses
Psychiatric Patients
Psychiatric Report
USE Psychological Report
Psychiatric Residency
USE Medical Residency AND Psychiatric Training

Psychiatric Social Workers
Psychiatric Symptoms
Psychiatric Training
Psychiatric Units
Child Psychiatric Clinics *USE Child Guidance Clinics*
Commitment **(Psychiatric)**
Evaluation (Psychiatric) *USE Psychiatric Evaluation*
Hospital Psychiatric Units *USE Psychiatric Units*
Outpatient Psychiatric Clinics *USE Psychiatric Clinics*
Psychiatrists
Psychiatry
Adolescent **Psychiatry**
Biological **Psychiatry**
Child **Psychiatry**
Community **Psychiatry**
Comparative Psychiatry *USE Transcultural Psychiatry*
Consultation Liaison **Psychiatry**
Cultural Psychiatry *USE Transcultural Psychiatry*
Forensic **Psychiatry**
Geriatric **Psychiatry**
Social **Psychiatry**
Transcultural **Psychiatry**
Psychic Healing *USE Faith Healing*
Psychoactive Drugs *USE Drugs*
Psychoanalysis
Psychoanalysts
Psychoanalytic Interpretation
Psychoanalytic Personality Factors
Psychoanalytic Theory
Psychoanalytic Therapy *USE Psychoanalysis*
Psychoanalytic Training
Freudian **Psychoanalytic** School
Psychobiology
Psychodiagnosis
Clinical Judgment (Psychodiagnosis) *USE Psychodiagnosis*
Psychodiagnostic Interview
Psychodiagnostic Typologies
Psychodrama
Psychodynamics
Woodcock Johnson **Psychoed** Battery
Psychoeducation
Psychogalvanic Reflex *USE Galvanic Skin Response*
Psychogenesis
Psychogenic Pain *USE Somatoform Pain Disorder*
Psychohistory
Psychoimmunology *USE Psychoneuroimmunology*
Psychokinesis
Illinois Test **Psycholinguist** Abil
Psycholinguistics
Psychological Abuse *USE Emotional Abuse*
Psychological Adjustment *USE Emotional Adjustment*
Psychological Assessment
Psychological Autopsy
Psychological Correlates *USE Psychodynamics*
Psychological Development *USE Psychogenesis*
Psychological Endurance
Psychological Interpretation *USE Theoretical Interpretation*
Psychological Needs
Psychological Reactance
Psychological Report
Psychological Screening Inventory
Psychological Stress
Psychological Terminology
Psychological Testing *USE Psychometrics*
Assessment (Psychological) *USE Psychological Assessment*
Boundaries **(Psychological)**
California **Psychological** Inventory
Incorporation (Psychological) *USE Internalization*
Nomenclature (Psychological) *USE Psychological Terminology*
Resilience (Psychological) *USE Hardiness*
Psychologist Attitudes
Psychologists
Clinical **Psychologists**
Counseling **Psychologists**
Educational **Psychologists**
Experimental **Psychologists**
Industrial **Psychologists**
Military **Psychologists**
School **Psychologists**
Social **Psychologists**
Psychology
Psychology Education
Adolescent **Psychology**
Analytic Psychology *USE Jungian Psychology*
Applied **Psychology**
Child **Psychology**
Clinical **Psychology**
Clinical **Psychology** Grad Training
Clinical **Psychology** Internship
Cognitive **Psychology**
Community **Psychology**
Comparative **Psychology**
Consumer **Psychology**
Counseling **Psychology**
Cross Cultural **Psychology**
Depth **Psychology**
Developmental **Psychology**
Eclectic Psychology *USE Theoretical Orientation*
Ecological **Psychology**
Educational **Psychology**
Engineering **Psychology**
Environmental **Psychology**
Experimental **Psychology**
Folk **Psychology**
Forensic **Psychology**
Gestalt **Psychology**
Graduate **Psychology** Education
Health Care **Psychology**
History of **Psychology**
Humanistic **Psychology**
Individual **Psychology**
Industrial **Psychology**
Jungian **Psychology**
Legal Psychology *USE Forensic Psychology*
Mathematical **Psychology**
Medical **Psychology**
Military **Psychology**
Organizational Psychology *USE Industrial Psychology*
Physiological **Psychology**
Political **Psychology**
School **Psychology**
Self **Psychology**
Social **Psychology**
Sport **Psychology**
Transpersonal **Psychology**
Psychometrics
Psychomotor Development
Psychomotor Processes *USE Perceptual Motor Processes*
Psychoneuroimmunology
Psychoneurosis *USE Neurosis*
Psychopath *USE Antisocial Personality*
Psychopathology
Psychopathy *USE Antisocial Personality*
Autistic Psychopathy *USE Aspergers Syndrome*
Psychopharmacology
Psychophysical Measurement
Psychophysics
Psychophysiologic Disorders *USE Psychosomatic Disorders*
Psychophysiology
Toxic **Psychoses**
Psychosexual Behavior
Psychosexual Development
Psychosis
Acute **Psychosis**

Affective **Psychosis**
Alcoholic **Psychosis**
Brief Reactive Psychosis *USE Acute Psychosis*
Childhood **Psychosis**
Chronic **Psychosis**
Experimental **Psychosis**
Infantile Psychosis *USE Childhood Psychosis*
Involutional Paranoid **Psychosis**
Korsakoffs **Psychosis**
Manic Depressive Psychosis *USE Manic Depression*
Paranoia **(Psychosis)**
Postpartum Psychosis *USE Postpartum Depression*
Process **Psychosis**
Reactive **Psychosis**
Senile **Psychosis**
Symbiotic Infantile **Psychosis**
Traumatic Psychosis *USE Reactive Psychosis*
Psychosocial Development
Psychosocial Factors
Psychosocial Mental Retardation
Psychosocial Readjustment
Psychosocial Rehabilitation
Psychosocial Resocialization
USE Psychosocial Readjustment
Psychosomatic Disorders
Psychosomatic Medicine
Psychosurgery
Psychotherapeutic Breakthrough
Psychotherapeutic Counseling
Psychotherapeutic Neutrality
Psychotherapeutic Outcomes
Psychotherapeutic Processes
Psychotherapeutic Resistance
Psychotherapeutic Techniques
Psychotherapeutic Transference
Insight **(Psychotherapeutic** Process)
Neutrality (Psychotherapeutic)
USE Psychotherapeutic Neutrality
Psychotherapist Attitudes
Psychotherapist Trainees
USE Therapist Trainees
Psychotherapists
Psychotherapy
Psychotherapy (Individual)
USE Individual Psychotherapy
Psychotherapy Training
Adlerian **Psychotherapy**
Adolescent **Psychotherapy**
Analytical **Psychotherapy**
Brief **Psychotherapy**
Child **Psychotherapy**
Eclectic **Psychotherapy**
Experiential **Psychotherapy**
Expressive **Psychotherapy**
Geriatric **Psychotherapy**
Group **Psychotherapy**
Individual **Psychotherapy**
Individual Psychotherapy (Adlerian)
USE Adlerian Psychotherapy
Interpersonal **Psychotherapy**
Jungian Psychotherapy
USE Analytical Psychotherapy
Person Centered Psychotherapy
USE Client Centered Therapy
Reconstructive Psychotherapy *USE Psychotherapy*
Short Term Psychotherapy *USE Brief Psychotherapy*
Supportive **Psychotherapy**
Time Limited Psychotherapy *USE Brief Psychotherapy*
Psychotic Depressive Reaction
USE Major Depression
Psychotic Episode (Acute)
USE Acute Psychosis
Psychotic Symptoms
USE Psychiatric Symptoms
Acute Psychotic Episode *USE Acute Psychosis*
Psychoticism
Psychotomimetic Drugs
Psychotropic Drugs *USE Drugs*
PTA *USE Parent School Relationship*

Puberty
Pubescence *USE Sexual Development*
Public Attitudes *USE Public Opinion*
Public Health
Public Health Service Nurses
Public Health Services
Public Opinion
Public Policy
USE Government Policy Making
Public Relations
Public School Education
Public Sector
Public Speaking
Public Transportation
Public Welfare Services
USE Community Welfare Services
Fear of Public Speaking *USE Speech Anxiety*
Retraction of **Publication**
Puerto Rican Americans *USE Hispanics*
Puerto Rico
Hair **Pulling**
Pulmonary Disorders *USE Lung Disorders*
Pulmonary Emphysema
Pulmonary Tuberculosis
Arterial **Pulse**
Punishment
Capital **Punishment**
Corporal Punishment *USE Punishment*
Pupil Dilation
Pupil (Eye)
Purdue Perceptual Motor Survey
Purkinje Cells
Puromycin
Rotary **Pursuit**
Putamen
Pygmalion Effect
USE Self Fulfilling Prophecies
Pygmy Chimpanzees *USE Bonobos*
Color Pyramid Test
USE Projective Personality Measures
Pyramidal Tracts
Pyramidotomy
Pyromania
Q Sort Testing Technique
Cochran **Q** Test
Quaalude *USE Methaqualone*
Quadriplegia
Quails
Leadership **Qualities**
Quality Circles
USE Participative Management
Quality Control
Quality of Care
Quality of Education
USE Educational Quality
Quality of Life
Quality of Services
Quality of Work Life
Educational **Quality**
Service Quality *USE Quality of Services*
Quartimax Rotation
Fund Interper Rela Orientat Beh **Ques**
Sixteen Personality Factors **Question**
Questioning
Childrens Personality **Questionnaire**
General Health **Questionnaire**
High Sch Personality **Questionnaire**
Questionnaires
Opinion Questionnaires *USE Attitude Measures*
Quinidine *USE Alkaloids*
Quinine
Quinpirole
Intelligence **Quotient**
Rabbis
Rabbits
Race and Ethnic Discrimination
Race (Anthropological)
Race Attitudes
USE Racial and Ethnic Attitudes

Race Relations
USE Racial and Ethnic Relations
Racial and Ethnic Attitudes
Racial and Ethnic Differences
Racial and Ethnic Relations
Racial Discrimination
USE Race and Ethnic Discrimination
Racial Integration *USE Social Integration*
Racial Segregation (Schools)
USE School Integration
Segregation (Racial) *USE Social Integration*
Racism
Radial Nerve *USE Spinal Nerves*
Radiation
Radiation Therapy
Radical Movements
Political **Radicalism**
Radio
Radiography *USE Roentgenography*
Radiology
Rage *USE Anger*
Railroad Trains
Consciousness **Raising** Groups
Random Sampling
Wide **Range** Achievement Test
Rank Difference Correlation
Rank Order Correlation
Wilcoxon Sign **Rank** Test
Rape
Acquaintance **Rape**
Date Rape *USE Acquaintance Rape*
Raphe Nuclei
Rapid Eye Movement
Rapid Eye Movement Dreams
USE REM Dreams
Rapid Eye Movement Sleep
USE REM Sleep
Rapid Heart Rate *USE Tachycardia*
Rapport *USE Interpersonal Interaction*
Rasch Model *USE Item Response Theory*
Rat Learning
Birth **Rate**
Cardiac Rate *USE Heart Rate*
Death Rate *USE Mortality Rate*
Heart **Rate**
Heart **Rate** Affecting Drugs
Learning **Rate**
Mortality **Rate**
Rapid Heart Rate *USE Tachycardia*
Response Rate *USE Response Frequency*
Speech **Rate**
X Rated Materials *USE Pornography*
Metabolic **Rates**
Rating
Rating Scales
Kupfer Detre Self Rating Scale
USE Nonprojective Personality Measures
Zungs Self **Rating** Depression Scale
Ratio Reinforcement
USE Fixed Ratio Reinforcement OR Variable Ratio Reinforcement
Fixed **Ratio** Reinforcement
Variable **Ratio** Reinforcement
Ratiocination *USE Logical Thinking*
Rational Emotive Therapy
Rationalization
Rats
Norway **Rats**
Rauwolfia *USE Alkaloids*
Raven Coloured Progressive Matrices
Raven Progressive Matrices
Cathode Ray Tubes *USE Video Display Units*
X Ray Diagnosis *USE Roentgenography*
X Ray Therapy *USE Radiation Therapy*
Raynauds Disease
USE Cardiovascular Disorders
RDC *USE Research Diagnostic Criteria*
Psychological **Reactance**
Reaction Formation
Reaction Time
Fugue **Reaction**
Negative Therapeutic **Reaction**
Neurotic Depressive **Reaction**
Psychotic Depressive Reaction *USE Major Depression*
Anniversary Reactions *USE Anniversary Events*
Crisis (Reactions to) *USE Stress Reactions*
Drug Adverse Reactions *USE Side Effects (Drug)*
Separation **Reactions**
Stranger **Reactions**
Stress **Reactions**
Reactive Attachment Disorder
USE Failure to Thrive
Reactive Depression
Reactive Psychosis
Reactive Schizophrenia
USE Reactive Psychosis AND Schizophrenia
Brief Reactive Psychosis *USE Acute Psychosis*
Cardiovascular **Reactivity**
Readability
Readaptation *USE Adaptation*
Basal Readers *USE Reading Materials*
Readiness Potential
USE Contingent Negative Variation
Metropolitan **Readiness** Tests
Reading **Readiness**
School **Readiness**
Reading
Reading Ability
Reading Achievement
Reading Aloud *USE Oral Reading*
Reading Comprehension
Reading Development
Reading Disabilities
Reading Education
Reading Materials
Reading Measures
Reading Readiness
Reading Skills
Reading Speed
Gates MacGinitie **Reading** Tests
Oral **Reading**
Remedial **Reading**
Silent **Reading**
Selected **Readings**
Psychosocial **Readjustment**
Readmission (Hospital)
USE Hospital Admission
Facility Readmission *USE Facility Admission*
Psychiatric Hospital **Readmission**
Realism (Philosophy)
Reality
Reality Testing
Reality Therapy
Virtual **Reality**
Self Realization *USE Self Actualization*
Home **Reared** Mentally Retarded
Animal **Rearing**
Reasoning
Inductive Deductive **Reasoning**
Syllogistic Reasoning
USE Inductive Deductive Reasoning
Sexual Reassignment *USE Sex Change*
Authoritarianism Rebellion Scale
USE Nonprojective Personality Measures
Rebuttal *USE Professional Criticism Reply*
Recall (Learning)
Cued **Recall**
Dream **Recall**
Free **Recall**
Serial **Recall**
Recency Effect
Receptive Fields
Cutaneous **Receptive** Fields
Visual **Receptive** Fields
Animal Sexual **Receptivity**
Receptor Binding
Neural **Receptors**

ROTATED ALPHABETICAL TERMS SECTION

Pain Receptors *USE Nociceptors*
Genetic **Recessiveness**
Recidivism
Reciprocal Inhibition Therapy
Reciprocity
Recognition (Learning)
Automated Speech **Recognition**
Automatic Speaker Recognition *USE Automated Speech Recognition*
Face Recognition *USE Face Perception*
Kinship **Recognition**
Object **Recognition**
Sex **Recognition**
Species **Recognition**
Word **Recognition**
Reconstruction (Learning)
Reconstructive Psychotherapy *USE Psychotherapy*
Graduate **Record** Examination
Kuder Preference **Record**
Tape **Recorders**
Videotape **Recorders**
Academic Records *USE Student Records*
Client **Records**
Medical **Records**
Patient Records *USE Client Records*
Student **Records**
Recovery (Disorders)
Spontaneous **Recovery** (Learning)
Recreation
Recreation Areas
Recreation Therapy
Summer Camps **(Recreation)**
Recreational Day Camps *USE Summer Camps (Recreation)*
Childrens **Recreational** Games
Parks (Recreational) *USE Recreation Areas*
Military **Recruitment**
Personnel **Recruitment**
Teacher **Recruitment**
Recurrence (Disorders) *USE Relapse (Disorders)*
Recurrent Depression
Red Blood Cells *USE Erythrocytes*
Red Nucleus *USE Mesencephalon*
Anxiety Reducing Drugs *USE Tranquilizing Drugs*
Reductionism
Reemployment
Reenactments *USE Enactments*
Reentry Students
Job Reentry *USE Reemployment*
Reference Groups
Self **Reference**
Criterion **Referenced** Tests
Objective Referenced Tests *USE Criterion Referenced Tests*
Referral (Self) *USE Self Referral*
Professional **Referral**
Self **Referral**
Court **Referrals**
Reflectiveness
Achilles Tendon **Reflex**
Acoustic **Reflex**
Babinski **Reflex**
Blink Reflex *USE Eyeblink Reflex*
Conditioned Reflex *USE Conditioned Responses*
Eyeblink **Reflex**
Flexion **Reflex**
Hoffmanns **Reflex**
Intra Aural Muscle Reflex *USE Acoustic Reflex*
Orienting **Reflex**
Psychogalvanic Reflex *USE Galvanic Skin Response*
Stapedius Reflex *USE Acoustic Reflex*
Startle **Reflex**
Unconditioned Reflex *USE Reflexes*
Reflexes
Educational **Reform**
Reformatories
Refraction Errors
Light **Refraction**
Reframing *USE Paradoxical Techniques*
Refugees
Political Refugees *USE Refugees*
Refusal (Treatment) *USE Treatment Refusal*
School **Refusal**
Treatment **Refusal**
Neural Regeneration *USE Neural Development*
Medical Regimen Compliance *USE Treatment Compliance*
Arctic **Regions**
Geographic Regions *USE Geography*
Regression Analysis *USE Statistical Regression*
Regression (Defense Mechanism)
Age **Regression** (Hypnotic)
Linear **Regression**
Multiple **Regression**
Nonlinear **Regression**
Statistical **Regression**
Rehabilitation
Rehabilitation Centers
Rehabilitation Counseling
Rehabilitation Counselors
Rehabilitation Education
Alcohol **Rehabilitation**
Cognitive **Rehabilitation**
Drug **Rehabilitation**
Neuropsychological **Rehabilitation**
Psychosocial **Rehabilitation**
Vocational **Rehabilitation**
Rehearsal *USE Practice*
Reinforcement
Reinforcement Amounts
Reinforcement Delay
Reinforcement Schedules
Reinforcement (Vicarious) *USE Vicarious Experiences*
Concurrent **Reinforcement** Schedules
Continuous Reinforcement *USE Reinforcement Schedules*
Differential **Reinforcement**
Fixed Interval **Reinforcement**
Fixed Ratio **Reinforcement**
Intermittent Reinforcement *USE Reinforcement Schedules*
Interval Reinforcement *USE Fixed Interval Reinforcement OR Variable Interval Reinforcement*
Negative **Reinforcement**
Noncontingent **Reinforcement**
Nonverbal **Reinforcement**
Partial Reinforcement *USE Reinforcement Schedules*
Positive **Reinforcement**
Primary **Reinforcement**
Ratio Reinforcement *USE Fixed Ratio Reinforcement OR Variable Ratio Reinforcement*
Secondary **Reinforcement**
Self **Reinforcement**
Social **Reinforcement**
Token Reinforcement *USE Secondary Reinforcement*
Variable Interval **Reinforcement**
Variable Ratio **Reinforcement**
Verbal **Reinforcement**
Vicarious Reinforcement *USE Vicarious Experiences*
Reinnervation *USE Neural Development*
Halstead **Reitan** Neuropsych Battery
Rejection (Social) *USE Social Acceptance*
Social Rejection *USE Social Acceptance*
Relapse (Disorders)
Relapse Prevention
Diagnosis **Related** Groups
Work **Related** Illnesses
Family **Relations**
Father Child **Relations**

ROTATED ALPHABETICAL TERMS SECTION

Fund Interper **Rela** Orientat Beh Ques
Human **Relations** Training
Intergenerational **Relations**
International **Relations**
Labor Management **Relations**
Male Female **Relations**
Marital **Relations**
Mother Child **Relations**
Object **Relations**
Parent Child **Relations**
Patient Therapist Sexual Relations
USE Professional Client Sexual Relations
Peer **Relations**
Professional Client Sexual **Relations**
Public **Relations**
Race Relations *USE Racial and Ethnic Relations*
Racial and Ethnic **Relations**
Sibling **Relations**
Therapist Patient Sexual Relations
USE Professional Client Sexual Relations
Relationship Termination
Relationship Therapy
Barrett Lennard **Relationship** Invent
Breakup (Relationship)
USE Relationship Termination
Family Work **Relationship**
Job Family Relationship
USE Family Work Relationship
Parent School **Relationship**
Work Family Relationship
USE Family Work Relationship
Relativism
Relaxation
Relaxation Therapy
Muscle **Relaxation**
Muscle Relaxation Therapy
USE Relaxation Therapy
Progressive **Relaxation** Therapy
Muscle **Relaxing** Drugs
Relearning
Institutional **Release**
ACTH Releasing Factor
USE Corticotropin Releasing Factor
Corticotropin **Releasing** Factor
Interobserver Reliability *USE Interrater Reliability*
Interrater **Reliability**
Statistical **Reliability**
Test **Reliability**
Pain Relieving Drugs *USE Analgesic Drugs*
Religion
Confession **(Religion)**
Ministers **(Religion)**
Rites (Religion) *USE Religious Practices*
Rituals (Religion) *USE Religious Practices*
Religiosity
Religious Affiliation
Religious Beliefs
Religious Buildings
Religious Education
Religious Experiences
Religious Groups
Religious Literature
Religious Occupations
USE Religious Personnel
Religious Organizations
Religious Personnel
Religious Practices
Religious Prejudices
Lay **Religious** Personnel
REM *USE Rapid Eye Movement*
REM Dream Deprivation
REM Dreams
REM Sleep
Remarriage
Remedial Education
Remedial Reading
Remembering *USE Retention*
Reminiscence
Remission (Disorders)
Spontaneous **Remission**
Symptom **Remission**
Remote Associates Test
Renal Diseases *USE Kidney Diseases*
Renal Transplantation
USE Organ Transplantation
Repairmen
USE Technical Service Personnel
Repeated Measures
Bannister **Repertory** Grid
Compulsive **Repetition**
Estrogen Replacement Therapy
USE Hormone Therapy
Experimental **Replication**
Professional Criticism **Reply**
Annual **Report**
Case **Report**
Psychiatric Report *USE Psychological Report*
Psychological **Report**
Self **Report**
Abuse **Reporting**
Child Abuse **Reporting**
Repressed Memory
Repression (Defense Mechanism)
Repression Sensitization
Repression Sensitization Scale
Sexual **Reproduction**
Reproductive Technology
Reptiles
Dominican **Republic**
East German Democratic Republic *USE East Germany*
Peoples **Republic** of China
United Arab Republic *USE Egypt*
West German Federal Republic *USE West Germany*
Republican Party *USE Political Parties*
Union of Soviet Socialist **Republics**
Reputation
Research *USE Experimentation*
Research Design
USE Experimental Design
Research Diagnostic Criteria
Research Dropouts
USE Experimental Attrition
Research Methods *USE Methodology*
Research Subjects
USE Experimental Subjects
Consumer **Research**
Cross Disciplinary Research *USE Interdisciplinary Research*
Interdisciplinary **Research**
Multidisciplinary Research *USE Interdisciplinary Research*
Parent Attitude **Research** Instrument
Family **Resemblance**
Resentment *USE Hostility*
Reserpine
Residence Halls *USE Dormitories*
Medical **Residency**
Psychiatric Residency *USE Medical Residency AND Psychiatric Training*
Residential Care Attendants
USE Attendants (Institutions)
Residential Care Institutions
Schizophrenia (Residual Type) *USE Schizophrenia*
Resilience (Psychological) *USE Hardiness*
Resistance
Basal Skin **Resistance**
Psychotherapeutic **Resistance**
Skin **Resistance**
Treatment **Resistant** Depression
Treatment **Resistant** Disorders
Tricyclic Resistant Depression
USE Treatment Resistant Depression
Psychosocial Resocialization
USE Psychosocial Readjustment
Conflict **Resolution**
Resonance *USE Vibration*
Magnetic **Resonance** Imaging
Resource Allocation
Resource Teachers
Allocation of Resources *USE Resource Allocation*

ROTATED ALPHABETICAL TERMS SECTION

Human Resources *USE Personnel Management*
Self Respect *USE Self Esteem*
Respiration
Respiration Stimulating Drugs
Artificial **Respiration**
Respiratory Distress
Respiratory System
Respiratory Tract Disorders
Respite Care
Respondent Conditioning
USE Classical Conditioning
Response Amplitude
Response Bias
Response Consistency
USE Response Variability
Response Cost
Response Duration
Response Frequency
Response Generalization
Response Lag *USE Reaction Time*
Response Latency
Response Parameters
Response Probability
Response Rate *USE Response Frequency*
Response Set
Response Speed *USE Reaction Time*
Response Time *USE Reaction Time*
Response Variability
Electrodermal Response *USE Galvanic Skin Response*
Galvanic Skin **Response**
Item **Response** Theory
Latency (Response) *USE Response Latency*
Oculomotor Response *USE Eye Movements*
RT (Response) *USE Reaction Time*
Set (Response) *USE Response Set*
Responses
Alarm **Responses**
Conditioned **Responses**
Conditioned Emotional **Responses**
Emotional **Responses**
Mediated **Responses**
Orienting **Responses**
Unconditioned **Responses**
Responsibility
Criminal **Responsibility**
Work **Rest** Cycles
Restlessness
Dietary **Restraint**
Emotional Restraint *USE Emotional Control*
Physical **Restraint**
Restricted Environmental Stimulation
USE Stimulus Deprivation
Cognitive **Restructuring**
Knowledge of **Results**
Retail Stores *USE Retailing*
Retailing
Retaliation
Borderline Mental **Retardation**
Cultural Familial Mental Retardation
USE Psychosocial Mental Retardation
Mental **Retardation**
Mental **Retardation** (Attit Toward)
Psychosocial Mental **Retardation**
Retarded Speech Development
Borderline Mentally Retarded *USE Slow Learners*
Educable Mentally **Retarded**
Home Reared Mentally **Retarded**
Institutionalized Mentally **Retarded**
Mentally **Retarded**
Mildly Mentally Retarded
USE Educable Mentally Retarded
Moderately Mentally Retarded
USE Trainable Mentally Retarded
Profoundly Mentally **Retarded**
Severely Mentally **Retarded**
Trainable Mentally **Retarded**
Retention
Retention Measures
Retention (School) *USE School Retention*

Benton Revised Visual **Retention** Test
School **Retention**
Reticular Formation
Retina
Ganglion Cells **(Retina)**
Retinal Eccentricity
Retinal Image
Retinal Vessels *USE Arteries (Anatomy)*
Retirement
Retirement Communities
Retraction of Publication
Automated Information **Retrieval**
Retroactive Inhibition
Retrospective Studies
Rett Syndrome
Return to Home *USE Empty Nest*
Return to Work *USE Reemployment*
Serotonin **Reuptake** Inhibitors
Revenge *USE Retaliation*
Directed **Reverie** Therapy
Reversal Shift Learning
Life **Review**
Literature **Review**
Peer Review *USE Peer Evaluation*
Benton **Revised** Visual Retention Test
Political **Revolution**
Reward Allocation
Rewards
External **Rewards**
Extrinsic Rewards *USE External Rewards*
Internal **Rewards**
Intrinsic Rewards *USE Internal Rewards*
Monetary **Rewards**
Preferred **Rewards**
Rh Incompatibility
Rheoencephalography
Rhetoric
Rheumatic Fever
Rheumatism *USE Arthritis*
Rheumatoid Arthritis
Spearman Rho *USE Rank Difference Correlation*
Rhodopsin
Rhombencephalon *USE Hindbrain*
Rhythm
Rhythm Method
Alpha **Rhythm**
Delta **Rhythm**
Speech **Rhythm**
Theta **Rhythm**
Animal Biological **Rhythms**
Animal Circadian **Rhythms**
Biological **Rhythms**
Circadian Rhythms (Human)
USE Human Biological Rhythms
Daily Biological Rhythms (Animal)
USE Animal Circadian Rhythms
Human Biological **Rhythms**
Ribonucleic Acid
RNA (Ribonucleic Acid) *USE Ribonucleic Acid*
Costa **Rica**
Puerto Rican Americans *USE Hispanics*
Puerto **Rico**
Right Brain
Right to Treatment
Civil **Rights**
Civil **Rights** Movement
Client **Rights**
Human **Rights**
Patient Rights *USE Client Rights*
Visitation Rights *USE Child Visitation*
Rigidity (Muscles)
USE Muscle Contractions
Rigidity (Personality)
Riots
Risk Analysis
Risk Management
Risk Perception
Risk Taking
At **Risk** Populations

High Risk Populations *USE At Risk Populations*
Sexual **Risk** Taking
Risky Shift *USE Choice Shift*
Risperidone
Ritalin *USE Methylphenidate*
Ritanserin
Rites (Nonreligious)
Rites of Passage
Rites (Religion) *USE Religious Practices*
Birth **Rites**
Death **Rites**
Initiation **Rites**
Marriage **Rites**
Rituals (Nonreligious)
USE Rites (Nonreligious)
Rituals (Religion) *USE Religious Practices*
Rivalry
RNA (Ribonucleic Acid)
USE Ribonucleic Acid
Robbery *USE Theft*
Robins
Robotics
Rock Music
Body **Rocking**
Rod and Frame Test
Rodents
Rods (Eye)
Roentgenography
Rogerian Therapy
USE Client Centered Therapy
Rogers (Carl)
Rokeach Dogmatism Scale
Role Conflicts
Role Expectations
Role Models
Role Perception
Role Playing
Role Satisfaction
Role Strain *USE Role Conflicts*
Role Taking
Bem Sex **Role** Inventory
Counselor **Role**
Gender Role Attitudes *USE Sex Role Attitudes*
Parental **Role**
Sex **Role** Attitudes
Therapist **Role**
Roles
Gender Roles *USE Sex Roles*
Sex **Roles**
Roman Catholicism
Romance
Romania
Roommates
Dorsal **Roots**
Ventral **Roots**
Rorschach Test
Rosenzweig Picture Frustration Study
Rotary Pursuit
Body Rotation *USE Rotational Behavior*
Equimax **Rotation**
Mental **Rotation**
Oblique **Rotation**
Orthogonal **Rotation**
Quartimax **Rotation**
Statistical **Rotation**
Varimax **Rotation**
Rotational Behavior
ROTC Students
Rote Learning
Rotter Incomplete Sentences Blank
Rotter Intern Extern Locus Cont Scal
RT (Response) *USE Reaction Time*
Rubella
Rule Learning
USE Cognitive Hypothesis Testing
Rumors *USE Gossip*
Runaway Behavior
Running
Runways (Maze) *USE Maze Pathways*

Rural Development
USE Community Development
Rural Environments
Rwanda
Saccadic Eye Movements
USE Eye Movements
Saccharin
Tay Sachs Disease
USE Amaurotic Familial Idiocy
SAD *USE Seasonal Affective Disorder*
Sadism
Sexual **Sadism**
Sadness
Sadomasochism
Sadomasochistic Personality
Safety
Safety Belts
Safety Devices
Safety Warnings *USE Warnings*
Automobile Safety *USE Highway Safety*
Aviation **Safety**
Driver Safety *USE Highway Safety*
Highway **Safety**
Industrial Safety *USE Occupational Safety*
Occupational **Safety**
Water **Safety**
Saint Lucia
Saint Vincent
Salamanders
Salaries
Sales Personnel
Stimulus **Salience**
Saliva
Salivary Glands
Salivation
Salmon
Saltiness *USE Taste Perception*
El **Salvador**
American **Samoa**
Western **Samoa**
Sample Size
Matching to **Sample**
Statistical **Sample** Parameters
Statistical **Samples**
Sampling (Experimental)
Biased **Sampling**
Random **Sampling**
Sanatoriums
Sarcomas *USE Neoplasms*
SAT
USE Coll Ent Exam Bd Scholastic Apt Test
Satiation
Satisfaction
Client **Satisfaction**
Consumer **Satisfaction**
Customer Satisfaction *USE Consumer Satisfaction*
Job **Satisfaction**
Life **Satisfaction**
Marital **Satisfaction**
Need **Satisfaction**
Patient Satisfaction *USE Client Satisfaction*
Role **Satisfaction**
Sexual **Satisfaction**
Work Satisfaction *USE Job Satisfaction*
Saturation (Color) *USE Color Saturation*
Color **Saturation**
Saudi Arabia
Idiot **Savants**
Authoritarianism Rebellion Scale
USE Nonprojective Personality Measures
Barron Welsh Art **Scale**
California F **Scale**
Cattell Infant Intelligence Scale *USE Infant Intelligence Scale*
Childrens Manifest Anxiety **Scale**
Columbia Mental Maturity **Scale**
Edwards Social Desirability **Scale**
Infant Intelligence **Scale**

Kupfer Detre Self Rating Scale
USE Nonprojective Personality Measures
Least Preferred Coworker **Scale**
Leiter Adult Intelligence Scale *USE Intelligence Measures*
Marlowe Crowne Soc Desirabil **Scale**
Repression Sensitization **Scale**
Rokeach Dogmatism **Scale**
Rotter Intern Extern Locus Cont **Scal**
Sensation Seeking **Scale**
Stanford Binet Intelligence **Scale**
Taylor Manifest Anxiety **Scale**
Temporal Spatial Concept Scale *USE Intelligence Measures*
Tennessee Self Concept **Scale**
Vineland Social Maturity **Scale**
Wechsler Adult Intelligence **Scale**
Wechsler Bellevue Intelligence **Scale**
Wechsler Intelligence **Scale** Children
Wechsler Memory **Scale**
Wechsler Preschool Primary **Scale**
White Betz A B Scale
USE Nonprojective Personality Measures
Wilson Patterson Conservatism **Scale**
Zungs Self Rating Depression **Scale**
Bayley **Scales** of Infant Development
Likert **Scales**
Rating **Scales**
Scaling (Testing)
Multidimensional **Scaling**
Scalp (Anatomy)
Scalp Disorders *USE Skin Disorders*
CAT Scan *USE Tomography*
Scandinavia
Animal **Scent** Marking
Diagnostic Interview **Schedule**
Edwards Personal Preference **Schedule**
Fear Survey **Schedule**
Concurrent Reinforcement **Schedules**
Learning **Schedules**
Reinforcement **Schedules**
Work **Scheduling**
Goldstein **Scheerer** Object Sort Test
Schema
Schizoaffective Disorder
Schizoid Personality
Schizophrenia
Schizophrenia (Disorganized Type)
USE Hebephrenic Schizophrenia
Schizophrenia (Residual Type)
USE Schizophrenia
Acute **Schizophrenia**
Catatonic **Schizophrenia**
Childhood **Schizophrenia**
Chronic Schizophrenia *USE Schizophrenia*
Fragmentation **(Schizophrenia)**
Hebephrenic **Schizophrenia**
Paranoid **Schizophrenia**
Process Schizophrenia *USE Process Psychosis AND Schizophrenia*
Pseudopsychopathic Schizophrenia *USE Schizophrenia*
Reactive Schizophrenia *USE Reactive Psychosis AND Schizophrenia*
Simple Schizophrenia *USE Schizophrenia*
Undifferentiated **Schizophrenia**
Schizophreniform Disorder
Schizophrenogenic Family
Schizophrenogenic Mothers
Schizotypal Personality
Scholarships
USE Educational Financial Assistance
Scholastic Achievement
USE Academic Achievement
Scholastic Aptitude
USE Academic Aptitude
Scholastic Aptitude Test
USE Coll Ent Exam Bd Scholastic Apt Test
Coll Ent Exam Bd **Scholastic** Apt Test

Preliminary Scholastic Aptitude Test
USE Coll Ent Exam Bd Scholastic Apt Test
School Accreditation
USE Educational Program Accreditation
School Achievement
USE Academic Achievement
School Adjustment
School Administration
USE Educational Administration
School Administrators
School Age Children
School and College Ability Test
USE Aptitude Measures
School Attendance
School Club Membership
School Counseling
School Counselors
School Dropouts
School Enrollment
School Environment
School Expulsion
School Facilities
School Federal Aid
USE Educational Financial Assistance
School Graduation
School Guidance *USE School Counseling*
School Integration
School Learning
School Leavers
School Libraries
School Nurses
School Organization
USE Educational Administration
School Phobia
School Principals
School Psychologists
School Psychology
School Readiness
School Refusal
School Retention
School Superintendents
School Suspension
School to Work Transition
School Transition
School Truancy
Elementary **School** Students
Elementary **School** Teachers
Freudian Psychoanalytic **School**
Graduation (School) *USE School Graduation*
High School Diplomas
USE Educational Degrees
High School Equivalency *USE Adult Education*
High **School** Graduates
High **Sch** Personality Questionnaire
High **School** Students
High **School** Teachers
Intermediate **School** Students
Junior High **School** Students
Junior High **School** Teachers
Middle **School** Education
Middle **School** Students
NeoFreudian School *USE Neopsychoanalytic School*
Neopsychoanalytic **School**
Nursery **School** Students
Parent **School** Relationship
Parochial School Education
USE Private School Education
Primary **School** Students
Private **School** Education
Public **School** Education
Retention (School) *USE School Retention*
Vocational **School** Students
Home **Schooling**
Schools
Alternative Schools *USE Nontraditional Education*
Boarding **Schools**
Elementary **Schools**
Graduate **Schools**

Grammar Schools *USE Elementary Schools*
High **Schools**
Institutional **Schools**
Junior High **Schools**
Magnet Schools *USE Nontraditional Education*
Military **Schools**
Nongraded **Schools**
Nursery **Schools**
Primary Schools *USE Elementary Schools*
Racial Segregation (Schools) *USE School Integration*
Technical **Schools**
Vocational Schools *USE Technical Schools*
Sciatic Nerve *USE Spinal Nerves*
Science Achievement
Science Education
Medicine (Science of) *USE Medical Sciences*
Sciences
Behavioral **Sciences**
Medical **Sciences**
Paramedical **Sciences**
Social **Sciences**
Scientific Communication
Scientific Methods *USE Experimental Methods*
Scientists
Sclera *USE Eye (Anatomy)*
Sclerosis (Nervous System)
Multiple **Sclerosis**
Scopolamine
Score Equating
Critical Scores *USE Cutting Scores*
Cutting **Scores**
Standard **Scores**
Test **Scores**
Z Scores *USE Standard Scores*
Scoring (Testing)
Scotland
Scotopic Stimulation
Scratching
Screening
Screening Tests
Breast Cancer Screening *USE Cancer Screening*
Cancer **Screening**
Drug Usage **Screening**
Health **Screening**
Job Applicant **Screening**
Prostate Cancer Screening *USE Cancer Screening*
Psychological **Screening** Inventory
Skin Cancer Screening *USE Cancer Screening*
Scripts *USE Schema*
Sculpturing
Sea Gulls
Seals (Animal)
Job **Search**
Visual **Search**
Computer **Searching**
Online Searching *USE Computer Searching*
Seasonal Affective Disorder
Seasonal Variations
Seat Belts *USE Safety Belts*
Seclusion (Patient) *USE Patient Seclusion*
Patient **Seclusion**
Secobarbital
Seconal *USE Secobarbital*
Second Language Education *USE Foreign Language Education*
Second Order Conditioning *USE Higher Order Conditioning*
English as **Second** Language
Secondary Education
Secondary Reinforcement
Secrecy
Secretarial Personnel
Clerical **Secretarial** Skills
Secretion (Gland)
Adrenal Gland **Secretion**
Endocrine Gland **Secretion**
Sectioning (Lesion) *USE Lesions*
Private **Sector**
Public **Sector**
Emotional **Security**
Job **Security**
Maximum **Security** Facilities
Social **Security**
Sedatives
Seduction
Seeing Eye Dogs *USE Mobility Aids*
Assistance Seeking (Professional) *USE Health Care Utilization*
Health Care **Seeking** Behavior
Help **Seeking** Behavior
Information **Seeking**
Novelty Seeking *USE Sensation Seeking*
Sensation **Seeking**
Sensation **Seeking** Scale
Stimulation Seeking (Personality) *USE Sensation Seeking*
Treatment Seeking Behavior *USE Health Care Seeking Behavior*
Segregation (Racial) *USE Social Integration*
Racial Segregation (Schools) *USE School Integration*
Seizures *USE Convulsions*
Audiogenic **Seizures**
Epileptic **Seizures**
Selected Readings
Selection Tests
Selection (Therapist) *USE Therapist Selection*
Animal Mate **Selection**
Employee Selection *USE Personnel Selection*
Habitat Selection *USE Territoriality*
Human Mate **Selection**
Job Selection *USE Occupational Choice*
Jury **Selection**
Mate Selection *USE Animal Mate Selection OR Human Mate Selection*
Natural **Selection**
Patient **Selection**
Personnel **Selection**
Therapist **Selection**
Toy **Selection**
Selective Attention
Selective Breeding
Self Acceptance *USE Self Perception*
Self Actualization
Self Analysis
Self Assessment *USE Self Evaluation*
Self Care Skills
Self Concept
Self Confidence
Self Congruence
Self Consciousness *USE Self Perception*
Self Control
Self Defeating Behavior
Self Defense
Self Destructive Behavior
Self Determination
Self Directed Learning *USE Individualized Instruction*
Self Disclosure
Self Efficacy
Self Employment
Self Esteem
Self Evaluation
Self Examination (Medical)
Self Fulfilling Prophecies
Self Handicapping Strategy
Self Help Techniques
Self Hypnosis *USE Autohypnosis*
Self Image *USE Self Concept*
Self Inflicted Wounds
Self Instruction *USE Individualized Instruction*
Self Instructional Training
Self Management
Self Medication

Self Monitoring
Self Monitoring (Personality)
Self Mutilation
Self Observation *USE Self Monitoring*
Self Perception
Self Preservation
Self Psychology
Self Realization *USE Self Actualization*
Self Reference
Self Referral
Self Reinforcement
Self Report
Self Respect *USE Self Esteem*
Self Stimulation
Self Talk
Academic **Self** Concept
Brain **Self** Stimulation
Child **Self** Care
Confidence (Self) *USE Self Confidence*
Control (Self) *USE Self Control*
Disclosure (Self) *USE Self Disclosure*
Ideal Self *USE Self Concept*
Intracranial Self Stimulation *USE Brain Self Stimulation*
Kupfer Detre Self Rating Scale *USE Nonprojective Personality Measures*
Referral (Self) *USE Self Referral*
Tennessee **Self** Concept Scale
Zungs **Self** Rating Depression Scale
Selfishness
Semantic Differential
Semantic Generalization
Semantic Memory
Semantic Priming
Semantics
Semicircular Canals
Seminarians
Seminaries
Semiotics
Senegal
Senescence *USE Aged*
Senile Dementia
Senile Psychosis
Senior Citizens *USE Aged*
Sensation *USE Perception*
Sensation Seeking
Sensation Seeking Scale
Pressure **Sensation**
Sense Organ Disorders
Sense Organs
Cutaneous **Sense**
Vomeronasal **Sense**
Sensitivity (Personality)
Sensitivity Training
Cultural **Sensitivity**
Drug **Sensitivity**
Ethnic Sensitivity *USE Cultural Sensitivity*
Spectral Sensitivity *USE Color Perception*
Sensitization (Protein) *USE Anaphylactic Shock*
Covert **Sensitization**
Protein Sensitization *USE Anaphylactic Shock*
Repression **Sensitization**
Repression **Sensitization** Scale
Sensorially Disabled
Sensorially Handicapped *USE Sensorially Disabled*
Sensorimotor Development *USE Perceptual Motor Development*
Sensorimotor Measures
Sensorimotor Processes *USE Perceptual Motor Processes*
Sensorineural Hearing Loss *USE Hearing Disorders*
Sensory Adaptation
Sensory Deprivation
Sensory Disabilities (Attit Toward)
Sensory Feedback
Sensory Gating
Sensory Handicaps (Attit Toward) *USE Sensory Disabilities (Attit Toward)*
Sensory Integration
Sensory Neglect
Sensory Neurons
Sensory Pathways *USE Afferent Pathways*
Sensory Preconditioning *USE Preconditioning*
Gating (Sensory) *USE Sensory Gating*
Sentence Completion Tests
Sentence Comprehension
Sentence Structure
Sentences
Rotter Incomplete **Sentences** Blank
Sentencing *USE Adjudication*
Separation Anxiety
Separation Individuation
Separation Reactions
Marital **Separation**
Septal Nuclei
Septum *USE Septal Nuclei*
Sequential Learning
Serial Anticipation (Learning)
Serial Learning
Serial Position Effect
Serial Recall
Time **Series**
Seriousness
Serotonin
Serotonin Agonists
Serotonin Antagonists
Serotonin Metabolites
Serotonin Precursors
Serotonin Reuptake Inhibitors
Serpasil *USE Reserpine*
Sertraline
Serum Albumin
Blood **Serum**
Civil Servants *USE Government Personnel*
Service Personnel
Service Quality *USE Quality of Services*
Domestic **Service** Personnel
Fee for **Service**
Health **Service** Needs
Health Service Utilization *USE Health Care Utilization*
Mental Health Service Needs *USE Health Service Needs*
Public Health **Service** Nurses
Technical **Service** Personnel
Volunteers in **Service** to America
Servicemen *USE Military Personnel*
Community **Services**
Community Mental Health **Services**
Community Welfare **Services**
Crisis Intervention **Services**
Emergency **Services**
Health Care **Services**
Hot Line **Services**
Information **Services**
Integrated **Services**
Interagency Services *USE Integrated Services*
Mental Health **Services**
Protective **Services**
Public Health **Services**
Public Welfare Services *USE Community Welfare Services*
Quality of **Services**
Social **Services**
Student Personnel **Services**
Welfare **Services** (Government)
Set (Response) *USE Response Set*
Fuzzy **Set** Theory
Response **Set**
Goal **Setting**
Severely Mentally Retarded
Severity (Disorders)
Sex
Sex Change

Sex Chromosome Disorders
Sex Chromosomes
Sex Differentiation Disorders
USE Genital Disorders
Sex Discrimination
Sex Drive
Sex Education
Sex Hormones
Sex Linked Developmental Differences
Sex Linked Hereditary Disorders
Sex Offenses
Sex Recognition
Sex Role Attitudes
Sex Roles
Sex Therapy
Animal **Sex** Differences
Bem **Sex** Role Inventory
Human **Sex** Differences
Sterilization **(Sex)**
Sexism
Sexual Abstinence
Sexual Abuse
Sexual Addiction
Sexual Arousal
Sexual Attitudes
Sexual Behavior
USE Psychosexual Behavior
Sexual Boundary Violations
USE Professional Client Sexual Relations
Sexual Compulsivity
USE Sexual Addiction
Sexual Delinquency *USE Promiscuity*
Sexual Development
Sexual Deviations
Sexual Disorders (Physiological)
USE Genital Disorders
Sexual Fantasy
Sexual Function Disturbances
Sexual Harassment
Sexual Identity (Gender)
USE Gender Identity
Sexual Intercourse (Human)
Sexual Masochism
Sexual Orientation
Sexual Reassignment *USE Sex Change*
Sexual Reproduction
Sexual Risk Taking
Sexual Sadism
Sexual Satisfaction
Affairs (Sexual) *USE Extramarital Intercourse*
Animal **Sexual** Behavior
Animal **Sexual** Receptivity
Boundary Violations (Sexual)
USE Professional Client Sexual Relations
Climax (Sexual) *USE Orgasm*
Compulsivity (Sexual) *USE Sexual Addiction*
Endocrine **Sexual** Disorders
Harassment (Sexual) *USE Sexual Harassment*
Hypoactive Sexual Desire Disorder
USE Inhibited Sexual Desire
Inhibited **Sexual** Desire
Patient Therapist Sexual Relations
USE Professional Client Sexual Relations
Perversions (Sexual) *USE Sexual Deviations*
Professional Client **Sexual** Relations
Therapist Patient Sexual Relations
USE Professional Client Sexual Relations
Sexuality
Sexually Transmitted Diseases
USE Venereal Diseases
Shamanism
Shame
Form and **Shape** Perception
Shared Paranoid Disorder
USE Folie A Deux
Sharing (Social Behavior)
Needle **Sharing**
Myelin **Sheath**
Sheep
Sheltered Workshops
Shelters
Choice **Shift**
Extradimensional Shift Learning
USE Nonreversal Shift Learning
Nonreversal **Shift** Learning
Reversal **Shift** Learning
Risky Shift *USE Choice Shift*
Population Shifts *USE Human Migration*
Workday **Shifts**
Shock
Shock Therapy
Shock Units
Anaphylactic **Shock**
Culture **Shock**
Electroconvulsive **Shock**
Electroconvulsive **Shock** Therapy
Insulin **Shock** Therapy
Shoplifting
Shopping
Shopping Centers
Short Term Memory
Short Term Potentiation
USE Postactivation Potentials
Short Term Psychotherapy
USE Brief Psychotherapy
Shoulder (Anatomy)
Shuttle Box Grids *USE Shuttle Boxes*
Shuttle Box Hurdles *USE Shuttle Boxes*
Shuttle Boxes
Shyness *USE Timidity*
Siamese Twins
Sibling Relations
Siblings
Sick Leave *USE Employee Leave Benefits*
Sickle Cell Disease
Motion **Sickness**
Side Effects (Drug)
Side Effects (Treatment)
Sierra Leone
Sight Vocabulary
Partially **Sighted**
Freud **(Sigmund)**
Sign Language
Sign Test
Wilcoxon **Sign** Rank Test
Signal Detection (Perception)
Signal Intensity *USE Stimulus Intensity*
Statistical **Significance**
Significant Others
Warning Signs *USE Warnings*
Silent Reading
Attitude **Similarity**
Stimulus **Similarity**
Simile *USE Figurative Language*
Simple Schizophrenia *USE Schizophrenia*
Herpes **Simplex**
Simulation
Simulation Games
Computer **Simulation**
Flight **Simulation**
Simulators *USE Simulation*
Sin
Sincerity
Singapore
Singing
Single Cell Organisms
USE Microorganisms
Single Fathers
Single Mothers
Single Parents
Single Persons
Sisters
Sixteen Personality Factors Question
Size
Size Constancy
Size Discrimination
Apparent **Size**
Body **Size**

Brain **Size**
Effect **Size** (Statistical)
Family **Size**
Group **Size**
Litter **Size**
Sample **Size**
Skeletomuscular Disorders
USE Musculoskeletal Disorders
Skewed Distribution
Skill Learning
Fine Motor **Skill** Learning
Gross Motor **Skill** Learning
Motor Skill Learning
USE Perceptual Motor Learning
Skilled Industrial Workers
Skills *USE Ability*
Basic Skills Testing
USE Minimum Competency Tests
Clerical Secretarial **Skills**
Communication **Skills**
Communication **Skills** Training
Employee **Skills**
Iowa Tests of Basic **Skills**
Motor **Skills**
Parenting **Skills**
Reading **Skills**
Self Care **Skills**
Social **Skills**
Social **Skills** Training
Study Skills *USE Study Habits*
Writing **Skills**
Skin (Anatomy)
Skin Cancer Screening
USE Cancer Screening
Skin Conduction *USE Skin Resistance*
Skin Disorders
Skin Electrical Properties
Skin Potential
Skin Resistance
Skin Temperature
Allergic **Skin** Disorders
Basal **Skin** Resistance
Galvanic **Skin** Response
Skinner Boxes
Skinner (Burrhus Frederic)
Skull
Slang
Sleep
Sleep Apnea
Sleep Deprivation
Sleep Disorders
Sleep Inducing Drugs
USE Hypnotic Drugs
Sleep Onset
Sleep Talking
Sleep Treatment
Sleep Wake Cycle
Nonrapid Eye Movement Sleep *USE NREM Sleep*
NonREM Sleep *USE NREM Sleep*
NREM **Sleep**
Paradoxical Sleep *USE REM Sleep*
Paroxysmal Sleep *USE Narcolepsy*
Rapid Eye Movement Sleep *USE REM Sleep*
REM **Sleep**
Slow Wave Sleep *USE NREM Sleep*
Sleeplessness *USE Insomnia*
Sleepwalking
Slosson Intelligence Test for Child
Slow Learners
Slow Wave Sleep *USE NREM Sleep*
Slums *USE Poverty Areas*
Smell Perception
USE Olfactory Perception
Smiles
Kolmogorov **Smirnov** Test
Smokeless Tobacco
Tobacco (Smokeless) *USE Smokeless Tobacco*
Smoking Cessation
Cigarette Smoking *USE Tobacco Smoking*
Tobacco **Smoking**
Snails
Snake Phobia *USE Ophidiophobia*
Snakes
Glue **Sniffing**
Snuff *USE Smokeless Tobacco*
Sobriety
Soccer
Sociability
Social Acceptance
Social Adaptation *USE Social Adjustment*
Social Adjustment
Social Anxiety
Social Approval
Social Behavior
Social Casework
Social Caseworkers *USE Social Workers*
Social Change
Social Class
Social Class Attitudes
USE Socioeconomic Class Attitudes
Social Cognition
Social Comparison
Social Control
Social Dating
Social Demonstrations
Social Density
Social Deprivation
Social Desirability
Social Development
USE Psychosocial Development
Social Discrimination
Social Drinking
Social Environments
Social Equality
Social Facilitation
Social Groups
Social Identity
Social Immobility *USE Social Mobility*
Social Influences
Social Integration
Social Interaction
Social Isolation
Social Issues
Social Learning
Social Maladjustment
USE Social Adjustment
Social Mobility
Social Movements
Social Networks
Social Norms
Social Perception
Social Phobia
Social Problems *USE Social Issues*
Social Processes
Social Programs
Social Psychiatry
Social Psychologists
Social Psychology
Social Reinforcement
Social Rejection *USE Social Acceptance*
Social Sciences
Social Security
Social Services
Social Skills
Social Skills Training
Social Stigma *USE Stigma*
Social Stress
Social Structure
Social Studies Education
Social Support Networks
Social Values
Social Work *USE Social Casework*
Social Work Education
Social Workers
Animal **Social** Behavior
Assistance **(Social** Behavior)
Clubs **(Social** Organizations)
Competence (Social) *USE Social Skills*

Control (Social) *USE Social Control*
Discrimination (Social) *USE Social Discrimination*
Edwards **Social** Desirability Scale
Equity **(Social)**
Marlowe Crowne **Soc** Desirabil Scale
Networks (Social) *USE Social Networks*
Psychiatric **Social** Workers
Rejection (Social) *USE Social Acceptance*
Sharing **(Social** Behavior)
Therapeutic **Social** Clubs
Trust **(Social** Behavior)
Vineland **Social** Maturity Scale
Socialism
Union of Soviet **Socialist** Republics
Socialization
Political **Socialization**
Socially Disadvantaged *USE Disadvantaged*
Society
Sociobiology
Sociocultural Factors
Socioeconomic Class Attitudes
Socioeconomic Status
Family **Socioeconomic** Level
Socioenvironmental Therapy *USE Milieu Therapy*
Sociograms
Sociolinguistics
Sociologists
Sociology
Sociometric Tests
Sociometry
Sociopath *USE Antisocial Personality*
Sociopathology *USE Antisocial Behavior*
Sociotherapy
Sodium
Sodium Ions
Sodium Lactate *USE Lactic Acid*
Sodium Pentobarbital *USE Pentobarbital*
Computer **Software**
Solvent Abuse *USE Inhalant Abuse*
Solvents
Anagram Problem **Solving**
Group Problem **Solving**
Problem **Solving**
Somalia
Somatization
Somatization Disorder *USE Psychosomatic Disorders*
Somatoform Pain Disorder
Atypical Somatoform Disorder *USE Dysmorphophobia*
Somatosensory Cortex
Somatosensory Evoked Potentials
Somatostatin
Somatotropin
Somatotypes
Somesthetic Perception
Somesthetic Stimulation
Somnambulism *USE Sleepwalking*
Sonar
Songs *USE Music*
Sons
Sorority Membership
Goldstein Scheerer Object **Sort** Test
Q **Sort** Testing Technique
Sorting (Cognition) *USE Classification (Cognitive Process)*
Wisconsin Card **Sorting** Test
Sound *USE Auditory Stimulation*
Sound Localization *USE Auditory Localization*
Sound Pressure Level *USE Loudness*
Sound Waves *USE Acoustics*
Noise (Sound) *USE Auditory Stimulation*
Sourness *USE Taste Perception*
South Africa
South America
South Korea
South Pacific
South Vietnam *USE Vietnam*
Southeast Asia
Union of **Soviet** Socialist Republics
Personal **Space**
Working **Space**
Spacecraft
Spaceflight
Spain
Attention **Span**
Digit **Span** Testing
Life Span *USE Life Expectancy*
Spanish Americans *USE Hispanics*
Spasms
Muscle **Spasms**
Spatial Ability
Spatial Discrimination *USE Spatial Perception*
Spatial Distortion
Spatial Frequency
Spatial Imagery
Spatial Learning
Spatial Memory
Spatial Neglect *USE Sensory Neglect*
Spatial Organization
Spatial Orientation (Perception)
Spatial Perception
Temporal Spatial Concept Scale *USE Intelligence Measures*
Visual Spatial Ability *USE Visuospatial Ability*
Visual Spatial Memory *USE Visuospatial Memory*
Automatic Speaker Recognition *USE Automated Speech Recognition*
Fear of Public Speaking *USE Speech Anxiety*
Public **Speaking**
Spearman Brown Test
Spearman Rho *USE Rank Difference Correlation*
Special Education
Special Education Students
Special Education Teachers
Special Needs
Information **Specialists**
Specialization (Professional) *USE Professional Specialization*
Academic **Specialization**
Hemispheric Specialization *USE Lateral Dominance*
Professional **Specialization**
Species Differences
Species Recognition
Sports **Spectators**
Spectral Sensitivity *USE Color Perception*
Speech *USE Oral Communication*
Speech and Hearing Measures
Speech Anxiety
Speech Characteristics
Speech Development
Speech Disabled
Speech Disorders
Speech Handicapped *USE Speech Disabled*
Speech Pauses
Speech Perception
Speech Pitch
Speech Processing (Mechanical)
Speech Rate
Speech Rhythm
Speech Therapists
Speech Therapy
Accelerated Speech *USE Speech Rate*
Articulation **(Speech)**
Automated **Speech** Recognition
Compressed **Speech**
Delayed Speech *USE Retarded Speech Development*
Figures of Speech *USE Figurative Language*
Filtered **Speech**
Inner Speech *USE Self Talk*
Retarded **Speech** Development

Synthetic **Speech**
Speechreading *USE Lipreading*
Speed *USE Velocity*
Cognitive Processing **Speed**
Information Processing Speed *USE Cognitive Processing Speed*
Reading **Speed**
Response Speed *USE Reaction Time*
Spelling
Sperm
Sperm Donation *USE Tissue Donation*
Spider Phobia *USE Phobias*
Spiders *USE Arachnida*
Spina Bifida
Spinal Column
Spinal Cord
Spinal Cord Injuries
Spinal Fluid *USE Cerebrospinal Fluid*
Spinal Ganglia
Spinal Nerves
Cranial **Spinal** Cord
Lumbar **Spinal** Cord
Spinothalamic Tracts
Spiperone *USE Spiroperidol*
Spirit Possession
Spirituality
Spiroperidol
Spleen
Split Brain *USE Commissurotomy*
Split Personality
USE Dissociative Identity Disorder
Spontaneous Abortion
Spontaneous Alternation
Spontaneous Recovery (Learning)
Spontaneous Remission
Sport Performance
USE Athletic Performance
Sport Psychology
Sport Training *USE Athletic Training*
Sports
Sports Spectators
Fans (Sports) *USE Sports Spectators*
Spouse Abuse *USE Partner Abuse*
Spouses
Cervical Sprain Syndrome *USE Whiplash*
Spreading Depression
Chi **Square** Test
Least **Squares**
Squirrels
Sri Lanka
Emotional **Stability**
Hospital Staff *USE Medical Personnel*
Psychiatric Hospital **Staff**
Stage Plays *USE Theatre*
Developmental **Stages**
Prenatal Developmental **Stages**
Stammering *USE Stuttering*
Competency to **Stand** Trial
Standard Deviation
Standard Error of Measurement
USE Error of Measurement
Standard Scores
Test **Standardization**
Standardized Tests
Professional **Standards**
Stanford Achievement Test
Stanford Binet Intelligence Scale
Stanines *USE Standard Scores*
Stapedius Reflex *USE Acoustic Reflex*
Starfish *USE Echinodermata*
Project Head **Start**
Startle Reflex
Starvation
State Board Examinations
USE Professional Examinations
State Dependent Learning
State Hospitals *USE Psychiatric Hospitals*
State Trait Anxiety Inventory
Mini Mental **State** Examination
Borderline **States**
Commonwealth of Independent **States**
Consciousness **States**
Emotional **States**
United **States**
Statistical Analysis
Statistical Correlation
Statistical Data
Statistical Estimation
Statistical Measurement
Statistical Norms
Statistical Power
Statistical Probability
Statistical Regression
Statistical Reliability
Statistical Rotation
Statistical Sample Parameters
Statistical Samples
Statistical Significance
Statistical Tables
Statistical Tests
Statistical Validity
Statistical Variables
Statistical Weighting
Diagnostic and **Statistical** Manual
Effect Size **(Statistical)**
Item Analysis **(Statistical)**
Magnitude of Effect (Statistical) *USE Effect Size (Statistical)*
Nonparametric **Statistical** Tests
Parametric **Statistical** Tests
Statistics
ANOVA (Statistics) *USE Analysis of Variance*
Confidence Limits **(Statistics)**
Interaction Analysis **(Statistics)**
Population **(Statistics)**
Status
Employment **Status**
Job Status *USE Occupational Status*
Marital **Status**
Occupational **Status**
Parenthood **Status**
Socioeconomic **Status**
Length of Stay *USE Treatment Duration*
Stealing *USE Theft*
Stelazine *USE Trifluoperazine*
Stellate Ganglion *USE Autonomic Ganglia*
Brain **Stem**
Twelve **Step** Programs
Stepchildren
Stepfamily
Stepparents
Stereopsis *USE Stereoscopic Vision*
Stereoscopic Presentation
Stereoscopic Vision
Stereotaxic Atlas
Stereotaxic Techniques
Stereotyped Attitudes
Stereotyped Behavior
Sterility
Sterilization (Sex)
Steroids
Adrenal Cortex Steroids *USE Corticosteroids*
Sticklebacks
Stigma
Social Stigma *USE Stigma*
Stimulants of CNS
USE CNS Stimulating Drugs
CNS **Stimulating** Drugs
Follicle **Stimulating** Hormone
Melanocyte **Stimulating** Hormone
Respiration **Stimulating** Drugs
Thyroid Stimulating Hormone *USE Thyrotropin*
Stimulation
Stimulation Seeking (Personality)
USE Sensation Seeking
Afferent **Stimulation**
Auditory **Stimulation**
Aversive **Stimulation**
Brain **Stimulation**
Brain Self **Stimulation**

Chemical Brain **Stimulation**
Dichoptic **Stimulation**
Dichotic **Stimulation**
Electrical **Stimulation**
Electrical Brain **Stimulation**
Intracranial Self Stimulation *USE Brain Self Stimulation*
Olfactory **Stimulation**
Perceptual **Stimulation**
Photopic **Stimulation**
Prismatic **Stimulation**
Restricted Environmental Stimulation *USE Stimulus Deprivation*
Scotopic **Stimulation**
Self **Stimulation**
Somesthetic **Stimulation**
Subliminal **Stimulation**
Tactual **Stimulation**
Taste **Stimulation**
Vestibular Stimulation *USE Somesthetic Stimulation*
Visual **Stimulation**
Stimulators (Apparatus)
Acoustic Stimuli *USE Auditory Stimulation*
Pictorial **Stimuli**
Verbal **Stimuli**
Stimulus Ambiguity
Stimulus Attenuation
Stimulus Change
Stimulus Complexity
Stimulus Control
Stimulus Deprivation
Stimulus Discrimination
Stimulus Duration
Stimulus Frequency
Stimulus Generalization
Stimulus Intensity
Stimulus Intervals
Stimulus Novelty
Stimulus Offset
Stimulus Onset
Stimulus Parameters
Stimulus Pattern *USE Stimulus Variability*
Stimulus Presentation Methods
Stimulus Salience
Stimulus Similarity
Stimulus Variability
Conditioned **Stimulus**
Discriminative Stimulus *USE Conditioned Stimulus*
Exposure Time (Stimulus) *USE Stimulus Duration*
Unconditioned **Stimulus**
Stipends
USE Educational Financial Assistance
Stochastic Modeling
Stomach
Automated Information **Storage**
Human Information **Storage**
Retail Stores *USE Retailing*
Storytelling
Mutual **Storytelling** Technique
Strabismus
Animal **Strain** Differences
Role Strain *USE Role Conflicts*
Stranger Reactions
Fear of Strangers *USE Stranger Reactions*
Strategies
Strategies (Learning)
USE Learning Strategies
Learning **Strategies**
Self Handicapping **Strategy**
Physical **Strength**
Stress
Stress Management
Stress Reactions
Environmental **Stress**
Occupational **Stress**
Physiological **Stress**
Posttraumatic **Stress** Disorder
Psychological **Stress**
Social **Stress**
Striate Cortex *USE Visual Cortex*
Corpus Striatum *USE Basal Ganglia*
Strikes
Film **Strips**
Stroboscopic Movement
USE Apparent Movement
Stroke (Cerebrum)
USE Cerebrovascular Accidents
Strong Vocational Interest Blank
Stroop Color Word Test
Stroop Effect
Structural Equation Modeling
Structuralism
Factor **Structure**
Family **Structure**
Group **Structure**
Household Structure *USE Living Arrangements*
Kinship **Structure**
Organizational **Structure**
Sentence **Structure**
Social **Structure**
Text **Structure**
Structured Overview
USE Advance Organizers
Strychnine
Student Activism
Student Adjustment
USE School Adjustment
Student Admission Criteria
Student Attitudes
Student Attrition
Student Characteristics
Student Personnel Services
Student Protest *USE Student Activism*
Student Records
Student Teachers
Student Teaching
Protest (Student) *USE Student Activism*
Teacher **Student** Interaction
Students
Business **Students**
College **Students**
Community College **Students**
Dental **Students**
Education **Students**
Elementary School **Students**
Foreign **Students**
Graduate **Students**
High School **Students**
Intermediate School **Students**
Junior College **Students**
Junior High School **Students**
Kindergarten **Students**
Law **Students**
Medical **Students**
Middle School **Students**
Nursery School **Students**
Nursing **Students**
Postgraduate **Students**
Preschool **Students**
Primary School **Students**
Reentry **Students**
ROTC **Students**
Special Education **Students**
Transfer **Students**
Vocational School **Students**
Followup **Studies**
Longitudinal **Studies**
Prospective **Studies**
Retrospective **Studies**
Social **Studies** Education
Study Habits
Study Skills *USE Study Habits*
Allport Vernon Lindzey Study Values *USE Attitude Measures*
Foreign **Study**
Independent Study *USE Individualized Instruction*
Rosenzweig Picture Frustration **Study**
Work Study Programs
USE Educational Programs
Stuttering
Cognitive **Style**

Leadership **Style**
Learning Style *USE Cognitive Style*
Perceptual **Style**
Subconscious
Subcortical Lesions *USE Brain Lesions*
Subculture (Anthropological)
Subcutaneous Injections
Subjectivity
Experimental **Subjects**
Research Subjects *USE Experimental Subjects*
Within Subjects Design *USE Repeated Measures*
Sublimation
Subliminal Perception
Subliminal Stimulation
Submarines
Submissiveness *USE Obedience*
Submucous Plexus
USE Autonomic Ganglia
Substance Abuse *USE Drug Abuse*
Substance Abuse Prevention
USE Drug Abuse Prevention
Substance P
Substantia Nigra
Subtests
Suburban Environments
Subvocalization
Success *USE Achievement*
Fear of **Success**
Occupational **Success**
Occupational **Success** Prediction
Successive Contrast *USE Afterimage*
Succinylcholine
Sucking
Sudan
Sudden Infant Death
Suffering
Suffocation *USE Anoxia*
Blood **Sugar**
Sugars
Suggestibility
Posthypnotic **Suggestions**
Suicidal Ideation
Suicide
Suicide Prevention
Suicide Prevention Centers
Assisted **Suicide**
Attempted **Suicide**
Sulpiride
Non Zero **Sum** Games
Summer Camps (Recreation)
Superego
School **Superintendents**
Superior Colliculus
Emotional **Superiority**
Superstitions
Supervising Teachers
USE Cooperating Teachers
Clinical Supervision *USE Professional Supervision*
Educational Supervision *USE Professional Supervision*
Practicum **Supervision**
Professional **Supervision**
Supervisor Employee Interaction
Employee Supervisor Interaction
USE Supervisor Employee Interaction
Supervisors *USE Management Personnel*
Medical Personnel **Supply**
Mental Health Personnel **Supply**
Personnel **Supply**
Support Groups
Child **Support**
Decision **Support** Systems
Social **Support** Networks
Supported Employment
Supportive Psychotherapy
Suppression (Defense Mechanism)
Conditioned **Suppression**
Dexamethasone **Suppression** Test
Progressive **Supranuclear** Palsy
Surgeons

Surgery
Cardiac Surgery *USE Heart Surgery*
Dental **Surgery**
Endocrine Gland **Surgery**
Heart **Surgery**
Operation (Surgery) *USE Surgery*
Pituitary Gland Surgery *USE Hypophysectomy*
Plastic **Surgery**
Surgical Complications
USE Postsurgical Complications
Surgical Patients
Surinam
Surrogate Parents (Humans)
Fear **Survey** Schedule
Guilford Zimmerman
Temperament **Surv**
Kuder Occupational Interest **Survey**
Opinion Attitude and Interest Survey *USE Attitude Measures*
Purdue Perceptual Motor **Survey**
Surveys
Consumer **Surveys**
Mail **Surveys**
Opinion Surveys *USE Attitude Measures*
Telephone **Surveys**
Survival Instinct *USE Self Preservation*
Survivors
Holocaust **Survivors**
Susceptibility (Disorders)
Hypnotic **Susceptibility**
School **Suspension**
Suspicion
Sustained Attention
Life **Sustaining** Treatment
Swallowing
Mate Swapping *USE Extramarital Intercourse*
Body **Sway** Testing
Swaziland
Sweat
Sweating
Sweden
Sweetness *USE Taste Perception*
Swimming
Code **Switching**
Switzerland
Nonsense **Syllable** Learning
Syllables
Syllogistic Reasoning
USE Inductive Deductive Reasoning
Biological **Symbiosis**
Symbiotic Infantile Psychosis
Symbolic Interactionism
Symbolism
Sympathectomy
Sympathetic Nervous System
Sympatholytic Drugs
Sympathomimetic Amines
Sympathomimetic Drugs
Sympathy
Professional Meetings and **Symposia**
Symptom Checklists
Symptom Prescription
USE Paradoxical Techniques
Symptom Remission
Symptoms
Extrapyramidal **Symptoms**
Negative and Positive Symptoms
USE Positive and Negative Symptoms
Positive and Negative **Symptoms**
Psychiatric **Symptoms**
Psychotic Symptoms *USE Psychiatric Symptoms*
Synapses
Syncope
Acquired Immune Deficiency **Syndrome**
Aspergers **Syndrome**
Battered Child **Syndrome**
Capgras **Syndrome**
Cervical Sprain Syndrome *USE Whiplash*
Chronic Fatigue **Syndrome**
Creutzfeldt Jakob **Syndrome**

Cri du Chat Syndrome *USE Crying Cat Syndrome*
Crying Cat **Syndrome**
Cushings **Syndrome**
Downs **Syndrome**
Fetal Alcohol **Syndrome**
Fibromyalgia Syndrome *USE Muscular Disorders*
Fragile X **Syndrome**
Ganser Syndrome *USE Factitious Disorders*
Hospital Addiction Syndrome *USE Munchausen Syndrome*
Irritable Bowel **Syndrome**
Klinefelters **Syndrome**
Munchausen **Syndrome**
Munchausen **Syndrome** by Proxy
Neuroleptic Malignant **Syndrome**
Prader Willi **Syndrome**
Premenstrual Syndrome *USE Premenstrual Tension*
Rett **Syndrome**
Temporomandibular Joint Syndrome *USE Musculoskeletal Disorders*
Testicular Feminization **Syndrome**
Turners **Syndrome**
Wernickes **Syndrome**
Syndromes
Organic Brain **Syndromes**
Drug Synergism *USE Drug Interactions*
Lunar **Synodic** Cycle
Synonyms
Syntax
Synthetic Speech
Syphilis
Syria
Autonomic Nervous **System**
Autonomic Nervous **System** Disorders
Cardiovascular **System**
Caste **System**
Central Nervous **System**
Central Nervous **System** Disorders
Central Nervous System Drugs *USE CNS Affecting Drugs*
Digestive **System**
Digestive **System** Disorders
Endocrine **System**
Gastrointestinal **System**
Hypothalamo Hypophyseal **System**
Hypothalamo Pituitary Adrenal **System**
Lemniscal **System**
Limbic **System**
Musculoskeletal **System**
Nervous **System**
Nervous **System** Disorders
Nervous **System** Neoplasms
Nervous System Plasticity *USE Neural Plasticity*
Parasympathetic Nervous **System**
Peripheral Nervous **System**
Respiratory **System**
Sclerosis (Nervous **System)**
Sympathetic Nervous **System**
Urogenital **System**
Systematic Desensitization Therapy
Systems
Systems Analysis
Systems Theory
Anatomical **Systems**
Classification Systems *USE Taxonomies*
Communication **Systems**
Decision Support **Systems**
Expert **Systems**
Human Machine **Systems**
Human Machine **Systems** Design
Information **Systems**
Knowledge Based Systems *USE Expert Systems*
Man Machine Systems *USE Human Machine Systems*
Man Machine Systems Design
USE Human Machine Systems Design
Management Information Systems *USE Information Systems*
Number **Systems**
Political Economic **Systems**
Telephone **Systems**
Systolic Pressure
Szondi Test
T Groups *USE Human Relations Training*

T Mazes
T Test
Statistical **Tables**
Taboos
Tachistoscopes
Tachistoscopic Presentation
Tachycardia
Tactual Discrimination
USE Tactual Perception
Tactual Displays
Tactual Maps *USE Mobility Aids*
Tactual Perception
Tactual Stimulation
Tailored Testing *USE Adaptive Testing*
Taiwan
Note **Taking**
Perspective Taking *USE Role Taking*
Risk **Taking**
Role **Taking**
Sexual Risk **Taking**
Test **Taking**
Talent *USE Ability*
Talented *USE Gifted*
Fairy Tales *USE Folklore*
Self **Talk**
Sleep **Talking**
Tantrums
Tanzania
Tape Recorders
Finger **Tapping**
Tardive Dyskinesia
Task Analysis
Task Complexity
Task Difficulty *USE Task Complexity*
Time On **Task**
Piagetian **Tasks**
Taste Aversion Conditioning
USE Aversion Conditioning
Taste Buds
Taste Discrimination
USE Taste Perception
Taste Perception
Taste Stimulation
Taurine
Taxation
Psychiatric Classifications (Taxon) *USE Psychodiagnostic Typologies*
Taxonomies
Tay Sachs Disease
USE Amaurotic Familial Idiocy
Taylor Manifest Anxiety Scale
Tea *USE Beverages (Nonalcoholic)*
Teacher Accreditation
USE Accreditation (Education Personnel)
Teacher Aides
Teacher Attitudes
Teacher Characteristics
Teacher Education
Teacher Effectiveness
USE Teacher Characteristics
Teacher Effectiveness Evaluation
Teacher Expectations
Teacher Personality
Teacher Recruitment
Teacher Student Interaction
Teacher Tenure
Teacher Training *USE Teacher Education*
Inservice **Teacher** Education
Minnesota Teacher Attitude Inventory
USE Attitude Measures
Teachers
College **Teachers**
Cooperating **Teachers**
Elementary School **Teachers**
High School **Teachers**
Junior High School **Teachers**
Preschool **Teachers**
Preservice **Teachers**
Resource **Teachers**
Special Education **Teachers**

Student **Teachers**
Supervising Teachers *USE Cooperating Teachers*
Technical Education Teachers *USE Vocational Education Teachers*
Vocational Education **Teachers**
Teaching
Teaching Internship *USE Student Teaching*
Teaching Machines
Teaching Methods
Discovery **Teaching** Method
Initial **Teaching** Alphabet
Student **Teaching**
Team **Teaching** Method
Team Teaching Method
Teams
Technical Education Teachers *USE Vocational Education Teachers*
Technical Personnel
Technical Schools
Technical Service Personnel
Holtzman Inkblot **Technique**
Mutual Storytelling **Technique**
Projective Testing **Technique**
Q Sort Testing **Technique**
Cognitive **Techniques**
Paradigmatic Techniques *USE Paradoxical Techniques*
Paradoxical **Techniques**
Personal Growth Techniques *USE Human Potential Movement*
Projective **Techniques**
Psychotherapeutic **Techniques**
Self Help **Techniques**
Stereotaxic **Techniques**
Technology
Nuclear **Technology**
Reproductive **Technology**
Teenage Fathers *USE Adolescent Fathers*
Teenage Mothers *USE Adolescent Mothers*
Teenage Pregnancy *USE Adolescent Pregnancy*
Teenagers *USE Adolescents*
Teeth (Anatomy)
Teeth Grinding *USE Bruxism*
Nocturnal **Teeth** Grinding
Ventral Tegmental Area *USE Tegmentum*
Tegmentum
Telecommunications Media
Teleconferencing
Telekinesis *USE Psychokinesis*
Telemetry
Telencephalon
Telepathy
Telephone Hot Lines *USE Hot Line Services*
Telephone Surveys
Telephone Systems
Televised Instruction
Television
Television Advertising
Television Viewing
Closed Circuit **Television**
Educational **Television**
Temperament *USE Personality*
Guilford Zimmerman **Temperament** Surv
Temperature Effects
Temperature Perception
Body **Temperature**
Skin **Temperature**
Tempo
Conceptual **Tempo**
Temporal Frequency
Temporal Lobe
Temporal Spatial Concept Scale *USE Intelligence Measures*
Temporomandibular Joint Syndrome *USE Musculoskeletal Disorders*
Temptation

Central **Tendency** Measures
Achilles **Tendon** Reflex
Tendons
Tennessee Self Concept Scale
Tennis
Tension Headache *USE Muscle Contraction Headache*
Premenstrual **Tension**
Occupational **Tenure**
Teacher **Tenure**
Teratogens
Long **Term** Care
Long **Term** Memory
Long Term Potentiation *USE Postactivation Potentials*
Short **Term** Memory
Short Term Potentiation *USE Postactivation Potentials*
Short Term Psychotherapy *USE Brief Psychotherapy*
Terminal Cancer
Terminally Ill Patients
Video Display Terminals *USE Video Display Units*
Employee Termination *USE Personnel Termination*
Personnel **Termination**
Relationship **Termination**
Treatment **Termination**
Terminology
Psychological **Terminology**
Territoriality
Terrorism
Night Terrors *USE Sleep Disorders*
Test Administration
Test Anxiety
Test Bias
Test Coaching
Test Construction
Test Difficulty *USE Difficulty Level (Test)*
Test Equating *USE Score Equating*
Test Forms
Test Interpretation
Test Items
Test Normalization *USE Test Standardization*
Test Norms
Test Reliability
Test Scores
Test Standardization
Test Taking
Test Tube Babies *USE Reproductive Technology*
Test Validity
Army General Classification **Test**
Bender Gestalt **Test**
Benton Revised Visual Retention **Test**
Blacky Pictures Test *USE Projective Personality Measures*
California **Test** of Mental Maturity
California **Test** of Personality
Cattell Culture Fair Intell Test *USE Culture Fair Intelligence Test*
Chi Square **Test**
Childrens Apperception **Test**
Cochran Q **Test**
Coll Ent Exam Bd Scholastic Apt **Test**
Color Pyramid Test *USE Projective Personality Measures*
Content Analysis **(Test)**
Cultural **Test** Bias
Culture Fair Intelligence **Test**
Dexamethasone Suppression **Test**
Difficulty Level **(Test)**
Draw A Man Test *USE Human Figures Drawing*
F **Test**
Franck Drawing Completion **Test**
Frostig Development **Test** Vis Percept
General Aptitude **Test** Battery
Goldstein Scheerer Object Sort **Test**
Goodenough Harris Draw A Person **Test**
Hidden Figures **Test**
Illinois **Test** Psycholinguist Abil

Incomplete Man **Test**
Item Analysis **(Test)**
Item Content **(Test)**
Kohs Block Design **Test**
Kolmogorov Smirnov **Test**
Lorge Thorndike Intelligence **Test**
Lowenfeld Mosaic **Test**
Mann Whitney U **Test**
Matching Test *USE Matching to Sample*
Memory for Designs **Test**
Miller Analogies **Test**
Modern Language Aptitude **Test**
Onomatopoeia and Images Test *USE Projective Personality Measures*
Peabody Picture Vocabulary **Test**
Porteus Maze **Test**
Preliminary Scholastic Aptitude Test *USE Coll Ent Exam Bd Scholastic Apt Test*
Remote Associates **Test**
Rod and Frame **Test**
Rorschach **Test**
Scholastic Aptitude Test *USE Coll Ent Exam Bd Scholastic Apt Test*
School and College Ability Test *USE Aptitude Measures*
Sign **Test**
Slosson Intelligence **Test** for Child
Spearman Brown **Test**
Stanford Achievement **Test**
Stroop Color Word **Test**
Szondi **Test**
T **Test**
Thematic Apperception **Test**
Vane Kindergarten Test *USE Intelligence Measures*
Welsh Figure Preference **Test**
Wepman **Test** of Auditory Discrim
Wide Range Achievement **Test**
Wilcoxon Sign Rank **Test**
Wisconsin Card Sorting **Test**
Zulliger Z **Test**
Testes
Testes Disorders *USE Endocrine Sexual Disorders*
Testicular Feminization Syndrome
Expert **Testimony**
Legal **Testimony**
Testing
Testing Methods
Adaptive **Testing**
AIDS Testing *USE HIV Testing*
Basic Skills Testing *USE Minimum Competency Tests*
Body Sway **Testing**
Cloze **Testing**
Cognitive Hypothesis **Testing**
Computer Assisted **Testing**
Digit Span **Testing**
Drug Testing *USE Drug Usage Screening*
Embedded Figures **Testing**
Essay **Testing**
Forced Choice **(Testing** Method)
Group **Testing**
HIV **Testing**
Hypothesis **Testing**
Hypothesis Testing (Cognitive) *USE Cognitive Hypothesis Testing*
Individual **Testing**
Multiple Choice **(Testing** Method)
Null Hypothesis **Testing**
Projective **Testing** Technique
Psychological Testing *USE Psychometrics*
Q Sort **Testing** Technique
Reality **Testing**
Scaling **(Testing)**
Scoring **(Testing)**
Tailored Testing *USE Adaptive Testing*
Testosterone
Tests *USE Measurement*
Ability Tests *USE Aptitude Measures*
Comprehension **Tests**
Criterion Referenced **Tests**
Differential Aptitude **Tests**
Employment **Tests**
Gates MacGinitie Reading **Tests**
Henmon Nelson Tests Mental Ability *USE Intelligence Measures*
Iowa **Tests** of Basic Skills
Mastery Tests *USE Criterion Referenced Tests*
Metropolitan Readiness **Tests**
Minimum Competency **Tests**
Nonparametric Statistical **Tests**
Objective Referenced Tests *USE Criterion Referenced Tests*
Parametric Statistical **Tests**
Performance **Tests**
Screening **Tests**
Selection **Tests**
Sentence Completion **Tests**
Sociometric **Tests**
Standardized **Tests**
Statistical **Tests**
True False Tests *USE Forced Choice (Testing Method)*
Verbal **Tests**
Testwiseness
Tetrabenazine
Tetrachoric Correlation
Tetrahydrocannabinol
Text Structure
Textbooks
Programed **Textbooks**
Texture Perception
Thailand
Thalamic Nuclei
Thalamotomy
Thalamus
Geniculate Bodies **(Thalamus)**
Thalidomide
Thanatology *USE Death Education*
Thanatos *USE Death Instinct*
Theatre
Theft
Thematic Apperception Test
Theology *USE Religion*
Theophylline
Bayes Theorem *USE Statistical Probability*
Theoretical Interpretation
Theoretical Orientation
Theories
Theories of Education
Theory Formulation
Theory of Evolution
Theory Verification
Chaos **Theory**
Communication **Theory**
Educational Theory *USE Theories of Education*
Fairbairnian Theory *USE Object Relations*
Fuzzy Set **Theory**
Game **Theory**
Information **Theory**
Item Response **Theory**
Latent Trait Theory *USE Item Response Theory*
Learning **Theory**
Personal Construct Theory *USE Personality Theory*
Personality **Theory**
Psychoanalytic **Theory**
Systems **Theory**
Winnicottian Theory *USE Object Relations*
Therapeutic Abortion *USE Induced Abortion*
Therapeutic Alliance
Therapeutic Camps
Therapeutic Community
Therapeutic Outcomes *USE Treatment Outcomes*
Therapeutic Processes
Therapeutic Social Clubs
Medical **Therapeutic** Devices
Negative **Therapeutic** Reaction
Organic **Therapies**

Therapist Attitudes
Therapist Characteristics
Therapist Effectiveness
USE Therapist Characteristics
Therapist Experience
USE Therapist Characteristics
Therapist Patient Interaction
USE Psychotherapeutic Processes
Therapist Patient Sexual Relations
USE Professional Client Sexual Relations
Therapist Personality
USE Therapist Characteristics
Therapist Role
Therapist Selection
Therapist Trainees
Patient Therapist Interaction
USE Psychotherapeutic Processes
Patient Therapist Sexual Relations
USE Professional Client Sexual Relations
Selection (Therapist) *USE Therapist Selection*
Therapists
Occupational **Therapists**
Physical **Therapists**
Speech **Therapists**
Therapy *USE Treatment*
Activity Therapy *USE Recreation Therapy*
Animal Assisted **Therapy**
Art **Therapy**
Aversion **Therapy**
Behavior **Therapy**
Bright Light Therapy *USE Phototherapy*
Client Centered **Therapy**
Cognitive **Therapy**
Cognitive Behavior Therapy *USE Cognitive Therapy*
Conjoint **Therapy**
Cooperative Therapy *USE Cotherapy*
Couples **Therapy**
Creative Arts **Therapy**
Dance **Therapy**
Directed Reverie **Therapy**
Drug **Therapy**
ECS Therapy
USE Electroconvulsive Shock Therapy
ECT (Therapy)
USE Electroconvulsive Shock Therapy
Educational **Therapy**
Electroconvulsive Shock **Therapy**
Electroshock Therapy
USE Electroconvulsive Shock Therapy
Encounter Group **Therapy**
Environmental Therapy *USE Milieu Therapy*
Estrogen Replacement Therapy *USE Hormone Therapy*
Existential **Therapy**
Exposure **Therapy**
Eye Movement Desensitization **Therapy**
Family **Therapy**
Feminist **Therapy**
Flooding Therapy *USE Implosive Therapy*
Gestalt **Therapy**
Group Therapy *USE Group Psychotherapy*
Gymnastic Therapy *USE Recreation Therapy*
Hormone **Therapy**
Illumination Therapy *USE Phototherapy*
Implosive **Therapy**
Individual Therapy *USE Individual Psychotherapy*
Insight **Therapy**
Insulin Shock **Therapy**
Maintenance **Therapy**
Marathon Group **Therapy**
Marital Therapy *USE Marriage Counseling*
Milieu **Therapy**
Morita **Therapy**
Movement **Therapy**
Multiple Therapy *USE Cotherapy*
Muscle Relaxation Therapy *USE Relaxation Therapy*
Music **Therapy**
Nondirective Therapy *USE Client Centered Therapy*
Occupational **Therapy**
Personal **Therapy**
Persuasion **Therapy**
Pet Therapy *USE Animal Assisted Therapy*
Physical **Therapy**
Play **Therapy**
Poetry **Therapy**
Pretraining (Therapy) *USE Client Education*
Primal **Therapy**
Progressive Relaxation **Therapy**
Psychoanalytic Therapy *USE Psychoanalysis*
Radiation **Therapy**
Rational Emotive **Therapy**
Reality **Therapy**
Reciprocal Inhibition **Therapy**
Recreation **Therapy**
Relationship **Therapy**
Relaxation **Therapy**
Rogerian Therapy *USE Client Centered Therapy*
Sex **Therapy**
Shock **Therapy**
Socioenvironmental Therapy *USE Milieu Therapy*
Speech **Therapy**
Systematic Desensitization **Therapy**
Triadic Therapy *USE Conjoint Therapy*
Vitamin **Therapy**
X Ray Therapy *USE Radiation Therapy*
Thermal Acclimatization
Thermal Factors
USE Temperature Effects
Thermoreceptors
Thermoregulation (Body)
Theta Rhythm
Thigh
Thinking
Autistic **Thinking**
Convergent Thinking
USE Inductive Deductive Reasoning
Divergent **Thinking**
Logical **Thinking**
Magical **Thinking**
Thiopental
Thioridazine
Thiothixene
Third World Countries
USE Developing Countries
Thirst
Thoracic Nerves *USE Spinal Nerves*
Thorax
Thorazine *USE Chlorpromazine*
Lorge **Thorndike** Intelligence Test
Thought Content *USE Cognitions*
Thought Control *USE Brainwashing*
Thought Disturbances
Fantasies **(Thought** Disturbances)
Threat
Threat Postures
Threshold Determination
Critical Flicker Fusion **Threshold**
Luminance Threshold *USE Brightness Perception AND Visual Thresholds*
Photic Threshold *USE Illumination AND Visual Thresholds*
Thresholds
Auditory **Thresholds**
Olfactory **Thresholds**
Pain **Thresholds**
Vibrotactile **Thresholds**
Visual **Thresholds**
Failure to **Thrive**
Thromboses
Coronary **Thromboses**
Project Follow **Through**
Thumb
Thumbsucking
Thymoleptic Drugs
USE Tranquilizing Drugs
Thyroid Disorders
Thyroid Extract *USE Thyroid Hormones*
Thyroid Gland
Thyroid Hormones

Thyroid Stimulating Hormone
USE Thyrotropin
Thyroidectomy
Thyrotoxicosis
Thyrotropic Hormone *USE Thyrotropin*
Thyrotropin
Thyroxine
Tibet
Tic Doloureux *USE Trigeminal Neuralgia*
Tics
Tigers *USE Felids*
Time
Time Disorientation
Time Estimation
Time Limited Psychotherapy
USE Brief Psychotherapy
Time Management
Time On Task
Time Out
Time Perception
Time Perspective
Time Series
Constant **Time** Delay
Exposure Time (Stimulus) *USE Stimulus Duration*
Interresponse **Time**
Leisure **Time**
Reaction **Time**
Response Time *USE Reaction Time*
Timers (Apparatus)
Timidity
Tinnitus
Tiredness *USE Fatigue*
Tissue Donation
Connective **Tissue** Cells
Tissues (Body)
Connective **Tissues**
Nerve **Tissues**
Toads
Tobacco (Drug) *USE Nicotine*
Tobacco (Smokeless)
USE Smokeless Tobacco
Tobacco Smoking
Chewing Tobacco *USE Smokeless Tobacco*
Smokeless **Tobacco**
Trinidad and **Tobago**
Toes (Anatomy) *USE Feet (Anatomy)*
Tofranil *USE Imipramine*
Toilet Training
Token Economy Programs
Token Reinforcement
USE Secondary Reinforcement
Tolerance
Tolerance for Ambiguity
Drug **Tolerance**
Toluene
Tomography
Positron Emission Tomography *USE Tomography*
Tone (Frequency) *USE Pitch (Frequency)*
Muscle **Tone**
Tonga
Tongue
Tonic Immobility
Tool Use
Animal Tool Use *USE Tool Use*
Top Level Managers
Topography
Torticollis
Tortoises *USE Turtles*
Torture
Totalitarianism
Touch *USE Tactual Perception*
Touching *USE Physical Contact*
Gilles de la **Tourette** Disorder
Towns
Toxic Disorders
Toxic Encephalopathies
Toxic Hepatitis
Toxic Psychoses
Toxic Waste *USE Hazardous Materials*

Toxicity
Toxicomania
Toxins *USE Poisons*
Toy Selection
Toys
Educational **Toys**
Memory **Trace**
Trachea
Tracking
Visual **Tracking**
Optic **Tract**
Respiratory **Tract** Disorders
Tractotomy
Extrapyramidal **Tracts**
Pyramidal **Tracts**
Spinothalamic **Tracts**
Traditionalism *USE Conservatism*
Air **Traffic** Accidents
Air **Traffic** Control
Motor **Traffic** Accidents
Trainable Mentally Retarded
Counselor **Trainees**
Psychotherapist Trainees *USE Therapist Trainees*
Therapist **Trainees**
Training *USE Education*
Training (Athletic) *USE Athletic Training*
Assertiveness **Training**
Athletic **Training**
Autogenic **Training**
Biofeedback **Training**
Childbirth **Training**
Clinical Methods **Training**
Clinical Psychology Grad **Training**
Communication Skills **Training**
Community Mental Health **Training**
Computer **Training**
Human Relations **Training**
Inservice **Training**
Job Training *USE Personnel Training*
Management **Training**
Memory **Training**
Mental Health Inservice **Training**
Military **Training**
Motivation **Training**
Omission **Training**
On the Job **Training**
Parent **Training**
Parent Effectiveness Training *USE Parent Training*
Personnel **Training**
Postgraduate **Training**
Psychiatric **Training**
Psychoanalytic **Training**
Psychotherapy **Training**
Self Instructional **Training**
Sensitivity **Training**
Social Skills **Training**
Sport Training *USE Athletic Training*
Teacher Training *USE Teacher Education*
Toilet **Training**
Work Adjustment **Training**
Railroad **Trains**
Latent Trait Theory *USE Item Response Theory*
State **Trait** Anxiety Inventory
Personality **Traits**
Major Tranquilizers *USE Neuroleptic Drugs*
Minor **Tranquilizers**
Tranquilizing Drugs
Transactional Analysis
Transaminases
Transcultural Psychiatry
Transducers
Transfer (Learning)
Transfer Students
Client **Transfer**
Interhemispheric Transfer *USE Interhemispheric Interaction*
Interocular **Transfer**
Negative **Transfer**
Patient Transfer *USE Client Transfer*
Positive **Transfer**

Transferases
Psychotherapeutic **Transference**
Transformational Generative Grammar
Blood **Transfusion**
Transgenerational Patterns
Transistors (Apparatus) *USE Apparatus*
School **Transition**
School to Work **Transition**
Transitional Objects
Career Transitions *USE Career Development*
Foreign Language **Translation**
Translocation (Chromosome)
Intergenerational Transmission
USE Transgenerational Patterns
Sexually Transmitted Diseases
USE Venereal Diseases
Transpersonal Psychology
Neural **Transplantation**
Organ **Transplantation**
Renal Transplantation
USE Organ Transplantation
Heart Transplants *USE Organ Transplantation*
Kidney Transplants *USE Organ Transplantation*
Transportation
Transportation Accidents
Air **Transportation**
Ground **Transportation**
Public **Transportation**
Water **Transportation**
Transposition (Cognition)
Transracial Adoption
USE Interracial Adoption
Transsexualism
Transvestism
Tranylcypromine
Birth **Trauma**
Emotional **Trauma**
Physical Trauma *USE Injuries*
Traumatic Brain Injury
Traumatic Neurosis
Traumatic Psychosis
USE Reactive Psychosis
Brain Injury (Traumatic) *USE Traumatic Brain Injury*
Commuting **(Travel)**
Traveling
Trazodone
Treatment
Treatment Client Matching
USE Client Treatment Matching
Treatment Compliance
Treatment Dropouts
Treatment Duration
Treatment Effectiveness Evaluation
Treatment Facilities
Treatment Outcomes
Treatment Planning
Treatment Refusal
Treatment Resistant Depression
Treatment Resistant Disorders
Treatment Seeking Behavior
USE Health Care Seeking Behavior
Treatment Termination
Treatment Withholding
Client **Treatment** Matching
Court Ordered Treatment *USE Court Referrals*
Cross Cultural **Treatment**
Day Care (Treatment) *USE Partial Hospitalization*
Dental **Treatment**
Electrosleep **Treatment**
Interdisciplinary **Treatment** Approach
Involuntary **Treatment**
Life Sustaining **Treatment**
Medical **Treatment** (General)
Multidisciplinary Treatment Approach
USE Interdisciplinary Treatment Approach
Multimodal **Treatment** Approach
Outpatient **Treatment**
Patient Treatment Matching
USE Client Treatment Matching
Physical **Treatment** Methods
Refusal (Treatment) *USE Treatment Refusal*
Right to **Treatment**
Side Effects **(Treatment)**
Sleep **Treatment**
Delirium **Tremens**
Tremor
Trends
Triadic Therapy *USE Conjoint Therapy*
Trial and Error Learning
Competency to Stand **Trial**
Triazolam
Tribes
Trichotillomania *USE Hair Pulling*
Tricyclic Antidepressant Drugs
Tricyclic Resistant Depression
USE Treatment Resistant Depression
Trifluoperazine
Triflupromazine
USE Phenothiazine Derivatives
Trigeminal Nerve
Trigeminal Neuralgia
Trigonum Cerebrale *USE Fornix*
Trihexyphenidyl
Triiodothyronine
Trinidad and Tobago
Triplets
Educational Field **Trips**
Trisomy
Trisomy 21
Trochlear Nerve *USE Cranial Nerves*
Truancy
School **Truancy**
Trucks *USE Motor Vehicles*
True False Tests
USE Forced Choice (Testing Method)
Trust (Social Behavior)
Tryptamine
Tryptophan
Tubal Ligation
Eustachian Tube *USE Middle Ear*
Test Tube Babies
USE Reproductive Technology
Tuberculosis
Pulmonary **Tuberculosis**
Cathode Ray Tubes *USE Video Display Units*
Tubocurarine
Tumors *USE Neoplasms*
Tunisia
Tunnel Vision
Turkey
Turners Syndrome
Employee **Turnover**
Personnel Turnover *USE Employee Turnover*
Turtles
Tutoring
Peer **Tutoring**
Tutors *USE Teachers*
Twelve Step Programs
Twins
Dizygotic Twins *USE Heterozygotic Twins*
Fraternal Twins *USE Heterozygotic Twins*
Heterozygotic **Twins**
Identical Twins *USE Monozygotic Twins*
Monozygotic **Twins**
Siamese **Twins**
Chorda Tympani Nerve *USE Facial Nerve*
Tympanic Membrane *USE Middle Ear*
Type A Personality
USE Coronary Prone Behavior
Type B Personality
USE Coronary Prone Behavior
Type I Errors
Type II Errors
Myers Briggs **Type** Indicator
Schizophrenia (Disorganized Type) *USE Hebephrenic Schizophrenia*
Schizophrenia (Residual Type) *USE Schizophrenia*

Body Types *USE Somatotypes*
Typing
Typists *USE Clerical Personnel*
Typologies (General) *USE Taxonomies*
Psychodiagnostic **Typologies**
Tyramine
Tyrosine
Mann Whitney **U** Test
Uganda
Ulcerative Colitis
Gastrointestinal **Ulcers**
Peptic Ulcers *USE Gastrointestinal Ulcers*
Ulnar Nerve *USE Spinal Nerves*
Ultrasound
Uncertainty
Unconditioned Reflex *USE Reflexes*
Unconditioned Responses
Unconditioned Stimulus
Unconscious (Personality Factor)
Collective **Unconscious**
Driving **Under** The Influence
Academic **Underachievement**
Underdeveloped Countries
USE Developing Countries
Undergraduate Degrees
USE Educational Degrees
Undergraduate Education
Undergraduates *USE College Students*
Underprivileged *USE Disadvantaged*
Understanding *USE Comprehension*
Underwater Effects
Underweight
Undifferentiated Schizophrenia
Unemployment
Union of Soviet Socialist Republics
Labor **Union** Members
Labor **Unions**
Unipolar Depression
USE Major Depression
United Arab Republic *USE Egypt*
United Kingdom
United States
Hospital Psychiatric Units *USE Psychiatric Units*
Psychiatric **Units**
Shock **Units**
Video Display **Units**
Words (Phonetic **Units)**
Universities *USE Colleges*
Open Universities *USE Nontraditional Education*
Unskilled Industrial Workers
Unwed Mothers
Upper Class
Upper Class Attitudes
Upper Income Level
Upward Bound
Upward Mobility *USE Social Mobility*
Urban Development
USE Community Development
Urban Environments
Urban Planning
Urbanization
Uric Acid
Urinalysis
Urinary Function Disorders
Urinary Incontinence
Urination
Urine
Urogenital Disorders
Urogenital System
Uruguay
Drug **Usage**
Drug **Usage** Attitudes
Drug **Usage** Screening
Intravenous Drug **Usage**
IV Drug Usage *USE Intravenous Drug Usage*
Marihuana **Usage**
Animal Tool Use *USE Tool Use*
Tool **Use**
Uterus
Health Care **Utilization**
Health Service Utilization *USE Health Care Utilization*
Vacation Benefits
USE Employee Leave Benefits
Vacationing
Vaccination *USE Immunization*
Vagina
Vaginismus
Vagotomy
Vagus Nerve
Concept Validity *USE Construct Validity*
Concurrent **Validity**
Construct **Validity**
Factorial **Validity**
Predictive **Validity**
Statistical **Validity**
Test **Validity**
Valium *USE Diazepam*
Valproic Acid
Values
Allport Vernon Lindzey Study Values *USE Attitude Measures*
Ethnic **Values**
Personal **Values**
Social **Values**
Heart **Valves**
Vandalism
Vane Kindergarten Test
USE Intelligence Measures
Variability Measurement
Response **Variability**
Stimulus **Variability**
Variable Interval Reinforcement
Variable Ratio Reinforcement
Dependent **Variables**
Independent **Variables**
Statistical **Variables**
Variance Homogeneity
Analysis of **Variance**
Error Variance *USE Error of Measurement*
Heterogeneity of Variance *USE Variance Homogeneity*
Interaction **Variance**
Contingent Negative **Variation**
Diurnal Variations *USE Human Biological Rhythms*
Seasonal **Variations**
Varimax Rotation
Vascular Dementia
Vascular Disorders
USE Cardiovascular Disorders
Cerebral Vascular Disorders
USE Cerebrovascular Disorders
Vasectomy
Vasoconstriction
Vasoconstrictor Drugs
Vasodilation
Vasodilator Drugs
Vasopressin
Vasopressor Drugs
USE Vasoconstrictor Drugs
Motor **Vehicles**
Veins (Anatomy)
Velocity
Venereal Diseases
Venezuela
Ventral Roots
Ventral Tegmental Area *USE Tegmentum*
Cerebral **Ventricles**
Heart **Ventricles**
Verapamil
Verbal Ability
Verbal Communication
Verbal Comprehension
Verbal Conditioning *USE Verbal Learning*
Verbal Fluency
Verbal Learning
Verbal Meaning
Verbal Memory
Verbal Reinforcement
Verbal Stimuli
Verbal Tests

Conditioning (Verbal) *USE Verbal Learning*
Verbalization *USE Oral Communication*
Verbs
Verdict Determination *USE Adjudication*
Vergence Movements
USE Eye Convergence
Theory **Verification**
Vernier Acuity *USE Visual Acuity*
Allport Vernon Lindzey Study Values
USE Attitude Measures
Vertebrates
Vertigo
Very Old
Blood **Vessels**
Coronary Vessels *USE Arteries (Anatomy)*
Retinal Vessels *USE Arteries (Anatomy)*
Vestibular Apparatus
Vestibular Nystagmus *USE Nystagmus*
Vestibular Stimulation
USE Somesthetic Stimulation
Military **Veterans**
Veterinary Medicine
Vibration
Vibrators (Apparatus)
Vibrotactile Thresholds
Vicarious Experiences
Vicarious Reinforcement
USE Vicarious Experiences
Reinforcement (Vicarious) *USE Vicarious Experiences*
Victimization
Crime **Victims**
Video Display Terminals
USE Video Display Units
Video Display Units
Video Games *USE Computer Games*
Videotape Instruction
Videotape Recorders
Videotapes
Vietnam
North Vietnam *USE Vietnam*
South Vietnam *USE Vietnam*
Vietnamese Cultural Groups
World **View**
Television **Viewing**
Vigilance
Saint **Vincent**
Vineland Social Maturity Scale
Boundary Violations (Sexual)
USE Professional Client Sexual Relations
Sexual Boundary Violations
USE Professional Client Sexual Relations
Violence
Client Violence *USE Patient Violence*
Domestic Violence *USE Family Violence*
Family **Violence**
Patient **Violence**
Viral Disorders
Epstein Barr **Viral** Disorder
Virgin Islands
Virginity
Virtual Reality
Human Immunodeficiency **Virus**
Vision
Vision Disorders
Binocular **Vision**
Central Vision *USE Foveal Vision*
Foveal **Vision**
Hysterical **Vision** Disturbances
Monocular **Vision**
Peripheral **Vision**
Stereoscopic **Vision**
Tunnel **Vision**
Visitation Rights *USE Child Visitation*
Child **Visitation**
Institution **Visitation**
Home **Visiting** Programs
VISTA Volunteers
USE Volunteers in Service to America
Visual Acuity
Visual Contrast
Visual Cortex
Visual Discrimination
Visual Displays
Visual Evoked Potentials
Visual Feedback
Visual Field
Visual Fixation *USE Eye Fixation*
Visual Hallucinations
Visual Masking
Visual Memory
Visual Neglect *USE Sensory Neglect*
Visual Perception
Visual Perspective
USE Linear Perspective
Visual Receptive Fields
Visual Search
Visual Spatial Ability
USE Visuospatial Ability
Visual Spatial Memory
USE Visuospatial Memory
Visual Stimulation
Visual Thresholds
Visual Tracking
Benton Revised **Visual** Retention Test
Focusing (Visual) *USE Ocular Accommodation*
Frostig Development Test **Vis** Percept
Visualization *USE Imagery*
Visually Disabled
Visually Handicapped
USE Visually Disabled
Visuospatial Ability
Visuospatial Memory
Vitamin C *USE Ascorbic Acid*
Vitamin Deficiency Disorders
Vitamin Therapy
Vitamins
In Vitro Fertilization
USE Reproductive Technology
Vocabulary
Peabody Picture **Vocabulary** Test
Sight **Vocabulary**
Words (Vocabulary) *USE Vocabulary*
Vocal Cords
Vocalization
Infant **Vocalization**
Animal **Vocalizations**
Vocational Adjustment
USE Occupational Adjustment
Vocational Aspirations
USE Occupational Aspirations
Vocational Choice
USE Occupational Choice
Vocational Counseling
USE Occupational Guidance
Vocational Counselors
Vocational Education
Vocational Education Teachers
Vocational Evaluation
Vocational Guidance
USE Occupational Guidance
Vocational Interests
USE Occupational Interests
Vocational Maturity
Vocational Mobility
USE Occupational Mobility
Vocational Preference
USE Occupational Preference
Vocational Rehabilitation
Vocational School Students
Vocational Schools
USE Technical Schools
Strong **Vocational** Interest Blank
Vocations *USE Occupations*
Voice
Voice Disorders *USE Dysphonia*
Voles *USE Rodents*
Volition
Volt Meters *USE Apparatus*

ROTATED ALPHABETICAL TERMS SECTION

Blood **Volume**
Volunteer Civilian Personnel
Volunteer Military Personnel
Volunteer Personnel
Volunteers in Service to America
Experiment **Volunteers**
VISTA Volunteers
USE Volunteers in Service to America
Vomeronasal Sense
Vomit Inducing Drugs *USE Emetic Drugs*
Vomiting
Voting Behavior
Vowels
Voyeurism
Deja Vu *USE Consciousness States*
Vygotsky (Lev)
Wages *USE Salaries*
Sleep **Wake** Cycle
Wakefulness
Wales
Walk In Clinics
Walking
Abdominal **Wall**
Wandering Behavior
War
Nuclear **War**
Prisoners of **War**
Warning Labels
Warning Signs *USE Warnings*
Warnings
Safety Warnings *USE Warnings*
Wasps
Toxic Waste *USE Hazardous Materials*
Water Deprivation
Water Intake
Water Safety
Water Transportation
Watson (John Broadus)
Slow Wave Sleep *USE NREM Sleep*
Sound Waves *USE Acoustics*
Weaning
Weapons
Weather *USE Atmospheric Conditions*
Wechsler Adult Intelligence Scale
Wechsler Bellevue Intelligence Scale
Wechsler Intelligence Scale Children
Wechsler Memory Scale
Wechsler Preschool Primary Scale
Work **Week** Length
Weight Control
Weight Perception
Birth **Weight**
Body **Weight**
Brain **Weight**
Low Birth Weight *USE Birth Weight*
Statistical **Weighting**
Weightlessness
Weightlifting
Welfare Services (Government)
Animal **Welfare**
Child **Welfare**
Community **Welfare** Services
Public Welfare Services
USE Community Welfare Services
Well Being
Wellness *USE Health*
Welsh Figure Preference Test
Barron **Welsh** Art Scale
Wepman Test of Auditory Discrim
Wernickes Syndrome
West Africa
West German Federal Republic
USE West Germany
West Germany
West Indies
Western Europe
Western Samoa
Whales
Wheelchairs *USE Mobility Aids*
Whiplash
Whistleblowing *USE Informants*
White Betz A B Scale
USE Nonprojective Personality Measures
White Blood Cells *USE Leucocytes*
White Collar Workers
White Noise
Whites
Mann **Whitney** U Test
Wholistic Health *USE Holistic Health*
Wide Range Achievement Test
Widowers
Widows
Wilcoxon Sign Rank Test
Wilderness Experience
Free Will *USE Volition*
Prader **Willi** Syndrome
James **(William)**
Willpower *USE Self Control*
Living Wills *USE Advance Directives*
Wilson Patterson Conservatism Scale
Wine
Winnicottian Theory *USE Object Relations*
Winter Depression
USE Seasonal Affective Disorder
Wisconsin Card Sorting Test
Wisdom
Witchcraft
Withdrawal (Defense Mechanism)
Withdrawal (Drug) *USE Drug Withdrawal*
Alcohol **Withdrawal**
Drug **Withdrawal**
Nicotine **Withdrawal**
Treatment **Withholding**
Within Subjects Design
USE Repeated Measures
Witnesses
Wives
Wolves
Women *USE Human Females*
Working **Women**
Womens Liberation Movement
Woodcock Johnson Psychoed Battery
Word Associations
Word Blindness *USE Alexia*
Word Deafness *USE Aphasia*
Word Frequency
Word Meaning
Word Origins *USE Etymology*
Word Processing
Word Recognition
Stroop Color **Word** Test
Words (Form Classes)
USE Form Classes (Language)
Words (Phonetic Units)
Words (Vocabulary) *USE Vocabulary*
Work Adjustment Training
Work (Attitudes Toward)
Work Environments
USE Working Conditions
Work Ethic *USE Work (Attitudes Toward)*
Work Family Relationship
USE Family Work Relationship
Work Load
Work Related Illnesses
Work Rest Cycles
Work Satisfaction *USE Job Satisfaction*
Work Scheduling
Work Study Programs
USE Educational Programs
Work Week Length
Family **Work** Relationship
Field Work (Educational)
USE Curricular Field Experience
Noise Levels **(Work** Areas)
Quality of **Work** Life
Return to Work *USE Reemployment*
School to **Work** Transition
Social Work *USE Social Casework*

Social **Work** Education
Workday Shifts
Workers *USE Personnel*
Agricultural **Workers**
Agricultural Extension **Workers**
Blue Collar **Workers**
Child Care **Workers**
Foreign **Workers**
Guest Workers *USE Foreign Workers*
Migrant Farm **Workers**
Psychiatric Social **Workers**
Skilled Industrial **Workers**
Social **Workers**
Unskilled Industrial **Workers**
White Collar **Workers**
Working Alliance
USE Therapeutic Alliance
Working Conditions
Working Memory
USE Short Term Memory
Working Space
Working Women
Workmens Compensation Insurance
Sheltered **Workshops**
World View
Third World Countries
USE Developing Countries
Worms
Worry *USE Anxiety*
Worship *USE Religious Practices*
Wounds
Self Inflicted **Wounds**
Wrist
Writers
Writing (Creative) *USE Creative Writing*
Writing Skills
Creative **Writing**
Cursive **Writing**
Written Communication
Written Language
Wryneck *USE Torticollis*
X Rated Materials *USE Pornography*
X Ray Diagnosis *USE Roentgenography*
X Ray Therapy *USE Radiation Therapy*
Fragile **X** Syndrome
Xenophobia *USE Stranger Reactions*
Xylocaine *USE Lidocaine*
Yawning
Yemen
Yoga
Yohimbine
Young Adults
Predelinquent **Youth**
Yugoslavia
Z Scores *USE Standard Scores*
Zulliger **Z** Test
Zaire
Zambia
New **Zealand**
Zen Buddhism
Non **Zero** Sum Games
Zidovudine
Zimbabwe
Zimeldine
Guilford **Zimmerman** Temperament Surv
Zinc
Zoo Environment *USE Animal Captivity*
Zoology
Zulliger Z Test
Zungs Self Rating Depression Scale

TERM CLUSTERS SECTION

Term Cluster/Subcluster Subject Areas

Disorders Cluster
- Antisocial Behavior & Behavior Disorders
- Diagnosis
- Disorder Characteristics
- Learning Disorders & Mental Retardation
- Physical & Psychosomatic Disorders
- Psychological Disorders
- Speech & Language Disorders
- Symptomatology

Educational Cluster
- Academic Learning & Achievement
- Curricula
- Educational Personnel & Administration
- Educational Testing & Counseling
- Schools & Institutions
- Special Education
- Student Characteristics & Academic Environment
- Student Populations
- Teaching & Teaching Methods

Geographic Cluster
- Africa
- Antarctica
- Asia
- Central America
- Europe
- Latin America
- North America
- Pacific Islands
- South America
- West Indies

Legal Cluster
- Adjudication
- Criminal Groups
- Criminal Offenses
- Criminal Rehabilitation
- Laws
- Legal Issues
- Legal Personnel
- Legal Processes

Neuropsychology & Neurology Cluster
- Assessment & Diagnosis
- Electrophysiology
- Neuroanatomy
- Neurological Disorders
- Neurological Intervention
- Neurosciences
- Neurotransmitters & Neuroregulators

Occupational & Employment Cluster
- Career Areas
- Employee, Occupational & Job Characteristics
- Management & Professional Personnel Issues
- Occupational Groups
- Organizations & Organizational Behavior
- Personnel Management

Statistical Cluster
- Design, Analysis & Interpretation
- Statistical Reliability & Validity
- Statistical Theory & Experimentation

Tests & Testing Cluster
- Academic Achievement & Aptitude Measures
- Attitude & Interest Measures
- Intelligence Measures
- Nonprojective Personality Measures
- Perceptual Measures
- Projective Personality Measures
- Testing
- Testing Methods

Treatment Cluster
- Alternative Therapies
- Behavior Modification
- Counseling
- Hospitalization & Institutionalization
- Medical & Physical Treatment
- Psychotherapy
- Rehabilitation
- Treatment (General)
- Treatment Facilities

DISORDERS CLUSTER

- Antisocial Behavior & Behavior Disorders
- Diagnosis
- Disorder Characteristics
- Learning Disorders & Mental Retardation
- Physical & Psychosomatic Disorders
- Psychological Disorders
- Speech & Language Disorders
- Symptomatology

Antisocial Behavior & Behavior Disorders

Abuse of Power
Acquaintance Rape
Acute Alcoholic Intoxication
Addiction
Alcohol Abuse
Alcoholism
Antisocial Behavior
Antisocial Personality
Arson
Attempted Suicide
Battered Child Syndrome
Battered Females
Behavior Disorders
Behavior Problems
Child Abuse
Child Neglect
Chronic Alcoholic Intoxication
Conduct Disorder
Crime
Criminals
Driving Under The Influence
Drug Abuse
Drug Addiction
Drug Dependency
Drug Distribution
Elder Abuse
Emotional Abuse
Exhibitionism
Family Violence
Female Criminals
Female Delinquents
Fetishism
Genocide
Glue Sniffing
Heroin Addiction
Homicide
Incest
Infanticide
Inhalant Abuse
Intravenous Drug Usage
Juvenile Delinquency
Juvenile Delinquents
Juvenile Gangs
Kidnapping
Kleptomania
Male Criminals
Male Delinquents
Oppositional Defiant Disorder
Partner Abuse
Pathological Gambling
Patient Abuse
Patient Violence
Pedophilia
Perpetrators
Physical Abuse
Polydrug Abuse
Pyromania
Rape
Sadomasochism
Sadomasochistic Personality
School Phobia
Sex Offenses
Sexual Abuse
Sexual Deviations
Sexual Masochism
Sexual Sadism
Shoplifting
Suicidal Ideation
Suicide
Theft
Transvestism
Truancy
Vandalism
Violence
Voyeurism

Diagnosis

Anatomically Detailed Dolls
Angiography
Biological Markers
Biopsy
Cancer Screening
Cardiography
Clinical Judgment (Not Diagnosis)
Cognitive Assessment
Comorbidity
Computer Assisted Diagnosis
Dexamethasone Suppression Test
Diagnosis
Diagnosis Related Groups
Diagnostic and Statistical Manual
Diagnostic Interview Schedule
Differential Diagnosis
Drug Usage Screening
Dual Diagnosis
Echoencephalography
Electro Oculography
Electrocardiography
Electroencephalography
Electromyography
Electronystagmography
Electroplethysmography
Electroretinography
Encephalography
Geriatric Assessment
Health Screening
HIV Testing
International Class of Diseases
Magnetic Resonance Imaging
Mammography
Medical Diagnosis
Medical Model
Misdiagnosis
Neuropsychological Assessment
Ophthalmologic Examination
Pain Measurement
Physical Examination
Plethysmography
Pneumoencephalography
Prenatal Diagnosis
Prognosis
Psychiatric Evaluation
Psychodiagnosis
Psychodiagnostic Interview
Psychodiagnostic Typologies
Psychological Assessment
Research Diagnostic Criteria
Rheoencephalography
Roentgenography
Screening
Symptom Checklists
Urinalysis

Disorder Characteristics

At Risk Populations
Chronicity (Disorders)
Client Attitudes
Client Characteristics
Comorbidity
Disease Course
Dual Diagnosis
Epidemiology
Ethnospecific Disorders
Etiology
False Memory
Health Complaints
Illness Behavior
Mortality Rate
Onset (Disorders)
Patient History
Positive and Negative Symptoms
Predisposition
Premorbidity
Recovery (Disorders)
Relapse (Disorders)
Remission (Disorders)
Repressed Memory
Seasonal Variations
Severity (Disorders)
Spontaneous Remission
Susceptibility (Disorders)
Symptom Remission
Symptoms
Syndromes
Treatment Resistant Disorders

Consult Relationship Section for more information

Learning Disorders & Mental Retardation

Acalculia
Alexia
Amaurotic Familial Idiocy
Anencephaly
Attention Deficit Disorder
Autism
Borderline Mental Retardation
Crying Cat Syndrome
Downs Syndrome
Dyslexia
Educable Mentally Retarded
Home Reared Mentally Retarded
Hyperkinesis
Idiot Savants
Institutionalized Mentally Retarded
Learning Disabilities
Learning Disorders
Mental Retardation
Mental Retardation (Attit Toward)
Mentally Retarded
Microcephaly
Profoundly Mentally Retarded
Psychosocial Mental Retardation
Reading Disabilities
Rett Syndrome
Severely Mentally Retarded
Trainable Mentally Retarded
Trisomy
Trisomy 21

Physical & Psychosomatic Disorders

Acquired Immune Deficiency Syndrome
Addisons Disease
Adrenal Gland Disorders
Adventitiously Disabled
Agnosia
Agraphia
AIDS (Attitudes Toward)
AIDS Dementia Complex
Allergic Disorders
Allergic Skin Disorders
Alopecia
Alzheimers Disease
Amblyopia
Amenorrhea
Amputees
Anaphylactic Shock
Anemia
Anencephaly
Aneurysms
Angina Pectoris
Anomie
Anorexia Nervosa
Anosmia
Anosognosia
Aphagia
Aphasia
Apnea
Apraxia
Arrhythmias (Heart)
Arteriosclerosis
Asthenia
Asthma
Ataxia
Atherosclerosis
Athetosis
Audiogenic Seizures
Aurally Disabled
Autonomic Nervous System Disorders
Autosome Disorders
Bacterial Disorders
Bacterial Meningitis
Barbiturate Poisoning
Benign Neoplasms
Birth Injuries
Blind
Blood and Lymphatic Disorders
Blood Pressure Disorders
Bone Disorders
Bradycardia
Brain Concussion
Brain Damage
Brain Damaged
Brain Disorders
Brain Neoplasms
Breast Neoplasms
Bronchial Disorders
Bulimia
Burns
Carbon Monoxide Poisoning
Cardiovascular Disorders
Catabolism
Catalepsy
Cataplexy
Cataracts
Central Nervous System Disorders
Cerebral Arteriosclerosis
Cerebral Hemorrhage
Cerebral Ischemia
Cerebral Palsy
Cerebrovascular Accidents
Cerebrovascular Disorders
Chorea
Chromosome Disorders
Chronic Fatigue Syndrome
Chronic Pain
Cirrhosis (Liver)
Cleft Palate
Colitis
Colon Disorders
Color Blindness
Congenital Disorders
Congenitally Disabled
Constipation
Coronary Prone Behavior
Coronary Thromboses
Creutzfeldt Jakob Syndrome
Crying Cat Syndrome
Cushings Syndrome
Cystic Fibrosis
Deaf
Deaf Blind
Dementia
Dermatitis
Developmental Disabilities
Diabetes
Diabetes Insipidus
Diabetes Mellitus
Diarrhea
Digestive System Disorders
Disabled
Disabled (Attitudes Toward)
Disorders
Drug Induced Congenital Disorders
Drug Induced Hallucinations
Dysarthria
Dyskinesia
Dysmenorrhea
Dysmorphophobia
Dyspareunia
Dyspnea
Ear Disorders
Eating Disorders
Eczema
Electrical Injuries
Embolisms
Encephalitis
Encephalomyelitis
Encephalopathies
Endocrine Disorders
Endocrine Neoplasms
Endocrine Sexual Disorders
Epilepsy
Epileptic Seizures
Epstein Barr Viral Disorder
Essential Hypertension
Ethnospecific Disorders
Eye Disorders
Failure to Thrive
Fecal Incontinence
Fetal Alcohol Syndrome
Fibrillation (Heart)
Food Allergies
Fragile X Syndrome
Frigidity
Gastrointestinal Disorders
Gastrointestinal Ulcers
General Paresis
Genetic Disorders
Genital Disorders
Gilles de la Tourette Disorder
Glaucoma
Goiters
Gonorrhea
Grand Mal Epilepsy
Gynecological Disorders
Hay Fever
Head Injuries
Headache

Consult Relationship Section for more information

Physical & Psychosomatic Disorders — (cont'd)

Health Impaired
Hearing Disorders
Heart Disorders
Hematoma
Hemianopia
Hemiplegia
Hemophilia
Hemorrhage
Hepatitis
Hermaphroditism
Herpes Genitalis
Herpes Simplex
Human Immunodeficiency Virus
Huntingtons Disease
Hydrocephaly
Hyperglycemia
Hyperkinesis
Hyperphagia
Hypersexuality
Hypersomnia
Hyperthyroidism
Hypochondriasis
Hypoglycemia
Hypogonadism
Hyponatremia
Hypopituitarism
Hypotension
Hypothyroidism
Immunologic Disorders
Impotence
Infectious Disorders
Infertility
Influenza
Injuries
Insomnia
Irritable Bowel Syndrome
Ischemia
Jaundice
Joint Disorders
Kidney Diseases
Klinefelters Syndrome
Labyrinth Disorders
Laryngeal Disorders
Lead Poisoning
Leukemias
Lipid Metabolism Disorders
Liver Disorders
Lung Disorders
Lupus
Malaria
Male Genital Disorders
Measles
Memory Decay
Memory Disorders
Menieres Disease
Meningitis
Menstrual Disorders
Mercury Poisoning
Metabolism Disorders
Microcephaly
Migraine Headache
Minimal Brain Disorders
Minimally Brain Damaged
Motion Sickness
Movement Disorders
Multi Infarct Dementia
Multiple Sclerosis
Multiply Disabled
Munchausen Syndrome
Munchausen Syndrome by Proxy
Muscle Contraction Headache
Muscle Spasms
Muscular Atrophy
Muscular Disorders
Muscular Dystrophy
Musculoskeletal Disorders
Myasthenia
Myasthenia Gravis
Myelitis
Myocardial Infarctions
Myoclonia
Myopia
Myotonia
Nail Biting
Narcolepsy
Narcosis
Neonatal Disorders
Neoplasms
Nervous System Disorders
Nervous System Neoplasms
Neuralgia
Neurasthenic Neurosis
Neurodermatitis
Neuromuscular Disorders
Neurosis
Neurosyphilis
Nocturnal Teeth Grinding
Nutritional Deficiencies
Nystagmus
Obesity
Obesity (Attitudes Toward)
Obstetrical Complications
Organic Brain Syndromes
Osteoporosis
Paralysis
Paraplegia
Parasitic Disorders
Parathyroid Disorders
Parkinsons Disease
Partially Hearing Impaired
Partially Sighted
Pellagra
Perceptual Disturbances
Peripheral Nerve Disorders
Petit Mal Epilepsy
Phantom Limbs
Pharyngeal Disorders
Phenylketonuria
Physical Disabilities (Attit Toward)
Physical Disfigurement
Physical Disorders
Physically Disabled
Pica
Picks Disease
Pituitary Disorders
Pneumonia
Poliomyelitis
Porphyria
Prader Willi Syndrome
Premature Ejaculation
Premenstrual Tension
Presenile Dementia
Progressive Supranuclear Palsy
Prosopagnosia
Protein Deficiency Disorders
Pruritus
Pseudodementia
Psychosomatic Disorders
Pulmonary Emphysema
Pulmonary Tuberculosis
Quadriplegia
Respiratory Distress
Respiratory Tract Disorders
Rett Syndrome
Rheumatic Fever
Rheumatoid Arthritis
Rubella
Sclerosis (Nervous System)
Self Inflicted Wounds
Senile Dementia
Senile Psychosis
Sense Organ Disorders
Sensorially Disabled
Sensory Disabilities (Attit Toward)
Sex Chromosome Disorders
Sex Linked Hereditary Disorders
Sexual Function Disturbances
Sickle Cell Disease
Skin Disorders
Sleep Apnea
Sleep Disorders
Somatoform Pain Disorder
Spina Bifida
Spinal Cord Injuries
Sterility
Sudden Infant Death
Syncope
Syndromes
Syphilis
Tachycardia
Terminal Cancer
Terminally Ill Patients
Testicular Feminization Syndrome
Thromboses
Thyroid Disorders
Thyrotoxicosis
Tinnitus
Torticollis
Toxic Disorders
Toxic Encephalopathies
Toxic Hepatitis

Consult Relationship Section for more information

Physical & Psychosomatic Disorders — (cont'd)

Toxic Psychoses
Toxicomania
Traumatic Brain Injury
Trigeminal Neuralgia
Tuberculosis
Tunnel Vision
Turners Syndrome
Ulcerative Colitis
Urinary Function Disorders
Urinary Incontinence
Urogenital Disorders
Vaginismus
Vascular Dementia
Venereal Diseases
Viral Disorders
Vision Disorders
Visually Disabled
Vitamin Deficiency Disorders
Wernickes Syndrome
Whiplash
Work Related Illnesses
Wounds

Psychological Disorders

Acrophobia
Acute Psychosis
Acute Schizophrenia
Adjustment Disorders
Affective Disturbances
Affective Psychosis
Agoraphobia
AIDS Dementia Complex
Alcoholic Hallucinosis
Alcoholic Psychosis
Alexithymia
Amnesia
Anaclitic Depression
Anorexia Nervosa
Anxiety Disorders
Aspergers Syndrome
Auditory Hallucinations
Autism
Autistic Children
Avoidant Personality
Body Image Disturbances
Borderline States
Bulimia
Capgras Syndrome
Castration Anxiety
Catatonic Schizophrenia
Childhood Neurosis
Childhood Psychosis
Childhood Schizophrenia
Chronic Mental Illness
Chronic Psychosis
Claustrophobia
Compulsive Repetition
Confabulation
Consciousness Disturbances
Conversion Neurosis
Cyclothymic Personality
Delirium Tremens
Delusions
Dementia
Dependent Personality
Depersonalization
Depression (Emotion)
Dissociative Identity Disorder
Dissociative Patterns
Dysfunctional Family
Dysmorphophobia
Dysthymic Disorder
Early Infantile Autism
Eating Disorders
Elective Mutism
Electra Complex
Emotionally Disturbed
Endogenous Depression
Erotomania
Explosive Personality
Factitious Disorders
Fantasies (Thought Disturbances)
Fetal Alcohol Syndrome
Folie A Deux
Fragmentation (Schizophrenia)
Fugue Reaction
Gender Identity Disorder
Global Amnesia
Hallucinations
Hallucinosis
Hebephrenic Schizophrenia
Homeless Mentally Ill
Hypnagogic Hallucinations
Hypomania
Hysteria
Hysterical Anesthesia
Hysterical Paralysis
Hysterical Personality
Hysterical Vision Disturbances
Impulse Control Disorders
Inadequate Personality
Infantilism
Inhibited Sexual Desire
Involutional Depression
Involutional Paranoid Psychosis
Judgment Disturbances
Koro
Korsakoffs Psychosis
Major Depression
Malingering
Mania
Manic Depression
Mental Disorders
Mental Illness (Attitudes Toward)
Mentally Ill Offenders
Munchausen Syndrome
Munchausen Syndrome by Proxy
Narcissistic Personality
Neuroleptic Malignant Syndrome
Neurosis
Neurotic Depressive Reaction
Obsessive Compulsive Neurosis
Obsessive Compulsive Personality
Occupational Neurosis
Oedipal Complex
Ophidiophobia
Oppositional Defiant Disorder
Organic Brain Syndromes
Panic Disorder
Paranoia (Psychosis)
Paranoid Personality
Paranoid Schizophrenia
Passive Aggressive Personality
Personality Disorders
Phobias
Postpartum Depression
Posttraumatic Stress Disorder
Presenile Dementia
Process Psychosis
Pseudocyesis
Pseudodementia
Psychosis
Reactive Depression
Reactive Psychosis
Recurrent Depression
Schizoaffective Disorder
Schizoid Personality
Schizophrenia
Schizophreniform Disorder
Schizophrenogenic Family
Schizophrenogenic Mothers
Schizotypal Personality
School Phobia
Seasonal Affective Disorder
Self Defeating Behavior
Self Destructive Behavior
Self Mutilation
Senile Dementia
Senile Psychosis
Separation Anxiety
Sexual Addiction
Social Phobia
Speech Anxiety
Spreading Depression
Stress Reactions
Symbiotic Infantile Psychosis
Syndromes
Tardive Dyskinesia
Thought Disturbances
Toxic Psychoses
Traumatic Neurosis
Treatment Resistant Depression
Undifferentiated Schizophrenia
Visual Hallucinations
Work Related Illnesses

Speech & Language Disorders

Alexia
Aphasia
Articulation Disorders

Consult Relationship Section for more information

Speech & Language Disorders — (cont'd)

Communication Disorders
Dysarthria
Dysphasia
Dysphonia
Echolalia
Glossolalia
Language Delay
Language Disorders
Mutism
Retarded Speech Development
Speech Disabled
Speech Disorders
Stuttering

Symptomatology

Acting Out
Agitation
Akathisia
Amnesia
Anhedonia
Anoxia
Aphagia
Apnea
Apraxia
Asthenia
Ataxia
Athetosis
Automatism
Back Pain
Behavior Change
Binge Eating
Body Rocking
Bruxism
Catalepsy
Catatonia
Chronic Pain
Coma
Convulsions
Craving
Delirium
Diarrhea
Extrapyramidal Symptoms
Fatigue
Hair Pulling
Head Banging
Headache
Health Complaints
Hematoma
Hemorrhage
Hypersomnia
Hyperthermia
Hyperventilation
Hyponatremia
Hypothermia
Insomnia
Mental Confusion
Nail Biting
Nausea
Nicotine Withdrawal
Pain
Parkinsonism
Positive and Negative Symptoms
Pruritus
Psychiatric Symptoms
Respiratory Distress
Restlessness
Scratching
Shock
Somatization
Spasms
Symptom Checklists
Symptom Remission
Symptoms
Syncope
Tics
Tremor
Vertigo
Vomiting
Wandering Behavior

EDUCATIONAL CLUSTER

- Academic Learning & Achievement
- Curricula
- Educational Personnel & Administration
- Educational Testing & Counseling
- Schools & Institutions
- Special Education
- Student Characteristics & Academic Environment
- Student Populations
- Teaching & Teaching Methods

Academic Learning & Achievement

Academic Achievement
Academic Achievement Motivation
Academic Achievement Prediction
Academic Aptitude
Academic Failure
Academic Overachievement
Academic Specialization
Academic Underachievement
Adult Learning
College Academic Achievement
Cooperative Learning
Discrimination Learning
Experiential Learning
Foreign Language Learning
Generalization (Learning)
Incidental Learning
Intentional Learning
Interference (Learning)
Latent Learning
Learning
Learning Ability
Learning Rate
Learning Schedules
Learning Strategies
Learning Theory
Mastery Learning
Mathematics Achievement
Metacognition
Nonsense Syllable Learning
Nonverbal Learning
Note Taking
Observational Learning
Overlearning
Paired Associate Learning
Perceptual Motor Learning
Probability Learning
Reading Achievement
Reading Readiness
Reading Skills
Reading Speed
Recall (Learning)
Recognition (Learning)
Reconstruction (Learning)
Relearning
Retention
Rote Learning
School Graduation
School Learning
Science Achievement
Sequential Learning
Serial Anticipation (Learning)
Serial Learning
Skill Learning
Social Learning
State Dependent Learning
Time On Task
Transfer (Learning)
Trial and Error Learning
Verbal Learning

Curricula

Adult Education
Affective Education
Art Education
Bilingual Education
Business Education
Career Education
Clinical Methods Training
Clinical Psychology Grad Training
Clinical Psychology Internship
Compensatory Education
Computer Training
Continuing Education
Cooperative Education
Counselor Education
Curriculum
Curriculum Development
Death Education
Dental Education
Driver Education
Drug Education
Education
Educational Program Accreditation
Educational Program Planning

Consult Relationship Section for more information

Curricula — (cont'd)

Educational Programs
Elementary Education
English as Second Language
Environmental Education
Equal Education
Extracurricular Activities
Family Life Education
Foreign Language Education
Foreign Study
Graduate Education
Graduate Psychology Education
Health Education
Higher Education
Home Schooling
Inservice Teacher Education
Language Arts Education
Literacy Programs
Mathematics Education
Medical Education
Middle School Education
Multicultural Education
Music Education
Nonstandard English
Nontraditional Education
Nursing Education
Paraprofessional Education
Phonics
Physical Education
Postgraduate Training
Preschool Education
Private School Education
Project Follow Through
Project Head Start
Psychology Education
Psychotherapy Training
Public School Education
Reading Education
Rehabilitation Education
Religious Education
Remedial Education
Remedial Reading
Science Education
Secondary Education
Sex Education
Social Studies Education
Social Work Education
Special Education
Spelling
Sports
Teacher Education
Undergraduate Education
Upward Bound
Vocational Education

Educational Personnel & Administration

Accreditation (Education Personnel)
Boards of Education
Budgets
College Teachers
Cooperating Teachers
Educational Administration
Educational Personnel
Educational Program Accreditation
Educational Psychologists
Educational Quality
Educational Reform
Elementary School Teachers
High School Teachers
Junior High School Teachers
Parent School Relationship
Preschool Teachers
Preservice Teachers
Resource Teachers
School Administrators
School Counselors
School Nurses
School Principals
School Psychologists
School Superintendents
Special Education Teachers
Student Teachers
Teacher Aides
Teacher Attitudes
Teacher Characteristics
Teacher Education
Teacher Effectiveness Evaluation
Teacher Expectations
Teacher Personality
Teacher Recruitment
Teacher Student Interaction
Teacher Tenure
Teachers
Vocational Counselors
Vocational Education Teachers

Educational Testing & Counseling

Adaptive Testing
Coll Ent Exam Bd Scholastic Apt Test
Computer Assisted Testing
Course Evaluation
Cultural Test Bias
Curriculum Based Assessment
Educational Counseling
Educational Diagnosis
Educational Financial Assistance
Educational Measurement
Educational Placement
Educational Program Evaluation
Educational Psychology
Educational Therapy
Entrance Examinations
Essay Testing
Grading (Educational)
Graduate Record Examination
Group Testing
Minimum Competency Tests
Posttesting
Pretesting
School Counseling
School Psychology
Student Admission Criteria
Student Personnel Services
Student Records
Teacher Effectiveness Evaluation
Test Coaching
Test Taking
Testing Methods
Testwiseness

Schools & Institutions

Boarding Schools
Campuses
Colleges
Community Colleges
Dormitories
Elementary Schools
Graduate Schools
High Schools
Institutional Schools
Junior High Schools
Kindergartens
Learning Centers (Educational)
Military Schools
Nongraded Schools
Nursery Schools
School Facilities
School Libraries
Schools
Technical Schools

Special Education

Acalculia
Agnosia
Agraphia
Alexia
Amaurotic Familial Idiocy
Anencephaly
Aphasia
Apraxia
Articulation Disorders
Ataxia
Attention Deficit Disorder
Aurally Disabled
Autism
Autistic Children
Behavior Disorders
Behavior Problems
Blind
Borderline Mental Retardation
Braille Instruction
Cleft Palate
Communication Disorders
Compensatory Education
Crying Cat Syndrome
Deaf
Deaf Blind
Delayed Development
Developmental Disabilities
Downs Syndrome
Dysarthria

Consult Relationship Section for more information

Special Education — (cont'd)

Dyskinesia
Dyslexia
Dysphasia
Dysphonia
Ear Disorders
Early Infantile Autism
Echolalia
Educable Mentally Retarded
Emotionally Disturbed
Gifted
Hearing Disorders
Home Reared Mentally Retarded
Hyperkinesis
Idiot Savants
Institutionalized Mentally Retarded
Language Disorders
Learning Disabilities
Learning Disorders
Literacy Programs
Mainstreaming (Educational)
Memory Disorders
Mental Retardation
Mentally Retarded
Microcephaly
Minimal Brain Disorders
Minimally Brain Damaged
Mutism
Partially Hearing Impaired
Perceptual Disturbances
Profoundly Mentally Retarded
Psychosocial Mental Retardation
Reading Disabilities
Remedial Education
Remedial Reading
Retarded Speech Development
Sensorially Disabled
Severely Mentally Retarded
Slow Learners
Special Education
Special Education Students
Speech Disabled
Speech Disorders
Stuttering
Trainable Mentally Retarded
Visually Disabled

Student Characteristics & Academic Environment

Ability Level
Academic Achievement
Academic Achievement Motivation
Academic Aptitude
Academic Environment
Academic Failure
Academic Overachievement
Academic Self Concept
Academic Specialization
Academic Underachievement
Artistic Ability
Athletic Participation
Classroom Behavior
Classroom Environment
Classrooms
Coeducation
Cognitive Ability
College Academic Achievement
College Environment
Computer Literacy
Declarative Knowledge
Educational Aspirations
Educational Attainment Level
Educational Background
Educational Degrees
Educational Incentives
Educational Objectives
Fraternity Membership
Grade Level
Learning Ability
Literacy
Mathematics Anxiety
Musical Ability
Nonverbal Ability
Performance Anxiety
Procedural Knowledge
Reading Ability
Reading Comprehension
Reading Skills
School Adjustment
School Attendance
School Club Membership
School Enrollment
School Environment
School Expulsion
School Graduation
School Integration
School Phobia
School Readiness
School Refusal
School Retention
School Suspension
School to Work Transition
School Transition
School Truancy
Sorority Membership
Special Needs
Student Activism
Student Attitudes
Student Attrition
Student Characteristics
Student Records
Study Habits
Teacher Student Interaction
Truancy
Verbal Ability
Writing Skills

Student Populations

Business Students
Classmates
College Athletes
College Dropouts
College Graduates
College Students
College Students
Community College Students
Dental Students
Dropouts
Education Students
Elementary School Students
Foreign Students
Gifted
Graduate Students
High School Graduates
High School Students
Intermediate School Students
Junior College Students
Junior High School Students
Kindergarten Students
Law Students
Medical Students
Middle School Students
Nursery School Students
Nursing Students
Postgraduate Students
Potential Dropouts
Preschool Students
Primary School Students
Reentry Students
ROTC Students
School Dropouts
School Leavers
Special Education Students
Students
Transfer Students
Vocational School Students

Teaching & Teaching Methods

Ability Grouping
Advance Organizers
Audiovisual Instruction
Braille Instruction
Classroom Behavior Modification
Classroom Discipline
Computer Assisted Instruction
Constant Time Delay
Cooperative Learning
Curricular Field Experience
Directed Discussion Method
Discovery Teaching Method
Education
Educational Audiovisual Aids
Educational Field Trips
Educational Incentives
Educational Laboratories
Educational Objectives
Educational Quality
Educational Television
Educational Toys
Experiential Learning
Feedback
Film Strips

Consult Relationship Section for more information

Teaching & Teaching Methods — (cont'd)

Group Discussion
Group Instruction
Home Schooling
Homework
Individualized Instruction
Initial Teaching Alphabet
Instructional Media
Language Laboratories
Lecture Method
Lesson Plans
Montessori Method
Motion Pictures (Educational)
Nondirected Discussion Method
Open Classroom Method
Peer Tutoring
Programed Instruction
Programed Textbooks
Prompting
Psychoeducation
Remedial Reading
Selected Readings
Self Instructional Training
Sight Vocabulary
Silent Reading
Student Teaching
Teaching
Teaching Machines
Teaching Methods
Team Teaching Method
Televised Instruction
Textbooks
Theories of Education
Tutoring
Videotape Instruction

GEOGRAPHIC CLUSTER

- Africa
- Arctic Regions
- Asia
- Central America
- Europe
- Latin America
- North America
- Pacific Islands
- South America
- West Indies

Africa

Africa
Algeria
Angola
Benin
Botswana
Cameroon
Congo
East Africa
Egypt
Ethiopia
Ghana
Guinea
Ivory Coast
Kenya
Liberia
Libya
Madagascar
Malawi
Mali
Morocco
Mozambique
Niger
Nigeria
Rwanda
Senegal
Somalia
South Africa
Sudan
Tanzania
Tunisia
Uganda
West Africa
Zaire
Zambia
Zimbabwe

Arctic Regions

Alaska
Antarctica
Canada
Union of Soviet Socialist Republics

Asia

Afghanistan
Asia
Bangladesh
Burma
Cambodia
Commonwealth of Independent States
Hong Kong
India
Indonesia
Iran
Iraq
Israel
Japan
Jordan
Korea
Kuwait
Laos
Lebanon
Malaysia
Mauritius
Middle East
Nepal
North Korea
Pacific Islands
Pakistan
Peoples Republic of China
Philippines
Saudi Arabia
Singapore
South Korea
South Pacific
Southeast Asia
Sri Lanka
Syria
Taiwan
Thailand
Tibet
Turkey
Union of Soviet Socialist Republics
Vietnam
Yemen

Central America

Belize
Central America
Costa Rica
El Salvador
Guatemala
Honduras
Nicaragua
Panama

Europe

Austria
Belgium
Bulgaria
Commonwealth of Independent States
Cyprus
Czechoslovakia
Denmark
East Germany
Eastern Europe
England
Europe
Finland
France
Germany
Great Britain
Greece
Hungary
Iceland
Ireland
Italy
Liechtenstein
Northern Ireland
Norway
Poland
Portugal
Romania
Scandinavia
Scotland
Spain
Sweden
Switzerland
Turkey
Union of Soviet Socialist Republics
United Kingdom
Wales

Consult Relationship Section for more information

Europe — (cont'd)

West Germany
Western Europe
Yugoslavia

Latin America

Latin America

North America

Alaska
Appalachia
Bermuda
Canada
Mexico
North America
United States

Pacific Islands

American Samoa
Australia
Fiji
Hawaii
New Zealand
Pacific Islands
Papua New Guinea
South Pacific
Tonga
Western Samoa

South America

Argentina
Bolivia
Brazil
Chile
Colombia
Ecuador
Guyana
Paraguay
Peru
South America
Surinam
Uruguay
Venezuela

West Indies

Bahama Islands
Barbados
Cuba
Dominican Republic
Haiti
Hispaniola
Jamaica
Puerto Rico
Saint Lucia
Trinidad and Tobago
Virgin Islands
West Indies

LEGAL CLUSTER

- Adjudication
- Criminal Groups
- Criminal Offenses
- Criminal Rehabilitation
- Laws
- Legal Issues
- Legal Personnel
- Legal Processes

Adjudication

Adjudication
Capital Punishment
Commitment (Psychiatric)
Competency to Stand Trial
Court Referrals
Crime Victims
Criminal Conviction
Criminal Justice
Criminal Responsibility
Defendants
Expert Testimony
Informants
Informed Consent
Insanity Defense
Juries
Jury Selection
Justice
Law Enforcement
Legal Arrest
Legal Decisions
Legal Detention
Legal Evidence
Legal Interrogation
Legal Processes
Legal Testimony
Parole
Polygraphs
Probation
Protective Services
Witnesses

Criminal Groups

Criminals
Defendants
Female Criminals
Female Delinquents
Juvenile Delinquency
Juvenile Delinquents
Juvenile Gangs
Male Criminals
Male Delinquents
Mentally Ill Offenders
Perpetrators
Predelinquent Youth
Prisoners

Criminal Offenses

Abandonment
Acquaintance Rape
Age Discrimination
Arson
Assisted Suicide
Battered Child Syndrome
Battered Females
Child Abuse
Child Neglect
Crime
Disability Discrimination
Driving Under The Influence
Drug Distribution
Elder Abuse
Family Violence
Fraud
Gambling
Genocide
Homicide
Incest
Infanticide
Kidnapping
Kleptomania
Obscenity
Pathological Gambling
Pedophilia
Persecution
Political Assassination
Pornography
Prostitution
Race and Ethnic Discrimination
Rape
Runaway Behavior
Sex Discrimination
Sex Offenses
Sexual Abuse
Sexual Deviations
Sexual Harassment
Sexual Sadism
Shoplifting
Social Discrimination
Terrorism
Theft
Torture
Vandalism
Victimization
Voyeurism

Criminal Rehabilitation

Correctional Institutions
Criminology
Forensic Psychiatry
Forensic Psychology
Incarceration
Institutional Release
Institutional Schools
Institutionalization
Maximum Security Facilities
Parole
Penology
Prisons

Consult Relationship Section for more information

Criminal Rehabilitation — (cont'd)

Probation
Recidivism
Reformatories

Laws

Abortion Laws
Abuse Reporting
Affirmative Action
Case Law
Child Abuse Reporting
Civil Law
Criminal Law
Disability Laws
Drug Laws
Equal Education
Government Policy Making
Gun Control Laws
Health Care Policy
Law (Government)
Laws
Legal Decisions
Legislative Processes
Marihuana Laws
Medicare
Social Security
Social Security
Taxation

Legal Issues

Affirmative Action
Age Discrimination
Assisted Suicide
Capital Punishment
Censorship
Child Care
Civil Rights
Cohabitation
Crime Prevention
Criminal Justice
Criminal Responsibility
Dangerousness
Drug Legalization
Drug Usage Screening
Employment Discrimination
Equal Education
Eugenics
Euthanasia
HIV Testing
Human Rights
Illegitimate Children
Informed Consent
Life Sustaining Treatment
Marihuana Legalization
Morality
Political Revolution
Privileged Communication
Professional Liability
Race and Ethnic Discrimination
Refugees
Right to Treatment
Riots
Safety Belts
Safety Devices
School Integration
School Truancy
Self Defense
Sex Discrimination
Social Discrimination
Social Equality
Social Integration
Surrogate Parents (Humans)
Treatment Withholding
Victimization
Warning Labels

Legal Personnel

Attorneys
Judges
Juries
Law Enforcement Personnel
Law Students
Legal Personnel
Parole Officers
Police Personnel
Prison Personnel
Probation Officers

Legal Processes

Abuse Reporting
Adoption (Child)
Advance Directives
Advocacy
Autopsy
Censorship
Child Abuse Reporting
Child Custody
Child Support
Child Visitation
Child Welfare
Citizenship
Civil Rights
Client Rights
Commitment (Psychiatric)
Conflict Resolution
Consumer Protection
Court Referrals
Crime Prevention
Criminology
Divorce
Forensic Evaluation
Forensic Psychiatry
Forensic Psychology
Foster Care
Guardianship
Immigration
Interracial Adoption
Involuntary Treatment
Joint Custody
Labor Management Relations
Labor Union Members
Labor Unions
Legal Processes
Marihuana Legalization
Marital Separation
Mediation
Organizational Merger
Outpatient Commitment
Professional Licensing
Protective Services
Psychiatric Evaluation
Social Integration
Strikes

NEUROPSYCHOLOGY & NEUROLOGY CLUSTER

- Assessment & Diagnosis
- Electrophysiology
- Neuroanatomy
- Neurological Disorders
- Neurological Intervention
- Neurosciences
- Neurotransmitters & Neuroregulators

Assessment & Diagnosis

Bender Gestalt Test
Echoencephalography
Electroencephalography
Halstead Reitan Neuropsych Battery
Luria Nebraska Neuropsych Battery
Magnetic Resonance Imaging
Magnetoencephalography
Memory for Designs Test
Mini Mental State Examination
Neuropsychological Assessment
Pain Measurement
Pneumoencephalography
Rheoencephalography
Wechsler Memory Scale
Wisconsin Card Sorting Test

Electrophysiology

Alpha Rhythm
Auditory Evoked Potentials
Contingent Negative Variation
Cortical Evoked Potentials
Delta Rhythm
Electrical Activity
Electroencephalography
Electrophysiology
Evoked Potentials
Kindling
Magnetoencephalography
Olfactory Evoked Potentials
Postactivation Potentials
Somatosensory Evoked Potentials
Theta Rhythm
Visual Evoked Potentials

Consult Relationship Section for more information

Neuroanatomy

Abducens Nerve
Acoustic Nerve
Adrenergic Nerves
Afferent Pathways
Amygdaloid Body
Auditory Cortex
Auditory Neurons
Autonomic Ganglia
Autonomic Nervous System
Axons
Baroreceptors
Basal Ganglia
Blood Brain Barrier
Brain
Brain Size
Brain Stem
Brain Weight
Caudate Nucleus
Central Nervous System
Cerebellum
Cerebral Blood Flow
Cerebral Cortex
Cerebral Dominance
Cerebral Ventricles
Cerebrospinal Fluid
Chemoreceptors
Cholinergic Nerves
Cones (Eye)
Cranial Spinal Cord
Cutaneous Receptive Fields
Cutaneous Sense
Dendrites
Diencephalon
Dorsal Horns
Dorsal Roots
Efferent Pathways
Extrapyramidal Tracts
Facial Nerve
Forebrain
Fornix
Fovea
Frontal Lobe
Ganglia
Ganglion Cells (Retina)
Geniculate Bodies (Thalamus)
Globus Pallidus
Gyrus Cinguli
Hindbrain
Hippocampus
Hypothalamo Hypophyseal System
Hypothalamo Pituitary Adrenal System
Hypothalamus
Inferior Colliculus
Interhemispheric Interaction
Lateral Dominance
Left Brain
Lemniscal System
Limbic System
Locus Ceruleus
Lumbar Spinal Cord
Mechanoreceptors
Medial Forebrain Bundle
Medulla Oblongata
Meninges
Mesencephalon
Motor Cortex
Motor Neurons
Myelin Sheath
Nerve Endings
Nerve Growth Factor
Nerve Tissues
Nervous System
Neural Analyzers
Neural Development
Neural Pathways
Neural Plasticity
Neural Receptors
Neurons
Nociceptors
Nucleus Basalis Magnocellularis
Occipital Lobe
Ocular Dominance
Olfactory Bulb
Olfactory Nerve
Optic Chiasm
Optic Lobe
Optic Nerve
Optic Tract
Parasympathetic Nervous System
Parietal Lobe
Periaqueductal Gray
Peripheral Nervous System
Photoreceptors
Pons
Preoptic Area
Proprioceptors
Purkinje Cells
Pyramidal Tracts
Raphe Nuclei
Receptive Fields
Receptor Binding
Reticular Formation
Retina
Right Brain
Rods (Eye)
Sense Organs
Sensory Neurons
Septal Nuclei
Somatosensory Cortex
Spinal Ganglia
Substantia Nigra

Neurological Disorders

Acalculia
Agnosia
Agraphia
Alcoholic Hallucinosis
Alcoholic Psychosis
Alexia
Alzheimers Disease
Anencephaly
Anoxia
Aphasia
Apraxia
Ataxia
Athetosis
Audiogenic Seizures
Autonomic Nervous System Disorders
Back Pain
Bacterial Meningitis
Brain Concussion
Brain Damage
Brain Damaged
Brain Disorders
Brain Neoplasms
Catalepsy
Cataplexy
Central Nervous System Disorders
Cerebral Arteriosclerosis
Cerebral Atrophy
Cerebral Hemorrhage
Cerebral Ischemia
Cerebral Palsy
Cerebrovascular Accidents
Cerebrovascular Disorders
Chorea
Chronic Pain
Coma
Convulsions
Creutzfeldt Jakob Syndrome
Delirium Tremens
Dementia
Dysarthria
Dyskinesia
Dyslexia
Dysphasia
Dysphonia
Encephalitis
Encephalomyelitis
Encephalopathies
Epilepsy
Epileptic Seizures
Extrapyramidal Symptoms
General Paresis
Gilles de la Tourette Disorder
Global Amnesia
Grand Mal Epilepsy
Head Injuries
Headache
Hemianopia
Hemiplegia
Huntingtons Disease
Hydrocephaly
Hyperkinesis
Korsakoffs Psychosis
Memory Disorders
Meningitis
Microcephaly
Migraine Headache
Minimal Brain Disorders
Minimally Brain Damaged
Movement Disorders

Consult Relationship Section for more information

Neurological Disorders — (cont'd)

Multi Infarct Dementia
Multiple Sclerosis
Muscle Contraction Headache
Muscular Dystrophy
Myasthenia Gravis
Myelitis
Myoclonia
Myofascial Pain
Narcolepsy
Nervous System Disorders
Nervous System Neoplasms
Neuralgia
Neuroleptic Malignant Syndrome
Neuromuscular Disorders
Neuropathology
Neurosyphilis
Organic Brain Syndromes
Pain
Paralysis
Paraplegia
Parkinsons Disease
Peripheral Nerve Disorders
Petit Mal Epilepsy
Picks Disease
Poliomyelitis
Presenile Dementia
Progressive Supranuclear Palsy
Quadriplegia
Sclerosis (Nervous System)
Senile Dementia
Senile Psychosis
Spasms
Spinal Cord Injuries
Tardive Dyskinesia
Tics
Torticollis
Toxic Encephalopathies
Traumatic Brain Injury
Tremor
Trigeminal Neuralgia
Vascular Dementia
Wernickes Syndrome

Neurological Intervention

Afferent Stimulation
Brain Lesions
Brain Self Stimulation
Brain Stimulation
Chemical Brain Stimulation
Commissurotomy
Decerebration
Decortication (Brain)
Electrical Brain Stimulation
Hemispherectomy
Hypothalamus Lesions
Kindling
Neural Lesions
Neural Transplantation
Neurosurgery
Psychosurgery
Pyramidotomy
Stereotaxic Techniques
Sympathectomy
Thalamotomy
Tractotomy
Vagotomy

Neurosciences

Neural Networks
Neural Transplantation
Neuroanatomy
Neurobiology
Neurochemistry
Neuroendocrinology
Neurolinguistics
Neurology
Neuropathology
Neurophysiology
Neuropsychiatry
Neuropsychology
Neurosciences
Neurosurgery
Psychoneuroimmunology
Psychopharmacology
Psychosurgery

Neurotransmitters & Neuroregulators

Acetylcholine
Acetylcholinesterase
Adenosine
Alanines
Angiotensin
Aspartic Acid
Bombesin
Catecholamines
Cholecystokinin
Choline
Cholinesterase
Dihydroxyphenylacetic Acid
Dihydroxytryptamine
Dopamine
Dopamine Metabolites
Dynorphins
Endogenous Opiates
Endorphins
Enkephalins
Epinephrine
Gamma Aminobutyric Acid
Glutamic Acid
Glycine
Histamine
Homovanillic Acid
Hydroxydopamine (6-)
Hydroxyindoleacetic Acid (5-)
Ibotenic Acid
Kainic Acid
Melanocyte Stimulating Hormone
Methoxyhydroxyphenylglycol (3,4)
Monoamine Oxidases
Neurokinins
Neurotensin
Neurotoxins
Neurotransmitters
Norepinephrine
Norepinephrine Metabolites
Oxytocin
Peptides
Phenethylamines
Serotonin
Serotonin Metabolites
Somatostatin
Substance P
Taurine
Tryptamine
Tyramine

OCCUPATIONAL & EMPLOYMENT CLUSTER

- Career Areas
- Employee, Occupational & Job Characteristics
- Management & Professional Personnel Issues
- Occupational Groups
- Organizations & Organizational Behavior
- Personnel Management

Career Areas

Advertising
Air Traffic Control
Behavioral Sciences
Business
Business Management
Child Care
Child Day Care
Community Psychology
Computer Programing
Consultation Liaison Psychiatry
Cross Cultural Psychology
Data Processing
Educational Administration
Educational Psychology
Entrepreneurship
Experimental Psychology
Forensic Psychiatry
Forensic Psychology
Geriatric Psychiatry
Gynecology
Health Care Administration
Health Promotion
Human Factors Engineering
Hypnotherapy
Industrial Psychology
Job Corps
Law Enforcement
News Media
Nontraditional Careers
Obstetrics

Consult Relationship Section for more information

Career Areas — (cont'd)

Occupational Therapy
Optometry
Paramedical Sciences
Pastoral Counseling
Pathology
Peace Corps
Pediatrics
Physical Therapy
Physics
Politics
Product Design
Psychiatry
Psychology
Psychotherapy
Public Relations
Rehabilitation
Rehabilitation Counseling
Retailing
School Psychology
Self Employment
Social Casework
Social Psychology
Sociology
Speech Therapy
Sport Psychology
Sports
Surgery
Veterinary Medicine
Vocational Rehabilitation
Word Processing
Zoology

Employee, Occupational & Job Characteristics

Career Change
Clerical Secretarial Skills
Disabled Personnel
Division of Labor
Dual Careers
Employability
Employee Absenteeism
Employee Attitudes
Employee Characteristics
Employee Efficiency
Employee Interaction
Employee Motivation
Employee Productivity
Employee Skills
Employee Turnover
Employer Attitudes
Employment History
Employment Status
Family Work Relationship
Health Personnel Attitudes
Impaired Professionals
Income Level
Industrial Accidents
Job Applicant Attitudes
Job Characteristics
Job Enrichment
Job Experience Level
Job Involvement
Job Knowledge
Job Performance
Job Satisfaction
Job Search
Job Security
Labor Union Members
Leadership Qualities
Mentor
Noise Levels (Work Areas)
Occupational Adjustment
Occupational Aspirations
Occupational Attitudes
Occupational Choice
Occupational Exposure
Occupational Interests
Occupational Mobility
Occupational Neurosis
Occupational Preference
Occupational Safety
Occupational Status
Occupational Stress
Occupational Success
Occupational Tenure
Organizational Characteristics
Organizational Commitment
Private Practice
Professional Competence
Professional Identity
Professional Specialization
Quality of Work Life
Reemployment
Retirement
Salaries
School to Work Transition
Supervisor Employee Interaction
Typing
Unemployment
Vocational Maturity
Work (Attitudes Toward)
Work Adjustment Training
Work Load
Work Related Illnesses
Work Rest Cycles
Work Scheduling
Work Week Length
Workday Shifts
Working Conditions
Working Space
Working Women

Management & Professional Personnel Issues

Affirmative Action
Budgets
Career Development
Entrepreneurship
Labor Management Relations
Leadership
Leadership Qualities
Leadership Style
Management
Management Decision Making
Management Methods
Management Personnel
Management Planning
Management Training
Middle Level Managers
Participative Management
Policy Making
Private Practice
Professional Certification
Professional Consultation
Professional Development
Professional Ethics
Professional Examinations
Professional Fees
Professional Identity
Professional Liability
Professional Licensing
Professional Referral
Professional Specialization
Professional Standards
Professional Supervision
Quality Control
Stress Management
Strikes
Supervisor Employee Interaction
Top Level Managers

Occupational Groups

Accountants
Aerospace Personnel
Agricultural Extension Workers
Agricultural Workers
Air Force Personnel
Aircraft Pilots
Anthropologists
Apprenticeship
Architects
Army Personnel
Artists
Astronauts
Athletes
Attendants (Institutions)
Attorneys
Blue Collar Workers
Business and Industrial Personnel
Chaplains
Child Care Workers
Clergy
Clerical Personnel
Clinical Psychologists
Clinicians
Coaches
Coast Guard Personnel
College Teachers
Commissioned Officers
Cooperating Teachers
Counseling Psychologists

Consult Relationship Section for more information

Occupational Groups — (cont'd)

Counselor Trainees
Counselors
Dentistry
Dentists
Disabled Personnel
Domestic Service Personnel
Draftees
Educational Personnel
Educational Psychologists
Elementary School Teachers
Engineers
Enlisted Military Personnel
Evangelists
Experimental Psychologists
Family Physicians
Fire Fighters
Foreign Workers
General Practitioners
Government Personnel
Gynecologists
Health Personnel
High School Teachers
Home Care Personnel
Hypnotherapists
Hypnotists
Industrial Foremen
Industrial Psychologists
Informants
Information Specialists
Internists
Interviewers
Job Applicants
Journalists
Judges
Junior High School Teachers
Labor Union Members
Law Enforcement Personnel
Lay Religious Personnel
Legal Personnel
Librarians
Management Personnel
Marine Personnel
Mathematicians
Medical Personnel
Mental Health Personnel
Middle Level Managers
Migrant Farm Workers
Military Medical Personnel
Military Personnel
Military Psychologists
Ministers (Religion)
Missionaries
Musicians
National Guardsmen
Navy Personnel
Neurologists
Noncommissioned Officers
Nonprofessional Personnel
Nuns
Nurses
Obstetricians
Occupational Therapists
Occupations
Optometrists
Paramedical Personnel
Paraprofessional Personnel
Parole Officers
Pathologists
Pediatricians
Personnel
Pharmacists
Physical Therapists
Physicians
Physicists
Police Personnel
Politicians
Preschool Teachers
Preservice Teachers
Priests
Prison Personnel
Probation Officers
Professional Personnel
Psychiatric Aides
Psychiatric Hospital Staff
Psychiatric Nurses
Psychiatric Social Workers
Psychiatrists
Psychoanalysts
Psychologists
Psychotherapists
Public Health Service Nurses
Rabbis
Rehabilitation Counselors
Religious Personnel
Resource Teachers
Sales Personnel
School Administrators
School Counselors
School Nurses
School Principals
School Psychologists
School Superintendents
Scientists
Secretarial Personnel
Seminarians
Service Personnel
Skilled Industrial Workers
Social Psychologists
Social Workers
Sociologists
Special Education Teachers
Speech Therapists
Student Teachers
Surgeons
Teacher Aides
Teachers
Technical Personnel
Technical Service Personnel
Therapist Trainees
Therapists
Top Level Managers
Unskilled Industrial Workers
Vocational Counselors
Vocational Education Teachers
Volunteer Civilian Personnel
Volunteer Military Personnel
Volunteer Personnel
Volunteers in Service to America
White Collar Workers
Working Women
Writers

Organizations & Organizational Behavior

Business Organizations
Choice Shift
Decentralization
Division of Labor
Entrepreneurship
Foreign Organizations
Government Agencies
International Organizations
Labor Unions
Nonprofit Organizations
Organizational Behavior
Organizational Change
Organizational Characteristics
Organizational Climate
Organizational Commitment
Organizational Crises
Organizational Development
Organizational Effectiveness
Organizational Merger
Organizational Objectives
Organizational Structure
Organizations
Professional Organizations
Religious Organizations
Teams

Personnel Management

Affirmative Action
Age Discrimination
Assessment Centers
Bonuses
Career Development
Career Education
Conflict Resolution
Disability Evaluation
Disability Management
Employee Assistance Programs
Employee Benefits
Employee Health Insurance
Employee Leave Benefits
Employee Pension Plans
Employee Turnover
Employer Attitudes
Employment Discrimination
Employment Tests
Inservice Training
Job Analysis
Job Applicant Interviews

Consult Relationship Section for more information

Personnel Management — (cont'd)

Job Applicant Screening
Job Search
Labor Management Relations
Management Training
Mediation
Medical Personnel Supply
Mental Health Inservice Training
Mental Health Personnel Supply
Military Recruitment
Military Training
Occupational Guidance
Occupational Success Prediction
On the Job Training
Personnel Evaluation
Personnel Management
Personnel Placement
Personnel Promotion
Personnel Recruitment
Personnel Selection
Personnel Supply
Personnel Termination
Personnel Training
Policy Making
Quality Control
Race and Ethnic Discrimination
Reemployment
Salaries
Sex Discrimination
Sexual Harassment
Social Security
Stress Management
Strikes
Supported Employment
Teacher Recruitment
Unemployment
Vocational Evaluation
Workmens Compensation Insurance

STATISTICAL CLUSTER

- Design, Analysis & Interpretation
- Statistical Reliability & Validity
- Statistical Theory & Experimentation

Design, Analysis & Interpretation

Algorithms
Analysis of Covariance
Analysis of Variance
Between Groups Design
Causal Analysis
Central Tendency Measures
Chi Square Test
Cluster Analysis
Cochran Q Test
Cohort Analysis
Content Analysis
Content Analysis (Test)
Equimax Rotation
Error Analysis
Error of Measurement
Experimental Design
F Test
Factor Analysis
Factor Analysis
Factor Structure
Fuzzy Set Theory
Goodness of Fit
Heuristic Modeling
Interaction Analysis (Statistics)
Interaction Variance
Item Analysis (Statistical)
Item Analysis (Test)
Item Response Theory
Kolmogorov Smirnov Test
Least Squares
Linear Regression
Mann Whitney U Test
Markov Chains
Mathematical Modeling
Maximum Likelihood
Mean
Median
Meta Analysis
Multidimensional Scaling
Multiple Regression
Multivariate Analysis
Nonlinear Regression
Nonparametric Statistical Tests
Oblique Rotation
Orthogonal Rotation
Parametric Statistical Tests
Path Analysis
Phi Coefficient
Point Biserial Correlation
Probability
Q Sort Testing Technique
Quartimax Rotation
Rank Difference Correlation
Rank Order Correlation
Repeated Measures
Scaling (Testing)
Score Equating
Sign Test
Spearman Brown Test
Standard Deviation
Standard Scores
Statistical Analysis
Statistical Correlation
Statistical Data
Statistical Estimation
Statistical Measurement
Statistical Norms
Statistical Probability
Statistical Regression
Statistical Rotation
Statistical Tables
Statistical Tests
Statistical Weighting
Stochastic Modeling
Structural Equation Modeling
T Test
Tetrachoric Correlation
Time Series
Variability Measurement
Variance Homogeneity
Varimax Rotation
Wilcoxon Sign Rank Test
Zulliger Z Test

Statistical Reliability & Validity

Concurrent Validity
Construct Validity
Content Analysis
Content Analysis (Test)
Error Analysis
Error of Measurement
Factorial Validity
Interrater Reliability
Item Analysis (Statistical)
Item Content (Test)
Predictive Validity
Statistical Power
Statistical Reliability
Statistical Validity
Test Reliability
Test Validity

Statistical Theory & Experimentation

Biased Sampling
Binomial Distribution
Chaos Theory
Confidence Limits (Statistics)
Conjoint Measurement
Consistency (Measurement)
Cutting Scores
Data Collection
Data Processing
Dependent Variables
Double Bind Interaction
Effect Size (Statistical)
Empirical Methods
Experiment Controls
Experimental Design
Experimental Replication
Experimental Subjects
Experimentation
Experimenter Bias
Followup Studies
Frequency Distribution
Fuzzy Set Theory
Halo Effect
Independent Variables
Knowledge of Results
Longitudinal Studies
Maximum Likelihood
Methodology
Normal Distribution
Null Hypothesis Testing
Population (Statistics)
Prediction Errors

Consult Relationship Section for more information

Statistical Theory & Experimentation — (cont'd)

Prospective Studies
Random Sampling
Retrospective Studies
Sample Size
Sampling (Experimental)
Skewed Distribution
Statistical Data
Statistical Sample Parameters
Statistical Samples
Statistical Significance
Statistical Tables
Statistical Variables
Statistics
Type I Errors
Type II Errors

TESTS & TESTING CLUSTER

- Academic Achievement & Aptitude Measures
- Attitude & Interest Measures
- Developmental Measures
- Intelligence Measures
- Neuropsychological Measures
- Nonprojective Personality Measures
- Perceptual Measures
- Projective Personality Measures
- Testing
- Testing Methods

Academic Achievement & Aptitude Measures

Achievement Measures
Aptitude Measures
Coll Ent Exam Bd Scholastic Apt Test
Comprehension Tests
Differential Aptitude Tests
Educational Measurement
Entrance Examinations
Gates MacGinitie Reading Tests
General Aptitude Test Battery
Graduate Record Examination
Iowa Tests of Basic Skills
Metropolitan Readiness Tests
Minimum Competency Tests
Modern Language Aptitude Test
Professional Examinations
Reading Measures
Retention Measures
Stanford Achievement Test
Verbal Tests
Wide Range Achievement Test
Woodcock Johnson Psychoed Battery

Attitude & Interest Measures

Attitude Measurement
Attitude Measures
Consumer Surveys
Interest Inventories
Kuder Occupational Interest Survey
Kuder Preference Record
Least Preferred Coworker Scale
Occupational Interest Measures
Parent Attitude Research Instrument
Preference Measures
Strong Vocational Interest Blank
Wilson Patterson Conservatism Scale

Developmental Measures

Bayley Scales of Infant Development

Intelligence Measures

Army General Classification Test
Benton Revised Visual Retention Test
California Test of Mental Maturity
Columbia Mental Maturity Scale
Creativity Measurement
Culture Fair Intelligence Test
Frostig Development Test Vis Percept
Goodenough Harris Draw A Person Test
Hidden Figures Test
Illinois Test Psycholinguist Abil
Infant Intelligence Scale
Intelligence Measures
Kaufman Assessment Battery Children
Kohs Block Design Test
Lorge Thorndike Intelligence Test
Lowenfeld Mosaic Test
Miller Analogies Test
Peabody Picture Vocabulary Test
Porteus Maze Test
Raven Coloured Progressive Matrices
Raven Progressive Matrices
Remote Associates Test
Slosson Intelligence Test for Child
Stanford Binet Intelligence Scale
Verbal Tests
Wechsler Adult Intelligence Scale
Wechsler Bellevue Intelligence Scale
Wechsler Intelligence Scale Children
Wechsler Memory Scale
Wechsler Preschool Primary Scale

Neuropsychological Measures

Bender Gestalt Test
Halstead Reitan Neuropsych Battery
Luria Nebraska Neuropsych Battery
Mini Mental State Examination
Wechsler Memory Scale
Wisconsin Card Sorting Test

Nonprojective Personality Measures

Bannister Repertory Grid
Barrett Lennard Relationship Invent
Barron Welsh Art Scale
Beck Depression Inventory
Bem Sex Role Inventory
California F Scale
California Psychological Inventory
California Test of Personality
Child Behavior Checklist
Childrens Manifest Anxiety Scale
Childrens Personality Questionnaire
Edwards Personal Preference Schedule
Edwards Personality Inventory
Edwards Social Desirability Scale
Embedded Figures Testing
Eysenck Personality Inventory
Fear Survey Schedule
Fund Interper Rela Orientat Beh Ques
General Health Questionnaire
Goldstein Scheerer Object Sort Test
Gough Adjective Check List
Guilford Zimmerman Temperament Surv
High Sch Personality Questionnaire
Kirton Adaption Innovation Inven
Learys Interpersonal Check List
Marlowe Crowne Soc Desirabil Scale
Maudsley Personality Inventory
Memory for Designs Test
Millon Clinical Multiaxial Inventory
Minn Multiphasic Personality Inven
Mooney Problem Check List
Myers Briggs Type Indicator
NEO Personality Inventory
Nonprojective Personality Measures
Omnibus Personality Inventory
Personal Orientation Inventory
Personality Measures
Psychological Screening Inventory
Repression Sensitization Scale
Rod and Frame Test
Rokeach Dogmatism Scale
Rotter Intern Extern Locus Cont Scal
Sensation Seeking Scale
Sixteen Personality Factors Question
State Trait Anxiety Inventory
Taylor Manifest Anxiety Scale
Tennessee Self Concept Scale
Vineland Social Maturity Scale
Welsh Figure Preference Test
Zungs Self Rating Depression Scale

Perceptual Measures

Perceptual Measures
Psychophysical Measurement
Purdue Perceptual Motor Survey
Sensorimotor Measures
Speech and Hearing Measures
Stroop Color Word Test
Wepman Test of Auditory Discrim

Projective Personality Measures

Bender Gestalt Test
Childrens Apperception Test

Consult Relationship Section for more information

Projective Personality Measures — (cont'd)

Franck Drawing Completion Test
Holtzman Inkblot Technique
Human Figures Drawing
Incomplete Man Test
Personality Measures
Projective Personality Measures
Projective Techniques
Projective Testing Technique
Rorschach Test
Rosenzweig Picture Frustration Study
Rotter Incomplete Sentences Blank
Sentence Completion Tests
Szondi Test
Thematic Apperception Test
Zulliger Z Test

Testing

Concurrent Validity
Consistency (Measurement)
Construct Validity
Content Analysis (Test)
Cultural Test Bias
Cutting Scores
Difficulty Level (Test)
Employment Tests
Factor Analysis
Factor Structure
Factorial Validity
Foreign Language Translation
Inventories
Item Analysis (Test)
Item Content (Test)
Item Response Theory
Measurement
Performance Tests
Piagetian Tasks
Predictive Validity
Profiles (Measurement)
Psychometrics
Rating Scales
Score Equating
Scoring (Testing)
Screening Tests
Selection Tests
Semantic Differential
Sociometric Tests
Sociometry
Standard Scores
Standardized Tests
Statistical Weighting
Subtests
Test Administration
Test Anxiety
Test Bias
Test Construction
Test Forms
Test Interpretation
Test Items
Test Norms
Test Reliability
Test Scores
Test Standardization
Test Taking
Test Validity
Testing
Testwiseness

Testing Methods

Adaptive Testing
Behavioral Assessment
Biographical Inventories
Body Sway Testing
Cloze Testing
Computer Assisted Testing
Criterion Referenced Tests
Digit Span Testing
Essay Testing
Forced Choice (Testing Method)
Group Testing
Individual Testing
Inventories
Likert Scales
Matching to Sample
Multiple Choice (Testing Method)
Neuropsychological Assessment
Posttesting
Pretesting
Q Sort Testing Technique
Questionnaires
Rating Scales
Scaling (Testing)
Surveys
Testing Methods

TREATMENT CLUSTER

- Alternative Therapies
- Behavior Modification & Therapy
- Counseling
- Hospitalization & Institutionalization
- Medical & Physical Treatment
- Psychotherapy
- Rehabilitation
- Treatment (General)
- Treatment Facilities

Alternative Therapies

Acupuncture
Aerobic Exercise
Alternative Medicine
Animal Assisted Therapy
Art Therapy
Autohypnosis
Communication Skills Training
Consciousness Raising Groups
Creative Arts Therapy
Dance Therapy
Encounter Group Therapy
Eye Movement Desensitization Therapy
Faith Healing
Folk Medicine
Holistic Health
Home Care
Home Visiting Programs
Hospice
Human Relations Training
Hypnosis
Hypnotherapy
Imagery
Meditation
Milieu Therapy
Morita Therapy
Motivation Training
Movement Therapy
Music Therapy
Outpatient Treatment
Pain Management
Partial Hospitalization
Phototherapy
Poetry Therapy
Primal Therapy
Recreation Therapy
Role Playing
Self Medication
Sensitivity Training
Sex Therapy
Sleep Treatment
Social Skills Training
Sociotherapy
Stress Management
Support Groups
Therapeutic Camps
Therapeutic Community
Therapeutic Social Clubs
Wilderness Experience

Behavior Modification & Therapy

Anger Control
Anxiety Management
Assertiveness Training
Aversion Therapy
Behavior Contracting
Behavior Modification
Behavior Therapy
Biofeedback Training
Contingency Management
Counterconditioning
Covert Sensitization
Exposure Therapy
Fading (Conditioning)
Implosive Therapy
Omission Training
Overcorrection
Progressive Relaxation Therapy
Reciprocal Inhibition Therapy
Relaxation Therapy
Self Help Techniques
Self Management

Consult Relationship Section for more information

Behavior Modification & Therapy — (cont'd)

Systematic Desensitization Therapy
Time Out
Token Economy Programs

Counseling

AIDS Prevention
Counseling
Counseling Psychology
Couples Therapy
Crisis Intervention
Crisis Intervention Services
Drug Abuse Prevention
Family Planning
Feminist Therapy
Genetic Counseling
Group Counseling
Health Promotion
Hot Line Services
Marriage Counseling
Pastoral Counseling
Peer Counseling
Premarital Counseling
Psychotherapeutic Counseling
Rehabilitation Counseling
Social Casework
Suicide Prevention
Suicide Prevention Centers

Hospitalization & Institutionalization

Deinstitutionalization
Discharge Planning
Emergency Services
Hospital Administration
Hospital Admission
Hospital Discharge
Hospital Environment
Hospital Programs
Hospitalization
Hospitalized Patients
Hospitals
Institution Visitation
Institutional Release
Institutionalization
Intensive Care
Nursing
Outpatient Treatment
Partial Hospitalization
Patient Seclusion
Psychiatric Hospital Admission
Psychiatric Hospital Discharge
Psychiatric Hospital Programs
Psychiatric Hospital Readmission
Psychiatric Hospitalization
Psychiatric Units
Therapeutic Community

Medical & Physical Treatment

Acupuncture
Adrenalectomy
Amputation
Artificial Pacemakers
Artificial Respiration
Biopsy
Blood Transfusion
Castration
Catheterization
Cochlear Implants
Colostomy
Commissurotomy
Dental Surgery
Dental Treatment
Dialysis
Diuresis
Drug Therapy
Electroconvulsive Shock Therapy
Electrosleep Treatment
Endocrine Gland Surgery
Family Medicine
Fertility Enhancement
Health Care Services
Health Maintenance Organizations
Heart Surgery
Hemispherectomy
Hemodialysis
Hormone Therapy
Hypophysectomy
Hysterectomy
Immunization
Induced Abortion
Insulin Shock Therapy
Intensive Care
Laser Irradiation
Male Castration
Mastectomy
Medical Therapeutic Devices
Medical Treatment (General)
Mobility Aids
Movement Therapy
Neural Transplantation
Neurosurgery
Organ Transplantation
Organic Therapies
Outpatient Treatment
Ovariectomy
Pain Management
Phototherapy
Physical Therapy
Physical Treatment Methods
Pinealectomy
Plastic Surgery
Postsurgical Complications
Prenatal Care
Preventive Medicine
Primary Health Care
Prostheses
Psychosomatic Medicine
Psychosurgery
Public Health Services
Pyramidotomy
Radiation Therapy
Self Medication
Sex Change
Shock Therapy
Sleep Treatment
Stereotaxic Techniques
Surgery
Sympathectomy
Thalamotomy
Thyroidectomy
Tractotomy
Tubal Ligation
Vagotomy
Vasectomy
Vitamin Therapy

Psychotherapy

Adlerian Psychotherapy
Adolescent Psychotherapy
Age Regression (Hypnotic)
Analytical Psychotherapy
Autogenic Training
Bibliotherapy
Brief Psychotherapy
Centering
Child Psychotherapy
Client Centered Therapy
Cognitive Restructuring
Cognitive Techniques
Cognitive Therapy
Conjoint Therapy
Consultation Liaison Psychiatry
Cotherapy
Countertransference
Couples Therapy
Crisis Intervention
Directed Reverie Therapy
Dream Analysis
Eclectic Psychotherapy
Existential Therapy
Experiential Psychotherapy
Expressive Psychotherapy
Family Therapy
Feminist Therapy
Geriatric Psychotherapy
Gestalt Therapy
Group Psychotherapy
Hypnotherapy
Individual Psychotherapy
Insight (Psychotherapeutic Process)
Insight Therapy
Interpersonal Psychotherapy
Logotherapy
Marathon Group Therapy
Marriage Counseling
Mirroring
Morita Therapy
Mutual Storytelling Technique
Outpatient Treatment

Consult Relationship Section for more information

Psychotherapy — (cont'd)

Paradoxical Techniques
Personal Therapy
Persuasion Therapy
Play Therapy
Primal Therapy
Psychoanalysis
Psychodrama
Psychotherapeutic Breakthrough
Psychotherapeutic Counseling
Psychotherapeutic Neutrality
Psychotherapeutic Outcomes
Psychotherapeutic Processes
Psychotherapeutic Resistance
Psychotherapeutic Techniques
Psychotherapeutic Transference
Psychotherapy
Rational Emotive Therapy
Reality Therapy
Relationship Therapy
Self Analysis
Self Help Techniques
Social Casework
Supportive Psychotherapy
Therapeutic Community
Transactional Analysis

Rehabilitation

Activities of Daily Living
Adaptive Behavior
Alcohol Rehabilitation
Alcoholics Anonymous
Augmentative Communication
Cochlear Implants
Cognitive Rehabilitation
Detoxification
Disability Management
Drug Rehabilitation
Habilitation
Halfway Houses
Mainstreaming
Memory Training
Methadone Maintenance
Occupational Therapy
Physical Therapy
Prostheses
Psychosocial Rehabilitation
Rehabilitation
Rehabilitation Centers
Rehabilitation Counseling
Sheltered Workshops
Smoking Cessation
Speech Therapy
Therapeutic Social Clubs
Twelve Step Programs
Vocational Evaluation
Vocational Rehabilitation
Work Adjustment Training

Treatment (General)

Adult Day Care
Advance Directives
Aftercare
AIDS Prevention
Assisted Suicide
Biological Psychiatry
Biopsychosocial Approach
Caregiver Burden
Caregivers
Child Psychiatry
Child Psychology
Childbirth Training
Client Education
Client Records
Client Transfer
Client Treatment Matching
Clinical Psychology
Community Mental Health
Cost Containment
Cross Cultural Treatment
Discharge Planning
Drug Abuse Prevention
Drug Education
Early Intervention
Fee for Service
Geriatric Psychiatry
Health Care Costs
Health Care Delivery
Health Care Policy
Health Care Psychology
Health Care Seeking Behavior
Health Care Services
Health Care Utilization
Health Education
Health Insurance
Health Promotion
Health Service Needs
Help Seeking Behavior
Holistic Health
Informed Consent
Intake Interview
Integrated Services
Interdisciplinary Treatment Approach
Involuntary Treatment
Life Sustaining Treatment
Long Term Care
Maintenance Therapy
Managed Care
Medicaid
Medical Patients
Medical Psychology
Medical Records
Medical Treatment (General)
Medicare
Multimodal Treatment Approach
Needs Assessment
Negative Therapeutic Reaction
Nonprescription Drugs
Optical Aids
Outpatient Commitment
Outreach Programs
Palliative Care
Patient Abuse
Patient History
Patient Seclusion
Patient Selection
Physical Examination
Posttreatment Followup
Prescribing (Drugs)
Prescription Drugs
Primary Mental Health Prevention
Private Practice
Professional Client Sexual Relations
Psychiatric Patients
Psychiatry
Psychoeducation
Psychotherapeutic Processes
Quality of Care
Quality of Services
Relapse Prevention
Respite Care
Right to Treatment
Self Examination (Medical)
Self Medication
Self Referral
Sex Education
Side Effects (Treatment)
Social Psychiatry
Social Services
Surgical Patients
Therapeutic Alliance
Therapeutic Processes
Therapist Selection
Treatment
Treatment Compliance
Treatment Dropouts
Treatment Duration
Treatment Effectiveness Evaluation
Treatment Outcomes
Treatment Planning
Treatment Refusal
Treatment Termination
Treatment Withholding

Treatment Facilities

Adult Day Care
Child Guidance Clinics
Clinics
Community Facilities
Community Mental Health Centers
Community Mental Health Services
Day Care Centers
Health Maintenance Organizations
Hospitals
Mental Health Programs
Mental Health Services
Nursing Homes
Orphanages
Psychiatric Clinics
Psychiatric Hospitals
Psychiatric Units

Consult Relationship Section for more information

Treatment Facilities — (cont'd)

Public Health Services
Rehabilitation Centers
Residential Care Institutions
Sanatoriums
Social Services
Suicide Prevention Centers
Therapeutic Community
Treatment Facilities
Walk In Clinics

Consult Relationship Section for more information

WITHDRAWAL